Private

Dispute

Settlement

Private
Dispute
Settlement

CASES AND MATERIALS ON ARBITRATION

Merton C. Bernstein

Professor of Law, THE OHIO STATE UNIVERSITY

 THE FREE PRESS, NEW YORK

COLLIER-MACMILLAN LIMITED, LONDON

For Benjamin Bernstein, Esq.
Who cleared the path and showed the way

PREFACE

This book is primarily designed to fill a gap in law school instructional materials. A minority of schools now offer a course in arbitration and then often limit it to labor arbitration. This volume should enable more schools to offer the subject and on a comprehensive basis. One thesis of the book is that there are many kinds of arbitration, and developments in one branch affect law and possibly practice in others.

In addition, this volume is designed to be of aid to practitioners and judges. The law of arbitration lacks a current treatise, and though growing rapidly, it suffers from insufficient information about practice and lack of a theoretical structure upon which to build. The book, it is hoped, is sufficiently comprehensive to fill that gap, although only partially. The law is galloping ahead too rapidly for a current treatise to be possible. This book can serve as a ready reference and a portable arbitration library. But, naturally enough, it does not purport to be encyclopedic.

Both cases and readings are edited, but omissions are not shown and footnotes are renumbered. Brackets usually enclose my editorial comments. In a few instances the bracketed material appeared that way in the original; the context indicates which is which. The aim is to present the main burden of information and argument in the shortest compass. But, even then, the extracts are more full than is commonly the case. These materials are designed for advanced courses and seminars, practitioners, and judges; hence, the frequent casebook approach of offering two or three cases and a few notes as the take-off point for a discussion is eschewed. Rather, the materials are designed to enable classes to select topics and study them in detail with whatever subtleties and confusions the decisions and commentaries contain. A few minor contextual matters are presented more sketchily.

Arbitration is an expanding area of the law, reaching constantly into new fields. It deserves serious study and discriminating use. It is my hope that this book makes a modest contribution to those ends.

Dublin, Ohio   M. C. B.

ACKNOWLEDGMENTS

Many minds and hands are needed to make a book, even if there is but one author.

My debts to many who write in this field cannot be adequately expressed. They are not limited to those who kindly consented to have portions of articles reproduced here (individually acknowledged where they appear). But anyone who works in this area must be conscious of the pioneering role of Wesley Sturges. In addition, he helped guide my earliest teaching in this field when he was in great distress. His kindness will always be remembered.

Over the years my understanding of arbitration has been deepened and sharpened by countless discussions with Professor Clyde Summers of Yale University Law School. Innumerable students there and at the College of Law, Ohio State University, have participated in testing out earlier versions of the materials and ideas contained here.

At Yale, former Dean Eugene V. Rostow lent indispensable support in the early stages of this volume, abetted by Isabel Malone, now Registrar. Dean Louis Pollack generously gave assistance thereafter. Former Yale Law Librarian Harry Bitner and his associates Jim Golden, Sam Smith, and Bob Brooks helped enormously. Dorothy Egan and Doris Moriarity rendered indispensable aid in the physical production process.

At Ohio State, Dean Ivan C. Rutledge scheduled two half quarters off and, with Assistant Dean Wharton, arranged to supply me with research assistants, Mark Kaufman and Harry Keith, who helped a great deal. My colleagues Howard Fink and Robert Nordstrom contributed in innumerable ways. Law Librarian Ervin Pollock, Reference Librarian Matthew Dee, and Gay Crumpler, Cheryl Hachman, and Jacqueline Kuyper made books and documents materialize when needed.

A special debt of gratitude is owed Mrs. Gladys Paulin, director of secretarial services at the College of Law, who painstakingly presided over three separate versions of this book. Mrs. Jane Welsch did a large portion of the work, ably and energetically assisted by Sheila Plants, Linda Philips, and Jean Smith.

To all these my hearty but inadequate thanks.

My wife claims that but for her, Johanna, Inga, Mac and Rachel this book would have been completed long ago. (The Supreme Court delayed me more.) The truth is that without them, this book would not have been done at all.

.

CONTENTS

Private Dispute Settlement

INTRODUCTION—THE VARIETIES OF ARBITRATION

No body of law can be understood without thorough familiarity with the institutions to which it applies. In the case of arbitration, where practice and law are developing rapidly, the need to relate law to practice is especially great. This is all the more true because arbitration operates in a context of law that becomes applicable, usually, when something goes wrong or is thought to have miscarried. Those who participate in arbitration, as lawyers often do, should know both the legal context of their activities and the institutional setting.

In addition, ascertaining the characteristics of arbitration serves three major purposes: determining the applicability of a statute or doctrine not specifically addressed to arbitration (e.g., a statute of limitations, a discovery procedure, or *Erie* and other conflicts doctrines); applying and shaping legal doctrines exclusively concerned with the arbitration process; and perhaps most important, enhancing the arbitral process by the conscious selection of rejection of various arbitral devices depending upon their considered potentialities, utility, or shortcomings.

For the greater part of its history, arbitration has persisted and grown without, and sometimes despite, the law. Indeed, law has been indifferent to arbitration, and even hostile, until the recent past. This institutional hardihood testifies to the utility and acceptability of arbitral processes and the comparative unimportance of legal doctrines. Commercial arbitration persisted with little legal support at least until the period beginning immediately after World War I. Labor arbitration similarly grew and proliferated with almost no common law or statutory under-pinnings until immediately after World War II. Perhaps the institutional forces that supported arbitration where it existed have diminished or been outgrown.

Whether or not statutory support is necessary or desirable seems, for the moment, to have become academic, in its most arid sense. State and federal legislation now validates a wide variety of arbitral institutions. This support, indeed preferential treatment, comes at a price—conformity to prescribed procedures and standards. Hence the current and future impact upon arbitration of law probably will be greater than in the past. Conceivably the effects may be limiting rather than strengthening.

If the law is to promote the beneficent aspects of arbitration and curb its undesirable potentialities, the institutions upon which the law impinges should be understood.

The first proposition of this volume is that arbitration is not unitary. Although it has been common to differentiate between labor arbitration and commercial arbitration, there seems to have been little appreciation of the many varieties within each of those two gross categories or of the several kinds of arbitration that do not fit within either, such as the thousands of uninsured-motorist claims and the fewer marital and custody disputes that are arbitrated.

The great variety of disputes and the differing forms of arbitral machinery raise the caution that in the formulation of any arbitration rule, account should be taken of the different contexts in which it may apply. It also raises the question as to whether *any* rules should be applied across-the-board.

Llewellyn has observed that constitutions and contracts often declare standards that may not be observed in the day to day conduct of affairs but are invoked when disputes arise.* In the subsequent adjudication the court consults the more-or-less fictitious standard in deciding the dispute. The great commercial judges, such as Mansfield, attempted to minimize the fictional element and to stir in as large a measure of realism as possible by using commercial men as jurymen and by consulting experienced businessmen. But the common law tries to resolve individual disputes in terms of fairly general propositions, although many cases are explicable only in terms of their peculiarities. Hence the fit between a court decision and the realities underlying a particular case may be rather poor.

Administrative agencies and quasi-judicial boards and commissions are attempts to introduce a larger element of realism derived from expertise in the affairs of an industry or a kind of activity (such as labor-management relations) because of the feeling that the courts often did not know what they were talking about. (This development was crowned by giving the courts some, and their taking more, authority to inquire whether the expert bodies know what they are talking about.) Such governmental agencies are concentrated in areas were private conduct and public activities or standards meet.

Outside the public agency realm, efforts such as the Uniform Commercial Code try to infuse a larger element of realism into the court disposition of commercial suits. If the advisers of potential litigants think the Code does achieve this, resort to the courts might be reduced where formerly a judge might accord relief or refuse it on a basis alien to business standards. But, although it tries to maximize the effect given to custom and practice, the Code is a statute of general application whose specific provisions may not accord with them because, for example, of difficulties of proof.

Perhaps the most important attribute of arbitration is that it can and often does involve dispute resolution with great emphasis upon the realities of the relationship and a result that is just in terms of the expectations of the particular parties or the standards of their groups, which often are unarticulated but nonetheless form the context of their contract or relationship. Although judges often seek such a result, arbitrators are more free of the restraints of law and even contract language, often have firsthand knowledge of such standards, and are less dependent upon the vagaries of rules of evidence. As with other institutions and, indeed, individuals, this strength is also a potential source of abuse. Other attributes of arbitration, some of which are not unmixed blessings, will be considered in this book.

This volume explores many institutional methods of using arbitration, their utility, and their drawbacks. The attempt is made to relate statutory and court-made law to the varying arbitration institutions. For it is a thesis of this volume that the law might be wise to take account of this variety if means can be found to do so. In all likelihood, differences among kinds of arbitration sometimes receive unexpressed recognition ; more explicit treatment may be more useful to those who must decide whether arbitration suits them and if so, what kind. Similarly, some differentiations commonly made —as between commercial and labor arbitration —may be too gross and thereby lead to improperly disparate treatment. It may also be that within classifications differentiations should be made so that potential disputants fully recognize their range of choice of arbitral arrangements and so that the courts may begin to understand, for whatever effect it may have upon their arbitration-related activities, how many different brands of arbitration there are.

Arbitration is now widely used as the apex of dispute settlement procedures in labor-management relations. Within the broad domain of labor relations, arbitration is used in many different industries, in large and small enterprises, by individual companies and local unions, by whole industries and aggregations of unions. Procedures include "permanent" umpireships and *ad hoc* arrangements, sole arbitrators, panels, or tripartite groups, perched atop grievance arrangements of differing scope and complexity. Less widely known are the several forms of commercial arbitration, usually used as *the* other category of arbitration but properly applicable

*Llewellyn, *What Price Contract*, 40 Yale L. J. 704, 730–31, 736–37 (1931).

only to proceedings to resolve disputes among businessmen. These forms include the arbitral arrangements of trade associations (sometimes limited to members but often involving transactions with nonmembers), commodity exchanges (usually limited to transactions between exchange members but with potential impact upon their customers), financial exchanges, intercompany claims by insurers, claims by insureds against insurers, parties to ship charters, small debt collection, parties to sales distribution agreements, construction contractors and subcontractors, stockholders of closed corporations. The arbitral machinery may be provided by an exchange or association, an institution like the American Arbitration Association or the International Chamber of Commerce, or it may be tailor-made by the parties to their own specifications, or it may be some combination of these elements. Procedures vary in many details even though only a few basic models exist.

Outside both major classifications—labor and commercial—are "arbitration" of small tort claims, adjudications of claims arising from accidents with uninsured motorists, and the not-yet-common custody and property problems in domestic relations, estate matters, and other non-commercial, nonlabor disputes.

This great variety of relations, issues, and procedures may be amenable to common doctrines, but one may be permitted to doubt it. At the least we should be wary of importing arbitral arrangements from one context to another and applying legal concepts and rules to situations with possibly major institutional differences and needs merely because they have a common last name: arbitration. For it may be that some judicial approaches are based upon arrangements different from those to which they are applied. And it may be that some arrangements now treated as arbitration should not have applied to them the standards, or indeed the statutes, fashioned for quite different arrangements. Although they are not so numerous as the tribes of Jones, Smith, Kelly, and the many "steins," the many arbitrations may have little or no relationship. One should also recognize that the common name leads, has led, and will lead to much common treatment. Whether and when common treatment is in order should be a matter of informed choice. That brings us to the point of beginning: an inquiry into the varieties of arbitration arrangements—and their law.

PART I

DEVELOPMENT, BASIC CONCEPTS, AND PROBLEMS—NON-LABOR ARBITRATION

CHAPTER I

INSTITUTIONAL SETTINGS AND CHARACTERIZATION OF ARBITRATION

A.

Institutional Settings

A NOTE ON COMMERCIAL ARBITRATION IN TRADE ASSOCIATIONS

Arbitration frequently occurs under the auspices of a trade association. Data on the arbitral machinery of trade associations and exchanges are not up to date.[1] Probably a majority of associations do not provide arbitral machinery for disputes among members but concentrate on governmental and employee relations, public relations, and trade promotion and statistical tasks. Quite a few, however, engage in attempts to improve "trade practices," both among members and with customers, using devices like standard-form contracts, statements of ethical or standard practices, and product standardization. Arbitration, sometimes under association auspices, often pursuant to provisions in the standard agreement, may be an adjunct of such activities. Among 1,244 associations studied by the TNEC a generation ago, 215 (17 per cent of the total) reported commercial arbitration as among their activities; 91 characterized that activity as one of the association's major activities.[2]

---

1. AMERICAN ARBITRATION ASSN., YEARBOOK OF COMMERCIAL ARBITRATION IN THE UNITED STATES (New York: Oxford University Press, 1927), the first (and last) of a series of annual surveys, set forth the detailed provisions of arbitration procedures of numerous trade groups. We stand in need of a similar survey today. An excellent 1925 study of trade associations presented a good disucssion of the reasons for and modes of arbitration under that form of organization. NATIONAL INDUSTRIAL CONFERENCE BOARD, TRADE ASSOCIATIONS: THEIR ECONOMIC SIGNIFICANCE AND LEGAL STATUS (1925). The latest edition of a standard reference on commodity exchanges elucidates their functions and organization and the role of arbitration. JULIUS BAER and O. GLENN SAXON, COMMODITY EXCHANGES AND FUTURES TRADING (New York: Harper & Row, 1949).

2. PEARCE, CONCENTRATION OF ECONOMIC POWER: TRADE ASSOCIATION SURVEY, Table 25 (TNEC Monograph No. 18, 1941). Not included in the study were commodity and security exchanges.

Some associations consists of all or several groups in a trade, including both buyers and sellers and perhaps brokers, commission merchants, and other such auxiliaries. Their standard form contracts (some containing arbitration clauses) frequently represent the outcome of accommodation among the various interest groups in the trade. Other associations comprise one segment (buyers, sellers, importers, exporters) of a larger trade. Their standard form contracts naturally tend to protect the interests peculiar to their group. If they contain an arbitration clause, they may provide for not wholly impartial procedures and tribunals to which other parties to the contract are supposed to submit. (Some resultant problems are considered hereafter.) The point here is that an association standard form clause may reach beyond the association.

Whereas trade associations typically consist of operating groups in an industry, commercial exchanges are much closer to financial institutions organized not simply to facilitate transfers of commodities but also to enable buyers and sellers to hedge their actual purchases and sales in order to protect against too great vagaries of the market. Exchange trading usually is limited to members, and members are limited to trade on the exchange. Exchange transactions are made by members but often on behalf of clients. As a result, nonmembers may be bound by the contracts entered into by members on their behalf. At the least, the members' contract with the nonmember will reflect the exchange form of agreement; whether this includes the arbitration clause is a question whose answer requires the kind of survey that has not been made for decades in the commercial area. (Only recently have similar data been assembled for labor-management agreements.)

In all likelihood, most commercial arbitration clauses occur in association and exchange agreements, in somewhat similar standard provisions promulgated by a professional group such as the American Institute of Architects, and in standard form contracts developed by individual firms. Although it is not demonstrable, the individually negotiated contract containing an individualized arbitration provision probably accounts for a minority of agreements with arbitration provisions and commercial arbitration proceedings (not taking account of the numerous noncommercial uninsured motorist contracts).

Some of these arrangements and others will be discussed in the text and cases hereafter. The effort is made to present available information about significant arbitral arrangements.

COMMERCIAL ARBITRATION*

SOIA MENTSCHIKOFF

I. Introduction

The first thing to be noted is that although commonly thought of as a single type phenomenon, both the structure and the process of commercial arbitration are determined by the different institutional contexts in which it arises. There are three major institutional settings in which commercial arbitration appears as a mechanism for the settlement of disputes.

The simplest is when two persons in a contract delineating a business relationship agree to settle any disputes that may arise under the contract by resort to arbitration before named arbitrators or persons to be named at the time of the dispute.† In this, which can be called individuated arbitration, the making of all arrangements, including the procedures for arbitration, rests entirely with the parties concerned. Although we do not know, we believe that the chief moving factors here are: (1) a desire for privacy as, for example, in certain crude oil situations where such arrangements exist; (2) the availability of expert deciders; (3) the avoidance of possible legal difficulties with the nature of the transaction itself; and (4) the random acceptance by many businessmen of the idea that arbitration is faster and less expensive than court action.

A second type of arbitration arises within the context of a particular trade association or exchange. The group establishes its own arbitration machinery for the settlement of disputes among its members, either on a voluntary or compulsory basis, and sometimes makes it available to nonmembers doing business in the particular trade. A particular association may also have specialist committees, which are investigatory in character, with the arbitration machinery handling only the private disputes involving nonspecialist categories of cases. Occasionally, when the volume of arbitration in a particular trade association is not large enough to warrant the

---

*Abridged from 61 COLUM. L. REV. 846 (1961). Reprinted with permission.

†[Others may view the submission of a single existing dispute as arbitration's simplest form. However, the agreement to arbitrate all or designated kinds of disputes during the life of a contract probably account for the greatest number of cases. So, for example, "All of the cases in the sample [of cases at the American Arbitration Association] involved some kind of contract and 81 per cent were based on a contract calling for arbitration of future disputes. The other 19 per cent were based on submissions signed by the parties after the dispute had arisen." Smith in article cited *infra*, p. 15.]

maintenance of its own machinery, or when the relevant trade association consists only of one segment of an entire industry, the association joins with other related associations in the organization of a confederated trade association system under which a single machinery for compulsory or voluntary use by persons in the related industries or trades is provided.

The third setting for commercial arbitration is found in administrative groups, such as the American Arbitration Association, the International Chamber of Commerce, and various local chambers of commerce, which provide rules, facilities, and arbitrators for any persons desiring to settle disputes by arbitration. Many trade associations with insufficient business to warrant separate organizations make special arrangements with one of these groups to process disputes that arise among their members.

In a survey, 34 per cent of the [trade] associations indicated that their members made individual arrangements for arbitration; 29 per cent indicated that they used some type of organized machinery, including the American Arbitration Association; and 26 per cent reported that their members never arbitrate. [Apparently] there were rational reasons for the existence of these differences.

A. FACTORS DETERMINING THE NEED FOR ARBITRATION

At this point it is useful to distinguish between those factors that can be said to produce a *need* for arbitration machinery in commercial groups and those factors that merely make it desirable. The reasons commonly given for arbitration—speed, lower expense, more expert decision, greater privacy—are appealing to all businessmen, and yet not all utilize arbitration. It seems reasonably clear, therefore, that for some trades these factors are of greater importance than for others, and that for some trades there must be countervailing values in not resorting to arbitration. We postulated three factors as being theoretically important in determining whether or not a particular trade needed institutionalized use of arbitration, and incorporated questions relating to these factors in our trade association questionnaire.

The first factor was the nature of the economic function being performed in relation to the movement of the goods by the members of the association. We postulated that persons primarily buying for resale, that is merchants in the original sense of the term, were much more likely to be interested in speed of adjudication, and that since price allowance would be a central remedy for defects in quality or, indeed, for nondelivery, the speed and low cost characteris-

tics of arbitration would be particularly attractive to them, thus leading to the creation of institutionalized machinery. The trade associations in which such merchants constitute all or part of the membership reported as follows: 48 per cent use institutionalized machinery, 34 per cent make individual arrangements for arbitration, and only 18 per cent never arbitrate. These figures are to be contrasted with the reports from those trade associations that stated that their memberships did not include any merchants. In those groups 23 per cent reported the existence of institutionalized arbitration, 44 per cent reported individual arrangements, and 33 per cent reported no arbitration whatever.

The second major factor that we thought would be important in determining the need for arbitration was the participation of the members of the association in foreign trade. Apart from the enhanced possibility of delay inherent in transnational law suits, when the parties to a transaction are governed by different substantive rules of law, resort to the formal legal system poses uncertainty and relative unpredictability of result for at least one of the parties. This uncertainty and unpredictability is increased by the fact that the very rules governing the choice of the applicable law are themselves relatively uncertain and are not uniform among the nations of the world. Faced with such an uncertain formal legal situation, any affected trade group is apt to develop its own set of substantive rules or standards of behavior as the controlling rules for its members. Obviously, when a trade group develops its own rules of law, it requires as deciders of its disputes persons who are acquainted with the standard it has developed. Since this knowledgeability does not reside in the judges of any formal legal system, the drive toward institutionalized private machinery is reinforced.

So far as American foreign trade associations are concerned, it is necessary to distinguish between associations whose members are primarily importers, and associations whose members are primarily exporters. The important thing to be noticed about this distinction is that in all cases of dispute other than those involving pure nondelivery, the documents or goods will be in the buyer's country when the dispute arises. Although the existence of an operative private law governing trade in particular commodities, with consequent administration by private adjudicatory machinery, means that such machinery can exist either in the buyer's or the seller's country, we postulated that in view of the normal location in the buyer's country of the documents or goods at the time of the dispute, a rule of convenience of forum would tend to place the situs of arbitration in the buyer's country.[1] It seemed reasonable to expect, therefore, that trade associations whose members included importers would show a higher incidence of organized arbitration than those that did not. Of the groups reporting an import relationship to foreign trade, 67 per cent did have organized machinery, 25 per cent made individual arrangements, and only 8 per cent reported they never arbitrated. Of groups that had both an import and export connection, 37 per cent reported that they had organized machinery, 45 per cent made individual arrangements, and 18 per cent never arbitrated. Of the groups which reported that the members dealt only in domestic trade or only in export, 25 per cent reported their own organized machinery, 40 per cent reported individual arrangements, and 35 per cent reported no arbitration.

The third factor that we thought would bear on the need for arbitration machinery relates to the kind of goods dealt with by the members of the association. One of the major areas of dispute among businessmen centers on the quality of the goods involved.[2] If, therefore, the goods are such as not to be readily susceptible of quality determination by third persons, arbitration or, indeed, inspection, is an unlikely method of settling disputes. If goods are divided into raws, softs, and hards, the differences in their suitability for third party adjudication becomes relatively clear. On the whole, raws are a fungible commodity, one bushel of #1 wheat being very much like another bushel of #1 wheat. On the other hand, hards, which consist of items like refrigerators and automobiles, are not viewed by their producers as essentially fungible, however they may appear to the layman. We did not believe that Ford would like to have General Motors sitting on disputes involving the quality of Ford cars, or vice versa. Moreover, quality differentials in raws can normally

be reflected by price differentials, but defects in hard goods frequently affect their usefulness and therefore price differential compensation is not feasible. Thus, the normal sales remedy for raws has come to be price allowance, whereas the normal sales remedy for hard goods has come to be repair or replacement. Raws, involving fungibility and ease of finding an appropriate remedy, are therefore highly susceptible to third party adjudication, whereas hard goods tend to move away from such adjudication. Soft goods, which are the intermediate category and range from textiles to small hardware, we thought would constitute a neutral category.

In our survey of exchanges dealing in grain and livestock, 100 per cent of those responding reported the use of institutionalized arbitration. There are, of course, other reasons for such a unanimous response by the exchanges, but the nature of the goods involved is a very important one. The trade association survey showed that of all the reporting associations dealing in raws, 46 per cent had machinery, 29 per cent made individual arrangements, and only 25 per cent never arbitrated. On the other hand, only 4 per cent of those reporting hards as their basic goods had machinery, 46 per cent made individual arrangements and 50 per cent never arbitrated. Of the soft goods associations reporting, 33 per cent had machinery, 41 per cent made individual arrangements, and 26 per cent never arbitrated.

To the extent that the factors leading to institutionalized machinery reinforce each other, as, for example, in the case of an association reporting that its members have an import relationship to foreign trade, deal in raws, and consist of merchants, the existence of arbitration machinery rises to approximately 100 per cent. When the contrary report is made, that is, that the membership consists of manufacturers of hard goods engaged only in domestic business, the percentage drops off to about 8 per cent.

B. RELATION OF ARBITRATION TO OTHER FORMALIZED PROCEDURES

Since commercial arbitration normally arises out of contracts between the parties to the dispute, and since the major issue is usually one of either interpretation of the contract or the measurement of performance, it is obvious that one of the factors enhancing predictability of result is the extent to which the arbitrator is aware of the trade meaning of the contract terms and the significance of the various aspects of performance under it. One would therefore expect that trades in which arbitration was a normal institutional way of life would realize rather early the prophylactic importance of generally under-

---

1. The situs might be in the seller's country if the sellers in the trade were in a heavily superior bargaining position or if the transaction were one governed by certain English trade associations that have traditionally decided all disputes in the particular trade without regard to nationality of the parties, place of making of the contract, or the place or places of performance.

2. At the American Arbitration Association, for example, quality disputes accounted for approximately 40 per cent of the sales cases. ["The Rubber Trade Association (New York), for example, arbitrates nearly 1,000 cases per year; about 90 per cent of these, however, are determinations of the quality of crude rubber. The same situation prevails in the New England Cotton Buyers (Boston) [sic] which arbitrates the quality of more than 25,000 bales of cotton each year, but arbitrates only a few technical disputes." Smith in article cited *infra*, page 15.]

stood and agreed upon standard contract clauses and quality specifications. Trade groups having institutionalized adjudicatory machinery do tend to develop standardization of contract terms. They also move towards standardization of quality and specialized provisions for adjudicating questions of quality. Finally, groups having institutionalized arbitration also show a tendency to have other important self-regulation committees, such as those on ethics and disciplinary proceedings, rules, form contracts, and the like.

We can thus say that the presence of institutionalized arbitration is a strong index of the existence of a generally self-contained trade association having its own self-regulation machinery and that the forces leading to institutionalized arbitration also, therefore, tend to lead to the creation of self-contained, self-governing trade groups.[3]

In addition to the institutionalized arbitration that takes place in the context of the trade associations, a great deal also occurs inside commodity and stock exchanges. The exchanges, of course, are much more tightly organized than are the trade associations and, in addition to an arbitration committee, frequently maintain various specialist committees among whose functions are the deciding of disputes arising out of contracts for commodities traded in the exchange under specific trade rules. In exchange groups, not only is resort to arbitration on the whole compulsory for members, but failure to abide by an award is frequently considered grounds for disciplinary proceedings against the recalcitrant party. In addition, the particular norms or standards by which such disputes are judged are frequently spelled out by special committees with a degree of particularity that is rarely matched by our statutes and only occasionally by regulations of administrative agencies.

II. The American Arbitration Association

The American Arbitration Association was the American response to the delays and difficulties that could result from procedural defects in the arbitration process in situations where the economic sanctions of some of the trade groups were not available. This organization from its beginning held itself out as an expert in matters that went to the enforceability of an award and set up its rules and regulations with the primary aim of rendering awards that would not be set aside by the courts. It has succeeded greatly in

the accomplishment of this goal, and as a result, it is now one of the most important forums for the determination of commercial disputes by arbitration.

Of the 128 trade associations reporting existence of institutionalized arbitration machinery, 73 per cent indicated that the machinery was organized and serviced either by the trade association itself or by one of the four federated associations.[4] The other 27 per cent indicated that they had made special arrangements with the American Arbitration Association; some allowed members a choice between their own and AAA machinery; and others used only the AAA.*

A. COMPARISON WITH THE SELF-CONTAINED TRADE GROUP ARBITRATION

Arbitration at the Association differs substantially from arbitration at the self-contained trade groups. The first and most significant difference between the two systems lies in the use of precedent. The decisions that are rendered by the arbitration committees of self-contained trade associations do have precedential value. This is achieved in two ways: in some associations opinions are written and circulated to the membership; in others awards can be appealed or referred to other committees for the establishment of general standards. Most important, however, in all of these associations there is a continuity in the membership of the deciders, which means that the system of precedent operates automatically, for a question decided in one case on the basis of consideration of competing norms is unlikely to be decided differently in the next case by the same people. However, the casual system of arbitration used by the American Arbitration Association, is designed to discourage the use of precedent. The Association puts enormous pressure on its arbitrators not to write opinions but to merely state the award in dollar amounts. It also tries very hard and very successfully not to have any one person sit as a[n] [commercial] arbitrator more than once or twice a year.

The second significant difference is that of the self-contained trade association groups, 40 per cent explicitly discourage or forbid the use of attorneys, and in the remaining 60 per cent

---

3. We do not believe, [based upon a survey of these factors] that the creation of self-contained trade groups rests in important part on the percentage of dollar volume or establishments represented by the association.

4. These are the General Arbitration Council, The National Federation of Textiles, Association of Food Distributors of New York, and the Uniform Plan of the National Canners Association.

*[Probably data on the number of cases would be more significant on the factor of the proportion of cases handled. Many of the association and exchange proceedings are brief —but numerous.]

attorneys very rarely appear. The American Arbitration Association, on the other hand, encourages the parties to use attorneys. This difference reflects the basic proposition that in the self-contained trade groups the norms and standards of the group itself are being brought to bear by the arbitrators, and the incursion of lawyers with their potential emphasis on general legal norms and standards is viewed as a factor deflecting expeditious hearing and wise decision. At the Association, theoretically, substantive legal rules are welcome as norms for decision, and therefore attorneys are welcome. In fact, however, relatively few arbitrators or counsel feel bound by the substantive rules of law, although most feel it should be "considered."

The third difference between self-contained trade association systems and the casual arbitration at the Association lies in the methods by which awards are enforced. The ultimate sanction in many of the self-contained associations and in almost all of the exchanges is a disciplinary proceeding and thus, potential legal problems with respect to procedure are not seriously considered in these groups. The ultimate sanction at the Association is the rendering of judgment on the award by a court of competent jurisdiction, and therefore problems of procedure are always uppermost in the minds of the tribunal clerks, who are charged with the duty of policing the arbitrators sufficiently, so [sic] that the award rendered will be legally enforceable.

B. WORKLOAD

During the years 1947–1950 the period of which we made an intensive study of the Association, a total of 1,883 commercial cases were filed and 1,740 cases were disposed of at the Association. The cases were disposed of as follows: 626 were settled or withdrawn before hearing; 82 were settled after hearing; and 1,032 went to award. Taking an average for the four years, the Association received 471 cases per year and held hearings on 279. Considering only the cases filed in New York City, the Association received about 420 cases each year and held hearings on 238. This number of arbitrations is somewhat greater than the number of cases of a comparable nature filed in the United States District Court for the Southern District of New York.[5]

---

5. Since our study was made the jurisdictional amount has been changed to $10,000. The cases filed at the Association have increased to an average of 700 per year over the past five years [*i.e.*, up to 1961].

C. PERSONNEL

1. *Use of lawyers.* The presence and participation of lawyers and law-trained judges in the trial of a case is one major characteristic of court action, especially of courts other than small claims courts. In almost all self-contained trade associations and exchanges, on the other hand, lawyer participation in the arbitration proceedings is either forbidden or discouraged, and very few of the arbitrators are lawyers or law-trained. The emphasis in these groups is on the utilization of norms and standards of the trade for deciding without regard to their similarity to or difference from the norms or standards that would be imposed by substantive rules of law. We frequently heard, both orally and in writing, that lawyer participation was not desired for two reasons: (1) lawyers did not understand the business usages and practices that were typically involved in adjudicating the dispute and were therefore not helpful; and (2) lawyers made the proceedings unduly technical and tended to create unnecessary delays. This second complaint about lawyers has some support in our analysis of the Assocation records. Both delays in the selection of arbitrators and postponements between hearings occur more frequently in cases in which the parties are represented by attorneys. Of course, the figures also showed that attorneys were more likely to be employed as the amount involved in the case became larger. Personal observation at the Association leads me to the reluctant conclusion that in the great majority of the cases observed, lawyer participation not only failed to facilitate decision but was so inadequate as to materially lengthen and complicate the presentation of the cases. Nonetheless, the Association encourages lawyer participation. Lawyers represent one or more of the parties in 80 per cent of the cases, and serve as arbitrators in about 30 per cent. The availability of legal norms or standards for utilization in the disposition of particular arbitrations at the Association is therefore theoretically present.

2. *Use of expert deciders.* Court actions are typified by the absence of expertise as to the particular business or trade involved, on the part of both the judge and the jury, but in the self-contained trade group arbitration mechanisms, the arbitrators all have this expertise. In 45 per cent of the cases at the Association, at least one of the arbitrators was a person from the trade or business in which the dispute arose. In many of the cases at the Association, therefore, the arbitrators have no peculiar expertise in the particular trade or business involved in the dis-

pute that is before them for decision. If lawyers be viewed as "expert" in knowledge of the rules of law, some utilization of this expert quality is made at the Association. As the cases move from sales to employment, agency contracts, royalties, leases, and the like, the use of lawyer arbitrators increases.

3. *Role attitudes.* The most important similarity of Association arbitration to the formal legal system, however, is found in the attitudes with which the arbitrators come to the proceedings. First and perhaps most significant, the Association explicitly urges its arbitrators to adopt a judicial attitude that will lead to decision on the merits rather than to a compromise award. "Compromise" is used here in its invidious sense of arriving at decision by, as one arbitrator expressed it, "giving a little and taking a little." It does not mean that legitimate clashes of interest are not resolved in a way that seems fairest to both sides, a process that lies at the foundation of any attempt to evolve a rule of law.

The efforts of the Association in propagating a judicial attitude on the part of its arbitrators are apparently highly successful. In the first place, in 50 per cent of the cases decided, the award was in full either for the plaintiff or for the defendant. Obviously such awards can not be the result of compromise. Secondly, many of the partial awards are arrived at in a judicial manner since they result from the striking of particular items of damage that the arbitrators believe are not justified under the facts or law of the particular case. Finally, more than two thirds [of the] arbitrators ... [studied] disagree [d] with the proposition that "arbitrators are expected to find a way of satisfying both parties in a dispute by finding compromise solutions ..." Over half accepted the following proposition: "An arbitrator should try to decide for one party or the other and not try to look for ways of compromising." Eighty per cent of the experimental arbitrators thought that they ought to reach their decisions within the context of the principles of substantive rules of law, but almost 90 per cent believed that they were free to ignore these rules whenever they thought that more just decisions would be reached by so doing. In other words, what they were saying is that rules of law were entitled to very heavy respect but could be reexamined in the interests of justice. This result is curiously parallel to the attitudes that seem to be implicit in our appellate courts.[6]

Although almost 100 per cent of the arbitrators polled thought that both parties should share the burden of proof to some extent, 75 per cent of them believed that in the ultimate analysis the burden should rest on the claimant. Again, the parallel to the formal legal structure is striking. This view of allocation of burden of proof is not an empty one; some cases in our field study were ultimately decided on this basis.

Finally, almost 70 per cent of the experimental arbitrators believed that they should decide the case "on the basis of the evidence available to them and not try to supplement the evidence by their own efforts." This attitude, of course, does not mean that the arbitrators believe that they may not request the parties to provide any additional information necessary to clear up ambiguous points. As to this, over 90 per cent believed that they were justified in making such a request.

4. *Prior knowledge of case.* At the Association the arbitrators, with rare exceptions, know no more about the dispute than can be told by an examination of the written claim of the petitioner and the answer of the respondent. Frequently, these are read immediately prior to the commencement of the arbitration. The elaborate pretrial techniques of the formal legal system are of doubtful availability in arbitration and are not in fact used. The equivalent of the pretrial conference that can be found in the sifting operations of many of the trade associations is not present, except as the arbitrators, after the commencement of hearings, may attempt to get the parties to agree on which issues are to be arbitrated. But this is not a material variation from court action so far as prior knowledge of the case by the decider is concerned since pretrial seems to be used primarily to force the parties into settlement, and very few jurisdictions assign cases so that the same judge operates both at its pretrial and its trial levels.

D. PROCEEDINGS PRIOR TO HEARINGS

Proceedings at the American Arbitration Association have three phases. The first deals with the filing of the case, the selection of arbitrators, and the setting of the hearing date. The second phase consists of the hearings themselves. The third phase consists of the deliberations among the arbitrators.*

The standard method of appointing arbitrators is for the Association to provide the parties with lists of names chosen from its panel of com-

---

6. See generally LLEWELLYN, THE COMMON LAW TRADITION: DECIDING APPEALS (1960).

*[These latter two aspects are considered later in the materials.]

mercial arbitrators. The original lists reflect any wishes the parties may have concerning particular occupations or kinds of persons. The parties then indicate the names to which they object on the list and express an order of preference for the others. The Association then selects the arbitrators from the names not objected to and, when possible, follows the preference of the parties. The parties are permitted to exhaust three lists in this way. If they do, the Association then appoints the arbitrators without further consultation with the parties. However, there is considerable flexibility, and, although the standard method of selection is used in 53 per cent of the cases, sometimes the Association is used only to appoint a third arbitrator or is asked to make the appointment without submission of lists.

The vital thing about the methods of selecting arbitrators that are used by the Association is the degree of party control possible both as to specification of the general qualifications that the arbitrators are to possess and as to the personal characteristics of the ones suggested by the Association. In view of the findings of our study that the prior experience of the arbitrators is an important factor in decision-making and decision consensus, this right to participate in and, in large measure, to control the selection of arbitrators affords persons using the arbitral procedure an enormous advantage over those using the courts, since in the courts, within narrow limits of tactical maneuvering, the parties have no say in the selection of the judge who will try the case.

E. THE DECISION-MAKING PROCESS

1. *Nature of disputes.* The nature of the disputes presented for adjudication at the Association is very similar to the nature of disputes settled in the courts. In commercial arbitration, unlike labor arbitration,* the issue in controversy is practically never what the terms of the contract should be, a question that is not justiciable. Commercial cases involve justiciable issues since they normally arise out of a contract or transaction that has occurred in the past and involve

---

*[Practitioners of labor arbitration probably would say that in this respect commercial and labor arbitration are alike, not unlike.]

7.

Nature of Issue	Number	Per cent
Fact alone	187	35
Contract interpretation alone	28	5
Law alone	2	—
Fact and contract interpretation	268	51
Fact and law	15	3
Contract interpretation and law	1	—
All three	26	5

either the question of what the contract means, or what has occurred, or both.[7]

2. *The arbitrators' job.* The basic task of arbitrators at the Association is to decide with fairness to the parties the merits of a controversy that arose in the past and is presented to them for the first time by the parties or their counsel. They do not have the two further tasks that are present both in the judicial organs of the self-contained trade groups and in the courts: because their decision is not intended to have precedential value, they are not compelled to either ascertain or judge the generalized situation that is typified by the particular case or to issue a rule that will have guiding value for parties in similar situations. Typically the product is limited in form to a "yes" or "no" answer or to a dollar amount. This, of course, makes it possible for both jurors in a court and commercial arbitrators at the Association to reach an agreed upon decision without reaching agreement on the reasons for the decision.

Any decision of the question of who is right in a dispute situation, however, requires the use by the deciders of a set of norms or standards against which the conduct involved in the dispute, as it is perceived by the deciders, is to be measured, because wrongness or rightness can never be a question of fact but is always a matter of judgment as to values. In both the formal legal and the arbitration systems the parties and their counsel can and frequently do suggest particular norms or rules of law as being *the* most relevant to the dispute involved, but the deciders are free to accept or reject the suggested norms. In the legal system, however, the instructions of the judge to the jury are a second source of norms. The norms provided by this source are theoretically not subject to rejection by the jury. This task of selecting the most relevant or appropriate norm, which is peculiarly the task of the judge in the formal legal system, is therefore a part of the total job of the commercial arbitrator.

A COMMENT ON "EXPERTISE"

More than one thing is meant by "expertise" in the arbitration context. It may mean technical competence required for the proper understanding of the evidence and issues in a specialized subject (such as accounting or various kinds of engineering) or familiarity with the methods of a particular trade or industry or group, including technical matters and business practice and mores. Both kinds of expertise are available in arbitration. It is in the latter sense that I shall use expertise in my editorial comments. Where technical competence is meant, that adjective will be employed.

THREE CENTURIES OF ARBITRATION IN NEW YORK*

WILLIAM C. JONES

In summary, it is clear that arbitration has been in constant use in New York from its beginnings to 1920. It did not suddenly come into being at that time because of the passage of a statute making agreements to arbitrate future disputes enforceable. Rather, it has existed with and without the benefit of statutes, and both separate from, and in connection with, court adjudication. For the more recent period,† its most important manifestation has been in connection with mercantile organizations such as exchanges and trade associations. It seems justified to believe that the New York development has not been entirely peculiar to that state. It is rare for an American state to retain important legal and economic features entirely different from those of its fellows. Further, New York has been for so long the commercial capital of the country that its example tends inevitably to be copied. There is, in any event, evidence to show that arbitration is in considerable use in other states.

However that may be, it is believed that the existence of the practice of extensive arbitration over so long a period of time in the mercantile community tends to show that, as used by merchants, arbitration is not really a substitute for court adjudication as something that is cheaper or faster or whatever, but is rather a means of dispute settling quite as ancient—for all practical purposes anyway—as court adjudication, and that is has, traditionally, fulfilled quite a different function. The primary function of arbitration is to provide for merchants fora where mercantile disputes will be settled by merchants. This, in turn, suggests that merchants wish to form, and have for a long time succeeded in forming, a separate, and, to some extent, self-governing community, independent of the larger unit. For law, this means that courts may perform, in the commercial field at least, a different function from that which we usually assign to them. In many cases, they may not be the primary fora for adjudication. If this is true, when they are called upon to decide a commercial case in one of these areas, it will be either after another adjudicatory agency has acted or because the other system cannot, or will not, cope with the case. In some areas, courts may almost never get a case. (What the influence of their decisions is on the arbitrators is a difficult question to answer.) Insofar as this area, in which arbitration is and—most importantly—has always been the primary dispute-settling agency, is an important one (and an area which includes stockbrokers, produce brokers, coffee merchants, etc., seems to be such an area), it cannot really be said that one has studied commercial law, in the sense of the rules that actually guide the settlement of disputes involving commercial matters, if he has studied only the reports of appellate courts and legislation.

Having gone so far with hypothesis, one may be forgiven for going a little farther and suggesting that the existence of a sufficient sense of community identity or separateness on the part of merchants to cause them to have a separate adjudicatory system tends to show that there is a mercantile community which is, to a considerable degree, self-governing. This community has existed in this form for centuries. Its existence suggests that there may be others—religious and educational communities come to mind.

COMMERCIAL ARBITRATION AT THE AMERICAN ARBITRATION ASSOCIATION‡

HAL M. SMITH

One of the chief advantages of arbitration as compared to court litigation is said to be the speed of decision. Typically the cases in the sample were disposed of in 60 to 90 days. Fifty-seven per cent of the cases were either withdrawn or went to final award in less than 90 days from the time of filing. This 57 per cent, however, gives an incomplete picture of the speed of arbitration because it does not allow for the delays requested by the parties. Many of the cases require more than one hearing, and there is often a long delay between hearings. These delays are typically requested by one of the parties, although the next hearing may be postponed for the convenience of the arbitrators. Of the cases which were not interrupted between hearings for more than 14 days, 77 per cent were disposed of in less than 90 days.

Besides postponements granted between hearings, an arbitration may be delayed because of difficulties in choosing arbitrators. The Association sedulously tries to appoint arbitrators who

---

*Excerpted from 1956 WASH. U.L.Q. 193, 218–219. Reprinted with permission.

†[1900–1920.]

‡Excerpted from 11 ARB. J. (n.s.) 3, 17–20 (1956). Reprinted with permission.

are acceptable to both parties. Thus several supplementary lists of possible arbitrators from the panel are sometimes sent to the parties before three men are found who are acceptable to both sides.

The case reports indicate whether the arbitrators were chosen from lists according to the standard method or were appointed by the AAA. It is probable that a large proportion of the Association appointment cases were cases in which the parties objected to most of the names on the lists submitted to them, time was spent sending additional lists which were also unsatisfactory to the parties, and the Association finally appointed the arbitrators under Rule 12. Consequently, Association appointment cases as a group would be expected to take longer than the cases in which the arbitrators were chosen from lists submitted to the parties. Of the cases in which one or all of the arbitrators were appointed by the AAA, only 36 per cent were decided within 90 days of filing, compared with 63 per cent in the remaining cases. Excluding these two types of delay, where the AAA was not called upon to appoint an arbitrator and there was no delay of more than 14 days between hearings, 83 per cent of the cases were decided in less than 90 days.

Both the delays incident to the selection of arbitrators and those occurring as postponements between hearings occur more frequently in cases in which the parties are represented by attorneys. Where both parties were represented by attorneys, 43 per cent of the cases were decided in less than 90 days and 21 per cent in less than 60 days. Where neither party brought an attorney, 78 per cent of the cases were decided in less than 90 days and 49 per cent in less than 60 days. The attorneys would seem to be bringing some of their court practices and skills to arbitration.

Decision of cases in less than 30 days is possible at the AAA, though it is not the general rule. Thirty-six cases in the sample, or 7 per cent, were decided in less than 30 days.* Under the arbitration procedures of the various commodity exchanges, such rapid decisions are apparently the usual practice. The rules of 17 of 39 commodity exchanges which have been studied require that arbitration cases come to hearing not more than ten business days after filing. Furthermore, the exchanges generally limit the time for which a case may be postponed after the first hearing without obtaining the arbitrators' consent to a longer postponement. While no accurate statistics have yet been collected, preliminary studies indicate that in most of the commodity exchanges arbitrations are decided in less than 30 days. This speed is undoubtedly favored by several facets of the operation of the exchanges. The members of the exchange are more easily assembled, whether they be parties or arbitrators. There is usually no problem of selection of arbitrators because a standing committee sits in all cases. Finally, in a majority of the exchanges, the arbitration rules exclude attorneys from the hearings.

In contrast to the speed of arbitration in the commodity exchanges, in one trade association studied in detail, namely the National Hay Association, the arbitrations take much longer than at the AAA. In 49 per cent of the hay cases more than six months elapsed between filing and award. This long delay exists despite the use of standing committees as arbitrators and the exclusion of attorneys. This delay in the Hay Association is probably due to their practice of calling a meeting of the Arbitration Committee to hear cases only after sufficient cases have accumulated to warrant the meeting, a practice followed in several trade associations. Furthermore, the delay is not as serious as it would be in some industries, since the hay is always disposed of quickly regardless of any disputes.

The AAA policies of seeking acceptable arbitrators, of allowing frequent postponements, and of allowing the parties to be represented by attorneys are all policies which tend to make the arbitrations fairer and therefore more acceptable to the parties. But these practices must also delay disposition of the cases.

Conclusion

From this general study of 545 cases arbitrated at the AAA, it is not possible to determine why certain disputes are taken to arbitration or why a certain party wins. But this study does show that the AAA is an important commercial tribunal and that arbitration is a faster method of adjudication than courts. The study also shows that the AAA arbitrators are apt to be experts in the matters involved; that the use of lawyers has some effect on the arbitrations, especially in favoring delays; and that the chance of successful outcome for a given party is related to the issues in the case rather than to a partiality of the tribunal towards certain occupational groups. The high rate of claimant wins in arbitration suggests that arbitration is often used as a collection mechanism, although accurate interpretation of this part of the study must await further

---

*For a description of a case completed in two hours, see 2 ARB. J. 131 (1938).

study. Further studies may also chart more accurately the effect which lawyers as counsel have on the outcome of the cases as well as examining in more detail the question of whether the presence of lawyers or experts as arbitrators makes any difference in the outcome of a case. Although there are many questions yet to be answered, it is clear that the AAA plays a major role in resolving commercial disputes in many industries. Whether because of the speed, economy or expert justice of the AAA arbitration, or all three, these industries indicate their satisfaction with the tribunal by continuing to bring their disputes to the AAA.

Table I-I. Major Categories of Arbitration Cases Administered by the American Arbitration Association 1957 to 1967 (Number of Cases)

Year	Uninsured Motorist	Commercial	Labor-Management	Elections	Total
1957	305	645	2598	14	3562
1958	384	710	2758	15	3867
1959	496	674	2816	13	3999
1960	681	783	3231	28	4723
1961	1727	800	3492	25	6044
1962	2711	887	3842	30	7470
1963	3910	985	4074	32	9001
1964	4823	1186	3932	33	9974
1965	6343	1276	4097	73	11,789
1966	7408	1449	4007	93	12,957
1967	8621	1588	4437	117	14,763

SOURCE: AMERICAN ARBITRATION ASSOCIATION, ARBITRATION NEWS No. 3, 1967, and No. 2, 1968. Reprinted with permission.

SOME OBSERVATIONS ON ARBITRATION*

EDWARD N. COSTIKYAN

The motto of the American Arbitration Association is "Speed, Economy, Justice." And for a generation arbitration has been sold to the profession on the premise that it achieves these objectives. A recent issue of TIME described the "agonizingly slow and annoyingly expensive" course of litigation of commercial quarrels as contrasted with the speedy economy and efficiency of arbitration.

But does arbitration live up to the AAA motto?

The consensus of many experienced litigators is that it achieves none of these objectives—at

*151 N.Y.L.J. (No. 40) 1, February 27, 1964. Reprinted with permission.

least not as well as traditional court procedures —unless both parties to the arbitration are eager for a speedy resolution. This, in our experience, is rare. The stronger the case on one side the more reluctant is the opposition to co-operate in a speedy decision. Indeed, our experience has been that arbitration, *except* in labor matters and as to technical questions of fact in a specialized area, such as quality of goods and industry standards, is uneconomical, slow and, as often as not, fails to achieve substantial justice.

Speed?

Are arbitrations speedier than court proceedings?

I doubt it.

First of all, there is the preliminary skirmishing as to whether there should be arbitration at all. And an adversary who wishes to delay an adjudication finds a ready obstacle to throw in the path of adjudication by arbitrators. For example, in one case involving the manufacturer of explosives that blew up a good part of a town in New Jersey, it was two years before there even was a final determination that there should be arbitration (Matter of Kilgore Mfg. Co., 280 App. Div. 332; aff'd, 305 N.Y. 815).

In another case, where there were a number of contracts between the parties, some with arbitration clauses, others without, and those with them differing one from another, there was lengthy litigation as to which, if any, arbitration clause was applicable. The matter ended with part of a controversy supposedly to be arbitrated and part of it not to be. Naturally, the parties then agreed to litigate the entire controversy in one tribunal (Levin v. Columbia Broadcasting System, 25 Misc. 2d 208).

Of course, where both sides are eager to reach a conclusion, such obstacles do not arise, but as noted above, it has been our experience that the clearer the claim of one party the more his adversary desires to delay an adjudication.

And what of the speed of the proceedings themselves once an arbitration has been directed or accepted? Here, again, a dilatory adversary can often stretch the proceedings indefinitely. In one case, to my knowledge, twenty-six sessions took two years to complete (Ballantine Books, Inc., v. Capital Distributing Co., 302 F. 2d 17).

The arbitrators were really not at fault in allowing the matter to drag along. They had their own business and professional activities. And, mindful of the mandate of the then Civil Practice Act that makes one of the grounds for setting aside an award the refusal to hear relevant evidence, and lacking a skilled judge who could rule on relevance instinctively, the arbitrators were content to hear most of the evidence that was adduced "for what it was worth."

The adjournments required by the arbitrators' principal activities resulted in repetition, forgetfulness as to what had been already established, and new obstacles to final adjudication, as ingenious counsel spent the adjourned time thinking up new issues.

The absence of pre-trial proceedings also tended to transform the arbitration hearings into discovery sessions.

The end result is that, perhaps if parties are eager to secure adjudication, arbitration can be speedy. But if one of the parties seeks to delay it—which is normally true—it offers an admirable vehicle to achieve that end.

Economy?

If speed is not a necessary characteristic of arbitration, what of economy?

In our experience, by and large, the cost of arbitration has been substantially higher than the cost of a proceeding in court. The reasons are the direct result of the informality of arbitration proceedings and the general tendency of arbitrators to hear every scrap of evidence "for what it is worth." The result is to permit arbitration proceedings to be drawn on interminably.

And since arbitrators cannot really be expected to sit from day to day, the cost of preparation for trial is multiplied immeasurably. Before each session the transcript must be reviewed. Before each session opposing counsel thinks up new ideas to prolong cross-examination. Before each session a substantial amount of time must be spent in refreshing recollections as to what has transpired.

And, notwithstanding such preparation, endless repetition is inevitable. Indeed, as the proceedings continue and the transcript grows and grows, indexes of the transcript are essential or else all sense of direction and movement is lost.

The result of all this is substantially higher legal fees. In the arbitration referred to above, what should have been no more than a week's trial continued for twenty-six sessions commencing in April of 1959 and terminating with final briefs in April of 1961. The cost of conducting a thirty-day trial over a two-year period instead of a one-week trial is obvious.

In addition, the basic costs of arbitrating are substantially higher than those of a lawsuit. For example, in the lengthy arbitration referred to above, filing fees were over $3,000; the arbitrators were paid $150 a day for 30 hearings,

for a total of $4,500, and the transcript, which ran to thousands of pages, was far more expensive than it would have been if the proceedings had been conducted in court, if only because three copies were needed for the arbitrators instead of one for a judge. With an impecunious or faint-hearted client, such financial burdens produce great pressure for settlement.

Moreover, the absence of pre-trial proceedings and pre-trial examinations meant that the arbitration hearings themselves were a form of discovery—an uneconomical form, since three arbitrators were required to sit and listen while counsel attempted to extract evidence from adversaries—in many cases evidence which does not exist.

In short, the claim that arbitration is economical is not borne out by actual experience if one includes in the cost of arbitration additional cost items which would not be present in a court proceeding.

Justice?

And what of justice?

Here it is more difficult to be precise. However, the quality of justice produced by arbitration must be the direct function of the person who happens to be selected as an arbitrator—a chancey business at best.

The problem of the method of selecting judges —by election or appointment—has concerned the political and governmental worlds for years. But no one has yet suggested the method used in selecting arbitrators be applied to the judiciary.

I happen to believe that professionals tend to be better at their jobs than amateurs. I tend to believe that those who spend their lives in the profession of judging tend to be better at that art than those who are occasional, part-time amateurs.

I tend to believe that a trial before a jury with a professional judge determining what is proper and what is not proper evidence is better than such a trial conducted with an amateur calling the shots.

It may be that the end result of arbitration is as good as the end result of a litigation in court, but I doubt it, for it seems to me that professional adjudication must inherently be preferable to adjudication by amateurs.

Conclusion

The experience described above has been shared by many of my partners and associates. While there have been exceptions, it has been our general experience that arbitrations have been slow, costly and unpredictable as to result, and we have finally prevailed upon our corporate brethren in our firm to eliminate arbitration clauses from agreements whenever possible. Instead, we have recommended that the simplified court procedure set forth in section 3031 of the CPLR be followed. To date, none of the contracts in which such proceedings are provided for have ended in litigation, so that as yet we have had no experience to measure the relative efficacy of this procedure.

But to those who fear the possibility of lengthy court proceedings, the simplified court procedure seems to offer the advantages that arbitration boasts for itself without its risks.

We have also pointed out to our hesitant brothers that in the event a dispute arises and both sides really desire a speedy-economic-just resolution of the dispute by arbitration, it is always possible to agree to arbitrate, after it is clear that both parties will co-operate in an effort to achieve that result.

So far, we haven't had that experience either.

B.

Characterization

ARBITRATION—WHAT IS IT?*

WESLEY A. STURGES

The identification of arbitration as it is constituted in legal lore is not very difficult. There is a near consensus of judicial utterance and statutory provision posing it as a process for hearing and deciding controversies of economic consequence arising between parties. It begins with and depends upon an agreement of the parties to submit their claims to one or more persons chosen by them to serve as their arbitrator.

Certain significant legal requirements governing the hearing and decision of the claims submitted attach unless the parties stipulate against them or otherwise waive them; they attach without any necessity of their stipulation. These minimum legal requirements assure:

1. Mutual rights of hearing. Each party is entitled to reasonable notice of time and place of hearing to be had before the arbitrators sitting in due quorum, an opportunity to present evidence in his own behalf relating to the matter in issue and an opportunity to cross-examine opposing evidence.

2. Mutual rights that, after hearing, the arbitrators shall render such award on the issues submitted to them as they deem fair and just—whether or not according to law. To the award attach legal finality, conclusiveness and enforceability subject only to limited causes to defeat or vacate the award.

This generic identification of arbitration does not, of course, reckon with the details of distinctions between common law and statutory

arbitration, nor with the declared distinctions between arbitration of commercial and labor-management causes. It does not take account of any precise similarities to or differences from processes of settling controversies frequently cited as "appraisals," "valuations" or miscellaneous methods of compromise or settlement. Nor does this identification comprehend so-called "compulsory arbitration."

In defining arbitration, it has been common in the law reports for judges to expand upon its general outline as set out above and to refer to it as a *substitute for litigation in the courts.* Thus:

> Arbitration is the submission of some disputed matter to selected persons, and the substitution of their decision or award for the judgment of the established tribunals of justice.

Again:

> Broadly speaking, arbitration is a contractual proceeding, whereby the parties to any controversy or dispute, in order to obtain an inexpensive and speedy final disposition of the matter involved, select judges of their own choice and by consent submit their controversy to such judges for determination, in place of the tribunals provided by the ordinary processes of law.

Similarly, "an arbitration is a substitute for proceedings in court";
also,

> An agreement to arbitrate is really an agreement between parties who are in controversy, or look forward to the possibility of being in one, to substitute a tribunal other than the courts of the land to determine their rights.

The New York Court of Appeals has carried the idea that arbitration is a *substitute* for litigation to the point of ruling that arbitration under the arbitration statute should be *limited*

---

*Abridged from 35 N.Y.U.L. REV. 1031 (1960). Reprinted with permission.

to "justiciable" controversies. It has been ruled from time to time that the parties' controversy must qualify more or less for litigation in the courts or it cannot be arbitrated under the statute. Said the court on one of these occasions:

> Arbitrators under the Arbitration Law deal with the same kinds of controversies that are dealt with by the courts ... The arbitration statute now in force is confined to controversies that are justiciable under the law as it exists today.[1]

It should be noted, if not emphasized, that in the foregoing identification of arbitration as a substitute for litigation, the substitute (arbitration) bears little resemblance to the litigation process. This is true, because the arbitral proceeding can be initiated and carried out without traditional pleadings. Accordingly, the validity and effect of such pleadings do not become of concern. Moreover, it is generally for the arbitrator to determine finally whether to receive or reject testimony or other evidence—subject to required deference for the parties' right of hearing. Traditional presumptions and burdens of proof of the law of pleading and of the law of evidence do not govern. Unless the parties require otherwise, the arbitrator generally may disregard (or estimate and follow) what might be the law of the case were it to be established in litigation; and distinctions between "issues of fact" and "issues of law" as conceived in the law of civil procedure have no comparable role in arbitration. In short, unless the parties require otherwise in the given case, arbitration displaces all significant aspects of civil litigation except the right of hearing as indicated above.

In contrast to the foregoing identification of arbitration as a *substitute* for litigation is a less prevalent identification whereby arbitration is advanced as a *part* of litigation. This has not proved reliable or helpful. A group of cases in the federal courts, involving the appealability to the court of appeals of orders by the district court under the United States Arbitration Act should be noted in this connection. Whether or not the actual decisions on appealability might plausibly be sustained on another rationale is not considered here. The identification of arbitration as an accessory to litigation is the point of present concern.

In Schoenamsgruber v. Hamburg-American Line[2] the Supreme Court, in an action in admiralty, ruled out the appealability of orders to proceed with arbitration and to stay trial pending arbitration entered by a district court under the United States Arbitration Act. The Court held that these orders of a district court were not "final"; nor were they "interlocutory injunctions" so as to qualify for appeal under pertinent statutes. In the course of its opinion the Supreme Court took the position that:

> The orders appealed from merely stay action in the court pending arbitration and filing of the award ... And plainly, so far as concerns appealability, *they are not to be distinguished from an order postponing trial of an action at law to await the report of an auditor.*

There is, however, no such reporting back by the arbitrator to the court as in the case of an auditor; and the course of the proceedings and the making of the award of the arbitrator are free from legal prescriptions governing reference to an auditor. Indeed any similarity of the situations seems to lie at best in the formal structure of the order of stay.

In Murray Oil Products Co. v. Mitsui & Co.,[3] Judge Learned Hand, dealing with a stay of trial pending arbitration under Section 3 of the United States Arbitration Act (on matters other than appealability of the order of stay of trial), went the foregoing opinion of the Supreme Court one better in making arbitration a function of the pending litigation. "Arbitration," he said, "is merely a form of *trial*, to be adopted in the action itself, in place of the *trial* at common law: it is like a reference to a master, or an '*advisory trial*' under Federal Rules of Civil Procedure, Rule 39(c), 28 U.S.C.A. following section 723c. That is the whole effect of § 3." This view was subsequently endorsed by the same court in 1953 in Stathatos v. Arnold Bernstein S.S. Corp.[4]

---

1. Matter of Buffalo & Erie Ry., 250 N.Y. 275, 279, 165 N.E. 291, 292 (1929). [This has been changed by statute. Ed.]

2. 294 U.S. 454 (1935).

---

3. 146 F.2d 381, 383 (2d Cir. 1944). (Emphasis added.)

4. 202 F.2d 525 (2d Cir. 1953). See also Bernhardt v. Polygraphic Co. of America, 218 F.2d 948 (2d Cir. 1955), rev'd, 350 U.S. 198 (1956). Similarly, in an earlier case, Hyman v. Pottberg's Ex'rs, 101 F.2d 262 (2d Cir. 1939), Judge Learned Hand had generalized that "however informal, an arbitration *is a kind of trial*, and the arbitrators do not ordinarily take sides." Id. at 265. (Emphasis added.) Again, Nolan, P. J., dissenting in Madawick Contracting Co. v. Travelers Ins. Co., 281 App. Div. 754, 118 N.Y.S.2d 115 (2d Dep't 1953) (mem.), rev'd, 307 N.Y. 111, 120 N.E.2d 520 (1954), urged that "A hearing before arbitrators, although informal, is nevertheless a trial." Id. at 756, 118 N.Y.S.2d at 118.

On the other hand, in Wilko v. Swan, 346 U.S. 427, reversing 201 F.2d 439 (2d Cir. 1953), respondent's argument that arbitration "is merely a form of trial to be used in lieu of a trial of law" failed him on the issues resolved by the majority in that case. Compare Frankfurter, J., dissenting, 346 U.S. at 439.

No authorities have been observed translating "a trial" into "an arbitration."

In 1956 we appear to have come to an end of this analogizing based on such remote resemblances—at least for the courts of the United States. In that year in Bernhardt v. Polygraphic Co. of America,[5] Justice Douglas, speaking for the Court, expressly disagreed with the foregoing rationale as set out in the Murray Oil Products case. And in the following year, in Goodall-Sanford, Inc. v. United Textile Workers,[6] Justice Douglas, for the majority of the Court, took occasion, after expressly passing over the Schoenamsgruber case,[7] to make the point that:

> Arbitration is not merely a step in judicial enforcement of a claim nor auxiliary to a main proceeding, but the full relief sought. A decree . . . ordering enforcement of an arbitration provision in a collective bargaining agreement is, therefore, a "final decision" [thereby qualifying for appeal] within the meaning of 28 U.S.C. § 1291.[8]

The differentiation of submissions to arbitration from submissions to "auditors," "masters," "referees" or the like long predated the novel analogies indulged in in the foregoing opinions in the Schoenamsgruber and Murray Oil Products cases. The distinction generally had come about in situations wherein the parties had started out in litigation but had come to agree upon the submission of their controversy to arbitration before the action or suit was concluded. Such submission of pending actions or suits to arbitration was generally recognized for its difference from reference of such causes to "auditors," "masters" or "referees." Thus, the Court of Appeals of Maryland commented upon such submissions to arbitration as follows:

> We think further, that the arbitrators were not bound to have stated in detail the grounds upon which they came to the conclusion, that nothing was due to the appellant. It was not their duty to perform the office of auditor or master in Chancery, and report facts for the decision of the Court; but to state the result of their examination, which according to the express terms of the submission, was to be final. Kyd on Awards, 345; where the distinction is taken between the duty of a master and that of an arbitrator, the latter is instituted judge of the facts without appeal; the former is only a minister to prepare something for the Court, which is really the judge; and when by agreement of the parties, the award of the referees is to be final, their power seems to be more of a judicial than a ministerial character.[9]

In line with the foregoing view disassociating arbitration from litigation, arbitration has generally been set apart from an "action," "suit" or "other proceeding" as well.[10] To identify arbitration as an "action," "suit" or "other proceeding" seems as unreliable as to identify it as any part of a litigation for any purpose. There being no court, pleadings or rules of civil procedure to govern and there being little constraint by the law of evidence or by what might be the substantive law of the cause were it in litigation, unless the parties agree otherwise, it is difficult to catch any substantial resemblance between arbitration and an "action," "suit" or "other proceeding."

---

5. 350 U.S. 198, 202 (1956).

6. 353 U.S. 550 (1957).

7. Id. at 551. See also Baltimore Contractors, Inc. v. Bodinger, 348 U.S. 176 (1955); In re Pahlberg, 131 F.2d 968 (2d Cir. 1942).

8. 353 U.S. at 551–52. The Supreme Court of Louisiana voiced like views in Housing Authority v. Henry Ericsson Co., 197 La. 732, 2 So. 2d 195 (1941), with respect to arbitration under the Louisiana arbitration statute, even though the given arbitration agreement provided that "The procedure and rules of evidence applicable to proceedings in the courts of the State of Louisiana shall apply to the proceedings of arbitration." Id. at 743, 2 So. 2d at 198. See also Snyder v. Superior Court, 24 Cal. App. 2d 263, 74 P.2d 782 (1937); In re Curtis and Castle Arbitration, 64 Conn. 501, 30 Atl. 769 (1894); Alderman v. Alderman, 296 S.W.2d 312 (Tex. Civ. App. 1956).

Holding that an order under the United States Arbitration Act appointing arbitrators was "final" and appealable, Judge Learned Hand had declared in Krauss Bros. Lumber Co. v. Louis Bossert & Sons, 62 F.2d 1004, 1005 (2d Cir. 1933), that: "The purpose of arbitration is essentially an escape from judicial trial . . . So far as the arbitration proceeding itself is concerned, the last deliberative action of the court is the appointment of the arbitrators, who thereupon take over the controversy and dispose of it." And in American Almond Prods. Co. v. Consolidated Pecan Sales Co., 144 F.2d 448, 451 (2d Cir. 1944), he generalized that "Arbitration may or may not be a desirable substitute for trials in courts; as to that the parties must decide in each instance. But when they have adopted it, they must be content with its informalities. . . . They must content themselves with looser approximations to the enforcement of their rights than those that the law accords them, when they resort to its machinery." To like effect, Dowling, J., in Matter of Interocean Mercantile Corp., 204 App. Div. 284, 197 N.Y. Supp. 706 (1st Dep't), aff'd mem., 236 N.Y. 587, 142 N.E. 295 (1923).

9. Caton v. MacTavish, 10 Gill & J. 192, 217 (Md. 1838). To like effect, see In re Curtis and Castle Arbitration, 64 Conn. 501, 30 Atl. 769 (1894); Gibson v. Burrows, 41 Mich. 713, 3 N.W. 200 (1879); Underwood v. McDuffee, 15 Mich. 361 (1867); Carpenter v. Bloomer, 54 N.J. Super. 157, 148 A.2d 497 (App. Div. 1959); Keener v. Goodson, 89 N.C. 273 (1883); Bollmann v. Bollmann, 6 S.C. 29 (1874); Boomer Coal & Coke Co. v. Osenton, 101 W. Va. 683, 133 S.E. 381 (1926).

10. N.Y. Civ. Prac. Act § 1459 declare[d] that the "arbitration of a controversy" under the statute "shall be deemed a special proceeding." This identification does not seem to pose arbitration as being more closely akin to litigation than otherwise. The utility or function of the provision is not clear; it is sometimes cited to court proceedings relating to the award—not to the arbitration. See Matter of Arbitration between Morris White Fashions, Inc. and Susquehanna Mills, Inc., 295 N.Y. 450, 68 N.E.2d 437 (1946) (special proceeding determined by court review of award). See also Accito v. Matmor Canning Co., 128 Cal. App. 2d 631, 276 P.2d 34 (1954).

Judicial refusal to include arbitration within these categories of litigation appears in various contexts in most of the American cases. Thus, an arbitration under the Alabama statute and proceedings thereunder to obtain entry of judgment on the award did not constitute a suit subject to an "act to regulate judicial proceedings." Arbitration, said the Alabama Supreme Court, "is a proceeding before triers chosen by the parties themselves. It is not an action commenced in any court, in which there may be an appearance term, a pleading term and a judgment term."[11] Similar ruling was made with respect to an arbitration and award under an arbitration statute which fashioned the arbitration after an amicable action. This statute was like some others of the older type under which the parties filed their submission agreement in a court and thereby invoked its jurisdiction to facilitate the arbitration, confirm the award and enter judgment or to vacate, modify or correct the award. The court held that neither a foreign corporation's participation in bringing on the arbitration nor its initiation of the proceedings in court to confirm the award and have judgment entered offended a statute providing that a foreign corporation without a license to do business in the state could not "maintain any suit or action, either legal or equitable, in any of the courts of this state, upon any demand." Said the Texas court:

It is our view that the court referred to in the statute from which foreign corporations were excluded is a court exercising judicial powers through officials selected to preside over established tribunals of justice, and before a court which can force a litigant to come for the adjudication of his rights. It does not mean a board or [sic] arbitration, created by agreement of the parties. . . . If the parties make an agreement to settle their dispute out of court, arising out of a legal contract, courts of this state will not interfere, especially when they follow a method conferred on them by the Legislature. We do not think a trial before arbitrators is a "suit of action" within the meaning of article 1318.[12]

It remains to take account of Madawick Contracting Co. v. Travelers Insurance Co., as decided by the New York Court of Appeals in 1954.[13] It involved an action for a declaratory judgment to determine whether or not the defendant insurer was required, under the terms of its policy, to defend the insured-plaintiff in an arbitration and pay any award that might be rendered against plaintiff. The plaintiff, a subcontractor, undertook in the subcontract to indemnify the general contractor against loss and expense incurred by reason of liability imposed on him by law for damages caused by or arising out of plaintiff's work in carrying out the subcontract, and further to provide various forms of liability insurance. The subcontract also included a general arbitration provision.

Pursuant to the subcontract, plaintiff procured the required indemnity insurance from defendant, Travelers Insurance Company. The insurer was advised of the foregoing provisions of the subcontract when it issued its policy to plaintiff. Furthermore, the insurer's representatives had read the contract before issuing the policy, under which the insurer undertook "to pay on behalf of the insured all sums which the insured shall become obligated to pay" under the subcontract, and also to "defend . . . any suit against the insured" seeking damages under the subcontract; but "no action shall lie against the company [insurer] . . . until the amount of the insured's obligation to pay shall have been finally determined either by judgment against the insured after actual trial or by written agreement of the insured, the claimant, and the company."

The general contractor made claim for property damages against the plaintiff, subcontractor under the subcontract, and demanded arbitration. Plaintiff called upon the insurer to defend in the arbitration; insurer refused, replying that it could not consent to the proposed arbitration, nor defend the insured in the arbitration proceeding nor be bound by the result of the arbitration, as it did not regard an arbitration proceeding as a suit against the insured within the meaning of the policy or an adverse finding

---

11. Crook v. Chambers, 40 Ala. 239, 243 (1866), enforcement of award enjoined, 42 Ala. 171 (1868). To like effect, Son Shipping Co. v. De Fosse & Tanghe, 199 F.2d 687 (2d Cir. 1952). See also The Ciano, 58 F. Supp. 65 (E.D. Pa. 1944); Matter of Arbitration between Republique Francaise and Cellosilk Mfg. Co., 124 N.Y.S.2d 93 (Sup. Ct. 1953), rev'd, 284 App. Div. 699, 134 N.Y.S.2d 470 (1st Dep't 1954), rev'd, 309 N.Y. 269, 128 N.E.2d 750 (1955).

In Weston v. City Council, 27 U.S. (2 Pet.) 448 (1829), Chief Justice Marshall voiced a definition of a civil "suit" which frequently has been quoted or paraphrased in whole or in part with approval. (The case involved an inquiry whether or not a writ of prohibition constituted a "suit" for the purpose at hand.) "The term," said the Chief Justice, "is certainly a very comprehensive one, and is understood to apply to any proceeding in a court of justice, by which an individual pursues that remedy in a court of justice which the law affords him. The modes of proceeding may be various, but if a right is litigated between parties in a court of justice, the proceeding by which the decision of the court is sought is a suit." Id. at 464.

12. Temple v. Riverland Co., 228 S.W. 605, 609 (Tex. Civ. App. 1921); see Everett v. Brown, 120 Misc. 349, 198 N.Y. Supp. 462 (Sup. Ct. 1923).

13. 307 N.Y. 111, 120 N.E.2d 520 (1954), reversing 281 App. Div. 754, 118 N.Y.S. 2d 115 (2d Dep't 1953) (mem.). The case, as decided in the appellate division, is noted in 27 St. John's L. Rev. 350 (1953).

as liability imposed by law. The New York Court of Appeals held that the insurer was obligated to defend plaintiff in the arbitration and to pay the amount of any award against plaintiff.

The court of appeals gave its attention chiefly to the point whether or not an arbitration should be held to constitute, under the terms of the policy, "any suit" which insurer had agreed to defend in the insured's name and behalf on the condition that no action should be brought on the policy until the amount of the insured's obligation to pay had been finally determined "by judgment against the insured after actual trial" or by compromise settlement.

The court translated the arbitration into "trial" and "judgment" as follows:

Here, by issuing an insurance policy to implement a construction contract which shows on its face that liability under the policy may result only through an award in arbitration proceedings, unless the adverse party elects to waive arbitration, the carrier is deemed to have meant the word "trial" as used in this policy to include arbitration proceedings, and to have intended that "judgment" shall include such judgments as are entered upon confirmation of arbitration awards pursuant to section 1464 of the Civil Practice Act, which by section 1466 are given the same force and effect after entry as a "judgment in an action."

The court came to this conclusion relying chiefly, it seems, upon the fundamental rule in the construction of all agreements, namely, ascertaining that mythical abstraction (used even when the parties are in dispute over the matter), "the substantial intent of the parties."

It is thought that a more plausible rationale for the result reached would involve (1) discarding translation of the arbitration into "any suit," "trial" and "judgment" as used in the policy, and (2) recognizing the insurer's policy as having been issued to cover the insured's stated obligations arising under the subcontract—including the arbitration provision therein—thereby making the insurer a party to the arbitration provision and subject to the rights and obligations relating thereto as provided in the arbitration statute.

The court of appeals was convinced that the insurer became a party to the arbitration provision in the subcontract, for

when an insurance company contracts to indemnify under such circumstances as to protect the insured against a particular liability imposed upon it by a construction contract, the insurer should be construed to have promised to do so in accordance with the requirements, terms and conditions of the agreement.

Accordingly, the proper and adequate remedy

of the insured in this case would have been, it seems, to have made application under the arbitration statute against the insurer for an order to proceed with arbitration.[14] Fit accompaniment would be a reading of the arbitration and award out of "any suit," "trial" and "judgment" as written in the policy.

In several cases the judiciary has considered whether or not the holding of arbitral hearings and the making of awards, or either, constitutes the carrying on of "judicial business" or "judicial proceedings" or the doing of "judicial acts" in violation of the Sunday laws. Here again the "judicializing" of arbitration has not been very persuasive in resolving the issue at hand. The general question has not been extensively litigated in recent times.

Sometimes arbitration is cited as being a "quasi-judicial tribunal" and arbitrators as being "judges" of the parties' choosing, "judicial officers" or officers exercising "judicial functions." Here, again, the presentation of arbitration or arbitrators in the role of courts or judiciary is necessarily based upon remote resemblances. "Quasi-judicial tribunal" and the other foregoing terms are not very meaningful. Opinions designating the courts or the judiciary as "quasi-arbitral tribunals" or the judiciary or jury as "arbitrators," or the like, have not been observed. It is true that as judges and juries hear and decide litigated matters, so do arbitrators hear and decide matters submitted to them by parties. But here the resemblance ends. Arbitrators, as distinguished from judges, are not appointed by the sovereign, are not paid by it, nor are they sworn to any allegiance. Arbitrators exercise no constitutional jurisdiction or like role in the judicial systems—state or national. As already indicated, they are generally not bound to follow the law unless the parties so prescribe and, as likely as not, they are laymen technically unqualified (and not disposed) to exercise the office of the professional judge.

As pointed out above, the Supreme Court of Alabama excluded arbitration from an "act to regulate judicial proceedings." That court also has ruled that arbitrators were not subject to a statute disqualifying "judge, chancellor, county commissioner or justice of the peace" from sitting in any cause or proceeding in which he was "related to either party within the fourth degree of consanguinity or affinity." Said the court in this connection:

Parties may be drawn against their consent before judges, chancellors, county commissioners and jus-

---

14. N.Y. Civ. Prac. Act § 1450.

tices of the peace; and usually they have little or no choice in the matter. These are officers appointed by the law, and suitors must submit to their orders. Arbitration, in this State, is never compulsory. Parties voluntarily elect this mode of adjustment, and appoint their own arbitrators. We know no reason why persons related to suitors within the fourth degree, may not, if chosen, act as arbitrators, and make a binding award. *Volenti non fit injuria.*[15]

In 1931, the New York Appellate Division summarized the disassociation of arbitrations, awards and arbitrators from judicial proceedings, judgments and the judiciary in refusing to grant an order of prohibition against a common law arbitration. Without reference to the earlier New York opinions on the applicability of the Sunday laws ... to arbitrations and awards, the court observed:

---

15. Davis v. Forshee, 34 Ala. 107, 109 (1859). Similarly, see Fisher v. Towner, 14 Conn. 26 (1840); White Eagle Laundry Co. v. Slawek, 296 Ill. 240, 129 N.E. 753 (1921); Underwood v. McDuffee, 15 Mich. 361 (1867). Compare Gallagher v. Kern, 31 Mich. 138 (1875).

This was an attempted common-law arbitration which is a contractual, not a judicial proceeding, and, if properly conducted, results, not in a judgment, but in a cause of action against the party who does not obey the award. The arbitrators do not constitute a judicial or quasi-judicial body whose proceedings are the subject of an order of prohibition.

The process of making judges of arbitrators and judicial proceedings of arbitrations seems to be at its best, when used *arguendo* to reaffirm the parties' right of hearing in arbitrations, to raise the finality and conclusiveness of awards to those of "a judgment" or to lend stature to some set of facts being made up in a given case as cause for disqualification of the arbitrator, as for insufficient "honesty" or "impartiality," undue "bias" or "misconduct."

As further litigation centers upon arbitrations and awards, so may the usages of analogy, metaphor and the making of classifications in the course of the judicial process confound and complicate the role of the arbitral process as presently conceived in legal tradition.

CHAPTER II

THE COMMON LAW

A.

Revocability of Agreements to Arbitrate

DEVELOPMENT OF COMMERCIAL ARBITRATION LAW*

PAUL L. SAYRE

At common law the authority of the arbitrator was based upon the submission, and since this was purely a private contract in any case, such submission could be revoked like powers generally, unless there was a public policy against it which took it out of the general rule of powers not coupled with an interest. [The rule is that a power must be coupled with the interest of the grantee of the power to be irrevocable.] Early common law arbitration did not regard the proceedings as a form of trial nor as a means of avoiding trial through negotiators who were the agents of the parties. It regarded arbitration as a partial substitute for trial secured through the formal grant of a power to arbitrators in the submission. The arbitrators could act only as long as their power remained unrevoked and their award, if made, was enforced by common law actions only. We must now consider whether submission to arbitration by private contract under a power to arbitrate delegated by the several parties was regarded at common law as such a delegation of authority as should be revocable, or whether it was considered as an exception to the general rule. Vynior's Case has usually been considered as the controlling authority which decided that submission to arbitration was revocable.

What, then, is the *ratio decidendi* of Vynior's Case? Few principles of the modern law have continued without change for three hundred years; yet we are told that Vynior's Case has such extraordinary vitality that its doctrine alone has limited the development of arbitration in commercial disputes in all common law countries. Are we to conclude that no one can fairly defend the case upon its merits except perhaps the old Scotchwoman who defended the devil himself on the ground that "Ye canna denie he is vurra persistent"? The pleadings are simple.

*Abridged from 37 YALE L. J. 595 (1928). Reprinted by permission of the Yale Law Journal Company and Fred B. Rothman & Company.

Robert Vynior brought an action against William Wilde on a bond for a hundred pounds and demanded twenty pounds' damages in addition for violation of the bond. The bond had been given by the defendant to insure his complying with an arbitration agreement which was made to cover disputes between him and plaintiff regarding the amount due for certain repair work on buildings. The defendant pleaded no award and the plaintiff rejoined that the defendant had revoked his authority to submit the matter to arbitration. The plaintiff set forth that such revocation was a violation of the defendant's agreement to "stand to and abide the award." To this the defendant demurred, and the court gave judgment for the plaintiff to recover both his bond and his alleged damages, setting forth three grounds for the decision.

The first ground is that,

> although William Wilde, the defendant, was bound in a bond to stand to, abide, observe, etc., the rule, etc., of arbitration, etc., yet he might countermand it, for one cannot by his act make such authority, power or warrant not countermandable which is by the law or of its own nature countermandable.[1]

Coke explains, where there is a suit on a bond given for a submission to arbitration, the submission is revocable, although the bond is forfeited, because, while a party has the power to revoke, he has broken the condition of his bond by such revocation. Coke points out that although the submission finds its authority in the very bond upon which the plaintiff is suing, nevertheless the defendant may revoke the submission in the bond and still be liable on the bond for such revocation. It is quite true that the recovery on the bond in this case does not prove that the submission itself was revocable, since there could be a recovery on the bond even though the defendant had neither the right under the contract nor the legal power to revoke his submission. Thus the case itself is a decision merely on the liability on the bond, and the opinion of the court to the effect that the submission is revocable is not necessary to the decision.

In modern times, Vynior's Case has generally been regarded as the original and controlling authority for revocability. This is unfortunate, since, as we have seen, the decision covers only recovery on the bond. This error has perhaps had no serious effects, since Coke's dictum that submission to arbitration was revocable correctly represents the common law at that time (1609).

There have been many charges that the courts took an unfriendly view toward arbitration, inasmuch as they upheld the revocability of submission. It is submitted that the earliest cases show no unfriendliness nor any will to preclude the fullest use of arbitration. In Vynior's Case itself there was recovery in the sum of 100 pounds with 20 pounds' damages on the bond. This was a large sum in those days and probably was much in excess of any fair recovery on the cause of action itself. It is surely absurd to say that the courts precluded the efficacy of submission to arbitration by admitting its technical revocability at a time when bonds were enforceable in their face value regardless of actual damages. It was the usual rule at the time of Vynior's Case to make the submission upon a bond, and suit upon the bond in a large sum was amply sufficient to insure arbitration. It seems clear, therefore, that the doctrine of revocability was a sound doctrine of powers in private contract and that the court's recognition of the doctrine did not indicate any unfriendliness toward arbitration. It is to be remembered further that at the time of Vynior's Case the entire law of contract was in its infancy and no such general rights of recovery upon promises as obtain today were then to be had. The almost invariable practice was to insure performance of any agreement through putting the obligee under bond. Then if he failed to perform, you had a straight suit upon the bond, which was made sufficiently large to protect you fully. When the courts allowed recovery on the bond they had done all that in practice was reasonably needed to make arbitration effective. It seems clear that if in fact the courts were jealous of their jurisdiction or were suspicious of arbitration, or for any other ulterior motive wished to prevent its efficacy, they would have declared directly that such agreements were against public policy and held any bond made as security for the performance of such an agreement a nullity. It was of course perfectly possible for the court to do this where it felt that the object of the bond was immoral or illegal or for any other reason was not to be countenanced by the law.

In modern times the doctrine of revocability is most generally based upon the principle that the courts cannot approve irrevocability, since it "ousts the jurisdiction of the court." Even to the present day this is so, and the old doctrine upon which Vynior's Case rested—namely, that of delegated powers—has been ignored. In fact, this theory of ousting the jurisdiction of the court is not referred to in any of the early cases and certainly has no conscious bearing upon Vynior's Case. The doctrine appears in Kill v.

---

1. 8 Co. 81b, 82a.

Hollister[2] for the first time without the citation of any authority.[3] Once asserted in that case, however, it is constantly quoted in subsequent cases. It is submitted that the introduction of this new doctrine into the law, based neither on court decisions nor on statute, is explained by the passing of the Statute of Fines and Penalties in (1687) 8 & 9 William III. This statute precluded the recovery of the face value of bonds where they had become single unless the actual damages justified it.* Under this statute and subsequent developments through the cases it has become the settled doctrine of the law that the court will look behind the sum stated in the bond, and while one may still sue on the bond and the obligor is liable up to the full amount of it, the court will not require him to pay in the particular case more than the estimated actual damages which the plaintiff has suffered. In view of this change in the law, it was no longer possible for parties to insure submission to arbitration. The courts in fact held that they would give only nominal damages on the theory that there could be no actual injury in forcing people to litigate in the King's own courts of justice. Litigation in the King's courts was assumed to be a high privilege and great advantage; and to recover damages because one had to try his case there was a little more than the courts could understand. Regardless of whether a rule of merely nominal damages is inherently fair or not, it is certain that any damages from such a breach of contract must be exceedingly speculative and that the plaintiff would have great difficulty in showing damages of any consequence. Hence, when plaintiffs came into court to enforce a submission to arbitration, they could no longer sue on their bond effectively, and it was felt that some added reason must be given to maintain the doctrine of revocability, since it could no longer be avoided by the use of the bonds. It seems that this is the origin of the doctrine of ousting the courts of their jurisdiction, and this doctrine should be attributed to the protection of the rights of the parties to the submission rather than to any unseemly cavilling by the courts themselves.

The courts' decision had not changed. They had held the submission revocable before and they continued to hold it so. The difference was that the legislature had so changed the law relating to bonds that the method of using a bond in submission was no longer effective. Nor had the situation so changed that the court could logically change the doctrine. It was still true that there was no developed system regulating arbitration tribunals as there is now in all countries. Hence the court had no further reason for making a power in the private law irrevocable when it was revocable before. As a matter of common law, the submission was based on a power which the grantor could revoke. The courts had no right to change this rule so long as arbitration proceedings were not regulated and the parties' only effective protection against an unfair or insufficient hearing by the arbitrators was in revoking the submission before the award was given. Common law arbitration was a system whose parts were highly interdependent. Many of the doctrines were strictly interpreted and exceedingly precise in their application. The statute of fines and penalties destroyed the working of the whole scheme. Quite reasonably it made some of the component rules seem ridiculous when used separately and in new relationships.

We note that parliament recognized its responsibility in destroying common law arbitration, since the year after the Statute of Fines and Penalties it passed the first arbitration act, (1698) 9 William III, c. 15. This statute did not provide for court review on questions of law. It aimed to make the submission irrevocable by making it a rule of court and providing that one who revoked would be subject to punishment for contempt of court. Even within these narrow limits the act could not be used extensively, since the submission was still revocable until a rule of court enforcing it had been obtained. It is significant to note in the first act, as in all subsequent arbitration acts in England, that no distinction is made between the submission of an existing dispute and any future dispute that may arise under a given contract. Both were

---

2. 1 Wils. 129 (1746). Kill v. Hollister involved a contract to submit future disputes to arbitration and it has sometimes been said that the doctrine of "ousting the courts of their jurisdiction" is incidental to contracts for the arbitration of future disputes rather than existing ones. It does not seem, however, that anything turns on this. Surely the courts are ousted of their jurisdiction in the sense intended by the use of this phrase whether the agreement be for existing or future disputes. It is merely a new phrase used in Kill v. Hollister in defense of the general doctrine of revocability where one elects to submit his dispute to some tribunal other than the regular courts when he has a common law right to the protection of the law.

3. Of course this doctrine of ousting the jurisdiction of the courts originated, not in any arbitration case, but in Coke's treatise upon Littleton where we find a comment under "waste."

*[The statute apparently was directed against "penal bonds" in general use prior to passage of the act. Overreaching by lenders and the imprudence of borrowers led to "oppressive exactions." McCORMICK, DAMAGES 600–603 (1935). A diligent search reveals no evidence that the use of the bond to enforce promises to arbitrate played any part in provoking the legislation.]

held to be proper subjects for arbitration at common law and both were assumed to be subject to all the English arbitration acts. This distinction thus appears only in American statutes. We must recognize further that the act of 1698 did not enable the parties to compel testimony or secure witnesses in the arbitration proceedings, nor did it have any other provisions aiming to secure a fair and adequate hearing. If the reader should ask here why it was that the courts recognized arbitration when made a rule of court under this statute even though the rights of the parties were not protected in the proceedings, although they did not hold a submission irrevocable where similarly at common law there was no security for a fair hearing, the answer is two fold. First, the statute of 1698 did give at least remedial protection to the parties, since the arbitration award was an order of court and would not be enforced if it involved fraud or did not conform to the terms in the submission. Second, we must remember that this first inadequate provision for arbitration by statute was the act of the legislature and not of the courts. Consequently, when submission had been made an order of court in strict compliance with the statute, the courts enforced it as they were bound to do, but where the submission did not come strictly within the terms of the statute the courts held it revocable in keeping with the common law rule, since there continued to be no protection for the rights of the parties at the hearings, and the courts consequently had no reason to change the common law rule that they had always upheld.

In 1833 the statute of (1698) 9 William III, c. 15 was extended and reinforced by the statute of 3 & 4 William IV, c. 42, which provided that any arbitration agreement which had been made a rule of court,

> in any action now brought or which shall be hereafter brought by or in pursuance of any submission to reference containing an agreement that such submission shall be made a rule of any of His Majesty's Courts of Record, shall not be revocable by any party to such reference without leave of court.

Thus, until action was brought in connection with an arbitration proceeding, it was still revocable, and the doctrine of common law revocability persisted. Its greatest improvement, however, was a provision by which the parties had compulsory legal process to compel the attendance of witnesses and the production of evidence at arbitration hearings. Thus the rights of the parties at the hearings were protected and the basis of a fair hearing for arbitration purposes was secured. With this protection there

would seem to be no objection to making the submission irrevocable, even on the original common law theory.

In 1854 came the Common Law Procedure Act, and section 17 of this act dealt with arbitration; but this too was insufficient to cover the usual case of voluntary submission in which the parties had not agreed that it might be made a rule of court. The previous arbitration act of 1833 applied only to cases where the arbitrator or umpire had been appointed, that is to say, where there had been a submission under an agreement that the submission might be made a rule of court. Section 7 of the act of 1854 provided further:

> Every agreement of submission to arbitration by consent whether by deed or instrument in writing not under seal may be made a rule of any one of the superior courts of law or equity at Westminster on the application of any party thereto unless such agreement or submission contain words purporting that the parties intend that it should not be made a rule of court.

This act made it possible for either party to make a submission irrevocable by applying to the court to make it a rule of court. The regular case of a private agreement to arbitrate without such application to a court was not yet covered, however.

The statutory relief for arbitration in England was completed by the statute of 1889, the first two sections of which made the following broad provisions:

> 1. A submission, unless a contrary intention is expressed therein, shall be irrevocable, except by leave of the Court or a judge, and shall have the same effect in all respects as if it had been made an order of court.
> 2. A submission, unless a contrary intention is expressed therein, shall be deemed to include the provisions set forth in the First Schedule to this Act, so far as they are applicable to the reference under the submission.[4]

Thus at the present time nearly all agreements for arbitration come within the terms of the statute.* The statute of 1889 was the first to provide for adequate court review of questions of law raised in the arbitration hearing itself, with the result that after that act statutory arbitration in England meant that the arbitrators could have final disposition on questions of fact only.

---

4. (1889) 52 & 53 Vict. c. 49, §§ 1, 2.

*[There has been subsequent English legislation.]

TOBEY v. COUNTY OF BRISTOL
(Cir. Ct. D. Mass. 1845)
[23 Fed. Cas. page 1313]

STORY, J. No one can be found, as I believe, and at all events, no case has been cited by counsel, or has fallen within the scope of my researches, in which an agreement to refer a claim to arbitration, has ever been specifically enforced in equity. So far as the authorities go, they are altogether the other way. The cases are divided into two classes. One, where an agreement to refer to arbitration has been set up as a defence to a suit at law, as well as in equity; the other, where the party as plaintiff has sought to enforce such an agreement in a court of equity. Both classes have shared the same fate. The courts have refused to allow the former as a bar or defence against the suit; and have declined to enforce the latter as ill-founded in point of jurisdiction.

It was suggested at the argument, that the ground upon which this doctrine of courts of equity is founded, is not solid or satisfactory. If this were admitted to be true, I do not know that any judge would now deem it correct or safe to depart from it, as he must content himself upon this, as many other occasions, to administer the established law, and walk in the footsteps of his predecessors, super antiquas vias. But, in truth, I do not well see, that the doctrine could have been otherwise settled. The two general grounds on which it rests belong to other branches of equity jurisprudence as well as this. What are they? The first ground is, that a court of equity ought not to compel a party to submit the decision of his rights to a tribunal, which confessedly, does not possess full, adequate, and complete means, within itself, to investigate the merits of the case, and to administer justice. The common tribunals of the country do possess these means; and although a party may have entered into an agreement to submit his rights to arbitration, this furnishes no reason for a court of equity to deprive him of the right to withdraw from such agreement, and thus to take from him the *locus penitentiae*; and to declare that the common tribunals of the country shall be closed against him, and he shall be compelled to submit all his rights and interests to the decision of another tribunal, however defective or imperfect it may be, to administer entire justice. The argument at the bar misconceived the doctrine of the court on this head. Courts of equity do not refuse to interfere to compel a party specifically to perform an agreement to refer to arbitration, because they wish to discourage arbitrations, as against public policy. On the contrary, they have and can have no just objection to these domestic forums and will enforce, and promptly interfere to enforce their awards when fairly and lawfully made, without hesitation or question. But when they are asked to proceed farther and to compel the parties to appoint arbitrators whose award shall be final, they necessarily pause to consider, whether such tribunals possess adequate means of giving redress, and whether they have a right to compel a reluctant party to submit to such a tribunal, and to close against him the doors of the common courts of justice, provided by the government to protect rights and to redress wrongs. One of the established principles of courts of equity is not to entertain a bill for the specific performance of any agreement where it is doubtful whether it may not thereby become the instrument of injustice, or to deprive parties of rights which they are otherwise fairly entitled to have protected. The specific performance of an agreement is, by no means, a matter of right which a party has authority to demand from a court of equity. So far from this, it is a matter of sound discretion in the court, to be granted or withheld, according to its own view of the merits and circumstances of the particular case, and never amounts to a peremptory duty. Now we all know that arbitrators, at the common law, possess no authority whatsoever, even to administer an oath, or to compel the attendance of witnesses. They cannot compel the production of documents, and papers and books of account, or insist upon a discovery of facts from the parties under oath. They are not ordinarily well enough acquainted with the principles of law or equity to administer either effectually, in complicated cases; and hence it has often been said, that the judgment of arbitrators is but *rusticum judicium*. Ought then a court of equity to compel a resort to such a tribunal, by which, however honest and intelligent, it can in no case be clear that the real legal or equitable rights of the parties can be fully ascertained or perfectly protected?

It has been said at the bar, that in modern times, most nations, and especially commercial nations, not only favor arbitrations, but in many instances make them compulsive. But in considering this point, two circumstances are important to be kept in view. In the first place, whenever arbitrations are made compulsive, it is by legislative authority, which at the same time, arms the arbitrators with the fullest powers to ascertain the facts, to compel the attendance of witnesses, to require discovery of papers, books and accounts, and generally, also, to compel the parties to submit themselves to examination under oath. In the next place, these arbitrations are never, or at least not ordinarily, made compulsive to the extent of excluding the jurisdiction of the regular courts of justice; but are instituted as mere preliminaries to an appeal to those courts, from the award of the arbitrators, if either party desires it, so that the law, and in many cases, the facts also, if disputed are reexaminable there. So that, in many cases, it will be found, that protracted litigation and very onerous expenses often follow as necessary results of the system. Indeed, so far as the system of compulsive arbitrations has been tried in America, the experiment has not, as I understand, been such as to make any favorable impression upon the public mind, as to its utility or convenience. At all events, it cannot be correctly said, that public policy, in our age, generally favors or encourages arbitrations, which are to be final and conclusive, to an extent beyond that which belongs to the ordinary operations of the common law. It is certainly the policy of the common law, not to compel men to submit their rights and interests to arbitration, or to enforce agreements for such a purpose. Nay, the common law goes farther, and even if a submission has been made to arbitrators, who are named, by deed or otherwise, with an express stipulation, that the submission shall be irrevocable, it still is revocable and countermandable, by either party, before the award is actually made, although not afterwards. This was decided as long ago as in Vynior's Case, 8 Coke, 8lb. The reason there given, is that a man cannot, by his act, make such authority, power, or warrant not countermandable, which is by law, and of its own nature, countermandable; as if a man should, by express words, declare his testament to be irrevocable, yet he may revoke it, for his acts or words cannot alter the judgment of law, to make that irrevocable, which is of its own nature revocable. This doctrine has been constantly upheld down to the present day.

And this leads me to remark in the second place, that it is an established principle of courts of equity never to enforce the specific performance of any agreement, where it would be a vain and imperfect act, or where a specific performance is from the very nature and character of the agreement, impracticable or inequitable, to be enforced. 2 Story Eq. Jur. § 959a. How can a court of equity compel the respective parties to name arbitrators; and a fortiori, how can it compel the parties mutually to select arbitrators, since each much, [sic] in such a case, agree to all the arbitrators? If one party refuses to name an arbitrator, how is the court to compel him to name one? If an arbitrator is named by one

party, how is the court to ascertain, if the other party objects to him, whether he is right or wrong in his objection? If one party names an arbitrator, who will not act, how can the court compel him to select another? If one party names an arbitrator not agreed to by the other, how is the court to find out what are his reasons for refusing? If one party names an arbitrator whom the other deems incompetent, how is the court to decide upon the question of his competency? Take the present case, where the arbitrators are to be mutually selected, when and within what time are they to be appointed? How many shall they be—two, three, four, five, seven, ten, or even twenty? The resolve is silent as to the number. Can the court fix the number, if the parties do not agree upon it? That would be doing what has never yet been done. If either party should refuse to name any arbitrator, or to agree upon any named by the other side, has the court authority, of itself, to appoint arbitrators, or to substitute a master for them? That would be, as Sir John Leach said in Agar v. Macklen, 2 Sim. & S. 418, 423, to bind the parties contrary to their agreement; and in Milnes v. Gery, 14 Ves. 400, 408, Sir William Grant held such an appointment to be clearly beyond the authority of the court. In Wilks v. Davis, 3 Mer. 507, 509, Lord Eldon referring to the cases of Cooth v. Jackson, 6 Ves. 34; Milnes v. Gery, 14 Vest. 400, 408; and Blundell v. Brettargh, 17 Ves. 232,—said:

> It has been determined in the cases referred to, that if one party agrees to sell and another to purchase, at a price to be settled by arbitrators named by the parties, if no award has been made, the court cannot decree respecting it.

In Cooth v. Jackson, 6 Ves. 34, Lord Eldon said:

> I am not aware of a case even at law, nor that a court of equity has ever entertained this jurisdiction, that where a reference has been made to arbitration and the judgment of the arbitrators is not given in the time and manner according to the agreement, the court have substituted themselves for the arbitrators and made the award. I am not aware that it has been done even in a case where the substantial thing to be done is agreed between the parties, but the time and manner in which it is to be done, is that which they have put upon others to execute.

The same learned judge, in Blundell v. Brettargh, 17 Ves. 232, 242, affirmed the same statement, substituting only the word "prescribe" for "execute." So that we abundantly see, that the very impracticability of compelling the parties to name arbitrators, or upon their default, for the court to appoint them, constitutes, and must forever constitute, a complete bar to any attempt on the part of a court of equity to compel the specific performance of any agreement to refer to arbitration. It is essentially, in its very nature and character, an agreement which must rest in the good faith and honor of the parties, and like an agreement to paint a picture, or to carve a statue, or to write a book, or to invent patterns for prints, must be left to the conscience of the parties, or to such remedy in damages for the breach thereof, as the law has provided.

SCOTT v. AVERY
5 H. L. C. 811 [1855–56]

Action on three policies of insurance effected on the ship *Alexander,* valued at £2,400, in three assurance companies, of which both the Plaintiff and Defendant were members. It will be sufficient to refer to the first only. The declaration, after stating in the usual form the making of the policy, alleged that it was mutually agreed that all rules and regulations of the association should be binding on the assurers and assured, as if they were inserted in the policy and formed part thereof, and that the said rules and regulations, so far as they relate to the Plaintiff's claim, are as follows:

> That any member, who shall prove to the committee of the said association that his ship is lost . . . will be entitled (at the expiration of two months from the date of the first quarterly settlement) to part payment for the same, but in no case to exceed 80 per cent on the sum insured, until a final account of the proceeds of the sale of the materials is furnished to the underwriters. That the sum to be paid by this association to any suffering member for any loss or damage shall, in the first instance, be ascertained and settled by the committee; and the suffering member, if he agrees to accept such sum in full satisfaction of his claim, shall be entitled to demand and sue for the same as soon as the amount to be paid has been so ascertained and settled, but not before, which can only be claimed according to the customary mode of payment in use by the society.

[If the claimant and committee disagreed, the claim was to be arbitrated. The right to sue was conditioned upon acceptance of either the amount set by the committee or the arbitrators. The method of selecting the arbitrators was specified; it precluded either party from preventing the arbitration.] Defendant demurred on two grounds: (1) that before the committee acted plaintiff and it had a disagreement and that no further action toward ascertaining the damage had taken place; and (2) the committee had placed a valuation upon the loss, but that plaintiff

was dissatisfied and that there had been no arbitration, plaintiff refusing to refer.

MR. ATHERTON AND MR. C. E. POLLOCK for the Plaintiff in Error.—The fifth plea is bad. It sets up an agreement which is in itself illegal, as ousting the jurisdiction of the courts of law, and which, if it could be good, is likewise inapplicable to the state of facts there set forth. The supposed agreement assumes the right of action in a suffering member when the committee shall have settled the claim, but denies that right if the member questions the amount thus settled. The effect of that would be to restrict the right of the member to sue for any sum except that which the committee might choose to award him. The law will not allow such a restriction; besides, the facts stated in the plea show such a supposed rule to be inapplicable, for they show that the committee never did come to a final decision as to the amount, so that the Plaintiff never was in the condition of a member who refused an amount settled by the committee. In that respect, therefore, the plea affords no answer to the action.

The declaration established a clear, complete, independent contract of insurance, and not a contract depending on what might be done on the intervention of a third party.

[LORD CAMPBELL.—All the rules and regulations are expressly made part of the contract.]

That is so, but the question is how far one of those rules, which contravenes a principle of law, can be operative. That rule professes to make an award a condition precedent to the right to sue, except for a sum awarded. Such a condition is illegal.

It is admitted that a mere agreement to refer cannot be a bar to an action. This is nothing more than a mere contract to refer; it is the ordinary arbitration clause, but it is not a submission, for the arbitrator is neither chosen nor appointed. If, therefore, the Plaintiff is deprived of his right of action the sum may never be settled, and he will never obtain compensation for his loss.

The words of the condition itself are, not merely any difference as to the amount, but also "any other matter relating to the insurance." That might involve questions of the most difficult nature in insurance, all which, it is contended on the other side, must be referred to arbitration, and absolutely decided by two out of the three arbitrators, without the assured being at liberty to bring them under the consideration of a court of law. That cannot be a valid agreement.

This is not a contract to pay the assured, in

the event of loss, so much as certain parties shall determine. It must be contended, on the other side, that nothing is due till a third person has intervened and settled the amount, but then it is clear, notwithstanding the machinery resorted to, that the intention is that the underwriter shall not make good a loss except after reference to arbitration. That intention cannot be carried into effect, for it is illegal. This is said to be nothing but an agreement to ascertain an amount, but then the reference to ascertain it must come after a difference, after a cause of action accrued, and consequently it is an agreement to exclude the courts from jurisdiction upon an existing cause of action. If so, the case cannot be brought within that class of cases in which work is to be done, and the sum due for it is to be ascertained by a third person previously nominated, for in those cases the cause of action only arises on the sum having been ascertained.

MR. BRAMWELL AND MR. MANISTY for the Defendant in Error:—There is no principle in law which prevents a man from agreeing to pay to another the sum which a third shall declare to be the fair value of goods sold, nor any which prevents a similar agreement as to the compensation to be paid for doing or not doing a particular act. If A. will build a house for B., the latter may agree to pay such sum as a third person shall award to be proper ; that is a good agreement and may be enforced: Thurnell v. Balbirnie (2 Mees. and Wels. 786). Suppose an agreement by A., that if he does not farm certain land in a particular way he shall pay to B., the landlord, such a sum as C. shall declare to be the difference occasioned by A.'s mode of farming ; that is the case of an action depending not on what A. has done, but on what C. shall find to be the amount of loss thereby occasioned. Such an agreement would be perfectly good, and the action would only arise when C. had settled the amount. That is exactly the case here ; and in the case supposed, C. would have to determine not only the amount, but the principle on which the amount was payable, and till C. had determined no action would lie.

Then is this an absolute covenant to pay the loss the Plaintiff claims, or to pay the sum which certain persons are to declare to be the amount of the loss. It is clearly the latter. In the declaration, the complaint is not only that the loss has been suffered, but that the amount of the loss has not been settled by the committee, and in truth no cause of action at all arises till the committee has ascertained the amount of the loss. The whole spirit of recent legislation has

been in favour of references, and there is no principle of law violated by an agreement of this kind.

This is not an absolute contract of insurance, but is a contract that, subject to the provisions thereinafter contained, the member shall be indemnified against loss. One of those provisions is that the amount of the loss shall be settled by the committee, or in case of dispute by reference. Such a provision is perfectly lawful.

This condition in the policy is good, and equity would interfere to restrain a party who, after a submission on a contract like this had been made a rule of Court, should proceed to bring an action at law in disregard of the condition.

MR. JUSTICE CROWDER: The fallacy of the argument on behalf of the Plaintiff lies in the assumption that there ever has arisen a cause of action in the present case. Collecting the substance of the contract from the allegations in the first count of the declaration and the sixth plea, it appears to me that no cause of action can arise before the sum to be paid is ascertained and settled by the arbitrator. Nor do I see how it can be held otherwise, without making a contract for the parties quite different from that which they really made in express terms for themselves ; for if this action is maintainable it must be so by rejecting the 25th rule as part of the contract, and by holding that a good contract of insurance remains, which has been broken. But the premium was not paid by the Plaintiff for such an absolute indemnity by the Defendant ; and it may well be that a less sum by way of premium was demanded by the Defendant, on the very ground that the contract of insurance was varied and modified by the 25th rule of the association.

MR. BARON MARTIN: It was asked, Were these conditions illegal? The answer is, They are not ; that they are of the same class of contracts as all submissions to arbitration were before the statute 3 and 4 Will. 4, c. 42, and as such submissions now which are not included within its provisions, viz., binding and operative if the parties choose to act upon them, but revocable at their will.

It was said that the parties, by express agreement between themselves, had made the decision or award of the arbitrators a condition precedent to the right of any member to maintain an action. This is so ; but if the matter be examined into, it will be found to be nothing more than what is included in every such contract. If the provision be binding, the consequences would be, in the event of a dispute, recourse must be had to an arbitrator, and an award made; but arbitrators have no power to enforce their awards; they cannot issue execution upon them; a court of law or equity must be called in aid to enforce an award adversely. Therefore, in every case, if the agreement to refer be binding, the award must be a condition precedent to maintaining an action, and such condition is tacitly implied.

LORD CAMPBELL. In the first place, I think that the contract between the shipowner and the underwriters in this case is as clear as the English language could make it, that no action should be brought against the insurers until the arbitrators had disposed of any dispute that might arise between them. It is declared to be a condition precedent to the bringing of any action. There is no doubt that such was the intention of the parties; and, upon a deliberate view of the policy, I am of opinion, that it embraced not only the assessment of damage, the contemplation of quantum, but also any dispute that might arise between the underwriters and the insured respecting the liability of the insurers, as well as the amount to be paid. If there had been any question about want of seaworthiness, or deviation, or breach of blockade, I am clearly of opinion that, upon a just construction of this instrument, until those questions had been determined by the arbitrators, no right of action could have accrued to the insured.

That being the intention of the parties, about which I believe there is no dispute, is the contract illegal? There is an express undertaking that no action shall be brought until the arbitrators have decided, and there is abundant consideration for that in the mutual contract into which the parties have entered; therefore, unless there is some illegality in the contract, the Courts are bound to give it effect. There is no statute against such a contract: then, on what ground is it to be declared illegal? It is contended, that it is contrary to public policy: that is rather a dangerous ground to go upon; but what pretence can there be for saying that there is anything contrary to public policy in allowing parties to contract, that they shall not be liable to any action until their liability has been ascertained by a domestic and private tribunal, upon which they themselves agree? Can the public be injured by it? It seems to me that it would be a most inexpedient encroachment upon the liberty of the subject if he were not allowed to enter into such a contract. Take the case of an insurance club, of which there are many in the north of England; a noble Lord

now present, who is connected with that part of the country, is probably aware of it: there are insurance clubs of this sort in Newcastle and in all the sea-ports of the north. Is there anything contrary to public policy in saying that the Company shall not be harassed by actions, the costs of which might be ruinous, but that any dispute that arises shall be referred to a domestic tribunal, which may speedily and economically determine the dispute? I can see not the slightest ill consequences that can flow from such an agreement, and I see great advantage that may arise from it. Public policy, therefore, seems to me to require that effect should be given to the contract.

Then, my Lords, when we come to the decided cases, if there had been any decision which had not been reviewed by your Lordships, which adjudged such a contract to be illegal, I should ask your Lordships to reverse it; for it would seem to me really to stand on no principle whatsoever. It probably originated in the contests of the different courts in ancient times for extent of jurisdiction, all of them being opposed to anything that would altogether deprive every one of them of jurisdiction. There is a saying of Lord Coke, which is the original foundation of this doctrine: it is this, "If a man makes a lease for life, and by deed grant that if any waste or destruction be done, that it shall be redressed by neighbours, and not by suit or plea; notwithstanding, an action and waste shall lie, for the place wasted cannot be recovered without a plea." Where an action is indispensable, you cannot oust the Court of its jurisdiction over the subject, because justice cannot be done without the exercise of that jursidiction. That is all, and there is no doubt about that. This is the foundation of the doctrine that Courts are not to be ousted of their jurisdiction.

But I am glad to think that there is no case that I am aware of that will be overturned by your Lordships' affirming the judgment now in dispute. Because all that has been hitherto decided in Thompson v. Charnock [8 T.R. 139], and the other cases referred to, is this, that if the contract between the parties simply contain a clause or covenant to refer to arbitration, and goes no further, then an action may be brought in spite of that clause, although there has been no arbitration. But there is no case that goes the length of saying, that where the contract is as it is here, that no right of action shall accrue until there has been an arbitration; then an action may be brought, although there has been no arbitration. Now, in this contract of insurance it is stipulated, in the most express terms, that until the arbitrators have determined, no action shall lie in any court whatsoever. That is not ousting the courts of their jurisdiction, because they have no jurisdiction whatsoever, and no cause of action accrues until the arbitrators have determined. Therefore, without overturning the case of Thompson v. Charnock, and the other cases to the same effect, your Lordships may hold that, in this case, where it is expressly, directly, and unequivocally agreed upon between the parties that there shall be no right of action whatever till the arbitrators have decided, it is a bar to the action that there has been no such arbitration.

Judgment for the Defendant in Error, with costs.

UNITED STATES ASPHALT REFINING CO. v. TRINIDAD LAKE PETROLEUM CO. LTD.
222 F. 1006 (S.D. N.Y. 1915))

[Actions for alleged breach of two charterparties made in London by libelant, a South Dakota corporation, and respondent, a British corporation. The chartered ships were used until the outbreak of war in 1914 when they allegedly were wrongfully withdrawn from the charterer's service. Respondent moved to stay prosecution of the suits.]

HOUGH, DISTRICT JUDGE: The charter party of each steamer contained the following very ordinary clause:

"19. Any dispute arising under this charter shall be settled in London by arbitration. For the purpose of enforcing any award, this agreement shall be made a rule of court."

There can be no doubt that this was a submission to arbitration, and for that reason was a contract between the parties to this action. It is equally plain that under the law of the place of the contract—i.e. England—this arbitration agreement was at the time of making the charterparties entirely valid, and any endeavor to do exactly what libelant has done by bringing these suits would have been restrained by the English courts, acting under authority of the English Arbitration Act of 1889.

Respondent urges that the contract for arbitration contained in the charterparties was valid and enforceable when and where it was made, and must consequently be enforced everywhere, unless some positive rule of the law of the forum prevents such recognition and enforcement. Libelant asserts that, whether the contract was or was not good at the time and place of making, it has always been invalid under the law of the United States and most of the states thereof,

with the admitted and asserted result that an American may make a solemn contract of this nature in England and repudiate it at will in America with the approbation of the courts of his own country.

There has long been a great variety of available reasons for refusing to give effect to the agreements of men of mature age, and presumably sound judgment, when the intended effect of the agreements was to prevent proceedings in any and all courts and substitute therefor the decision of arbitrators. The remarkably simple nature of this libelant's contract breaking has led me to consider at some length the nature and history of the reasons adduced to justify the sort of conduct, by no means new, but remarkably well illustrated by these libels.

It has never been denied that the hostility of English-speaking courts to arbitration contracts probably originated (as Lord Campbell said in Scott v. Avery) "in the contest of the courts of ancient times for extension of jurisdiction—all of them being opposed to anything that would altogether deprive every one of them of jurisdiction."

A more unworthy genesis cannot be imagined. Since (at the latest) the time of Lord Kenyon, it has been customary to stand rather upon the antiquity of the rule than upon its excellence or reason: "It is not necessary now to say how this point ought to have been determined if it were res integra—it having been decided again and again," etc. Per Kenyon, J., in Thompson v. Charnock, 8 T.R. 139.

There is little difference between Lord Kenyon's remark and the words of Cardozo, J., uttered within a few months in Meacham v. Jamestown, etc., R. R. Co., 211 N.Y. at page 354, 105 N.E. at page 656. "it is true that some judges have expressed the belief that parties ought to be free to contract about such matters as they please. In this state the law has long been settled to the contrary."

Nevertheless the legal mind must assign some reason in order to decide anything with spiritual quiet, and the causes advanced for refusing to compel men to abide by their arbitration contracts may apparently be subdivided as follows:

(a) The contract is in its nature revocable.

(b) Such contracts are against public policy.

(c) The covenant to refer is but collateral to the main contract, and may be disregarded, leaving the contract keeper to his action for damages for breach of such collateral covenant.

(d) Any contract tending to wholly oust the court of jurisdiction violates the spirit of the laws creating the courts, in that it is not competent for private persons either to increase or diminish the statutory juridical power.

(e) Arbitration may be a condition precedent to suit, and as such valid, if it does not prevent legal action, or seek to determine out of court the general question of liability.

THE DOCTRINE OF REVOCABILITY

This seems to rest on Vynior's Case, 8 Coke, 8lb, and is now somewhat old-fashioned, although it appears in Oregon, etc., Bank v. American, etc., Co. (C.C.) 35 Fed. 23, with due citations of authority; and in Tobey v. County of Bristol, 3 Story, 800, Fed. Cas. No. 14,065, it is treated at great length.

THE PUBLIC POLICY DOCTRINE

No reason for the simple statement that arbitration agreements are against public policy has ever been advanced, except that it must be against such policy to oust the courts of jurisdiction. This is hardly a variant of the reasoning ascribed by Lord Campbell to the "courts of ancient times": "Such stipulations [for arbitration] are regarded as against the policy of the common law, as having a tendency to exclude the jurisdiction of the courts." Hurst v. Litchfield, 39 N.Y. 377.

"Such agreements have repeatedly been held to be against public policy and void." Prince Co. v. Lehman (D.C.) 39 Fed. 704, 5 L.R.A. 464.

The above are two examples of the cruder forms of statement; but of late years the higher courts have been somewhat chary of the phrase "public policy," and in Insurance Co. v. Morse, 20 Wall. 457, 22 L. Ed. 365, Hunt, J., quotes approvingly from Story's Commentaries, thus:

> Where the stipulation, though not against the policy of the law, yet is an effort to divest the ordinary jurisdiction of the common tribunals of justice, such as an agreement in case of dispute to refer the same to arbitration, a court of equity will not, any more than a court of law, interfere to enforce the agreement, but will leave the parties to their own good pleasure in regard to such agreements.

But neither the court nor the commentator pointed out any other method by which an arbitration agreement could be against the policy of the law, unless it were by seeking to divest the "ordinary jurisdiction of the common tribunals of justice."

Having built up the doctrine that any contract which involves an "ouster of jurisdiction" is invalid, the Supreme Court of the United States has been able of late years to give decision without ever going behind that statement. Thus in Insurance Co. v. Morse, *supra*, it is said: "Agreements in advance to oust the courts of the

jurisdiction conferred by law are illegal and void."

In Doyle v. Continental Insurance Co., 94 U.S. 535, 24 L. Ed. 148, the case last cited is distinctly reaffirmed. The lower courts have followed, and in Perkins v. United States, etc., Co. (C.C.) 16 Fed. 513 Wallace, J., said: "It is familiar doctrine that a simple agreement inserted in a contract, that the parties will refer any dispute arising thereunder to arbitration, will not oust courts of law of their ordinary jurisdiction."

Even a partial ouster was held "evidently invalid" when inserted in a bill of lading, in The Etona (D.C.) 64 Fed. 880, citing Slocum v. Western Assurance Co. (D.C.) 42 Fed. 236, and the Guildhall (D.C.) 58 Fed. 796.

THE DOCTRINE THAT THE COVENANT TO REFER IS COLLATERAL ONLY

This idea is set forth with his customary clearness by Jessel, M. R., in Dawson v. Fitzgerald, 1 Ex. D. 257. It was repeated in Perkins v. United States, etc., Co., *supra,* and accepted in Crossley v. Connecticut, etc., Co. (C.C.) 27 Fed. 30. The worthlessness of the theory was amply demonstrated in Munson v. Straits of Dover (D.C.) 99 Fed. 787, affirmed 102 Fed. 926, 43 C.C.A. 57, where Judge Brown, accepting without query or comment the doctrine that any agreement which completely ousted the courts of jurisdiction was specifically unenforceable, found himself unable to award more than nominal damages for the breach of the collateral agreement. The opinion for affirmance (102 Fed. 926, 43 C.C.A. 57) is written by Wallace, J., who had himself pointed out in Perkins v. United States, etc., Co., *supra* that the action for breach of the collateral agreement to refer was a remedy against the contract breaker who sued when he had promised not to. Comment seems superfluous upon any theory of law (if law be justice) that can come to such conclusions.

THE THEORY THAT ARBITRATION AGREEMENTS VIOLATE THE SPIRIT OF THE LAWS CREATING THE COURTS

This is the accepted doctrine in New York, as shown in Meacham v. Jamestown, etc. Railroad, *supra.* Yet it is surely a singular view of juridical sanctity which reasons that, because the Legislature has made a court, therefore everybody must go to the court.

THE THEORY THAT A LIMITED ARBITRATION, NOT OUSTING THE COURTS OF JURISDICTION, MAY BE VALID

This is thought to be the doctrine of Delaware

etc., Co. v. Pennsylvania, etc., Co., 50 N.Y. 265, and it is plainly accepted by the Supreme Court of the United States. Hamilton v. Liverpool, etc., Insurance Co., 136 U.S. at page 255, 10 Sup. Ct. 945, 34 L. Ed. 419, shows the familiar proviso in an insurance policy by which the *amount* of loss or damage to the property insured shall be ascertained by arbitrators or appraisers, and further that, until such an award should be obtained, the loss should not be payable and no action should lie against the insurer. This makes the appraisal or partial arbitration a condition precedent to suit. Gray, J., said:

> Such a stipulation, not ousting the jurisdiction of the courts, but leaving the general question of liability to be judicially determined, and simply providing a reasonable method of estimating and ascertaining the amount of the loss, is unquestionably valid, according to the uniform current of authority in England and in this country.

In Hamilton v. Home Insurance Co., 137 U.S. at page 385, 11 Sup. Ct. at page 138, 34 L. Ed. 708, the same learned Justice said (of a somewhat similar proviso in an insurance policy): "If the contract . . . provides that no action upon it shall be maintained until after such an award, . . . the award is a condition precedent to the right of action."

But persons who would thus far avail themselves of compulsory arbitration must be careful, for it has been said:

> While parties may impose, as a condition precedent to applications to the courts, that they shall first have settled the amount to be recovered by an agreed mode, they cannot entirely close the access to the courts of law. . . . Such stipulations are repugnant to the rest of the contract and assume to divest courts of their established jurisdiction. As conditions precedent to an appeal to the courts, they are void. Stephenson v. Insurance Co., 54 Ma. 70, cited in Insurance Co. v. Morse, *supra*.

Finally, in Guaranty, etc., Co. v. Green Cove, etc., R. R. Co., 139 U.S. at page 142, Brown, J., considered a proviso in a mortgage to the effect that a sale by the trustee should be "exclusive of all other" methods of sale, and he laid down the law thus:

> This clause, . . . is open to the objection of attempting to provide against a remedy in the ordinary course of judicial proceedings, and oust the jurisdiction of the courts, which (as is settled by the uniform current of authority) cannot be done.

This decision was filed in 1890. The latest opinion in this circuit known to me is Gough v. Hamburg, etc., Co. (D.C.) 158 Fed. 174, where Adams, J., lays down the rule without comment

that any limitation upon the jurisdiction of courts contained in a contract is void.

Whatever form of statement the rule takes, the foregoing citations show that it always amounts to the same thing, viz.: The courts will scarcely permit any other body of men to even partially perform judicial work, and will never permit the absorption of all the business growing out of disputes over a contract by any body of arbitrators, unless compelled to such action by statute. Even such cases as Mittenthal v. Mascagni, 183 Mass. 19, 66 N.E. 425, show no more than a belated acceptance of the right to confine litigation by contract to a particular court, for even that opinion does not recognize the right of mankind to contract themselves out of all courts.

The English Arbitration Act, *supra*, is such a statute. It has compelled the courts of that country to abandon the doctrine that it is wrong or wicked to agree to stay away from the courts when disputes arise. It is highly characteristic of lawyers that, when thus coerced by the Legislature, the wisdom of previous decision begins to be doubted. In Hamlyn v. Talisker Distillery [1894] App. Cas. 202, Lord Watson said:

> The rule that a reference to arbitrators not named cannot be enforced does not appear to me to rest on any essential considerations of public policy. Even if an opposite inference were deducible from the authorities by which it was established, the rule has been so largely trenched upon by the *legislation* of the last 50 years . . . that I should hesitate to affirm that the policy upon which it was originally based could now be regarded as of cardinal importance.

Neither the Legislature of New York nor the Congress has seen fit thus to modernize the ideas of the judges of their respective jurisdictions.[1]

The question presented by these motions is to be regarded as one of general law; *i.e.,* one wherein the courts of the United States are not bound to follow or conform to the decisions of the state jurisdiction in which they may happen to sit.

Furthermore the question is one of remedy, and not of right. Such was substantially the holding in Mitchell v. Dougherty, *supra*; and in Stephenson v. Insurance Co., *supra*, it is pointed out that:

> The law and not the contract prescribes the remedy; and parties have no more right to enter into stipulations against a resort to the courts for their remedy, in a given case, than they have to provide a remedy prohibited by law.

---

1. It has not seemed necessary to pursue this subject beyond the courts of the United States, New York, and Massachusetts; but, with the possible exception of Pennsylvania, the result would not, I think, be different.

Finally it has been well said by Cardozo, J., in Meacham v. Jamestown, etc., R. R. Co., *supra,* that: "An agreement that ... differences arising under a contract shall be submitted to arbitration relates to the law of remedies, and the law that governs remedies is the law of the forum."

It follows that the final question for determination under these motions is whether the law as laid down by the Supreme Court of the United States permits the enforcement as a remedy of the arbitration clause contained in a contract, assuming that such clause (as here) is intended to oust the courts and all courts of their jurisdiction.

I think the decisions cited show beyond question that the Supreme Court has laid down the rule that such a complete ouster of jurisdiction as is shown by the clause quoted from the charter parties is void in a federal forum. It was within the power of that tribunal to make this rule. Inferior courts may fail to find convincing reasons for it; but the rule must be obeyed, and these motions be severally denied.

KULUKUNDIS SHIPPING CO. v.
AMTORG TRADING CORP.
126 F. 2d 978 (2d Cir. 1942)

FRANK, CIRCUIT JUDGE: It became fashionable in the middle of the 18th century to say that [arbitration] agreements were against public policy because they "oust the jurisdiction" of the courts. But that was a quaint explanation, inasmuch as an award, under an arbitration agreement, enforced both at law and in equity, was no less an ouster; and the same was true of releases and covenants not to sue, which were given full effect. Moreover, the agreement to arbitrate was not illegal, since suit could be maintained for its breach. Here was a clear instance of what Holmes called a "right" to break a contract and to substitute payment of damages for nonperformance; as, in this type of case, the damages were only nominal, that "right" was indeed meaningful.

An effort has been made to justify this judicial hostility to the executory arbitration agreement on the ground that arbitrations, if unsupervised by the courts, are undesirable, and that legislation was needed to make possible such supervision.[1] But if that was the reason for

unfriendliness to such executory agreements, then the courts should also have refused to aid arbitrations when they ripened into awards. And what the English courts, especially the equity courts, did in other contexts, shows that, if they had had the will, they could have devised means of protecting parties to arbitrations. Instead, they restrictively interpreted successive statutes intended to give effect to executory arbitrations.[2] No similar hostility was displayed by the Scotch courts. Lord Campbell explained the English attitude as due to the desire of the judges, at a time when their salaries came largely from fees, to avoid loss of income.[3] Indignation has been voiced at this suggestion; perhaps it is unjustified.[4] Perhaps the true explanation is the hypnotic power of the phrase, "oust the jurisdiction." Give a bad dogma a good name and its bite may become as bad as its bark.

In 1855, in Scott v. Avery, 5 H.C.L. [sic] 811, the tide seemed to have turned. There it was held that if a policy made an award of damages by arbitrators a condition precedent to a suit on the policy, a failure to submit to arbitration would preclude such a suit, even if the policy left to the arbitrators the consideration of all the elements of liability. But, despite later legislation, the hostility of the English courts to executory arbitrations resumed somewhat after Scott v. Avery, and seems never to have been entirely dissipated.

That English attitude was largely taken over in the 19th century by most courts in this country. Indeed, in general, they would not go as far as Scott v. Avery, *supra,*[5] and continued to use the "ouster of jurisdiction" concept. An executory agreement to arbitrate would not be given specific performance or furnish the basis of a

---

1. Sayre argues that if the courts had really been unfriendly to arbitrations they would not have enforced arbitrators' awards. The real truth, however, seems to be that they were unfriendly but did not carry out their hostility to its logical conclusion.

2. Annotation, 47 L.R.A., N.S., 436.

3. "The doctrine," he said, "had its origin in the interests of the judges. There was no disguising the fact that, as formerly, the emoluments of the Judges depended mainly, or almost entirely, upon fees, and as they had no fixed salaries, there was great competition to get as much as possible of litigation into Westminster Hall, and a great scramble in Westminster Hall for the division of the spoil.... And they had great jealousy of arbitrations whereby Westminster Hall was robbed of those cases which came not into Kings Bench, nor the Common Please, nor the Exchequer. Therefore they said that the courts ought not to be ousted of their jurisdiction, and that it was contrary to the policy of the law to do so. That really grew up only subsequently to the time of Lord Coke, and a saying of his was the foundation of the doctrine." Scott v. Avery, 25 L. J. Ex. 308, 313; the report of his remarks in 5 H.C.L. [sic] 811 is more meager.

4. Yet able historians have stressed this pecuniary motive as an important factor in the struggles for jurisdiction between the several English courts.

5. See, *e.g.*, Whitney v. National Masonic Accident Ass'n, 52 Minn. 378, 54 N.W. 184; Annotation, 47 L.R.A., N.S., at page 448.

stay of proceedings on the original cause of action. Nor would it be given effect as a plea in bar, except in limited instances, i.e., in the case of an agreement expressly or impliedly making it a condition precedent to litigation that there by an award determining some preliminary question of subsidiary fact upon which any liability was to be contingent. Hamilton v. Liverpool, 1890, etc., Ins. Co., 136 U.S. 242, 255, 10 S. Ct. 945, 34 L. Ed. 419. In the case of broader executory agreements, no more than nominal damages would be given for a breach.

Generally speaking, then, the courts of this country were unfriendly to executory arbitration agreements. The lower federal courts, feeling bound to comply with the precedents, nevertheless became critical of this judicial hostility. There were intimations in the Supreme Court that perhaps the old view might be abandoned, but in the cases hinting at that newer attitude the issue was not raised.[6] Effective state arbitration statutes were enacted beginning with the New York Statute of 1920.[7]

Associated, and sometimes confused, with the doctrine of revocability of executory agreements to arbitrate, was the doctrine—grounded in the "ouster of jurisdiction" rationale—that an agreement to submit all questions arising under a contract was void. This was an erroneous outgrowth of the doctrine that an agreement to condition suit upon the determination of arbitrators of subsidiary questions but not questions of liability was valid and enforceable as a condition precedent. (This despite the fact that in the policy in Scott v. Avery all questions were subject to determination by the committee and, in the event of differences with it, to arbitration as a condition precedent to the right to bring suit.) So at common law in some jurisdictions agreements to submit all disputes to arbitration were not only revocable but, said the courts—in dubious reliance upon English cases—"void." It was such a line of cases that was declared overruled in Park Construction Co. v. Independent School Dist., 299 Minn. 182, 296 N.W. 475 (1941).

6. The Atlanten, 1920, 252 U.S. 313, 315, 40 S. Ct. 332, 64 L. Ed. 586; Red Cross Line v. Atlantic Fruit Co., 1924, 264 U.S. 109, 123, 124, 44 S. Ct. 274, 68 L. Ed. 582.

7. For a discussion of the earlier American state legislation, see CHAFFEE and SIMPSON, 1 CASES ON EQUITY (1934) 552–553; STURGES, COMMERCIAL ARBITRATION (1930) Sections 1–6.

Apparently the sole companion to *Park Construction* is United Ass'n of Journeymen of the Plumbing and Pipefitting Indus. v. Stine, 76 Nev. 189, 351 P. 2d 965 (1960), in which, despite the reception of the common law by statute, the state supreme court declined to follow the common law doctrine of revocability, giving as its reason the dubious origin of the doctrine and the thoroughly changed situation in present day labor-management relations as compared with conditions prevailing when the doctrine was promulgated and the common law was received.

LATTER v. HOLSUM BREAD CO.
108 Utah 364, 160 P. 2d 421 (1945)

It is almost the universal rule that in the absence of a statute to the contrary, an agreement to arbitrate all future disputes thereafter arising under the contract does not constitute a bar to an action on the contract involving such dispute, on the ground that it seeks to deny to the parties judicial remedies and therefore is contrary to public policy. Johnson v. Brinkerhoff, 89 Utah 530, 57 P. 2d 1132; Blodgett Company v. Bebe Company, 190 Cal. 665, 214 P. 38, 26 A.L.R. 1070; McCullough v. Clinch-Mitchell Construction Company, 8 Cir., 71 F. 2d 17; Gates v. Arizona Brewing Company, 54 Ariz. 266, 95 P. 2d 49; see annotation in 135 A.L.R. 79. Defendant concedes that this is the rule and that we have no statute to the contrary but contends that, notwithstanding the holding of Gates v. Arizona Brewing Company, *supra*, to the contrary, in labor cases a different rule should apply. He points out that by Section 49-1-9, U.C.A. 1943 we approved collective bargaining and contends that arbitration is a necessary part thereof. He refers us to an article entitled "The Function of Arbitration" by Philip G. Phillips, 33 COLUMBIA LAW REVIEW 1366.

That article does not support defendant's contention. It does not discuss what is or ought to be the common law rule but what is the most desirable statutory policy. It states that the Draft State Arbitration Act authorizes contracts to arbitrate future disputes and poses the question whether arbitration agreements in labor trade contracts are specifically enforceable and whether statutes should attempt to make them so. The author points out that there are two theories of arbitration: One, that the arbitrators are the agents of the parties and as such are formulating contracts for the parties; the other, that the arbitrators are judges and determine problems of a judicial nature. He concludes that the statutes in question adopt the theory that the arbitrators are performing a judicial function; that ordinarily a labor dispute involves the making of a contract rather than determining the right of parties under a contract and therefore do not present a judicial problem but rather one of conciliation and mediation; and that such matters should be left to boards and commissions rather than to arbitrators authorized to perform judicial functions.

Here we are not concerned with an ordinary labor dispute. There is here no question of formulating a contract or agreeing upon terms. The contract has been made and fully performed by the employees and the only question to be determined is how much money is owing to the employees under its terms. This is purely a judicial question and in no sense one of collective bargaining. There does not appear to be any reason why there should be a different rule in this case and any other case involving the construction of a contract. Whether a new policy shall be established is for the legislature and not for the courts.

B.

Revocation

WILLIAMS v. BRANNING MFG. CO.
153 N.C. 7, 68 S.E. 902 (1910)

Civil action for damages for breach of contract in writing in which plaintiffs obligated for certain consideration to operate defendant's lumber plant at Ahoskie, in Hertford County, and to cut into logs the standing timber of defendant and manufacture them into lumber at said plant.

In October, 1904, these parties entered into another contract, modifying and changing some of the provisions of the contract of 1901. In the contract of 1904 the following provision is incorporated:

> Section 9. It is further understood and agreed, in the event of any future misunderstanding or disagreement between the parties hereto as to the contract of 1 March, 1901, or as to any modifications of the same herein contained, that the matter shall be settled by arbitrators, to be selected, one by the Branning Manufacturing Company and one by the said J. T. Williams & Bro., and the third by the two, who shall hear and determine the same, and whose award shall be accepted as final between the parties and faithfully performed by each.

Disagreements having arisen the matters in controversy were submitted to arbitrators on 20 February, 1906, in accordance with the agreements.

After the controversy had been heard by the arbitrators, but before they rendered their award, to-wit, 1 January, 1907, this action was commenced to recover the damages for the breach of the aforesaid contract. It is admitted in the "facts agreed" that several matters of difference submitted to arbitration are those set out in the complaint in this action, which complaint was not filed until 18 January, 1908. It is admitted in the case agreed,

5th. That said arbitrators, thereafter, on the 25th day of January, 1907, rendered their award, passing on the matters submitted to them, and shortly thereafter the same was sent to plaintiffs and defendant, and which the plaintiffs ignored.

[The lower court held that the award did not bar this action.]

BROWN, J. It is unnecessary to review the conclusions of the Superior Court that the provision in the contract agreeing to submit all matters of difference to arbitration is no bar to this action, for the reason that the plaintiffs and defendant did voluntarily submit such matters to arbitration in manner and form as provided in the contract and the arbitrators in due time rendered their award. It is common learning that a valid award operates as a final and conclusive judgment, as between the parties to the submission, or within the jurisdiction of the arbitrators, respecting all matters determined and disposed of by it.

But it is contended that the fact that a summons in this action was issued some days before the rendering of the award revoked the submission, and deprived the arbitrators of the right to make an award.

No other form of revocation is contended for.

At common law a submission might be revoked by any party thereto at any time before the award was rendered. Bacon Abridgment, Arb. B., Comyns Dig., Arb. D., 5; Vinyor's case 8 Coke, 82.

Some courts of this country have held to the contrary (Berry v. Carter, 19 Kan., 135, and cases cited), but this Court has followed the doctrine of the common law. Tyson v. Robinson, 25 N.C., 333; Carpenter v. Tucker, 98 N.C., 316.

The revocation to be effective must be express

unless there is a revocation by implication of law, and in case of express revocation, in order to make it complete, notice must be given to the arbitrators. It is ineffective until this has been done. Allen v. Watson, 10 Johns, 205 ; Brown v. Leavitt, 26 Maine, 251 ; Morse on Arb. and Award, p. 231 ; Vin Ab., Authority E., 3, 4 ; Vinyor's case, supra, 2 Am. & Eng., 600.

It is contended that commencing an action is a revocation by legal implication. Such revocations arise from the legal effect of some intervening happening after submission, either by act of God or caused by the party, and which necessarily puts an end to the business.

The death of a party, or arbitrator, marriage of a *feme sole*, lunacy of a party, or the utter destruction and final end of the subject matter, are of this description. But whether the bringing of an action for the subject matter of an arbitration after submission and before award is an implied revocation, is a matter about which the courts differ.

In New York it is held that it is no revocation in law (Lumber Co. v. Schneider, 1 N.Y. Supp., 441 ; Smith v. Bard, 20 Barb, 262). To same effect are the decisions in New Jersey and Vermont (Knores v. Jenkins, 40 N.J.L., 288 ; Sutton v. Tyrrell, 10 Vt., 91). The courts of Kentucky, Illinois, Georgia and New Hampshire hold the contrary. (Peters v. Craig, 6 Dana, 307 ; Paulser v. Manske, 24 Ill. App., 95 ; Leonard v. House, 15 Ga., 473 ; Kimball v. Gilman, 60 N.H., 54). The conclusion of Judge Collamer in the Vermont case is that "The entry and continuance of an action was, obviously, not an express revocation, nor was it such an act as put an end to the subject matter of the submission nor did it prevent the arbitration from proceeding with effect. It occasioned the defendant no cost, and, indeed, it was no more than an ordinary act of caution to keep the action in existence should the opposite party revoke or decline to attend. This, then, was not a revocation in law." Nevertheless it is plainly deducible from all the cases that the action when commenced must cover the subject matter submitted to arbitration ; otherwise, it cannot be construed as a revocation or notice to the party or to the arbitrators.

In the case at bar the summons was issued some days before the award was made, but the complaint was not filed until a year after. The summons gave no indication as to the character of the action except that it was a civil action.

Until a complaint is filed the defendant has no legal notice of the cause of action and the arbitrators had a right to proceed with the pending arbitration and to render their award. Assuming that the bill of particulars furnished upon defendant's demand is notice of the character of the action, that was not furnished until after 1 August, 1908, several months after the award had been rendered.

The judgment of the Superior Court upon the "case agreed" is Reversed.

Claims by the same plaintiff that were held not to be covered by the arbitration award in the principal case were said not to be barred by the very same arbitration clause, which the court observed was like those declared "void" in other cases. (N.C.) 70 S.E. 290 (1911). If this clause were void, it is difficult to see why revocation would be necessary. The court did not declare it void, however, noting only that in the later case the arbitration clause had not in fact been invoked by the defendant in regard to these claims and that it therefore need not decide what effect the provision would have if steps had been taken to invoke it. This is some further indication of the confusion in American common-law doctrine in which revocability of agreements to arbitrate was, in some jurisdictions, translated into the doctrine that "all dispute" clauses that "ousted the courts" of jurisdiction were contrary to public policy and hence void.

MORRISON DEPARTMENT STORE CO. v. LEWIS
96 W.Va. 277, 122 S.E. 747 (1924)

McGINNIS, JUDGE: This is an action of assumpsit brought in the Circuit Court of Cabell County.

The declaration contains the common counts in assumpsit, and a special second count on a contract entered into between O. J. Morrison and others and C. W. Campbell and others, bearing date June 1, 1924, which contract is [omitted].

Said special count of the declaration substantially charges that said contract was executed by the parties thereto, and duly recorded in the office of the Clerk of the County Court of Cabell County, on the 16th day of December, 1914, and that at the time the contract was entered into, the contracting parties, mentioned therein, were the owners of the respective properties therein described.

The said special count also alleges that the plaintiff and the defendant are the respective owners of the lot described in said contract, and each are mutually bound by the covenants contained in said contract; that the plaintiff and its predecessors in title, namely O. J. Morrison and others mentioned in said contract as parties of the first part, after said contract had been executed, erected and completed a party wall between the respective lots of the plaintiff and defendant by constructing a four story brick building, the west wall of which constitutes the party wall referred to in said contract, and that the cost of labor and material expended and used on said wall was $9952.92; that after the said wall had been constructed by plaintiff, the defendant erected a five story brick building on his lot Number 7, and that said party wall is the eastern wall of the defendant's said building; that the plaintiff demanded of the defendant payment of one-half of the cost of construction of said party wall as provided in the third article of said contract, and that said plaintiff and defendant disagreed in reference to said amount and the existence of said contract, and that owing to said disagreement arbitrators were appointed as provided in article 7 of said contract, and the manner in which said arbitrators were appointed is set forth in the declaration from which it appears that the defendant, although notice was given him, refused to take any part in said arbitration or in the appointment of the arbitrators; however, the declaration alleges that these arbitrators met and heard evidence and fixed the cost of said party wall at $9952.92 and that the defendant should pay the one-half of that amount to the plaintiff, to-wit: the sum of $4976.46, that demand has been made on the defendant by the plaintiff for the payment of said sum and the defendant refused to pay said sum, and declared that he did not recognize the amount fixed and awarded by said arbitrators, as an obligation against him, and refused and still refuses to pay said amount.

The defendant filed certain off-sets amounting to $3400.00, for clearing his lot of debris, from fire which destroyed the Morrison Building, $1200.00, and $2200.00 for rent on his lot for one year while the debris remained thereon. The case was tried on the plea of non-assumpsit and the jury rendered a verdict for the plaintiff for $4679.50, and on motion of the defendants said verdict was set aside and the case comes here upon a writ of error.

The plaintiff introduced the contract between O. J. Morrison and others and Campbell, Brown and Davis of June 1, 1915, and a deed from O. J. Morrison and others to the plaintiff bearing date January 5, 1915; a deed from Campbell, Brown and Davis to W. H. Lewis of July 22, 1919, conveying lot number 7 to said Lewis and a deed from said W. H. Lewis to M. Cohen et

al., of June 23, 1920, conveying a one-half interest in said lot No. 7, and a deed from Cohen, et al., to W. H. Lewis of January 13, 1921. The plaintiff also introduced the award of arbitration set forth in the record, and after showing that the award was honestly and fairly made and the amount so found by the arbitrators to be fair and impartially arrived at the plaintiff rested its case.

The defendant, claiming that the contract of June 1, 1914, was no longer in force, proved that he notified the plaintiff's attorney and the arbitrators that he refused to enter into the arbitration, denied the validity of the appointment of the arbitrators and their jurisdiction to arbitrate any amount due from him to the plaintiff, he refused to offer any testimony before the arbitrators and at no time recognized their authority to act as such arbitrators.

The serious question in the case is as to whether or not the defendant revoked the arbitration clause in the contract. The written notice was given and directed to the arbitrators, and accepted by the plaintiff's counsel. The defendant was notified by the arbitrators of the time, place and purpose of this meeting, and the defendant, on the day that the arbitrators met, served the notice in question whereby he denied the validity of the appointment of the arbitrators under the contract and the right, power, authority and jurisdiction to hear evidence and determine the amount due from defendant to plaintiff, which notice closes with the following statement: "This notice being only for the purpose of informing you as to the want of any right, power, authority or jurisdiction in you or any of you as aforesaid, and for no other purpose." It is signed by the defendant, but there is no seal attached to it. It does not mention the revocation of the arbitration clause of the contract, nor does it express any intention to revoke the submission or the authority of the arbitrators. The notice denies the authority and jurisdiction of the arbitration but expresses no intention of revoking their authority.

Mere intention to revoke an arbitration clause does not suffice, to be effective it must be expressed. There can be no implied revocation here.

So long as the intention to revoke the submission is clearly expressed and the revocation is of the same dignity as the submission and the arbitrators have been notified of the revocation, and it is plain in its intent, the revocation will be upheld but not otherwise.

A submission by deed can be revoked by deed only. See note to Williams v. Branning Mfg. Co., 138 A. S. R. 646, citing many cases.

The arbitration clause in question in this case is contained in a sealed instrument and the notice here in question, not being under seal, is ineffective and does not meet the requirements of the law.

Shaver v. Bush, 57 Ind. 349 ; Brown v. Levatt, 26 Me. 251 ; Wallice v. Carpenter, 13 Allen (Mass.) 19 ; Dexter v. Young, 40 N.H. 130 ; Van Antwerp v. Stewart, 8 John (N.Y.) 25.

The West Virginia cases cited by the defendant: Kohlsatt v. Coal Company, 90 W. Va. 656 ; King v. B. & O. Ass'n., 35 W. Va. 385 ; Turner v. Stuart, 51 W. Va. 493 ; Lawson v. Williamson, 61 W. Va. 669 ; Flaville v. Coal Company, 82 W. Va. 295, have no application to the question now under consideration. In neither of these cases did the question of express revocation arise. They all hold that unless the arbitration clause in the contract provides that the contract makes the arbitration a condition precedent to the right of action, a suit may be brought without submitting the question to arbitration. In the present case there was an arbitration strictly in conformity with article 7 of the contract and under the terms thereof it is binding upon the defendant.

We are therefore of the opinion that the lower court erred in setting aside the verdict of the jury and the order of the court setting it aside will be reversed, the verdict re-instated and judgment thereon entered here.

Reversed, verdict reinstated, and judgment entered.

Written notice to the arbitrators and the claimant declaring that two parties to the agreement "object and protest against any action taken [by the] arbitrators ... while the [protesting parties who had withdrawn their arbitrator] remain without representation on the board of arbitration" did not in terms revoke. The court, however, did not decide the issue, the case going off on other grounds. Ames Canning Co. v. Dexter Seed Co., 195 Ia. 1285, 190 N.W. 167 (1922).

CHAPTER III

ARBITRATION UNDER STATUTE

A.

The Early Acts

SOME COMMENTS ON ARBITRATION LEGISLATION AND THE UNIFORM ACT*

MAYNARD E. PIRSIG

The task of arbitration statutes is to remedy defects of the common law principles. Such statutes have existed in this country from earliest times. Among the first were those patterned on the English act of 1698. Thus the New York act of 1791 provided that the parties might agree that their submission of their dispute to arbitrators he made a rule of court. On proof of the agreement, a rule of court was to issue

> that the parties shall submit to, and finally be concluded by the arbitration ... and in case of disobedience to such arbitration or umpirage, the party refusing or neglecting to perform and execute the same, or any part thereof, shall be subject to all the penalties of contemning a rule of court, when he is a suitor or defendant in such court ... unless it shall be made appear on oath to such court, that the arbitrators or umpire misbehaved themselves, and

such award, arbitration, or umpirage, was procured by corruption or other undue means.

A similar act was passed in Virginia in 1789 but with important modifications. The contempt provisions were omitted and instead the award could be entered as the judgment or decree of the court. The award could be avoided if it "was procured by corruption or other undue means, or that there was evident partiality or misbehavior in the arbitrators or umpires, or any of them."

New Jersey adopted a similar act in 1794, but retained the contempt provision.

Under [the Massachusettes] act parties could agree "to have the dispute determined by referees, mutually chosen by the parties," and submit a statement thereof to a justice of the peace who was then obligated to prepare an agreement in the form set out in the statute to be subscribed and acknowledged by the parties. The agreement provided that the persons chosen as referees were to report to the court, "judgment thereon to be final." The act provided further that

---

*Excerpted from 10 VAND. L REV. 685 (1957). Reprinted with permission.

the Court of Common Pleas, to whom the report of the referees may be made as aforesaid, shall have cognizance thereof, in the same way and manner, and the same doings shall be had thereon, as though the same had been made by referees appointed by a rule of the same court.

Referees so appointed were "vested with all the authority and power that referees have been, or may hereafter be vested with, who have been, or shall be appointed by a rule of court." Provision was also made for summoning of witnesses.

The statutes had limited objectives. They were confined to agreements to arbitrate existing disputes as distinguished from disputes arising after the agreement was made. They did not abrogate common law principles applicable to those agreements not coming within the terms of the statutes.

It was against this background that a new, and, for the times, a radically different arbitration statute appeared in the New York revision of 1829. This statute undertook to present a rather comprehensive code on the subject. The success of the venture is indicated by the fact that it has served as a model for legislation in many other states which still survives to this day.

The objectives of the revisors are indicated by their note to section 1:

Instead of enforcing an award by process of contempt, in cases where such process is not applicable, (Section 18 limited contempt proceedings to judgments on awards requiring an act other than the payment of money.) it is proposed to authorize a regular judgment to be entered, filed and docketed, and an execution to be issued against the property or person, conformably to the laws of Massachusetts, 1 v. p. 266; of Virginia, v. 1, p. 454; of Missouri, v. 1, 137. By this means, the parties will be saved the necessity of an expensive and perplexing action, on the bond or the award; and the object of the statute "to contribute much to the ease of parties, in the determining their differences," as expressed in its preamble, will be more effectually obtained. The remedies for relief will be found to be as ample as by the existing law, or as are afforded by an action.

The act provided that the parties

may, by an instrument in writing, submit to the decision of one or more arbitrators, any controversy existing between them, which might be the subject of an action at law, or of a suit in equity . . . and, may, in such submission, agree that a judgment of any court of law and of record, to be designated in such instrument, shall be rendered upon the award made pursuant to such submission.

It excluded certain actions relating to real estate, incorporating the common law in this respect. It provided for the hearing and its post-ponement in language which has survived in many present day statutes, prescribed an oath for the arbitrators, provided for subpoenas, and required the award to be in writing subscribed by the arbitrators and attested by a subscribing witness. On proof of the submission "by the affidavit of a subscribing witness" and similarly of the award, within one year, the court by rule in open court was to confirm the award.

The act then provided in terms common in present-day statutes, including those of New York, for the vacation of an award or for its modification. On confirmation, the award was to be reduced to judgment to be filed and docketed. The grounds for vacation were those which the revisors thought represented the common law on the subject. The grounds for modification were intended to remedy the defect of the common law which did not give such power to the court.

Applications to vacate or modify an award were to be by motion. On such motions the court could direct a rehearing by the arbitrators.

But the revisors were unwilling to break very far with common law principles. The Act was not to

be construed to impair, diminish, or in any way affect the power and authority of the court of chancery over arbitrators, awards, or the parties thereto; nor to impair or affect any action upon any award, or upon any bond or other engagement to abide by an award.

Also common law revocability of any submission to arbitration was recognized but with liability for "all the costs, expenses, and damages which (the opposing party) may have incurred in preparing for such arbitration." Likewise, recovery on any bond given to insure against revocation was permitted.

The act was thus an interesting mixture of earlier statutes of New York and other states, of common law principles and of some wholly new and progressive provisions.

The act remained practically unchanged until 1880 when there was considerable clarification of procedure, some additions such as the effect of death of a party, some changes deemed needed to conform the act to the existing judicial procedure and some modifications of substance such as the requirement that submissions and awards be acknowledged "in like manner as a deed to be recorded." But in general, the basic structure of the 1829 act remained unchanged. It was incorporated in substantially this form in the Civil Practice Act of 1920, and is still the basis of the present New York act on the subject.

Aside from some of its overly technical features, the basic defect of the 1829 act and its successors was their failure to encompass agreements to arbitrate disputes arising subsequent to the agreement. Such an act failed to meet the needs of twentieth century trade and industry. In 1920 New York adopted a short act of major significance specifically directed at validating agreements to arbitrate future disputes and providing a simple and summary procedure for their enforcement.

B.

The Modern Arbitration Acts

Judge Hough's opinion demonstrates that by 1915 (and, indeed, earlier) the common law rules of revocability of agreements to arbitrate future disputes had engendered a considerable adverse reaction. Commercial groups, such as the New York Chamber of Commerce, had become aroused by the lack of court aid for agreements to arbitrate and had advocated legislative change.

The first of the "modern acts" was enacted in New York in 1920. Although it did not extend to rewriting of the earlier legislation, a draft embodying and systematizing the New York provisions was drawn by the American Arbitration Association and used as the model for other states and the federal government.

The major features of the acts patterned after the New York law were that agreements to arbitrate future disputes were made "valid, irrevocable and enforceable," and procedural means were provided to obtain relatively speedy specific enforcement of the promise to arbitrate or to bar suit on the same subject matter; and, where the agreement to arbitrate omitted a means of selecting the arbitrator or the selected means failed, courts were empowered to appoint the arbitrator, thus overcoming a common method of frustrating arbitration agreements. Most acts also empowered arbitrators to issue subpoenas for witnesses and documentary evidence, in response to a criticism that the arbitral process would often be ineffective without it. The new statutes specified, as did the earlier ones, the formalities for the agreement (usually a writing and sometimes more), the powers of arbitrators (to issue notices of hearing, to administer oaths), the requisites of the award (sometimes fairly detailed and formal, *e.g.,* requiring execution in the form of a deed), when and how an award would be enforced in an expedited proceeding leading to entry of judgment, when and how an award could be vacated or modified (generally continuing the grounds that equity courts used before the statutes), and a few other formalities. (The New York law, as codified in the Civil Practice Act, set forth in Appendix C, is fairly typical of the state acts

adopted in the twenties and thirties with some amendments.) A number of the otherwise modern acts limit their scope to agreements to arbitrate disputes that would be justiciable. Some state acts exclude labor agreements, and some, following the common law, do not cover agreements to arbitrate controversies over interests in land (an exclusion dating from feudal times and based upon the suspicion that collusive awards might be used to make dispositions of land inconsistent with fedual tenure rules). A few laws exclude insurance agreements (apparently because of the suspicion that the procedure favored insurers).

By 1955 about sixteen states had enacted some form of "modern" act. In 1955 a Uniform Arbitration Act was promulgated, again based upon the New York pattern but also embodying refinements growing out of experience. As amended in 1956, the Uniform Act has been adopted—with variations—in five states (Florida, Illinois, Maryland, Minnesota and Wyoming). In 1965 Texas enacted a comprehensive act that derived many of its features from the new Uniform Act but, naturally, added many peculiarities of its own. The 1961 California Act, which is the most detailed of all, also drew upon the Uniform Act. And in 1962 the New York legislature codified and amended its statute; the new act, Article 75 of the Civil Practice Law and Rules, became effective in 1963.

The Uniform Act treats equally agreements to arbitrate existing and future disputes. In addition to enforcing agreements specifically and staying suits, it also provides for staying arbitration on the ground that no agreement to arbitrate was effected.

A number of the statutes direct courts to order arbitration without regard to the merits of the asserted claims. And several, following the Uniform Act, provide that the fact that a court could not or would not give the relief afforded by the award is not a ground for refusing confirmation of the award.

Some of the modern acts also provide a means of obtaining modifications or corrections from the arbitrator after award, an impossibility under common law because with the issuance of the award an arbitrator's powers came to an end. Some of the statutes also empower a court to remand the case to new arbitrators or, in some circumstances, to the original arbitrators, rather than leaving an invalid award and no arbitral resolution to the dispute. The latest modern acts, by and large, are not limited to justiciable controversies, and few contain the old exclusions, although some still provide that labor agreements are excluded unless the parties specifically adopt the act as applicable.

Many of the foregoing provisions contain the germs of controversy and will receive some further study hereafter.

About half the states do not have statutes making clauses to arbitrate future disputes enforceable. Hence, there the common law governs unless the Federal Arbitration Act applies. And even in states with modern acts, the common law exists side by side with the statutory system and governs when the statute is inapplicable (usually because of a departure in form of agreement or prescribed procedure).

Unique among the jurisdictions is Washington, which does not recognize or permit common-law arbitration but rather, views arbitration as a proceeding entirely governed by statute. RCWA 7.04.010 *et. seq.* The only exception to this concerns collective-bargaining agreements, in which the parties still have the option to provide by specific agreement for the statutory procedure or may agree upon procedures different from those available under the Act. RCWA 7.04.010. Irrespective of whether the statutory or their own procedures are followed, however, arbitration clauses agreed on by the parties and inserted in collective-bargaining agreements are not subject to the common-law rule permitting revocation at the will of the parties. Greyhound Corp. v. Division 1384 of Amalgamated Ass'n, 44 Wn. 2d 808, 271 P.2d 689 (1954).

The Appendices contain the United States Arbitration Act, the present New York Act (from the Civil Practice Law and Rules) and its predecessor (from the Civil Practice Act). Their early and repeated study are necessary for an understanding of much of the material that follows.

C.

Validity and Applicability of Statutes Making Agreements to Arbitrate Enforceable

LOUIS COCALIS v. EUGENE NAZLIDES
308 Ill. 152, 139 N.E. 95 (1923)

MR. JUSTICE CARTWRIGHT delivered the opinion of the court.

Upon a trial by the court without a jury the municipal court of Chicago rendered judgment in favor of Louis Cocalis, appellee, against Eugene Nazlides, appellant, for $25 liquidated damages for refusal by the appellant to submit to arbitration two controversies between the parties, under an agreement that each would submit to arbitration any controversy that might arise between them or pay $25 damages. Questions of constitutional right being involved, an appeal of this court was allowed and perfected.

In 1922 the Chicago Association of Commerce distributed printed forms of an agreement to submit to arbitration future disputes or controversies which might arise between persons who should sign such papers. The form for such agreement, signed by S. J. Whitlock, chairman, and J. Kent Greene, manager, showing such purpose to provide beforehand for the settlement of controversies which might arise in the future and advising that the best time would be before discord was even threatened. It was not required that parties should sign the same agreemen nor that they should know what other person might sign it, but the plan was that any signer could compel any other signer to submit to arbitration any controversy that might arise between them. It was intended that the Association of Commerce should keep an index list of all who should sign agreements and deposit them with the association. The contract was in the following form:

> The undersigned, contracting with each other and with all others, jointly and severally that have heretofore contracted, do now or may hereafter contract by executing any other or different instrument containing the same language and bearing the same date (no matter when actually executed) as this instrument, each in consideration of one dollar and other good and valuable considerations to him, her, it, them, paid, the receipt of which is hereby acknowledged, and in consideration of the mutual and

several promises of each and all of the parties, not only to this contract but to all said other contracts containing the same language and bearing the same date, hereby agree with each other, and with all the other parties to all said contracts, that if any one or more controversies growing out of contract shall arise at one or successive times between them or any of them, or any parties to any of said contracts during the year 1922 or 1923, growing out of any other contract, whether written, verbal, express or implied, now existing or that may be entered into between them or any of said parties, or growing out of the dealings between any of said parties, the same shall be submitted to arbitration from time to time on demand of any such party under the Arbitrations and Awards statute of Illinois and the rules of arbitration of the Chicago Association of Commerce.

Any party to any such controversy or controversies refusing for the space of ten days after such demand so to submit any such controversy or controversies to arbitration shall be held to have broken this contract, and for so doing shall pay to the other the sum of twenty-five dollars ($25) for each and every controversy so offered to be submitted, as liquidated damages justly incurred through such refusal: *Provided,* such breach of this contract shall not in any way affect the rights of the parties other than to make the one guilty of such breach liable for the payment of said liquidated damages.

It is understood that from time to time other parties will execute this and other instruments containing the same language. All such instruments shall together be construed as one continuing contract executed for the benefit of all. The names and addresses of all parties signed to any of said instruments may be published for the benefit of all whom it may concern.

Witness the hands and seals of the parties hereto this fourteenth day of July, 1922.

The appellee signed one of these agreements and the appellant signed another. In August and September, 1922, controversies arose between the appellant and appellee, and appellee demanded that appellant should submit the controversies to arbitration in accordance with the agreement, which appellant refused to do. Appellee brought this action for the $25 named in the contract, and in his statement of claim set forth a copy of the agreement and the fact that controversies arose and the refusal of the appellant to comply with his contract.

The municipal court refused to hold propositions of law submitted by the appellant that the agreement to submit to arbitration future controversies not existing at the time of its execution was void, and that the promise of the appellant to pay $25 damages for a breach of the void contract was therefore void.

Section 3 of the statute revising the law in relation to arbitration and awards now provides that a submission to arbitration shall, unless a contrary intention is expressed therein, be irrevocable. That provision does not violate any constitutional right, and the common law rule that either party might revoke a submission at any time before an award was made and take from the arbitrator all power to make a binding award has been modified in that particular. White Eagle Laundry Co. v. Slawek, 296 Ill. 240.

Inasmuch as the arbitration of controversies avoids the formalities, delay and expense of litigation in court, the courts, speaking from an economic standpoint, have approved and recommended that method of settlement. The question, however, to be decided is not whether the courts would advise the appellant to submit his controversies with the appellee to arbitration, but whether he shall be compelled to do it because he signed an agreement that he would. The constitution has created courts for the adjustment of rights, the settlement of controversies and the redress of grievances, with all the necessary powers to enforce their judgments and decrees, and has preserved the right of citizens to invoke their jurisdiction. Parties, generally, in dealing with each other adjust their differences without the intervention of any authority, but if they do not, they may refer any such matter to arbitration or may call upon a court to enforce alleged rights or redress alleged grievances. If there is a submission to arbitration the law has always been that there must be an existing controversy between the parties. It is essential to the very idea of an arbitration that there should have been an antecedent dispute or an existing matter of difference to be adjudicated and determined, so as to conclude the parties as to the matter in issue between them. Even in a case where there is an executory contract, an agreement that any dispute that may arise under it shall be submitted to arbitration, by which the individual citizen renounces his right to resort to the courts provided by the constitution for the redress of grievances and the settlement of disputes, is void.

This agreement says that the future disputes shall be submitted to arbitration under the arbitrations and awards statute of Illinois. That statute does not authorize any agreement to submit future controversies to arbitration under it. It has not changed the law or enlarged it, but provides that all persons having requisite legal capacity may by an instrument in writing signed by them submit to one or more arbitrators, to be named in the manner indicated by such writing, any controversy existing between them. The statute plainly requires an existing controversy and is permissive to the parties when the controversy exists.

The law as above stated, holding agreements to submit future disputes or controversies to arbitration to be void has been applied where such agreements have been contained in existing executory contracts as a condition or part of such contracts, and no case has been found like this one, where there has been no existing contract, but an agreement, if there should be one, that any dispute or controversy that might arise under it shall be submitted to arbitration. One of the agreements signed by any person was a proposition to anyone who might sign another that if they should have any business relations they would each waive and forego the right guaranteed by the constitution to resort to a court for the determination of rights. Such a proposition, although accepted by some other person by signing a similar agreement, is unquestionably void.

The agreement was void and the judgment is reversed.

Judgment reversed.

HARDWARE DEALERS MUTUAL FIRE INSURANCE CO. v. GLIDDEN CO.
284 U.S. 151 (1931)

MR. JUSTICE STONE delivered the opinion of the Court.

This case is here on appeal, § 237a of the Judicial Code, from a judgment of the Supreme Court of Minnesota, upholding the constitutionality of the arbitration provisions of the standard fire insurance policy prescribed by Minnesota statutes. 181 Minn. 518 ; 233 N.W. 310.

Appellant, a Wisconsin corporation licensed to carry on the business of writing fire insurance in Minnesota, issued, within the state, its policy insuring appellees' assignor against loss, by fire, of personal property located there. The policy was in standard form, the use of which is enjoined by statutes of Minnesota on all fire insurance companies licensed to do business in the state. Mason's Minn. Stat. 1927, §§ 3314, 3366, 3512, 3515, 3711. Failure to comply with the command of the statute is ground for revocation of the license to do business, § 3550, and wilful violation of it by any company or agent is made a criminal offense, punishable by fine or imprisonment. §§ 3515, 9923.

A fire loss having occurred, the insured appointed an arbitrator and demanded of appellant that the amount be determined by arbitration as provided by the policy.[1] The appellant having refused to participate in the arbitration, the insured, in accordance with the arbitration clause procured the appointment of an umpire to act with the arbitrator designated by the insured. The arbitrator and umpire thus selected proceeded to determine the amount of the loss and made their award accordingly.

In the present suit, brought to recover the amount of the award, the appellant set up by way of defense, the single point relied on here, that so much of the statutes of Minnesota as requires the use by appellant of the arbitration provisions of the standard policy infringes the due process and equal protection clauses of the Fourteenth Amendment. In rejecting this contention and in sustaining a recovery of the amount of the award, the Supreme Court of Minnesota, consistently with its earlier decisions, ruled that the authority of the arbitrators did not extend to a determination of the liability under the policy, which was a judicial question, reserved to the courts, but that their decision as to the amount of the loss is conclusive upon the parties unless grossly excessive or inadequate, or procured by fraud. See Glidden Co. v. Retail Hardware Mut. Fire Ins. Co., 181 Minn. 518, 521, 522 ; 233 N.W. 310 ; Abramowitz v. Continental Ins. Co., 170 Minn. 215 ; 212 N.W. 449 ; Harrington v. Agricultural Ins. Co., 179 Minn. 510 ; 229 N.W. 792.

This type of arbitration clause has long been

---

[1]. Mason's Minn. Stat. 1927, § 3512. " . . . In case of loss, except in case of total loss on buildings, under this policy and a failure of the parties to agree as to the amount of the loss, it is mutually agreed that the amount of such loss shall, as above provided, be ascertained by two competent, disinterested and impartial appraisers who shall be residents of this state, the insured and this company each selecting one within fifteen days after a statement of such loss has been rendered to the company, as herein provided, and in case either party fail to select an appraiser within such time, the other appraiser and the umpire selected, as herein provided, may act as a board of appraisers, and whatever award they shall find shall be as binding as though the two appraisers had been chosen: and the two so chosen shall first select a competent, disinterested and impartial umpire; provided, that if after five days the two appraisers cannot agree on such an umpire, the presiding judge of the district court of the county wherein the loss occurs may appoint such an umpire upon application of either party in writing by giving five days' notice thereof in writing to the other party. Unless within fifteen days after a statement of such loss has been rendered to the company, either party, the assured or the company, shall have notified the other in writing that such party demands an appraisal, such right to an appraisal shall be waived; the appraisers together shall then estimate and appraise the loss, stating separately sound value and damage, and, failing to agree, shall submit their differences to the umpire; and the award in writing of any two shall determine the amount of the loss. . . ."

commonly used in fire insurance policies, both in Minnesota and elsewhere, and, when voluntarily placed in the insurance contract, compliance with its provisions has been held to be a condition precedent to an action on the policy. Gasser v. Sun Fire Office, 42 Minn. 315; 44 N.W. 252; Hamilton v. Liverpool, London & Globe Ins. Co., 136 U.S. 242; Scott v. Avery, 5 House of Lords 811, 854; see Red Cross Line v. Atlantic Fruit Co., 264 U.S. 109, 121.

Appellees insist that the use of the clause here was voluntary, since the appellant was not compelled to write the policy, and that in any case appellant, by long acquiesence in the statute, is estopped to challenge, after the loss, the right of the insured to rely upon it. Without stopping to examine these contentions, we assume that appellant's freedom of contract was restricted by operation of the statute, and pass directly to the question decided by the state court, whether the Fourteenth Amendment precludes the exercise of such compulsion by the legislative power.

The right to make contracts embraced in the concept of liberty guaranteed by the Fourteenth Amendment is not unlimited. Liberty implies only freedom from arbitrary restraint, not immunity from reasonable regulations and prohibitions imposed in the interests of the community. Chicago, Burlington & Quincy R. Co. v. McGuire, 219 U.S. 549, 567. Hence, legislation otherwise within the scope of acknowledged state power, not unreasonably or arbitrarily exercised, cannot be condemned because it curtails the power of the individual to contract. McLean v. Arkansas, 211 U.S. 539; Schmidinger v. Chicago, 226 U.S. 578; German Alliance Insurance Co. v. Lewis, 233 U.S. 389; Erie R. Co. v. Williams, 233 U.S. 685; Keokee Cons. Coke Co. v. Taylor, 234 U.S. 224.

The present statute substitutes a determination by arbitration for trial in court of the single issue of the amount of loss suffered under a fire insurance policy. As appellant's objection to it is directed specifically to the power of the state to substitute the one remedy for the other, rather than to the constitutionality of the particular procedure prescribed or followed before the arbitrators, it suffices to say that the procedure by which rights may be enforced and wrongs remedied is peculiarly a subject of state regulation and control. The Fourteenth Amendment neither implies that all trials must be by jury, nor guarantees any particular form or method of state procedure. See Missouri ex rel. Hurwitz v. North, 271 U.S. 40. In the exercise of that power and to satisfy a public need, a state may choose the remedy best adapted, in the legislative judgment, to protect the interests concerned, provided its choice is not unreasonable or arbitrary, and the procedure it adopts satisfies the constitutional requirements of reasonable notice and opportunity to be heard.

The record and briefs present no facts disclosing the reasons for the enactment of the present legislation or the effects of its operation, but as it deals with a subject within the scope of the legislative power, the presumption of constitutionality is to be indulged. O'Gorman & Young, Inc., v. Hartford Fire Ins. Co., 282 U.S. 251; see Standard Oil Co. v. Marysville, 279 U.S. 582, 584; Ohio ex rel. Clarke v. Deckebach, 274 U.S. 392, 397. We cannot assume that the Minnesota legislature did not have knowledge of conditions supporting its judgment that the legislation was in the public interest, and it is enough that, when the statute is read in the light of circumstances generally known to attend the recovery of fire insurance losses, the possibility of a rational basis for the legislative judgment is not excluded.

Without the aid of the presumption, we know that the arbitration clause has long been voluntarily inserted by insurers in fire policies, and we share in the common knowledge that the amount of loss is a fruitful and often the only subject of controversy between insured and insurer; that speedy determination of the policy liability such as may be secured by arbitration of this issue is a matter of wide concern, see Fidelity Mut. Life Assn. v. Mettler, 185 U.S. 308; Farmers' & Merchants' Ins. Co. v. Dobney, 189 U.S. 301; that in the appraisal of the loss by arbitration, expert knowledge and prompt inspection of the damaged property may be availed of to an extent not ordinarily possible in the course of the more deliberate processes of a judicial proceeding. These considerations are sufficient to support the exercise of the legislative judgment in requiring a more summary method of determining the amount of the loss than that afforded by traditional forms. Hence the requirement that disputes of this type arising under this special class of insurance contracts be submitted to arbitrators, cannot be deemed to be a denial of either due process or equal protection of the laws.

Granted, as we now hold, that the state, in the present circumstances, has power to prescribe a summary method of ascertaining the amount of loss, the requirements of the Fourteenth Amendment, so far as now invoked, are satisfied if the substitute remedy is substantial and efficient. See Crane v. Hahlo, 258 U.S. 142, 147. We cannot say that the determination by arbitrators, chosen as provided by the present statute, of the single issue of the amount of loss under a fire insurance policy, reserving all other issues for trial in court, does not afford such a remedy, or that in this respect it falls short of due process, more than the provisions of state workmen's compensation laws for establishing the amount of compensation by a commission, New York Central R. Co. v. White, 243 U.S. 188, 207–208 ; Mountain Timber Co. v. Washington, 243 U.S. 219, 235; or the appraisal by a commissioner of the value of property taken or destroyed by the public, made controlling by condemnation statutes, Dohany v. Rogers, 281 U.S. 362, 369; Long Island Water Supply Co. v. Brooklyn, 166 U.S. 685, 695 ; Crane v. Hahlo, *supra,* p. 147 ; or findings of fact by boards or commissions which, by various statutes, are made conclusive upon the courts if supported by evidence, Tagg Bros. & Moorhead v. United States, 280 U.S. 420; Interstate Commerce Comm. v. Union Pacific R. Co., 222 U.S. 541; Virginian Ry. Co. v. United States, 272 U.S. 658, 663; Silberschein v. United States, 266 U.S. 221; Ma-King Products Co. v. Blair, 271 U.S. 479.

Affirmed.

MATTER OF BERKOVITZ v. ARBIB and HOULBERG
230 N.Y. 261, 130 N.E. 288 (1921)

CARDOZO, J. The validity of the Arbitration Law (L. 1920, ch. 275 ; Consol. Laws, ch. 72), and its application to existing contracts and pending actions, are the questions here involved.

In one case (Matter of Berkovitz & Spiegel), a contract for the sale of goatskins was made in November, 1919. It provides that the skins shall "be the usual quality of their kind, and claims in regard thereto shall not invalidate this contract, but shall be settled amicably or by arbitration in the usual manner." The skins, which came from India, arrived in New York on April 12, 1920. The Arbitration Law took effect on April 19 of the same year. The buyer, after inspection of the goods, gave notice of rejection. The seller demanded arbitration, and moved, under the statute, for the appointment of an arbitrator. The appointment was refused at Special Term and at the Appellate Division, the latter court holding that the Arbitration Law did not apply to pre-existing contracts.

In the second case (Spiritusfabriek Astra v. Sugar Products Company), a contract for the sale of molasses was made in July 1914. One of its provisions is: "The regular arbitration and force majeure clauses are to form part of this contract.... It is agreed in the event of an arbitration being called, it is to sit in London." The plaintiff, the buyer, brought action against the seller in July, 1916. The defendant answered with defenses and counterclaims. Between July, 1916, and April 19, 1920, there was active litigation. One phase of the controversy, a motion by the defendant for judgment on the pleadings, came as far as this court (221 N.Y. 581). Plaintiff expended several thousand dollars for fees and disbursements. In June, 1920, on the eve of the trial, the defendant moved for a stay of proceedings until the matters in difference were arbitrated. The Special Term denied the motion, and the Appellate Division affirmed.

(1) We think the Arbitration Law is applicable to pre-existing contracts, but not to pending actions.

Section 2 of the statute (L. 1920, ch. 275 ; Consol. Laws, ch. 72) declares a new public policy, and abrogates an ancient rule.

> A provision in a written contract to settle by arbitration a controversy thereafter arising between the parties to the contract, or a submission hereafter entered into of an existing controversy to arbitration pursuant to title eight of chapter seventeen of the code of civil procedure, shall be valid, enforcible and irrevocable, save upon such grounds as exist at law or in equity for the revocation of any contract (Arbitration Law, section 2).

Sections 3 and 4 prescribe the procedure for the enforcement of the contract and the naming of the arbitrator.

Section 5 directs a stay of proceedings "if any suit or proceeding be brought" when arbitration should be ordered.

The common-law limitation upon the enforcement of promises to arbitrate is part of the law of remedies (Meacham v. Jamestown, F. & C. R. R. Co., 211 N.Y. 346, 352 ; Aktieselskabet K. F. F. v. Redieri Aktiebolaget Atlanten, 232 Fed. Rep. 403, 405 ; 250 Fed. Rep. 935 ; U.S. Asphalt Refining Co. v. Trinidad Lake Petroleum Co., 222 Fed. Rep. 1006, 1011). The rule to be applied is the rule of the forum. Both in this court and elsewhere, the law has been so declared. Arbitration is a form of procedure whereby differences may be settled. It is not a definition of the rights and wrongs out of which differences grow. This statute did not attach a new obligation to sales already made. It vindicated by a new method the obligation then existing.

In thus classifying its purpose, we have gone far in determining its effect. Changes in the form of remedies are applicable to proceedings thereafter instituted for the redress of wrongs already done. They are retrospective if viewed in relation to the wrongs. They are prospective if viewed in relation to the means of reparation (Lazarus v. Metr. E. R. Co., 145 N.Y. 581, 585 ; Laird v. Carton, 196 N.Y. 169 ; Brearley School, Ltd., v. Ward, 201 N.Y. 358, 363). A different problem arises when proceedings are already pending. There is then a distinction to be noted. The change is applicable even then if directed to the litigation in future steps and stages (Lazarus v. Metr. E. R. Co., supra ; Lamport v. Smedley, 213 N.Y. 82, 86). It is inapplicable, unless in exceptional conditions, where the effect is to reach backward, and nullify by relation the things already done (Maxwell Interpretation of Statutes [5th ed.], pp. 348, 370 ; Reid v. Mayor, etc., of N.Y., 139 N.Y. 534 ; U.S. Fidelity & G. Co. v. Struthers Wells Co., 209 U.S. 306 ; Attorney-General v. Chandler, 108 Mich. 569, 571). There can be no presumption, for illustration, that a statute regulating the form of pleadings or decisions is intended to invalidate pleadings already served, or decisions already filed (Gen. Construction Law [Cons. Laws, ch. 22], secs. 93, 94). We speak, of course, of the principles that govern in default of the disclosure by the legislature of a different intent. Nice distinctions are often necessary (Jacobus v. Colgate, 217 N.Y. 235). The word "remedy" itself conceals at times an ambiguity, since changes of the form are often closely bound up with changes of the substance (Jacobus v. Colgate, supra, at p. 244 ; Isola v. Weber, 147 N.Y. 329). The problem does not permit us to ignore gradations of importance and other differences of degree. In the end, it is in considerations of good sense and justice that the solution must be found (Maxwell, supra, pp. 348, 370).

Applied to the case of Berkovitz & Spiegel, these principles and presumptions require that arbitration be enforced. The statute was enacted after the contract had been made, but before a remedy was invoked. The range of choice is governed by the remedies available at the time when choice is made. We are told that the promise to arbitrate when made was illegal and a nullity. Even before the statute, this was not wholly true. Public policy was thought to forbid that the promise be specifically enforced. Public policy did not forbid an award of damages if it was broken (Haggart v. Morgan, 5 N.Y. 422, 427 ; Finucane Co. v. Bd. of Education, 190 N.Y. 76, 83). The result would not be changed, however, if the right to damages were denied. A promise that differences will be arbitrated is not illegal and a nullity without reference to the law in force when differences arise. Since it is directed solely to the remedy, its validity is to

be measured by the public policy prevailing when a remedy is sought. In that respect, it is not different from a promise that future controversies shall be submitted to a court. The jurisdiction of the court at the time of the submission will determine whether the promise is to be rejected or enforced. This is so whether jurisdiction in the interval has been diminished or enlarged. Of course, we exclude cases where the contract is inherently immoral or in contravention of a statute. General contracts of arbitration were never subject to that reproach. In these circumstances, public policy does not speak as of the date of the promise that the parties shall have a remedy then unknown to the law. Public policy speaks as of the hour and the occasion when the promise is appealed to, and the remedy invoked.

Our decision in Jacobus v. Colgate (217 N.Y. 235), much relied upon by counsel, has little pertinency here. We dealt there with a statute which gave a remedy for a wrong where there had been no remedy before. Right and remedy coalesced, and took their origin together. Finding them so united, we construed the statute which defined them as directed to the future (Cf. Winfree v. No. Pac. Ry. Co., 227 U.S. 296). Here the wrong to be redressed is the rejection of merchandise in violation of a contract. Such a wrong had a remedy for centuries before the statute. All that the statute has done is to make two remedies available when formerly there was one.

We think the promise to arbitrate must be held within the statute, and the subject-matter of the controversy within the purview of the promise.

Different considerations apply to the second of the cases, in which demand is made by the Sugar Products Company after four years of litigation that proceedings in the cause be stayed. That action, as we have seen was begun in July, 1916. The plaintiff then elected to disregard the arbitration clause, and seek a remedy in the courts. The defendant did, it is true, demand the benefit of the clause, but at the date of the joinder of issue the defense was insufficient in law. To hold that the Arbitration Law of 1920 applies in such condition is to nullify a cause of action by relation, and by relation again to establish a defense. Years of costly litigation will thus be rendered futile. Nothing in the language of the statute gives support to the belief that consequences so harsh and drastic were intended by the legislature: "If any suit or proceeding be brought," its progress shall be stayed (Arbitration Law, section 5). Full effect is given to this provision when it is limited to suits or proceedings brought thereafter. We are not to presume a willingness that rights already accrued through actions lawfully initiated are to be divested or impaired (Lazarus v. Metr. E. E. Co., at p. 584; General Construction Law, secs. 93, 94). In such circumstances, it is impossible to apply the statute to the stages of the litigation that remain without applying it at the same time, at least in some degree, and with some extent of prejudice, to those that have gone by.

(2) The validity of the statute remains to be considered.

(a) The statute is assailed as inconsistent with article I, section 2, of the Constitution of the state, which secures the right of trial by jury. The right is one that may be waived (People v. Quigg, 59 N.Y. 83; People ex rel. McLaughlin v. Bd. Police Commissioners, 174 N.Y. 450, 456; Boyden v. Lamb, 152 Mass. 416, 419; Constitution, art. I, sec. 2). It *was* waived by the consent to arbitrate. We are told that the consent must be disregarded as illusory because the parties could not be held to it till this statute was adopted. A consent, none the less, it was, however deficient may once have been the remedy to enforce it. Those who gave it, did so in view of the possibility that a better remedy might come. They took the chances of the future. They must abide by its vicissitudes.

(b) The statute is assailed again as abridging the general jurisdiction of the Supreme Court, which article VI, section 1, of the Constitution of the state continues unimpaired.

Jurisdiction exists that rights may be maintained. Rights are not maintained that jurisdiction may exist. The People, in establishing a Supreme Court to administer the law, did not petrify the law which the court is to administer (Matter of Stillwell, 139 N.Y. 337, 342; Clapp v. McCabe, 84 Hun, 379; 155 N.Y. 525; Constitution, art. I, sec. 16). Article VI, section 1, preserves the existence of the court "with general jurisdiction in law and equity," but the same article in section 3 secures to the legislature "the same power to alter and regulate the jurisdiction and proceedings in law and equity that it has heretofore exercised." When change shall be held to trench on jurisdiction in a prohibited degree, cannot be known with certainty in advance of the event as the result of general definition. "The process of judicial inclusion and exclusion" must serve to trace the line. Power lodged in the Supreme Court is not to be withdrawn merely that it may be transferred and established somewhere else. Power, though not transferred, is still not to be withdrawn, if fundamental or inherent in the conception of a court with general jurisdiction in equity and law. Changes, we may

assume, will be condemned if subversive of historic traditions of dignity and power. Such is not the change effected by this statute. The Supreme Court does not lose a power inherent in its very being when it loses power to give aid in the repudiation of a contract, concluded without fraud or error, whereby differences are to be settled without resort to litigation. For the right to nullify is substituted the duty to enforce. Contending parties have contracted that the merits of their controversy shall be conditioned upon the report of arbitrators, as upon any other extrinsic fact which agreement might prescribe. Whether they have so contracted is a question which the court must still determine for itself (Arbitration Law, section 3). If the contract has not been made or is invalid, the court will proceed, as in any other case, to a determination of the merits. If it has been made and is valid, the court will stay its hand till the extrinsic fact is ascertained, and the condition thus fulfilled. That done, its doors are open for whatever measure of relief the situation may exact (Hamlyn & Co. v. Talisker Distillery, 1894, A.C. 202; Wilson v. Glasgow Tramways & O. Co., 5 Session Cases [Scot.], 4th series, 981, 992, quoted by Cohen, COMMERCIAL ARBITRATION AND THE LAW, pp. 262, 263). The award will be enforced if valid, and for cause will be annulled. "In common language where no attempt is made at logical accuracy," it is sometimes said that the contract of arbitration "ousts the jurisdiction" of the judges (Wilson v. Glasgow Tramways & O. Co., supra). "In strictness, however, it does not oust the jurisdiction, but merely introduces a new plea into the cause" on which the judge as at common law is under a duty to decide (Wilson v. Glasgow Tramways & O. Co., supra). The situation is the same in substance as when effect is given to a release or to a covenant not to sue. Jurisdiction is not renounced, but the time and manner of its exercise are adapted to the convention of the parties restricting the media of proof. Long before the statute there was a like withholding of relief whenever the subject-matter of arbitration, instead of extending to all differences, was limited to some (Prest., etc., D. & H. C. Co. v. Pa. Coal Co., 50 N.Y. 250; Scott v. Avery, 5 H. L. [sic] 811; Hamilton v. Liverpool, L. & G. Ins. Co., 136 U.S. 242, 255). There was a like refusal to permit the litigation of the merits when the contract though general, was no longer executory but had ripened into an award. The change resulting from the statute is one of measure and degree.

We think there is no departure from constitutional restrictions in this legislative declaration of the public policy of the state. The ancient rule, with its exceptions and refinements, was criticized by many judges as anomalous and unjust (D. & H. C. Co. v. Pa. Coal Co., supra, at p. 258 ; Fudickar v. Guardian Mutual Life Ins. Co., 62 N.Y. 392, 399 ; U.S. Asphalt Refining Co. v. Trinidad Lake Petroleum Co., 222 Fed. Rep. 1006, and cases there cited). It was followed with frequent protest, in deference to early precedents. Its hold even upon the common law was hesitating and feeble. We are now asked to declare it so imbedded in the very foundations of our jurisprudence and the structure of our courts that nothing less than an amendment of the Constitution is competent to change it. We will not go so far. The judges might have changed the rule themselves if they had abandoned some early precedents, as at times they seemed inclined to do. They might have whittled it down to nothing, as was done indeed in England, by distinctions between promises that are collateral and those that are conditions (Scott v. Avery, supra ; London Tramways Co. v. Bailey, L. R. Q. B. D. 217, 221 ; Spackman v. Plumstead Dist. Bd. of Works, L. R. 10 App. Cas. 229 ; Trainor v Phœnix Fire Assur. Co., 65 L. T. Rep. 825). No one would have suspected that in so doing they were undermining a jurisdiction which the Constitution had charged them with a duty to preserve. Not different is the effect of like changes when wrought by legislation (Alexander v. Bennett, 60 N.Y. 204, 206, 207).

(c) Finally, the statute is said to violate article I, section 10, of the Constitution of the United States on the ground that it impairs the obligation of a contract. There is no merit in the contention. The obligation of the contract is strengthened, not impaired.

HISCOCK, CH. J., HOGAN, POUND, McLAUGHLIN and ANDREWS, JJ., concur ; CRANE, J., dissents on opinion of DOWLING, J., at Appellate Division.

MARINE TRANSIT CORP. v. DREYFUS
284 U.S. 263 (1931)

MR. CHIEF JUSTICE HUGHES delivered the opinion of the Court.

The petitioner, Marine Transit Corporation, entered into a written booking agreement with the respondents, Louis Dreyfus & Company, to furnish insurable canal tonnage for about 200,000 bushels of wheat, to be carried from Buffalo to New York. The contract provided that it should be "subject to New York Produce Exchange Canal Grain Charter Party No. 1 as amended." That charter party contained the following provision as to disputes: "All disputes arising under this contract to be arbitrated before the Committee on Grain of the New York Produce Exchange whose decision shall be final and binding."

Under this contract, the Marine Transit Corporation, in September, 1928, provided the barge *Edward A. Ryan* to carry 19,200 bushels of the above-stated amount. This was a shipment, as the bill of lading of the Marine Transit Corporation shows, to the order of the Bank of Nova Scotia and was from Fort William, Ontario, "in bond, for export," to be delivered "on surrender of original Lake bill of lading properly endorsed." While in tow of the petitioner's tug *Gerald A. Fagan* on the New York Barge Canal, and approaching the federal lock at Troy, the *Edward A. Ryan* struck the guide wall and sank with its cargo. The respondents, Louis Dreyfus & Company, filed a libel in admiralty against the Marine Transit Corporation *in personam,* and against the tug *Gerald A. Fagan, in rem,* to recover damages for the loss of the wheat. The libel was also against a barge *John E. Enright,* one of the boats in the tow, but the action as to that boat was subsequently discontinued. A claim for the tug *Gerald A. Fagan* was made by the Marine Transit Corporation and a stipulation for value was filed by it, as claimant, in the sum of $26000, with the usual provision that the stipulation should be void if the claimant and the stipulator (the Continental Casualty Company) should abide by all orders of the court and pay the amount awarded by its final decree, and that otherwise the stipulation should remain in full force.

After answer to the libel had been filed by the Marine Transit Corporation, as respondent and as claimant of the tug *Gerald A. Fagan*, the libellants moved for a reference of the dispute to arbitration in accordance with the provision of the booking contract. This motion was granted "only as to the issues raised by the contract between the libellants and the Marine Transit Corporation," and the latter was ordered to submit to arbitration as to these issues before the Committee on Grain of the New York Produce Exchange. The arbitration proceeded and resulted in an award against the Marine Transit Corporation for the sum of $23,016, with interest and the costs and expenses of the arbitration. The award was confirmed by the District Court and an order—in substance, a final decree—was entered for the recovery by the libellants against the Marine Transit Corporation of the amount of the award, with the further provision that, if payment was not made within ten days, execution should issue against the Marine Transit Corporation and the stipulator. A motion to restrain the libellants from recovering from the claimant or its stipulator on behalf of the tug *Gerald A. Fagan* was denied. The decree entered upon the award was affirmed by the Circuit Court of Appeals, 49 F. (2d) 215, and the case comes here on writ of certiorari.

There is no question that the controversy between the petitioner and the respondents was within the arbitration clause of the booking contract. That provision was valid, Red Cross Line v. Atlantic Fruit Co., 264 U.S. 109, 122, and, as it related to all disputes arising under the contract, it applied to the controversy with the Marine Transit Corporation as operating owner of the tug *Gerald A. Fagan*, which was used for the agreed transportation. The questions presented are (1) whether the action of the District Court was authorized by the United States Arbitration Act,[1] and (2) whether that Act, as thus applied, is constitutional.

First. In construing the statute, we deal only with the questions raised by the present record. The loss occurred upon a waterway which was part of the navigable waters of the United States, The Robert W. Parsons, 191 U.S. 17, and while the cargo was being transported by the petitioner under a maritime contract. The subject matter of the controversy thus lay within the jurisdiction of admiralty. The ambiguities of the statute have been stressed in argument, but we think that its provisions embrace a case such as the one before us[2] and it is not necessary to discuss others. Section 4 authorizes a court, which would otherwise have jurisdiction in admiralty 'of the subject matter of a suit arising out of the controversy between the parties' to a written agreement for arbitration, to "make an order directing the

parties to proceed to arbitration in accordance with the terms of the agreement." Section 8 explicitly provides that where a cause of action is "otherwise justiciable in admiralty, then, notwithstanding anything herein to the contrary, the party claiming to be aggrieved may begin his proceeding hereunder by libel and seizure of the vessel or other property of the other party according to the usual course of admiralty proceedings," and the court may then "direct the parties to proceed with the arbitration and shall retain jurisdiction to enter its decree upon the award."

In this instance, the libel against the vessel came directly within the provision of § 8. But the petitioner insists that the Distrct Court "had no power under that section to make an order for arbitration of the proceeding against the Marine Transit Corporation, *in personam*." Section 8, it is said, applies "only to proceedings *in rem* or proceedings *in personam* where there has been an attachment of the property of the respondent," and there was no such attachment in this case. And it is contended that, aside from § 8, the Act does not provide for the granting of an order for arbitration "in a pending suit." With respect to the last contention, it may be observed that § 3 provides for a stay in a pending suit until arbitration has been had in accordance with the terms of the agreement, and it would be an anomaly if the court could grant such a stay and could not direct the arbitration to proceed, although the court, admittedly, could have made an order for the arbitration if no suit had been brought. We think that the petitioner's argument is based upon a misconception of the statute. The intent of § 8 is to provide for the enforcement of the agreement for arbitration, without depriving the aggrieved party of his right, under the admiralty practice, to proceed against "the vessel or other property" belonging to the other party to the agreement. The statutory provision does not contemplate "the vessel or other property," which may be seized, as being the party to the arbitration agreement. By the express terms of § 8, the libel and seizure are authorized as an initial step in a proceeding to enforce the agreement for arbitration, and it is the parties to that agreement who may be directed to proceed with the arbitration. Here, the Marine Transit Corporation was the party to the arbitration agreement. It had used the tug as a facility for the transportation of the libellants' wheat, and the dispute as to liability was within the promise to arbitrate. If there was to be an order for arbitration, it would appropriately run against the Marine Transit Corporation to enforce that obligation. It was not necessary or

---

1. "Sec. 8. That if the basis of jurisdiction be a cause of action otherwise justiciable in admiralty, then, notwithstanding anything herein to the contrary, the party claiming to be aggrieved may begin his proceeding hereunder by libel and seizure of the vessel or other property of the other party according to the usual course of admiralty proceedings, and the court shall then have jurisdiction to direct the parties to proceed with the arbitration and shall retain jurisdiction to enter its decree upon the award."

2. The Committee on the Judiciary of the House of Representatives, in its report upon the bill, which with the senate amendment became the Act in question, said:

"The purpose of this bill is to make valid and enforcible agreements for arbitration contained in contracts involving interstate commerce or within the jurisdiction of admiralty, or which may be the subject of litigation in the federal courts. ... The remedy is founded also upon the federal control over interstate commerce and over admiralty." HOUSE REP, No. 96, 68th Cong., 1st sess. See, also, CONG. REC., vol. 66, pt. 3, 68th Cong., 2d sess., pp. 3003, 3004.

proper that the order should run against the tug. Nor was it necessary that the court in directing the arbitration should attempt to split the proceeding with respect to the demand in the suit *in personam* against the corporation and that *in rem* against the tug. The Marine Transit Corporation was before the court both as respondent and as owner and claimant of the vessel seized, and the agreement to arbitrate bound the corporation in both capacities. We conclude that the order directing the arbitration of the issues arising under the contract between the libellants and the Marine Transit Corporation was authorized by the statute.

We do not conceive it to be open to question that, where the court has authority under the statute, as we find that it had in this case, to make an order for arbitration, the court also has authority to confirm the award or to set it aside for irregularity, fraud, *ultra vires* or other defect. Upon the motion to confirm the award in this case, objections to the proceedings before the arbitrators were overruled by the District Court and are not pressed here.

The petitioner also insists that, under § 9, a judgment may be entered upon the award only if the parties have so agreed in their contract for arbitration and that the agreement here does not so provide. But the agreement for arbitration stipulated that the award should be "final and binding." The award was accordingly binding upon the Marine Transit Corporation both as respondent and as the owner and claimant of the tug, and the District Court entered its decree upon the award against that corporation under the authority expressly conferred by § 8.

The Circuit Court of Appeals also upheld the decree as against the stipulator, as its stipulation conformed to Admiralty Rule 8 of the Southern District of New York[3] and the decree was in accord with the stipulation and admiralty practice. The Palmyra, 12 Wheat. 1, 10 ; The Wanata, 95 U.S. 600, 611. We express no doubt as to the correctness of this conclusion, which the petitioner contests, but we have no occasion to deal with the question, as the stipulator has taken no steps to obtain a review of the decree in this Court.

We find no ground for disturbing the decree as unauthorized by the statute.

Second. The constitutional question raised by this application of the statute, is whether it is compatible with the maintenenace of the judicial power of the United States as extended to cases of admiralty and maritime jurisdiction (Const. Art. III).

In Red Cross Line v. Atlantic Fruit Co., *supra* (at pp. 122, 123), this Court pointed out that in admiralty "agreements to submit controversies to arbitration are valid," and that "reference of maritime controversies to arbitration has long been common practice." "An executory agreement," said the court, "may be made a rule of court" and the "substantive right created by an agreement to submit disputes to arbitration is recognized as a perfect obligation." The question, then, is one merely as to the power of the Congress to afford a remedy in admiralty to enforce such an obligation. It was because the question was one of remedy only, that this Court decided that a State, by virtue of the clause saving to suitors "the right of a common law remedy,"[4] had the power "to confer upon its courts the authority to compel parties within its jurisdiction to specifically perform an agreement for arbitration, which is valid by the general maritime law, as well as by the law of the State," and is contained in a maritime contract made within the State and there to be performed. Red Cross Line v. Atlantic Fruit Co., *supra*, at p. 124. The general power of the Congress to provide remedies in matters falling within the admiralty jurisdiction of the federal courts, and to regulate their procedure, is indisputable. The petitioner contends that the Congress could not confer upon courts of admiralty the authority to grant specific performance. But it is well settled that the Congress, in providing appropriate means to enforce obligations cognizable in admiralty, may draw upon other systems. Thus the Congress may authorize a trial by jury in admiralty, as it has done in relation to certain cases arising on the Great Lakes. Courts of admiralty may be empowered to grant injunctions, as in proceedings for limitation of liability. Similarly, there can be no question of the power of Congress to authorize specific performance when that is an appropriate remedy in a matter within the admiralty jurisdiction. As Chief Justice Taney said in The Genesee Chief, 12 How. 443, 460:

> The Constitution declares that the judicial power of the United States shall extend to "all cases of admiralty and maritime jurisdiction." But it does not direct that the court shall proceed according to ancient and established forms, or shall adopt any other form or mode of practice. . . . In admiralty and maritime cases there is no such limitation as to

---

3. This rule is as follows: "Such stipulation shall contain the consent of the stipulators, that if the libellant or petitioner recover, the decree may be entered against them for an amount not exceeding the amount named in such stipulation and that thereupon execution may issue against their goods, chattels, lands, and tenements or other real estate."

4. Judicial Code, § 24 (3); U.S.C., Tit. 28, § 41 (3).

the mode of proceeding, and Congress may therefore in cases of that description give either party right of trial by jury, or modify the practice of the court in any other respect that it deems more conducive to the administration of justice.

In this instance a remedy is provided to fit the agreement. The Congress has authorized the court to direct the parties to proceed to arbitration in accordance with a valid stipulation of a maritime contract, and to enter a decree upon the award found to be regular and within the terms of the agreement. We think that the objection on constitutional grounds is without merit.

Decree affirmed.

MATTER OF BULLARD (GRACE CO.)
240 N.Y. 388, 148 N.E. 559 (1925)

The facts herein are as follows: Shipments under two contracts were to be made by Grace Company to Bullard Company during November, 1923, from the Argentine. The contracts were each for the sale of 500 cases of Argentine best creamery butter—salted—which contained a provision that the Argentine government inspection certificate certifying that the shipment is of first grade and free from preservatives, together with inspector's certificate certifying free from mold, and weight certificate to be attached to documents were to be final. Each contract also contained a provision that any dispute under the contracts was to be settled by arbitration before the New York Mercantile Exchange. The c.i.f. contracts read: "Price: 32c per lb. c.i.f. New York."

Bullard Company made a claim on Grace Company that the butter did not come up to the quality called for by the contract and demanded an arbitration. The respondent, Grace Company, claimed that the question of quality of the butter on its arrival in New York could not be arbitrated, because there was no dispute arising under the contract since the contract provided that certificates should be final on the subject of quality. The appellant, Bullard Company, asserted that it was entitled to an allowance by reason of the defective quality of the butter and that such claim constituted a dispute to be settled by arbitration under the terms of the contract.

A submission was made which stated the matters submitted to arbitration as follows:

> Whether or not 500 cases of Argentine Best Creamery Butter, contract November 13th, 1923, and 500 cases Argentine Best Creamery Butter, contract

November 27th, 1923, are a good delivery per terms of said contracts.

The parties then proceeded to the holding of the arbitration before arbitrators selected. On the hearing of the arbitration the appellants' representative claimed the right to arbitrate the quality of the butter. The respondent's representative stated that the certificates were final and that the quality of the butter was not the subject of the arbitration. The chairman of the arbitrators ruled that the Argentine inspection was not final and that the quality of the butter must be taken into consideration by the arbitrators.

Before any testimony was taken on this branch of the case, Grace Company, the respondent, together with one of the arbitrators, withdrew, refused to carry out the arbitration proceedings and took no further part therein. Two arbitrators thereafter signed findings and an award, dated January 11, 1924, making an allowance to Bullard Company on each contract for the loss occasioned by the alleged inferior quality of the butter on arrival. The Special Term confirmed the award and denied a motion to revoke it, and judgment was entered thereon. The Appellate Division reversed the order and judgment.

POUND, J. A preliminary question involved in this appeal is as follows: When a submission to arbitration by three arbitrators has been entered into pursuant to the terms of a contract to settle all disputes thereunder by arbitration and one of the arbitrators formally withdraws and refuses to take part therein before all the proofs of the parties have been heard, may two arbitrators proceed with the hearing and make a valid award?

Civil Practice Act, section 1453, provides

> All the arbitrators selected as prescribed in this article must meet together and hear all the allegations and proofs of the parties; but an award by a majority of them is valid unless the concurrence of all is expressly required in the submission.*

When an arbitrator withdraws before the allegations and proofs of the parties have been heard, the filling of the vacancy by appointment of a substitute arbitrator either under the terms of the contract or under Arbitration Law (§§ 3, 4) becomes a prerequisite to further proceedings under the submission. (Bulson v Lohnes, 29 N.Y. 291.) The purpose of the statute was to

---

*[The quoted provision is to be found in Section 1456 of the CPA as it existed in 1952. See Appendix C. Compare CPLR § 7506(e) and (f).]

change the common-law rule which permitted two arbitrators to hear when the third was notified and refused to attend or was willfully absent (Crofoot v. Allen, 2 Wend. 494) and its plain mandate may not be ignored, whether an arbitrator at this stage of the proceedings withdraws for good cause or arbitrarily. (See, however, Matter of Am. Eagle Fire Ins. Co. v. N.J. Ins. Co., 240 N.Y. 398, decided herewith.)

A decision on this point alone might dispose of the appeal but the question of the right of a party to withdraw from a submission to arbitration is also presented and a determination of this question is essential to the complete disposition of the case. Appellant contends that it may go on with the arbitration without application to the court because a submission is irrevocable except as other contracts are revocable. (Arbitration Law, § 2.) Respondent says, you may go on with the arbitration over our withdrawal only when the court says that you are proceeding under the terms of the submission and that we are in default in refusing to arbitrate the question submitted. An analysis of the Arbitration Law becomes helpful at this stage. It makes no change in the law as it stood at the time of its enactment except to make arbitration agreements and submissions irrevocable and to provide the judicial remedy in case of a default. (Berizzi Co. v. Krausz, 239 N.Y. 315, 318, 319.)

Arbitration Law, section 2, provides:

> Validity of arbitration agreements. A provision in a written contract to settle by arbitration a controversy thereafter arising between the parties to the contract, or a submission hereafter entered into of an existing controversy to arbitration pursuant to title eight of chapter seventeen of the code of civil procedure, or article eighty-three of the civil practice act, shall be *valid, enforceable and irrevocable, save upon such grounds as exist at law or in equity for the revocation of any contract.*

But neither the agreement to arbitrate nor the submission is self-executory. A party to an arbitration agreement may break his contract. A remedy is provided in case of his default by Arbitration Law, section 3. A party aggrieved by the failure, neglect or refusal of another to perform either under a contract or a submission providing for arbitration may petition the Supreme Court for an order directing that the arbitration proceed. On such an application, the other party may put in issue (a) the making of the contract to arbitrate the questions sought to be submitted to arbitration, or (b) the submission of such questions to arbitration, or (c) the failure to comply therewith. If the making of the contract or the submission or the default

be in issue the issue thus joined shall be tried. A jury trial may be demanded. It is only when it is found by the court that a written contract of arbitration has been made or a submission has been entered into covering the question sought to be included in the arbitration and that a party is in default in the performance thereof that the court will order the parties to the contract or submission to proceed with the arbitration in accordance with the terms thereof. The question arises in this case whether there was a default in the performance of the arbitration agreement or the submission. Grace Company contends that it made no contract to arbitrate and no submission to arbitrate the question of the quality of the butter on its arrival in New York. The question is at least arguable. When it withdrew Bullard Company became a party aggrieved. It could not proceed with the arbitration on the question of quality although arbitrators had been chosen and the hearing had begun.

Much reliance is placed by the appellants on the English case of Bankers & Shippers Insurance Co. v. Liverpool Marine & General Insurance Co., Ltd. (N.Y.L.J. Mar. 4, 1925). The contract in question in that case was a New York contract and the English courts undertook to apply the New York Arbitration Law. The arbitration clause contained a provision that in default of either party appointing any arbitrator within one month of the other party requesting it to do so, the latter should name both arbitrators and they should elect an umpire. One party denied the authority of arbitrators thus named and declined to take any part in the arbitration. Arbitrators were named and proceeded to make an award. Action was brought thereon. Much the same question was presented as when, as in this case, the arbitrators were named and the hearing begun. May the arbitration proceed without judicial sanction? It was held by the Court of Appeal that by reason of the provisions of the contract for the appointment of a full board of arbitrators without the consent of the party in default the active party was not "aggrieved" by the conduct of the other party and might proceed without obtaining the sanction of the court. The learned court held that the constitutional right of trial by jury was waived by the agreement to refer. In reaching this conclusion it overlooked the scheme of the New York Arbitration Law which reserves to a party to an arbitration or submission the right to a judicial hearing before the arbitration shall proceed. True, the contract and the submission are irrevocable, but the terms of the contract and of the submission are open to judicial inquiry. Did the party agree to arbitrate or submit the questions sought to be arbitrated? Is he in default under the contract or the submission in refusing to arbitrate or to proceed with an arbitration once begun?

Repudiation by one party of the contract to arbitrate does not, therefore, leave the other party in position to proceed without the sanction of the court. The withdrawing party might still assert that it had made no contract to submit to arbitration the questions contained in the submission ; that it was not in default under the contract. Mr. Justice Bailhache, on the trial of the English action, aptly stated the proper rule as follows:

> It seems to me the section of the act treats such a party, the party who desires to go to arbitration, as a party aggrieved if the other party fails, neglects or refuses to perform his obligation under the contract. That seems to me the definition of the party aggrieved, and his grievance is the failure, neglect or refusal of another to perform under the contract ... Prior to the act of 1920 there was no remedy when a person refused to submit to arbitration. The act of 1920 does provide a remedy but that remedy is, if the person still desires to go to arbitration that he shall do so after first obtaining the sanction of the court to that effect.

So with a submission. Agreements to arbitrate and submissions to arbitrate are on the same footing (Arbitration Law, §§ 2, 3). Arbitrators must observe their commission and keep within their jurisdiction. If a *bona fide* question arises as to the proper construction of the submission agreement, a party may raise the question by withdrawing from the arbitration. If the party aggrieved then desires to go on with the arbitration he must apply to the court and the court will determine whether or not the withdrawing party was in default in refusing to proceed to arbitrate a question covered by the submission agreement.

Such construction of the Arbitration Law prevents a party or the arbitrators from proceeding to arbitrate and decide questions which the other party never agreed to submit to arbitration. Arbitrations should be encouraged but arbitration tribunals may not determine for themselves, over the objection of a party, to include within the scope of the arbitration questions which were never submitted to arbitration.

The rules of the Dried Fruit Association of New York, which governed the arbitration, were not produced to sustain the award in the Special Term, the Appellate Division or in this court. The Civil Practice Act controls unless the party seeking to uphold the award establishes that it is inconsistent with the terms of the submission.

The award herein and the judgment entered thereon were properly vacated under Civil Practice Act, section 1457.*

The order should be affirmed, with costs.

HISCOCK, CH. J., MCLAUGHLIN, CRANE, ANDREWS and LEHMAN, JJ., concur ; CARDOZO, J., not voting.

Order affirmed.

FINSILVER, STILL & MOSS (GOLDBERG, M. & CO.) 253 N.Y. 382, 171 N.E. 579 (1930)

CARDOZO, CH. J. The defendant in this arbitration proceeding, Goldberg, Maas & Co., Inc., signed and delivered to the plaintiff, Finsilver, Still & Moss, Inc., an order for the purchase of twenty-five pieces of merchandise, described as style number 195, the price to be six dollars and ninety-five cents per yard, and delivery to be made at stated times. There was an arbitration clause as follows:

> All claims, demands, disputes, differences, controversies and misunderstandings arising under, out of, or in connection with, or in relation to this contract, shall be submitted to and to be determined by arbitration, pursuant to the Arbitration Law of the State of New York, in The Tribunal of Justice known as the Court of Arbitration established and conducted by the American Arbitration Association and in accordance with its Rules.

The plaintiff, upon receipt of the order, notified the defendant in writing of its acceptance, adding a description of the merchandise as "Karavan Kamel Kloth," forty-eight inches in width and thirty to thirty-five in length.

A dispute arising thereafter as to the width of goods delivered, the defendant gave notice to the plaintiff that future deliveries would be rejected. Upon this the plaintiff made demand for arbitration. A proceeding, based upon a submission, went forward to the stage of an award, but in the end was abortive for lack of an acknowledgment. That proceeding have failed, another was begun. In default of a new submission, there was adherence to the forms prescribed by the executory agreement. Under this the rules of the American Arbitration Association were to govern the procedure. The defendant was notified by the association that arbitration was demanded, and was requested to join in the selection of an arbitrator. The request

---

*[§ 1462 in Appendix C contains the provision formerly in § 1457.]

having been ignored, the association, in adherence to its rules, made its own choice of an arbitrator from the members of a panel, and so notified the defendant, informing it also of the time and place of hearing. Again the defendant paid no attention to the warning. Upon its failure to respond, the arbitration proceeded in its absence. The arbitrator made an award of damages in favor of the plaintiff, upon which judgment was thereafter entered pursuant to an order of the court. The court at the same time denied a motion by the defendant for a perpetual injunction, or in the alternative for the submission to a jury of the question of the existence of a contract. Upon appeal to the Appellate Division the judgment and order were reversed on the ground that there had been an unconstitutional denial of due process of law.

The Arbitration Law of this State, as first enacted in 1920 (Cons. Laws, ch. 72), declared agreements for the arbitration of future differences to be valid and irrevocable, but did not set up any machinery whereby an award would be effective in the absence of an order that arbitration should proceed (Arbitration Law, § 3 ; Matter of Bullard v. Grace Co., 240 N.Y. 388). The workings of the statute were thought to have disclosed inconveniences as a result of that omission. Thus, where one of three arbitrators withdrew before the proofs had been submitted, there was need of a new order to give validity to the proceeding continued by the others (Matter of Bullard v. Grace Co., *supra*). Still more hapless was the plight of a party to a controversy if his adversary was a nonresident, without the jurisdiction. The process of the court could not reach the recalcitrant opponent to coerce response to a petition that the arbitration should proceed. In a much litigated case, a claimant so situated tried the experiment of an arbitration without preliminary judicial sanction. The adverse party, resident in England, was notified of the proceeding, but refused to have a part in it, and later contested the jurisdiction when sued on the award abroad. On the authority of our decision in Matter of Bullard v. Grace Co. (*supra*), the House of Lords decided that the award was ineffective, though declaring at the same time that according to its own view of the law and the practice in Great Britain, an antecedent order was not an indispensable condition (Liverpool Marine & Gen. Ins. Co., Ltd., v. Bankers & Shippers Ins. Co., Jan. 29, 1926, reported in 24 Ll. L. Rep. 85, H. L., reversing a decision of the Court of Appeal reported in the New York Law Journal of March 4, 1925, *sub nom.* Bankers & Shippers Ins. Co. v. Liverpool Marine & Gen. Ins. Co.,

Ltd. ; cf. Matter of Bullard v. Grace Co., *supra*, p. 396.)

Faced by these mischiefs, the Legislature by an amendment adopted in 1927 added to the Arbitration Law a section, designated 4-a, which reads as follows:

> Where pursuant to a provision in a written contract to settle by arbitration a controversy thereafter arising between the parties to the contract, or a submission described in section two hereof, an award has been, or is hereafter rendered, without previous application to the supreme court, or a judge thereof, as required by section three hereof, such award shall notwithstanding anything contained in section three hereof be valid and enforceable according to its terms, subject, nevertheless to the provisions of this section. At any time before a final judgment shall have been given in proceedings to enforce any such award whether in the courts of the state of New York, or elsewhere, any party to the arbitration who has not participated therein may apply to the supreme court, or a judge thereof, to have all or any of the issues hereinafter mentioned determined, and if, upon any such application the court, or a judge thereof, or a jury, if one be demanded, shall determine that no written contract providing for arbitration was made, or submission entered into, as the case may be, or, that such party was not in default by failing to comply with the terms thereof, or that the arbitrator, arbitrators and, or umpire was, or were not appointed or did not act, pursuant to the written contract, then and in any such case, the award shall thereupon become invalid and unenforceable. Where any such application is made any party may demand a jury trial of all or any of such issues, and if such a demand be made, the court or a judge thereof shall make an order referring the issue or issues to a jury in the manner provided by law for referring to a jury issues in an equity action.

This section of the statute has been condemned by the Appellate Division as a denial of due process. Arbitration presupposes the existence of a contract to arbitrate. If a party to a controversy denies the existence of the contract and with it the jurisdiction of the irregular tribunal, the regular courts of justice must be open to him at some stage for the determination of the issue. The right to such a determination, either at the beginning or at the end of the arbitration or in resistance to an attempted enforcement of the award, is assured by the Constitution as part of its assurance of due process of law. In the view of a majority of the Appellate Division, the statute nullifies this right, or burdens it unreasonably, by attaching a condition that if the contract be upheld, the party unsuccessfully disputing its existence shall be deemed to have waived the benefit of a hearing before the arbitrators, though the proceeding be still pending.

We think the holding has its origin in a mis-construction of the statute, its aim and its effect. What the amendment seeks to do is to give validity to the practice which in the opinion of the English judges or most of them was permissible already without the aid of an amendment. A

> party might not wish to enter upon an expensive arbitration which might be a nullity, and he was given power to get the validity of the arbitration determined beforehand by the court. But this ... still left it free to a party whose arbitration tribunal was duly constituted under the contract, to proceed at his risk, and enforce his award, if no objection could be raised to it

(Scrutton, L. J., in Bankers & Shippers Ins. Co. of N.Y. v. Liverpool Marine & Gen. Ins. Co., Ltd., Court of Appeal, *supra*). This being the aim, the question is whether there has been any infringement of constitutional guaranties in making it effective. Two classes of parties are covered by the statute, those who stay out of the arbitration, and those who go in. A party to a controversy, informed by his adversary that there is to be a hearing by an arbitrator, may choose to stay out of the arbitration altogether. If he does, the statute is explicit in the protection of his rights. He may be heard by a court or judge in support of his contention that the arbitration is of no effect in that he never bound himself to arbitrate, and may have the issues of fact, if any, submitted to a jury. Even then, it is not too late to have a part in the arbitration if the proceeding is still open. There is no suggestion in the statute that as a penalty for resistance he shall forfeit any rights that would otherwise be his. The proceeding will often be kept open by a stay or by adjournments. If so, the unsuccessful denial of the jurisdiction of the arbitrators will not prejudice the opportunity to go before them on their merits.

So much for the party who stays out of the arbitration altogether, or who seeks a hearing in the court, with the right to trial by jury, before electing to go in. Rights substantially as great, however, are assured to the party who is in from the beginning. Nothing in the statute denies to one so situated the right to participate in the arbitration, and still contest the jurisdiction. On the contrary, the section opens with the declaration that the award shall be valid, though made without previous application to the court, in those cases and in those only where the arbitration is "pursuant to" the provisions of a contract. If it is not pursuant to a contract, if in truth there is no contract at all or none calling for arbitration, the self-constituted tribunal is a nullity, without power to bind or loose by

force of its decision. We assume that circumstances may exist in which a party to an arbitration, joining in its proceedings without protest or disclaimer, may be found to have joined by implication in the appointment of the arbitrators, and to have confirmed their jurisdiction, if otherwise defective. The limits of this implication and its effect may be postponed for definition until the event creates the need. On the other hand, the rule is well established and of general validity that where there is seasonable protest or disclaimer in response to a claim of jurisdiction, the protest or disclaimer is not nullified by proceeding thereafter to a hearing on the merits (Harkness v. Hyde, 98 U.S. 476, 479 ; Southern Pac. Co. v. Denton, 146 U.S. 202, 209 ; Hassler, Inc., v. Shaw, 271 U.S. 195 ; Jones v. Jones, 108 N.Y. 415, 425). We see no reason to doubt that the rule applies as fully to a proceeding before an arbitrator (Kent v. French, 76 Iowa, 187) as to one before a referee or before any board or officer who asserts the right to judge. The decision in Christman v. Moran (9 Penn. St. 487), to the effect that participation in the hearing is to be deemed a waiver of the protest was made many years ago (1848), before the underlying principle was clearly understood. It cannot be accepted in this State as embodying existing law. In the light of existing law we approach the amendment and determine its effect. Certain it is that in the terms of the statute there is no express denial of the right to join in the proceeding under protest and then contest the jurisdiction. If denial was intended, it has been left to doubtful implication. The implication should be clear before a right so fundamental will be held to have been lost. In the absence of a contract expressing a consent to arbitrate, an award by an arbitrator is an act of usurpation. Nowhere does the statute say that its quality shall be different. As an act of usurpation, it is subject to be challenged whenever and wherever it is put forward by the usurper as a source of rights and duties. Till there is an adjudication of its validity by a competent judicial officer, as for example upon a motion after due notice to confirm or to vacate it, the issue of jurisdiction is open at the instance and for the benefit of any litigant aggrieved.

We are not forgetful in all this of the element of obscurity introduced into the statute by the description of the remedy available to a litigant who does not fight the arbitration from within, but keeps out from the beginning. Why say that such a one may attack the jurisdiction of the arbitrators if others may do the same? The task of judicial construction would be easier if statutes were invariably drafted with unity of plan and precision of expression. Indeed, adherence to the same standards would be useful also in opinions. The ideal being unattainable, we must not exaggerate the significance of deviations from the perfect norm. Very possibly the description of the remedy had its origin in excess of caution. More probably the purpose was to assure to one so situated the privilege of a jury trial, which was then explicitly conceded. By contrast, one who fights from within, and has had a part in the proceeding, may lose the privilege of a jury in his attack on jurisdiction and be forced to abide by the decision of a judge. The motion to confirm is equivalent to a suit in equity to carry into effect the terms of the agreement and the arbitration had thereunder. In suits for specific performance there is no constitutional right to the verdict of a jury, though the existence of a contract be the basis of the controversy.

We hold that a party who joins in an arbitration after seasonable protest has the right, none the less, to contest by appropriate forms of challenge the jurisdiction of the arbitrators, and that this right has not been taken away by reasonable implication through the concession of a particular remedy to a party who stays out. In so holding we are not to be understood as assenting to the view that there would be a denial of due process of law if the right had been withheld. There is no need to inquire whether due process of law will permit the Legislature to say that a party to such a controversy, failing in his challenge to the jurisdiction of the arbitrators after a contest in the court, shall be penalized thereafter by forfeiting the right to a hearing before the arbitrators while the proceeding is still open. It is a very different thing to say that to take voluntary part before the arbitrators in a trial upon the merits shall operate thereafter as a waiver of the right to contest the jurisdiction. Such a result has been worked out, in one State at least, without the aid of any statute (Christman v. Moran, *supra*). The conclusion may have been wrong, but there is little reason to believe that it was also unconstitutional. Such cases as York v. Texas (137 U.S. 15, 20, 21); Western Life Ind. Co. v. Rupp (235 U.S. 261, 271, 272), and Chicago Life Ins. Co. v. Cherry (244 U.S. 25, 29) are sign posts pointing us with distinctness along another route. The party who contests the jurisdiction may keep out. If he chooses to go in, the Legislature may say to what extent the going shall be interpreted as a waiver of other rights. In this case it has been generous, and has said that though in, he may wage the contest as if out.

The question remains as to the remedy, if any, that should have been accorded to the defendant upon its motion for an injunction and for alternative relief. It had refrained from taking part in the hearings before the arbitrator. That being so, by the very terms of the statute, it was entitled to a jury trial as to the existence of a contract, if any issue of fact was raised by the petition and the answer. We think an issue, not frivolous, remains to be determined. The order for the goods, it will be remembered, calls for twenty-five pieces of style No. 195, and does not otherwise describe them. The acceptance adds to the description a statement of the width and length. The break between the parties had its origin in a dispute about the width. Whatever the merits of the dispute, there was a variance in form at least between offer and assent. The plaintiff insists that the variance was unsubstantial, that it was one in form only (Williston, Contracts, § 78). There was, so it insists, a standard length and width, which were identified with certainty by the style number without more (Mesibov, etc., Inc., v. Cohen Bros. Mfg. Co., Inc., 245 N.Y. 305, 312). Whether this is so in a question that must be determined after trial. A suggestion, too, there is that the defendant assented to the variance, if there was any, by going forward with performance and accepting a delivery (Pettibone v. Moore, 75 Hun, 461, 464 ; WILLISTON, CONTRACTS, § 90), but this in turn is met by explanation or denial. Again a trial is necessary for choice between conflicting claims. The arbitration clause falls if a contract was never made.

The judgment of the Appellate Division vacating the award should be reversed and the judgment of the Special Term affirmed without costs to either party.

The order of the Appellate Division perpetually enjoining the enforcement of the award should be modified by directing a trial by jury of the existence of a contract, and staying the enforcement of the judgment until the hearing and determination of the issues so referred.

POUND, CRANE, LEHMAN, KELLOGG, O'BRIEN and HUBBS, JJ., concur.

Judgment accordingly.

SCHAFRAN & FINKEL, INC. v. LOWENSTEIN & SONS, INC.
280 N.Y. 164, 19 N.E. 2d 1005 (1939)

CRANE, CH. J. This appeal presents a drastic rule, if it be legal, relating to arbitration. One who has never made a contract to arbitrate, upon receiving an informal letter directing him to arbitrate a purchase of goods which he never made, may be mulcted in damages by an award unless, within ten days after receiving such notice, he applies to the court for an injunction or a stay. Should the notice have been misunderstood or too vague and indefinite or, if through a mistake or unavoidable lapse of time, a party cannot or does not reach a judge within the ten days, there is absolutely no relief, not even in a court of equity.

The facts, briefly, are these, taking, as we must, the allegations of the complaint at their face value. The plaintiff, on October 29, 1937, received from the defendant an invoice for goods alleged to have been sold to Schafran & Finkel. On November 1, 1937, the plaintiff notified the defendant that it had never ordered any merchandise nor received any merchandise, and was returning the invoice. On December 8, 1937, there was delivered at the office of Schafran & Finkel, Inc., the following letter:

DEAR SIRS:

Please be advised that the undersigned, M. Lowenstein & Sons, Inc., of Nos. 37–45 Leonard Street, New York City, hereby demands, pursuant to the provisions of the written agreement between said M. Lowenstein & Sons, Inc. and yourselves, dated June 29, 1937, that you submit to arbitration before the General Arbitration Council of the Textile Industry of No. 320 Broadway, New York City, the controversy arising out of your failure and refusal to accept the goods called for by said agreement.

"Upon said arbitration M. Lowenstein & Sons, Inc., will request that you be directed to pay to it the sum of $1500 with interest thereon, representing the difference between the contract price and the market price of said goods at the time of your refusal to accept the same.

"You are hereby notified that it is the intention of M. Lowenstein & Sons, Inc. to conduct such arbitration pursuant to the provisions of the said agreement dated June 29, 1937. To that end a copy of said agreement and this notice and demand will be filed with the General Arbitration Council of the Textile Industry, with the request that it proceed to put its rules into effect.

"Very truly yours,

"M. LOWENSTEIN & SONS, INC.
"By IRVING D. LIPKOWITZ (Sgd)
"*Attorney.*"

Apparently no attention was paid to it. The plaintiff did not buy goods of the defendant; it did not agree to any submission to arbitration; it signed no contract to arbitrate; in fact, the alleged agreement of arbitration contained in the record is a paper relating to the sale of merchandise signed solely by M. Lowenstein & Sons, Inc. Later, in January of 1938, the plaintiff was

notified that an award had been made against it of $1500, and that a motion would be made at Special Term of the Supreme Court on the 28th day of January, 1938, to confirm the award and directing entry of judgment for the amount.

The plaintiff finds itself in this position: under the arbitration law, as it stands, it has no relief whatever, for, on the motion to confirm, it cannot plead or show lack of jurisdiction, or that no contract was entered into, or any equities requiring relief. The plaintiff is also barred by the decisions below from maintaining any action in equity to meet the situation. In other words, the plaintiff lost all rights of a litigant, either at law or in equity, or in the arbitration proceeding, when it failed to meet the lawyer's letter or notice to apply to the Supreme Court for a stay or injunction. We doubt very much whether article 84 of the Civil Practice Act, relating to arbitration, intended to go as far as this, or whether it would be constitutional, to deprive one of property upon such informal notice as the lawyer's letter in this case.

The plaintiff, faced with this situation, brought an action in equity to restrain the entry of any judgment upon the alleged award, for the reasons here stated; the defendant countermoved by asking that the complaint be dismissed as not stating a cause of action. The complaint has been dismissed on the ground that no remedy whatever existed, except that provided by the arbitration law. This, we think, is error.

The arbitration law, as it exists today, says this:

Two or more persons . . . may contract to settle by arbitration a controversy thereafter arising between them and such submission or contract shall be valid, enforceable and irrevocable, *save upon such grounds as exist at law or in equity for the revocation of any contract.* (Civ. Prac. Act, § 1448.)

Now we turn to section 1458, added by the Laws of 1937, chapter 341, in effect September first of that year.

An award shall be valid and enforceable . . . without previous adjudication of the existence of a submission or contract to arbitrate, subject, nevertheless, to the provisions of this section:

2. A party who has not participated in the selection of the arbitrators . . . and who has not made or been served with an application to compel arbitration under section fourteen hundred fifty may also put in issue the making of the contract . . . either by a motion for a stay of the arbitration or in opposition to the confirmation of the award. If a notice shall have been personally served upon such party of an intention to conduct the arbitration pursuant to the provisions of a contract or submission specified in such notice, then the issues specified in this subdivision may be raised only by a motion for a

stay of the arbitration, notice of which motion must be served within ten days after the service of the notice of intention to arbitrate.

By section 1462 of the Civil Practice Act a motion to vacate an award may be made: "5. If there was no valid submission or contract, and the objection has been raised under the conditions set forth in section fourteen hundred fifty-eight."

There is a saving clause, however, to this arbitration article, found in section 1469, which reads:

> This article does not affect any right of action in affirmance, disaffirmance, or for the modification of a submission or contract, made either as prescribed in this article or otherwise, or upon an instrument collateral thereto, or upon an award made or purporting to be made in pursuance thereof. And, except as otherwise expressly prescribed therein, this article does not affect a submission or contract, made otherwise than as prescribed therein, or any proceedings taken pursuant to such a submission or contract, or any instrument collateral thereto.

These are the pertinent provisions of this arbitration article, and may be summarized as follows: A party who has not been served with an application to compel arbitration may put in issue the making of the contract in opposition to the confirmation of the award, but a person who has been personally served with a notice of an intention to conduct arbitration, pursuant to the provisions of a contract, can only put in issue the making of the contract by a motion for a stay, notice of which must be served within ten days after the service of the notice of intention to arbitrate. Unless this notice is served within ten days, then, according to section 1462, the award may not be set aside on the ground that there was no valid contract. Thus, the one and only move that may be made by a person who signed no contract, is to apply to the court for a stay and, if he fails to move within the ten days, he is thereafter prevented from bringing any action or any proceeding in equity to be relieved of his default, or question the validity of the contract.

If the plaintiff made no contract to submit, or signed and executed no submission to arbitrate, how, by any possibility, can it be bound by an award of arbitrators who had no jurisdiction? (Finsilver, Still & Moss v. Goldberg, Maas & Co., 253 N.Y. 382.) The answer, as given by the respondent in the court below, is "The Lipkowitz letter." It was personally served; the plaintiff failed to go to court for a stay within ten days, and, therefore, is barred from ever raising the question of jurisdiction of the arbitrators or the lack of any contract to arbitrate. If this be

the meaning of the law, it fails, for lack of due process. Other statutes which provide that a money judgment may be taken against a man unless he makes a move require far more specific notice. Title II of the New York City Municipal Court Code (Laws of 1915, ch. 279) furnishes a good example. There it is provided that a summons may be served stating the amount for which demand is made, and that in default of an answer judgment will be taken. (See, also, Rules Civ. Prac., rule 46.) The form of the summons is given and the notice is specific as to what the defendant must do. The clerk of the court issues the summons, which is uniform in all cases, except as to the amount and the nature of the transaction. Here is a process of the court, notifying that a judgment results in case of default; here is an opportunity to answer and be heard, after due notice. This constitutes due process of law.

What have we in the arbitration case? Section 1458 of the Civil Practice Act simply says a notice shall be personally served of an intention to conduct an arbitration, pursuant to the provisions of a contract. It does not give the form of notice nor require time and place and consequences of a default to be stated, nor that the notice should tell what should or must be done. A mere letter from a lawyer saying he demands arbitration of a contract before some board seems to be sufficient—nothing more. And the consequence? If the party does not proceed to get a stay within ten days no court of equity nor any other court can afford him any relief; and all this in face of the fact that he never made any contract to arbitrate. This is going too far, in my estimation.

For instance, in this case the plaintiff writes that it never ordered any such goods as it had been billed for. A lawyer thereupon writes a letter demanding that the plaintiff submit to arbitration before the General Arbitration Council of the Textile Industry, at 320 Broadway, of the controversy arising out of a failure to accept goods. He further says in his letter that $1500 is demanded. This is the extent of the notice. This is no way to conduct a proceeding resulting in a money judgment. The notice should state where and at what time the party is to proceed and the consequences of his failure to act as the law specifies. We do not say that all these things are necessary, but we do say that the proceedings for arbitration cannot be left so vague and uncertain that people may be mulcted in judgment without being sufficiently warned of their rights. The notice here was insufficient, and the plaintiff cannot be deprived of an opportunity to show that it never entered into any contract at all to arbitrate. Awards cannot stand upon such flimsy procedure. Under these circumstances the plaintiff's cause of action to set this award aside or to restrain further proceedings should not have been dismissed. Equity can afford relief if that under the arbitration law has failed. We review upon this appeal only the judgment of dismissal. The court at Special Term must determine whether the plaintiff has shown facts sufficient to entitle him to an injunction either permanent or temporary.

For these reasons the judgments should be reversed, with costs in all courts, and the motion of the defendant to dismiss the complaint denied. (See 280 N.Y. 687.)

LEHMAN, O'BRIEN, HUBBS, LOUGHRAN, FINCH and RIPPEY, JJ., concur.

Judgments reversed, etc.

MATTER OF CULINARY EMPLOYEES (SCHIFFMAN)
272 App. Div. 491, 71 N.Y.S. 2d 160 (First Dept. 1947)

PECK, J. Appellant is a union of restaurant employees and respondent is a restaurant proprietor. They are parties to a contract governing the terms and conditions of employment in respondent's restaurant and providing for arbitration of all disputes by an arbitrator named in the agreement. The agreement provides that in the event either party shall willfully default in appearing before the arbitrator at the time and place fixed by him, then the arbitrator may hear the testimony and evidence of the party appearing and render his decision as if both parties had appeared.

An arbitration proceeding was instituted by the union in reference to the discharge of two employees. Written notice of the arbitration was given to respondent on April 5, 1946, calling for a hearing on April 8, 1946. Respondent wrote to the arbitrator asserting that in his opinion there was no arbitrable claim, and defaulted in appearing on the day set. The arbitrator thereupon advised respondent by letter dated April 8, 1946, that he could not pass upon the conflicting claims except by hearing them and accordingly set the arbitration for April 11, 1946. Two further adjournments were had after conversations between the respondent and the arbitrator and at the request of an attorney for respondent. On the day finally set for arbitration respondent again defaulted.

The arbitrator's award contains a notation

that during the interval a second notice had been sent by the union demanding arbitration for the discharge of another member, and that the two proceedings were joined.

The arbitrator took the evidence, only appellant appearing, and made an award in respect to the three discharged employees.

Upon motion to confirm, the court vacated the award and named another arbitrator of its own selection to hear the matter anew. The grounds for vacating the award were that notice of the arbitration was not given in the manner provided by law for personal service of a summons, as required by section 1450 of the Civil Practice Act, and that the arbitrator exceeded his authority in making an award in respect to the third employee, when the notice of arbitration was limited to the claimed unlawful discharge of two employees, and in other details.

The principal question presented by this appeal is whether a notice of arbitration must be given in accordance with section 1450 of the Civil Practice Act. That section provides that a party aggrieved by the failure of another to perform under a contract providing for arbitration may petition the Supreme Court for an order directing arbitration and that notice of the application shall be served in the manner specified in the contract and if no manner be specified then in the manner provided by law for personal service of a summons. No manner of service was specified in the contract, so respondent contends that service of the notice of arbitration had to be by personal service as of a summons.

It must be noted that the only issue which the court may pass upon in a proceeding instituted under section 1450 is whether there is a contract or submission to arbitrate and a failure to comply therewith. If so, the court is obliged to make an order directing arbitration.

Section 1454 of the Civil Practice Act provides that the arbitrator must appoint a time and place for the hearing and cause notice to be given to each of the parties. That this is all that is necessary when an arbitrator has been named by the parties, and that the notice need not be personally served is made manifest by section 1458 of the Civil Practice Act. That section provides that an award shall be valid and enforcible without a previous adjudication of the existence of a submission or contract to arbitrate, such as would be made under section 1450 of the Civil Practice Act, but that a party who has not been served with an application to compel arbitration under section 1450 may put in issue the making of the contract or submission, or the failure to comply therewith, either by motion for a stay of arbitration or in opposition to confirmation of the award. The section goes on to provide that if notice of the arbitration shall have been personally served, then the issues may be raised only by motion for a stay.

Sections 1450, 1454 and 1458 of the Civil Practice Act together form a pattern which makes clear that neither an application to the Supreme Court to compel arbitration nor personal service of a notice of arbitration is necessary to institute an arbitration proceeding, that the only consequence or personal service of such notice is to require an objectant to arbitration to raise the issue of a submission or failure to comply therewith by motion for a stay instead of waiting to raise objections upon a motion to confirm the arbitrator's award, and that the only issues as to the propriety of arbitration which may be raised in any event are whether there has been a contract or submission to arbitrate and a failure to comply therewith. Failure to institute the proceeding in the first instance by application to the court or by personal service of the notice of arbitration under section 1450 is not a ground for attacking the award. It may be necessary, as a practical matter, where the opposing party is obliged to do something, such as appointing an arbitrator, to complete the institution of an arbitration proceeding, that the proceeding be instituted in the absence of his co-operation by an application to the court under section 1450. There is no necessity for such application, however, where the arbitration agreement names the arbitrator, and it certainly should not be required, and is not required, in such event or in every case to commence an arbitration proceeding with a Supreme Court proceeding.

Respondent had due notice of the proceeding at least in respect to two of the employees, and the record bears out the arbitrator's conclusion that the respondent's default was willful and deliberate after every reasonable opportunity was granted to the respondent to appear. The only question which remains open and not satisfactorily answered on the record is what notice the respondent had of the arbitration as to the third employee, Sherri Reyes. All that appears as to this notice is a reference in the arbitrator's award to a "second notice" having been sent. The other objections to the award go to the merits and we find the award in all those respects to come within the province of the arbitrator.

The order appealed from should be modified to confirm the award in all respects except in respect to Sherri Reyes, as to whom the matter is remanded to Special Term to determine whether respondent received due notice of the arbitration as to her. If Special Term so finds, the award shall be confirmed as to Sherri Reyes. If Special Term finds that due notice of the arbitration was not given to respondent, the matter of Sherri Reyes shall be remanded to the arbitrator named in the contract for arbitration on due notice. The award in all other respects should be confirmed, with $20 costs and disbursements to appellant.

GLENNON, DORE and COHN, JJ., concur.

A NOTE ON DEFAULT IN ARBITRATION

Note that under both the AAA Commercial (§ 29) and Labor (§ 27) Rules the arbitration may proceed in the absence of a party who has been notified of the proceeding. But an award cannot be granted on the basis of default alone. "The arbitrator shall require the party who is present to submit such evidence as he may require for the making of an award."

Given the lack of pleadings and the frequent generality of the statement of the issue in demands for arbitration, some evidence would seem to be absolutely necessary. Some arbitrators require that the party seeking arbitration put on his entire case and prove the essential elements of the claim made; this seems to be desirable practice.

KENTUCKY RIVER MILLS v. JACKSON
206 F.2d 111 (6th Cir.)
cert. denied, 346 U.S. 887 (1953)

McALLISTER, C. J. [The contract provided:

23. Arbitration: Any dispute arising out of this contract of [sic] its interpretation shall be settled by arbitration in New York in the customary manner, buyer and seller each naming his arbitrator, whose award, or that of the umpire whom the arbitrators may appoint, shall be final and binding upon both parties. If either party fails to appoint an arbitrator within seven (7) days after receiving the other party's nomination of an arbitrator, the one arbitrator nominated may act as sole arbitrator . . . the seller and buyer consent that the arbitration shall be enforceable under and pursuant to the laws of the State, Country or Government having jurisdiction and that judgment upon the award may be entered in any court of any such jurisdiction.

After dispute arose the plaintiff appointed an arbitrator and requested the defendant to do so, but the defendant refused, declaring that he regarded the contract as a nullity because of alleged fraudulent inducement. The plaintiff-appointed arbitrator rendered an award for plaintiff; the report does not show the nature or extent of the proceedings.]

What appears to be the principal claim of appellant with respect to the award is that it is invalid because it is the award of only one arbitrator. The above mentioned contract between the parties, however, provided that if either party failed to appoint an arbitrator within seven days after receiving the other party's nomination of an arbitrator, the one arbitrator nominated might act as sole arbitrator. The award of the single arbitrator was, therefore, entirely in accordance with the agreement of the parties, as evidenced by their written contract.

Appellant, however, submits that the agreement to arbitrate is not self-executory; that where, under a contract providing for arbitration, one of the parties is aggrieved by the refusal of another to arbitrate, the recourse of the party aggrieved is to petition the court for an order directing that the arbitration proceed; and it is argued that an *ex parte* arbitration is contrary to the ordinary concepts of fairness. It is to be said that an arbitration by an arbitrator appointed by one of the parties only may well result in a degree of advantage to the other party, for mere personal friendship with one of the parties does not disqualify an arbitrator, and an arbitration carried on by such an arbitrator would not be contrary to ordinary concepts of fairness, although one would hardly be considered vigilant of his interests if he failed to appoint an arbitrator himself when he was entitled to do so. But it is the proof of bias or unfairness or partiality on the part of an arbitrator that results in unjust advantage, and calls for the setting aside of the award. See Davy v. Faw, 7 Cranch 171, 3 L.Ed. 305; American Guaranty Co. v. Caldwell, 9 Cir., 72 F. 2d 209. For arbitrators are selected to act in a quasi-judicial capacity, in the place of a court, and must be fair and impartial so as to render a faithful, honest, and disinterested opinion, in carrying out their obligation to do justice to the parties through their award. Davy v. Faw, *supra*; American Eagle Fire Ins. Co. v. New Jersey Insurance Co., 240 N.Y. 398, 148 N.E. 562.

Both parties agree that the state law does not govern either the matter of the validity or the enforcement of the award in this case. Appellant declares there is no question as to the fact that Congress, in the enactment of the United States Arbitration Act, entered into the field of regulating the enforcement of the arbitration clauses contained in contracts evidencing transactions in interstate commerce, and, also, in such cases where one of the parties to such a contract

refuses to arbitrate. However, appellant insists that Congress did not thereby sanction *ex parte* proceedings by one arbitrator, but provided the remedy where one party refuses to arbitrate in accordance with his contract by a procedure in which the federal court, on petition and hearing, can compel arbitration, and, in case of refusal of one of the parties to appoint an arbitrator, can appoint an arbitrator who would act under the agreement with the same effect as though he had been appointed by the contracting party. Title 9 U.S.C.A. §§ 2 and 4.

Section 2 of the Act provides that a written provision in a contract evidencing a transaction involving interstate commerce to settle by arbitration a controversy thereafter arising out of such contract or transaction shall be valid, irrevocable, and enforceable, save upon such grounds as exist at law or in equity for the revocation of any contract.

Section 4 of the Act provides that a party aggrieved by the failure, neglect, or refusal of another to arbitrate under a written agreement for arbitration may petition any court of the United States which, save for such agreement, would have jurisdiction under the judicial code of the subject matter of a suit arising out of the controversy between the parties, for an order directing that such arbitration proceed in the manner provided for in such agreement.

An *ex parte* arbitration was permissible at common law where provided for by the terms of the arbitration agreement; and, as is evident upon its face, Section 4 of the Act uses permissive language only, and does not, by its terms, require resort to the enforcement provisions thereof, if an *ex parte* arbitration is permitted by the terms of the arbitration agreement.

To sustain its contention that the *ex parte* award in this case was not valid, appellant relies upon the authority of Bullard v. Morgan H. Grace Co., Inc., 240 N.Y. 388, 148 N.E. 559, 562, decided under Section 3 of the State Arbitration Law, of New York, which is comparable to Section 4 of the United States Arbitration Act.

In the *Bullard* case, the controversy arose between the arbitrators as to whether or not there was an agreement to arbitrate a particular question. The jurisdiction of the arbitrators depended upon the existence of an agreement to arbitrate the question to be decided by them, and at the arbitration hearing, challenge was made to their jurisdiction to consider the particular question that was then in dispute. It is not clear that the court, by its holding that the award was invalid, intended to declare that all awards rendered in *ex parte* statutory arbitrations were invalid except where the party desiring the arbitration procured an enforcement order under Section 3 of the State Arbitration Law. In STURGES ON COMMERCIAL ARBITRATION AND AWARDS, pages 448/9, where extensive comment is made upon the *Bullard* case, the observation is made that it appears that it was the purpose of the court therein to announce that resort to enforcement proceedings under Section 3 was a prerequisite to an *ex parte* statutory arbitration when a question of jurisdiction of the arbitrators under the contract was placed in issue ; and this view would seem to be borne out by the following statement of the court on that subject:

> Arbitrators must observe their commission and keep within their jurisdiction. If a *bona fide* question arises as to the proper construction of the submission agreement, a party may raise the question by withdrawing from the arbitration. If the party aggrieved then desires to go on with the arbitration, he must apply to the court, and the court will determine whether or not the withdrawing party was in default in refusing to proceed to arbitrate a question covered by the submission agreement.

It seems doubtful that the court in the *Bullard* case intended to include within the scope of its ruling cases where a party to an agreement to arbitrate refused to appear, when duly notified, or where he appeared and withdrew pending the hearing, giving no reason therefor or giving a reason that did not involve the authority of the arbitrators to act. For in such cases, there would to present no *bona fide* questions as to the construction of the submission agreement, nor the objection that the arbitration tribunal was determining for itself, over the protest of a party, to include within the scope of the arbitration questions that had not, in fact, been submitted to arbitration—all factors which were deemed to be of importance by the court in the *Bullard* case. See STURGES ON COMMERCIAL ARBITRATION AND AWARDS, *supra*.

In Finsilver, Still & Moss, Inc. v. Goldberg, Maas & Co., Inc., 253 N.Y. 382, 171 N.E. 579, 69 A.L.R. 809, the Court of Appeals of New York had occasion to discuss an amendment to the State Arbitration Law which had become effective subsequent to the decision in the Bullard case. In the course of the opinion, Chief Judge Cardozo, speaking for the court, pointed out that in an English case involving a New York contract providing for arbitration the House of Lords held that it was bound by the decision in the Bullard case, and that, accordingly, an award which had been made under a provision for arbitration was ineffective since one of the parties had refused to take part in it. At the same time, however, the House of Lords de-

clared that, according to its own view of the law and the practice, an enforcement order was not indispensable, and an action on an award so made could be maintained. Liverpool Marine & General Ins. Co., Ltd. v. Bankers & Shippers Ins. Co. of New York, 24 Ll.L. Rep. 85, H.L. It is curious that in the *Bullard* case, which was decided on July 15, 1925, the Court of Appeals of New York adopted the reasoning of the trial judge in the above English case (*sub nom.* Bankers' & Shippers' Ins. Co. of New York v. Liverpool Marine & General Ins. Co., Ltd.) which was decided March 4, 1925. Yet, subsequent to the decision in the *Bullard* case, both the English Court of Appeal, and, afterward, on January 29, 1926, the House of Lords, on the appeal of the *Liverpool Insurance* case, adopted a view of the law entirely contrary to that of the trial judge, which was quoted approvingly in the *Bullard* case, and, then, solely because of the decision in the *Bullard* case construing the law in New York, held that the award was, in the case before it, invalid.

Regardless of whether the *Bullard* case constituted a holding to the effect that every *ex parte* arbitration was invalid except where the party desiring arbitration procured an enforcement order under the statute, we are of the opinion that the award in the instant case was a valid award. The parties explicitly contracted for arbitration of any dispute arising out of the contract or its interpretation, and agreed that if one of them failed to appoint an arbitrator within seven days after receiving the other party's nomination of an arbitrator, the one arbitrator nominated might act as sole arbitrator. There was nothing in the terms of the contract that invalidated it. It was not contrary to public policy, for such *ex parte* arbitrations were permitted under the common law. International Brotherhood of Teamsters v. Shapiro, 138 Conn. 57, 82 A.2d 345 ; Caldwell v. Caldwell, 121 Ala. 598, 601, 25 So. 825 ; Couch v. Harrison, 68 Ark. 580, 60 S.W. 957 ; Whitlock v. Redford, 82 Ky. 390, 393 ; Sanborn v. Paul, 60 Me. 325, 327 ; Gowen v. Pierson, 166 Pa. 258, 263, 31 A. 83. Appellant in the suit upon the award could have raised any defenses which it could have raised under the statutory proceeding for an order directing arbitration to proceed in accordance with the contract, under Section 4 of the Act. Such defenses would include the invalidity of the contract, duress, and fraud in its procurement. In fact, the defense of fraud in the procurement of the contract was raised by the appellant in this case and passed upon by the district court on the trial. Moreover, the terms of Section 4 of the Act are permissive, not mandatory. See International Brotherhood of Teamsters v. Shapiro, *supra*. Our conclusion is that it was not necessary for Smith & Bird to resort to Section 4 of the Act before proceeding to arbitration in this case by the single arbitrator.

Accord: Standard Magnesium Corp. v. Fuchs, 251 F.2d 455 (10th Cir. 1957) (affirming an award rendered in Norway); Kanmak Mills, Inc. v. Society Brand Hat Co., 236 F.2d 240, (8th Cir. 1956); Brink v. Allegro Builders, Inc., 25 Cal. Rptr. 556, 375 P.2d 436 (1962); Battle v. General Cellulose Co., 23 N.J. 538, 129 A.2d 865 (1957).

However, where one party named its arbitrator

a few days after the contract-specified time for doing so and the other party's arbitrator, named within the period, proceeded *ex parte* the resultant award was held invalid. Texas Eastern Transmission Corp., v. Barnard, 285 F.2d 536 (6th Cir. 1960).

California Code of Civil Procedure § 1282.2 provides:

> (e) If a court has ordered a person to arbitrate a controversy, the arbitrators may hear and determine the controversy upon the evidence produced notwithstanding the failure of a party ordered to arbitrate, who has been duly notified, to appear.
>
> (f) If an arbitrator, who has been duly notified, for any reason fails to participate in the arbitration, the arbitration shall continue but only the remaining neutral arbitrator or neutral arbitrators may make the award.

D.

The Agreement to Arbitrate

MATTER OF HUXLEY
(REISS AND BERNHARD, INC.)
294 N.Y. 146, 61 N.E. 2d 419 (1945)

LOUGHRAN, J. Transactions in respect of a sale of merchandise are the subject matter of the controversy. The parties are the seller and the buyer. The dispute concerns the quality of the goods. The present proceeding is one which the seller brought for a stay against a demand by the buyer for arbitration of their differences. Whether there exists a valid antecedent contract for arbitration thereof is the question for decision. After trial at an Equity Term, the court found that no such agreement was in force and thereupon the seller's application for a stay was granted. In that disposition of the matter, the Equity Term was affirmed by a judgment of the Appellate Division from which the buyer has appealed to this Court.

The affair in issue was negotiated by a corporate merchandise broker employed for the purpose by the seller. Over its signature, this broker supplied to the parties statements of its handling of the matter which they retained without comment. The material items of the statement received by the seller (which bore the label *"Sold Note"*) were these:

> Sold to Reiss & Bernhard, Inc. [the buyer] ... For account of F. B. Huxley & Son [the seller] ... Terms net cash payable on receipt of invoice. Swell guarantee 4 per cent ... If incorrect please advise

immediately ... Quantity 1000cs. Article 6/10 Fancy cut beets ... Price 3.72 doz. .... Any controversy or claim arising out of or relating to this contract or the breach thereof, shall be settled by arbitration, in accordance with the rules then obtaining, of the Association of Food Distributors, Inc., New York, and judgment upon the award rendered may be entered in the highest court of the forum, state or federal, having jurisdiction. Seller to conform with National Pure Food Laws. This memorandum shall be subordinate to more formal contract when and if such contract is executed. In the absence of such contract this memorandum represents the contract of the parties.

The statement received from the broker by the buyer was a *"Bought Note"* wherein the same particulars were recited.

After the receipt by the parties of these statements of the broker, the seller transmitted to the buyer and to the broker other writings which in the material parts thereof are exemplified by the following specimen:

> Reiss & Bernhard [the buyer] ... To B. F. Huxley & Son [the seller] Dr. ... 1000 cases 6/10 Cut Beets 500 doz 3.72 $1860. Less ¼ of 1 per cent swells 4.65. $1855.35 ... Conditions of Sale ... 1½ per cent discount allowed if invoice is paid within ten days of date of invoice ... Swells guaranteed only six months after delivery ... Other claims of whatever kind must be made five days after receipt of goods. ... No allowance will be made for goods lost or damaged in transit. ...

These writings from the seller were held by the buyer without dissent therefrom.

In that condition of things the goods were delivered and paid for.

The foregoing, we believe, is an adequate statement of the fact situation. The main contest is upon this issue. Did the documents which the broker delivered to the parties (with the provision therein for arbitration) constitute the contract of sale, with the result that the buyer's demand for arbitration was justified; or, did the writings which thereafter went forth from the seller to the buyer annul such earlier documents (arbitration clause and all), with the result that the buyer cannot prevail, since a contract for arbitration of a future dispute must be in writing? (See Civ. Prac. Act, § 1449.)

The documents which the broker delivered to the parties were bought and sold notes—instruments which have long been used in the marketing of commodities through merchandise brokers. Four forms of these notes have been recognized. (4 AMER. & ENG. ENCY. OF LAW [2d ed.] 751.) The first (which was employed in the present case) is one in which the broker professes to act for both parties whose names are disclosed in the notes. An acceptance by the parties of bought and sold notes of that type makes a contract in the terms thereof, inasmuch as thereby each party admits that the broker was his agent in the transaction. (Benjamin on Sale [7th ed.], 293–294.) The bought and sold notes in question were still in the possession of the parties when the goods were delivered and paid for. Under such circumstances, these notes necessarily became a contract binding upon the buyer and seller respectively. (Newberry et al. v. Wall, 84 N.Y. 576; Childs v. Riley Co., 186 App. Div. 775. See Remick v. Sanford, 118 Mass. 102.)

We inquire, then, as to the effect of the writings from the seller which the buyer retained after the bought and sold notes had become operative. The Equity Term said that these later writings "operated in law to nullify the arbitration clauses contained in the documents issued by the broker." Upon that proposition, we are of the opposite opinion.

At the top of each of these later writings, the buyer is described by the seller as being indebted to him—the seller—and next comes a statement of the quantity and price of the merchandise. This much was no more than a bill rendered. The "Conditions of Sale" (which were printed on the reverse side) did indeed make references to something which is not mentioned in the bought and sold notes, viz. "1½ per cent discount allowed if invoice is paid within ten days of date of invoice." Even so, this new item is accounted for by uncontradicted expert testimony in this phrase: "One and one-half per cent is the customary canned goods discount." But beyond all this, the seller was a business man who must be presumed to have known what was essential to a valid contract (Newberry et al. v. Wall, 84 N.Y. 576, 581); hence it is most significant that his so-called conditions of sale made neither provision nor place for any signature by the buyer—whose confirmation as the party to be charged was necessary to the validity of a contract of sale under the Statute of Frauds. (Personal Property Law, § 85.) Clearly, as we think, these later writings of the seller were at best mere invoices which did not affect the earlier bought and sold notes in any way. (See Matter of Tanenbaum Textile Co. v. Schlanger, 287 N.Y. 400.)

The orders should be reversed and the proceedings dismissed, with costs to the appellant in all courts.

LEHMAN, CH. J., LEWIS, CONWAY, DESMOND, THACHER and DYE, JJ., concur.

Orders reversed, etc.

At common law oral agreements to arbitrate were neither more nor less enforceable than written agreements. They could support an enforceable award. The American statutes require that agreements to arbitrate be reduced to writing. New York CPA § 1449 required that future dispute agreements be in writing and that submissions of existing disputes be subscribed. CPLR § 7501 only requires a writing for either kind of agreement. Quite a few states prescribe subscription for at least some kinds of agreements. See e.g. Conn. Gen. Stat, § 52–408. Cal. Code of Civ. Proc. § 1281 employs the Uniform Act form:

> A written agreement to submit to arbitration an existing controversy or a controversy thereafter arising is valid, enforceable and irrevocable save upon such grounds as exist for the revocation of any contract.

In addition § 1280(f) declares: " 'Written agreement' shall be deemed to include a written agreement which has been extended or renewed by an oral or implied agreement." The New York Court of Appeals has reached the same result by interpretation of former CPA § 1449. Matter of Acadia Co. (Edlitz) 7 N.Y. 2d 348, 197 N.Y.S. 2d 457 (1960).

The Rhode Island Arbitration Act (to be distinguished from three acts governing arbitration in labor relations and firemen's and policemen's employment) validates agreements to arbitrate "when clearly written and expressed and contained in a separate paragraph placed immediately before the testimonium clause or the signatures of the parties ...' General Laws of Rhode Island 10–3–2.

MATTER OF ALBRECHT CHEMICAL CO. (ANDERSON TRADING CORP.) 298 N.Y. 437, 84 N.E.2d 625 (1949)

FULD, J. In May of 1948, Anderson Trading Corp., as seller, and Albrecht Chemical Co., Inc., as buyer, arranged over the telephone for the sale and purchase of 10,000 pounds of a certain dye. Thereafter, Albrecht sent the seller two "purchase orders", each for 5,000 pounds of dye. In addition to describing the merchandise and specifying their quantity and price, each order bore on its face the notation "KINDLY SIGN AND RETURN ONE COPY FOR OUR RECORDS," and, on its reverse side, eleven separately numbered terms and conditions. One of these conditions provided for the arbitration of any controversy or claim that might arise between the parties (¶ 11), and another recited that the "order and the terms and conditions thereof shall be deemed accepted" by the seller if he should fail to advise the buyer to the contrary within ten days (¶ 9).

The seller neither signed nor returned the purchase orders. Instead, it sent its own memoranda of sale to the buyer, and in them made no reference to the buyer's purchase order or to any provision of it. About ten days later, on May 21st, Albrecht purchased a further quantity of the dye; on this occasion, the only document issued was the seller's memorandum of sale. During the course of the following month, Albrecht, complaining that the goods were defective, demanded that the matter be arbitrated as provided in its purchase order. Anderson refused to accede to the request, maintaining that it had never agreed to arbitrate.

The purchaser thereupon initiated the present proceeding. The court at Special Term, holding that the seller's explicit consent to arbitrate was unnecessary in view of its failure to indicate disagreement, directed arbitration, and the Appelate Division affirmed. We see no alternative but to reverse, for the seller never agreed or bound itself to arbitration.

In the first place, considering the affidavits which are before us, it may be that a contract was consummated by telephone, and, if that is so, nothing more need be said. Clearly, such an oral contract could not have created a binding agreement to arbitrate future differences, even if the parties had so intended. "A contract to arbitrate a controversy thereafter arising between the parties must," the Civil Practice Act is explicit, "be in writing" (Civ. Prac. Act, § 1449).

We go further, however, and hold that, even if the terms of the agreement were not finally fixed by the oral communications over the telephone and remained open to further negotiation, the subsequent written exchanges did not commit the seller to arbitrate. The buyer's purchase order was at best merely an offer or a counter-offer, and its retention by the seller without objection may not be deemed ratification of, or acquiescence to, the terms which it contained.

This follows from the settled rule that, where the recipient of an offer is under no duty to speak, silence, when not misleading, may not be translated into acceptance merely because the offer purports to attach that effect to it. (See Matter of Tanenbaum Textile Co. v. Schlanger, 287 N.Y. 400, 404; Poel v. Brunswick-Balke-Collender Co., 216 N.Y. 310, 318 et seq.; More v. New York Brewery Fire Ins. Co., 130 N.Y. 537, 545, 547; see, also, 1 WILLISTON ON CONTRACTS [Rev. ed.], § 91, pp. 279–280; RESTATEMENT, CONTRACTS, § 72, [1].) That fundamental principle we stated in the *Tanenbaum* case (*supra*), which also concerned the binding effect of an arbitration clause (287 N.Y. at p. 404):

> A party cannot be held to contract where there is no assent. Silence operates as an assent and creates an estoppel only when it has the effect to mislead.... When a party is under a duty to speak, or when his failure to speak is inconsistent with honest dealings and misleads another, then his silence may be deemed to be acquiescence.

It is to be observed that, in the cases wherein acceptance has been thrust upon a party as the result of his silence, something more than here was present. For example, the parties may have been advised and warned by a previous course of dealings that inaction would be taken as assent (see Matter of Catz Amer. Sales Corp. [Holleb & Co.], 298 N.Y. 504, affg. 272 App. Div. 689; see, also, 1 WILLISTON ON CONTRACTS, op cit., § 91B; RESTATEMENT, CONTRACTS, § 72 [1], subd. [c], or, acting through a common agent they may have impliedly authorized him to bind them without more to various provisions, including one on arbitration. (See Matter of Catz Amer. Sales Corp. [Holleb & Co.], *supra*.)

In the present case, there is no basis for finding that the seller had a duty to speak out and reject the arbitration clause in the buyer's purchase order. Those orders were not issued by an agent acting for both parties; and obviously the seller's silence could not have been misleading. Indeed, on each occasion, instead of heeding the direction to "SIGN AND RETURN" the order, the seller dispatched its own memorandum. In whatever light we view that document—as affirmation of an agreement closed over the telephone, as an offer based upon previous negotiations, or as a counteroffer to the purchase order—it did not amount to acceptance of the arbitration provision. Implicit in the seller's conduct in sending its own memorandum was notice that it did not accede to the buyer's terms; no positive rejection was necessary to avoid them. In point of fact, there is strong indication that the buyer could not have harbored any expectation that arbitration had been assented to, for the third transaction, that of May 21st, was executed without any purchase order from the buyer and with no mention whatever of a provision to arbitrate.

In short, neither expressly nor impliedly, neither directly nor indirectly, did the parties ever discuss arbitration or bargain about it, and certainly they reached no agreement thereon. (See Matter of Kahn [Nat. City Bank], 284 N.Y. 515, 523; Matter of Bullard [Grace Co.], 240 N.Y. 388, 395.) The buyer's only recourse for alleged breach is to the courts.

The orders appealed from should be reversed, and the petition dismissed, with costs in all courts.

LOUGHRAN, CH. J., LEWIS, CONWAY, DESMOND and DYE, JJ., concur.

Orders reversed, etc.

MATTER OF LEVEL EXPORT CORP.
(WOLZ, AIKEN and CO.)
305 N.Y. 82, 111 N.E. 2d 218 (1953)

[Special Term granted a stay of arbitration, an order unanimously affirmed by the Appellate Division, First Department.]

LEWIS, J. Incidental to a commercial transaction between the parties to this proceeding, there has emerged the question, now decisive in this litigation, whether each of the two contracts, which fixed the obligations of the parties, validly incorporated an agreement that "Any controversy arising under, or in relation to, this contract, shall be settled by arbitration."

As to facts: The petitioner-respondent, Level Export Corporation, to which reference will be made as the buyer, is engaged in the purchase and export of a variety of commodities including textiles. On January 22 and February 14, 1951, the buyer executed two written contracts, practically identical in text, by which it agreed to purchase from the respondent-appellant, Wolz, Aiken & Co., hereinafter referred to as the seller, a total quantity of 135,000 yards of leno—a light-weight cotton fabric used in making summer garments. Each of the two agreements contained the names of the parties, the quantity of fabric sold, the delivery dates and the terms of payment. The balance of each contract—covering a substantial portion of the single page upon which the agreement was printed—consists of the following two paragraphs.

> This Salesnote is subject to the provisions of STANDARD COTTON TEXTILE SALESNOTE which, by this reference, *is incorporated as a part of this agreement and together herewith constitutes the entire contract between buyer and seller. No variation therefrom shall be valid unless accepted in writing.*
> Prices on any undelivered portion of this contract are subject to any further increase or decrease due to Governmental action and any present or future Federal or State legislation affecting the seller's costs, and deliveries may be modified to the extent necessitated by any such Governmental action or legislation affecting production. (Emphasis supplied.)

The standard cotton textile salesnote which—by the words italicized above—is incorporated by reference in each of the two agreements here involved, contains ten subdivisions which, by their titles, relate to—"I. CONSTRUCTION," "II. PASSING OF TITLE," "III. STORAGE AND INSURANCE," "IV. TERMS OF COLLECTION AND CREDIT," "V. CANCELLATIONS, REJECTIONS AND CLAIMS," "VI. DEFAULTS IN PAYMENT," "VII. FURNISHING SPECIFICATIONS," "VIII. CASUALTY," "IX. OTHER CONTINGENCIES," and "X. ARBITRATION." The tenth subdivision, relating to "ARBITRATION," provides as follows:

> Any controversy arising under, or in relation to, this contract, shall be settled by arbitration. If the parties are unable to agree respecting time, place, method, or rules of the arbitration, then such arbitration shall be held in the City of New York in accordance with the laws of the State of New York and the rules then obtaining of the General Arbitration Council of the Textile Industry and the parties consent to the jurisdiction of the Supreme Court of said State and further consent that any process or notice of motion or other application to the Court or a Judge thereof may be served outside the State of New York by registered mail or by personal service, provided a reasonable time for appearance is allowed.

When a dispute subsequently arose between the parties with regard to performance under the two purchase agreements, the seller instituted arbitration proceedings in accord with the rules of the General Arbitration Council of the Textile Industry. Thereupon the buyer, when requested to do so, refused to appoint an arbitrator and has thus far successfully opposed arbitration by motion for a stay made at Special Term upon the ground that no aggreement to arbitrate exists between the parties (Civ. Prac. Act, § 1458, subd. 2).

The buyer admits that it executed the contracts of purchase mentioned above, each of which by its terms incorporates the standard cotton textile salesnote containing the provision upon which is based the seller's demand for arbitration. The ground upon which the buyer resists arbitration, viz., that no arbitration agreement exists between the parties, is stated in the affidavit by the buyer's secretary and treasurer, read in support of its motion in this proceeding, as follows:

> At no time was the petitioner informed in any way that the provisions of the Standard Cotton Textile Salesnote contained any provision requiring arbitration of any controversy between the parties.
>
> Neither the petitioner nor any of its officers or directors is a member of any association or any textile group; none of us has ever seen the Worth Street Rules; we have never been provided with a copy thereof. Arbitration was mentioned for the first time by the attorneys for the respondent on September 14, 1951, which was several months after the controversy arose. At the time that the petitioner signed the contracts . . . neither the petitioner nor any of its officers or directors was aware of any provision requiring arbitration under the contracts. . . .
>
> The petitioner [buyer] did not know, if it is the fact, that by signing the agreements annexed hereto that it had agreed to arbitrate any disputes with respondent. No arbitration clause was ever called to the attention of the petitioner.

The question thus presented is whether the factual allegations contained in the buyer's affidavit, quoted in part above, serve to raise "a substantial issue as to the making of the contract," thereby entitling the buyer to a stay of arbitration. (Civ. Prac. Act, § 1458, subd. 2) That question is one of law. (Matter of General Elec. Co. [United Elec. Radio & Mach. Workers of America], 300 N.Y. 262, 264 ; Alpert v. Admiration Knitwear Co., 304 N.Y. 1, 3.)

Mindful that "No one is under a duty to resort to arbitration unless by clear language he has so agreed" (Matter of Lehman v. Ostrovsky, 264 N.Y. 130, 132), we are unable to find in the record legal justification for the buyer's present claim that it is not obligated, by each of the purchase agreements to which it was a party, to arbitrate the disputes which have arisen in the course of performance of those agreements.

Each of those contracts contains the statement that it is made "subject to the provisions of STANDARD COTTON TEXTILE SALESNOTE" which, as we have seen, was expressly "incorporated as a part of this agreement and together herewith constitutes the entire contract between buyer and seller." Difficult it would be to find words more clearly to express the contractual intent of the parties. There is no evidence that an attempt was made to limit the application of the standard cotton textile salesnote ; nor was there indication that any one of the ten subdivisions of the salesnote was not intended to apply. Indeed, a contrary intention is indicated by the sentence which immediately follows the contract provision last quoted above "No variation therefrom shall be valid unless accepted in writing."

The effect of the foregoing contract provisions was to adopt, and to integrate into each purchase agreement, the terms of the standard cotton textile salesnote. Among those provisions is the tenth subdivision, bearing the caption "ARBITRATION," beneath which is the printed statement "Any controversy arising under, or in relation to, this contract, shall be settled by arbitration," followed by procedural provisions in the event arbitration should become necessary.

In view of the documents to which reference has been made—which, when integrated, form the contracts executed by buyer and seller (see 3 WILLISTON ON CONTRACTS [Rev. ed.], § 628) we regard the buyer's contention—that no contract to arbitrate exists between the parties—as being at variance with the plain language of its agreements.

There is no allegation by the buyer of misrepresentation by the seller either with respect to the effect of the two purchase agreements, or with respect to provisions of the standard cotton textile salesnote. Nor does the buyer claim to have been innocently misled by words or conduct of the seller which indicated that disputes between the contracting parties would be settled by means other than by arbitration. The buyer's sole contention is that through its own ignorance of the provisions contained in the standard cotton textile salesnote it failed to understand the significance and effect of those provisions of the purchase contracts to which reference has been made. Upon that phase of the case we note in the record a statement by an officer of the buyer that the business of that corporation "consists of the purchase of commodities and their export to customers throughout the world" and that the commodities purchased and exported comprise a wide variety of items including textiles. In those circumstances we may assume that the buyer—an exporter of wide experience—dealt with the seller with knowledge that the provisions of the purchase agreements here involved were to have legal effect and were thus enforcible.

In Metzger v. Aetna Ins. Co., 227 N.Y. 411, 416, this court had occasion to state the rule which we believe to be applicable to the present case:

> ... when a party to a written contract accepts it as a contract he is bound by the stipulations and conditions expressed in it whether he reads them or not. Ignorance through negligence or inexcusable trustfulness will not relieve a party from his contract obligations. He who signs or accepts a written contract, in the absence of fraud or other wrongful act on the part of another contracting party, is conclusively presumed to know its contents and to assent to them and there can be no evidence for the jury as to his understanding of its terms.

We regard as inapplicable to our present problem the decisions in Matter of General Silk Importing Co. (Gerseta Corp.), 198 App. Div. 16, and Matter of Bachmann, Emmerich & Co. (Wenger & Co.), 204 App. Div. 282, cited by the Appellate Division in support of its ruling herein. In each of those cases the contract under which arbitration was sought provided that " 'Sales are governed by raw silk rules adopted by the Silk Association of America.' " In refusing to direct arbitration, the court, in Matter of General Silk Importing Co. (Gerseta Corp.) indicated that the parties had not clearly expressed an intention that the raw silk rules should apply to anything more than to the completion of sales under the agreement. In Matter of Bachmann, Emmerich & Co. (Wenger & Co.) involving the identical contract provision, the case was decided upon the authority of Matter of General Silk Importing Co. (Gerseta Corp.).

Our examination of the present record leads us to conclude that it does not raise a "substantial issue" as to the making of the two purchase agreements in suit so as to avoid their legal consequences (Civ. Prac. Act, § 1458, subd. 2).

Accordingly, the orders should be reversed and the matter remitted to Special Term for further proceedings not inconsistent with this opinion, with costs to appellant in all courts.

DESMOND, J. (dissenting). I dissent and vote to affirm.

Whether respondent ever consented to arbitration was, on this record, a question of fact, and the negative answer to that question given by both courts below, leaves us powerless to reconsider it. No one can be forced into arbitration unless by plain language he actually agrees to arbitrate (Matter of Lehman v. Ostrovsky, 264 N.Y. 130, 132), and such an agreement is not established, conclusively and as matter of law, by a showing that he signed a contract which incorporated by reference only and with no mention of arbitration, another document which, although he did not know it, contained a consent to arbitration. Decisions in cases where a party signed a contract without reading it, are not helpful here. Respondent, so it has been found as fact by both courts below, never saw the document "incorporated by reference" into the contract he did see and sign, never knew that appellant desired an agreement on arbitration, and never in fact knew that the other, or "incorporated," document prescribed arbitration. In legal effect, the situation is identical with that in the two cases cited by the Appellate Division (Matter of General Silk Importing Co. [Gerseta Corp.], 198 App. Div. 16, and Matter of Bachmann, Emmerich & Co. [Wenger & Co.], 204 App. Div. 282) where the arbitration provision was in the rules of the Silk Association, by which rules the sales involved in the two cited cases were "governed."

LOUGHRAN, CH. J., CONWAY, DYE and FROESSEL, JJ., concur with LEWIS, J.; DESMOND, J., dissents in opinion in which FULD, J., concurs.

Orders reversed, etc.

MATTER OF RIVERDALE FABRICS CORP. (TILLINGHAST-STILES CO.)
306 N.Y. 288, 118 N.E. 2d 104 (1954)

VAN VOORHIS, J. The question is whether the contract entered into between these parties contains an arbitration clause, precluding resort to actions at law or in equity.

There is a substantial distinction between this contract and the one which was involved in the *Level* case. The rule is that a party is not to be compelled to surrender his right to resort to the courts, with all of their safeguards, unless he has agreed in writing to do so (Matter of Philip Export Corp. [Leathertone, Inc.], 275 App. Div. 102, 104), and by clear language (Matter of Lehman v. Ostrovsky, 264 N.Y. 130, 132). Although one may by contract bargain away his right to resort to the courts in matters which might be the subject of a civil action (Civ. Prac. Act, § 1448), "the agreement to do so will not be extended by construction or implication" (Western Assur. Co. v. Decker, 98 F. 381, 382).

This controversy turns on a sales memorandum of yarn, which contained a printed sentence: "This contract is also subject to the

Cotton Yarn Rules of 1938 as amended." This language evidently referred to regulatory rules adopted by certain well-known trade associations of cotton yarn dealers in the United States. This contract contains no arbitration clause, nor does it mention the settlement of disputes by arbitration. The clause in question is similar to the one in the contract involved in Matter of General Silk Importing Co. (Gerseta Corp.) (198 App. Div. 16) wherein the following statement was made in the sales memoranda: "Sales are governed by Raw Silk Rules adopted by the Silk Association of America." The raw silk rules, to which reference was made, contained exclusive arbitration articles and many other detailed provisions concerning the sale of such merchandise. The court held that this language failed to show with sufficient definiteness that the minds of the parties met on arbitration, or that they intended to adopt the rules of the Silk Association of America "not merely to insure performance of the contract in accordance with those rules, but that in the event of a controversy, it should be arbitrated in accordance therewith." (Pp. 20–21.) The court said further:

> The parties could have provided for such arbitration without setting forth all or any of the rules of the Silk Association of America if they had merely added to the provision incorporated in the contract to the effect that the *sales* are to be governed by those rules a provision that in the event of a controversy between the parties it should be arbitrated as provided by the rules, or if the contract had provided in any manner by appropriate phraseology that the reference to the rules was intended to include those providing for arbitration.

(P. 21. Italics from original.) The Special Term order denying application to compel arbitration in the raw silk case was affirmed (198 App. Div. 16), but it contained leave to renew. On removal, and on a full record showing that the rules provided that "All differences arising between buyer and seller must be submitted to the Arbitration Committee of the Silk Association of America" and that both parties were members of the Association, the petition to compel arbitration was again denied at Special Term, and its order was unanimously affirmed by the Appellate Division (200 App. Div. 786) and by the Court of Appeals (234 N.Y. 513).

That case is in point here. It was distinguished in the opinion in the *Level* case, by stating that the phraseology in the sales note in the *General Silk Importing Co.* case "indicated that the parties had not clearly expressed an intention that the raw silk rules should apply to anything more than the completion of sales under the agreement." (305 N.Y. 88.) The *Level* contracts were

in the form of salesnotes, each of which contained a clause reading: "This Salesnote is subject to the provisions of STANDARD COTTON TEXTILE SALESNOTE which, by this reference, is incorporated as a part of this agreement and together herewith constitutes the entire contract between buyer and seller." The standard cotton textile salesnote was thus incorporated verbatim by reference, which contained an exclusive arbitration clause. The *Level* opinion pointed up this distinction by stating further at page 86: "The effect of the foregoing contract provisions was to adopt, and to integrate into each purchase agreement, the terms of the standard cotton textile salesnote."

The present contract contains no "incorporation" clause, and is almost identical with the language of the memorandum in Matter of General Silk Importing Co. (Gerseta Corp.), which was distinguished in the *Level* case. Paraphrasing what was there said of the Silk Association contract, these parties are not deemed necessarily to have contemplated anything more than that the cotton yarn rules should apply to the completion of sales under the agreement.

The intent must be clear to render arbitration the exclusive remedy; parties are not to be led into arbitration unwittingly through subtlety. The intention to do that is reasonably clear from the draftsmanship of the cotton yarn rules, which aimed to avoid mentioning arbitration in the sales memoranda themselves, where the contracting parties could see it. This could have been done briefly, since no set form of words is required if the intent to arbitrate is made clear. Nevertheless, these rules were elaborately drafted so as to state that a clause contained in a sales memorandum which says " 'This Contract is subject to the provisions of the Cotton Yarn Rules,' " means that "such rules become a part of the contract," and that "By this reference the 'Cotton Yarn Rules' are incorporated as a part of an agreement and altogether therewith constitutes the entire contract between buyer and seller. No variation therefrom shall be valid unless accepted in writing." Rule 31 contains an elaborate exclusive arbitration clause. All of this awaited the unwary trader if he assented to the clause that the contract would be subject to the Cotton Yarn Rules.

If this clause, or a much simpler one, had been set forth in the memorandum of sale, unquestionably arbitration would have been the exclusive remedy. If part of the care exhibited in drafting the rules had been used in mentioning arbitration in the contract, there would be no difficulty in affirming the order appealed from. Instead, the form of words favored by these trade associations appears to have been designed to avoid any resistance that might arise if arbitration were brought to the attention of the contracting parties as the exclusive remedy in case of disputes.

The order of the Appellate Division and that of Special Term should be reversed, and appellant's motion to stay arbitration granted, with costs in all courts.

DESMOND, J. (dissenting). My dissent is not prompted by any dissatisfaction with the result arrived at here—I unsuccessfully urged a similar result, from construction of similar language, in my dissent, a year ago, in the Matter of Level Export Corp. (Wolz, Aiken & Co.) case (305 N.Y. 82). What troubles me about this present decision is that this court, without any reargument or overruling of that very recent *Level* case ruling, now puts the opposite construction on language, in the contract between these parties, which has the same meaning as the language in the salesnote in the *Level* case. What is now the law as to whether a businessman can make his agreement subject to arbitration by general references therein to trade association rules which, in fact, make all disputes arbitrable?

We now have three decisions of this court on the subject: Matter of General Silk Importing Co. (Gerseta Corp.) (234 N.Y. 513), Matter of Level Export Corp. (Wolz, Aiken & Co.) (305 N.Y. 82, *supra*), and this case. The *Gerseta* contract said: "Sales are governed by Raw Silk Rules adopted by the Silk Association of America" and these "Raw Silk Rules" made arbitration compulsory, but the courts said that this reference to the rules did not bind to arbitration. In the *Level* case, more words were used, but to the very same effect: "This Salesnote is subject to the provisions of STANDARD COTTON TEXTILE SALESNOTE which, by this reference, is incorporated as a part of this agreement and together herewith constitutes the entire contract between buyer and seller." The "STANDARD COTTON TEXTILE SALESNOTE" provided, in one of its terms, for arbitration of disputes. Although that *Level* salesnote did not mention arbitration, any more than did the contract in *Gerseta*, this court held that the parties had agreed to arbitration, and must arbitrate. Now, in the present case, we have this form of reference to outside rules which require arbitration: "This contract is also subject to the Cotton Yarn Rules of 1938 as amended."

In none of the three contracts (*Gerseta, Level* and the one here) was there any actual mention of arbitration, but each contract was in terms made subject to an outside, unattached document which, on inspection, would have been found to contain a conventional arbitration clause. In each instance, by variant phraseology, the contracting party was warned that the transaction expressed in the contract was subject to certain identified but not otherwise described rules.

The *Level* case salesnote failed, just as did the contract here, to include "clear language" (Matter of Lehman v. Ostrovsky, 264 N.Y. 130) binding the parties to arbitrate. The words used in one instance were no more or less subtle, artful or devious than in the other. If one set of words was a trap for the unwary or if, on the contrary, it was a fair warning to look at the rules, then, whichever of those two views we take, we should take the same as to the same-meaning words in the other instance. In short, we should either overrule the *Level* case, or follow it.

The order should be affirmed, with costs.

FROESSEL, J. (dissenting). I concur with Judge DESMOND for affirmance. In Matter of General Silk Importing Co. (Gerseta Corp.) (234 N.Y. 513) decided in 1922, the crucial provision read: "*Sales* are governed by Raw Silk Rules adopted by the Silk Association of America." (Emphasis supplied.) In Matter of Level Export Corp. (Wolz, Aiken & Co.) (305 N.Y. 82) where the "Salesnote" was made "subject to the provisions of STANDARD COTTON TEXTILE SALESNOTE," we pointed out (p. 88) that the court in the *Gerseta* case "indicated that the parties had not clearly expressed an intention that the raw silk rules should apply to anything more than to the completion of *sales* under the agreement" (emphasis supplied). Here, the reference is not to "sales" but to "This contract," a far broader term, which in my opinion brings it within the holding of the *Level* case.

LEWIS, CH. J., CONWAY and FULD, JJ., concur with VAN VOORHIS, J.; DESMOND, J., dissents and votes for affirmance in an opinion in which DYE, J., concurs; FROESSEL, J., dissents and votes for affirmance in a separate memorandum.

Orders reversed, etc.

MATTER OF AMERICAN RAIL AND STEEL CO. (INDIA SUPPLY MISSION)
308 N.Y. 577, 127 N.E. 2d 562 (1955)

DYE, J. The issue here is whether a contract for the purchase and sale of a quantity of used steel rails and angle bars bound the parties to settle disputes arising therefrom exclusively by arbitration. Whether it did or not depends on purchase order language providing viz.: "This Contract is placed in accordance with the conditions of contract Form ISM 826 Rev. Copy attached and can be modified or supplemented only in writing and signed by both parties hereto."

Paragraph 25 of the aforementioned form provided: "ARBITRATION: All questions and controversies arising in connection with this contract shall be submitted to arbitration in New York, N.Y., in accordance with the rules of arbitration of the American Arbitration Association."

When a dispute arose as to whether the used rails delivered corresponded in quantity and quality to those called for in the purchase order, the purchaser demanded that it be settled by arbitration. The seller then made the within motion for a stay claiming that arbitration was not called for by the contract documents since the purchase order did not mention it and that Form ISM 826 Rev., on which the purchaser relies, was not attached or that its contents were otherwise brought to the seller's attention. While respondent attempts to deny this assertion by saying that it was their practice to attach said form, it, nonetheless, takes the position that its omission "does not change the situation." The motion for stay was denied in Special Term on authority of Matter of Level Export Corp. (Wolz Aiken & Co.) (305 N.Y. 82, revg. 280 App. Div. 211). Upon appeal, such denial was unanimously affirmed in the Appellate Division, First Department, and the parties were directed to proceed to arbitration. We granted leave in order that the controversy might be examined in light of our subsequent decision in Matter of Riverdale Fabrics Corp. (Tillinghast-Stiles Co.) (306 N.Y. 288). That case dealt with a salesnote for cotton yarn containing a clause reading: "This contract is also subject to the Cotton Yarn Rules of 1938 as amended." Rule 31 of those rules contained an arbitration clause. We deemed such reference was ineffective "to render arbitration the exclusive remedy", because the intention to do so was not clearly expressed. This distinguished the holding in the *Level* case (*supra*) for there the verbatim reference in the main contract to the salesnote provision did not, as a matter of law, raise any substantial issue as to the making of the agreement to arbitrate (Civ. Prac. Act, § 1458, subd. 2). In our view this case more closely resembles *Riverdale* (*supra*) than *Level* and, accordingly, a court cannot say that the intent to arbitrate was so clearly expressed as to warrant a direction that parties proceed to settle their dispute by arbitration.

The order should be reversed and the motion to stay arbitration granted, with costs.

The order of the Appellate Division and that of Special Term should be reversed, with costs in all courts, and the matter remitted to Special Term for further proceedings in accordance with the opinion herein.

CONWAY, CH. J., DESMOND, FULD, FROESSEL, VAN VOORHIS and BURKE JJ., concur.

Orders reversed, etc.

MATTER OF CENTRAL STATES PAPER AND BAG CO. (CHICOPEE MILLS, INC.) 132 N.Y.S. 2d 69 (1954) (S. Ct. N.Y. Cty.)

[Seller's "confirmation" was signed by the buyer.]

The notation in bold type upon the front of the confirmation form and across its entire width that "This order is subject to the provisions ... on the reverse side" sufficiently called to the attention of Central the arbitration provision which was set forth on the reverse side. It is thus distinguishable from the case of Matter of Arthur Philip Exp. Corp. (Leathertone, Inc.), 275 App. Div. 102 [87 N.Y.S. 2d 665], upon which petitioner relies. In the latter case there appeared in small print on the right side at the lower center of the face of the order the legend "(See also back)."

Central chose John O'Neil as its agent to sign the confirmation form and is estopped from denying his authority.

The application is denied.

[On motion for reargument, motion was denied. Ed.]

MATTER OF STEIN, HALL & CO. (NESTLE-LeMUR CO.) 13 Misc. 2d 547, 177 N.Y.S. 2d 603 (S. Ct. N.Y. Cty. 1958)

In other words, the arbitration clause did not become part of the contract between the parties to the instant proceeding for two reasons: (1) instead of checking one of the boxes preceding the statements referring to the terms and conditions on the reverse side, respondent sent an accompanying letter referring to the document, in effect, as an acceptance of the movant's order (rather than as a counter offer) and (2) the references on the face of the document to the terms and conditions on the other side did not apprise the movant that the terms and conditions included a provision for arbitration of all disuptes.

Motion granted.

In Matter of Emerson Radio & Phonograph Corp. (Illustrated Technical Products Corp.), 12 Misc. 2d 1000, 178 N.Y.S. 2d 277 (N.Y. Cty. 1958) another Supreme Court judge in New York County observed: "A provision for arbitration may not ... be incorporated by reference to an extrinsic document which is neither exhibited nor attached to the contract itself," citing *inter alia Riverdale* but making no mention of *Level Export*, in which the document containing the arbitration clause was not appended and, indeed, was never seen by the buyer.

After taking orders by phone, seller shipped goods and sent invoices to factory, which, after checking their accuracy, forwarded the invoices to the buyer. Seller's invoices were stamped "All controversies arising from the sale of these goods are to be settled by arbitration." The buyer retained the invoices without comment. Unanimously held that no agreement to arbitrate was concluded. Although "acceptance of a document which plainly purports to be a contract gives rise to an implication of assent to its terms despite ignorance thereof ... an invoice is no contract." Matter of Tanenbaum Textile Co. v. Schlanger, 287 N.Y. 400, 40 N.E. 2d 225 (1942).

MATTER OF HELEN WHITING, INC. (TROJAN TEXTILE CORP.)
307 N.Y. 360, 121 N.E. 2d 367 (1954)

DESMOND, J. Petitioner-appellant Helen Whiting, Inc., is a garment manufacturer with offices in New York City, while respondent Trojan Textile Corporation is a manufacturer of textiles with offices in the same city. On July 10, 1953, at petitioner's office, there was a discussion between persons representing the two corporations which discussion, according to respondent Trojan, resulted in an oral agreement by Whiting to buy from Trojan a total of about 83,000 yards of three different kinds of goods, all at the one price of 52½c per yard. Trojan claims that, on that same day, three written contracts

were delivered by hand by Trojan to Whiting, that, three days later, on July 13, 1953, Trojan sent Whiting invoices for parts of each lot of goods, and that, on July 14, 1953, Whiting requested and got delivery of five yards against each of the three contracts, but that, on July 16, 1953, petitioner Whiting notified respondent Trojan, orally and by letter, that Whiting could use only one kind of the merchandise, and signed and sent back one only of the three contracts. Trojan, considering this as an effort by Whiting to cancel two of three contracts already made, refused to agree to it. On the back of each of the three original writings prepared by Trojan, there is a general arbitration clause, and Trojan demanded arbitration thereunder. Whiting, however, brought this proceeding to stay the arbitration, alleging that the negotiations between the parties never reached the stage of contract. Trojan, opposing the stay and praying for an order requiring Whiting to proceed to arbitration, took the position, in an affidavit, that there was, on July 10, 1953, a completed oral contract for all the three kinds of goods, that written forms of agreement covering the whole transaction were immediately sent to Whiting, that Whiting held them for several days without returning them, that there was delivery of part of the quantity specified in each contract pursuant to order by Whiting, that Whiting had no right to cancel any of the three contracts, and that, so far as arbitration is concerned, there was no necessity for a signing by Whiting of the three papers containing the arbitration clauses, and that Whiting has never objected to the inclusion of arbitration clauses but has merely insisted on its alleged right to take one of the lots of goods on one of the written documents, and reject the other two.

Since there was thus set up an issue "as to the making of the contract" to arbitrate (Civ. Prac. Act, § 1450), Special Term made an order sending that issue to trial before Official Referee Isidor Wasservogel. The trial was had before the Official Referee, who held, as fact, that the parties had, on July 10, 1953, agreed on a purchase and sale of about 80,000 yards of these three kinds of cloth at 52½c per yard, that the agreement was, at the request of Whiting, that Trojan "bill and hold" all the goods, two of the quantities to be billed at once and the third to be billed on September 1, 1953, that, on the same day, Trojan sent Whiting three written confirmations, one for each lot, that Whiting held these three papers without signing or returning them until July 16th, and, in the meantime, ordered and got delivery of one five-yard piece against each of the three contracts, which three pieces Whiting accepted and has never returned, that these three deliveries, while small, satisfied the requirements of the Statute of Frauds (Personal Property Law, § 85), and that Whiting is bound to the arbitration agreement although it failed to sign two of the contracts. The Referee made an order adjudging that the contracts contained arbitration clauses which are binding upon the parties, and Special Term, on the Referee's report, made an order directing petitioner to proceed to arbitration. On petitioner's appeal to the Appellate Division, First Department, there was a three-to-two affirmance with no opinion by the majority but a brief dissent which expressed the view of two Justices that there was no enforcible written contract to arbitrate, no partial delivery, and that the Statute of Frauds applies. Petitioner then appealed to this court as of right.

Petitioner argues here that the alleged contracts were unenforcible under the Statute of Frauds because not signed by petitioner, that the three small deliveries did not constitute partial deliveries under the Statute of Frauds, and that there was no enforcible contract to arbitrate. In the light of these contentions, we will examine briefly the proofs before the Referee. One Ozdoba, sales manager of Trojan but produced as a witness by Whiting, testified that on July 10, 1953, he called on Sterngold, president of Whiting, at the latter's office, with the purpose of selling Sterngold some merchandise, that Ozdoba showed Sterngold a number of samples, and that Sterngold picked out three and said that he would take the whole lot, that is, all that Trojan had of these three kinds, if he could get a special price for the whole, and, as a result of bargaining, the parties then and there came to an agreement for the sale and purchase of the whole of the three kinds at 52½c per yard for all, which, according to Ozdoba, was a large reduction in price. Ozdoba testified that, at Sterngold's request, and since the goods were for next year's manufacture and Sterngold did not have storage space, Ozdoba agreed to "bill ... and hold" the goods, that is, charge them to Whiting on dates agreed upon, but hold them until called for. The arrangement, according to Ozdoba, was that he would go back to his office and prepare and send to Sterngold written contracts on the goods. There was no discussion about arbitration. Later the same day, Ozdoba prepared the three contracts and sent them over to Sterngold's office by delivery boy. The delivery boy confirmed the testimony of Sterngold that these contracts were not handed to Sterngold personally on Friday, July 10th. They did not reach Sterngold's hands until the Monday

following. On Tuesday, July 14th, according to Ozdoba, Sterngold telephoned and asked for samples of each of the three kinds of merchandise, that is, five-yard pieces of each, which were delivered on Wednesday, July 15th, Sterngold meanwhile holding the three contracts or proposed contracts. It is, we think, significant that on July 13th, which was Monday and three days after the conversation at Whiting's office, Trojan invoiced to Whiting substantial quantities of two of the three kinds of goods, apparently under the "bill and hold" arrangement, and that, on July 14th, four days after the contracts had been delivered to Whiting, Trojan billed Whiting for the three five-yard pieces, assigning those deliveries by number, to the three contracts in question. Sterngold, in his testimony, admitted that he read the face of each of these contracts but denied that he had read the reverse side on which appeared the arbitration clauses.

Sterngold, in his testimony on behalf of Whiting, confirmed that Ozdoba had come to Sterngold's office to sell the merchandise, that they decided on three patterns and on a reduced price of 52½c per yard for the three lots, but Sterngold's version was that the sale was subject to the approval of Sterngold's designer and that sample cuts were to be sent to Sterngold who would agree finally to the sale if the designer approved. Of course, since the Referee and Special Term accepted Trojan's version of this conversation, and the Appellate Division affirmed, we are bound by those holdings as to this issue of fact. Sterngold testified further that the sale on the part of Trojan was made contingent on price approval by someone at Trojan's office, which Ozdoba denied and which is not important since, obviously, Trojan, by sending on the contract, approved the price. Thus, the only substantial dispute between the parties as to the oral arrangements of July 10th was as to whether the sale was contingent on Whiting's later approval of samples—this was denied by Trojan, and the Referee found that there was no such condition of sale but that the three five-yard pieces were not samples for inspection but were partial deliveries against the contracts. We are bound by those findings.

As aforesaid, Whiting, on July 16th, six days after the written contracts had been sent and received, notified Trojan, orally and by letter, that it could not use two of the patterns, but was signing and sending to Trojan the signed contract for the other pattern, the letter expressing regret for any inconvenience. On July 20th, Trojan wrote a letter, in which it replied to Whiting's letter of July 16th by saying that it (Trojan) would not accept the "cancellation" of the two patterns. That letter repeated Trojan's version of the oral arrangements, stated that the low price was based on Whiting taking the whole lot, and demanded that Whiting honor the contracts and pay the invoices.

There are really two questions here: first, whether Whiting made any binding agreement at all to purchase the three lots, and, second, if the first question be answered in the affirmative, whether Whiting bound itself to arbitrate in case of dispute. As to the first question, it seems clear that the facts as found and affirmed below establish, as of July 10, 1953, an agreement to buy and sell which was to be, and was, memorialized by written contracts sent out on the same day. That such was the arrangement is established not only by testimony as to the conversation at Whiting's office but by the fact that Whiting held these contracts for six days without returning them and, meanwhile, received invoices for some of the goods and received actual delivery of the three five-yard pieces which Whiting never did return, and that, even when writing the letter of July 16th, Whiting did not really deny having made a deal for the three lots but expressed its regret that it could not use two of them. Perhaps, we do not have to decide on this appeal whether or not these contracts would be, in a suit at law, unenforcible. This is not such a suit at law but an arbitration proceeding and it may be that a failure to comply with the Statute of Frauds would not help Whiting. However, if we assume that the Statute of Frauds is applicable, its provisions are satisfied here, since the Referee held, on sufficient evidence, that the three five-yard pieces were not samples sent for approval but were "part of the goods" accepted and received by the buyer (Personal Property Law, § 85). Of course, they were very small deliveries but they were billed as deliveries under the contracts.

The other question is as to whether there is sufficient proof here to justify the findings below that the parties agreed on arbitration. We think that finding is amply justified by the showing that Whiting retained, for several days, the contracts containing arbitration clauses, and that Whiting never, at any time, objected to there being arbitration clauses and, in fact, signed one of the contracts containing an arbitration clause. From our own experience, we can almost take judicial notice that arbitration clauses are commonly used in the textile industry, and Sterngold testified that he was familiar with them. Cases like Matter of Albrecht Chem. Co. (Anderson Trading Corp.) (298 N.Y. 437) and Matter of Tanenbaum Textile Co. v. Schlanger (287 N.Y. 400) are not at all in point here since they involve situations where there was nothing to show an agreement to arbitrate but, rather, rejection of proposals for arbitration clauses. Here, the retention of the agreements containing arbitration clauses and the return, signed, of one of them was, we hold, sufficient evidence of an agreement on arbitration (see Matter of Japan Cotton Trading Co. v. Farber, 233 App. Div. 354, 355).

The court's observation that *Albrecht* and *Tanenbaum* involved "rejections of proposals for arbitration clauses" seems unwarranted by the facts and reasoning of those cases. Nonetheless, both may be distinguished from *Helen Whiting* on other grounds.

MATTER OF PERFECT FIT PRODUCTS MFG. CO. (PANTASOTE CO.)
5 Misc. 2d 348, 161 N.Y.S. 2d 376 (1957)

SAMUEL C. COLEMAN, J. Matter of Helen Whiting, Inc. (Trojan Textile Corp.) (307 N.Y. 360) determines the issue in favor of the respondent seller and calls for arbitration of the controversy between buyer and seller. In a period of over five months the buyer placed about 15 separate orders with the seller for the purchase of substantial quantities of goods, over $50,000 worth. The orders were oral or in writing, the writing in some instances "confirming" orders that had been placed orally with the seller's salesman. The order forms said nothing about arbitration. On receipt of each other the seller sent its printed form incorporating the substance of the seller's order (due to changes in some of the orders as the transactions went on there were about 20 of these forms). This was done apparently without reference to a written "confirmation"; it was sometimes sent on receiving an oral order and before receiving a "confirmation." The seller refers to its form as an "acknowledgment" but that term does not appear on it. What does appear—not in conspicuous type but in a conspicuous place—is a statement, the first sentence of which declares that orders are subject to acceptance at the seller's office. But as no further acceptance followed and as the goods were shipped, this declaration is of no legal significance. Indeed the orders were reviewed immediately on receipt and none was rejected. The statement in substance continues: The buyer agrees to be bound by the conditions printed on the reverse side of the form either by accepting the goods when delivered or by not rejecting those conditions in writing within 10 days. The conditions on the back are clearly printed ; one of them provides for the arbitration of controversies. There was no rejection, orally or in writing, but each of the orders was filled in the sense that the goods were delivered and accepted ; and payments were made for all of the merchandise, except that shipped under the last few orders. The controversy relates to these last orders and as to the merchandise covered by them complaint was made a substantial time after delivery.

The buyer says that it did not read the statement on the face of the "acknowledgment" or the conditions on the back of the seller's document. In any case, it maintains that there was no agreement to accept the terms, no agreement to arbitrate, and that the seller's "acknowledgment" adds nothing to an agreement already made. But I think it is bound by those terms, including the one as to arbitration.

This is not a case of an offeror presenting an offeree with the alternative of a compelled acceptance or breaking silence (cf. Matter of Albrecht Chem Co. [Anderson Trading Corp.], 298 N.Y. 437) nor, again as in the *Albrecht* case, of an offeree objectively accepting neither alternative by proposing his own form in answer to that of the offeror which omits a reference to arbitration. Speaking of the *Albrecht* case and of Matter of Tannenbaum Textile Co. v. Schlanger (287 N.Y. 400), the court in the *Whiting* case said that in each of the two earlier cases there was rejection in fact of the proposals for arbitration.

The situation is different here. Experienced, competent businessmen had staked out the ground in which they were carrying out their dealings and their conduct within that area can be resorted to to indicate agreement. They need not formally vocalize offer and acceptance of arbitration. In the *Whiting* case, retaining three separate orders for six days, signing and returning one of them (and accepting a token delivery under each of the orders) was held to be sufficient evidence of the making of an agreement to arbitrate as to all three contracts. There is much more here. The transactions covered a long period of time. Each order was followed by a document which contained an arbitration clause and which was received without demur, a document that in the buyer's view now is altogether meaningless and has no place at all in the transaction ; and deliveries under all the orders were accepted and payments made as to most. As to the buyer's contention that the seller's form is without significance, the fact is that on receiving

them he "checked it to see whether it conformed to our orders." What was on them was for him to read. Nor do I believe that the order alone was intended to be the contract.

All in all, the evidence indicates acceptance, by a course of conduct, of the conditions under which the transactions were to be carried on (*cf.* Matter of Catz American Sales Corp. [Holleb & Co.], 272 App. Div. 689, affd. 298 N.Y. 504 ; Matter of Japan Cotton Trading Co. v. Farber, 233 App. Div. 354). "Parties are not to be led into arbitration unwittingly through sublety" (Matter of Riverdale Fabrics Corp. [Tillinghast-Stiles Co.], 306 N.Y. 288, 291), but they should not be permitted to avoid it when an established course of conduct indicates familiarity with the conditions upon which transactions were to be and were being carried on (*cf.* Matter of Continental Nut Co. [Banner Mfg. Corp.], 286 App. Div. 1088, affd., 1 N.Y. 2d 705.) The controversy is subject to arbitration and the matter should proceed to arbitration. The stay is vacated. Settle order.

In an extended series of transactions, plaintiff submitted its form order with a designated place for acceptance. On most orders defendant indicated acceptance as the form required. In addition, defendant submitted its form of contract (with an arbitration clause on its reverse side and the notation "subject to the general terms and conditions set forth on back hereof" appeared on its face) ; defendant insisted that its forms be signed and plaintiff obliged. The court held that both documents constituted the contract between the parties and that the arbitration clause was operative and prevented suit.

Oregon-Pacific Forest Products Corp. v. Welsh Panel Co. 248 F. Supp. 903 (Ore. 1965).

MATTER OF DOUGHBOY INDUSTRIES (PANTASOTE CO.)
17 App. Div. 216, 233 N.Y.S. 2d 488
(First Dept. 1962)

BREITEL, J. This case involves a conflict between a buyer's order form and a seller's acknowledgment form, each memorializing a purchase and sale of goods. The issue arises on whether the parties agreed to arbitrate future disputes. The seller's form had a general arbitration provision. The buyer's form did not. The buyer's form contained a provision that only a signed consent would bind the buyer to any terms thereafter transmitted in any commercial form of the seller. The seller's form, however, provided that silence or a failure to object in writing would be an acceptance of the terms and conditions of its acknowledgment form. The buyer never objected to the seller's acknowledgment, orally or in writing. In short, the buyer and seller accomplished a legal equivalent to the irresistible force colliding with the immovable object.

Special Term denied the buyer's motion to stay arbitration on the ground that there was no substantial issue whether the parties had agreed to arbitrate. For the reasons to be stated, the order should be reversed and the buyer's motion to stay arbitration should be granted. As a matter of law, the parties did not agree in writing to submit future disputes to arbitration (Civ. Prac. Act, §§ 1448, 1449).

Of interest in the case is that both the seller and buyer are substantial businesses—a "strong" buyer and a "strong" seller. This is not a case of one of the parties being at the bargaining mercy of the other.

The facts are:

During the three months before the sale in question the parties had done business on two occasions. On these prior occasions the buyer used its purchase-order form with its insulating conditions, and the seller used its acknowledgment form with its self-actuating conditions. Each ignored the other's printed forms, but proceeded with the commercial business at hand.

The instant transaction began with the buyer, on May 6, 1960, mailing from its office in Wisconsin to the seller in New York City two purchase orders for plastic film. Each purchase order provided that some 20,000 pounds of film were to be delivered in the future on specified dates. In addition, further quantities were ordered on a "hold basis," that is, subject to "increase, decrease, or cancellation" by the buyer. On May 13, 1960 the seller orally accepted both purchase orders without change except to suggest immediate shipment of the first part of the order. The buyer agreed to the request, and that day the seller shipped some 10,000 pounds of film in partial fulfillment of one purchase order. On May 16, 1960, the buyer received the seller's first acknowledgment dated May 13, 1960, and on May 19, 1960 the seller's second acknowledgment dated May 16, 1960. Although the purchase orders called for written acceptances and return of attached acknowledgments by the seller no one paid any attention to these requirements. Neither party, orally or in writing, objected to the conditions printed on the other's commercial form. Later, the buyer sent change

orders with respect to so much of the orders as had been, according to the buyer, on a "hold basis."

The dispute, which has arisen and which the parties wish determined, the seller by arbitration, and the buyer by court litigation, is whether the buyer is bound to accept all the goods ordered on a "hold basis." The arbitration would take place in New York City. The litigation might have to be brought in Wisconsin, the buyer's home State.

The buyer's purchase-order form had on its face the usual legends and blanks for the ordering of goods. On the reverse was printed a pageful of terms and conditions. The grand defensive clause reads as follows:

> ALTERATION OF TERMS—None of the terms and conditions contained in this Purchase Order may be added to, modified, superseded or otherwise altered except by a written instrument signed by an authorized representative of Buyer and delivered by Buyer to Seller, and each shipment received by Buyer from Seller shall be deemed to be only upon the terms and conditions contained in this Purchase Order except as they may be added to modified, superseded or otherwise altered, notwithstanding any terms and conditions that may be contained in any acknowledgment, invoice or other form of Seller and notwithstanding Buyer's act of accepting or paying for any shipment or similar act of Buyer.

The buyer's language is direct; it makes clear that no variant seller's acknowledgment is to be binding. But the seller's acknowledgment form is drafted equally carefully. On its front in red typography one's attention is directed to the terms and conditions on the reverse side; and it advises the buyer that he, the buyer, has full knowledge of the conditions and agrees to them unless within 10 days he objects in writing.

The seller's clause reads:

> IMPORTANT
>
> Buyer agrees he has full knowledge of conditions printed on the reverse side hereof; and that the same are part of the agreement between buyer and seller and shall be binding if either the goods referred to herein are delivered to and accepted by buyer, or if buyer does not within ten days from date hereof deliver to seller written objection to said conditions or any part thereof.

On the reverse side the obligations of the buyer set forth above are carefully repeated. Among the conditions on the reverse side is the general arbitration clause.

This case involves only the application of the arbitration clause. Arguably, a different principle from that applied here might, under present law, govern other of the terms and conditions in either of the commercial forms. The reason is the special rule that the courts have laid down with respect to arbitration clauses, namely, that the agreement to arbitrate must be direct and the intention made clear, without implication, inveiglement or subtlety (Matter of Riverdale Fabrics Corp. [Tillinghast-Stiles Co.], 306 N.Y. 288, 289, 291 ; Matter of Lehman v. Ostrovsky, 264 N.Y. 130, 132 ; see, also, Matter of Amer. Rail & Steel Co. [India Supply Mission], 308 N.Y. 577, 579–580 ; Matter of Princeton Rayon Corp. [Gayley Mill Corp.], 309 N.Y. 13, involving conflicting forms). The severability of arbitration clauses from other provisions in commercial documentation would, of course, follow, if it be true that the threshold for clarity of agreement to arbitrate is greater than with respect to other contractual terms (see Matter of General Silk Importing Co., 198 App. Div. 16, 200 App. Div. 786, affd. 234 N.Y. 513 ; see, also, Matter of Arthur Philip Export Corp. [Leathertone, Inc.], 275 App. Div. 102, 104–105; but cf. Matter of Albrecht Chem. Co. [Anderson Trading Corp.], 298 N.Y. 437, 440–441).

It should be evident, as the buyer argues, that a contract for the sale of goods came into existence on May 13, 1960 when the seller made a partial shipment, especially when following upon its oral acceptance of the buyer's purchase order (RESTATEMENT, CONTRACTS, § 63; 1 WILLISTON, SALES [rev. ed.], § 5b; Personal Property Law, § 85, subd. 1, par. [b]). The contract, at such time, was documented only by the buyer's purchase-order form. However, that is not dispositive. It is equally evident from the prior transactions between these parties, and general practices in trade, that more documents were to follow. Such documents may help make the contract, or modify it (12 AM. JUR., CONTRACTS, § 405; 10 N.Y. JUR., CONTRACTS, §403). Whether the subsequent documents were necessary to complete the making of the contract (as would be true if there had been no effective or valid acceptance by partial shipment), or whether they served only to modify or validate the terms of an existing contract (as would be true if there had been a less formal written acceptance, merely an oral acceptance, or an acceptance by partial shipment of goods) is not really too important once the commercial dealings have advanced as far as they had here. By that time, there is no question whether there was a contract, but only what was the contract.

Recognizing, as one should, that the business men in this case acted with complete disdain for the "lawyer's content" of the very commercial forms they were sending and receiving, the question is what obligation ought the law to attach to the arbitration clause. And in determining

that question the traditional theory is applicable, namely, that of constructive knowledge and acceptance of contractual terms, based on prior transactions and the duty to read contractual instruments to which one is a party (Matter of Level Export Corp. [Wolz, Aiken & Co.], 305 N.Y. 82, 86-87 ; Matter of Wachusett Spinning Mills [Blue Bird Silk Mfg. Co.], 7 A. D. 2d 382, affd. 6 N.Y. 2d 848 ; cf. Matter of Riverdale Fabrics Corp. [Tillinghast-Stiles Co.], 306 N.Y. 288, supra).

But, and this is critical, it is not only the seller's form which should be given effect, but also the buyer's form, for it too was used in the prior transactions, and as to it too, there was a duty to read. Of course, if the two commercial forms are given effect, they cancel one another. (Certainly, the test is not which is the later form, because here the prior form said the buyer would not be bound by the later form unless it consented in writing. It needs little discussion that silence, a weak enough form of acceptance, effective only when misleading and there is a duty to speak, can be negatived as a misleading factor by announcing in advance that it shall have no effect as acceptance [RESTATEMENT, CONTRACTS, § 72 ; 1 CORBIN, CONTRACTS, §§ 72–75; 9 N.Y. JUR., Contracts, §§ 34, 45].

As pointed out earlier, an agreement to arbitrate must be clear and direct, and must not depend upon implication, inveiglement or subtlety (Matter of Riverdale Fabrics Corp. [Tillinghast-Stiles Co.], 306 N.Y. 288, 289, 291, supra ; Matter of Lehman v. Ostrovsky, 264 N.Y. 130, 132, supra). It follows then that the existence of an agreement to arbitrate should not depend solely upon the conflicting fine print of commercial forms which cross one another but never meet (cf. Matter of Princeton Rayon Corp. [Gayley Mill Corp.], 309 N.Y. 13, supra ; Matter of American Rail & Steel Co. [India Supply Mission], 308 N.Y. 577, supra).

Matter of Wachusett Spinning Mills (Blue Bird Silk Mfg. Co.) (7 A.D. 2d 382, affd. 6 N.Y. 2d 948, supra) provides no applicable rule. There the seller's acknowledgment of the buyer's purchase order (which included an arbitration clause) expressly accepted the purchase order by reference and designation. Although the acknowledgment contained additional terms, the specific reference to the purchase order was held determinative that the acknowledgment was an acceptance of the purchase order with all its terms. Thus, it was said (per Rabin, J., p. 383):

> The position of the petitioners might be sound if the confirmation orders made no reference to the original orders containing the arbitration clause. On the contrary however, the confirmation orders were

in such form as to show an intent to incorporate all the terms of the original orders—except, of course, as to specific changes stated.

In this case, the supposed condition happened, the acknowledgment made no reference to the purchase order, and, moreover, the prior purchase order disavowed the future application of any subsequent differing acknowledgment. And, the arbitration clause was one of the "specific changes" from the purchase order, which even under the rule in the *Wachusett* case would not be binding on the other party.

Consequently, as a matter of law there was no agreement to arbitrate in this case, if one applies existing principles.*

But the problem of conflicting commercial forms is one with which there has been much concern before this, and a new effort at rational solution has been made. The new solution would yield a similar result. The Uniform Commercial Code (L. 1962, ch. 553) takes effect in this State September 27, 1964 (§ 10–105). It reflects the latest legislative conclusions as to what the law ought to be. It provides:

§ 2–207. Additional Terms in Acceptance or Confirmation.

(1) A definite and seasonable expression of acceptance or a written confirmation which is sent within a reasonable time operates as an acceptance even though it states terms additional to or different from those offered or agreed upon, unless acceptance is expressly made conditional on assent to the additional or different terms.

(2) The additional terms are to be construed as proposals for addition to the contract. Between merchants such terms become part of the contract unless:

(a) the offer expressly limits acceptance to the terms of the offer;

(b) they materially alter it; or

(c) notification of objection to them has already been given or is given within a reasonable time after notice of them is received.

(3) Conduct by both parties which recognizes the existence of a contract is sufficient to establish a contract for sale although the writings of the parties do not otherwise establish a contract. In such case the terms of the particular contract consist of those terms on which the writings of the parties agree,

together with any supplementary terms incorporated under any other provisions of this Act.

While this new section is not in its entirety in accordance with New York law in effect when the events in suit occurred (see 1 Report of N.Y. Law Rev. Comm. on Uniform Commercial Code [1955], p. 627 *et seq*.), in its particular application to the problem at hand it is quite useful. The draftsmen's comments to section 2–207 are in precise point (Uniform Commercial Code [U. L. A.], § 2–207, comments 3 and 6). Thus, it is said:

3. Whether or not additional or different terms will become part of the agreement depends upon the provisions of subsection (2). If they are such as materially to alter the original bargain, they will not be included unless expressly agreed to by the other party. If, however, they are terms which would not so change the bargain they will be incorporated unless notice of objection to them has already been given or is given within a reasonable time. . . .

6. If no answer is received within a reasonable time after additional terms are proposed, it is both fair and commercially sound to assume that their inclusion has been assented to. Where clauses on confirming forms sent by both parties conflict each party must be assumed to object to a clause of the other conflicting with one on the confirmation sent by himself. As a result the requirement that there be notice of objection which is found in subsection (2) is satisfied and the conflicting terms do not become a part of the contract. The contract then consists of the terms originally expressly agreed to, terms on which the confirmations agree, and terms supplied by this Act, including subsection (2).

On this exposition, the arbitration clause, whether viewed as a material alteration under subsection (2), or as a term nullified by a conflicting provision in the buyer's form, would fail to survive as a contract term. In the light of the New York cases, at least, there can be little question that an agreement to arbitrate is a material term, one not to be injected by implication, subtlety or inveiglement. And the conclusion is also the same if the limitation contained in the offer (the buyer's purchase order) is given effect, as required by paragraph (a) of subsection 2 of the new section.

Accordingly, the order denying petitioner-appellant buyer's motion to stay arbitration should be reversed, on the law, with costs to petitioner-appellant and the motion should be granted.

Botein, P. J., Valente, McNally, and Eager, JJ., concur.

Order, entered on April 13, 1962, denying petitioner-appellant buyer's motion to stay arbitration, unanimously reversed, on the law,

---

*The parties have not argued which law, that of New York or elsewhere, should be applied in this case, but have assumed that it is the law of New York. This assumption is followed here, in the absence of contrary suggestion by either of the parties. The assumption, moreover, is supported by the fact that the arbitration clause provided for arbitration in the City of New York; required the parties' consent to jurisdiction of the State and Federal courts sitting in the State of New York; the buyer's offer was orally accepted in New York and, assuredly, the arbitration agreement, if effective, would be governed by the law of New York.

with $20 costs and disbursements to appellant, and the motion granted.

ARBITRATION AND THE UNIFORM COMMERCIAL CODE*

DANIEL G. COLLINS

The subject of arbitration is not mentioned in the text of the Uniform Commercial Code or, in any significant way, in its draftsmen's comments. From the viewpoint of codification of commercial law, the desirability of this omission is debatable. The omission is not without some logic, however, in the case of the Uniform Commercial Code, given certain of that document's tenets. The Code, first of all, does not purport to be a codification of *all* matters that bear on the commercial transaction. Even more important, a principal stated aim of the Code is "to permit the continued expansion of commercial practices" by bargain and custom. This being so, there is something to be said for the Code's leaving arbitration—a prime vehicle for achieving the goal of commercially moulded legal devices—to develop with as little interference as possible.

It is also true, though, that the Uniform Commercial Code ranges broadly over the commercial area and, in addition, concerns itself to a much greater extent than the statutes it is intended to supersede with basic principles of contract law. Since arbitration is essentially a matter of contract, it would be remarkable if the Code did not have some bearing on the law of arbitration as it relates to commercial transactions. In point of fact the Code interacts in a number of significant ways with established principles of arbitration.

The Code's greater liberality in approaching the question of when a "deal" is on, including particularly its pronounced reliance on trade custom and course of dealing or performance, is at least philosophically at odds with statutory requirements that agreements to arbitrate be in writing, as well as with those rules of decision that establish a higher "threshold of clarity" for arbitration undertakings. It is clear, too, that the Code has important implications as to the duty of arbitrators to apply substantive law, and as to the basis on which judicial review of awards may be predicated. Thus, though there may be some justification for the Code draftsmen's failure to take up the matter of arbitration, it

would appear more likely that an essential opportunity was missed.

Contract Formation and the Agreement To Arbitrate

A. Traditional doctrine. Contract-formation rules are extremely significant for commercial arbitration in view of the latter's consensual character. Essentially, the common-law approach to contract formation is rigid and, as a result, often reaches commercially unrealistic results. For the common law, the keynotes are definiteness and responsiveness, the offeree's "acceptance" seldom being allowed to deviate from the offeror's terms. This rule is subject to the caveat that once the common law finds a responsive offer and acceptance on "essential" terms, it normally is not unwilling to "construct" other terms. That caveat, however, has no applicability to the arbitration clause—for the reasons set forth below, courts will not impute an undertaking to arbitrate.

The common law was notoriously reluctant to enforce undertakings to arbitrate future disputes. For the most part this posture has now been changed, most frequently by legislation and sometimes by decision, but it is still the rule that agreements to arbitrate, even when part of a larger commercial understanding, must surmount a "higher threshold" of articulation than is required of other contract terms. It is not necessary to be as acutely distrustful of the arbitral process as is Professor Kronstein to appreciate, though not necessarily to approve, the higher threshold requirement. An undertaking to arbitrate normally means that the parties have largely forsaken their access to judicial proceedings including, perhaps, jury trial. Whatever its rationale, though, the higher threshold for formation of undertakings to arbitrate goes a step beyond even the normally strict common-law notions concerning contract formation.

B. The Code's Approach

The Code seeks to give effect to the businessman's understanding of when a "deal is closed." Basic to the achievement of that goal is section 2-204, which provides that a sales contract "may be made in any manner sufficient to show agreement, including conduct by both parties which recognizes the existence of such a contract." Section 1-201(3) supplements this by defining "agreement" as: "[T]he bargain of the parties in fact as found in their language or by implication from other circumstances including course of dealing or usage of trade or course of performance as provided in this Act."

The thrust of these provisions is that use is

*Excerpted from 41 N.Y.U.L. Rev. 736 (1966). Reprinted with permission.

to be made not only of the expressions of the parties, but also of the commercial context, to determine whether a deal has been struck and, if it has, what its terms are.

There is no suggestion in the Code that an undertaking to arbitrate that is part of a larger commercial understanding must surmount any higher formation threshold than other aspects of the deal. On the contrary, any such suggestion is negatived by the Code's singling out the quantity term as the only one requiring formal clarity of expression. In this respect the Code draftsmen have stated.

> All that is required is that the writing [necessary to satisfy the Code's Statute of Frauds] afford a basis for believing that the offered oral evidence rests on a real transaction. . . . It need not indicate which party is the buyer and which the seller. The only term which must appear is the quantity term which need not be accurately stated but recovery is limited to the amount stated. The price, time and place of payment or delivery, the general quality of the goods, or any particular warranties may all be omitted.

To be sure, the Code's "commercial" perspective is not the only possible way of viewing contract formation as it relates to arbitration. Through the eyes of those intimately involved with the arbitral process, the undertaking to arbitrate seems to take on special significance. This becomes apparent when the foregoing comments of the Code draftsmen are compared with the statement, contained in a brochure recently published by the Abitration Committee of the Association of the Bar of the City of New York in conjunction with the American Arbitration Association, that

> under the [N.Y. Civ. Prac. Law] . . . no distinction is made between submissions to arbitration of existing controversies and contracts to settle by arbitration controversies thereafter arising. The simple language rendering written arbitration agreements enforceable places them on the same footing as any other enforceable agreement. The present law requires only that the agreement be in writing.

The Arbitration Committee's statement is unobjectionable if the agreement to which it refers constitutes a separate undertaking to resolve, by arbitration, an existing controversy. In the context, though, of an undertaking to arbitrate future disputes that, typically, constitutes but one term of a commercial deal, the Committee's conclusion is fraught with difficulty. Viewed in the latter context, the clear implication of the Arbitration Committee's statement is that the requirement that the underaking to arbitrate be in writing does no violence to the standard for enforceability of the larger, commercial contract.

But in the context of the Code's approach to

contract formation, the mere introduction of a writing requirement for the arbitral undertaking cannot help but be troublesome. Any need, whether based on arbitration statutes or judicial decisions, to surmount a higher threshold of formal clarity for an undertaking to arbitrate may have the effect of making this important term of the contract unenforceable. In other words, if the higher threshold for enforceability of arbitration clauses has survived enactment of the Uniform Commercial Code, the Code's liberalization of contract formation rules may actually increase the risk that a party may find himself bound to a contract lacking a material term for which he bargained or a term that he assumed, by virtue of trade custom or practice, to be a part of his deal.[1]

There is one way in which the problem that has been posed might be avoided. It could be concluded that the mere enactment of the Code modifies any statute in the jurisdiction requiring a written undertaking to arbitrate. This proposition finds conceptual support in the New York Court of Appeals' decision in Matter of Arbitration between Ruppert and Egelhofer,[2] which upheld a labor arbitrator's award granting injunctive relief, in the face of Section 876-a of the Civil Practice Act (now Section 807 of the Labor Law)—the state's "Little Norris-LaGuardia Act"—on the ground that arbitration and anti-injunction statutes had to be accommodated to each other. In the court's words,

> once we have held that this particular employer-union agreement not only did not forbid but contemplated the inclusion of an injunction in such an award, no ground remains for invalidating this injunction. Section 876-a, like its prototype, the Federal Norris-LaGuardia Act, . . . was the result of union resentment against issuance of injunctions in labor strifes. But arbitration is voluntary and there is no reason why unions and employers should deny such powers to the special tribunals they themselves create. Section 876-a and article 84 (Arbitration) are both in our Civil Practice Act. Each represents a separate public policy and by affirming here we harmonize those two policies.

Emulating this approach, it could be said that the requirement for a writing in the case of an arbitration agreement is primarily intended to serve a cautionary purpose. It would not do

---

1. The unlikely, but equally objectionable, alternative is that a court might not only refuse to "sever" the unenforceable arbitration undertaking but also refuse enforcement of the entire contract. Normally, courts will sever the unenforceable clause. See 6A CORBIN, CONTRACTS § 1436 (1962). But see the discussion of materiality of arbitration clauses in the text accompanying notes 27–33 infra.

2. 3 N.Y. 2d 576, 148 N.E. 2d 129, 170 N.Y.S. 2d 785 (1958).

violence to that policy, therefore, to enforce arbitration undertakings, without a writing, where the transaction was between merchants in the context of established trade custom and practice. The Code, after all, is not opposed to higher thresholds as such, and in fact creates quite a few. But absent explicit adoption of such higher thresholds it would seem that they should not be imposed on Code transactions unless the policy they serve is of compelling importance.

The proposition that the Code impliedly modifies special arbitration legislation finds further support in New York in the inclusion of a supremacy clause in the New York enactment of the Code.[3] Whether the implied modification theory would fare well outside New York, in jurisdictions that have adopted the Code, while leaving intact the "General Repealer" in the "official" text,[4] is problematical.[5]

It seems considerably easier to make the point, based on the foregoing considerations, that the Code effects a change in the higher standard of clarity for enforcement of undertakings to arbitrate when that standard rests upon judicial rules rather than upon legislation. Nevertheless, one distinguished New York jurist (Justice Breitel) indicated in a recent case that the judicially created higher threshold for arbitration clauses had survived enactment of the Code.[6] His conclusion on this point was not necessary to the decision, however, and its full implications may not have been apparent.

---

3. N.Y. Uniform Commercial Code § 10–103. A local rule against general repeal of legislation precluded New York from adopting the language of § 10–103 of the official text providing for repeal of all "inconsistent" "acts and parts of acts."

4. Uniform Commercial Code § 10–103.

5. Relative enactment dates might be significant. In New York the Code was enacted after the last reenactment of the state's arbitration law. Compare N.Y. Uniform Commercial Code § 10–105, with N.Y. Civ. Prac. Law § 10005. Of course, "harmonization" may sometimes be viewed as impossible or undesirable. See Wilko v. Swan, 346 U.S. 427, 438 (1953) (agreement to arbitrate invalid because restrictions on judicial review in United States Arbitration Act could not be reconciled with Securities Act prohibition against waiver of judicial proceedings). It might be argued, too, that there is some implication of intent *not* to amend arbitration legislation in the draftsmen's solitary reference to arbitration, contained in comment 3 to § 2–515. The comment states that the statutory text, dealing with "Preserving Evidence of Goods in Dispute," "suggests the use of arbitration, where desired, of any points left open, but nothing in this section is intended to repeal or amend any statute governing arbitration." It seems clear though that in no sense is this a considered or comprehensive commentary on the relationship of the Code and arbitration.

6. See Matter of Arbitration between Doughboy Indus., Inc. and Pantasote Co., 17 App. Div. 2d 216, 223 N.Y.S. 2d 488, 495–96 (1st Dep't 1962), discussed in Domke, Arbitration, 1963 Ann. Survey Am. L. 131, 132 (1964).

THE IMPACT OF THE UNIFORM COMMERCIAL CODE UPON ARBITRATION: REVOLUTIONARY OVERTHROW OR PEACEFUL COEXISTENCE?*

MERTON C. BERNSTEIN

This textual gloss† is quite unappealing. Moreover, the gloss also may be confusing because it tends to lump two separate, albeit related, problems. Code Section 2–204 addresses itself to "contract formation," *i.e.* what events and conduct will produce a contract. The policy of the section is that contracts will be governed by business norms not the conceptualistic notions of the common law. Separately treated is the *formality* required of a contract if it is to be enforced. Code § 2–201 requires a writing "signed by the party against whom enforcement is sought," with specified exceptions. One could observe that the omission or incorrect statement of a term is not fatal to an agreement and only a quantity term is indispensable; this is not the same thing as saying that all omitted terms will be enforced. After all, the Code deals specifically with several kinds of omitted terms, such as price, delivery, time of payment. Other unwritten terms, although their absence is not fatal to the existence of a contract, may not be enforceable.

In view of the Code's Article 2 Statute of Frauds (requiring a writing to be "signed" by the party to be charged—albeit with "signed" accorded an extremely broad definition (Sec. 1–201(39))—what he seems to be arguing for is a *lesser* requirement to establish the existence of the undertaking to arbitrate. Some writing must substantiate the overall deal unless there is partial performance. However, " 'partial performance' as a substitute for the required memorandum can validate the contract only for the goods which have been accepted or for which payment has been made and accepted." Comment to Code § 2–201. This makes eminent good sense. But Professor Collins apparently would validate the arbitration clause even if oral although such a result does not fit the rationale of the partial performance rule; the arbitration clause cannot be so apportioned.

That the arbitration law writing requirement, only refined into its present form in the same session of the Legislature should fall, practically by accident, before this catch-all scythe requires

---

*Excerpted from 42 N.Y.U.L. Rev. 8 (1967). Reprinted with permission.

†[In the preceding excerpt from the Collins article.]

a formalistic approach to legislation that has quite gone out of style.

Professor Collins suggests: "Relative enactment dates might be significant. In New York the Code was enacted after the last reenactment of the states 'arbitration law.' " They may indeed be significant but do not support an argument that the Code modified the arbitration act. CPLR §§ 7501 et. seq., became law on April 4, 1962. (N.Y. Sess., Laws 1962, Ch. 308); the Code became law at the same session on April 18, 1962 (N.Y. Sess. Laws 1962, Ch. 553). The former was no mere reenactment but the product of many years of active and searching consideration. The Code also was considered painstakingly over many years. To deduce that the Legislature had changed its mind within a few days of enacting CPLR § 7501 is to elevate formality over reality. No mention of arbitration appears in the Code, and only a fleeting and inconclusive reference is to be found in the comments; the inference seems reasonably clear that no intent to modify arbitration law was harbored by the Code draftsmen. What went into both statutes derived from the studies by the respective committees and professional and interest groups working with and upon them. Dramatic changes were not made in the last few minutes of play.

As a treatise on New York statutes observes:

> Should the Legislature intend to repeal an act passed during the same session, it is reasonable to suppose that such intent would not be left to implication. The presumption is strong that the Legislature would not repeal an act which is fresh in their minds, without making an express reference to it, and the general rule that repeals by implication are not favored, applies with peculiar force as between two statutes passed at the same session of Legislature. McK. Statutes § 393.

Elsewhere Professor Collins argues that arbitration agreements must not be permitted to "subvert" the national uniformity which the Code is designed to achieve. Yet he questions whether the uniform section 10–103 would have the same effect in other states. If he is correct,[1] the goal of uniformity hardly is served by his suggested interpretation. Moreover, the Uniform Act Section 10–103 could be construed as directed at statutory provisions dealing with subject matter covered by the Code; if read more expansively,

it should also be read very carefully because it embodies so amorphous an "intent."

More importantly,[2] Professor Collins suggested dismantling of the arbitration law based upon the standards of section 2–204 does not accord with either Code or arbitration act patterns.

Parsing this Code language may be exhilarating (or dull depending upon one's taste), but clearly more productive would be achieving the results sought by the Code's enactment. Section 2–201 exacts a writing signed by the party to be charged, but the details required are minimal. The section requires some but not much physical evidence of the sales transactions, but even that is unnecessary if partial performances or other conduct evidencing a contractual arrangement exists. Section 2–204 also serves the policy of recognizing as contractual whatever is "sufficient to show agreeement, including conduct by both parties" The second subsection of section 2–204 relieves the party seeking enforcement from establishing some magical moment when the parties' minds met. And the third subsection makes even more clear what section 2–201 already indicates, that the omission of some terms is not fatal. All of these provisions recognize that the formal requirements of the offer exact-counterpart-acceptance framework for contract simply could not bear the weight of modern commercial transactions. As to the terms that the parties bargain about, the Code declares that they can be dickered and agreed in the actual manner in which such terms are bargained in their business context. This liberal, realistic approach applies to the terms about which parties *do* bargain— price, quality, delivery dates, and the like—all performance terms.

But it may be appropriate to subject to different standards those terms the parties usually do not bargain about—those which come into play when the transaction miscarries. Absent certain minimal formalities, there is no assurance that the parties did come to an agreement about them.

Section 2–204 is designed to salvage those arrangements which at common law would have failed as contracts because of no "meeting of the minds" or omitted terms. In most cases in which the section makes a difference, specific performance would not be the usual remedy.

---

1. The differences between § 10–103 in the New York and Uniform Act do not seem to warrant results so markedly different. The New York version is meant to achieve the same purposes as that in the Uniform Act; its more precise language reflects New York legislative policy against the technique of using the term "repeal" in superseding inconsistent statutes. McK. Statutes, § 394.

2. I pass as unimportant the attempt to find an analogy in the "harmonization" of New York's "Little Norris-LaGuardia Act" with court enforcement of an arbitrator's order to a union enjoining a slow down (Matter of Ruppert (Egelhofer)). Suffice it to say that the decision left intact all of the anti-injunction act's normal applications. That is quite different from employing the Code to obliterate a normal requirement of the arbitration act.

And the last clause[3] carries the strong implication that something less than specific performance is contemplated. While Code section 2–716(1) does provide for specific performance ("where the goods are unique or in other proper circumstances"), the catalogue of remedies[4] indicates that in the usual case the relief accorded by the Code will be directed to preventing or rectifying a particular item of damage rather than commanding the entire promised performance. But a prime purpose of the "modern" arbitration statute is to make the agreement to arbitrate specifically enforceable. That was the great innovation of the 1920 New York Act and those patterned after it, including the Federal Arbitration Act of 1925, and most other comprehensive state arbitration statutes.

Unlike the Code, which is primarily the handiwork of lawyers seeking to promote commercial realism in law, the early modern arbitration acts were shaped and fought into law by commercial groups, notably the New York Chamber of Commerce which championed the New York and Federal arbitration acts. This fact and the widespread commercial support for the other modern acts—all of which exact a written agreement, and sometimes more as the price of specific enforcement—argue for the commercial realism of the requirement.

For four decades a writing has been the minimal requirement for an enforceable arbitration clause. The recent Texas and California acts, passed after detailed consideration, also include it, although the latter permits oral extentions. Perhaps the requirement's rationale should be reviewed.

Two major justifications for the writing requirement and the "higher threshold of articulation" exacted by the New York courts for arbitration agreements as compared with other undertakings suggest themselves. In the first place, arbitration entails so many departures from court litigation (practically no pleadings, no jury, no need to follow rules of evidence, non-lawyers may decide disputes, and no need to follow substantive law) that a party to an arbitration agreement should be on notice of what he is getting into. Perhaps it is significant that comment on these great differences comes from lawyers. Noting these variances from what

we lawyers regard as the norm may carry the implication that unsuspected hazards lurk in the alien procedure (we know the hazards of the game we play). And they may. Those who fashion and adopt arbitral machinery may shape it to their own ends which do not coincide with the interests of outsiders. The designated arbitrators may be impartial among members of their own group but, perhaps unconsciously, may be biased toward their fellows when in controversy with an outsider ; indeed, they may have interests similar to the group member vis-a-vis the non-member. The possibilities recommend that adoption of the arbitral arrangement for future (usually unanticipated) disputes be conscious or at least on notice. The writing may serve this function (although if not conspicuous it may be overlooked while specific mention of arbitration in oral bargaining may be superior). Similar considerations support the judicially fashioned requirement that the writing be prominent or references to it quite clear.

Secondly, arbitration does not mean just one thing. The scope of the agreement to arbitrate may vary from disputes over only specified issues to all contract issues or even all controversies related to the transaction. On this count, a writing serves the notice function more adequately than the necessarily less exact oral discussion. Testimony based on memory of what was said may be approximate where the precise phraseology of the undertaking may be crucial. I suggest that price, quantity, quality, dates of performance, and the normal dickered elements of a sales transaction may be remembered and reproduced more reliably than a description of what is to be arbitrated. If *everything* is to be arbitrated and an existing procedure is adopted by name, this argument is inapplicable if both parties know the procedure thus adopted. However, the incorporation of an arbitration clause by reference where one party may be a relative stranger does not satisfy the spirit of the notice requirement.

If this reasoning is correct, at least some oral agreements to arbitrate may be unobjectionable, *i.e.,* where the party resisting arbitration had actual notice and was familiar with the contemplated arbitral arrangements. Such a formula, however, fits trade and exchange members, those least likely to contest a demand for arbitration. The adequacy of notice and extent of knowledge of non-members or of those dealing in less structured situations would be difficult to establish.

If exceptions to the writing and notice requirements were to be made, I suggest that it would require more complete and precise knowledge

---

3. "Even though one or more terms are left open a contract for sale does not fail for indefiniteness if the parties have intended to make a contract and there is a reasonably certain basis for giving an appropriate remedy."

4. §§ 2–702 through 2–721. Of course, some of the Code "remedies" do not emanate from a court. For example, when a seller finds a buyer is insolvent he can refuse delivery except for cash and may stop delivery.

about the extent and methods of arbitration than we now possess. Our data are several decades out of date. To effect such a change through such an unintended device as the Code seems quite precipitate. The legislative process seems the appropriate method for considering whether there is a demand for such a change (apparently none reached the threshold of audibility during the many years of active drafting, consultation, article writing, speech making, and symposia on both the CPLR and the Code), who would be helped and who hindered, the situations in which the suggested changes would be desirable and those in which their use might be unfortunate. Not only should we update our knowledge about arbitration clauses and formal machinery, but we should know more about practice and the incidence of different kinds of arbitration and the volume and nature of appeals to the courts. (In New York especially, unreported cases may run into significant numbers.) If the justification for change is commercial utility, the business community, not notably diffident, has yet to speak. Should it begin to do so, we probably would discover several differing interests whose harmonization might be better effected by a legislature before whom all groups contend than by litigated cases which arise so haphazardly.

MATTER OF DRACHMAN AND CO. (WULWICK)
20 Misc. 2d 912, 195 N.Y.S. 2d 399 (1959)

MORRIS E. SPECTOR, J. Petitioner moves for an order directing arbitration and designating the Board of Arbitration of the New York Stock Exchange as arbitrator.

The dispute arises out of a claimed wrongful discharge with respect to an employment alleged to have commenced on July 1, 1955. Petitioner urges that it is a member of the New York Stock Exchange, conducting its business as regulated by the constitution and rules of the Exchange. It is further charged that, to secure employment with a member of the Exchange, the prospective employee must file with the Exchange an application for approval of employment as a registered representative. By the signed application, it is alleged that the applicant submits himself to the jurisdiction of the Exchange and agrees to be bound by the constitution and rules of the governors.

Petitioner alleges that employment commenced on January 5, 1956, and that on January 26, 1956, petitioner and respondent signed the application for approval of employment. The application contains the following statement:

> I hereby certify that I have read and understand the foregoing statements and that each of my responses thereto is true and complete. In consideration of the New York Stock Exchange's receiving and considering this application.
>
> (d) I have read the Constitution and Rules of the Board of Governors of the New York Stock Exchange and, if approved, I hereby pledge myself to abide by the Constitution and Rules of the Board of Governors of the New York Stock Exchange as the same have been or shall be from time to time amended, and by all rules and regulations adopted pursuant to the Constitution, and by all practices of the Exchange.

At page 3590, rule 345 is set forth, the substance of which is contained as quoted above in the application. Rule 345 contains also the following provision:

> (10) I agree that any controversy between me and any member or member organization arising out of my employment or the termination of my employment by and with such member or member organization shall be settled by arbitration at the instance of any such party in accordance with the Constitution and rules then obtaining of the New York Stock Exchange.

But no reference whatever is said to be contained in the application or in any existing written agreement of employment.

Further reference is made to arbitration of controversies in rule 347b.

Absent any reference to arbitration in the application or in the employment agreement, it is not established that the respondent in undertaking the employment gave his assent to any provision for arbitration of disputes, and no triable issue is raised with respect thereto.

The motion is denied.

E.

The Effect of Later Events upon the Agreement to Arbitrate— Who Decides?

MATTER OF LIPMAN
(HAUESER SHELLAC CO).
289 N.Y. 76, 43 N.E. 2D. 817 (1942)

FINCH, J. The petition alleges that on September 18, 1940, Acme Shellac Products Corp., hereinafter referred to as Acme, entered into a written contract with the Haeuser Shellac Company, Inc., hereinafter referred to as Haeuser, by which Haeuser agreed to sell and deliver to Acme 150 barrels of bone dry white shellac at twenty-three cents per pound, delivery by December 31, 1940. The contract contained the following clause: "Any and all controversies in connection with, and/or arising out of, this contract shall be exclusively settled by arbitration by the Arbitration Committee of the American Bleached Shellac Manufacturers Association, Inc., in accordance with the rules of said Association." Petition also alleges that Haeuser failed and refused to deliver, although demand was duly made.

On October 1, 1940, Acme entered into a new contract with Haeuser for the sale of 150 barrels of shellac to Acme at twenty-two cents a pound. This contract was sent to Acme by Haeuser enclosed in a letter which read:

> We are enclosing herewith our contract in duplicate covering your purchase of 150 barrels of bone dry white shellac.
> "Will you please sign both copies and return for our signature. We will then send you one copy for your files. . . .
>
>   Yours very truly,
>   HAEUSER SHELLAC COMPANY, INC.

Haeuser claims that this contract of October 1, 1940, by agreement of the parties, was substituted in place of the contract dated September 18, 1940, and that pursuant to this agreement the contract dated September 18, 1940 was thereby cancelled. It is to be noted that nothing in the contract of October 1, 1940, or in the accompanying letter indicated an intention to cancel the contract of September 18, 1940, nor was this contract ever surrendered for cancellation.

On December 31, 1940, petitioner Harry Lipman, who was president of Acme, discontinued business as a corporation and commenced operating the corporate business individually, doing business as Acme Shellac Products Co. In consequence Acme assigned the contract dated September 18, 1940, to Lipman individually, who in turn assumed the performance of all the terms of said contract. Petition further alleges that Haeuser, however, although promising to deliver, never in fact delivered any of the goods under this contract of September 18, 1940, although constant demand was made for such delivery between September and December, 1940, as well as between January and July, 1941. Lipman thereupon demanded that Haeuser proceed to arbitrate the differences arising out of this contract, but Haeuser refused. In consequence petitioner moved at Special Term pursuant to section 1450 of the Civil Practice Act to compel Haeuser to proceed to arbitration in accordance with the terms of the contract.

At Special Term an order was entered directing that the making of the contract of September 18, 1940, be submitted to a jury and if the jury found that the contract was made, then was it thereafter cancelled and annulled by the parties? If not, Haeuser was directed to submit forthwith to arbitration. Upon appeal to the Appellate Division the order was modified by striking therefrom the submission to the jury so as to compel arbitration forthwith.

As to the making of the contract, there is no issue, since that is, in effect, admitted not only in the answer of defendant but also in its brief in this court.

Upon this appeal appellant stresses that the issue of the cancellation of the contract is one which must be determined by the court before it may compel arbitration. A different question would be here if the issue was whether the contract never came into existence and hence was void, or if, although the contract was made, there arose an issue of fraud, duress or other impediment which rendered the contract voidable, or if there were any conditions precedent. But since appellant in the case at bar admits the making of the contract of September 18, 1940, and its failure to proceed to arbitration in accordance with that portion of the contract which provides therefor, sufficient has been shown to make applicable that part of section 1450 of the Civil Practice Act which reads as follows:

> Upon being satisfied that there is no substantial issue as to the making of the contract . . . or the failure to comply therewith, the court . . . hearing such application, shall make an order directing the parties to proceed to arbitration in accordance with the terms of the contract.

While it must ever be borne in mind that a court has no power to grant a motion to compel arbitration unless the subject-matter is comprised within the agreement to arbitrate made by the parties, yet when once an agreement to arbitrate has been made, such an agreement must be considered in the light of the broad language used in the above arbitration statute. (Civ. Prac. Act, § 1450.) This language seems to imply that all acts of the parties subsequent to the making of the contract which raise issues of fact or law, lie exclusively within the jurisdiction of the arbitrators. It is to be noted that, contrary to the contention of appellant, the statute only requires the contract to have been made and does not require that it shall continue to be in existence. The language of the agreement to arbitrate, of course, must be sufficiently broad so as to permit of the application of the general principle that all issues subsequent to the making of the contract are not for the court but for the arbitrators. Where, however, as here, the language of the provision providing for arbitration uses not only the phrase "any and all controversies arising out of the contract" but also "any and all controversies in connection with the contract," this language would appear sufficiently broad to express the intention of the parties to include within the exclusive jurisdiction of the arbitrators as a general rule all acts by the parties giving rise to issues in relation to the contract, except the making thereof.

So in Matter of Kahn (284 N.Y. 515, 523), where the agreement for arbitration was much narrower than in the case at bar and the question presented was "whether the court, before it may compel arbitration, must in this case pass upon an issue of whether the depositor has breached the agreement of settlement," we held that before compelling arbitration it was not necessary for the court to determine that the contract was either performed by one party or breached by the other. The question of performance goes to the merits, and that, the parties have consented to have decided by the arbitral tribunal. (Matter of Wenger & Co. v. Propper Silk Hosiery Mills, Inc., 239 N.Y. 199.) The issue arising from the defense of cancellation, therefore, must be submitted for decision to the arbitrators.

Defendant also urges as a defense to the motion to compel arbitration that, since Lipman was not a party to the contract but is an assignee, he may not compel Haeuser to submit to arbitration. The argument of appellant is based on the premise that the arbitration clause may not be taken advantage of by an assignee. We have heretofore held, however, with reference to a contract similar to that in the case at bar, that the arbitration clause is an integral part of the contract and may be availed of, not only by the original parties but also by assignees. (Matter of Lowenthal, 199 App. Div. 39; affd., 233 N.Y. 621; Matter of Hosiery Manufacturers Corp. v. Goldston, 238 N.Y. 22). These cited cases thus negative the contention that a contract for the sale of merchandise containing an arbitration clause may not be taken advantage of by an assignee.

Haeuser urges secondly that the contract is not assignable because it is a personal contract since Haeuser was obliged to sell the merchandise on credit and hence, while it might be satisfied with the credit standing of Acme, it might be unwilling to extend credit to Lipman. This contention is untenable. Since Haeuser did not refuse to arbitrate or to deliver the goods upon the ground that the credit of Lipman was not satisfactory, it may not now make such claim for the first time. Moreover, this contract provided that, if the credit of the buyer was such that in the judgment of the seller, payment ought to be made in advance, upon notification by the seller to the buyer to this effect, the terms of payment were to be deemed amended so as to provide for payment in advance of delivery.

LEWIS and CONWAY, JJ. concur with FINCH, J.; LEHMAN, CH., J., and DESMOND, J., concur in the result for the reasons stated in the dissenting opinion in Matter of Kramer & Uchitelle, Inc. (288 N.Y. 467), decided herewith; LOUGHRAN and RIPPEY, JJ., dissent.

Order affirmed.

CHECKER CAB MFG. CO v. HELLER
241 N.Y. 148, 149 N.E. 333 (1925)

POUND, J. The application for an arbitration arises out of a written contract between the parties. The portion thereof relating to arbitration is as follows:

This contract shall continue and be in force until

December Thirty-first, Nineteen Hundred and Twenty-four (December 31, 1924) during all of which time it shall not be cancelled by either of the parties hereto, unless the other parties violate the provisions thereof, but neither the first nor second parties shall have the right to cancel on account of any violation by the other of them; and, in the event a violation is charged, *the party violating shall have the right* to immediately purge itself of such violation or submit the question of such violation to arbitration, in which event the first and second parties shall select one arbitrator, the third party shall select an arbitrator, and the two jointly shall select a third; and in the event the said arbitrators find that the contract has been violated, and the violator does not immediately purge itself of such violation, then if either the first or second party has violated the same, the third party may terminate, or if the third party has violated same, either the first or second party may terminate same upon giving notice in writing of the intention to cancel by a letter addressed to the other parties, and sent by registered mail, providing the notice of such intention to cancel shall be given ninety (90) days before the time fixed for cancellation.

The allegations of the petition are in substance as follows:

On September 28, 1922, the Checker Cab Manufacturing Corporation and Weiss Polansky Becker Corporation and Albert Heller entered into the agreement containing the foregoing provisions for arbitration; subsequent to the 28th of September, 1922, the Mogul Finance Corporation assumed the obligations thereof; Checker Cab Manufacturing Corporation and Weiss Polansky Becker Corporation duly performed the said agreement on their parts; on or about the 12th day of July, 1923, Albert Heller and Mogul Finance Corporation violated the terms of the said agreement on their part in that they failed and refused to pay to the Checker Cab Manufacturing Corporation moneys then due and owing and refused to accept notes for discount which under the terms of the said agreement they were obligated to do; upon this breach of the contract the petitioners demanded that they purge themselves of their breach, which they refused to do. Petitioners demanded pursuant to the terms of the said contract, but after the expiration of the term of the contract and on January 8, 1925, that the question of the violation thereof be submitted to arbitration but Heller and Mogul Finance Corporation failed, refused and declined to name any arbitrator or submit the question of their breach of the said agreement to arbitration. The question is whether the court may under Arbitration Law, section 3, order appellants to proceed to arbitration on the question as to whether there has been a violation of the contract.

The moving parties rely on an alleged violation occurring on the 12th day of July, 1923, but they delayed to apply for arbitration until January 8, 1925. Meanwhile they had, as they allege in the petition, rescinded the contract. The contract expired by its terms on December 31, 1924. Although they rescinded the contract "without prejudice to all rights on the part of the Checker Cab Manufacturing Corporation and the Weiss Polansky Becker Corporation because of the violation and repudiation and expressly reserving them" and although the contract provides that it "shall be automatically extended from year to year after December 31, 1924, unless either of the parties hereto advises the others thirty days before December 31, 1924, and each subsequent year of their intention to cancel on said December 31," it cannot be claimed by respondents that the contract was in force after December 31, 1924. It was terminated either when they rescinded or attempted to rescind it or on December 31, 1924. We do not understand that either party contends that the contract was in force after the latter date.

The clause for arbitration limits the inquiry to the question whether there has been a violation and so limits it for a specific purpose. The purpose of obtaining a decision of arbitrators on that question is to lay the foundation for a termination of the contract before it expires by its terms in case of a finding that the contract had been violated. As the case now presents itself, the question of violation, so far as the purpose of the arbitration agreement is concerned, has become academic and abstract. The parties aggrieved cannot terminate the contract under the arbitration clause after its term has expired. A determination of arbitrators that appellants had violated the contract would now create no right to terminate under the contract. Termination is already a fact. The parties agreed to settle a controversy as to a violation of the contract only in connection with a claim of right to rescind the contract while it was still operative. Respondents now seek to have the bare question of their right to rescind determined. Such a determination might be useful in connection with future litigation between the parties.

The only question before the court is as to the right of the respondents to go to arbitration on the question of violation and no other question has been considered. We hold merely that the court is now without power to compel arbitration after that question has become an incidental element of the entire controversy between the parties.

Orders reversed, with costs in all courts, and application denied, with ten dollars costs.

HISCOCK, CH. J., CARDOZO, MCLAUGHLIN, CRANE, ANDREWS and LEHMAN, JJ., concur.

MATTER OF TERMINAL AUXILIAR MARITIMA (WINKLER CREDIT CORP.)
6 N.Y. 2d 294, 160 N.E. 2d 526 (1959)

Petitioner Terminal, charterer, sought stay of suit brought by assignee (Winkler) of corporation arranging for the ship. Winkler's suit alleged breach of charter party by Terminal. Terminal had entered into an arrangement directly with the shipowner after Winkler's assignor failed to obtain shipowner's performance. Winkler's suit was instituted by attachment of Terminal's subcharterer in New York and Rotterdam. Terminal agreed to enter a general appearance in Winkler's suit, without prejudice to any of its rights, if attachment of subcharter's property were released. This was agreed to, and Terminal appeared generally and posted a bond as agreed. Terminal then began this proceeding to stay the suit pending the arbitration called for by the charterparty which Terminal charged Winkler's assignor had breached. Winkler opposed the stay on two main grounds: (1) that by making alternative arrangements for performing the charter Terminal had "cancelled" the agreement and with it the agreement to arbitrate ; and (2) the general appearance constituted a waiver of the right to arbitrate.

Held: Stay granted. (1) Both parties allege breach—charter provides for arbitration of such disputes. Terminal's "cancellation" or "termination" was due to Winkler's assignors alleged breach. Indeed, Winkler does not regard charter cancelled—he's suing on it. Terminal's "termination" did not end right to arbitrate, for if it did agreements to arbitrate would seldom, if ever, be carried out. "It is settled that under a broad provision for arbitration, such as we have here, arbitration may be had as to all issues arising subsequent to the making of the contract." (2) Court found it unnecessary to decide because the stipulation makes it clear that no waiver was intended.

The court purportedly followed *Lipman* in Sontone Corp. v. Ladd, 17 Wis. 2d 580, 117 N.W. 2d 591 (1962). There the plaintiff Sonotone sought replevin alleging termination of Ladd's contract as its district manager. Ladd made a plea in abatement asking for arbitration alleging that the ground of termination, failure to meet quota, was Sonotone's fault. The agreement called for arbitration of any "difference, dispute or controversy arising between the parties with respect to this contract or performance hereunder while this contract is in effect and prior to any termination thereof" shall be settled by arbitration. The Wisconsin Supreme Court reversed the dismissal of the plea in abatement and held that a stay pending arbitration should be granted if the defendant "satisfi[es] the court at a hearing ... that the dispute can reasonably be said to have arisen before" the date of the purported termination. Is this an application of *Lipman*?

MATTER OF STEIN-TEX (IDE MFG. CO.)
9 A.D. 2d 288, 193 N.Y.S. 2d 719
(First Dept. 1959)

PER CURIAM. Involved in this appeal is whether a general release, the generality of which is disputed between the parties, prevents arbitration of disputes arising under contracts which antedated the general release.

The rule would now seem to be settled that subsequent acts or documents purporting or claimed to terminate an agreement containing a broad arbitration clause, if in dispute, raise issues for the arbitrators and not for the court (Matter of Lipman [Haeuser Shellac Co.], 289 N.Y. 76 ; Matter of Aqua Mfg. Co. [Warshow & Sons], 179 Misc. 949, affd. 266 App. Div. 718).

This has been so held specifically as to a release (Matter of City Sewing Center [Portman Sewing Mach. Co.], 279 App. Div. 784, motion for leave to appeal denied 279 App. Div. 893, motion for leave to appeal denied 304 N.Y. 986). In that case this court affirmed, without opinion, the holding of Mr. Justice Rabin, then at Special Term, to the effect that "The question whether the release terminated the contract containing the arbitration clause and ended all liability of the movant to City Sewing Center, Inc., is one to be decided by the arbitration tribunal and not by the court [citing the *Lipman* and *Aqua Mfg. Co.* cases, *supra*]."

Quite different is the situation, as pointed out by Special Term, where there is undisputed cancellation of the agreement and the issue raised is fraud in the inducement of such cancellation. (Matter of Minkin [Halperin], 279 App. Div. 226, affd. 304 N.Y. 617.)

Accordingly, the orders denying petitioner's

motion to stay arbitration should be affirmed, on the law and the facts, with costs to respondent-respondent.

BOTEIN, P. J., BREITEL, M. M. FRANK, VALENTE and STEVENS, JJ., concur.

Orders unanimously affirmed, on the law and on the facts, with $20 costs and disbursements to the respondent.

MATTER OF MINKIN (HALPERIN)
279 App. Div. 226, 108 N.Y.S. 2d 945
(Second Dept. 1951)

JOHNSTON, J. On June 16, 1950, appellants agreed in writing with respondent and others, as sellers, to purchase certain corporate stock, and paid $10,000 on account of the purchase price. The agreement contained a clause that "Any controversy or claim arising out of, or relating to this agreement or the breach thereof, shall be settled by arbitration."

On October 24, 1950, the same parties contracted in writing: (1) that the $10,000 paid by appellants on June 16, 1950, be returned to them; (2) that the agreement of June 16, 1950, "is hereby canceled and declared of no further force or effect, and said agreement shall be interpreted as though it had not been executed"; (3) that "Each of the parties does hereby release the other from any and all obligations arising as a result of the execution of the aforesaid agreement."

On March 7, 1951, respondent (one of the sellers of the corporate stock) served a demand for arbitration under the above-quoted provision of the June 16, 1950, agreement with respect to damages for the alleged breach by appellants of that agreement.

Appellants moved for a stay of arbitration on the ground that no contract to arbitrate was in existence. Respondent opposed the motion, claiming. (1) that the execution of the October 24, 1950, contract had been induced by coercion and duress and, hence, it was invalid and does not operate as a cancellation or release of the June 16th agreement; (2) that whether the second contract operated to cancel the first agreement was a matter to be submitted to and decided by the arbitrators. Special Term denied the motion and directed that arbitration proceed. The purchasers appeal.

In my opinion the order should be reversed and the motion granted.

"Arbitration presupposes the existence of a contract to arbitrate" (Finsilver, Still & Moss v. Goldberg, Maas & Co., 253 N.Y. 382, 389); and "proceedings to enforce arbitration under article 84 of the Civil Practice Act presuppose the existence of a valid and enforceable contract at the time the remedy is sought." (Matter of Kramer & Uchitelle, Inc., 288 N.Y. 467, 471.) Here the contract to arbitrate was cancelled by express agreement of the parties, an act which was within their power to do. Even if the Legislature should attempt to prevent parties from modifying or canceling their agreement to arbitrate, "it would be such an abridgement of the right of citizens to contract that the constitutionality of the law might well be doubted." (Matter of Zimmerman v. Cohen, 236 N.Y. 15, 20.)

Respondent seeks to revive the agreement of June 16th, providing for arbitration, by the mere assertion—unsupported by a single evidentiary fact—that the cancellation contract is invalid because his consent thereto was procured by coercion and duress. But such a result may not be reached until the cancellation contract is set aside by action in equity brought for that purpose. (Matter of Remeny, Inc. [Jolico Textile Co.], 274 App. Div. 916, motion for leave to appeal to the Court of Appeals denied, 274 App. Div. 985; Matter of Binger [Thatcher], 279 App. Div. 650; Matter of Worcester Silk Mills Corp., 50 F. 2d 966.) The issue of coercion and duress in inducing the October 24th contract is not an issue which the parties may be said to have intended to arbitrate under the June 16th agreement. That issue is not a controversy or claim arising out of, nor does it have relation to, the agreement of June 16th. It is an issue which relates solely to the validity of the contract of October 24th.

Matter of Remeny, Inc. (Jolico Textile Co.) (*supra*) is directly in point. There petitioner contracted—the contracts containing arbitration clauses—to purchase certain goods from respondent. After more than half the goods were delivered and $4,000 were paid on account of the purchase price of the goods delivered, petitioner, complaining of the quality of the merchandise that had been delivered, claimed that the contracts were cancelled, and demanded the return of the money it had paid on account. Following extended conferences, the matter was settled, the original purchase and sale contracts were cancelled and general releases were exchanged. Thereafter petitioner, alleging that it had been induced by respondent's fraud to enter into the settlement agreement and to deliver its general release, and relying upon the arbitration clauses contained in the original purchase and sale contracts, instituted a proceeding to compel arbitration of the controversies between the parties. Respondent claimed that there was no existing, valid and enforcible contract or contracts to arbitrate because the original purchase and sale contracts containing the arbitration clauses had been cancelled and terminated and petitioner had delivered to respondent a general release discharging and terminating all contracts between the parties, including agreements to arbitrate. The application to compel arbitration was denied at Special Term and the order was affirmed by the Appellate Division in the First Department. Exactly the same situation exists in the case at bar, and the same determination should be made. To the same effect is Matter of Binger (Thatcher) (*supra*.)

Matter of Lipman (Haeuser Shellac Co.) (289 N.Y. 76), cited by Special Term, and upon which respondent primarily relies, does not require a different holding. Examination of the record in that case shows there were three contracts for the purchase and sale of shellac—one on September 18, 1940, for 150 barrels at twenty-three cents a pound; one on October 1, 1940, for 150 barrels at twenty-two cents a pound, and one on November 8, 1940, for 300 barrels at twenty-two cents a pound. Each contract contained an arbitration clause providing that "'Any and all controversies in connection with, and/or arising out of, this contract shall be exclusively settled by arbitration.'" (P. 78.) Delivery was made by the seller under the October 1st and November 8th contracts. Almost a year later, when the market price of shellac had risen about 50 per cent, Lipman, the purchaser's assignee, claiming that the seller failed to deliver the merchandise covered by the September 18th contract, demanded arbitration under that contract, but the seller refused. In consequence, Lipman moved to compel the seller to proceed to arbitration. In opposition to the application, the seller contended that the September 18th contract was no longer in existence because, after the purchaser had complained about the price, by oral agreement of the parties the October 1st contract was *substituted* for the September 18th contract. The Court of Appeals held that that was an issue to be determined by the arbitrators because it was a matter which not only arose out of the September 18th contract, but also was a controversy "in connection with" that contract. Obviously that case is readily distinguished from the case at bar. There the issue was whether the September 18th contract had been performed. In other words, whether or not the parties in fact agreed that there should be performance by the substitution of the October 1st contract for the September 18th contract and by delivery pursuant to the October 1st contract

was a matter properly to be determined by the arbitrators. (Cf. Moers v. Moers, 229 N.Y. 294, 300.) As stated in Matter of Wenger & Co. v. Propper Silk Hose Mills (239 N.Y. 199, 202–203): "where a *bona fide* dispute in fact arises over the performance of a contract of purchase and sale it does not devolve upon the court to say that as matter of law there is nothing to arbitrate." In the case at bar there is not present either the issue of performance or breach of the original contract of purchase and sale. Here the sole issue is whether or not the cancellation contract was invalid because of alleged coercion and duress in inducing that contract. That is a matter which does not arise out of the original contract, nor does it have any relation or connection therewith. It should be noted that in Matter of Lipman (Haeuser Shellac Co.) (289 N.Y. 76, 78–79, *supra*) the court emphasized "that nothing in the contract of October 1, 1940, or in the accompanying letter indicated an intention to cancel the contract of September 18, 1940," while in the case at bar the parties, by the written contract of October 24, 1950, expressly provided that the agreement of June 16, 1950, "is hereby canceled and declared to be of no further force or effect, and said agreement shall be interpreted as though it had not been executed."

Nor is Alpert v. Admiration Knitwear Co. (278 App. Div. 841), cited by respondent, helpful. That case concerned a contract for the sale of goods. The contract contained an arbitration clause and also a provision that, "if at any time, in the sole opinion of the Seller, the financial responsibility of the Purchaser shall become impaired or unsatisfactory to the Seller cash payments in advance of delivery may be required," and "Upon failure to pay any amount due to the Seller," it may at its option terminate the contract. The seller demanded payment in advance of delivery, but the buyer refused to comply with the demand. The seller terminated the contract and refused to deliver the goods. The buyer moved to compel arbitration. The seller opposed the application on the ground that the contract had been terminated (not as in the instant case by mutual agreement of the parties but solely by the seller); and, therefore, there was no longer in existence any binding contract to arbitrate. By a divided court we held that the application for arbitration should be granted because there was an issue as to whether the parties intended that the seller should have the right to cancel the contract even if the demand for the advance cash payment were not made in good faith, and if the parties intended that the demand was required to be made in good faith, whether or not the demand by the seller was so made. In that case there also was an issue as to whether the seller had breached the contract before demanding the cash advance payment, it appearing that the contract was made on May 12, 1950, and required delivery of the goods "at once," whereas the demand for the cash advance payment was not made until June 8, 1950, after the buyer had demanded delivery of the goods or that the matter be submitted to arbitration. The majority of the court held that these were controversies arising out of or relating to the contract which were required to be settled by arbitration. In the case at bar there is no ambiguity in the purchase and sale contract, or in the cancellation contract and, hence, the interpretation of either contract is not at issue. The only issue is whether the cancellation contract of October 24th was induced by coercion and duress. In my opinion, that is not a matter for arbitration because the subject matter is not comprised within the arbitration agreement of June 16th.

The foregoing has been written on the assumption that facts are set forth in the affidavit in opposition to the motion for a stay of arbitration sufficient to raise an issue of fact with respect to the coercion and duress claimed to have induced the contract of cancellation. However, the affidavit is clearly insufficient. It is made, not by the respondent, one of the sellers, but by his attorney in fact, who also executed the contract of cancellation on behalf of respondent. None of the other three sellers, who also executed the contract of cancellation, ever demanded arbitration or claimed that the June 16th agreement was breached or that the contract of cancellation is invalid. All that respondent's attorney in fact states in the opposing affidavit is that the execution by him of the cancellation contract was "procured by coercion and duress because of the fear of petitioners' [appellants'] threats to use illegal and improper means which would result in a considerable loss and damage to the respondent". These allegations are mere conclusions of law. (Crossways Apts. v. Amante, 213 App. Div. 430, 435–436 ; Talcott v. City of Buffalo, 125 N.Y. 280, 284 ; Knapp v. City of Brooklyn, 97 N.Y. 520, 523.) Where an application is made to compel arbitration, the statute requires that evidentiary facts be set forth raising a substantial issue as to the making of the contract or submission or the failure to comply therewith before there may be a preliminary trial of those issues. (Civ. Prac. Act, § 1450.) Obviously the same rule should be applied where a party desiring arbitration asserts that there is an issue with respect to the making of a contract which expressly cancels the arbitration contract. There being no such factual showing in opposition to the motion for a stay of arbitration the cancellation contract must be given full force and effect.

The order should be reversed, with $10 costs and disbursements, and the motion to stay arbitration granted, with $10 costs.

NOLAN, P. J. (concurring). In a proceeding such as this the only issues which may be decided by the court are those which arise as to the making of the contract to arbitrate, and the failure to comply therewith. (Civ. Prac. Act, §§ 1450–1458.) Every other issue, whether of fact or law, if it is comprised within the agreement to arbitrate, is within the exclusive jurisdiction of the arbitrators. (Matter of Lipman [Haeuser Shellac Co.], 263 App. Div. 880, affd. 289 N.Y. 76.) If any other issue exists, which is not comprised within the agreement to arbitrate, it may not be decided over objection, either by arbitrators (Matter of Lipman [Haeuser Shellac Co.], *supra* ; Matter of Bullard v. Grace Co., 240 N.Y. 388) or by the court in an arbitration proceeding. (Cf. Matter of Worcester Silk Mills Corp., 50 F. 2d 966.) If one of the issues to be determined is whether or not an agreement containing an arbitration clause has been cancelled, it must be determined by arbitrators if the language of the arbitration clause is sufficiently broad to express such an intention. (Matter of Lipman [Haeuser Shellac Co.], *supra*.) On the other hand, if, as in the instant case, a claim is made under such an agreement, and there is no dispute as to the fact that it has been cancelled and that all the parties have been released from their obligations thereunder, there are no issues relating to the agreement which remain to be decided, by arbitration or otherwise. (Cf. Matter of Kramer & Uchitelle, Inc., 288 N.Y. 467.) Arbitration may be resorted to only to settle controversies. If no issue of fact or law exists in relation to a matter sought to be submitted to arbitration, there is, obviously, no controversy to be settled, and the matter is not one which may be comprised within an agreement to arbitrate. (Civ. Prac. Act, § 1448.)

Respondent contends that a controversy has arisen as to whether or not the contract of June 16th was cancelled. This controversy, he asserts, should be settled by arbitration, since it is one which relates to that contract and the parties agreed to arbitrate any controversy or claim arising out of or relating to it. If that were the controversy to be settled, it could be settled only by arbitrators. The issue is not one which may be decided by the court in this proceeding, and it does fall within the broad provisions of the arbitration agreement. (Cf. Matter of Lipman [Haeuser Shellac Co.], *supra*.)

It is apparent, however, that respondent has not correctly stated the issue to be determined. There is no dispute between the parties as to the effect of the agreement of October 24th, if that is a valid agreement, and there can be no dispute that, unless that agreement is void or may be avoided, the contract of June 16th has ceased to exist and has no force or effect whatever. Respondent asserts that the agreement is void because it was induced by coercion and duress. As Mr. Justice JOHNSTON has pointed out, that assertion creates no controversy which relates to the contract of June 16th. If any controversy exists by reason of that assertion it is one which relates solely to the agreement of October 24th. Moreover, if the agreement of October 24th was induced by duress, it is not necessarily void. A contract obtained by duress is not ordinarily void but is merely voidable, and a party seeking to avoid such a contract must act promptly to repudiate it, and must return, or offer to restore, what he has received under it. (Oregon Pacific R. R. Co. v. Forrest, 128 N.Y. 83.) Respondent must establish, therefore, before he may assert any claim under the contract of June 16th, not only that his later agreement was induced by duress, but also that he is entitled, under existing circumstances, to avoid it. Since these issues were not comprised within the agreement to arbitrate, they may not be decided by arbitrators, nor may they be decided by the court, in this proceeding. (Civ. Prac. Act, §§ 1450, 1458 ; Matter of Worcester Silk Mills Corp., 50 F. 2d 966 *supra*.)

SNEED and MACCRATE, JJ., concur with JOHNSTON, J. ; NOLAN, P. J., concurs in separate opinion in which SNEED and MACCRATE, JJ., concur ; ADEL, J., concurs with the following memorandum : Perforce the terms of the release agreement there is no existing agreement to arbitrate. The affidavit submitted on behalf of respondent is insufficient to tender to the court any issue as to the validity of the release.

Order denying petitioners' motion to stay an arbitration proceeding reversed, with $10 costs and disbursements, and motion granted, with $10 costs.

This disposition was affirmed, 304 N.Y. 617, 107 N.E. 2d 94 (1952), Judges Desmond and Fuld dissenting:

... on the ground that sufficient appears in the papers to show an issue of fact, triable by the arbitrators, as to the existence of a valid release.

IN RE WORCESTER SILK MILLS CORPORATION
50 F. 2d. 966 (S.D.N.Y. 1927)

THACHER, District Judge. This is a proceeding under the United States Arbitration Act of February 12, 1925, c. 213, § 4, 43 Stat. 883, U.S.C. Title 9 (9 USCA § 4), in which the petitioner seeks to compel the respondent to submit to arbitration a dispute arising under a contract for the sale of 200 pieces of georgette. In May of this year a dispute arose between the parties concerning the merchantable quality of 80 pieces of merchandise delivered under the contract. The respondent claimed that the merchandise was not in accordance with the contract and that he was entitled to a credit by reason of the return thereof. The petitioner disputed this claim, asserting that the merchandise was in accordance with the contract when delivered, but was spoiled by the dyer and finisher to whom respondent delivered the same, and that the respondent was not entitled to a credit by reason of the return thereof. The petitioner alleges failure and refusal to arbitrate under the agreement, which contains a clause for arbitration, and prays an order directing that such arbitration proceed in the manner provided for in the agreement. The respondent has answered under oath, setting forth in particularity negotiations between the parties which resulted in an adjustment and settlement of the entire controversy, and in this connection has set forth an agreement to settle the controversy, confirmed by correspondence, pursuant to which the merchandise claimed to have been defective in quality was to be returned and credited to the respondent, a credit allowed to the petitioner on account of its claim of damage by the dyer, and the balance of the account paid by the respondent. The answer further shows payment of the balance thus adjusted, by check which upon its face recites the transaction and states that the indorsement of the payee will constitute a receipt in full. It is alleged that this check was accepted and deposited by the petitioner, and the amount thereof paid to the petitioner by the respondent's bank on which it was drawn. None of these allegations in the answer, all of which are verified by the respondent's oath, have been denied by the petitioner. If true, these facts constitute a complete settlement, and an accord and satisfaction, and no dispute between the parties remains to be adjusted under the arbitration clause contained in the agreement.

The statute requires such an application as this to be heard in the manner provided by law for the making and hearing of motions. Section 6, Title 9, U.S.C. (9 USCA § 6). The petition and answer must therefore be regarded as affidavits submitted in support of a motion, and, there being no denial of any of the statements contained in the answer, I must accept these statements as true, and accordingly deny the application.

On Reargument of Petitioner's Application for an Order Requiring Arbitration

Upon reargument of the above motion upon additional affidavits, I have concluded that the denial of the motion must stand. Section 4 of the Arbitration Act of February 12, 1925, c. 213, 43 Stat. 883, U.S.C. Title 9 (9 USCA § 4), contemplates the summary trial of two issues only. These are: (1) The making of the arbitration agreement; and (2) the failure, neglect, or refusal to perform the same. Neither of these issues is presented here. Respondent confesses the making of the arbitration agreement and his refusal to arbitrate, but alleges that all disputes which he agreed to arbitrate have been settled by agreement under which there has been accord and satisfaction. Petitioner, in turn, confesses the agreement to settle, and payment thereunder, but alleges by way of confession and avoidance that the settlement was induced by fraud and has been rescinded. Respondent denies fraud and rescission.

The issue thus presented cannot be summarily tried under section 4 of the Arbitration Act, which provides. "If the making of the arbitration agreement or the failure, neglect, or refusal to perform the same be in issue, the court shall proceed summarily to the trial thereof." Thus the statute authorizes a special statutory proceeding in which the issues to be tried are quite narrowly defined, and the court is entirely without jurisdiction to summarily try issues other than those defined. The issues of fraud and rescission raised at bar are quite clearly beyond the court's jurisdiction as defined by the statute. There has been no agreement to arbitrate the dispute which now arises over the right to rescind, and the respondent is entitled to insist that the issues raised by the assertion of any such right be tried and determined in a plenary suit.

The petition must therefore be dismissed.

The current vitality of the foregoing ruling and reasoning are open to question, although the case has not been overruled; nor has it been cited with approval by federal courts on this point. Galveston Maritime Assn. v. South Atlantic & Gulf Coast Dist., Int'l Longshoremen's Assn., 234 F. Supp. (250, S. D. Tex. 1964) noted:

> The first assertion [in support of the motion to dismiss motion to compel arbitration] is that any dispute once existing between the parties is now moot due to an alleged accord and satisfaction. The Court views this assertion as an answer to the merits rather than a fact to be considered in determinining jurisdiction.

This was a case involving § 301 of the Labor-Management Relations Act of 1947 (Taft-Hartley) and this point was made without reference to any case or the Federal Arbitration Act.

IN RE UTILITY OIL CORPORATION
69 F.2D. 524 (2d Cir. 1934)

Before MANTON, AUGUSTUS N. HAND, and CHASE, CIRCUIT JUDGES.

MANTON, CIRCUIT JUDGE. The petition filed alleged that on August 6, 1928, the Petroleum Navigation Company chartered the steamship *Papoose* to the appellant for as many consecutive voyages as the vessel could make between Trinidad, British West Indies, and United States ports, north of Cape Hatteras, between January, 1929, and December, 1933. Under clause 23, the charterer might cancel, at its option, three voyages in any one year. On December 5, 1932, it gave notice to the owner canceling three consecutive voyages for the year 1933, the first of which was to take effect on the expiration of the notice of cancellation forty-five days later. This cancellation notice expired January 19, 1933. The petition states that three Trinidad voyages of the ship would have consumed fifty-four days and therefore the vessel was bound to report at Trinidad to load her next cargo March 14, 1933. She did not report on that day; she was then sailing between New York and the Gulf of Mexico, not for the account of the charterer. The petition alleges that the failure to have the vessel at the loading port March 14, 1933, was a breach of the charter. It is also suggested that, even though the cancellation period might not be regarded as beginning until the vessel completed an entire voyage for Gulf ports, not under the charter, beginning January 18, 1933, and ending at Providence, R. I., January 27, 1933, the cancellation period expired March 22, 1933.

In that event, it is claimed, there was a breach of the charter by the owner because the vessel did not report for loading on or before March 22, 1933. On March 28, 1933, the appellant advised the appellee that it would not deliver any further cargoes to the vessel. Thereafter a demand was made by the appellee for damages for breach of the charter, which the appellant refused to pay.

The charter contained an arbitration clause reading: "Any dispute arising during performance of this Charter Party shall be settled by arbitration in New York, Owner and Charterer each appointing an Arbitrator, and the two thus chosen, if they cannot agree, nominating a third whose decision shall be final. Should one of the parties neglect or refuse to appoint an Arbitrator within twenty-one days after receipt of request from the other party, the single Arbitrator appointed shall have the right to decide alone, and his decision shall be binding on both parties. For the purpose of enforcing any award this agreement shall be made a Rule of Court."

The appellee filed a libel in admiralty against the appellant and refuses to arbitrate the dispute. Thereupon this petition was filed. In support of the petition, the appellant invokes section 4 of the United States Arbitration Act (U.S.C. section 4, title 9 [9 USCA § 4]) which provides.

> A party aggrieved by the alleged failure, neglect, or refusal of another to arbitrate under a written agreement for arbitration may petition any court of the United States which, save for such agreement, would have jurisdiction under the judicial code at law, in equity, or in admiralty of the subject matter of a suit arising out of the controversy between the parties, for an order directing that such arbitration proceed in the manner provided for in such agreement.

It further provides:

> The court shall hear the parties, and upon being satisfied that the making of the agreement for arbitration or the failure to comply therewith is not in issue, the court shall make an order directing the parties to proceed to arbitration in accordance with the terms of the agreement.

The petition sufficiently sets forth the refusal to arbitrate and the grievance of the appellant thereby under the terms of the agreement so to do.

It is to be noted that the agreement to arbitrate was for a dispute arising during the performance of the charter party. The parties had entered into the performance of this contract. According to the appellant's petition, the denial of which raises the issue, there was a termination of performance by the appellant, on breach of the

appellee; thus the question presented is whether, on the shipowner's breach of the charter during performance, the charterer is entitled to have the respective rights of the parties determined by an arbitration under the arbitration clause.

The court below, resting its decision on The Atlanten, 252 U.S. 313, 40 S. Ct. 332, 333, 64 L. Ed. 586, held that the appellant was not entitled to an order directing arbitration. In that case the owner repudiated the contract before performance, and the court held that the arbitration clause did not apply. The owner refused to proceed with the voyage there contracted for. The court approved the reasoning in the District Court (232 F. 403), and said that

> ... the withdrawal was before the voyage began and it is absurd to suppose that the captain, who might be anywhere in the world, was to be looked up and to pick an arbitrator in such a case. The clause obviously referred to disputes that might arise while the parties were trying to go on with the execution of the contract—not to a repudiation of the substance of the contract, as it is put by Lord Haldane in Jureidini v. National British & Irish Millers Ins. Co., Ltd. [1915] A.C. 499, 505.

The Atlanten, *supra*, was decided before the effective date of the United States Arbitration Act (February 12, 1925). Prior thereto an agreement to arbitrate was not recognized as a valid defense to an action, nor was it specifically enforceable in admiralty. Red Cross Line v. Atlantic Fruit Co., 264 U.S. 109, 123, 44 S. Ct. 274, 68 L. Ed. 582. The United States Arbitration Act (9 USCA § 1 et seq.) was intended to change this view. Marine Corp. v. Dreyfus, 284 U.S. 263, 52 S. Ct. 166, 76 L. Ed. 282. See Report 96 Congressional Committee on H.R. 646. It is quite apparent that Congress intended, by the United States Arbitration Act, to validate arbitration agreements as affirmative defenses in admiralty as well as in other courts.

There is sufficient averment in the petition that the vessel did not report unloaded as required under the terms of the charter, and a breach on the part of the owner is thereby alleged. It is sufficiently alleged that the ship should have been at Trinidad, British West Indies, ready for loading not later than March 22, 1933, but instead she was engaged on business other than the charterer's, between New York and Gulf ports. There is no provision of the charter which granted an exception of this kind to the vessel owner which would avoid a breach by the owner of the entire engagement. Hasler v. West India S. S. Co., 212 F. 862 (C.C.A. 2). The petition proceeds further in stating that, as a result of this breach by the owner, the charterer elected to terminate further performance and advised the owner accordingly; no further cargoes were to be received. In this situation the claim is that further performance was terminated by the charterer on the breach by the owner.

It is not a repudiation of the contract, as was the case in The Atlanten, *supra*. A dispute arose under the contract, for here one of the parties, in the opinion of the other, failed to perform. Arbitration clauses are designed to provide remedies for such situations. The fact that the appellant did not continue performance after breach by the appellee did not deprive it of the right to rely on the arbitration clause. Matter of General Footwear Corp. v. Lawrence Leather Co., 252 N.Y. 577, 170 N.E. 149; Matter of Wenger & Co. v. Propper S. H. Mills, 239 N.Y. 199, 146 N.E. 203. But it is argued that the appellant terminated performance and therefore the arbitration clause does not apply. The parties clearly intended to arbitrate "any dispute arising during the performance of this charter party." Their intention so to do should be strictly observed. Matter of Marchant v. Mead-Morrison Mfg. Co., 252 N.Y. 284, 169 N.E. 386. The arbitration clause must be regarded as covering any dispute which arose after performance began. The whole clause should be considered, and not parts of it. O'Brien v. Miller, 168 U.S. 287, 18 S. Ct. 140, 42 L. Ed. 469.

Nothing in the clause requires performance to continue during the dispute or during the arbitration. Performance by the appellant did not end until it exercised its right to terminate performance by the alleged breach of the appelle. It is clear that the parties intended the words "arising during performance" to attach to all disputes arising although performance on both sides had terminated. This dispute arose during performance and is within the scope of the clause.

No sufficient reason is advanced why the purposes of this arbitration clause should not be carried out and the appelle held bound by its agreement.

Order reversed.

THE WILJA
113 F.2D. 646 (2d Cir. 1940)

Before SWAN, AUGUSTUS N. HAND, and PATTERSON, CIRCUIT JUDGES.

AUGUSTUS N. HAND, CIRCUIT JUDGE. The libellant, a French copartnership doing business in New York, filed its libel to recover damages for breach of a contract, entered into August 17, 1939, in London, England, whereby the owner of the Finnish Steamship *Wilja* chartered her to the libellants to proceed from New York to Montreal, Sorel, Quebec or Three Rivers and there load grain and carry it to Cardiff, Barry, Swansea, London, Hull, Antwerp or Rotterdam, with an option of additional ports of destination, all in the British Isles. The rates of freight were specified in the charterparty.

Article 15 of the charter provided as follows:

> Owner to declare laydays and cancelling dates to Louis Dreyfus & Co., London, as soon as he is in a position to do so. On receipt of such declaration, Messrs. Louis Dreyfus & Co. London to declare whether they will execute or whether they cancel this Charterparty.

The charter also provided at Article 16 as follows: "16. Canadian Water Carriage Goods Act, 1936 ... and Arbitration Clause No. 39 of the Centrocon C/Party to apply to this Charterparty."

Arbitration Clause No. 39 of the Centrocon Charterparty incorporated by the foregoing reference read thus:

> 39. All disputes from time to time arising out of this contract shall, unless the parties agree forthwith on a single arbitrator, be referred to final arbitrament of two arbitrators carrying on business in London who shall be members of the Baltime and engaged in the shipping and/or grain trades.

The amended libel alleged that the need of libellants for the steamship to transport their cargo became so great that they afterwards agreed, conditional upon prompt performance of the contract of carriage, to pay approximately twice the original freight rates for the transportation of their cargo and on or about November 18, 1939, entered into a supplemental agreement with the respondent which provided that the charter should be so amended that they should pay the higher rates for freight and that the lay days and cancelling dates should be November 20, 1939, and November 28, 1939, respectively and that the respondent should cause the *Wilja* to proceed forthwith from New York to the St. Lawrence loading ports provided for in the original charter dated August 7, 1939, as amended November 18, 1939. The libel further alleged that the respondent neglected and refused to cause the *Wilja* to sail forthwith but instead caused her to stay at New York until about noon of November 20, 1939, and then to sail from New York but to return to that port within a few days. The libel finally alleged that the respondent violated its warranty that the *Wilja* was "tight, staunch and strong and in every way fitted for the voyage agreed upon" and that by reason of the failure and refusal of the respondent to perform its agreement the libellants were compelled to secure other transportation for the cargo at a rate greatly in excess of the rates agreed upon and thereby suffered damages in the amount of $60,000.

The libellants acquired jurisdiction of the *Wilja* by seizing her in the Eastern District of New York through process of foreign attachment. The vessel was thereupon released on bond and afterwards proceeded to sea under another charter and was sunk. After her return to New York in November she was under repair until the end of December, 1939.

The respondent moved that the court decline jurisdiction of the suit and also dismiss the libel on the ground that it did not state facts sufficient to constitute a cause of action and that the court lacked jurisdiction of the suit.

The affidavit of Fernand Leval was submitted on the argument and showed that on December 15 the proctors for the respondent had notified the proctors for libellants as follows:

> In response to your inquiry, we are instructed by owner to inform you that as United States ports are not within the range of the above charter party, owner declines to permit the vessel to load at New York or other U.S. Atlantic port.
>
> It seems to us that inasmuch as Montreal, the port to which the vessel was originally ordered and to which she proceeded, is now closed, performance under the above charterparty has become impossible and that, accordingly, it should be agreed upon between both parties that the charter party is terminated.

It also appears by the affidavit of libellants' proctor Henry E. Otto verified January 2, 1940, that the *Wilja* had been chartered to Messrs. Isbrandtsen-Moller at a higher rate than that agreed upon between the libellants and the owner for a voyage from New York to Antwerp/Rotterdam.

The District Judge, after argument of the motion, filed an opinion declining jurisdiction and relegating the parties to arbitration in London.

It seems clear to us that the libellants have shown that this is not a case in which the arbitration provided for in the charterparty can be regarded as a condition upon the maintenance of the cause of action. The record indicates that there was a repudiation of the amended charterparty by the respondent which was evidently doing everything it could to get higher freight rates on a rising market. Moreover it had already repudiated the original charterparty of August 17, 1939 for supposed lack of considera-

tion and had entered into the amended one of November 18, 1939, upon obtaining from the libellants an agreement to pay about double the original freight rates. Even after obtaining this great concession the respondent soon began to insist that performance was impossible because it could not load the ship at Montreal as that port was closed for the winter and shortly afterwards took the technical position that it would not accept libellants suggestion that it load their cargo at New York because under the terms of the charter it was not required to do so. It followed this by entering into engagements with a new charterer for another European voyage. Under such circumstances it seems clear that the arbitration clause had no application to the right of the libellants to maintain the present suit. The decision of the Supreme Court in The Atlanten, 252 U.S. 313, 40 S. Ct. 332, 64 L.Ed. 586, and the rulings of the House of Lords in Jureidini v. National British and Irish Millers Insurance Company, Limited (1915) A.C. 499, and Hirji Mulji v. Cheong Yue Steamship Company Limited (1926) A.C. 497, indicate that the parties should not have been relegated to London for arbitration. Before the libel was filed the charterparty had already been repudiated by the respondent, and the latter had insisted that the voyage was frustrated by the closing of the St. Lawrence River for the winter. Accordingly the arbitration clause became wholly inapplicable to the case.

It is argued on behalf of the respondent that the motion of libellants in the District Court for a rehearing in order that they might obtain an order requiring security from the respondent that it would proceed to arbitrate in London estops it from questioning the latter's right to arbitration, but we can see no basis for such a contention. The making of the motion caused no prejudice to the respondent and worked no estoppel. Nor did it constitute an election which enlarged the scope of the clause for arbitration in the charterparty. As Holmes, J., said in The Atlanten, 252 U.S. 313, at page 316, 40 S.Ct. 332, 333, 64 L.Ed. 586: "The clause obviously referred to disputes that might arise while the parties were trying to go on with the execution of the contract—not to a repudiation of the substance of the contract...."

In view of the foregoing, we think there can be no doubt that the District Court has power to retain jurisdiction of the dispute even though between citizens of foreign states and to dispose of the litigation on the merits. In view of the widespread conflict in Europe and the chaotic conditions there it would seem a great hardship to the libellants for our courts to decline jurisdiction and thereby to require them to bring suit either in Finland or England. Proof of damages could apparently be readily obtained in New York. The repudiation of the charterparty occurred there and, if the seaworthiness of the vessel should become a factor in the litigation, proof of her condition could be most easily secured from New York witnesses, since the repairs were conducted there in November and December, 1939, and the condition of the *Wilja* must have been there known. But in order that the question of the propriety of retaining jurisdiction may be passed on by the District Court with all the proof on the subject which the parties may choose to present, we think it best, upon this reversal of the decree for error of law in relegating the parties to arbitration in London, to remand the cause to the District Court with directions to exercise its discretion in regard to retention of jurisdiction, and, if it should determine to retain jurisdiction, to decide the cause on the merits. This is in accord with the rule laid down by the Supreme Court in Charter Shipping Company v. Bowring, Jones & Tidy, Limited, 281 U.S. 515, 50 S.Ct. 400, 74 L.Ed. 1008, and Canada Malting Co. v. Paterson Co., 285 U.S. 413, 52 S.Ct. 413, 76 L.Ed. 837.

Decree reversed.

KULUKUNDIS SHIPPING CO. v. AMTORG TRADING CORPORATION
126 F. 2D. 978 (2d Cir. 1942)

Before L. Hand, Chase, and Frank, Circuit Judges.

Frank, Circuit Judge. The libel alleged that appellant (respondent) had, through its authorized representatives, agreed to a charter party with appellee (libellant). Appellant's answer in effect denied that anyone authorized to act for it had so agreed. After a trial, the district court made the following

FINDINGS OF FACT

1. Libellant, Kulukundis Shipping Co. S/A, employed Blidberg Rothchild Co. Inc. as a broker and the respondent, Amtorg Trading Corporation employed Potter & Gordon, Inc. as its broker in the negotiations for the chartering of the ship "Mount Helmos" for a trip to Japan. On March 15, 1940, Rothchild, of the firm of Blidberg Rothchild Co. Inc., and Gordon, acting on behalf of Potter & Gordon, Inc., agreed upon a charter and closed by Gordon executing and delivering to Rothchild a fixture slip which is the usual trade practice, indicating the conclusion of charter negotiations in the trade of ship brokerage. All the material terms of the bargain are set forth in the fixture slip excepting demurrage, dispatch, and the date of the commencement of the charter term which all had been agreed on but were omitted by an oversight. A number of the terms, including the War Risks Clause of 1937, were fixed by the incorporation of a reference to an earlier charter of the steamer "Norbryn." Gordon acted with authority.

2. Thereafter respondent refused to sign the charter but instead repudiated it.

CONCLUSIONS OF LAW

1. Respondent has breached a valid contract and is liable in damages to the libellant.

Pursuant to the foregoing, the court entered an order that appellee recover from appellant the damages sustained, and referred to a named commissioner the ascertainment of the damges, to be reported to the court.

The errors assigned on this appeal by appellant (with an exception we shall discuss later) relate to the admissibility of certain letters, the weight and sufficiency of the evidence, and the credibility of witnesses. The letters, for reasons adequately stated in the district court's opinion, were properly admitted in evidence.

But there is an error assigned which is of a different character. The appellant, in its answer originally filed, pleaded that no contract had been made. No steps of any importance having meanwhile occurred in the suit, some nine months later and two months before the trial, it sought to amend its answer by including, as a separate defense, the fact that the alleged charterparty upon which appellee was suing contained an arbitration clause, that appellee had not at any time asked appellant to proceed to arbitration, and that therefore the suit had been prematurely brought. This motion to amend was denied. If the amendment should have been allowed, the additional defense can now be urged.

The arbitration clause reads as follows:

> 24. Demurrage or despatch is to be settled at loading and discharging ports separately, except as per Clause 9. Owners and Charterers agree, in case of any dispute or claim, to settle same by arbitration in New York. Also, in case of a dispute of any nature whatsoever, same is to be settled by arbitration in New York. In both cases arbitrators are to be commercial men.

In 1925 Congress enacted the Arbitration Act, U.S.C.A., Title 9. Pertinent sections of that statute read as follows: [Sections 2, 3, and 4 are omitted]

Appellant admits—as it must—that the district court had jurisdiction to determine whether the parties had made an agreement to arbitrate.[1] Appellant contends, however, that, once the court determined in this suit that there was such an arbitration agreement, the court lost all power over the suit beyond that of staying further proceedings until there had been an arbitration as agreed to;[2] in that arbitration, argues appellant, the arbitrators will have jurisdiction to determine all issues except the existence of the arbitration clause. This jurisdiction, it is urged, is broad enough to permit an independent determination, by the arbitrator, that the contract itself is not valid or binding. Appellee asserts that the defendant had repudiated the charterparty, and that, therefore, the arbitration clause must be wholly disregarded.

In considering these contentions in the light of the precedents, it is necessary to take into account the history of the judicial attitude towards arbitration: [appears earlier in this volume in Chapter II].

The United States Arbitration Act of 1925 was sustained as constitutional, in its application to cases arising in admiralty. Marine Transit Corp. v. Dreyfus, 1932, 284 U.S. 263, 52 S.Ct. 166, 76 L.Ed. 516. The purpose of that Act was deliberately to alter the judicial atmosphere previously existing.

In the light of the clear intention of Congress, it is our obligation to shake off the old judicial hostility to arbitration. Accordingly, in a case like this, involving the federal Act, we should not follow English or other decisions which have narrowly construed the terms of arbitration agreements or arbitration statutes. With this new orientation, we approach the problems here presented. They are twofold: (a) Does the arbitration provision here have the sweeping effect ascribed to it by appellant? (b) Is it, as appellee contends, wholly without efficacy because appellant asserted that there never was an agreement for a charter party? We shall consider these questions in turn.

To the appellant's sweeping contention there are several answers.

(a) Appellant, as we saw, concedes that, in such a case as this, before sending any issue to arbitrators, the court must determine whether an arbitration provision exists. As the arbitration clause here is an integral part of the charter-

party, the court, in determining that the parties agreed to that clause, must necessarily first have found that the charterparty exists.[3] If the court here, having so found, were now to direct the arbitrators to consider that same issue, they would be traversing ground already covered in the court trial. There would thus result precisely that needless expenditure of time and money (the "costliness and delays of litigation") which Congress sought to avoid in enacting the Arbitration Act. In the light of that fact, a reasonable interpretation of the Act compels a repudiation of appellant's sweeping contention.

(b) If the issue of the existence of the charter party were left to the arbitrators and they found that it was never made, they would, unavoidably (unless they were insane), be obliged to conclude that the arbitration agreement had never been made. Such a conclusion would (1) negate the court's prior contrary decision on a subject which, admittedly, the Act commits to the court, and (2) would destroy the arbitrator's authority to decide anything and thus make their decision a nullity. Cf. Phillips, *The Paradox in Arbitration Law*, 46 HARV. L.REV. (1933) 1258, 1270–1272; Phillips, *A Lawyer's Approach to Commercial Arbitration*, 41 YALE L.J. (1934) 31; 6 WILLISTON, CONTRACTS (Rev. ed. 1938), Section 1920 (pp. 5369–5379).

(c) The Arbitration Act does not cover an arbitration agreement sufficiently broad to include a controversy as to the existence of the very contract which embodies the arbitration agreement. Section 2 of the Act describes only three types of agreement covered by the Act: One type is "an agreement ... to submit to arbitration an existing controversy arising out of ... a contract, transaction," etc.; thus the parties here, after a dispute had arisen as to the existence of the charter party, might have made an agreement to submit to arbitration that "existing" controversy. But that is not this case. Section 2 also includes a "provision in ... a contract evidencing a transaction ... to settle by arbitration a controversy thereafter arising out of such contract or transaction ..." Plainly such a provision does not include a provision in a contract to arbitrate the issue whether the minds of the parties ever met so as to bring about the very contract of which that arbitration clause is a part; a controversy relating to the denial that the parties ever made a contract is not a controversy arising out of that contract. Nor is it a controversy "arising out of a transaction evidenced by a contract," for if no contract existed

---

1. Under Section 3 of the Act, the court cannot grant a stay until it is "satisfied that the issue involved in such suit is referable to arbitration under" an "agreement in writing for ... arbitration." Clearly the court cannot be thus "satisfied" without a determination that the parties made such an agreement to arbitrate.

2. Or, if plaintiff had so requested, then under Section 4, directing the parties to proceed with the arbitration.

---

3. The situation would be different if a separate arbitration agreement had been made.

then there was no such transaction evidenced by a contract and, therefore, no controversy arising out of that transaction. The third type of arbitration agreement described in Section 2 of the Act is a provision in a contract to settle by arbitration "a controversy thereafter arising out of ... the refusal to perform the whole or any part thereof." This is familiar language ; it refers to a controversy, which parties to a contract may easily contemplate, arising when a party to the contract, without denying that he made it, refuses performance ; it does not mean a controversy arising out of the denial by one of the parties that he ever made any contract whatsoever.

It is clear then that, even assuming, arguendo, that a contract could be drawn containing an arbitration clause sufficiently broad to include a controversy as to whether the minds of the parties had ever met concerning the making of the very contract which embodies the arbitration clause, such a clause would not be within the Arbitration Act. Accordingly, it perhaps would not be immunized from the prestatutory rules inimical to arbitration, i.e., would not serve as the basis of a stay of the suit on the contract, leaving the parties to the arbitration called for by their agreement. Were the arbitration clause here sufficiently broad to call for arbitration of the dispute as to the existence of the charter-party, it would, therefore, perhaps be arguable that it was entirely outside of the Act and, accordingly, irrelevant in the case before us ; we need not consider that question, as we hold that the breadth of the arbitration is not so great and it is within the terms of Section 2 of the Act.

We conclude that it would be improper to submit to the arbitrators the issue of the making of the charter party.

But it does not follow that appellant was not entitled to a stay of the suit, under Section 3, until arbitration has been had as to the amount of the damages.[4] Here it is important to differentiate between Sections 3 and 4 of the Act. Under Section 4, the proceeding—as the Supreme Court observed in Marine Transit Corp. v. Dreyfus, 284 U.S. 263, 278, 52 S.Ct. 166, 76 L.Ed. 516—is one for specific performance : One of the parties seeks "an order directing that ... arbitration proceed in the manner provided for" in the arbitration clause or agreement. It may well be that in a proceeding under Section 4, there are open many of the usual defenses avail-

able in a suit for specific performance. It would seem that a court, when exercising equity powers, should do so on the basis of a fully informed judgment as to all the circumstances. We recognize that some authorities have held to the contrary under similarly worded state arbitration statutes, interpreting them to require the courts automatically to decree specific performance without regard to the usual equitable considerations. It is difficult for us to believe that Congress intended us so to construe Section 4, although we do not here decide that question. However that may be, the same equitable considerations should surely not be applicable when a defendant asks a stay pursuant to Section 3. For he is not then seeking specific performance (i.e., an order requiring that the parties proceed to arbitration) but merely a stay order of a kind long familiar in common law, equity and admiralty actions. His position is that when the court (to quote Section 3) is "satisfied that the issue involved in such suit ... is referable to arbitration," the court must "stay the trial of the action until such arbitration has been had in accordance with the terms of the agreement." There is a well recognized distinction between such a stay and specific performance: The first merely arrests further action by the court itself in the suit until something outside the suit has occurred ; but the court does not order that it shall be done. The second, through the exercise of discretionary equity powers, affirmatively orders that someone do (or refrain from doing) some act outside the suit.

The Supreme Court has made just this distinction between Sections 3 and 4. In Shanferoke Corp. v. Westchester Corp., 1935, 293 U.S. 449, 452, 453, 55 S.Ct. 313, 315, 79 L.Ed. 583, in which it sustained this court in granting a stay when the arbitration clause provided for specific performance by the New York courts of the agreement to arbitrate, the Supreme Court said:

> Whether it [the contract] should be construed so as to exclude the bringing of a suit in the federal court to compel specific performance of the agreement to arbitrate, we have no occasion to decide. For the District Court was not asked, in the proceedings now under review, to compel specific performance. The motion was to stay the action until arbitration shall have been had ; and the direction of the Court of Appeals was limited to granting a stay. Section 3 of the United States Arbitration Act ... provides broadly that the court may "stay the trial of the action until such arbitration has been had in accordance with the terms of the agreement." We think the Court of Appeals was clearly right in concluding that there is no reason to imply that the power to grant a stay is conditioned upon the existence of power to compel arbitration in accordance with section 4 of

---

4. While it is not literally so worded, we treat, as an application for a stay, the new matter in the amended answer which appellant asked leave to file.

the act. . . . There is . . . strong reason for construing the clause as permitting the federal court to order a stay even when it cannot compel the arbitration.

In the case at bar, so far as the arbitration was concerned, it was the first duty of the court, under Section 3, to determine whether there was an agreement to arbitrate and whether any of the issues raised in the suit were within the reach of that agreement. The appellant contested the existence of the charterparty which contained that agreement, but also alternatively[5] pleaded that, if it existed, then there should be a stay pending arbitration of the appropriate issues. We see no reason why a respondent should be precluded from thus pleading in the alternative.

It is suggested, however, that there is a difference in the position of (1) a defendant who, even if he has no excuse to offer, refuses wholly to perform a contract containing an arbitration clause which he sets up as a condition precedent and (2) one who, like appellant, defends on the ground that no contract was ever made and, alternatively, similarly sets up an arbitration clause. The latter, it is urged, is somehow guilty of a greater moral wrong and, therefore, entitled to less relief. We cannot agree. For we have already shown that equitable factors have slighter bearing where defendant asks a stay under Section 3 and not specific performance under Section 4. But even if such factors were fully pertinent under Section 3, it would not be true that there is more equity in the position of a person who, admitting that he has made a contract, wilfully refuses all performance without excuse than in that of one who, in good faith, raises a question of fact as to whether a contract was ever made.[6]

The arbitration clause here was clearly broad enough to cover the issue of damages; "a clause of general arbitration does not cease to be within the statute when the dispute narrows down to damages alone."[7] It has been suggested that the arbitration clause calls for arbitrators who are "commercial men," that they are not appropriate persons to compute damages in this case where appellant has not merely breached but denied the existence of the charter party, and that,

therefore, it must follow that the parties did not contemplate arbitration of such damages. But that argument is untenable, since it rests upon an unsound assumption, *i.e.,* that damages are to be differently computed in those two kinds of situations. In truth, it is precisely this sort of case where arbitration of damages by "commercial men" may be peculiarly useful, as they are likely to be more familiar than the average lawyer who serves as special master with the relevant background of international shipping in the state of world affairs as of the period covered by the charterparty.[8]

There remains to be considered the language of Section 3 of the Act that, "on application," such a stay shall be granted "providing the applicant for the stay is not in default in proceeding with such arbitration." We take that proviso to refer to a party who, when requested, has refused to go to arbitration or who has refused to proceed with the hearing before the arbitration once it has commenced. The appellant was never asked by appellee to proceed with the arbitration indeed, it is the appellee who has objected to it. In Shanferoke Coal & Supply Corp. v. Westchester S. Corp., 2 Cir., 1934, 70 F. 2d 297, plaintiff alleged that defendant, after part performance, materially breached the contract. The defendant in its answer denied the allegations and, as a special defense, set up an arbitration clause in the contract, alleged that it was willing to arbitrate, and moved for a stay under Section 3 of the Arbitration Act. Answering plaintiff's contention that defendant was "in default in proceeding with such arbitration," we held that the fact that defendant may have breached the contract was not a "default" within that statutory provision; we said that the initiative as to proceeding with the arbitration rested upon plaintiff, adding: "If it did not but sued instead, it was itself the party who fell 'in default in proceeding with such arbitration,' not the defendant."[9] Our decision was affirmed in Shanferoke Co. v. Westchester Co., 1935, 293 U.S. 449, 55 S.Ct. 313, 79 L.Ed. 583.

Accordingly, we conclude that the defendant here was not in default within the meaning of the proviso in Section 3. It follows that the district court should have stayed the suit, pending arbitration to determine the damages.

Our conclusion is not inconsistent with our

---

5. That is, it tried so to plead in its amended answer. Since we hold that it should have been allowed to amend, we deal with the case as if it had so pleaded.

6. Although we do not disturb the findings of the trial judge, they were based on a record containing conflicting testimony and it cannot be said that appellant was in bad faith in contesting the making of the charterparty. Presumably, in so doing, it relied on its counsel, a reputable member of the bar.

7. Shanferoke Coal & Supply Corp. v. Westchester S. Corp., 2 Cir., 1954, 70 F.2d 297, 299.

8. The chartered vessel here was to travel from New York to the Orient.

9. In line with this interpretation, we directed that the stay be granted but said that "the District Court will be free . . . to vacate it at any time, should it appear that the defendant is in default in proceeding with the arbitration."

decision in The Wilja, 2 Cir., 1940, 113 F.2d 646, properly interpreted. There is a dictum in that opinion intimating that there was a "repudiation of the contract" which nullified the arbitration clause, because the respondent ship-owner had completely refused performance, so that it could not ask for a stay based on that clause. But the facts of that case were that, due to war conditions, it had become impossible to carry out the arbitration, which, by its terms, was to take place in London. Moreover, there the libellant, under what came close to being coercion on the part of respondent, had agreed to an amendment of the original contract increasing the freight rates to twice the amount originally agreed upon ; and respondent had then flagrantly breached even this amended contract. There was thus the impossibility of complying with the arbitration clause coupled with impressive unfairness by respondent.... We do not say that impossibility will always excuse non-compliance with an arbitration clause, but merely that it did in The Wilja, on the facts there present.

The phrase "repudiation of the contract," as used by Lord Haldane in the *Jureidini* case, was incidentally referred to in The Atlanten, 1920, 252 U.S. 313, 40 S.Ct. 332, 64 L.Ed. 586, which arose before the enactment of the Arbitration Act of 1925. That was a suit against a Swedish corporation, owner of a steamship, for a breach of a charter party made in Denmark. Before any voyage was made, the owner refused to perform, and, when sued, set up the arbitration clause of the agreement which read: "If any dispute arises the same to be settled by two referees, one to be appointed by the Captain and one by charterers or their agents, and if necessary, the arbitrators to appoint an Umpire." It was alleged that by the laws of Denmark and Sweden such a provision was binding as an effective condition precedent.[10] The court said that the refusal to perform "was not a 'dispute' of the kind referred to in the arbitration clause" because "the withdrawal was before the voyage began and it is absurd to suppose that the captain, who might be anywhere in the world, was to be looked up and to pick an arbitrator in such a case." Due to that fact—the provision for selection of an arbitrator by the captain—the court said, "The clause obviously

referred to disputes that might arise while the parties were trying to go on with the execution of the contract," and added, "not to a repudiation of the substance of the contract, as it is put by Lord Haldane in Jureidini v. National British & Irish Millers Co., Ltd., [1915] A.C. 499, 505." That reference to the *Jureidini* case was thus made merely in passing, and was not at all necessary to the court's reasoning or decision. The Atlanten, then, turned on the construction of the particular arbitration clause involved in that case which was markedly different from that we have before us in the case at bar. In Shanferoke Coal & Supply Corp. v. Westchester S. Corp., 2 Cir., 1934, 70 F.2d 297, 299 affirmed 293 U.S. 449, 55 S.Ct. 313, 79 L.Ed. 583, in which we discussed and applied the Arbitration Act of 1925, we expressly said that we were leaving open the question whether the "repudiation" idea expressed in the *Jureidini* case was correct.

The order of the district court is reversed and the cause is remanded with directions to proceed in accordance with the foregoing opinion.

ASTER v. JACK ALOFF CO.
190 Pa. Super. 615, 155 A. 2d 627 (1959)

The appellant's contract was terminated by appellee in accordance with its terms prior to completion of the work ; appellant contended that this action also terminated the arbitration provisions of the agreement. Held: the subsequent arbitration of the dispute which arose during the contract term was proper ; the agreement to arbitrate had not been impaired.

IN re PAHLBERG PETITION
131 F.2D. 968 (2d Cir. 1942)

Before SWAN, AUGUSTUS N. HAND and CHASE, CIRCUIT JUDGES.

AUGUSTUS N. HAND, CIRCUIT JUDGE. This is an appeal from an order granting the petition of Rud Pahlberg to compel the respondent, Bulk Carriers Corporation, to proceed with arbitration pursuant to Section 4 of the United States Arbitration Act, U.S.C.A. Title 9, § 4.

The owners of the Estonian Steamship "Hildur" agreed to let the steamship, and Bulk Carriers Corporation, to hire her for a period of three consecutive months at the rate of $2.50 per ton on the vessel's total deadweight carry-

---

10. The court said (252 U.S. at page 315, 40 S.Ct. at page 333 64 L.Ed. 586), "With regard to the arbitration clause we shall not consider the general question whether a greater effect should not be given to such clauses than formerly was done, since it is not necessary to do so in order to decide the case before us."

ing capacity, represented to be about 3,000 tons. Under the terms of the charterparty she was to be placed at the disposal of the charterer not before January 5, 1940, and not later than May 15, 1940, but was never delivered to the charterer.

The charterparty contained an abitration clause which read as follows:

> That should any dispute arise between Owners and the Charterers, the matter in dispute shall be referred to three persons at New York, one to be appointed by each of the parties hereto, and the third by the two so chosen, their decision or that of any two of them, shall be final, and for the purpose of enforcing any award, this agreement may be made a rule of the Court. The Arbitrators shall be commercial men.

The charterer filed a libel against the owners of the vessel to recover $25,000 damages for failure of the latter to perform its contract by delivering the "Hildur" to the libellant for the carriage of merchandise within the range of limits set forth in the contract. After vainly demanding an arbitration, the owners of the "Hildur" moved in the District Court on October 24, 1941, for an order staying the pending action until arbitration could be had pursuant to Section 3 of the Arbitration Act, 9 U.S.C.A. § 3. This motion was denied upon the authority of The Wilja, 2 Cir., 113 F.2d 646, and the denial was affirmed on reargument. Thereafter, and on or about January 29, 1942, Rud Pahlberg, the petitioner-appellee, and one of the alleged owners of the "Hildur," filed an independent petition to compel arbitration pursuant to Section 4 of the United States Arbitration Act and his petition was granted.

The denial of the motion for a stay under Section 3 of the Arbitration Act resulted in an order which, because it was interlocutory, was not res judicata in respect to the later order directing the charterer to proceed to arbitration pursuant to Section 4. Joseph T. Ryerson & Son v. Bullard Machine Tool Co., 2 Cir., 79 F.2d 192.

Aside from the fact that the order denying a stay was interlocutory, it is entirely clear from the decision of the Supreme Court in Shanferoke Coal & Supply Corp. v. Westchester Service Corp., 293 U.S. 449, 452, 55 S.Ct. 313, 79 L.Ed. 583, that the power given by Section 3 of the Arbitration Act to grant a stay until arbitration is not confined to cases in which arbitration may be compelled under Section 4 of the Act. Therefore, application for a stay under Section 3 did not exclude the right to proceed under Section 4 of the Act to enforce arbitration. See, also, In re Utility Oil Corporation, 2 Cir., 69 F.2d 524.

The statement in The Wilja, 2 Cir., 113 F.2d 646, that the arbitration clause there being considered could not be invoked because the charter had been repudiated was not the ground on which that decision properly rested, but the proper ground, as was noted in Kulukundis Shipping Company v. Amtorg Trading Corp., 2 Cir., 126 F.2d 978, was the actual impossibility of arbitration. In view of the discussion in Kulukundis Shipping Company v. Amtorg Trading Corp., and the recent decision of the House of Lords in Heyman v. Darwins (1942), A.C. 356, we think that the dictum in The Wilja, *supra*, was not controlling upon the court below and that under the language of the arbitration clause in the charterparty before us the repudiation of the charter by the owners, by failure to deliver the ship, was to be fairly regarded as a dispute arising between the parties referable to arbitration within Section 17 of the charter party. The somewhat confused interpretation of the British Arbitration Act in various decisions of the British Courts has been recently clarified by the House of Lords in Heyman v. Darwins, *supra*, which reached a conclusion similar to the one this court arrived at in Kulukundis Shipping Company v. Amtorg Trading Corp., namely, that under a clause providing for arbitration of "any dispute ... between the parties ... in respect of this agreement or any of the provisions herein contained or anything arising hereout ... arbitration may be compelled except as to the issue whether the contract containing the clause was ever made or was void for fraud or other illegality." In Heyman v. Darwins, the Lord Chancellor remarked:

> An arbitration clause is a written submission, agreed to by the parties to the contract, and, like other written submissions to arbitration, must be construed according to its language and in the light of the circumstances in which it is made. If the dispute is whether the contract which contains the clause has ever been entered into at all, that issue cannot go to arbitration under the clause, for the party who denies that he has ever entered into the contract is thereby denying that he has ever joined in the submission. Similarly, if one party to the alleged contract is contending that it is void ab initio (because, for example, the making of such a contract is illegal), the arbitration clause cannot operate, for on this view the clause itself also is void. But, in a situation where the parties are at one in asserting that they entered into a binding contract, but a difference has arisen between them whether there has been a breach by one side or the other, or whether circumstances have arisen which have discharged one or both parties from further performance, such differences should be re-

garded as differences which have arisen "in respect of," or "with regard to," "under" the contract, and an arbitration clause which uses these, or similar, expressions should be construed accordingly. (1942) A.C. 356, 366.

The foregoing language of the Lord Chancellor in Heyman v. Darwins, and the reasoning of this court in Kulukundis Shipping Company v. Amtorg Trading Corp., justify the conclusion of the District Court that the refusal of the owners to deliver the "Hildur," pursuant to the terms of the charterparty, even though it amounted to a total nonperformance of the contract, did not prevent the petitioner from resorting to arbitration under Clause 17. We think that Section 2 of the Arbitration Act, covers just such arbitrations as were provided for by that clause.

We have doubtless gone somewhat afield in discussing the merits of the present appeal. We have done this in order to define the limits of our decision in The Wilja, *supra*, for litigations over the scope of arbitration clauses which are likely to arise in the future. Under the ruling of the Supreme Court in Schoenamsgruber v. Hamburg Line, 294 U.S. 454, 55 S.Ct. 475, 79 L.Ed. 989, an order directing parties to proceed to arbitration was held not appealable because interlocutory. Accordingly no appeal lies from the order sought to be reviewed, since it is interlocutory, and the pending appeal must be dismissed.

F.

Stay of Suit Pending Arbitration

SHANFEROKE COAL & SUPPLY CORP. v. WESTCHESTER SERVICE CORP.
293 U.S. 449 (1935)

Mr. Justice Brandeis delivered the opinion of the Court.

This action was brought by the Shanferoke Coal & Supply Corporation, a citizen of Delaware, in the federal court for southern New York against the Westchester Service Corporation, a citizen of the latter State. The declaration alleged that the defendant had by a contract in writing agreed to purchase from the plaintiff a large quantity of coal to be taken in instalments throughout a period of years; and that the defendant had, after accepting part of the coal, repudiated the contract. The defendant set up in its answer, as a special defense, that prior to the commencement of the action a dispute had arisen concerning the construction of the contract, the rights and duties of the respective parties thereunder and its performance; that the contract contained an arbitration clause; and that prior to the commencement of the action the defendant had notified the plaintiff of its readiness and willingness to submit the dispute to arbitration and ever since had been ready and willing to do so; but that the plaintiff had refused to proceed with the arbitration. The defendant then moved that the action, and all proceedings therein, be stayed until an arbitration should be had in accordance with the terms of the contract sued on. The motion was heard on affidavits and counter affidavits.

The arbitration clause is as follows:

In case any dispute should arise between the Buyer and Seller as to the performance of any of the terms of this agreement, such dispute shall be arbitrated and the cost thereof shall be borne equally by both parties, The Buyer and the Seller shall each appoint one arbitrator and the two arbitrators so appointed shall select a third arbitrator and the decision of a majority of the three arbitrators shall be final and conclusive on both parties. In case for any reason any such arbitration shall fail to proceed to a final award, either party may apply to the Supreme Court of the State of New York for an order compelling the specific performance of this arbitration agreement in accordance with the arbitration laws of the State of New York.

The District Court interpreted the clause as making the arbitration enforceable only in state courts of New York; and on that ground denied the stay. On an appeal from the order of denial, the Court of Appeals held that even if the clause should be so interpreted, § 3 of the United States Arbitration Act authorized the stay. It, therefore, reversed the order and directed the District Court to grant the stay, with leave to that court "to vacate it at any time, should it appear that the defendant is in default in proceeding with the arbitration." 70 F. (2d) 297. This Court granted certiorari.

Second. The plaintiff contends that the District Court was without power to grant the stay, because the contract provides that arbitration can be compelled only by proceedings in a state court of New York. The provision is that "either party may apply to the Supreme Court of the

State of New York for an order compelling specific performance of this arbitration agreement in accordance with the arbitration law of the State of New York." The contract does not in terms prohibit proceedings in the federal court. Whether it should be construed so as to exclude the bringing of a suit in the federal court to compel specific performance of the agreement to arbitrate, we have no occasion to decide. For the District Court was not asked, in the proceedings now under review, to compel specific performance. The motion was to stay the action until arbitration shall have been had; and the direction of the Court of Appeals was limited to granting a stay. Section 3 of the United States Arbitration Act provides broadly that the court may "stay the trial of the action until such arbitration has been had in accordance with the terms of the agreement." We think the Court of Appeals was clearly right in concluding that there is no reason to imply that the power to grant a stay is conditioned upon the existence of power to compel arbitration in accordance with § 4 of the Act.[1] Marine Transit Corp. v. Dreyfus, 284 U.S. 263, 274, is not to the contrary. There is, on the other hand, strong reason for construing the clause as permitting the federal court to order a stay even when it cannot compel the arbitration. For otherwise, despite congressional approval of arbitration, it would be impossible to secure a stay of an action in the federal courts when the arbitration agreement provides for compulsory proceedings exclusively in the state courts; since only in exceptional circumstances may a state court enjoin proceedings begun in a federal court. See Central National Bank v. Stevens, 169 U.S. 432. Compare § 265 of the Judicial Code; Kline v. Burke Construction Co., 260 U.S. 226.

Affirmed.

MANNESMANN ROHRLEITUNGSBAU v. S.S. BERNHARD HOWALDT
254 F. Supp. 278 (S.D. N.Y. 1965)

WYATT, DISTRICT JUDGE.
This is a motion by respondent Transamerican Steamship Corporation ("Transamerican") to dismiss the libel because this forum is inconvenient or, in the alternative, for a stay under 9 U.S.C. § 3 pending arbitration.

The motion to dismiss is plainly without merit.

On the other hand, nothing has been shown to defeat the right of Transamerican to a stay under 9 U.S.C. § 3.

The contract made by the parties clearly provided for arbitration in Rotterdam.

The argument for libelant appears to be that for a variety of reasons in Dutch law it cannot go into a *Dutch* court and *compel* Transamerican to arbitrate. This seems beside the point. Apparently no move has been made by libelant to have arbitration in Rotterdam. Under the contract, the first move would be to try to agree with Transamerican on a single arbitrator. If this cannot be done in a reasonable time, libelant should "nominate" an arbitrator. Whether Transamerican will then refuse to proceed with arbitration in Rotterdam remains to be seen, but if it should so refuse, a stay of this suit can of course be vacated. Transamerican cannot have it both ways; it cannot maintain a stay of this suit and also delay or frustrate arbitration. An applicant for a stay under 9 U.S.C. § 3 is, by the terms thereof, required to be "not in default in proceeding with such arbitration." There is nothing to show that Transamerican is presently in default.

The circumstance that the arbitration is to take place in a foreign country does not affect the right to a stay under 9 U.S.C. § 3. The Quarrington Court, 25 F.Supp. 665, 666 (S.D.N.Y. 1938); reversed on other grounds, 102 F.2d 916 (2d Cir.), cert. denied Court Line v. Isthmian, 307 U.S. 645, 59 S.Ct. 1043, 83 L.Ed. 1525 (1939). See also Shanferoke Coal & Supply Corp. v. Westchester Service Corp., 293 U.S. 449, 452–453, 55 S.Ct. 313, 79 L.Ed. 583 (Brandeis, J.; 1935).

The motion for a stay is accordingly granted and the trial of this suit is hereby stayed until arbitration has been had in accordance with the terms of the agreement between the parties dated February 18, 1963, and libelant has leave to move to vacate this stay upon a showing that respondent Transamerican is delaying or frustrat-

---

1. In the lower federal courts there has been some difference of opinion as to whether a stay should be granted when the court is not in a position to compel arbitration. Compare Danielsen v. Entre Rios Ry. Co., 22 F. (2d) 326, 328, with The Silverbrook, 18 F. (2d) 144. See, too, The Beechwood, 35 F. (2d) 41; The Volsinio, 32 F. (2d) 357, 358; Ex parte De Simone, 36 F. (2d) 773; The Fredensbro, 18 F. (2d) 983. Interpretations of the English arbitration statutes are in accord with the view adopted here. See Law v. Garrett, L. R. 8 Ch. Div. 26 (C. A.); Austrian Lloyd S. S. Co. v. Gresham Life Assurance Society, [1903] 1 K. B. 249; Kirchner & Co. v. Gruban, [1909] 1 Ch. Div. 413; *The Cap Blanco*, [1913] Pro. Div. 130.

ing the arbitration provided for in said agreement.

The motion to dismiss the libel is denied.

So ordered.

In Bruno v. Pepperidge Farm, Inc., 256 F. Supp. 865 (E.D. Pa. 1966) plaintiff sued for improper termination of his franchise, unreasonably short notice of termination entailing loss of a month's profit (plaintiff set a reasonable time at 30 days), loss of value of merchandise on hand, and the value of the franchise. Defendant moved for a stay of suit pending arbitration under a provision that read:

> Upon termination pursuant to this paragraph the Bakery [the defendant] will pay to the distributor [the plaintiff] a sum equal to the fair market value of this franchise on the termination date plus 25 per cent of such value, such value to be determined either by agreement between [the parties] or, *if they shall be unable to agree, by three arbitrators, one of whom shall be chosen by the Bakery and one by the Distributor and the third by the first two chosen.* (Emphasis supplied by the court.)

The district judge praised arbitration and the beneficent purposes of the Federal Arbitration Act and noted "the danger of allowing a party to avoid arbitration by merely casting his complaint in tort." But he deduced that the ambit of the arbitration clause was quite restricted and declined the request to dismiss or stay the suit. (Precisely how the matter was disposed of on this point is unclear because the court allowed 90 days for the plaintiff to employ discovery to ascertain facts sufficient to plead adequately on the question of jurisdictional amount.) Note that the Federal Act does not have language comparable to New York's CPLR § 7503(a):

> If an issue claimed to be arbitrable is involved in an action pending in a court having jurisdiction to hear a motion to compel arbitration, the application [to compel arbitration] shall be made by motion in that action. If the application is granted, the order shall operate to stay a pending or subsequent action, or so much of it as is referable to arbitration.

And the California statute provides in C.C.P. § 12 81.4:

> If the issue which is the controversy subject to arbitration is severable, the stay may be with respect to that issue only.

G.

The Interplay of the United States Arbitration Act and State Law—The Cases

BERNHARDT v. POLYGRAPHIC COMPANY OF AMERICA, INC.
350 U.S. 198, 76 S.Ct. 273 (1956)

Mr. Justice Douglas delivered the opinion of the Court.

This suit, removed from a Vermont court to the District Court on grounds of diversity of citizenship, was brought for damages for the discharge of petitioner under an employment contract. At the time the contract was made petitioner was a resident of New York. Respondent is a New York corporation. The contract was made in New York. Petitioner later became a resident of Vermont, where he was to perform his duties under the contract, and asserts his rights there.

The contract contains a provision that in case of any dispute the parties will submit the matter to arbitration under New York law by the American Arbitration Association, whose determination "shall be final and absolute." After the case had been removed to the District Court, respondent moved for a stay of the proceedings so that the controversy could go to arbitration in New York. The motion alleged that the law of New York governs the question whether the arbitration provision of the contract is binding.

The District Court rules that under Erie R. Co. v. Tompkins, 304 U.S. 64, the arbitration provision of the contract was governed by Vermont law and that the law of Vermont makes revocable an agreement to arbitrate at any time before an award is actually made. The District Court therefore denied the stay, 122 F. Supp. 733. The Court of Appeals reversed, 218 F.2d 948. The case is here on a petition for certiorari which we granted, 349 U.S. 943, because of the doubtful application by the Court of Appeals of Erie R. Co. v. Tompkins, *supra*.

A question under the United States Arbitration Act, 43 Stat. 883, as amended, 61 Stat. 669,

9 U.S.C. §§ 1–3, lies at the threshold of the case. Section 2 of that Act makes "valid, irrevocable, and enforceable" provisions for arbitration in certain classes of contracts ; and § 3 provides for a stay of actions in the federal courts of issues referable to arbitration under those contracts. Section 2 makes "valid, irrevocable, and enforceable" only two types of contracts : those relating to a maritime transaction and those involving commerce. No maritime transaction is involved here. Nor does this contract evidence "a transaction involving commerce" within the meaning of § 2 of the Act. There is no showing that petitioner while performing his duties under the employment contract was working "in" commerce, was producing goods for commerce, or was engaging in activity that affected commerce, within the meaning of our decisions.

The Court of Appeals went on to hold that in any event § 3 of the Act stands on its own footing. It concluded that while § 2 makes enforceable arbitration agreements in martime transactions and in transactions involving commerce, § 3 covers all arbitration agreements even though they do not involve maritime transactions or transactions in commerce. We disagree with that reading of the Act. Sections 1, 2, and 3 are integral parts of a whole. To be sure, § 3 does not repeat the words "maritime transaction" or "transaction involving commerce," used in §§ 1 and 2. But §§ 1 and 2 define the field in which Congress was legislating. Since § 3 is a part of the regulatory scheme, we can only assume that the "agreement in writing" for arbitration referred to in § 3 is the kind of agreement which §§ 1 and 2 have brought under federal regulation. There is no intimation or suggestion in the Committee Reports that §§ 1 and 2 cover a narrower field than § 3. On the contrary, S. Rep. No. 536, 68th Cong., 1st Sess., p. 2, states that § 1 defines the contracts to which "the bill will be applicable." And H. R. Rep. No. 96, 68th Cong., 1st Sess., p. 1, states that one foundation of the new regulating measure is "the Federal control over interstate commerce and over admiralty." If respondent's contention is correct, a constitutional question might be presented. Erie R. Co. v. Tompkins indicated that Congress does not have the constitutional authority to make the law that is applicable to controversies in diversity of citizenship cases. Shanferoke Coal & Supply Corp. v. Westchester Service Corp., 293 U.S. 449, applied the Federal Act in a diversity case. But that decision antedated Erie R. Co. v. Tompkins ; and the Court did not consider the larger question presented here—that is, whether arbitration touched on substantive rights, which Erie R. Co. v. Tompkins held were governed by

local law, or was a mere form of procedure within the power of the federal courts or Congress to prescribe. Our view, as will be developed, is that § 3, so read, would invade the local law field. We therefore read § 3 narrowly to avoid that issue. Federal Trade Commission v. American Tobacco Co., 264 U.S. 298, 307. We conclude that the stay provided in § 3 reaches only those contracts covered by §§ 1 and 2.

The question remains whether, apart from the Federal Act, a provision of a contract providing for arbitration is enforceable in a diversity case.

The Court of Appeals, in disagreeing with the District Court as to the effect of an arbitration agreement under Erie R. Co. v. Tompkins, followed its earlier decision of Murray Oil Products Co. v. Mitsui & Co., 146 F. 2d 381, 383, which held that, "Arbitration is merely a form of trial, to be adopted in the action itself, in place of the trial at common law: it is like a reference to a master, or an 'advisory trial' under Federal Rules of Civil Procedure...."

We disagree with that conclusion. We deal here with a right to recover that owes its existence to one of the States, not to the United States. The federal court enforces the state-created right by rules of procedure which it has acquired from the Federal Government and which therefore are not identical with those of the state courts. Yet, in spite of that difference in procedure, the federal court enforcing a state-created right in a diversity case is, as we said in Guaranty Trust Co. v. York, 326 U.S. 99, 108, in substance "only another court of the State." The federal court therefore may not "substantially affect the enforcement of the right as given by the State." Id., 109. If the federal court allows arbitration where the state court would disallow it, the outcome of litigation might depend on the courthouse where suit is brought. For the remedy by arbitration, whatever its merits or shortcomings, substantially affects the cause of action created by the State. The nature of the tribunal where suits are tried is an important part of the parcel of rights behind a cause of action. The change from a court of law to an arbitration panel may make a radical difference in ultimate result. Arbitration carries no right to trial by jury that is guaranteed both by the Seventh Amendment and by Ch. 1, Art. 12th, of the Vermont Constitution. Arbitrators do not have the benefit of judicial instruction on the law ; they need not give their reasons for their results ; the record of their proceedings is not as complete as it is in a court trial ; and judicial review of an award is more limited than judicial review of a trial—all as discussed in

Wilko v. Swan, 346 U.S. 427, 435–438. We said in the *York* case that

> The nub of the policy that underlies Erie R. Co. v. Tompkins is that for the same transaction the accident of a suit by a non-resident litigant in a federal court instead of in a State court a block away should not lead to a substantially different result.

326 U.S., at 109. There would in our judgment be a resultant discrimination if the parties suing on a Vermont cause of action in the federal court were remitted to arbitration, while those suing in the Vermont court could not be.

The District Court found that if the parties were in a Vermont court, the agreement to submit to arbitration would not be binding and could be revoked at any time before an award was made. He gave as his authority Mead's Admx. v. Owen, 83 Vt. 132, 135, 74 A. 1058, 1059, and Sartwell v. Sowles, 72 Vt. 270, 277, 48 A. 11, 14, decided by the Supreme Court of Vermont. In the *Owen* case the court, in speaking of an agreement to arbitrate, held that "either party may revoke the submission at any time before the publication of an award." 83 Vt., at 135, 74 A., at 1059. That case was decided in 1910. But it was agreed on oral argument that there is no later authority from the Vermont courts, that no fracture in the rules announced in those cases has appeared in subsequent rulings or dicta, and that no legislative movement is under way in Vermont to change the result of those cases. Since the federal judge making those findings is from the Vermont bar, we give special weight to his statement of what the Vermont law is. See MacGregor v. State Mutual Co., 315 U.S. 280 ; Hillsborough v. Cromwell, 326 U.S. 620, 630 ; Steele v. General Mills, 329 U.S. 433, 439. We agree with him that if arbitration could not be compelled in the Vermont courts, it should not be compelled in the Federal District Court. Were the question in doubt or deserving further canvass, we would of course remand the case to the Court of Appeals to pass on this question of Vermont law. But, as we have indicated, there appears to be no confusion in the Vermont decisions, no developing line of authorities that casts a shadow over the established ones, no dicta, doubts or ambiguities in the opinions of Vermont judges on the question, no legislative development that promises to undermine the judicial rule. We see no reason, therefore, to remand the case to the Court of Appeals to pass on this question of local law.

Respondent argues that since the contract was made in New York and the parties contracted for arbitration under New York law, New York arbitration law should be applied to the enforcement of the contract. A question of conflict of laws is tendered, a question that is also governed by Vermont law. See Klaxon C. v. Stentor Co., 313 U.S. 487. It is not clear to some of us that the District Court ruled on that question. We mention it explicitly so that it will be open for consideration on remand of the cause to the District Court.

The judgment of the Court of Appeals is reversed and the cause is remanded to the District Court for proceedings in conformity with this opinion.

Reversed and remanded.

MR. JUSTICE FRANKFURTER, concurring.

It is my view that the judgment of the Court of Appeals should be reversed and the case remanded to that court and not to the District Court.

This action was brought in the Bennington County Court of the State of Vermont by petitioner, a citizen of Vermont, against respondent, a corporation of the State of New York. Respondent removed the case to the United States District Court for the District of Vermont. The subject matter of the litigation is a contract made between the parties in New York, and the sole basis of the jurisdiction of the District Court is diversity of citizenship. Not only was the contract made in New York, but the parties agreed to the following provision in it:

> Fourteenth: The parties hereto do hereby stipulate and agree that it is their intention and covenant that this agreement and performance hereunder and all suits and special proceedings hereunder be construed in accordance with and under and pursuant to the laws of the State of New York and that in any action special proceeding or other proceeding that may be brought arising out of, in connection with or by reason of this agreement, the laws of the State of New York shall be applicable and shall govern to the exclusion of the law of any other forum, without regard to the jurisdiction in which any action or special proceeding may be instituted.

Respondent invoked another provision of the contract whereby disputes under the agreement were to be submitted to arbitration subject to the regulations of the American Arbitration Association and the pertinent provisions of the New York Arbitration Act. It did so by a motion to stay the proceeding in the District Court pending arbitration.

The District Court denied the stay because, on its reading of the Vermont cases, Vermont law, while recognizing the binding force of such an agreement by way of a suit for damages does not allow specific performance or a stay pending arbitration. It rested on a decision rendered by the Supreme Court of Vermont in a bill for an accounting evidently between two Vermonters and relating wholly to a Vermont transaction, *i.e.,* a controversy about personal property on a Vermont farm. Mead's Admx. v. Owen, 83 Vt. 132, 74 A. 1058. This case was decided in 1910 and, in turn, relied on Aspinwall v. Tousey, 2 Tyler (Vt.) 328, decided in 1803, authorizing revocation of a submission to arbitration at any time before the publication of an award.

The Court of Appeals found it unnecessary to consider what the Vermont law was today, for it held that the arbitration provision did not concern a matter of "substantive" law, for which in this diversity case, Vermont law would be controlling on the United States District Court sitting in Vermont. It held that the arbitration provision fell within the law of "procedure" governing an action in the federal court, whatever the source of the jurisdiction. So holding, the Court of Appeals found § 3 of the United States Arbitration Act, 9 U.S.C. § 3, applicable and, accordingly, directed the District Court to heed that Act and allow the matter to go to arbitration. 218 F. 2d 948.

This Court explained in Guaranty Trust Co. v. York, 326 U.S. 99, why the categories of "substance" and "procedure" are, in relation to the application of the doctrine of Erie R. Co. v. Tompkins, 304 U.S. 64, less than self-defining. They are delusive. The intrinsic content of what is thought to be conveyed by those terms in the particular context of a particular litigation becomes the essential inquiry. This mode of approaching the problem has had several applications since the *York* decision. I agree with the Court's opinion that the differences between arbitral and judicial determination of a controversy under a contract sufficiently go to the merits of the outcome, and not merely because of the contingencies of different individuals passing on the same question, to make the matter one of "substance" in the sense relevant for Erie R. Co. v. Tompkins. In view of the ground that was taken in that case for its decision, it would raise a serious question of constitutional law whether Congress could subject to arbitration litigation in the federal courts which is there solely because it is "between Citizens of different States," U.S. Const., Art. III, § 2, in disregard of the law of the State in which a federal court is sitting. Since the United States Arbitration Act of 1925 does not obviously apply to diversity cases, in the light of its terms and the relevant interpretive materials, avoidance of the constitutional question is for me sufficiently compelling to lead to a construction of the Act

as not applicable to diversity cases.[1] Of course this implies no opinion on the constitutional question that would be presented were Congress specifically to make the Arbitration Act applicable in such cases. Furthermore, because the Act is not here applicable, I abstain from any consideration of the scope of its provisions in cases which are in federal courts on a jurisdictional basis other than diversity of citizenship.

Vermont law regarding such an arbitration agreement as the one before us, therefore, becomes decisive of the litigation. But what is Vermont law? One of the difficulties, of course, resulting from Erie R. Co. v. Tompkins, is that it is not always easy and sometimes difficult to ascertain what the governing state law is. The essence of the doctrine of that case is that the difficulties of ascertaining state law are fraught with less mischief than disregard of the basic nature of diversity jurisdiction, namely, the enforcement of state-created rights and state policies going to the heart of those rights. If Judge Gibson's statement of what is the contemporary Vermont law relevant to the arbitration provision now before him were determinative, that would be that. But the defendant is entitled to have the view of the Court of Appeals on Vermont law and cannot, under the Act of Congress, be foreclosed by the District Court's interpretation.

As long as there is diversity jurisdiction, "estimates" are necessarily often all that federal courts can make in ascertaining what the state court would rule to be its law. See Pomerantz v. Clark, 101 F. Supp. 341. This Court ought not to by-pass the Court of Appeals on an issue which, if the Court of Appeals had made a different estimate from the District Court's, of contemporaneous Vermont law regarding such a contract as the one before us, this Court, one can confidently say, would not have set its view of Vermont law against that of the Court of Appeals. For the mere fact that Vermont in 1910 restated its old law against denying equitable relief for breach of a promise to arbitrate a contract made under such Vermont law, is hardly a conclusive ground for attributing to the Vermont Supreme Court application of this equitable doctrine in 1956 to a contract made in New York with explicit agreement by the parties that the law of New York which allows such a stay as was here sought, New York Civil

---

1. Shanferoke Coal & Supply Corp. v. Westchester Service Corp., 293 U.S. 449, was a diversity case wherein § 3 of the Arbitration Act was applied. But the case was pre-Erie, and the Court's attention was not directed toward the question.

Practice Act, § 1451, should govern. *Cf.* Brown v. Perry, 104 Vt. 66, 156 A. 910. Law does change with times and circumstances, and not merely through legislative reforms.[2] It is also to be noted that law is not restricted to what is found in Law Reports, or otherwise written. See Nashville, C. & St. L. R. Co. v. Browning, 310 U.S. 362, 369. The Supreme Court of Vermont last spoke on this matter in 1910. The doctrine that it referred to was not a peculiar indigenous Vermont rule. The attitude reflected by that decision nearly half a century ago was the current traditional judicial hostility against ousting courts, as the phrase ran, of their jurisdiction. See the adverse comments of Judge Hough in United States Asphalt Refining Co. v. Trinidad Lake Petroleum Co., Ltd., 222 F. 1006, against what he assumed to be the law in the federal courts, and compare with the shift in judicial attitude reflected by the reservation of this question in Mr. Justice Brandeis' opinion for the Court in Red Cross Line v. Atlantic Fruit Co., 264 U.S. 109. To be sure, a vigorous legislative movement got under way in the 1920's expressive of a broadened outlook of view on this subject. But courts do not always wait for legislation to find a judicial doctrine outmoded. Only last Term, although we had no statute governing an adjudication, we found significance in a relevant body of enactments elsewhere: "A steady legislative trend, presumably manifesting a strong social policy, properly makes demands on the judicial process." National City Bank of New York v. Republic of China, 348 U.S. 356, 360.

Surely in the light of all that has happened since 1910 in the general field of the law of arbitration, it is not for us to assume that the Court of Appeals, if it had that question for consideration, could not have found that the law of Vermont today does not require disregard of a provision of a contract made in New York, with a purposeful desire to have the law of New York govern, to accomplish a result that today may be deemed to be a general doctrine of the law. Of course if the Court of Appeals versed in the general jurisprudence of Vermont and having among its members a Vermont lawyer should find that the Vermont court would despite the New York incidents of the contract apply Vermont law and that it is the habit of the Vermont court to adhere to its precedents and to leave changes to the legislature it would not be for the federal court to

gainsay that policy. I am not suggesting what the Court of Appeals' answer to these questions would be still less what it should be. I do maintain that the defendant does have the right to have the judgment of the Court of Appeals on that question and that it is not for us to deny him that right.

I would remand the case to the Court of Appeals for its determination of Vermont law on matters which the basis of its decision heretofore rendered it needless to consider.

MR. JUSTICE HARLAN concurring.

I concur in the opinion of the Court except insofar as it undertakes to review and affirm the District Court's interpretation of Vermont law. I agree with Mr. Justice Frankfurter that the review of questions of state law should ordinarily be left to the Courts of Appeals and would remand the case to the Court of Appeals for that purpose.

Mr. Justice Burton dissenting.

Whether or not § 3 of the Federal Arbitration Act is applicable to this contract the judgment of the Court of Appeals should be affirmed.

Assuming the validity of the arbitration clause in the New York contract here involved I regard the procedure which it prescribes as a permissible "form of trial." See Murray Oil Products Co. v. Mitsui & Co., 146 F. 2d 381. Accordingly, the United States District Court for the District of Vermont may stay its own proceedings to await completion of the arbitration proceedings, although a state court of Vermont would not do likewise. I do not interpret Erie R. Co. v. Tompkins, 304 U.S. 64, or Guaranty Trust Co. v. York, 326 U.S. 99, as requiring the contrary.

ROBERT LAWRENCE CO., v. DEVONSHIRE FABRICS, INC.
271 F. 2d 402 (2d Cir. 1959)
[cert. granted 362 U.S. 909; appeal dismissed per stipulation, 364 U.S. 801 (1960)]

MEDINA, CIRCUIT JUDGE.

Devonshire Fabrics, Inc. (Devonshire) appeals from an order denying its motion for a stay of proceedings pending arbitration pursuant to the United States Arbitration Act, 9 U.S.C. Section 3.

Plaintiff in this action, Robert Lawrence Company, Inc. (Lawrence) is seeking damages for allegedly fraudulent misrepresentations made by Devonshire inducing it to purchase and pay for a quantity of woolen fabric. The transaction

---

2. The Vermont Supreme Court does not obstinately adhere to its past decisions [citations omitted].

out of which this case arose was initiated on August 4, 1955 when Lawrence, a Massachusetts corporation, ordered through its New York City office 36 pieces of a certain style of wool. Devonshire, a New York corporation, upon receipt of the order issued a confirmation which differed in several respects from the terms of the order. While the parties disagree as to which document embodies the final contract, each of the two documents contains the following provision for arbitration:

> Any complaint, controversy, or question which may arise with respect to this contract that cannot be settled by the parties thereto, shall be referred to arbitration. If the controversy concerns the condition or quality of merchanidise it shall be referred to the Mutual Adjustment Bureau of the cloth and garment trades pursuant to the rules and regulations thereof. All other controversies shall be submitted to the American Arbitration Association.

Delivery of the goods, originally scheduled for October 1, 1955 was postponed at Lawrence's request until June 1956 when shipment to Boston was made. Lawrence paid the purchase price of $9,062.43 in July 1956. According to Lawrence, whose version of the fraud we must accept in the present posture of the case, certain latent defects were subsequently discovered and the merchandise proved not to be "first quality" as called for by the agreement. It is disputed whether Lawrence "rescinded" the contract or whether it waived its right to do so by later inconsistent acts.

The court below denied the stay of proceedings pending arbitration and held: "The question whether or not there is a valid agreement to arbitrate must be decided by the court prior to the issuance of a stay and cannot be submitted to arbitration 'as a controversy thereafter arising out of such contract' within section 2. ... If the contract was fraudulent in its inception and therefore voidable at the option of the plaintiff and plaintiff has disaffirmed such contract, then there is no valid agreement to arbitrate which would justify a stay."

I. Questions of the Validity and Interpretation of an Arbitration Agreement "In Any Maritime Transaction or a Contract ... Involving Commerce" Are Governed by Federal Not by Local Law

The case involves questions left open by the Supreme Court in Bernhardt v. Polygraphic Co. of America, Inc., 1956, 350 U.S. 198, and these questions are interesting and important. The basic inquiry must be whether the validity and interpretation of the arbitration clause of the contract in this case is governed by Federal law, *i.e.* the Federal Arbitration Act, or by local law. But this critical issue is imbedded in a proliferation of collateral questions, and all must be considered against the background of the concurring opinion of Mr. Justice Frankfurter in *Bernhardt* to the effect that, in order to avoid vexing constitutional questions under Erie R.R. v. Tompkins, 1938, 304 U.S. 64, the Arbitration Act must be held wholly inapplicable in a diversity case. We are reluctant to disagree with so eminent a jurist whose views are so widely respected but feel compelled to reach a different conclusion, not only because the exclusion of diversity cases would emasculate the federal Arbitration Act, but because we find a reasonably clear legislative intent to create a new body of substantive law relative to arbitration agreements affecting commerce or maritime transactions. Thus we think we are here dealing not with state-created rights but with rights arising out of the exercise by the Congress of its constitutional power to regulate commerce and hence there is involved no difficult question of constitutional law under *Erie*.

The arbitration agreement before the Court in *Bernhardt* did not involve commerce nor did it affect a maritime transaction. But the defendant in that case moved for a stay pending arbitration on the theory that the federal Arbitration Act was applicable because the limitations of Section 2 were said not to affect Section 3, and, even if the Act was not applicable, that arbitration was a mere mode of procedure and a federal court should follow its own practice rather than that of Vermont because in matters of procedure the law of the forum controls. This reasoning would have by-passed certain old Vermont cases holding arbitration agrements to be revocable prior to the making of an award and unenforceable. But such a result ran into *Erie v. Tompkins* head-on for the obvious reason that, had the case not been removed from the Vermont state court by reason of the diversity of citizenship of the parties, the determination of the merits of the controversy between the parties in the federal court might well have been just the opposite to the one that would have been reached had the case been permitted to remain in the state court. So the Court decided the case by holding: (1) that the federal Arbitration Act was inapplicable because the limitation to commerce and maritime matters in Section 2 applied as well to Section 3 and the rest of the Act; and, (2) that the enforceability of an arbitration agreement, apart from the Arbitration Act, "substantially affects the cause of action created by the State" and, because the dispute between the litigants was sufficiently substantive to bring into operation the *Erie* doctrine, the Court refused to apply the rule that the law of the forum governs matters of procedure. The Court flatly disagreed with the statement that arbitration "is merely a form of trial." Instead, the Court held that it was dealing with "a right to recover that owes its existence to one of the States, not to the United States"; and the view of the federal District Judge in Vermont as to the Vermont law relative to the enforceability of arbitration agreements was adopted. This conclusion was reached notwithstanding the fact that in several other contexts the enforceability of an arbitration agreement had generally been considered to be procedural only.[1] But the constitutional difficulties Justice Frankfurter feared only become operative if the Arbitration Act is regarded as exclusively procedural in character and scope. And, if the Congress had relied solely on its power to regulate procedure in the federal courts to make arbitration agreements valid and enforceable, it might well be doubted whether the constitutional base provided adequate support for the legislative structure. But see STURGES AND MURPHY, SOME CONFUSING MATTERS RELATING TO ARBITRATION UNDER THE UNITED STATES ARBI-

TRATION ACT, 17 LAW & CONTEMP. PROBS. 580, 587 (1952).

We think it is reasonably clear that the Congress intended by the Arbitration Act to create a new body of federal substantive law affecting the validity and interpretation of arbitration agreements. In the first place Section 2 of the Arbitration Act specifically limits its applicability to "any maritime transaction or a contract evidencing a transaction involving commerce." This indicates a congressional intention to rely on the admiralty power implied from Article III, Clause 2 and the commerce power, Article I, Section 8, Clause 3. Such intention is confirmed by the legislative history. See H. R. Rep. 96, 68th Cong., 1st Sess., p. 1 (1924). Moreover, the *Bernhardt* ruling is specifically to the effect that the maritime or commerce requirements had to be met before any other section of the Act could be applied. It is true that an additional reason for construing the Act "narrowly" was that such a construction avoided a constitutional difficulty arising out of the *Erie* doctrine; but we think this does not lessen the force of the principal basis for the ruling which is that the Congress intended the maritime or commerce requirements to permeate the Act in its entirety.

It is also clear that the Congress intended to exercise as much of its constitutional power as it could in order to make the new Arbitration Act as widely effective as possible. One of the dark chapters in legal history concerns the validity, interpretation and enforceability of arbitration agreements. From the standpoint of business men generally and of those immediately affected by such agreements they were beneficial and salutary in every way. But to the courts and to the judges they were anathema. In England and in America the courts resorted to a great variety of devices and formulas to destroy this encroachment on their monopoly of the administration of justice, protecting what they called their "jurisdiction." An attempt to enumerate the ways in which arbitration agreements were declared to be against public policy and void, or revocable or unenforceable would now serve no useful purpose. See Kulukundis Shipping Co., S/A v. Amtorg Trading Corp., 2 Cir., 1942, 126 F. 2d 978, 982. Suffice it to say for a considerable time prior to the passage of the Arbitration Act in 1925[2] the Congress had come to the conclusion that an effort should be made to legislate on the subject of arbitration

---

1. For choice of law purposes it has been generally held that the forum is free to apply its own "remedy" and is not compelled to enforce an arbitration agreement by applying the law of the State with the controlling contracts. See Meacham v. Jamestown Franklin & Clearfield Ry., 1914, 211 N.Y. 346, 105 N.E. 653; Gantt v. Felipe Y Carlos Hurtado & Cia, Ltda, 1948, 297 N.Y. 433, 79 N.E. 2d 815; Vitaphone Corp. v. Electrical Research Products, 1933, 19 Del. Ch. 247, 166 Atl. 255. For the purpose of determining whether a state act enforcing arbitration is constitutional or an intrusion upon federal admiralty jurisdiction, the Supreme Court held arbitration to be "remedial." Red Cross Line v. Atlantic Fruit Co., 1924, 264 U.S. 109. A similar characterization was also made to determine if the New York Act could constitutionally apply retroactively. Matter of Berkovitz v. Arbib & Houlberg, 1921, 230 N.Y. 261, 130 N.E. 288. In pre-*Erie* diversity cases the enforcement of an arbitration agreement was deemed "procedural" and state statutes upholding the agreements were accordingly held inapplicable. California Prune & Apricot Growers' Ass'n v. Catz American Co., 9 Cir., 1932, 60 F. 2d 788; Lappe v. Wilcox, N.D. N.Y., 1926, 14 F. 2d 861. And the federal judicial power in admiralty was deemed not to have been unduly extended by the new enforcement provisions of the Act but was a valid exercise of congressional power "to provide remedies in matters falling within the admiralty jurisdiction of the federal courts, and to regulate their procedure." Marine Transit Corp. v. Dreyfus, 1932, 284 Y.S. 263. Indeed, even in the *Erie* context to *Bernhardt* the dominant view was that the enforceability of arbitration agreements was procedural. Compare Murray Oil Products Co. v. Mitsui & Co., 2 Cir., 1944, 146 F. 2d 381; Parry v. Bache, 5 Cir., 1942, 125 F. 2d 493; Pioneer Trust & Savings Bank v. Screw Mach. Products Co., E. D. Wis., 1947, 73 F. Supp. 578 with Tejas Development Co. v. McGough Bros., 5 Cir., 1947, 165 F. 2d 276.

---

2. The federal Arbitration Act, Title 9 of the United States Code, was first enacted in 1925, 43 Stat. 883. It was repealed and substantially reenacted in codified form in 1947, 61 Stat. 669.

in such fashion as to remove the hostility of the judiciary and make the benefits of arbitration generally available to the business world. See Sen. Rep. 536 *supra*. At that time and even today, in various states judge-made law still stands as an obstacle to the enforceability of arbitration agreements, as was illustrated in *Bernhardt*. It was not assumed that this hostility could be easily overcome, despite certain encouragement in the ranks of those in opposition. See Red Cross Line v. Atlantic Fruit Co., 1924, 264 U.S. 109; Atlantic Fruit Co. v. Red Cross Line, S.D.N.Y., 1921, 276 Fed. 319, affirmed, 2 Cir., 1924, 5 F. 2d 218; United States Asphalt Refining Co. v. Trinidad Lake Petroleum Co., S.D.N.Y., 1915, 222 Fed. 1006. Hence the Congress took pains to utilize as much of its power as it could and by doing so it sought to reduce to a minimum the danger of judicial rejection on constitutional grounds.

Thus we think the text of the Act and the legislative history demonstrate that the Congress based the Arbitration Act in part on its undisputed substantive powers over commerce and maritime matters. To be sure much of the Act is purely procedural in character and is intended to be applicable only in the federal courts. But Section 2 declaring that arbitration agreements affecting commerce or maritime affairs are "valid, irrevocable, and enforceable" goes beyond this point and must mean that arbitration agreements of this character, previously held by state law to be invalid, revocable or unenforceable are now made "valid, irrevocable, and enforceable." This is a declaration of national law equally applicable in state or federal courts. See Kochery, *The Enforcement of Arbitration Agreements in the Federal Courts. Erie v. Tompkins,* 39 CORN. L. Q. 74, 78 (1953). This conclusion flows directly from the realization by the Congress that nothing of significance would have been accomplished without tapping these substantive sources of power. It is these that put teeth into the statute and make it accomplish the salutary and beneficial ends the Congress had in mind. It matters not that in the interval of years since the passage of the Act this point has only rarely been noticed. See Standard Magnesium Corp. v. Fuchs, 10 Cir., 1957, 251 F. 2d 455; Kentucky River Mills v. Jackson, 6 Cir., 1953, 206 F. 2d 111, 117–18, cert. denied, 346 U.S. 887. What does matter is whether or not this reasoning is sound. And we believe it to be sound if the Congress intended to use to the fullest possible extent its powers to regulate commerce as it was affected by arbitration agreements and to do the same thing in the field of maritime law.

Nor do we think there is any tenable distinction between the holding in *Bernhardt* that the enforceability of an arbitration agreement is sufficiently substantive to call into play the *Erie* doctrine and our holding in this case that the questions of the validity and interpretation of the arbitration agreement before us are substantive questions. In any event, it seems safe to say that those who drafted the Arbitration Act and supervised its progress through the House and Senate Committees had not the least suspicion that there might at some future day be raised the constitutional question referred to in Mr. Justice Frankfurter's concurring opinion in *Bernhardt*, the avoidance of which led him to the view that the Arbitration Act was wholly inapplicable to cases where the jurisdiction of the federal court was based on diversity of citizenship. *Erie* still was hidden in the mist of the future.

Mere catchwords, labels and cliches no longer smooth the path of justice as they so often did in the past. As noted above, arbitration has often been described as pertaining to the law of remedies, but this tendency is losing much of its fascination in these modern times. See Ross v. Twentieth Century-Fox Film Corp. 9 Cir. 1956, 236 F. 2d 632; Jackson v. Atlantic City Electric Co., D. N. J., 1956, 144 F. Supp. 551; Miller v. American Insurance Co., W. D. Ark., 1954, 124 F. Supp. 160; Kochery, *The Enforcement of Arbitration Agreements in the Federal Courts; Erie v. Tompkins, supra;* Note, 56 COLUM. L. REV. 902 (1956); 41 VA. L. REV. 379 (1955); Comment 27 TEX. L. REV. 218 (1948). The opinion of Mr. Justice Douglas in *Bernhardt* summarizes nicely the manifold effects of such agreements. We need not belabor them here. The crucial point is that the "nature of the tribunal where suits are tried is an important part of the parcel of rights behind a cause of action." See 350 U.S. at 203. Whether the bargain evidenced by the contract or agreement is or is not valid cannot differ essentially from the question of whether any other meeting of the minds of the parties will be recognized as having created certain rights. And the same may be said of the rules or principles to be evolved in connection with the construction and interpretation of the agreement.

It is interesting to note that though new substantive federal rights were created, suits involving the application of the Arbitration Act do not furnish an independent basis of federal jurisdiction under 28 U.S.C. Section 1331. Krauss Bros. Lumber Co. v. Louis Bossert & Sons, Inc., 2 Cir., 1933, 62 F. 2d 1004; In re Woerner, 2 Cir., 1929, 31 F. 2d 283; Mengel Co. v. Nashville Paper Products and Specialty Workers Union, 6 Cir., 1955, 221 F. 2d 644. But see Local 19, Warehouse Union v. Buckeye Cotton Oil Co., 6 Cir., 1956, 236 F. 2d 776, 781, cert. denied, 1957, 354 U.S. 910. This is evident upon consideration of the Act as a whole as the Congress under its Article III powers sought to prevent the federal courts from becoming unduly snarled by this far-reaching law. Section 4 relating to the filing of a petition to compel arbitration provides for such filing only in "any court of the United States which, save for such agreement, would have jurisdiction under the judicial code at law, in equity, or in admiralty of the subject matter of a suit arising out of the controversy between the parties." And proceedings on motion for a stay pursuant to Section 3 are authorized only in "the court in which ... suit is pending," which must mean a suit in which the court already has jurisdiction over subject matter. Section 8 also seems to presuppose a basis of jurisdiction other than the Arbitration Act. The explicitness with which the Congress indicated that the assertion or denial of a right arising under the Act is not sufficient to give the federal court jurisdiction over subject matter constitutes further proof that something more than mere "procedural" rules were intended. For if the Act were entirely "procedural" in character, it plainly could not furnish a basis of federal jurisdiction.

While the jurisdiction under either Section 3 or Section 4 may doubtless in some instances be federal question jurisdiction, based upon rights alleged to arise out of some federal statute other than the Arbitration Act, it would seem that the most numerous class of cases in which it was anticipated that resort would be made to the federal courts for the enforcement of arbitration agreements was diversity cases.

We, therefore, hold that the Arbitration Act in making agreements to arbitrate "valid, irrevocable and enforceable" created national substantive law clearly constitutional under the maritime and commerce powers of the Congress and that the rights thus created are to be adjudicated by the federal courts whenever such courts have subject matter jurisdiction, including diversity cases, just as the federal courts adjudicate controversies affecting other substantive rights when subject matter jurisdiction over the litigation exists.[3] We hold that the body of law

thus created is substantive not procedural in character and that it encompasses questions of interpretation and construction as well as questions of validity, revocability and enforceability of arbitration agreements affecting interstate commerce or maritime affairs, since these two types of legal questions are inextricably intertwined.

In the case before us there can be little doubt that the transaction in question relates to an interstate shipment of goods and involves "commerce" within the meaning of Sections 1 and 2.[4] Kentucky River Mills v. Jackson, 6 Cir., 1953, 206 F. 2d 111, cert. denied, 346 U.S. 887; Petition of Prouvost Lefebvre, S. D. N.Y., 1952, 105 F. Supp. 757; Wilson & Co. v. Fremont Cake & Meal Co., D. Neb., 1948, 77 F. Supp. 364, affirmed, 8 Cir., 1950, 183 F. 2d 57. We, therefore, find federal law as derived from the Arbitration Act to be controlling.

II. Formulation and Application of Substantive Rules Governing Arbitration Agreements Involving Commerce

We now turn to the decision of this case and the formulation of the principles of federal substantive law necessary for this purpose.

The District Court held that there could be no finding of an "agreement to arbitrate" until it was judicially resolved whether or not there was fraud in the inception of the contract as alleged by Lawrence. But surely this is oversimplification of the problem. For example, it would seem to be necessary to answer the following questions before we can decide to affirm or reverse the order appealed from: (1) is there anything in the Arbitration Act or elsewhere to prevent the parties from making a binding agreement to arbitrate any disputes thereafter arising between them, including a dispute that there had been fraud in the inception of the contract; (2) is the exception of Section 2, "save upon such grounds as exist at law or in equity for the revocation of any contract" applicable if such an agreement to arbitrate has been made and the only fraud charged is fraud in inducing the purchase of the goods, rather than fraud in connection with the making of the agreement to arbitrate; (3) did the parties in the case before us make a binding agreement to arbitrate; and (4) is the arbitration clause broad enough to cover the charge of fraud.

That the Arbitration Act envisages a distinc-

---

3. We think the court in Ross v. Twentieth Century-Fox Film Corporation, 9 Cir., 1956, 236 F. 2d 632, misconstrued *Bernhardt* when it held that the contract in that case, which involved commerce, was required by the *Bernhardt* reasoning to be interpreted according to California law.

---

4. Section 1 of the Act provides in part:
" 'commerce,' as herein defined, means commerce among several States or with foreign nations, . . .

tion between the entire contract between the parties on the one hand and the arbitration clause of the contract on the other is plain on the face of the statute. Section 2 does not purport to affect the contract as a whole. On the contrary, it makes "valid, irrevocable, and enforceable" only a "written provision in any maritime transaction or a contract evidencing a transaction involving commerce to settle by arbitration a controversy thereafter arising out of such contract or transaction"; and Section 3 provides for the granting of a stay in any suit or proceeding in the federal courts "upon an issue referable to arbitration under an agreement in writing for such arbitration."

Our construction of Section 2 treating the agreement to arbitrate as a separable part of the contract is based not only upon the clear wording of the text but is buttressed by several other pertinent considerations. Historically arbitration clauses were treated as separable parts of the contract, although such treatment generally meant the agreement was being deprived of its efficacy. Hamilton v. Home Insurance Co., 1890, 137 U.S. 370; Gattliff Coal Co. v. Cox, 6 Cir., 1944, 142 F. 2d 876; United States Asphalt Refining Co. v. Trinidad Lake Petroleum Co., S.D. N.Y., 1915, 222 Fed. 1006. And since the passage of the Arbitration Act, the courts have similarly held that the illegality of part of the contract does not operate to nullify an agreement to arbitrate. Wilko v. Swan, 2 Cir., 1953, 201 F. 2d 439, reversed on other grounds, 346 U.S. 427; Watkins v. Hudson Coal Co., 3 Cir., 1945, 151 F. 2d 311, cert. denied, 327 U.S. 777; Petition of Prouvost Lefebvre, S.D. N.Y., 1952, 105 F. Supp. 757. Nor does the alleged breach or repudiation of the contract preclude the right to arbitrate. Kulukundis Shipping Co. v. Amtorg Trading Corp., 2 Cir., 1943, 126 F. 2d 978; Almacenes Fernandez, S.A. v. Golodetz, *supra,* 2 Cir., 148 F. 2d 625; In re Pahlberg Petition, 2 Cir., 1942, 131 F. 2d 968.

Finally, any doubts as to the construction of the Act ought to be resolved in line with its liberal policy of promoting arbitration both to accord with the original intention of the parties and to help ease the current congestion of court calendars. Such policy has been consistently reiterated by the federal courts and we think it deserves to be heartily endorsed. See Shanferoke Coal & Supply Corp. v. Westchester Service Corp., *supra,* 293 U.S. 449, 453; Kulukundis Shipping Co. v. Amtorg Trading Corp., *supra,* 2 Cir., 126 F. 2d 978; Signal-Stat Corp. v. Local 475, 2 Cir., 1956, 235 F. 2d 298, cert. denied, 1957, 354 U.S. 911. See also Wabash Ry. v. American Refrigerator Transit Co., 8 Cir., 1925,

7 F. 2d 335, 351, cert. denied, 1926, 270 U.S. 643.

It would seem to be beyond dispute that the parties are entitled to agree, should they desire to do so, that one of the questions for the arbitrators to decide in case the controversy thereafter arises, is whether or not one of the parties was induced by fraud to make the principal contract for the delivery of the merchandise. Surely there is no public policy that would stand as a bar to an agreement of such obvious utility, as is demonstrated by the facts of this case. The issue of fraud seems inextricably enmeshed in the other factual issues of the case. Indeed, the difference between fraud in the inducement and mere failure of performance by delivery of defective merchandise depends upon little more than legal verbiage and the formulation of legal conclusions. Once it is settled that arbitration agreements are "valid, irrevocable, and enforceable" we know of no principle of law that stands as an obstacle to a determination by the parties to the effect that arbitration should not be denied or postponed upon the mere cry of fraud in the inducement, as this would permit the frustration of the very purposes sought to be achieved by the agreement to arbitrate, *i.e.* a speedy and relatively inexpensive trial before commercial specialists.

The saving clause of Section 2 fits perfectly into the framework disclosed by the above analysis. The agreement described in Section 2 is the arbitration "provision" or clause of the principal contract. If this arbitration clause was induced by fraud, there can be no arbitration; and if the party charging this fraud shows there is substance to his charge, there must be a judicial trial of that question before a stay can issue in a case of the type with which we are now dealing. It is not enough that there is substance to the charge that the contract to deliver merchandise of a certain quality was induced by fraud.

Did the parties in the case before us make a binding agreement to arbitrate? While this narrow issue was obscured in the court below by the miscellaneous and varied contentions of the parties, we think it clear that there exist no grounds "at law or in equity" for the revocation of the arbitration clause of the contract between Lawrence and Devonshire. Indeed, there is no dispute on the point. Lawrence does not allege that the arbitration provision was induced by fraud. Nor could it do so with any show of reason as its own order contained this identical clause. What Lawrence does claim is that the entire transaction was induced by fraud and that the arbitration provision necessarily falls with the rest. This contention we reject as above stated, because the facts of this case do not support the argument.

Accordingly, there is no reason why we should not now decide this preliminary issue and we hereby find that the parties did agree upon the arbitration clause quoted in the early part of this opinion and that such agreement is valid and binding.

It may well be that such charges of fraud may in some cases postpone arbitration because there is so little to support the finding that the parties agreed to arbitrate as to make necessary a preliminary trial of the issue of alleged fraud, to be followed by another trial before the arbitrators, if there is found by the court to have been no fraud. As has been shown, this case is different. And we would suppose that generally where the arbitration provision of the contract is sufficiently broad to encompass the issue of fraud, the mutual promises to arbitrate would form the *quid pro quo* of one another and constitute a separable and enforceable part of the agreement. We do not decide this point, however, as it is not necessarily before us.

Certainly this is not a case like Kulukundis Shipping Co. v. Amtorg Trading Corp., *supra*, 2 Cir., 126 F. 2d 978, where the defendant denied ever agreeing to anything. Naturally such a question had first to be settled before arbitration could be directed. But it is remarkably similar to Almacenes Fernandez, S.A. v. Golodetz, 2 Cir., 1945, 148 F. 2d 625, where "fraud in the performance" was held to be an arbitrable question. See also Reynolds Jamaica Mines, Ltd. v. La Societe Navale Caennaise, 4 Cir., 1956, 239 F. 2d 689 ; McElwee-Courbis Construction Co. v. Rife, M. D. Pa., 1955, 133 F. Supp. 790. The issue of fraud in the procurement of the contract was evidently litigated by consent in Kentucky River Mills v. Jackson, *supra*, 6 Cir., 206 F. 2d 111, 120, cert. denied, 346 U.S. 887, but the broad dictum at page 120 would seem to indicate that the charge of fraud must in every case be judicially tried and disposed of. If this be a fair interpretation of the language of the opinion we think it too broad and we disagree with it.

In the view we take of the case before us it is immaterial that Lawrence claims to have rescinded the contract and that Devonshire disputed this claim and asserts that Lawrence by later inconsistent acts waived any right to rescind. We say there was a valid agreement to arbitrate, that all that remains is to construe the agreement and that the controversy over fraud in the inducement, whether Lawrence affirmed or disaffirmed the contract and attempted to or did rescind it, is a "complaint, controversy or question" which arose "with respect to this contract."

What is the proper construction and interpretation of the arbitration clause? Did the parties intend the arbitration proceedings to encompass a charge of fraud in the inducement to make the principal contract for delivery of the merchandise? We think it is clear that the parties did just that. It would be hard to imagine an arbitration clause having greater scope than the one before us. Certainly fraud in the inducement is a "complaint, controversy or question which may arise with respect to this contract that cannot be settled by the parties thereto." And we fail to perceive any rational basis for thinking that the issue is of such a character that only the courts can resolve it. We think that the charge of fraud in the inducement comes squarely within the phraseology of this particular agreement and that nothing short of a renascence of the old judicial hostility to arbitration could evolve a contrary ruling.

We note that were we compelled to apply New York law to the problems involved in this case, we would have been forced to arrive at a contrary conclusion. Had this not been so, we would not have given such detailed consideration to the choice of the applicable law. But the pattern and substance of New York law appear to be different than what we have found the federal law to be.

This seems to have been made clear in the 1957 decision of the New York Court of Appeals in Matter of Wrap-Vertiser Corp. (Plotnick), 3 N.Y. 2d 17, 143 N.E. 2d 366. Plotnick claimed that he had been induced to pay $6,000 when the agreement was executed "for the purchase of supplies for distribution, on the strength of misrepresentation respecting the past business of the manufacturer, respecting a patent which the manufacturer claimed to have had but did not have, and with regard to the nature of the product." The arbitration clause which provided for the arbitration of any question "as to the validity, interpretation or performance of this agreement," was held not to encompass the question of fraud in the inducement. There was a strong dissent by Judge Burke, in which Judge Fuld and Judge Foressel concurred. There was no discussion of the separability of the arbitration agreement. Perhaps the Court of Appeals would have arrived at a different result had it been construing the somewhat broader language of the arbitration clause now before us. But with all due respect to a distinguished and able court, we think the approach to the problem by the New York Court of Appeals is too narrow. This restrictive New York policy is also reflected in the opinions in several other cases. Manufacturers Chemical Co. v. Caswell, 1 Dep't, 1940, 259 App. Div. 321, 19 N.Y.S. 2d 171, appeal dismissed, 283 N.Y. 679, 28 N.E. 2d 404 ; Cheney Bros. v. Joroco Dresses, Inc., 1 Dep't, 1926, 218 App. Div. 652, 219 N.Y. Supp. 96, reversed on other grounds, 245 N.Y. 377, 157 N.E. 272 ; Reo Garment, Inc. v. Jason Corp., Sup. Ct. Spec. T., 1958, 9 Misc. 2d 521, 170 N.Y.S. 2d 412 ; Greenspan v. Greenspan, Sup. Ct., Spec. T., 1954, 129 N.Y.S. 2d 258.

III. There Was No Waiver

One more point in this fascinating case remains to be disposed of. Lawrence asserts that Devonshire has waived its right to arbitrate or was "in default in proceeding with such arbitration" under Section 3 of the Act. The complaint was filed May 9, 1957 and in its answer filed June 13, 1957 Devonshire demanded arbitration. The motion for the stay of proceedings was made almost nine months later, March 4, 1958. During this time settlement was discussed and Devonshire consented to an examination before trial of its President. Such examination was adjourned repeatedly and has not yet been taken. Lawrence also maintains it released certain information to Devonshire otherwise unavailable and that Devonshire tested the disputed goods. The delay in moving for a stay and these various intervening acts are asserted to constitute the waiver or default. Such a contention, however, is without merit under the decided cases. Devonshire has at no time acted in a manner inconsistent with its right to arbitrate. Lawrence was apprised of Devonshire's intention to arbitrate from the time the answer was filed and the intervening steps taken with a view toward settlement can in no way affect Devonshire's rights. Indeed, considerably more significant intervening steps have not been regarded as amounting to a waiver. See Farr & Co. v. Cia Intercontinental De Navegacion De Cuba, S.A., 2 Cir., 1957, 243 F. 2d 342 ; Almacenes Fernandez, S.A. v. Golodetz, *supra* ; Kulukundis Shipping Co. v. Amtorg Trading Corp., *supra* ; Reynolds Jamaica Mines Ltd. v. La Societe Navale Caennaise, *supra*. In the instances where a waiver has been found the party seeking the arbitration generally first brought up the subject only after long delay or when the trial was near at hand. American Locomotive Co. v. Chemical Research Corp., 6 Cir., 1948. 171 F. 2d 115, cert. denied, 1949, 336 U.S. 909 ; Radiator Specialty Co. v. Cannon Mills, Inc., 4 Cir., 1938, 97 F. 2d 318 ; La Nacional Plantanera, S.C.L. v. North American F. & S.S. Corp., 5 Cir., 1936, 84 F. 2d 881. The claim that Devonshire's rejection of an offer by Lawrence to arbitrate also constituted a waiver is likewise lacking in substance in view of the conditional nature of the offer.

Reversed with a direction to grant the stay.

Affidavit of Hugo M. Prince Read in Support of Motion

UNITED STATES DISTRICT COURT

SOUTHERN DISTRICT OF NEW YORK

[SAME TITLE]

STATE OF NEW YORK,
COUNTY OF NEW YORK, SS:

HUGO M. PRINCE, being duly sworn, deposes and says:

I am the President of the defendant, Devonshire Fabrics, Inc. I make this affidavit in support of a motion by the defendant to stay all proceedings in this action and for summary judgment in favor of the defendant, pursuant to Rule 56 of the Federal Rules of Civil Procedure.

The complaint alleges that on or about August 4, 1955, plaintiff ordered from defendant 37 pieces of fabric ; that defendant falsely and fraudulently represented that such goods were to be delivered ready for the needle, sponged, examined, specially finished and of first quality ; that the fabric was delivered to it in May 1956 and a total purchase price of $9,062.43 was paid by plaintiff.

Plaintiff further alleges that the representations made by defendant were false in that the goods were not ready for the needle, sponged and examined, and were not of first quality. As a result of its alleged reliance upon the representations, plaintiff claims that it was induced to order the goods, accept delivery thereof and pay over the purchase price. Plaintiff claims as its damages the sum of $25,000.

Defendant's answer admits that plaintiff ordered the fabric and that defendant delivered the same to the plaintiff who paid therefor, but otherwise denies the material allegations of the complaint.

Defendant further alleges as affirmative defenses (1) that plaintiff agreed to arbitrate any claims against defendant, and (2) that any demand for arbitration must be made within thirty (30) days after delivery of the merchandise.

The transaction out of which the action arose

was initiated on August 4, 1955. Charles Freiman, an independant salesman who carried merchandise in defendant's line, obtained an order from plaintiff for 36 pieces of defendant's fabric, style 910. The order was taken by Mr. Freiman at plaintiff's New York City office located at 200 Fifth Avenue. Robert L. Cohen signed the order on behalf of plaintiff, and a copy thereof is annexed hereto as Exhibit "1" and made a part hereof.

I acknowledged receipt of the order on behalf of defendant on August 10, 1955, and sent plaintiff a confirmation of the order of 37 pieces of fabric. The confirmation form used was that of H. M. Prince Textiles, Inc., the parent corporation to defendant, Devonshire Fabrics, Inc. I am president and a director of both corporations. Copies of my letter of August 10, 1955 and of the order confirmation designated AP # 5, are annexed hereto marked Exhibit "2" and Exhibit "3" respectively and made a part hereof.

The order confirmation, setting forth on its face the terms under which it was made, stated:

> This order is given subject to the terms herein stated and those on the reverse side hereof including arbitration which are hereby accepted by the buyer and shall become a contract only when signed and delivered by the buyer to the seller and accepted in writing by the seller, or when buyer has accepted delivery of the whole or any part of the goods herein described.

On the reverse side, the form, among other things, provided as conditions of sale that:

> 9. Any complaint, controversy, or question which may arise with respect to this contract that cannot be settled by the parties thereto, shall be referred to arbitration. If the controversy concerns the condition or quality of merchandise it shall be referred to the Mutual Adjustment Bureau of the cloth and garment trades pursuant to the rules and regulations thereof. All other controversies shall be submitted to the American Arbitration Association.

> 15. Any demand for arbitration covering any controversy or claim arising out of or relating to this contract must be made within thirty days after delivery of the merchandise.

Receipt of defendant's order confirmation AP # 5 dated August 4, 1955, was acknowledged by a representative of plaintiff. A copy of plaintiff's letter of acknowledgment, dated August 16, 1955, is annexed hereto as Exhibit "4" and made a part hereof.

The questions concerning an additional charge of 8¢ for sponging and examining raised by the last two (2) paragraphs of plaintiff's letter were clarified by defendant's salesman, Charles Freiman, in a conversation he had in New York City with Robert L. Cohen, who had placed the order for plaintiff. Plaintiff's Boston office was notified of this conversation by Mr. Freiman, a copy of his letter, dated August 19, 1955, being annexed hereto as Exhibit "5" and made a part hereof.

As indicated on the face of the order confirmation, delivery of the goods to plaintiff was supposed to be made in August, 1955. Following the making of the sale, the fabric was held at the factory of defendant's sponger, Eastern Textile Shrinkers, Inc., at 880 Broadway in the Borough of Manhattan, City of New York, subject to plaintiff's shipping instructions. No instructions having been issued by the middle of October, I wrote to plaintiff on October 14, 1955 for authority for the sponger to hold the fabric for plaintiff's account. A copy of my letter is annexed hereto as Exhibit "6" and made a part hereof.

I received no response from plaintiff and on October 27, 1955 notified plaintiff that unless instructions or a letter of authorization to the spongers was received by October 31st, the spongers would ship the fabric to plaintiff in Boston. A copy of my letter is annexed hereto as Exhibit "7" and made a part hereof.

My letter produced results and on October 31st, plaintiff telegraphed instructions to "hold our goods at Eastern Textile until further notice letter follows." In the letter which followed, a copy of which is annexed hereto as Exhibit "8" and made a part hereof, plaintiff gave as the reason for its delay, the curtailment of production in its factories in the New England area. The letter indicated that plaintiff anticipated using the cloth for the 1956 fall season instead of the 1955 season as planned. Plaintiff, at the same time, requested swatches of the cloth and these were promptly sent.

Plaintiff let the sponger retain the fabric for its account until June 1956. Upon information and belief, it was delivered to a common carrier in New York City on or about June 13, 1956 for delivery to plaintiff in Boston. Plaintiff advised defendant of its receipt of the shipment by a letter dated June 20, 1956. Plaintiff paid for the goods in July 1956.

The first indication that plaintiff had any complaint about the quality of the fabric delivered to it was made seven (7) months later. Robert L. Cohen telephoned me in December 1956 and made the claim which is now alleged in the complaint. I advised him then, and I still believe, that the claim coming at that late date was untimely and unwarranted. Plaintiff had more than six (6) months to examine and inspect the cloth and during that time had, I understand, cut and manufactured it into finished garments.

Paragraph 4 of the order confirmation expressly provided that no allowance shall be made after fifteen (15) days from receipt, nor after goods are sponged, cut or otherwise processed.

In its complaint, plaintiff relies upon the sales order it signed on August 4, 1955, Exhibit "1" annexed hereto. This order was superseded by the order confirmation dated the same day, Exhibit "2" annexed hereto. Both documents explicitly and clearly provided that any complaint, controversy, or question which may arise with respect to this contract that cannot be settled by the parties thereto, shall be referred to arbitration.

At no time prior to, or since, the commencement of this action has plaintiff demanded arbitration in accordance with the terms of the contract. For that reason alone, I believe defendant is entitled to a stay of all proceedings. Since the action was begun, the sole additional step taken after service of the pleadings was the demand by plaintiff to take my deposition upon oral examination. I have not submitted to such examination.

Moreover, my attorneys advise me that the conditions of sale printed on the order confirmation, Exhibit "2", constitute the contract governing this transaction. Under the terms of the confirmation, any demand for arbitration had to be made within thirty (30) days after delivery of the goods. No demand for arbitration having ever been made by plaintiff, much less within that time, I believe that plaintiff has waived whatever rights it may have had.

It is, therefore, respectfully requested that plaintiff be stayed from proceeding further with the claim asserted in this action and that summary judgment against plaintiff be granted to the defendant.

HUGO M. PRINCE

(Sworn to March 3, 1958.)

Affidavit of Robert L. Cohen Read in Opposition to Motion

UNITED STATES DISTRICT COURT

SOUTHERN DISTRICT OF NEW YORK

[SAME TITLE]

STATE OF NEW YORK,
COUNTY OF NEW YORK, ss.:

ROBERT L. COHEN, being duly sworn, deposes and says:

I am the President of the plaintiff corporation and make this affidavit in opposition to the motion by defendant to stay all proceedings in this action until all the issues raised herein have been submitted to arbitration.

The basis of the complaint is fraud and misrepresentation on the part of defendant in inducing me to enter into a contract to purchase blended fabric then in existence from the defendant. The relationship between my company and Mr. Prince's was established through fraud and misrepresentation, and the complaint with respect thereto refers to misrepresentations all made prior to the signing of the order by me.

Significantly in his affidavit Mr. Prince at no point denies that the goods were not "first quality" as represented.

The goods in question were received at our Boston factory in late June, 1956. Since they were allegedly sponged and "ready for the needle" no further inspection by us or by our sponger was called for under trade practice. "Ready for the needle" in the trade means that I did not have to sponge or inspect the goods and that they are perfect goods ready to use without further preparation. Consequently my factory people properly relying on defendant's representations held the goods after checking the fact that the correct number of pieces had arrived and that they were properly labelled. When we came to use the goods in the fall of 1956 the fraud practiced upon us was first discovered and we then sent the goods to our sponger.

The order I signed (attached to defendant's affidavit) was prepared by defendant's salesman and states on its face: "These goods are sold as first quality." That they are not so is a fact which even defendant must admit as its own tests of some of the pieces as recently as December, 1957 so demonstrate. Moreover, defendant does not deny the defects in his affidavit. These defects, evidence of which has been submitted to defendant by plaintiff in addition to defendant's own recent tests are so considerable and serious that one is led inescapably to the conclusion that defendant could never have intended to deliver "first quality" goods.

I am advised by my attorney that the full extent of the fraud and misrepresentations by reason of the very nature of fraud cannot be brought to full light without an examination of defendant which he has been resisting through delaying tactics more fully spelled out infra.

On December 13, 1956, after discovery of the fraud practiced by defendant, my attorney in Boston wrote to defendant stating our position as per Exhibit 1 attached hereto. Therein we offered to return the goods to defendant. Defendant rejected our view to which reply was made on December 17, 1956, as per Exhibit 2, reiterating our position and stating that the goods were being held for defendant's account. No communication was thereafter received from defendant.

Defendant in his affidavit in support of this motion makes several statements of fact which are incomplete and though perhaps not germane to the specific issue at hand must be pointed out to the Court lest they be accepted as true.

1. Defendant refers to a confirmation. But it is an incomplete document because it omits items 13 and 14 on the back thereof, whatever they may be. This alleged confirmation which was attached to the answer does not bear plaintiff's signature or defendant's. My attorney called this fact to the attention of the then counsel for defendant who stated that he would rectify the oversight by furnishing us with a signed copy of the confirmation. This has never been done. This is not to deny that I ordered the goods but the inducements for the purchase are the oral statements made to me and the representations made on the order prepared by defendant's salesman and signed by me on August 4, and not the alleged unilateral confirmation. Defendant also relied on the order as a contract in a letter written to us in February, 1956—Exhibit 3. I would not have bought the goods unless guaranteed to be first quality.

2. Defendant states that the only additional step in this action since the filing of the answer has been the notice of examination served by me. The complete picture is as follows:

On July 26, 1957 the notice to examine was served on the attorney for defendant by mail. Pursuant to agreement, the examination was set for August 20, 1957. If my recollection serves me right it was between the date of service of the answer and July 26th that counsel for defendant told my lawyer that the defendant was planning to substitute counsel at that time. He did not do so however until February, 1958 which change was then, after earlier numerous adjournments, used as the basis for a further adjournment of plaintiff's examination of defendant.

Before the examination of August 20, 1957 could take place, defendant through its counsel requested an adjournment to September 5, 1957 to allow for a conference to discuss the issues and possible settlement. That conference was held at the office of counsel for defendant on or about August 27, 1957. No settlement resulted. At this conference, in an effort to expedite settlement and be open and frank, my lawyer exhibited to defendant reports from our own sponger on the goods sold to us. We again offered to return the goods to defendant.

A second adjournment was requested by defendant until September 19th.

Defendant then indicated that it elected to exercise the option, requested at the August 27th meeting, or shortly thereafter, of testing the goods themselves, the other alternative, and also acceptable to us, being to visit our factory. As a consequence, adjournments were granted to October 10, 1957 and November 12, 1957 and even into December.

The goods were tested by defendant. In December I attended a conference at the office of counsel for defendant at which time he stated that some of the goods had tested bad and some tested acceptable. Significantly defendant did not reciprocate by furnishing us with copies of his test although we had furnished him with copies of ours. Possible settlement was again discussed and rejected. My lawyer then again renewed his demand for a prompt examination and was told that Hugo Prince, President of defendant, was in Mexico. Further adjournments were necessarily granted for that reason and again in late December and January, 1958 because of the illness of defendant's counsel.

Ultimately, at my insistence, the examination was set by telephone for the first week in February. At this juncture the defendant's counsel requested by telephone a further delay to February 17th until Mr. Prince returned from an out-of-town trip. Shortly thereafter, defendant substituted new counsel who asked for and received another adjournment until February 20, 1958 for which examination Mr. Prince did not appear.

Mr. Prince in his affidavit argues on the basis of these facts that he has not waived his right to have the matter settled by arbitration, if indeed he has ever had such right. The facts do show that on May 28, 1957 counsel for both parties together reviewed the question of arbitrability of the dispute, and my lawyer furnished counsel with such authorities. This fact is borne out by the attached copy of a letter dated May 29, 1957 from defendant's attorney (Exhibit 3).

At no time subsequent to that letter did defendant revive the question of arbitration except by reference in his answer on which no action was subsequently taken or suggested throughout the meetings or numerous telephone conversations on this matter with my attorney or with me.

Proceeding on the theory that the matter would be tried in a court of law and relying on counsel's failure to seek a stay after the mutual review of the law, my attorney advised me to cooperate with defendant in giving information which could have been obtained only on an examination before trial by defendant, thus saving time for both parties and expense for defendant. Defendant has now ascertained that there is substantial validity to plaintiff's contentions and is attempting to resort to procedural devices because of my cooperation and the information it could not have otherwise obtained from us had it insisted on arbitration from the outset of this action.

I believe that if the motion is granted defendant will be allowed to convert delaying tactics and my cooperation with his counsel, as well as my attorney's frankness, into unfair advantage.

Had defendant been interested in expediting this matter he could have avoided the many delays caused by the adjournments and sought arbitration himself which even now he does not seek, or he could have accepted the proffer of arbitration made by my attorney in May, 1957 —Exhibit 4.

Under all these circumstances defendant has waived whatever right to arbitration it may have had.

3. Mr. Prince states in his affidavit, page 5. "Plaintiff ... had, I understand, cut and manufactured it (the cloth) into finished goods" prior to December 6, 1956. This, of course, is not a fact. Mr. Prince has chosen to forget my counsel's letters of December 13 and 17, in which it was plainly stated that we wanted to return the merchandise. Likewise, he forgets that we so told him at the confereence of August 27, 1957 and that we subsequently sent him swatches from 23 pieces for testing as requested by him. After his rejection of our offer of December 13th we made about 300 coats to fill a commitment to customer (sic), which commitment was made prior to our learning of the fraud and relying on the representations of defendant. Our customer because of the inferior quality of the goods insisted on a very low price and the coats were sold without recourse at a loss by us. All of this including the fact that over two-thirds (⅔) of the fabric is still on hand is well known to Mr. Prince and his prior counsel.

It is therefore respectfully requested that defendant's motion be denied in all respects.

ROBERT L. COHEN

(Sworn to March 11, 1958.)

From the opinion, what do you deduce the issues would be in reaching a decision on the merits? From the affidavits, of the parties in the Record, what would the issues be? Are they issues of law? of fact? mixed law and fact? Which forum—court or arbitrator—is most competent to decide them? Why? Should that competence be a determinative factor in the court's decision as to where the issue of fraud should be resolved?

Here the court decided that the issue was for the arbitrator. (In fact, if the plaintiff was correct—as he seems to have been—that he had lost the opportunity to arbitrate because a timely demand had not been made, the plaintiff had no forum in which to litigate his claim.) Assume that arbitration in a case like this is had and results in an award. On a motion to enforce the award or to vacate it, the issue of fraud might be tendered to the court. We shall deal with questions of impeachment of the award hereafter. At that point you should consider again the problems of "fraud in the inducement."

In the Comment, *Limitations on Freedom to Modify Contract Remedies,* 72 YALE L. J. 723 (1963) it was observed at 761:

But commentators have long argued that the agreement to arbitrate is "separable" from the rest of the contract, that mutual promises to arbitrate are consideration for each other and should be enforced, without any court investigation into the validity of the underlying contract. Underlying the separability argument, which is also a semantic one, is a more basic struggle. The issues which go to the existence or validity of the contract—presence of consideration, mutuality, fraud in the inducement—overlap or are identical with the arbitrable questions, for instance, of what constitutes adequate performance or what was promised by the parties. Thus, a decision on the merits by a court on the former issues often pre-empts the arbitrator's jurisdiction. Judicial control over these basic issues, therefore, has a great effect on recovery in arbitration. Most questions relating to whether there is adequate performance can be framed in terms of failure of consideration or fraud in the inducement. Thus, a court's decision on mutuality or on the existence of the contract may also answer the question whether arbitration is a suitable remedy in a particular case. The general refusal of courts to accept the logic of the separability argument evidences their determination to retain this control over the granting of arbitration.

But compare with this the opinion expressed in 6A CORBIN, CONTRACTS § 1444 (1962):

Suppose, however, that the agreement to arbitrate disputes is a component part of the very bargaining transaction that is now asserted to be void for want of mutual assent, consideration, or capacity, or to be voidable for fraud, duress, lack of capacity or mistake. It would seem that if the alleged defect exists, it affects the provision for arbitration just as much as it affects the other provisions. Even if, for some purposes, the provision for arbitration is declared to be independent and collateral, the factor that makes the rest of the transaction void or voidable would affect that transaction as a whole. If one party failed to express assent to the terms proposed by the other, no contract has been made. The proposal for arbitration lacks acceptance just as fully as do the other proposed terms. Insanity and infancy affect the validity of the acceptance as to all terms alike. The fraud of one party, inducing the other's assent to the whole, makes the whole voidable at the latter's option ; after a proper avoidance, the right to an arbitration falls along with all other rights created by the other promises that were made. In cases within this paragraph, the remedies for enforcement of arbitration agreements are not available, including the enforcing order authorized by an arbitration statute. Before issuing such an order the court must know that a legal duty to arbitrate exists ; this is an issue that the court itself must decide.

MOSELEY v. ELECTRONIC & MISSILE FACILITIES, INC., ET AL.
374 U.S. 167 (1963)

Mr. Justice Clark delivered the opinion of the Court.

The primary issue in this case is whether a claim under the Miller Act, 40 U.S.C. §§ 270a–270d, as amended, based upon arbitration clauses in two subcontracts providing for arbitration of any dispute arising thereunder, is enforceable under the provisions of the United States Arbitration Act. 9 U.S.C. §§ 1, 2 and 3. The institution of this suit was directed toward the recovery of compensation alleged to be due under two subcontracts between the petitioner, a plumbing and heating contractor, and the respondent Electronic & Missile Facilities, Inc., who was the prime contractor under a contract with the United States Corps of Engineers, Savannah District, covering certain Nike Hercules missile installations at Robins Air Force Base Defense Area and Turner Air Force Base Defense Area, both of which are located in the State of Georgia The subcontracts provided for arbitration in New York, and, disputes having arisen there-

under, the respondent filed suit in the Supreme Court of New York seeking an order directing arbitration in accordance with the arbitration provisions. Petitioner then filed this suit in the Middle District of Georgia, where the work under the subcontracts was performed, seeking (1) recovery of the amounts alleged to be due under the subcontracts ; (2) rescission of the subcontracts—on grounds of fraud—and recovery on a *quantum meruit* basis ; (3) in the alternative, failing in both of these claims, recovery of the reasonable value of the labor and materials furnished ; and (4) an injunction enjoining the respondent from proceeding with its arbitration efforts in New York. Neither party sought to compel specific performance of the arbitration agreement. The District Court, holding (1) that the Miller Act gave petitioner the right to sue in the District Court where the subcontracts were performed and (2) that the arbitration clause, if induced by fraud on the part of respondent, would be vitiated, made permanent its prior restraining order directed at the arbitration proceedings in New York. The Court of Appeals reversed, holding that petitioner must arbitrate in New York under New York law. 306 F. 2d 554. We granted certiorari. 371 U.S. 919. Petitioner attacks the subcontracts, as well as the arbitration agreement, as being fraudulent, and this issue, we conclude, must be first determined by the District Court. We therefore reverse the judgment and remand the case to the Court of Appeals with directions to remand to the District Court for further proceedings not inconsistent with this opinion.

I.

We need not elaborate at length on the involved factual situation since it is detailed in the opinions of the Court of Appeals and the District Court. As we have said, petitioner filed suit in the United States District Court for the Middle District of Georgia, the district in which the subcontracts were performed, alleging breach of contract for refusal to pay and seeking recovery for work which had been performed and, alternatively, rescission of the subcontracts on grounds of fraud. The suit was brought under the provisions of the Miller Act, which provides in pertinent part:

> Every suit instituted under this section shall be brought in the name of the United States for the use of the person suing, in the United States District Court for any district in which the contract was to be performed and executed and not elsewhere, irrespective of the amount in controversy. 40 U.S.C. § 270b (b).

It further provides that parties included within the Act "shall have the right to sue ... and to prosecute said action to final execution and judgment" *Id.,* at § 270b (a). Respondent moved to dismiss the suit or stay the same so that the New York arbitration suit might proceed under the terms of both subcontracts, each of which provided that "[a]ny controversy or claim arising out of or relating to" the subcontracts or their breach would be submitted to arbitration in New York City under New York law. In denying these motions the District Court held that the Arbitration Act did not apply here since any other holding would nullify the provisions of the Miller Act. It also concluded that the allegations of fraud, if sustained, would, under Georgia law, rescind the subcontracts, including the agreement for arbitration.

The Court of Appeals, with one judge dissenting, reversed on the theory that the Miller Act was not enacted for the benefit of plaintiffs in the selection of a forum, but rather for the convenience of the defendant, and that this is the type of dispute that is and should be subject to arbitration. As to the issue of fraud, it held that federal law controls in determining whether an allegation of fraud precludes arbitration of a dispute arising under the subcontracts and concluded that, in order to bar arbitration under federal law, the allegation of fraud must be specifically directed to the arbitration clause rather than to the entire contract. Thus, it reversed the District Court on both points.

II.

At the outset we note, as we have indicated, that no request has been made here for the enforcement of the arbitration agreement included within the subcontracts. Indeed, the petitioner has attacked not only the subcontracts, but also the arbitration clauses contained therein, as having been procured through fraud. With the pleadings in this posture, we are obliged to pass upon the priority in determination of that issue in the trial of the case. In essence, petitioner alleges that the subcontracts with him, as well as other subcontractors, were a fraudulent scheme to obtain a great amount of work and material from petitioner and the other subcontractors without making payment therefor and to "browbeat" petitioner and his fellow subcontractors into accepting much less than the value of their claims. One of the means used to effect such scheme was alleged to be the insertion in the subcontracts of an arbitration clause requiring arbitration of disputes in New York.

Under either the Miller Act or the Arbitration Act, it seems clear that the issue of fraud should first be adjudicated before the rights of the parties under the subcontracts can be determined. It appears necessary, therefore, that the District Court proceed first to trial of this issue. In considering the question of the sufficiency of the pleadings with reference to the allegation of fraud, we believe that, as alleged here, the issue goes to the arbitration clause itself, since it is contended that it was to be used to effect the fraudulent scheme. If this issue is determined favorably to the petitioner, there can be no arbitration under the subcontracts.

In view of our holding here, it is not necessary to reach the issues relating to arbitrability of disputes arising under these subcontracts. In fact, disposition of the fraud issue may dispose of the entire suit. In the event the fraud issue is decided favorably to the respondent, and the United States District Court for the Middle District of Georgia should be called upon to decide the question of arbitrability of such disputes and related problems in Miller Act cases, its decision on that point would then, of course, be subject to review.

We therefore reverse the judgment of the Court of Appeals and remand the case to it with instructions that it remand the same to the District Court for further proceedings not inconsistent with this opinion.

It is so ordered.

MR. JUSTICE STEWART would affirm the judgment substantially for the reasons stated in Chief Judge Tuttle's opinion for the Court of Appeals. 306 F. 2d 554.

THE CHIEF JUSTICE and MR. JUSTICE BLACK, concurring.

We agree with the Court that fraud in the procurement of an arbitration contract, like fraud in the procurement of any contract, makes it void and unenforceable and that this question of fraud is a judicial one, which must be determined by a court. To allow this question to be decided by arbitrators would be to that extent to enforce the arbitration agreement even though steeped in the grossest kind of fraud. Compare Robert Lawrence Co. v. Devonshire Fabrics, 271 F. 2d 402 (C. A. 2d Cir. 1959). For this reason we acquiesce in the Court's present disposition of the case on this single issue. But we point out that this disposition leaves open questions of great importance to laborers and materialmen who under the Miller Act are entitled to have their controversies settled in independent courts of law:

(1) Can a member of the special class of

laborers and materialmen which Congress, in the public interest, has protected by fixing the venue for their claims under the Miller Act in a particular federal court deprive himself of that kind of remedy as a condition of his obtaining the employment or the purchase of his materials?

(2) Can any person, before any dispute has arisen, agree to arbitrate all future disputes he may have and thereby lose his right to go into court to try his claim according to due process of law?

(3) Can the Arbitration Act, in light of its language and legislative history, be applied to laborers and materialmen or to construction projects subject to the Miller Act?

(4) Is a construction project, like the one in this case, one "involving commerce" so as to come within the restricted scope of the Arbitration Act?

PRIMA PAINT CORP. v.
FLOOD AND CONKLIN MFG. CO.
388 U.S. 395, 87 S.Ct. 1801 (1967)

MR. JUSTICE FORTAS delivered the opinion of the Court.

This case presents the question whether the federal court or an arbitrator is to resolve a claim of "fraud in the inducement," under a contract governed by the Federal Arbitration Act of 1925,[1] where there is no evidence that the contracting parties intended to withhold that issue from arbitration.

The question arises from the following set of facts. On October 7, 1964, respondent Flood & Conklin Manufacturing Company, a New Jersey corporation, entered into what was styled a "Consulting Agreement," with petitioner Prima Paint Corporation, a Maryland corporation. This agreement followed by less than three weeks the execution of a contract pursuant to which Prima Paint purchased F & C's paint business. The consulting agreement provided that for a six-year period F & C was to furnish advice and consultation "in connection with the formulae, manufacturing operations, sales and servicing of Prima Trade Sales accounts." These services were to be performed personally by F & C's chairman, Jerome K. Jelin, "except in the event

of his death or disability." F & C bound itself for the duration of the contractual period to make no "Trade Sales" of paint or paint products in its existing sales territory or to current customers. To the consulting agreement were appended lists of F & C customers, whose patronage was to be taken over by Prima Paint. In return for these lists, the covenant not to compete, and the services of Mr. Jelin, Prima Paint agreed to pay F & C certain percentages of its receipts from the listed customers and from all others, such payments not to exceed $225,000 over the life of the agreement. The agreement took into account the possibility that Prima Paint might encounter financial difficulties including bankruptcy, but no corresponding reference was made to possible financial problems which might be encountered by F & C. The agreement stated that it "embodies the entire understanding of the parties on the subject matter." Finally, the parties agreed to a broad arbitration clause, which read in part:

> Any controversy or claim arising out of or relating to this agreement, or the breach thereof, shall be settled by arbitration in the City of New York in accordance with the rules then obtaining of the American Arbitration Association. . . .

The first payment by Prima Paint to F & C under the consulting agreement was due on September 1, 1965. None was made on that date. Seventeen days later, Prima Paint did pay the appropriate amount, but into escrow. It notified attorneys for F & C that, in various enumerated respects their client had broken both the consulting agreement and the earlier purchase agreement. Prima Paint's principal contention, so far as presently relevant, was that F & C had fraudulently represented that it was solvent and able to perform its contractual obligations, whereas it was in fact insolvent and intended to file a petition under Chapter XI of the Bankruptcy Act shortly after execution of the consulting agreement. Prima Paint noted that such a petition was filed by F & C on October 14, 1964, one week after the contract had been signed. F & C's response, on October 25, was to serve a "notice of intention to arbitrate." On November 12, three days before expiration of its time to answer this "notice," Prima Paint filed suit in the United States District Court for the Southern District of New York, seeking rescission of the consulting agreement on the basis of the alleged fraudulent inducement. The complaint asserted that the federal court had diversity jurisdiction.

Contemporaneously with the filing of its complaint, Prima Paint petitioned the District Court

---

1. Although the letter to F & C's attorneys had alleged breaches of both consulting and purchasing agreements, and the fraudulent inducement of both, the complaint did not refer to the earlier purchase agreement, alleging only that Prima Paint had been "fraudulently induced to accelerate the execution and closing of the [consulting] agreement from October 21, 1964, to October 7, 1964."

for an order enjoining F & C from proceeding with the arbitration. F & C cross-moved to stay the court action pending arbitration. F & C contended that the issue presented—whether there was fraud in the inducement of the consulting agreement—was a question for the arbitrators and not for the District Court. Cross-affidavits were filed on the merits. On behalf of Prima Paint, the charges in the complaint were reiterated. Affiants for F & C attacked the sufficiency of Prima Paint's allegations of fraud, denied that misrepresentations had been made during negotiations, and asserted that Prima Paint had relied exclusively upon delivery of the lists, the promise not to compete, and the availability of Mr. Jelin. They contended that Prima Paint had availed itself of these considerations for nearly a year without claiming "fraud," noting that Prima Paint was in no position to claim ignorance of the bankruptcy proceeding since it had participated therein in February of 1965. They added that F & C was revested with its assets in March of 1965.

The District Court, 262 F.Supp. 605, granted F & C's motion to stay the action pending arbitration, holding that a charge of fraud in the inducement of a contract containing an arbitration clause as broad as this one was a question for the arbitrators and not for the court For this proposition it relied on Robert Lawrence Co. v. Devonshire Fabrics, Inc., 271 F.2d 402 (C.A.2d Cir. 1959), cert. granted, 362 U.S. 909, 80 S.Ct. 682, 4 L.Ed. 2d 618, dismissed under Rule 60, 364 U.S. 801 (1960). the Court of Appeals for the Second Circuit dismissed Prima Paint's appeal, 2 Cir., 360 F.2d 315. It held that the contract in question evidenced a transaction involving interstate commerce ; that under the controlling *Robert Lawrence Co.* decision a claim of fraud in the inducement of the contract generally—as opposed to the arbitration clause itself—is for the arbitrators and not for the courts ; and that this rule—one of "national substantive law"—governs even in the face of a contrary state rule.[2] We agree, albeit for somewhat different reasons, and we affirm the decision below.

The key statutory provisions are §§ 2, 3, and 4 of the United States Arbitration Act of 1925. Sec-

tion 2 provides that a written provision for arbitration in any maritime transaction or a contract evidencing a transaction involving commerce ... shall be valid, irrevocable, and enforceable, save upon such grounds as exist at law or in equity for the revocation of any contract." Section 3 requires a federal court in which suit has been brought "upon any issue referable to arbitration under an agreement in writing for such arbitration" to stay the court action pending arbitration once it is satisfied that the issue is arbitrable under the agreement. Section 4 provides a federal remedy for a party "aggrieved by the alleged failure, neglect, or refusal of another to arbitrate under a written agreement for arbitration," and directs the federal court to order arbitration once it is satisfied that an agreement for arbitration has been made and has not been honored.

In Bernhardt v. Polygraphic Co., 350 U.S. 198, 76 S.Ct. 273, 100 L.Ed. 199 (1956), this Court held that the stay provisions of § 3, invoked here by respondent F & C, apply only to the two kinds of contracts specified in §§ 1 and 2 of the Act, namely those in admiralty or evidencing transactions in "commerce." Our first question, then, is whether the consulting agreement between F & C and Prima Paint is such a contract. We agree with the Court of Appeals that it is. Prima Paint acquired a New Jersey paint business serving at least 175 wholesale clients in a number of States, and secured F & C's assistance in arranging the transfer of manufacturing and selling operations from New Jersey to Maryland. The consulting agreement was inextricably tied to this interstate transfer and to the continuing operations of an interstate manufacturing and wholesaling business. There could not be a clearer case of a contract evidencing a transaction in interstate commerce.[3]

---

2. Whether a party seeking *rescission* of a contract on the ground of fraudulent inducement may in New York obtain judicial resolution of his claim is not entirely clear. Compare Exercycle Corp. v. Maratta, 9 N.Y. 2d 329, 334, 214 N.Y.S. 2d 353, 174 N.E. 2d 463 (1961), and Amerotron Corp. v. Maxwell Shapiro Woolen Co., 3 A.D. 2d 889, 162 N.Y.S. 2d 214 (1957), aff'd, 4 N.Y. 2d 722 (1958), with Fabrex Corp. v. Winard Sales Co., 23 Misc. 2d 26, 200 N.Y.S. 2d 278 (N.Y. Co. 1960). In light of our disposition of this case, we need not decide the status of the issue under New York law.

3. It is suggested in dissent that, despite the absence of any language in the statute so indicating, we should construe it to apply only to "contracts between merchants for the interstate shipment of goods." Not only have we neither the desire nor the warrant so to amend the statute, but we find persuasive and authoritative evidence of a contrary legislative intent. See, *e.g.*, the House Report on this legislation which proclaims that "the control over interstate commerce [one of the bases for the legislation] reaches not only the actual physical interstate shipment of goods but also contracts related to interstate commerce. H.R.Rep. No. 96, 68th Cong., 1st Sess., 1 (1924). We note, too, that were the dissent's curious narrowing of the statute correct, there would have been no necessity for Congress to have amended the statute to exclude certain kinds of employment contracts. See § 1. In any event, the anomaly urged upon us in dissent is manifested by the present case. It would be remarkable to say that a contract for the purchase of a single can of paint may evidence a transaction in interstate commerce, but that an agreement relating to the facilitation of the purchase of an entire interstate paint business and its reestablishment and operation in another State is not.

Having determined that the contract in question is within the coverage of the Arbitration Act, we turn to the central issue in this case: whether a claim of fraud in the inducement of the entire contract is to be resolved by the federal court, or whether the matter is to be referred to the arbitrators. The Courts of Appeals have differed in their approach to this question. The view of the Court of Appeals for the Second Circuit, as expressed in this case and in others is that—*except where the parties otherwise intend*—arbitration clauses as a matter of federal law are "separable" from the contracts in which they are embedded, and that where no claim is made that fraud was directed to the arbitration clause itself, a broad arbitration clause will be held to encompass arbitration of the claim that the contract itself was induced by fraud.[4] The Court of Appeals for the First Circuit, on the other hand, has taken the view that the question of "severability" is one of state law, and that where a State regards such a clause as inseparable a claim of fraud in the inducement must be decided by the court. Lummus Co. v. Commonwealth Oil Ref. Co., 280 F.2d 915, 923–924 (C.A. 1st Cir.), cert. denied, 364 U.S. 911, 81 S.Ct. 274, 15 L.Ed.2d 225 (1960).

With respect to cases brought in federal court involving maritime contracts or those evidencing transactions in "commerce," we think that Congress has provided an explicit answer. That answer is to be found in § 4 of the Act, which provides a remedy to a party seeking to compel compliance with an arbitration agreement. Under § 4, with respect to a matter within the jurisdiction of the federal courts save for the existence of an arbitration clause, the federal court is instructed to order arbitration to proceed once it is satisfied that "the making of the agreement for arbitration or the failure to comply [with the arbitration agreement] is not in issue:" Accordingly, if the claim is fraud in the inducement of the arbitration clause itself—an issue which goes to the "making" of the agreement to arbitrate—the federal court may proceed to adjudicate it.[5] But the statutory language does

not permit the federal court to consider claims of fraud in the inducement of the contract generally. Section 4 does not expressly relate to situations like the present in which a stay is sought of a federal action in order that arbitration may proceed. But it is inconceivable that Congress intended the rule to differ depending upon which party to the arbitration agreement first invokes the assistance of a federal court. We hold, therefore, that in passing upon a § 3 application for a stay while the parties arbitrate, a federal court may consider only issues relating to the making and performance of the agreement to arbitrate. In so concluding, we not only honor the plain meaning of the statute but also the unmistakably clear congressional purpose that the arbitration procedure, when selected by the parties to a contract, be speedy and not subject to delay and obstruction in the courts.

There remains the question whether such a rule is constitutionally permissible. The point is made that, whatever the nature of the contract involved here, this case is in federal court solely by reason of diversity of citizenship, and that since the decision in Erie R. Co. v. Tompkins, 304 U.S. 64, 58 S.Ct. 817, 82 L.Ed. 1188 (1938), federal courts are bound in diversity cases to follow state rules of decision in matters which are "substantive" rather than "procedural," or where the matter is "outcome determinative." Guaranty Trust Co. of New York v. York, 326 U.S. 99, 65 S.Ct. 1464, 89 L.Ed. 2079 (1945). The question in this case, however, is not whether Congress may fashion federal substantive rules to govern questions arising in simple diversity cases. See Bernhardt v. Polygraphic Co., *supra*, 350 U.S. at 202 and at 208, 76 S.Ct. at 275 and at 279. Rather, the question is whether Congress may prescribe how federal courts are to conduct themselves with respect to subject matter over which Congress plainly has power to legislate. The answer to that can only be in the affirmative. And it is clear beyond dispute that the federal arbitration statute is based upon and confined to the incontestable federal foundations of "control over interstate commerce and over admiralty." H.R.Rep. No. 96, 68th Cong., 1st

---

4. The Court of Appeals has been careful to honor evidence that the parties intended to withhold such issues from the arbitrators and to reserve them for judicial resolution. See El Hoss Engineer. & Transport Co. v. American Ind. Oil Co., *supra*. We note that categories of contracts otherwise within the Arbitration Act but in which one of the parties characteristically has little bargaining power are expressly excluded from the reach of the Act. See § 1.

5. This position is consistent both with the decision in

Moseley v. Electronic & Missile Facilities, 374 U.S. 167, 171, 172, 83 S.Ct. 1815, 1817, 1818, 10 L.Ed. 2d 818 (1963), and with the statutory scheme. As the "saving clause" in § 2 indicates, the purpose of Congress in 1925 was to make arbitration agreements as enforceable as other contracts, but not more so. To immunize an arbitration agreement from judicial challenge on the ground of fraud in the inducement would be to elevate it over other forms of contract—a situation inconsistent with the "saving clause."

Sess., 1 (1924); S.Rep. No. 536, 68th Cong., 1st Sess., 3 (1924).[6]

In the present case no claim has been advanced by Prima Paint that F & C fraudulently induced it to enter into the agreement to arbitrate "any controversy or claim arising out of or relating to this agreement, or the breach thereof." This contractual language is easily broad enough to encompass Prima Paint's claim that both execution and acceleration of the consulting agreement itself were procured by fraud. Indeed, no claim is made that Prima Paint ever intended that "legal" issues relating to the contract be excluded from arbitration, or that it was not entirely free so to contract. Federal courts are bound to apply rules enacted by Congress with respect to matters—here, a contract involving commerce—over which it has legislative power. The question which Prima Paint requested the District Court to adjudicate preliminarily to allowing arbitration to proceed is one not intended by Congress to delay the granting of a § 3 stay. Accordingly, the decision below dismissing Prima Paint's appeal is affirmed.

Affirmed.

MR. JUSTICE HARLAN:

In joining the Court's opinion I desire to note that I would also affirm the judgment below on the basis of Robert Lawrence Co. v. Devonshire Fabrics, Inc., 271 F.2d 402 (C.A.2d Cir. 1959), cert. granted, 362 U.S. 909, 80 S.Ct. 682, 4 L.Ed.2d 618, dismissed under Rule 60, 364 U.S. 801, 81 S.Ct. 27, 5 L.Ed.2d 37 (1960).

MR. JUSTICE BLACK, with whom MR. JUSTICE DOUGLAS and MR. JUSTICE STEWART join, dissenting.

The Court here holds that the Federal Arbitration Act, as a matter of federal substantive law, compels a party to a contract containing a written arbitration provision to carry out his

"arbitration agreement" even though a court might, after a fair trial, hold the entire contract—including the arbitration agreement—void because of fraud in the inducement. The Court holds, what is to me fantastic, that the legal issue of a contract's voidness because of fraud is to be decided by persons designated to arbitrate factual controversies arising out of a valid contract between the parties. And the arbitrators the Court holds are to adjudicate the legal validity of the contract need not even be lawyers, and in all probability will be nonlawyers, wholly unqualified to decide legal issues, and even if qualified to apply the law, not bound to do so. I am by no means sure that thus forcing a person to forgo his opportunity to try his legal issues in the courts where, unlike in arbitration, he may have a jury trial and right to appeal, is not a denial of due process of law. I am satisfied, however, that Congress did not impose any such procedures in the Arbitration Act. And I am fully satisfied that a reasonable and fair reading of that Act's language and history shows that both Congress and the framers of the Act were at great pains to emphasize that nonlawyers designated to adjust and arbitrate factual controversies arising out of valid contracts would not trespass upon the courts' prerogative to decide the legal question of whether any legal contract exists upon which to base an arbitration.

The Court today affirms this holding [that the validity of the contract is to be decided by the arbitrator] for three reasons, none of which is supported by the language or history of the Arbitration Act. First, the Court holds that because the consulting agreement was intended to supplement a separate contract for the interstate transfer of assets, it is itself a "contract evidencing a transaction involving commerce," the language used by Congress to describe contracts the Act was designed to cover. But in light of the legislative history which indicates that the Act was to have a limited application to contracts between merchants for the interstate shipment of goods, and in light of the express failure of Congress to use language making the Act applicable to all contracts which "affect commerce," the statutory language Congress normally uses when it wishes to exercise its full powers over commerce,[1] I am not at all certain

6. It is true that the Arbitration Act was passed 13 years before this Court's decision in Erie R. Co. v. Tompkins, *supra*, brought to an end the regime of Swift v. Tyson, 16 Pet. 1. 10 L.Ed. 865 (1842), and that at the time of enactment Congress had reason to believe that it still had power to create federal rules to govern questions of "general law" arising in simple diversity cases—at least, absent any state statute to the contrary. If Congress relied at all on this "oft-challenged" power, see Erie R. Co., 304 U.S., at 69. 58 S.Ct., at 818, it was only supplementary to the admiralty and commerce powers, which formed the principal bases of the legislation. Indeed, Congressman Graham, the bill's sponsor in the House, told his colleagues that it "only affects contracts relating to interstate subjects and contracts in admiralty." 65th CONG. REC. 1931 (1924). The Senate Report on this legislation similarly indicated that the bill "[relates] to maritime transactions and to contracts in interstate and foreign commerce." S.Rep. No. 536, 68th Cong., 1st Sess., 3 (1924). Non-congressional sponsors of the legislation agreed.

1. In some Acts Congress uses broad language and defines commerce to include even that which "affects" commerce. Federal Employers' Liability Act, 45 U.S.C. § 51; National Labor Relations Act, 29 U.S.C. § 152(7). In other instances Congress has chosen more restrictive language. Fair Labor Standards Act, 29 U.S.C. § 206. Prior to this case, this Court has always made careful inquiry to assure

that the Act was intended to apply to this consulting agreement. Second, the Court holds that the language of § 4 of the Act provides an "explicit answer" to the question of whether the arbitration clause is "separable" from the rest of the contract in which it is contained. Section 4 merely provides that the court must order arbitration if it is "satisfied that the making of the agreement for arbitration ... is not in issue." That language, considered alone, far from providing an "explicit answer," merely poses the further question of what kind of allegations put the making of the arbitration agreement in issue. Since both the lower courts assumed that but for the Federal Act, New York law might apply and that under New York law a general allegation of fraud in the inducement puts into issue the making of the agreement to arbitrate (considered inseparable under New York law from the rest of the contract), the Court necessarily holds that federal law determines whether certain allegations put the making of the arbitration agreement in issue. And the Court approves the Second Circuit's fashioning of a federal separability rule which overrides state law to the contrary. The Court thus holds that the Arbitration Act, designed to provide merely a procedural remedy which would not interfere with state substantive law, authorizes federal courts to fashion a federal rule to make arbitration clauses "separable" and valid. And the Court approves a rule which is not only contrary to state law, but contrary to the intention of the parties and to accepted principles of contract law—a rule which indeed elevates arbitration provisions above all other contractual provisions. As the Court recognizes, that result was clearly not intended by Congress. Finally, the Court summarily disposes of the *Erie* problem, recognized as a serious constitutional problem in Bernhardt v. Polygraphic Co., 350 U.S. 198, 76 S.Ct. 273, 100 L.Ed. 199, by insufficiently supported assertions that it is "clear beyond dispute" that Congress based the Arbitration Act on its power to regulate commerce and that "if Congress relied at all on" its power to create federal law for diversity cases, such reliance "was only supplementary."

It is clear that had this identical contract dispute been litigated in New York courts under its arbitration act, Prima would not be required to present its claims of fraud to the arbitrator if the state rule of nonseparability applies. The Court here does not hold today, as did Judge Medina,[2] that the body of federal substantive law created by federal judges under the Arbitration Act is required to be applied by state courts. A holding to that effect—which the Court seems to leave up in the air—would flaunt the intention of the framers of the Act. Yet under this Court's opinion today—that the Act supplies not only the remedy of enforcement but a body of federal doctrines to determine the validity of an arbitration agreement—failure to make the Act applicable in state courts would give rise to "forum shopping" and an unconstitutional discrimination that both *Erie* and *Bernhardt* were designed to eliminate. These problems are greatly reduced if the Act is limited, as it should be, to its proper scope: the mere enforcement in federal courts of valid arbitration agreements.

The potential effects of *Prima* are considered further in Chapter XV, "Choosing Applicable Law."

---

itself that it is applying a statute with the coverage that Congress intended, so that the meaning *in that statute* of "commerce" will be neither expanded nor contracted. The Arbitration Act is an example of carefully limited language. It covers only those contracts "involving commerce," and nowhere is there a suggestion that it is meant to extend to contracts "affecting commerce." The Act not only uses narrow language, but is also completely without any declaration of some national interest to be served or some nationwide comprehensive scheme of regulation to be created, and this absence suggests that Congress did not intend to exert its full power over commerce.

2. "This is a declaration of national law equally applicable in state or federal courts." 271 F.2d, at 407.

CHAPTER IV

THE PROCEEDINGS

WOOD v. HELME
14 R.I. 325 (1884)

The evidence submitted at the trial disclosed the following state of facts, namely:

1. That the arbitrators named in the submission, after hearing the parties in the premises, were unable to agree upon an award, and thereupon called in a third person as provided.

2. That after said third person was called in, he and one of the original arbitrators met, and in the absence of the other arbitrator visited and inspected the two houses mentioned in the submission, and then and there, in the absence of the complainants and without any notice to them of said meeting, heard the defendant's brother, who was acting in her interest, with regard to the defects in the construction of the houses and her grievances in the premises.

3. That during said examination and hearing, one of said arbitrators absented himself therefrom, leaving the other to complete the same, and that the man called in as the third arbitrator did remain and further examine said houses with the defendant's brother, and then and there heard the defendant and her brother as to her complaints and grievances in the premises, she and her said brother being the only persons present with said arbitrator.

4. That the information thus received by said third arbitrator was the only information which he obtained on the side of the defendant as to her claim, and that it was used by him in determining the amount of said award.

5. That after hearing the defendant and her witness in the manner aforesaid, all of the arbitrators met at the office of said Reed, where they heard the complainants in the premises, without the knowledge of or any notice to the defendant. These were the only hearings which were had after calling in the third arbitrator.

6. That said arbitrators thereupon made and published their award.

Under this state of facts the award cannot be sustained, for two reasons, namely: first, because no notice was given of the meeting of the arbitrators at which the houses were examined and evidence submitted by the defendant as to her claim in the premises; and, second, because the arbitrators did not all act together.

Without question it was the duty of the arbitrators under the submission in this case to give due notice to the parties of the time and place for hearing the cause before proceeding therein. The right to such notice was clearly implied in the agreement to submit, and the nature of the inquiry also, by the arbitrators, was such as to render notice necessary. Furthermore, the plainest principles of justice require this. It was a judicial proceeding, directly affecting the interests of both parties to the submission; and the very first step in all proceedings of this sort is to give proper notice to the parties of the time and place of hearing or trial; and until this is done, no jurisdiction to act is acquired. And this rule is held with great strictness in all proceedings of this sort where testimony is to be taken, whether under oath, or, as in this case, in the form of statements of the parties which amount to the same thing. In Knowlton v. Mickles, 29 Barb. S.C. 465, the arbitrators proceeded to examine the premises in dispute in the absence of the defendant, attended part of the time by the plaintiff in person, and then and there made various inquiries of, and called for and listened to the statements of other persons as to their knowledge of the damage and the cause thereof, and without the knowledge and in the absence of the defendant. The court, Emott, J., condemned the proceeding and affirmed the judgment below setting aside the award.

And it makes no difference in this respect that there has been a regular hearing in the case before the two arbitrators originally chosen, who were unable to agree, and thereupon called in a third person; for the proceeding then commences *de novo*, and the parties are entitled to the same notice as though no proceedings had been previously had. Selby v. Gibson, 1 Har. & J. 362, note; Lutz v. Linthicum, 8 Pet. 165.

The rule which the authorities make upon the question of notice is well stated in 6 Wait's Actions and Defences, 522, 523, and is, that

> unless the submission expressly shows that the parties intended that the arbitrators should decide the questions in dispute without the aid or presence of the parties, or it is evident that such was the intention, as where the matter is merely one of appraisal, Bushey v. Culler, 26 Md. 534; Collins v. Vanderbilt, 8 Bosw, 313, the arbitrators must give both parties notice of the time and place of meeting, and they have no authority to proceed *ex parte*; Bullitt v. Musgrave, 3 Gill, 31; Webber v. Ives, 1 Tyler, 441; Frey v. Vanlear, 1 Serg. & R. 435; and where the parties are entitled to notice in the first instance, they are entitled to notice of the time and place of any subsequent hearing, and it is improper, and will invalidate the award, if the arbitrators make an examination, or hear testimony, at the request of one of the parties without notice to the other.

Chaplin v. Kirwan, 1 Dall. 187; Peters v. Newkirk, 6 Cow. 103; Banton v. Gale, 6 B. Mon. 260.

The reasoning of this court in the case of Cleland et al v. Hedly, 5 R.I. 163, with regard to the illegality of receiving any *ex parte* evidence in cases of this sort, without notice to the opposite party, is abundantly supported by the authorities, and we are content with the law as therein stated. It is decisive of the case at bar upon that point.

The second reason why the award in this case cannot be sustained is that the arbitrators did not act together. It is a well settled rule that where the submission is to the several arbitrators jointly, all must act and act together. And this rule obtains as well in those cases where the majority are authorized to make an award which shall be binding upon the parties to the submission, as where entire unanimity is required. Said Mr. Justice Nelson, in Harris v. Norton, 7 Wend. 534: "Referees have no power to act unless all attend. The concurrence of two, had the third been present, would have been enough; but only two attending, they could do no act affecting the rights of the parties."

And the law is the same with regard to arbitrators as to referees.

In Hoff v. Taylor, 5 N.J. Law, 829, the court states the rule as follows: "All are to deliberate, consult, reason; but the weight or majority of opinion is the rule. The whole court is to hear, but the claim which gains the most suffrages is to prevail."

Says Mr. Justice Breese, in Smith v. Smith, 28 Ill. 56, 60:

> They must each be present at every meeting, and the witnesses and the parties must be examined in the presence of them all; for the parties are entitled to have recourse to the arguments, experience, and judgment of each arbitrator at every stage of the proceedings brought to bear on the minds of his fellow judges, so that by conference they shall mutually assist each other in arriving at a just conclusion.

To the same effect are both the English and American decisions almost without exception. See KYD ON AWARDS, 105, 106; RUSSELL ON ARBITRATION, 209; MORSE ON ARBITRATION AND AWARD, 152, 153; Thompson v. Mitchell, 35 Me 281; In re Plews & Middletown, 6 Q.B.N.S. 845; Little v. Newton, 9 Dowl. P.C. 437; Lord v. Lord, 5 El. & B. 404; Lyon v. Blossom, 4 Duer, 318, 325; M'Inroy v. Benedict, 11 Johns. Rep. 402.

In the case at bar this important and salutary rule was not observed, owing, doubtless, to the misapprehension on the part of the arbitrators of their duty in the premises; for we do not find that they were guilty of any intentional wrong doing in the attempted performance of the duty which they assumed. The entire proceedings, after the calling in of the third arbitrator, were wholly irregular and illegal, and consequently of no binding force upon any one. It is unnecessary to consider the question raised as to whether the award set out in the bill and signed by the arbitrators was or was not arrived at in an improper manner by them, as in either event it was a nullity, owing to the illegality of the previous proceedings.

The award must be set aside, and the defendant enjoined from pleading the same in bar of the complainant's said suit at law.

Decree accordingly, but without costs.

Typically arbitrators or the parties are required to give notice of the proceedings, and opportunity for a hearing before the arbitrators in the presence of the parties must be approved. See, *e.g.,* C.P.L.R. § 7506 (a) and (b). Even where the statutes are not specific on these points, almost without exception notice and hearing are deemed indispensable to a valid proceeding.

In re Arbitration Puget Sound Bridge Co. v. Lake Washington Shipyards 1 Wash. 2d 401, 96 P.2d 257 (1939) the appellant, Puget Sound Bridge & Dredging Company, employed respondent Lake Washington Shipyards as contractor to do certain work and furnish materials in the repair and equipment of appellant's ship. Upon the completion of the work a dispute arose as to the amount owing on the contract, and the parties entered into a written agreement to arbitrate the matter. The agreement contained no specific directions as to how the arbitrators were to proceed other than providing that the arbitration should be conducted according to the laws of the State of Washington except where the agreement expressly included the contrary. The arbitrators filed their oaths and carried out an informal and *ex parte* investigation and examination, inspecting invoices, work orders, job specifications, and the ship itself. No representative of the other party was present at any of the investigations or conferences with either party although each party was aware of the nature of the arbitrators' investigation. After finishing their investigation, the arbitrators prepared and filed in court their award granting the respondent the full amount of his claim less a credit of $259.36 in favor of the appellant. The appellant filed exceptions to the award, alleging that the arbitrators had misbehaved themselves and the award procured by undue means, in that the arbitrators had not held meetings at fixed or specified times according to law. The court here affirmed a judgment of the superior court enforcing the award, holding that although under the statute a hearing must be had

in the presence of both parties, if the parties agree or consent to the reception of evidence *ex parte* or informally, they cannot afterwards maintain that there has been a deprivation of their right to a proper hearing.

For a similar result see Waller v. Atkinson (Ohio Court of Common Pleas, Franklin County, 1966) 64 LRRM 2259.

For a similar result in a proceeding characterized by great informality and private consultations by the arbitrators among themselves and one of them with the parties, see Lambert Bros. Lumber Co. v. Jake Lampert Yards, Inc., 176 Minn. 622, 224 N.W. 248 (1929).

IN THE MATTER OF THE ARBITRATION BETWEEN NORMA BRILL, PETITIONER, AND MULLER BROTHERS, INC., RESPONDENT.
40 Misc. 2d 683, 243 N.Y.S. 2d 905 (1962).

MATTHEW M. LEVY, J. The petitioner moves for vacatur of an arbitration award upon the grounds (1) that it was procured by corruption, fraud, or other undue means and (2) that there was evident partiality in the arbitrator. The usual prayer for other relief is included in the notice.

The petitioner had stored certain furniture, furnishings and clothing with the respondent, a storage warehouse concern in New York City. She thereupon left the city, allegedly giving the respondent the address of a friend as the place to which her mail was to be sent. Upon returning to the city several months later, the petitioner called the respondent, informing it that she wished her chattels back, only to learn that that very day her property was being auctioned off, apparently for unpaid storage charges. The petitioner claims that this was the first notice she had of the sale. According to the petitioner, the property was worth $30,000. She rushed over to the warehouse with $600 in cash (the storage charges were less than that) and tendered full payment to the respondent's president. Allegedly, he refused to accept the payment and insisted upon proceeding with the sale, notwithstanding personal protests by the petitioner and telephonic objections thereto by lawyers on her behalf. Moreover, she asserts, the auctioneer and the respondent refused to take any bids from the petitioner herself. The property was sold in the auction for a few hundred dollars.

The matter went to arbitration, pursuant to the contract of storage. In full settlement of the petitioner's claim of $30,000, the arbitrator awarded her $483.04, and required her to pay $60, half of the arbitration fee. The allegations made by the petitioner—as to breach of the storage agreement on the part of the respondent, as to the conduct of the auctioneer during the sale, that personalty of substantial value was deliberately sold for a mere pittance, and that this was all a part of a scheme to defraud her of her property—are charges with which we are not now concerned. Since the parties submitted their controversy to arbitration, it is the procedure in the arbitration that concerns us, not the merits of the basic dispute as flowing from the evidence adduced before the arbitrator.[1] This is true even though the witnesses may have differed as to what had occurred in respect of notice, tender or auction. For the available bases for vacatur are not issues as to the merits, but rather the claimed corruption, fraud, or other undue means in the procurement of the arbitration award or alleged partiality in the arbitrator or of any other misbehavior by which the rights of a party have been prejudiced (Civ. Prac. Act, § 1462).

The first ground presented by the petitioner to set aside the award is that the attorney for the respondent, it is said, was apparently favorably known to the arbitrator and had business transactions with him. This appearance, it is asserted by the petitioner in her affidavit, stemmed from the alleged fact that the respondent's attorney started to say something to the arbitrator "off the record" about recent business transactions that he and the arbitrator had been engaged in, when the attorney "shut up" abruptly upon a warning look from the arbitrator. When the petitioner asked what it was about, she was told that it was nothing and that it had nothing to do with the arbitration. Counsel advises her, the petitioner states, that this is evidence of the use of undue means to effect a result and of the arbitrator's partiality. Concerning this "off the record" conversation with the arbitrator, the respondent's attorney responds:

> Petitioner's allegations at page 4 of her affidavit to the effect that I started to say something "off the record" to Mr. Hill about "recent business transactions" that he and I had engaged in, is [are?] a figment of petitioner's imagination conjured up at this late date as a last resort in an attempt to influence the Court. I emphatically deny that I knew or had any business dealings of any kind whatsoever with B. Douglas Hill prior to the hearings in the instant matter. Mr. Hill was chosen by the parties hereto as an impartial arbitrator pursuant to the rules of the American Arbitration Association. I have had absolutely no other business dealing with Mr. Hill prior to, during, or since the close of the hearings.

Is this a denial of the existence of any business dealings with the arbitrator, or is it a denial that there was an off-the-record conversation about business dealings? If this does not constitute an explicit denial that there was an in-camera off-the-record conversation between the arbitrator and the respondent's counsel, it seems to me that it does not matter what was said in the conversation in the absence of the petitioner or not in her hearing.

An off-the-record conference by the arbitrator with both counsel[2] is not in the least impermissible (see Ballantine Books v. Capital Distr. Co., 302 F. 2d 17 [C.A. 2d]). But, unless the other party consent thereto, I take it that an arbitrator should not, during the arbitration proceedings (any more than should a Judge during a trial in a court of law), converse *sotto voce* with one of the parties or his counsel—that is, behind the back, so to speak, of the other party. To hold otherwise would, I think, render quite innocuous what is already a rather narrow sphere of judicial review of the proceedings leading to an arbitrator's award. For, how, otherwise—as an example—is a judicial tribunal, when called upon to vacate or confirm an award, to know whether the arbitrator has or has not received

---

1. On the argument of the motion, the following minute was made:

"THE COURT: The moving party raises the issue that stenographic minutes were taken of the arbitration proceedings, and they have not been presented by the respondent, and that in consequence I should draw some inference resulting from that omission.

"The respondent states that it deliberately refrained from presenting the voluminous record before the arbitrator because the respondent does not want to relitigate the matters which were before and properly before the arbitrator under the contract.

"Decision reserved."

There are other factors on this motion, aside from the merits of the controversy, that might have been clarified one way or the other by having the transcript of the arbitration proceedings and hearings before me. But, of course, the burden is on the moving party to justify the vacatur of the award, and she might have subpoenaed the minutes (Civ. Prac. Act, § 406) or asked for admissions (Civ. Prac. Act, § 322) or taken the testimony of the arbitrator or stenographer (Civ. Prac. Act, § 307) if she did not (or were unable to) obtain a transcript of her own—which is not indicated in her affidavit.

The correct "inference" that I might draw because of the respondent's non-production is more fully set forth in Mitler v. Friedeberg (32 Misc 2d 78, 90–91). But, in any case, in arriving at my determination of the basic issue on this application, I do not rely upon any inference because of the unwillingness of the respondent to submit the entire record to the court.

---

2. Or, as would be the situation in the case at bar, with respondent's counsel and the petitioner in person, since she does not appear to have been represented in the arbitration hearing by an attorney.

ex parte "evidence" of which the other party is entitled to be aware and perhaps rebut. It is my belief that, in arbitration, just as in a court of law, it is not alone requisite to administer justice but so to conduct the proceedings as to make the parties feel that they are indeed being accorded justice.

It may be, however, that what was hereinbefore quoted from the respondent's attorney's affidavit was intended to be a denial—though somewhat obscurely expressed—of the petitioner's assertion that there was any *sub rosa* conversation whatsoever, and that what now remains for consideration on this issue is that the petitioner has merely alleged, without attempting to bring forward any proof thereof, that the arbitrator had had business dealings with the counsel for the respondent and was therefore biased in the respondent's favor. The counsel has categorically denied this.

Even were the petitioner's allegation true, however, it would not in itself necessarily constitute a basis for disqualification of the arbitrator or for vacatur of the award (Matter of Cross Props. [Gimbel Bros.], 15 A D 2d 913 ; Matter of Meinig Co. [Katakura & Co.], 241 App. Div. 406, affd. 266 N.Y. 418 ; Matter of Atlantic Rayon Corp. [Goldsmith], 277 App. Div. 554, mot. for lv. to app. den. 278 App. Div. 567 ; Matter of Newburger v. Rose, 228 App. Div. 526, affd. 254 N.Y. 546), unless the nature and extent of such dealings would justify such action (see BOTEIN, J., in Matter of Knickerbocker Textile Corp. [Donath], 22 Misc 2d 1056, affd. 282 App. Div. 680 ; McNALLY, J., in Matter of Dukraft Mfg. Co. [Bear Mill Mfg. Co.], 22 Misc 2d 1057, 1059), and unless there was nondisclosure of such dealings to the complaining party (Matter of Milliken Woolens [Weber Knit Sportswear], 11 A D 2d 166, 168, affd. 9 N.Y. 2d 878). The state of the present affidavit record, pro or con, being inconclusive on this point, I would normally direct a hearing to take testimony thereon.

But I have come to the conclusion that the award should be vacated upon another ground altogether, which is presented on the record before me and therefore does not require the taking of testimony. That ground is that the respondent offered and the arbitrator received in evidence, over the petitioner's protest, a certain written statement which should not have been in the case at all. That evidence consisted of a report prepared for the respondent by the Pinkerton Detective Agency. It is comprised of the several buff-colored pages attached to the moving affidavit. Contained therein are various highly unfavorable comments about the peti-

tioner presumably gathered from her former neighbors, and a record of various lawsuits in which the petitioner was involved, and other data about her financial standing. It is conceded in the respondent's answering affidavit that the petitioner made timely objection to the introduction of this report as evidence, and that she did not waive her right to object now. The respondent's contentions are a denial that the arbitrator was in any way partial or biased or that he was guilty of misconduct in accepting the Pinkerton report, which was, it is said, introduced merely to impeach the petitioner's credibility ; and the respondent argues that it is elementary that the legal rules of evidence do not apply in arbitration proceedings, so that the inadmissibility of the report upon a trial in a court of law does not affect the propriety of its acceptance by an arbitration tribunal.

By way of preface, I want to state that the issue here is an unusual one, for which I have found no precedents. For this reason, it may be useful to review the common-law evidentiary problems involved before proceeding to the question of whether the award is immune from attack because it was a determination in arbitration and not a judgment at law.

The Pinkerton report admitted in evidence—allegedly to impeach plaintiff's credibility—is defective testimony by any test that would apply in a court of law. The narrative portions of the report are annexed as an exhibit hereto. They consist mostly of a dime-novel series of stories about the petitioner and her behavior, said to be gathered from former neighbors. It is hearsay of the most flagrant character. Indeed, it is hearsay on hearsay, consisting of statements made by neighbors to a detective as to what they had heard about the petitioner. The investigator put these statements in the report, but neither he nor his informants testified personally before the arbitrator. Neither he nor any of the persons who provided or recorded the alleged facts and opinions was put under oath or was made available for cross-examination in the arbitration proceeding.[3] All of the valid reasons for the hear-

---

3. A point not raised by the petitioner is worthy of mention—certainly by way of footnote, for the sake of complete presentation, if for no other.

Neither the contract nor the submission nor the minutes of the hearing before the arbitrator were presented to me. It appears, however, to be implicit from the record that is before me—such as some of the statements in the affidavits and the reporter's stamp on the exhibits—that the proceedings were conducted in accordance with the Rules of the American Arbitration Association. If so, it would seem that the testimony of the Pinkerton detective should have been submitted in person, and if not that, at least by way of affidavit, rather than as an unsworn statement.

say exclusionary rule come into play. (See 5 WIGMORE, EVIDENCE [3d ed.], §§ 1361, 1362, for discussion of the lack of opportunity for cross-examination as the basis for the rule.)

Moreover, the report does not fall under any exception to the hearsay rule under our law. It was not competent as evidence to impeach credibility. A witness may be impeached by evidence that he has a bad reputation for truth and veracity in his neighborhood (Carlson v. Winterson, 147 N.Y. 652, 656). But a stranger sent out by the adverse party may not, for the purpose of impeaching credibility, testify as to the result of his investigation about a witness' reputation for truth (People v. Loris, 131 App. Div. 127, 129). And such testimony must be confined strictly to the reputation of the witness for veracity; the impeaching witness may not testify to specific instances of want of veracity on the part of the witness whose credibility is in question (Theodore v. Daily Mirror, 282 N.Y. 345, 347; People v. Rodawald, 177 N.Y. 408, 424). Nor may specific instances of vicious, immoral or criminal conduct, which might tend to render one unworthy of belief, be testified to by the impeaching witness (Conley v. Meeker, 85 N.Y. 618). Yet, here, the evidence offered defied all of these rules: it was an investigator's second- and third-hand report detailing specific acts of alleged avarice, malice and chicanery, not as such necessarily relevant to the issue of the petitioner's credibility, but capable of placing plaintiff in a highly unfavorable light.

In short, as the most cursory examination of the report will indicate, it was prejudicial to the petitioner in the extreme, and was entirely inadmissible by any test in a court of law. It is perfectly correct, as the respondent argues, that, ordinarily, the rules of evidence do not apply to an arbitration proceeding. The books abound in such statements. But the cases do not, I believe, embrace the instant situation. For there is a substantial difference between the receipt of merely incompetent or irrelevant evidence, and the receipt of thoroughly unfair evidence. None of the precedents that I have been able to dis-

cover deals squarely with the problem where, as here, evidence objected to is not only technically incompetent, but also entirely irrelevant and completely immaterial, and, in addition, inflammatory and prejudicial to the highest degree.

I recognize that, under existing law, an arbitration award may be set aside by the court only upon the bases specified in the statute (Civ. Prac. Act, §§ 1462, 1462-a; Matter of French Textiles Co. [Senor], 7 A D 2d 896; but, see, the intimation in the opinion at Special Term of Associate Judge FROESSEL of the Court of Appeals in Matter of Rosenberg [Wolfe], 180 Misc. 500, 503, that "the interest of justice" is an independent test of the validity of an arbitrator's award, apart from the enumerated statutory grounds for vacatur). Limiting my sights to the statutory provisions referred to, it is my view that the award here is tainted because it was "procured" by the respondent by "undue means" when the respondent offered the offending exhibit in evidence and that the arbitrator, in accepting the proffer, was "guilty of misbehavior" to such an extent as to "prejudice" the rights of the petitioner (Civ. Prac. Act, § 1462, subds. 1, 3).

I have found no helpful cases—one way or the other—defining, in the present context, what is meant by "undue means", "misbehavior" or "prejudice." And, in saying this, I have not overlooked the holding in Matter of Deering Milliken & Co. [Boepple Sportswear Mills] (4 A D 2d 652, affd. 4 N.Y. 2d 956). In that case, the contract giving rise to the arbitration limited the seller's liability for breach in a certain way and provided further that the buyer shall not be entitled to claim consequential damages. The court declined to review the admission of evidence of consequential damages, as it was not apparent either from the award or the record that the arbitrators departed from the fixed formula for determining damages or that they allowed consequential damages. The court said (p. 653) that it "certainly cannot ordinarily review the admission of evidence by arbitrators and cannot assume from the admission of irrelevant evidence that the award made was responsive to that evidence rather than to the standard of judgment provided by the contract." But, as I have said, the offending evidence in the instant case obviously goes far beyond the merely irrelevant. It is my considered opinion that the submission of the Pinkerton report could have had no other purpose but improperly and adversely to affect the petitioner in her right to a fair hearing and determination on the issue to be arbitrated, and that the admission into evidence of the report was prejudicial to the petitioner.

Rule 31 of the Commercial Arbitration Rules of the American Arbitration Association provides that: "The Arbitrator may receive and consider the evidence of witnesses by affidavit, but may give it only such weight as he deems it entitled to after consideration of any objections made to its admission" (see Matter of Milliken Woolens [Weber Knit Sportswear], 20 Misc 2d 504, 509, revd. 11 A D 2d 166, affd. 9 N.Y. 2d 878).

This would appear—without question—to preclude the receipt in evidence of the investigator's unsworn report, even were an affidavit of the data, comments and opinions contained in the present exhibit admissible (as urged by the respondent) on the question of the petitioner's credibility.

The issue before the arbitrator was a simple, narrow one, stated by the respondent in the answering affidavit on this motion as follows, quoting from the petitioner's claim in the arbitration: "The claimant is seeking damages for the conversion and unlawful sale of a quantity of furniture, silverware, household effects, linens and wearing apparel, and other items stored by the respondent and wrongfully sold by the respondent." What possible relevance or materiality the principal statements contained in the report had to this issue I cannot see.

I shall take the liberty of paraphrasing and adding to what Judge Cardozo had to say in another connection (Berizzi Co. v. Krausz, 239 N.Y. 315, 319, *supra*): The declaration of policy embodied in the Arbitration Act does not call for a complete relaxation of all restraints upon the presentation of proof before nonlawyer arbitrators or upon the conduct of arbitrators generally insofar, at least, as those restraints have relation to the fundamentals of a trial and the primary conditions of a fair hearing.

The motion to vacate the award is granted, and the matter is remitted to arbitration anew in accordance with the terms of the contract or submission.

Exhibit

Pinkerton's National Detective Agency, Inc.

Client Muller Brothers		Character of Case Inv. Mrs. Norma Brill
Office of Origin New York	File No. S 838	Status Continuing
Reporting Office New York	Report Made By H. L. K.	Date of Report Thursday, October 13, 1960

Identification

Norma Brill is about 55 years of age, has been married but her present marital status not known.

Resided at 112–35—69th Road, Flushing, L.I., N.Y., from early 1951 until April 1960. Neighbors interviewed call her a "Terrible Woman." These neighbors stated she is a shrewd calculating and shifty person, who would stop at nothing to make money. They say she was married but do not know Mr. Brill's business or what became of him, or if he is still alive or divorced or just separated from Mrs. Brill.

She talked about being in the fur business in Midtown Manhattan and said she was fairly successful.

She arrived in this neighborhood in Queens in 1951, when a man named Charles H. Leger about 65 years old, who was said to be a friend of Norma Brill (whom she met in the fur business in New York City) came over here and he bought the house located at 112–35—69th Road, Forest Hills, N.Y.

The price at that time was said to be $32,000.00. No one knew the exact financial arrangements made at the time, but all neighbors agree that this man Leger, paid a down payment for the house whatever amount was required at the time. The neighbors say "Leger" bought this house because Norma Brill had promised him she would marry him, if he bought the house, showing his good intentions of really getting married to her.

It is said that she persuaded him to come and live with her in this house on the promise she would marry him later. However somehow he confided in her about holding out some financial items he should have noted in his Federal Income Tax returns and after that she used this information to threaten him, and finally persuaded him to sign the house over to her in her name. This was done about January, 1952.

On New Year's Eve and Day, 1/1/1952 she locked him out of the house he bought for her. He was unable to get in and he walked around front of the house and finally was let in by a neighbor Mr. and Mrs. Philip Kelly and he told them a sad story of a scheming woman using him to get a $32,000.00 house and then getting rid of him, although he said he was firmly resolved to marry her. Said she had promised to take care of him and look after him as long as he lived and that he would never have to worry about his old age, that she would always look after him, but that instead she had thrown him out of the very home he had bought because she had asked him to buy it for her to show her he really loved her. After he bought the house, she told him she would not marry him until he turned the deed of the house over to her, to show his sincerity so he signed the house over to her, and a couple of months later she locked him out of the house. She packed a suitcase with his belongings and left them outside the basement entrance to the house. He walked the street until about 3:00 A.M. and he finally rang the bell of the Kellys home at 112–29—69th Road. They let him in and let him sleep there that night. The following day he told the Kelly family that Norma Brill threw him out of his own home and which he had bought, and that he was aware she had another man visit her on week-ends. That she made a good deal of trouble for him. He told the Kellys that he was an investigator for the New York City Board of Education and was employed in the Legal Department, Specializing in Professional Law. He then left the Kellys saying he was going to give this matter of the "House" to the courts and try and get the house back again. After that she (Norma Brill) had her two daughters live there, one was named Janet who also got into a good deal of trouble about debts. Janet lived there for a time then Norma Brill threw her out of the house one night, and Janet also slept with the Kellys that night. The following morning Janet had to call the local police to get her personal belongings out of the house.

Janet is said to be about 30 years of age, her present whereabouts are unknown.

The other daughter Betty (now about 19 years of age) also left one day, and was never seen around the neighborhood again.

Norma Brill rented some of the rooms and at one time had a refined German woman roomer who had a son about six years old. This woman went to work and left the boy with Norma Brill. She was there a few months and Norma Brill accused her of not paying her rent for several weeks and threw her out. This woman also had a problem in getting her personal belongings out of the Brill house.

A short time later Norma Brill rented most of the house to a Brazilian family with two children. Asked $450.00 rent for her place and demanded three months rent as security in advance. These people paid her $1,350.00 and Norma later accused them of not paying this money in advance. These people moved out and later took this case to court in Municipal Court, Non Jury Part at 8 Reade Street, New York. Norma Brill was represented by attorneys Rosoff and Rosoff of 29 Broadway, New York. Norma Brill then kept renting part of the house, furnished, to a number of people, however, none of whom remained long. She then ran out of money, secured a National City Bank loan and gave some place of employment as a reference located on lower Park Avenue, New York. It seems she gave a fictitious employer, and received the loan. The bank had difficulty trying to collect this money, and had to go to court several times. Mrs. Brill tried to get another mortgage (already having two mortgages on the house) and went around to several of the neighbors with negative results. By this time she owed a lot of money, dealers were taking cases to court and banks threatened foreclosure and she finally sold the house to a Mr. Nathan H. Wadler, who has a doctor degree in teaching. He taught at Columbia University and was later sent to Israel to teach there. He is the present owner of the house. He rented the house to a Rabbi Mordecai A. Stern. The Rabbi had no information about Norma Brill.

There was a fire at Brill's house the day after she left to go to Miami, Florida. Neighbors believe she had something to do about this fire. However, no proof or evidence was found by the Fire department, that it was of incendiary origin. She had the whole house refurnished with some fine furniture and after selling the house, she stored the furniture with Muller Brothers. There was some dispute about the sale of the house and the present owner Mr. Wadler had to go to court.

Her furniture was auctioned by Muller Bros. Storage and Warehouse people at 67 Drive and Queens Boulevard, Queens. Sale was held on 4/16/60. She (Norma Brill) attended the sale and was bidding on her own furniture which it was said, was an attempt on her part to bid each item up and in this way derive more money from this sale. She was told by the auctioneer not to bid on her own furniture and this caused quite a disturbance at the time, threatening to sue everybody including Mayor Wagner.

A statement made by a Pinkerton's National Detective Agency uniformed guard, Mr. Hillel Valentine who was on duty on day of the auction sale is attached to this report.

There is a list of suits and judgments against Norma Brill.

October 14, 1960

Mr. Kenner
Investigating Department
Dear Sir:

In accordance with our telephone conversation on the morning of October 14th, I arrived at your office approximately 1:15 PM. Since no-one knew when you were expected to return, I thought it best to type out what I remembered about the case in question. (I would have waited for you but I had my family waiting for me in my car downstairs).

As I remember the case, it was in early spring ... a storage company was auctioning off furniture at one of their warehouses on Queens Boulevard. My duty was to guard the articles that were to be auctioned off.

During the afternoon, after the bidding commenced, a lady approached me and mentioned that one of the bidders was bidding for her own furniture; she knew the bidder ... in fact, if my memory serves me correctly, she and her husband purchased the house from the bidder and were therefore on personal terms with her. They (informant and husband) were aware of the furniture at the warehouse and made up their minds to bid for them. The lady (informant) said that she knew that the bidder had no intentions of living up to the bids she was making.

I informed the auctioneer who stated that he had become aware of the situation. He spoke to the bidder. She stated that the auction of her furniture was against the law and that she was going to sue everyone connected with the unlawful venture. There was an approximate 15 minute interruption during which time the bidder was loud and boisterous. I do not remember her using any vile language but she did manage to disrupt the proceedings. The auctioneer finally persuaded her to report to the office of the Storage Co. (Muller Bros.) to make a formal complaint. I escorted her to the main office, When I returned, the auctioning continued without any further interruption.

Hillel J. Valentine
Security Guard
Shield #2213

NOTE: Bidder mentioned above was Norma Brill. (HJL)
Witnessed by H. L. Kenner

IN THE MATTER OF THE ARBITRATION BETWEEN NORMA BRILL, APPELLANT, AND MULLER BROTHERS, INC., RESPONDENT.
13 N.Y. 2d 776, 192 N.E. 2d 34 (1963)

Order affirmed, without costs, in the following memorandum: The action of an arbitrator in receiving upon the arbitral hearing evidence which would not be admissible in the trial of an action in court does not constitute "corruption, fraud or undue means" or "misbehavior" within the sense and meaning of subdivisions 1 and 3 of section 1462 of the Civil Practice Act.

Concur: CHIEF JUDGE DESMOND and JUDGES DYE, FULD and SCILEPPI. JUDGE VAN VOORHIS dissents in the following opinion in which JUDGES BURKE and FOSTER concur:

VAN VOORHIS, J., dissenting. In this arbitration under a storage contract petitioner sought $30,000 for the conversion of furniture and other items of personal property which the respondent sold at public auction. The arbitrator awarded petitioner $483.04.

Special Term vacated the award on the ground that the receipt in evidence of a report by the Pinkerton Detective Agency which was disparaging of the petitioner's character resulted in procuring the award by "undue means" within the meaning of subdivision 1 of section 1462 of the Civil Practice Act and constituted "misbehavior" by the arbitrator within the meaning of subdivision 3 of section 1462 of the Civil Practice Act.

The Appellate Division held that while receipt of the report may have been unwise it did not constitute a ground for vacatur of the award, that the propriety of the admission of the report into evidence was not for the courts to review, and, in any event, there was no proof that the award resulted from consideration of the report.

The Pinkerton report contained a list of lawsuits in which appellant was presumably involved and a report by the private detective of what neighbors purportedly said about appellant, including matters which they said they had heard others say, or had heard from others that still others had heard about appellant. According to the present respondent's brief in the Appellate Division, its purpose in putting this Pinkerton report into evidence before the arbitrators was to portray appellant as possessing a highly litigious nature and to impair her credibility.

Such procedure, in our view, can hardly be countenanced even in arbitration. The report of a detective agency employed to dredge up whatever defamatory or derogatory things may be said justly or unjustly, accurately or untruthfully, by enemies or neighbors or whatever persons may be discovered or imagined, identified or unidentified, based on hearsay and multiple hearsay has no place in the judicial process in court or by arbitration. Special Term correctly characterized this as "an investigator's second and third hand report detailing specific acts of alleged avarice, malice, and chicanery, not as such necessarily relevant to the issue of the petitioner's credibility, but capable of placing petitioner in a highly unfavorable light." After stating that this was prejudicial to the petitioner in the extreme, and entirely inadmissible by any test, Special Term noted correctly that "there is a substantial difference between the receipt of merely incompetent or irrelevant evidence, and the receipt of thoroughly unfair evidence" which "goes far beyond the merely irrelevant", from which Special Term concluded: "It is my considered opinion that the submission of the Pinkerton report could have had no other purpose but improperly and adversely to affect the petitioner in her right to a fair hearing and determination on the issues to be arbitrated, and that the admission into evidence of the report was prejudicial to the petitioner."

This constituted, in our opinion, "undue means" within the meaning of subdivision 1 of section 1462 of the Civil Practice Act requiring the award to be set aside. The admission of this report also in our opinion, constituted "misbehavior" by the arbitrator within the meaning of subdivision 3 of section 1462 of the Civil Practice Act.

The order appealed from should be reversed and the matter remanded for a hearing before another arbitrator to be selected, if possible, by agreement between the parties, but, if they are unable to agree, then as otherwise provided by the Arbitration Article of the Civil Practice Act.

Order affirmed.

For informed discussions of questions concerning evidence in labor arbitration, see DALLAS JONES, ed., PROBLEMS OF PROOF IN ARBITRATION (1967) and Edgar Jones, *Evidentiary Concepts in Labor Arbitration: Some Modern Variations on Ancient Legal Themes,* 13 U.C.L.A. L. REV. 1241 (1966).

A NOTE ON PRE-HEARING AND HEARING ARRANGEMENTS

Few arbitral arrangements provide for pre-hearing formalities whose purpose is to enable the other side to prepare for the hearing. Of course, in a labor-management dispute the parties presumably have explored each other's reasons and proof during the several stages of the grievance procedure. But even that does not enable the other to anticipate and plan for the witnesses and proof actually adduced. This can mean that hearings are less compact and the proof less orderly than if parties exchanged witness lists and brief summaries of testimony to be proffered. On occasion, adjournments may be necessary to overcome "surprise" or the colorable claim of it (a particular problem where state statutes—assuming they could be applied— make improper refusal to grant continuances a ground for vacating an award).

The parties can avoid postponements and generally improve the quality of the hearing by having it conducted where relevant records and potential witnesses (for both sides) are, usually— in labor cases—the work place, rather than some technically neutral site. Such an arrangement also makes it possible to keep potential witnesses at work until shortly before they are needed rather than gathering everyone "for the duration" of the entire proceeding.

Nor is it common to enlighten the arbitrator before the hearing about the issues of the dispute (beyond advising him, if he is chosen *ad hoc*, when seeking his services of the general nature of the case, *e.g.* discharge, contract interpretation, wage classification). Hence the arbitrator starts the hearing with little notion of the issues, without having read critical documents or the disputed passages of the agreement, and without any advance reflection about potential secondary issues. This almost complete innocence makes it difficult for him to aid the parties in framing the issues early in the hearing. And his own appreciation of contentions and evidence may be incomplete until he learns enough about the dispute to focus upon the issues he must decide.

My own frequent practice is to ask each party to provide in advance of the hearing a statement of his version of the basic facts, issues, and agreement provisions in controversy. I can then at least study the contract. Some may object that such a study may lead to erroneous impressions. But at the hearing each side has the opportunity to present only its version, and that is not regarded as inappropriate. An arbitrator must surely know how to familiarize himself with each party's version without making up his mind before all the story and arguments are in.

Indeed, such prestudy enables the arbitrator to formulate his own questions in time for the hearing, when they can be discussed in the presence of all parties.

CHAPTER V

THE ARBITRATOR

SELECTION

The parties control the selection of the arbitrator. They can name him in their agreement, specify the method of selection, or adopt the procedures of some institution, such as the American Arbitration Association, the International Chamber of Commerce, or the Federal Mediation and Conciliation Service. The AAA and FMCS rules in the appendices describe their procedures. Some association and most exchange rules provide for institutional designation of the arbitrator.

Different arbitrators and procedures may be desirable according to the nature of the issue in dispute. For example, controversies over quality may be better decided by an association panel or individuals with technical expertise whereas contract interpretation issues may call for business management or trading expertise. There seems to be no reason for parties to limit themselves to but one arbitrator, tribunal, or procedure, if different kinds of questions can arise and warrant differing treatment. With forethought, they could provide for various arbitral methods and combinations according to the claims made. Where the parties differ as to the essential nature of the dispute, a neutral arbitrator expert in each aspect claimed to be relevant should serve. Lest this procedure prove

more expensive than the parties believe warranted, they could limit the multi-arbitrator arrangement to claims involving in excess of stipulated amounts. No reason appears to prevent providing for procedures which differ according to the amount in controversy.

A "profile" of AAA arbitrators can be found in STEVEN LAZARUS et al., RESOLVING BUSINESS DISPUTES 68–69 (1965). A similar description of the age and vocation of AAA labor arbitrators is provided by Robert Coulson, "Spring Check-up on Labor Arbitration Procedure," 16 LAB. L. J. 259 (1965).

COMMERCIAL ARBITRATORS—
THE ISSUE OF COMPENSATION

Arbitrators in commercial cases under the auspices of the AAA serve without fee, as do many panelists in trade association and exchange arbitrations. Arbitrators selected individually by the parties, however, often are compensated, some very well indeed. One set of commentators summarizes the major arguments:

> Compensation of commercial arbitrators is a subject which has been debated for years. Proponents argue that adequate compensation would foster the development of a cadre of professional commercial arbitrators who would be widely reputed, experienced, and well qualified. Opponents argue that the neces-

sity for compensation would eliminate one of the principal advantages of commercial arbitration— economy.

There are further questions. Would a financial incentive attract a more capable arbitrator than would a social incentive? Is it practical to institutionalize the commercial arbitrator's role? While in labor arbitration there is a cadre of professional, paid arbitrators, there are basic differences which inhibit us from generalizing from the labor experience. First, businessmen arbitrators who are expert in their fields are often allowed by their companies to serve because such service contributes to the public or industry good. This public-service motivation might be eliminated if commercial arbitrators were paid, and there might actually occur a reduction in the number of arbitrators available, Secondly, commercial cases in particular fields could arise so infrequently that it would not be feasible to attempt to maintain professional commercial arbitrators in each of these areas.

Lazarus et al., RESOLVING BUSINESS DISPUTES 79 (1965). Some critics of labor arbitration question the wisdom of paying arbitrators on the ground that this gives them an interest in gaining the favor of future potential patrons. Critics of nonpayment question the wisdom of expecting from volunteers the degree of attention and diligence required for important cases.

STRONG v. STRONG
12 Cush. (66 Mass.) 135 (1853)

SHAW, C. J. This case was formerly before the court, on the exceptions of the defendant to a verdict for the plaintiff, in a suit on a bond to abide an award of arbitrators. Strong v. Strong, 9 Cush. 560. All the exceptions were overruled except one; and the verdict was so far set aside as to permit the defendant to go to trial on a point stated in the fifth item of the answer, and which was not submitted to the jury. That fifth specification of defence was thus stated in the answer: 5. "Because Luther Edwards, one of the arbitrators, was not a disinterested person, and in making said award, conducted himself with partiality to the plaintiff."

This case has again been tried upon this issue, and a verdict returned for the plaintiff. It appears by the report in this case, that it was left to the jury upon all the evidence, with directions, that if they believed, on the evidence, that Edwards was not distinterested, or that he conducted himself with partiality to the plaintiff, the award was void, and they would so find; otherwise they would find for the plaintiff. These instructions were right, and we think sufficient.

In the former case there was evidence tending to show that the arbitrator was influenced by the consideration that he was selected by the plaintiff, and felt himself rather committed as the plaintiff's man. These were explicitly denied by the arbitrator in his testimony on this trial; and it was for the jury to weigh the evidence and pass on the credit of witnesses.

It was certainly extremely reprehensible for the plaintiff to talk privately to the arbitrator before the award was made, on the matters in controversy between him and his father, which the arbitrators were judicially to act upon; but we are not disposed to say, that this circumstance alone, against any and all counteracting evidence, is sufficient proof of culpable partiality to set aside the unanimous award of five arbitrators.

Exceptions overruled, and judgment on the award.

FIRST NAT. BANK IN CEDAR FALLS v. CLAY 231 Iowa 703, 2 N.W. 2d 85 (1942)

[Plaintiff, the Bank, sued to vacate award; judgment for defendant; plaintiff appealed.]

BLISS C. J.: In support of its first proposition, appellant states its position to be that when there is a communication between a party and an arbitrator in the absence of the other parties, the award should be set aside even though no wrong was intended. We have found no sound authority supporting such rule. It is in clear conflict with the pronouncements of this court from its organization. Such a rule condemns what the appellant did when its president, vice-president and counsel met its arbitrator in conference in its directors' room to notify him of his selection. We are not criticizing them for this conference, but it would hardly justify the setting aside of an award favorable to the plaintiff had it received one.

As said by Morse in his work "On the Law of Arbitration and Award" page 535:

> But it is not misconduct on the part of a person to whom application is made to act as arbitrator, and who afterwards consents to do so, if at the time of the request he inquires of the party preferring it as to the general nature of the controversy in relation to which his services are wanted. This is only what usually and perfectly proper occurs in such cases. A person cannot be expected to accept such an office with no idea as to the character of the duties which it will involve, or whether it may be

within the scope of his powers or knowledge to fulfill them.

Campbell v. Western, 3 Paige, N.Y. 124.

AMERICAN EAGLE FIRE INS. CO. v. NEW JERSEY FIRE INS. CO.
240 N.Y. 398, 148 N.E. 562 (1925)

The facts herein are as follows: In the year 1920, pursuant to an agreement made in the latter part of December, 1919, New Jersey Insurance Company, appellant, issued one or more policies of re-insurance to American Eagle Fire Insurance Company, The American Insurance Company, Fidelity-Phenix Fire Insurance Company, Glens Falls Insurance Company and Hanover Fire Insurance Company.

New Jersey Insurance Company refused to pay losses under the re-insurance policies, claiming that they were invalid because of alleged misrepresentation and concealment. Accordingly, under date of August 22, 1922, the parties executed an agreement and submission to arbitration in which the dispute as to the validity of the policies was submitted to three arbitrators. Two of the arbitrators, Mr. Osborn and Mr. Ullman, were named in the arbitration agreement, and the third arbitrator, Mr. Cox, was later appointed by written agreement between the parties.

The arbitration agreement provided that an award should be made on or before November 1, 1922. This date was extended to December 1 by written agreement. The first hearing before the arbitrators was held on November 2 and hearings continued thereafter from time to time to December 4, 1922. A large number of witnesses were examined, approximately four hundred pages of testimony were taken and a large number of exhibits were submitted. At the request of the arbitrators the time within which the award might be made was first extended to December 15 and was later extended to December 22, 1922. Briefs were submitted to the arbitrators on December 16 and several sessions were held by them to discuss their decision. On the afternoon of December 21, the day before the date on which the award was required pursuant to the last extension, the arbitrators held a meeting and requested that the parties agree to a further extension of the time within which an award might be rendered. This was agreed to by the five companies but was refused by New Jersey Insurance Company. Mr. Osborn, one of the three arbitrators, then stated at this meeting on December 21, in the presence of the other

two arbitrators and of counsel for both parties, that he felt he could not do justice to the case in the short time remaining, namely, prior to midnight of the following day, and that unless a further extension were granted he would resign. Meanwhile, Mr. Osborn had been in touch with respondents' attorneys and was obtaining cases from them to sustain their side of the controversy. A further meeting was held on the morning of December 22, at which Mr. Cox and Mr. Ullman, two of the arbitrators, were present. At this meeting was presented and read a letter from Mr. Osborn in which he said: "I must and do therefore resign." Mr. Osborn was not present at this meeting and took no part in any of the proceedings after the meeting of December 21. After discussion Mr. Cox stated that he and Mr. Ullman would spend the rest of the day in going over the evidence, exhibits and briefs and that if he and Mr. Ullman, the other arbitrator, could concur in a decision they would render an award. An award was made and signed by them.

The first paragraph of the arbitration agreement provided as follows:

First. The parties hereto name and appoint Frank H. Osborn and Albert Ullman as two of the three arbitrators herein provided for. In the event that Frank H. Osborn shall refuse to act as such arbitrator, or having accepted the appointment hereunder *shall later cease to act as such arbitrator through death, resignation or otherwise, the parties of the first part shall elect an arbitrator from among the individuals* named in the list of "Proposed Arbitrators," annexed hereto, and so as to each of the other arbitrators.

Fourth. It is understood and agreed that the arbitrators, or a majority of them, are to determine whether or not the said policies are unenforcible by reason of any misrepresentation or concealment of material facts by the agent or agents of the parties of the first part or any of them.

In the event that the arbitrators, or a majority of them, shall find and determine that the said policies are so unenforcible they shall find in their awards that nothing is due from any of the parties hereto to any of the other parties hereto, arising out of the issuance of said policies.

Fifth. . . . The awards shall be in writing, shall be subscribed by all of the arbitrators *unless only two of the arbitrators shall agree upon said award,* in which case it shall be signed by the two arbitrators so agreeing. . . . *An award by a majority of the arbitrators shall be valid and binding.*

On December 20, 1923, New Jersey Insurance Company brought on for hearing before Special Term a motion to confirm the purported award made by the two arbitrators following the resignation of Mr. Osborn. The Special Term denied the motion, holding that under the express provisions of the first clause of the arbitration agreement, the two remaining arbitrators were without power to make the award, in view of the fact that Mr. Osborn, the third arbitrator, had resigned or ceased to act and held that the purported award was a nullity and vacated it. On appeal the Appellate Division unanimously affirmed without opinion the order of Special Term. The matter is now before this court as the result of leave to appeal granted by this court.

POUND, J. The question is whether, after the final submission of an arbitration, one of three arbitrators may by his resignation prevent the other two arbitrators from making a valid award under a submission providing for an award by a majority and for the filling of vacancies in case an arbitrator resigns. It is contended on one hand that, while the final award may unquestionably be made by a majority of the arbitrators, nevertheless in case of a vacancy by resignation before the final award is made, the agreement requires literally the choice of a substitute arbitrator before an award can be made; it is contended on the other hand that the arbitration proceedings proper, which require all the arbitrators to act, end when the case is finally submitted to the arbitrators for their decision and that the withdrawal of an arbitrator thereafter is of no more importance than the equivalent of a dissent.

The Legislature by the enactment of the Arbitration Law of 1920, and this court by upholding broadly the constitutionality of the statute (Matter of Berkowitz v. Arbib & Houlberg, Inc., 230 N.Y. 261), have given a new importance to arbitration tribunals set up by the parties as a substitute for the courts in the settlement of controversies. To approach the consideration of the question we may, therefore, properly bear in mind the development of the common law of arbitration through the statutes to its present stage.

But first, the practice of arbitrators of conducting themselves as champions of their nominators is to be condemned as contrary to the purpose of arbitrations and as calculated to bring the system of enforced arbitrations into disrepute. An arbitrator acts in a quasi-judicial capacity and should possess the judicial qualifications of fairness to both parties so that he may render a faithful, honest and disinterested opinion. He is not an advocate whose function is to convince the umpire or third arbitrator. He should keep his own counsel and not run to his nominator for advice when he sees that he may be in the minority. When once he enters into an arbitration he ceases to act as the agent of the party who appoints him. He must lay aside all bias and approach the case with a mind open to conviction and without regard to his previously formed opinions as to the merits of the party or the cause. He should sedulously refrain from any conduct which might justify even the inference that either party is the special recipient of his solicitude or favor. The oath of the arbitrators is the rule and guide of their conduct. Civil Practice Act, section 1452, prescribes the form of oath as follows:

> Before hearing any testimony, arbitrators selected either as prescribed in this article or otherwise must be sworn, by an officer authorized by law to administer an oath, *faithfully and fairly to hear and examine the matters in controversy and to make a just award according to the best of their understanding.* . . .

The oath may be waived, but the obligation remains. Although a known interest does not disqualify and the parties may not complain merely because the arbitrators named were known to be chosen with a view to a particular relationship to their nominator or to the subject-matter of the controversy, they are entitled to expect the arbitrators thus chosen will proceed with indifference and impartiality.

Viewed with this background, the law forbids the arbitrator, even though he acts with good intentions, so to conduct himself as to defeat the purpose of the arbitration by acting either for his own convenience or in the supposed interests of the party by whom he is named, except as he has, under Civil Practice Act, section 1453, the naked power to withdraw before all the proofs and allegations are heard. (Matter of Bullard v. Grace Co., 240 N.Y. 388, decided herewith.) He accepts responsibilities to which convenience and favor must defer. We may assume that Mr. Osborn's conduct was inspired by the best of reasons and with no intention to frustrate the arbitration for ulterior ends. Another might follow the same course of conduct that he followed with an eye single to his own convenience or the interest of his nominator to avoid an adverse decision. Such an untoward result should be avoided unless the law applicable to arbitrations permits the arbitration to be brought to so impotent a conclusion.

The provisions of the Civil Practice Act so far as practicable and consistent apply to arbitration agreements. Material provisions are as follows:

> § 1451. Hearings by arbitrators. Subject to the terms of the submission, if any are specified therein, the arbitrators selected as prescribed in this article must appoint a time and place for the hearing of the matters submitted to them, and must cause notice

thereof to be given to each of the parties. They, or a majority of them, may adjourn the hearing from time to time upon the application of either party for good cause shown or upon their own motion, *but not beyond the day fixed in the submission for rendering their award, unless the time so fixed is extended by the written consent of the parties to the submission or their attorneys.*

§ 1453. Power of arbitrators. The arbitrators selected either as prescribed in this article or otherwise, or a majority of them, may require any person to attend before them as a witness; and they have, and each of them has, the same powers with respect to all the proceedings before them which are conferred upon a board or a member of a board authorized by law to hear testimony. *All the arbitrators selected as prescribed in this article must meet together and hear all the allegations and proofs of the parties, but an award by a majority of them is valid unless the concurrence of all is expressly required in the submission.*

The scheme of the law thus divides the arbitration proceedings into two parts: (a) the hearing, and (b) the decision and award. All the arbitrators must hear the allegations and proofs of the parties but an award by a majority of them is valid unless the submission otherwise provides. Even when prior to the enactment of the Arbitration Law of 1920 agreements to arbitrate and submissions were arbitrarily revocable up to a certain stage in the proceedings, the Code of Civil Procedure, section 2383, drew the line thus indicated between the hearing and the award. It read: "A submission to arbitration . . . cannot be revoked by either party, after the allegations and proofs of the parties have been closed, and the matter finally submitted to the arbitrators for their decision." Now that agreements to arbitrate are no longer revocable at the will of a party but may be enforced by a party who is aggrieved by a refusal to proceed to arbitration, this limitation no longer has a place in the law and has been repealed, but it is significant that even under the earlier practice a party who stayed in until the final submission to the arbitrators for their decision could no longer trim his sails to shift his course when the wind of defeat began to rise.

At common law more latitude was allowed as to the hearing. Where the submission was to three with power to two to make the award, two had power to hear where the third was notified and refused to attend or was willfully absent (Crofoot v. Allen, 2 Wend, 494), but by the Revised Statutes (now Civil Practice Act) all the arbitrators were required to hear all the proofs and allegations of the parties, otherwise the award was a nullity. (Bulson v. Lohnes, 29 N.Y. 291.) No further change was made in the

common law. It is not said that all the arbitrators must participate in making the award. That is an exception to the general rule which may be expressly stipulated for by the parties. All the arbitrators should be notified to meet for deliberation so that opportunity for full consultation is furnished but it is not the rule that one may then by wilful absence,—and resignation at this stage is no less than wilful absence, —prevent an award by a majority. All should meet and hear the proofs but the report of two is valid unless the third has been excluded from participation in their deliberations without fault on his part. The refusal of the third arbitrator to attend after final submission ceases to be material when its effect would be to juggle one of the parties out of the benefit of the arbitration. (Carpenter v. Wood, 42 Mass. 409.) If an arbitrator may resign at the last moment, if concert of action in reaching a decision as distinguished from the award itself is necessary, no award could be reached in any case if at the eleventh hour one of the three found himself in the minority and sought to serve his own interests or those of the party naming him by resigning. The law does not contemplate that the edifice thus elaborately raised should be toppled over by such an untimely explosion from within. The salutary purpose of an arbitration is the summary and extrajudicial settlement of controversies between parties. The court should pause before permitting a technical and strained construction of the law or the agreement of the parties to defeat that purpose. If the law or the parties contemplate the possibility of an endless chain of frustrated arbitrations or the summary termination of the submission when the pen is in the hand of two of the arbitrators to sign an award, the meaning should be unmistakably expressed. It is highly improbable that any arbitration agreement or submission to arbitration would be made if it would involve the parties in such absurd consequences. Laws should be construed sensibly and plain purposes should not be defeated by narrow interpretations.

It follows that the withdrawal of one of the arbitrators on the threshold of a formal award does not end the authority of the other two unless the terms of the arbitration submission take the case out of the general rule governing majority awards. The arbitration agreement and the Civil Practice Act should be read in harmony where harmony is possible. Literally, the agreement provides that if an arbitrator ceases to act a substitute arbitrator shall be chosen. But the substitute clause need not be read so crabbedly as to permit an unreasonable result in flat contradiction of the common and statute law.

The letter should be enlarged within legitimate bounds, rather than limited, when the end in view may thereby be more effectually accomplished.

Under a fair and equitable interpretation of the submission agreement, a vacancy caused by the withdrawal of an arbitrator need not be filled after the case has been heard, considered and practically decided. The withdrawal at that point does not prejudice the rights of the parties to a hearing before a full board and an award by a majority or make necessary a rehearing of all the allegations and proofs of the parties before a substitute arbitrator.

The orders should be reversed, with costs in all courts, and application to confirm award granted, with ten dollars costs.

CRANE, J. dissenting. The Arbitration Law is based on contract. There can be no arbitration enforced upon the parties by the courts in the absence of contract. The contract of arbitration is to be construed like any other contract and all its terms and conditions given force and effect unless they are against public policy or illegal. (Matter of Zimmerman v. Cohen, 236 N.Y. 15.)

Article 2, sections 3 and 4 of the Arbitration Law are based upon a previous existing contract. If the contract provides how an arbitrator shall be appointed in case of failure or neglect of one to act, this method must be pursued. The court acts only on failure of the parties to live up to the contract. There is nothing in the law that prevents the parties from contracting for the appointment of three arbitrators, and that if one should resign after the hearings were closed, and before decision, another should be appointed in his place. In fact, this is what happens in case of death. Should one of three arbitrators die at the end of the hearings and before decision, another arbitrator, in my opinion, would have to be appointed to take his place. An award by the two living arbitrators would be void.

The result is the same when one of the arbitrators ceases to exist as such by resignation. He is actually dead to the proceeding. The case would be different if his resignation was brought about by the action of the party appointing him, or was done in bad faith. We must assume in this case, after the unanimous affirmance, that Osborn's resignation was in the utmost good faith ; and it is conceded that the respondents are not the cause, but the sufferers. They contracted for just such an emergency in the very first paragraph of the arbitration agreement.

In the event that Frank H. Osborn shall refuse to act as such arbitrator or, having accepted the appointment hereunder, shall later cease to act as such arbitrator through death, resignation or otherwise, the parties of the first part shall (1) elect an arbitrator from among the individuals named in the list of "Proposed Arbitrators," annexed hereto.

The opinion of this court in my judgment amends and modifies this contract. The resignation of Osborn, it says, must take place before the hearings have ended and not after. There is no such limitation in the contract. The parties have agreed otherwise, and as I have before stated, I do not think the law prevents them from making such an agreement. Such a limitation does not apply, I take it, in case of Osborn's death after a hearing and before decision. Why should there be this limitation in the one instance and not in the other? Of course we must assume that there was the utmost good faith in the resignation. Bad faith changes all things. The cases where an arbitrator deliberately resigns in order to prevent an adverse decision can be dealt with when they arrive. This is not such a case.

The contract having provided for an arbitration, the decision was as important as the hearings. The respondents were entitled to an arbitrator appointed by them to discuss the case and present his views, whatever they were, and both parties were entitled to their arbitrators able to act and functioning as such at the time of the decision, although the majority vote of the three could make the decision. (Civ. Prac. Act, sect. 1453.)

Such is the contract as I read it, which the parties have made. For these reasons I dissent.

A NOTE ON THE USE OF MULTI-ARBITRATOR PANELS AND TENTATIVE AWARDS

Until the recent past "the arbitrator" usually was three persons rather than one. Quite commonly submissions to arbitration called for each party to select an arbitrator and for the two thus selected to choose the third. Of course, in many institutional arrangements panels of three or even more were often used and still are.

The use of more than one arbitrator increases costs, however, and may also make the proceeding more slow moving as all three (or five or seven) arbitrators consult and vote on procedural questions. (That difficulty could be obviated by conferring the power to rule upon the chairman. But the resulting rulings might not satisfy the other panel members, especially if evidence is excluded that anyone believed pertinent.) And scheduling problems, often a sticky detail of arbitration where parties, lawyers, and arbitrators have packed schedules, are multiplied.

As a result, arbitration by a single arbitrator has become standard. Some state statutes provide that in the absence of the specification in the agreement of the number of arbitrators, one will be deemed intended. Section 15 of the American Arbitration Association's Voluntary Labor Arbitration Rules is to the same effect, but the Commercial Rules are silent on the point although Rules 12 and 13 seem to assume a single arbitrator.

However, multi-arbitrator panels frequently have their uses.

The expected issues may pose difficulties requiring the expertise of several specialized skills. While this need might be met by "expert" witnesses, the common tendency of experts to diverge along the lines of the interests of the parties frequently requires expertise by an arbitrator to assess the experts' presentations. For example, take the situation of a claim against an oil-well driller by an oil prospector for allegedly improper drilling. The direct evidence is several hundred or thousand feet in the earth. Surely an engineer familiar with oil-well drilling would be useful on the panel. So would an oil geologist. And to deal with the allocation of risks and burdens, a businessman (or possibly a lawyer) with experience in the field would be desirable.

An arbitrator selected by one party alone may be useful in insuring that an *ad hoc* neutral arbitrator fully understands the view and situation of each party. In order to be useful in this way the party-selected arbitrator must be familiar with them, otherwise he may be partisan but uninformative. It would be duplicative to have the party-appointed arbitrators merely argue again what was argued at the hearing. But the neutral arbitrator can test his understanding of the significance of evidence or the tenability of a contract interpretation upon a fellow arbitrator who knows enough to offer guidance and assessment. The arbitrator may not fully understand or appreciate evidence or contentions made early in the hearing before he got his bearings. Many arbitrators attest that not infrequently the issues do not emerge with any clarity until quite late in the proceedings. Posthearing consultation with the party-appointed arbitrators can fill in the resulting gaps.

On occasion, the rationales offered by the parties at the hearing prove equally unsatisfactory. An arbitrator who undertakes a resolution of the dispute without knowledge of whether his theory, which emerges after the hearing, will work with at least one of the parties runs a high risk of making a mistake. The arbitrator's solution may prove to be objectionable to both parties and was not put forward for that very reason. In the ordinary case, if it is a contract rather than a fact issue, the interpretation should coincide with the understanding of at least one party as to what the contract means. Otherwise, one achieves the anomalous result of giving the contract a meaning not intended or desired by either contracting party, which would be carrying the objective theory of contract formation rather far. With *informed* partisan arbitrators present and available, the tie-breaking neutral can test out his views. If they prove "wrong," they can be withdrawn and reworked, whereas the solo arbitrator must decide either on grounds unacceptable to him or run considerable risk of making a mistake.

The tripartite format can be misused for a secret "sell-out" by a partisan arbitrator, which might be difficult to distinguish from a candid admission that his side's view lacked merit.

An alternative to the multi-arbitrator format that also makes the parties' views available to the arbitrator before his decision becomes final is the "tentative award." The arbitrator can state his views orally or in writing for comment by the parties. I can attest to the utility of this device because I have used it often and have made some changes in awards and many changes in opinions after submitting tentative awards to party criticism.

If the parties must meet for the critique, there is the problem of time consumed and the possibility of an unproductive rehash of arguments. For those who believe in the cathartic value of arbitration, even such an argument may not be totally useless.

Given the fact that so many arbitrators are strangers to the parties and issues involved, the "tentative award" can be a useful device to guard against unwitting arbitral error.

MATTER OF LIPSCHUTZ (GUTWIRTH)
304 N.Y. 58, 106 N.E. 2d 8 (1952)

CONWAY, J. This is an appeal, as of right, from an order of the Appellate Division, First Department, unanimously modifying on the law and the facts an order of Special Term of Supreme Court, New York County, directing that the parties proceed to arbitration and appointing an arbitrator.

Appellants, Isidore Lipschutz and Charles Gutwirth, and respondent, Albert Gutwirth, nephew of Isidore and son of Charles, are parties to a partnership agreement. An arbitration clause in that agreement provides for the arbitration of disputes by three arbitrators—"the First Party [Isidore Lipschutz] shall select his arbitrator, and the Second and Third Parties [Charles and Albert Gutwirth, father and son] jointly shall select their arbitrator ; and the two arbitrators shall thereupon select a third arbitrator.

Controversies arose between appellants and respondent due to the latter's alleged lack of concern for the welfare of the partnership. Pursuant to the arbitration clause Isidore demanded that the controversy be submitted to arbitration and designated his arbitrator. Albert and Charles could not, however, agree upon a joint arbitrator—due, among other things, to Albert's insistence that he be permitted to select an arbitrator independently since the interests of Charles and Isidore in the controversy were identical and adverse to his. Upon motion made by appellants and pursuant to sections 1450 and 1452 of the Civil Practice Act, Special Term appointed a joint arbitrator for Charles and Albert and directed that arbitration proceed. That joint arbitrator together with the arbitrator selected by Isidore chose a third person as provided by the agreement of the parties. Respondent thereupon appealed to the Appellate Division which was of the opinion that because of the change in alignment of the partners, not contemplated when the agreement was entered into, the contract providing for arbitration "should be construed as though no method [for appointing arbitrators] were provided therein." (278 App. Div. 132, 133.) That court then entered an order appointing a single arbitrator and directing that arbitration proceed before such person.

The sole question presented on this appeal is whether, under the circumstances presented, it was error for the Appellate Division to disregard the provisions of the contract of the parties which provided for the settlement of disputes by a panel of three arbitrators, one of whom was to be selected by appellant Isidore.

Appellants contend that the Appellate Division, in appointing a single arbitrator, has rewritten the contract of the parties. Respondent, on the other hand, argues that the designation of a single arbitrator was a proper exercise of discretion, especially since appellants allegedly seek to deprive respondent of his interest in the firm.

The present statutory provisions regarding arbitration are to be found in article 84 of the Civil Practice Act (L. 1937, ch. 341, as amd.). The purpose of that article is to give effect to contracts providing for the settlement of disputes before tribunals of the parties' own choosing by rendering such agreements irrevocable and, in effect, subject to specific enforcement. The provisions of article 84 are intended to strengthen—not change—the rights and obligations of parties to arbitration agreements. The law "does not bring the contract into being, but adds a new implement, the remedy of specific performance, for its more effectual enforcement." (Matter of Marchant v. Mead-Morrison Mfg. Co., 252 N.Y. 284, 293.)

The spirit of the arbitration law being the fuller effectuation of contractual rights, the method for selecting arbitrators and the composition of the arbitral tribunal have been left to the contract of the parties. Sections 1450, 1453, and 1462 of article 84 bear witness to the fact that the Legislature in enacting that article intended that the Supreme Court give due regard to the method and procedure prescribed by the contract of the parties. However, at times parties, for one reason or another, fail to make provision for a method of naming arbitrators or fail to designate in their contract the panel of arbitrators or the arbitrator who is to settle their dispute. An order directing the parties to agree on the matter in dispute would be impractical since an agreement, by its very nature, is dependent upon the concurrence of free wills and cannot be brought into existence by coercion. Moreover, even though a method has been provided, a party may refuse to avail himself of his right, under the contract, to select an arbitrator. In the absence of statutory provision for the appointment of arbitrators under those circumstances, the plan for arbitration could be thwarted and the right of the other party or parties rendered valueless. Section 1452 of the Civil Practice Act, conferring power upon the Supreme Court to designate arbitrators, was enacted to cover such situations. It is apparent from a reading of section 1452 that it is but part of the overall plan of article 84 of the Civil Practice Act to honor the contractual rights and obligations of the parties. That section is entitled, *"Provision in case of failure to name arbitrator or umpire"* and provides:

> If, in the contract for arbitration . . . provision be made for a method of naming or appointing an arbitrator or arbitrators or an umpire, such method shall be followed; but if no method be provided therein, or if a method be provided and any party thereto shall fail to avail himself of such method, or for any reason there shall be a lapse in the naming of an arbitrator or arbitrators or umpire, or in filling a vacancy, then, upon application by either party to the controversy, the supreme court, or a judge thereof, shall designate and appoint an arbitrator or arbitrators or umpire, as the case may require, who shall act under the said contract . . . with the same

force and effect as if he or they had been specifically named therein; and unless otherwise provided, the arbitration shall be by a single arbitrator.

From the plain wording of that section it will be seen that if the parties have provided for a method of naming or appointing an arbitrator the Supreme Court shall follow such method and is empowered to designate an arbitrator only if "any party thereto shall fail to avail himself of such method, or for any reason there shall be a lapse in the naming of an arbitrator or arbitrators." It is also clear that the power of the court to provide for arbitration by a single arbitrator is limited to those cases where the parties have not provided otherwise—"*unless otherwise provided,* the arbitration shall be by a single arbitrator." (Emphasis supplied.)

The right to have disputes adjusted by several rather than one arbitrator is not to be lightly regarded. The widespread practice of parties to arbitration agreements of making provision for those rights indicates the value placed upon them. Our appellate systems are a result of the general view that there is less possibility for error where the question for decision is· to be considered by a tribunal consisting of more than one person.

Here the contract of the parties provides for a panel comprised of three persons. Appellant Isidore has the *contract right to appoint one arbitrator.* Appellant Charles and respondent Albert have the *contract right to appoint a second arbitrator.* The two arbitrators thus selected have the *contract power* to select a third arbitrator. Despite those facts the Appellate Division has sought to compel the parties to submit their controversy to a single arbitrator. Clearly since Charles and Albert cannot agree upon an arbitrator the Supreme Court, under the provisions of section 1452, has the *statutory power* to appoint an arbitrator for Charles and Albert jointly. However, that is the limit of the court's power. The arbitrator so selected and the one chosen by Isidore will select a third.

Undoubtedly the Supreme Court in acting in arbitration matters does act as a court of equity —it applies equitable principles and enjoys a certain latitude of discretion. (Matter of Feuer Transp., Inc. [Local No. 445], 295 N.Y. 87; Western Union Tel. Co. v. Selly, 295 N.Y. 395.) Furthermore, it is familiar law that equitable relief may be tailored to the demands of circumstances and that the granting of the remedy of specific performance rests in the broad discretion of the court. (2 STORY, EQUITY JURISPRUDENCE [14th ed.], §§ 1026–1027 pp. 407–408.) However, it is also well established that equitable discretion is limited to the necessities of the situation. In addition in matters arising under article 84 that discretion must be exercised in consonance with the agreement made by the parties and to that extent it may be said that the discretion of the court in arbitration matters is not as broad and untrammeled as that of equity generally. The court should unless there exists a real probability that injustice will result, adhere to the method established by the contract and forego the rewriting of the contract for the parties. No such probability exists here.

Let us assume for the purpose of discussion a situation where a dispute arises and the alignment remains the same as that supposedly contemplated at the time the contract was drawn viz., Charles and his son Albert arrayed against Isidore. It is conceivable that Charles and Albert, though their interests in the dispute be identical, would be unable to agree on the joint arbitrator. Upon petition of one of the parties, the court acting under section 1452 would, presumably, appoint a joint arbitrator for Charles and Albert. The effect would be the same as that resulting from Special Term's order in the instant matter: One "side"—Isidore—would be permitted to choose one arbitrator and the other arbitrator would be appointed by the court. If in that situation the court could appoint a single arbitrator the result would be that Isidore's right to appoint an arbitrator and to have disputes decided by three arbitrators for which he had contracted could be defeated at any time by his partners' actual or feigned inability to agree upon their joint arbitrator. Certainly under those circumstances the court would not have the power to so disregard the contract of the parties. We are unable to perceive any good reason why the result should be any different simply because the alignment of the partners has changed. The fact that one "side" will be able to appoint its arbitrator whereas the other "side" will be required to accept the court's choice does not work such injustice that contractual rights may be disregarded.

The view that an arbitrator chosen by a party is merely that party's agent and will act in a partial manner, as suggested by respondent, may not be accepted. Under section 1455 of the Civil Practice Act arbitrators swear "faithfully and fairly to hear and examine the matters in controversy and to make a just award according to the best of their understanding." If that oath be violated and an award procured by fraud or corruption or if an award be tainted by partiality or interest of an arbitrator, it will be vacated. (Matter of Shirley Silk Co. [American Silk Mills], 260 App. Div. 572; Matter of Friedman, 215 App. Div. 130; Civ. Prac. Act, § 1462.)

Upon a showing that there is reason to believe that an arbitrator is incapable of discharging his duties in an impartial manner he may be removed. (Western Union Tel. Co. v. Selly, 295 N.Y. 395, *supra*.) Thus it is clear that the law provides adequate protection for the interests of Albert.

Of course the right to designate an arbitrator is as valuable to Albert as it is to Isidore. But Isidore contracted for the right to do so independently and Albert did not. We do not see that harm may result from honoring the contractual right of Isidore to select an arbitrator or that any useful purpose will be served by altering the framework within which the parties have agreed that their disputes be settled.

The order of the Appellate Division should be reversed and that of Special Term affirmed, with costs in this court and in the Appellate Division.

LOUGHRAN, CH. J., LEWIS, DYE, FULD and FROESSEL, JJ., concur with CONWAY, J.; DESMOND, J., dissents for the reasons stated by the Appellate Division in its *Per Curiam* opinion.

Ordered accordingly.

———————

Is the court's view of the arbitrator appointed by the party compatible with a later holding of the Appellate Division, Second Department: "We are also of the opinion that petitioner's attorney, by reason of that relationship standing alone, is not disqualified from being designated as petitioner's arbitrator."? Matter of Karpinecz (Marshall), 14 App. Div. 2d 569, 218 N.Y.S. 2d 88 (1961).

———————

MATTER OF ASTORIA MEDICAL GROUP (HIP OF NEW YORK)
11 N.Y. 2d 129, 227 N.Y.S. 2d 401 (1962)

FULD, J. The intensely practical question presented by this appeal revolves about the attempt of one party to a typical tripartite arbitration agreement to have the court intervene, before an award has been made, and disqualify the arbitrator designated by the other party because of his asserted personal interest and partiality.

The appellant Health Insurance Plan (HIP), a nonprofit corporation organized under this State's Insurance Law (art. IX-C), is engaged in writing policies of insurance which provide complete medical care. And, to assure such care to its policyholders, HIP enters into contracts with a number of partnerships of physicians, called Medical Groups, whereby they agree to furnish the necessary medical services. In identical contracts made by HIP with those Medical Groups which are the respondents herein, it was agreed that each of them would be paid a fixed sum, or "capitation," for each insured person receiving the services of the particular Group. In addition to such "capitation," HIP agreed to pay each Group an additional sum—termed "supplemental capitation"—in an amount depending upon criteria and standards which were to be established in the future.

The contract further recited that, if the parties were unable to agree upon such criteria by a specified date, "the unresolved issues [were] to go to arbitration" in accordance with the arbitration clause of the contract. This provided, in part, that "One arbitrator shall be appointed by HIP and another by the GROUP, who jointly shall appoint a third arbitrator" and that, if the third arbitrator could not be agreed upon, either party was to request the American Arbitration Association to select him. The decision of two of the three arbitrators was to be final and binding upon both parties.

When the parties failed to agree on the essential criteria for "supplemental capitation," the Medical Groups demanded arbitration and appointed an attorney, Samuel Seligsohn, Esq., as their arbitrator. HIP, in turn, designated, as its arbitrator, Dr. George Baehr, a physician with a long and distinguished career in medicine. The Groups objected to the designation of Dr. Baehr. Noting that he was one of the incorporators of HIP and its president from 1950 to 1957 and that he is, currently, a member of its board of directors and one of its paid consultants, they moved for an order (1) disqualifying him on the ground of personal interest, bias and partiality arising out of his relationship with HIP and (2) requiring HIP "to designate an impartial arbitrator." The justice at Special Term granted the motion and the Appellate Division affirmed by a divided court, granting leave to appeal to us on certified questions. Since the order here involved is a final order (*cf.* Matter of Lipschutz [Gutwirth], 304 N.Y. 58; Matter of Delma Eng. Corp. [K & L Constr. Co.], 5 N.Y. 2d 852), "there was neither need nor authorization for the certification of questions, and we dispose of the appeal without answering them." (Matter of Associated Metals & Minerals Corp. [Kemikalija], 10 N.Y. 2d 298, 301.)

Although we recognize that a strong argument may be advanced, in reliance upon our statute (Civ. Prac. Act, § 1462, subd. 2), to support the appellant HIP's contention that the court lacks authority to intervene until after the arbitrators have made an award (see Matter of Franks [Penn-Uranium Corp.], 4 A.D. 2d 39; see, also, Matter of Dover S.S. Co., 143 F. Supp. 738, 740–741; San Carlo Opera Co. v. Conley, 72 F. Supp. 825, affd. 163 F. 2d 310), we are persuaded that, in an appropriate case, the courts have inherent power to disqualify an arbitrator before an award has been rendered. (Cf. Western Union Tel. Co. v. Selly, 295 N.Y. 395; Gaer Bros. v. Mott, 144 Conn. 303.) However, the present is not such a case.

Arbitration is essentially a creature of contract, a contract in which the parties themselves charter a private tribunal for the resolution of their disputes. The law does no more than lend its sanction to the agreement of the parties, the court's role being limited to the enforcement of the terms of the contract. We have had before us numerous cases in which we have been asked to decide whether the parties had contracted to arbitrate their disputes. We have had many other cases in which we have examined the contract to determine the scope of the arbitration and the nature and extent of the arbitrators' jurisdiction. In the case now before us, we are called upon to interpret the contract in order to resolve a question as to who may sit on the arbitral tribunal.

It is indisputable, as a general proposition, that the parties to an arbitration contract are completely free to agree upon the identity of the arbitrators and the manner in which they are to be chosen. Indeed, our statute so provides, declaring as it does that, "If, in the contract for arbitration ... provision be made for a method of naming or appointing an arbitrator or arbitrators ... such method shall be followed" (Civ. Prac. Act, § 1452). And, in interpreting the provision, this court has expressed the view that "The spirit of the arbitration law being the fuller effectuation of contractual rights, the method for selecting arbitrators and the composition of the arbitral tribunal have been left to the contract of the parties." (Matter of Lipschutz [Gutwirth], 304 N.Y. 58, 61–62, supra; see, also, Matter of Amtorg Trading Corp. [Camden Fibre Mills], 304 N.Y. 519, affg. 277 App. Div. 531.)

In order to determine, therefore, whether HIP's choice of Dr. Baehr was permissible or impermissible, we look to the agreement between the parties. It provides, as we have seen, that "One arbitrator shall be appointed by HIP and another by the GROUP, who jointly shall appoint a third arbitrator."

This type of tripartite arbitration provision, requiring each side to name its own arbitrator and such party-designated arbitrators to agree upon a third neutral arbitrator, is one which has been widely used in both labor and commercial arbitration. Arising out of the repeated use of the tripartite arbitral board, there has grown a common acceptance of the fact that the party-designated arbitrators are not and cannot be "neutral," at least in the sense that the third arbitrator or a judge is. And, as might be expected, the literature is replete with references both to arbitrators who are "neutrals" and those who are "partial," "partisan" or "interested" and to arbitration boards composed entirely of "neutrals" and those contrastingly denominated "tripartite in their membership."

In short, usage and experience indicate that, in the type of tripartite arbitration envisaged by the contract before us, each party's arbitrator "is not individually expected to be neutral."

In fact, the very reason each of the parties contracts for the choice of his own arbitrator is to make certain that his "side" will, in a sense, be represented on the tribunal. And, it was with that thought in mind that this court held the choice of an arbitrator to be a "valuable" contractual right not lightly to be disregarded. (Matter of Lipschutz [Gutwirth], 304 N.Y. 58, 65, supra.) In the Lipschutz case, the several parties had agreed that two of them would jointly choose one arbitrator, that the third party to the contract would choose another and that the two party appointees would select a third. When the first two contracting parties could not agree on their joint arbitrator, one of them moved the court to name a single neutral arbitrator to replace the tripartite tribunal agreed upon in the contract. Although the Appellate Division approved this proposal, we reversed and decided, instead, that the court should appoint an arbitrator for the two contracting parties who could not agree, but that the third party should be allowed the right to choose his own arbitrator.

In thus enforcing the party's contractual right to designate an arbitrator of his own choice, we implicitly recognized the partisan character of tripartite arbitration. The right to appoint one's own arbitrator, which is of the essence of tripartite arbitration and which was vindicated in the Lipschutz case, would be of little moment were it to comprehend solely the choice of a "neutral." It becomes a valued right, which parties will bargain for and litigate over, only if it involves a choice of one believed to be sympathetic to his position or favorably disposed to him.

Turning to the case before us, there can be no doubt that, when HIP and the Medical Groups agreed upon the use of a tripartite tribunal, they must be taken to have contracted with reference to established practice and usage in the field of arbitration. (See Bolles v. Scheer, 225 N.Y. 118, 121; see, also, CARDOZO, THE NATURE OF THE JUDICIAL PROCESS, pp. 62–64.) In the light of accepted practice, which sanctions and contemplates two non-neutral arbitrators on a tripartite board, the parties must be deemed to have intended that each was to be free to appoint any arbitrator desired, however close his relationship to it or to the dispute.[1] Moreover, this conclusion is reinforced by the fact that the provision relating to arbitration contains no word of limitation on the identity, status or qualifications of the arbitrators; had the parties intended that their appointees be completely impartial or disinterested, they could have readily so provided.

It is hardly necessary to observe that we enforce the tripartite arbitration clause before us because it is the one chosen by the parties, not because we favor it or regard it as ideal or even desirable. We are, in effect, mandated by the policy, no less than by the terms, of our statute to give life to the tribunal which the parties themselves create. (Civ. Prac. Act, § 1452.) If they choose to have their disputes resolved by a body consisting of two partisan arbitrators, and a third neutral arbitrator, that is their affair. We may not rewrite their contract. (See Matter of Lipschutz [Gutwirth], 304 N.Y. 58, 61–62, supra.)

Nor do we perceive any public policy which condemns or forbids this arrangement. On the contrary, this court many years ago recognized that, although every arbitrator must act fairly and impartially in arriving at a decision and making an award, "a known interest does not disqualify and the parties may not complain merely because the arbitrators named were known to be chosen with a view to a particular relationship to their nominator or to the subject-matter of the controversy." (Matter of American Eagle Fire Ins. Co. v. New Jersey Ins. Co., 240 N.Y. 398, 405; see, also, Matter of Amtorg Trading Corp. [Camden Fibre Mills], 277 App. Div. 531, 532–533, affd. 304 N.Y. 519, supra.; Matter of Linwood [Sherry], 14 Misc 2d 495, 496,

affd. 7 A.D. 2d 757, motion for leave to app. den. 5 N.Y. 2d 711; Matter of Dover S. S. Co., 143 F. Supp. 738, 741, supra.) In point of fact, even in cases where the contract expressly designated a single arbitrator who was employed by one of the parties or intimately connected with him, the courts have refused to disqualify the arbitrator on the ground of either interest or partiality. (See, e.g., Matter of Amtorg Trading Corp. [Camden Fibre Mills], 304 N.Y. 519, affg. 277 App. Div. 531, supra; Jackson v. Barry Ry. Co., [1893] 1 Ch. 238; Eckersley v. Mersey Docks & Harbour Bd., [1894] 2 Q.B. 667; Perry v. Cobb, 88 Me. 435; Nelson v. Atlantic Coast Line R. R. Co., 157 N.C. 194; Barclay v. Deckerhoof, 171 Pa. 378; see, also, Board of Educ. v. Frank, 64 Ill. App. 367, cited with approval in Giddens v. Board of Educ., 398 Ill. 157, 167.)

It is urged that the inclusion of non-neutral arbitrators is alien to the judicial process, with its stricture that judges be completely impartial and dissociated from both litigant and dispute. And so it is. However, although the courts have, on occasion, "judicialized" arbitration (see, e.g., Madawick Contr. Co. v. Travelers Ins. Co., 307 N.Y. 111, 119; Matter of Brody, 259 App. Div. 720, 721) and referred to an arbitration board as a "quasi-judicial tribunal" and to arbitrators as "judges of the parties' choosing" or "officers exercising judicial functions" (see, e.g., Fudickar v. Guardian Mut. Life Ins. Co., 62 N.Y. 392, 399), we are reminded by Dean Sturges that such references are based on nothing more than "remote resemblances" and are "not very meaningful." Sturges, Arbitration—What Is It?, 35 N.Y.U.L. REV. 1031, 1045–1046.)

Our decision that an arbitrator may not be disqualified solely because of a relationship to his nominator or to the subject matter of the controversy does not, however, mean that he may be deaf to the testimony or blind to the evidence presented. Partisan he may be, but not dishonest. Like all arbitrators, the arbitrator selected by a party must (unless the requirement is waived) take the prescribed oath that he will "faithfully and fairly ... hear and examine the matters in controversy and ... make a just award according to the best of [his] understanding" (Civ. Prac. Act, § 1455). And, if either one of the party-appointed arbitrators fails to act in accordance with such oath, the award may be attacked on the ground that it is the product of "evident partiality or corruption" (Civ. Prac. Act, § 1462, subd. 2). Such an attack, however, must be based on something overt, some misconduct on the part of an arbitrator, and not simply on his interest in the subject matter of

---

1. This is not to say that, under an arbitration provision such as the one before us, a person may serve as his own arbitrator. When the agreement authorizes a party to "appoint" an arbitrator, it is implicit in that very provision that he may not appoint himself. Contrary to the contention advanced by the respondents, however, a member of the board of directors of a corporation is not the corporation either in law or fact, and we would be doing violence to both reason and reality were we to say that Dr. Baehr is HIP, or should be so regarded, simply because he is one of a number of persons on its board.

the controversy or his relationship to the party who selected him. (See Matter of Milliken Woolens [Weber Knit Sportswear], 9 N.Y. 2d 878 ; Matter of Lipschutz [Gutwirth], 304 N.Y. 58, 64–65, *supra* ; Matter of American Eagle Fire Ins. Co. v. New Jersey Ins. Co., 240 N.Y. 398, *supra* ; Matter of Friedman, 215 App. Div. 130, 136–137.)[2]

It may well be that there is greater danger that party-designated arbitrators will overstep the bounds of propriety than will those who are disinterested neutrals. But this risk, quite apart from being one to which the parties submitted, is thought by many to be more than offset by certain benefits gained from use of the tripartite board. One such benefit is that arbitrators selected by the parties, are, generally speaking, experts on the subject in controversy and bring to their task a wealth of specialized knowledge. As one commentator has indicated, "the expert guidance" furnished by "partisan" arbitrators "can be of assistance to the neutral member, who is not in a position to appreciate the problem and the fine points of its setting." (Lesser, *Tripartite Boards or Single Arbitrators in Voluntary Labor Arbitration?*, 5 ARB. J. [n.s.] 276, 279 ; see, also, Bell Aircraft Corp., 13 L.A. 813, 820–821 ; Note, 68 HARV. L. REV. 293, 297 *et seq.*) Consequently, to disqualify an arbitrator because of his relationship to, or association with, his nominator would be to withhold from the arbitration board a source of the specialized knowledge which contributes to the unique value of the arbitration process. Moreover, any personal advantage to be derived from the power to select as arbitrator anyone he wishes is available to each party and, experience tells us, is ordinarily availed of by both.

In brief, it is our view that, since both parties, by agreeing upon tripartite arbitration, have necessarily accepted the idea of "partisan" appointees, neither may object to the other's designation of someone associated with his interest or related to him.

The order appealed from should be reversed

---

2. As previously indicated the Advisory Committee on Practice and Procedure took "cognizance of the common practice of each party appointing his own arbitrator who is not individually expected to be neutral" and declared that "partiality of such arbitrators should not be a ground for vacating the award" (Second Preliminary Report of the Advisory Committee on Practice and Procedure [N.Y. LEGIS. DOC., 1958, No. 13], p. 146). To carry out its recommendations, the Advisory Committee introduced a bill at this 1962 session of the Legislature (S. Int. 26, Pr. 26), now awaiting action by the Governor, which permits a vacatur of an award only where the "partiality" is that "of an arbitrator appointed as a neutral" (CPLR, § 7511, subd. [b], par. 1, cl. [ii]).

and the petitioners' motion denied, with costs in all courts. The questions certified are not answered.

CHIEF JUDGE DESMOND dissenting. On these facts the arbitrator was correctly held to be disqualified and subject to removal. The appeal does not present the broader and more general question as to whether a party may validly nominate as one of three arbitrators a person whose business or personal relationship to the party is so close as presumably to predispose him in favor of his sponsor. Here the interest of the nominee is not presumed but actual, the conflict direct. It is ancient wisdom not lightly to be discarded that "No one should be judge in his own cause" (Maxims of Publilius Syrus, 42 B.C.). Dr. Baehr is a director and paid consultant and former president of HIP. As the Appellate Division majority wrote: "He is, therefore, essentially a 'party' to the dispute because he is now asked to sit as an arbitrator to determine the propriety or fairness of a decision in the making of which he participated." If there is anything left of the idea that a director is an agent of the trustee for his corporation (Continental Securities Co. v. Belmont, 206 N.Y. 7, 16) or anything left of the concept that an arbitrator is "a judge appointed by the parties" (Fudickar v. Guardian Mut. Life Ins. Co., 62 N.Y. 392, 399) and that he "acts in a quasi-judicial capacity" (Matter of American Eagle Fire Ins. Co. v. New Jersey Ins. Co., 240 N.Y. 398, 405), Dr. Baehr is as matter of law not qualified to sit on this arbitration board. Only by so holding can we preserve a concept which is rooted not in naïveté or impracticality but in integrity and principle. If Dr. Baehr can be an arbitrator when his own corporation is a party, then an individual party can name himself as his own arbitrator-judge and the whole affair becomes a cynical travesty of the arbitral process, "calculated to bring the system of enforced arbitrations into disrepute" (Matter of American Eagle Fire Ins. Co. v. New Jersey Ins. Co., *supra*).

There is in this court no authority precisely in point but such decisions as there are show that arbitrators have been held disqualified because of relationships to the parties or to the controversy, or because of "interest" much more remote than demonstrated here (see Western Union Tel. Co. v. Selly, 295 N.Y. 395 ; Matter of Milliken Woolens [Weber Knit Sportswear], 11 A.D. 2d 166, affd. 9 N.Y. 2d 878 ; and for a general statement of the rule, Matter of Lipschutz [Gutwirth], 304 N.Y. 58, 65). As to the equitable power of the court (see Matter of Lipschutz [Gutwirth], *supra,* p. 63; Matter of Feuer Transp. [Local No. 445], 295 N.Y. 87, 91) to remove an unqualified arbitrator before the hearings, there should be no doubt (Western Union Tel. Co. v. Selly, 295 N.Y. 395, *supra*). That is the time to pass on such a clause of ineligibility since if the party knowing the disqualifying facts as to his opponent's nominee nevertheless participates in an arbitration without applying for the nominee's removal his inaction will constitute a waiver (Matter of Newburger v. Rose, 228 App. Div. 526, affd. 254 N.Y. 546).

We are, of course, not dealing here with arbitration agreements, if any such there be, where the parties have expressly or by necessary implication consented that a party's nominee may be a director, officer, employee, agent or attorney of that party.

The order should be affirmed, with costs.

JUDGES VAN VOORHIS, BURKE and FOSTER concur with JUDGE FULD; CHIEF JUDGE DESMOND dissents in an opinion in which JUDGES DYE and FROESSEL concur.

Order reversed, with costs in all courts, and matter remitted for further proceedings in accordance with the opinion herein. Questions certified not answered.

Does the majority opinion's characterization of the *Lipschutz* case square with your reading of that case?

Western Union Tel. Co. v. Selly, 295 N.Y. 395, 68 N.E. 2d 183, affg, 270 App. Div. § 839, mem., 61 N.Y.S. 2d 911, affg, 60 N.Y.S. 2d 411 (1946), approved the replacement of an arbitrator whom the judge originally appointed. The Court of Appeals, in a memorandum decision, merely noted that

> The removal of the arbitrator was within the discretion of the Special Term [the lower court which initially appointed and then removed the arbitrator] and was not an abuse of that discretion, although, as the dissent pointed out, "The parties concede his honesty and ability."

The opinion accompanying the order of removal and replacement indicates that the arbitrator's social and political views were pro-labor, implying that he also counseled an especially militant strike policy. In an earlier passage of his opinion the judge expressed his disapproval of the widespread postwar (1946) strike activity. How much this element affected the decision it

is hard to say, although the dissenter in the Court of Appeals stated that "he was removed solely because he holds and had expressed certain social, economic and political views." See Note, 46 COLUM. L. REV. 845 (1946).

MATTER OF KNICKERBOCKER TEXTILE CORPORATION AND SHEILA-LYNN, INC.
172 Misc. 1015, 16 N.Y.S. 2d 435
(N.Y. Cty. 1939)

COLLINS, J. Sheila-Lynn, Inc., moves to vacate the unanimous arbitration award in favor of Knickerbocker Textile Corporation, on the grounds (1) that there was evident partiality on the part of one of the three arbitrators, and (2) that such arbitrator was guilty of misbehavior which prejudiced the rights of Sheila-Lynn.

The motion poses an important and uncommon question in the law of arbitration. Important, because the invocation of the machinery of arbitration is encouragingly increasing and the issue here bears significantly on the proper conduct of arbitrators; novel, inasmuch as no precise New York pattern for this case has been offered.

The facts are free from entanglement; no dispute concerning them is presented.

Differences having arisen between the parties over a contract for the sale of fabric, arbitration was resorted to under the aegis and rules of the National Federation of Textiles, Inc. Each party designated an arbitrator and the two thus chosen selected the third, Ellis Arnoff, whose alleged partiality and misbehavior constitute the foundation for this proceeding. Any two could have rendered a binding award. The arbitration proceeding was initiated on October 14, 1938, and Arnoff was notified of his selection on or about October twenty-seventh. After taking testimony, a unanimous decision was made on November 11, 1938, in favor of Knickerbocker for $9,891.70, and Knickerbocker was required to cancel the undelivered portion of the goods purchased by Sheila-Lynn under the contract. Sheila asserts that Knickerbocker's victory was complete; Knickerbocker counters that its victory was but partial. Sheila paid the award on November 21, 1938, and Knickerbocker made the cancellation of the remainder of the goods.

On February 10, 1939, this proceeding was instituted on the basis that on January 9, 1939, Sheila discovered that in an arbitration between American Silk Mills, Inc., and Shirley Silk Co., Inc., of which latter company Arnoff was and is treasurer, Jacob Granowitz, Knickerbocker's president, was designated by the Shirley Company as its arbitrator. The American Silk Mills–Shirley Silk Co. arbitration was commenced September 13, 1938, the hearing therein occurred on October 24, 1938, and on the same day a two to one award was made in favor of Shirley, Granowitz being one of the majority. Thus, three days after Granowitz had decided an arbitration proceeding in favor of Shirley, of which Arnoff was treasurer, Arnoff received notice of his selection as an arbitrator in a proceeding to which Knickerbocker, Granowitz's concern, was a party. Granowitz decided for Arnoff's Company and Arnoff, in turn, decided for Granowitz's.

It is not contradicted that there was no disclosure of Granowitz's participation in the other arbitration proceeding prior to January 9, 1939. Nor is it disputed that Sheila-Lynn had no knowledge of such participation prior to that time.

Naturally enough, Arnoff disavows any bias, undue influence or other improper conduct. He affirms:

The fact that Mr. Granowitz, President of Knickerbocker Textile Corporation, had been an arbitrator in my company's case with American Silk Mills, Inc., in no way affected my judgment in the present matter. The award was unanimous. In signing the award with my co-arbitrators, Burgess and Sondheim, I did what I believed to be fair and just under the evidence as presented to the Arbitration Board. I was not influenced by any extraneous considerations in reaching that decision.

For the purpose of the discussion we shall accept the disclaimer of Arnoff at its face value. We shall assume, too, that the award was justified by the evidence. The merits of the award, however, are not presently in issue.

The principle involved is broader than the correctness of the arbitrator's decision. The concern here is with policy rather than expediency; with the fundamental spirit and objective of the law rather than a punctilious adherence to its letter.

Assuming that both sides have stated the truth, what then?

Arbitration is a salutary device. That it has become increasingly valuable and popular is explicable. It is a time and expense economizer. It relieves the courts. It is simple, expeditious and free from the myriad technicalities which beset and protract litigation. Its decisions possess a finality not inherent in lawsuits. It is a business-like method of resolving differences. *Ergo,* arbitration is to be encouraged. Arbitration awards should not be disturbed for trivial, captious or technical reasons; the causes must be cardinal.

But just because the practice is increasingly common, and just because arbitration awards have a sense of absolutism, the more scrupulous should be the conduct of arbitrators.

The doctrine is admirably stated by the First Department in Matter of Friedman [215 App. Div. 130, 136], thus:

During recent years arbitration has been more and more resorted to for the settlement of business controversies. It, therefore, becomes of the utmost importance that in statutory proceedings of this character where the rights of parties are adjudicated, not by trained lawyers and judges, but by fellow-businessmen, every safeguard possible should be thrown about the proceeding to insure the utmost fairness and impartiality of those charged with the determination of the rights of the parties. Nothing should be permitted to throw suspicion even upon the entire impartiality of arbitrators. The finality of an award of arbitrators as compared with the reviewable decision of a judge or a referee makes this all the more important, and that the tribunal which is to pass upon the rights of the parties be not subject to the slightest suspicion as to its fairness.

Granowitz's opposing affidavit declares:

In the silk and rayon industry the practice of arbitrating disputes under the arbitration rules of the National Federation of Textiles, Inc. and its predecessor, the Silk Association of America, Inc., has been established for many years. It has been the custom in the industry to select arbitrators from among the heads of the various concerns engaged in the industry and its affiliated branches. Thus it is not unusual for an arbitrator to serve on cases where both parties and arbitrators are connected with concerns with which the arbitrator or his company have done or are doing business, or whose officers have been arbitrators in cases involving his company. Such inter-relationships are inevitable because of the method of arbitration used in the industry, and they have never been regarded as a basis for disqualifying an arbitrator in the absence of any showing that the arbitrator was actually biased.

There is force and cogency to Granowitz's argument; but it is far from conclusive. To be sure, proof of business relations between parties and arbitrators, standing alone, is not sufficient to vitiate an award.

But this situation goes beyond that of mere business relations. Here we have an additional question: was Arnoff obliged to reveal his connection with the other arbitration proceeding so as to give Sheila an opportunity to object to his serving as arbitrator?

Before proceeding with the arbitration, the director of the arbitration bureau introduced the arbitrators to the parties and witnesses, and inquired: "Is there any objection to these arbitrators serving on this case or does either party believe that the past, present or future dealings of any of these arbitrators with either of the parties will prevent the rendering of a fair and just award?"

No objection was voiced. Indeed, ignorant of the facts, Sheila could raise none. Here was Arnoff's chance to make known the fact of Granowitz's connection with the first arbitration. Though asked to speak out, he remained mute.

It behooved Arnoff, I think, to make a disclosure. (O'Brien v. Long, 49 Hun, 80, 82 ; Kimberley v. Dick, 13 Eq. Cas. 1.).

By reason of his connection with Granowitz, unknown to Sheila, Arnoff, in my opinion, was disqualified to serve as an arbitrator in the arbitration proceeding here assailed.

Matter of Shirley Silk Co., Inc., v. American Silk Mills, Inc. (257 App. Div. 375), involved the arbitration of Arnoff's Company, above alluded to. That decision restates some of the principles to which reference has been made. As indicated, the award reviewed by the Appellate Division was by a two to one vote. The appellate tribunal designated "an official referee to take proof and report to the Special Term upon the question of the relationship existing between the arbitrator Granowitz and appellant and as to the knowledge of respondent with respect to such relationship." The official referee found that "(a) The Arbitrator Granowitz was entirely impartial and was not disqualified from rendering an award. (b) There was no relationship between the arbitrator Granowitz and the petitioner Shirley Silk Co. Inc." However, the official referee's report is of little significance here because the inquiry before the official referee was restricted and, what is more, here, as distinguished from the American Silk Mills case, there was a relationship between the arbitrator Arnoff and Knickerbocker ; here, because of such relationship, Arnoff *was* disqualified from rendering an award.

I am satisfied that were this a two to one award, with Arnoff on the majority side, the award would indubitably have to be vacated.

We approach, therefore, the pivotal point, which is whether or not the unanimity of the award compels a different conclusion.

There is authority for the rule that although one arbitrator may have acted fraudulently and corruptly, if the other two acted honestly the award must stand. (Plummer v. Saunders, 55 N.H. 23 ; Davis v. Forshee, 34 Ala. 107.) But no New York case upholding this rule has been called to my attention.

In 6 Corpus Juris Secundum (§ 104, p. 249) the rule is given thus:

Where there are several arbitrators, partiality or misconduct on the part of one only who acts with the others is ground for setting aside the award, although it was unanimous, and although an award by the others alone would have been valid.

The Corpus Juris pronouncement is based on the provocative and luminous case of Moshier v. Shear (102 Ill. 169) where a unanimous arbitration award was vacated because one of the arbitrators, Hubbell, had spoken to Stephens, an arbitrator in a previous set-aside arbitration, of the same matter. Some of the observations of the court there are so apposite here that they bear quoting. It was said (at p. 173):

After being selected, it is the duty of an arbitrator, like a juror, to act fairly and impartially between the parties and on the evidence adduced before them on the trial, and entirely independent of all outside influences, and what will be misconduct on the part of a juror will, as a general rule, be such on the part of an arbitrator.

And the court added (at pp. 174–176):

It is true that there is no positive proof that the arbitrator was influenced in his opinions by the conversation, but we have no reason to expect such proof in such cases, However much he may have been influenced, it is scarcely probable that he would be aware of the fact. Such effects are seldom perceptible or consciously produced. They are usually imperceptible, and unknown to the subject of their influence. However honest and upright Hubbell may be, and however he may feel from influence produced by his conversation with Stephens, still it is almost impossible to believe that such a conversation with a friend of long standing, and for whom the arbitrator had a high regard, did not produce strong, if not controlling, convictions on his mind, and *however desirable it may be to terminate protracted contention, it is more desirable that justice shall be administered, free from all improper or corrupting influences,—that the mode of settling contests by arbitration shall be kept pure, and free from improper influences.* Here, whatever the motive of the arbitrator, he was subjected to improper influences, and whether or not it operated to the injury of plaintiff in error, it was calculated to operate to the prejudice of the parties, and *to sanction it would form a dangerous precedent.* We can not know what influence it may have exerted in this case. *It is sufficient that it was calculated to produce improper results.*

To sustain this award would be to sanction and justify the means by which the whole system of arbitration would be perverted and corrupted. If we hold that the party thus objecting must prove that undue influence actually resulted, then the objection would seldom be available, however corrupt the influence. Such things can seldom, owing to precautions taken by those engaged in such practices for concealment, be shown by positive evidence, hence *the safer rule is, to hold that when it appears there has been conduct calculated to result, and which has probably resulted, perniciously, to set aside the award.* It is clear that had Shear done what Stephens did, or had he procured another to do the same thing, there could not have been the slightest hesitation in setting aside the award, and yet the influence of Stephens was equal to, if not more potent than that of Shear would have been, on the mind of the arbitrator, who was his intimate friend, and whom he held in high esteem. What more powerful influence could have been exerted? If we sustain this award we shall license every person, whether a partisan or not to the contest, to enter into the conflict, and exercise his full influence, whether inspired by friendship or hatred of the parties to the contest, only excluding the unseemly and improper conduct of the parties themselves, their attorneys or agents. We must therefore hold that the conduct of Hubbell was improper, to an extent that rendered him incompetent to act in the case.

The final paragraph of the Moshier opinion pierces to the vitals of the current case:

It is, however, urged, that the submission was to three arbitrators named, or to any two of them, and the award published by the three, or any two of them, should be binding on the parties to the submission, and that it was signed and published by all three, and hence the award is made and published by two of the arbitrators, against whom there is no charge of misconduct of any kind. This reason is more apparent than real. The misconduct of a juror has always been held ground for setting aside a verdict, notwithstanding the other eleven concurred with him in the finding; and it is because it is impossible to know the extent of his influence over the minds of the other jurors, and because that fact is incapable of proof, and can not be known, the courts, to avoid the probability that the misconduct of one has influenced the others, to keep the stream of justice certainly pure will set the verdict aside. So, here, no one can know the extent of Hubbell's influence over the minds of the other two. For aught we can know, it may have controlled in making up the award that was published. *Plaintiff in error had the right to have all who acted, free from bias and improper influences produced after their selection. Had but the other two acted, then we can see no objection to the award.* But all of the members who did act were not free from improper influences, and he was thus deprived of an essential right secured to him by the law, and for that reason the award should be set aside, and the Circuit Court committed no error in the decree it rendered, but the Appellate Court erred in reversing it. (Italics mine.)

True, the *Moshier* precedent is an old one—1882—and derives from another State. But I have not perceived that time has depreciated juridical standards or that such standards are loftier in Illinois than in New York. In fact, the *Moshier* case is approvingly cited by Judge Cardozo in Berizzi Co., Inc. v. Krausz (239 N.Y. 315, 318).

My conclusion is that the award should be vacated and another arbitration held in accordance with the arbitration agreement.

I am convinced that the unanimity of the three does not dissolve and clear the cloud of disqualification of the one. I confess that this determination was not easily or unhesitatingly reached, *first*, because the query is not entirely removed from the zone of debate, and, *second*, because of the general reluctance of courts—a reluctance in which I share—to sustain a challenge to an arbitration award. I am satisfied, however, that a new arbitration will better serve the cause of justice than to permit the sullied cloud to remain. This is, I am sure, a just disposition, if not technically free from doubt. To stand on just ground is, I feel, safer than to rest on the tenuous security of technicality.

I do not hold that Arnoff was corrupt or that he willfully misbehaved. Indeed, the presumption of innocence from intentional wrongdoing is accorded him. But good faith alone is of insufficient strength to repel the finding of misbehavior. (Cardozo, J. Berizzi Co., v. Krausz, *supra*, p. 318.) I am persuaded that Arnoff's participation in the arbitration, without disclosing his connection, was not in consonance with right or with the principles of fair play. It may well be that the award was a righteous one. And it is possible that Knickerbocker did not retrieve all it was entitled to. But I am quite sure that neither Granowitz's company, Knickerbocker, nor Arnoff's, Shirley, would wish a case of theirs tried by a judge who had been the recent beneficiary of an arbitration proceeding in which the opposing litigant sat as an arbitrator, unless, of course, the judge first made known his connection, and the parties stipulated to proceed before him notwithstanding. And I am equally certain that an adverse decision of such a judge, in such a case, under such circumstances, would experience a fight for survival.

The conclusion here reached is not to be construed as an invitation to every disgruntled party to an arbitration to move for redress. We are concerned here with a particular situation and the decision is grounded on that situation. The citadel of arbitration remains inviolate.

No virtue would ensue, as I see it, from sending any of the issues to a referee, as was done in Matter of Wersba v. Cobb (254 App. Div. 481) and Matter of Shirley Silk Co., Inc., v. American Silk Mills, Inc. (*supra*). As observed, no facts are in dispute. The question here propounded is a legal, not a factual one.

Knickerbocker's solvency not having been questioned, it shall remain in custody of the fund and hold it in escrow pending, and to abide the result of, the new arbitration. Finally, Knickerbocker should welcome the opportunity to reassert its claim in full.

The motion to vacate and set aside the award is granted to the extent herein indicated. Settle order accordingly.

EDWARDS v. EMPLOYERS MUT. LIABILITY INS. CO. OF WISC.
219 Ga. 121, 132 S.E. 2d 39 (1963)

CANDLER, JUSTICE.

The Employers Mutual Liability Insurance Company of Wisconsin issued a policy of insurance to James O. Edwards. It obligates the company to pay him or his legal representative damages not in excess of $10,000 for bodily injury, including his death, resulting from the negligent operation of an uninsured automobile by a third party. The policy also provides that if the company and the insured or his legal representative are unable to agree on the question of liability for such an injury or death, or the amount of damages which should be paid by the company for such injury or death, the matter in dispute will be submitted to and settled by arbitration in accordance with the rules of the American Arbitration Association. The insured was killed when an uninsured truck belonging to Lyman Austin which James Heard was operating for him in the prosecution of his business collided with a pickup truck he was driving. The collision occurred in Floyd County about 4½ miles west of Rome on Georgia Highway No. 20, commonly known as the West Alabama Road. Mrs. Edwards, as widow of the insured, and the insuring company were unable to agree on a settlement, and Mrs. Edwards asked for arbitration specifying therein the several acts of negligence charged against the driver of such truck. Hugh F. Newberry, an attorney of Atlanta, Georgia, was named sole arbitrator by the American Arbitration Association. After hearing all of the evidence offered by the parties, he rendered a decision that Mrs. Edwards was not entitled to any amount as damages for the death of her husband, the insured. His decision was rendered on December 5, 1961.

Mrs. Edwards on June 16, 1962, filed a petition in the Superior Court of Floyd County to set aside the decision of Mr. Newberry on the ground that he was a partisan arbitrator, partisan in favor of the insurer and that she and her counsel had no knowledge of that fact until after he had rendered a decision against her.

Respecting her position of his partisanship, her petition as amended alleges that Newberry had, until a few weeks immediately prior to the hearing of her case, been a claims examiner for several insurance companies from which employment he received his sole means of livelihood; that he was at the time of hearing and deciding her case representing a client who was asserting a claim against an insured of the defendant company and did not disclose such fact to her or to her counsel prior to the hearing of her case; and that the evidence introduced on the hearing of her case demanded a finding in her favor that her husband was killed because of the negligence of the driver of the uninsured truck. She attached to her petition as exhibits a copy of her application for arbitration and the evidence which the arbitrator heard. The defendant answered her amended petition and denied all allegations thereof relating to his [sic] disqualification and that a finding in her favor was demanded by the evidence.

The defendant moved for a summary judgment and in support of it introduced an affidavit by the arbitrator Newberry in which he said he was admitted to the bar of the State of Georgia in 1958 and began a general practice of law on May 19, 1959 in Atlanta, Georgia. Prior to entering the general practice of law, he worked for two insurance companies. First, from February 1950 to June 1956, he worked for Motors Insurance Corporation in Atlanta, Georgia, Chattanooga, Tennessee and Augusta, Georgia, starting as an adjuster and ultimately serving as manager of that company's district office in Augusta. That company writes only first party automobile physical damage coverage and does not provide liability coverage. From June 1956 until the time of beginning a general practice of law, he was a claim examiner for Allstate Insurance Company in Atlanta. In this position he worked primarily with third party or liability claims, both automobile and general liability. His work consisted largely of examining and supervising liability claim files and training and supervising adjusters. At the time he began a general practice of law, he had no regular insurance company clients, with the exception of Motors Insurance Corporation which work was confined to subrogation cases. He first opened an office in the William-Oliver Building, Atlanta, Georgia. In this office he was a lone practitioner, not associated in any way with any firm. He remained in that situation until February 1, 1962. During such period, he engaged in an assorted practice taking what work was available including domestic and criminal matters. The tort cases he handled, save subrogation cases, were largely confined to plaintiff's personal injury cases against defendants carrying liability insurance. On February 1, 1961, affiant joined a firm of attorneys in Atlanta. He brought no liability insurance clients to that firm. That firm by virtue of the relationship of several of the partners did and does now represent regularly several liability insurance companies, primarily Aetna Casualty & Surety Company, Cotton States Mutual Insurance Company, St. Paul-Mercury Insurance Company, and Government Employees Insurance Company. On occasion the firm has represented on defense Allstate Insurance Company, Great Central Insurance Company and International Service Insurance Company. By reason of his association with the firm, he has worked on cases involving all of the above mentioned insurance companies. Since joining that law firm, he has not been restricted in his acceptance of plaintiff's cases. He has continued to receive and handle plaintiff's [sic] damage cases. At the present time his work is probably evenly divided between plaintiff's cases and defendant's cases. At the time he heard Mrs. Edwards' case as arbitrator his work was probably divided two-thirds plaintiff and one-third defendant. He has handled two substantial claimant's cases against insurance companies under the uninsured motorist coverage before the American Arbitration Association. He has handled one case for the insurance company in which arbitration was demanded, that case being settled before hearing. He has never represented the defendant insurance company in any particular and was not acquainted with any of its personnel at the time of his award in Mrs. Edwards' case. The only dealing he ever had with that company was in representing a plaintiff against an insured of such company and that case was pending at the time of the hearing and award in the Edwards' case and is still pending. The defendant's motion for summary judgment was granted and plaintiff excepted.

Held. An arbitrator's finding or award may be set aside for any unfair advantage given to either party in the hearing of the case or in the rendition of his finding or award, or for fraud on the part of the arbitrator or of either party in obtaining the award. Code § 7–111. Partisanship of the arbitrator as to one of the parties to the proceeding, unknown to the other party, is a ground for setting aside his finding or award; and that question when properly raised by one against whom an adverse finding or award has been made is an issue which should be submitted to a jury for its determination. Orme v. Birney, 95 Ga. 418, 22 S.E. 633. Under an act

which the legislature passed in 1959 (Ga. L. 1959, p. 234 ; Code Ann. § 110–1203) a summary judgment may be rendered on proper motion therefor if the pleadings, depositions and admissions on file, together with affidavits, if any, show that there is no genuine issue as to any material fact and that the moving party is entitled to a judgment as a matter of law, but nothing in the act should be construed as denying to any party the right to trial by jury where there is a substantial issue of fact to be determined. "In arriving at a verdict, the jury, from facts proved, and sometimes from the absence of counter evidence, may infer the existence of other facts reasonably and logically consequent on those proved." Code § 38–123. Beall v. State, 68 Ga. 820 ; Castleberry v. City of Atlanta, 74 Ga. 164 (2) ; White v. Hammond, 79 Ga. 182, 4 S.E. 102. In the instant case there are facts and circumstances shown by the record which would in our opinion authorize a jury to infer that the arbitrator who rendered the award sought to be set aside was disqualified to serve as an arbitrator in the instant cause. This being true, the court erred in granting a summary judgment in favor of the defendant. In other words, the record shows a substantial issue of fact respecting the fairness and impartiality of the arbitrator which the court should have submitted to a jury for determination.

> Partiality on the part of arbitrators is a well-recognized ground for the setting aside of awards. It is not necessary, in order to warrant the intervention of equity, that the partiality be evidenced by an unjust award. It has been held sufficient that the relationship between the arbitrators and one of the parties is of such a nature as to give clear grounds for suspicion of their proceedings and render it unlikely that they constituted the fair and impartial tribunal to which the other party is entitled.

5 AM. JUR. 2d 652, § 181. Common justice requires that he be entirely fair to and absolutely impartial between the parties involved in the controversy submitted to him for decision.

Judgment reversed.

All the Justices concur.

BALLANTINE BOOKS, INC. v. CAPITAL DISTRIBUTING CO.
302 F. 2d 17 (2d Cir. 1962)

Before LUMBARD, CHIEF JUDGE, and MOORE and HAYS, CIRCUIT JUDGES.

LUMBARD, CHIEF JUDGE.

Capital Distributing Company appeals from a

judgment of the District Court for the Southern District of New York which confirmed the award of three arbitrators in favor of Ballantine Books, Inc. for $151,343.84. The proceeding to confirm was brought in the district court by Ballantine, a New York corporation with its principal place of business in New York City, against Capital, a Connecticut corporation with its business headquarters in Derby, Connecticut, pursuant to the United States Arbitration Act, 9 U.S.C. § 1 et seq.

Capital's appeal claims that the federal court was without jurisdiction as the New York courts had previously taken jurisdiction by reason of Capital's motion there to disqualify the chairman of the arbitration board. It also alleges that the district court should have vacated the award because of the evident partiality of the chairman, and because the award was incomplete and went beyond the powers of the arbitrators. We affirm the district court as it had jurisdiction to pass upon the award, and we find no merit in Capital's claims of improper conduct by the chairman and imperfections in the award itself.

In 1954 Ballantine, a publisher of paperbacks contracted with Capital to distribute its publications. Capital was to pay Ballantine 15 per cent of the invoice value of Ballantine's shipments to Capital's wholesalers' inventory twenty days after the end of the month in which shipments were made, and an additional 40 per cent thirty days later. Because the wholesalers had the right to return books, the remainder (less a further 3 per cent "settlement account") was not payable until six months after a specific title had been called in from the wholesalers. As Capital was paid by the wholesalers, it therefore acquired sums of money as reserves against returns from wholesalers for which it was required to account to Ballantine from time to time.

All went well until May and June 1958, when Capital refused to pay Ballantine approximately $175,000 claimed to be due, stating that this was in accordance with its right to maintain additional reserves against future returns. In June, 1958, Ballantine served a demand for arbitration pursuant to the terms of the contract. Arbitration hearings finally commenced on April 29, 1959, and continued with adjournments and frequent delays until January 11, 1961; on May 29, 1961 the award in favor of Ballantine was filed.

On the ninth day of the hearing, October 8, 1959, Chester B. McLaughlin, Jr., the chairman of the arbitration panel, asked the attorneys for the parties, off the record, whether there was any possibility of settlement. After being advised that there had been unfruitful talks, the chairman said that on the basis of the record as it then stood it was his tentative view that there should be an award for Ballantine. This session continued, and what was expected to be the final session was arranged for November 5.

On November 4, Capital moved before the arbitrators for disqualification of the chairman, on account of his off-the-record comments on October 8. The arbitrators denied the motion on November 5, and a special Committee on Challenge of the American Arbitration Association also passed on the matter with the same result on December 17, 1959. The Association scheduled the resumption of the arbitration for January 11, 1960.

We find no merit in the claim that the district court should have set aside the award because of the alleged "partiality and misbehavior" of the chairman of the arbitration panel. Appellant's claims fall under two heads: First, it renews its attack, ultimately rejected by the state courts as premature, on Chairman McLaughlin's off-the-record discussion with counsel indicating his tentative views and encouraging settlement. Second, it claims that throughout the hearing Mr. McLaughlin continually favored Ballantine's position, discriminated against Capital's counsel, and in effect "usurped the office of counsel for Ballantine."

Capital's broadside attack upon Mr. McLaughlin in its brief is imprecise as to the standards of judicial review on these grounds, and includes claims of violation of various unofficial pronouncements by the American Arbitration Association. In actuality, our review is limited to a determination whether, in the language of the United States Arbitration Act, there was "evident partiality or corruption in the arbitrators," or "any other misbehavior by which the rights of any party have been prejudiced," or whether the Commercial Arbitration Rules of the American Arbitration Association, which the contract explicitly made applicable, were violated.

It is clear at the outset that there was no violation of the Rules in this respect. Sections 11 and 18 of the Rules, in which the only reference to bias is made, refer only to an arbitrator's financial interest in the outcome of a dispute or personal or business relationship with a party, and no claim has been made that any of these conditions existed in this case. Thus we are left to a judicial assessment of the fairness of the conduct of the proceedings, based upon our own reading of the transcript of the arbitration hearings. Such a reading does not convince us that the district judge was wrong in finding no "evident partiality."

Chairman McLaughlin's conduct of the hearing was wholly consistent with those standards of informality and expedition appropriate to arbitration proceedings. Indeed, we doubt that there would be any reason for questioning his actions had he been the judge at a trial in a district court. A judge is not wholly at the mercy of counsel, and would be remiss if he did not participate in questioning to speed proceedings and eliminate irrelevancies. *E.g.,* Peckham v. Ronrico Corp., 288 F. 2d 841 (1 Cir., 1961). *A fortiori* an arbitrator should act affirmatively to simplify and expedite the proceedings before him, since among the virtues of arbitration which presumably have moved the parties to agree upon it are speed and informality. American Almond Prods. Co. v. Consolidated Pecan Sales Co., 144 F. 2d 448, 154 A.L.R. 1205 (2 Cir., 1944); Compania Panemena Maritima v. J. E. Hurley Lumber Co., 244 F. 2d 286 (2 Cir., 1957); see generally Mentschikoff, *Commercial Arbitration,* 61 COLUM. L. REV. 846 (1961).

We agree with Mr. Justice Steuer's oral opinion in the New York Supreme Court that Chairman McLaughlin's off-the-record discussion with the parties neither constituted prejudicial misbehavior nor demonstrated evident partiality.

It is to be expected that after a judge or an arbitrator has heard considerable testimony, he will have some view of the case. As long as that view is one which arises from the evidence and the conduct of the parties it cannot be fairly claimed that some expression of that view amounts to bias. By October 8, 1959, the arbitration had been under way for over five months, something over one thousand pages of testimony had been taken and many exhibits had been introduced and examined. On that same day, Capital's counsel told the arbitrators that it would take him no more than fifteen or twenty minutes of additional testimony to complete his defense. Under these circumstances, it is not to be wondered at that the chairman had reached a tentative conclusion.

While it is better in most cases for arbitrators to be chary in expressing any opinion before they reach their ultimate conclusion, and to avoid discussing settlement, it does not follow that such expressions are proof of bias. Mr. McLaughlin's remarks had no effect whatever on the hearings at the subsequent sessions. In summary, we can find no prejudice to Capital in his conversation with counsel.

ATLANTIC RAYON CORP. v. GOLDSMITH
277 App. Div. 554, 100 N.Y.S. 2d 849
(1st Dept. 1950)

PER CURIAM. While an arbitrator is not a judge in the strict sense, his functions are quasi-judicial in character and he must be a person in a position to act impartially, one who is not biased or prejudiced in favor of or against either side to the controversy.

Where arbitrators are selected under the auspices of a trade organization and where their special skill and experience in the trade are invoked, it is, in and of itself, no disqualification that they have had business dealings with either party to the arbitration. Here, however, it appears that originally the controversy between the parties was made the basis of an action at law. That action was discontinued and the parties proceeded to arbitration. Under the practice of the trade organization which supervised the arbitration, neither of the two arbitrators (who later chose the third arbitrator) knew which party to the arbitration selected him. One of the arbitrators and the corporations in which he had a substantial interest had, as their regular attorney, the lawyer who acted in that capacity for the successful party to the arbitration. The attorneys themselves did not participate in the proceedings before the arbitrators.

The arbitrator now sought to be disqualified claims that he did not know that his attorney also represented one of the parties to the arbitration. If he had such knowledge, it was his duty under the circumstances of this case to have disclosed it before he proceeded to act as arbitrator.

There is a further question as to whether the party now claiming to be aggrieved knew or should have known of the relationship complained of before the arbitration was concluded.

Courts are loath to sustain belated claims of disqualification after an adverse award but, considering all of the circumstances, substantial issues have here been raised concerning the knowledge of one of the arbitrators of the relationship of his attorney, to the submitted controversy and of the appellants' prior knowledge of this situation. Those issues should be referred to an official referee to hear and report thereon with his recommendations to the Special Term.

The order confirming the award and the judgment entered thereon and the order denying petitioners' motion to renew their motion to vacate the award herein should be reversed with $20 costs and disbursements to the appellants to abide the event. Settle order.

Order confirming the award and the judgment

entered thereon and the order denying petitioners' motion to renew their motion to vacate the award herein reversed with $20 costs and disbursements to the appellants to abide the event.

Settle order on notice.

PECK, P. J., and CALLAHAN and SHIENTAG, JJ. concur.

GLENNON and VAN VOORHIS, JJ., dissent and vote to affirm.

MATTER OF MILLIKEN WOOLENS (WEBER KNIT SPORTSWEAR)
11 A.D. 2d 166, 202 N.Y.S. 2d 431
(1st Dept. 1960)

VALENTE, J. Presented upon this appeal is the validity of an arbitration award assailed by appellant because of certain disqualifying relationships of the two arbitrators who signed the award —the third arbitrator dissented.

The arbitration proceeding was initiated in November, 1956, based on appellant's claim of a breach of warranty in the purchase of orlon yarns intended for the manufacture of sweaters. Appellant sought damages of $41,983, while respondents, in addition to denying any breach of warranty, counterclaimed for $13,481, the unpaid balance of the purchase price of the yarns. The arbitrators, by a divided vote, rejected appellant's claim and allowed respondents' counterclaim of $13,481. Thereafter, respondents moved to confirm and appellant applied to vacate the award. Holding that appellant's claim of disqualification of the arbitrators created triable issues as to credibility, Special Term directed a trial. The trial was held before a judge without a jury, who found appellant's claims to be "baseless and without merit." The motion to vacate the award was thereupon denied, and a motion to renew upon newly discovered evidence was likewise denied.

Among other grounds, section 1462 of the Civil Practice Act provides that an arbitration award must be vacated where there was "evident partiality" in the arbitrators or the arbitrators were guilty of any misbehavior by which the rights of any party have been prejudiced. In the case before us there has been no attempt to prove actual partiality; but appellant contends that the award must be vacated because of certain relationships—unknown and undisclosed to it—between the arbitrators and respondents and their attorneys which disqualified two of the arbitrators from acting in the matter.

An arbitrator's functions are quasi-judicial. But unlike a judge, he is not subject to disqualification for all of the grounds set forth in section 14 of the Judiciary Law. (See Matter of Amtorg Trading Corp. [Camden Fibre Mills], 277 App. Div. 531, 532–533, affd. 304 N.Y. 519.) With the development of arbitrations in commercial matters, particularly among persons in the same trade, arbitrators have been permitted to function who have had prior business dealings with one or both parties. (Matter of Atlantic Rayon Corp. [Goldsmith], 277 App. Div. 554, 555.) Hence, it has been held that mere proof of prior business relations with one party is insufficient to disqualify an arbitrator where that relationship is known to the opposing party.

Thus knowledge, on the part of a party, of the existence of a disqualifying relationship between the opposition and an arbitrator, coupled with a failure to make timely objection, will be deemed a waiver of the right to press the objection. Actual partiality, however, may not be deemed waived. (Matter of Miller v. Weiner, 260 App. Div. 444.)

Since waiver is a matter of intention (Matter of City of Rochester, 208 N.Y. 188, 197), the touchstone in these arbitration cases is the knowledge, actual or constructive, in the complaining party of the tainted relationship or interest of the arbitrator. Thus, in Matter of Dukraft Mfg. Co. (Bear Mill Mfg. Co.) (22 Misc. 2d 1057). McNally, J. set aside an award because no disclosure was made that business transactions between the arbitrator and one of the parties had increased considerably during the pendency of the arbitration proceeding. In Matter of Shirley Silk Co. v. American Silk Mills (260 App. Div. 572) an award was vacated where the arbitrator designated by the respondent failed to reveal to appellant that, prior to the arbitration, the firm of which the arbitrator was president had received a substantial award (in another arbitration) from a board of arbitrators of which the president of respondent was a member. (See, also, Matter of Knickerbocker Textile Corp. v. Sheila-Lynn, Inc., 172 Misc. 1015, affd. 259 App. Div. 992, supra.)

We have concluded that the record herein amply demonstrates the existence of certain relationships on the part of two of the arbitrators and respondents which would disqualify the arbitrators from acting; that those disqualifying relationships were not known by, or adequately disclosed to, appellant; and that appellant may not be deemed to have waived them. Consequently the award should have been vacated because appellant was not accorded that complete impartiality and indifference which it was entitled to expect from a disinterested board of arbitrators.

In the case of one of the arbitrators, who is an attorney, it appeared that he had been on the staff of the same law firm with respondents' trial counsel up to a time two and one-half years before the arbitration was held. Not only was that relationship not disclosed to appellant, but appellant may well have been misled by the innocuous statement in a letter written by the arbitrator, at the time of his appointment, that he was "acquainted with each of the attorneys representing the respective parties." Moreover, after the award had been made, appellant discovered that the law firm representing respondents and the arbitrator's law firm had served as co-counsel in a number of matters, one of which was pending at the time of the arbitration. Unquestionably, the foregoing relationships disqualified the attorney arbitrator from acting in this case in the absence of a waiver by appellant. Since the record negatives disclosure or knowledge by appellant of the disqualifying relationships, there was no waiver.

As to the second arbitrator, a businessman, the record establishes that, as one who was responsible for buying textiles for an affiliate of his present company, he had for many years purchased a substantial part of his requirements from respondent companies or their affiliates. These purchases constituted a regular course of dealings running into transactions amounting to millions of dollars. They may not be regarded as the casual and occasional dealings which might be expected where arbitrators are chosen because of familiarity with an industry (see Matter of Knickerbocker Textile Corp. [Donath], 22 Misc 2d 1056 [Botein, J.] affd. 282 App. Div. 680; Matter of Weavecraft, Inc. [Mil-Jay], 22 Misc 2d 1054 [Breitel, J.]). Moreover, it was shown that this arbitrator had served as arbitrator in three prior cases in which respondents' counsel represented a party, and in which the arbitrator had joined in a favorable award to respondents' counsel. Finally, it was established that a substantial claim which respondents' counsel was prosecuting against this arbitrator's company at the time of the arbitration was settled immediately after the award herein was made. The mere statement of the foregoing relationships is sufficient to show a disqualification to act as arbitrator. The absence of disclosure or waiver makes disqualification imperative.

However, added to the undisclosed disqualifying relationships of the two arbitrators, alluded to above, the circumstances of the selection of these arbitrators, which came to light after the award, create another basis for impugning the award. Their designation by the tribunal clerk of the American Arbitration Association was in the nature of administrative appointments when the parties could not agree. But the record shows that a former tribunal clerk, who had processed some part of this matter and who had thereafter become associated with respondents' counsel, suggested the names of these two arbitrators to his successor. There was testimony on behalf of respondents that the fact that the names of the arbitrators had been suggested by respondents' counsel had been communicated to appellant's counsel in a telephone conversation before their appointment. From the evidence, we must accept appellant's counsel's denial of the receipt of any such information. Present in the record is a letter written by respondents' counsel on February 26, 1957, objecting to the third arbitrator because he had been nominated by appellant's counsel. In view of this letter, it is incredible that appellant would have consented to the respondents naming two out of the three arbitrators, had there been a disclosure that they were suggested by respondents. Hence, in addition to the disqualifying interests of the two arbitrators, the record sustains a conclusion that there was covert influence in the selection of the arbitrators and a failure to disclose that their nomination stemmed from respondents.

Under the circumstances, the order appealed from should be reversed on the law and the facts, with costs to appellant, the motion to confirm the award denied and the motion to vacate the award granted. The parties must proceed to a new arbitration. The appeal from the order denying a renewal of the motion to vacate should be dismissed as moot.

RABIN, J. P., McNALLY and BASTOW, JJ., concur; M. M. FRANK, J., deceased.

CROSS PROPERTIES, INC v. GIMBEL BROTHERS, INC.
15 A.D. 2d 913, 225 N.Y.S. 2d 1014
(1st Dept. 1962)

PER CURIAM. In this arbitration proceeding the appellant appeals from an order confirming an arbitrators' award and denying appellant's application to vacate the said award.

The vacatur was sought on four grounds. One of the grounds, charging that one of the arbitrators made independent visits to the building whose construction was the subject matter of the arbitration, is frivolous. The arbitrator explains those visits by saying that they were simply normal shopping visits made by him and his wife from their home in the neighboring vicinity. There is no reason to believe otherwise since prior to such shopping excursions there had already been several official visits by the arbitrators to the site.

A second objection is that two of the arbitrators entered into a business relationship during the proceeding. We see nothing wrong in that relationship in so far as this arbitration is concerned. Apparently neither did the appellant because it had full knowledge thereof and raised no objection until after an adverse award had been rendered. Having such knowledge and not having objected they waived the right to do so after the rendition of the award.

It is also urged that the method of selection of the arbitrators was unfair. This argument is without merit. The method of selection had been agreed upon between the parties and the arbitration tribunal. If in fact there were any deviations from the agreed-upon procedure they were insignificant, nonprejudicial and, in any event, justifiable under the circumstances.

The only ground advanced in support of vacatur that deserves more than a summary disposition is that concerning the relationship between the arbitrator, Spear, and the respondent. We agree that where there are undisclosed dealings between a party and an arbitrator which impart a lack of impartiality and fairness, the award made is subject to vacatur (Matter of Friedman, 215 App. Div. 130, 137, 213 N.Y.S. 369, 376; Matter of Milliken Woolens [Weber Knit Sportswear], 11 A.D. 2d 166, 202 N.Y.S. 2d 431, aff'd 9 N.Y. 2d 878, 216 N.Y.S. 2d 696, 175 N.E. 2d 826). However, this is not to say that any undisclosed relationship, no matter how peripheral, superficial or insignificant, compels the same result. "Courts are loath to sustain belated claims of disqualification after an adverse award" (Matter of Atlantic Rayon Corp. [Goldsmith], 277 App. Div. 554, 556, 100 N.Y.S. 2d 849, 850), and particularly should this be so where the arbitration proceeding is a lengthy and involved one extending over a period of several years as in this case. The type of relationship which would appear to disqualify is one from which it may not be unreasonable to infer an absence of impartiality, the presence of bias or the existence of some interest on the part of the arbitrator in the welfare of one of the parties.

While there was a "relationship" here between the respondent and the arbitrator, we find it not to be a disqualifying one. The transactions between them were isolated and involved nothing of such a nature as would cause Spear to act other than with the requisite impartiality. The nature and magnitude of the real estate company with which Spear was affiliated would make it most likely that at one time or another there would be some contact with one of the largest department stores in the City of New York. Whether or not Spear disclosed such relationship to the tribunal clerk is of no consequence. The rules of the arbitration association required a disclosure only if the circumstances were "likely to create a presumption of bias" or were such as would make the arbitrator believe "might disqualify him as an impartial arbitrator." In the light of the nature of the relationship a failure to disclose would not have been violative of the rules.

In view of the great reliance placed by appellant upon the case of *Matter of Milliken, supra,* it should be noted that there the relationship between one of the arbitrators and the attorneys for one of the parties was such that there could be no question but that it could reasonably be inferred that there was present partiality or bias. In addition, there the arbitrator had not only failed to disclose the true relationship but had also made affirmative statements concerning the same which were less than the truth and—one must conclude—were designed to mislead. Not so in this case.

We can apply to this case the language of this Court in Matter of E. Richard Meinig Co. v. Katakura & Co., Ltd., 241 App. Div. 406, 407, 272 N.Y.S. 735, 736, aff'd 266 N.Y. 418, 195 N.E. 134, where it was stated: "If we were to give heed to the contentions of every unsuccessful litigant, based upon the flimsy ground[s] assigned here, it would be well-nigh impossible to carry out that part of the contract pertaining to arbitration."

Accordingly, the order entered on June 28, 1961 granting respondent's motion to confirm the arbitrators' award and denying the appellant's cross motion to vacate the said award should be affirmed, with costs.

Order and judgment affirmed with costs to respondent.

All concur except VALENTE, J., who dissents.

VALENTE, JUSTICE dissenting. I dissent. I would reverse the order confirming the award of the arbitrators and the judgment entered thereon and would vacate the award. The award was assailed upon four grounds: (1) that the arbitrator Spear failed to disclose his former relationships with respondent; (2) that Spear, during the course of the arbitration, employed Caverly, a fellow arbitrator, to act as a business associate in matters as to which Caverly expected substantial compensation ; (3) that the third arbitrator, Reinhard, made independent visits to the property involved in the arbitration ; and (4) that the method of selecting the arbitrators was unfair.

I find it necessary to go no further than the first objection to vitiate the award. In Matter of Milliken Woolens (Weber Knit) [sic] 11 A.D. 2d 166, 202 N.Y.S. 2d 431, aff'd 9 N.Y. 2d 878, 216 N.Y.S. 2d 696, 175 N.E. 2d 826, this Court announced a firm policy on the maintenance of the integrity of the arbitration process by insisting that no award should stand where disqualifying relationships between an arbitrator and a party are not adequately disclosed.

———————

Arbitrators to decide "value of ore developed" employed expert assistants as contemplated by the submission. Held: no right in party to cross-examine such expert assistants on their reports to the arbitrators. They were not, as contended, in the nature of witnesses nor their reports like testimony at a hearing.

Continental Materials Corp. v. Gaddis Mining Co. 306 F. 2d 952 (10th Cir. 1962), citing for same point Twin Lakes Reserve & Candle Co. v. Platt Rogers, Inc. 112 Colo. 155, 147 P. 2d 828 (1944).

———————

HILL v. ARO CORPORATION
263 F. Supp. 324 (N.D. Ohio W.D. 1967)

DON J. YOUNG, DISTRICT JUDGE. Plaintiff was discharged from employment by defendant Aro Corporation on March 8, 1965. A grievance was thereafter filed on his behalf by the defendant union. Subsequently, the defendant arbitrator was selected by the company and union from a list of nine candidates submitted by the Federal Mediation and Conciliation Service and on September 21, 1965 an award was entered affirming the company's action. This suit followed. Jurisdiction is purportedly found in the National Labor Relations Act, 29 U.S.C. § 185 (1964), the Labor Management Reporting & Disclosure Act, 29 U.S.C. § 412 (1964), and diversity of citizenship, 28 U.S.C. § 1332 (1964).

The complaint charges the arbitrator with various acts alleged to be inconsistent with the duties of an arbitrator. Many of the charges are petty and none need be dignified by repetition here. All are based upon the conduct of the defendant in his capacity as an arbitrator. The defendant arbitrator now moves pursuant to Rule 12(b) (6) for dismissal in that the com-

plaint fails to state a claim upon which relief may be granted. The arbitrator contends he is immune from civil liability for all acts done in his arbitral capacity. The Court agrees.

The history of litigation aimed at arbitrators is easily reviewed, for there are few reported cases. In 1836 an English writer succinctly summed up the English experience at that point: "It has been said that an arbitrator is liable to an action, if he misconduct himself ; but I cannot find any case in which such an action has ever been brought."[1] Since then a few such actions have been brought, but none have so far been successful.

In Jones v. Brown, 54 Iowa 74, 6 N.W. 140 (1880), an arbitrator who attempted to collect a modest fee of $240 for 24 days of labor was confronted with a counterclaim which charged him and his fellow arbitrators with corruption and fraud. The Iowa Supreme Court, noting that arbitrators "are in a certain sense a court," held that arbitrators are clothed with the same immunity as the judiciary. A few years later, in Hoosac Tunnel Dock and Elevator Co. v. O'Brien, 137 Mass. 424, 50 Am. Rep. 323 (1884), the Massachusetts Supreme Court came to the same conclusion. An arbitrator was alleged to have conspired with a tort claimant's attorney and to have "fraudulently induced and persuaded" his two fellow members of a court-appointed panel to "unite in an award against plaintiff." The Court's reasoning in sustaining a demurrer to the complaint has often been quoted:

> An arbitrator is a quasi judicial officer, under our laws, exercising judicial functions. There is as much reason in his case for protecting and insuring his impartiality, independence, and freedom from undue influences, as in the case of a judge or juror. The same considerations of public policy apply, and we are of opinion that the same immunity extends to him. Id. at 426, 50 Am. Rep. at 324.

Other cases may be found involving parties whose functions the courts have characterized as quasi-arbitral. In Hutchins v. Merrill, 109 Me. 313, 84 A. 412, 42 L.R.A., N.S., 277 (1912), a surveyor, whose appraisal of plaintiffs' timber was binding on the parties to a service contract, was charged with negligence in scaling the logs. In Melady v. South St. Paul Live Stock Exchange, 142 Minn. 194, 171 N.W. 806 (1919), the board of directors of an exchange empowered by statute to arbitrate matters concerning its membership, was charged with "wanton, malicious, and willful" action in finding a member guilty of "uncommercial conduct." In both

———————

1. WATSON, "A Treatise on the Law of Arbitration and Awards," 11 L. LIBRARY 36 (1836).

cases the rule of immunity applied. Architects, when acting pursuant to an agreement between owner and contractor, are also protected from suits, although their immunity in many jurisdictions does not extend to charges of fraud. Lundgren v. Freeman, 307 F. 2d 104, 118 (9th Cir. 1962).

Apparently, the first reported case involving a labor arbitrator is a decision by a judge of the New York Supreme Court. Babylon Milk & Cream Co. v. Horvitz, 151 N.Y.S. 2d 221 (Sup. Ct. 1956), aff'd, 4 A.D. 2d 777, 165 N.Y.S. 2d 717 (1957). An employer, unhappy with an arbitrator's award and alleging "collusion among the defendants," sued various union officials and an arbitrator. Noting that the question was one of first impression in New York, the court dismissed the cause against the arbitrator. The opinion contains the following significant language:

> Arbitrators exercise judicial functions and while not *eo nomine* judges they are judicial officers and bound by the same rules as govern those officers. Matter of Friedman, 215 App. Div. 130, 213 N.Y.S. 369; Matter of American Eagle Fire Ins. Co. v. New Jersey Ins. Co., 240 N.Y. 398, 148 N.E. 562. Considerations of public policy are the reasons for the rule and like other judicial officers, arbitrators must be free from the fear of reprisals by an unsuccessful litigant. They must of necessity be uninfluenced by any fear of consequences for their acts. Id. at 224.

Cahn v. International Ladies' Garment Union, 203 F.Supp. 191 (E.D.Pa. 1962) is the only other reported case involving a labor arbitrator. Charges of conspiracy were again leveled against an arbitrator and other defendants and the court again invoked the immunity rule in favor of the arbitrator. The Court of Appeals for the Third Circuit affirmed. 311 F. 2d 113 (1962).

Plaintiff attempts to counter this persuasive, albeit not voluminous, case law authority with a strange mixture of theories: the arbitrator's actions are said to be in excess of his jurisdiction; plaintiff claims to be a third-party beneficiary of the arbitrator's implied contract with the Federal Mediation & Conciliation Service requiring the arbitrator to comply with its regulations; the fact that neither Congress nor the Ohio legislature have granted immunity to arbitrators is supposed to have some weight with this Court; the Ohio and federal constitutions and the federal civil rights act are alleged to have been violated; and finally, if the common law grants defendant immunity, then it is time for a change. The problem with all of these theories is that they require a result directly contrary to and inconsistent with the very thrust of modern labor jurisprudence. Although there may exist some disagreement among the states, there is not the slightest doubt about the all-important role of the labor arbitrator in the developing federal common law of labor relations. "Under federal law it is now a clearly established national policy to encourage the use of arbitration." Rhine v. Union Carbide Corp., 343 F. 2d 12, 16 (6th Cir. 1965). "The federal policy of settling labor disputes by arbitration would be undermined if courts had the final say on the merits of the awards ... the arbitrators under these collective agreements are indispensable agencies in a continuous collective bargaining process." United Steelworkers of America v. Enterprise Wheel & Car Corp., 363 U.S. 593, 596, 80 S.Ct. 1358, 1360, 4 L.Ed.2d 1424 (1960). If national policy encourages arbitration and if arbitrators are indispensable agencies in the furtherance of that policy, then it follows that the common law rule protecting arbitrators from suit ought not only to be affirmed, but, if need be, expanded. The immunity rule was sound when announced by two state supreme courts over eighty years ago; it is still sound today.[2]

Defendant's dismissal motion will be sustained.

In a suit by a contractor against an architect alleging innumerable acts of misconduct by the arbitrator that caused damage and expense to the plaintiff-contractor, the trial court dismissed the complaint on the grounds that "an architect is an arbitrator or a quasi arbitrator and as such is immune from private actions against him for damages resulting from his act as an arbitrator or quasi arbitrator." The appellate court declared:

> With that rule we have no quarrel.... The immunity in question ... is one bestowed by public policy on those people who by office or by contract, are called upon to act as judges. It is in every sense a judicial immunity. It attaches to every act done in the judicial capacity, but to no other. Thus the architect has no immunity as an architect.... He may in the construction of a building assume many roles—planner, designer, supervisor, arbitrator, arbitrator and owner's agent. In the role of arbitrator, and in that role alone, goes the cloak of immunity.

Craviolini v. Scholer and Fuller, 89 Ariz. 24, 357 P. 2d 611 (1961).

---

2. Insofar as the court's jurisdiction is based on diversity of citizenship, no authority has been shown which would indicate that an Ohio court would rule otherwise.

CHAPTER VI

REVIEW OF AWARDS—MOTIONS TO CONFIRM, VACATE, AND MODIFY

A.

Scope of Review

WILKINS v. ALLEN
169 N.Y. 494, 62 N.E. 575 (1902)

MARTIN, J. The questions of law involved upon this appeal relate to a submission and award determining the rights of the parties under certain leases of property in the city of New York, made between them or their respective grantors, immediate or remote. The first lease was made in 1833, the second in 1854, and the third in 1875. The term of each was for 21 years, so that the full term under the several leases finally terminated in 1896. Only questions of law were submitted for arbitration, which included the interpretation or construction of the leases, and a determination of the legal rights of the parties under them. The submission was in writing, stated plainly the questions to be decided, and provided that a judgment in the supreme court should be entered upon the award. The parties obviously understood that only questions of law were involved, and hence

it was that they submitted them to an eminent and distinguished member of the legal profession, in whose ability and fairness they evidently had complete and perfect confidence. That they were fully and fairly considered, and that the arbitrator determined all the questions submitted, is not, and cannot be successfully, denied. No motion was made to vacate, modify, or correct the award upon any of the grounds mentioned in the statute. The appellant, however, excepted to the award, and to each conclusion thereof,—a procedure authorized neither at common law nor by statute, and hence the exceptions presented no question for review by an appellate court. He also opposed its confirmation, but not upon any of the statutory grounds, which were the only grounds upon which the action of the arbitrator could in any manner be considered or reviewed. The award was confirmed, and judgment thereon subsequently entered. From the judgment and order the appellant appealed to the appellate division, where both were affirmed. A judgment of affirmance was subsequently entered, from which an appeal to this court was taken.

The first and only question this court is called upon to determine is whether the decision of the appellate division can be sustained, which was to the effect that the appeal to that court did not bring up for review the question of the correctness of the award upon the merits, either as to the law or facts, but presented only such questions as would be involved in an application to vacate, modify, or correct it as provided by the Code. Where the merits of a controversy are referred to an arbitrator selected by the parties, his determination, either as to the law or the facts, is final and conclusive ; and a court will not open an award unless perverse misconstruction or positive misconduct upon the part of the arbitrator is plainly established, or there is some provision in the agreement of submission authorizing it. The award of an arbitrator cannot be set aside for mere errors of judgment either as to the law or as to the facts. If he keeps within his jurisdiction, and is not guilty of fraud, corruption, or other misconduct affecting his award, it is unassailable, operates as a final and conclusive judgment, and, however disappointing it may be, the parties must abide by it.

But it is claimed that section 2381 of the Code furnishes express authority for an appeal from a judgment entered upon such an award, and that that right is unlimited by the other provisions of the Code relating to the subject of arbitration and award. That section is practically a re-enactment of the law as it previously existed, and confers no right or authority which was not given by the Revised Statutes. In construing that section we must consider the provisions of title 8 of the Code, which contains the existing law upon the subject, and of which that section forms only a part. That title, after declaring in what cases a submission to arbitration cannot be made, what controversies may be submitted and how, and after providing for the appointment of arbitrators, for the hearing, for the attendance of witnesses, how the award shall be made and authenticated, provides that a motion may be made to confirm the award, and that the court "must" grant an order confirming it, unless it is vacated, modified, or corrected as prescribed therein. Thus, at the outset, we find that, as to the merits of a controversy submitted, the successful party has an absolute right to an order confirming the award, and to enter a judgment thereon, unless it is vacated, modified, or corrected for the reasons and in the manner therein prescribed. Section 2374 provides

that the court "must" make an order vacating an award, where it is procured by corruption, fraud, or undue means, where the arbitrators are partial or corrupt, or guilty of misconduct or other misbehavior which prejudiced the rights of any party, or where they have exceeded their powers or imperfectly executed them. Section 2375 declares that the court "must" make an order modifying or correcting the award, where there has been an evident miscalculation of figures, or mistake in the description of any person, thing, or property, where they have awarded upon a matter not submitted and not affecting the merits of the decision, or where the award is imperfect in form. The statute also provides within what time such a motion shall be made ; makes provision as to costs, and as to the judgment to be awarded. Code, §§ 2376–2378. Then follows a provision as to what the judgment roll shall contain. It must contain the submission ; the selection of arbitrators or umpire ; each written extension of time, if any, within which to make the award ; the award ; each notice, affidavit, or paper used upon an application to confirm, modify, or correct the award ; a copy of each order of the court upon such application ; and also a copy of the judgment. Section 2379. Following this is a provision as to the effect of the judgment, and the manner of its enforcement. Section 2380. Then follows the section relied upon by the appellant, which declares: "An appeal may be taken from an order vacating an award, or from a judgment entered upon an award, as from an order or judgment in an action. The proceedings upon such an appeal, including the judgment thereupon, and the enforcement of the judgment, are governed by the provisions of chapter twelfth of this act, as far as they are applicable." Section 2381.

This examination of the various provisions of the statute relating to this subject, and the decisions of the courts of this state as to the conclusiveness of an award upon the merits, discloses that the only method of attacking or reviewing an award is by motion to vacate, modify, or correct it for the reasons mentioned in the statute. Previous to any statute, a court of law had no jurisdiction to examine into an award made by an arbitrator selected by the parties, and even a court of equity could award relief in such a case only upon the ground of corruption. A statute was, however, subsequently enacted providing that for certain specified reasons an award might be vacated, modified, or corrected. Since its adoption it has been uniformly held in this state that the power of the court to review or vacate an award is limited to the power expressly conferred by the plain words of the enactment, and that an award is conclusive and final as to the questions decided unless it is modified, corrected, or vacated in the manner and upon the specific grounds provided by the statute. The conclusiveness of awards is based upon the principle that, the parties having chosen judges of their own and agreed to abide by their decision, they are bound by their agreement, and compelled to perform the award.

The claim of the appellant that section 2381 furnishes authority for an appeal from a judgment entered upon an award, whereby the merits of the award may be reviewed, is in direct conflict with the authorities cited, most of which arose under the Revised Statutes, of which title 8 is a substantial re-enactment. Therefore the principle of the cases arising and decided under that statute is clearly in point, and the cases uniformly establish the doctrine that the merits of an award cannot be reviewed by the court, and that it can review an award only upon the grounds, to the extent, and in the manner specified in the statute. Moreover, when the provisions of the Code relating to arbitration are read together, and the section relied upon is construed in the light of the entire statute, it is manifest that the only method of attacking an award is by motion to vacate, modify, or correct for the reasons enumerated in sections 2374 and 2375. Where such an application has been made and determined, the provisions of section 2381 are applicable, but not otherwise. In such a case, if the application be granted, then, under that section, the defeated party may appeal from the order, and thus review the action of the court that granted it. If it be denied, then, after the judgment is entered, the party conceiving himself aggrieved by such denial may appeal from the judgment, and thus review the action of the court in that respect. It is very obvious that the provisions of that section relating to an appeal apply only to an appeal from the action of the court, and were never intended to authorize an appellate court to review the action of arbitrators in the first instance. This is further indicated by the fact that the judgment roll must contain all the papers used upon such an application, the evident purpose being to enable the appellate court to examine and pass upon the action of the court below. But where there has been no such application, then, as the provisions of the Code requiring the court to enter a judgment are mandatory, so that it can exercise no official judgment or judicial discretion, there is nothing which an appellate court can review. If the legislature had intended to confer upon a defeated party the right to appeal from an award upon the merits and thus change the law as it has existed for more than a century, that purpose would have been plainly stated in the statute, and the legislature would have employed language which would have clearly indicated its purpose, especially in view of the fact that no such right existed under the common law. To hold that any court, appellate or other, has the right to review the action of an arbitrator upon the merits of a controversy submitted to him, would entirely subvert the whole system and principle of arbitration, and transfer to courts powers which the parties themselves have expressly confided to arbitrators, and that, too, without their consent. Hence we are of the opinion that the learned appellate division correctly held that an appeal from a judgment entered upon the award of an arbitrator, to whom questions of law were submitted under an agreed statement of facts, presented for review only such questions as were raised by a motion under sections 2374 and 2375 of the Code, and that, as no such application was made in this case, the award of the arbitrator could not be reviewed.

It follows that the judgment should be affirmed, with costs.

PARKER, C. J., and GRAY, O'BRIEN, BARTLETT, HAIGHT, and VANN, JJ., concur.

Judgment affirmed.

HARRELL v. DOVE MFG. CO., 234 Ore. 321, 381 P. 2d 710 (1963)

[Appellant Dove contended:

> The Arbitrator erred in holding that respondent forfeited its right to rescind the contract upon the specification of fraud alleged because the respondent remained in possession and control of the assets herein involved and is still in possession and control, where respondent had knowledge or was charged with the duty of inquiry into all the facts, because the contract (Exhibit 1) placed on all of the subject matter of the contract in question in escrow with the attorney for respondent and there is no evidence in the record to show that respondent had knowledge or that any evidence was introduced from which knowledge could be inferred.

> The Arbitrator erred in holding that petitioner did not breach his covenant not to compete because there was no evidence that petitioner competed in any way with respondent.

The statutory grounds for excepting to an award were:

> (1) The award was procured by corruption, fraud or undue means.

(2) There was evident partiality or corruption on the part of the arbitrators, or any of them.

(3) The arbitrators were guilty of misconduct in refusing to postpone the hearing, upon sufficient cause shown, or in refusing to hear evidence pertinent and material to the controversy; or of any other misbehavior by which the rights of any party were prejudiced.

(4) The arbitrators exceeded their powers, or so imperfectly executed them that a mutual, final and definite award upon the subject-matter submitted was not made.

(5) There was an evident material miscalculation of figures or an evident material mistake in the description of any person, thing or property referred to in the award.

(6) The arbitrators awarded upon a matter not submitted to them, unless it was a matter not affecting the merits of the decision upon the matters submitted.

(7) The award was imperfect in matter of form not affecting the merits of the controversy.

In rejecting Dove's attack upon the award the Oregon Supreme Court said]:

We quote the following from Jacob v. Pacific Export Lumber Company, 136 Or. 622, 297 P. 848 (1931): "It is not the province of the courts to substitute their judgment for that of an honest impartial, and competent arbitrator.... Neither a mistake of fact or law vitiates an award." See also, Rueda v. Union Pacific Railroad Co., 180 Or. 133, 175 P. 2d 778 (1946) at page 168. The quoted statement is in accord with the provisions of ORS 33.210 through ORS 33.340 which regulate arbitration proceedings in Oregon. The latter section provides for appeals from judgments based upon awards of arbitrators. The scope of such appeals, however, is necessarily limited by the provisions of ORS 33.320 which sets forth the grounds upon which exceptions to awards may be filed with the circuit court. That section does not provide for judicial review on the merits of arbitrators' awards. This court is limited in its consideration of awards to exceptions which have been submitted to the circuit court in accordance with the provisions of ORS 33.320.

These provisions of our statute are rooted in reasons of policy. One of the primary purposes for which parties agree to arbitrate their disputes is to avoid what they fear may be costly and time-consuming litigation. See generally, Note, 63 HARV. L. REV. 681 (1950). It would be patently unfair to allow a party to an arbitration proceeding for which both parties have voluntarily contracted to turn the proceedings into a lawsuit in the event the arbitrator's decision is unfavorable to him. Through the provisions of ORS 33.320 our legislature has undertaken to

guarantee that the proceedings will be conducted in a fair and honorable manner. It has not undertaken to authorize the courts to substitute their judgment for that of an arbitrator whose actions do not fall within the purview of that section. Were the courts to assume this privilege they would defeat the very purposes for which disputes are submitted to arbitrators. In the absence of an arbitration clause in the contract the parties are free to settle their disputes in court. But where they have contracted not to do so the courts are authorized to interfere only where statutory grounds for such interference appear.

We have noted that the exceptions submitted by the respondent to the circuit court raised grounds approved by ORS 33.320. But we have also seen that it abandoned those exceptions upon this appeal in favor of two assignments of error which would necessitate a decision on the merits. Such a decision would be beyond the authority conferred upon this court by the legislature.

The judgment of the circuit court is affirmed.

Pennsylvania has five systems of arbitration: common law, statutory under provisions enacted in the 18th and 19th provisions; "compulsory"— at the option of either party in common law actions, but not in Philadelphia county; a special brand of "compulsory" arbitration for small claims on a county option basis; modern statutory arbitration; and references by agreement to attorneys.

For the second category (old statutory arbitration) it is provided:

It shall be lawful also for the parties to any suit to consent as aforesaid to a rule of court, for referring all matters of fact in controversy in such suit to referees, as aforesaid, reserving all matters of law arising thereupon for the decision of the court, and the report of such referees, setting forth the facts found by them, shall have the same effect as a special verdict, and the court shall and may proceed thereupon in like manner as upon a special verdict, and either party may have a writ of error to the judgment entered thereupon, as in the case of a judgment entered upon special verdict. 1836, June 16, P.L. 715, § 3.

The California Code of Civil Procedure provides:

§ 1286.2 Grounds for vacation of award

Subject to Section 1286.4, the court shall vacate the award if the court determines that:

(a) The award was procured by corruption, fraud or other undue means;

(b) There was corruption in any of the arbitrators;

(c) The rights of such party were substantially prejudiced by misconduct of a neutral arbitrator;

(d) The arbitrators exceeded their powers and the award cannot be corrected without affecting the merits of the decision upon the controversy submitted; or

(e) The rights of such party were substantially prejudiced by the refusal of the arbitrators to postpone the hearing upon sufficient cause being shown therefor or by the refusal of the arbitrators to hear evidence material to the controversy or by other conduct of the arbitrators contrary to the provisions of this title. (Added Stats. 1961, c. 461, p. 1546, § 2.)

§ 1286.6 Grounds for correction of award

Subject to Section 1286.8, the court, unless it vacates the award pursuant to Section 1286.2, shall correct the award and confirm it as corrected if the court determines that:

(a) There was an evident miscalculation of figures or an evident mistake in the description of any person, thing or property referred to in the award;

(b) The arbitrators exceeded their powers but the award may be corrected without affecting the merits of the decision upon the controversy submitted; or

(c) The award is imperfect in a matter of form, not affecting the merits of the controversy. (Added Stats. 1961, c. 461, p. 1546, § 2.)

The Illinois Arbitration Act provides:

Ch. 10 § 112. Vacating an award

(a) Upon application of a party, the court shall vacate an award where:

(1) The award was procured by corruption, fraud or other undue means;

(2) There was evident partiality by an arbitrator appointed as a neutral or corruption in any one of the arbitrators or misconduct prejudicing the right of any party;

(3) The arbitrators exceeded their powers;

(4) The arbitrators refused to postpone the hearing upon sufficient cause being shown therefor or refused to hear evidence material to the controversy or otherwise so conducted the hearing, contrary to the provisions of Section 5,[1] as to prejudice substantially the rights of a party; or

(5) There was no arbitration agreement and the issue was not adversely determined in proceedings under Section 2[2] and the party did not participate in the arbitration hearing without raising the objection; but the fact that the relief was such that it could not or would not be granted by a court of law or equity is not ground for vacating or refusing to confirm the award.

(b) An application under this Section shall be made within 90 days after delivery of a copy of the award to the applicant, except that if predicated upon corruption, fraud or other undue means, it shall be made within 90 days after such grounds are known or should have been known.

(c) In vacating the award on grounds other than stated in clause (5) of subsection (a) the court may order a rehearing before new arbitrators chosen as provided in Section 3,[3] or if the award is vacated on grounds set forth in clauses (3) and (4) of subsection (a) the court may order a rehearing before the arbitrators who made the award or their successors appointed in accordance with Section 3. The time within which the agreement requires the award to be made is applicable to the rehearing and commences from the date of the order.

(d) If the application to vacate is denied and no motion to modify or correct the award is pending, the court shall confirm the award.

(e) Nothing in this Section or any other Section of this Act shall apply to the vacating, modifying, or correcting of any award entered as a result of an arbitration agreement which is a part of or pursuant to a collective bargaining agreement; and the grounds for vacating, modifying, or correcting such an award shall be those which existed prior to the enactment of this Act. 196 Aug. 24, Laws 1961, p. 3844, § 12.

1 Section 105 of this chapter.
2 Section 102 of this chapter.
3 Section 103 of this chapter.

[Sec. 2 covers proceedings to compel or stay arbitration.]

Note that the statutes provide a shorter period during which a party may move to vacate, modify, or correct as compared with the period allowed for moving to confirm. Nonetheless, on motion to confirm, the grounds available for vacating may be asserted in defense.

In a proceeding under motion to confirm "the party opposing may apparently object upon any ground which constitutes a sufficient cause under the statute to vacate, modify, or correct although no such formal motion has been made. See Matter of Picker, 130 App. Div. 88, 114 N.Y.S. 289; Matter of Conway [179 App. Div. 108, 166 N.Y.S. 182]; Matter of Wilkins, 169 N.Y. 494, 62 N.E. 575; STURGES, COMMERCIAL ARBITRATIONS AND AWARDS, 874." The Hartbridge, 57 F. 2d 672 (2d Cir. 1932).

Indeed, some courts have held that on a motion to confirm the resisting party must assert all grounds of objection. He may not later institute a separate proceeding to vacate or modify. The latter procedure is only arguably possible in labor-management disputes where the time limits of the United States Arbitration Act and state statutes may not apply. (On this latter point see Chapter XV, "Choosing Applicable Law", Part B.)

AMICIZIA SOCIETA NAVE GAZIONE, v. CHILEAN NITRATE AND IODINE SALES CORPORATION
184 F. Supp. 116 (S.D.N.Y., 1959)

Petitioner, an Italian corporation, is the owner of two ships which, while still under construction, it chartered to respondent, a corporation of Chile. The two charterparties were negotiated in New York City and dated September 6, 1955. Clause 29 of the charterparty provided that hatches 2, 3 and 5 should be "double-rigged". It was later provided by Addendum No. 1 that all six hatches should be "double-rigged". The controversy arises over the meaning of "double-rigged". Petitioner-owner claims that "double-rigged" means two winches and two booms at each hatch and this is how the ship was outfitted. Respondent-charterer claims that "double-rigged" means four winches and four booms at each hatch. Pursuant to the arbitration clause of the charterparties the controversy went before three arbitrators—one selected by each side, and the third selected by the two first chosen. The arbitrators, one dissenting, found that the express [sic] "double-rigged" has two meanings in New York City and found in favor of the petitioner-owner.

It should be noted that New York law is cited because of the scarcity of federal cases directly in point, and because 9 U.S.C. §§ 9, 10 and 11 were taken from Sections 1461, 1462 and 1462a of the New York Civil Practice Act.

"The federal act in respect to the sections now under consideration is almost verbatim like the corresponding provisions of the New York statute, so that the state practice may be regarded as highly persuasive, if not controlling." The Hartbridge, 2 Cir., 1932, 57 F. 2d 672, 673.

Courts cannot rejudge the decision of arbitrators on the merits. If the courts could rejudge the decision then the value of arbitration would be lost. However, the decision of arbitrators can be upset if it was procured by fraud or corruption, if there was evident partiality, if the arbitrators exceeded their powers, or if their decision is a perverse misconstruction of the law. As was stated in Matter of Wilkins, 169 N.Y. 494, 62 N.E. 575,

> Where the merits of a controversy are referred to an arbitrator selected by the parties, his determination, either as to the law or the facts is final and conclusive, and a court will not open an award unless perverse misconstruction or positive misconduct upon the part of the arbitrator is plainly established, or there is some provision authorizing it. The award of an arbitrator cannot be set aside for mere errors of judgment, either as to the law or as to the facts.

It should be pointed out that courts are extremely hesitant about vacating or modifying arbitrators' decisions. All the cases stated that it can be done if the error is a manifest disregard of the law or a perverse misconstruction, but they hesitate to set aside the arbitrators' decision. In Fudickar v. Guardian Mutual Life Insurance Co., 62 N.Y. 392 the court found that the arbitrator had a misconception about the law but upheld the arbitrator's decision because it was not apparent that the decision was based solely on the misconception. The court said that—

> The party alleging error of law must be able to point to the award and say that the arbitrator, as appears from the award itself, intended to decide the case according to law, and has mistaken it, and that except for this mistake his award would have been different.

On appeal, it was observed, 274 F. 2d 807 (2d Cir. 1960):

Were we empowered to view the matter *de novo*, we would find much to persuade in the arguments advanced by the dissenting arbitrator. But as respondent recognizes, the court's function in confirming or vacating an arbitration award is severely limited. If it were otherwise, the ostensible purpose for resort to arbitration, *i.e.,* avoidance of litigation, would be frustrated. See Note, *Judicial Review of Arbitration Awards on the Merits,* 63 Harv. L. Rev. 681 (1950). The statutory provisions, 9 U.S.C. §§ 10, 11, in expressly stating certain grounds for either vacating an award or modifying or correcting it, do not authorize its setting aside on the grounds of erroneous finding of fact or of misinterpretation of law. It is true that an award may be vacated where the arbitrators have "exceeded their powers." 9 U.S.C. § 10(d). Apparently relying upon this phrase, the Supreme Court in Wilko v. Swan, 346 U.S. 427, 436–437, 74 S. Ct. 182, 98 L. Ed. 168, suggested that an award may be vacated if in "manifest disregard" of the law. But *cf.* Bernhardt v. Polygraphic Co. of America, 350 U.S. 198, 203 note 4, 76 S. Ct. 273, 276, 100 L. Ed. 199: "Whether the arbitrators misconstrued a contract is not open to judicial review," citing The Hartbridge, 2 Cir., 62 F. 2d 72, certiorari denied [sic] Munson Steamship Line v. North of England Steamship Co., 288 U.S. 601, 53 S. Ct. 320, 77 L. Ed. 977. See also Krauss Bros. Lumber Co. v. Louis Bossert & Sons, 2 Cir., 62 F. 2d 1004; James Richardson & Sons v. W. E. Hedger Transp. Corp., 2 Cir., 98 F. 2d 55, certiorari denied W. E. Hedger Transp. Corp. v. James Richardson

& Sons, 305 U.S. 657, 59 S. Ct. 357, 83 L. Ed. 426.

Respondent contends that the arbitrators' reliance upon the principle that ambiguous language is to be construed against the author constitutes a "manifest disregard" of the law, since petitioner had reason to know the meaning respondent gave to the expression "double-rigged." But if labels are to be applied to the issues involved, we deem the question of what each party had reason to know to be one of fact. Further, an examination of the arbitrators' opinion has not disclosed to us any finding as to what the parties had reason to know, as opposed to what they did in fact understand. While the evidence perhaps does suggest that petitioner had notice of respondent's meaning, the arbitrators may have been of the view that respondent, which proposed the term, had reason to know of the ambiguity. Or, as appears quite likely, the issue may not have been considered. But in any event, the misapplication—if it be that—of such rules of contract interpretation does not rise to the stature of a "manifest disregard" of law.

Cert. denied, 363 U.S. 843 (1960).

For a discussion of the possibility of review to ascertain whether Code standards have been observed, see Daniel Collins, *Arbitration and the Uniform Commercial Code,* 41 N.Y.U. L. REV. 736 (1966) (pro) and Merton C. Bernstein, *The Impact of the Uniform Commercial Code upon Arbitration: Revolutionary Overthrow or Peaceful Coexistence?,* 42 N.Y.U. L. REV. 8 (1967) (anti).

In Matter of Grace Line, Inc. (National Marine Engineer's Beneficial Association), 38 Misc. 2d 909. N.Y.S. 2d 293 (N.Y. Cty. 1963), the court bemoaned the necessity of enforcing an award it said "runs counter to one's sense of fairness" and possibly turned on too literal a reading of a prior arbitrator's earlier award, which had been incorporated into the collective agreement. But the court confirmed and its action was affirmed ; mem. 20 A.D. 2d 759, 246 N.Y.S. 2d 994 (1st Dep't.), leave to appeal denied, 14 N.Y. 2d 484, 200 N.E. 2d 220, cert. denied, 379 U.S. 843 (1964).

Subsequently the association of which the company losing this case was a member refused to continue the arbitrator in office when negotiating a new contract. Reportedly a major issue in the ensuing strike was the union's demand that the arbitrator be renamed as "permanent umpire" for the new contract term. Whether this decision played any part in the dispute is not known.

LOCAL 1078, UNITED AUTOMOBILE WORKERS OF AMERICA v. ANACONDA AMERICAN BRASS COMPANY
149 Conn. 687, 183 A. 2d 623 (1962)

BALDWIN, C. J., KING, MURPHY, SHEA and ALCORN, JJ.

SHEA, J. The plaintiff applied to the Superior Court for an order vacating an award made in an arbitration between the plaintiff and the defendant. The court granted the application and vacated the award. The defendant has appealed.

In October, 1956, the parties entered into a collective bargaining agreement with respect to rates of pay, hours of work and other conditions of employment for the employees of the defendant who were represented by the plaintiff. In 1957, the defendant began to equip a small area in one of its mills for the production of copper tubing. At the outset, a five-die drawbench was used. The plaintiff claimed that a foreman was doing certain tasks which, in other parts of the mill, were usually performed by section men. Section men are in the bargaining unit, while foremen are not. The plaintiff filed a grievance, claiming that the defendant was violating article VI, § 9, of the contract, which reads as follows:

> It is understood that the services of non-bargaining unit personnel will in no case be used to deprive bargaining unit employees of overtime work or for the purpose of replacing bargaining unit employees. It is the intention of the Company not to have non-bargaining unit employees perform duties customarily performed by bargaining unit employees.

The defendant replied to the grievance as follows:

> After considerable discussion regarding the charge in this grievance, it was brought out that the main reason for the grievance is the activity of salaried foremen in the vicinity of the new five die bench. As more operations are started up, other arrangements will be made.

Disposition of the grievance was held up pending the addition of new equipment. This took place the following summer, when a three-die drawbench was installed. The plaintiff again requested the defendant to assign a section man, but the request was rejected, reactivating the grievance which the parties designated as "grievance No. 80." Thereupon, the parties submitted the following issue to arbitration: "Under the terms of the applicable Collective Bargaining Agreement is the Company's present operating practice in the bay which includes Benches 69 and 70 and associated equipment of the East Tube Mill in violation of Article VI, Section 9." The arbitrator rendered the following award.

> The Company's present operating practice in the bay which includes Benches 69 and 70 and associated equipment of the East Tube Mill does not violate Article VI, Section 9 so long as the work involved does not occupy the major portion of the foreman's time. Grievance No. 80 is dismissed.

The court vacated the award on the ground that the arbitrator had exceeded his powers by rendering a decision outside the scope of the question submitted. It is a truism frequently stated by this court that the charter of an arbitrator is the submission, and no matter outside the submission may be included in the award. The basic test of the validity of an award lies in its conformity to the terms of the submission.

Article X of the contract gave to an arbitrator jurisdiction over the interpretation as well as the application of the agreement, and his decision was to be "final and binding on both parties." However, in making his award, the arbitrator could not exceed his powers. General Statutes § 52–418 (d) ; International Brotherhood v. Trudon & Platt Motor Lines, Inc., 146 Conn. 17, 23, 147 A. 2d 484. The question submitted by the parties was specific in form and could have been answered with precision and exactitude. It required a clear, unequivocal answer as to "the Company's present operating practice." The arbitrator was not requested to give any opinion concerning other possible practices, nor was he called on to furnish the parties with a guide for their future operations. The award, when it stated that the present operating practice "does not violate ... [the contract] so long as the work involved does not occupy the major portion of the foreman's time," went beyond the question submitted. The arbitrator not only answered the question submitted but he also defined a course of conduct which could be followed in the future. Since the award exceeded the scope of the submission, it cannot be upheld. Local 63, Textile Workers Union v. Cheney Bros., *supra*.

The defendant concedes that a portion of the award contains unnecessary statements but suggests that the court should modify or correct the award by rejecting the imperfect portion of it. As authority for such an action, the defendant relies on § 52–419 (c) of the General Statutes. Although it is true that this statute authorizes the correction of an award by the Superior Court, correction is made only on the timely application of a party to the arbitration. Here, the defendant failed to apply to the Superior Court for relief under § 52–419 (c). The correc-

tion which it now suggests cannot be made. See General Statutes § 52–420.

There is no error.

In this opinion KING, MURPHY and ALCORN, JJ., concurred.

BALDWIN, C. J. (concurring). I do not understand the opinion of the majority to mean that every award of an arbitrator which looks to the future relationship of the parties to a collective bargaining agreement is necessarily invalid for that reason. We have long endorsed a policy favoring arbitration as a means of resolving labor-management disputes. Arbitration of such disputes involves the resolution of many detailed problems of the labor-management relationship. These problems are often not specifically foreseen, or at least they are often not expressly provided for by the contract negotiators. The negotiators, however, are presumed to have left these problems to be resolved by reference to the long-standing practices of the industry and the shops covered by the contract. So far as these practices, the "common law of the shop," are not inconsistent with the express provisions of the contract, they are an equally valid source of law for the arbitrator. United Steelworkers v. Warrior & Gulf Navigation Co., 363 U.S. 574, 580–82, 80 S. Ct. 1347, 1363, 4 L. Ed. 2d 1409, 1432 ; Posner v. Grunwald-Marx, Inc., 56 Cal. 2d 169, 177, 363 P. 2d 313. Logically, then, an award, to render explicit what the contract negotiators have left implicit, should not only settle present disputes but serve, if possible, as a guide to avoiding future ones.

The difficulty in the present case is that the submission by its terms prevented the arbitrator from looking to the future. As the majority point out, the submission called for an answer to the question whether "the Company's present operating practice" violated the terms of the agreement. It required a precise answer of "Yes" or "No," not a determination of what might in the future constitute a violation of the agreement.

SYDNOR CO. v. COUNTY SCHOOL BOARD
182 Va. 156 28 S.E. 2d 33 (1943)

GREGORY, J., delivered the opinion of the court.

The appellant, Sydnor Pump and Well Company, Inc., was the complainant below, and filed its suit in equity against the County School Board of Henrico County, J. W. Atkinson and W. F. Gerhardt as defendants. The purpose of the suit was to have declared void an alleged arbitration award which grew out of a certain school building contract between the County

School Board, on the one hand, and J. W. Atkinson, general contractor, on the other. If the award is held valid, then the prayer is that it be held not binding on the complainant, and, further, the complainant asks for a judgment against W. F. Gerhardt for $1,212.20 with interest and costs.

The court below denied every ground of relief. It held the award of the arbitrators valid and binding upon all the parties including the complainant and that the complainant was not entitled to a judgment against Gerhardt. Costs were awarded against the complainant.

There is no dispute about the material facts. The contract was made between the County School Board and J. W. Atkinson, general contractor. It comprehended that portions of the work would be let to subcontractors. W. F. Gerhardt was a subcontractor, agreeing to perform all of the plumbing including the drilling of a well. The appellant for many years had operated a business which was that of drilling wells and it became a sub-subcontractor under Gerhardt for the drilling of the well required under the original contract. Its contract consisted of certain proposals embraced in the specifications for the construction of the school building. These proposals were the basis upon which the appellant made its bid and read thus:

WELL:
GENERAL: It is the intent to drill a well at Virginia Randolph School to furnish ten [sic] (15) gallons of water per minute. It is estimated that to secure this amount of pure water the well is to be 200 ft. deep and a minimum diameter of 6".

If the well is drilled deeper than 200 ft. the extra depth shall be determined and fixed by the Architect with the approval of the School superintendent.

LOCATION: Well shall be located at a point designated in the plans and specifications of the Virginia Randolph School.

SIZE OF WELL: The casing of the well shall be 6 inches.

It is not anticipated that any rock will be encountered when driving the well, but if rock is encountered the well shall be cased to rock, and the contractor will be paid for drilling through the rock at price bid in his proposal. Payment will be made at price bid in proposal—requirements to be made from existing surface of ground at well sites to the greatest depth drilled.

DEPTH: It is intended to drive the casing approximately 200 ft. in depth and secure if possible a supply of 15 gallons per minute from the well. If, however, a suitable supply of water can be obtained at a less depth and below 100 ft. from the surface, the well will not be driven deeper. Should the contractor fail to secure a satisfactory supply of water at a depth of 200 ft. he shall drill deeper, if required to do so by the County School Board.

The general contractor will be required to set up in his proposal the following segregated items:

Additional cost per lineal foot for a depth beyond 200 ft. from surface of ground.

Additional cost per lineal foot for drilling 6" inside diameter hole through rock if encountered.

These proposals were considered by the appellant and through its proper agents a bid was made for the job of drilling the well. It was in writing addressed to Gerhardt and in this language:

Gentlemen:
We have examined the specifications covering the well with its extras and pumping unit and the proposal form, and we desire to submit the following figures which it will be necessary for you to have for the preparation of your bid:

6" x 200 ft. specification well $200.00
Extra drilling well in rock, per foot . .   6.00
Extra drilling well beyond 200 ft.
    well depth specified, per foot 6.00

The bid of the appellant was duly accepted and the contract closed. Special attention is directed to the proposals which required the appellant to segregate (a) the cost per lineal foot for a depth beyond 200 feet from the surface and (b) the additional cost per lineal foot "for drilling 6" inside diameter hole through rock if encountered" because the appellant's claim, as we will see later, has its background in those extra items. In response to those directions the appellant did segregate those items in its bid as will be observed by a reference to it.

The two events which the parties hoped would not happen actually did happen. First, the well had to be drilled more than 200 feet. Actually it was drilled to a depth of 393 feet and 9 inches, in order to obtain the required flow. Secondly, rock was encountered at a depth of 23 feet and 6 inches, and from that point to completion it was drilled through rock for 370 feet and 3 inches. Accordingly, the appellant billed Gerhardt as follows:

SOLD TO
W. F. Gerhardt,
2007 West Broad Street,
Richmond, Virginia.

To drilling, casing and testing
    well as per specifications at
    Virginia Randolph School. .$ 200.00
Extra for drilling in rock from
    23'6" to 393'9" 370'3" @
    $6.00 per foot. 2,221.50
Extra for drilling beyond
    200 ft. well depth specified
    from 200' to 393'9" 193'9"
    @ $6.00 per foot 1,162.50
                                              ————————
                                              $3,584.00
Credit by check April 25 . . . .   498.93
                                              ————————
                                              $3,085.07

Bills in like amount were sent by Gerhardt to the general contractor, Atkinson, and by him sent to the School Board. All but $1,212.20 has been paid on the account. Payment of that balance was refused by the School Board, Atkinson and Gerhardt, though Gerhardt in his letter transmitting the account to Atkinson expressed satisfaction with the account. He wrote that the well complied with the plans and specifications and with his contract. He also wrote that the extras shown on the account for drilling through rock and for drilling below 200 feet were correct. He requested that the account be paid.

The reason assigned by the School Board for its refusal to pay the account is contained in a letter from the Director of School Buildings to J. W. Atkinson. The Director construed the appellant's contract with Gerhardt to mean that appellant was to receive only $6.00 per foot below the 200 feet regardless of whether the drilling was through solid rock or through earth without any rock.

The appellant looked to Gerhardt for payment of the account. It was made to him because the contract was with him. The appellant, failing in his efforts to collect the account, elected to arbitrate the matter in accord with the terms of the dominant contract between the School Board and Atkinson, general contractor. Atkinson agreed to represent the appellant in the arbitration and to present his account. The arbitration, in form was to be between Atkinson and the School Board, but in substance it was to be between the appellant and Gerhardt. However, if an award had been made against Gerhardt, he, in turn, would have looked to Atkinson, and the latter to the School Board. Atkinson, therefore, to some extent at least, had an adverse interest to that of appellant.

The arbitrators were selected and the appellant delivered all of his papers to the one selected by him prior to the time of the meeting. Later, the meeting was held and the attorney for the School Board was allowed to state the case for the School Board first, because he had another important engagement and desired to be excused as soon as convenient. Mr. Atkinson, the formal party to the arbitration and the representative and spokesman for the appellant, did not arrive until after the counsel for the School Board had stated its side of the case. No evidence was offered by the School Board and none was heard by the arbitrators.

During the presentation of counsel for the School Board, Garland Sydnor, an officer of the appellant, present at the meeting, interrupted several times. He was told by the arbitrators that "he wasn't supposed to talk" and that his turn would come later. After the attorney for the School Board left, Mr. Atkinson arrived and he was called upon to state his claim against the School Board. He stated that he had no disagreement with the School Board. Thereupon, Mr. Sydnor reminded him of the understanding whereby he, Atkinson, had agreed to represent the appellant in the arbitration and that appellant did have a controversy to be settled by the arbitration. Mr. Atkinson persisted in stating that he had no disagreement with the School Board. The arbitrators then requested all the witnesses to leave. Immediately afterwards Sydnor and Atkinson discussed the matter and returned to the arbitrators and Atkinson asked to be heard. This was denied though the arbitrators were still present and, so far as the record discloses, had not made their award. Mr. Sydnor was never allowed to testify, though the arbitrators, from the papers and from the statement of counsel for the School Board, should have known that the sole purpose of the arbitration was to settle a controversy between his company, the appellant, and Gerhardt, who had refused to pay his account.

Later the arbitrators made an award drawn in legal form as follows:

> The undersigned Arbitrators duly appointed to arbitrate a certain controversy between J. W. Atkinson & Company and Henrico County School Board, arising out of claim for extras for digging a well on the above project, met in the offices of R. Stuart Royer on Wednesday, November 15, 1939, at 2 o'clock P.M., and after hearing evidence reached a unanimous decision that the amount owed J. W. Atkinson & Co. by the Henrico County School Board for extras on the above project is as follows:
>
> For drilling well through rock
> for a distance of 176.4′ @
> $6.00 per foot (above 200′)..$1,058.40
> For drilling well (below 200′)
> a distance of 193.9′ @ $6.00
> per foot 1,163.40
> _____
> Total...........$2,221.80
>
> The Arbitrators, in view of the work and time involved in this case, have set their fee at $50.00 each or a total of $150.00, and herewith submit to the County of Henrico and to J. W. Atkinson & Co. their joint bill for $75.00 each.
>
> Respectfully submitted,
> JN. J. WILLIAMS, JR.
> C. W. ROPER
> R. STUART ROYER

After the purported award no other meeting of the arbitrators was held. As already indicated, the court below held that the award was valid and bound the appellant. The amount found due under the award has been paid the appellant and accepted by it without prejudice to its right to sue for the $1,212.20 claimed.

The appellant insists with great earnestness that there was no arbitration and no valid award; that even if the award is valid, it does not bind because the arbitrators were guilty of misconduct in not allowing Mr. Sydnor to testify; and that, in any event, the appellant was not a party to the arbitration which was between the School Board and Mr. Atkinson.

The procedure before the arbitrators was very informal and irregular. The very matter which was the subject of the arbitration, to-wit: Whether the appellant was entitled to the $1,212.20 was never inquired into, nor was there introduced any evidence, documentary or otherwise, touching that claim. This fact is not only established by Mr. Sydnor but it is expressly testified to by two of the arbitrators. One arbitrator did not take the stand. The two arbitrators unhesitatingly state that they heard no evidence on the appellant's claim. They heard only the statement of counsel for the School Board and the statement of Atkinson (who had an adverse interest to appellant), that he had no disagreement with the School Board. The arbitrators stated freely that there was no disagreement and nothing to arbitrate.

The arbitrators evidently misconceived their duties and departed from the submission. A mistake as to the purpose of the arbitration is perfectly obvious. They were called upon to arbitrate the appellant's claim but through mistake or misconception they failed to arbitrate it. They acted just as though they were hearing only a contest between the School Board and Atkinson when, as a matter of fact, there was no issue between them. When Atkinson stated that he had no disagreement with the School Board, this alone was conclusive that there was nothing to arbitrate between them. So there being no disagreement between them, and the arbitrators failing to consider the appellant's claim, no valid award could have been made that would bind any of the parties.

An award must decide what is submitted. It must be construed liberally so as to uphold it, if possible, and all fair presumptions are in its favor, but if the award is outside of the submission, it is invalid. BURKS, PLEADING AND PRACTICE (3rd ed.) p. 16.

The general rule is that an award will not be set aside for a mistake of law or fact where the arbitrators are made the judges of the law and fact by the submission. 3 AM. JUR., Arbitration and Award, section 147. However, there are exceptions to the general rule. A notable one is where the mistake has thwarted the intention of the arbitrators. If the award is to operate in a way not intended by them or if the mistake is a palpable one, admitted by them, and occurring through misapprehension or inadvertence, it will be set aside. 3 AM. JUR., Arbitration and Award, section 149. Again the same author, at section 150, states the rule, that an award will be set aside when the arbitrators have mistaken their powers and duties so as to do a real injustice to one of the parties even though no mistake appears on the face of the award.

It certainly cannot be said that the arbitrators intended to arbitrate controverted claims when two of them now testify that there was nothing to arbitrate. The award, under the circumstances, was bound to have been made under a mistaken conception of their duties and against their intent. If it was, it is invalid.

The general rule on this subject is found in 6 C. J. S., Arbitration and Award, sec. 105, at page 253, where this is said:

> According to many decisions, whenever, in a proper proceeding, it is made plainly to appear, either by the face of the award or properly by matter extrinsic thereto, that the arbitrators have fallen into such an error, either of fact or of law, as will make the award operate prejudicially against the complaining party, as to a material matter, in a manner in which they manifestly did not intend it to operate, the award will not conclude the parties as to such matter, and if the entire award is so infected by such a mistake or if the inoperative portion is not clearly severable from the remainder the award is thereby vitiated and may be set aside. Other decisions recognize the general principle stated, but require that the mistake or error appear on the face of the award or by documents properly a part thereof so that it can be ascertained therefrom that the intention of the arbitrators has miscarried, unless the mistake is admitted by the arbitrators; and this principle has been held to apply both at law and in equity.

If it plainly appears by "matter extrinsic thereto" or upon the face of the award that the arbitrators have made an award through palpable error or mistake and one they did not intend to make, it will be declared invalid in a court of equity.

Awards that do not conform to the submission are void. The agreement of submission is the arbitrator's charter of authority. An award made under a total misapprehension of the function assigned them by the agreement of submission is a departure from the submission justifying annulment of the award by a court of equity. See DIGEST OF VIRGINIA AND WEST VIRGINIA REPORTS (MICHIE) Vol. 1, Arbitration and Award, pp. 600 and 601.

In Shipman v. Fletcher, 82 Va. 601, the principle is stated thus:

> This court, chosen by the parties, can exercise all the

powers granted to them by the submission. This is the charter of their existence; they must proceed upon the fullest notice to all, and act only after hearing the evidence adduced before them in due course. Each party is not only entitled to present his own case, both by evidence and argument before the arbitrators but he is also entitled to be present whenever witnesses or argument are heard on behalf of his opponent.

As was said by a learned judge in an early case in this country, "both parties should have an opportunity of being heard, and that in the presence of each other, that they may be enabled to apply their testimony to the allegations. The witnesses on both sides are likewise to give their testimony in the presence of the parties, that they may have an opportunity of cross-examining them."

These rules or similar ones are founded in natural justice, and are absolutely necessary for the due administration of justice in every form whatever." Hollingsworth v. Liper, 1 Dallas, 161.

In the case at bar, as already indicated, no evidence of any kind was heard by the arbitrators. The statement of counsel for the School Board was not evidence, and the admission of Atkinson that there was no disagreement between him and the School Board did not throw any light upon the correct decision of the sole issue that was before arbitrators, namely whether the appellant was entitled to $1,212.20. His statement was not evidence.

In Shipman v. Fletcher, *supra*, the court said:

> Numerous cases upon this point are cited by the counsel, and citations might be multiplied, but it is unnecessary. It obviously lies at the foundation of justice that, in any forum where the rights of any person are to be judicially determined, he has a right to be present, and to be heard through his own witnesses and by counsel, and to hear the testimony of his adversary's witnesses, to cross-examine them, and rebut their testimony. Any trial which excludes him, and tries his case in his absence, is but a mock trial, and should be set aside.

As a general rule the arbitrators are not allowed to impeach their award when called as witnesses. In this case two of them were examined as witnesses. Their testimony was corroborative of that of Mr. Sydnor. The latter testified, without contradiction, that no evidence was heard by the arbitrators, either oral or documentary, and that he was not permitted to testify in behalf of the appellant.

Generally, extrinsic evidence cannot be admitted to alter an award and their award itself is the best evidence of the matters determined by the arbitrators. It is said to be conclusive of all matters contained in it, provided the arbitrators have not exceeded the powers delegated to them by the submission.

However, the arbitrators may testify and extrinsic evidence may be admitted to show that the award was a nullity. Here such testimony was proper to show that the arbitrators were mistaken in their view of the extent of their powers; that they received no evidence whatever; that they mistakenly relied solely, as a basis for the award, upon the statement of counsel for the School Board and Mr. Atkinson, neither of whom were witnesses, that inasmuch as there was no disagreement there was nothing to arbitrate. This testimony conclusively shows that no valid award could have been made.

In 6 C. J. S., Arbitration and Award, sec. 131, the rule is stated thus:

> Although the submission and award may be in writing and available, it often becomes necessary in determining what questions are concluded by the award, or whether the award is in itself binding on the parties, to show, by parol evidence, what took place before the arbitrators, what was in controversy, and what matters entered into the decision. Accordingly, extrinsic evidence is admissible to show the existence of a real controversy between the parties, and where it does not certainly appear from the submission or award what matters were submitted to, and decided by, the arbitrators, parol evidence is admissible to show that fact, even though the submission and the award were in writing or under seal, or though a judgment has been rendered on the award. Where an award, under a general submission of all matters in difference, is regarded as merging such matters only as were actually presented to the arbitration, parol evidence is admissible to show what matters were in fact presented, provided the terms of the award are not varied thereby; but where all matters in difference are regarded as merged, whether brought forward or not, parol evidence is, of course, inadmissible....
>
> In other words, parol evidence is always admissible to show that an award is a mere nullity, as, for instance, that the arbitrators failed to pursue their authority by considering matters that were not submitted....
>
> So long as no attempt is made to impeach an award by showing his own fraud or misconduct, an arbitrator's testimony is generally admissible to prove matters of fact in connection with the arbitration, in any case where other parol evidence can be received; and this is true, whether the purpose of the testimony is to sustain the award, or to show that it is a mere nullity....
>
> Notwithstanding the rule against impeachment, it is usually held that testimony of arbitrators is admissible to show a mistake on their part.

A great deal is said about the appellant, through its agent, placing a "trick bid" for drilling the well, and that therefore it is in a court of equity without clean hands.

The bid is in direct response to the proposal. Both are in writing and complete. The bid is clear, unambiguous, and in terms that are not difficult to understand. For instance, the proposal required the specific cost of drilling the well to a depth beyond 200 feet. On this item, the bid of the appellant was $6.00 per foot for drilling beyond the 200 feet. There is nothing indefinite or ambiguous about that item. It means precisely what is stated: that is, for every foot drilled beyond 200 feet the appellant was to be paid $6.00.

The proposal also required the bid to specifically state the cost if the drilling were through rock. The bid did state this cost to be $6.00 per foot. Therefore, the appellant was to receive $6.00 per foot for drilling beyond the 200 feet. It was also to receive, in the event the drilling was through rock either above or below the 200 feet, an additional $6.00 per foot. The proposal and bid so state in clear language. From the account rendered, as shown above, the appellant drilled beyond the 200 feet, to obtain the required flow of water, 193 feet and 9 inches. This, at $6.00 per foot, is $1,162.50. The appellant drilled through rock for a distance of 370 feet and 3 inches, and for this at $6.00 per foot he was entitled to $2,221.50, and for drilling the first 200 feet the appellant was entitled to $200.00. The total due the appellant was $3,584.00. All but $1,212.20 has been paid. That the appellant is now due that amount is entirely free from doubt. If the bid was a "trick" one then the proposal was of like character.

We are not impressed with the argument that the appellant is in a court of equity without clean hands.

We attribute no bad faith to the arbitrators. They innocently misconceived their powers and duties. They failed to follow the terms of the submission and found an award which we must conclude was actully founded upon a misconception of their duties. For these reasons the award is invalid and does not bind any of the parties.

The award being invalid, the court must decide what disposition should be made of the case, and whether a final disposition of it should be made here or the case should go back to the trial court with directions.

This court, upon excellent authority, has not the power to recommit a case to arbitrators, in the absence of an authorizing statute or an agreement between the parties for that purpose. WILLISTON ON CONTRACTS (Revised ed.) Vol. 6, sec. 1927A and note. After a purported award has been made the arbitrators become *functi officio*. They cannot remedy a defective award, or conduct further proceedings, in the absence of agreement or statute. (See also 6 C. J. S., Arbitration and Award, sections 51 and 113). In Virginia,

there is no such statute and the parties have not indicated any agreement to recommit in the event the award in this case be set aside.

Gerhardt has admitted in his letter to Atkinson that the appellant's account rendered was in accord with the plans and specifications and correct. Gerhardt recommended that it be paid. He is obligated to pay it, and a judgment is now entered against him in favor of the appellant for $1,212.20, with interest from May 15, 1939.

Ultimate liability for the amount of the judgment rendered against Gerhardt should properly rest upon the School Board, but the pleadings are not broad enough to permit this court to fix the liability upon the School Board. For that purpose the cause is remanded to the lower court with directions that Gerhardt, if he be so advised, may amend his pleadings and seek to recover of the School Board the amount he is required to pay upon the judgment here rendered.

So it now appears that the purpose of the arbitration, which was to eliminate litigation and its attendant costs and delay, has been defeated. The parties are now, and already have been for three years, in litigation. What they thought would be a quick and inexpensive way of settling the issues of law and fact between them perhaps has resulted in more delay and costs than would have been incurred if they had sought to settle their differences in a court in the first instance. The Supreme Court of Pennsylvania in Pierce Steel Pile Corp. v. Flannery, 319 Pa. 332, 179 A. 558, 104 A. L. R. 706, using language which is fitting here, aptly concluded:

> The parties elected to submit their disputes to arbitration. This method of trying issues of fact and law is now somewhat in fashion. It may well be that after other experiences such as the present litigants have had, it will be determined that the ancient method of trial in duly constituted courts of law is a more satisfactory way to settle controversies. This is for further experience to demonstrate.

The decree of the lower court is reversed, a decree in favor of the appellant against Gerhardt for $1,212.20 with interest from May 5, 1939 is here rendered, and the cause is remanded for Gerhardt to take such further proceedings as he may deem advisable.

Reversed and remanded.

JUDICIAL REVIEW OF ARBITRATION AWARDS ON THE MERITS*

In general, the courts are reluctant to reconsider the merits of arbitrators' awards whether

---

*Excerpted from 63 HARV. L. REV. 681 (1950). Reprinted with permission.

governed by common law procedure or by the statutory system of arbitration which in many jurisdictions exists parallel to the common law. It is sometimes stated that the parties, in submitting to arbitration, took the risk that the arbitrators might depart from some legal rules or make some errors.[1] Where the arbitration agreement contains a stipulation restricting the arbitrator's discretion, the intention-of-the-parties argument fails, and the courts review freely despite the arguments based on judicial convenience. In addition, regardless of these arguments against review, the courts ought to interfere when an award directs or allows the parties to depart from a law which operates notwithstanding a contrary consensual arrangement.[2] Finally, if a particular jurisdiction has an exclusively statutory procedure as distinguished from those states which have parallel common law and statutory arbitration, a so-called arbitration which takes place outside that procedure is ineffective to limit judicial review.[3]

Under the statutory systems in a few jurisdictions, arbitration does not have the status of a bargain to avoid litigation, for the court is granted, or has taken on itself, power to set aside any arbitration award when it would have reversed a judgment at law reaching the same result. This, in effect, is the interpretation put by the Georgia court on a statute authorizing it to set aside an "illegal" award. And under the statute in Alabama, while the lower courts appear to be limited in their power to disturb an arbitrator's decision,[4] the appellate court has construed the statutory language "an appeal shall

lie as in other cases" as empowering it to review the merits as though the award "were originally the judgment of the trial court itself." By the [pre-1955] Uniform Arbitration Act[5] and statutes in England and elsewhere,[6] the arbitrator is permitted, and can be forced by a party, to obtain a judicial decision on a question of law arising before he makes an award, or to state an award which sets out the facts so that the court of first instance can give judgment as it would on special findings of a jury. In addition, both statutory and common law arbitration awards are reviewable in particular situations discussed below.

Award against the Evidence.—Since the courts often refuse to review the evidence presented in an arbitration proceeding, they may not reach the question of whether there was enough, or any, evidence to support the arbitrator's findings. In some states, however, the court reviews the evidence as a matter of course, inspecting the record if one is available or receiving other proof of what took place at the arbitration proceeding, and vacates the award if it decides that there was no evidence to support the arbitrator's findings.[7] Under a few state statutes, the court appears to be authorized to disturb an award even though there was some slight evidence in its favor, so that an award occupies roughly the same position as a jury verdict.[8]

---

1. See Pine Street Realty Co. v. Coutroulos, 233 App. Div. 404, 407, 253 N.Y. Supp. 174, 177 (1st Dep't 1931), leave to appeal denied, 258 N.Y. 609, 180 N.E. 354 (1932). In compulsory arbitration nonreview cannot be justified on this ground. *Cf.* Texoma Natural Gas Co. v. Oil Workers Int'l Union, 58 F. Supp. 132 (N.D. Tex. 1943), aff'd, 146 F.2d 62 (5th Cir. 1944), cert. denied, 324 U.S. 72 (1945) (arbitration ordered by WLB). Several statutes compel arbitration in public service labor disputes. See collection in 22 LAB. REL. REP. (Ref. Man.) 3088 (1948).

2. *Cf.* Western Union Tel. Co. v. American Communications Ass'n, 299 N.Y. 177, 86 N.E.2d 162 (1949), 63 HARV. L. REV. 347 (award construed basic contract so as to allow party to violate penal law). [More material on this issue appears below. Ed.]

3. Glens Falls Ins. Co. v. Gulf Breeze Cottages, Inc., 38 So.2d 828 (Fla. 1949); Jung v. Gwin, 174 La. 111, 139 So. 774, cert. denied, 286 U.S. 561 (1932). Washington's statute, which was exclusive, Dickie Mfg. Co. v. Sound Construction & Engineering Co., 92 Wash. 316, 159 Pac. 129 (1916), has been superseded, WASH. REV. STAT. ANN. §§ 430–1 to 430–23 (Supp. 1943), but the new act does not expressly sanction common law arbitration.

4. ALA. CODE ANN. tit. 7, § 842 (1940) (award cannot be impeached if it determines controversy and is final except in case of arbitrator's fraud, partiality, or corruption).

5. Section 13. The only cases in which the Act permits review, as such, on the merits are mathematical error and misdescription. Section 17(a). The Act was placed on the inactive list in 1943. HANDBOOK OF NAT. CONFERENCE OF COMM'RS 73 (1943).

6. ILL. REV. STAT. c. 10, § 6 (1949) (review as such authorized for "legal defects," § 11); MASS. GEN. LAWS c. 251, § 20 (1932) (without judicial action, award is equivalent to award by referees appointed by rule of court, § 10). Under one statute the arbitrator has sole discretion to obtain a judicial decision, PA. STAT. tit. 5, § 177 (1936) (declaratory judgment) (otherwise, award equivalent to verdict, § 171(d)). Under another statute both parties must agree. CONN. REV. STAT. § 8158 (1949) (review as such authorized only for mathematical error or misdescription, § 8162).

7. Barnes v. Avery, 192 Ga. 874, 16 S.E.2d 861 (1941) (alternative holding) ("evident miscalculation of figures"). In England, when the award states all the evidence offered, the court can upset an award which is wrong as a matter of "law." Meiklejohn v. Campbell, 162 L.T. 357 (K.B.), appeal dismissed, *ibid.* (C.A. 1940). See United Farmers Ass'n v. Klein, 41 Cal. App.2d 766, 769, 107 P.2d 631, 633 (1940). As to review for errors of law on the face of the award, see *infra.*

8. In Pennsylvania the court can modify the award whenever it would have entered judgment notwithstanding a verdict to the same effect as the award. PA. STAT. tit. 5, § 271(d) (1936). See also IOWA CODE §§ 679.12–13 (1946) and NEB. REV. STAT. §§ 25–2115 to 25–2116 (1943) (award can be rejected for "any legal and sufficient" reason and has "same force and effect as the verdict of a jury"); MINN. STAT. § 572.05(5) (Henderson 1945) (award can be vacated if con-

There is a disposition in several cases to vacate an award if the arbitrator has acted on an unconscious and erroneous assumption as to a relevant fact, as when he has unwittingly used false weights or measures[9] or when he has ignored the possibility that some property insured against fire might have been stolen rather than burned.[10] Such a failure to exercise judgment has been stigmatized as fatal "mistake," rather than nonfatal "error of judgment."[11] But the mere fact that no evidence was introduced on a submitted issue does not mean that the arbitrator failed to exercise his judgment on the point, for he may have made a conscious decision as to the burden of coming forward with the evidence; and, even where it can be shown that the arbitrator did not consider that burden, the dissatisfied party does not deserve a second opportunity to put in evidence merely because he neglected his first. Where evidence was submitted, it can seldom be proved that the arbitrator failed to exercise any judgment on the issue, unless the arbitrator himself testifies to that effect.[12] Finally, even when there is direct proof that the arbitrator failed to exercise judgment on a disputed issue and that the issue, had been presented to him by means of evidence, an argument against disturbing the award can be made that the parties took the risk of their arbitrator's inadvertence.

Another criterion for judicial interference cuts across the distinctions based on the existence of supporting evidence or on the exercise of judgment by the arbitrator: a few courts reverse the award when the court's and the arbitrator's views of the amount of damage differ widely.[13] This standard can be justified on the ground that, as part of the price for avoiding litigation, the parties contemplated that the arbitrator might deviate somewhat from the result that would be reached by a court but did not assume the risk of very large deviation; but this is at best an uncertain rule, for the court must determine in each case whether the error is of a magnitude sufficient to pass a threshold newly constructed for each occasion. If the courts were to apply the notion of sizable deviation where the arbitrator's finding is not susceptible of variation by degrees but must be correct or incorrect, their emphasis on the size of the discrepancy would then seem to be only an insistence that, for reversal, the arbitrator's error must make a material difference in the amount of the ultimate liability, and a smaller difference would probably suffice for interference.

Normally, the size of the error is used, if at all, as a basis for a finding that the arbitrator is biased or has acted in bad faith.[14] When the court is really concerned with the arbitrator's state of mind, the size of the error is a relevant but not necessarily determinative consideration. But some of the courts, unwilling to acknowledge gross error explicitly as an independent ground for reversal, have created categories of "legal" or "constructive" fraud.[15]

Award Based on Erroneous Rule.—In those jurisdictions where the courts have blanket authority to set aside arbitration awards when they would have reversed an inferior judgment at law,[16] any rule used by the arbitrator that varies from the one a trial judge ought to use will not survive review where it leads to a different result from that which would have been reached at law—whether or not the court specifically criticizes the arbitrator's rule. Moreover, at least one court has relied on the broad language, found in several statutes, which permits the court to modify an award to "effect

---

trary to "law and evidence"). *Cf.* Industrial Elec. Co. v. Meyers, 85 N.E.2d 415 (Ohio App. 1949) (award vacated; alternative ground, mentioned in passing, that it was manifestly against the weight of evidence).

9. *See* Boston Water Power Co. v. Gray, 47 Mass. (6 Metc.) 131, 169 (1843).

10. Kaufman Jewelry Co. v. Insurance Co. of Pa., 172 Minn. 314, 215 N.W. 65 (1927). See also Barrows v. Sweet, 143 Mass. 316, 9 N.E. 665 (1887). The arbitrator may be aware of the issue of fact but may lack enough evidence to exercise informed judgment. Aetna Ins. Co. v. Hefferlin, 260 Fed. 695 (9th Cir. 1919).

11. The authority for this distinction is reviewed in Sturges 787–93. "Mistake" is a category of old origin, see Knox v. Symmonds, 1 Ves. 369, 370, 30 Eng. Rep. 390, 391 (Ch. 1791), which appears in many current cases, see, *e.g.*, Standard Construction Co. v. Hoeschler, 245 Wis. 316, 321, 14 N.W.2d 12, 14 (1944). A few statutes also contain the category. Fla. Stat. Ann. § 57.07 (1943); Ga. Code Ann. § 7–219 (1936); Iowa Code § 679.18 (1946); W. Va. Code Ann. § 5502 (1949).

12. The tendency is to prohibit arbitrators from so testifying as to impeach the award.

13. Baldinger v. Camden Fire Ins. Ass'n, 121 Minn. 160, 141 N.W. 104 (1913); Perry v. Insurance Co., 137 N.C. 402, 49 S.E. 889 (1905). [Note that these cases pre-date a modern statute. Ed.]

14. See Hyman v. Pottberg's Ex'rs, 101 F.2d 262, 265 (2d Cir. 1939); Boomer Coal & Coke Co. v. Ostenton, 101 W. Va. 683, 694, 133 S.E. 381, 385 (1926).

15. See Putterman v. Schmidt, 209 Wisc. 442, 451, 245 N.W. 78, 81 (1932). A similar practice is criticized in Kaufman Jewelry Co. v. Insurance Co. of Pa., 172 Minn. 314, 317–18, 215 N.W. 65, 67 (1927). See Sturges 802 (doubts if fraud necessary part of sizable-error doctrine).

16. For statutory sources of this power, see Ga. Code Ann. §§ 7–111, 7–219 (1936) (two arbitration systems—award can be set aside for "palpable mistake of law" or if award is "illegal") and the statutes cited *supra*.

the intent thereof and promote justice between the parties,"[17] and has altered the award on the express ground that the relief granted by the arbitrator, a mild compromise solution, was not the "legal conclusion."[18] Finally, in a few insurance cases—apparently not governed by an arbitration statute—involving only the determination of the amount of loss, the court has upset an award because it disapproved of the rule which the arbitrator used to estimate the amount of damage, such as whether or how depreciation should be taken into account.[19] Aside from these few cases, the general view, both at common law and by statute, is that the courts will not review for its wisdom or soundness the principle selected by the arbitrator, unless his discretion in making that selection is limited by the terms of the submission agreement. Where the arbitrator's rule is adjudged to be not merely erroneous but totally unreasonable, the award should be set aside if the error is prejudicial[20] unless it can be shown that the parties intended to take even this risk. As in all such tests, it is difficult to describe the blurred border between nonreversible error and reversible unreason ; but unless the arbitrator has made his decision capriciously, as by the toss of a coin—which would be in itself a failure to exercise judgment as to the rule he should apply[21]—a court should hesitate to place his action on the wrong side of that border.

The few courts that do review for errors of law apply the doctrine frequently to cases involving the construction of contracts,[22] which is traditionally a "matter of law" only because the judge is thought to be better able than a jury to decide the meaning of terms in a written instrument.[23] In arbitration, where the reviewing judge is usually less familiar than the arbitrator with trade usage that bears on interpretation, the analogy which is in effect drawn by a few courts between an arbitrator and a jury is particularly inept.[24]

In England, errors of law are not reviewed except when they appear on the face of the award. A few American cases have similar expressions, now chiefly in dicta. As applied in England to the construction of contracts, this limitation confines review to cases where sufficient data appeared from the award itself, and from documents on which the arbitrator has relied expressly in the award, to enable the court to say with certainty that it would have interpreted the contract differently than the arbitrator. Even as thus limited, the practice of reviewing an award for errors of law has long been criticized in dicta ; and one court has narrowed the effect of the rule still further by indicating that it would be slow to find that the contract underlying an arbitration dispute had been incorporated by reference into the face of the award. Even when the contract is found to be incorporated and thus accessible to the reviewing court, the English cases give the arbitrator the benefit of the doubt if the court is not certain of the proper construction, as where the language is ambiguous, or if the award does not set out enough of the facts to enable the court to infer what construction the arbitrator adopted. If a court is to review an arbitration award for any errors "of law," it is preferable to confine its scrutiny to the face of the award and related documents, as is done in England, so as at least to limit the time consumed in each case of review ; but even the English practice, like all interference with arbitration awards, contributes to undermining the effectiveness of arbitration as a bargain to avoid litigation.[25]

---

17. N.Y. CIV. PRAC. ACT § 1462-a. In section 11 of the Draft State Arbitration Act (sponsored by the American Arbitration Ass'n, see YEARBOOK ON COMMERCIAL ARBITRATION 23–27 (1927)), three specific causes for which the court must modify the award are listed, and it is next stated that the court "must" modify and correct the award to effect its intent and do justice. However, New York's statute reads "may," indicating, perhaps, that this power is not limited to the preceding three specific categories. [I doubt that such a reading is correct. The corresponding provision of the CPLR, § 7511 (c), omits the language quoted in the text.—Ed.]

18. Modernage Furniture Corp. v. Weitz, 64 N.Y.S.2d 467 (Sup. Ct. 1946). In two other cases the matter has been remitted to the arbitrator without modification by the court. Simon v. Stag Laundry, Inc., 259 App. Div. 106, 18 N.Y.S.2d 197 (1st Dep't 1940); Campe Corp. v. Pacific Mills, 87 N.Y.S.2d 16 (Sup. Ct. 1949).

19. McIntosh v. Hartford Fire Ins. Co., 106 Mont. 434 78 P.2d 82 (1938); Providence Wash. Ins. Co. v. Board of Educ., 49 W. Va. 360, 38 S.E. 679 (1901).

20. See Stowe v. Mutual Home Builders Corp., 252 Mich. 492, 233 N.W. 391 (1930); Raleigh Coal & Coke Co. v. Mankin, 83 W. Va. 54, 97 S.E. 299 (1918). [These cases did not arise under statutes and involved a departure from the agreed standards of valuation and the agreed method of procedure, respectively—Ed.].

21. See GA. CODE ANN. § 7–111 (1936). See also p. 684 *supra*. Conceivably, an arbitrator who decides an issue by chance may have exercised his judgment in coming to a decision not to weigh the merits.

22. *E.g.*, Navarro Corp. v. School Dist., 344 Pa. 429, 25 A.2d 808 (1942); Philadelphia Housing Authority v. Turner Construction Co., 343 Pa. 512, 23 A.2d 426 (1942).

23. See 3 WILLISTON, CONTRACTS § 616 (rev. ed. 1936).

24. The general view, of course, is that the arbitrator's construction is not subject to review. See, *e.g.*, Mutual Benefit Health & Acc. Ass'n v. United States Cas. Co., 142 F.2d 390 (1st Cir.), cert. denied, 323, U.S. 729 (1944).

25. Although the English practice permits the arbitrator to prevent review by keeping data out of the award, the practice tends to encourage the parties to choose arbitrators with legal training. *Cf.* Nordon, *British Experience with Arbitration*, 83 U. OF PA. L. REV. 314, 318–19 (1935).

Award Defectively Executing Arbitrator's Intent.—In the jurisdictions denying review for errors of law, one of the distinctions drawn between nonfatal "errors of judgment" and fatal "mistake" is that, although an award cannot be upset merely because the arbitrator's guiding principle is itself unsound, it can be upset if he made a logical error in applying his own principle.[26] This power to interfere is justified in the decisions as a means to prevent an award from achieving an effect which the arbitrator, as can be seen from his own theory, really did not intend.[27] Of course, the courts should correct a scrivener's error in committing the ultimate conclusion to writing. But the only circumstance where the court should interfere because of an arbitrator's logical inconsistency is that of mathematical error, which many statutes allow the court to correct. Otherwise, what appears to be a mistake in logic is just as likely to be an inexpert statement of the basic premise, and this uncertainty should preclude a syllogistic inquiry if the court in general does not reverse for selection of the wrong rule. Of the authority which seems to point toward the logical inconsistency rule, the relatively recent expressions are in the form of dicta, and perhaps review on this head will soon cease to be recognized except with reference to mathematical error.

Under the common law of some states, the courts are said to be able to vacate an arbitrator's decision when the arbitrator intended to apply the law of the jurisdiction but his conclusions are not ones which the court would reach.[28] This basis for judicial review can result in an award's being overturned either because the arbitrator selected the wrong legal rule or because he misapplied some correct legal rule; it also, like some of the statutes providing for judicial decision on a stated case, permits an arbitrator to provoke judicial review on his own motion. Some of the courts have indicated that the intention to follow the law must appear from the face of the award, but at least one court will also allow the arbitrator to testify that he meant

to reach a legal result.[29] Probably, the courts would hesitate to infer the requisite intent from the language of the award; this would go far to prevent judicial interference on such a ground when the arbitrator's reference to legal materials was only by way of makeweight. Moreover, even though the arbitrator attempted and failed to reach the legal result, the award should not be vacated if the point of law is a doubtful one.

Stipulations in the Submission Agreement.—Sometimes the parties either stipulate that the arbitrator should decide the matter according to a specific standard, or provide that the law of the jurisdiction shall govern. The courts generally—even in those jurisdictions which otherwise strictly limit review on the merits—are quick to upset an award which does not conform to the stipulation.[30] Occasionally, the courts have held that a submission agreement contains an implied limitation on the arbitrator's discretion as to the standard by which he may decide an issue expressly submitted; for instance, that a submission agreement in a sales contract dispute implicitly forbade the arbitrator to assess consequential damages.[31] In some of these cases, the reviewing court may be imputing an intent to the parties only for the sake of criticizing the arbitrator's rule.[32] It would seem better to infer that the parties have not agreed on a standard unless they have seen fit to stipulate one in their submission agreement. Even where the agreement does contain a standard which relates to one part of the case, such as whether there was any liability at all, the court should not infer that the arbitrator's discretion is restricted as to a different part of the case, such as the amount of damage.

It is not yet settled what effect will be given to stipulations against judicial review, which, be-

26. See Liggett v. Torrington Building Co., 114 Conn. 425, 431, 158 Atl. 917, 919 (1932). See Sturges 792–93.

27. See Goddard v. King, 40 Minn. 164, 168, 41 N.W. 659, 661 (1889).

28. Reid & Yeomans, Inc. v. Drug Store Employees Union, 29 N.Y.S.2d 835 (Sup. Ct. 1941), aff'd mem., 265 App. Div. 870, 37 N.Y.S.2d 911 (2d Dep't 1942); see Held v. Comfort Bus Line, Inc., 136 N.J.L. 640, 641–42, 57 A.2d 20, 22 (Sup. Ct. 1948). Cf. SEC v. Chenery Corp., 318 U.S. 80 (1943), 62 Harv. L. Rev. 478 (1949) (same doctrine applied to decision of administrative tribunal).

29. See Hoboken Manufacturers' R.R. v. Hoboken R.R. Warehouse and S.S. Connecting Co., 132 N.J. Eq. 111, 119, 27 A.2d 150, 154–55 (Ch. 1942), aff'd, 133 N.J. Eq. 270, 31 A.2d 801 (Ct. Err. & App. 1943).

30. Western Union Tel. Co. v. American Communications Ass'n, 299 N.Y. 177, 86 N.E.2d 162 (1949), 63 Harv. L. Rev. 347 (stipulation that arbitrator had no authority to modify express provisions of contract). The court's insistence on adherence to stipulated standards is akin to their reviewing to see whether the arbitrator decided issues which were not submitted. As to the interpretation of the submission agreement generally, see Sturges § 75.

31. Marchant v. Mead-Morrison Mfg. Co., 252 N.Y. 284, 169 N.E. 386 (1929), appeal dismissed per curiam, 282 U.S. 808 (1930); cf. Bierlein v. Johnson, 73 Cal. App.2d 728, 166 P.2d 644 (1946); McKay v. McKay, 187 Minn. 521, 246 N.W. 12 (1932).

32. See Marchant v. Mead-Morrison Mfg. Co., criticized in Sturges 602–07. See also Goff v. Goff, 78 W. Va. 423, 89 S.E. 9 (1916).

cause they furnish clear proof of the intent of the parties, test the extent of the courts' willingness to free arbitration from litigation. When the submission agreement stipulates against all judicial review,[33] it would seem preferable to give the provision full effect as to review on the merits except when the result of the award contravenes public policy. The courts have seldom declared these stipulations invalid,[34] but they tend to ignore them, even while setting them out in their opinions. Judicial resistance to provisions against review may be compared to the reluctance which was, and even continues to be, manifested when courts refuse to enforce an executory agreement to arbitrate because it constitutes an "ouster of jurisdiction." One statute apparently invalidates stipulations against review.[35] Moreover, even when statutes provide that no appeal to the courts will lie unless expressly provided for,[36] the courts are loath to give up their power entirely and have created exceptions to the statutory rule, such as review for gross error.[87] Somewhat greater deference is paid to the parties' desires under the English practice, whereby the parties can refer a question of law specifically to the arbitrator for decision ; this will normally prevent judicial review even for errors on the face of the award,[38] provided that, before the award, a special case has not been stated for judicial decision.[39]

If the parties do not wish to stipulate against all review, but have some general and perhaps undefined notion that there is some limit to the arbitral errors they will tolerate, they cannot fairly expect to keep out of the courts completely. However, draftsmen of submission agreements can help the parties avoid litigation in part at least by clarifying their ideas of the risks they are willing to assume and by advising them, as the case may be, to provide (1) that the award shall not be reviewed for lack of supporting evidence ; (2) that legal rules are not to be binding on the arbitrator ; (3) that the arbitrator is not empowered to provoke judicial review merely by exhibiting an intention to follow the law of the jurisdiction ; or (4) that in case the award is reviewed a court is not to find any restrictions on the arbitrator's discretion implied in the submission agreement. The respect accorded to stipulations giving the arbitrator authority to interpret the submission agreement[40] gives some indication that specific provisions may be more effective than sweeping stipulations against all review, which may be ignored or even, conceivably, condemned regardless of their particular application.

MATTER OF COLLETTI (MESH)
23 A.D. 2d 245, 260 N.Y.S. 2d 130
(First Dept. 1965)

PER CURIAM. Disputes arose among the five shareholders of a close corporation, Colonial Farms, Inc. (Colonial), which operated a milk processing company in Maspeth, Queens, New York. Of those five shareholders all but Mr. Schwartz were interested in milk distributing companies which were customers of Colonial. Essentially, the main point of controversy among the five stockholders concerned charges that the four stockholders who had interests in milk distributing companies were giving preferential treatment and prices to their respective companies to the detriment of Colonial. At the time arbitration was demanded under the stockholders' agreement Mr. Schwartz and petitioner Colletti were aligned on one side while respondents, Emanuel Mesh, Joseph Mesh and Louis Rosasco,

---

33. See provision against any appeal from award in Ford-UAW collective bargaining agreement, 5 CCH LAB. LAW REP. (4th ed.) 54,073 (1948).

34. *See* McCullough v. Clinch-Mitchell Construction Co., 71 F.2d 17, 21 (8th Cir.), cert. denied, 293 U.S. 582 (1934) (declared invalid). *Contra:* Daniels v. Willis, 7 Minn. 374 (1862) (stipulation against review effective in absence of fraud or misbehavior). In two cases where the court could have reached the same result by invalidating stipulations against review as being contrary to public policy, the court relied on another ground without questioning the general validity of such stipulations. See Edward Thompson & Co. v. Moulton, 20 La. Annual 535 (1868); Seaboard Surety Co. v. Commonwealth, 345 Pa. 147, 27 A.2d 27 (1942).

35. ORE. COMP. LAWS ANN. § 11–610 (1940).

36. ARIZ. CODE ANN. § 27–306 (1939) and TEX. STAT., REV. CIV. art. 233 (1948).

37. *See* Evans v. De Spain, 37 S.W.2d 231, 232 (Tex. Civ. App. 1930).

38. See Government of Kelantan v. Duff Development Co., [1923] A.C. 395 (but dictum, p. 409, that some errors of law would be reviewable even when the question had been specifically referred); Hitchins v. British Coal Refining Processes, Ltd., [1936] 2 All. E.R. 191 (K.B.). To the same effect see Barnes v. Avery, 192 Ga. 874, 879–80, 16 S.E.2d 861, 865 (1941).

39. In England, the parties cannot waive their right to obtain a judicial decision before the award, and probably cannot waive their right to have the award stated in the form of a special case. See HOGG, LAW OF ARBITRATION 113–14 (1936).

40. Willesford v. Watson, L.R. 8 Ch. 473 (1873); Freydberg Bros., Inc. v. Corey, 177 Misc. 560, 31 N.Y.S.2d 10 (Sup. Ct.), aff'd mem., 263 App. Div. 805, 32 N.Y.S.2d 129 (1st Dep't 1941); see B. Fernandez & Hnos., S. En. C. v. Rickert Rice Mills, Inc., 119 F.2d 809, 814 (1st Cir. 1941). See STURGES 234.

were on the other. As a result of this internal friction, there arose increasing difficulty in the proper operation of Colonial.

The stockholders' agreement contained a broad arbitration clause reading as follows:

> Should at any time any dispute arise between any one or more of the parties hereto with respect to his or their rights, obligations, duties, and requirements under and by virtue of the provisions of this agreement, shall be referred to, and consent and approval of each of the parties hereto is expressly given to refer said dispute for determination to the American Arbitration Association, whose determination and/ or decision shall be final and binding upon the parties hereto, and there shall be no appeal from said decision.

It was pursuant to that clause that the respondents, the Meshes and Rosasco, finally demanded arbitration to resolve the deadlock in Colonial. Schwartz and petitioner, Colletti, submitted a counterclaim. In the demand for arbitration by respondents, they asked that "A figure be established, fair and equitable to all, at which either group can buy or sell their stock and property interest as they choose." Petitioner-appellant did not object to that demand.

The arbitrators heard evidence on the charges and counter charges of the respective stockholders. In an award—to which one of the arbitrators dissented—that the arbitrators stated was "in full settlement of all claims and counterclaims submitted to arbitration herein," it was determined that Schwartz should have the option to purchase the stock of the Meshes and Rosasco at $700 per share and, should Schwartz not exercise the option, Rosasco shall purchase Colletti's stock at $700 per share and so much of Schwartz' stock as Rosasco may desire at $1,400 per share. Finally, should Rosasco fail to purchase Schwartz' stock, the Meshes jointly or severally shall purchase all or the balance of Schwartz' stock at $1,400 per share.

Petitioner attacked the award at Special Term on the ground that the arbitrators had exceeded their powers. In our opinion, the award was properly confirmed.

It is contended that the award does not determine the controversies submitted regarding the management of the corporation. On its face, the award specifically states that it was "in full settlement of all claims and counterclaims submitted to arbitration." There is no showing that the arbitrators did not go into all of the matters which were submitted. It was unnecessary for the arbitrators in their award specifically to mention the particular issues they had decided. They were not required to set forth their findings.

In Matter of Bay Ridge Med. Group v. Health Ins. Plan of Greater N.Y. (22 A.D. 2d 807, 808) the court said:

> The validity of an award is unaffected by the absence of a recital of the reasons for the award (Matter of Willow Fabrics [Carolina Frgt. Carriers Corp.], 20 A.D. 2d 864); and an award may not be vacated because the arbitrators did not give their reasons for the award nor set forth their calculations to justify the award (Matter of Linwood [Sherry], 16 Misc 2d 488, 491, affd. 7 A.D. 2d 757; Matter of Weiner Co. [Freund Co.], *supra*; Matter of Big-W Corp. [Horowitz], 24 Misc 2d 145, 156, affd. 14 A.D. 2d 817). "Inquisition of an arbitrator for the purpose of determining the processes by which he arrives at an award, finds no sanction in law" (Matter of Weiner Co. [Freund Co.], 2 A.D. 2d 341, 342, *supra*).

Nor should the award be disturbed because the arbitrators arrived at a different figure for Schwartz' stock than for the stock of the other shareholders. Appellants argue that the arbitrators imperfectly executed their powers and that no final and definite award was made. In particular, it is claimed that the arbitration demand called for the arbitrators establishing one figure for the stock—which would be fair and equitable to all shareholders—and that the arbitrators, in arriving at two figures instead of one figure, imperfectly executed their power.

We do not read the arbitration demand in so restrictive a fashion. The demand is that "A figure be established, fair and equitable to all, at which either group can buy or sell their stock and property interest, as they choose." Under such a demand the arbitrators had a broad discretion to resolve the issues before them. Whatever ambiguity there may be in this portion of the demand was for the arbitrators to resolve. An arbitration award is not reviewable by a court for errors of law or fact. (Matter of S & W Foods [Office Employees Int. Union] 8 A.D. 2d 130, affd. 7 N.Y. 2d 1018 ; Matter of Weiner Co. [Freund Co.] 2 A.D. 2d 341, affd. 3 N.Y. 2d 806.)

Neither is the conclusion reached by the arbitrators herein a "perverse misconstruction" (see Matter of Wilkins, 169 N.Y. 494) nor an "irrational" one (see Matter of National Cash Register Co. [Wilson], 8 N.Y. 2d 377, 383). In point of fact, the fixing of a different price at which the stockholder Schwartz would be required to sell his interest from that of the other shareholders was a plausible recognition of Schwartz' position, vis-a-vis the other stockholders. Schwartz was the only one of the stockholders who did not own or control a business which was a customer of the corporation. On the other hand, the remaining stockholders had gained certain financial advantages by virtue of their joint ownership of both Colonial and their own distributing companies. In any event, the question of whether the arbitrators were wrong or right in their conclusion is not one for the courts. Certainly, the award was final and the arbitrators did not imperfectly execute their powers in making the determination assailed by appellant.

We do not consider—since it was not raised—the interesting question as to whether the clause in the arbitration provision, that there shall be no appeal from the decision of the arbitrators, foreclosed petitioner's attack on the award in the courts in the absence of a claim of partiality, fraud, corruption or misconduct of the arbitrators. (See STURGES, COMMERCIAL ARBITRATION AND AWARDS, p. 798.)

The judgment should, therefore, be affirmed, with costs and disbursements to respondents.

EAGER, J. (dissenting). I would reverse and vacate the judgment entered upon the award and remand the issues for determination before new arbitrators. The arbitrators have "so imperfectly executed" their powers "that a final and definite award upon the subject matter submitted was not made." (See CPLR 7511, subd. [b], par. 1, cl. [iii].)

"The arbitrator's award must be a complete determination of the issues presented." (Matter of Ritchie Bldg. Co. [Rosenthal], 9 A.D. 2d 880; see, also, Matter of Schwartz Silk Co. [Granowitz], 224 App. Div. 705.) Furthermore, it is clear that arbitrators are bound by the clear and unambiguous terms of the submission and may not dispose of the controversies submitted to them by disregarding them and rendering an award which is neither authorized by the terms nor by the contract of the parties.

The agreement between the parties, as stockholders of a closely held corporation, provided that no action should be taken by them or the directors except upon a unanimous vote and it contained a broad arbitration clause for reference to arbitration of "any dispute ... between any one or more of the parties hereto with respect to his or their rights, obligations, duties and requirements under and by virtue of the provisions of this agreement." The demand for arbitration, served by a majority group of stockholders upon a minority group, demanded the arbitration of disputes concerning management, and no one questions but that the disputes sought to be arbitrated were within the scope of the arbitration clause. The relief sought was "[t]o compel the said minority to act in conformity with the plans and suggestions of the majority" in certain detailed respects, including "(2) A figure be established, fair and equitable to all,

at which either group can buy or sell their stock and property interest, as they choose." The minority group served a counterdemand or counterclaim for arbitration, listing several matters in dispute with respect to the management of the corporation and requested certain relief.

The arbitrators' award, however, except for the fixing of the rental to be paid by a certain tenant of the corporation, does not on its face purport to determine any of the controversies submitted in management matters. Instead, without any provision in the contract for a compulsory sale of the stock or the real property interests of a stockholder within his lifetime, and beyond the scope of the submission, the award in effect provides for certain stock options, including a provision whereby one of the majority group of stockholders shall purchase the stock of the petitioner, Colletti, one of the minority stockholders.

Furthermore, the parties proceeded to arbitrate the disputes with respect to management within the framework of a demand for arbitration which stated that the arbitrators could establish "[a] figure ... fair and equitable to all, at which either group can buy or sell their stock and property interest, as they choose." Not only does the award fail to fix a figure purporting to be "fair and equitable to all, at which either group can buy or sell their stock and property interest," but instead fixes two figures—providing in effect that Schwartz, one of the minority stockholders, shall receive $1,400 a share for his stock, in the event he does not buy out the majority stockholders, and then provides that one of the majority stockholders shall purchase the stock of the petitioner, Colletti, the other minority stockholder, and his property interest, at the price of $700 per share of stock.

Finally, the arbitrators have not set a figure at which the members of either group may "choose" to buy or sell their stock and property interest; this is contrary to the submission in that, under the plain terms of the demand, a choice to buy or sell at the figure to be fixed by the arbitrators was to be left to "either group."

This is a case where the arbitrators "gave a completely irrational construction" to the plain terms of the submission. (Matter of National Cash Register Co. [Wilson], 8 N.Y. 2d 377, 383.) Instead of making "a final and definite award upon the subject matter submitted" (CPLR 7511, subd. [b]), within the framework of the agreement of the parties and the controversies described in the demand and counterdemand, the arbitrators have failed to determine the disputes between the stockholders that were submitted to them and, instead, have provided for an unauthorized purchase and sale of stockholders' interests.

The award should be vacated because it is not only imperfect but, in effect, it has made a new contract between the parties, and this is not permitted.

BREITEL, J. P., RABIN, VALENTE and STEUER, JJ., concur in PER CURIAM opinion; EAGER, J., dissents in opinion.

Judgment affirmed, with $50 costs to respondents.

Under the majority's view how many of the grounds for vacating an award described in the preceding note could be entertained?

B.

Requisites of Award

MATTER OF HUNTER (PROSER)
First Dept. 274 App. Div. 311, 83 N.Y.S. 2d 345 (1948) [aff'd without opinion, 298 N.Y. 828, 84 N.E. 2d 143 (1949)]

PER CURIAM. The arbitrators' award in this matter, except for item E, is a clear and definite determination of the rights and obligations of the parties and is final and enforceable as any similar judgment would be in an action. The fact that certain computations will have to be made week by week to carry the award into effect does not render the award ineffective for the present or for the future. The formulae for the computations are so clear and specific that the determination of the amounts owing to the petitioner week by week is merely an accounting calculation. Neither arbitrators nor further arbitration are required to make such calculations. Indeed, the box office statements routinely issued by respondents will serve the purpose.

In this light, the attack of respondents upon the finality of the award and their claim that each week's computation of their indebtedness to petitioner must be the subject of a new arbitration is plainly an effort to avoid the determination made and defeat petitioner's rights by making their enforcement impractical. The words of Medalie, J., speaking for the Court of Appeals in Matter of Feuer Transportation, Inc. (Local No. 445) (295 N.Y. 88, 91-92) should be read in this connection:

> To work well it [arbitration] must operate with a minimum of delay and with all the flexibility which equity can give it. . . . If the relief to which a party is entitled is not granted and he is remitted to a new proceeding, the purposes of the reforms intended by the Arbitration Law of 1920 would be defeated. Instead of relief from legal technicality, the parties to an arbitration are given delay and a surfeit of legal

procedure. Proceedings of this kind are equitable in character, and the practice of equity as to relief should be followed.

Perhaps the judgment should not have provided for the appointment of a referee as a reference is unnecessary if respondents will simply do what they should do pursuant to the judgment. The court may do whatever is necessary to enforce the judgment, however, employing all the provisions of law relating to a judgment in an action (Civ. Prac. Act, § 1466) and we think, if necessary, might appoint a referee under section 467 of the Civil Practice Act.

MATTER OF PYRAMID PRODUCTIONS (NATIONAL TELEFILM ASSOCIATES)
40 Misc. 2d 675, 243 N.Y.S. 2d 170 (New York Cty. 1963)

HENRY CLAY GREENBERG, J. The petitioner moves to confirm and the respondent cross moves to vacate the award of the arbitrator. The relief sought in the petitioner's demand for arbitration was an accounting by the respondent, in detail, respecting all activities of the three television series involved, a determination of the fair and reasonable value of the television rights, and a direction that the respondent pay all sums found due and owing. The arbitrator's award provides that the respondent account to the petitioner for the period from December 14, 1953 "up to a recent date (April 30, 1963 or later)" in sufficient detail to permit a satisfactory audit by "a national firm of independent certified public accountants."

The award further provides that if, in the opinion of the independent accountants, the respondent's accounting is not fair, "the indepen-

dent accountants shall submit an accounting, in their opinion fair and such accounting shall be binding." and the "respondent shall pay to claimant . . . any amounts shown in said report . . . shown to be owing by respondent to claimant. . . ." The award is not final and definite upon the subject matter submitted and therefore should be vacated (Section 7511 CPLR). This is not a case where the formula for computation is so clear that the determination of the amounts owing is merely an accounting calculation (see Matter of Hunter (Proser), 274 App. Div. 311, 83 N.Y.S. 2d 345, aff'd 298 N.Y. 828, 84 N.E. 2d 143).

In order to arrive at the amount due, the award requires an explanation of allocations of receipts from "block bookings" or "package deals," dispositions of spots or other consideration received in barter transactions and a "complete accounting of transactions of NTA Film Network, Inc., or any other affiliated organization" pertaining to the television series. As aforementioned, these records cover a period of approximately ten years. It is obvious that a determination of any amounts owed requires more than mere arithmetical computations. In effect, the arbitrator has delegated his power to decide the amount due to independent accountants and this he may not do (Publishers' Ass'n of New York City, on Behalf of Brooklyn Daily Eagle v. New York Typographical Union No. 6, 168 Misc. 267, 274, 5 N.Y.S. 2d 847, 853). "Businessmen and accountants can well disagree as to what a set of books show as being 'due' to a party. An award must be clear enough to indicate unequivocally what each party is required to do." (Matter of Overseas Distributors Exchange, Inc. (Benedict Bros.), 5 A.D. 2d 498,

173 N.Y.S. 2d 110). The determination of amounts due was for the arbitrator, and "[t]he absence of a mutual, final and definite award upon the subject matter submitted requires a remand to the arbitrators for further action." (Matter of Overseas Distributors Exchange, Inc. (Benedict Bros.), *supra*). The arbitrator here, having heard all the evidence and being the one most familiar with the issues would be the proper party to make this determination, and the respondent's bare assertions are insufficient to show that such impropriety as would require a substitution. Accordingly the motion is denied and the cross motion is granted. The matter is directed to be resubmitted to the same arbitrator to fix the obligations of the parties in a definite manner.

In Kramer v. Gough, 310 Ky. 299, 220 S.W. 2d 577 (1949) the court observed, in dictum: "In a dispute over the loss of or damages to property, an award by arbitrators is void for uncertainty where the value in money is left open for dispute."

In this case the asserted agreement conferred power on the arbitrators "to ascertain the *amount* of corn damaged or destroyed" and were without authority "to fix the liability or to determine pecuniary damage." (Emphasis added)

See also International Longshoremen's Association, Local 1291 v. Philadelphia Marine Trade Association, 389 U.S. 64 (1967) set out below, p. 630.

C.

Uninsured Motorist Claims

NEW YORK'S MVAIC*

Traffic victims suffering injuries at the hands of unknown or financially irresponsible motorists have been the subject of increasing legislative concern. While this regard for the plight of the

remediless victim has yielded a variety of statutory solutions, none has provided sufficiently broad coverage. Compulsory insurance omits from its protection those injured by uninsured non-residents, hit-and-run drivers, operators of stolen or unregistered vehicles, and drivers of

---

*Excerpted from Comment, 65 COLUM. L. REV. 1075 (1965). Reprinted by permission. In addition to the descriptive material presented here, the comment raises the question whether the required arbitration unconstitutionally denies jury trial to claimants, the issue dealt with earlier in *Matter of Berkovitz*, and concludes that the provision might very well

be unconstitutional. For a contrary view, see Stone, *A Paradox in the Theory of Commercial Arbitration*, 21 ARB. J. (n.s.) 156 (1966). The author is a vice president of the American Arbitration Association. Uninsured-motorist claims comprise the largest and fastest growing category of cases now administered by the AAA.

registered but somehow uninsured automobiles. Statutes requiring that uninsured motorist coverage be offered to all persons purchasing automobile liability insurance fail to protect the still significant number of residents who do not own a motor vehicle. Even narrower in scope are the financial responsibility laws, which require proof of ability to compensate future accident victims only after the motorist has either been involved in an accident or committed a traffic violation. The unsatisfied judgment fund, offering indemnity to all victims of unknown or financially irresponsible motorists, provides the broadest coverage, but has been frequently criticized as involving unwarranted state entry into the insurance field.

Recognizing the limitations inherent in both its financial responsibility and compulsory insurance provisions, New York State enacted the Motor Vehicle Accident Indemnification law. Combining the coverage of the uninsured motorist and unsatisfied judgment plans, the statute is a significant attempt to widen the scope of protection for victims of traffic accidents.

The Motor Vehicle Accident Indemnification Corporation was created in 1958 to compensate innocent traffic victims or their survivors for personal injuries or death arising from accidents with uninsured or hit-and-run vehicles. The Corporation is composed of all motor vehicle liability insurers authorized to do business within New York State; these members, in turn, elect the board of directors, which is responsible for the management of the Corporation. Functioning as an insurer, the MVAIC is authorized to investigate claims and to appear on behalf of the unidentified or financially irresponsible motorist. Its liability is limited to $10,000 for injury or death of one person and $20,000 in the case of an accident injuring two or more persons; no provision is made for compensating property damage.

While the statute's coverage is quite broad, several classes of potential claimants are excluded from its protection. For example, New York residents injured in accidents in other states have no recourse to the Corporation. Other accident victims disqualified from recovery are owners of uninsured vehicles and their spouses, if injured while in the vehicle; those operating a vehicle in violation of orders suspending or revoking their licenses; those settling with the wrongdoer without permission from the MVAIC; and those whose recovery would benefit any workmen's compensation or disability benefits carrier.

The statute creates two categories of eligible claimants—"qualified" and "insured." While the "qualified" claimant derives his rights solely from this legislation, the "insured's" rights flow from the New York Motor Vehicle Accident Indemnification Endorsement, which is included by law in every automobile liability policy within the state.

1. *The "Qualified" Claimant.* The statute designates two kinds of claimants as "qualified." The first class embraces all residents of New York State, omitting, however, those designated elsewhere by the statute as "insured" and those residents or their spouses suffering injury while riding in their own uninsured vehicle. The second class of "qualified" claimants includes accident victims who are residents of states affording "substantially similar" remedies to New York residents suffering injury within their borders.

2. *The "Insured" Claimant.* As defined in the endorsement, the "insured" category includes the named insured and his spouse, and any of their relatives living with them; any other person occupying an automobile that is owned by the insured or his spouse and used with permission of either; and any person who has a derivative cause of action for care or loss of services arising from bodily injury to a third person eligible to recover under the endorsement. While coverage of the "insured" would seem to depend upon the existence of a valid insurance policy, the endorsement has been broadly construed to embrace the occupant of a car, in situations where the insurer has disclaimed liability.

As a condition to recovery, a "qualified" claimant must submit to the MVAIC notice of an intention to file a claim within ninety days of the accrual of his cause of action.

Having filed notice, the "qualified" claimant's path to recovery—absent a settlement with the Corporation—depends upon the identity of the party allegedly at fault. In cases involving a known but financially irresponsible motorist, the claimant must first institute an action against the motorist. If a judgment is secured, but remains fully or partially unsatisfied despite the "qualified" person's exhaustion of his remedies, he may apply to the court in which judgment was rendered for an order directing payment by the MVAIC. With respect to unidentified motorists, however, the claimant must apply to the supreme court for an order permitting him to bring an action directly against the MVAIC; he must also demonstrate that he has complied with all conditions precedent. If leave to use is granted, the Corporation is deemed to be the defendant and therefore has available any defenses which would have been available to the hit-and-run driver. Whether the motorist causing the accident is uninsured or unknown, he is liable to the MVAIC for any payments made by the Corporation to the claimant.

The "insured" claimant's method of recovery, as defined by the endorsement, is limited strictly to arbitration. If the "insured" and the MVAIC fail to agree upon his eligibility to recover damages from the "owner or operator of the uninsured vehicle because of bodily injury to the insured, or do not agree to the amount of payment," then the matter is submitted to arbitration in accordance with the rules of the American Arbitration Association [which has promulgated a special set of rules for this category of case].

Nonmandatory endorsements are becoming more common. The California act provides that questions concerning entitlement to damages and their amount are to be settled by agreement and, failing agreement, by arbitration. Cal. Ins. Code § 11580 2(e). However, the coverage may be "deleted" by an agreement in writing. Some other states, e.g. Ohio, use this "elective" form with the initiative to avoid the endorsement falling to the purchaser of automobile liability insurance. Some states specifically or by common law will not honor the arbitration clause now standard in this endorsement.

The American Arbitration Association has established a special panel of lawyers to act as arbitrators of liability and damage disputes arising under this endorsement. Under the AAA rules the potential arbitrator may not be interested in the outcome and must declare any possible ground of bias. Their awards are not accompanied by opinions and are not published. *Uninsured Motorist Coverage: A Guide to MVAIC and Arbitration,* 15 ARB. J. 166 (1960).

Matter of Phillips (American Casualty Co.) arose as a claim under the uninsured-motorist coverage. The insured, when killed, was 42 years old, in good health, earning $13,000 annually, and contributing to the support of an invalid mother and unmarried sister. The award of the arbitrators was $2,000 in addition to funeral expenses. Special Term vacated the award (unreported). The Appellate Division reinstated the award, mem., 10 A.D. 2d 689, 198 N.Y.S. 2d 538 (First Dept. 1961). The Court of Appeals confirmed without opinion, the lone dissenter noting that under the circumstances the award "is so shockingly inadequate as to be tantamount to

evident partiality." 9 N.Y. 2d 873, 216 N.Y.S. 2d 694 (1961).

MATTER OF WAINWRIGHT (GLOBE INDEMNITY CO.)
25 Misc. 2d 212, 210 N.Y.S. 2d 186
(Madison Cly S.Ct 1960)

HOWARD A. ZELLER, J. Petitioner Charles R. Wainwright moves pursuant to section 1462 of the Civil Practice Act for an order vacating and setting aside an arbitration award of damages arising from the death of his daughter, Connie Ann Wainwright, on a claim made by him under his own automobile liability insurance policy issued by the respondent. The respondent, Globe Indemnity Company, has cross-moved for an order confirming the arbitration award and directing entry of judgment thereon.

Connie Ann Wainwright's death on October 10, 1959 was caused by carbon monoxide poisoning while a passenger in an uninsured automobile whose owner-operator had removed a substantial portion of its exhaust pipe and allowed the muffler to remain in a rusted and corroded condition. Mr. Wainwright's own automobile liability insurance policy issued by Globe Indemnity Company contained an endorsement providing indemnity for injuries or loss sustained by him or members of his family caused by accident arising out of the negligent maintenance, operation or use of an uninsured vehicle. After having been appointed administrator of his daughter's estate, Mr. Wainwright sought indemnity from Globe Indemnity Company, which rejected his claim upon the ground that the incident which caused his daughter's death was not covered by the endorsement.

Pursuant to a requirement of the endorsement, the dispute was submitted to arbitrators. After a hearing and deliberation, two of the arbitrators, a majority, awarded Mr. Wainwright $1,145, an amount exactly equal to the undisputed bills for funeral and burial expenses of his daughter. One of the arbitrators dissented from the award but neither gave nor was required to give a reason for his decision. Matter of Weiner Co. (Freund Co.). 2 A.D. 2d 341, 155 N.Y.S. 2d 802, affirmed no opinion, 3 N.Y. 2d 806, 166 N.Y.S. 2d 7.

Mr. Wainwright claims the arbitration award should be vacated and set aside because (1) there was evident partiality in the arbitrators; (2) there was an obvious mistake made by the arbitrators in the assessment of damages; and (3) the arbitrators so imperfectly executed their powers that a mutual, final and definite award upon the subject matter submitted was not made.

The basic reason for the attack on the award is that it granted no more than so-called special damages and made absolutely no award for pecuniary loss to Miss Wainwright's next of kin as permitted by the Decedent's Estate Law.

The evidentiary facts are either conceded or uncontested. At the time of her death, Miss Wainwright was 17 years and eight months old. For a year and a half preceding her death she had worked without salary as such for 50 to 60 hours a week in a restaurant owned by her parents but operated primarily by her mother and herself. Miss Wainwright was an industrious and ambitious girl with a genuine interest in restaurant operation. Competent restaurant help, as Miss Wainwright was characterized, would be paid $1.25 per hour locally. The Wainwrights provided their daughter with a home, her clothing and all other necessaries, whatever funds she required, and also furnished and maintained a car for her. Miss Wainwright's character and habits were beyond reproach, she had not been keeping steady company with any young man, and had no immediate plans for marriage insofar as her parents knew. Much of her off-duty time was spent at home looking after several younger sisters whose ages ranged down to six years.

The applicable statutory grounds for vacating an arbitration award by this court are contained in the following provisions of Section 1462 of the Civil Practice Act:

> . . . 1. Where the award was procured by corruption, fraud or other undue means.
>
> 2. Where there was evident partiality or corruption in the arbitrators or either of them.
>
> 3. Where the arbitrators were guilty of misconduct in refusing to postpone the hearing upon sufficient cause shown, or in refusing to hear evidence pertinent and material to the controversy; or of any other misbehavior by which the rights of any party have been prejudiced.
>
> 4. Where the arbitrators or other persons making the award exceeded their powers, or so imperfectly executed them, that a mutual, final and definite award upon the subject-matter submitted was not made. . . .

Despite the general rule that the powers of this court to vacate an arbitration award are derived solely from the statute, "the court will not lend its power to the enforcement of the kind of a decision in arbitration which it would neither allow nor enforce as the subject of an action maintained before it directly." Matter of Publishers' Ass'n (Newspaper Union) 280 App. Div. 500, 507, 114 N.Y.S. 2d 401, 407; see Matter of Weiner Co. (Freund Co.), 2 A.D. 2d 341, 155 N.Y.S. 2d 802 affirmed no opinion, 3 N.Y. 2d 806, 166 N.Y.S. 2d 7; Matter of Garnett (Kassover), 8 A.D. 2d 631, 185 N.Y.S. 2d 435; Matter of French Textiles Co. (Senor), 7 A.D. 2d 896, 182 N.Y.S. 2d 282; 21 Carmody Wait 566. This statement of principle is not to be interpreted as permitting judicial interference with mere errors of judgment on the part of the arbitrators concerning the law or the facts of a submitted matter. Matter of Wilkins, 169 N.Y. 494, 62 N.E. 575. Nor is the statement construable as confining an arbitration award to the forms of relief common to law or in conformity with the precepts of equity. Matter of Transpacific Trans. Corp. (Sirena Co.), 9 A.D. 2d 316, 193 N.Y.S. 2d 277. However, the principle does support the vacation of awards in instances which are beyond or outside the scope of the existing statutes. Thus the equitable jurisdiction of the courts in matters of arbitration (Matter of Lipschutz (Gutwirth), 304 N.Y. 58, 62, 106 N.E. 2d 8, 10) has been invoked to vacate awards which transgress a particular statute (Western Union Tel. Co. (ACA), 299 N.Y. 177, 86 N.E. 2d 162), which are illegal in result or their contractual inception (Metro Plan, Inc. v. Miscione, 257 App. Div. 652, 15 N.Y.S. 2d 35), which otherwise violate public policy, as in matters of infant custody and support (Matter of Michelman (Michelman), 5 Misc. 2d 570, 135 N.Y.S. 2d 608), which are legally erroneous on the face of the award (Fudickar v. Guardian Mutual Life Ins. Co., 62 N.Y. 392), and those which are punitive or excessive as to the damages awarded (Matter of Publishers' Ass'n (Newspaper Union), 280 App. Div. 500, 114 N.Y.S. 2d 401; Van Cortlandt v. Underhill, 17 Johns. 405, 410).

The award implicitly, and with ample support in the record, finds liability on the part of the uninsured owner-operator and establishes the obligation of Globe Indemnity Company to pay damages consequent to Miss Wainwright's death. To then award only the special damages arising from her death and grant no damages to her next of kin for the value of her life to them is such a grossly unjust result as to both assault the equitable conscience of this court and to invoke its inherent powers. True, the quantum of damages awarded in arbitration ordinarily is not subject to judicial review. It is equally true that the pecuniary loss sustained in money or money's worth by next of kin in a wrongful death action is greatly speculative. But to hold that this young lady's life had no monetary value to her father and mother is so grave an injustice and so contrary to the case proved that this court should not lend its powers of enforcement to such portion of the arbitration decision. Van Cortlandt v. Underhill, *supra*, 17 Johns. 405, 410, 416.

Apart from the aspects of the equitable jurisdiction of the courts to vacate or confirm awards in arbitration, the award as made is considered neither final nor definite as to all matters submitted to the arbitrators. Despite the general language in the award that it was "in full settlement of all claims submitted", the absence of any clear monetary recognition for the pecuniary losses to the next of kin arising from wrongful death renders the award incomplete and non-final within the intent of Section 1462, subd. 4 of the Civil Practice Act. See, Jones v. Welwood *et al.,* 71 N.Y. 208.

That portion of the award which establishes by implication the basic right of Mr. Wainwright for full indemnity and determines the amount of the special damages is considered separable and should be confirmed. Herbst v. Hagenaers, 137 N.Y. 290, 33 N.E. 315 ; Jones v. Welwood *et al., supra,* 71 N.Y. 208 ; Shrump v. Parfitt, 84 Hun 341, 33 N.Y.S. 409 ; Keep v. Keep, 17 Hun 152. The question of the value of the damages accruing to Miss Wainwright's next of kin for her wrongful death should be referred for a hearing and determination to another and different panel of arbitrators selected as before. To the extent that the present award fails to grant any such damages it should be vacated.

In view of the foregoing disposition Mr. Wainwright's other contentions need not be considered.

An order may be submitted accordingly.

This decision was reversed, 14 A.D. 2d 971, 221 N.Y.S. 2d 409 (Third Dept. 1961) in a memorandum opinion that cited the *Phillips* case.

For a critical commentary on these two cases see Kronstein, *Arbitration is Power,* 38 N.Y.U. L. REV. 661, 669-676 (1963), who insists that the arbitrators are supposed to determine legal rights and hence that what he regards as their obvious mistakes should be subject to judicial supervision. He argues further that it is specious to claim that the parties are getting what they bargained for because there is no bargaining, inasmuch as the uninsured motorist's clause is prescribed by statute. The Columbia Committee for Effective Justice is studying the arbitration of claims under the uninsured motorist coverage. When published, its report may provide a basis for assessing the fairness of the procedure.

What policies argue for applying the usual limitations upon review to uninsured motorist claims?

What arguments are there for more extensive review? Are the arguments different under the New York statute and the California type? Should either or both be treated differently from "commercial arbitration"?

CHAPTER VII

THE ARBITRABLE ISSUE

A.

Justiciability

MATTER OF FLETCHER
237 N.Y. 440, 143 N.E. 248 (1924)

LEHMAN, J. On or about February 3, 1917, Stanley Fletcher and Grosvenor Nicholas entered into a written contract which contained a provision that Grosvenor Nicholas should deposit in escrow with three named persons stock of the par value of $40,000 of the corporation of Grosvenor Nicholas & Co., Inc., to be held for Mr. Fletcher upon the condition that in certain contingencies

> Mr. Nicholas shall have the right to purchase the said $40,000 aggregate par value of stock of Grosvenor Nicholas & Company, Inc., held for Mr. Fletcher as aforesaid at the fair value thereof, to be determined as of the date of November 1st, 1917, and may take and pay therefor within thirty days after the said fair value thereof shall have been determined as hereinafter provided in paragraph Fifth hereof. *Fifth.* The said fair value of the said stock on November 1st, 1917 at which Mr. Nicholas may purchase the same shall be determined by an appraisal thereof made by three arbiters, one to be appointed by Mr. Fletcher or his representative,

another to be appointed by Mr. Nicholas or his representative and a third to be appointed by the other two.

It was further provided in the contract that "if Mr. Nicholas shall not so purchase the same within the said thirty (30) days then the certificates for the said stock shall be immediately thereafter delivered to Mr. Fletcher to be held or disposed of by him as he may see fit." On November 1, 1917, the contingency had arisen upon which it was agreed that Mr. Nicholas should have the right to purchase the stock but no third arbiter has ever been selected and no appraisal has been had as provided in the contract between the parties. Apparently Mr. Fletcher or his representative has made some attempts, at least during the last two or three years, to secure the selection of a third arbiter by the other arbiters and when these attempts failed he made application to the court for the appointment of an arbiter under section 4 of the Arbitration Law, chapter 275 of the Laws of 1920. This appeal brings up for review the order granting that application.

Section 4 of the Arbitration Law (Cons. Laws, ch. 72) authorizes the appointment of an arbitrator by the court where for any reason "there shall be a lapse in the naming of an arbitrator or arbitrators or umpire, or in filling a vacancy" in connection with an arbitration provided for "in the contract for arbitration or in the submission, described in section two." Section 2 of the Arbitration Law provides that

> a provision in a written contract to settle by arbitration a controversy thereafter arising between the parties to the contract, or a submission hereafter entered into of an existing controversy to arbitration pursuant to title eight of chapter seventeen of the Code of Civil Procedure, or article eighty-three of the Civil Practice Act, shall be valid, enforcible and irrevocable, save upon such grounds as exist at law or in equity for the revocation of any contract.

No contention is made that except as provided in the Arbitration Law the courts have any power to appoint an arbitrator where the parties have provided for the appointment of arbitrators directly or indirectly by themselves, and the Arbitration Law applies only to contracts or submissions "described in section two." The agreement of the parties in the present case constitutes no actual "submission to arbitration" pursuant to the provisions of the Code of Civil Procedure or the Civil Practice Act even if it could conceivably be regarded as a submission to arbitration at common law. (See Wurster v. Armfield, 175 N.Y. 256.) Moreover though the Arbitration Law applies to all written *contracts to settle* by arbitration a controversy thereafter arising, including contracts made before the passage of the Arbitration Law (Matter of Berkovitz v. Arbib & Houlberg, 230 N.Y. 261); yet by its express terms it applies only to such *submissions* as are "hereafter entered into." The exercise of the power of the court to appoint an "arbitrator" in this special proceeding must, therefore, rest upon a finding that the provision of the contract providing for the determination of the value of corporate stock by three "arbiters" constitutes a provision "to settle by arbitration a controversy thereafter arising" within the meaning of the statute.

It is to be noted at the outset that the contract under consideration does not provide for a determination of damages for which one of the parties may be liable in law; it does not provide for a determination of any question after disagreement of the parties upon that question; it does not attempt to substitute a tribunal created by contract for a court of justice in a dispute which would otherwise be justiciable by the courts. It merely substituted the determination of a particular matter affecting contractual rights, by persons selected by the parties, in place of the determination of that question by the parties themselves in some other manner. If such a provision brings the contract within the application of the Arbitration Law then it would seem that every contract which provides for an appraisal, a valuation or the determination of any fact affecting contractual rights, by one or more persons, either named or thereafter to be selected likewise comes within the provisions of that law.

Even prior to the Arbitration Law the courts have held that a provision in a contract that before a right of action arises certain facts shall be determined or amounts and values ascertained is valid and not against public policy (President, etc., D. & H. Canal Co. v. Pennsylvania Coal Co., 50 N.Y. 250), and it cannot be doubted that the provision of the contract under consideration comes within this rule. The primary purpose of the Arbitration Law was to make valid and enforcible provisions for arbitration which had previously been regarded as contrary to public policy but it also provides a practical method for the enforcement of such provisions and both the letter and spirit of the statute require the courts to hold that this method was intended to apply to all contracts "to settle by arbitration a controversy thereafter arising;" both those which were regarded as valid before the Arbitration Law as well as those which were regarded as contrary to public policy. On the other hand, the language of the statute should not be stretched to cover contracts which do not come within its plain intent where the application of the method of procedure provided in the statute is not practicable.

> In order to constitute a submission to arbitration there must be some difference or dispute, either existing or prospective, between the parties and they must intend that it should be determined in a quasi-judicial manner. Therein lies the distinction between an agreement for a valuation and a submission to arbitration, for in the case of a valuation there is not as a rule any difference or dispute between the parties and they intend that the valuer shall without taking evidence or hearing argument, make his valuation according to his own skill, knowledge and experience. (HALSBURY, LAWS OF ENGLAND, vol. I, p. 440.)

See also, Matter of Carus-Wilson & Greene (18 Q.B.D. 7), where the court held that the valuation of property by appraisers, to be selected, as in the present case, to determine the price to be paid upon a sale constitutes no arbitration and the distinction is drawn between the appointment of a person "to ascertain some matter for the purpose of preventing differences from arising" and the appointment of a person to settle or determine differences after they have arisen. In the present case no difference or controversy can be said to have arisen between the parties as to the fair value of the stock or the amount to be paid by Mr. Nicholas if he decides to buy it—perhaps because the parties in order to avoid the possibility of such differences arising have left the determination of the question in the first instance to presumably disinterested and expert persons. The Arbitration Law is by its terms made applicable only to contracts "to settle by arbitration a controversy" and we cannot hold that the contract under consideration comes within the terms of the statute unless we give the words "to settle a controversy" a construction so extraordinarily broad as to cover a provision intended to permit third persons to determine any question which affects the contractual rights of the parties.

Even should we assume that such a construction would in a proper case be permissible in order to effectuate the purpose of the legislature, if such purpose clearly appeared from a reading of the entire statute in the light of the conditions which led to its enactment, it seems clear that no such legislative purpose appears in this case. Arbitrations have always been regarded as proceedings by which controversies otherwise cognizable by the courts are submitted to the decision of persons selected by the parties to the dispute. The provisions of the Code of Civil Procedure now embodied in the Civil Practice Act permitted submissions to arbitration even before the Arbitration Law was passed and regulated the procedure upon such submission. These provisions require hearing upon notice and the taking of an oath by the arbitrators. They confer upon the arbitrators all the powers which are "conferred upon a board or a member of a board authorized by law to hear testimony" including the power to require the attendance of witnesses. They give the arbitrators the right in their awards to require the payment by either party of fees and expenses. They fix the form of an award. They provide for motions to confirm, vacate, modify or correct an award and they permit the entry of a judgment after the confirmation of an award. That judgment "may be enforced as if it had been rendered in an action in the court in which it is entered" and "an appeal may be taken from an order vacating an award, or from a judgment entered upon an award, as from an order or judgment in an action." These provisions are appropriate to proceedings where parties substitute judges of their own choice for judges chosen by the state in the determination of disputes otherwise cognizable

by the courts alone; they can have no application to proceedings through which disinterested persons are authorized to settle questions which would otherwise be left to the determination of the parties to the contract. If we hold that the contract under consideration comes within the purview of the Arbitration Law, then by force of Section 8, the provisions of the Code of Civil Procedure and of the Practice Act above referred to "so far as practicable and consistent with this chapter, shall apply to an arbitration agreement under this chapter, and for such purpose the arbitration agreement shall be deemed a submission to arbitration." Since the legislature has expressly confined the application of the Arbitration Law to contracts "to settle by arbitration a controversy thereafter arising between the parties" and has conferred upon the arbitrators powers appropriate only to the decision of matters otherwise cognizable by the courts, it seems to us that it was the plain intent of the legislature not to include mere valuations, appraisals or other determination of matters which except for the provisions of the contract would be settled not by the courts after a judicial inquiry but by the parties themselves without such inquiry. The present contract is not one to settle a controversy between the parties but is one to avoid a possible controversy by leaving the settlement of a question to third parties; the third parties are not expected to settle the matter in a quasi-judicial manner and it seems to us that it, therefore, does not come within the letter or the spirit of the statute.

It is urged that since the courts have decided in many cases that they will not enforce by a decree of specific performance provisions in a contract for the determination by third parties of questions arising thereunder, the parties are left helpless or at best must resort to a cumbersome remedy by suit. Assuming but by no means deciding both that the rule against specific performance of such provisions has survived the enactment of the Arbitration Law and that in spite of the language of the statute, consideration of convenience could be given any weight, such considerations seem to have little foundation in fact. The courts have always enforced such contracts where as in this case the provision for an appraisal could be regarded as incidental and subsidiary to the substantive part of the agreement and "treating the method as a matter of form rather than substance, the courts have by a reference or otherwise determined the value for the purpose of enforcing the contract according to its real spirit and purpose." (Mutual Life Ins. Co. of N.Y. v. Stephens, 214 N.Y. 488, at p. 495, and cases there cited.) The effect of failure to act by persons selected, under the provisions of a contract, to determine particular matters as a prerequisite to the assertion of rights under the contract and the effect of misconduct which vitiates a determination have been frequently considered by the courts, especially in connection with insurance or construction contracts. In such contingency a party to the contract may enforce his rights thereunder by action as if there were no requirement for a prior determination of any fact which the court could itself determine in the action. We cannot hold that either party may in such a case compel an appraisal, valuation or other determination of fact preliminary to the assertion of a right, as an "arbitration" within the purview of the Arbitration Law, without at the same time bringing confusion into the law and inconvenience to the parties to the contract. No party to such a contract would know till the courts have passed upon the question whether in any given case the application of any particular section of the Civil Practice Act would be practicable. At his peril a party would be obliged to determine for himself whether the so-called arbitrator should be sworn, whether he must hold hearings upon notice and make a formal award. The award would be ineffective unless confirmed ; if confirmed no appeal could be taken unless a judgment is entered, yet sometimes as in the present case it would be difficult to decide what judgment could be appropriately entered upon the determination of the particular question settled by the "arbitrator." A party would be required to make a motion vacating the award in case of misconduct of the "arbitrator," and then to enter upon a new "arbitration" instead of being permitted to disregard a determination improperly made and to assert his rights without any further prior determination. The present case in my opinion aptly illustrates the clumsiness of the proposed remedy when applied to contracts of this type. The real purpose of the contract was to give Mr. Nicholas the right to purchase the stock at its fair value, the provision for valuation constituted merely the agreed method of arriving at the fair value and was purely incidental and subsidiary to the substantive part of the contract. Such a valuation would serve no purpose except to enable Mr. Nicholas to decide whether to exercise his right to buy the stock and to enable Mr. Fletcher to fix a definite time when that right must be exercised or lost. No so-called award would settle the ultimate rights of the parties, for all the parties have agreed to do is to permit "arbiters" to determine one question of fact upon which the assertion of rights may thereafter be based. If both parties are willing to have such determination made in accordance with the terms of the contract, no resort to the court is necessary. If the determination has not been made because of wrongful acts or refusal to proceed on the part of Mr. Nicholas, it might well be held that he has waived or forfeited any rights under the contract which might be based upon such valuation, and that Mr. Fletcher is entitled to the delivery of the stock free from any rights of Mr. Nicholas thereto ; but only the court could pass upon this question. Only if the prior determination has failed for any other reason, such as the wrongful acts, disability or failure to proceed on the part of either or both arbiters or the umpire, would the right of Mr. Nicholas to purchase still be in existence and any necessity exist for the determination of the value of the stock. In such an event, in an action brought by either for the enforcement of his rights, the court upon allegation and proof of such failure to make a valuation as provided in the contract, would have the power to determine itself the fair value of the stock as an incident to the enforcement of the rights of the parties, "treating the method as a matter of form rather than substance." (Mutual Life Ins. Co. of N.Y. v. Stephens, *supra*.)

MATTER OF BUFFALO & ERIE RY. CO. (AMALGAMATED ASS'N OF STREET RY. EMPLOYEES)
250 N.Y. 275, 165 N.E. 291 (1929)

CRANE, J. The Special Term of the Supreme Court for the county of Erie on the 29th day of June, 1927, designated an arbitrator or umpire, pursuant to section 4 of the Arbitration Law (Cons. Laws, ch. 72), under an agreement or contract between the Buffalo and Erie Railway Company and the Amalgamated Association of Street and Electric Railway Employees of America, Division No. 592 of Fredonia, N.Y. and Division No. 624 of Buffalo, N.Y. The Appellate Division has unanimously affirmed the order and has certified that in its opinion a question of law is involved which ought to be reviewed by this court.

The question, briefly stated, is whether the matter in controversy comes within the provisions of the Arbitration Law of this State.

The agreement made between the railway and the Amalgamated Association in May of 1926, provided for the hours of work of the men, and for their rate of wages and many other details which are usually contained in this class of agreement between a railroad and its operatives. Article XII and article XVI are the only two provisions necessary to state here. Article XVI I will quote first:

> This agreement and the provisions thereof shall continue in force and be binding upon the respective parties hereunto until the first day of May, 1927, and from year to year thereafter unless changed by parties hereunto. Either of the parties hereunto desiring a change in any section or sections of this Agreement, shall notify the other party in writing of the desired change, thirty days prior to the end of each year, which is the first day of April. After such notice the agreement shall be opened up and the change or changes shall be considered. Upon the failure to reach a mutual agreement upon any changes desired by the parties hereunto, the same shall be arbitrated as provided in this agreement, and this agreement shall be modified to conform to the decision of the arbitration.

The provision relating to arbitration is article XII.

> All matters that cannot be adjusted between the Company and the Association shall be submitted to a temporary Board of Arbitration. Either party to this agreement shall, upon being notified in writing by the other party that arbitration is desired, name its arbitrator, within forty-eight hours from the date of receiving such notice. The Board of Arbitration shall be composed of three persons, the Company to select one, the Association to select one, and the two thus selected shall within five days from the date of their appointment, select a third arbitrator. At the Hearing before the Board of Arbitration, either side may be represented by anyone whom they may desire, and after all evidence and arguments have been heard by the Board, they shall, within fifteen days, formulate their award in writing and submit the same to both parties of this agreement. The findings of the majority of the Board shall be final and binding upon both parties of this agreement.

Prior to May 1, 1927, the railroad found it necessary in view of reduction in the volume of business carried over its line, compared with the volume of business carried by it in preceding years, to make a ten per cent reduction in the compensation of substantially all its employees of whatever kind and character, and announced such proposed reduction in wages as effective on May 1, 1927. The railway desired a change in the contract. The Amalgamated Association objected to said reduction and demanded arbitration. To this the railroad company acceded, and arbitrators were appointed by the respective parties, pursuant to article XII of the agreement. The two arbitrators, however, were unable to agree upon a third. Thereupon, application was made to the Special Term by the railroad company for the appointment of the third arbitrator or umpire, pursuant to section 4 of the Arbitration Law.

Attention is immediately directed to the fact that no dispute has arisen between the parties to the contract over the terms or provisions of the contract, or any difficulty arising thereunder. The men have been paid the wages agreed upon, and they have worked for and accepted those wages. The railroad company desires to make a new contract. It desires to reduce wages ten per cent and seeks arbitration under the Arbitration Law for the purpose of arriving at new terms and agreements as to the rate of wages. No power exists in the courts to make contracts for people. They must make their own contracts. The courts reach their limit of power when they enforce contracts which parties have made. A contract that the court shall determine what an agreement shall be for the future is unenforcible, unless the lines of the agreement have been laid out by the parties. The most a court may do is to determine some incidental fact, as for example the reasonable value of property or services, and thereupon enforce the agreement, by judgment for damages, if not specifically, with such value written into it. Such is not the nature of the question that has been left open for decision here. The rate of wages to be fixed is not the fair or market value, the value measured by an objective standard, as in action on a *quantum meruit,* but such compromise value as may be chosen as a substitute. Indeed the contract is not limited to a change in the rate of wages, but extends to any provision that has become distasteful to one or other of the parties. Whenever one or other desires a change in some respect and agreement is impossible, there may be a reference to third parties who are to say what the agreement ought to be. Arbitrators under the Arbitration Law deal with the same kinds of controversies that are dealt with by the courts. This was decided in Matter of Fletcher (237 N.Y. 440). The controversy between this employer and its men is not of such an order. Whether or not it is possible for the Legislature to provide for the arbitration of such differences hereafter, fixing the rate of wages which an employer ought to pay, is not the question we are called upon to decide. Arbitration upon these matters has been attempted to a certain extent by Congress in dealing with interstate commerce. (U.S. Compiled Statutes, 1916, Annotated, No. 8, §§ 8666–8676.) Conceivably the class of justiciable controversies may be enlarged by legislation. The arbitration statute now in force is confined to controversies that are justiciable under the law as it exists today.

No power is given to the courts to change or modify existing contracts or to make new ones for the parties.

The order of the Appellate Division should, therefore, be reversed and the petition dismissed, with costs in all courts.

POUND, J. (dissenting). We have a "written contract" and a provision therein "to settle by arbitration a controversy arising between the parties to the contract." We have such a controversy. The agreement to arbitrate is a valid one under the language of Arbitration Law, § 2.

The decision of Matter of Fletcher (237 N.Y. 440) is not controlling. While the language of the opinion may be unnecessarily broad for general application, the decision rests wholly on the distinction between a valuation and an arbitration. The agreement for valuation was inserted in the contract in that case to prevent a controversy, not to settle one. The distinction is pointed out by ESHER, M. R., in Matter of Carus-Wilson and Greene (18 Q. B. D. 7, at p. 9) as follows:

> If it appears from the terms of the agreement by which a matter is submitted to a person's decision, that the intention of the parties was that he should hold an enquiry in the nature of a judicial enquiry, and hear the respective cases of the parties, and decide upon evidence laid before him, then the case is one of an arbitration. The intention in such cases is that there shall be a judicial enquiry worked out in a judicial manner. On the other hand, there are cases in which a person is appointed to ascertain some matter for the purpose of preventing differences from arising, not of settling them when they have arisen, and where the case is not one of arbitration but of a mere valuation. There may be cases of an intermediate kind, where, though a person is appointed to settle disputes that have arisen, still it is not intended that he shall be bound to hear evidence or arguments. In such cases it may be often difficult to say whether he is intended to be an arbitrator or to exercise some function other than that of an arbitrator. Such cases must be determined each according to its particular circumstances.

The arbitrators in this case are to proceed judicially and reach a determination based on evidence. The controversy is made arbitrable by the agreement of the parties. It is not a compulsory arbitration. The court makes no contract for the parties. It enforces one already in existence. The court should enforce true arbitration contracts rather than permit the parties to disregard them.

It by no means follows that the findings of the arbitrators may be enforced by the court by the remedy of specific performance. No man may be compelled to work for another or to continue another in his employment. I hold merely that industrial disputes as to future wages may be submitted to arbitration where the parties so agree. The incapacity of a court of law to effectuate justice by enforcing the agreements of parties should not be readily admitted. The court should be keen to enable the parties to ascertain their rights in the mode prescribed by them for that purpose.

The order should be affirmed, with costs.

CARDOZO, CH. J., LEHMAN, KELLOGG and O'BRIEN, JJ., concur with CRANE, J.; POUND, J., dissents in opinion; HUBBS, J., not sitting.

Order reversed, etc.

In Matter of Burkin (Katz), 1 N.Y. 2d 570, 136 N.E. 2d 862 (1956), the Court of Appeals reversed an order refusing a stay of arbitration where the ouster of a minority stockholder was sought in the arbitration proceeding. No action had been taken by the stockholders because their agreements required unanimous stockholder action on all questions. The removal thus could not be "the subject of an action" and was therefore, under CPA § 1448, not a subject for arbitration under the statute. The CPLR omits the justiciability requirement, however, thereby making enforceable arbitration available in a wide variety of intracorporate disputes.

For discussions of procedures and problems in arbitration of internal problems of closely held corporations, consult Kessler, *Arbitration of Intra-Corporate Disputes under New York Laws,* 19 ARB. J. 1 (1964); Hornstein, *Arbitration in Incorporated Partnerships,* 18 ARB. J. 229 (1963); Note, *Arbitration as a Means of Settling Disputes Within Close Corporations,* 63 COLUM. L. REV. 267 (1963).

AMALGAMATED ASS'N, ETC. v. SOUTHERN BUS LINE
189 F. 2d 219 (5th Cir. 1951)

Before HUTCHESON, CHIEF JUDGE, and McCORD and BORAH, CIRCUIT JUDGES.

BORAH, CIRCUIT JUDGE. The plaintiffs-appellants, Amalgamated Association of Street, Electric Railway and Motor Coach Employees of America, Division No. 1127, a labor organization, brought this action for the benefit of the plaintiff R. E. Harper, and all other union members and employees of defendant Southern Bus Lines, Inc., who are similarly situated, to compel the defendant-appellee to arbitrate proposed changes in an alleged existing contract of employment. The appellee moved to dismiss the complaint for want of jurisdiction and for failure to state a claim upon which relief could be granted. The District Court held that the allegations in the complaint did not state a ground for relief, and from the ensuing judgment of dismissal, this appeal was taken.

While the assignments of error relate to the court's dismissal of the case on the merits, the question of jurisdiction has been raised in argument and must be first considered.

As grounds for jurisdiction, the complaint alleges that

> this suit is based upon facts arising out of Interstate Commerce and under a contract between the plaintiffs and the defendant involving interstate transportation and, therefore comes within the provisions of the statutes of the United States of America governing the interstate transportation of passengers, freight and other commodities, and is controlled by the laws of the United States and the contract hereinafter referred to which was made pursuant to the obligations of all of the parties to contract for the interstate transportation above referred to.

The complaint then alleges that the Union, acting for and on behalf of its members, entered into a contract with the defendant effective May 16, 1947; that under the terms of the agreement if modification or termination of the contract was desired, it was the duty of either party to give notice in writing to the opposite party of that desire at least thirty days prior to May 16, 1947, the expiration date of the original year of the contract; that on the 14th day of April, 1947, the plaintiffs gave proper notice to the defendant of their desire to have certain modifications made in the contract[1] and the defendant countered with a like proposal; that plaintiffs and the defendant negotiated for many days on the subject of the modifications of the existing contract and when it became apparent that no agreement could be reached, the plaintiffs demanded arbitration of the issues, in conformity with the contract, but the defendant refused and still refuses to accede to this request and because of this consistent refusal plaintiffs are entitled to a mandatory injunction, requiring the defendant to arbitrate with the plaintiffs all issues between them.

Upon the allegations of the complaint, we think it clear that the court below did not have jurisdiction over this controversy. No facts are alleged upon which the conclusion can legitimately be based that the District Court independently of the arbitration agreement would have jurisdiction of the "subject matter of a suit arising out of the controversy between the parties" as required by Section 4 of the Federal Arbitration Act, 9 U.S.C.A. § 4.[2] Agostini Bros. Building Corporation v. United States, 4 Cir., 142 F. 2d 854, 857. No allegation is made that the amount in controversy exceeds $3,000, and more important, the complaint admits that there is no diversity of citizenship between the parties. The litigation therefore is halted at the threshold by the lack of facts which open the door to federal litigation unless there are to be found in the complaint sufficient allegations to disclose that the controversy is one which arises "under the Constitution, laws or treaties of the United States," Title 28, § 1331, U.S.C.A., and "the matter in controversy exceeds the sum or value of $3,000."

Nowhere in the complaint is it alleged that any provision of the federal constitution or a federal treaty or a law of the United States is involved. Nor is it alleged that there is a substantial dispute between the parties respecting the validity, construction or effect of some law of the United States, upon the determination of which the result depends.

"It is not enough that grounds of jurisdiction other than diverse citizenship may be inferred argumentatively from the statements in the bill, for jurisdiction cannot rest on any ground that is not affirmatively and distinctly set forth." Shulthis v. McDougal, 225 U.S. 561, 569, 32 S.Ct. 704, 706, 56 L.Ed. 1205. The question of jurisdiction must be determined from the face of the complaint. City Railway Co. v. Citizens' Street Ry. Co., 166 U.S. 557, 17 S.Ct. 653, 41 L.Ed 1114; Cuyahoga-River Power Co. v. City of Akron, 240 U.S. 462, 36 S.Ct. 402, 60 L.Ed. 743. The jurisdiction of a federal court is never to be presumed, but must be made to affirmatively appear. Grace v. American Central Ins. Co., 109 U.S. 278, 283, 3 S.Ct. 207, 27 L.Ed. 932; Neel v. Pennsylvania Co., 157 U.S. 153, 15 S.Ct. 589, 39 L.Ed. 654.

> A suit to enforce a right which takes its origin in the laws of the United States is not necessarily, or for that reason alone, one arising under those laws, for a suit does not so arise unless it really and substantially involves a dispute or controversy respecting the validity, construction, or effect of such a law, upon the determination of which the result depends.

---

1. These changes were over forty in number, and among other things requested the establishment of a pension plan by the defendant, the establishment of a sick leave plan, liberalized vacations and wage increases.

2. Appellants contend that the Federal Arbitration Act, 9 U.S.C.A. § 1 et seq., is controlling.

Shulthis v. McDougal, *supra*.

In Gully v. First National Bank, 299 U.S. 109, 112, 57 S.Ct. 96, 97, 81 L.Ed. 70, the Supreme Court re-affirmed the same doctrine and speaking through Mr. Justice Cardozo said

> How and when a case arises "under the Constitution or laws of the United States" has been much considered in the books. Some tests are well established. To bring a case within the statute, a right or immunity created by the Constitution or laws of the United States must be an element, and an essential one, of the plaintiff's cause of action. Starin v. [City of] New York, 115 U.S. 248, 257, 6 S.Ct. 28, 29 L.Ed. 388; First National Bank [of Canton, Pa.] v. Williams, 252 U.S. 504, 512, 40 S.Ct. 372, 374, 64 L.Ed. 690. The right or immunity must be such that it will be supported if the Constitution or laws of the United States are given one construction or effect, and defeated if they receive another. Id.; King County [Wash.] v. Seattle School District, 263 U.S. 361, 363, 364, 44 S.Ct. 127, 128, 68 L.Ed. 339.

Viewing the case at bar against this background of established principle, we do not find in it the elements of federal jurisdiction. What is here involved is merely a controversy between the parties as to the construction of a contract which allegedly arises out of the laws of the United States respecting collective bargains between employer and employees in interstate commerce; but the right of action asserted does not arise out of those laws but only arises from the subsequent contractual relations of the parties. The wrongful breach of such relations does not confer federal court jurisdiction unless there is diverse citizenship. Barnhart v. Western Maryland Ry. Co., 4 Cir., 128 F. 2d 709.

Since the court was without jurisdiction, it is unnecessary to consider whether the complaint states a claim upon which relief could be granted The judgment of the District Court is vacated and set aside and the case is remanded to that court with instructions to dismiss for want of jurisdiction.

Also consult Greenwich Marine, Inc. v. S.S. Alexandra, (2d Cir. 1965) 339 F. 2d 901. Particular attention should be paid to note 1 at 904.

SHEETS v. SHEETS
22 A.D. 2d 176, 254 N.Y.S. 2d 320
(1st Dep't 1964)

APPEAL from an order of the Supreme Court at Special Term (Frederick Backer, J.), entered April 6, 1964 in New York County, which granted a motion by plaintiff for an order staying arbitration of paragraphs 3, 4 and 5 of defendant's amended demand for arbitration.

VALENTE, J. This appeal presents the question as to what extent parties to a separation agreement may effectively contract for arbitration of disputes concerning the beneficial interests of the children of the marriage.

The parties entered into a separation agreement in January, 1962. Thereafter, the wife took up residence in Florida, where she obtained a decree of divorce approving the separation agreement. Paragraph 3 of that agreement provided that the wife shall have custody of the children and control and supervision of their upbringing, subject to specified visitation rights to the husband. It also provided for consultation by the wife with the husband on all matters of importance relating to the children's health, welfare and education, for notification to the husband in the event of serious injury or illness to any child, and for the encouragement of respect and love for both parents.

Insofar as is pertinent at this time, the agreement provided that "[i]f the parties cannot reach an agreement as to any matter within the scope of Paragraph 3 ... the dispute shall be settled by arbitration in accordance with the Rules of the American Arbitration Association."

The husband served a demand for arbitration seeking, among other things, damages for violation of the agreement with respect to visitation, with respect to the secular and religious education of the children, and as to a claimed alienation of the children's affection for their father. The husband has appealed from an order staying arbitration of such demands.

It is now settled law in this State that provisions in separation agreements for the arbitration of disputes regarding the amount the husband is to pay for the support of the wife and children will be enforced. (Matter of Robinson, 296 N.Y. 778; Matter of Luttinger, 294 N.Y. 855; Matter of Lasek, 13 A. D. 2d 242.) But it has been held that there may be no arbitration of a dispute between parents as to rights of visitation (Matter of Michelman [Michelman], 5 Misc. 2d 570) or as to custody and visitation (Matter of Hill [Hill], 199 Misc. 1035).

Yet, there seems to be no clear and valid reason why the arbitration process should not be made available in the area of custody and the incidents thereto, *i.e.* choice of schools, summer camps, medical and surgical expenses, trips and vacations. In fact, the American Arbitration Association is now equipped to arbitrate marital disputes arising out of separation agreements.

(Marital Disputes Arbitration [Memorandum, Nov. 1963].) (For a general discussion of the subject, see LINDEY, SEPARATION AGREEMENTS AND ANTE-NUPTIAL CONTRACTS, [Rev. ed., 1961], § 14–29; *Committee Decision of Child Custody, Disputes and the Judicial Test of 'Best Interests,'* 73 YALE L. J., 1201.)

There should be some clarification and re-statement of the proper position to be taken by courts as to arbitration provisions in separation agreements which affect matters of custody and visitation of children. Courts will, as a general rule, enforce an agreement between a husband and wife regarding custody of children so long as the agreement is in the best interests and welfare of the children. The inherent power of the courts to safeguard the welfare of children would not, however, be dissipated by a separation agreement that provided for settlement of custody disputes and related matters by some arbitration tribunal. Necessarily, an award rendered upon a voluntary submission of any such disputes to arbitration would still be subject, in a direct proceeding affecting the child alone, to the supervisory power of the court in its capacity as *parens patriae* to the child. (Finlay v. Finlay, 240 N.Y. 429; People ex rel. Herzog v. Morgan, 287 N.Y. 317.)

To the extent that such an award conflicted with the best interests of the child, courts would treat it as a nullity insofar as the child is concerned, irrespective of what binding effect it may have on the parents. An arbitration award under such circumstances could no more infringe the paternal duty of the court to guard the child's welfare, than a foreign decree of a court rendered before the child became subject to our courts' jurisdiction. (Matter of Bachman v. Mejias, 1 N.Y. 2d 575; Matter of Hicks v. Bridges, 2 A.D. 2d 335, 339; *cf.* Ford v. Ford, 371 U.S. 187.) The controlling factor would be, as always, what was for the best interests of the child; and the provisions of any award could be challenged in court on that basis at the instance of a parent, a grandparent, an interested relative, or the child himself by a friend. (See 6 WEINSTEIN-KORN-MILLER, N.Y. CIV. PRAC., par. 7002.14.) The challenge might take the form of opposition to confirmation of the award, of a cross application invoking the court's paternal jurisdiction, or an independent summary proceeding.

Thus, the best interest of the child is assured protection by this omnipresent judicial check against arbitration awards in custody matters attaining the unassailable finality of awards in other arbitrations. Nor could any such award in a custody matter be given any *res judicata* con-

sequences against the child, who was not a party to the arbitration. However, such an award would effectively bind the parents of the child to the extent that it settled their disputes, but only insofar as the award did not adversely affect the substantial interest of the child.

Hence, upon any showing that a provision of an award might be adverse to the best interests of a child, the court could take such action that was necessary for the best interest of the child. Once the court's paternal jurisdiction is invoked, it would examine into the matter, *de novo*, and in doing so could utilize the proof adduced before the arbitration tribunal, could call for new proof, or could employ a combination of both. The court could then determine what was necessary for the best interest of the child.

However, the award could not be effectively attacked by a dissatisfied parent merely because it affected the child. Obviously every such award will have that effect. What must be shown to evoke judicial intervention is that the award adversely affects the welfare and best interest of the child—clearly a much narrower issue. Thus, for example, an award might provide (1) that a father have visitation rights on one particular day of the week instead of another day; (2) that the child wear clothes purchased from some high-priced tailoring establishment rather than another in a lower-price range; (3) that the child should be accompanied to school by a parent or governess; (4) that the child should have no, or a particular, religious training; or (5) that the child go to a summer camp in the mountains rather than one located at sea level. For our purpose, these examples, which could be multiplied indefinitely, will suffice to clarify the distinction sought to be drawn.

All of the above situations present determinations which affect the child; yet the only one which could be deemed to have an adverse effect is the one dealing with religious training. It might be that the provision regarding the proper camp to attend would also fall into the category of adverse effects if it were shown that a summer camp at a high altitude would be inimical to the child's health. An arbitration award which purported to adjudicate the latter two items could successfully be attacked in court, as hereinabove indicated, by opposition to a motion to confirm the award or by an independent proceeding. However, as to the other examples, a court could confirm the award upon the theory that while they affected the child they could not reasonably be deemed to have any substantial effect on the child's best interest and welfare.

Since only with the coming in of an arbitration

award can the court initially rule on the question as to whether any direction adversely affects the best interest and welfare of the child, it would seem that on any application to stay an arbitration demanded by a parent or to compel arbitration, the court would be concerned, at that preliminary stage, only with whether the agreement between the parties provided for arbitration of the dispute.

With these caveats, submission of disputes in custody and visitation matters to voluntary arbitration need no longer receive general interdiction, and such procedure should be encouraged as a sound and practical method for resolving such disputes. But as indicated hereinabove, arbitration awards which may adversely affect the best interest of the child will be disregarded by the courts whose paternal jurisdiction is paramount. As a consequence, there may in certain instances be a duplication in effort, where the court decides to look into the matter *de novo* and reaches the same or different result.

The general discussion has been prompted by the fact that the separation agreement, *sub judice*, contains a broad provision for arbitration of disputes as to control, supervision and upbringing of children, visitation rights and of the general welfare of the children. While we hold that the demands for arbitration before us do not fall within the scope of the arbitration provision—broad as it is—we do not want to foreclose the parties from seeking arbitration upon proper demands consistent with this opinion.

The demands of the appellant husband do not fall within the purview of the arbitration provision. The husband does not seek to remedy any alleged grievances claimed to be in violation of the agreement, but seeks money damages which are to be set off against his obligation to pay alimony under the agreement. There is nothing in the separation agreement which can reasonably be construed as obligating either party to submit to arbitration the matter of assessment of punitive damages for a violation of any of the provisions of paragraph 3 of the agreement.

The arbitration clause in issue is not an agreement to arbitrate any dispute under the contract. In commercial cases it has been held that an agreement to arbitrate all controversies under the contract confers jurisdiction on arbitrators to assess damages. (Matter of Utility Laundry Serv. [SKLAR], 300 N.Y. 255 ; Matter of General Footwear Co. v. Lawrence Leather Co., 252 N.Y. 577.) The intent of the parties is the governing consideration. Here the arbitration clause merely provides for the settlement of the dispute "[i]f the parties cannot reach an agreement as to any matter within the scope of Paragraph 3." Since paragraph 3 is concerned only with the custody, visitation rights and other matters affecting the welfare of the children, there could be no warrant, were arbitration permissible, for any award of punitive damages for failure to comply with the agreement. Therefore, apart from any conclusion as to whether there may be arbitration as to the matters affecting the custody and welfare of the children, we would have, in any event, stayed the demanded arbitration as not within the scope of the arbitration clause.

The order should, therefore, be affirmed, without costs and without prejudice to the service of a proper demand for arbitration as to any disputes, consonant with this opinion.

BOTEIN, P. J., BREITEL and RABIN, JJ., concur ; McNALLY, J., concurs in result.

For a discussion putting the case into context consult Note, *Domestic Relations—New York Court Approves of Arbitration in Custody Disputes,* 33 FORDHAM L. REV. 726 (1965). For a thoughtful and informed discussion of methods of deciding custody problems, see Kubie, *Provisions for the Care of Children of Divorced Parents: A New Legal Instrument,* 73 YALE L. J. 1197 (1964). What Dr. Kubie recommends is not the equivalent of arbitration, although some have interpreted his proposals as such an equivalent.

It is, of course, the multiple *dictum* of Sheets v. Sheets that is of interest. One can readily see some advantages to arbitration of custody and similar problems of children when their parents fall out. The court does not say explicitly that it would give the arbitrator's award any weight when it was not binding. In any event, privacy, informal procedure—sparing children court appearances and possible cross-examination—and an informed, sensitive, and skillful dispute-decider all make arbitration attractive. Moreover, the parents can select an arbitrator who generally shares their cultural pattern and standards, whereas judges may have religious, ethnic, social, and financial backgrounds and criteria for evaluating conduct that differ decidedly from those of the parents.

Whereas under the Civil Practice Act provisions a nonlabor dispute had to be justiciable in order to be arbitrable, the CPLR omission of such a requirement, opens up a considerable range of "domestic relations" disputes to arbitration.

B.

Tenability of the Claim

ALPERT v. ADMIRATION KNITWEAR CO.
304 N.Y. 1, 105 N.E. 2d 561 (1952)

LEWIS, J. We are to determine whether in the commercial transaction which gave rise to this proceeding there remains between the parties an arbitrable dispute. That question is one of law. (Matter of General Elec. Co. [United Elec. Radio & Mach. Workers], 300 N.Y. 262, 264.)

On May 12, 1950, the petitioners-respondents—to whom reference will be made as the purchasers—entered into a written contract for the purchase by them from the appellant—the seller—of a quantity of woolen material. The fact is of some importance that in preparing the written contract to contain a recital of terms upon which agreement had been reached, the purchasers chose one of their own contract forms formerly used by them in transactions where they were sellers. The adaptation was accomplished by one of the purchasers, who struck from the form their name as sellers and in place thereof wrote in the name of the appellant. It is thus made clear that, by adapting one of their own contract forms to the requirements of the agreement here involved, the purchasers were fully aware of the terms thereof and the purpose to be served thereby. It was also noted on the front of the agreement that the sale was to be F.O.B. at Philadelphia and that shipment was to be "at once."

Over the signatures of the two parties, which appear on the front of the single sheet upon which the contract was written, there was printed the following:

THE CONDITIONS OF SALE PRINTED ON THE BACK HEREOF ARE HEREBY MADE PART OF THIS CONTRACT.

The undersigned hereby orders the above goods upon terms as stated, including the terms and conditions printed on the back of this contract and forming a part hereof.

On the back of the contract were printed fifteen "CONDITIONS OF SALE", among which is the following:

2. . . . if *at any time, in the sole opinion of the Seller*, the financial responsibility of the Purchaser shall become impaired *or unsatisfactory to the Seller* cash payments in advance of delivery may be required. Upon failure to pay any amount due to the Seller under this . . . contract, the Seller may at its option

terminate this contract . . . as to further deliveries, *and no forbearance or course of dealings shall affect this right of the seller.* (Emphasis supplied.)

Exercising the arbitrary right which the parties to the transaction, by their written agreement, had seen fit to accord to the seller, the following letter was sent to the purchasers by the seller under date of June 8, 1950:

ADMIRATION KNITWEAR CO., INC.
347–5th Avenue
New York 16, New York
June 8th, 1950

Z. Alpert & Sons
220–4th Avenue
New York 3, New York
Gentlemen:

In reference to our contract of May 12th, 1950 it is my opinion that your financial responsibility is unsatisfactory under all the circumstances of this sale.

I am therefore demanding that you pay in advance of any shipment of the woolens that may come from Philadelphia. Will you kindly contact me immediately relative to a disposition of this matter as I am ready, willing and able to deliver the goods upon payment.

Unless I hear from you relative to these arrangements on or before June 16th, 1950, I shall deem the contract abandoned and will proceed to dispose of the goods in other channels.

Yours very truly,
(signed) DAVID SCHWARTZ
DAVID SCHWARTZ
President

Following failure by the purchasers to comply with the seller's letter demanding cash payment in advance of shipment, the purchasers applied at Special Term for an order directing that the controversy, thus created between them and the seller, proceed to arbitration under the following "condition" in their contract:

8. Any complaint, controversy or question which may arise with respect to this contract that cannot be settled by the parties thereto, shall be referred to arbitration in the following manner: . . .

(b) All other controversies arising out of or relating to this contract, or breach thereof, shall be settled by arbitration in accordance with the Rules, then obtaining of the American Arbitration Association, and judgment upon the award rendered may be entered in the highest court of the forum, State or Federal, having jurisdiction.

At Special Term the order for which the purchasers applied was denied. At the Appellate Division the order of Special Term was reversed —two Justices dissenting—and an order was granted in accord with the purchasers' original application. The case comes to us upon the seller's appeal taken as of right.

We read the decisive "condition" numbered "2" of the contract (quoted *supra*) as a plain provision whereby the purchasers gave to the seller the absolute right to require "cash payments in advance of delivery" whenever, in its "sole opinion," the financial responsibility of the purchasers became "impaired or unsatisfactory to the Seller." In the exercise of that contract right the record shows that the seller, by its letter of June 8, 1950—concededly received by the purchasers—demanded payment in advance of any shipment, the ground of such demand being that in the seller's opinion the financial responsibility of the purchasers was unsatisfactory. Such letter also gave notice to the purchasers that the seller was then "ready, willing and able" to make delivery of the goods upon advance payment therefor ; that the purchasers would have eight days within which to arrange for such payment, and that upon a failure by the purchasers within that time to comply with the seller's demand, the contract would be deemed abandoned and the seller would make other disposition of the woolens.

Concluding, as we do, that the seller's demand and notice to the purchaser, contained in its letter of June 8, 1950, was in accord with its right expressly provided by the contract, we think the case falls within the rule stated in Matter of General Elec. Co. (United Elec. Radio & Mach. Workers) (300 N.Y. 262, 264, *supra*):

> If, under the unambiguous terms of an agreement calling for arbitration, there has been no default, the court may not make an order compelling a party to proceed to arbitration (Matter of International Assn. of Machinists [Cutler-Hammer, Inc.], 271 App. Div. 917, affd. 297 N.Y. 519). Whether or not a bonafide dispute exists is a question of law (Matter of Wenger & Co. v. Propper Silk Hosiery Mills, 239 N.Y. 199, 202–203). If there is no real ground of claim, the court may refuse to allow arbitration, although the alleged dispute may fall within the literal language of the arbitration agreement.

The record before us does not support the suggestion that, in view of the contract phrase "ship at once," the seller was in default on June 8, 1950, by reason of nondelivery. From a provision in the contract giving the seller an option of one week to repurchase, the inference may fairly be drawn that delivery would not be made before the expiration of that option. We also are informed by the reply affidavit filed at Special Term by the purchasers in support of their application, that in "the first part of June, I [Leon Alpert] ... asked him [the seller's president] to . . . ship the merchandise. . . ." It thus appears that early in June the buyer still desired the seller to perform its obligation under the contract. In other words, the purchasers did not at that time—"the first part of June"— consider the seller in default, nor had they elected to cancel the contract for that reason. As we have seen it was shortly thereafter—on June 8, 1950, still in the "first part of June"— that the seller made his demand under the contract for payment in advance of delivery, with which the purchasers have failed to comply. In those circumstances, there is no support for the suggestion that the seller had breached the contract by its failure to deliver. On the contrary it was the purchasers' failure to tender payment —properly requested by the seller pursuant to the terms of the contract—which has resulted in the termination of the contract.

The assertion in the purchasers' reply affidavit that their financial rating in the field of commerce is "a good safe credit risk" has not escaped our attention. It is, however, in our view, irrelevant in the light of the unequivocal language in the contract by which the purchasers gave the seller the absolute right "*at any time*" to require cash payment in advance of delivery of the woolens if "*in the sole opinion of the Seller,* the financial responsibility of the Purchaser shall become ... *unsatisfactory to the Seller.*" (Emphasis supplied.)

Absent any showing of a tender by the purchasers pursuant to the seller's demand, no conclusion is warranted by the record before us other than that, after June 16, 1950, the contract no longer was in existence. Accordingly, we agree with the court at Special Term that no issue remained which properly could be submitted for decision to arbitrators. (Matter of Kramer & Uchitelle, Inc., 288 N.Y. 467, 471 ; Matter of General Elec. Co. [United Elec. Radio & Mach. Workers], *supra* ; and see Matter of International Assn. of Machinists [Cutler-Hammer, Inc.], 297 N.Y. 519.)

The order of the Appellate Division should be reversed and that of Special Term affirmed, with costs in this court and in the Appellate Division.

LOUGHRAN, CH. J., CONWAY, DYE, FULD and FROESSEL, JJ., concur with LEWIS, J. ; DESMOND, J., dissents for the reasons stated by the Appellate Division in its memorandum decision here, as amplified by its reference to the present case in Matter of Minkin (Halperin) (279 App. Div. 226, 230, 231).

Ordered accordingly.

The Appellate Division's memorandum was not revealing. In another case, however, the following explanation of the majority's view was set forth before the Court of Appeals reversed it.

MATTER OF MINKIN (HALPERIN)
279 App. Div. 226, 230, 108 N.Y.S. 2d 945, 949 (1951)

Nor is Alpert v. Admiration Knitwear Co. (278 App. Div. 841), cited by respondent, helpful. That case concerned a contract for the sale of goods. The contract contained an arbitration clause and also a provision that, "if at any time, in the sole opinion of the Seller, the financial responsibility of the Purchaser shall become impaired or unsatisfactory to the Seller cash payments in advance of delivery may be required," and "Upon failure to pay any amount due to the Seller," it may at its option terminate the contract. The seller demanded payment in advance of delivery, but the buyer refused to comply with the demand. The seller terminated the contract and refused to deliver the goods. The buyer moved to compel arbitration. The seller opposed the application on the ground that the contract had been terminated (not as in the instant case by mutual agreement of the parties but solely by the seller) and, therefore, there was no longer in existence any binding contract to arbitrate. By a divided court we held that the application for arbitration should be granted because there was an issue as to whether the parties intended that the seller should have the right to cancel the contract even if the demand for the advance cash payment were not made in good faith, and if the parties intended that the demand was required to be made in good faith, whether or not the demand by the seller was so made. In that case there also was an issue as to whether the seller had breached the contract before demanding the cash advance payment, it appearing that the contract was made on May 12, 1950, and required delivery of the goods "at once," whereas the demand for the cash advance payment was not made until June 8, 1950, after the buyer had demanded delivery of the goods or that the matter be submitted to arbitration.

INTERNATIONAL ASS'N OF MACHINISTS
v. CUTLER-HAMMER, INC.
271 App. Div. 917, 67 N.Y.S. 2d 317
(First Dept. 1947)

PER CURIAM. The clause of the agreement that "The Company agrees to meet with the Union early in July 1946 to discuss payment of a bonus for the first six months of 1946" can only mean what it says, that the parties will *discuss* the subject. While the contract provides for arbitration of disputes as to the "meaning, performance, non-performance or application" of its provisions, the mere assertion by a party of a meaning of a provision which is clearly contrary to the plain meaning of the words cannot make an arbitrable issue. It is for the court to determine whether the contract contains a provision for arbitration of the dispute tendered, and in the exercise of that jurisdiction the court must determine whether there is such a dispute. If the meaning of the provision of the contract sought to be arbitrated is beyond dispute, there cannot be anything to arbitrate and the contract cannot be said to provide for arbitration.

The union does not contend that a discussion was not had here. It admits that there was a discussion as to *whether* a bonus should be paid, but takes the position that the contract provision meant that a bonus must be paid and that all there was to discuss was the amount of the bonus to be paid. Logically, the union then contends that in the absence of an agreement between the parties as to the amount of the bonus to be paid, the arbitrator shall determine the amount. In the last analysis that is what the union seeks and is the ultimate result of accepting the union's interpretation of the contract. The case, altogether frankly and fairly, has been presented in its actualities rather than in any academic aspects. The union does not seek any further discussion, but the payment of a bonus under an interpretation of the contract which would require a payment rather than discussion of a payment and permit the arbitrator to order a payment in an amount to be determined by him. Unless the contract can possibly mean what the union contends for, there is no occasion for arbitration.

In the union's view the bonus was an integral part of the wage, but clearly the parties never submitted the amount of wages to arbitration, nor did they submit the amount of a bonus to arbitration. All the bonus provision meant was that the parties would discuss the payment of a bonus. It did not mean that they had to agree on a bonus or that failing to agree an arbitrator would agree for them. Nor did it mean that a bonus must be paid and only the amount was open for discussion. So clear is this and so untenable any other interpretation that we are obliged to hold that there is no dispute as to meaning of the bonus provision and no contract to arbitrate the issue tendered.

The order appealed from should be reversed, with $20 costs and disbursements, and the motion of petitioner-respondent to compel arbitration denied and the motion of appellant for a stay of arbitration granted.

DORE, J. (dissenting). The parties expressly agreed to arbitrate *any* dispute as to the meaning of "performance, non-performance or application" of the contract provisions. On this appeal there are presented at least preliminary questions as to (1) the meaning of the clause in question, and (2) performance by the company. The union claims that no "discussion" was had but only an announcement made by the company.

At this state we need not pass upon other issues.

Accordingly, I dissent and vote to affirm.

MARTIN, P. J., GLENNON, CALLAHAN and PECK, JJ., concur in PER CURIAM opinion; DORE, J. dissents in opinion.

Order reversed, with $20 costs and disbursements to the appellant, the motion to compel arbitration denied and the motion for a stay of arbitration granted.

Settle order on notice.

Affirmed, PER CURIAM, 297 N.Y. 519, 74 N.E. 2d 464 (1947).

B. FERNANDEZ & HNOS, S. EN C. v. RICKERT RICE MILLS, INC.
119 F. 2d 809 (1941)

The seller shipped certain rice by steamer November 4, 1940, which duly arrived in San Juan. Immediately after the discharge of the rice from the ship it was examined by the buyer. The latter thereupon notified the seller in writing that it refused to accept or pay for the rice which had been shipped because it was "Fancy Japan" rice and not "Extra Fancy Japan" rice as had been ordered, and that therefore it was not bound to accept and pay for it. The certificate of the Rice Millers' Association which was furnished by the seller pursuant to the contract showed the grade of the rice shipped to be "Fancy Japan Milled Rice" which is a grade inferior to "Extra Fancy Japan" rice.

The seller maintained that even though the Rice Millers' Association certificate showed the rice shipped to be of an inferior grade or quality, the buyer was required by the contract to submit to arbitration the question of the difference in value between the rice ordered and that shipped. If the difference were one-fifth of a cent per pound or less, the seller claimed that the buyer had to accept it at the allowance made. On the other hand, the buyer insisted that the contract made the certificate of the Rice Millers' Association conclusive and that the contract did not require it to submit the question of difference in value to arbitration or to accept an inferior grade of goods at an allowance when the shipment was accompanied by a Rice Millers' Association certificate. Therefore, the buyer steadfastly refused to accept the goods or to request arbitration, claiming that there was nothing to arbitrate.

The seller then submitted to the Arbitration Committee of the Chamber of Commerce at San Juan the question whether the matter in dispute between the parties was a controversy which they were bound to arbitrate. The buyer did not submit to the arbitration but objected in writing before the Committee that there was no question in controversy to be determined by the Committee under the terms and conditions of the contract. The Committee considered the matter on the seller's petition and the buyer's objections and decided that there was a controversy between the parties which they had agreed to arbitrate not only in accordance with the rules and regulations of the Chamber of Commerce, of which they were both members, but also according to the signed contract.

> " 'Art. No. 1 Chapt. No. 1 of our Rules and Regulations concerning arbitration, under title "Arbitration" reads:
> " ' " * * * All members of the Chamber of Commerce of P.R. promise to solicit and accept arbitration on any question or dispute that may come up between them."
> " 'Also on reverse side of the contract, clause (D), says as follows:
> " '(D) Arbitration, both buyer and seller hereby agree to submit all questions of quality, complaints and/or controversies that may arise out of or in conection with this contract, in the following manner: (here follows details).
> " 'It is the opinion of this Committee, that beyond any doubt there is a controversy between these two members. And that both parties have agreed to arbitrate, not only according with the Rules and Regulations of our Chamber of Commerce but also according with the signed contract. The fact that one party or the other party believes he is right in his contention does not mean that there is not a controversy between them. In all controversies one of the parties is right and the other not.' "

It is now well settled that the question of the

construction of a contract to determine what questions the parties thereto agreed to submit to arbitration is one for the court to decide and not for the arbitrators. Lehigh Coal & Navigation Co. v. Central R. of New Jersey, D.C.E.D. Pa. 1940, 33 F. Supp. 362, 367; Pumphrey v. Pumphrey, 1937, 172 Md. 323, 191 A. 235; Bullard v. Morgan H. Grace Co., 1925, 240 N.Y. 388, 148 N.E. 559 (1926) 35 YALE L. J. 369; In re Kelley, 1925, 240 N.Y. 74, 147 N.E. 363; Walker v. Walker, 1864, 60 N.C. 255; Piercy v. Young, 1879, 14 Ch. D. 200; see STURGES, COMMERCIAL ARBITRATIONS AND AWARDS 144-145 (1930); *cf.* Parsell, *Arbitration of Fraud in the Inducement of a Contract,* (1927) 12 CORN. L. Q. 351, 359. To allow the arbitrators conclusively to decide what questions were submitted to arbitration is to allow them finally to determine the extent of their own jurisdiction. If the parties intended that the arbitrators should have the power finally to decide what was to be submitted to them, there is no objection to their doing so, but the courts do not readily infer such an agreement. In re Kelley, *supra;* Piercy v. Young, *supra,* at 208; cf. Willesford v. Watson, [1873] L.R. 8 Ch. App. 473; see STURGES, op. cit.; Baum & Pressman, *The Enforcement of Commercial Arbitration Agreements in the Federal Courts,* (1930) 8 N.Y. U.L.Q. REV. 238, 240. We find nothing to indicate that these parties intended to allow the Arbitration Committee to decide what disputes they had agreed to submit to arbitration.

Paragraph (d) of the contract provides that "Both buyer and seller hereby agree to submit [to arbitration] all questions of quality, complaints, disputes and/or controversies that may arise out of or in connection with this contract, in the following manner:" and also that "Differences in quality and all other differences as regarding the terms of this contract, including time of shipment, shall be arbitrated ..." It is on these clauses that the seller relies. He insists that whether the parties agreed to arbitrate this question is a dispute or controversy arising "out of or in connection with this contract" and is a difference "regarding the terms of this contract" and, therefore, must be submitted to arbitration. In brief, the seller's argument is that these words make it obligatory to submit to arbitration the question whether the parties agreed to submit this particular question to arbitration. We do not believe this was the intention.

A party is never required to submit to arbitration any question which he has not agreed so to submit, and contracts providing for arbitration will be carefully construed in order not to force a party to submit to arbitration a question which he did not intend to be submitted. Pumphrey v. Pumphrey, *supra;* Marchant v. Mead-Morrison Mfg. Co., 1929, 252 N.Y. 284, 299, 169 N.E. 386, 391; Eagar Construction Corp. v. Ward Foundation Corp., 1st Dept. 1938, 255 App. Div. 291, 7 N.Y.S. 2d 450. In view of the reluctance of courts to find that the parties to a contract agreed to submit to arbitrators the question of what they agreed to arbitrate, we do not believe the language here used intended such an agreement. The agreement was to arbitrate "all questions of *quality,* complaints, disputes and/or controversies" and "all other differences as regarding the terms of this contract, *including time of shipment.*" (Italics supplied.) The italicized words tend to show that the questions which the parties intended to submit were questions of the construction of the commercial terms of the contract, such as quality and time of shipment, and not problems of reconciling seemingly inconsistent provisions to decide whether a certain question had been submitted to them. It is probable that the parties never had any intention at all as to whether they wished a court or the arbitrators to decide what questions they had agreed to arbitrate. More likely it was not until the actual situation arose that either one considered the problem. It is impossible to say in such situation that they intended to allow the arbitrators to decide what they had agreed to submit.

ENGINEERS ASS'N v. SPERRY GYROSCOPE CO., ETC.
251 F. 2d 133 (2d Cir. 1957)

Under New York law, the law which would govern this dispute were it not for the power granted the federal courts by Section 301, arbitration will not be compelled unless the party demanding it introduces evidence of the existence of an arbitrable dispute. General Electric Co. v. United Electrical Radio & Machine Workers, 1949, 300 N.Y. 252, 90 N.E. 2d 181; Application of Berger, 1948, 191 Misc. 1043, 78 N.Y.S. 2d 528. The difficulty in the present case, as the court below recognized, is that a determination of the arbitrability of the grievance depends upon the same facts relevant to a decision by an arbitrator upon the merits of the grievance. If the wage increases granted by Sperry were "on a merit basis only," then Sperry has not only not violated the contract, but the present dispute is not arbitrable. If, on the other hand, the increases were granted on the basis of considerations other than merit, Sperry has violated the contract and the dispute is arbitrable. But, merely because there is an identity of issues in the two proceedings, the court is not relieved of its duty to determine whether an arbitrable dispute exists. In construing the provisions of the Federal Arbitration Act, we have stated that after determining that the parties have entered into an arbitration agreement, the duty of the court is to determine "whether any of the issues raised in the suit were within the reach of that agreement." Kulukundis Shipping Co. v. Amtorg Trading Corp., 2 Cir., 1942, 126 F. 2d 978, 988. This duty cannot be adequately performed unless the court examines the facts upon which the demand for arbitration is based as those facts relate to the language of the agreement. See Industrial Trades Union v. Woonsocket Dyeing Co., D.C.R.I. 1954, 122 F. Supp. 872. To make out a case for arbitration, Sperry's alleged breach must be "put in issue by facts, as distinguished from unsupported charges." Application of Berger, *supra*, 78 N.Y.S. 2d at page 532; General Electric Co. v. United Electrical Radio and Machine Workers, *supra*.

It should be observed, however, that even in a case such as the present one, where the same facts are determinative of both arbitrability and the merits of the controversy, an order compelling the parties to submit to arbitration does not impinge upon the power of the arbitrator to decide the merits of the dispute. The difference between the two proceedings is in the quantum of proof necessary for the moving party to obtain relief. In the arbitration hearing, the party seeking relief must fully establish his claim that the opposing party has violated the contract. Determination of arbitrability only requires that the moving party produce evidence which tends to establish his claim. Once the tendency of the evidence to support the claim has been established, it is then the function of the arbitrator to weigh all the evidence and to then determine whether the contract was broken.

I. S. JOSEPH COMPANY v. GOLDE
185 F. Supp. 521 (D.C. Minn. 1960)

DEVITT, C. J. The petitioner Minnesota corporation seeks an order to compel arbitration under the Federal Arbitration Act, 9 U.S.C. § 4 (1958), against the respondent New York partnership in a matter alleged to involve more than $10,000.

The controversy arises from petitioner's contract to sell five thousand tons of sugar beet pulp to respondents. Included as the last provision in the contract was an arbitration clause which provided that arbitration at Minneapolis, Minnesota would be final for both parties "for all discrepancies which might eventually arise from this contract." No delivery was made under the contract and each side contends the other party either repudiated or breached the contract.

The principal issue is whether a contract clause submitting to arbitration "all discrepancies which might eventually arise from this contract" covers a dispute involving repudiation or rescission of the contract before delivery.

The contract of October 16, 1959 provided a detailed description of the goods to be delivered. It also specified three price and delivery options for the respondents. Prior to the contract amendment, respondents were required to notify petitioner before close of business on October 19, 1959 as to their election of one price and delivery option and failure to do so would be a default of contract. On October 19, 1959, this portion of the contract was amended. The deadline for selecting the price and delivery option was deleted but the petitioner would have ten days after receipt of respondents' option election to assemble the merchandise. The contract also provided that the petitioner had the option of requiring payment by sight draft bill of lading or letter of credit valid until November 30, 1959.

On November 4, 1959 petitioner sent the following telegram to respondents:

> Pursuant Our Contract October 16 Subheading Payment As Amended We Elect Establishment By You Of Letter Of Credit As Described Stop To Fix The Amount Of Credit You Must At This Time Provide Us With Shipping Instructions Pursuant To Your Price-shipping Option.

Petitioner on November 12, 1959 sent another telegram to respondents as follows:

> In View Of Your Breech (*sic*) Contract Dated October 16 We Are Commencing Sale For Your Account To Minimize Damages Stop First Indication $31 Short Ton Baltimore Difference For Your Account.

Respondents replied by telegram the next day, November 13, 1959 as follows:

> Shocked Your Arbitrary And High-Handed Conduct In Selling Our Authorization The Beetpulp Contracted For Of October 16th Consider This An Unwarranted Breach On Your Part, And Are Compelled To Disaffirm The Contract For This Reason We Hereby Elect To Rescind The Contract And Consider All Our Obligations Thereunder At An End.

Petitioner contends that respondents breached the contract prior to petitioner's telegram of

November 12 but has not specifically identified the substance of the breach. Apparently the alleged breach involved the failure of respondents to provide a letter of credit. The respondents claim that petitioner repudiated the contract by the November 12 telegram.

The petitioner urges that this dispute as to which party originally repudiated or breached the contract is an arbitrable issue within the meaning of "all discrepancies which might eventually arise from this contract." The respondents assert that the word "discrepancies" does not include this dispute. Respondents also contend that even assuming this dispute to be an arbitrable issue, petitioner can no longer rely on the arbitration clause after its alleged repudiation of the contract.

The first issue is whether this court should interpret the meaning and extent of the arbitration clause. Petitioner relies on a portion of The Federal Arbitration Act, 9 U.S.C. § 4 (1958), in its assertion that the court should not decide this question. A part of that section reads as follows:

> The court shall hear the parties, and upon being satisfied that the making of the agreement for arbitration or the failure to comply therewith is not in issue, the court shall make an order directing the parties to proceed to arbitration in accordance with the terms of the agreement.

Petitioner contends that the interpretation of the arbitration clause should be passed along to the arbitrator because there's no controversy concerning the fact that the arbitration agreement was made and that the respondents refuse to arbitrate.

It is fundamental initially, however, that the court determine whether the parties have agreed to submit a particular dispute to arbitration. Refinery Employees Union of Lake Charles Area v. Continental Oil Company, 5 Cir., 268 F. 2d 447, 451, certiorari denied 1959, 361 U.S. 896, 80 S.Ct. 199, 4 L.Ed. 2d 152 ; Engineers Ass'n v. Sperry Gyroscope Co., 2 Cir., 251 F. 2d 133, 137, certiorari denied 1958, 356 U.S. 932, 78 S.Ct. 774, 2 L.Ed. 2d 762 ; B. Fernandez & Hnos., S. En C. v. Rickert Rice Mills, Inc., 1 Cir., 1941, 119 F. 2d 809, 814, 136 A.L.R. 351. The controlling principle in situations of this kind was stated in Local 205 United Electrical, etc. v. General Electric Company, 1 Cir., 233 F. 2d 85, 101, affirmed 353 U.S. 547, 77 S.Ct. 921, 1 L.Ed. 2d 1028, as follows:

> Arbitrability is a question which the district court must pass on in the first instance. . . . The scope of an arbitration pledge is solely for the parties to set, and thus the determination of whether a particular

dispute is arbitrable is a problem of contract interpretation. . . . However, an arbitration clause, either expressly or by broadly stating its scope to include interpretations of any contract term, may refer the very question of arbitrability to the arbitrator for decision. . . . Thus the district court must first determine whether the contract in suit puts matters of arbitrability to the arbitrator or leaves them for decision by the court.

This court must under the general rule proceed to determine as a matter of law whether the dispute involved herein was covered by the arbitration clause.

The next issue is whether the word "discrepancies" in the arbitration clause means "all disputes" or only those relating to quantity or quality of the goods delivered.

The petitioner urges that dictionary synonyms for the word "discrepancy" are "disagreement" or "difference" and that these words should be substituted into the arbitration clause by interpretation. Petitioner also points to the words "all" and "arising from the contract" and the location of the arbitration clause at the end of the agreement as evidencing an intention to make the clause all-inclusive.

The respondents, on the other hand, attempt to establish a more restrictive meaning of "discrepancy" as a difference arising from a comparison of two things. In view of the detailed requirements in the contract for quality, color, protein content, sugar content, nitrogen content, fat content and packaging, the respondents argue the "discrepancies" naturally refer to any variations between these contract standards and the character of the pulp as actually delivered.

I agree with the respondents' interpretation in the context of this contract, see Barash v. State, 1956, 2 Misc. 2d 686, 154 N.Y.S. 2d 317, 321; State ex rel. Doyle v. Superior Court, 1926, 138 Wash. 488, 244 P. 702, 703 ; In re Barrett, 1924, 209 App. Div. 217, 222, 204 N.Y.S. 705, 709 ; Smith v. Board of Canvassers, 1915, 92 Misc. 607, 611, 156 N.Y.S. 837, 841 ; and conclude that the arbitration clause is restrictive and does not cover a dispute arising prior to performance of the contract. The word "discrepancies" does not indicate clearly the scope of the arbitration clause. Respondents should not be forced to submit to arbitration a dispute they did not intend to submit. Accord, B. Fernandez & Hnos., S. En C. v. Rickert Rice Mills, Inc., 1 Cir., 1941, 119 F. 2d 809, 815, 136 A.L.R. 351.

Having decided that the dispute herein is not within the ambit of the arbitration clause, we need not consider the further problem of whether the petitioner lost or waived its right to proceed under the arbitration clause after repudiating the contract. See generally, 3 A.L.R. 2d 383.

The petition seeking to compel arbitration is denied.

MATTER OF DE LAURENTIIS (CINEMATOGRAFICA DE LAS AMERICAS)
9 N.Y. 2d 503, 174 N.E. 2d 736 (1961)

DESMOND, C. J. We granted petitioner leave to appeal so that we might consider certain problems in the law of arbitration.

In 1957 petitioner De Laurentiis, an Italian producer of motion pictures, respondent Cinematografica, a Panamanian corporation which distributes films, and respondent Enrique Campos Menendez, an author (herein called "Campos"), made a written agreement whereby the three parties covenanted to do what was necessary for the production and distribution of a motion picture to be based on Campos' biography of the South American patriot Bolivar. De Laurentiis, as producer, was to begin photography within 15 months from the date of the writing and was to complete production within 8 months more and was to devote to the enterprise the major part of his time and effort beginning at the date of the agreement. He was required to engage a writer or writers of the first rank to prepare a story outline, a "screen treatment" and thereafter a final scenario. Campos and De Laurentiis were to consult during the preparation of the story outline and scenario. De Laurentiis was to complete a scenario in final form within three months from the date of the agreement and if Cinematografica did not approve that script De Laurentiis was to revise it. De Laurentiis undertook to make all necessary arrangements for financing, for the hiring of actors and a director and for world distribution of the completed picture, all this to be subject to the prior approval of Cinematografica which promised not to withhold such approval unreasonably. Cinematografica made certain other commitments as to financing and distribution. Other provisions required De Laurentiis and Cinematografica to share expenses up to a total of $150,000. Campos was to act as consultant and give his consent to the use of his book for a fee of $75,000. There were in the contract elaborate provisions whereby, if the final scenario should be unacceptable to De Laurentiis, Cinematografica should have the right to take over the whole project by reimbursing De Laurentiis for his expenditures.

Paragraph 14 of the contract required that any dispute arising thereunder should be submitted to arbitration in New York City under the rules and regulations of the American Arbitration Association and the laws of New York State, and in connection thereto each of the parties designated residents of New York City to act as their respective agents for the receipt of process in the State of New York. The motion picture has never been produced and respondents charge that De Laurentiis has never engaged a writer for the scenario or performed any of his other obligations under the agreement. On June 20, 1960 New York City attorneys who had been designated as representatives of respondents sent on their behalf to American Arbitration Association a demand for arbitration of the disputes which had arisen out of the contract between their clients and De Laurentiis and sent a copy of this demand to the agent (Serpe) designated by De Laurentiis.

The letter which demanded arbitration stated that the disputes had arisen from a breach by De Laurentiis of "numerous provisions of the said contract of November 1, 1957, specifically paragraphs 2, 3, 4, 5, 6 and 8 and his resultant breach of other provisions of the contract dependent for their operations on performance of the obligations imposed by the specified paragraphs." The paragraphs so specified describe all the obligations undertaken by petitioner De Laurentiis and so the demand for arbitration (read with respondents' affidavits) charged De Laurentiis with having failed to perform any of the obligations undertaken by him. In the letter of demand, damages of Cinematografica were claimed in a total of $1,105,000 broken down as follows: advanced to De Laurentiis, $75,000; expenditures for travel and other necessary expenses, $85,000; legal expenses, £20,000; loss of business reputation of Cinematografica, $150,000 and loss of its profits, $600,000. Damages of respondent Campos (Menendez) were set forth as: loss of his $75,000 fee as consultant and $100,000 damage to his business and professional reputation.

De Laurentiis responded to this demand for arbitration by commencing the present proceeding for a stay. His petition says that his agreement with Cinematografica and Campos was unenforcible because the promises therein contained were illusory. Also, says he, even assuming the agreement to be valid, the issues and the damages should be limited by the court to those arising directly out of the alleged breach of the agreement.

Special Term denied the application for a stay. The court's opinion held that petitioner was barred from litigating the validity of the contract because, so the court found, petitioner had participated in the selection of arbitrators and in the arbitration proceeding itself. On appeal the Appellate Division, while agreeing with Special Term that the participation of De Laurentiis had debarred him from litigating any alleged invalidity of the contract, went further and examined into his other allegations: that the contract was illusory and that the demand for arbitration was not sufficiently definite. The Appellate Division ruled against him on both these issues.

The holdings below that petitioner so participated that he can no longer contest the validity of the agreement nor the arbitrability of the dispute were based on a series of letters written on behalf of petitioner to respondents' representatives in June, July and August, 1960, after receipt by Serpe, petitioner's designated representative, of respondents' demand for arbitration. We do not think that the mere requests by petitioner's agent Serpe for extensions of time were "participation" in the arbitration within the meaning of subdivision 2 of secton 1458 of the Civil Practice Act, construed by us in Matter of National Cash Register Co. (Wilson) (8 N.Y. 2d 377). Reasonably read, the various applications made by Serpe were no more than successive requests for time to allow petitioner to decide whether to participate in the selection of arbitrators and in the arbitration proceedings or to begin court proceedings for a stay of arbitration. At the time these letters were written neither party had done anything about selecting the arbitrators. It would be unfair to construe careless language by Serpe (whose authority was limited to receiving process) to mean that petitioner was agreeing to go forward in the arbitration.

We turn now to petitioner's arguments for a stay. The first of his positions is that the agreement on its face is so lacking in mutuality that it bound neither party and could not produce an arbitrable dispute. This, however, seems to be completely answered by our decision in Matter of Exercycle Corp. (Maratta) (9 N.Y. 2d 329). The Exercycle Corporation had argued that its contract with Maratta was illusory since the latter had not specifically agreed to work for life or any other definite period. We pointed out in the *Exercycle* opinion that the resolution of such a dispute depended primarily on a construction of the agreement and that, when there were permissible differences of interpretation, the issue was for the arbitrators and not for the court. The present agreement, as petitioner points out, does leave to future agreement the approval of the story outline and scenario and failure to approve might put an end to all the obligations. However, De Laurentiis and Campos expressly promised each other to consult at reasonable times and places during the preparation of the outline and of the scenario "to the end that both De Laurentiis and Campos may make every effort in good faith to cause to be created, within the period specified herein, a story outline, screen treatment and final scenario acceptable to both." Thus, in addition to the implication of good faith read into every contract (see Wood v. Duff-Gordon, 222 N.Y. 88), we had an express promise of consultation and of good-faith effort to bring to completion a scenario of such form and quality as to be acceptable. It is for the arbitrators to decide what, under all the circumstances, these covenants contemplated and whether petitioner did all that he was thereby required to do.

As his other ground for a stay petitioner attacks the sufficiency of the demand for arbitration, arguing that the issues and damages are stated in much too general terms and that some of the round figure damage items are outside any possible scope of the arbitration clause. We are told that the claim for "Loss of business reputation" and "Damage to personal and business reputation" as well as the items for legal expense and travel and secretarial expenditures describe purely consequential damages not recoverable under the rule of Matter of Marchant v. Mead-Morrison Mfg. Co. (252 N.Y. 284) and De Lillo Constr. Co. v. Lizza & Sons (7 N.Y. 2d 102). As to the alleged failure of the demand for arbitration to set forth with definiteness any dispute or disputes, we think the demand (plus the affidavits) is to be read as alleging that petitioner took none of the steps required of him by the agreement and did none of the things he had promised to do. As to whether damages of the kind listed are recoverable, it must be remembered that the parties agreed not only to arbitrate their differences but to do so under the rules of the American Arbitration Association, one of which rules (No. 42) says that the arbitrator in his award "may grant any remedy or relief which he deems just and equitable and within the scope of the agreement of the parties." The arbitration agreement here called for the submission of "Any dispute arising under this agreement" and was not otherwise limited. When we incorporate rule 42 into that clause we have a grant of power to the arbitrators so broad that it would be inappropriate to determine in advance of an arbitration that there must be eliminated from any award any items of damage which the arbitrators might consider "just and equitable" under the facts as developed before the arbitrators (see Matter of Transpacific Transp. Corp. [Sirena Shipping Co., S.A.], 9 A.D. 2d 316, affd. 8 N.Y. 2d 1048).

The order should be affirmed, with costs.

FROESSEL, J. (concurring). I concur in the result. In my opinion, the contract is not illusory, and arbitration is, therefore, the appropriate remedy. As to any consequential damages, the arbitrators are bound by our decisions in Matter of Marchant v. Mead-Morrison Mfg. Co. (252 N.Y. 284) and De Lillo Constr. Co. v. Lizza & Sons (7 N.Y. 2d 102).

VAN VOORHIS, J. (dissenting). It is familiar law that courts will not permit arbitrators to change unambiguous contracts nor to make awards of damages which are of so speculative a nature as to be outside of the province of a court of law. There has to be an arbitrable dispute in order to permit arbitration (Matter of International Assn. of Machinists [Cutler-Hammer], 271 App. Div. 917, affd. 297 N.Y. 519; Matter of General Elec. Co. [United Elec. Radio & Mach. Workers], 300 N.Y. 262; Matter of Essenson [Upper Queens Med. Group], 307 N.Y. 68; Matter of Sarle [Sperry Gyroscope Co.] 4 A.D. 2d 638, affd. 4 N.Y. 2d 917).

The position of respondent and of the courts below is, in effect, that when parties to a contract containing an arbitration clause get into argument, if any element of the dispute is arbitrable, then the arbitrators have power without limitation by the courts to decide not only the arbitrable element of the controversy but all other matters in difference regardless of whether of themselves these would have constituted arbitrable disputes. In other words, if the contestants disagree about six items, five of which would not be arbitrable if presented alone, all may be submitted to arbitration if one dispute is of an arbitrable nature. Absent that one, nothing could be arbitrated, so the argument runs, under the cases which have been cited; but with that one present, everything else can be arbitrated which the parties choose to disagree about, beyond the control of the courts.

It was held otherwise as recently as Matter of Sarle (Sperry Gyroscope Co.) (4 A.D. 2d 638, affd. 4 N.Y. 2d 917, supra). There is no valid reason, it seems to me, on account of which what is arbitrable cannot be submitted to the arbitrators at the same time restraining them from trying or deciding other questions in conjunction therewith which, of themselves, are not

subject to arbitration. Neither is there any occasion in my judgment for awaiting the confirmation of the arbitrators' report if it appears in advance that they have no jurisdiction to try such aspects of the controversy.

This is not just a question of the arbitration of consequential damages. The improbability that parties intend to submit consequential damages to arbitration is so strong that they were held to be excluded from the submission in Matter of Marchant v. Mead-Morrison Mfg. Co. (252 N.Y. 284, 301) in an opinion by Chief Judge Cardozo, in which he said:

We think there would be surprise and consternation in the trade if under cover of such a clause an architect or engineer could hold a contractor liable for the bankruptcy of the owner, and assess the damages accordingly. The precedents are apt that no such power is conferred (Somerset Borough v. Ott, 207 Penn. St. 539; Young v. Crescent Dev. Co., 240 N.Y. 244).

The Marchant case was followed as recently as De Lillo Constr. Co. v. Lizza & Sons (7 N.Y. 2d 102, 106), in which the opinion states by Judge Froessel:

The instant dispute between Lizza and De Lillo had its origin in the contract and prominently raises issues concerning the rights and obligations of the parties under the contract and in the performance thereunder. It is, therefore, arbitrable, in accordance with the fair meaning of their agreement, except, on the basis of our holding in Matter of Marchant v. Mead-Morrison Mfg. Co., with regard to one aspect of the claim for consequential damages asserted in the fourth cause of action. As to that claim, the issue of breach of contract is within the scope of the instant submission, but the assessment of damages is not.

Apart from the fact that an affirmance would, as it seems to me, overrule both the Marchant and De Lillo cases (supra) by injecting the question of consequential damages where neither the arbitration clause nor the rules of the American Arbitration Association contain any reference to them, this is not a case of even consequential damage. Here several items of the damages claimed, which comprise the bulk of the amount for which judgment is sought, are so attenuated that they are not even consequential. The item of $600,000 claimed for loss of profits, for example, and the $150,000 for loss of the business reputation of Cinecam [sic] could not possibly have been incurred unless under the terms of the agreement the parties had made a further agreement which legally they were entirely free to accept or reject. An agreement to agree is not a binding contract (St. Regis Paper Co. v. Hubbs & Hastings Paper Co., 235 N.Y. 30). In this instance I agree that, in view of the allegation that De Laurentiis did nothing, an arbitrable question is presented concerning whether he should be compelled to return the $75,000 deposit advanced to him and the travel expense of $85,000 plus legal expense and possibly other items incurred on the faith of his taking steps to engage a writer of the first rank to prepare the story outline and to do some other things necessary to launch the project.

Upon the other hand, in view of the terms of the contract and the nature of the undertaking, it is pure speculation to assume that even if De Laurentiis had done everything which he was required to do the venture would have been successful. The contract states that the scenario is to be based on Campos' book, but the story outline and screen treatment are subject to the mutual agreement of Campos, Cineam [*sic*] and De Laurentiis. The contract expressly states that work shall not proceed on the preparation of the final scenario until such approval shall have been given. A veto is provided in case the final scenario deviates from the story outline or treatment in various respects. "Upon the completion and mutual approval by the parties hereto of the final scenario, De Laurentiis undertakes to do all things necessary to the production of the motion picture described in Paragraph '1' hereof."

These are questions about which the parties were yet to agree relating to artistic production. Campos had an absolute veto on whether the dramatization conformed to the theme of his story. Moreover, all of the parties reserved to themselves, under the language above quoted, the right not to proceed unless, after the dramatization had been completed, it seemed to them that it was sufficiently likely to succeed to warrant the further expenditure of time and money.

In Rockcliffe Realty Corp. v. Mutual Life Ins. Co., it was said by Justice Pecora:

> In 3 WILLISTON, CONTRACTS, Revised Ed. 1936, § 675A, p. 1947, the author suggests that in determining the construction to be given contracts containing provisions for satisfactory performance, the subject matter of the bargain should be looked into. Where the approval involves "an affair of individual judgment" upon which there can be no standard of reasonableness, there must be personal satisfaction. Wynkoop Hallenbeck Crawford Co. v. Western Union Tel. Co., 268 N.Y. 108, 196 N.E. 760. The contract here falls in the category of those requiring the exercise of individual judgment. (50 N.Y.S. 2d 851, 853.)

In the case cited it was said in the opinion for the court by Judge Loughran (268 N.Y. 108, 112–113, *supra*):

We may assume with the referee that in all this there is no element of taste or fancy in a strict sense. It is here demonstrated, that the allocation of "administrative and overhead charges" to one of many separate undertakings in a single business is in large degree an affair of individual judgment,—an interpretation which is not matter of general agreement in the business community. Under settled principles, therefore, the contract phrase "satisfactory to the Electric Company" is to be read, not as a stipulation for what court or jury would pronounce satisfactory to a reasonable man, but literally as meaning actually satisfactory to defendant personally. (Duplex Safety Boiler Co. v. Garden, 101 N.Y. 387, 390; Crawford v. Mail & Express Pub. Co., 163 N.Y. 404; American Law Institute, Restatement of the Law of Contracts, § 265.)

The latter quotation from the *Wynkoop* case in the excerpt from Judge Loughran's opinion shows that this rule requiring actual literal satisfaction, not what a court or jury would pronounce satisfactory to a reasonable man, is not confined to situations involving an element of taste or fancy. In the present appeal, however, that is definitely what the clause requiring future consent does cover. It would be difficult to find a situation where that was more literally true than in the determination of whether a scenario follows the theme of a novel in the opinion of the author.

Consequently there could be no profit and no injury to reputation of any one in case of failure to which liability could extend, even though De Laurentiis had engaged the scenario writer of first rank and taken the other preliminary steps to set this venture in motion. No one could know with any certainty, not even enough to spell out consequential damages, whether the scenario would have been accepted by the parties under this clause giving each of them an express veto.

To permit arbitrators to say that they would or would not have accepted and approved of a scenario that was never written is the antithesis of the rule of law. If issues which could not be adjudicated in a court of law on account of the speculative nature of the damage can be the subject of arbitration, a lawyer who understands his duty would not be likely to permit a client to sign a contract of this nature containing an arbitration clause. The majority opinion concludes by saying "we have a grant of power to the arbitrators so broad that it would be inappropriate to determine *in advance of an arbitration* that there must be eliminated from any award any items of damage which the arbitrators might consider 'just and equitable' under the facts as developed before the arbitrators (see Matter of Transpacific Transp. Corp.

[Sirena Shipping Co., S.A.], 9 A.D. 2d 316, affd. 8 N.Y. 2d 1048)." (Italics supplied.)

This language contains a broad inference that whatever the arbitrators consider just and equitable by way of loss of profits, reputation or anything else about which the parties have argued would be final and conclusive in any event. The Courts and the Bar are deeply interested, I think, in knowing whether if arbitrators go out of bounds in a matter of this kind it is premature to raise the point before the arbitration begins and too late to raise it afterwards. The questions to be submitted to the arbitrators should be limited, it seems to me, by eliminating at least the claim for $600,000 loss of profits and the damages for loss of personal and business or professional reputation by reason of the non-production of the scenario. Nothing can be gained by protracted litigation of those matters before the arbitrators who are incapacitated by the contract from awarding any sum to be recovered by reason thereof.

Judges DYE, FULD, BURKE and FOSTER concur with CHIEF JUDGE DESMOND; JUDGE FROESSEL concurs in result in a separate memorandum; Judge VAN VOORHIS dissents in an opinion.

Order affirmed.

In Wyatt Earp Enterprises v. Sackman (D.C. S.D. N.Y. 1958) 157 F. Supp. 621, plaintiff sought to enjoin the use of the "name, mark and symbol of Wyatt Earp" after an agreement licensing its use by defendant had expired. The defendant cross-moved for a stay of the court proceedings and to compel arbitration under a clause in the licensing agreement which the court characterized as calling for arbitration of any dispute between the parties "arising out of or *relating to*" the licensing contract. (Emphasis added.) The court observed:

> Section 3 of Title 9 U.S.C. authorizes the court to grant a stay "upon being satisfied that the issue involved . . . is referable to arbitration." The written agreement between the parties provides for the arbitration of any dispute or disagreement between the parties "arising out of or relating to" the licensing contract. But the controversy between the parties, certainly the claim of the plaintiff, is one involving the issue of unfair competition. The action sounds not in contract but in tort, and the issue is not defined by the question of the rights of the parties under the agreement. If the dispute were confined to issues of whether or not the contract was violated, it would be referable to arbitration. But "*the issue involved*", see International Union, United Automobile Aircraft v. Benton Harbor

Malleable Industries, 6 Cir., 242 F. 2d 536, 539, 542, is much broader in scope, requiring a consideration of facts and factors beyond the contract. Even if any existing subordinate contract issues were resolved by arbitration, "*the issue involved*" would remain. Indeed, in the absence of a license agreement and of defendant's operation under it, the broad issue would remain. No arbitration decision interpreting the contract could determine the controversy at bar. To delay the suit for injunctive relief and require arbitration would merely add to the "costliness and delays of litigation" it was the purpose of the Arbitration Act to eliminate. 68 Cong., 1st Sess., House of Rep. Report No. 96. For the controversy between the parties would still have to be decided by this court. Whether or not defendant has competed unfairly with the plaintiff presents an issue far transcending one merely "arising out of or relating to" the contract between the parties, and it is inconceivable that they intended such a dispute to be settled by arbitration. While the parties have made an agreement to arbitrate, the filing of suit for injunctive relief does not constitute a failure, neglect or refusal of the respondent-plaintiff to perform its agreement under 9 U.S.C. § 4. The motion for a stay and to compel arbitration will be denied.

MATTER OF UDDO (TAORMINA)
21 A.D. 2d 402, 250 N.Y.S. 2d 645
(First Dept. 1964)

STEUER, J. The parties to this dispute are stockholders and directors of nine affiliated corporations. The corporations, each in a distinct phase, are engaged in the food processing business on a large scale. The business was originally in the hands of an individual, the progenitor of the Uddo family. He took in as a partner his son-in-law, the respondent Frank G. Taormina. Subsequently, the three Uddo sons and five relatives of Taormina became partners. In 1958 the business was incorporated, nine corporations being formed. Each corporation had two classes of stock: the A stock, held by the Uddos; and the B stock, held by the Taorminas. Each class of stock elected five directors to the corporate boards. An eleventh director was A. E. Krackov, the attorney for all of these people. After some months Mr. Krackov severed his connection with the families and an agreement was entered into between all the stockholders as to the method for the conduct of the affairs of the corporations. The number of directors was reduced to ten, elected as before. It was provided that if the board of directors was unable to take effective action on any issue, the matter should be resolved by Frank J. Uddo and Frank G. Taormina jointly. These latter were the executive officers of the corporations and, in a sense, the heads of the respective families. In the event these two were unable to agree, each was to designate an outside person. If their choice fell on the same person, he should resolve the difference. If they made designations of different persons, those two should decide. And if they were unable to reach a conclusion, they should designate a third person whose decision would be final.

In 1963 the managing officers were not in entire accord as to proposals for a public offering of stock. In addition, there were differences between various members as to several minor matters of management, particularly concerning employment of relatives. In this situation the petitioner herein, Frank Uddo, demanded of respondent, Frank Taormina, that they arbitrate some eight issues. Instead, Taormina called a special meeting of each of the boards of directors. Proper notice was given. The meetings were attended by all of the Taormina directors and one of the Uddo directors, namely, Salvador Uddo. All of the eight matters were considered by the boards, and all were unanimously resolved; whereupon Frank Uddo instituted this proceeding demanding arbitration.

Special Term granted the motion to compel arbitration on the ground that the agreement, indisputably made, provided for arbitration in the event that the board of directors was unable to take effective action. Special Term decided that whether effective action was taken is a matter for the arbitrators to decide. The validity of this ruling depends on the meaning of the words "effective action." Ordinarily this would mean resolution by the board of the question before it. And it is quite obvious from the undisputed history of the corporate organizations that this is what is meant. Prior to the making of the agreement the boards consisted of equal numbers of representatives of each of the two families, with an independent extra director. This arrangement for a built-in umpire insured against action being frustrated by tie votes. When the umpire disappeared from the scene, a tie vote became a contingency which had to be provided against. The arbitration provision was designed in order to meet that situation and only became binding if the situation, or one allied to it, such as a failure to obtain a quorum, arose. It may be noted that this interpretation is advanced by the petitioner who concedes that the original provision for an umpire and the succeeding one for arbitration are to obviate the situation arising from a deadlock caused by the directors voting along strict family lines.

It is argued that even if this be the fact, and the claim of an arbitrable question entirely specious, that question is nevertheless for the arbitrators and not for the court. Support for this contention is based on CPLR § 7501, directing that the "court shall not consider whether the claim with respect to which arbitration is sought is tenable, or otherwise pass upon the merits of the dispute." This revokes the prior existing rule that the court could refuse to order arbitration of a claim which was patently frivolous (Matter of International Assn. of Machinists, Dist. No. 15, Local No. 402 v. Cutler-Hammer, Inc., 297 N.Y. 519, 74 N.E. 2d 464). But this rule applied to matters which under the terms of the arbitration agreement were arbitrable (Alpert v. Admiration Knitwear Co., 304 N.Y. 1, 105 N.E. 2d 561). It does not affect the axiomatic proposition that one can only be compelled to arbitrate when one has agreed to do so, nor its necessary concomitant that whether one has so agreed is a question for the court. Confusion may arise from the holdings interpreting broad clauses in agreements which provide as arbitrable any question that may arise under or in connection with the making, meaning or performance of the particular contract. Under such clauses any question beyond the physical execution of the contract would by its terms be one for the arbitrators (Matter of Lipman, 289 N.Y. 76, 43 N.E. 2d 817, 142 A.L.R. 1088). But this does not affect the basic rule that what the parties agreed to and whether they agreed is for the court. It merely means that where they have agreed to arbitrate everything there is nothing for the court to decide beyond that they have so agreed. It would follow that a mere claim, no matter how frivolous, is sufficient to invoke the process.

The agreement to arbitrate in this family-corporate complex as distinct from being all embracing is very limited. It is confined to issues before the board of directors. It does not apply to any dispute that may arise between the family members or even such of them as are stockholders. And it may be observed that when the original demand was made there were no issues before any of the boards of these corporations. Apart from this consideration, it only applies where the board is "unable" to take effective action. There is no showing of any such inability. Actually, the board did take action and there is no question that a majority voted upon and resolved all of the questions upon which arbitration is sought. Far from showing inability, the exact contrary is shown. To put the situation into its legal framework, the petitioner has not shown any issue which is arbitrable under the agreement. The contention he raises is quite different, namely, whether the condition under which an agreement to arbitrate depends has come to pass. Under the restricted agreement to arbitrate, this issue is not arbitrable. It being for the court, no impediment exists for a determination that it is specious.

In order for the petitioner to sustain his position he must, and he does, ignore the action actually taken by the boards. There is no claim that the meetings were illegal. In fact, protest in this regard is very odd indeed. It is pointed out that this meeting was conducted formally, in strict accord with corporate practice, whereas usually meetings were conducted informally. Also, it is claimed that some of the matters considered were not really in dispute, but that the board merely passed resolutions which had been agreed upon. Further, it is asserted that four of the Uddo directors found it difficult to attend and an adjournment was refused. It is not claimed that the failure to grant the adjournment invalidated the meetings. Lastly, the real reason which explains the absence of the Uddo directors is asserted. The Taorminas had prevailed on one of the Uddos, Salvador, who attended the meeting, to vote in advance with them. This was known to the Uddos in advance so they knew that their attendance would be ineffective. It is further claimed that Salvador's votes at the directors' meeting were illegal as in breach of an agreement he had with the other members of his family. It is contended that had Salvador voted as his obligations required, and had the other Uddo directors attended as they would have, a deadlock would have resulted. This would, in turn, have given the right to invoke arbitration.

But this whole house of cards, defective legally in practically every step in the argument, rests upon a false assumption. Salvador was not bound by any agreement to vote in any way on any proposition before the board. Salvador was one of the three brothers, sons of the founder. The three had entered into a written agreement. This agreement refers to the action to be taken by Frank Uddo in the event he and Frank Taormina are called upon to resolve a question that the board is unable to pass upon. It was agreed that a majority of the three should control Frank's actions, and in the event Frank was in the minority the other two should take his place. Clearly this agreement does not affect Salvador's freedom to vote as a director in any way he deemed proper, assuming that an agreement to vote against his better judgment would be legal.

The minority opinion relies on an arbitration clause in a prior agreement. This agreement, dated April 25, 1958, was modified by the present agreement of May 10, 1960. The particular aspects in which the earlier agreement was modified had to do with the control of the corporations and, specifically, with the manner in which a possible deadlock was to be resolved. It changed the former procedure and the former provisions for arbitration. We find it difficult to understand how it can be urged that the discarded provision still retains vitality even to the extent of leaving to the arbitrators there provided for whether it in fact survives. The difficulty is further enhanced by considering the method of control adopted in the May, 1960, superseding agreement. Recalling that in the event of a block of action by the directors resolution is to be made by Frank Uddo and Frank Taormina, this provision becomes entirely inoperative if any of the persons entitled to demand arbitration under earlier agreements could enforce his rights. Instead of control being vested in the two representatives of the two families, it would be in the power of others to frustrate that control by transferring their power of decision to outside arbitrators.

In a related application one of the Taorminas asked leave to intervene. We believe the denial of this application to have been proper.

Order directing arbitration to proceed and order denying reargument reversed on the law and the facts, with costs to appellant, and order denying leave to intervene affirmed with costs to respondent.

Orders, entered on October 1, 1963 and January 3, 1964, reversed, on the law and on the facts, with $20 costs and disbursements to appellant, the motion to direct arbitration denied, and the petition dismissed.

Order, entered on January 3, 1964, unanimously affirmed with $20 costs and disbursements to respondent.

All concur except BREITEL, J. P., and VALENTE, J., who dissent and vote to affirm in a dissenting opinion by VALENTE, J.

VALENTE, J. (dissenting). I dissent and would affirm the order compelling appellant to arbitrate.

The result reached by the majority may fairly be considered as a subtle revenant of the Cutler-Hammer doctrine (Matter of International Assn. of Machinists, Dist. No. 15, Local No. 402, v. Cutler-Hammer, Inc., 271 App. Div. 917, 67 N.Y.S. 2d 317, affd. 297 N.Y. 519, 74 N.E. 2d 464) which, presumably, was thoroughly and effectively exorcized by former section 1448–a of the Civil Practice Act and the present CPLR § 7501. These sections specifically preclude the Court from considering "whether the claim with respect to which arbitration is sought is tenable, or otherwise pass upon the merits of the dispute."

The majority opinion succinctly traces the growth and development of the corporate empire and the concomitant equal division of control between the Uddos and the Taorminas. From a simple partnership between petitioner and his son-in-law, Frank G. Taormina, the business burgeoned into a complex of nine corporations. Initially, a stockholders' agreement of April 25, 1958, provided for joint control by the two family factions. That agreement was subsequently amended and modified by two agreements, dated July 17, 1958 and May 10, 1960.

The specific arbitration clause of the modification agreement of May 10, 1960 (Paragraph 5), in its first sentence, reiterates the primary intent of the parties, viz: "It is intended that control of all nine corporations be vested in Frank J. Uddo and Frank G. Taormina jointly." There follows the provision for arbitration "if the Board of Directors is unable to take effective action on any issue."

As already noted, the May 10, 1960 agreement was a modification, in a limited area, of the two prior agreements of April 25, 1958 and July 17, 1958. Except as modified, the provisions of the antecedent agreements remained unaffected. The agreement of April 25, 1958 contained a broad arbitration clause. It provided (Paragraph 24) that "all disputes arising out of, under, in connection with or in relation to this agreement, as any alleged breach thereof, shall be submitted to arbitration." The majority opinion recognizes that under such a broad clause "any question beyond the physical execution of the contract would by its terms be one for the arbitrators." Yet, completely ignoring this broad arbitration clause, the majority trenches on the function of arbitrators in imposing its interpretation of the specific clause of the modification contract of May 10, 1960, as being "confined to issues before the board of directors." But even if it were assumed that such interpretation were sound, is not this process of construction of a term of the contract an invasion of the province of arbitrators under the general arbitration clause of the April 25, 1958 contract?

The main thrust of the majority opinion is that "when the original demand was made there were no issues before any of the boards of these corporations," that there was no showing of any inability of the boards to take effective action, and that in fact the boards did take effective action, and, by a majority vote, "resolved all

of the questions upon which arbitration is sought." I completely disagree with these conclusions.

In the first place, the record shows (Pet. Exh. D) that the demand for arbitration was dated July 10, 1963—which antedated the meeting of the Boards of Directors—and it states that it is made pursuant to all three agreements. Respondent-appellant's affidavit in opposition to the motion to compel arbitration avers:

> As of July 30, 1963 the Boards of Directors of the nine corporations were deadlocked and, therefore, were unable to take effective action on the issues as outlined in petitioner's Exhibit "D".

The admissions in the record refute a major premise of the majority's opinion. Thus, it uncontrovertibly appears that when the demand for arbitration was made, there was a deadlock in the Boards of Directors and that they were unable to take action.

Finally, whether "effective action" was taken by the meetings of the Boards of Directors in August, 1963 is not for the Court to determine, but for the arbitrators. The contracts among the stockholders, expressly and impliedly, provided for joint control of the corporations by two family groups. Since there was equal division of control provision was made for arbitration to settle differences which might arise where neither group could prevail. Whether upon the occurrence of a deadlock, either side may, through action not contemplated by the agreement, and in fact contrary to the underlying purposes of the agreement, take any effective action is a matter of the interpretation of the contracts which must be left to arbitration. Considering the entire background of the agreements, I cannot agree with the majority that a claim by petitioner that no effective action under the contract was taken by the Boards of Directors in August, 1963, after the demand for arbitration was served, is "specious." I would hold that the claim is substantial and must be decided by arbitration, not only under the modification agreement of May 10, 1960, but also pursuant to the original agreement of April 25, 1958. The modification agreement covered only disputes between the chiefs of the two family groups in the event of a deadlock in the board of directors. The arbitration clause of the original agreement survived to confer jurisdiction over all other disputes, inclusive of the interpretation and effect of the modification agreement.

BREITEL, J. P., concurs.

MATTER OF LIPSKY
(FASHION ART CORP.)
23 A.D. 2d 775, 258 N.Y.S. 2d 530
(Second Dept. 1965)

The notice of intention to arbitrate which was served by the respondent upon the petitioners failed to state any claim against the petitioner Anna Lipsky. Accordingly, there is no reason for her to be a party to the arbitration. With respect to the proceeding on behalf of Morris Lipsky, the record is inconclusive; it may not be determined therefrom whether the dispute in question is arbitrable under the agreement between the parties. Indeed, the contract containing the arbitration clauses is not set forth or described, nor are we informed as to the nature of the business in which the parties were engaged or of the "understanding" respecting insurance involved in the dispute. Under the circumstances, the court below should have required the submission of additional proof and upon such submission, if no triable issues of fact were raised, should have made a summary determination as to whether the dispute between the parties is arbitrable (CPLR 409). If triable issues of fact were raised, they should have been tried forthwith and the court should have made a final determination thereon (CPLR 410). Such procedures may now be adopted on the remission. We do not agree with the court below that the arbitrability of the dispute is an issue to be decided by the arbitrators (CPLR 7501, 7503; Matter of Carey v. Westinghouse Elec. Corp., 11 N.Y. 2d 452, 456; Matter of Dairymen's League Coop. Assn. [Conrad], 18 A.D. 2d 321, 325–326; Matter of Uddo [Taormina], 21 A.D. 2d 402; Matter of Empire State Master Hairdressers Assn. [Journeymen Barbers], 18 A.D. 2d 808; Matter of Camhi [Undergarment, etc., Union], 13 A.D. 2d 752).

UGHETTA, Acting P. J., BRENNAN, HILL, RABIN, and HOPKINS, JJ., concur.

MATTER OF NEWMEYER
(BILL CHAN'S INC.)
23 A.D. 2d 836, 259 N.Y.S. 2d 419
(First Dept. 1965)

By the language of the arbitration clause the parties agreed to arbitrate virtually everything arising out of, relating to, or connected with the business in which they were engaged. In respect to this dispute it is not for the courts to decide if the claim is tenable, or to attempt to

pass upon the merits (CPLR 7501); all of that is for the arbitrator. (Matter of Exercycle Corp. [Maratta], 9 N.Y. 2d 329, 334; cf. Matter of Uddo [Taormina], 21 A.D. 2d 402.)

BREITEL, J. P., RABIN, VALENTE, McNALLY and STEVENS, JJ. concur.

MATTER OF TRIPLE P REALTY CORP.
(PEORIA PENNY PARK)
34 Misc. 2d 355, 228 N.Y.S. 2d 175
(N.Y. Cty. 1962).

HECHT, J. This is a motion to stay arbitration. The parties hereto entered into a contract for the purchase of real estate, the construction of a garage thereon, and a long-term net lease to be given back as part of the package deal.

The contract contains an arbitration clause as follows: "In the event that there is any dispute between the parties hereinto *pertaining* to the terms of this agreement, then the parties." (Emphasis supplied.)

The respondent is not seeking under arbitration to have an award as to any of the terms of the contract, but requests to have incorporated into the contract different terms or changes in terms as required by a change in the circumstances between the parties, in accordance with the express agreement that if they could not agree on any dispute pertaining to the terms of the agreement, then the matter was to be arbitrated. The respondent urges that the practical construction the parties themselves have given to the contract, the embryonic nature of the entire venture, the fluidity of the positions, the changes agreed to, and the wide scope of the arbitration clause, bring this case within established authorities supporting arbitration as to the changes sought.

None of the cases cited support the main relief sought by respondent, which is, in simple language, the right to vary the terms of the written contract through the intervention of arbitration.

Whether the court would allow such variance if it had been brought before the court in the first instant, or whether the arbitrators could modify the contract under the existing law even if the matter were rightfully before them, are not the principal questions at this stage of an application to stay arbitration.

The petitioner urges that there is no dispute arising within the terms of the contract. Respondent concedes that, but states that it is not asking for an award against the clear terms of the contract. The court cannot compel arbitration as to controversies beyond the scope of those specifically stated in the contract (Belding Hemingway Co. [Wholesale & Warehouse Worker's Union] 295 N.Y. 541). The key is that the issue must be referable to the arbitration agreement, or else there is no compulsion to arbitrate that issue. The issue herein would cover the variance of the terms of the contract as to 18 features therein. It is a well-established rule that "No one is under a duty to resort to arbitration unless by clear language he has so agreed (Matter of Lehman v. Ostrovsky, 264 N.Y. 130, 131). Though the principle of arbitration in commercial transactions is a sound one, and should be encouraged, no one may be compelled to give up his right to resort to established judicial tribunals with all their safeguards unless he has agreed by a writing to do so. (Matter of Philip Export Corp. [Leathertone, Inc.], 275 App. Div. 102). Respondent claims that there are broad terms within the arbitration clause. Whether broad or limited, the language is not specific enough to permit a change of the terms of the contract itself.

To the extent to which the respondent seeks to change the contracts, even though the arbitrators may not grant all the requests, the principles heretofore stated compel the conclusion that respondent has failed to prove that such changes were subject to arbitration. Accordingly, the application to stay arbitration on the submitted matter is granted. Cross motion is denied.

LAYNE-MINNESOTA CO. v. REGENTS OF UNIVERSITY OF MINNESOTA
266 Minn. 284, 123 N.W. 2d 371 (1963)

ROGOSHESKE, J. Appeal from an order denying plaintiff's motion to compel arbitration under Minn. St. 572.09 of the Uniform Arbitration Act adopted by Minnesota in 1957.[1]

On March 9, 1961, plaintiff, a contractor, after acceptance of its bid, entered into a construction contract with the defendant to construct caisson foundations for two buildings to be erected on the west campus of the University of Minnesota.

A caisson is a column of concrete and steel upon which the building rests. The contract called for a total of 56 caissons with varying diameters of 4, 5 or 6 feet. Each caisson extends from the ground surface to whatever depth was necessary to get an 8-inch penetration into bedrock which was approximately 25 feet below the surface. After excavation to bedrock was completed the holes were filled with concrete and reinforcing steel to form a set of reinforced concrete legs upon which the buildings would rest.[2]

Attached to the specifications, pursuant to which the plaintiff made its bid, were reports on preconstruction borings which had been conducted for defendant by the Minnesota Test Boring Company. These reports were provided for what value they might have to the contractor but were not guaranteed by defendant as accurate or indicative of all soils at the site. The contract included a modification clause and an arbitration clause hereafter quoted. During the course of the construction plaintiff encountered boulders, limestone slabs, and underground water in amounts and at locations not indicated by the plans and specifications. Plaintiff claims that a requested modification of the contract and a claim for additional compensation was made and denied. We are not informed whether this occurred before or after completion of the work.[3] Defendant does not deny that a request was made, but the particulars concerning the time, nature, and manner of the request, and of defendant's denial, are not disclosed by the record. We assume that the request was denied and that plaintiff completed the work notwithstanding this controversy.[4] In any event, after a denial, the plaintiff, on February 8, 1962, served a written request for arbitration of the claim for additional compensation because of unanticipated difficulties. Defendant refused this request on the ground that such claim was not a dispute intended to be referable to arbitration under the language of the arbitration clause of the contract. The controversy as to whether the claim of the contractor was a dispute subject to

---

1. This act was drafted and approved by the National Conference on Uniform Laws and thereafter approved by the American Bar Association in 1955. In 1957, under the sponsorship of the Minnesota State Bar Association, Minnesota was the first state to adopt the act. Wyoming, Massachusetts, Illinois, and Arizona have subsequently adopted it. 9 Uniform Laws Annotated, pocket part p. 36.

2. The record does not disclose these facts concerning the nature of the work but this statement, taken from plaintiff's brief, is not challenged by defendant.

3. Apart from the moving papers, the record contains only the written request for arbitration and those parts of the contract which the parties deemed pertinent.

4. Plaintiff's written request for arbitration includes this statement: "That this claim was presented to owner's representative and on January 17, 1962, the same was denied." In an opposing affidavit submitted on defendant's behalf there is this statement: "That a prerequisite to arbitration would be a decision of the architect/engineer, and that no decision has been made." This apparent conflict was not presented to nor resolved by the trial court.

arbitration apparently continued and remained unresolved until April 24, 1962, on which date the defendant commenced a declaratory judgment action seeking a construction of the provisions of the contract relating to arbitration. Thereafter, pursuant to § 572.09(a) of the Uniform Arbitration Act, plaintiff made application for an order compelling arbitration and staying the declaratory judgment action until its motion to compel arbitration was heard and determined. Under § 572.09(d) of the act, the parties agreed to stay the action for declaratory judgment, and the plaintiff's application was heard and denied. The court held that the dispute involved was not one within the meaning of section 1–23 of the contract. This appeal from the order denying an application to compel arbitration is expressly authorized by § 572.26, subd. 1(1) of the act.

The pertinent provisions of the contract are as follows:

SECTION 1–16 CHANGES, EXTRAS, ETC.

Should the Contractor find at any time during the progress of the work that in his judgment existing conditions demand or make desirable or beneficial a modification in the requirements covering any particulars or items, it shall be his duty and he is required to promptly report in writing each such matter to the Supervising Engineer for his decision and instruction.

SECTION 1–23 DISPUTES.

If during progress of the work, any disputes, claims or questions arise between the owner and the contractor concerning the work, the architect/engineer shall be consulted and his decision shall be final. However, decision may be submitted to arbitration.

SECTION 1–24 ARBITRATION.

All disputes, claims or questions subject to arbitration under this contract shall be submitted to arbitration in accordance with the provisions, then obtaining of the Uniform Arbitration Act. Chapter 633, Laws of Minnesota, 1957, and this Agreement shall be specifically enforceable under the prevailing arbitration law, and judgment upon the award rendered may be entered in the court of the forum, state or federal, having jurisdiction. It is mutually agreed that the decision of the arbitrators shall be a condition precedent to any right of legal action that either party may have against the other.

Essentially the question presented to the trial court and here is whether or not the parties intended by their contract to submit to arbitration a dispute arising over a claim for additional compensation occasioned by unanticipated difficulties in performing the work required by the contract.

As the question was submitted to the trial court and here, the arguments of the parties were primarily directed toward seeking a final judicial determination of whether the claim presents an issue referable to arbitration. We are urged, as was the trial court, to decide the question under the rules relating to the construction of contracts without reference to any specific provisions of the Uniform Arbitration Act. This emphasis overlooks section 1–24 of the contract which makes the act an integral part of the contract, thereby requiring a consideration of those provisions of the act which were intended to apply and control a judicial determination of the very question presented.

One of the fundamental objectives of the act was to encourage and facilitate the arbitration of disputes by providing a speedy, informal, and relatively inexpensive procedure for resolving controversies arising out of commercial transactions, including the labor-management field. The language of the act emphasizes an intention to change the common-law policy of judicial hostility toward arbitration to one favoring arbitration. Contrary to decisions found in many states, it specifically makes a written agreement to arbitrate effective whether relating to existing or future disputes.[5] By invoking the aid of courts, the legal rights of parties to such an agreement are protected. Summary procedures are provided to compel[6] or prevent[7] arbitration and to review awards with express provisions relating to judicial vacation,[8] modification, and correction of awards,[9] as well as for the enforcement of the results of the arbitration process.[10] Even though resort to courts is authorized, the basic intent of the act is to discourage litigation and to foster voluntary resolution of disputes in a forum created, controlled, and administered by the

---

5. Although in the minority, Minnesota as early as 1943 adopted the policy of favoring arbitration and held that an agreement to arbitrate a future dispute could be specifically enforced and repudiated the common-law doctrine of revocability. Park Construction Co. v. Independent School District, 216 Minn. 27, 11 N.W. 2d 649; Zelle v. Chicago & North Western Ry. Co., 242 Minn. 439, 65 N.W. 2d 583. Section 572.08 of the Uniform Act clearly reverses the common-law rule of nonenforceability by providing: "A written agreement to submit any existing controversy to arbitration or a provision in a written contract to submit to arbitration any controversy thereafter arising between the parties is valid, enforceable and irrevocable, save upon such grounds as exist at law or in equity for the revocation of any contract. ..." See, also, Pirsig, *The Minnesota Uniform Arbitration Act and the Lincoln Mills Case*, 42 MINN. L. REV. 333; RESTATEMENT, CONTRACTS, § 550 (1932).

6. Minn. St. 572.09(a).

7. Minn. St. 572.09(b).

8. Minn. St. 572.19.

9. Minn. St. 572.20.

10. Minn. St. 572.18 and 572.21.

written agreement. Thus, contracting parties, desiring to avail themselves of the benefits of arbitration, retain control over the arbitration process by the language of their agreements. In contracts providing for arbitration of future controversies, the parties may narrowly limit arbitrability or they may comprehensively provide that all disputes, whether arising under the terms of the contract or growing out of their relationship—even though not cognizable in a court of law or equity—may be referable to arbitration.[11] Where the intention of the parties in this respect is not clearly expressed, problems relating to judicial interference with the arbitration process inevitably arise.[12]

In this case the plaintiff vigorously contends that its claim for additional compensation is a controversy which arose during the progress of the work; that it concerns the work; and is one which the parties clearly agreed to arbitrate. Defendant, with equal vigor, contends that the claim is not a controversy concerning the work, and that it is clearly not one intended to be arbitrable. These conflicting contentions demonstrate most forcibly that the language of the contract does not clearly express the intention of the parties. Moreover, our determination would have to be based solely on the language of the contract since no other evidence relevant to the question presented was submitted to the trial court. We conclude that from the language alone a reasonable basis exists for arguing either contention. This the parties concede.

We believe that where upon application to compel arbitration the court is unable to ascertain the clear intent of the parties as to the scope of the arbitration clause in a contract, the sole issue is whether or not an agreement to arbitrate exists. Minn. St. 572.09 provides:

> (a) On application of a party showing an agreement described in section 572.08, and the opposing party's refusal to arbitrate, the court shall order the parties to proceed with arbitration, but if the opposing party denies the existence of the agreement to arbitrate, the court shall proceed summarily to the determination of the issue so raised and shall order arbitration if found for the moving party, otherwise, the application shall be denied.
>
> (b) On application, the court may stay an arbitration proceeding commenced or threatened on a showing that there is no agreement to arbitrate.

Such an issue, when in substantial and bona fide dispute, shall be forthwith and summarily tried and the stay ordered if found for the moving party. If found for the opposing party, the court shall order the parties to proceed to arbitration.

> *   *   *   *   *   *
>
> (e) An order for arbitration shall not be refused on the ground that the claim in issue lacks merit or bona fides or because any fault or grounds for the claim sought to be arbitrated have not been shown.

Section 572.19, subd. 1, provides:

> Upon application of a party, the court shall vacate an award where:
>
> *   *   *   *   *   *
>
> (3) The arbitrators exceeded their powers;
>
> *   *   *   *   *   *
>
> (5) There was no arbitration agreement and the issue was not adversely determined in proceedings under section 572.09 and the party did not participate in the arbitration hearing without raising the objection; . . .

So far as we can find, the construction and application of these provisions to the question presented is a matter of first impression. There are no legislative records which disclose the specific legislative intent underlying these provisions at the time the act was adopted in this state. However, the records of the National Conference of Commissioners on Uniform Laws, and particularly the writings of the chairman of the subcommittee that undertook the drafting of the act, disclose that the problem of judicial interference with the question of arbitrability was intended to be governed by § 2 of the Uniform Act, now Minn. St. 572.09.[13] Apart from these writings, the language of § 572.09(a, b) expressly authorizes a court to interfere and protect a party from being compelled to submit to arbitration proceedings where no arbitration agreement exists, either in fact or because the

---

11. Minn. St. 572.19, subd. 1(5).

12. The draftsmen of the Uniform Act had this problem in mind because it had arisen under the New York arbitration law which, with its prototypes in other states, served as a base for the committee's effort to draft a modern, simplified act. Pirsig, *Some Comments on Arbitration Legislation and the Uniform Act*, 10 VAND. L. REV. 685, 692 to 699.

13. Pirsig, *The Minnesota Uniform Arbitration Act and The Lincoln Mills Case*, 42 MINN. L. REV. 333; Pirsig, *Some Comments on Arbitration Legislation and the Uniform Act*, 10 VAND. L. REV. 685, 692. The intent of the draftees of the act becomes the legislative intent upon enactment. Only in this manner can uniformity be achieved. Minn. St. 645.22 provides: "Laws uniform with those of other states shall be interpreted and construed to effect their general purpose to make uniform the laws of those states which enact them." See, also, Minn. St. 572.28; People's Savings & Trust Co. v. Munsert, 212 Wis. 449, 249 N.W. 527, 250 N.W. 385, 88 A.L.R. 1306. Where a provision of the uniform state law is ambiguous resort may be had to notes of the Commissions. Colby v. Riggs National Bank, 67 App. D.C. 259, 92 F. 2d 183, 114 A.L.R. 1065; 82 C.J.S., Statutes, § 356. A review of the available notes leaves no doubt that § 572.09 is intended to govern the question of arbitrability and was designed to limit judicial interference in such cases as the one before us.

controversy sought to be arbitrated is not within the scope of the arbitration clause of the contract. Such construction does no violence to the purpose of the act since a party should not be compelled to go to the expense, trouble, and hazard of the arbitration process when he has clearly not agreed to do so. The difficulty lies in applying this rule when the intention of the parties is not clearly expressed. Where the parties are in conflict as to the scope of the provision for arbitration, and the question of the parties' intention as to such scope is reasonably debatable, the problem arises as to whether the court or the arbitrators shall decide the question. We believe in such cases the rule should be, and we hold, that the issue of arbitrability be initially determined by the arbitrators subject to a party's right reserved in § 572.19, subd. 1 (3, 5), to challenge such determination subsequent to any award. Such a rule is consistent with the purpose and objectives of the Uniform Act. It would also be more likely to coincide with the intent of the parties who, by failing to precisely delineate the controversies to be arbitrated, probably chose broad language for the purpose of extending arbitration to unforeseeable disputes. To construe § 572.09(a) to authorize a preliminary judicial determination of whether or not the applicant presented an issue referable to arbitration would be to add nonexistent language. Such a construction, in many instances, might be destructive of the arbitration clause itself. The contents of the written request for arbitration would take on the aspects of a pleading; and where no evidence was submitted to the court, technicalities never intended to be used in arbitration proceedings could be controlling.

This case illustrates the difficulties of determining the true intent of the parties. We do not have before us any of the facts that most certainly would be presented in submitting the issue of arbitrability to the arbitrators. One of the claims made by plaintiff in its request for arbitration is that defendant withheld information concerning the condition of the soil, thus forcing plaintiff to rely solely on the prebidding exploration report of the Minnesota Test Boring Company. The particulars prompting this claim, and the evidence, if any, which may support plaintiff's contention that this is part of the dispute arising "during progress of the work" and "concerning the work," are not before us.[14]

---

14. If plaintiff by this claim charges fraud in the inducement of the contract, it might be observed that it is difficult to understand how such a dispute could arise "during progress of the work."

The fact that the act directs the court to "summarily" determine the issue of arbitrability was not intended to foreclose the taking of testimony relevant to that issue where the intent of the parties can be determined from the language of the contract. When that is not possible or even probable, practical considerations alone would, in most cases, indicate that the issue of arbitrability be referable to arbitration.

Minn. St. 572.09(e) reinforces our conclusion. The act intended that arbitrators decide both questions of law and fact.[15] Arbitration is not to be refused because a party seeks to establish that the "claim in issue lacks merit or bona fides or because any fault or grounds for the claim ... have not been shown." On the preliminary application to compel arbitration a court is barred from examining into the merits of that defense. No such limitation is imposed on the court upon application of a party to vacate the award under § 572.19. By express provision the court is directed to vacate the award if the "arbitrators exceeded their powers." These provisions of the act persuasively demonstrate its policy as applied to our problem. If parties voluntarily agree to submit disputes to arbitration, the arbitration process should go forward unimpeded by judicial interference. Where the process has failed to dispose of the controversy, the rights of the parties to litigate the issue of arbitrability is not only unimpaired but both the court and the parties will be immeasurably aided by what has occurred. Where litigation follows arbitration, the cost to the parties is increased and one of the benefits claimed by proponents of arbitration is defeated. However, it must be remembered that this cannot be charged to the act but to the contract over which the parties alone had control.

Defendant argues finally that the contract requires arbitration only if both parties consent. Although the contract uses the word "may" in section 1-23, in section 1-24 it requires that disputes "shall be submitted to arbitration in accordance with the provisions" of the act. Unmistakably, the parties intended that any arbitration would be statutory and not governed by common-law principles. Minn. St. 572.08 expressly declares that an agreement to arbitrate shall be "irrevocable, save upon such grounds as exist at law or in equity for the revocation of any contract." When the parties incorporated the act into their contract, the agreement to arbitrate became irrevocable by force of this section unless the contract expressly provides for revoca-

---

15. Pirsig, *Some Comments on Arbitration Legislation and the Uniform Act*, 10 VAND. L. REV. 685, 695.

tion. Under principles relating to contracts, a provision reserving the right of revocation is enforceable and by the language of § 572.08 such a provision in an agreement would be enforceable as an exception to irrevocability. However, we are not persuaded that the terms of the contract before us include any such provision.

Reversed with instructions to enter an order directing the parties to proceed with arbitration.

SCHOOL DISTRICT NO. 46 v. A. J. DEL BIANCO AND ASSOCIATES
68 Ill. A. 2d 145, 215 N.E. 2d 25 (1966)

DAVIS, J. This case involves the propriety of the order of the Circuit Court denying defendant's motion, pursuant to section 2 of the Uniform Arbitration Act (Ill. Rev. Stat. 1963, Chap. 10, sec. 102), for an order to plaintiff and defendant to proceed to arbitration and to stay proceedings in said cause, and the appealability of such order. [The court decided that the order directing arbitration was appealable.]

Plaintiff, a School District, on March 1, 1962, entered into a standard form owner-architect agreement with defendant architect, whereby the defendant was to perform professional services in connection with the erection of the Streamwood Elementary School. The agreement outlined the basic services to be rendered by defendant; specified the extra services of the architect and the plaintiff's responsibilities; defined construction costs as well as the architect's expense; provided for payments to the architect and other routine matters; and provided for arbitration, as follows:

> Arbitration of all questions in dispute under this Agreement shall be at the choice of either party and shall be in accordance with the provisions, then obtaining of the Standard Form of Arbitration Procedure of The American Institute of Architects. This Agreement shall be specifically enforceable under the prevailing arbitration law and judgment upon the award rendered may be entered in the court of the forum, state or federal, having jurisdiction. The decisions of the arbitrators shall be a condition precedent to the right of any legal action.

The Standard form of Arbitration Procedure of The American Institute of Architects, by agreement of the parties, established the procedure to govern any arbitration conducted pursuant to the agreement.

Plaintiff filed a three count complaint against the general contractor, the architect and the bonding company in connection with the construction of the Streamwood Elementary School. Count II, against the defendant architect, alleged the execution of the aforesaid agreement; performance by plaintiff; the duty of defendant to exercise the degree of skill and diligence contracted for in preparing plans, specifications and in superintending the construction of the building; his negligence in so doing to the extent that the building settled, causing cabinets, doorways and floors to become uneven and plumbing facilities to malfunction; that the school building has never been completed as a result of defendant's failure to exercise such reasonable skill and diligence; demanded of defendant that he rectify such defective and improper work; alleged his failure and refusal to make repairs or replacements; and stated that plaintiff would be obliged to employ labor and procure materials to complete said school under proper plans and specifications, to its damage in the sum of $150,000.

To our knowledge, there are neither Illinois legislative records disclosing specific legislative intent underlying these statutory provisions, nor cases construing this Uniform Act with reference to the conflicting contentions of the parties concerning the arbitrability of disputes such as the one in litigation. Under such circumstances, it has been properly held that

> the records of the National Conference of Commissioners on Uniform Laws, and particularly the writings of the chairman of the subcommittee that undertook the drafting of the act, disclose that the problem of judicial interference with the question of arbitrability was intended to be governed by § 2 of the Uniform Act.

Layne-Minnesota Co. v. Regents of Univ. of Minn., 266 Minn. 284, 123 N.W. 2d 371, 376 (1963).

In the case at bar, the parties expressly agreed to submit to arbitration "all questions in dispute under this Agreement." However, plaintiff argues that the agreement to arbitrate does not require it to submit those controversies arising out of the relationship of the parties, and that the questions in dispute so arose and are not within the terms of the arbitration agreement. This case is before us on Count II of the complaint and the aforesaid motions, and under this posture it may be said that the intention of the parties, as to the scope of the arbitration agreement, is fairly debatable. This poses a question of construction of section 2 of the Act and the contract as to whom, under these circumstances —the Court or the arbitrators—shall make this determination.

If the dispute is clearly within the arbitration clause, the court should order arbitration. However, if the dispute is clearly not within the clause—as in the case where the agreement was limited to disputes as to the quantity requirements of the purchaser, and the claim sought to be arbitrated was for damages due to the inferior quality of merchandise delivered—then there is no agreement to arbitrate, and the court should deny arbitration.

However, if the dispute is over the scope of the issues intended to be submitted to arbitration and they are not clearly defined in the arbitration clause or agreement, as in the case at bar, then a construction by the court of the clause or contract in the light of section 2 would end in destroying the agreement of the parties that a specific term or the terms and meaning of the arbitration clause should be determined by the arbitrators. See: *Arbitrability and the Uniform Act,* Maynard E. Pirsig, 19 ARB. J. 154 (1964) ; and [Pirsig] *Some Comments on Arbitration Legislation and the Uniform Act.*

If such terms and meaning are determined by the court in defining the scope of the issues to be arbitrated, then there is only the limited factual question left for the arbitrators to consider. We believe it within the contemplation of section 8 of the Act (Ill. Rev. Stat. 1963, Chap. 10, par. 108), unless the arbitration agreement provides otherwise, that the parties are presumed to agree that everything—both as to law and fact—necessary to a decision, is included within the authority of the arbitrators. See: Continental Materials Corp. v. Gaddis Min. Co., 306 F. 2d 952, 954 (CA 10 1962).

Where there is an agreement to arbitrate and its scope is reasonably in doubt, the issue of arbitrability should be initially determined by the arbitrators, subject to the protective reservations of section 12 of the Act—under which the court may vacate an award under the varying conditions therein specified. Layne-Minnesota Co. v. Regents of Univ. of Minn., *supra,* 123 N.W. 2d 377, 378.

This view is further buttressed by the fact that under section 11 of the prior Act (Ill. Rev. Stat. 1959, Chap. 10, par. 11), fraud, corruption or other undue means, misbehavior by the arbitrators, and legal defects, were the only grounds

for vacating an award, while under section 12(a) (5) of the new Uniform Act (Ill. Rev. Stat. 1963, Chap. 10, par. 112(a) (5)), upon application of a party, the court shall vacate an award where: "There was no arbitration agreement and the issue was not adversely determined in proceedings under Section 2 and the party did not participate in the arbitration hearing without raising the objection." If it was intended that the Court should initially determine such issue of arbitrability, there would be little reason for placing authority in the Court to vacate an award where the arbitrators, in making an award, exceeded the scope of the arbitration agreement.

It is also significant that section 2(b) of the Act provides that upon preliminary application, the Court shall summarily determine the issue of arbitrability, and section 2(e) specifies that the Court is barred from refusing arbitration "on the ground that the claim in issue lacks merit or bona fides or because any fault or grounds for the claim sought to be arbitrated have not been shown," while upon application to vacate the award under section 12(a) (3)—which provides for the vacation of an award where the "arbitrators exceed their powers"—there is no statutory restriction upon the power of the court.

The foregoing provisions of the Act militate against the contention that a party to an arbitration agreement may choose between the judicial or arbitration forum. The sole issue under the Act on the preliminary hearings to compel or stay arbitration, is whether there is an agreement to arbitrate. If so, the Court should order arbitration ; if not, arbitration should be refused. Upon this simple formula, the preliminary hearings on such issue should be determined. See: *Some Comments on Arbitration Legislation* and the *Uniform Act, supra.*

If arbitration fails to dispose of the controversy, the parties may then litigate the issues of arbitrability, and the arbitration proceeding which took place should be an aid to both the litigants and the Court in the subsequent court hearings. Layne-Minnesota Co. v. Regents of Univ. of Minn., *supra* 377.

Reversed and remanded with instructions.

C.

Some Problems Concerning the Validity of the Agreement to Arbitrate—Before Arbitration

MATTER OF KRAMER AND UCHITELLE, INC. (EDDINGTON FABRICS CORP.) 288 N.Y. 467, 43 N.E. 2d 493 (1942)

RIPPEY, J. Although the foregoing were separately instituted and separately prosecuted proceedings under article 84 of the Civil Practice Act, argument thereof was consolidated in the court below and in this court, the same questions are involved in all of them and they will be treated as one consolidated proceeding in our opinion here.

On June 18 and 19, 1941, the petitioner-respondent, Kramer & Uchitelle, Inc., entered into four separate written contracts severally with appellants, Eddington Fabrics Corporation, M. Lowenstein & Sons, Inc., and Classic Mills, Inc., affiliated corporations, generally similar in form as to all features affecting the decision here, by which appellants agreed to buy and the petitioner agreed to sell 365,000 yards of plaincloths, woven cuts as far as practicable, of specified count, width, weight and quality at 8.9375 cents per yard for 40,000 yards, 9 cents per yard for 150,000 yards and at 9.8 cents per yard for the balance, net ten days, F.O.B. mill, delivery to be made on order by installments during the months of August and September, 1941, subject to the provisions of Standard Cotton Textile Sale Note (with Specification G), which was made a part of the agreement. The "plaincloths" referred to in the contracts were "Cotton Gray Goods." Each contract contained a clause that

> any controversy arising under or in relation to this contract shall be settled by arbitration. If the parties are unable to agree respecting time, place, method or rules of the arbitration, then such arbitration shall be held in the city of New York in accordance with the laws of the State of New York and the rules then obtaining of the General Arbitration Council of the Textile Industry.

On April 11, 1941, the President of the United States, in accordance with authority vested in him by the Congress as affecting the emergency, issued Executive Order No. 8734, establishing the Office of Price Administration and Civilian Supply (OPACS) in the Executive Office of the President and defined its duties and functions and, pursuant thereto, appointed Mr. Leon Henderson as Administrator. On June 27, 1941, Administrator Henderson, by due authority, issued Price Schedule No. 11, which pertained to "Cotton Gray Goods," effective June 28, 1941, which read in part as follows:

> 1316.2 Maximum Prices Established for Cotton Grey Goods. (a) On and after June 30, 1941, regardless of any commitment theretofore entered into, no person shall sell or deliver, or offer to sell or deliver, any Cotton Grey Goods, and no person shall buy or accept delivery of or offer to buy or accept delivery of any Cotton Grey Goods at a price exceeding the maximum prices set forth in 1316.7.

The price established in 1316.7 was 8.037 cents per yard. No party here challenges the validity of the order and all parties construe it as applicable to existing contracts.

When the delivery dates arrived, the seller refused the demands of the purchasers to make deliveries at the "maximum price set forth" in the order of the Price Administrator on the grounds that performance of the contract had been forbidden by law and non-performance had been excused. The buyers served demands on the seller that it submit the matter to arbitration. Thereupon the seller moved in each case for a stay of arbitration pursuant to section 1458 of the Civil Practice Act upon the grounds that by the order of the Price Administrator performance of the contracts had been frustrated and that such frustration terminated the whole contract including the incidental provisions for arbitration. The notice of motion in each case contained a statement that the court would be asked to order an immediate trial of the issues. In the first motion returnable an order was granted ordering a trial but upon a reargument requested by purchaser, the court held that no trial was necessary and stayed arbitration permanently upon the motion papers. Petitioner's motions in the subsequent cases were granted upon the authority of the first. A separate order was entered in each case at Special Term and in the Appellate Division. Upon appeal, the Appellate Division unanimously affirmed in each case, without opinion, but granted leave to appeal to this court.

Arbitration clauses in contracts such as those under consideration are directed solely to the remedy—not to the validity or existence of the contract itself. Thus proceedings to enforce arbitration under article 84 of the Civil Practice Act presuppose the existence of a valid and enforceable contract at the time the remedy is sought. (Matter of Berkovitz v. Arbib & Houlberg, Inc., 230 N.Y. 261, 271 ; Mulji v. Cheong Yue Steamship Co., Ltd [1926] A.C. 497.) Seasonable challenge may be made to the court to the existence of such a contract by one who stays out of the arbitration and, if no issue of fact is presented on such challenge, the issue is properly determinable by the court as matter of law. (Matter of Finsilver, Still & Moss, Inc., v. Goldberg Maas & Co., 253 N.Y. 382.) There is no issue of fact raised by the record. The affidavits are in agreement as to all material facts and no reason for a trial was shown to the court. If a trial had been ordered, there would have been no issue to decide. Both parties to each proceeding admit the making of the contract, that the contract price was higher than that fixed as the maximum by the Price Administrator, that the ceiling was fixed before delivery was required by the contract and that the contract was not performed.

As of the precise time when the remedy was invoked, it was to be determined whether public policy prohibited enforcement of the contracts according to their terms. The price at which the goods were to be sold as of the time of delivery was as much of the essence of the contract as any of its other provisions and controlling public policy barred delivery at that price. By act of government there was complete frustration of performance excusing the seller from performance as matter of law. (Mulji v. Cheong Yue Steamship Co., supra ; Varagnolo v. Partola Mfg. Co., 239 N.Y. 621 ; Nitro Powder Co. v. Agency of Canadian Car & Foundry Co., 233 N.Y. 294 ; Mawhinney v. Millbrook Woolen Mills Inc., 231 N.Y. 290 ; 6 WILLISTON ON THE LAW OF CONTRACTS, §§ 1759, 1938.)

Arbitration was the method agreed to between the parties to determine controversies in connection with the obligations of the seller and buyers to deliver and pay for cotton gray goods at a stipulated price. The question was not whether the seller could be compelled to deliver the goods at the price fixed as the maximum by the Price Administrator. It was whether delivery could be compelled according to the terms of the contracts of sale and the Price Administrator put an end to that question and to the contract itself before time for delivery arrived or any dispute as to delivery arose. Thus there was no

"controversy arising under or in relation to" the contracts. The arbitration clause was only an incidental part of an indivisible contract of purchase and sale and when the contract was at an end the arbitration provision no longer existed or had any force whatsoever (Mulji v. Cheong Yue Steamship Co., supra ; RUSSELL ON ARBITRATION AND AWARD, p. 78) except as to rights and wrongs which had already come into existence as to which the contract still remained in effect.

The orders should be affirmed, with costs.

LEHMAN, CH. J. (dissenting).
I shall state as briefly as I can the reasons why I cannot concur in that conclusion. I do not pause to consider the legal effect of the order of the Price Administrator. That is the question which the buyer demands should be submitted to arbitration. We do not reach that question if the parties have agreed that it should be determined by arbitration, not by the court. The court, upon the motion to stay arbitration, has power to decide only an issue "as to the making of the contract ... or the failure to comply therewith." (Civ. Pr. Act. § 1450.) As I have said, there is no issue as to the making of the contract for arbitration. The only issue in this case is as to the failure to comply therewith. There is failure to comply with the contract of arbitration, which is, I concede, only an incidental part of the contract to sell and pay for goods, if the controversy as to whether the principal contract has been terminated by impossibility of performance in exact accordance with its terms falls within the scope of the agreement to arbitrate. The primary question to be determined upon this appeal concerns the scope of the agreement to arbitrate.

Doubtless, since the contract for arbitration is only an incidental part of an indivisible contract of purchase and sale, it can apply only to a controversy in regard to the obligation of the seller to deliver the goods or the obligation of the buyer to accept and pay for them. If, then, it appeared without dispute that these obligations had been terminated either by act of the parties or from some other cause, it would be plain that no controversy exists which the parties agreed to submit to arbitration. Here there is no dispute concerning the facts, but there is dispute about the effect of those facts upon the obligations assumed by the buyer and the seller. The seller asserts that as matter of law neither party can or may lawfully perform the obligation it assumed at a time when performance was lawful. The buyer asserts that the obligation of the seller to *deliver* the goods may be performed without violation of the order of the Price Administrator, and that the effect of the order is only to relieve the buyer of obligation to pay for the goods the part of the stipulated price in excess of the price fixed by the order. I assume, *arguendo* but only *arguendo* and without further consideration or attempt to decide, that a court of law applying legal rules and principles would be constrained to sustain the contention of the seller. I cannot assume that arbitrators might not sustain the contention of the buyer, and to me it seems clear that by agreement of the parties any controversy concerning the existence, scope or effect of the obligations assumed under the contract is a controversy "arising under" the contract and also "in relation" to the contract, and that such a controversy must be "settled by arbitration" in accordance with the contract made by the parties.

In the affidavit of the seller upon the motion for a stay of arbitration the demand of the buyer for arbitration is characterized as

> a very clever move because arbitrators in the textile industry—invariably laymen who are untrained in the distinctions of the law—might be deluded into thinking that Mr. Henderson's price ruling was intended to benefit the buyer and thus make some kind of an award to it.

In that statement the seller, it seems to me, supplies an incontrovertible reason why the arbitration should proceed. The parties have agreed to abide by the judgment of business men in *all* disputes concerning the interpretation of their contract or the scope of the obligations they have assumed, and disputes concerning the effect of subsequent words, acts or events upon these obligations are not excluded. It has been said that

> the conditions that rendered performance impossible do not terminate the contract *ab initio*, and vitiate what has been done and what remains to be done that is capable of execution. The conditions may be of such an extent as to amount to a substantial abrogation of the entire contract, or they may relate to an insignificant part of the contract, but they excuse performance only to the extent to which performance is impossible, and leave what has been done valid permitting a recovery therefor, and may not excuse performance of the remaining work. No general rule can be laid down which will apply to all cases, but each case must be decided upon its own facts, and that this course can be taken and justice done according to the facts in each case unhampered by written rules is due to the great flexibility of the common law which is its chief merit.

(Kinser Construction Co. v. State, 125 N.Y. Supp. 46, at p. 55; affd., 145 App. Div. 41; affd., 204 N.Y. 381; quoted with approval, 6

Williston on The Law of Contracts [1938], § 1956.) Professor Williston there states the applicable rule: "Since the qualification of the literal terms of the promise is imposed by the law, on principles of justice, not because of the expressed intention of the parties, the extent of the qualification depends merely on what is just." The parties have agreed to submit question of what is just to business men "untrained in the distinctions of the law." The courts should not assume to decide according to legal principles a controversy which the parties have agreed should be decided otherwise. The order should be reversed, etc.

LOUGHRAN, FINCH, LEWIS and CONWAY, JJ., concur with RIPPEY, J.; LEHMAN, Ch. J., dissents in opinion in which DESMOND, J., concurs.

Orders affirmed.

Compare Behrens v. Feuerring, 296 N.Y. 172, 71 N.E. 2d 454 (1947) and see Reconstruction Finance Corp. v. Harrisons and Crosfield, (2d Cir. 1953) 204 F. 2d 366, 368, n. 7.

MATTER OF EXERCYCLE CORP. (MARATTA)
9 N.Y. 2d 329, 174 N.E. 2d 463 (1961)

FULD, J. In March of 1955, James Maratta entered into an employment agreement with Exercycle Corporation. It provided that "Exercycle employs Maratta as its Vice-President in charge of sales" and that he hereby "shall have general charge and supervision of the selling activities for Exercycle." And, the agreement went on to recite, "Maratta accepts the employment and agrees to devote his best efforts and full time to Exercycle's sales activities." The employment was to continue "until he voluntarily leaves the employ of Exercycle or dies", with Exercycle retaining the right to terminate the contract, if sales fell below specified levels. The agreement further stated that "Any dispute arising out of or in connection with this agreement shall be settled by arbitration in accordance with the rules of the American Arbitration Association."

Prior to entering into his agreement with Exercycle, Maratta had been associated with several large and successful enterprises and thereafter became an independent direct sales consultant. In early 1955, he was approached by the then president and controlling stockholder of Exercycle and asked to join that company as a direct sales specialist in improving its business and sales which were then at a low ebb. After a period of negotiation and study, Maratta agreed to give up his work as an independent consultant and, in the words of the contract, "to devote his best efforts and full time to Exercycle's sales activities." He was fearful, however, that, once he had developed Exercycle's sales to the point where his compensation, based on commissions, was substantial, a new management might attempt to deprive him of the fruits of his efforts. For this reason, he insisted upon and was given a life employment contract.

Maratta worked for the corporation for some four years and, apparently, the fact that he devoted all of his time, his efforts and his imagination to the enterprise, revitalized the company and improved its business. In 1959, differences arose between Maratta and the corporation—control of which had been acquired by a Mr. Little—and Maratta resigned as president, to which office he had succeeded, but continued in his employment under the 1955 arrangement. Some time later, Mr. Little expressed displeasure with Maratta's contract and the latter, having come to believe that the new management was interfering with his supervision of sales, advised Mr. Little, by letter dated January 12, 1960, that he had "started" to seek employment elsewhere. Three days later, an officer of Exercycle responded. Treating the letter as one of resignation, he expressed regret at Maratta's "decision to terminate [his] relationship with the Exercycle Corporation."

Relying upon the broad arbitration provision in the contract, namely, to arbitrate any dispute "arising out of or in connection with" the agreement, Maratta sought arbitration. Exercycle thereupon brought this proceeding for a stay on the ground that the alleged contract of employment "is void and unenforceable in that ... is lacking in mutuality by obligating Petitioner [Exercycle] to employ Respondent [Maratta] for a definite term *i.e.* for Respondent's life and permitting Respondent to terminate his employment and said alleged contract at will." Exercycle also objected to the arbitration on the further ground that, irrespective of its validity, the contract "is no longer in existence" by reason of Maratta's having terminated the contract and resigned as an employee.

The court at Special Term denied the motion for a stay and the Appellate Division affirmed by a three-to-two vote. Both the majority and the minority, to support their respective conclusions, proceeded to construe the contract. It was the majority's view that the contract was one to employ the respondent for life and that the provision "that the employment was to continue until the respondent 'voluntarily leaves the employ of Exercycle or dies' did not as a matter of law make the contract illusory or just an agreement terminable at will." On the other hand, it was the dissenters' opinion that the contract was "illusory" since the employee did not agree to work for life or for any other definite period.

We, too, agree that there should be arbitration, but we reach our conclusion by a route quite different from that taken by the courts below. In our view, the question whether the contract lacked mutuality of obligation, depending as it does primarily on a reading and construction of the agreement, and involving, as is obvious from the disagreement amongst the judges of this court and the courts below, substantial difficulties of interpretation, is to be determined by the arbitrators, not the court. Once it be ascertained that the parties broadly agreed to arbitrate a dispute "arising out of or in connection with" the agreement, it is for the arbitrators to decide what the agreement means and to enforce it according to the rules of law which they deem appropriate in the circumstances.

It has long been this State's policy that, where parties enter into an agreement and, in one of its provisions, promise that any dispute arising out of or in connection with it shall be settled by arbitration, any controversy which arises between them and is within the compass of the provision must go to arbitration. (Civ. Prac. Act, § 1448 ; see *e.g.* Matter of Kelley, 240 N.Y. 74, 79 ; Matter of Marchant v. Mead-Morrison Mfg. Co., 252 N.Y. 284, 298 ; Matter of Lipman [Haeuser Shellac Co.], 289 N.Y. 76 ; Matter of Terminal Auxiliar Maritima [Winkler], 6 N.Y. 2d 294.) As the court wrote in Matter of Marchant (252 N.Y., at p. 298).

> Parties to a contract may agree, if they will, that any and all controversies growing out of it in any way shall be submitted to arbitration. If they do, the courts of New York will give effect to their intention.

As exceptions to this general policy, however, we have held that a court will enjoin arbitration (1) where fraud or duress, practiced against one of the parties, renders the agreement voidable (see Matter of Lipman [Haeuser Shellac Co.], 289 N.Y. 76, 79, *supra* ; cf. Matter of Behrens [Feuerring], 296 N.Y. 172, 178 ; Matter of Wrap-Vertiser Corp. [Plotnick], 3 N.Y. 2d 17 ; Matter of Metro Plan v. Miscione, 257 App. Div. 652, 655) ; (2) where there is no "bonafide dispute" between the parties, that is, where the asserted claim is frivolous (see Alpert v. Admiration Knitwear Co., 304 N.Y. 1, 6 ; Matter of General Elec. Co. [United

Elec. Radio & Mach. Workers], 300 N.Y. 262; Matter of International Assn. of Machinists [Cutler-Hammer], 297 N.Y. 519; Matter of Wenger & Co. v. Propper Silk Hosiery Mills, 239 N.Y. 199); (3) where the performance which is the subject of the demand for arbitration is prohibited by statute (see Matter of Kramer & Uchitelle [Eddington Fabrics Corp.], 288 N.Y. 467); or (4) where a condition precedent to arbitration under the contract or an applicable statute has not been fulfilled. (See Matter of Board of Educ. [Heckler Elec. Co.], 7 N.Y. 2d 476; Matter of Lipman [Haeuser Shellac Co.], 289 N.Y. 76, 79, *supra*; Matter of Cauldwell-Wingate Co. [New York City Housing Auth.], 262 App. Div. 829, motion for leave to appeal denied 287 N.Y. 853.)

Applying these principles to the case before us, there can be no doubt that Maratta and Exercycle made a contract in which they promised each other to arbitrate any differences which might arise out of or in connection with it. In fact, the agreement, entered into in March of 1955, was continued in force, its terms and provisions complied with and carried out, until January, 1960, a period of almost five years. It may hardly be said, therefore, that the making of the present agreement is in issue under section 1450 of the Civil Practice Act.

Nor is the agreement which was entered into "void and unenforceable" within the meaning of Matter of Kramer (288 N.Y. 467, *supra*), as Exercycle contends. In that case, performance of an agreement had been rendered illegal by Federal price control regulations, and we stayed arbitration of the claim, based on a failure to deliver the goods contracted for, on the ground that "controlling public policy barred delivery" at the contract price (288 N.Y., at p. 472). The present case is patently dissimilar. In Matter of Kramer, public policy as embodied in a Federal statute forbade the performance which was the subject of dispute and that policy and statute were as binding on the arbitrators as on the courts. No statute or public policy, as reflected in a legislative act, is here involved to render the employment contract unenforcible and, absent one or the other, it has long been firmly established that arbitrators may disregard the strict and traditional rules of law. (See Fudickar v. Guardian Mut. Life Ins. Co., 62 N.Y. 392, 399–400; STURGES, COMMERCIAL ARBITRATION AND AWARDS 793-798 [1930].) In other words, since there is no statute or public policy which prohibits the performance of a promise to employ one "until he voluntarily [quits] or dies," enforcement of performance by the arbitrators in this case is not rendered unlawful or legally impermissible.

Maratta's claim is not frivolous or insubstantial (cf., *e.g.* General Elec. Co. [Elec. Workers], 300 N.Y. 262, *supra*) and there is no suggestion of fraud (cf., *e.g.,* Matter of Lipman [Haeuser Shellac Co.] 289 N.Y. 76, 79, *supra*) or an unfilled condition precedent to arbitration. (Cf., *e.g.,* Matter of Board of Educ. [Heckler Elec. Co.], 7 N.Y. 2d 476, *supra*.) Under these circumstances, where there is a broad provision for arbitration, such as we have here, arbitration may be had as to all issues arising under the contract. (See Matter of Terminal Auxiliar Maritima [Winkler], 6 N.Y. 2d 294, 298, *supra*; Matter of Paloma Frocks [Shamokin Sportswear Corp.], 3 N.Y. 2d 572, 574; Matter of Lipman [Haeuser Shellac Co.], 289 N.Y. 76, 80, *supra*; Fudickar v. Guardian Mut. Life Ins. Co., 62 N.Y. 392, 399–400, *supra*.)

Exercycle's claim is that no court of law would enforce the promise which it made to employ Maratta for life. Obviously, however, once having agreed to eschew recourse to courts of law and have its disputes with Maratta settled by arbitrators, Exercycle cannot urge, in opposition to arbitration, that a court of law would not enforce the agreement. If the issue involved was solely one of construction or interpretation, it would, without a doubt, be for the arbitrators to decide. The mere fact that its determination involves a mixed question of the agreement's meaning and of law should not lead to a different result. Whether the issue is one involving interpretation or law or fact or all three, it is for the arbitrators and, as long as they remain within their jurisdiction and do not reach an irrational result, they may fashion the law to fit the facts before them. (See Matter of National Cash Register Co. [Wilson], 8 N.Y. 2d 377, 383; Matter of Wenger & Co. v. Propper Silk Hosiery Mills, 239 N.Y. 199, 203, *supra*; Fudickar v. Guardian Mut. Life Ins. Co., 62 N.Y. 392, 399, *supra*.) So this court said in the *Fudickar* case (62 N.Y., at p. 399):

> The arbitrator is a judge appointed by the parties; he is by their consent invested with judicial functions in the particular case; he is to determine the right as between the parties in respect to the matter submitted, and all questions of fact or law upon which the right depends are . . . deemed to be referred to him for decision. The court possesses no general supervisory power over awards, and if arbitrators keep within their jurisdiction their award will not be set aside because they have erred in judgment either upon the facts or the law.

In short, the issue before us is not whether a court of law would enforce Maratta's claim, but rather whether, as part of their agreement, the parties mutually promised to resolve all controversies "arising out of or in connection with" their agreement by arbitration. If the arbitrators could rationally and legitimately make an award in favor of Maratta, a court is not justified in staying the arbitration even if the claim would not be enforcible at law. In point of fact, we have declined to enjoin an arbitration even where an arbitrator has been asked to do what a court of law would clearly not do. (See Matter of Staklinski [Pyramid Elec. Co.], 6 N.Y. 2d 159; cf. Matter of Grayson-Robinson Stores [Iris Constr. Corp.], 8 N.Y. 2d 133.) To paraphrase what this court wrote in the *Staklinski* case (6 N.Y. 2d, at pp. 163–164), since the parties agreed to arbitration, it is beside the point to consider whether or not in a case such as the present a court of law would enforce the employer's promise to employ Maratta for life.   ,

Since Exercycle's further claim that Maratta had resigned and thereby brought his employment to an end turns on the construction of the letter written by him and on an appraisal of his conduct, the issue of termination must also be decided by the arbitrators. (See Matter of Terminal Auxiliar Maritima [Winkler], 6 N.Y. 2d 294, 298, *supra*; Matter of Lipman [Haeuser Shellac Co.], 289 N.Y. 76, *supra*.)

The order of the Appellate Division should be affirmed, with costs.

FROESSEL, J. (concurring). I am in agreement with the majority that there should be an affirmance here. I do not agree, however, with their reasoning that it was error for the Appellate Division to pass on the question of the alleged lack of mutuality of the contract or its illusory nature. The notice of motion for a stay was made upon the ground that the contract "is void and unenforceable on its face." Should there in fact be an absence of mutuality of obligation, or illusoriness—which in essence means an absence of consideration—the purported contract would be invalid and unenforcible, as petitioner contends (Schlegel Mfg. Co. v. Cooper's Glue Factory, 231 N.Y. 459; Bintz v. City of Hornell, 268 App. Div. 742, 747, affd. 295 N.Y. 628; 1 CORBIN, CONTRACTS, §§ 152, 145). In that case, as Professor Corbin puts it, no "contract was made" (p. 499)—it never came into existence. Determination of that issue, under well-established principles, is a threshold matter for determination by the court.

The rule is succinctly stated in Matter of Kramer & Uchitelle (Eddington Fabrics Corp.) (288 N.Y. 467, 471) as follows:

> Arbitration clauses in contracts such as those under consideration are directed solely to the remedy—not to the validity or existence of the contract itself.

Thus, proceedings to enforce arbitration under article 84 of the Civil Practice Act *presuppose the existence of a valid and enforceable contract* at the time the remedy is sought. (Matter of Berkovitz v. Arbib & Houlberg, Inc., 230 N.Y. 261, 271; Mulji v. Cheong Yue Steamship Co., Ltd. [1926], A.C. 497.) Seasonable challenge may be made to the court to the existence of such a contract by one who stays out of the arbitration and . . . *the issue is properly determinable by the court as matter of law*. (Matter of Finsilver, Still & Moss, Inc. v. Goldberg, Maas & Co., 253 N.Y. 382.) (Emphasis supplied.)

In Matter of Lipman (Haeuser Shellac Co.) (289 N.Y. 76) we acknowledged that the issue of "whether the contract never came into existence" is for the court (*id.*, at p. 79); and in Matter of Sarle (Sperry Gyroscope Co.) (4 A.D. 2d 638, affd. 4 N.Y. 2d 917) the distinction between questions of "performance under the contract" and "the contract itself" was stressed (4 A.D. 2d, at p. 640), the former being for the arbitrators and the latter for the court (see, also, Matter of Wrap-Vertiser Corp. [Plotnick], 3 N.Y. 2d 17, 20, 22).

The logic of this rule is forcefully stated in Matter of Finsilver, Still & Moss v. Goldberg, Maas & Co. (253 N.Y. 382) where Chief Judge Cardozo, writing for a unanimous court, said (pp. 390–391):

> If in truth there is *no contract at all or* none calling for arbitration, the self-constituted tribunal is a nullity, without power to bind or loose by force of its decision. . . . In the absence of a *contract* expressing a consent to arbitrate, an award by an arbitrator is an act of usurpation. (Emphasis supplied.)

Simply put, the legal existence of the arbitral tribunal depends on contract. It is from that agreement between the parties that their very being, or jurisdiction and power to act, derives. Unless such contract, when seasonably challenged is declared valid and enforcible, therefore, the arbitral tribunal can never legally come into being. As the court stated in Matter of Gruen v. Carter (173 Misc. 765, 766, affd. 259 App. Div. 712, motion for rearg. den. 259 App. Div. 813), "It is not for the arbitrators to decide upon the validity of the very agreement upon which their own status as arbitrators is predicated"; or, as Judge Burke well put it in Matter of Wrap-Vertiser Corp. (Plotnick) (3 N.Y. 2d 17, 22, *supra*), "Obviously, parties cannot agree, in an invalid contract, to arbitrate the validity of the contract."*

---

*The majority did not disagree with this premise in the *Wrap-Vertiser* case. Judge Van Voorhis there stated: "Even if he had rescinded or asked for rescission, such an issue would have had to have been decided in court *before* it could be known that an agreement existed supplying a foundation for the jurisdiction of the arbitrators" (p. 20; italics supplied).

The majority in this case, without purporting to overrule these well-established principles and their underlying logic, state the applicable rule to be that

> where parties enter into an agreement and, in one of its provisions, promise that any dispute arising out of or in connection with it shall be settled by arbitration, any controversy which arises between them and is within the compass of the provision, must go to arbitration.

This statement of the allegedly established law in this State contains its own refutation. If it has not been determined whether "an agreement" was entered into, what basis is there for the existence of the arbitrators and their jurisdiction in the matter? Again, if mutuality of obligation is lacking, there is no agreement—or, as Chief Judge Cardozo stated in *Finsilver* (*supra*), "no contract at all"—and the existence of such an agreement when seasonably challenged must be determined preliminarily by a court of law in order to legally constitute the arbitral tribunal, and afford them jurisdiction over the controversy between the parties arising out of the agreement.

Conceivably, the only rationale which can justify the position of the majority is that the arbitration clause is an agreement separate and apart from the main agreement, supported by its own consideration. But the majority does not proceed on that basis. They recognize—as our decisions from *Finsilver* through Matter of Sarle (*supra*) clearly demonstrate—that in this jurisdiction the promise to arbitrate is considered to be but a clause or part of the over-all contract, for they state there is "an agreement," and "one of *its provisions*" (emphasis supplied) contains a "promise" to arbitrate. Consequently, if the over-all contract is lacking in consideration—*i.e.* illusory or lacking in mutuality—or is otherwise invalid, it is unenforcible, and the right to arbitrate, which is a part of it and contingent thereon, falls. Unless we determine this preliminarily as a matter of law, the jurisdiction of the arbitrators has not been established. If there be no contract, they are a "self-constituted" "nullity."

It is no answer, as the majority state, that, since "the question whether the contract lacked mutuality of obligation" depends "primarily on a reading and construction of the agreement" and involves "substantial difficulties of interpretation," a basis for arbitration has been established. It is rather our function to resolve these questions since they bear on the validity, enforcibility and existence of the contract, upon which the right to arbitrate and the jurisdiction of the arbitrators in turn depend. If no agreement conferring that right and jurisdiction exists,

there is nothing for the arbitrators to read and construe; and the happenstance that the question may be difficult does not permit us to pass the problem on to the arbitral tribunal—which as yet has no legal being.

Inasmuch as I am in agreement with the majority of the Appellate Division that the contract here at issue is not lacking in mutuality of obligation, the arbitrators may be properly constituted and adjudicate the controversies between the parties arising out of the agreement, and on that basis I would affirm.

DYE, J. (dissenting). In dealing with controversies concerning the enforcibility of arbitration, the initial question is whether the underlying contract is valid and enforcible. If it is, then we may pass to the question of whether the contract, by its terms, makes provision for the settlement of disputes arising thereunder by arbitration. If not, then we do not enforce arbitration since its vitality depends, in the first instance, on the existence of a valid contract (Civ. Prac. Act, art. 84, § 1450). Whether the term "contract" refers to the entire agreement in which the provision for arbitration is contained, or it refers, by a loose construction of that term, solely to the clause permitting arbitration is at the heart of this controversy.

While there is a school of thought favoring the view that the power of the court is limited to a determination of whether or not an agreement to arbitrate has been made (cf. 36 YALE L. J. 866; Note, 24 N.Y.U.L. Q. REV. 429), our decisions, until now, have uniformly held that an arbitration clause fails if a contract was never made (Matter of Wrap-Vertiser Corp. [Plotnick], 3 N.Y. 2d 17; Matter of Finsilver, Still & Moss v. Goldberg, Maas & Co., 253 N.Y. 382; Matter of Levinsohn Corp. [Joint Bd. of Cloak Makers' Union], 299 N.Y. 454; 38 Cornell L. Q. 391; 6 Corbin, Contracts, § 1444).

Here, there is a real dispute between the parties concerning the existence of a contract. This, under the authorities, is for the court to determine before proceeding to the question of arbitration. On its face, the ability of this contract to survive the scrutiny of a court of law is indeed dubious. It lacks mutuality and is illusory. It provides that the employment of Maratta shall continue until he voluntarily leaves the employ of Exercycle or dies. Maratta is thus privileged in language which includes no restrictive conditions to quit his employment without obligation to respond in damages. Exercycle's promise is to retain Maratta for as long as he wishes to continue, provided only that he maintain sales above a specified minimum. Maratta promised to devote his full time and best efforts to the business. He promised nothing with respect to continuation of employment, for he was at liberty to leave voluntarily at any time.

When Maratta's promise to put forth his best efforts on a full-time basis is read together with the option to quit at any time, it becomes an unenforcible promise—and amounts to no more than a mere gratuitous statement, furnishing the company with nothing more than a hope that it will come about and as such is an illusion of a promise. So viewed, the entire agreement is unenforcible for lack of mutuality of obligation. It follows then that all the provisions contained therein, including the arbitration clause, are likewise unenforcible.

DURST v. ABRASH
22 A.D. 2d 39, 253 N.Y.S. 2d 351
(First Dept. 1964)

BREITEL, J. P. In an action for a declaratory judgment to determine that a certain purported stock sale transaction was in fact a disguise for a usurious loan agreement defendant appeals from an order denying her motion to compel arbitration (CPLR 7503, subd. [a]). Special Term denied the motion but directed a preliminary trial of the issues upon which arbitrability depends. The issue is whether the agreement to arbitrate has independent viability apart from the alleged usurious transactions so that all the issues, including the claim of usury, are for the arbitrators to determine rather than the court.

The order should be affirmed. The subsidiary agreement to arbitrate is subject to the alleged illegality of the principal agreement.

The transaction, as described by plaintiff, was a loan to plaintiff of $30,000, disguised in the form of a sale by him to defendant of 10,000 shares of Class A common stock in a close corporation. Plaintiff was required to repurchase the stock some 15 months later at a price of $5.40 per share. In addition, defendant was to receive the dividends payable on the stock, amounting to 60 cents per share, or a total of $6,000 in dividends. Consequently, under the transaction, if it was what plaintiff alleges it to be, defendant would receive interest at the rate of 80 per cent per annum.

Simultaneously with the execution of the principal agreement in suit the parties also executed, under the same date, a paper which read as follows:

> It is hereby agreed among the undersigned that any dispute, claim, or controversy arising under or pursuant to letter agreements between them dated this day, shall be settled by arbitration in New York City pursuant to the rules of the American Arbitration Association then obtaining.

The statute provides that "[w]here there is no substantial question whether a valid agreement was made or complied with ... the court shall direct the parties to arbitrate" (CPLR 7503, subd. [a]). Whether the statute, which was adopted in its present form in 1962 and became effective September 1, 1963 (CPLR 10005), changed the law as it existed under the Civil Practice Act (§ 1450) need not be dispositive of the issue in this case. The law under the Civil Practice Act had been that a contract for the doing of an act the performance of which was prohibited by statute or was otherwise "void and unenforceable" was not enforceable in arbitration (Matter of Exercycle Corp. [Maratta], 9 N.Y. 2d 329, 334–335 ; Matter of Kramer & Uchitelle [Eddington Fabrics Corp.], 288 N.Y. 467, 471). In this case, concededly, there are various statutes affecting the legality or validity of usurious transactions.

If, on the other hand, CPLR changed the law then defendant's situation is the worse. The Civil Practice Act provided for the preliminary determination of a "substantial issue as to the making of the contract or submission or the failure to comply therewith" (§ 1450). The language was always troublesome and there was decisional law that the court was to decide as a preliminary matter not merely the fact of making an agreement but also whether the parties had succeeded in effecting an enforceable contract to arbitrate (see concurring and dissenting opinions in Matter of Exercycle Corp., *supra*, and the cases cited).

The language in CPLR, on the other hand, makes explicit that the preliminary question for the court is whether there is a substantial question of the existence of a "valid agreement" to arbitrate. If the statute intended the meaning normally attributed to those words there is no question that a preliminary question for the court to determine is whether or not there is a valid arbitration agreement in the first instance. Certainly, if the new statute was intended to change the law, that is the only direction in which the change points. In that case, *a fortiori,* an agreement to arbitrate subject to a claim of infirmity for illegality in the principal agreement involves a preliminary question to be determined by the court and not by the arbitrators.

There is some authority that the new statute, which was enacted after the *Exercycle* case, was not intended to change the pre-existing law (8 WEINSTEIN-KORN-MILLER, N.Y. Civ. Prac., par.

7503.02). The commentators, in supporting that view, however, cite the Second Advisory Committee Report (2d Preliminary Rep. of Advisory Comm, on Practice and Procedure, p. 135, 1958 Report of Temporary Comm. on Courts, N.Y. Legis. Doc., 1958, No. 13, p. 135). In fact, the Second Report draft of the statute did not expressly refer to the "validity" of the agreement but only to "the existence of the agreement." This language continued unchanged through the 1962 drafts even after the section had received its present designation "§ 7503" (6th Report Sen. Finance Comm., N.Y. Legis. Doc., 1962, No. 8, p. 648). It was much later in the 1962 legislative session that the language was changed to its present form referring to validity of the agreement. This, therefore, may suggest an argument that the new statute was intended to change the law, or, at least, restate the rule as generalized in the *Kramer* case (*supra*).

The rule in the *Kramer* case (referring generally to the necessity of there being a valid and enforcible contract before there can be arbitration under a subsidiary clause) was cast in some doubt by the opinion in the *Exercycle* case (*supra*). The holding in the *Exercycle* case certainly was that common-law contract invalidity, as distinguished from public policy illegality, of a principal agreement containing an otherwise viable arbitration clause was not a preliminary matter to be determined by the court. Whether the language in CPLR was intended to overrule the holding in the *Exercycle* case, a matter which is not relevant to the issues in this case, is quite another question. It is this last question with which the commentators were primarily concerned, namely, whether technical common law contract rules (*e.g.* mutuality, consideration, and the like) which might leave a substantive agreement unenforcible at law did not also render a subsidiary agreement to arbitrate unenforcible.

As for the form of the agreement, it is undisputed law that a usurious agreement is invalid regardless of the form it takes and regardless of the rules governing integrated agreements. It is always possible to show that any transaction and the documents which are a part of it are illegal and unenforcible as a usurious transaction. RESTATEMENT, CONTRACTS, § 229, *Comment b* ; § 529 ; cf. Hartley v. Eagle Ins. Co., 222 N.Y. 178, 184–185 ; Thurston v. Cornell, 38 N.Y. 281, 285.) In such an inquiry the issue is not the interpretation of the language used but what are the facts behind the facade of language.

There is no need to consider the subtleties in the line of cases discussing whether a usurious agreement is void or voidable. That question

may be important when the interest of a third party is involved. Indeed, the distinction is not important when duress or fraud is involved, although these result only in voidable agreements ; the preliminary issue is still for the court (Matter of Exercycle Corp., *supra*).

Nor does any sound distinction rest on the obvious fact that different kinds of illegality may involve a lesser or greater degree of public harm. The fact is that there are many kinds of public policy illegality, other than usury, which require a positive election or an affirmative defense to render agreements subject to the infirmity unenforcible (17A C. J. S., Contracts, § 559).

In this case no third party is involved and a party to the alleged usury is asserting the illegality and unenforcibility of the agreements, both as to the principal agreement and the subsidiary agreement to arbitrate. No precedent suggests that illegality may be waived in advance. If so, such waiver would be accomplished indirectly by inserting an arbitration clause in the otherwise illegal agreement, thus precluding court control of the public policy issue.

The separate execution of the one-sentence agreement to arbitrate any disputes which might arise under the principal agreements does not, of course, present a separable question. The papers being executed simultaneously and as part of the same transaction are to be construed together (Nau v. Vulcan Rail & Constr. Co., 286 N.Y. 188, 197 ; 10 N.Y. JUR., Contracts, § 213 ; RESTATEMENT, CONTRACTS, § 235, subd. [c]). If the main purpose of the transaction was illegal then the subsidiary agreements, if they are truly subsidiary, are rendered invalid by the invalidity of the principal agreement (Manson v. Curtis, 223 N.Y. 313, 324).

What the situation would be with respect to a prior general agreement between parties to arbitrate all disputes which might arise between them in a variety of transactions need not now be decided.

In Matter of Metro Plan v. Miscione (257 App. Div. 652) the precise question involved in this case was decided as an alternative holding. It was held that a principal agreement, if usurious, would render unenforcible stipulations for arbitration contained within it. It was said flatly that such a question was for the court to decide and not the arbitrators.

The most significant aspect of the matter, however, is that in *Matter of Exercycle (supra)*, the court referred to the *Metro Plan* case. It was cited under the first category of cases described by the court as one in which arbitration would be preliminarily enjoined with respect to certain allegedly voidable agreements. While the category was denominated as involving fraud or duress, the *Metro Plan* case was included with a comparative reference, p. 334. Consequently, not only is the *Metro Plan* case a binding precedent upon this court but its rule is one which appears to have been expressly excepted from the principle laid down in the *Exercyle* case.

Matter of Gale (Hilts) (262 App. Div. 834) did not hold contrary to the *Metro Plan* case, and therefore does not impair the precedental standing of the *Metro Plan* case. There the question of illegality was raised only after award by the arbitrators. This is quite a different matter; the grounds for vacatur of an award are not identical with those which will warrant a stay of arbitration (Civ. Prac. Act, § 1462; cf. CPLR 7503, subd. [b]; 7510, 7511, subd. [b]). The award, on the facts in that case, was then supportable on the ground that the arbitrators could have found on the facts that there was no usurious transaction.

There is nothing in the decisional law or in the usury statutes which blanket the Anglo-American jurisdictions which suggests that usury involves an illegality of a lesser degree than others for the purpose of determining the enforcibility of agreements. But even this should not be critical to the determination of this case. If usurious agreements could be made enforcible by the simple device of employing arbitration clauses the courts would be surrendering their control over public policy in a way in which the Court of Appeals in the *Exercyle* case made very clear could not happen. Moreover, any one desiring to make a usurious agreement impenetrable need only require the necessitous borrower to consent to arbitration and also to arbitrators by name or occupation associated with the lending industry (cf. Matter of Astoria Med. Group [Health Ins. Plan], 11 N.Y. 2d 128). In this way the statutes and, where they exist, licensing agencies, would all be facilely by-passed.

The problems of usury extend well beyond larger commercial transactions to small business situations and to personal loans for those without capital. If the arbitration clause device could be thus used, all the complicated legislative distinctions in the statutes, civil and criminal, as well as the authority of the administrative regulating agencies, would be avoided by the simplest draftsmanship. The welter of legislation in this area makes clear that the concern is one of grave public interest and not merely a regulation with respect to which the immediate parties may contract freely.

Accordingly, the order denying defendant's motion to compel arbitration pending a trial of the issues of whether the written agreements are usurious and invalid should be affirmed, with costs to plaintiff-respondent.

STEUER, J. (dissenting). We disagree to the extent that we believe all the issues are determinable by the arbitrators and that consequently Special Term should have granted the motion to compel arbitration.

We agree with the majority that two questions are presented, namely, whether CPLR changed the existing law as to the respective functions of the court and the arbitrators and whether, assuming there was no change applicable to the present situation, the question is for the court or the arbitrator. We further agree that if either of these questions is to be answered as the respondent contends, Special Term's disposition is correct. As to the first question, as we read the majority opinion the court found it unnecessary to decide, merely calling attention to respondent's position and stating that if it is correct it provides an additional ground for affirmance. While this disposition is eminently proper, it does not dispense with the necessity of our establishing our position on this phase of the legal issue presented.

Prior to the enactment of Civil Practice Law and Rules it was quite clear that before arbitration could be directed it was the duty of the court to determine whether the parties had agreed to arbitrate (Matter of Rosenbaum [Amer. Sur Co.], 11 N.Y. 2d 310). This would involve a court-made determination of such questions as whether there was a meeting of the minds, and whether an apparent agreement was vitiated by fraud in the factum, duress or any other element which interdicted an offer and its acceptance (see Matter of Lipman [Haeuser Shellac Co.], 289 N.Y. 76, 79). As most agreements to arbitrate are terms in the contract which gives rise to the controversy, it was also the province of the court to determine whether that term was so understood by the parties that it could be said that they had agreed to it (Matter of Riverdale Fabrics Corp. [Tillinghast-Stiles Co.], 306 N.Y. 288). Other questions are for the arbitrators.

> Once it be ascertained that the parties broadly agreed to arbitrate a dispute "arising out of or in connection with" the agreement, it is for the arbitrators to decide what the agreement means and to enforce it according to the rules of law which they deem appropriate in the circumstances.

(Matter of Exercyle Corp. [Maratta], 9 N.Y. 2d 329, 334.)

The *Exercyle* case was decided pursuant to the statutory directions contained in section 1450 of the Civil Practice Act, which limited court inquiry to any "substantial issue as to the making of the contract." The current statutory provision (CPLR 7503) is whether there is any "substantial question whether a valid agreement was made." The distinction between the succeeding provision and its predecessor is in the use of the word "valid." This may refer to the making of the contract, that is, that all steps necessary to formalize an agreement were taken and nothing was done to negate the effect of those steps, or it may refer to the agreement itself—whether it is such that no legal obstacle to its enforcement can prevail. This would embrace such questions as lack of consideration, mutuality of obligation and all other situations which can serve to render what purports to be a contract obligation into a *nudum pactum*. Either interpretation is possible under the language used. If the first represents the legislative intent, no substantial change in the law was effected.[1] If the latter, there has been a very substantial change indeed, not only in procedure but in substance. In very many instances the question of whether the instrument is legally enforcible or not depends on the interpretation to be put on it and this, in turn, depends most frequently on subsidiary issues of fact. The resolution of these issues determines the right to recovery. It is just those issues that the parties agreed to submit to arbitrators. If these issues are to be determined by the court, the role of the arbitrators is written out of the contract, or at least reduced to a calculation of damages. While the Legislature could, no doubt, achieve such a result if they so wished, we cannot believe that they would undertake to effect so material a change by the use of a single word in a practice statute.

We turn now to the more difficult question of whether illegality under the rule of the *Exercycle* case is arbitrable or whether, when such a claim is asserted, the court must first find the claim unjustified before arbitration can be ordered. The general rule is, and always was, that illegality negates the existence of the contract and hence there is nothing to arbitrate (Matter of Kramer & Uchitelle, 288 N.Y. 467). However, illegality is a very broad term and when applied to contracts is used to cover a multitude of situations. These vary from agreements which are intended to carry out a criminal result (*i.e.* an agreement to divide the spoils of a robbery) to one that runs counter to a statute regulating trade. The nature of the illegality involved can and does have some effect on the rights created by the contract and the ability to enforce it. Every contract to which a claim of illegality in the broad meaning of that word might be asserted is not, *ipso facto*, a nullity, nor is arbitration of questions arising out of it interdicted. That result only attends such contracts whose performance would call for acts which run counter to our public policy. (See Matter of Exercycle, *supra*, p. 335.) And this limitation of the effect of the generic term "illegality" fits in perfectly with our legal concepts. As noted, arbitrators, where they are empowered to act, may enforce an agreement under any rule of law that they deem appropriate. It would be an unthinkable travesty to allow them to apply a rule which directed enforcement of acts, or to give damages for the failure to perform acts which our public policy forbade. No such difficulty is presented where the acts called for do not offend against our public policy.

So it becomes necessary to determine whether the collection of a usurious rate of interest is such an act. We submit it is not. Usury means a stipulation for interest in excess of a statutory rate. A contract tainted with usury occupies, in the law of this State at least, a rather peculiar situation. By statute, certain, but not all, such contracts, are declared to be void (General Business Law, § 373[2]). Nevertheless, from the earliest times it has been stated that "[t]he contract is not absolutely *void*, but only *voidable* at the election of the borrower, or those who are privies ... with him: hence, no other party can make the objection." (Williams v. Tilt, 36 N.Y. 319, 325.) The Court of Appeals has repeatedly reaffirmed this proposition, even to the quotation, long after usurious contracts were declared void by statute (Lipedes v. Liverpool & London & Globe Ins. Co., 184 App. Div. 332, affd. 229 N.Y. 201, citing Chapuis v. Mathot, 91 Hun 565, affd. 155 N.Y. 641, which cites the quotation with approval). That the defense is peculiar to the borrower is still the law (Broad & Wall Corp. v. O'Connor, 13 A.D. 2d 462). Furthermore, our courts are not wedded to the principle that they will throw out all cases where a rate in excess of our statutory rate is called for. If the obligation arises outside the State, it can be enforced here despite the fact that the interest called for is in excess of our legal rate (City Nat. Bank in Miami v. Lake Constr. Co.,

---

1. While there is very little proof of the legislative intent dehors the statute, Professor Weinstein states that no change in the substantive law was intended (8 WEINSTEIN-KORN-MILLER, N.Y. Civ. Prac., p. 75–62). (But see Thornton, Practice Commentary, § 7503, McKinney's Cons. Laws of N.Y., Book 7B, CPLR, p. 488; Falls Jr., *Arbitration Under the Civil Practice Law and Rules in New York*, IX N.Y. L. FORUM 335.)

2. This section will very shortly become part of the General Obligations Law, § 5–511.

227 App. Div. 85). It has also long been our policy, as it is that of many States, that where a contract calling for interest has relation to several States, the law of the State which will sustain the contract (*i.e.* allows a rate of interest equal to or exceeding the contract rate) will be applied (Cutler v. Wright, 22 N.Y. 471 ; LEFLAR, CONFLICT OF LAWS, § 131 ; Ann. 125 A. L. R. 482, Conflict of Laws as to Usury). These considerations are no mere subtleties as to whether a contract is void or voidable. They present a very clear picture of our public policy. They show that the making of an agreement that calls for interest in excess of our statutory rate does not contravene our public policy but that in certain of these contracts the court will not, under certain circumstances, enforce their performance. It would follow that there would be no objection to allow such contracts to go to arbitration.

In reaching this conclusion we are not unaware of the holding in Matter of Metro Plan v. Miscione (257 App. Div. 652). As pointed out in the majority opinion, this is an alternative holding. It was also held that the contract did not, under the limited arbitration clause, provide for arbitration of the question. We submit that at the time the case was decided the law as to what was arbitrable had not been developed to its present degree. As to its citation in the *Exercycle* case, the manner is fairly set out in the majority opinion, but we do not conclude from that that the Court of Appeals intended to approve the specific holding.

Our courts have increasingly adopted the principle that where the parties have agreed upon arbitration as the forum for their disputes, the courts will not place obstacles in the way of that agreement. The nature of the contract here is in dispute. It is not controverted that this very question, the nature of the contract, is left to arbitration. If we can, we should give recognition to this agreement. If it should eventuate that the arbitrators find an agreement that contravenes our policy but, nevertheless, decree enforcement, any resulting question can be determined on the motion to confirm the award (Matter of Gale, 262 App. Div. 834). But the factual

questions upon which the legality or illegality of the contract depends are for the arbitrators (Matter of Goodman v. Lazrus, 15 A.D. 2d 530). This is exactly what the parties contracted for. Moreover, it is the only way consonant with our existing procedure in which their indisputable agreement to arbitrate the underlying questions of fact—which will determine whether this is in fact a usurious contract—can be given effect.

In the view we take it is unnecessary to decide whether the agreement to arbitrate should be considered separate and apart from the agreement in dispute. Naturally, if it is considered separate, the first question is obviated (17A C. J. S., Contracts, § 515[5]). No doubt exists that the agreement to arbitrate is a valid agreement.

Order denying motion for arbitration pending a trial of certain issues should be reversed and the motion granted.

VALENTE and McNALLY, JJ., concur with BREITEL, J. P. ; STEUER, J., dissents in opinion in which EAGER, J., concurs.

Order, entered June 15, 1964, denying defendant's motion to compel arbitration pending a trial of the issues of whether the written agreements are usurious and invalid, affirmed, with $30 costs and disbursements to respondent.

[The Court of Appeals affirmed in a memorandum opinion, 17 N.Y. 2d 445, 213 N.E. 2d 887 (1965).]

One lower New York Court has held that if the issue of contract illegality is raised before the arbitrator, it cannot be raised thereafter before the court. Einiger Mills, Inc. v. Clyde Fashions, Ltd., N.Y.L.J., June 28, 1962, p. 6, col. 8. Other New York Courts have entertained the issue of illegality after award. *E.g.*, Matter of Mencher (B. Geller and Sons), 276 App. Div. 556, 96 N.Y.S. 2d 13 (1st Dep't. 1950). The precise grounds for such a procedure are unclear.

CHAPTER VIII

THE INTERRELATION OF ARBITRATION WITH OTHER LAWS

A.

The Problem of Illegality or Public Policy—After Arbitration

LOVING & EVANS v. BLICK
33 Cal. 2d 603, 204 P. 2d 23 (1949)

[Plaintiff copartnership sought enforcement of an arbitration award for amounts due under a repair contract. Although Loving was a licensed contractor, Evans was not, nor was the copartnership. A California statute declared it unlawful for any "person" (including a copartnership) to act as a contractor without a license, and the court concluded that Loving & Evans had been in violation of this provision while performing the repair work in dispute.]

There now remains the question of the premise of appellant's objection to the enforcement of the award in favor of respondents. It must be conceded at the outset that ordinarily with respect to arbitration proceedings "the merits of the controversy between the parties are not subject to judicial review" (Pacific Vegetable Oil Corp. v. C. S. T., Ltd., 29 Cal. 2d 228, 233 [174 P. 2d 441]) and that "arbitrators are not

bound by strict adherence to legal procedure and to the rules on the admission of evidence expected in judicial trials." (*Ibid.,* p. 241.) But, as will hereinafter appear, the rules which give finality to the arbitrator's determination of ordinary questions of fact or of law are inapplicable where the issue of illegality of the entire transaction is raised in a proceeding for the enforcement of the arbitrator's award. When so raised, the issue is one for judicial determination upon the evidence presented to the trial court, and any preliminary determination of legality by the arbitrator, whether in the nature of a determination of a pure question of law or a mixed question of fact and law, should not be held to be binding upon the trial court.

The foregoing conclusion is entirely in harmony with the provisions of section 1288 of the Code of Civil Procedure, which recites the grounds upon which the trial court "must make an order vacating the award." Section (d) thereof specifies that the award must be vacated "where the arbitrators exceeded their powers." It seems clear that the power of the arbitrator to determine the rights of the parties is dependent upon the existence of a valid contract under which such rights might arise.

In the absence of a valid contract no such rights can arise and no power can be conferred upon the arbitrator to determine such nonexistent rights. The question of the validity of the basic contract being essentially a judicial question, it remains such whether it is presented in a proceeding "for an order directing ... arbitration" under section 1282 of the Code of Civil Procedure or in a proceeding "for an order confirming" or "vacating an award" under sections 1287 and 1288 of said code. If it is presented in a proceeding under said section 1282 and it appears to the court from the uncontradicted evidence that the contract is illegal, the court should deny the petition "for an order directing the parties to proceed to arbitration." If it is presented in a proceeding under said section 1287 or 1288 and similar uncontradicted evidence is offered, the court should deny confirmation and should vacate any award granting relief under the illegal contract upon the ground that the arbitrator exceeded his powers in making such award.

Section 1281 of the Code of Civil Procedure, providing for submission to arbitration of "any controversy ... which arises out of a contract," does not contemplate that the parties may provide for the arbitration of controversies arising out of contracts which are expressly declared by law to be illegal and against the public policy of the state. So it is generally held that "a claim arising out of an illegal transaction is not a proper subject matter for submission to arbitration, and that an award springing out of an illegal contract, which no court can enforce, cannot stand on any higher ground than the contract itself." (6 C.J.S., § 12, p. 160.) Aptly illustrative of this well-settled principle is the fairly recent case of Smith v. Gladney, 128 Tex. 354 [98 S.W. 2d 351], where a dispute arose between the parties as a result of trading in "futures" upon the Chicago Board of Trade. The matter was submitted to arbitration. When suit was brought upon the award it was affirmed "on the theory that [it] was final," the appellate court, in reversing the judgment, said at pages 351–352 [98 S.W. 2d]: "It appears to be almost universally recognized that a claim arising out of an illegal transaction, such as a speculation in futures, is not a legitimate subject of arbitration, and an award based thereon is void and unenforceable in courts of the country. Tandy v. Elmore-Cooper Livestock Commission Co., 113 Mo. App. 409 [87 S.W. 614, 618]; Benton v. Singleton, 114 Ga.

548 [40 S.E. 811, 58 L.R.A. 181]; Lum v. Fauntleroy, 80 Miss. 757 [32 So. 290, 92 Am.St. Rep. 620]; Hall y. Kimmer, 61 Mich. 269 [28 N.W. 96, 1 Am.St.Rep. 575]; Polk v. Cleveland Railway Co., 20 Ohio App. 317 [151 N.E. 808] ... A claim that cannot be made the basis of a suit cannot be made the basis of an arbitration. The mere submission of an illegal matter to arbitrators and reducing it to an award does not purge it of its illegality." (See, also, In re Gale, 176 Misc. 277 [27 N.Y.S. 2d 18, 21–23].)

[The order enforcing the award was reversed. On the same day the court reached the same conclusion in a similar case. Franklin v. Nat'l. Goldstone Agency, 33 Cal. 2d 628, 204 P. 2d 37 (1949).]

MATTER OF WESTERN UNION TELEGRAPH CO. (AMERICAN COMMUNICATIONS ASS'N)
299 N.Y. 177, 86 N.E. 2d 162 (1949)

LEWIS, J. Our inquiry upon this appeal goes to the legal sufficiency of an award made by an arbitrator named in a collective bargaining agreement between the appellant, American Communications Association, C.I.O.—to which reference will be made as the union—and the respondent, Western Union Telegraph Company.

At Special Term—where an application by the union for confirmation of the award was met by a cross motion by Western Union for vacatur —the award was confirmed and vacatur denied. Upon appeal by Western Union the Appellate Division by a divided court reversed the order of confirmation "upon the law, the questions of fact not having been considered." The present appeal by the union is taken as of right.

Since its merger in 1943 with the Postal Telegraph Cable Company Western Union has been the only landlines telegraph carrier operating in the United States.

It thus comes about that Western Union's landlines division acts as a connecting carrier— within the United States—for its own separate cable division and for all other competing international carriers according to rates, routing and regulations promulgated by the Federal Communications Commission under the Federal Communications Act. By that act (U.S. Code, tit. 47, § 201) Western Union is required—"to furnish such communication service upon reasonable request therefor" (subd. [a]). In payment for its service as a connecting carrier Western Union landlines division collects from its separate cable division and from competing international carriers according to tariffs established by the Federal Communications Commission and may not accord preferential treatment of any kind to any international carrier.

Important to our inquiry is the fact that the 7,000 employees of Western Union's landlines division within the metropolitan area of New York have as their agent in matters relating to collective bargaining the appellant union's Local No. 40. The employees of Western Union's cable division—approximately 350 in number—are represented by the appellant union's Local No. 11.

On June 18, 1947, Western Union entered into a collective bargaining agreement with the appellant union covering employees who are members of that union's Local No. 40. Included in that agreement was the following provision:

> SECTION 31. Since *the Company's business is one of serving the public* and *it is the mutual desire to both the Company and the Union to provide uninterrupted and continuous public service,* to promote industrial peace and to provide for stable labor relations, the Company agrees that there shall be no lockouts and *the Union agrees that there shall be no strikes or other stoppages of work during the life of this contract.* (Emphasis supplied.)

On January 2, 1948—contemporaneously with other locals affiliated with the appellant union and representing employees of competing international cable companies—Local No. 11 called a strike of employees in Western Union's cable division which strike prevailed until March 31, 1948. At a "special membership meeting" held January 3, 1948, the day following the onset of the strike called by Local No. 11 and other locals, Local No. 40—*which was not on strike* and which, as we have seen, comprised *landlines* employees of Western Union in the metropolitan area of New York—passed unanimously a formal resolution which provided in part "we will take every action necessary to force the Mackay Radio, Commercial Cable, All America, and the Western Union Cable Companies to bargain in good faith with Locals 10, 11, and 15. *To accomplish this purpose we will not handle struck traffic*" (emphasis supplied).

Although Local No. 40 did not strike, a substantial number of its members—employees of Western Union's landlines division—complied with the resolution quoted in part above and refused to handle "hot traffic," viz., cable messages which had been transmitted by or were destined for any of the international companies in which strikes prevailed. The refusal to handle "hot traffic"—concededly practiced by such employees—interrupted and delayed the forwarding of messages which Western Union was re-

quired by law to transmit, disarranged a system of work designed by Western Union to assure the quick dispatch of those messages, and made idle those employees who, although trained in the technique of such work, refused to transmit messages which were within their prescribed duties in the performance of an ordinary day's work. The arbitrator found that

> On January 9th the Company began advising employees who were refusing to handle "hot traffic" that they would be suspended for four months if they did not perform all of their customary duties. Warnings which were ignored were followed by suspensions. On January 23rd the Union requested the instant arbitration and hearings were held on January 26th and 27th.

By the award made following those hearings it was determined that section 31 of the collective bargaining agreement (quoted *supra,* p. 181), when read in the light of a "custom of trade" which the arbitrator found existed, viz., the refusal by nonstriking employees in the telegraph industry to handle "hot traffic," did not prohibit the union from directing employees not to handle such traffic or the employees from following such directions. The award also directed Western Union to submit to the union for future action by the arbitrator a list of employees whom the company claimed had hidden or mutilated cablegrams which had come into their hands and whose suspension it claimed was justified by such misconduct. The company was further directed to reinstate, with back pay, all suspended employees whose names did not appear on such list. The award also provided—

> It is possible that some employees, because of their unwillingness to handle struck traffic, may not be occupied full time. If the Company [Western Union] sees fit, it may make a proportionate deduction from the salary of any such employee.

Against this background we are to determine as a matter of law whether, as held by the Justice at Special Term, it was "within [the arbitrator's] power to construe and interpret the [collective bargaining] contract in the light of its language and the background of the industry in which the agreement was operating," or, as ruled by the Appellate Division, the award herein

> must be set aside on the ground that the arbitrator exceeded the powers conferred upon him, and, on the further ground that the controversy submitted to arbitration involved the right of telegraph employees to conduct themselves in a manner expressly forbidden by statute. (274 App. Div. 754.)

We agree with the bases upon which rests the decision of the Appellate Division. The collective bargaining contract under which the arbitrator acted contains the following provision:

> SECTION 6. (a) In the event that an agreement cannot be reached between the Union and the Company with respect to the application or interpretation of this contract, or with respect to any grievances as defined in Section 5(h), it is agreed that such matters shall be submitted on the request of either party to Max Meyer, as impartial arbitrator. . . . *The arbitrator shall not have the authority to alter or modify any of the express provisions of the contract*, nor shall he have the power to make a ruling contrary to any agreement reached by the parties in the course of negotiations for this contract. (Emphasis supplied.)

In view of the clearly expressed agreement by the parties that in the event of their disagreement with respect to the interpretation of their contract an arbitrator shall have no authority to modify its express provisions, and in view of the express provision in section 31 of the contract that "there shall be no strikes or other stoppages of work during the life of this contract," the award before us, as we view it, amply demonstrates that the arbitrator exceeded the power granted to him (Civ. Prac. Act, § 1462, subd. 4).

Where, as in the contract which the arbitrator was here called upon to interpret, "the language is unambiguous, the words plain and clear, conveying a distinct idea, there is no occasion to resort to other means of interpretation. Effect must be given to the intent as indicated by the language employed" (Settle v. Van Evrea, 49 N.Y. 280, 281). Upon that subject this court has said that "Evidence of custom is permitted for the purpose of qualifying the meaning of a contract *where otherwise ambiguous* and of providing for incidents not in contradiction of the fundamental provisions of the contract and of supplying omissions under certain circumstances which have occurred in the agreement of the parties. Evidence of it is not permitted for the purpose of contradicting the agreements which the parties have made or for the purpose of accomplishing an unfair or immoral construction of their contract" (emphasis supplied). (Gravenhorst v. Zimmerman, 236 N.Y. 22, 33–34, and see Gearns v. Commerical Cable Co., 293 N.Y. 105, 109; Green v. Wachs, 254 N.Y. 437, 440–441). That no provision in section 31 of the contract impressed the arbitrator as ambiguous is indicated by his statement—"If we were to construe that language in vacuo we might well find that the Union's direction to the employees not to handle 'hot traffic' violated the letter if not the spirit of the clause." Although the record is clear that "stoppages of work" did result from refusal by employees of Western Union's landlines division to handle "hot traffic," the arbitrator found that such refusal conformed to a practice generally prevalent in the telegraph industry. Thereupon, despite his own disclaimer of ambiguity in the contract, he concluded that "the language of Section 31 must be read in the light of this practice and that so read it does not prohibit the Union from directing employees not to handle 'hot traffic' or the employees from following such directions."

By that conclusion, as we view it, the arbitrator—entering a field of decision from which the parties had expressly excluded him—modified an express provision of the contract by which the union had agreed that "there shall be no . . . stoppages of work during the life of this contract." As the language employed to express the union's agreement leaves no doubt as to its meaning "there is no occasion to resort to other means of interpretation" (Settle v. Van Evrea, *supra*, p. 281; and see Brainard v. New York Central R. R Co., 242 N.Y. 125, 133).

We know of no case where a court, in construing a contractual obligation expressed in language as clear as is the clause here in controversy, has found it necessary to employ extrinsic means to ascertain a party's obligation thereunder. The lack of such authority may well be due to the early rule in Collender v. Dinsmore (55 N.Y. 200, 208-209):

> Custom and usage is resorted to only to ascertain and explain the meaning and intention of the parties to a contract when the same could not be ascertained without extrinsic evidence, but never to contravene the express stipulations; and if there is no uncertainty as to the terms of a contract, usage cannot be proved to contradict or qualify its provisions. . . . Usage is sometimes admissible to add to or explain, but never to vary or contradict, either expressly or by implication, the terms of a written instrument, or the fair and legal import of a contract.

The modification of the contract here accomplished, being, as we believe, in excess of the arbitrator's authority as limited by the parties, serves to vitiate the award (Civ. Prac. Act, § 1462, subd. 4).

We come then to the effect which certain provisions of the Penal Law have upon section 31 of the contract *as interpretated [sic] by the arbitrator and by Special Term.*

On this branch of the case we note at the outset the statement by Dean Wesley A. Sturges, in his text COMMERCIAL ARBITRATIONS AND AWARDS at page 202 (§ 61): "It may be stated generally that controverted claims which are not enforceable for illegality cannot be submitted to arbitration either at common law or under an arbitration statute." (See, also, 6 C.J.S., Arbitration and Award, § 12 ; 3 Am. Jur., Arbitration and Award, § 11.)

By section 552 of the Penal Law it is provided:

> A person who: . . .
>
> 2. *Being such clerk, operator, messenger or other employee*, wilfully divulges to anyone but the persons for whom it was intended, the contents or the nature thereof of a telegraphic or telephonic message or dispatch intrusted to him for the transmission or delivery, or of which contents he may in any manner become possessed, or *occupying such position in a telegraph office shall wilfully refuse or neglect duly to transmit or deliver messages received at such office* . . . is punishable by a fine of not more than one thousand dollars or by imprisonment for not more than two years, or by both such fine and imprisonment. (Emphasis supplied.)

A further penal provision is found in section 1423 of the Penal Law:

> A person who wilfully or maliciously displaces, removes, injures, or destroys: . . .
>
> 6. A line of telegraph or telephone . . . or who *shall wilfully prevent, obstruct or delay*, by any means or contrivance whatsoever, the sending, transmission, conveyance or delivery, in this state of any authorized message, communication or report by or through any telegraph or telephone line, wire or cable, under the control of any telegraph or telephone company doing business in this state; or who *shall aid, agree with, employ or conspire with any person or persons to unlawfully do, or permit or cause to be done, any of the acts hereinbefore mentioned.*
>
> 9. . . . is punishable by imprisonment for not more than two years. (Emphasis supplied.)

No one has suggested that the collective bargaining agreement with which we are concerned is illegal as drawn. However, if, as the award before us and the decision by Special Term would indicate, we are warranted as a matter of law in reading section 31 of that contract in the light of a "practice of the trade" which permits a telegraph employee, without leaving his job, to refuse to forward a telegram or cablegram which comes to his hand in the ordinary course of business, then judicial sanction will be given to such conduct by an employee who "occupying such position in a telegraph office shall wilfully refuse or neglect duly to transmit or deliver messages received at such office". That, however, is precisely the act which the Legislature by section 552 of the Penal Law (*supra*) has declared to be a crime and has made punishable by fine or imprisonment or both.

Likewise if we are to read section 31 of the contract in accord with the award herein and the decision by Special Term—which would permit a telegraph employee while remaining on his job in good standing to refuse to transmit a telegram or cablegram—then judicial sanction will be given to the acts of any such employee who

> shall wilfully prevent, obstruct or delay, by any means or contrivance whatsoever, the sending, transmission, conveyance or delivery, in this state of any authorized message . . . or who shall aid, agree with, employ or conspire with any person or persons to unlawfully do, or permit or cause to be done, any of the acts hereinbefore mentioned.

That, however, is precisely the conduct which the Legislature by section 1423 of the Penal Law (*supra*) has declared to be a crime, punishable by imprisonment for not more than two years.

The penal statutes quoted above do not deprive an employee of his right to leave his position and to engage in a strike. Nor can it be said, as suggested by counsel for the union, that those statutes are intended to apply only to employees who have tampered with telegraphic messages for personal gain. The manifest purpose of the Legislature was to preserve for public use the service which a telegraph company is required to furnish.

To that end and in line with established public policy the Legislature chose penal measures as means to avoid disruption of the *public service* furnished by a telegraph company.

Obviously the function which Western Union's landlines division is required by law to perform as the sole connecting carrier for the several international cable companies, is a service affected by a public interest. In that connection the fact is again noted that by section 31 of the collective bargaining agreement here invoked (quoted *supra*, p. 181), the parties thereto expressly agreed that "the Company's business is one of *serving the public* and *it is the mutual desire to both the Company and the Union to provide uninterrupted and continuous public service*" (emphasis supplied). From those circumstances it follows that any construction of the terms of the contract in suit which tends to restrict the free and general use of telegraph lines and the public service those facilities afford is invalid (Central New York Tel. & Tel. Co. v. Averill, 199 N.Y. 128, 134, 135 ; and see Public Service Law, art. 5).

It is difficult to understand how Western Union can discharge those duties required of it by both Federal and State statutes if it is also required to *retain* in its service employees whose duty it is to transmit telegraph messages but who refuse to handle messages offered by the public which happen to be routed over facilities of a telegraph company where a strike prevails. To approve such a practice would to that extent oust the employer company from control of its own business and to that extent would prevent it from performing duties to the public required by law.

The award herein as confirmed by Special Term approves of action taken by the appellant union's Local No. 40 pursuant to its resolution adopted January 3, 1948. We are not disposed to approve that award which would permit Western Union's landlines employees, *while still occupying positions in that company's offices,* to determine—for reasons of their own and contrary to the company's demand upon them for the maintenance of standard service—that messages routed to and from certain cable companies should not be transmitted. "The law will not presume an agreement void as illegal or against public policy when it is capable of a construction which would make it consistent with the laws and valid."

The order should be affirmed, with costs.

DESMOND, J. (dissenting). These parties agreed (§ 6, subd. [a]) to send to the named arbitrator for determination, all disputes "with respect to the application or interpretation of this contract." A dispute arose between them as to the application or meaning of so much of section 31 of the agreement as provided that "there shall be no strikes or other stoppages of work during the life of this contract." The union, in connection with a strike called by another union, had refused to handle "struck traffic." The arbitrator, after hearings, held that, in view of the tradition and customs of the industry, which he felt he could not ignore and in the light of which the language "stoppages of work" had to be construed, the phrase did not prohibit employees refusing to handle "hot" or "struck" messages. That was a pure question of interpretation and application, and the very kind of question which the parties themselves had agreed should be decided by the arbitrator alone. Accordingly, his decision must stand (Matter of Wenger & Co. v. Propper Silk Hosiery Mills, 239 N.Y. 199, 202). Whether we consider that decision to be "right" or "wrong" is beside the point. "The courts in this State have adhered with great steadiness to the general rule that awards will not be opened for errors of law or fact on the part of the arbitrator." (Fudickar v. Guardian Mut. Life Ins. Co., 62 N.Y. 392, 400.) "The conclusiveness of awards is based upon the principle that the parties having chosen judges of their own and agreed to abide by their decision, they are bound by their agreement and compelled to perform the award." (Matter of Wilkins, 169 N.Y. 494, 496, 499 ; see Matter of

Marchant v. Mead-Morrison Mfg. Co., 252 N.Y. 284, 300, 302 ; Matter of Morris White Fashions (Susquehanna Mills), 295 N.Y. 450, 456.) "It is the duty of the court to enforce their agreement rather than to undertake itself to settle the dispute or to narrow the field of arbitral disputes." (Matter of Wenger & Co. v. Propper Silk Hosiery Mills, *supra,* p. 202.)

The second ground asserted for vacating the award is that it would, we are told, condone or legalize violations of sections 552 and 1423 of the Penal Law, which make it criminal for telegraph employees willfully to refuse or neglect to transmit or deliver messages, or willfully to prevent, obstruct or delay such transmission or delivery. To refuse confirmation on this ground is to hold, as matter of law, that any refusal by a telegraph company employee, for any reason whatever, to handle a message, is a crime, even though the message is forthwith handled by another employee, after the first employee's refusal. I think that goes much too far. No decision anywhere upholds it.

If the arbitrator was within his powers in holding, as to the first point, that the employees' refusal to handle the struck traffic was within the rights of their employment, then, of course, it could not possibly be that their action was *criminal* as matter of law.

The order of the Appellate Division should be reversed and the order of Special Term affirmed, with costs in this court and in the Appellate Division.

CONWAY, DYE and BROMLEY, JJ., concur with LEWIS, J. ; DESMOND, J., dissents in opinion in which LOUGHRAN, CH. J., and FULD, J., concur.

Order affirmed.

STURGES, COMMERCIAL ARBITRATION AND AWARDS, 202–203 (1930) observes: Thus, if A and B have participated in a robbery or larceny, clearly a dispute between them concerning the division of the spoils is not subject to arbitration. It seems equally clear that controverted claims predicated upon a contract which violates a criminal or penal statute, or is otherwise too great shock to a standard of good morals invoked by a court in a particular case, cannot be made the subject of an arbitration.

On the other hand, it is no objection to a submission and award that the claim submitted is based upon such misconduct of a party as would constitute sufficient basis for a criminal prosecution of that party. The private or civil consequences of conduct can be arbitrated notwithstanding that the conduct constitutes a criminal offense by the wrongdoer. Thus, controverted claims for damages for an assault can be submitted with the same effect as submission of other disputes, although the assault is also a violation of criminal law. Disputed claims against a party for damages to property can be submitted although they are based upon facts which may render the party liable to a criminal prosecution for maintaining a public nuisance.

In Matter of Publishers' Ass'n of New York City (Newspaper and Mail Deliverers' Union) 280 App. Div. 500, 114 N.Y.S. 2d 401 (First Dept. 1952) the court refused to enforce an award of $2,000 actual damages and $5,000 "penalty" damages for the union's breach of its no-strike clause. The "penalty" was to be payable if the arbitral board found a subsequent violation. The majority held that the imposition of penalties for breach of contract was inimical to long-established common law contract damage doctrine and against public policy. The majority and dissenting opinions appear hereafter where arbitrators' remedy powers are considered.

BLACK v. CUTTER LABORATORIES
43 Cal. 2d 788, 278 P. 2d 905
cert. denied, 351 U.S. 292 (1955)*

SCHAUER, J.—Cutter Laboratories, Inc., appeals from a judgment entered upon the granting of an order confirming the award of an arbitration board. (See Code Civ. Proc., §§ 1291–1293.) By the award, rendered by two of the three arbitrators with the third dissenting, it was held that appellant (hereinafter sometimes termed the company) had discharged one of its employes in violation of a collective bargaining agreement between appellant and the Bio-Lab Union (hereinafter sometimes called the union) of Local 225, United Office and Professional Workers of America, and that the employe was entitled to reinstatement and to back pay limited by the bargaining agreement to eight weeks regular pay less any outside earnings or unemployment com-

pensation received during such period. We have concluded that, upon the undisputed evidence and upon the facts found by the arbitration board, the company is correct in its contention that the arbitrators exceeded their powers, that the award is contrary to law, that it would contravene public policy for the courts of this state to enforce reinstatement of the discharged employe, and that the judgment must therefore be reversed.

From extensive findings made by the arbitration board it appears that the employer, Cutter Laboratories, Inc., with offices and laboratories located in Berkeley, manufactures and sells throughout the United States and certain foreign countries vaccines, serums, antitoxins and other antibiotics for both civilian and military use. During World War II the company was subject to stringent security control by federal authorities, and its products and processes are said to be peculiarly subject to sabotage. Since World War II the company has been under no specific contract obligation to any governmental agency to discharge employes who are "bad security risks"; any obligation to take such steps grows out of the duties it owes generally to its customers, its dealers, its employes, and its stockholders.

The Bio-Lab Union of Local 225, United Office and Professional Workers of America C.I.O., was recognized in February, 1944, by the company pursuant to a National Labor Relations Board election. It is a union "generally denominated as 'left-wing'" and it as well as the U.O.P.W.A. was expelled from the C.I.O. in March, 1950.

The discharged employe, Mrs. Doris Walker, graduated from the University of California School of Jurisprudence in 1942, and is an active member of The State Bar of California. She was elected to Phi Beta Kappa and to the editorial board of the California Law Review. From 1942 to 1944 she was employed as an enforcement attorney with the federal Office of Price Administration in San Francisco and from 1944 to 1946 as an attorney with a firm of lawyers in the same city. She left the law firm and secured employment as a cannery worker sorting and trimming vegetables in three canneries in Oakland and San Francisco and (later in 1946) as an organizer for the Food and Tobacco and Agricultural Workers Union. She testified that she went to law school "because I was interested in becoming a labor lawyer" and that she left the law firm because her "time was spent on routine civil matters ... and I became dissatisfied with my work and felt that I would rather take a more active role in the field in which I was

---

*A divided Supreme Court held that the decision went off on an adequate state ground, construction of a contract, which made it unnecessary to reach the constitutional issue posed. Of course, labor agreement construction where the employer's activities affect commerce is now regarded as posing issues of federal law.

interested and so I quit in order to take a job in a plant."

In October, 1946, Mrs. Walker sought employment at Cutter Laboratories and filled out an application form supplied by the company, on which under the heading of "Education" she concealed her attendance at law school, her law degree, and her admission to practice law in this state. Under the heading "Previous Employment" she concealed her entire previous employment record and showed a false employment as file clerk for six or eight months in 1939 by "John Tripp Att'y," which the company later discovered to be a fictitious name. Mrs. Walker also gave a dentist and a lawyer in San Francisco as references, but at her request their letters of recommendation to the company did not reveal her subterfuge. She states that she intentionally deceived the company because of her belief it would not employ her if she were truthful. The company hired her as label clerk in its production planning department, and in April, 1949, she became a clerk typist in the purchasing department.

At the company plant Mrs. Walker became active in union affairs and in April, 1947, was elected shop chairman and also a member of the executive board of Local 225. Late in 1948 she was elected chief shop steward; her duties as steward took her to all departments in the plant except the executive and administrative departments and primarily entailed representing the union in grievances arising under its collective bargaining agreement with the company. In the spring of 1949 she was elected president of Local 225; her term expired December 15, 1949, and a new president was elected.

Meanwhile, in May, 1946, following proceedings before the National Labor Relations Board, the company and the union entered into a contract; in January, 1947, the wage provisions thereof were opened and a 10 cent hourly wage increase agreed upon. In April, 1947, Mrs. Walker had been elected shop chairman and during the same month she and another union official learned that they were being investigated by the company as to past employment, character, and Communist affiliation. In June, 1947, the union served notice of intention to amend the contract and at the same time filed with the National Labor Relations Board an unfair labor practice charge against the company based on the investigations. A week-long strike ensued in August, 1947, which was settled following the intervention of Harry Bridges and as a result of negotiation with him. June 9, 1949, the contract was again opened, solely as to wages, and November 30, 1949, a two-year contract was

agreed upon; on October 6, 1949, during the negotiations and at a time when company officials were angry at certain activities of Mrs. Walker purportedly in connection with union demands, the company's discharge of Mrs. Walker which is here involved took place.

At the time of the discharge a company official read to Mrs. Walker the following notice:

Mrs. Walker: As you are aware, the company has known for some time that when you applied for work with Cutter Laboratories on October 4, 1946, you made a number of false representations on your "Application for Employment."

As we know now, you falsified the statement of your education so as to conceal the fact that you had completed a law shcool [sic] course at the University of California's School of Jurisprudence at Berkeley in May, 1942. You concealed the facts that you received the degree of Bachelor of Laws in May, 1942, and that you were admitted to the State Bar of California on December 8, 1942. You concealed that since that date you have at all times been admitted and entitled to practice as an attorney before all of the Courts of California.

We know now that by falsification of the name of a previous employer, you concealed the fact that from June, 1942 to February, 1944 you were employed by the Federal Government's Office of Price Administration, including employment as an Enforcement Attorney at a salary of about $3,200.00 a year.

We know now that you deliberately concealed from us that from February 1944 to December, 1945 you were employed as an attorney by Gladstein, Grossman, Sawyer and Edises, a well-known firm of lawyers specializing in labor cases.

You know that a few weeks ago the "Labor Herald", the official CIO newspaper, stated that the National Labor Relations Board had sustained a cannery firm that had discharged you for refusing to answer whether or not you were a Communist.

We have checked the records. We know now that you deliberately concealed that in 1946, just before you applied for work here, you were employed by a series of canneries and had been discharged by them.

Ordinarily, an employee of the Company would be discharged immediately for falsifying material facts on an "Application for Employment". Because you were an officer of the Union we kept you on the pay roll rather than open ourselves to a charge of persecuting a union officer. We have given your case careful consideration because we know very well that no matter how strong the case against you there will be a claim of discrimination because of union activities.

Because no employer wants to become involved in a dispute of that kind we have been patient and deliberate in our consideration of your misconduct.

On October 1, 1948, when you testified under oath before a Trial Examiner of the National Labor Relations Board, you refused to answer the question as to whether or not you were a member of the Communist Party.

You refused to answer under oath the question as to whether or not you were or had been a member of the Federal Workers' Branch No. 3 of the Communist Party.

You refused to testify under oath whether or not you were or had been a member of the South Side Professional Club of the Communist Party.

We are convinced now, that you were and still are a member of the Communist Party, that you were a member of the Federal Workers' Branch No. 3 of the Communist Party, and that you were a member of the South Side Professional Club of the Communist Party.

Our recent investigation of your past record has uncovered previously unknown conduct that goes far beyond a mere concealment of material facts. We have just completed a thorough investigation and have a full report upon your past activities. We realize now the importance of the facts that you concealed from us. We realize the full implications of your falsification and misrepresentations. A follow-up and investigation of the "Labor Heralds" recent revelations has uncovered a situation far more grave than we expected.

We are convinced now that for a number of years, you have been and still are a member of the Communist Party. We are convinced beyond any question that for a number of years you have participated actively in the Communist Party's activities.

The nature of our company's business requires more than the usual precaution against sabotage and subversion. Upon a disclosure that any employee is a member of the Communist Party, or has participated in other subversive or revolutionary activity, we conceive it to be the responsibility of management to take action.

Confronted with such a situation, any inclination to be lenient or to grant a union official special consideration is out. In the face of your record there is no alternative open to us except to terminate your services at once. Accordingly, you are notified now that you are discharged for the causes mentioned. You will be paid the full amount due to you promptly.

"Shortly after" the notice was read to Mrs. Walker, it was likewise read to plant employees at a meeting called by the company. At the meeting statements were made by company officials "either to the entire group or in private discussion afterward, advising employees 'to get out of that left-wing union' and telling them that 'nothing but a left-wing union would press for wage increases at this time.'" Following the discharge of Mrs. Walker negotiations between the union and the company continued, and as already mentioned a two-year contract was agreed upon on November 30, 1949; it provided for wage increases and other contract changes. The company also agreed to, and did, pending the holding of a union-shop election,

join the union in urging all eligible employes and all newly-hired eligible employes to become and remain members in good standing of the union.

The arbitration board further found that on October 5, 1949, following a grievance meeting with union representatives earlier in the day and prior to discharging Mrs. Walker on October 6, officials of the company met with its attorneys and considered evidence which the attorneys had marshalled and which may be summarized as follows:

a. State Bar records showed no California lawyer named John Tripp (a name given by Mrs. Walker to the company, as a previous employer), but that there was such a lawyer with the given names of John Tripp; it developed that he was Mrs. Walker's supervisor in the O.P.A. (1942–1944).

b. A transcript of N.L.R.B. hearings of September 30 and October 1, 1948, in proceedings by discharged cannery workers, including Mrs. Walker, for reinstatement with back pay, showed a refusal by Mrs. Walker to answer the question, "are you or were you ever a member of the Communist Party?"

c. Statements to the following effect which appeared in certain of the Reports of the Joint Fact-Finding Committee on Un-American Activities in California for the years 1943, 1945, 1947, 1948 and 1949: That Mrs. Walker's O.P.A. supervisor associated with persons said to be "members of the Communist Party organization"; that "attorneys for the Communist Party are" the firm of labor lawyers by whom Mrs. Walker was employed in 1944 to 1946; reporting the identity of the Communist Political Association with the Communist Party despite a change of name "for strategic reasons May 20–23 1944"; giving a biography of one Archie Brown, an admitted Communist Party member and a candidate for various public offices on that ticket and mentioning sponsors of his from various unions including the United Office and Professional Workers of America; and indicating that the *People's Daily World,* a newspaper, is "the official organ of the Communist Party on the west coast."

d. Four issues of the *People's Daily World* contained items concerning Mrs. Walker: her employment by the labor law firm in February, 1944, was mentioned; she was listed as a 1944 alternate delegate to a State Committee of "the Communist Political Association"; and in October, 1946, a radio program was noted which she conducted on behalf of a committee "for Archie Brown for Governor ... the Communist write-in candidate."

e. A photostatic copy of an unaddressed hand-written letter dated "7/10/46" and signed with Mrs. Walker's maiden name discussed the propriety of the introduction of a resolution on the maritime strike at the Cannery Workers Club by the writer and another, and stated that "I tried to evaluate my action, as I try to evaluate whatever I do, from the point of view of the welfare of the working class and the strengthening of the Party."

f. Two "unidentified undated documents contained biographical material" about Mrs. Walker and stated, among other things, that she was issued 1945 Communist Party membership card No. 40360, that she joined the Communist Party in 1942 and had held various positions in various clubs and sections of the party including the "Cannery Club," that her present husband was a Communist Party member and organizer, and that in February, 1946, she listed on a Communist Party interview form the information that "she gave up law practice because it was frustrating to work with people she had to work with (namely, professional people)."

Mrs. Walker was not shown the above described evidence when she was discharged, but was confronted with it at the arbitration board hearing, and company attorneys asked her a series of questions concerning it and her Communist affiliations and activities, including the questions, "Are you now or have you ever been a member of the Communist Party?" and

> Isn't it a fact, Mrs. Walker ... that the reason why you sought employment ... at Cutter Laboratories was because you felt and believed, and had it in mind, that by obtaining that employment at that plant you could more actively and more effectively carry on the program and the activities of the Communist Party?

Mrs. Walker's attorney objected to the questions on the grounds, among others, that the political affiliations of an employe are immaterial and that by not acting more promptly the company had waived the Communism issue as a ground for discharge. The board overruled the objections but also announced that Mrs. Walker would not be instructed to answer the questions "if she did not care to do so, but that if she refused to answer we would draw all justifiable inferences from the refusal." Mrs. Walker thereupon refused to answer the questions as an "unwarranted invasion into my private beliefs." The evidence as to her Communist membership and acceptance of party principles, with all the implications that flow therefrom, thus stands unchallenged and uncontradicted by her and clearly supports the board's finding that the company honestly

and correctly believed her to be a knowing and deliberately acting Communist.

It was further found by the board that the company's 1947 investigation of Mrs. Walker indicated that she was a Communist and also disclosed most of the omissions and falsifications in her application for employment, that "a strong case" had been made out that in 1948 the company learned of her cannery activities and of the cannery hearings, and that there was "at least a general indifference on the part of the Company about Doris Walker's activities until the autumn of 1949 and a specific indifference about obvious ... clues to her background." The company stated that the reason they did not discharge Mrs. Walker in 1947 was because of a desire to "lean over backward" rather than to be accused of harassing union officials and because company attorneys advised that there was at that time insufficient evidence to support a discharge.

Under the provisions of the collective bargaining agreement in effect when Mrs. Walker was discharged, the company had agreed not to interfere with, restrain or coerce employes or discriminate against them because of *membership or lawful activity* in the union. It further agreed that, except for personnel reductions for lack of work or to effect economies, it would not discharge an employe "except for just cause." Both the union and the company also agreed that they will not discriminate against "a present or prospective employee or member because of race, color, creed, national origin, religious belief, or Union affiliation"; formerly "political" as well as "religious belief" was listed in this contract provision, but by negotation the word "political" was amended out of the agreement. The board held that although removal of the word "political" seemed to authorize the practice of discrimination because of "political belief," "we are unable to conclude" that the company's agreements not to discriminate because of union activity and not to discharge except for just cause were thereby limited or modified "in such a way as to dispose of this dispute." In this connection it is to be noted that the old hoax that the Communist Party is but a political party has been effectively exposed, as is hereinafter shown in some detail.

The company at the board hearings advanced two grounds as the basis for discharging Mrs. Walker: "the omissions and falsifications in the Application for Employment and membership in the Communist Party with the full implications of dedication to sabotage, force, violence and the like, which Party membership is believed to entail." Although finding that the company "honestly believed all of these things," and that the "accuracy of those beliefs is established in the record," the board further found that the company had not satisfactorily explained the delay of two years (from 1947 to 1949) in asserting the grounds for discharge presented to the board and that such grounds were therefore stale. Finally, it was found by the board that the reasons assigned by the company were not its real reasons for discharging Mrs. Walker, and that actually the discharge, which occurred during wage negotiations, was "retaliatory in nature" and "interfered with, restrained and coerced an employee because of participation as an officer and negotiator on behalf of the Union in a wage negotiation." As already stated, the board's award, based on the above findings, was that the company's discharge of Mrs. Walker violated the collective bargaining contract provisions against discrimination *because of union activity* and against discharging *except for just cause,* and that she is entitled to reinstatement and to limited back pay. The company failed to comply with the award, the union petitioned the superior court for its confirmation, and the company asked the court that it be vacated. (See Code Civ. Proc., §§ 1287, 1288.) After a hearing the trial court confirmed the award, and this appeal by the company followed.

Section 1288 of the Code of Civil Procedure provides, so far as here material, that

> In either of the following cases the superior court ... must make an order vacating the award, upon the application of any party to the arbitration: ...
> (d) Where the arbitrators exceeded their powers,

As ground for reversal the company contends, among other things and as it contended before the trial court in seeking vacation of the award, that an arbitration award which directs that a member of the Communist Party who is dedicated to that party's program of "sabotage, force, violence and the like" be reinstated to employment in a plant which produces antibiotics used by both the military and civilians is against public policy, as expressed in both federal and state laws, is therefore illegal and void and will not be enforced by the courts. With this contention we agree.

In the case of Loving & Evans v. Blick (1949), 33 Cal. 2d 603 [204 P. 2d 23], this court reversed a judgment confirming an arbitrator's award of a disputed sum owing under a building contract where it appeared that only one of the partners of the contracting firm was licensed as required by statute, and that neither the other partner nor the partnership held such a license. After referring to the principles that (p. 607)

"a contract made contrary to the terms of a law designed for the protection of the public and prescribing a penalty for the violation thereof is illegal and void, and no action may be brought to enforce such contract" and that (p. 609)

> ordinarily with respect to arbitration proceedings "the merits of the controversy between the parties are not subject to judicial review" [citation] and that "arbitrators are not bound by strict adherence to legal procedure and to the rules on the admission of evidence expected in judicial trials,

it was held (p. 610) that the "power of the arbitrator to determine the rights of the parties is dependent upon the existence of a valid contract under which such rights might arise," that

> Section 1281 of the Code of Civil Procedure, providing for submission to arbitration of "any controversy ... which arises out of a contract," does not contemplate that the parties may provide for the arbitration of controversies arising out of contracts which are expressly declared by law to be illegal and against the public policy of the state,

that (p. 611) "an unlawful transaction cannot be given legal vitality by the arbitration process," that (p. 614) "the only evidence before the trial court showed without contradiction that the contract upon which the award was based was illegal and void because of respondents' failure to comply with the licensing requirements," and that therefore that court had erred in confirming the award. And in Franklin v. Nat C. Goldstone Agency (1949), 33 Cal. 2d 628, 630–633 [204 P. 2d 37], a judgment confirming an arbitration award in favor of unlicensed contractors was likewise reversed upon the ground that the basic contract was illegal because in violation of the statutes and of "the public policy of this state."

It is at once apparent that the controversy now before us presents an even stronger case for refusal to confirm the award than was involved in the *Loving & Evans* and in the *Franklin* cases. There the illegality was held to exist in the contracts upon which the awards were based, while here the very award itself is illegal in that it orders reinstatement as an employe of one whose dedication to and active support of Communist principles and practices stands proved and unchallenged in the record. As is hereinafter shown, the true implications of knowing membership in and support · of the Communist Party are no longer open to doubt, and the long overworked party line theme that Communism is but a political activity has been exposed as a false and fraudulent stratagem designed particularly as a device for securing, in the free nations having government by law, legal support for the "party" in carrying on to the end of its illegal objectives.

The Congress of the United States, in adopting the Internal Security Act of 1950, declared the dangers of the Communist movement in the following terms (Act of Sept. 23, 1950, ch. 1024, tit. I, § 2, 64 Stats. 987; 50 U.S.C.A. § 781):

> As a result of evidence adduced before various committees of the Senate and House of Representatives, the Congress finds that—
>
> (1) There exists a world Communist movement which in its origins, its development, and its present practice, is a world-wide revolutionary movement whose purpose it is, by treachery, deceit, infiltration into other groups (governmental and otherwise), espionage, sabotage, terrorism, and any other means deemed necessary, to establish a Communist totalitarian dictatorship in the countries throughout the world through the medium of a world-wide Communist organization.
>
> (2) The establishment of a totalitarian dictatorship in any country results in the suppression of all opposition to the party in power, the subordination of the rights of individuals to the state, the denial of fundamental rights and liberties which are characteristic of a representative form of government, such as freedom of speech, of the press, of assembly, and of religious worship, and results in the maintenance of control over the people through fear, terrorism, and brutality . . .
>
> (9) In the United States those individuals who, knowingly and willfully participate in the world Communist movement, when they so participate, in effect repudiate their allegiance to the United States, and in effect transfer their allegiance to the foreign country in which is vested the direction and control of the world Communist movement . . .
>
> (15) The Communist movement in the United States is an organization numbering thousands of adherents, rigidly and ruthlessly disciplined. Awaiting and seeking to advance a moment when the United States may be so far extended by foreign engagements, so far divided in counsel, or so far in industrial or financial straits, that overthrow of the Government of the United States by force and violence may seem possible of achievement, it seeks converts far and wide by an extensive system of schooling and indoctrination. Such preparations by Communist organizations in other countries have aided in supplanting existing governments. The Communist organization in the United States, pursuing its stated objectives, the recent successes of Communist methods in other countries, and the nature and control of the world Communist movement itself, present a clear and present danger to the security of the United States and to the existence of free American institutions, and make it necessary that Congress, in order to provide for the common defense, to preserve the sovereignty of the United States as an independent nation, and to guarantee to each State a republican form of government enact appropriate legislation recognizing the existence of

such world-wide conspiracy and designed to prevent it from accomplishing its purpose in the United States.

And in the Smith Act (Act of June 25, 1948, ch. 645, 62 Stats. 808; 18 U.S.C.A. § 2385) it was provided that

> Whoever knowingly or willfully advocates, abets, advises, or teaches the . . . overthrowing or destroying the government of the United States or . . . of any State . . . by force or violence, or . . . Whoever organizes or helps or attempts to organize any society, group, or assembly of persons who . . . encourage the overthrow or destruction of any such government by force or violence; or becomes or is a member of, or affiliates with, any such . . . assembly of persons, knowing the purposes thereof

is guilty of a crime.

More recently, in adopting the Communist Control Act of 1954 (Public Law 637, ch. 886, approved August 24, 1954), our Congress further expressed its, and necessitates our, awareness of the true nature of the party program and methods, in these findings of fact:

> Sec. 2. The Congress hereby finds and declares that the Communist Party of the United States, although purportedly a political party, is in fact an instrumentality of a conspiracy to overthrow the Government of the United States. It constitutes an authoritarian dictatorship within a republic, demanding for itself the rights and privileges accorded to political parties, but denying to all others the liberties guaranteed by the Constitution. Unlike political parties, which evolve their policies and programs through public means, by the reconciliation of a wide variety of individual views, and submit those policies and programs to the electorate at large for approval or disapproval, the policies and programs of the Communist Party are secretly prescribed for it by the foreign leaders of the world Communist movement. Its members have no part in determining its goals, and are not permitted to voice dissent to party objectives. Unlike members of political parties, members of the Communist Party are recruited for indoctrination with respect to its objectives and methods, and are organized, instructed, and disciplined to carry into action slavishly the assignments given them by their hierarchical chieftains. Unlike political parties, the Communist Party acknowledges no constitutional or statutory limitations upon its conduct or upon that of its members. The Communist Party is relatively small numerically, and gives scant indication of capacity ever to attain its ends by lawful political means. The peril inherent in its operation arises not from its numbers, but from its failure to acknowledge any limitation as to the nature of its activities, and its dedication to the proposition that the present constitutional Government of the United States ultimately must be brought to ruin by any available means, including resort to force and violence. Holding that doctrine, its role as the agency of a hostile foreign power ren-

ders its existence a clear present and continuing danger to the security of the United States. It is the means whereby individuals are seduced into the service of the world Communist movement, trained to do its bidding, and directed and controlled in the conspiratorial performance of their revolutionary services. Therefore, the Communist Party should be outlawed.

A similar awareness was shown by the President of the United States in his State of the Union message delivered before a joint session of the Senate and the House of Representatives on January 7, 1954 (100 Congressional Record 62, H. Doc. 251), wherein he declared,

> The subversive character of the Communist Party in the United States has been clearly demonstrated in many ways, including court proceedings. We should recognize by law a fact that is plain to all thoughtful citizens—that we are dealing here with actions akin to treason—that when a citizen knowingly participates in the Communist conspiracy he no longer holds allegiance to the United States.

And in this state the courts have recognized that the type of activity found by the board here to have been engaged in by Mrs. Walker—*i.e.* membership "in the Communist Party with the full implications of dedication to sabotage, force, violence and the like, which Party membership is believed to entail"—constitutes a violation of the California Criminal Syndicalism Act. (Pen. Code, §§ 11400–11402, formerly Deering's Gen. Laws, Act 8428 ; see People v. McCormick (1951), 102 Cal. App. 2d Supp. 954, 962 [228 P. 2d 349] ; People v. Chambers (1937), 22 Cal. App. 2d 687, 709–713 [72 P. 2d 746].)

The Legislature of California itself has found as facts, and has so declared in section 1027.5 of the Government Code, that

> (a) There exists a world-wide revolutionary movement to establish a totalitarian dictatorship based upon force and violence rather than upon law . . .
>
> (d) Within the boundaries of the State of California there are active disciplined communist organizations presently functioning for the primary purpose of advancing the objectives of the world communism movement, which organizations promulgate, advocate, and adhere to the precepts and the principles and doctrines of the world communism movement. These communist organizations are characterized by identification of their programs, policies, and objectives with those of the world communism movement, and they regularly and consistently cooperate with and endeavor to carry into execution programs, policies and objectives substantially identical to programs, policies, and objectives of such world communism movement . . .
>
> There is a clear and present danger, which the Legislature of the State of California finds is great and imminent, that in order to advance the program,

policies and objectives of the world communism movement, communist organizations in the State of California and their members will engage in concerted effort to hamper, restrict, interfere with, impede, or nullify the efforts of the State and the public agencies of the State to comply with and enforce the laws of the State of California . . .

Further evidencing the implications of membership in the Communist Party and the policy of the state in respect thereto, the Legislature has declared that (Gov. Code, § 1028):

> It shall be sufficient cause for the dismissal of any public employee when such public employee advocates or is knowingly a member of the Communist Party or of an organization which during the time of his membership he knows advocates overthrow of the Government of the United States or of any state by force or violence.

(See also Board of Education v. Wilkinson (1954), 125 Cal. App. 2d 100 [270 P. 2d 82].) A private employer, particularly one largely engaged in supplying manufactured products to the government, to its armed forces, and to retailers for distribution through hospitals and doctors to the public at large, should not be required by state action through its courts (see Shelley v. Kraemer (1948), 334 U.S. 1 [68 S.Ct. 836, 92 L.Ed. 1161, 3 A.L.R. 2d 441] ; Hurd v. Hodge (1948), 334 U.S. 24 [68 S.Ct. 847, 92 L.Ed. 1187]) to retain in or restore to employment a person who would not be entitled to state employment and who is known to have dedicated herself to the service of a foreign power and to the practice of sabotage to the end of overthrowing our government.

Graphically depictive of the nature of the Communist conspiracy and of the extremes to which it is prepared to resort are the following statements by Mr. Justice Jackson, concurring in Dennis v. United States (1951), 341 U.S. 494, 564–565 [71 S.Ct. 857, 95 L.Ed. 1137, 1181]:

> The Communist Party, nevertheless, does not seek its strength primarily in numbers. Its aim is a relatively small party whose strength is in selected, dedicated, indoctrinated, and rigidly disciplined members. From established policy it tolerates no deviation and no debate. It seeks members that are, or may be, secreted in strategic posts in transportation, communications, industry, government, and especially in labor unions where it can compel employers to accept and retain its members. It also seeks to infiltrate and control organizations of professional and other groups. Through these placements in positions of power it seeks a leverage over society that will make up in power of coercion what it lacks in power of persuasion.
>
> The Communists have no scruples against sabotage, terrorism, assassination, or mob disorder; but violence is not with them, as with the anarchists, an

end in itself. The Communist Party advocates force only when prudent and profitable. Their strategy of stealth precludes premature or uncoordinated outbursts of violence, except, of course, when the blame will be placed on shoulders other than their own. They resort to violence as to truth, not as a principle but as an expedient. Force or violence, as they would resort to it, may never be necessary, because infiltration and deception may be enough.

Force would be utilized by the Communist Party not to destroy government but for its capture. The Communist recognizes that an established government in control of modern technology cannot be overthrown by force until it is about ready to fall of its own weight. Concerted uprising, therefore, is to await that contingency and revolution is seen, not as a sudden episode, but as the consummation of a long process.

Other instances of recognition by the courts of the clear and present danger to this country and to its institutions presented by the Communist Party and its adherents may be found in decisions upholding the provisions of the Labor Management Relations Act of 1947, also known as the Taft-Hartley Act, (Act, June 23, 1947, ch. 120, § 1 et seq.; 61 Stat. 136 et seq.; 29 U.S.C.A. § 141 et seq.), which deny the privilege of being chosen as exclusive bargaining agent to a union whose officers have not filed with the National Labor Relations Board their affidavits denying membership or affiliation with the Communist Party and denying belief in the overthrow of the United States Government by force (see American Communications Assn., C.I.O. v. Douds (1950), 339 U.S. 382, as well as in cases sustaining other legislation or Congressional inquiry directed at exposing and controlling Communist activities in this country.

We are of the view, further, that the type of activity engaged in by the employe here—membership in the Communist Party and sustained participation in its activities—is one which as a matter of public policy the company should not be held to have waived by its failure to discharge her earlier than it did. In the first place, it is an established principle that parties cannot be estopped from relying on defenses based on considerations of public policy, such as illegal contracts. (See Fewel & Dawes, Inc. v. Pratt (1941), 17 Cal. 2d 85, 91 [109 P. 2d 650]; American Nat. Bank v. A. G. Sommerville, Inc. (1923), 191 Cal. 364, 371 [216 P. 376].) In the second place, the employe's party membership was not shown or even asserted by her to have been an instance of past error but appears, rather, to have been the studied and calculated choice of a person of some intellectual attainment, and to have been persisted in on an active and devoted basis even at the time of the board hearings. Thus an entirely adequate ground for refusing to employ her (whether by original refusal to hire or by discharge) was a continuing one which was available to the employer at any time during its existence. In this connection it may also be noted that the employer had not only the right to protect itself and its customers against the clear and present danger of continuing a Communist Party member in its employ, but also the duty to take such action as it deemed wise to preserve order in its plant and to protect its other employes, both union and nonunion, against the same danger and the possibility of "sabotage, force, violence and the like." The company properly stated in its notice of discharge, as related above,

> The nature of our company's business requires more than the usual precaution against sabotage and subversion. Upon a disclosure that any employe is a member of the Communist Party . . . we conceive it to be the responsibility of management to take action.

Knowing the facts which the company knew, it is difficult to conceive of any tenable defense which it could make, or which would be entertained in this court, as against an action for damages in a personal injury or wrongful death case arising from the wilful adulteration of any of its products by Mrs. Walker if it continued her in its employ and she should thereafter take that means of party activity. That acts of sabotage by Communists are reasonably to be expected at any time such acts may be directed by the party leader is not open to question, as has already been shown.

The fact that the company was not specifically obliged by any governmental regulation to discharge Mrs. Walker affects in nowise its right to do so or the impelling public policy which militates against the order for her reinstatement; in this country, built as it has been upon the initiative and self-reliance of its citizens, the government is expected to step in only where the employer has failed or is unable to act for himself, and he is not obligated to await a governmental decree before taking steps to protect himself or to exercise his right to discharge employes who upon the established facts are dedicated to be disloyal to him, to be likewise disloyal to the American labor union they may purport to serve, and who constitute a continuing risk to both the employing company and the public depending upon the company's products.

Lastly, in the light of the undisputed evidence and of the specific findings of fact made by the arbitration board, it clearly appears that the conclusional finding that Mrs. Walker was discharged because of her labor union activities is untenable. We have here an exemplification of that which Justice Jackson (in Dennis v. United States (1941), *supra,* 341 U.S. 494, 564 [71 S.Ct. 857, 95 L.Ed. 1137, 1181]) so clearly envisaged when he said of the Communist Party:

> From established policy it tolerates no deviation and no debate. It seeks members that are, or may be secreted in strategic posts in . . . industry . . . and especially in labor unions where it can compel employers to accept and retain its members,

and of that to which the court referred when it stated in American Communications Assn., C.I.O. v. Douds (1950), *supra,* 339 U.S. 382, 389 [70 S.Ct. 674, 94 L.Ed. 925]:

> Congress [in enacting the Taft-Hartley Act] had a great mass of material before it which tended to show that Communists and others proscribed by the statute had infiltrated union organizations not to support and further trade union objectives . . . but to make them a device by which commerce and industry might be disrupted.

The issue of labor union activity herein is manifestly a false one, a subterfuge injected not to promote the cause of American labor but to further the Communist Party line. Mrs. Walker, as a Communist, was not at any time or in any of her activities truly serving the cause of an American labor union or the interests of an American laboring man; she was but doing the bidding and serving the cause of her foreign master who "tolerates no deviation and no debate." Her activities, therefore, upon any reasonable view of the evidence and the specific findings of fact, were not in truth union labor activities but were Communist Party activities.

Of no small significance in this connection is the fact that at the arbitration board hearing Mrs. Walker was asked, and she refused to answer the question,

> Isn't it a fact, Mrs. Walker . . . that the reason why you sought employment . . . at Cutter Laboratories was because you felt and believed, and had it in mind, that by obtaining that employment at that plant you could more actively and more effectively carry on the program and the activities of the Communist Party?

It is, we think, indisputable that if Mrs. Walker sought and obtained employment at Cutter Laboratories so that she "could more actively and more effectively carry on the program and the activities of the Communist Party," her reinstatement in that employment would serve no cause save that of the Communist conspiracy. The courts of this country by making such an order would be but aiding toward destruction of the government they are sworn to uphold.

The contract between Cutter Laboratories and the Bio-Lab Union cannot be construed, and will not be enforced, to protect activities by a Communist on behalf of her party whether in the guise of unionism or otherwise.

The judgment is reversed and the cause is remanded for further proceedings not inconsistent with the views herein expressed.

SHENK, J., EDMONDS, J., and SPENCE, J., concurred.

TRAYNOR, J., Dissenting.—All the members of the court agree that we are bound by the determination of the arbitrators[1] that for two and one-half years Doris Walker's communist affiliations were a matter of indifference to Cutter, that Cutter therefore waived her communist affiliations as a ground for discharging her, that it discharged her solely because of her lawful

---

1. "While there is a work stoppage and a strike in this collective bargaining history [during Doris Walker's employment], both were directed at wage and contract issues. There is no evidence of any work stoppage, strike or other interference with production, the avowed objective of which was political, philosophical, subversive or revolutionary. . . .

"It is admitted that Doris Walker's conduct and the quality of her work were no different in 1949 from what they were in 1947. It is uncontradicted on the record that all of the essential facts upon which the discharge was based were in existence in 1947 and some years before. And finally, it is established to our satisfaction, by admission of the Company and by proof, that the reasons assigned in 1949 by the Company for the discharge were both known and believed by the Company in 1947.

"This state of the record raises a doubt that the Company ever took the assigned grounds for discharge seriously. . . .

"Finally, it appears, by admission of the Company, that notwithstanding the 1947 investigative report, there was no further investigation until the autumn of 1949. This is inexplicable to us if there was real concern about the combination of Communist Party membership and the omissions and falsifications disclosed by the 1947 investigative report.

"From all of this we are unable to find any satisfactory excuse for the Company's delay of over two years in asserting the grounds for discharge presented here. Contract relationships lose effectiveness if grievances about performance are not promptly discussed, settled or brought to an issue. This cuts both ways: unadjusted dissatisfactions of either employer or employees cumulate and exaggerate the importance of ensuing minor dissatisfactions. It seems to us that a commonplace of any 'just' system of discipline is the swift imposition of the penalty upon the heels of discovery of the offense. Under an agreement like this one, an employer should not be entitled to carry mutually known grounds for discharge in his hip pocket indefinitely for future convenient use.

"In view of the foregoing considerations, we find that the grounds asserted by the Company for the discharge were stale. . . .

"The discharge of a top Union official and negotiator at a passionate climax in the middle of a stubbornly contested wage negotiation, standing alone, raises an inference that the discharge is retaliatory in nature and designed to restrain, coerce or interfere with the employee because of lawful Union activity. And we find convincing circumstantial evidence to support this inference.

union activity, and that in doing so it violated its collective bargaining agreement with the Union. (Code Civ. Proc., §§ 1280–1293 ; Pacific Vegetable Oil Corp. v. C.S.T., Ltd., 29 Cal. 2d 228, 233 [174 P. 2d 441] ; Sapp v. Barenfeld, 34 Cal. 2d 515, 523 [212 P. 2d 233] ; Crofoot v. Blair Holdings Corp., 119 Cal. App. 2d 156, 185 [260 P. 2d 156], see Loving & Evans v. Blick, 33 Cal. 2d 603, 609 [204 P. 2d 23].) It would seem necessarily to follow that we should affirm the judgment of the superior court confirming the award. The majority opinion holds, however,

> that an arbitration award which directs that a member of the Communist Party who is dedicated to that party's program of "sabotage, force, violence and the like" be reinstated to employment in a plant which produces antibiotics used by both the military and civilians is against public policy, as expressed in both federal and state laws, is therefore illegal and void and will not be enforced by the courts.

Thus, even though an employer is indifferent to the fact that an employee is a Communist and is therefore no longer free under a collective bargaining contract to discharge him for being a Communist, it can nevertheless violate its contract not to discharge him for lawful union activity and use the fact that he is a Communist as an excuse for its unlawful action. It can do so because this court holds that the employment of a Communist poses such a threat to the security of the country that a contract by an employer with a union to keep a known Communist in its employ is against public policy and is therefore illegal. *A fortiori* such a contract by an employer with the employee is illegal. Thus by judicial fiat, but without the temerity to declare that Communists are deprived of civil rights (see Civ. Code, § 1556), the court abrogates not only the right of employers and unions to contract for the employment of Communists, but the right of Communists as a class to enter into binding contracts. It does so by invoking public policy in violation of clearly stated policies of the Legislature (Civ. Code, § 1556 ; Lab. Code, § 923 ; Code Civ. Proc., §§ 1280–1293) and in a field in which Congress and the Legislature have clearly indicated their competence to deal with the problems involved.

Section 1556 of the Civil Code provides that "All persons are capable of contracting, except minors, persons of unsound mind, and persons deprived of civil rights." (See also 1 WILLISTON ON CONTRACTS [rev. ed.] § 222, pp. 669–670.) To deny persons other than those mentioned in this section the right to enter into employment contracts is to repeal *pro tanto* its provisions with

respect to the class of contracts of greatest importance to those who must work for a living. Even if this court were at liberty so to repeal the statute, there are compelling reasons why it should not do so.

It is true that in this case only an employment contract is involved. There is nothing in the rationale of the majority opinion, however, that limits its application to such contracts. If it is illegal to employ a Communist, is it illegal to allow a Communist unemployment benefits? If the threat of communist activity makes an employment contract with a known Communist illegal as against public policy, does it not also invalidate other contracts?

If breaches of contract can be defended on the ground that one of the parties is a Communist, certainly a hearing will not be denied the alleged Communist on the issue of whether or not he is a Communist. The communist problem, which the court has thus injected into private litigation, may therefore dominate all such litigation and become one of the principal preoccupations of courts. To what end? Certainly private litigation does not lend itself to the formulation of a solution to the problem of what to do with Communists. It is a rash assumption that Congress and the Legislature have been inept in their consideration of the problem, or are incapable of meeting it, or that astride the "unruly horse" of public policy (National Auto. Ins. Co. v. Winter, 58 Cal. App. 2d 11, 22 [136 P. 2d 22]) courts are better able to meet it.

It is obvious that Cutter cannot properly invoke public policy on its own behalf. Doris Walker's work was satisfactory and her union activities were consistent with legitimate trade-union objectives. Her presence at Cutter presented at most a threat that she might attempt to use her position for subversive activities. That risk, however, was one that Cutter itself did not consider serious enough to disqualify her for employment, and it has been materially lessened by the fact that her communism has been thoroughly exposed. As an afterthought, Cutter now uses this threat as an excuse not only for discharging her for lawful union activity in violation of its contract, but for attacking an arbitration award that it had agreed should be "final and binding" upon it. By sanctioning these violations of Cutter's contract this court not only defeats the public policy in favor of employee organization free of employer interference and coercion (Lab. Code, § 923 ; National Labor Relations Act, 29 U.S.C.A. § 151 et seq.) and the public policy in favor of the settlement of disputes by arbitration (Code Civ. Proc., §§ 1280–1293) but needlessly introduces confusion into a field in which Congress has already undertaken to formulate a workable policy. (50 U.S.C.A. § 781 et seq.)

It is true that there are sensitive areas in which no Communist should be employed. We cannot assume, however, that the security system established by the federal government is not adequate to protect these areas from subversive persons. As the very authorities cited in the majority opinion make clear, neither Congress in enacting subversive control legislation nor the executive department in enforcing it has been insensitive to the nation's security. To date, however, Congress has not seen fit to make mere membership in the Communist Party a crime or to prohibit persons from entering into employment or other contracts with Communists. Similarly, the executive department has not undertaken to prosecute all Communists under the Smith Act. (18 U.S.C.A. § 2385.) It is not the policy of the United States that all Communists are without legal rights and should be interned. So long as they may legally remain at large they should be allowed to earn a living. Even resident enemy aliens, whose activities have not been restricted by Congress or the President, may engage in time of war in ordinary activities and make binding contracts of employment or other contracts.

It must be obvious that in passing on the validity of ordinary employment contracts in litigation between private parties, courts are in no position effectively to evaluate the security factors that should determine what jobs Communists should or should not hold. In its finding of necessity for the enactment of the Internal Security Act of 1950 (50 U.S.C.A. § 781 et seq.) Congress demonstrated its awareness of the communist problem and specifically established in that act the policy of the United States with respect to the employment of Communists. It did not prohibit all hiring of Communists nor did it leave to the courts the decision as to what jobs Communists might hold. It provided instead that the Secretary of Defense should determine and designate the defense facilities in which members of Communist-action organizations should not be employed. Cutter has not been so designated, and we may therefore assume that the employment of a Communist at Cutter poses no threat to the security of the country. I see no evidence of congressional incompetence or of executive negligence in this respect, nor do I see any evidence of superior wisdom, facilities, or techniques available to this court that would justify its intrusion into policy making in this field. It is my opinion that we can still safely leave to the legislative branch of the government

the formulation of policies for the security of the country, and I would therefore affirm the judgment.

GIBSON, C. J., and CARTER, J., concurred.

Respondents' petition for a rehearing was denied February 16, 1955. GIBSON, C. J., CARTER, J., and TRAYNOR, J., were of the opinion that the petition should be granted.

In Baltimore Transit Co., 47 Lab. Arb. 62 (1966), the arbitrator upheld the discharge of a bus driver who, after 13 years of employment, was publicized as Grand Dragon of the Ku Klux Klan in Maryland. The company's fear of violence because of his continued employment was "good cause" although such membership was legal and the dischargee had not engaged in KKK activity on company time nor acted improperly toward Negro bus drivers or patrons. On a motion to vacate the award, what should the ruling be?

LOCAL 453, INT'L UNION OF ELECTRICAL WORKERS v. OTIS ELEVATOR CO.
314 F. 2d 25 (2d Cir.) [cert. denied 373 U.S. 949 (1963)]

Before FRIENDLY, KAUFMAN and MARSHALL, CIRCUIT JUDGES.

MARSHALL, C. J. This is an appeal by the plaintiff below, Local 453, International Union of Electrical Workers, from an order entered by the United States District Court for the Southern District of New York, Cashin, J., granting summary judgment in favor of the defendant, Otis Elevator Company. The effect of the order was to vacate, set aside, and deny enforcement to an arbitration award which had directed Otis to reinstate an employee whom it had discharged for violating a company rule prohibiting gambling. The facts underlying the controversy are not in dispute.

Joseph Calise, an employee of Otis who was represented by Local 453, was convicted on December 1, 1960, in the County Court of Westchester County on two counts of knowingly possessing policy slips in the Otis plant in Yonkers on December 28, and 29, 1959, in violation of New York Penal Law, § 974, which makes such conduct a misdemeanor. He was fined a total of $250. There was testimony at the trial that four other Otis employees were "working for" Calise in handling policy slips within the plant, but apparently none of the four was prosecuted by the public authorities or disciplined by Otis.

During the eleven months that elapsed between the date of Calise's arrest and the date of his conviction, Otis took no disciplinary action against him and he remained on the job without evidence of further transgression. However, on December 5, 1960, four days after Calise's conviction was entered, he was discharged for violating the company's rule against gambling on its premises during working hours. The union challenged the discharge and after the exhaustion of grievance procedures under the collective bargaining agreement the parties submitted the dispute to arbitration.

The applicable provisions of the collective bargaining agreement gave the employer "the right to discharge any employee for just cause" and the union "the right to challenge the propriety of the discharge of any employee" as a grievance. The agreement further provided that when an issue was submitted to arbitration, the decision of the arbitrator "shall be final and binding upon the parties." In submitting the present controversy to arbitration, the parties stipulated that the question for decision was, "Has Joseph Calise been discharged for just cause, and if not what shall the remedy be?"

The arbitrator concluded that under all of the circumstances Calise had not been discharged for just cause. He ordered Otis to reinstate Calise to his former position on July 3, 1961, but without back pay or accrual of seniority or other benefits flowing from the collective agreement for the seven-month period of disciplinary layoff, although his prior-accrued seniority and pension rights were to be preserved and not to be affected by the layoff.

The arbitrator made plain that Calise had been guilty of serious misconduct and that his award was in no way to be taken as condoning "such illegal activities as policy numbers gambling." Substantial disciplinary action sufficient to serve as a deterrent would have been permissible, he said, but "outright and final discharge is a disciplinary action with effects too harsh upon the grieving employee." He based his decision upon the facts that Calise had already been punished once for his offense by the public authorities, that he had undergone a seven-month layoff without pay or unemployment compensation, that he had 24 years of unbroken seniority and satisfactory service at the company, that he had "heavy family obligations involving four young innocent children and a wife," that as a result of discharge he would lose considerable pension rights "built up after decades of service," and that the company had not disciplined the four other men who "were guilty also of violating the same rule against gambling in the plant."

The union subsequently brought suit in the United States District Court for the Southern District of New York to confirm the arbitration award and to compel Otis to comply with it, asserting jurisdiction under Section 301 of the Labor Management Relations Act, 29 U.S.C.A. § 185. By an order to show cause, the union moved for a preliminary injunction to compel compliance pending final disposition of the action. The motion was denied by the District Court, MacMahon, J., in an opinion reported at 201 F.Supp. 213 (S.D.N.Y. 1962), on the ground that the arbitrator's award was "void and unenforceable" because violative of an "overriding public policy." The court said that the award "indulges crime, cripples an employer's power to support the law, and impairs his right to prevent exposure to criminal liability." Id. at 218.

The union then moved for summary judgment pursuant to Rule 56 of the Federal Rules of Civil Procedure. The District Court, Cashin, J., in an opinion reported at 206 F.Supp. 853 (S.D.N.Y. 1962), denied the motion. At the same time, since there was no genuine issue of fact, it exercised its right to grant summary judgment to the defendant, vacating and setting aside the arbitration award, without the filing of a formal cross-motion.

In entering summary judgment for the defendant, Judge Cashin said that he agreed with "Judge MacMahon's determination that the arbitrator had the power to settle the dispute involved. I also agree that this court is foreclosed [by the arbitrator's decision] from considering the question of whether or not the commission of a crime by an employee upon the premises of the employer is just cause for discharge as a matter of law." 206 F.Supp. at 854. But he nevertheless felt bound to deny enforcement to the arbitrator's award.

> However, as Judge MacMahon found, the misconduct involved here is not just an infraction of a company rule. It is a misdemeanor under § 974, McK. Consol. Laws, c. 40, of the N.Y. Penal Law. This same statute also provides that a "person who . . . is the owner . . . of any place . . . where policy playing or the sale of what are commonly called "lottery policies" is carried on with his knowledge or after notification that the premises are so used, permits such use to be continued, or who aids, assists, or abets in any manner, . . . is a common gambler, and guilty of a misdemeanor." Thus, the responsibility for the observance of this law rests upon the owner of the premises and exposes him to criminal prosecution.

In the instant case, Calise was not just gambling himself, but he was carrying an organized professional gambling and had four other employees working for him. Under these circumstances I cannot compel the defendant to comply with the arbitration award. *Id.* at 855.

It is from the decision of Judge Cashin that the union has taken this appeal.

The decision of Judge Cashin expressly adopted the conclusions of Judge MacMahon that the grievance that arose between Local 453 and Otis over the discharge of Calise was an arbitrable one and that the arbitrator had the power to settle the dispute involved. These conclusions were clearly correct. The terms of the collective bargaining agreement provide that the employer may discharge an employee for "just cause" and that the union may challenge the "propriety" of a discharge as a grievance. They further provide that the arbitrator shall have the authority to make a "final and binding" decision on all grievances between the parties. The agreement nowhere defines what conduct constitutes "just cause" for discharge or what criteria shall govern the "propriety" of a discharge. That the parties intended to leave such definition to the arbitrator is made plain both by the "plenary grant" of power made to him, 201 F.Supp. at 217, and by the broad scope of the stipulated question, framed only in terms of "just cause," which accompanied the submission. Although the scope of an arbitrator's authority is not unlimited, Textile Workers Union of America v. American Thread Co., 291 F. 2d 894 (4 Cir., 1961), the terms of the contract and of the submission in the present case, underscored by the rule that courts must uphold the arbitrator in the exercise of the broadest jurisdiction in the absence of specific contractual limitations on that jurisdiction, clearly bespeak arbitrability.

Having bargained for the decision of the arbitrator on the question of whether Calise's conduct and criminal conviction constituted "just cause" for discharge, the parties are bound by it, even if it be regarded as unwise or wrong on the merits; "so far as the arbitrator's decision concerns construction of the contract, the courts have no business overruling him because their interpretation of the contract is different from his." United Steelworkers of America v. Enterprise Wheel & Car Corp., 363 U.S. 593, 599, 80 S.Ct. 1358, 1362, 4 L.Ed. 2d 1424 (1960). To separate the just causes for discharge from the injust [*sic*] was precisely what the parties clothed the arbitrator with the authority to do. If the employer wanted the automatic right to discharge an employee for violation of certain company rules or for the commission of certain crimes,

whether on or off the company premises, it had the opportunity to seek such an explicit exclusion from the general arbitration clause when the collective agreement was negotiated, as it may do when the collective agreement expires. In the absence of such a clause, the decision of the arbitrator in the present case must be taken as conclusively establishing as a matter of contract interpretation that the discharge of Calise was not for just cause and as foreclosing judicial review of the merits of the question.

Despite his recognition of the force and applicability of these principles, Judge Cashin nevertheless concluded, for the same reasons for which Judge MacMahon had concluded, that the award of the arbitrator was judicially unenforceable because of its repugnance to public policy. The precise nature of the public policy which the award was thought to offend is not made clear by either opinion in the District Court. Apparently the Court was concerned with the fact that the possession of policy slips "is regarded by responsible law enforcement officials, state and federal, as the incubator of most, and more sinister, organized crime," 201 F.Supp. at 218, and with the fact that since an employer is responsible for knowingly permitting policymaking on his premises, "[t]o deny him the power to discharge for the commission of such a crime upon his property exposes him to criminal prosecution." Id. at 217. See 206 F.Supp. at 855. We think that the District Court's analysis of the public policy issue was inadequate. Accordingly, we reverse, with instructions that an order issue compelling the employer to comply with the terms of the arbitrator's award.

It is no less true in suits brought under § 301 to enforce arbitration awards than in other lawsuits that the "power of the federal courts to enforce the terms of private agreements is at all times exercised subject to the restrictions and limitations of the public policy of the United States." Hurd v. Hodge, 334 U.S. 24, 34–35, 68 S.Ct. 847, 852–853, 92 L.Ed. 1187 (1948). The public policy to be enforced is a part of the substantive principles of federal labor law which federal courts, under the mandate of Textile Workers Union of America v. Lincoln Mills, 353 U.S. 448, 77 S.Ct. 912, 1 L.Ed. 2d 972 (1957), are empowered to fashion. Cf. Local 174, Teamsters, etc., v. Lucas Flour Co., 369 U.S. 95, 82 S.Ct. 571, 7 L.Ed. 2d 593 (1962). Thus, when public policy is sought to be interposed as a bar to enforcement of an arbitration award, a court must evaluate its asserted content.

Of course there is a public policy which condemns gambling by an employee on the premises of his employer; it is a policy expressed by the section of the New York Penal Law which Calise was convicted of violating. But that policy has been vindicated in the present case in the very manner that the State of New York contemplated, by a criminal conviction and the judicial imposition of a penalty. Parenthetically, it may further have been vindicated, beyond any demands of the State of New York, by the seven-month layoff without compensation or accrual of seniority benefits which Calise sustained and which the arbitrator upheld. There is no federal policy that requires greater vindication of the public condemnation of gambling than this. The law is not that Draconian. To enforce the arbitrator's award in these circumstances cannot fairly be looked upon as judicial condonation of Calise's offense.

Moreover, in light of the important role which employment plays in implementing the public policy of rehabilitating those convicted of crime, there can hardly be a public policy that a man who has been convicted, fined, and subjected to serious disciplinary measures, can never be ordered reinstated to his former employment, particularly when the conviction was for his first offense and when the arbitrator found no indication that reinstatement would result in repetition of the illegal activity. Indeed, the arbitrator in effect took into account the importance of rehabilitation when he concluded that the criminal conviction, the sentence imposed as a result of that conviction, and the seven-month layoff without pay or unemployment compensation were appropriate punishment under the circumstances.

The argument, persuasive to the District Court, that reemployment of Calise may subject Otis to prosecution under New York Penal Law, § 974 if Calise resumes his criminal activity is open to serious doubt. As one commentator has said in criticizing the result reached by the District Court in the present case,

> It is hard to imagine that an employer who had specifically indicated his disapproval of gambling on the premises, had penalized the employee found guilty, and had warned the employee against any such conduct in the future could be found guilty of violating the statute.

Fleming, *Arbitrators and the Remedy Power*, 48 VA. L. REV. 1199, 1209 (1962).

The award of the arbitrator was regular in every respect. There is no substantive principle of federal labor law which authorizes denial of enforcement on the present facts for reasons of public policy. Accordingly, the judgment below is reversed, with instructions that an order issue compelling Otis to comply with the terms of the arbitration award.

Reversed.

Avco Corp. v. Preteska, 22 Conn. Supp. 475, 174 A. 2d 684 (Super Ct. 1961) presented quite similar facts. The court there held that the order to reinstate the confessed gambler violated public policy. "Awards which contravene the public policy of a state exceed the powers of an arbitrator and are illegal and unenforceable." (Citing *Cutter Laboratories*). Jenkins Bros v. Local 5623, United Steelworkers of America, 341 F. 2d 987 (2d Cir. 1965) rejected the argument that *Avco* could be harmonized with *Otis*.

B.

Interaction with Other Statutes

WILKO v. SWAN
346 U.S. 427 (1953)

REED, J. This action by petitioner, a customer, against respondents, partners in a securities brokerage firm, was brought in the United States District Court for the Southern District of New York, to recover damages under § 12 (2) of the Securities Act of 1933.[1] The complaint alleged that on or about January 17, 1951, through the instrumentalities of interstate commerce, petitioner was induced by Hayden, Stone and Company to purchase 1,600 shares of the common stock of Air Associates, Incorporated, by false representations that pursuant to a merger contract with the Borg Warner Corporation, Air Associates' stock would be valued at $6.00 per share over the then current market price, and

---

1. 48 Stat. 74, 15 U.S.C. § 77a *et seq.* § 12 (2), 48 Stat. 84, 15 U.S.C. § 77*l* (2), provides: "Any person who . . .

"(2) sells a security (whether or not exempted by the provisions of section 77c of this title, other than paragraph (2) of subsection (a) of said section 77c), by the use of any

means or instruments of transportation or communication in interstate commerce or of the mails, by means of a prospectus or oral communication, which includes an untrue statement of a material fact or omits to state a material fact necessary in order to make the statements, in the light

that financial interests were buying up the stock for the speculative profit. It was alleged that he was not told that Haven B. Page (also named as a defendant but not involved in this review), a director of, and counsel for, Air Associates was then selling his own Air Associates' stock, including some or all that petitioner purchased. Two weeks after the purchase, petitioner disposed of the stock at a loss. Claiming that the loss was due to the firm's misrepresentations and omission of information concerning Mr. Page, he sought damages.

Without answering the complaint, the respondent moved to stay the trial of the action pursuant to § 3 of the United States Arbitration Act until an arbitration in accordance with the terms of identical margin agreements was had. An affidavit accompanied the motion stating that the parties' relationship was controlled by the terms of the agreements and that while the firm was willing to arbitrate petitioner had failed to seek or proceed with any arbitration of the controversy.

Finding that the margin agreements provide that arbitration should be the method of settling all future controversies, the District Court held that the agreement to arbitrate deprived petitioner of the advantageous court remedy afforded by the Securities Act, and denied the stay. A divided Court of Appeals concluded that the Act did not prohibit the agreement to refer future controversies to arbitration, and reversed.

The question is whether an agreement to arbitrate a future controversy is a "condition, stipulation, or provision binding any person acquiring any security to waive compliance with any provision" of the Securities Act which § 14 declares "void." We granted certiorari, 345 U.S. 969, to review this important and novel federal question affecting both the Securities Act and the United States Arbitration Act. Cf. Frost & Co. v. Coeur D'Alene Mines Corp., 312 U.S. 38, 40.

As the margin agreement in the light of the complaint evidenced a transaction in interstate commerce, no issue arises as to the applicability of the provisions of the United States Arbitration Act to this suit, based upon the Securities Act.

9 U.S.C. (Supp. V, 1952) § 2. Cf. Tejas Development Co. v. McGough Bros., 165 F. 2d 276, 278, with Agostini Bros. Bldg. Corp. v. United States, 142 F. 2d 854. See Sturges and Murphy, *Some Confusing Matters Relating to Arbitration,* 17 Law & Contemp. Prob. 580.

In response to a Presidential message urging that there be added to the ancient rule of *caveat emptor* the further doctrine of "let the seller also beware," Congress passed the Securities Act of 1933. Designed to protect investors, the Act requires issuers, underwriters, and dealers to make full and fair disclosure of the character of securities sold in interstate and foreign commerce and to prevent fraud in their sale. To effectuate this policy, § 12 (2) created a special right to recover for misrepresentation which differs substantially from the common-law action in that the seller is made to assume the burden of proving lack of scienter.[2] The Act's hope for its usefulness both in controversies based on statutes or on standards otherwise created. This hospitable attitude of legislatures and courts toward arbitration, however, does not solve our question as to the validity of petitioner's stipulation by the margin agreements, set out below, to submit to arbitration controversies that might arise from the transactions.[3]

Petitioner argues that § 14 shows that the purpose of Congress was to assure that sellers could not maneuver buyers into a position that might weaken their ability to recover under the Securities Act. He contends that arbitration lacks the certainty of a suit at law under the Act to enforce his rights. He reasons that the arbitration paragraph of the margin agreement is a stipulation that waives "compliance with" the provision of the Securities Act, set out in the margin, conferring jurisdiction of suits and special powers.

Respondent asserts that arbitration is merely a form of trial to be used in lieu of a trial at law, and therefore no conflict exists between the Securities Act and the United States Arbitration

---

2. See note 1, *supra.* "Unless responsibility is to involve merely paper liability it is necessary to throw the burden of disproving responsibility for reprehensible acts of omission or commission on those who purport to issue statements for the public's reliance. . . . To impose a lesser responsibility would nullify the purposes of this legislation." H.R. Rep. No. 85, 73d Cong., 1st Sess. 9–10.

3. "Any controversy arising between us under this contract shall be determined by arbitration pursuant to the Arbitration Law of the State of New York, and under the rules of either the Arbitration Committee of the Chamber of Commerce of the State of New York, or of the American Arbitration Association, or of the Arbitration Committee of the New York Stock Exchange or such other Exchange as may have jurisdiction over the matter in dispute, as I may elect. Any arbitration hereunder shall be before at least three arbitrators."

---

of the circumstances under which they were made, not misleading (the purchaser not knowing of such untruth or omission), and who shall not sustain the burden of proof that he did not know, and in the exercise of reasonable care could not have known, of such untruth or omission, shall be liable to the person purchasing such security from him, who may sue either at law or in equity in any court of competent jurisdiction, to recover the consideration paid for such security with interest thereon, less the amount of any income received thereon, upon the tender of such security, or for damages if he no longer owns the security."

Act either in their language or in the congressional purposes in their enactment. Each may function within its own scope, the former to protect investors and the latter to simplify recovery for actionable violations of law by issuers or dealers in securities.

Respondent is in agreement with the Court of Appeals that the margin agreement arbitration paragraph, note 4, *supra*, does not relieve the seller from either liability or burden of proof, note 1, *supra*, imposed by the Securities Act.[4] We agree that in so far as the award in arbitration may be affected by legal requirements, statutes or common law, rather than by considerations of fairness, the provisions of the Securities Act control. This is true even though this proposed agreement has no requirement that the arbitrators follow the law. This agreement of the parties as to the effect of the Securities Act includes also acceptance of the invalidity of the paragraph of the margin agreement that relieves the respondent sellers of liability for all "representation or advice by you or your employees or agents regarding the purchase or sale by me of any property. . . ."

The words of § 14 void any "stipulation" waiving compliance with any "provision" of the Securities Act. This arrangement to arbitrate is a "stipulation," and we think the right to select the judicial forum is the kind of "provision" that cannot be waived under § 14 of the Securities

---

4. "Paragraph 3 of the margin agreement provides that all transactions 'shall be subject to the provisions of the Securities Exchange Act of 1934 and present and future acts amendatory thereto [15 U.S.C.A. § 78a et seq.].' It contains no express mention of the Securities Act of 1933. If reference to the 1934 Act were construed as excluding the 1933 Act, it might be argued that the agreement did not provide for arbitration of a controversy as to the liability of Hayden, Stone & Co. under section 12 (2) of the 1933 Act. But we do not think the principle of *expressio unius est exclusio alterius* is here applicable. It may well be that the phrase 'present . . . acts . . . supplemental' to the 1934 Act should be construed to include the 1933 Act. In any event the sale transaction would necessarily be subject to that Act. Therefore the *amicus* does not regard it as material whether or not the agreement purports to make that statute applicable. We agree, and shall proceed to a consideration of the question decided below, namely, whether the 1933 Act evidences a public policy which forbids referring the controversy to arbitration." 201 F. 2d, at 443.

The paragraph of the agreement referred to by the Court of Appeals as "3" reads as follows:

"All transactions made by you or your agents for me are to be subject to the constitutions, rules, customs and practices of the exchanges or markets where executed and of their respective clearing houses and shall be subject to the provisions of the Securities Exchange Act of 1934 and present and future acts amendatory thereof or supplemental thereto, and to the rules and regulations of the Federal Securities and Exchange Commission and of the Federal Reserve Board insofar as they may be applicable. . . ."

Act. That conclusion is reached for the reasons set out above in the statement of petitioner's contention on this review. While a buyer and seller of securities, under some circumstances, may deal at arm's length on equal terms, it is clear that the Securities Act was drafted with an eye to the disadvantages under which buyers labor. Issuers of and dealers in securities have better opportunities to investigate and appraise the prospective earnings and business plans affecting securities than buyers. It is therefore reasonable for Congress to put buyers of securities covered by that Act on a different basis from other purchasers.

When the security buyer, prior to any violation of the Securities Act, waives his right to sue in courts, he gives up more than would a participant in other business transactions. The security buyer has a wider choice of courts and venue. He thus surrenders one of the advantages the Act gives him and surrenders it at a time when he is less able to judge the weight of the handicap the Securities Act places upon his adversary.

Even though the provisions of the Securities Act, advantageous to the buyer, apply, their effectiveness in application is lessened in arbitration as compared to judicial proceedings. Determination of the quality of a commodity[5] or the amount of money due under a contract is not the type of issue here involved.[6] This case requires subjective findings on the purpose and knowledge of an alleged violator of the Act. They must be not only determined but applied by the arbitrators without judicial instruction on the law. As their award may be made without explanation of their reasons and without a complete record of their proceedings, the arbitrators' conception of the legal meaning of such statutory requirements as "burden of proof," "reasonable care" or "material fact," see note 1, *supra*, cannot be examined. Power to vacate an award is limited. While it may be true, as the Court of Appeals thought, that a failure of the arbitrators to decide in accordance with the provisions of the Securities Act would "constitute grounds for vacating the award pursuant to section 10 of the Federal Arbitration Act," that failure would need to be made clearly to appear. In unrestricted submissions, such as the present

---

5. Campe Corp. v. Pacific Mills, 87 N.Y.S. 2d 16, reversed, 275 App. Div. 634, 92 N.Y.S. 2d 347.

6. Evans v. Hudson Coal Co., 165 F. 2d 970; Donahue v. Susquehanna Collieries Co., 160 F. 2d 661; Watkins v. Hudson Coal Co., 151 F. 2d 311; Donahue v. Susquehanna Collieries Co., 138 F. 2d 3; Agostini Bros. Bldg. Corp. v. United States, 142 F. 2d 854; American Almond Prod. Co. v. Consolidated Pecan S. Co., 144 F. 2d 448.

margin agreements envisage, the interpretations of the law by the arbitrators in contrast to manifest disregard are not subject, in the federal courts, to judicial review for error in interpretation. The United States Arbitration Act contains no provision for judicial determination of legal issues such as is found in the English law. As the protective provisions of the Securities Act require the exercise of judicial direction to fairly assure their effectiveness, it seems to us that Congress must have intended § 14, *supra*, to apply to waiver of judicial trial and review.

This accords with Boyd v. Grand Trunk Western R. Co., 338 U.S. 263. We there held invalid a stipulation restricting an employee's choice of venue in an action under the Federal Employers' Liability Act. Section 6 of that Act permitted suit in any one of several localities and § 5 forbade a common carrier's exempting itself from any liability under the Act. Section 5 had been adopted to avoid contracts waiving employers' liability. It is to be noted that in words it forbade exemption only from "liability." We said the right to select the "forum" even after the creation of a liability is a "substantial right" and that the agreement, restricting that choice, would thwart the express purpose of the statute. We need not and do not go so far in this present case. By the terms of the agreement to arbitrate, petitioner is restricted in his choice of forum prior to the existence of a controversy. While the Securities Act does not require petitioner to sue, a waiver in advance of a controversy stands upon a different footing.

Two policies, not easily reconcilable, are involved in this case. Congress has afforded participants in transactions subject to its legislative power an opportunity generally to secure prompt economical and adequate solution of controversies through arbitration if the parties are willing to accept less certainty of legally correct adjustment. On the other hand, it has enacted the Securities Act to protect the rights of investors and has forbidden a waiver of any of those rights. Recognizing the advantages that prior agreements for arbitration may provide for the solution of commercial controversies, we decide that the intention of Congress concerning the sale of securities is better carried out by holding invalid such an agreement for arbitration of issues arising under the Act.

Reversed.

JACKSON, J. concurring. I agree with the Court's opinion insofar as it construes the Securities Act to prohibit waiver of a judicial remedy in favor of arbitration by agreement made before any controversy arose. I think thereafter the parties could agree upon arbitration. However, I find it unnecessary in this case, where there has not been and could not be any arbitration, to decide that the Arbitration Act precludes any judicial remedy for the arbitrator's error of interpretation of a relevant statute.

FRANKFURTER, J. dissenting, joined by MINTON, J. If arbitration inherently precluded full protection of the rights § 12 (2) of the Securities Act affords to a purchaser of securities, or if there were no effective means of ensuring judicial review of the legal basis of the arbitration, then, of course, an agreement to settle the controversy by arbitration would be barred by § 14, the anti-waiver provision, of that Act.

There is nothing in the record before us, nor in the facts of which we can take judicial notice, to indicate that the arbitral system as practiced in the City of New York, and as enforceable under the supervisory authority of the District Court for the Southern District of New York, would not afford the plaintiff the rights to which he is entitled.

The impelling considerations that led to the enactment of the Federal Arbitration Act are the advantages of providing a speedier, more economical and more effective enforcement of rights by way of arbitration than can be had by the tortuous course of litigation, especially in the City of New York. These advantages should not be assumed to be denied in controversies like that before us arising under the Securities Act, in the absence of any showing that settlement by arbitration would jeopardize the rights of the plaintiff.

Arbitrators may not disregard the law. Specifically they are, as Chief Judge Swan pointed out, "bound to decide in accordance with the provisions of section 12(2)." On this we are all agreed. It is suggested, however, that there is no effective way of assuring obedience by the arbitrators to the governing law. But since their failure to observe this law "would ... constitute grounds for vacating the award pursuant to section 10 of the Federal Arbitration Act," 201 F. 2d 439, 445, appropriate means for judicial scrutiny must be implied, in the form of some record or opinion, however informal, whereby such compliance will appear, or want of it will upset the award.

We have not before us a case in which the record shows that the plaintiff in opening an account had no choice but to accept the arbitration stipulation, thereby making the stipulation an unconscionable and unenforceable provision in a business transaction. The Securities and Exchange Commission, as *amicus curiae,* does not contend that the stipulation which the Court of Appeals respected, under the appropriate safeguards defined by it, was a coercive practice by financial houses against customers incapable of self-protection. It is one thing to make out a case of overreaching as between parties bargaining not at arm's length. It is quite a different thing to find in the anti-waiver provision of the Securities Act a general limitation on the Federal Arbitration Act.

On the state of the record before us, I would affirm the decision of the Court of Appeals.

An award, pursuant to a submission agreement entered into after a dispute with a securities dealer arose and the purchaser was aware of her rights to pursue her remedies in court, is enforceable. Moran v. Paine, Webber, Jackson and Curitis, 442 Pa. 66, 220 A. 2d 624 (1966).

WATKINS v. HUDSON COAL CO.
151 F. 2d 311 (3rd Cir. 1945)

GOODRICH, C. J. This is a civil action based on the "Fair Labor Standards Act of 1938," to recover unpaid overtime wages claimed under § 7 (a)[1] and liquidated damages, reasonable attorney's fee and court costs claimed under § 16(b). Defendant is the owner and operator of certain coal mines in Pennsylvania in and around which plaintiffs are employed. That these employees are within the Act is not disputed.

Thirty-eight employees filed complaint seeking recovery as indicated. Defendant coal company in answer to the complaint made application for stay of suit until arbitration had been had. Plaintiff's reply to the application was that the contracts set out in defendant's answer and upon which defendant affirmatively relied were illegal and void as against public policy and contrary to the Act. The District Court ordered that trial be "stayed until arbitration has been had in

accordance with the terms of the agreements." This is the order appealed from. A brief has also been filed for the Administrator of the Wage and Hour Division, United States Department of Labor as *amicus curiae*. Certain matters of fact were stipulated by the parties, which will be considered later in conjunction with the requirements of the Act. Our conclusion is that the matter should proceed to arbitration, but only in accordance with the rulings of law as hereinafter set out.

The events separate naturally into three distinct time periods, each of which centers upon a different problem under the Act. The first period extends from the effective date of the Act, October 24, 1938, until November 1, 1939, when an alleged formula method for overtime was announced. The second period extends from November 1, 1939, until May 1, 1941, when the Union-Operators Agreement of that day went into effect. The third period covers time subsequent to May 1, 1941.

The evidence already marshalled is clearly indicative that the formulae were directed only to one goal, *i.e.*, to continue the old methods of payment for work while ostensibly meeting the requirements of the Act technically and technicalities are not enough.

Our final problem has to do with the question of arbitration. As stated above the District Court stayed the lawsuit until arbitration could be had. The provision in the contract of the parties for arbitration goes clear back to the year 1903 following the settlement in the famous anthracite coal strike of that period. There are three points with regard to the arbitration here.

The first point has to do with the question whether the formula and the waiver provisions which we have found to be insufficient under the Act so completely vitiate the contract for illegality that no reference to arbitration can be made. We think this question must be answered in the negative. The sufficiency of the wage formula and the provision for waiver are entirely separable elements of the contract between the parties. We do not refer to arbitration the question of legality of the formula. That is a question of law which the Court must take responsibility in answering. All we are saying upon this point is that the arbitration provision is not rendered ineffective because the contract contains one clause, setting out the formula, and another clause setting forth a provision for waiver which we deem insufficient under the statute.

The next point is whether there is anything to refer to arbitration. We think the answer to this question is yes. After the rights of claimants have been determined as a matter of law there is

---

1. § 207(a) of Title 29 U.S.C.A. provides:

"No employer shall, except as otherwise provided in this section, employ any of his employees who is engaged in commerce or in the production of goods for commerce—

"(1) for a workweek longer than forty-four hours during the first year from the effective date of this section,

"(2) for a workweek longer than forty-two hours during the second year from such date, or

"(3) for a workweek longer than forty hours after the expiration of the second year from such date, unless such employee receives compensation, for his employment in excess of the hours above specified at a rate not less than one and one-half times the regular rate at which he is employed."

still the not inconsiderable problem of determining how much each claimant is entitled to. That involves his identity as an employee of the defendant, the question of the days and hours on which he worked and the calculation of the amount of money to which he may be entitled under the Act. It is the kind of problem which is properly referable either to a special master or an arbitrator, and since the parties by contract have provided for arbitration we think the reference is appropriate in this instance.

DONAHUE v. SUSQUEHANNA COLLIERIES CO.
160 F. 2d 661 (3rd Cir. 1947)

It is necessary to comment upon the broad authority assumed by the District Court in specifying the issue for arbitration and directing the findings of the arbitrators. Under Sections 3 and 4 of the Arbitration Act, the Court is directed to give effect to an arbitration agreement on the application of a non-defaulting party by staying the judicial proceeding, in the one case, and by specific enforcement, in the other, when it finds that there exists an issue referable to arbitration according to the terms of the written agreement between the parties. The Court may determine questions relating to enforcement, but that is a far cry from such supervision and control of the arbitration proceeding as was here attempted. Force is added to this conclusion by Sections 10 and 11 of the Act which provide for recourse to the court in the proper case. We find nothing in the arbitration agreement here in controversy on this score, and it would certainly seem that the arbitrators may hear and decide any issue referable to them under the agreement which the parties care to submit. In any event, we see no reason for the exercise of such restrictions here and now. As this Court said in disposing of the prior appeal, 138 F. 2d 3, at page 7, 149 A.L.R. 271, "we should not choke the arbitration process which has been given congressional approval." In the Watkins case, *supra*, we merely decided the issues which were not for arbitration and noted that there remained other matters for arbitration.

EVANS v. HUDSON COAL CO.
165 F. 2d 970 (5th Cir. 1948)

If the arbitration process proceeds to an award which is not in accordance with the pro-

visions of the Fair Labor Standards Act or any other applicable statute, Sections 10 and 11 of the Arbitration Act provide means for its vacation, rehearing, modification or correction. The court below will be open for those ends.

In re Pennsylvania Electric Co. and System Council U-12, Int'l Bhd of Electrical Workers, 47 LAB. ARB. 526 (1966), involved a dispute over employee time spent in traveling to and from an "educational institute." The company contended that the contract and practice should control, while the Union argued that the Fair Labor Standards Act provided the criteria for decision. The arbitrator agreed that the Act governed. He then proceeded to decide the issue on the basis of language in Interpretive Bulletins issued by government agencies, among which was the following:

> Attendance at lectures, meetings, training programs and similar activities need not be counted as working time if the following four criteria are met: (a) attendance is outside of the employee's regular working hours; (b) attendance is in fact voluntary; (c) the course, lecture, or meeting is not directly related to the employee's job; and (d) the employee does not perform any productive work during such attendance.

Although he found that practice favored the company's interpretation of the contract, the arbitrator held for the grievants on the basis of his interpretation of the government bulletins.

What are the advantages and disadvantages of having such an issue decided by an arbitrator?

After a strike the company recalled men employees with less seniority than four women; the women grieved, and the union took the dispute to arbitration. The arbitrator ordered that the women be given the opportunity, in order of seniority, to perform eight designated jobs, and those whose performances proved satisfactory were to be reinstated with back pay. Upon the employer's refusal to follow the award, the union brought suit to enforce and moved for judgment on the pleadings; the company moved to dismiss on the grounds that Michigan law made the award unenforceable. Primarily at issue was the award's alleged inconsistency with a state statute providing that "No female shall be assigned any task disproportionate to her strength."

At least some of the jobs required lifting materials weighing fifty pounds or more. The arbitrator had not found that specific grievants could perform the jobs in dispute; rather, he expressed the belief that among the grievants there would be individuals capable of performing or that several working together could perform the necessary tasks without strain.

The court declared that it would not consider the correctness of the arbitrator's award but had to consider whether its enforcement would require the employer to violate the Michigan statute. As the record did not show that enforcement would not be violative, the district judge denied the union's motion for judgment on the pleadings; as the record did not show that enforcement of the award would require violation, he denied the employer's motion to dismiss. Local 985, United Auto Workers v. Chace Co., (E. D. Mich. 1966) F.Supp. (64 LRRM 2098). Presumably the issue would be tried by the court. Does any other procedure suggest itself?

SCHNEIDER v. SCHNEIDER
17 N.Y. 2d 123, 216 N.E. 2d 318 (1966)

DESMOND, C. J. The parties had made a separation agreement which contained provisions for payments to the wife for alimony and for the support of the child, totaling $142 per week (with an increase if the husband's income should go above $22,500 a year) and this agreement was approved by the Alabama divorce court.

The husband remarried after the Alabama divorce and the wife remarried in 1964. The 1960 separation agreement (not later amended in this respect) said that, if the wife should remarry, the defendant's obligation to support her would cease but his obligation to support the child would continue during the latter's minority and, if the parties could not agree on the amount for the child, the matter should be arbitrated in a manner described.

After plaintiff remarried, the parties could not agree on the amount to be paid by defendant for the support of the child (now seven years old). The wife, asserting that the arbitration provisions as to the child were illegal, moved the Supreme Court in the divorce action for an order fixing an amount to be paid to plaintiff for the child's support and maintenance, and for an order restraining defendant from initiating an arbitration.

Special Term granted plaintiff's motion holding that arbitration would be illegal under CPLR 1209 and under Chernick v. Hartford Acc. & Ind. Co., 8 N.Y. 2d 756, 201 N.Y.S. 2d 774, 168 N.E. 2d 110. The Appellate Division held at the contrary as had the First Department

in a thorough and convincing opinion in Sheets v. Sheets, 22 A.D. 2d 176, 254 N.Y.S. 2d 320. (See, also, Matter of Lasek, 13 A.D. 2d 242, 215 N.Y.S. 2d 983.)

Plaintiff argues that CPLR 1209 and section 240 of the Domestic Relations Law, Consol. Laws c. 14, require that the amount for the infant's support must be fixed by a court, not by an arbitrator.

Let us first take up CPLR which reads thus:

> § 1209. Arbitration of controversy involving infant or judicially declared incompetent. A controversy involving an infant or person judicially declared to be incompetent shall not be submitted to arbitration except pursuant to a court order made upon application of the representative of such infant or incompetent.

In Matter of Robinson, 296 N.Y. 778, 71 N.E. 2d 214 (1947) we, reversing the Appellate Division, held properly arbitrable a dispute under a separation agreement which fixed support payments for a wife and children at $105 per week for one year and provided that, if at the end of the year the amount of future payments could not be agreed on, there should be an arbitration. In this court's brief memorandum in *Robinson* no stress was put on the fact that payment for a child was involved, but the court of course knew that fact. The *Robinson* memorandum cited Matter of Luttinger, 294 N.Y. 855, 62 N.E. 2d 487 where there was a wife but no child. *Luttinger, Robinson, Sheets* and the present Appellate Division holding all recognize that a separation agreement like this one is a contract between husband and wife only and that the child or children are not parties (although beneficially interested therein) to any litigation or arbitration thereunto appertaining. All the authorities seem to say that a cause of action for payments like these for a child belongs not to the child but to the mother (Yates v. Yates, 183 Misc. 934, 937, 51 N.Y.S. 2d 135, 138 [Van Voorhis, J.]; Kendall v. Kendall, 200 App. Div. 702, 705, 193 N.Y.S. 658, 661; Percival v. Luce, 9 Cir., 114 F. 2d 774, 775).

Plaintiff says, however, that the settled law as to arbitrability of such support provisions was changed when the Legislature, in enacting new CPLR, changed section 1448 of the old Civil Practice Act which said that "A controversy cannot be arbitrated" where "one of the parties to the controversy is an infant" and substituted CPLR 1209 which says that there can be no arbitration of a controversy "involving an infant." No one has found any explanation of the change in verbiage but the Revision Committee's Report to the Legislature (N.Y. Legis. Doc., 1958

No. 13, p. 385) said that new CPLR 1209 was "derived from subdivision 1 of section 1448 of the civil practice act with only language changes which do not affect the substance of the provision." Our court has held that where the Legislature votes a general revision of a code with hundreds of changes we will not interpret a minor change in language to indicate a meaning unless legislative purpose so to change the meaning is clear (Henavie v. New York Cent. & H. R. R. R. Co., 154 N.Y. 278, 281, 48 N.E. 525, 526; Lynk v. Weaver, 128 N.Y. 171, 177, 28 N.E. 508, 509).

Plaintiff cites section 240 of the Domestic Relations Law. This is a long, involved statute which gives the courts broad powers as to custody and support of children, including continuing right to annul or modify previous orders. There is nothing in it to change the well-settled rule that parties may agree to arbitrate their differences as to the amount of support money. The substance of section 240 was in old sections of the Civil Practice Act such as 1169, 1170 and 1170–a and no court ever held or suggested that those laws prohibited such arbitrations. To affirm here we need not hold that an award made by an arbitrator is final and beyond court review. As the late Justice Valente wrote in Sheets v. Sheets, 22 A.D. 2d 176, 178, 254 N.Y.S. 2d 320, 324, *supra*).

> Thus, the best interest of the child is assured protection by this omnipresent judicial check against arbitration awards in custody matters attaining the unassailable finality of awards in other arbitrations. Nor could any such award in a custody matter be given any *res judicata* con-

sequences against the child, who was not a party to the arbitration. However, such an award would effectively bind the parents of the child to the extent that it settled their disputes, but only insofar as the award did not adversely affect the substantial interest of the child.

The only decision cited by Special Term was Chernick v. Hartford Acc. & Ind. Co., 8 N.Y. 2d 756, 201 N.Y.S. 2d 774, 168 N.E. 2d 110, *supra*. *Chernick* held (under Civ. Prac. Act, § 1448) that an insurance policy arbitration clause could not be enforced as to an infant's own claim for personal injury damages.

The order should be affirmed, without costs.

FULD, VAN VOORHIS, BURKE, SCILEPPI, BERGAN and KEATING, JJ., concur.

Order affirmed.

The second major point in the preceding opinion, that an arbitration award for a child's maintenance (as with the earlier like determination as to custody) is subject to court review, demonstrates that courts will, on occasion, modify "normal" arbitration doctrine to make it harmonize with other legal policies. Obviously such a flexible approach can be overdone to the detriment of reliability in arbitration law. Yet, to this editor, it seems decidedly preferable to following inflexibly the same course whenever the label "arbitration" becomes involved. Here is one example of court recognition that different kinds of arbitration may, on occasion, warrant different kinds of judicial treatment.

PART II

ARBITRATION IN LABOR RELATIONS

CHAPTER IX

THE GRIEVANCE-
ARBITRATION PROCESS

A.

Introduction

Every working day of the year millions of employees spend about one third of their time, roughly half their waking hours, at their jobs. Tens of thousands more plan and direct employee activities. Some fifteen million men and women and their thousands of foremen, supervisors, and other managers operate under the regime of collective-bargaining agreements that declare their rights and duties in relation to this vital function—work. Every day disagreements arise as to what may, must, or cannot be done by employees, unions, and management. The bulk are settled informally when and where they arise. Every year thousands of these disagreements, some seemingly petty, some obviously substantial, require more discussion and handling.

They are channeled through grievance procedures negotiated by union representatives and management and reduced to written form as sections of the collective bargaining agreement. Grievance procedures usually require several "steps," and most culminate in some form of arbitration—but not for all grievances. The de-

tails and variations are manifold. More about them shortly.

Usually only a very small percentage, and in many situations none, of the grievances reach arbitration. How the arbitration machinery works can have a vital impact upon how well the grievance procedures operate. Perhaps even more important, how well the grievance procedures function will determine whether arbitration can function satisfactorily. The two processes must be considered, understood, shaped and conducted as interacting parts of a process. Hence, this chapter starts with a consideration of grievances and the procedures employed to handle them.

With or without a union, employees become dissatisfied with existing situations or specific events and sometimes seek what they consider to be appropriate redress. On occasion, resentments flare into a spontaneous stoppage or less dramatic or observable "job action," such as a slowdown. Unionization makes two major differences in regard to grievances: it erects an institutional framework to channel grievances in a comparatively orderly process, and it provides a set of norms, embodied in a collective bargaining agreement, defining employee rights. Both factors facilitate and probably encourage the overt expression of grievances, and if the system works at all satisfactorily, they also reduce the resort to spontaneous self-help.

Grievances express dissatisfaction. The explosive force they can generate must be appreciated. In the best of circumstances, men and women at work are subject to innumerable pressures and dissatisfactions, some personal and some rooted in their jobs. Commonly the work place involves tensions and frictions among employees, between employee groups, and with supervisors. The latter often are caught between the desires, needs, and sensibilities of the people they supervise and the demands of superiors for more production, greater efficiency or closer observance of company routine. These powerful forces alone contain the potential for disagreement, sometimes dramatically expressed. Not infrequently the detonating occasion is only tangentially related to the grievances that built the pressure. So, for example, several years ago a Boston bus driver was ordered to take a run involving overtime work; his refusal led to his suspension from work. The suspension led to a spontaneous walkout that left Boston without bus service for several days. Pretty clearly, the employee response was out of all proportion to the provocation, even assuming that the driver's refusal was warranted. Such disproportion suggests an accumulation of unresolved, unrelieved dissatisfaction. In 1967 the suspension of a crane operator and a helper who refused to handle work they claimed to be improperly subcontracted led to a wildcat walkout at an automobile parts plant; the shutdown necessitated the cessation of operations at more than two dozen other plants employing some 80,000 workers.

Added to the grievances that originate in working conditions (which may or may not be affected by collective agreement provisions) are the controversies stemming from the administration of the collective-bargaining contract. The agreement's language may be incomplete or ambiguous, changing circumstances raise new questions of meaning or application, and additions and modifications occur in bargaining; all these factors, and others, can lead to disputes over the proper interpretation or application of the agreement. Inasmuch as the employer has the initiative in the employment situation, disputes commonly, but not invariably, arise from company activities or requirements that are challenged by employees or the union or both.

In addition, institutional problems arise. When a union enters a plant, shop, or office, pre-existing relationships change. Union officials, especially those in the work place, such as stewards, acquire power and often privileges vis-a-vis supervisors as well as a political-representative relation with other employees. Supervisors become subject to limitations imposed by the collective agreement and are bound to observe new procedures, such as those governing the handling of grievances. Adjustments in these new relationships occur frequently, if not continuously, especially as changes in the union and management hierarchy take place. Questions of the prerogatives of both union and management arise that the agreement may not answer beyond dispute.

All these gripes and problems make grievances. The grievance provisions of the collective agreement lay down the procedure to be followed in their handling. Often the first step is consultation between grievant and immediate supervisor, sometimes in the presence of a union shop steward, sometimes not. Early in the procedure, sometimes at the first step, the grievance is reduced to writing, with certain identifying data included, often on a prescribed form. The pattern (more detail follows) calls for grievance by employee or union and answer by management representatives at higher and higher levels if the answers prove unsatisfactory to the party with the power to appeal (sometimes the employee, sometimes the union). Often each move must be made within prescribed time limits. Most grievance procedures today culminate in arbitration if a party wants to take it there, but (as will be seen) arbitration clauses do not always have the same reach as grievance procedures.

It is of vital importance that the interrelationship of the two procedures—grievance and arbitration—be borne in mind by those who study and practice arbitration. A grievance procedure in which few disputes are settled inevitably overloads arbitral machinery. Arbitration procedures and awards that undermine the grievance machinery by permitting serious disregard of its prescribed procedures can invite more arbitration and fewer settlements by negotiation. Or arbitration that encourages overemphasis on technical procedural requirements will thwart settlement on the merits so that pressure builds for resort to self-help. Obviously the balance to be struck requires judgment, preeminently on the part of the representatives of unions and management, who have initial and primary responsibility. How they discharge their functions may be affected by what arbitrators do. Arbitration is a powerful tail that can, on occasion, send reverberations through the larger organism, the grievance procedure and shop and office relations.

B.

Grievance Procedures

PATTERNS OF GRIEVANCE PROCEDURES*

Extent of Use of Provisions

Procedures for handling disputes arising out of workers' grievances during the term of the contract were provided for in virtually all major agreements. Of the 1,717 contracts examined, covering a total of 7,438,400 workers, only 20, with 50,800 workers, made no reference to a method of settling grievances. All of these 20 were multiemployer agreements, and in these instances, some formal method of settling grievances may have been in effect at the plant or work level. Nine of the 20 agreements were in the construction industry; most of these 9 provided for a job or shop steward but did not define his duties or refer to processing disputes.

Scope of Grievance Procedure

In general usage, any complaint of an employee relating to his job, pay, working conditions, or treatment, may be considered a grievance. Use of formal grievance procedures, however, is not necessarily available upon all such complaints. In contract language, a grievance may be defined as any complaint or dispute that a regular employee, group of employees, or the union may submit to a management representative, to seek an adjustment through part or all of the contract grievance procedure. Management complaints were also included in the grievance definition in a few agreements; that is, they were admissible into the formal grievance setup.

---

*Abridged from U.S. Dep't of Labor, MAJOR COLLECTIVE BARGAINING AGREEMENTS: GRIEVANCE PROCEDURES, Bureau of Labor Statistics Bulletin No. 1425–1 (1964).

This study is based on an analysis of 1,717 collective bargaining agreements, each covering 1,000 workers or more, representing almost all agreements of this size in the United States, exclusive of railroad, airline, and government agreements. The 7.4 million workers covered by these agreements accounted for slightly less than half of all workers estimated to be covered by collective bargaining agreements in the United States, exclusive of railroad, airline, and government workers. Manufacturing establishments accounted for 1,045 agreements, covering 4.4 million workers; nonmanufacturing establishments, for 672 agreements applying to 3 million workers. Multiemployer groups negotiated 616 of the 1,717 agreements, covering 3.1 million workers. All statistical data presented in this report relate to agreements in effect in 1961–62.

Some agreements made allowances for all complaints but did not define a complaint or dispute as a formal grievance at the initial stage.

Generally, complaints involving proposed changes or additions to the contract were not subject to the grievance procedure. In some agreements, disputes relating to changes in the contract were explicitly defined as matters for collective bargaining negotiations rather than for grievance settlement.

For purposes of this study, grievance definitions in major collective bargaining agreements were classified either as (1) unrestrictive, in that they expressed or implied that any dispute or complaint could be processed as a grievance, or (2) restrictive, in that they limited the grievance process to disputes arising under or relating to the specific terms of the contract. Some agreements in each category separately excluded one or more specific issues from the grievance process, but such exclusions were not set forth as essential limitations of the general grievance definition.

The definition of a grievance within the two broad classifications varied from inferred inclusions to a specific listing of issues which can be presented as grievances. Usually, the degree of formality of the grievance definition matched that of the contract grievance procedure. The less formal definition was often found in multiemployer agreements covering small firms and in single-employer master agreements where a summary of the grievance procedure was sometimes given, with an indication that details were to be negotiated at the local level.

The grievance definition was unrestricted (any and all disputes) in approximately 47 per cent of the contracts, extending to 52 per cent of the total worker coverage. In nearly 6 per cent, the contracts listed one or more specific issues that were excluded from the grievance procedure.

Only disputes arising under or relating to the specific provisions of the agreement were defined as grievances in about 53 per cent of the agreements. Approximately 4 per cent of these also excluded disputes over one or more specific provisions in the agreement.

Restrictive grievance definitions, like the unrestrictive definitions, varied widely in degree of formality. Sometimes, the agreement simply stated that disputes arising under the agreement would be processed as a grievance. In other agreements the wording was even less precise, as in the use of the general expression, "disputes referring to the contract," in explaining the procedure mechanics.

More often the grievance definition was more specific, using such terms as interpretation, application, compliance, or other synonymous terms, either singularly or in combination, to describe what would constitute a grievance subject to the procedures established. The most frequent definition was a combination worded in the following manner:

> In the event that any difference arises between the company and the union, or any employee, concerning the interpretation, application or compliance with the provisions of this agreement, such difference shall be deemed to be a grievance and shall be settled only in accordance with the grievance procedure set forth herein.

Restrictions on the admissibility of grievances may have been designed, in part, to avoid overloading the grievance mechanism with trivial matters. Such restrictions may also be designed to limit the authority and responsibility of the unions, although differences between restrictive and unrestrictive provisions in this regard may dissolve into differences among unions in the ingenuity they exercise in handling grievances. The ultimate arbitrability of formal grievances is another factor that influences the scope of the grievance provision. In the long run, as the history of labor-management relations demonstrates, any substantial accumulation of grievances not covered by the contract and not admissible into the grievance procedure will very likely work itself out, either in open conflict or in a revision of the contract to accommodate the issue or the type of grievance.

In approximately 5 per cent of the agreements, covering 9 per cent of the workers, including substantial numbers in the primary metals and transportation equipment industries, the procedures listed one or more specific issues that were excluded from the grievance process. These excluded issues were generally found in the section of the contract to which the exclusion was applicable, rather than in the definition in the grievance procedure.

Including multiple exclusions, the issues excluded and the number of agreements from which they were to be excluded were as in Table IX-1.

Many agreements supplemented a broadly defined grievance procedure by specifically mentioning in other sections of the agreement the right to raise grievances. These specific mentions were made either to eliminate doubt as to whether

Table IX-1

Issues	Agreements
Wage adjustments	53
Seniority or promotion	5
Employee benefit plans	9
Plant administration matters	9
Strikes/lockouts	9
Other	8

the overall definition included such issues, or to emphasize the right to submit complaints to the grievance procedure.

Frequently, the specific inclusions pertained to new or changed operations, or to changed production standards.

Parties Initiating Grievances

The parties permitted to submit a complaint to the grievance procedure were identified in 395 agreements, more than 9 out of 10 of the 416 examined in detail, as follows. All of those that did not indicate who presented grievances were multiemployer agreements. (See Table IX-2.)

Table IX-2

Parties identified	Agreements	Workers
Number studied	416	2,600,100
Initial presentation by:		
Employee and/or union steward[1]	238	1,625,700
Union	71	516,000
Steward	37	94,300
Employee	20	67,400
Business agent	15	132,900
Grievance committee	11	55,800
Business agent and/or steward	3	8,300
Not clear, or varies by local agreement	3	4,800
Not indicated	18	95,100

1. Includes 2 agreements which specified the steward, but required the employee's presence; and 8 which specified the employee, but required the union representative's presence.

NOTE: Because of rounding, figures may not equal totals.

Almost two-thirds (238) of the 395 agreements which definitely identified the initiating parties involved both the employee and the union representative. Nearly all of the clauses in this group either allowed the steward, at the employee's option, to accompany the employee; permitted either the aggrieved employee or the union representative or both to present the grievance; required the employee and the union representative to present the grievance; or allowed the employee to accompany the steward on presentation.

Initial presentation of the grievance by union representatives (including grievance committee), without mention of employee participation, was specified in approximately a third (137) of the provisions. One-half of these provisions just indicated the union in general.

In the other half, a specific representative of the union (steward, business agent, or grievance committee) was identified.

Only 20 agreements made provision for initiation by the employee without mentioning the union.

Initial presentation of grievances in the vast majority of single- or multi-plant agreements of a single company involved the employee and the union representative. By contrast, the majority of multiemployer agreements named the union or a union representative as the grievance initiator. However, multiemployer agreements which referred to individual supplements usually did not specify the initiating party; appeal at the association level was often indicated.

Some agreements, in addition to including a clause specifying presentation by the employee and/or steward, included a clause which allowed higher officials of the union to initiate grievances of a general nature or grievances relating to interpretation of the agreement.

The company, as well as the union and the employee, could initiate a grievance under some agreements.

Other agreements also allowed the union to initiate and process employee grievances without action on the part of the employee.

A ban on initiation of grievances by either the company or the union was included in only a few agreements.

In most agreements, once the union took charge of processing the grievance, the right to appeal was vested with the union.

Some agreements, however, have explicitly preserved the right of the employee to request the union to appeal if he was not satisfied.

In some cases, the employee could independently exercise this right up to a certain level only.

Although in some agreements no provision was made for the employee to appeal a grievance; he was allowed to be present during part or all of the grievance process.

On the other hand, in some agreements employee participation was limited to presenting the facts, not to adjudicating the complaint.

Employee Grievance Representatives

Agreements frequently included detailed provisions relating to the grievance representatives designated or appointed to handle grievances. The number and type of grievance representatives were often specified. Details included number and/or proportion of representatives, method of selection, qualifications, duties, and restrictions and privileges.

The grievance representatives at the earlier stages of the grievance procedure were most often employees of the company, although, at times, a business agent or international representative took part in the discussions.

The first representative was frequently the shop steward or department steward. The shop steward often handled grievances at successive steps along with the chief steward or other union representatives. Sometimes the shop steward or department steward was included in the union grievance committee, which was frequently used to adjust matters not settled in the early stages.

In addition, some agreements designated the types of grievances various representatives were to handle.

The duties of grievance representatives, which include investigation of complaints, examination of records, and representation at hearings, were sometimes included in the agreement.

Generally, grievance representatives were permitted to leave their regular work to investigate and process grievances, subject to various restrictions. Common restrictions included those which concerned keeping records of time spent, as well as setting the maximum time which could be devoted to grievance handling. Other restrictions dealt with notification to and permission of the foreman, especially when it was necessary to leave the work area. A few agreements specifically prohibited representatives from soliciting grievances.

Processing Grievances

The process through which unresolved disputes move from the complaining worker to ultimate settlement, through arbitration if necessary, varies considerably among agreements, reflecting different plant and company organizational or decisionmaking structures. The size of the plant or company is a key factor; that is, the larger the unit the more formalized the grievance procedure tends to become. Since this study deals with agreements covering 1,000 workers or more, the procedures described here are generally appropriate to large units. In multiemployer agreements, however, the procedures are usually less formal, with a typically small employer at one end and, in many cases, a large association at the other end of the grievance line.

Contracts generally listed the successive procedural steps through which a dispute is to be processed if agreement is not reached. These procedures ranged from simple informal to highly formalized ones of six steps or more; most contracts specified three or four steps.

In a simple one-step procedure, the employee takes his complaint to the union, and the union deals directly with the employer or his representative; if no agreement is reached, the dispute goes to arbitration, or is dropped, or perhaps becomes a strike issue. A three-step procedure, such as that provided in the agreement between the Ohio Brass Co. and International Association of Machinists, comprise the following:

Step	For employee	For company
1	Employee and/or departmental steward	Foreman
2	Shop committee	Factory manager or representative from the personnel department
3	Officer(s) of the union or any authorized representative(s)	President of the company

(Arbitration)

Provisions for informal procedures were frequently found in multiemployer agreements covering small retail, wholesale trade, and construction companies. This type of procedure usually called for the union or a grievance committee to negotiate with the company representatives on grievances, with no mention of participation of the employee and steward or the foreman.

In multistep procedures, usually the employee, the steward, or both, and the foreman were to participate in the initial stage of the grievance process. The number of additional steps and the parties who were to participate at each step were related to some extent to delegation of authority within the company and the union. Appeal of a grievance from one step to the next nearly always involved submitting the issue to a higher level of authority in the company. Some agreements required that at each step, also, the union participant represent a higher level of authority; other agreements required the same union representative to participate at some or all intermediate steps of the procedure. In the longer multistep procedures, agreements often provided for a change in union participation, from local representation to some higher body of the union in the last or next-to-last step of the procedure.

In many contracts, the one- and two-step procedures did not indicate participation of union representatives other than those on the local level.

Multiemployer association agreements frequently listed a three-step procedure. Participation in the second stage was usually open to a representative of the association, with a joint union-association committee provided for in the third step of the procedure.

Procedures of four steps or more were usually established under large single-plant or multiplant single employer agreements. Generally, the procedural steps closely followed the authority structure of the company. Illustrative of this is the following excerpt from a multiplant agreement which specified movement of the dispute from plant floor level, to plant personnel supervisory level, to plant management, to company management:

...All grievances will be settled in the following manner:

First stage: Between the employee and one department shop steward and/or one grievance committeeman, and the foreman or the department supervisor...

Second stage: Between members of the grievance committee...and the personnel supervisor...

Third stage: Between members of the grievance committee...and the plant manager or his authorized representative or representatives...

Fourth stage: Between representatives of the international union along with the local grievance committee and officials of the company...

Arbitration

In the event the grievance shall not have been settled satisfactorily, the matter may be referred to arbitration...

Multiplant master agreements frequently outlined the general framework of a grievance procedure but left the steps of the procedure to be fixed at the local plant level or permitted adjustment of steps to fit local needs.

For specific types of grievances, many agreements also provided for deviation from the procedural steps prescribed in the general procedure. Usually, these were disputes relating to company-union policy, discipline-discharge, problems of an emergency nature, or other disputes which were outside the limited authority of stewards, foremen, or other lower echelon personnel. Special handling of these disputes included initiation at some intermediate step, and omitting or adding other steps in the general grievance procedure.

Some agreements specifically stated that procedural steps of the grievance process must be followed. In other agreements, full utilization of the grievance procedure was a prerequisite to submittal to arbitration:

> ... [the aggrieved employee or the union] ... shall be required to follow the procedure hereinafter set forth in presenting the grievance and having the grievance investigated and the merits thereof determined ...
>
> If, after the procedure for settling disputes as set forth in the preceding steps has been followed, there still remains any question of construction or interpretation or application of the provisions of this agreement, such question shall be referred to an arbitrator ...

Under many agreements, failure to utilize the steps of the grievance procedure could result in waiving of the strike/lockout ban:

> The union and the company, respectively, agree that there shall be no stoppage of work either by strike or lockout, and no intentional and concerted slowdown of work or production, because of any dispute arising during the life of this agreement, or under the terms of this agreement or any proposed modifications or amendments thereof: provided, however, that this article shall not be binding upon one party if the other shall have failed or refused to comply with the grievance procedure hereunder or any decision or award of the arbitrators made thereunder.

Time Limits

Time limits aimed at expeditious processing of grievances, while still allowing adequate time for investigation of relevant facts, were found in many agreements. Where no time limits were specified, some agreements stated that a mutual attempt for prompt settlement of an issue should be made.

Nearly 5 out of every 6 of the 416 agreements examined in detail set forth time limits on some or all steps of the grievance procedure.

Approximately 1 out of 6 of these 416 agreements, by setting a time limit for each action, fixed the limit from the time the act took place until the terminal point of the grievance procedure (prior to submittal to arbitration or other action). The remaining provisions varied considerably, ranging from time limits on certain phases of the procedural steps, such as a time limit on management's answer in each step, to limits on all steps except initiation and/or the final step.

Limits on the initiation of a dispute varied in both length of time and the effective starting date. Some of the more common limitations stated that the grievance must be filed within a specified time beginning with the occurrence or termination of the act on which the grievance was based, at the time the aggrieved party became aware of the act, or provided a combination of these qualifications.

The amount of time in which the aggrieved party was allowed to initiate a grievance ordinarily ranged from 2 weeks to 2 months, but intervals as low as 3 days and as high as 1 year were found.

Exceptions to the regular initiation time limits were often specified for discharge and discipline grievances. Here, more stringent time limits, usually ranging from 1 day to 1 week, were found.

Agreements often excluded Saturdays, Sundays and holidays from time limitations, or specified that only working days would be counted. Others merely stated the number of days, without indicating whether nonworkdays were to be excluded. Less frequently, the number of "calendar days" was specified.

Time spent on vacation, sick leave, or leaves of absence was also excluded from initiation time limits in some agreements; usually a limitation was placed on this excluded time.

Usually any grievance that was not filed within the initiation period was considered dropped. Noncompliance with other time limits of the procedure resulted in settlement of the grievance in favor of the last party to act, or the grievance was dropped, or, in some cases, the grievance was to be processed at the next step.

In some contracts, the same time limit on appeals or management answers applied throughout the entire grievance procedure. Where variations occurred, usually the time limits increased for the later steps of the procedure.

Overall time limits (from the time action took place to the decision) ranged from less than 1 week to over 1 year. Periods of 1 week through 2 months, however, were most common. Obviously, more complex multistep procedures involved longer overall time limits than informal one- or two-step procedures. Among exceptions to this were occasional agreements which granted from 6 months to a year for initiation, but which limited processing to a few days or weeks.

In most formal procedures, the agreements established overall time limits by specifying maximum time granted for each appeal and reply under each step. Under informal procedures, as a rule, the contracts merely set time limits for presentation of grievances and for final adjustment after presentation.

Form

Written presentation of the grievance at some stage of the grievance procedure was indicated in most agreements. Although a few required a written submission at the first step of the procedure, most agreements required it at the second step, while some specified another intermediate or the final step of the procedure.

Specifications for a written submittal ranged from a mere statement that the complaint be submitted in writing, or that a statement of the grievance be filed, to a request that all data concerning the issue be included.

Special Grievance Procedures

For purposes of this study, grievance procedures which deviated from the regular procedure by skipping or adding steps, providing special time limits or special representatives, as well as completely separate procedures, were classified as special grievance procedures.

Provisions for the use of a special grievance procedure were found in over half of the 416 agreements studied in detail. The major reasons for the employment of special procedures were to expedite the handling of issues that required immediate attention, to handle grievances of a general nature that did not require the participation of lower step representatives, or to provide technical assistance for issues which could not be handled by the regular grievance representatives.

Many agreements provided more than one special procedure for different issues. The issue most frequently found to require a special procedure (113 agreements) was discharge and/or discipline. Other issues were company-union grievances (77 agreements), plantwide-areawide grievances (32), safety and health (14), incentives (8), job evaluation (8), hiring (8), issues requiring technical assistance (7), benefit plans (6)* and a variety of other special problem areas.

The special procedure most commonly found called for skipping some of the regular steps. This accelerated procedure was predominately used for matters that required urgent attention, such as discharge, safety and health, and company-union grievances. Skipping of steps applied to the initiation of grievances at a higher level, to intermediate steps, and to final steps, in order to refer the disputes directly to arbitration.

Additional steps in the grievance procedure were sometimes provided where technical assistance or top level negotiations were involved. Shorter time limits were frequently set for the initiation of grievances involving certain issues ; a few agreements extended this time. A limited

---

*Does not include procedures set forth in separate documents (*i.e.*, benefit plan booklets).

number extended the time limits for other steps of the procedure. Only 1 of the 416 agreements examined specified shorter time limits for processing after initiation, and this involved discharge cases only. However, under the agreements which required initiation of certain issues at higher levels, or bypassing of other steps, the overall time limits for processing such grievances were, of course, tightened.

Completely separate procedures, where all the representatives and all the steps were different, were found only in agreements which included detailed benefit plans, and applied only to those plans.

Under some agreements, company and union grievances of a general nature, which affect a large number of employees or more than one plant, or involve policy or interpretation of the agreement, were to be initiated at a higher level. The grieving party occasionally was permitted to determine the initiating step.

Where both multiplant and local agreements were involved, an additional step was sometimes provided for unsettled disputes involving interpretation and application of the master agreement. This permitted negotiation by top level management and union officials.

Disputes involving technical issues were frequently to be submitted to a special committee or individual for review, or to an impartial agency for study before final determination. Usually a union representative was to participate in the study.

Settlement of grievance disputes through nonbinding mediation by an outside agency was provided in 45, or 2.6 per cent, of the 1,717 major agreements in this study, the 45 agreements covering 84,700 workers, or 1.1 per cent of all workers covered by the 1,717 agreements.

Grievance Decisions

Settlements arrived at jointly by labor and management at any step in the grievance procedure were generally final and binding on the parties concerned.

Some agreements stipulated whether decisions were applicable to similar cases, or only to the case in dispute.

Many agreements provided that a grievance would be considered settled unless it was appealed within specified time limits.

This description does not reveal the informal practices sometimes employed to settle grievances before the arbitration stage. Under the UAW-General Motors agreement, for example, if an appeal to the umpire is filed after exhaustion of the grievance procedure, international representatives of the union visit the plant and investigate the grievance to determine whether it should be appealed or withdrawn or an attempt made to settle. The company also conducts an inquiry and may advise local management to attempt to settle rather than carry the case to the umpire. Locally, management and union meet to discuss all appealed cases although the contract does not call for such a procedure. General Motors v. Mendicki (10th Cir. 1966) 367 F. 2d 66, citing Alexander, *Impartial Umpireships,* in ARBITRATION AND THE LAW (1959).

REPAS, *Grievance Procedure Without Arbitration,* 20 IND. AND LAB. REL. REV. 381 (1967) analyzes such an arrangement and suggests that it may be quite useful in small units where arbitration costs may be too high for the expected benefit. It is interesting to note that in the situation studied it was primarily the union that resisted use of arbitration.

Tactics in the Use of Grievance-Arbitration Procedures

While the employer generally holds the initiative on all aspects of the conduct of operations, the union or employees, or both, usually hold the initiative on the invocation of the grievance procedure and on moving all decisions unsatisfactory to them through its stages, including arbitration. These positions of initiative confer considerable power.

By and large, employees may not refuse to obey management directions even if the orders are contractually improper. Except for improper orders found to imperil employees, the employee must obey and his sole recourse is to grieve. The abuse of such power could bring employee retribution of many kinds, including slowdown.

Employees can use the grievance procedure to press grievances that lack merit or to try to obtain concessions not granted by the collective agreement. Processing grievances can impinge on the work time of both supervisors and employees. Employees can deluge a supervisor to extract treatment that is their due or that may go beyond their contractual rights. In either case, the pressure upon the supervisor is very real. The eventual loss, or more frequently withdrawal,

of the bogus grievances means little to the employees or union.

Supervisors often have considerable leeway in granting or withholding cooperation or favors from particular employee groups or representatives. The interests of employee groups frequently differ, and shop stewards, business agents, and other elected officials frequently need to obtain favors or score grievance victories to bolster or advance their union-political fortunes.

A fascinating detailed account of a tangled set of demands and relationships lurking behind a grievance is to be found in KUHN, BARGAINING IN GRIEVANCE SETTLEMENT (1961); Chapter IV, "Appearance and Realities," in particular will repay reading.

DETERMINANTS OF GRIEVANCE RATES*

The most striking finding from a review of grievance rates in many plants is that the satisfaction of individual workmen has relatively little to do with the grievance rate. The chief determinants appear to be organizational and institutional conditions. An exceptionally low grievance rate does not necessarily mean that employees are satisfied with conditions, and an exceptionally high rate does not mean that they are very dissatisfied. When very low or very high grievance rates are found, they are usually associated with one or more of the following conditions: (1) The state of relations between the union and the employer, (2) the experience of the union and the employer in dealing with each other, (3) the personalities of key union and company representatives, (4) methods of plant operation, especially methods of wage payment, (5) changes in operating methods or conditions, (6) union policies, (7) union politics, (8) grievance adjustment procedures, and (9) management policies.

---

*From S. SLICHTER, J. HEALY, and R. LIVERNASH THE IMPACT OF COLLECTIVE BARGAINING ON MANAGEMENT 701 (1960).

[The literature on labor arbitration tends to stress union-employee concerns and institutional problems to the neglect of management problems and organizational and political considerations. The Slichter, Healy, Livernash volume concentrates on management interests but does not exclude union and employee factors. Study of labor arbitration requires a livelier appreciation and more conversancy with management aspects of labor-management relations. Of course, really expert arbitrators have or develop these elements of expertise.]

C.

Arbitration Procedures

PATTERNS OF ARBITRATION*

All but a small proportion of major agreements providing for a grievance procedure, also provide for final and binding arbitration of grievance disputes. This widespread reliance upon voluntary arbitration to resolve grievance disputes, characteristic of the American system of collective bargaining, is unparalleled among other industrialized countries. Thousands of disputes are arbitrated in the United States each year under these procedures, and even in companies in which no disputes reach the stage of arbitration the availability of the procedure undoubtedly exercises a stabilizing influence.

In contrast, all but a small proportion of major agreements avoid any prior commitment to arbitrate disputes arising out of the negotiation of new contracts or out of contract reopening provisions. The instances in which such arbitration is invoked, or even mutually agreed to on an *ad hoc* basis, are still more uncommon in any year. The arbitration of jurisdictional disputes is confined almost entirely to the construction industry, the handling of complaints and appeals in the administration of employee-benefit plans often is excluded from the regular grievance-arbitration machinery, as is the arbitration of disagreements between union and management trustees of multiemployer plans.

Provision for arbitration of some or all grievance disputes was incorporated in 1,609 (94 per cent) of the 1,717 agreements [covering 16 million employees] analyzed, covering 96 per cent of the workers. The proportion of agreements providing for grievance arbitration reflects a steady increase in prevalence. In 1944, 1949, and 1952 Bureau studies, arbitration provisions were found in 73, 83, and 89 per cent of the agreements, respectively.

Twenty of the 108 agreements without provision for grievance arbitration were multiemployer agreements which also failed to provide for a formal grievance procedure.

---

*Abridged from Bureau of Labor Statistics, MAJOR COLLECTIVE BARGAINING AGREEMENTS, ARBITRATION PROCEDURES, B.L.S. Bull. No. 1425–6 (1966). [The study covered practically all collective bargaining agreements for large units (1,000 employees or more), excluding those in the railroad and airline industries and government. Hereafter this study is referred to as the "BLS Arbitration Study."]

All agreements providing for a grievance procedure and for arbitration of grievance disputes either explicitly or implicitly define the scope of the grievance and arbitration procedures, and the jurisdiction of the arbitrator. Only a small minority of agreements open the doors wide to admit any and all possible grievances into the grievance procedure and any and all grievance disputes to arbitration. Most agreements impose a restriction or exclusion in the grievance procedure, or in arbitration, or in both. The intent of the parties, their day-to-day decisions, their exercise of reasonableness and responsibility, cannot be assessed in agreement analysis, and it is well for the reader to bear these limitations in mind, particularly in the discussion that follows.

In 7 out of 10 agreements calling for grievance arbitration, all grievance disputes not satisfactorily resolved at the last step in the grievance procedure could be referred to arbitration.

The clause can be simply worded, as in the following example:

> In the event the dispute shall not have been satisfactorily settled in the preceding steps, the matter shall then be appealed to an impartial umpire.

The tendency to exclude certain grievance issues from arbitration was particularly pronounced in the chemical, machinery, electrical equipment, transportation equipment, and communication industries. In industries in which multiemployer bargaining predominates (*e.g.* apparel, mining, transportation, construction) a single standard for formal grievance settlement and arbitration prevailed.

The nature of the limitation on arbitration as against the grievance procedure is revealed when the scope of the grievance procedure is taken into account. Significantly, half of the agreements that opened the grievance procedure to any grievance restricted the scope of arbitration. On the other hand, only about 1 out of 8 agreements that limited grievance processing to complaints involving the interpretation, application, or violation of the agreement cut back the jurisdiction of the arbitrator. A total of 340 agreements out of the 1,717 studied, provided what may be considered the ultimate in the handling of workers' complaints—every grievance was guaranteed a hearing and every grievance dispute a settlement.

Examples of agreement clauses defining [*i.e.* limiting] the jurisdiction of the arbitrator follow:

> In the event that any grievance or dispute arising out of the interpretation or application of any clause of this contract remains unsettled after the steps provided by the grievance procedure have been taken, either party, within 2 weeks, may refer the matter to a tripartite arbitration panel . . .

> The term "grievance" as hereinafter used in this agreement shall mean any alleged violation of the terms or provisions of this agreement, or difference of opinion as to its interpretation and/or application . . .

> A grievance not settled in step 4 may be certified to arbitration by the party initiating the grievance so advising the other party in writing within 5 working days after the date of the last meeting held as required under step 4.

> At the request of either party, as provided above, a dispute, grievance, or difference involving a violation of this agreement that cannot be satisfactorily settled between the parties, or grievances based on discharges shall be submitted to arbitration.

> Whenever any complaint or misunderstanding arises as to wages, hours, working conditions, layoffs or discharges of individuals affected by this agreement, such complaints or misunderstandings shall be discussed with the foreman . . .

> If the grievance is not settled . . . the individual, the company or the union shall have the right to have the grievance submitted to arbitration . . .

In 433 agreements, any dispute between the parties could be brought to arbitration, except for specified excluded issues, as in the following examples:

> Any dispute or controversy arising during the life of this agreement, which cannot be settled to the mutual satisfaction of both parties, shall be submitted for arbitration . . . within 48 hours after the request of either party that such dispute or controversy be arbitrated.

> It is agreed that, should any dispute arise in any plant of a member of the association, such dispute shall be adjusted . . . If the [grievance] board fails to come to an agreement, it shall select an arbiter not connected with this industry . . . This arbiter shall review the case, and his decision shall be final and binding.

> Should grievances arise between the company and the union as to the application of this agreement, or of the policies of the company, as set forth herein, or should any dispute or trouble arise, an earnest effort shall be made to settle such differences during which time there shall be no suspension of work. . . . In the event the dispute shall not have been satisfactorily settled in the preceding steps, the matter shall then be appealed to an impartial umpire.

Issues Excluded From Arbitration

A total of 348 agreements, covering 2.2 million workers, identified one or more dispute issues as nonarbitrable. The reasons for such exclusions usually were not indicated by the agreements and, although they may have been fully understood by the parties, they are not always clear to outsiders reading the agreements. Some exclusions undoubtedly were intended to preserve certain management prerogatives, others to preserve union prerogatives. Some were necessary because the parties had agreed upon other methods of handling certain problems, and possibly some were motivated by a mutual desire not to overburden the arbitration machinery with trivialities. Exclusions in some cases appeared to represent a signal to workers in the bargaining unit that it would be pointless to raise a grievance over the designated issue. It seems reasonable to assume, however, that underlying many exclusions was a strongly held belief of one or both parties that the issue in question was too important or too subtle to be entrusted to a decision of a third party.

A number of the 348 contracts with specific exclusions listed more than one issue as nonarbitrable, resulting in a total of 456 exclusions. Almost half related to wage adjustments (other than general wage changes), and slightly over a fourth to plant administration disputes. The other exclusions principally related to job security, administration of employee benefit plans, and union security provisions.*

A few agreements which excluded specific issues also listed all issues subject to arbitration (the excluded issues were tabulated in the appropriate categories discussed previously). Included in this group were the General Motors national agreements with the UAW and IUE.

Arbitral Forum

Arbitration was to be conducted by a single impartial arbitrator in over one-half (858) of the 1,609 contracts; and by a tripartite board in over two-fifths (670). The parties were allowed the option of using either a single arbitrator or a board in 42 contracts. In 26 contracts, provision was made for use of a single arbitrator for certain issues and a board for others. The remaining 13 contracts either did not indicate the type of agency or provided for local plant negotiation.

The arbitration agency, whether a single arbitrator or tripartite board, was to be selected on

---

*Defined in the study as promotion or demotion, training, retraining, layoff, recall or transfer.

an *ad hoc* (temporary) basis in over four-fifths (1,348) of the contracts. Under these arrangements, selection must be made each time a dispute is referred to arbitration. Worker coverage under *ad hoc* arrangements was greatest in contracts negotiated by single plant employers, accounting for 85 per cent of the employees in this group. There was only a slight difference in worker coverage under multiplant-single employer contracts (67 per cent of the employees) and in multiemployer contracts (71 per cent). [In all, 4.7 of the 7.1 million employees were under agreements with arbitration clauses, calling for *ad hoc* arbitration.]

Permanent, rather than *ad hoc*, arbitration machinery was provided in 222 contracts. Under these arrangements, the arbitrators or boards hear all disputes arising during their term of office. In terms of worker coverage, permanent arbitration was most predominant in multiplant contracts of single employers (31 per cent of the workers), and in multiemployer contracts (22 per cent). Such arrangements in single plant contracts accounted for only 13 per cent of the workers. [In all 2.5 million employees were under agreements providing permanent arbitration, or about one third of the employees under agreements sampled.*]

The largest concentration of workers under permanent arbitration was in association contracts in the apparel industry and in multiplant contracts in the transportation equipment industry. In apparel, nearly two-thirds of the employees were covered by permanent arrangements established in three-quarters of the contracts; all but one specified a single arbitrator. In transportation equipment, over one-half of the workers were under permanent arrangements, all of which also specified a single arbitrator; these provisions were established in a relatively small number of contracts but they covered large numbers of workers. Other industries in which permanent arbitration was prevalent included primary metals, machinery, hotels and restaurants, and services.

---

*[This portion of the BLS study was done by sampling one fourth the collective agreements, proceeding by size groups. The elimination of three fourths of the agreements with the greatest coverage may have the effect of understating the number of employees under contract with permanent arbitrators or umpires because such arrangements are quite common in the largest companies. Moreover, the study classified as an *ad hoc* arrangement those in which the parties were to make their selection from a panel named by the parties in the agreement, which I would classify either as a permanent arbitrator provision or mixed *ad hoc*-permanent, depending upon how frequently the panel members were used. If all are often selected, as happens in some arrangements, the procedure comes closer to a permanent-arbitrator arrangement.]

Selection of the Arbitrator

Various methods were outlined for selection of the arbitrator, either directly by the two parties, or with the assistance of governmental or private agencies or individuals, or, less frequently, by outside agencies only. Although many agreements took the necessary precautions to prevent a deadlock over the selection of the arbitrator, at least half did not.

Most agreements indicated that some help would be sought from outside agencies (chiefly the Federal Mediation and Conciliation Service or the American Arbitration Association) in the selection of arbitrators, and in a substantial proportion of agreements the selection was to be made or could be made by the outside agency. Of 416 agreements examined in detail, 30 per cent made no reference to outside assistance; these were typically large agreements in such industries as apparel, transportation equipment, primary metals, and transportation where considerable experience with arbitration had been accumulated. In about a fourth of the agreements, a list of suitable arbitrators was to be requested from outside agencies, in most cases only if the parties could not reach a decision on their own. A few of these agreements provided for the submission of more than one list, or for final selection by the outside agency if the parties could not agree. Provision for breaking a deadlock over the selection of the arbitrator was incorporated into almost 30 per cent of the agreements, while slightly more than 10 per cent relied in the first instance on the outside agency to select. A few contracts merely provided for selection in accordance with American Arbitration Association (AAA) rules. In general, these rules require submission of an identical list to each of the parties, with the final appointment made by the AAA from the names approved by each party, in order of preference.

Provisions designating the Federal Mediation and Conciliation Service or the American Arbitration Association as the participating outside agencies were most predominant, each accounting for over two-fifths of the contracts providing for outside participation. The FMCS was specified more frequently where arrangements called for submission of a panel for selection if the parties were unable to agree on a choice. The AAA was specified more frequently where the outside agency made the selection in event of disagreement. A few agreements permitted the parties to select either the FMCS or AAA; a few others permitted a choice of FMCS or a State mediation agency.

Outside participants other than FMCS or AAA included State or city mediation agencies, a Federal or State judge, and the Secretary of Labor.

Selecting a Temporary (Ad Hoc) Arbitrator

Arrangements which gave the parties complete responsibility for the selection of an *ad hoc* single arbitrator, with no provision for outside participation in event of a deadlock, usually did not include a detailed procedure for selection.

Provisions for outside participation either called for submission of a panel from which the parties were to make the selection, or for direct appointment by the designated agency.

A number of agreements provided for submission of more than one list in the event the parties could not agree on a selection from the first panel:

> The parties shall jointly request the American Arbitration Association and the Federal Mediation and Conciliation Service to furnish lists of available arbitrators.
>
> After receipt of such lists and an opportunity to consider the names thereon the parties, . . . [shall] determine which of such mutually acceptable arbitrators shall be deemed to be named.
>
> If the foregoing does not result in a designation of a mutually acceptable arbitrator the procedure shall be repeated with respect to additional lists until such a designation results.

The most predominant type of arrangement for outside participation called for assistance only in the event the parties were unable to agree on their own. Either the AAA or the FMCS was the designated agency in nearly all of these agreements. Provisions for submission of a panel more frequently designated the FMCS; those requesting the agency to appoint the arbitrator specified the AAA more often.

> Should the . . . [labor management grievance committee] fail to reach agreement on the matter in dispute . . . they shall select a disinterested third party to act as arbitrator.
>
> In the event the committee fails to agree on an [arbitrator] . . . the Director of the Federal Mediation and Conciliation Service shall be called upon to provide a panel of seven experienced arbitrators . . . and each party shall alternately strike a name from the panel until one remains. The person whose name remains shall serve as the arbitrator.

> In the event the grievance has not been settled in the third step, the matter may then be appealed to an impartial umpire to be appointed by mutual agreement of the parties hereto.
>
> In the event no agreement on the choice of an umpire can be reached, then after a 10-day period, the American Arbitration Association shall be requested to appoint the umpire.

A few of the agreements specified selection under the AAA procedure, if the parties could not agree on an arbitrator.

State mediation agencies or public officials were designated in a few other contracts. One of these varied the procedure by requesting the parties to attempt to select an agency or person to appoint the arbitrator if they could not agree on a choice. If they still could not agree, a judge was designated, either to appoint an arbitrator or to act as one.

Provisions for outside participation at the time arbitration is requested, without any initial attempt by the parties to select an arbitrator, usually followed the same pattern as those discussed in the preceding paragraphs. In nearly all cases, the outside agency either was to submit a panel for selection by the parties or appoint an arbitrator directly.

Selecting an Ad Hoc Board of Arbitration

The most common type of board was composed of an equal number of management and union representatives, with an impartial member acting as chairman. Relatively few contracts specified a board composed entirely of nonpartisan members, that is, persons who were not company or union officials. Frequently the board consisted of three members. However, a number of contracts specified five or seven members, and a few specified more.

Partisan members selected by management generally were required to be officials or employees of the company. Those to be selected by the union were usually employee union members or nonemployee union officials. A number of agreements did not require union representatives to be company employees or union officials; rather, the choice was left to the union.

A common practice where arbitration boards included partisan members was for the union and management representatives to attempt to settle the disputed issue before calling in an impartial chairman to form a tripartite board. Thus, the partisan representatives, in effect, served as grievance negotiators in another step of the grievance procedure, after arbitration had been requested.

Included in the 623 contracts providing for an *ad hoc* board were 73 which required selection of a temporary chairman for each case, although the partisan members served permanently. The permanent partisan members also served as a joint grievance adjustment board; an *ad hoc* chairman was appointed only if the partisan members were unable to settle the dispute.

Most of the contracts provided for selection

of the impartial chairman by the union and management members. In the event of failure to agree on a choice, usually either party could request an outside agency to appoint an impartial chairman, or to submit a panel of names for selection by the parties.

Another variation, designed to forestall the union or management from barring arbitration, permitted either party to request an outside agency to designate the opposing party's board member if the appointment was not made within a specified time.

Selecting a Permanent Arbitrator

Selection of the arbitrator was the responsibility of management and the union. Most frequently, the arbitrator was named in the contract.

Outside participation in the selection was sometimes provided for in event of a deadlock.

While most permanent arbitrators were appointed for the duration of the contract, a few specified shorter periods, and in some instances the arbitrator was subject to removal by either party, upon proper notification.

To insure continuity in the event an arbitrator was removed, resigned, or was unable or unwilling to serve for other reasons, a number of contracts either designated one or more alternates or provided for appointment of another arbitrator by the parties.

Outside assistance if the parties could not agree on a successor also was provided in a few contracts.

An interesting variation provided for selection of a new permanent arbitrator by the parties in event of a vacancy, and, in addition, named five substitute arbitrators, one of these to be chosen each time arbitration was requested, until a new permanent arbitrator was appointed.

Another method used to insure continuity provided for a permanent panel of three or more arbitrators, named in the contract, one of which was to be selected whenever arbitration was requested.

Selecting a Permanent Arbitration Board

The union and management members, selected by the parties, were often members of a permanent bipartisan adjustment board; the chairman acted only if the adjustment board could not resolve the dispute.

Provision was made for an alternate chairman in a number of the contracts, usually following the same procedure specified for selection or designation of the permanent chairman. Outside participation was provided for in some contracts

if the parties were unable to agree on the arbitrator or his alternate.

One agreement, which provided for participation by the American Arbitration Association if the parties could not agree on a selection, specified a 6-month appointment and shortened this to 4 months if the AAA made the appointment.

The short-term appointment illustrated above was an exception to the general practice of appointing the impartial arbitrator for the duration of the contract. Appointment of the union and management members for the duration generally was expressed or implied, although some contracts reserved to either party the right to change its members from time to time.

Only 1 of the 47 contracts provided for a permanent chairman with *ad hoc* union-management members, to be selected each time arbitration was requested.

Special Arbitration Procedures

Twenty-six agreements provided for separate arbitration machinery for disputes involving technical problems or health, welfare, and pension issues. These either specified a single arbitrator for regular grievances and a board for other issues, or reversed the procedure. A number of others provided special procedures for arbitrating such disputes. Provisions for these specialized cases generally specified that an arbitrator with special training or experience was to be used, or, in the case of an arbitration board, a specially qualified chairman.

Among the technical issues cited for special arbitration were incentive and piece-rate systems, job rates, job evaluation, production standards, and work assignments. Some contracts did not list the issues, merely specifying grievances involving technical problems or those requiring specialized knowledge.

Frequently, where contracts included health, welfare, and pension plans, two types of special machinery were provided—one for technical problems and another for disputes involving administration of the benefit plans. A few contracts permitted the parties either to designate a special arbitrator for technical issues or to employ an impartial expert to assist an arbitrator. Where the question of physical disability was to be resolved, provision often was made for a physician, or a board composed of physicians, to arbitrate the dispute.

Some contracts did not require a special arbitrator, but provided for the employment of technical or medical experts to assist the arbitrator when needed, as in the following:

When an arbitrator is requested to consider a case

within one of the above exclusions [production standards—safety and health], it is understood that he may need to call on expert or technical witnesses to assist him. The company and the union agree to share equally the expenses of such experts as the arbitrator considers necessary to a fair and equitable decision.

Said commission [tripartite arbitration board] shall further have the power, duty and authority to: Engage or secure auxiliary experts for advice or research, subject to prior concurrence in and approval of any expenditure in excess of $500 for such purposes by both the union and the company representatives . . .

Qualification of Arbitrators

Except in contracts which provided for special arbitrators for certain issues, eligibility requirements for arbitrators were not often specified. Qualifications imposed for arbitrators of regular grievances usually were designed to prevent selection of an individual whose neutrality was in doubt. The most common requirement prohibited selection of an arbitrator who was affiliated in any way with the company, association, or union ; a few specifically excluded stockholders. A few contracts required residence within the State, while others prohibited appointment of anyone residing or in business within a certain radius of the company's plant.

Although generally no restrictions were placed on the union or management in the selection of their representatives, a few contracts, as noted earlier, called for appointment of impartial representatives by each party. One contract specifically banned appointment of legal advisers of either party.

Time Limits on Selection of Arbitrators

Most contracts set time limits on the selection of the arbitrators. If the parties were not able to agree on a choice within the specified time, the contracts usually provided for outside participation. Under AAA rules, 7 days are allowed for appointment of the arbitrator if no period of time is specified by the parties. The FMCS allows 15 days after mailing a panel to the parties. Under these rules, the agency is authorized to make the appointment if either party fails to do so within the allotted time.

Time limits were necessarily longer where an *ad hoc* board was involved, frequently ranging from 20 to 30 days for the selection of all members. Usually, separate time limits were set for selection of the union and management representatives and for the impartial chairman.

Cost of Arbitration

Provisions for apportioning arbitration costs were included in 360 of the 416 contracts examined in detail. In all but 10 of these contracts, the employer and the union agreed to share equally the cost (fees and expenses) of the arbitrator or of the impartial chairman of a tripartite board. Where arbitration boards were involved, the contracts generally stipulated that each party would bear the expenses of its appointed member ; in others, this was implied.

Only 7 of the 360 contracts required the losing party to pay the cost of the arbitrator or impartial chairman. The contracts either defined the arbitrator's costs to include his fees and expenses or merely referred to arbitration cost or expenses. One contract permitted the arbitrator to apportion the cost. Another required each party to share the cost in event of a compromise.

One contract left the matter of allocation of expenses to the determination of the arbitrator.

A limited number of contracts specifically stated that time spent by union representatives, and occasionally by witnesses, in arbitration proceedings during working hours would be paid for by the employer. A few of these placed a limit on the number of employees to be paid. Conversely, another contract stipulated that employees representing the union in arbitration proceedings would not be paid for time lost.

Most of the contracts did not stipulate the arbitrator's fee, nor indicate how the fee would be determined. However, where contracts provided for arbitration with the assistance of, or under the rules of, the AAA of the FMCS, it may be assumed that the rules of these organizations regarding arbitration fees were followed. The FMCS permitted its nominees or appointees to charge a maximum of $150 per day.* The AAA rules do not prescribe a minimum or maximum fee, but the procedures are such that the parties are notified of the fee set by the arbitrator when the list of names is furnished.

PROCEDURE AND PRACTICE

Based upon a survey of a large sample of cases—almost all of which went to award in 1954—the American Arbitration Association reports that the overwhelming majority were instituted by a demand for arbitration under agreements providing for arbitration of future disputes arising under the agreement (about 70 per cent)

---

*This limit is expected to be raised before long.

and the remainder were submissions of existing disputes. Most cases were heard by single arbitrators (81.6 per cent), a smattering by boards composed of three neutrals, and the bulk of the remainder (16.5 per cent) by three-man tripartite boards. Among the tripartite boards most awards were decided by majority vote (84.5 per cent); a large portion of the unanimous awards were due to one party-appointed arbitrator "going along," as a matter of tradition or for the good effect it would have upon the parties' relationship.

Only in a few cases did the parties directly select the arbitrator. In most cases (88 per cent) the arbitrator was selected by the Association's "standard procedure": identical lists submitted to the parties who then cross out those unacceptable and rank the remaining names in order of preference. Guided by the lists, the AAA selects the individual who comes closest to satisfying both disputants. [The British call this method of selection "knocking the brains out of the panel."] *Procedural and Substantive Aspects of Labor-Management Arbitration: An AAA Research Report,* 12 ARB. J. 67 (1957).

The Federal Mediation and Conciliation Service assists in the administration of arbitration arrangements that call for the selection of arbitrators for individual cases as they arise [See Appendix F for a statement on the Service's arbitration procedures.] Tables IX-3 and IX-4 give some indication of some of the characteristics and issues of cases involving arbitrators drawn from the Service.

Table IX-4—Issues Most Frequently Adjudicated by Arbitrators From Service-Provided Panels, Fiscal Years 1963 and 1964

	1964	1963	Numerical increase or decrease in 1964
Disciplinary	854	846	8
Job classification and work assignment	592	548	44
Overtime and hours of work	357	355	2
Management rights	320	307	13
Seniority in demotion	238	202	36
Seniority in promotion	284	255	29
Vacations and holidays	132	136	−4
Pay for time not worked	168	147	21
Arbitration, jurisdiction and grievance	153	152	1
Incentive rates—standards	114	141	−27
Union security	58	49	9
Auxiliary pay	46	32	14
Job evaluation and workloads	72	61	11
Working conditions	46	42	4
Health and welfare	57	46	11
Guaranteed employment	35	10	25
Miscellaneous or unclassified issues	1,269	1,145	124
Totals	4,795	4,474	321

Table IX-3—Averages† for Fiscal Year 1963— Arbitration Cases*

Average number of grievances per case	1.09
Average hearing time in days	1.07
Average travel time in days	.31
Average study time in days	1.7
Average fee per case	$384.47
Average expenses per case	$51.18
Average total charges per case	$433.77
Average days between date of filing of grievance and request for panel	82.9
Average days between date request for panel and date list sent	3.8
Average days between date list sent and date of appointment	27.1
Average days between appointment and hearing	49.9
Average days between hearing and award	43.9
Average total days between date request for panel and award	124.8

†Based on 394 cases out of 1,332 included in the study.

*U.S. Federal Mediation and Conciliation Service, 17th ANNUAL REPORT 58 (1964). The fee and expense items are for arbitrators. Other items, such as attorney fees, transcripts, charges for space in which to conduct the hearing, are not covered in this table.
For further information on labor arbitration costs see R. FLEMING, THE LABOR ARBITRATION PROCESS, Ch. II 1966).

ARBITRATION COSTS AND TACTICS

As noted, in addition to the arbitrator's fee, there are costs for attorneys, a hearing room, transcripts, and possibly transportation costs for all those involved. The greater the cost the less attractive and useful arbitration is. Indeed, some parties shrink from arbitration because of cost considerations, and this fear is exploited by some employers who refuse to change grievance dispositions. Whether prevailing temporarily is worth the resulting resentment and possibly unrest is at least open to question.

As Fleming points out, arbitration can be done deluxe or coach. One expensive dispensable item is the transcript. But in a long and complicated case the saving may be penny wise. The hearing can be held at the plant or office (which is helpful because both witnesses and records are readily available). Briefs may be dispensed with. In short, arbitration can be more or less costly as the parties decide and according to the needs of the particular case.

D.

The Labor Arbitrator

PERMANENT ARBITRAL ARRANGEMENTS: A STUDY IN VARIETY*

CHARLES KILLINGSWORTH AND SAUL WALLEN

In 1940 General Motors and the UAW set up a permanent arbitration system. This was a great landmark in the modern history of labor arbitration because General Motors was the first major corporation in heavy manufacturing to agree to such a system. But it would be erroneous to regard 1940 as "Year One" in labor arbitration. The fact is that in 1940 there were two distinctly different types of permanent arbitration systems in the United States, both with quite long histories and strong advocates. These two types merit our close attention because the failure to distinguish between them has been a source of a great deal of confusion in discussions of arbitration over the last twenty or twenty-five years.

The Impartial Chairman System

The first type was the impartial chairman system. The first successful system was established in 1911 in the Hart, Schaffner & Marx factory in Chicago. The architects of this system were Sidney Hillman of the Amalgamated Clothing Workers and Joseph Schaffner, a civic-minded businessman. The man that they chose as their impartial chairman was John Williams, a one-time coal miner who had had some experience as an arbitrator in the bituminous coal industry in Illinois.

The basic characteristics of this system were the following: (1) the collective bargaining agreement was quite brief and was stated in general terms; (2) the scope of arbitration was very broad, in that *any* problem arising between labor and management could be submitted to the impartial chairman; and (3) the settlements were achieved primarily by a process of mediation.

A contemporary of John Williams has written

*Abridged from C. Killingsworth and S. Wallen, *Constraint and Variety in Arbitration Systems*, in LABOR ARBITRATION—PERSPECTIVE AND PROBLEMS, 56 (1964). Reprinted with the permission of the Bureau of National Affairs, Inc.

an excellent summary of the procedures and approach developed by this pioneer:

> His method was primarily that of a court of equity rather than a court of law; but, though acting as a judge, he functioned as the administrator of the law as much as its interpreter. In other words, he saw the duties of industrial arbitrators as much the same as those of a Workmen's Compensation Board or a Public Utilities Commission. Their functions are quasi-judicial, partaking both of a court and an administrative officer. He would not decide cases merely on the merits of the briefs or arguments of the parties, for it would not help the industry or either party to have the other party lose a case if it was right but happened to present its case poorly or had its arguments wrong. He would make investigations on his own initiative, get all the facts in the situation, and then decide on the basis of those facts regardless of what might have been presented or omitted in the argument of the case. In making these investigations he often consulted each party separately and in confidence. He found it necessary to do this to get the real truth in industrial cases, which as in ordinary law cases are often hidden by the trial. But it was also necessary at the same time to retain the confidence of both parties in his honesty and impartiality. He was able to accomplish both these things; and thus he laid the basis for a successful industrial jurisprudence.

Other accounts make it clear that the purpose of the "consultation" mentioned in the foregoing description was usually mediation of the issues involved in particular cases. Williams also participated actively in the contract negotiations of the parties. In a few years, as the union extended its organization, most of the men's clothing industry in Chicago was brought under this impartial chairmanship. Similar systems were subsequently established in other major men's clothing centers and in other branches of the garment industry.

We conclude this description of the impartial chairman system by suggesting that it be defined as follows: An impartial chairmanship is a system for resolving all problems that arise during the life of a contract, utilizing a technique of continuous negotiation, and centering on a mediator who is vested with the reserved power to render a final and binding decision.

The Umpire System

The other distinct type of permanent arbitration system that had become well-established by 1940 was the umpire system, which originated in the anthracite coal industry. This system was not established by an agreement between management and labor; rather, it originated in an award promulgated by the Anthracite Strike Commission in 1903. Even the Commission had not been voluntarily accepted by the coal companies. It had been forced on them by President Theodore Roosevelt with the assistance of the elder J. P. Morgan.

We stress the following basic characteristics of the umpire system: (1) the collective bargaining agreement is detailed and, to the extent possible, specific; (2) the scope of arbitration is restricted to the interpretation and application of existing agreements between the parties, and disputes not covered by such agreements are not to be arbitrated; and (3) the umpire disposes of those problems that fall within his jurisdiction by a process of adjudication, which means that he promulgates a decision based on the formal record of a hearing.

These characteristics suggest the following definition of the umpireship. it is a system of adjudication of those rights and duties which are recognized by the language of an existing agreement between the disputing parties.

Development of Arbitration Systems After 1940

THE GENERAL MOTORS–UAW SYSTEM

Let us now return to those "pioneers" of 1940, General Motors and the UAW. While permanent grievance arbitration systems were unknown in heavy manufacturing industries at that time, GM and the UAW were clearly not embarking on uncharted seas. And there is evidence which suggests that both parties had studied the available charts. Company executives had had extensive discussions of the anthracite umpire system with Charles Neill, who had filled that umpireship from 1905 to 1928. General Motors also sent a representative to spend two months with George Taylor in order to observe the operation of the impartial chairman system in the hosiery industry. The Company also studied the impartial chairmanship in the men's clothing industry in Chicago. Harry Millis of the University of Chicago was the chairman at that time. The UAW had two excellent sources of first-hand information concerning the impartial chairman and the umpire systems in Sidney Hillman and Philip Murray, who both had roles in the 1940 GM-UAW negotiations. As we have noted, Hillman was one of the architects of the impartial chairmanship in men's clothing. Murray had served for many years as an officer of the United Mine Workers and was familiar with the anthracite umpireship.

In the 1940 negotiations, General Motors took the initiative in submitting a draft proposal which clearly contemplated the establishment of an umpire system rather than an·impartial chairmanship. GM proposed that the new permanent arbitrator—to be called "the umpire"—should have sharply limited authority. Only alleged violations of certain specified clauses of written agreements between the parties were to be subject to arbitration. A separate procedure, culminating in possible strike action, was provided for disputes over certain matters such as production standards and health and safety. GM also proposed that all cases should be presented to the arbitrator in writing and that a hearing would be held only at the arbitrator's option—apparently an adaptation of the long-distance arbitration of the anthracite industry. The UAW objected to the proposed limitations on the authority of the arbitrator, apparently preferring the much broader scope of an impartial chairman system. But GM stood firm, and its proposal was incorporated in the parties' agreement without substantial change.

Any possible doubt that General Motors had made a deliberate choice between the two types of permanent arbitration systems is dispelled, we believe, by the press announcement which GM issued after agreement had been reached on the new system. The announcement emphasized that "The umpire will not be an impartial chairman, but rather a judge, in that he cannot make new regulations but can only decide questions under the rules and regulations agreed to between the corporation and the union."

Having established an umpire system resembling the anthracite model, these parties then chose their first umpire from among the ranks of the impartial chairmen. They called Harry Millis from the impartial chairmanship of the Chicago men's clothing industry. This choice suggests the possibility that the parties may have reached an interesting compromise in their bargaining over the arbitration system: the union accepted the umpire system proposed by the corporation, but the corporation agreed to appoint as umpire a man who had many years of experience in an impartial chairmanship. The tenure of Millis was quite brief; shortly after the parties appointed him, President Roosevelt called him to Washington to be chairman of the National Labor Relations Board. Thereupon,

GM and the UAW appointed another well-known impartial chairman, George Taylor, as their umpire.

Everyone who is familiar with the writings of George Taylor can readily infer that his enthusiasm for the umpire system was not unbounded. But in his early months in the GM-UAW system he conformed to what he understood was the parties' conception of the proper role of the umpire in their system. Soon the parties were expressing surprise and even dismay at some of the umpire decisions. Taylor received a delegation of corporation executives and listened to their complaints. His reply was that an umpire system inevitably produced some decisions which one side or the other found unacceptable, and that this was why decisions were mediated rather than adjudicated in impartial chairman systems. Thereafter, with the consent of both parties, Taylor mediated the key decisions in the GM-UAW system. We should emphasize, however, that his role was considerably more limited than in the hosiery chairmanship because his jurisdiction was limited. As already noted, the parties had agreed to arbitrate only claims of violation of specified clauses of their agreement, not "all disputes" arising during the life of the agreement. In many cases, therefore, mediation consisted of informal discussion of a proposed decision with representatives of the parties prior to its issuance. On some vital points, however, such as proper cause for discipline, the agreement provided no real guideposts for decision, and the necessary principles were developed by consensus of the parties under Taylor's guidance.

Taylor issued 245 decisions before he was called to Washington in 1942 to serve on the War Labor Board. His successor as GM-UAW umpire was G. Allan Dash, Jr., who had been associated with Taylor in the hosiery chairmanship. Dash continued the Taylor practice of discussing his decisions with the key representatives of the parties prior to their issuance. But toward the end of his tenure, the practice faded away. The parties did not specifically discuss this change with the umpire; rather, the key representative of one of the parties was transferred to another assignment and no successor was designated, and obviously the umpire could not continue his discussion of proposed decisions with only one of the parties. Ralph Seward succeeded Dash as umpire in 1944. Seward had gained the impression, in meetings with representatives of both parties prior to his appointment, that they wanted their new umpire to follow a "strictly judicial approach—*i.e.*, to base his decisions entirely on the formal hearing record without recourse to informal discussions with the parties. Seward adopted this approach, and ever since there has been an unwritten rule in the GM-UAW system that there is no communication whatever between the umpire and the parties concerning a case that has been heard until a decision has been issued.

Thus General Motors and the UAW, after agreeing to establish an umpire system, accepted for a time one of the principal elements of the impartial chairman system—mediated decisions—while retaining the other elements of the umpire system, particularly the restricted scope of arbitration. We can only speculate concerning the reasons why both parties had come to prefer the "strictly judicial" approach to the mediation approach in decision-making by 1944. One apparent reason was that many of the basic principles had been hammered out by then. Another was that arbitration had become a more routine operation by 1944 and the responsibility for representing the parties had been delegated to lower echelons of officialdom than at the beginning. Taylor frequently dealt with top-level officials on both sides; but by 1944 both parties had developed permanent staffs of arbitration specialists. Finally, we have gathered from discussions with some of the participants in this system that the officials of this big union and this big corporation found that their own relations with their respective constituencies were easier if the umpire had sole responsibility for his decisions. The relatively brief tenure of most of the early umpires suggests that one of the important functions served by the incumbents was to bear the onus for unpalatable decisions.

THE CHRYSLER AND FORD SYSTEMS

While General Motors pioneered the permanent arbitration system in the automobile industry, the other two members of the "Big Three" of the industry followed the GM example in 1943. The Chrysler-UAW system was ordered by a War Labor Board directive. It is interesting that the author of the WLB directive was George Taylor. The directive instructed Chrysler and the UAW to appoint an "impartial chairman" for their appeal board, which up to that time had not included a neutral member but nevertheless had been the terminal step in the grievance procedure. The directive specified that "The impartial chairman shall have the right ... to participate in all discussions and meetings of the appeal board and shall also have the duty of assisting the parties in resolving particular questions." No doubt we may justifiably assume that when George Taylor used the term, "impartial chairman," and provided that the incumbent of this position should *assist the parties* in settling disputes, he had in mind a system of continuous negotiations presided over by a mediator with ultimate decision-making authority.

Ironically, despite the apparent intent of this directive, Chrysler and the UAW proceeded to establish arbitration machinery that was almost an exact duplicate of the anthracite umpire system. In the Chrysler system, the partisan members of the appeal board developed a voluminous written record in each case, without any participation by the impartial chairman. When the appeal board found itself unable to dispose of a case, the chairman was invited to meet with the partisan members of the board. There were no hearings in the usual sense. The board members presented the written record to the chairman and argued their respective positions. The chairman then retired, studied the record, and issued his decision without further consultation with the parties. David A. Wolff, who served as impartial chairman in this system from 1943 to 1962, often pointed out that he had never heard a witness or made a plant inspection under this procedure. His role was more that of an appellate judge than a trial judge. As in the GM-UAW system, the impartial chairman had a carefully circumscribed jurisdiction; he was authorized only to rule on alleged violations of certain specified provisions of the parties' agreements.

The Chrysler-UAW system retained essentially its original form until 1962. By then, some new faces had appeared on both sides of the bargaining table. The parties decided that they wanted broader participation in their arbitration proceedings, particularly by those directly involved in particular cases. They revamped their procedure to provide for the appearance at hearings of witnesses and other company and union representatives who had previously been excluded from the appeal board meetings with the impartial chairman. Obviously, this revision was not a move in the direction of the clothing and hosiery type of impartial chairmanship; rather, it conformed the Chrysler-UAW system more closely to the GM-UAW system. Interestingly, Chrysler and the UAW chose as their first arbitrator under the revised system a former GM-UAW umpire, Gabriel N. Alexander.

The Ford-UAW arbitration system was established by the parties themselves in 1943 without a WLB directive. The contract language which established the system was similar to that which GM and the UAW had adopted in 1940. But for the first ten years of the Ford-UAW system, most of the important decisions were the product of mediation rather than adjudication. The main reason was that Harry Shulman was the umpire during that period. Most people interested in arbitration know well the name and works of Harry Shulman. His decisions and his essays on arbitration are perhaps more widely quoted than those of any other arbitrator. As a reading of his essays and decisions suggests, the man himself was eloquent, persuasive, and self-assured. He originally entered the Ford-UAW relationship as a special War Labor Board mediator. His assignment was to help the parties to improve a labor-management relationship that was so tumultuous that it was hindering war production. Shulman found a union badly divided by factionalism and a management which generally lacked clear lines of authority. In this situation both sides appear to have welcomed the forceful personality of Shulman. We may never know the precise extent of his influence in the development of what is now a good working relationship between Ford and the UAW. But we do know that scores of people in the UAW and in Ford management still regard Shulman as one of the closest personal friends they ever had, and that he advised them on a great many matters, including labor relations policies.

Shulman's approach to arbitration was highly informal. Often he disposed of cases with a one-sentence award after a hearing of a few minutes. Several hundred cases were presented to him which he thought should remain undecided, and he consigned them to what he termed his "graveyard," without a decision. When a case presented a basic issue, he often deferred a decision until other cases presenting other facets of the same issue had been heard, and then he would mediate the terms of a broad decision. If he felt that a case had been inadequately presented by one side or the other, he would undertake his own investigation to obtain the facts that he thought were necessary for a sound decision. He felt no inhibitions about discussing past, pending, or potential arbitration cases with grievance committeemen, individual grievants, or line supervision.

Despite Shulman's remarkable abilities and the great respect which both parties had for him personally, there was a growing undercurrent of resistance to his approach to the umpire function during the closing years of his tenure. Key representatives of the company and the union appear to have concluded that they had "outgrown" the Shulman approach. Factionalism in the Ford Department of the union had greatly decreased with a consequent reduction in leadership turnover, and under Henry Ford II the company management had been thoroughly rationalized. Both parties had developed a considerable degree of sophistication and confidence in their dealings with each other. Hence, there was a growing desire on both sides for the umpire to interpret the language of their contract and stop at that, instead of counseling and advising them on all aspects of their relationship. Shulman's tenure as umpire was ended by his death in 1955. The parties appointed as his successor Harry Platt, who already had several years of service in the system as one of the "temporary umpires" who were needed to handle the extremely heavy case load. As a temporary umpire, Platt had been expected to hear cases and decide them without resort to the mediation techniques so extensively utilized by Shulman. As the chief umpire, Platt has continued to resolve cases by the techniques of adjudication rather than mediation. It is our strong impression that the parties have welcomed this change.

We have described the evolution of the GM, Chrysler and Ford arbitration systems in some detail because we believe that the pattern of development is significant. We see initial diversity and ultimate uniformity. Today, the points of similarity in the three systems far outweigh the points of difference. Does this trial-and-error progression toward the same basic arbitration system in this industry represent a kind of Darwinian adaptation to environmental necessities? We suggest that it does. But we defer further consideration of the point while we briefly survey the development of permanent arbitration systems in several other major industries since 1940.

THE STEEL INDUSTRY

The initial agreements which the Steel Workers Organizing Committee signed in 1937 with United States Steel and three other major producers included provisions for *ad hoc* arbitration as the terminal point of the grievance procedure. It is perhaps self-evident that a provision for *ad hoc* arbitration almost automatically rules out the mediation approach to decision making. And it is clear that in those early days the steel companies were quite wary of any kind of arbitration. They did not relish the prospect of binding decisions by outsiders who "knew nothing about the steel industry." The first contracts provided that the *ad hoc* arbitrators would be selected by mutual agreement of the parties and there was no procedure for breaking a deadlock. The result was that few arbitrators were appointed and few cases were heard in the early years.

After the beginning of World War II, there was growing pressure to cut down the backlog of cases appealed to arbitration but not heard, and the companies and the unions began to discover arbitrators that were acceptable to both. Some of the decisions undoubtedly confirmed the worst fears of company representatives concerning the ignorance of outsiders about the steel industry. In 1945, United States Steel decided that a permanent arbitration system would be a lesser evil than *ad hoc* arbitration. The union had reached that conclusion some time previously. Therefore, these parties established in 1945 what they named the Board of Conciliation and Arbitration. To help remedy the ignorance of outsiders concerning the steel industry, this Board included one permanent, full-time member representing the company and another representing the union, in addition to the permanent neutral chairman. At first glance, it might seem that this structure would encourage the resolution of disputes by mediation—an impression strengthened by the inclusion of the word "conciliation" in the name of the Board. But as the system developed, very little conciliation or mediation was possible. The partisan members were advocates, not principals; their chief function was to win decisions, not to negotiate. Executive sessions of the Board became what amounted to rehearings of the important cases. Draft decisions of the chairman were also discussed at length in many cases. Finally, the partisan members of the board often issued dissenting opinions couched in strong language.

U.S. Steel and the union substantially modified this system in 1951. They eliminated the provision for partisan members of the board and deleted the "conciliation" part of the title. The permanent neutral is still called the "chairman," even though he is now the sole member of the "board." Despite the "chairman" title, this arbitration machinery remains essentially an umpire system rather than an impartial chairman system as we have used those terms in this discussion. There is one significant difference, however, between this umpire system and the GM-UAW model. Since 1951, the chairman of the U.S. Steel-Steelworkers board has regularly reviewed and discussed his draft decisions with designated representatives of the company and the union. But, unlike the old system, the representatives of the parties do not devote their full time to this function; they do not attend the arbitration hearings; they are at a considerably higher policy level in their respective organizations than were the former full-time board members; and they appear to function primarily as consultants to the arbitrator rather than as advocates. This system is clearly different from the impartial chairmanships that we have already described, but it is also a significant modification of the old anthracite umpire system in which the neutral's only contacts with the parties were through the post office. The U.S. Steel-Steelworkers system now appears to be working to the satisfaction of both parties. The present chairman, Sylvester Garrett, has served continuously since 1951, which suggests that the parties have not only found the right man for the job but have also evolved a system which meets their needs.

Like U.S. Steel, and probably for the same reasons, the other major companies in the basic steel industry first relied on *ad hoc* arbitration. Most of them have switched to the single permanent umpire system, generally omitting the intermediate step of a tripartite permanent board. In 1947, Bethlehem established a permanent three-man rotating panel of neutrals; but this arrangement proved to be a transitional step to a single permanent umpire. In 1952, Bethlehem and the Steelworkers designated Ralph Seward as their sole umpire, and his tenure has been continuous since that date. Some of the smaller steel producers have stayed with *ad hoc* arbitration. In several of the companies in more recent years, the union has successfully pressed for the establishment of permanent umpireships.

OTHER INDUSTRIES

Although collective bargaining agreements were signed by the Rubber Workers Union and the major firms in the rubber industry in the late thirties, there was virtually no arbitration in this industry prior to World War II. The reason was stated in familiar terms by a student of the industry writing in 1941: "It is the general sentiment of most management and union representatives in the rubber industry that arbitration by an outsider is not desirable because no outsider understands the problems of a particular concern as well as the local management and employees."

When the war-time no-strike pledge made strikes and slow-downs contrary to national policy, the major companies and the union somewhat reluctantly accepted *ad hoc* arbitration. After several years of *ad hoc* experience, Goodyear, Goodrich, and U.S. Rubber each agreed to the establishment of permanent umpireships with company-wide jurisdiction. Firestone tried this kind of system for a time but reverted to a permanent panel of arbitrators. In 1963 Goodyear also replaced a single umpire with a panel, in part because the case load in this company is so heavy that it is difficult for a single umpire to keep up with it. Several of the rubber companies have utilized tripartite boards, with the neutral member functioning essentially as an umpire, but the trend in this industry appears clearly to be away from this arrangement.

We will not attempt a detailed survey of arbitration systems in the remainder of American industry. The major thrust of union organizing activities in the thirties and forties was in the mass-production industries. We believe that we can safely put forth these rather broad generalizations: *ad hoc* arbitration is the most widely used system in most of these industries; where permanent arbitration systems have been established in these industries, the umpire model has been followed rather than the impartial chairman model, without any important exceptions known to us. The impartial chairman system has been retained in those industries such as clothing where it was established many years ago. The jurisdictional disputes board in the construction industry also functioned as an impartial chairmanship during the many years that John Dunlop headed it. In recent years Ted Kheel has developed what appears to be essentially the impartial chairman system in several industries or segments of industries in which he is active as a neutral.

Conclusions

We have said that impartial chairmanships are usually established in a largely unstructured decision-making environment in which the principal constraint on the arbitrator is the necessity to achieve a consensus of the parties. Yet the process of problem-solving and decision-making inevitably creates precedents. In some systems, efforts have been made to preserve flexibility by the adoption of agreement provisions that past decisions have no precedent value—but even in these systems, the impartial chairmen and the parties themselves have gradually come to place some reliance on the precedents of the past. No doubt most people regard reasonable consistency as an essential attribute of fairness. Hence, the development of a body of past decisions almost inevitably adds to the constraints on the impartial chairman and reduces his room for maneuver in mediation. There also appears to be a general tendency in all types of industrial relations systems to develop more rather than less detailed agreements. Therefore, as arbitration systems mature, the guideposts for decision-making tend to become more numerous, more detailed, and more explicit.

This elaboration of the intellectual structure for decision-making has two important effects on the arbitration process. One is that arbitrators tend to become interchangeable. In many present day umpireships with heavy case loads, a number of arbitrators are employed to decide cases with a minimum of coordination with each other.

The implied assumption is that any reasonably competent arbitrator is likely to decide a given case in the same way that any other competent arbitrator would. The proliferation of guideposts makes decisions more predictable.

When this stage is reached, it becomes easier for the parties themselves to settle their own disputes by reference to the applicable guideposts. In some of the industries which have had impartial chairmanships for many years, there is by now little or no arbitration. And in some of the major umpireships, there have been dramatic reductions in case loads since the early years. In the GM-UAW umpireship, more than 200 cases per year were arbitrated at the outset; the current volume is only 10 or 15 per cent of the earlier figure. In the Ford-UAW system, five or six hundred cases per year were arbitrated for many years; since 1958, the average has been less than a hundred a year. Goodyear and the Rubber Workers have reduced their case load by about 50 per cent in the past several years. Many other similar examples could be cited.

On the other hand, there are many arbitration systems in which the case load has remained stable or has even increased over the years. Many of these systems must hold some latent possibilities for reducing the volume of arbitration and thereby cutting its costs. We suggest that in some of these systems, the failure of the parties themselves to apply the available guideposts is probably attributable to the political structure of the union or the company or both; it may be "safer" to put the burden of decision on the arbitrator even when the answer is obvious. In other words, we believe that excessive case loads today are less often the result of ignorance of the guideposts, or the unavailability of guideposts, than they are the result of insecurity or lack of authority on the part of the company or union representatives who must decide whether to settle or to arbitrate.

REASON, CONTRACT AND LAW IN LABOR RELATIONS

HARRY SHULMAN*

The parties' bargaining normally results in a collective labor agreement for a stated term or for an indefinite period. The agreement is made on the understanding and with the expectation that both parties will respect it as a com-

*Abridged from 68 HARV. L. REV. 999 (1955). This classic was Dean Shulman's Oliver Wendell Holmes Lecture in 1955. Copyright 1955 by the Harvard Law Review Association and reprinted with its permission.

mitment binding upon them. In the business world such commitments are called contracts. And the collective labor agreement itself comes to be called the contract even by the workers—as, for example, in the slogan "no contract, no work." Does it not naturally follow, then, that the law which provides remedies for breaches of contract generally should also provide remedies for breaches of collective labor agreements? If the parties are entrusted by law with the responsibility of determining conditions of employment, should they not be held to their responsibility and their agreements be given the sanction of legal enforcement? This is the line of reasoning which apparently persuaded the Congress to invest the federal courts with jurisdiction over actions for breach of contract between employers and labor organizations.

Again, if the collective agreement provides for resort to voluntary arbitration, it is argued that the law should enforce the agreement; and provision is made for suits to enjoin or compel the arbitration or to enjoin or enforce the resulting awards. This limited intervention by the law, it is argued, is not an impairment of the freedom of contract but rather a means of making it effective.

In my judgment, these are unwise limitations on the parties' autonomy. For me this conclusion follows from the analysis which I propose to make of the rule of law and reason which the parties' contract—the collective agreement—establishes. But the analysis has validity, whether or not you draw the same conclusion.

While what I shall say may have wider application, my archetype is a large industrial enterprise employing many thousands of organized workers in one or more plants. It is necessary to bear in mind that such an enterprise involves not only large groups of organized workers but also an employer who acts through many hundreds or thousands of representatives at various levels of authority from the job foreman through the superintendents and managers to the vice-presidents and president and board of directors. While the organization on the employer side is more monolithic than on the worker side, the fact that many people exercise its authority in various ways is of great practical significance.

Collective bargaining today is not concerned merely with the return for the employees' services that Holmes talked about. That is, of course, one important concern. On occasion all attention seems to be focused on it. But wages are negotiated only periodically, once in six months, or twelve months, or perhaps even at longer intervals. Even when wages appear to be the chief or only matter in controversy, there is a great deal more involved—more which is not only of at least equal importance but which also affects the wage negotiations.

Collective bargaining is today, as Brandeis pointed out, the means of establishing industrial democracy as the essential condition of political democracy, the means of providing for the workers' lives in industry the sense of worth, of freedom, and of participation that democratic government promises them as citizens. The modern industrial worker is not engaged to produce a specific result and left to himself for the performance. He is hired to work under continuous and detailed direction and supervision, in close association with hundreds or thousands of fellow workers, each of whom performs a very minute portion of the work that ultimately results in a finished product. The enterprise requires the continuous co-ordination of the work of this multitude of employees; and this poses numerous daily problems whether or not the employees are organized. So elementary a matter as leaving the job for a few minutes "to service the body," as they say in the shop, poses a serious problem which must be carefully analyzed and provided for, otherwise one might find the work of a hundred men held up every time one of them had to leave. Every day a number of employees may be absent or report late. Daily or almost daily some employees have to be laid off for a short period or indefinitely; some employees must be hired; changes must be made in job assignments, either by way of promotion or demotion or otherwise. And daily there are thousands of occasions for friction between employee and supervisor which may erupt in disciplinary action against the employee or a stoppage of work.

These and a host of similar problems are inherent in the necessity of co-ordinating the work of thousands of persons into an efficient operation. Even where there is no union, the employer needs statements of policy to guide the hundreds of persons through whom he must act, though he may be ready to invest them with large powers of discretion. Addition of the union alters the situation in at least two ways: First, the employees, through the union, must participate in the determinations. Second, the acceptance of unions and collective bargaining has increased the employee's confidence and his sense of dignity and importance; where previously there may have been submission, albeit resentful, there is now self-assertion.

One might conceive of the parties engaging in bargaining and joint determination, without an agreement, by considering each case as it arises and disposing of it by *ad hoc* decision. But this is, of course, a wholly impractical method, particularly for a large enterprise. So the parties seek to negotiate an agreement to provide the standards to govern their future action.

In this endeavor they face problems not unlike those encountered wherever attempt is made to legislate for the future in highly complex affairs. The parties seek to foresee the multitude of variant situations that might arise, the possible types of action that might then be available, the practicalities of each and their anticipated advantages or disadvantages. Choice between the suggested possibilities is rendered more difficult by the very process of bargaining and the expected subsequent administration of the bargain. The negotiations are necessarily conducted by representatives removed in variant degrees from direct confrontation with the anticipated situations. They act on the basis partly of their own experience and partly of the more or less incomplete or clashing advice of constituents—the resolutions of councils, subcouncils, unit and departmental meetings in the case of the union, and the suggestions from individuals at the various levels of management in the case of the employer. While each area of problems —vacations, overtime, promotions, layoffs, and the like—must be separately and carefully considered, each is nevertheless but a small part of the total negotiation. The pressure for trade or compromise is ever present.

No matter how much time is allowed for the negotiation, there is never time enough to think every issue through in all its possible applications, and never ingenuity enough to anticipate all that does later show up. Since the parties earnestly strive to complete an agreement, there is almost irresistible pressure to find a verbal formula which is acceptable, even though its meaning to the two sides may in fact differ. The urge to make sure of real consensus or to clarify a felt ambiguity in the language tentatively accepted is at times repressed, lest the effort result in disagreement or in subsequent enforced consent to a clearer provision which is, however, less favorable to the party with the urge. With agreement reached as to known recurring situations, questions as to application to more difficult cases may be tiredly brushed aside on the theory that those cases will never—or hardly ever—arise.

Then there is never, of course, enough time to do an impeccable job of draftsmanship after substantive agreement is reached—apart from the hazard that such an effort might uncover troublesome disagreement. Though the subject matter is complex and the provisions intricate, the language must nevertheless be directed to laymen whose occupation is not interpretation—the workers in the plant, the foremen, the clerks in the payroll office. For it is they whose actions must be guided by the agreement; and indeed, in the case of the union, the membership is asked to ratify or reject what is prior to its action only a proposed agreement. While the interpretations or explanations made at the membership meetings can hardly bind the employer, it is nevertheless important that the agreement be not such as to become a promise to the ear but a disappointment to the hope of the membership.

To be sure, the parties are seeking to bind one another and to define "rights" and "obligations" for the future. But it is also true that, with respect to nonwage matters particularly, the parties are dealing with hypothetical situations that may or may not arise. Both sides are interested in the welfare of the enterprise. Neither would unashamedly seek contractual commitments that would destroy the other. Each has conflicts of interests in its own ranks. Both might be content to leave the future to discretion, if they had full confidence in that discretion and in its full acceptance when exercised. And even when the negotiating representatives have full confidence in each other as individuals, they recognize that it will be many others, not they, who will play major roles in the administration of the agreement. So they seek to provide a rule of law which will eliminate or reduce the areas of discretion. The agreement then becomes a compilation of diverse provisions: some provide objective criteria almost automatically applicable; some provide more or less specific standards which require reason and judgment in their application; and some do little more than leave problems to future consideration with an expression of hope and good faith.

The parties recognize, when they make their collective agreement, that they may not have anticipated everything and that, in any event, there will be many differences of opinion as to the proper application of its standards. Accordingly the agreement establishes a grievance procedure or machinery for the adjustment of complaints or disputes during its term. The autonomous rule of law thus established contemplates that the disputes will be adjusted by the application of reason guided by the light of the contract, rather than by force or power.

While the details of the grievance procedure differ from one enterprise to another, its essence is a hierarchy of joint conferences between designated representatives of the employer and the union. But joint conferences even at the highest levels of authority may not, and frequently do not, result in agreement. In the absence of provision for resolution of stalemate, the parties are left to their own devices. Since grievances are almost always complaints against action taken or refused by the employer, a stalemate means that the employer's view prevails. Of course, in the absence of some restraint by contract or otherwise, the union is free to strike in order to reverse the employer's choice. But the union can hardly afford an all out strike every time it feels that a grievance has been unjustly denied. The consequence is either that unadjusted grievances are accumulated until there is an explosion, or that groups of workers, less than the entirety, resort to job action, small stoppages, slowdowns, or careless workmanship to force adjustment of their grievances.

The method employed by almost all industry today for the resolution of stalemates in the adjustment of grievances under the private rule of law established by the collective agreement is private arbitration by a neutral person. The largest enterprises provide for a standing umpire or arbitrator to serve for a stated period of time or so long as he continues to be satisfactory to both sides. The great majority of agreements provide for separate appointment of an arbitrator in each case. And the appointments in any case are made by the parties or by a method agreed upon by them. The wide acceptance of arbitration as a terminal step in the grievance procedure—as contrasted with its relatively limited use in the making of the contract in the first place—is explained generally on the grounds, first, that grievances involve interests of lesser importance than those in contract negotiation and, second, that the discretion of the arbitrator is confined by the agreement under which the grievances arise. Both statements require qualification. As umpire under one collective agreement, I have arbitrated cases ranging all the way from the claim of a single employee for fifteen minutes' pay to that of more than sixty thousand employees for a paid lunch period the direct cost of which was between seven and eight million dollars a year. And the restraining bonds of the collective agreement are found on occasion to be elastic indeed.

The parties do not generally restrict their own joint powers in the grievance procedure. But it is customary for the collective agreement to limit the arbitrator's jurisdiction with apparent strictness. Apart from the specific exclusion of certain subjects, as, for example, rates for new jobs or production standards, he is commonly confined to the resolution of grievances or disputes as to "the interpretation or application of the agreement," or of claims of "violation of the agreement." And quite frequently he is further enjoined not to "add to, subtract from, or modify any of the terms of the agreement." In the agreement with which I am most familiar he is admonished also that he has "no power to substitute his discretion for the Company's discretion in cases where the Company is given discretion" by the agreement, and no power "to provide agreement for the parties in those cases where they have in their contract agreed that further negotiations shall or may provide for certain contingencies."

Doubtless these are wise, perhaps even necessary, safeguards—at least before the parties develop sufficient confidence in their private rule of law to enable them to relax the restriction. And an arbitrator worthy of appointment in the first place must conscientiously respect the limits imposed on his jurisdiction, for otherwise he would not only betray his trust, but also undermine his own future usefulness and endanger the very system of self-government in which he works. But these are hardly provisions which would be inserted in the agreement to control the courts in an action on the contract. The judge, too, must decide only "according to law." Unlike the case of the arbitrator, however, the judge's authority and the law which he must interpret and apply do not derive entirely from the agreement of the litigants before him.

Let me consider some of the difficulties and limitations of the arbitrator's function. Suppose the collective agreement is completely silent on a matter in dispute. Suppose, for example, that the agreement is silent on the question whether acceptance of overtime work is mandatory or optional with the employee. This very issue was reported as the cause of the recent extensive and vexing strikes on the English docks. It is an issue which a number of arbitrators have had to decide under collective agreements. Now it is easy enough to say that the matter is not covered by the agreement. But what follows? May the employer, therefore, require the employees to accept the overtime assignments on pain of disciplinary penalties, such as layoff or discharge, or may the employees properly refuse the assignments? Answer would be aided, of course, if there were a common presupposition as to the effect of the collective agreement. In constitutional law terms, but without pushing the metaphor far, is it a grant of limited powers or is it a set of restrictions on otherwise unlimited powers? If it is the former and the employer is not given the power to command overtime work, then his attempt to discipline employees for failure to accept would be a violation of the contract; if it is the latter, then, since by hypo-

thesis the agreement contains no relevant restriction, the employer would have the "reserved power" to enforce the command.

Partly for the purpose of meeting this difficulty many agreements now include what is generally called a "management prerogative" clause, sometimes more accurately and tactfully called a "management responsibility" or "management functions" clause. This normally lists certain matters as "the sole right" of management or for "sole determination" by management, subject, however, to such restriction as may be provided in the agreement. The inclusion of the management provision in some agreements may raise a question as to the significance of its exclusion in others; and it focuses attention on the precise language of the provision with possible reference to the maxim *inclusio unius est exclusio alterius*. Apart from its specification of items as to which there is normally no question, such as the products to be manufactured, the provision is normally couched in broad phrases like "the right to manage the business" or to "direct the working forces." One may wonder about the chances of the adoption of an agreement, in some enterprises at least, if it states in unmistakable language that the employer shall have the right to do anything at all with respect to the work of the employees except as he is expressly limited by the agreement.

Courts, if confronted with this problem, would doubtless declare a general principle, whether or not it squared with the conception of the parties in the particular case. But the power of the arbitrator to do so is at least questionable. The obvious alternative is for the arbitrator to refrain from affirmative decision and to remand the dispute to the parties on the ground that it is outside of his jurisdiction. But would not that be in effect a decision supporting the employer's freedom of action? If the validity of the employer's order requiring the overtime work is beyond the arbitrator's jurisdiction, he would seem to have no power to restrain the disciplinary action taken by the employer to enforce the order. On the other hand, if he does restrain the disciplinary action, is he not in effect denying validity to the employer's order? Again, the denial of jurisdiction presumably leaves the dispute for resolution by the parties. But whether the union may properly resort to economic pressure in the effort at resolution may depend upon the construction of the "no strike" provision of the agreement. The obligation not to strike may or may not be coextensive with the arbitrator's jurisdiction.

The question of fundamental presuppositions

arises in another way. The parties rarely start with an enterprise from scratch ; generally they negotiate an agreement for a going enterprise which has been in operation for some time and which has developed practices or precedents of varying degrees of consistency and force. What is the significance of the claimed "prior practice"?

For example, in the overtime case we have been considering, suppose that evidence is tendered that the employer never sought to compel acceptance of overtime assignments, or that the employees never refused such assignments without good excuse. Or suppose that, though the agreement is silent on the matters, the employer had been giving the employees a rest period of ten minutes in each half of the shift, or a lunch period on the employer's time, or a five minute wash-up period before lunch or at the end of the shift, or a money bonus at Christmas. Or, to vary the nature of the example, suppose the claim is that it had been customary for the employer to assign a rigger to assist pipefitters when they were required to lift pipe of four inches or more in diameter, or to assign an employee to hold the pieces which a welder had to weld. Now suppose that, during the term of the agreement, the employer changes these claimed practices over the union's strenuous objections, which are then carried through the grievance procedure to the umpire. In these cases it is the union which relies on the prior practice. But frequently the position is reversed. For example, an employer directs a punch press operator to paint his press when he has no punching to do ; or he asks a crib attendant to paint the walls of his crib. In either case, the employee refuses on the ground that painting is not work in his classification, but rather in that of a painter. And the employer points to a claimed prior practice in accord with his direction.

Again the fundamental question may be asked : Is the agreement an exclusive statement of rights and privileges or does it subsume continuation of existing conditions? And again it may be ventured that courts, if confronted with the question, would probably give a general answer for all cases. For the arbitrator, particularly if his jurisdiction is limited to "interpretation" with a prohibition against "adding to, subtracting from or modifying" the terms of the agreement, a general answer is not so clear.

Some have urged that established practices, at least if they were in existence at the time of the negotiation of the agreement and were not considered in any way during the negotiations, are binding upon the parties and must be continued for the duration of the agreement. This, it is said, is implied in the agreement itself—or in the "logic" of the agreement or in the collective bargaining relationship. Lawyers are familiar with "implied" terms. We used to differentiate between implications "in fact" and implications "in law." Now scholars say the differentiation is not quite valid and the implication in any event is based on morality, common understanding, social policy, and legal duty expressed in tort or quasi-contract. The common understanding of the litigants in the particular action is only one factor in the implication—and not the most important. But the judges' authority for imposing the implication is not the party's will ; it is the superior authority of the law, which transcends the party's will.

The arbitrator of whom we are talking does not have such superior authority to impose implied conditions. The implications which he may find are only those which may reasonably be inferred from some term of the agreement. Is there an implication "in fact" in the collective agreement that existing practices must be continued until changed by mutual consent? It may be said parenthetically that the legal duty to bargain is not quite relevant because, apart from the question whether the arbitrator may enforce that duty, the issue is whether the practice may be changed without mutual consent when bargaining has failed to achieve consent.

It is more than doubtful that there is any general understanding among employers and unions as to the viability of existing practices during the term of a collective agreement. There may be some agreements which are negotiated upon a real or tacit assumption of continuance of existing practices except as modified by the agreement. There are certainly some agreements which specifically provide for the continuance of existing practices with variant limitations. But I venture to guess that in many enterprises the execution of a collective agreement would be blocked if it were insisted that it contain a broad provision that "all existing practices, except as modified by this agreement, shall be continued for the life thereof unless changed by mutual consent." And I suppose that execution would also be blocked if the converse provision were demanded, namely, that "the employer shall be free to change any existing practice except as he is restricted by the terms of this agreement." The reasons for the block would be, of course, the great uncertainty as to the nature and extent of the commitment, and the relentless search for cost-saving changes. The larger the enterprise the more varied its operations, the more dependent it is on technological change, and the keener the competition the greater this uncertainty and search. The agreement between Bethlehem Steel and the United Steelworkers steers a middle course. It provides that if management changes any local practice or custom, an affected employee may file a grievance and in "the disposition of the grievance the burden shall be on Management to justify its action." The agreement does not state, however, what is to constitute justification. That little question is left to future judgment.

Assuming the prior practice to be at least relevant, we may find ourselves in further trouble. I have spoken of the practice as an ascertained or readily ascertainable matter. But commonly it is only a question. Commonly there is widely conflicting evidence as to what was in fact done in the past. Ascertaining the facts with respect to an alleged practice is a difficult task not suggested by the assurance implicit in the word "practice." Nor is it a task which can fortunately be cast on the broad shoulders of a jury. But even after the facts are ascertained, what is their significance? When do they add up to a practice? And what practice?

Suppose that in the pipefitters' case, the employer says: "Sure we've used a rigger in the instances cited. But we did that because we had a rigger available with free time and used him to expedite the work. We still do that. But we never had any notion that we would supply a rigger in other circumstances or that the pipefitters can't be required to work without him." Or take the Christmas bonus. The employer says: "Of course we've paid the bonus. We did it in our discretion when we thought we could afford it and accomplish some good for our business. This year we are convinced that we cannot afford the bonus and, in any event, that it will do us no good." Or consider the union's reply to the company's claim that crib attendants always painted their cribs: "Sure they have. But that was their individual choice—not a collective determination. The union is not out to stir up trouble. So long as nobody objected, we did not look into the question. But when a crib attendant did object, we then took our position. And we say that the attendant has the choice of accepting or rejecting the assignment." Such are the limitations commonly claimed for alleged practices, and their reality cannot be gainsaid merely because they were not recorded at the time or communicated to the other side. One cannot accompany his every act in the course of a busy day with explanations which would avoid prejudice for the future.

I have been discussing situations where the agreement is silent on important phases of the parties' dispute. But frequently the silence so assumed is a conclusion as to the very question in dispute. Generally one or the other of the parties urges strongly that while the agreement may not speak to the issue directly, it speaks to it indirectly but clearly.

A fairly common recurring dispute relates to the employment of independent outside contractors to do work which has been or can be done by the employer's own employees. For example, an employer may decide to engage an independent outside painting contractor to paint the plant, though he has painters in his own work force. Or he may decide to employ an outside contractor to make an electrical installation in the plant though he has his own electricians available for the work. The fact that some of his own employees may be on layoff while the outside contractor is working aggravates the situation, but is not necessarily controlling on the issue of interpretation involved. The employer's defense of his action in these cases normally runs along these lines: He contends that the determination whether to have particular work done by his own employees or by an outside contractor is part of his reserved "prerogative" which is either unrestrained by the agreement or recognized in the agreement by a provision of the kind mentioned above, leaving to him the "management of the business," the choice of "products to be manufactured," "the schedules of production," the "direction of the working forces," and the like. And he may add, with or without full disclosure of the supporting evidence, that he chose to engage an independent contractor for reasons of economy and business expediency.

The union's reliance is on the agreement. It points to the section, normally called recognition, which usually states that the employer recognizes the union as the collective bargaining agent for his employees in stated categories of work, such as production, or maintenance, or shop clerical and the like. This means, it argues, that work of the stated categories must be done by employees represented by the union. Its representation, it maintains, is not of any specified individuals as of any one time, but of the categories of work in the plant. Unless this meaning is accepted, the argument runs, the employer could drastically reduce or destroy the bargaining unit for which the union was designated.

Of course, if this meaning is accepted, the considerations of economy and business expediency upon which the employer relies become irrelevant. But another possibility is suggested. The recognition clause, it is said, merely establishes the bargaining unit. But good faith, which must be an obligation in all agreements, requires that the employer refrain from deliberately impairing that unit without sufficient justification. In this view the recognition clause is violated only if the letting of the work to the outside contractor is without sufficient business justification.

But if this is the view found to be required by the agreement, then it launches an inquiry for which the agreement provides no guides at all: What is sufficient business justification? To what extent is the employer's own assertion of business judgment significant? How much or what kind of evidence is necessary to bolster his judgment? How much or how little economy is necessary to justify the assumed impairment of the bargaining unit?

Or take the example of employee discipline discussed above. The agreement may be quite clear that the employer has the power to discharge or discipline for cause. It may be quite clear in empowering the arbitrator to pass on grievances protesting the employer's action and even to reduce or modify penalties. But what and where are the guides for his decision? With the advent of grievance procedures and arbitration, discharge has ceased to be regarded as the only available disciplinary measure. Layoffs for various periods are now in general use; and suggestion is made of disciplinary demotions, transfers, reduction of seniority, and the like. What is proper cause for disciplinary action, and more particularly, for discharge rather than for some other penalty? May such measures as demotion or reduction in seniority be properly used for disciplinary purposes? How much weight is to be attached in each case to the employer's judgment, particularly in view of the fact that it is precisely that judgment which is sought to be curbed by the grievance procedure? What significance is to be attached to the personality of the individual employee, his age, his seniority, his prior record, his promise? What consideration, if any, is to be given to probable effects on plant "morale," the morale of supervisors as well as of the workers, and the effects at the time the decision is to be made as well as at the time the penalty is imposed? The frequent instances of stoppage of work in a department or a whole plant because of a disciplinary penalty imposed on a single employee indicates that what is involved is not merely the case of an individual but a group dispute. Factors of this kind should be and doubtless are considered by the parties in the other stages of the grievance procedure. Do they become irrelevant when the case is appealed to the arbitrator?

Here is, of course, the clearest illustration of the arbitrator's role as creative more than interpretive. It would be folly to suggest that all his work is of that character. Despite all platitudes as to the inherent ambiguity of language, there are cases in which the language of the agreement appears compelling and leaves no room for consideration of other evidence of meaning; cases in which the dispute seems frivolous or captious, or patently designed to shift the onus of decision from the party to the arbitrator, or a desperate effort to recapture a concession made in negotiations and subsequently regretted. Assuming, however, a real difference of opinion, what criteria may the arbitrator look to for the choice between conflicting interpretations, each of which is more or less permissible?

Answer in the form of rules or canons of interpretation is neither practical nor helpful. Long experience with statutory interpretation has failed to produce such answer. In the last analysis, what is sought is a wise judgment. It is judgment, said Holmes, that the world pays for. And we can only seek to be aware of the kind of care and preparation that is necessary in forming and pronouncing this judgment.

A proper conception of the arbitrator's function is basic. He is not a public tribunal imposed upon the parties by superior authority which the parties are obliged to accept. He has no general charter to administer justice for a community which transcends the parties. He is rather part of a system of self-government created by and confined to the parties. He serves their pleasure only, to administer the rule of law established by their collective agreement. They are entitled to demand that, at least on balance, his performance be satisfactory to them, and they can readily dispense with him if it is not.

To the extent that the parties are satisfied that the arbitrator is properly performing his part in their system of self-government, their voluntary cooperation in the achievement of the purposes of the collective agreement is promoted. When I speak of the satisfaction of the parties, I do not mean only the advocates who may present the case to the arbitrator, or the top echelons of management or union representatives. I mean rather all the persons whose cooperation is required—all the employees in the bargaining unit and all the representatives of management who deal with them, from the job foreman up.

Ideally, the arbitrator should be informed as fully as possible about the dispute which he is asked to resolve. He should hear all the contentions with respect to it which either party desires to make. For a party can hardly be satisfied that his case has been fully considered if he is not permitted to advance reasons which to him seem relevant and important.

The more serious danger is not that the arbitrator will hear too much irrelevancy, but rather that he will not hear enough of the relevant. Indeed, one advantage frequently reaped from wide latitude to the parties to talk about their case is that the apparent rambling frequently discloses very helpful information which would otherwise not be brought out. Rules of procedure which assure adequate opportunity to each party to prepare for and meet the other's contentions, or rules designed to encourage full consideration and effort at adjustment in the prior stages of the grievance procedure may be quite desirable. But they should not be such as to prevent full presentation of the controversy to the arbitrator before he is required to make final decision. For that would not only limit his resources for sound judgment, but would tend also to create dissatisfaction with the system.

The arbitrator may have to take a more active part in the investigation than does a trial court. This is not merely because, being charged with the responsibility for decision, he should be satisfied that he knows enough to be able to decide. A judge starts with some legal premises as to burden of proof or burden of going forward, which are presumably known to the lawyers who conduct the litigation and are binding on their clients. Even there these burdens are considerably eased by the modern practice of pretrial examination and discovery. But a collective agreement—the arbitrator's law— rarely states any burden of proof ; and the presentation to the arbitrator is not always in the hands of skilled advocates having the same training for the work and operating on common premises. A court's erroneous findings of fact in a particular litigation may work an injustice to the litigants but with one voice at the hearing, the fact is that there may be considerable difference of opinion among the many people who make up the artificial entity called the party.

The important question is not whether the parties agree with the award but rather whether they accept it, not resentfully, but cordially and willingly. Again, it is not to be expected that each decision will be accepted with the same degree of cordiality. But general acceptance and satisfaction is an attainable ideal. Its attainment depends upon the parties' seriousness of purpose to make their system of self-government work, and their confidence in the arbitrator. That confidence will ensue if the arbitrator's work inspires the feeling that he has integrity,

independence, and courage so that he is not susceptible to pressure, blandishment, or threat of economic loss ; that he is intelligent enough to comprehend the parties' contentions and empathetic enough to understand their significance to them ; that he is not easily hoodwinked by bluff or histrionics ; that he makes earnest effort to inform himself fully and does not go off halfcocked ; and that his final judgment is the product of deliberation and reason so applied on the basis of the standards and the authority which they entrusted to him.

An important factor tending toward such general acceptance is the opinion accompanying the arbitrator's award. It has been urged by some that an arbitrator's award should be made without opinion or explanation in order to avoid the dangers of accumulating precedents and subjecting arbitration to the rigidities of *stare decisis* in the law. Perhaps this view has merit when the particular arbitration is regarded as solely a means of resolving the particular stalemate and nothing else. It is an erroneous view for the arbitration which is an integral part of the system of self-government and rule of law that the parties establish for their continuing relationship.

In this system opinions are necessary, first, to assure the parties that the awards are based on reason applied to the agreement in the manner I have described. To be sure, the opinions may convince the parties that their arbitrator is inadequate and should be replaced. This may work a hardship, and at times even an injustice, on the arbitrator. But that is a risk which the parties are entitled to impose on his occupation and which is a necessary feature of the system.

Secondly, in this system a form of precedent and *stare decisis* is inevitable and desirable. I am not referring to the use in one enterprise, say United States Steel, of awards made by another arbitrator in another enterprise, say General Motors. Because the publishing business has made arbitration awards generally available, they are being used in this way both by the parties and by arbitrators. But they are not so used in the belief that they are entitled to any particular precedential value, for they are not so entitled. Their value, if any, lies rather in their suggestion of approach or line of argument, or perhaps in their character of evidence as to practice in other enterprises. As such evidence, it must be used, of course, with great circumspection because of its limited character, and with ample opportunity for the parties to consider it.

But the precedent of which I am now speaking refers to the successive decisions within the same enterprise. Even in the absence of arbitration, the parties themselves seek to establish a form of *stare decisis* or precedent for their own guidance—by statements of policy, instructions, manuals of procedure, and the like. This is but a means of avoiding the pain of rethinking every recurring case from scratch, of securing uniformity of action among the many people of coordinate authority upon whom each of the parties must rely, of assuring adherence in their action to the policies established by their superiors, and of reducing or containing the possibilities of arbitrary or personal discretion.

When the parties submit to arbitration in the system of which I speak, they seek not merely resolution of the particular stalemate, but guidance for the future, at least for similar cases. They could hardly have a high opinion of the arbitrator's mind if it were a constantly changing mind. Adherence to prior decisions, except when departure is adequately explained, is one sign that the determinations are based on reason and are not merely random judgments.

The arbitrator's opinion can help in rationalizing the agreement and the parties' contentions with respect to it and in fostering greater appreciation by them of each other's views and needs with respect to the problem at hand. Its greatest utility lies in its effect, not merely on the advocates who presented the case or the higher authorities in the enterprise, but on what might be called the rank and file—the workers in the shop and their supervisors. It is the rank and file that must be convinced. For the temptation to resort to job action is ever present and is easily erupted. The less their private rule of law is understood by the workers and the more remote from their participation are the decisions made on their grievances, the greater is the likelihood of wildcat stoppages or other restraints on productivity. The likelihood can be decreased by bringing the arbitration close to the shop, not only in the hearings and investigations, but also in the opinion which explains the award.

The awards must necessarily set precedents for recurring cases and the opinions must necessarily provide guidance for the future in relating decision to reason and to more or less mutually accepted principle. Consistency is not a lawyers' creation. It is a normal urge and a normal expectation. It is part of the ideal of equality of treatment. The lawyer's contribution, indeed, is his differentiation of rational, civilized consistency from apparent consistency. Let me give you an example. In many appeals from disciplinary penalities imposed by the employer, I heard the union argue earnestly that the penalty should be reduced because of the employee's long service record. I was persuaded and held

that the employee's seniority should be considered in fixing the size of his penalty. Then came a case in which two employees committed the same offense at the same time, and one was given a larger penalty than the other. The union protested the larger penalty as being an obvious impairment of the principle of equality. This was not necessarily conscious opportunism, although there is always a good deal of that. A period of education was required to effect the realization, not only by the advocates, but by the rank and file that the equality for which they themselves contended in the area of discipline necessitated different penalties for the same offense whenever factors other than the offense itself were considered.

The arbitrator's opinions may thus be a valuable means of seating reason in labor relations. But the opinions must be carefully restrained. I venture to think that the greater danger to be guarded against is that too much will be said rather than too little. If the opinion wanders too far from the specific problem, in order to rationalize and guide, it runs great risk of error and subsequent embarrassment to the arbitrator himself. Even more unfortunately, it may lead the parties to distrust him because he has gone beyond the necessities of the case and has assumed to regulate their affairs in excess of their consent.

The danger of deciding too much or too early appears in another way. The parties themselves, each confidently expecting a decision its way, may press the arbitrator to decide issues which might better be left undecided or at least delayed until time and experience provide greater assurance of wise judgment. To the dogmatic and the partisan, there is no need for delay; their minds are made up and, to them, delay is confusing and exasperating. The United States Supreme Court has seen the dangers of premature decision and has developed standards for avoiding it, such as the insistence upon a "case or controversy" and the refusal to pass upon a constitutional question when a narrower ground will suffice for the case in hand. The conscientious arbitrator sometimes yearns for similar means of avoiding or delaying decision on issues which he feels unready to decide. For it must be remembered that the arbitrator's decision has a strength and a carry-over which does not exist in the case of an adjustment made by the parties in the lower stages of the grievance procedure.

Consider this example: The agreement sets forth certain classifications with attached rates of pay—ironworker, millwright, crib builder, sashman, belt repairman, and the like. The work of all these classifications is related by features common to all of them. In some plants all the work might be covered by perhaps one or two classifications rather than by a half-dozen. The agreement contains no job descriptions outlining the work of each classification, or if there are job descriptions they are either unilaterally adopted, or sketchy and expressly not exhaustive, or both. Disputes arise as to whether particular assignments made on certain days by supervision fall properly within one or another of the classifications. The particular cases may come to the arbitrator on appeal of disciplinary penalties imposed on employees who refused the assignments on the ground that they were not within the classifications of these employees; or they may come on the grievances of employees claiming that they were deprived of work belonging to their classification when the work was assigned to others. Such cases are vexing indeed, for the parties as well as the arbitrator. Even after long experience, he may find it practically impossible to draw clear and fine lines of demarcation between the several classifications. If he attempts to prick points in a future line by deciding the individual cases as they arise, his task is not much easier because he lacks confidence as to the direction in which he is going and knows that each case may be a prelude to many others. To decide that the issues are beyond his jurisdiction, because the agreement does not demarcate the classifications, is unsatisfactory because that may in effect be a decision for one of the parties and because the fact is that the dispute relates to a provision of the agreement.

In cases of this character, and others in which the arbitrator conscientiously feels baffled, it may be much wiser to permit him to mediate between the parties for an acceptable solution. I do not suggest it for all cases; nor do I urge that settlement is always better than decision. I suggest it only for those cases where decision with confidence seems impossible and where the arbitrator is quite at sea with respect to the consequences of his decision in the operation of the enterprise. In such cases, an adjustment worked out by him with the parties is the most promising course. And the possibility of adjustment is enhanced if he is able to exert the gentle pressure of a threat of decision. In this activity, as in the case of the arbitrator's socializing or meeting with the parties separately, the dangers envisaged with respect to judges or other governmental personnel are not equally applicable. For the parties' control of the process and their individual power to continue or terminate the services of the arbitrator are adequate safeguards against these dangers.

The example I cited comes from my own ex-perience. With the parties' indulgence, though not with their prior consent, I withheld decision and let numerous cases accumulate, meanwhile gaining more illustrations of the scope of the problem and encouraging the parties to search for solution. We finally came up with a mutual understanding which amalgamated the several classifications into one with an appropriate adjustment of rate, reclassified the affected employees, disposed of the accumulated cases, and eliminated the problem for the future. To avoid certain internal difficulties the understanding was recorded not as a signed agreement, but rather as a decision of the umpire, the parties having waived for this case the normal limitations on his jurisdiction.

I have attempted in this paper to sketch the autonomous rule of law and reason which the collective labor agreement establishes. It has, of course, its limitations and its faults. It relies upon wholehearted acceptance by the parties and requires a congenial and adequate arbitrator, as I have explained, who is neither timid nor rash and who feels a responsibility for the success of the system. The arbitration may be resented by either party as an impairment of its authority or power. It is susceptible of use for buck-passing and face-saving. And it may sometimes encourage litigiousness. But when the system works fairly well, its value is great. To consider its feature of arbitration as a substitute for court litigation or as the consideration for a no-strike pledge is to take a foreshortened view of it. In a sense it is a substitute for both—but in the sense in which a transport airplane is a substitute for a stagecoach. The arbitration is an integral part of the system of self-government. And the system is designed to aid management in its quest for efficiency, to assist union leadership in its participation in the enterprise, and to secure justice for the employees. It is a means of making collective bargaining work and thus preserving private enterprise in a free government. When it works fairly well, it does not need the sanction of the law of contracts or the law of arbitration. It is only when the system breaks down completely that the courts' aid in these respects is invoked. But the courts cannot, by occasional sporadic decision, restore the parties' continuing relationship; and their intervention in such cases may seriously affect the going systems of self-government. When their autonomous system breaks down, might not the parties better be left to the usual methods for adjustment of labor disputes rather than to court actions on the contract or on the arbitration award? I suggest that the law stay out—but, mind you, not the lawyers.

COLLECTIVE BARGAINING AND THE ARBITRATOR*

LON L. FULLER

One conception of the role of the arbitrator is that he is essentially a judge. His job is to do justice according to the rules imposed by the parties' contract, leaving the chips to fall where they may. He decides the controversy entirely on the basis of arguments and proofs presented to him "in open court" with the parties confronting one another face to face. He does not attempt to mediate or conciliate, for to do so would be to compromise his role as an adjudicator. He will strictly forego any private communication with the parties after the hearing. The friends of this conception see it as casting the arbitrator in the role of a man of principle, a man who respects the institutional limits of his task, a man who conscientiously refuses to exploit his powers for ulterior purposes, however benign. The critics of this conception have a less flattering view. To them it is unrealistic, prudish, purist, legalistic, an abandonment of common sense, a chasing after false models motivated perhaps by a secret hankering for the glamour and security of judicial office.

The opposing conception expects the arbitrator to adapt his procedures to the case at hand. Indeed, in its more extreme form it rejects the notion that his powers for good should be restrained at all by procedural limitations. By this view the arbitrator has a roving commission to straighten things out, the immediate controversy marking the occasion for, but not the limits of, his intervention. If the formal submission leaves fringes of dispute unsettled, he will gladly undertake to tidy them up. If the arguments at the hearing leave him in doubt as to the actual causes of the dispute, or as to what the parties really expect of him, he will not scruple to hold private consultations for his further enlightenment. If he senses the possibility of a settlement, he will not hesitate to step down from his role as arbitrator to assume that of mediator. If despite his conciliatory skill negotiations become sticky, he will follow Harry Shulman's advice and—with an admonitory glance toward the chair just vacated —"exert the gentle pressure of a threat of decision" to induce agreement.[1]

The critics of this view are seldom charitable

in describing it. They say that arbitrators who accept it think they can "play God," though the actual motive of their actions is usually a base instinct to meddle in other people's affairs. The conception that encourages this intermeddling rests essentially on hypocrisy, for it enables a man who pretends to be a judge to enjoy the powers of his office without accepting its restraints. It is a Messianic conception, a patent abuse of power, a substitution of one-man rule for the rule of law. So the castigations mount. There is need for a neutral term. As the nearest approach I suggest that we describe this view as one that sees the arbitrator, not as a judge, but as a labor-relations physician.

The other major controversy is, as I have said, that which relates to the interpretation of the collective bargaining agreement. By one view a labor contract is like any other legal document and ought to be subject to the same principles of interpretation. If, as it commonly does, it states that the arbitrator shall have no power to add to or to detract from its terms, the arbitrator must accept this limitation. His object is not to do justice, but to apply the agreement. If the agreement imposes hardships, it is no business of the arbitrator to alleviate them. His powers and his duties lie wholly within the four corners of the written document.

The opposing view stresses the unique quality of the collective bargaining agreement. It is not quite like any other document ever conceived by the mind of man. It is at once a constitution and the written record of an economic trade. It is a charter of the parties' rights and a set of resolutions never really expected to be fully realized in practice. From the curiously mixed nature of the collective bargaining agreement there is derived (by a logic that is certainly not obvious) the conclusion that it must be construed freely. Unlike judges, arbitrators must eschew anything like a "literal" interpretation. Their task is not to bend the dispute to the agreement, but to bend the agreement to the unfolding needs of industrial life.

In presenting these two controversies I have purposely thrown the contending sides into a sharper opposition than commonly exists in practice. In reality the matter is never so black and white as I have just painted it. Even those arbitrators who purport to adhere to a fairly extreme position at one end or the other of the scale seldom practice entirely what they preach.

The two controversies I have outlined are to some extent two aspects of a single dispute. One can generally predict that the arbitrator with strong instincts toward mediation will also be likely to favor free principles of contract con-

---

*Abridged from KAHN, ed., COLLECTIVE BARGAINING AND THE ARBITRATOR'S ROLE, 8 (1962). Reprinted with the permission of the Bureau of National Affairs, Inc.

1. Shulman, *Reason, Contract, and Law in Labor Relations*, 68 HARV. L. REV. 999 (1955).

struction. This is not necessarily so, however. There is no compelling reason why the strict constructionist should not, on occasion at least, undertake the role of mediator. Indeed, he is in an especially favorable position to coax an agreement by "the gentle threat of a decision," for in his case this threat may be fortified by a reputation for stiff interpretations. But with this allowance it still remains true that where one will take his position on each of the two controversies is likely to be influenced by a single disposition.

This affinity of views comes to clear expression in Mr. Justice Douglas's remarks in United Steelworkers v. Warrior & Gulf Nav. Co.:

> Arbitration is a means of solving the unforeseeable by molding a system of private law for all the problems which may arise and to provide for their solution in a way which will generally accord with the variant needs and desires of the parties. . . . The labor arbitrator performs functions which are not normal to the courts. . . . The parties expect that his judgment of a particular grievance will reflect not only what the contract says but, insofar as the . . . agreement permits, such factors as the effect on productivity of a particular result, its consequence to the morale of the shop, his judgment whether tensions will be heightened or diminished.[2]

Here by a single stroke the arbitrator-physician is largely relieved both of the restraints of judicial office and of any undue concern to find justification for what he does in the words of the agreement.

It is time now to undertake an analysis of the merits of the controversies I have so far been merely describing. It will be convenient to start with that concerning interpretation.

II

No one has seriously contended, I believe, that formal legal principles of interpretation ought to govern the construction of a labor contract. In a labor arbitration they would be a needless encumbrance and would probably make no difference in the result. As is often pointed out, these principles tend to come in off-setting pairs. One can find a maxim according to which when you say "trees" you must mean shrubs also, shrubs being so much like trees. By another maxim one can argue that when you say "trees" you must mean to exclude shrubs because if you had meant shrubs you would have said so; shrubs being so much like trees, and so naturally suggested by them you couldn't have forgotten about them when you said "trees" and stopped.

Latin expressions of these contradictory truths may lend a certain dignity to judicial opinions. They can hardly serve any purpose in an arbitration award.

There is one legal principle affecting interpretation that might be thought to have a proper bearing on the arbitrator's task of construing the collective bargaining agreement. I have heard arbitrators say that they wish they felt free to invoke the parol evidence rule to cut off certain kinds of testimony with which hearings are often burdened. What they have in mind generally is testimony along this line: One of the parties wants to testify to what *he* meant by a phrase in the agreement. He may add, "I wrote that part myself." He is generally puzzled that his explanations are not received with more enthusiasm. When he is asked whether he communicated his interpretation to the other party, he replies that of course he did not. When he is asked if he is prepared to testify to any fact that will tend to show that the other party ought reasonably to have put the same interpretation on the phrase that he did, he replies that he does not understand the question. At this point the arbitrator will probably be well-advised to let the witness proceed on his own, meanwhile suspending the taking of notes until the testimony takes a more propitious turn. In actual fact, however, the testimony just described is not excluded by the parol evidence rule. It is excluded by the more fundamental rule of relevance, the common sense rule that the testimony received ought to have some bearing on the dispute.

The parol evidence rule comes into question only when the party seeks to testify to some *communicated* expression of intention, some expression that passed between the parties. If the intention so communicated finds no expression in the written contract, testimony concerning it may be offered for the purpose of altering the construction that would otherwise be put on it. Here the possible exclusionary effect of the parol evidence rule becomes relevant. Unfortunately the answer it yields is not simple. The rule's apparent exclusionary force is greatly reduced by two qualifications: (1) errors in the written document may be corrected by a resort to parol evidence, and (2) matters deliberately left to "side agreement" generally do not come within the rule. With these qualifications the rule largely reduces itself to a rebuttable presumption that when some intention expressed during negotiations fails to get into the written document, it was omitted because it was not intended to stand as a part of the total agreement of the parties. If this is a correct appraisal of the effect

---

2. 363 U.S. at 581–82.

of the rule, then it is apparent that its use in labor arbitrations would accomplish little that cannot be achieved by a common sense appraisal of the testimony received and the probabilities to which it points.

These remarks are, however, a digression from our subject. The real controversy hinges, not on specific rules of interpretation, but on the general spirit with which the task of assigning meaning to the contract is conducted. Here the field is cluttered with a good many clichés that have done great harm. The most common of these asserts that judges construe contracts strictly and literally, while arbitrators play fast and loose with them. I don't believe that there is anything in this at all, and that if any generalization were to be made, it ought to run in the opposite direction.

In the first place courts have been rather free in reading obligations into contracts that are not expressed in the writing, and that sometimes directly contradict the writing. A enters a contract with B to render a performance scheduled to begin July 1. On May 15, A repudiates his agreement and tells B he is not going to perform. B brings suit on May 16. A alleges that the suit is premature. His promise was to begin performance on July 1. Until that date arrives he cannot be guilty of a breach of contract for he has promised nothing before then. For more than a century British and American courts have generally allowed B to recover. Why, they ask, should B have to wait around for July 1 to arrive when A has already told him he is not going to perform? If a promise is needed, we can say that in committing himself to begin performance on July 1, A impliedly promised not to repudiate his obligation meanwhile. This result has often been criticized by legal scholars as an unprincipled rewriting of the words of the contract. It has become, however, accepted law.

A father has two children, a son and a daughter. Before his death the father conveys most of his property to his son and exacts from the son a promise that he will provide for the daughter during her life. The father makes the son the executor of his will. After the father's death, the son refuses to carry out the agreement to provide for his sister. The sister brings suit against him. It is argued that she cannot sue on the contract since she was not a party to it. The promise ran to the father, not to her. Again, for at least a century the courts have generally found some way to allow the daughter to recover on the contract. If we say that only a person to whom a promise is made can sue on it, the father has departed and his representative is now the son, who obviously has no interest in suing himself. There being no machinery of public enforcement available, the only solution is to allow a suit by the daughter herself. This result has also been criticized by scholars, who have seen in it a loose addiction by the courts to doing justice at the cost of legal principle. Again, however, the result stands as law.

My third illustration is somewhat more extreme. In an individual contract of employment, an employer promises his employee a bonus if the employee will remain on the job for a certain period of time. The contract states "the provision herein concerning a bonus is to be understood as a gratuity and shall impose on the employer no legal liability whatsoever." The employee complies with the stipulated conditions for securing the bonus. The employer refuses to pay it. The courts have held in cases like this that the stipulation against legal liability does not relieve the employer of an obligation to pay the bonus. The employer cannot have his cake and eat it too. He cannot induce the employee to remain with him by holding a bonus before his eyes, obtain in this way the employee's loyalty and the benefit of his services, and then cut the ground from under him by invoking a clause against legal liability.

The three cases I have just described—and I could expand the list many times over—witness a willingness by courts to add to and subtract from the language of contracts that would seem strange indeed in a labor arbitrator. The reason for this difference is not far to seek. The labor arbitrator is himself a creature of the contract. It is the charter, not only of the parties' rights, but of his powers as well. The courts on the other hand, have a commission broader than that of the enforcement of contracts. They have, accordingly, claimed the power to interpret contracts broadly in terms of their evident purpose and to disregard certain kinds of provisions deemed unduly harsh.

To emphasize this contrast let me recall an arbitration award that has been widely regarded as a particularly bold piece of interpretation, reaching toward the limit of what is appropriate in labor arbitration. In this case, though there was no provision making discharges subject to the grievance procedure (including arbitration), the arbitrator held that such a provision was necessary implied.[3] He reasoned that this implication was essential to maintain the integrity of the rest of the contract, which contained the

---

3. In the Matter of Coca-Cola Bottling Co. (1949), reported in Cox & Bok, Cases on Labor Law 530 (5th ed. 1962).

usual grievance and seniority procedures. He observed that giving a man a right to present and arbitrate grievances is of little value if, at the first stirrings of discontent, his boss is free to throw him out of the plant. When we compare this award with the judicial holdings just passed in review—and I want to emphasize that the list could be expanded many times over—it seems odd indeed that the award should be regarded as involving any unusual standard of interpretation. The principle that you read into a contract those obligations that are essential to achieve its principal objectives is almost a judicial commonplace.

When the question is not that of infusing a contract with unexpressed implications, but rather that of construing particular words, I believe it can again be asserted that courts by and large proceed more freely than arbitrators —and I would again say, properly so. Arbitrators are especially likely to put a fairly strict interpretation on provisions that confer on individuals what may be called earned or acquired rights, like seniority and vacation benefits. These are a species of property. Now it is obvious that the courts themselves approach the law of property in a somewhat different spirit than they do, say, the law of torts. There is in property law a certain conceptual rigor, a willingness to draw black and white distinctions, that would be out of place in most areas of law, including that of ordinary contracts. The only thing peculiar in this respect about the collective bargaining agreement is that it has the side effect of establishing a system of earned privileges or rights—essentially property rights—in individuals. This is a quality not shared by contracts generally. In administering this aspect of the collective bargaining agreement, arbitrators proceed much as judges do in administering the law of property generally. This works toward a stricter type of interpretation than would be appropriate for contracts generally.

At this point it may be objected that the comparisons I have been making are irrelevant. If a meaningful comparison of interpretation by courts and by arbitrators is to be made, it ought not to be as to contracts generally, but with respect to the same kind of contract. Is it not true that in those cases where courts have had occasion to interpret collective bargaining agreements—chiefly in passing on the issue of arbitrability—they have favored a more literal and strict interpretation than have arbitrators? And does not this judicial inclination toward a strict and word-bound interpretation underlie the now widely felt concern lest the institution of arbi-

tration be impaired by an expanding judicial control over it?

These are questions that deserve careful consideration. In attempting to answer them, let us start by accepting the word "literal" in a sense frankly pejorative—for surely all would agree that an interpretation can be too "literal." What produces such an interpretation? One thing that can bring it about is an animosity toward the purpose of the document being interpreted. A perversely literal interpretation is one of the surest ways of making a contract unworkable. The classic example is the judgment in *Shylock's Case*. There are those who discern something similar in the carefree literalness with which courts sometimes approach the construction of labor contracts. One cannot dismiss this suspicion as wholly without warrant. Perhaps indeed there are judges who would be flattered by the comparison with Portia, who in their private moments like to think of themselves as rescuing the Merchant from the knife. The tone of occasional judicial utterances suggests as much.

The most common cause of an inept literalness, however, likes not in bias but in a lack of understanding. The innocent who asked why a player was permitted to continue in a baseball game after the umpire had told him he was "out," was not actuated by bias. He simply did not understand the game.

Labor relations have today become a highly complicated and technical field. This field involves complex procedures that vary from industry to industry, from plant to plant, from department to department. It has developed its own vocabulary. Though the terms of this vocabulary often seem simple and familiar, their true meaning can be understood only when they are seen as parts of a larger system of practice, just as the umpire's "You're out!" can only be fully understood by one who knows the objectives, the rules and the practices of baseball. I might add that many questions of industrial relations are on a level at least equal to that of the infield fly rule. They are not suitable material for light dinner conversation.

In the nature of things few judges can have had any very extensive experience in the field of industrial relations. Arbitrators, on the other hand, are compelled to acquire a knowledge of industrial processes, modes of compensation, complex incentive plans, job classifications, shift arrangements, and procedures for layoff and recall.

Naturally not all arbitrators stand on a parity with respect to this knowledge. But there are open to the arbitrator, even the novice, quick methods of education not available to courts. An arbitrator will frequently interrupt the examination of witnesses with a request that the parties educate him to the point where he can understand the testimony being received. This education can proceed informally, with frequent interruptions by the arbitrator, and by informed persons on either side, when a point needs clarification. Sometimes there will be arguments across the table, occasionally even within each of the separate camps. The end result will usually be a clarification that will enable everyone to proceed more intelligently with the case. There is in this informal procedure no infringement whatever of arbitrational due process. On the contrary, the party's chance to have his case understood by the arbitrator is seriously impaired if his representative has to talk into a vacuum, if he addresses his words to uncomprehending ears.

The education that an arbitrator can thus get, say, in a half an hour, might take days if it had to proceed by qualifying experts and subjecting them to direct and cross examination. The courts have themselves recognized the serious obstacle presented by traditional methods of proof in dealing with cases involving a complex technical background. In March of 1960 the Judicial Conference approved a *Handbook of Recommended Procedures for the Trial of Protracted Cases*. The text of this *Handbook* makes it clear that by "protracted cases" the Conference has in mind cases that are likely to be indefinitely protracted if difficult technical questions, say, of economics or engineering, are dealt with by conventional methods of proof. There is an analysis in the *Handbook* of the difficulties encountered by courts in anti-trust and patent cases. I believe that every item in this analysis has an equal application to complicated labor cases. I only regret that there is no explicit recognition of this fact in the *Handbook*. We would have gone a long way toward better understanding if we could think of the labor arbitrator performing a function much like that of the court-appointed referee or special master in cases involving patents, antitrust problems, water diversion issues and the like.

There is a second—and to my mind even more important—reason why courts are at a distinct disadvantage in dealing with problems involving industrial relations. The question they chiefly have to decide, that of arbitrability, is the most difficult question of all, and is virtually unanswerable within the frame of its usual submission for judicial decision. Let me explain what I mean.

In the first place the questions of the merits and that of arbitrability are generally—to put it mildly—closely intertwined. There are, to be sure,

cases of highly specific limitations on the arbitrator's power, such as an express stipulation that no question relating to pensions shall be arbitrated. Here there is no real penumbra of doubt and a straight-forward ruling on arbitrability is possible without trespassing on the merits. Unfortunately for the courts questions like these don't go to litigation. Usually you can't answer the question either of arbitrability or of the merits without answering another question: "Is there any provision of the contract that could be or has been broken?" Unfortunately, this question does not readily break into two pieces, one part of which determines arbitrability, the other the decision on the merits.

Let us examine how the matter typically comes up when arbitrability is passed on by the arbitrator himself, at least in the first instance. At the very outset of the hearing the company interposes the objection that the question submitted by the union is not arbitrable. Arguments are then heard on that issue. If the arbitrator had then to decide the case, he might rule either for or against arbitrability. But he would feel insecure in any such ruling. The language and facts adduced before him seem to add up to a prima facie case for or against arbitrability, but he knows from experience that things which seem simple at the outset often turn out to be complicated. Language that seems to mean one thing may have acquired a different meaning in the practice of the plant. The arbitrator cannot in good conscience rule until he has a chance to probe more deeply. Accordingly, he suggests that the question of arbitrability be reserved and that the parties proceed to the merits. He then hears the same story told a second time, but this time in three dimensions, as it were. When he comes to make his award, he may rule against arbitrability, in which case there is no occasion to discuss the merits, or he may rule in favor of arbitrability and then proceed to decide the merits. But in deciding on arbitrability he has the advantage of the testimony he heard on the merits.

I can imagine these remarks causing a chill of horror to run down the spines of those who are convinced in advance that all arbitrators are unprincipled triflers insensitive to procedural due process. But let us recall the peculiar intertwining of the merits and the question of arbitrability under the usual labor contract. The arbitrator has jurisdiction to decide the case only if there is some provision in the contract that might reasonably be thought to have been broken. The grievant wins on the merits only if the contract has been broken.

The arbitrator's reservation of a decision on

arbitrability as he goes into a hearing on the merits is not an empty form or an act of hypocrisy. Let me spell the thing out procedurally a little more precisely than is customary in practice. Suppose after hearing the arguments on arbitrability the arbitrator says, "I rule tentatively that the company is right in its contention that this dispute is not arbitrable ; it involves no provision of the contract that could be broken." The union says it wants a chance to show the history of the contract, to go into the way in which it has been administered and how the parties have in practice construed its provisions. The conscientious arbitrator cannot refuse to hear such evidence. But such evidence is equally relevant on both the merits and arbitrability and it would be a shameful waste of time, as well as a source of confusion, to go through it twice. But if this evidence does not suffice to overcome the tentative ruling against arbitrability, then the arbitrator will make that ruling absolute. He gives the union a chance to rebut the prima facie case against arbitrability. If it fails, the decision on arbitrability goes against it. Viewed in this light, proceeding to the merits while a final decision on arbitrability is reserved involves no prejudgment at all, but simply the adoption of an expeditious procedure in the interest of all concerned.

Contrast this procedure with that which is imposed on the parties and the court when arbitrability is judicially decided before the case goes to an arbitrator. A union, let us say, demands specific performance of an agreement to arbitrate contained in a collective bargaining agreement. The company defends on the ground that the grievance in question is not subject to arbitration. This frame of argument puts all concerned in a quandary. If the lawyer for either side attempts to go too deeply into such matters as the history of the contract, the practices that have arisen under it or the manner in which the particular grievance came up and how it was treated at earlier steps, he is likely to be reminded that he cannot argue the merits but must stick to arbitrability. The result is an abstractly presented case, a skeleton of the real facts. If the court decides on the basis of this presentation, it runs the risk of not really knowing what it is deciding. If the court itself seeks to go more deeply into the facts, it arouses the suspicion of being influenced by its views of the merits in making its decision on arbitrability.

Let me illustrate these points by reference to a much discussed case, that of Local 149, Am. Fed'n of Technical Eng'rs v. General Electric

Co.[4] This case is all the more significant because it was decided by a court which entered with evident reluctance upon a task it considered to be imposed on it by law.

In this case the union claimed that four men were improperly classified, that, in other words, they were performing duties falling within a classification higher than that actually assigned to them by the company. The suit was a petition for a decree of specific performance directing the company to arbitrate. The company defended on the ground that the grievance was not subject to arbitration under the contract. The contract contained a schedule of the rates to be paid to the various classifications, and contained no clause suggesting that the propriety of the classification assigned to a worker was beyond arbitration.

The district judge held for the company. It appeared that the jobs in question were "newly created." There was a provision in the contract that the arbitrator should have no power to establish a new wage rate or a new job classification. Therefore, the judge reasoned, if an arbitrator were to declare the classification assigned to the grievants improper he would be creating a new classification. This holding was rather patently based on a misunderstanding of the meaning of a job classification system. What the union wanted was a chance to urge the arbitrator to put the men in a slot different from that into which the company had put them, but the slot itself would not be created by the arbitrator but was one already created by agreement between the union and the company.

The court of appeals indicated its disagreement with the reasoning of the district judge. It upheld the refusal of specific performance, however, on a different ground. It relied on a general provision limiting the arbitrator to the function of interpreting and applying the agreement. There was in this case, so the court considered, nothing to interpret and apply. It was true that the contract referred to a system of job classifications, but the table purporting to set forth the classifications consisted merely of figures,— a vertical column of labor grades, and a horizontal column of appropriate rates. Nowhere was there any verbal description of the duties appropriate to the different labor grades. There was therefore nothing to interpret or apply.

I venture the opinion that if the contract had set forth, not numerical labor grades, but job titles, the decision would have been different. If the quarrel had been not whether the men should

---

4. 250 F. 2d 922 (1st Cir. 1957). Some of the assertions in the discussion of this case are based on the record.

be assigned Labor Grade No. 13 instead of No. 12, but should be classified as Methods Planners, Grade A, instead of Methods Planners, Grade B, the court would have perceived the possibility that these titles, though they were accompanied by no verbal description of the duties that went with them, might easily have gained content from the practice of the parties. It is easy to see that words need interpretation. Faced with the numeral "12" there seems no occasion for interpretation at all. But it is of course perfectly possible for a number indicating a labor grade to take on a specific meaning in much the same way that a verbal title can, especially since the company had obligated itself to provide the employee on hiring or transfer with a card designating his job classification.

What I have said is not in criticism of the court in this case, which, as I have said, evidenced a reluctance to assume a task it considered imposed on it by statute. My criticism is directed to the whole frame within which issues of this sort are presented to the court.

As I have said, the court in a case presented as this one was faces the hardest task of all. An arbitrator with a very wide experience in cases involving draftsmen and the various methods of classifying their jobs, might have decided the case with some assurance on the basis of the evidence before the court. But no one whose experience fell short of that standard could possibly do so.

A good many of the cases involving arbitrability contain suggestions of the argument that the apparent meaning of the contract's language has been modified by practice under it. In this connection I would recall that courts have held (1) that written contracts may be modified by subsequent oral agreements, (2) that such oral agreements may be effective even though the written contract expressly states that it can only be altered by an agreement written and signed,[5] and (3) that conduct as well as words may evidence an intention to change the terms of a contract.[6] I might add that to determine when a contractual provision has in fact been modified by practice is a subtle question requiring an intimate knowledge of the whole structure of the parties' relations. It is not a question that can be decided on the basis of a factual skeleton.

Another harmful cliché is that the courts mistakenly tend to treat collective bargaining agreements as if they were commercial contracts. In this case the cliché may contain an ironic element of unintended truth. Courts have in fact had difficulty with complicated commercial litigation. The problems here are not unlike those encountered in dealing with labor agreements. There are really few outstanding commercial judges in the history of the common law. The greatest of these, Lord Mansfield, used to sit with special juries selected from among experienced merchants and traders. To further his education in commercial practice he used to arrange dinners with his jurors. In Greek mythology it is reported that Minos prepared himself for a posthumous career as judge of shades by first exposing himself to every possible experience of life. It is not only in labor relations that the impracticability of such a program manifests itself.

At this point one remedy may suggest itself for the difficulties confronted by courts when they undertake to interpret collective bargaining agreements. Why, it may be asked, should they not use the device of the special master, as they do in other complicated litigations? The answer is that in labor relations there is usually already a special master—the arbitrator himself —who has been appointed by the parties or who is ready to be appointed through procedures established by agreement of the parties. To displace him from his appointed function is to destroy an essential element in the whole structure of industrial self-government.

There will be occasion later to return to the problem of interpretation for the purpose of relating it more closely to the problem of the role of arbitration generally in labor relations. Meanwhile it will be helpful to summarize the three relatively simple conclusions I have so far sought to support. *First*, there is nothing ineffably peculiar about the job of interpreting collective bargaining agreements. Such agreements are complicated and they contain provisions foreign to most contracts, such as those establishing a framework for industrial self-government. But we find similar provisions in long-term supply contracts, percentage leases and other specialized legal documents. Such documents may also involve what may be called constitutional aspects, establishing a private system of adjudication and providing procedures for accommodating the contract to changing circumstances. *Second,* intelligent interpretation of collective bargaining agreements requires an understanding of a complex and changing body of industrial practice. This understanding is not as a practical matter accessible to courts through ordinary procedures of proof. *Third*, in most cases there is and can be no sharp distinction between testimony bearing on the merits of a dispute and testimony

---

5. 6 WILLISTON, CONTRACTS § 1828 n.8 (rev. ed. 1938).
6. RESTATEMENT, CONTRACTS § 235, comment on (e) (1932).

bearing on the arbitrator's jurisdiction to hear the dispute. For this reason to determine the question of arbitrability on the basis of a fraction of the facts relevant to the case as a whole is to take a shot in the dark, a proceeding all the more dangerous when the marksman mistakenly thinks, as he often does, that he sees the target clearly.

III

Let me now turn to the other major controversy surrounding labor arbitration, that of the proper role of the arbitrator himself. Is his office essentially judicial, with all the restraints that term implies? Or shall we assign to him a freer role, something like that suggested by the term "labor-relations physician"?

Here we encounter the difficulty of defining the restraints of the judicial role in the case of one who does not hold public office in the ordinary sense of the word. Even the most ardent advocate of the view that the arbitrator's function is essentially judicial would hardly argue that his procedures should be patterned precisely after those applicable to courts of law. The problem then becomes that of defining in some more general sense what it means to act like a judge.

At this point one is tempted to discern the essence of the judicial function in a requirement that the decision reached be *informed* and *impartial*. This will not do, however. The expectation that judgments should be informed and impartial applies to many social roles: that of supervisors toward those under their direction, of teachers toward pupils, of parents toward children, and so forth. The essence of the judicial function lies not in the substance of the conclusion reached, but in the procedures by which that substance is guaranteed. One does not become a judge by acting intelligently and fairly, but by accepting procedural restraints designed to insure—so far as human nature permits—an impartial and informed outcome of the process of decision.

I believe there is open to us a relatively simple way of defining the procedural restraints to which the judicial role is subject. We can do this by looking at adjudication, not through the eyes of the judge, but through the eyes of the affected litigant. Adjudication we may define as a social process of decision which assures to the affected party a particular form of participation, that of presenting proofs and arguments for a decision in his favor.

Viewed in this light, adjudication is only one form of social decision in which the affected party is afforded an institutionally guaranteed participation. Elections grant to the affected party participation through voting; contracts grant to him participation through negotiation, either in person or through representatives. No procedure of decision guarantees any particular outcome and least of all an outcome favorable to any particular participant. But the essence of the rule of law lies in the fact that men affected by the decisions which emerge from social processes should have some formally guaranteed opportunity to affect those decisions.

Within this frame of thought we may say, then, that adjudication is a process of decision in which the affected party—"the litigant"—is afforded an institutionally guaranteed participation, which consists of the opportunity to present proofs and arguments for a decision in his favor. Whatever protects and enhances the effectiveness of that participation, advances the integrity of adjudication itself. Whatever impairs that participation detracts from its integrity. When that participation becomes a matter of grace, rather than of right, the process of decision ceases to deserve the name of adjudication.

From the analysis just presented can be derived, I believe, all of the restraints usually associated with an adjudicative role. Thus, interest or bias on the part of the adjudicator constitutes an obvious impairment of the interested party's participation through presenting proofs and arguments. So does the holding of private conferences, for the party not included in such a conference cannot know toward what he should be directing the presentation of his case. Matters are not squared when both parties are separately consulted, for then both are dependent on the candor and intelligence of the adjudicator in learning what the other side is saying, not to mention the more usual objections, such as the lack of an opportunity to cross-examine.

The test here suggested by no means coincides with popular prejudice concerning the judicial role. In this country there is a strong inclination to identify judicial behavior with passiveness, the judge being viewed as an umpire over a game in which he takes no active part until called upon by one of the parties to do so. The test here proposed renders a quite different judgment. If the arbiter of a dispute judges prematurely without hearing what both sides have to say, he obviously impairs the effectiveness of the parties' participation in the decision by proofs and arguments. On the other hand, that participation may be equally impaired if the parties are given no inkling at any time as to what is happening in the arbiter's mind. One cannot direct an effective argument into a vacuum. Accordingly it is the part of the wise arbitrator at some time, usually toward the end of the hearing, to convey to the parties some notion of the difficulties he finds in supporting or in answering certain of the arguments that have been addressed to him. He may find it useful also to summarize the arguments on each side, asking the parties to make corrections or additions so that he may be sure he fully grasps what each is contending for. Such discussions, initiated by the arbitrator himself, take him out of a purely passive role. It is plain, however, that they enhance meaningful participation by the parties in the decision and thus enhance the integrity of adjudication itself.

Perhaps the crassest infringement of adjudicative integrity consists in what has been called the "rigged award." In its most extreme form this means that although the affected parties think their case is being submitted to arbitrational decision, in fact their representatives have already agreed on the outcome to be incorporated in the award. It might seem that this procedure involves not so much an abuse of arbitration as a fraud by representatives on their constituents. But it should not be forgotten that the object of the whole manipulation is to secure the moral force of adjudication for what is in fact not adjudicated at all. The apparent participation of the affected party—through proofs and arguments presented on his behalf—is an empty sham. This problem of the "rigged," or more politely, the "informed" award deserves some analysis. Such an analysis will reveal that, while in some cases to clothe an agreement with the trappings of an award will constitute a plain abuse of adjudicative power, in other instances the appraisal is less obvious.

Let me take two extreme cases, beginning with an instance where the practice is presented in its most innocent form. Six grievances are scheduled for hearing over a three-day period. These grievances are all closely related, involving, let us say, a series of work-load or machine-assignment problems. Late on the third day the sixth case has still not been heard. If it is to be heard at all, a new hearing will have to be scheduled and this will be difficult. Though the arbitrator has as yet rendered no formal award in any of the cases heard, the drift of his mind has become apparent during the hearing of the first five cases, and the disposition of the sixth is not hard to predict. The parties' representatives agree on a solution of it and ask the arbitrator to incorporate their settlement in an award. If the first five cases were reported to the membership as settled by arbitration, while the sixth

was reported as settled by agreement, quite unjustified suspicions and doubts would be aroused. Hence the arbitrator is willing to put the agreed settlement "in series," as it were, with its five companions. It would take a purist indeed to discern any real wickedness in this action.

At the other extreme is the case where an arbitrator is paid handsomely to hold extended hearings, where a parade of witnesses is heard, where lawyers plead with heart-stirring eloquence, when all the while the whole thing has been rigged and fixed from the beginning and the whole hearing is a farce from start to finish. I agree with Willard Wirtz that even if awards rendered in cases like this always produced a short-run advantage judged from the standpoint of public welfare, the long-run cost would be too high to pay. Such an arbitrational practice is essentially parasitic. It takes advantage of the fact that most awards are honest, for if all awards were known to be fixed there would be no point in masquerading an agreement as the decision of an arbitrator. One recalls here the remark of Schopenhauer, that the prostitute owes her bargaining power to the restraint of virtuous women.

It should be observed that in cases like that just suggested, the "fixed" award may involve a by-passing of procedural guarantees surrounding the negotiation of the collective bargaining agreement itself. Those representing the union in an arbitration would seldom possess the power acting by themselves to negotiate a contract binding on the union. Thus, in the typical case where the arbitration involves the wages to be paid under a new contract, the arbitrator becomes an accomplice in circumventing limitations on the agency of the union's representatives.

At the extremes, passing judgment on the "agreed" award is relatively easy. In the middle area of gray, arriving at a valid appraisal requires a greater exercise of individual responsibility. One thing seems to me clear, however. In deciding what he should do the arbitrator is not entitled to take the easy way out by saying, "After all, the purpose of arbitration is to promote good labor relations. If I can head off an unjustified and futile strike by issuing as an arbitrator's decision what is really an agreed settlement, then my conscience is clear." Before taking this escape the arbitrator should reflect that he is trustee for the integrity of the processes of decision entrusted to his care. He should ask himself whether the argument for bending his powers for good is not like that of the man who, in order to give to a worthy charity, embezzles funds entrusted to his care for an undeserving nephew. In practice the temptation to take short cuts in order to do good is a much greater threat to the integrity of arbitration than the temptation to use its forms for evil purposes.

Before leaving this question of the "informed" award—so that none of its nuances may be left unnoticed—it should be remarked that the problem can arise within the framework of an arbitration wholly conducted within the strictest judicial restraints. Effective advocacy sometimes suggests that the advocate give some intimation in his argument of the most acceptable form of an adverse decision in the event such a decision should be rendered. It needs hardly to be said that such intimations, though conveyed "in open court" and in the presence of all affected, are not always perceived by an inattentive audience. This tincturing of the argument with intimations of settlement, instead of employing more direct and reliable channels of communication, may seem to some the essence of hypocrisy. To others it will represent that deference for symbolism without which social living is impossible.

There remains the difficult problem of mediation by the arbitrator, who instead of issuing an award, undertakes to persuade the parties to reach a settlement, perhaps reinforcing his persuasiveness with "the gentle threat" of a decision. Again, there is waiting a too-easy answer: "Judges do it." Of course, judges sometimes mediate, or at least bring pressure on the parties for a voluntary settlement. Sometimes this is done usefully and sometimes in ways that involve an abuse of office. In any event the judiciary has evolved no uniform code with respect to this problem that the arbitrator can take over ready-made. Judicial practice varies over a wide range. If the arbitrator were to pattern his conduct after the worst practices of the bench, arbitration would be in a sad way.

Analysis of the problem as it confronts the arbitrator should begin with a recognition that mediation (or conciliation, the terms being largely interchangeable) has an important role to play in the settlement of labor disputes. There is much to justify a system whereby it is a prerequisite to arbitration that an attempt first be made by a skilled mediator to bring about a voluntary settlement. This requirement has at times been imposed in a variety of contexts. Under such systems the mediator is, I believe, invariably someone other than the arbitrator. This is as it should be.

Mediation and arbitration have distinct purposes and hence distinct moralities. The morality of mediation lies in optimum settlement, a settlement in which each party gives up what he values less, in return for what he values more.

The morality of arbitration lies in a decision according to the law of the contract. The procedures appropriate for mediation are those most likely to uncover that pattern of adjustment which will most nearly meet the interests of both parties. The procedures appropriate for arbitration are those which most securely guarantee each of the parties a meaningful chance to present arguments and proofs for a decision in his favor. Thus, private consultations with the parties, generally wholly improper on the part of the arbitrator, are an indispensable tool of mediation.

Not only are the appropriate procedures different in the two cases, but the facts sought by those procedures are different. There is no way to define "the essential facts" of a situation except by reference to some objective. Since the objective of reaching an optimum settlement is different from that of rendering an award according to the contract, the facts relevant in the two cases are different, or, when they seem the same, are viewed in different aspects. If a person who has mediated unsuccessfully attempts to assume the role of arbitrator, he must endeavor to view the facts of the case in a completely new light, as if he had previously known nothing about them. This is a difficult thing to do. It will be hard for him to listen to proofs and arguments with an open mind. If he fails in this attempt, the integrity of adjudication is impaired.

These are the considerations that seem to me to apply where the arbitrator attempts to mediate before hearing the case at all. This practice is quite uncommon, and would largely be confined to situations where a huge backlog of grievances seemed to demand drastic measures toward an Augean clean-up. I want now to pass to consideration of the case where the arbitrator postpones his mediative efforts until after the proofs are in and the arguments have been heard. In doing so I pass over the situation where the arbitrator interrupts the hearing midway in order to seek a voluntary settlement. The standards properly applicable to this intermediate situation may be derived from those governing the two cases that lie on either side of it.

One might ask of mediation first undertaken after the hearing is over, what is the point of it? If the parties do not like the award, they are at liberty to change it. If there is some settlement that will effect a more apt adjustment of their interests, their power to contract for that settlement is the same after, as it is before, the award is rendered. One answer would be to say that if the arbitrator undertakes mediation after the hearing but before the award, he can use "the gentle threat" of a decision to induce settlement, keeping it uncertain as to just what the decision will be. Indeed, if he has a sufficiently Machiavellian instinct, he may darkly hint that the decision will contain unpleasant surprises for both parties. Conduct of this sort would, however, be most unusual. Unless the role thus assumed were played with consummate skill, the procedure would be likely to explode in the arbitrator's face.

There is, however, a more convincing argument for mediative efforts after the hearing and before the award. This lies in the peculiar fact —itself a striking tribute to the moral force of the whole institution of adjudication—that an award tends to resist change by agreement. Once rendered it seems to have a kind of moral inertia that puts a heavy onus on the party who proposes any modification by mutual consent. Hence if there exists the possibility of a voluntary settlement that will suit both parties better than the award, the last chance to obtain it may occur after the hearing and before the award is rendered. This may in fact be an especially propitious moment for a settlement. Before the hearing it is quite usual for each of the parties to underestimate grossly the strength of his adversary's case. The hearing not uncommonly "softens up" both parties for settlement.

What, then, are the objections to an arbitrator's undertaking mediative efforts after the hearing and before rendering the award, this being often so advantageous a time for settlement? Again, the objection lies essentially in the confusion of role that results. In seeking a settlement the arbitrator turned mediator quite properly learns things that should have no bearing on his decision as an arbitrator. For example, suppose a discharge case in which the arbitrator is virtually certain that he will decide for reinstatement though he is striving to keep his mind open until he has a chance to reflect on the case in the quiet of his study. In the course of exploring the possibilities of a settlement he learns that, contrary to the position taken by the union at the hearing, respectable elements in the union would like to see the discharge upheld. Though they concede that the employee was probably innocent of the charges made by the company, they regard him as an ambitious trouble maker the union would be well rid of. If the arbitrator fails to mediate a settlement, can he block this information out when he comes to render his award?

It is important that an arbitrator not only respect the limits of his office in fact, but that he also *appear* to respect them. The parties to an arbitration expect the arbitrator to decide the dispute, not according to what pleases the parties, but by what accords with the contract. Yet as a mediator he must explore the parties' interests and seek to find out what would please them. He cannot be a good mediator unless he does. But if he has then to surrender his role as mediator to resume that of adjudicator, can his award ever be fully free from the suspicion that it was influenced by a desire to please one or both of the parties?

Finally, in practice, the settlement mediated after the hearing will seldom be free from some taint of being "rigged." Indeed, when an agreement is reached under the express or implied threat of an award, the distinction between agreement and award is lost; the "rigged award" blends into the coerced settlement, and it may at a given time be uncertain which will emerge from the discussions. During these discussions it is most unusual for all affected to know at all times just what is going on.

These, then, are the arguments against the arbitrator's undertaking the task of mediation. They can all be summed up in the phrase, "confusion of role."

In practice departures from the strict judicial role are most common in the case of the so-called permanent umpire, who may preside over disputes between the same parties for many year. In such a situation success in combining the role of arbitrator with that of mediator attests not only to the arbitrator's professional skill, but to the depth of trust imposed in him by the parties. The role of arbitrator-mediator thus becomes doubly satisfying and the temptation to assume it correspondingly greater. Furthermore, with the permanent umpire, departures from the judicial role tend to become cumulative. As the parties discover his willingness to resolve all controversies—including those unsuited to decision within the restraints of a judicial role—they are likely to become more and more dependent upon him. He becomes in effect a kind of super-manager. In the short run this role can relieve both union and management of many inconvenient responsibilities. The cost in the long run is that the moral force of the judicial role has been forfeited. It is no longer available as a reserve for meeting an eventual crisis. Meanwhile, the parties' capacity for unaided self-government may have suffered a serious decline through disuse.

The picture just drawn may lean a little toward the dismal. At the same time it is vitally important, I believe, that the apparent successes of mediative arbitration by permanent umpires be appraised with a full understanding of the situations in which they have occurred. Was the industry in question, for example, economically sick? Sick industries may need, not judges, but physicians, though, as with individuals, a sign of returning health would be a restored capacity to dispense with medical care. Again, did the apparent successes of mediative arbitration entail hidden costs not revealed in reports that confine themselves to the disposition of disputes? In this respect it is most unfortunate that readers of Harry Shulman's famous Holmes Lecture do not have available to them a careful appraisal of the effects of the philosophy therein expounded upon the total labor relations of the Ford Motor Company. Without that appraisal any judgment is bound to be one-sided.

Sometimes judgment on the issues here under discussion is influenced by a kind of slogan to the effect that an agreed settlement is always better than an imposed one. As applied to disputes before they have gone to arbitration this slogan has some merit. When the case is in the hands of the arbitrator, however, I can see little merit in it, except in the special cases I have tried previously to analyse. After all, successful industrial self-government requires not only the capacity to reach and abide by agreements, but also the willingness to accept and conform to disliked awards. It is well that neither propensity be lost through disuse. Furthermore, there is something slightly morbid about the thought that an agreement coerced by the threat of decision is somehow more wholesome than an outright decision. It suggests a little the father who wants his children to obey him, but who, in order to still doubts that he may be too domineering, not only demands that they obey but insists that they do so with a smile. After having had his day in court, a man may with dignity bend his will to a judgment of which he disapproves. That dignity is lost if he is compelled to pretend that he agreed to it.

The *ad hoc* arbitrator, called in to decide a single case, will usually be most strongly moved to undertake mediation when it becomes apparent to him that what the parties really need is not someone to judge their dispute, but a labor relations adviser. For example, a company, inexperienced in collective bargaining and perhaps generally inept in labor relations, may be insisting on its pound of flesh—which, to be sure, it is entitled to under the contract—without being aware of the price it will pay for its victory in worsened labor relations. There is no easy way out of such a predicament for the arbitrator. In most cases he will do well to proceed with his assigned role, consoling himself with the thought that there is no better teacher than experience. He should think long and hard before employing the written opinion as an outlet

for his pedagogical inclinations. Perhaps later on, after the award has been rendered, some discussion might be in order if his relationship with the party concerned seems to suggest it might be useful.

Throughout this paper I have asserted that adjudication is a *social* process of decision. This is true not only in the sense that it is a process of decision in which the affected party is afforded an institutionally guaranteed form of participation. It is also true in the sense that the success of adjudication, and the maintenance of its integrity, depend not only on the arbitrator, but on everyone connected with the process as a whole. It has been said that it is impossible for a judge to rise above the level of the bar practicing before him. So it may become virtually impossible for the arbitrator to perform his proper role if the parties—through ignorance, ineptness or selfish interest—are constantly pushing him out of that role. Unions not uncommonly come to view arbitration as a kind of general-purpose facility, ready to solve their internal problems or to lend a friendly hand winning over doubtful workers. Management, in turn, has its special techniques for bending arbitration to its own ends. A company that has never really accepted collective bargaining may, by refusing to settle anything, overload arbitration to the point of breakdown. Naturally in such a situation it will demand of the arbitrator the strictest judicial properties, a circumstance that has much embarrassed the struggle to preserve the integrity of the arbitrator's role.

A viable system of law requires that parties be willing to settle the great bulk of disputes out of court. It requires not only a willingness to settle cases that are reasonably certain to be decided against the conceding party, but also to settle at least some cases he could be quite certain of winning if they were taken to litigation. The decision of a dispute by law is not always the same thing as a wise disposition of it. People who are always demanding their "rights" can be a menace to any society. One of the responsibilities of the parties to a collective bargaining agreement is to ease the strains on arbitration by not litigating cases where there is an obvious tension between the result demanded by the terms of the contract and that which accords with practical wisdom in labor relations.

I have just been asserting that a large part of the responsibility for maintaining the integrity of arbitration rests with the parties. I do not wish to be understood as suggesting, however, that the arbitrator is entitled to thrust on the parties the whole responsibility for his role. I emphatically reject the contention made by Harry Shulman that in appraising such practices as "meeting with the parties separately" the "dangers envisaged with respect to judges and other governmental personnel are not equally applicable" to the arbitrator, for, "the parties' control of the process and their individual power to continue or terminate the services of the arbitrator are adequate safeguards against these dangers."

The democratic principle does not require us, I submit, to indulge in the fiction that whatever institutions develop in a particular situation must be viewed as approved by those affected by them. There is generally no real sense, for example, in which it can be said that the workers in a particular factory have approved either a loose or a strict interpretation of the arbitrator's role. In such a matter only a few key figures, chiefly the arbitrator himself, have that sense of alternatives which is required for intelligent choice.

Successful arbitration obviously depends upon successful collective bargaining. It is from the collective bargaining agreement that arbitration derives its standards. If those standards are clearly and properly set, they will shape the award toward the needs of industrial self-government as seen by those most directly in contact with its problems. Reasonably clear standards contractually established are also essential for the integrity of arbitration. Without them the bond of participation that characterizes adjudication may be lost. Carelessly drawn agreements invite, may indeed demand, a departure by the arbitrator from his proper role. In this case the damage done becomes cumulative, since arbitration is almost certain to become overloaded if there are no standards to govern the settlement of grievances short of arbitration.

Conversely, the institution of collective bargaining can be undermined if the arbitrator casts off all restraints, assumes a variety of discordant roles, and presides generally over a process of decision from which may emerge, almost indifferently, a half-coerced agreement or a half-agreed award. In any such procedural chaos the guideline of the agreement is inevitably forfeited. When the agreement ceases to play a significant role in arbitration, the incentive to draft it carefully and fairly is lost.

CHAPTER X

LABOR ARBITRATION AND THE LAW—BASIC ISSUES AND DOCTRINES

As with commercial arbitration, the practice of labor arbitration predated statutes that made arbitration agreements enforceable. Some unions and employers found it useful without the coercive power of law to enforce the promise to arbitrate. In a few highly unionized industries arbitration became common after the First World War, although the construction industry, one of the few organized, hardly used it.

In states with "modern" acts, some cases found their way into court, primarily for the enforcement of awards. The statutes' subpoena powers may have been useful in giving arbitration clauses some coercive force. But by and large, the statutes were not a major force in spreading the use of arbitration, possibly because unionization itself was so limited before the constitutionality of the Wagner Act was upheld in 1937 and the consequent organization of some of the major industries in the very late thirties and early forties.

World War II created conditions favorable to unionization, and it spread. At the same time, work stoppages due to grievances and disputes were considered intolerable. The War Labor Board encouraged the use of arbitration as an alternative to its own mandatory procedures; the arbitrators were WLB staff, neutral members of regional boards, or their appointees. Although thus rooted in coercion, the institution apparently gained favor because the end of the war saw continued widespread use of labor arbitration, quite often with the use of the same neutrals as during the war. Indeed, WLB alumni form the core of the labor arbitration fraternity, including many party representatives.

The 1947 enactment of the Taft-Hartley Act had no immediate impact upon arbitration despite provisions for suit for violation of contract in section 301, a Congressional declaration favoring "final adjustment by a method agreed upon by the parties . . . for settlement of disputes arising over the application or interpretation of an existing collective-bargaining agreement" in section 203(d), and a provision in section 10(k), governing jurisdictional disputes, that the National Labor Relations Board would hold a hearing to determine the dispute unless the parties settled it or had agreed upon a method of "voluntary adjustment." These statutory provisions had a profound effect although not wholly the expected ones and not very quickly.

Although section 301 was designed to make labor organizations more observant of contract undertakings not to strike, unions soon sought specific enforcement of agreements to arbitrate under it, alleging that the refusal was a violation of the contract. Many federal courts agreed, but the constitutionality of the section came into question.

A.

Section 301, LMRA:* Procedural or Substantive?

ASS'N OF WESTINGHOUSE EMPLOYEES v. WESTINGHOUSE ELECTRIC CORP.
348 U.S. 437 (1955)

FRANKFURTER, J. (plurality opinion): The Court of Appeals for the Third Circuit, sitting *en banc*, three judges dissenting, vacated the district courts order dismissing the complaint on the merits, and directed a dismissal for lack of jurisdiction. After stating that § 301 "is a grant of federal-question jurisdiction and thus creates a federal, substantive right" and reviewing various theories explaining the relationship between union, employer and employees under a collective bargaining agreement, the court adopted an "eclectic theory," based primarily upon language in J. I. Case Co. v. Labor Board, 321 U.S. 332. The bargaining contract, said the Court, obligates the employer to include in the contracts of hire with each employee the terms and conditions which had been settled between the union and the employer, but the collective contract itself is not a contract of hire. Not until an employee enters into an individual contract of hire and performs services does the employer become bound to pay the particular employee the specified wages. It follows, said the Court, that if there was a breach in this case, it was a breach of the employment contracts with the individual employees who were not paid. Section 301, on the other hand, grants jurisdiction to federal courts only over cases involving breaches of the collective bargaining contract between the union and the employer. Therefore, it was concluded, the district court was without jurisdiction of the suit. 210 F. 2d 623.

1. In dealing with an enactment such as § 301 of the Labor Management Relations Act, it is necessary first to ascertain its jurisdictional scope, more particularly, whether it extends to the suit at hand. Here, as may not infrequently be the case, this question turns in large measure on what sources a federal court would be required to draw upon in determining the underlying substantive rights of the parties—in this case, in deciding whether the union has the contract right which it asserts. If Congress has itself defined the law or authorized the federal courts to fashion the judicial rules governing this question, it would be self-defeating to limit the scope of the power of the federal courts to less than is necessary to accomplish this congressional aim. If, on the other hand, Congress merely furnished a federal forum for enforcing the body of contract law which the States provide, a serious constitutional problem would lie at the threshold of jurisdiction. Moreover, if the function of § 301 is merely that of providing a federal forum for state law, there are good reasons for finding that, despite the broad wording of § 301, Congress did not intend to confer jurisdiction over this type of suit.

If the section is given the meaning its language spontaneously yields, it would seem clear that all it does is to give procedural directions to the federal courts. "When an unincorporated association that happens to be a labor union appears before you as a litigant in a case involving breach of a collective agreement," Congress in effect told the district judges, "treat it as though it were a natural or corporate legal person and do so regardless of the amount in controversy and do not require diversity of citizenship."

Since a statute like the Taft-Hartley Act is an organism, § 301 must be placed in the context of the legislation as a whole. So viewed, however, the meaning which the section by itself affords is not affected. While some sections of the Act in certain instances may be relevant in actions for breach of contract and as such binding also on the States, no provision suggests general application of defined or theretofore available federal substantive law in actions arising under § 301.

Congressional concern with obstacles surrounding union litigation began to manifest itself as

---

*The text appears in Appendix D.

early as 1943. In the first session of the 78th Congress and thereafter numerous bills were introduced proposing various solutions, including federal incorporation, denial of rights under the Wagner Act to contract violators, creation of a cause of action for strikes and other acts in violation of the collective bargaining contract, and grants of federal jurisdiction similar to the present § 301. Only one of these, the so-called "Case bill," was acted upon. This bill, which passed both Houses in 1946, only to fail through President Truman's veto, included as § 10 a provision somewhat similar to the present section. That section passed the House in the following form:

> *Sec. 10. Binding Effect of Collective-Bargaining Contracts.*—All collective-bargaining contracts shall be mutually and equally binding and enforceable against each of the parties thereto, any other law to the contrary notwithstanding. In the event of a breach of any such contract or of any agreement contained in such contract by either party thereto, then, in addition to any other remedy or remedies existing, a suit for damages for such breach may be maintained by the other party or parties in any State or United States district court having jurisdiction of the parties. H.R. 4908, 79th Cong., 2d Sess.

Discussion in that chamber was not enlightening, due perhaps to the fact that the Case bill had been substituted on the House floor for the text of a very different bill and thus had never been considered in committee. Section 10 was presented as necessary to achievement of "mutuality" of obligation between employer and union, but there was no guiding explanation of the nature of the obstacle to mutuality. The language of the section, however, gave support to the view that a federal cause of action was to be created.

After the bill passed the House, hearings were held on it by the Senate Committee on Education and Labor, during which Senator Taft pointed out to Representative Case that, in his view, the section as written failed to deal with the real problem, which was not substantive enforceability but procedural difficulty in obtaining jurisdiction over unincorporated labor organizations. Mr. Case agreed that the section should be redrafted to reach that problem. The Committee reported the bill without § 10, asserting that as it passed the House the section was "based upon a misapprehension as to the legal responsibility of the parties under such contracts," that such contracts "are at present legally enforceable in the courts," and that to promote litigation concerning them would be undesirable.

Senators Ball, Taft and H. Alexander Smith filed a minority report conceding that collective agreements "theoretically are legally enforceable contracts" but contending that action was necessary to overcome practical obstacles to enforcement arising from the status of unions as unincorporated associations. They proposed a differently worded section later adopted in substance by both Houses, which closely approximated the wording of the present § 301.

In introducing this proposed amendment, Senator Taft stated.

> All we provide in the amendment is that voluntary associations shall in effect be suable as if they were corporations, and suable in the Federal courts if the contract involves interstate commerce and therefore involves a Federal question. 92 Cong. Rec. 5705.

This rather casual *non sequitur* seems to suggest reliance not on the existence or establishment of any substantive federal law governing collective bargaining contracts to create a "federal question" in the technical sense relevant to jurisdiction of district courts, but on the mere power of Congress to enact such law. While some statements on the Senate floor by opponents of the amendment are ambiguous, all authoritative materials indicate the strictly procedural aim of the section. The aim was to open the federal courts to suits on agreements solely because they were between labor organizations and employers without providing federal law for such suits.

In the first session of the 80th Congress, bills introduced independently in both Houses contained sections strikingly similar to the final version of § 10 of the Case bill. Discussion was more analytical. While generalities in praise of mutuality and enforceability reappear, it was evident that the specific desire was to remove procedural obstacles to suit by and against the union. Senator Pepper and Secretary of Labor Schwellenbach deemed the measure one "to provide a Federal forum" for suits on contracts based on local law. It was assumed that this would result in mutual enforceability, which in turn would further labor harmony. The testimony of Secretary Schwellenbach (who together with the labor unions opposed § 301, minority reports in both Houses, and opposition statements on the floor of the Senate directed attention to the fact that state law would govern actions under § 301 and that this, diversity jurisdiction apart, would raise a substantial constitutional question. No denial of the first of these assertions appears. Senator Taft did not justify § 301 as dependent on federal substantive law governing interpretation of collective bargaining contracts:

> Mr. President, title III of the bill . . . makes unions suable in the Federal courts for violation of contract. As a matter of law unions, of course, are liable in theory on their contracts today, but as a practical matter it is difficult to sue them. They are not incorporated; they have many members; in some States all the members must be served; it is difficult to know who is to be served. But the pending bill provides they can be sued as if they were corporations and if a judgment is found against the labor organization, even though it is an unincorporated association, the liability is on the labor union and the labor-union funds, and it is not on the individual members of the union, where it has fallen in some famous cases to the great financial distress of the individual members of labor unions. 93 Cong. Rec. 3839.

Legislative history, in its relevant aspects, thus reinforces the meaning conveyed by the statute itself as a mere procedural provision.

2. From this conclusion inevitably emerge questions regarding the constitutionality of a grant of jurisdiction to federal courts over a contract governed entirely by state substantive law, a jurisdiction not based on diversity of citizenship yet one in which a federal court would, as in diversity cases, administer the law of the State in which it sits. The scope of allowable federal judicial power that this grant must satisfy is constitutionally defined as

> Cases, in Law and Equity, arising under this Constitution, the Laws of the United States, and Treaties made, or which shall be made, under their Authority. Art. III, § 2.

Almost without exception, decisions under the general statutory grants of jurisdiction strikingly similar to the constitutional wording, have tested jurisdiction in terms of the presence, as an integral part of plaintiff's cause of action, of an issue calling for interpretation or application of federal law. Although it has sometimes been suggested that the "cause of action" must derive from federal law, it has been found sufficient that some aspect of federal law is essential to plaintiff's success. The litigation-provoking problem has been the degree to which federal law must be in the forefront of the case and not be remote, collateral or peripheral.

It has generally been assumed that the full constitutional power has not been exhausted by these general jurisdictional statutes. And in two lines of decision, under special jurisdictional grants for actions by or against federally incorporated organizations and trustees in bankruptcy, federal jurisdiction has been sustained despite the fact that the traditional "federal question" theory of jurisdiction has considerable latitude if satisfied by the contingent likelihood of presentation of a federal question. Analysis of these cases in terms of that theory reveals analogies to § 301. For federal law is, in certain respects, in the background of any action on a collective bargaining agreement affecting commerce: § 301 vests rights and liabilities, which under state law are distributed among the union members, in a legal "entity" recognized by federal law for purposes of actions on collective bargaining agreements in the federal courts; in such actions, the validity of the agreement may be challenged on federal grounds—that the labor organization negotiating it was not the representative of the employees involved, or that subsequent changes in the representative status of the union have affected the continued validity of the agreement.

3. In an effort to avoid these problems, lower federal courts have given discordant answers. Most have ascribed to § 301 the creation of "substantive federal rights" or the subjection of collective agreements to a body of federal common law. We must, of course, defer to the strong presumption—even as to such technical matters as federal jurisdiction—that Congress legislated in accordance with the Constitution. Legislation must, if possible, be given a meaning that will enable it to survive. This rule of constitutional adjudication is normally invoked to narrow what would otherwise be the natural but constitutionally dubious scope of the language. *E.g.,* United States v. Delaware & Hudson Co., 213 U.S. 366; United States v. Rumely, 345 U.S. 41. Here the endeavor of lower courts has resulted in adding to the section substantive congressional regulation even though Congress saw fit not to exercise such power nor to give the courts any concrete guidance for defining such regulation.

To be sure, the full scope of a substantive regulation is frequently in dispute and must await authoritative determination by courts. Congress declares its purpose imperfectly or partially and the judiciary rounds it out compatibly. But in this case we start with a provision which is wholly jurisdictional and as such bristles with constitutional problems under Article III. To avoid them, interpolation of substantive regulation has been proposed. From what materials are we to draw a determination that § 301 is something other than what it clearly appears to be? The problem is particularly vexing in view of the very difficult choice of policy that the alternatives of state or federal law present and the uncertainty as to the consequences of the choice. Is the Court justified in creating all these difficult problems of choice in matters of delicate legislative policy without any direction from Congress and merely for the sake of giving effect to a provision which seems to deal with a different subject? How far are courts to go in reshaping or transforming the obvious design of Congress in order to achieve validity for something Congress has not fashioned? In the words of Mr. Justice Cardozo, speaking for the whole Court:

> We think the light is so strong as to flood whatever places in the statute might otherwise be dark. Courts have striven mightily at times to canalize construction along the path of safety. . . . When a statute is reasonably susceptible of two interpretations, they have preferred the meaning that preserves to the meaning that destroys. . . . "But avoidance of a difficulty will not be pressed to the point of disingenuous evasion." . . . "Here the intention of the Congress is revealed too distinctly to permit us to ignore it because of mere misgivings as to power." Hopkins Federal Savings & Loan Assn. v. Cleary, 296 U.S. 315, 334–335.

But assuming that we would be justified in proceeding further, the suggestion that the section permits the federal courts to work out without more a federal code governing collective bargaining contracts does not free us from difficulties.

Such a task would involve the federal courts in multiplying problems which could not be solved without disclosing that Congress never intended to raise them. Application of a body of federal common law would inevitably lead to one of the following incongruities. (1) conflict in federal and state court interpretations of collective bargaining agreements; (2) displacement of state law by federal law in state courts, not only in actions between union and employer but in all actions regarding collective bargaining agreements; or (3) exclusion of state court jurisdiction over these matters. It would also be necessary to work out a federal code governing the inter-relationship between the employee's rights and whatever rights were found to exist in the union. Moreover, if the general unfolding of such broad application of federal law were designed, the procedural objectives of Congress would have been accomplished without the need of any special jurisdictional statute. Federal rights would be in issue, and, under 28 U.S.C. § 1331 and Federal Rule 17 (b), the suit could be brought in any district court by or against the union as an entity. The only effect of § 301 would then be to dispense with the requirement of amount in controversy and to adopt certain other minor procedural rules.

It has been suggested that a more modest role might be assigned to federal law. The suggestion

is that, in view of the difficulties which originally plagued the courts called upon to identify the nature of the legal relations created by a collective contract[1] and in view of the generalized statements in the legislative history of § 301 in favor of enforceability of collective agreements, § 301 may be viewed as a congressional authorization to the federal courts to work out a concept of the nature of the collective bargaining contract, leaving detailed questions of interpretation to state law.

This is an excessively sophisticated attribution to Congress. Evidence is wholly wanting that Congress was aware of the diverse views taken of the collective bargaining agreement or, in any event, that they were interfering with any federal objective. Moreover, once the right of the union to enter into contracts is granted by state law, these problems are really questions of interpretation of the language of ambiguously drawn contracts. If federal law undertook to resolve these ambiguities, it would become inextricably involved in questions of interpretation of the language of contracts. Discrepancies between federal and state court treatment, while not so inevitable as where federal law undertook the entire task of interpretation, would result. And any difference between state and federal theories of enforceability would present opportunities for forum-shopping.

To turn § 301 into an agency for working out a viable theory of the nature of a collective bargaining agreement smacks of unreality. Nor does it seem reasonable to view that section as a delivery into the discretionary hands of the federal judiciary, finally of this Court, of such an important, complicated and subtle field. These difficulties may be illustrated by a discussion of the holding of the Court of Appeals in the present case. Its "eclectic theory" of the nature of a collective agreement has no support in the statute, and, on the contrary, it is in some ways repugnant to it. (1) For example, the National Labor Relations Act seeks in § 9 (a) to preserve the "right" of an individual employee to take up grievances with his employer; but no

---

1. The collective agreement was variously viewed as: (1) the mere formulation of usage or custom relevant to the interpretation of the individual employment contract; (2) a contract between the employer and the individual member-employees, negotiated by the union as the employees' agent; (3) a contract between the union and employer for the benefit of the individual employees; and (4) as held by the court below, a contract between the union and employer giving the union certain rights, including the right to insist that the employer contract with his employees consistently with the terms of the agreement, but giving the union no right to enforce obligations running to individuals under their contracts of hire.

one has ever suggested that these grievances may not be taken up by the union. (2) It excludes from the court stage the party that is recognized in the required preliminary stages. The union that is empowered to negotiate and settle the controversy before suit is barred from bringing suit when settlement is not reached. (3) This would tend to impair the union's power to negotiate a mutually satisfactory settlement. As a practical matter, the employees expect their union not just to secure a collective agreement but more particularly to procure for the individual employees the benefits promised. If the union can secure only the promise and is impotent to procure for the individual employees the promised benefits, then it is bound to lose their support. And if the union cannot ultimately resort to suit, it is encouraged to resort to strike action.

Perhaps the prime example of an individual cause of action, as distinguished from a union cause, under the Court of Appeals' "eclectic theory," would be the case of the discharge of a single employee. To make the situation vivid, assume that there is no dispute whatever as to the propriety of the alleged ground for the discharge and that the only matter in controversy is the question of fact whether the employee did or did not commit the offense alleged. Yet precisely such incidents often pull the trigger of work stoppages. When stoppages do occur, they most frequently involve a grievance with respect to one employee or a few employees much smaller in number than those involved in the stoppage. That such stoppages are wildcat and officially unauthorized merely emphasizes the fact of group interest in the incident. It is a matter of industrial history that stoppages of work because of disciplinary penalties against individuals, or because of failure to pay the rates claimed, or because of the promotion or layoff of one employee rather than another, or for similar reasons, have been frequent occurrences. A legal rule denying standing to the union to protect individual rights under what is to be deemed a contract with individuals would encourage such indiscipline. And this is true even though the ultimately desirable social policy is to make it a matter of industrial habit to rely for a remedy for such grievances not on stoppage of work or on lawsuits but on the grievance procedure within an industry. There is in fact a strong group interest in procuring for the employee the benefit promised as well as the promise in the collective agreement. If the union can represent and press that group interest, the stoppage may be avoided; if it cannot, the group resorts to wildcat self-help. The holding below

cannot eliminate this group interest; it can stimulate its manifestation by way of a strike.

Is the line which the Court of Appeals has drawn the result of interpretation of the particular contract or of a rule of law beyond the power of the parties to alter? If it is the former, then the line can be obliterated by express language in the contract; and the unions can be trusted to find suitable language. They were quick to secure amendment to their constitutions or statutes in order to avoid the decision of this Court in Elgin, Joliet & Eastern R. Co. v. Burley, 325 U.S. 711, 327 U.S. 661. If it is the latter, what is the basis for the rule? It is not to be found in fear that the employee may not be able to sue. To hold that the union may sue, it is not necessary to hold that the employee may not sue in any forum, and vice versa. At least when the union and the employee are in agreement, there is no reason why either or both should not be permitted to sue. Such is the situation under § 9 (a) of the National Labor Relations Act with respect to the adjustment of grievances without suit. When the employee and the union are in disagreement, the question is not which may sue, but rather the extent to which the one may conclude the other.

Speculative reflection reveals other possible substantive additions which might be made to § 301. When tested against the limitations which must restrict judicial elaboration of legislation, however, all meritorious possibilities are either too specialized to reach this case or too insignificant an addition to dissipate the constitutional doubts which have revealed themselves.

4. In the present case, however, serious constitutional problems may be avoided, and indeed must be, through the orthodox process of limiting the scope of doubtful legislation. We cannot adopt the reasoning of the Court of Appeals in reaching our conclusion that § 301 does not extend jurisdiction to the present case. That court relied upon an assumed federal concept of the nature of a collective bargaining agreement which is not justified either in terms of discoverable congressional intent or considerations relevant to the function of the collective agreement in the field of labor relations. The same objections do not, however, prevail against the view that whether or not the applicable substantive law—in our view state law—would recognize a right in the union, Congress did not intend to burden the federal courts with suits of this type.

Considering the nature of a collective bargaining contract, which involves the correlative rights of employer, employee *and* union, we might be disposed to read § 301 as allowing the union to sue in this case. With due regard to the constitutional difficulties which would be raised, and in view of the fact that such an interpretation would bring to the federal courts an extensive range of litigation heretofore entertained by the States, we conclude that Congress did not will this result. There was no suggestion that Congress, at a time when its attention was directed to congestion in the federal courts, particularly in the heavy industrial areas, intended to open the doors of the federal courts to a potential flood of grievances based upon an employer's failure to comply with terms of a collective agreement relating to compensation, terms peculiar in the individual benefit which is their subject matter and which, when violated, give a cause of action to the individual employee. The employees have always been able to enforce their individual rights in the state courts. They have not been hampered by the rules governing unincorporated associations. To this extent, the collective bargaining contract has always been "enforceable."

Nowhere in the legislative history did Congress discuss or show any recognition of the type of suit involved here, in which the union is suing on behalf of employees for accrued wages. Therefore, we conclude that Congress did not confer on the federal courts jurisdiction over a suit such as this one.

Affirmed.

MR. JUSTICE HARLAN took no part in the consideration or decision of this case.

MR. CHIEF JUSTICE WARREN, with whom MR. JUSTICE CLARK joins, concurring.

We agree with the decision but not with all that is said in the opinion. The only question we see here is one of statutory interpretation. For us the language of § 301 is not sufficiently explicit nor its legislative history sufficiently clear to indicate that Congress intended to authorize a union to enforce in a federal court the uniquely personal right of an employee for whom it had bargained to receive compensation for services rendered his employer. Thus viewed, it becomes unnecessary for us either to make labor policy or to raise constitutional issues.

[MR. JUSTICE DOUGLAS' dissent is omitted.]

Even after the *Lincoln Mills* case, which follows, resolved the constitutional issue, the "uniquely personal" categorization plagued arbitration litigation for a considerable period until finally laid to rest—in a footnote—many years later.

The *Lincoln Mills* case marks the beginning of the present era of labor arbitration law.

TEXTILE WORKERS UNION OF AMERICA
v.
LINCOLN MILLS OF ALABAMA
353 U.S. 448 (1957)

MR. JUSTICE DOUGLAS delivered the opinion of the Court.

Petitioner-union entered into a collective bargaining agreement in 1953 with respondent-employer, the agreement to run one year and from year to year thereafter, unless terminated on specified notices. The agreement provided that there would be no strikes or work stoppages and that grievances would be handled pursuant to a specified procedure. The last step in the grievance procedure—a step that could be taken by either party—was arbitration.

This controversy involves several grievances that concern work loads and work assignments. The grievances were processed through the various steps in the grievance procedure and were finally denied by the employer. The union requested arbitration, and the employer refused. Thereupon the union brought this suit in the District Court to compel arbitration.

The District Court concluded that it had jurisdiction and ordered the employer to comply with the grievance arbitration provisions of the collective bargaining agreement. The Court of Appeals reversed by a divided vote. 230 F. 2d 81. It held that, although the District Court had jurisdiction to entertain the suit, the court had no authority founded either in federal or state law to grant the relief. The case is here on a petition for a writ of certiorari which we granted because of the importance of the problem and the contrariety of views in the courts. 352 U.S. 821.

The starting point of our inquiry is § 301 of the Labor Management Relations Act of 1947, 61 Stat. 156, 29 U.S.C. § 185, which provides:

(a) Suits for violation of contracts between an employer and a labor organization representing employees in an industry affecting commerce as defined in this chapter, or between any such labor organizations, may be brought in any district court of the United States having jurisdiction of the parties, without respect to the amount in controversy or without regard to the citizenship of the parties.
(b) Any labor organization which represents employees in an industry affecting commerce as defined in this chapter and any employer whose activities affect commerce as defined in this chapter shall be bound by the acts of its agents. Any such labor

organization may sue or be sued as an entity and in behalf of the employees whom it represents in the courts of the United States. Any money judgment against a labor organization in a district court of the United States shall be enforceable only against the organization as an entity and against its assets, and shall not be enforceable against any individual member or his assets.

There has been considerable litigation involving § 301 and courts have construed it differently. There is one view that § 301 (a) merely gives federal district courts jurisdiction in controversies that involve labor organizations in industries affecting commerce, without regard to diversity of citizenship or the amount in controversy.[1] Under that view § 301 would not be the source of substantive law ; it would neither supply federal law to resolve these controversies nor turn the federal judges to state law for answers to the questions. Other courts—the overwhelming number of them—hold that § 301 (a) is more than jurisdictional—that it authorizes federal courts to fashion a body of federal law for the enforcement of these collective bargaining agreements and includes within that federal law specific performance of promises to arbitrate grievances under collective bargaining agreements. Perhaps the leading decision representing that point of view is the one rendered by Judge Wyzanski in Textile Workers Union v. American Thread Co., 113 F. Supp. 137. That is our construction of § 301 (a), which means that the agreement to arbitrate grievance disputes, contained in this collective bargaining agreement, should be specifically enforced.

From the face of the Act it is apparent that § 301 (a) and § 301 (b) supplement one another. Section 301 (b) makes it possible for a labor organization, representing employees in an industry affecting commerce, to sue and be sued as an entity in the federal courts. Section 301 (b) in other words provides the procedural remedy lacking at common law. Section 301 (a) certainly does something more than that. Plainly, it supplies the basis upon which the federal district courts may take jurisdiction and apply the procedural rule of § 301 (b). The question is whether § 301 (a) is more than jurisdictional.

The legislative history of § 301 is somewhat cloudy and confusing. But there are a few shafts of light that illuminate our problem.

The bills, as they passed the House and the Senate, contained provisions which would have made the failure to abide by an agreement to arbitrate an unfair labor practice. S. Rep. No. 105, 80th Cong., 1st Sess., pp. 20–21, 23 ; H. R. Rep. No. 245, 80th Cong., 1st Sess., p. 21. This feature of the law was dropped in Conference. As the Conference Report stated, "Once parties have made a collective bargaining contract the enforcement of that contract should be left to the usual processes of the law and not to the National Labor Relations Board." H. R. Conf. Rep. No. 510, 80th Cong., 1st Sess., p. 42.

Both the Senate and the House took pains to provide for "the usual processes of the law" by provisions which were the substantial equivalent of § 301 (a) in its present form. Both the Senate Report and the House Report indicate a primary concern that unions as well as employees should be bound to collective bargaining contracts. But there was also a broader concern—a concern with a procedure for making such agreements enforceable in the courts by either party. At one point the Senate Report, *supra*, p. 15, states:

> We feel that the aggrieved party should also have a right of action in the Federal courts. Such a policy is completely in accord with the purpose of the Wagner Act which the Supreme Court declared was "to compel employers to bargain collectively with their employees to the end that an employment contract, binding on both parties, should be made."

Congress was also interested in promoting collective bargaining that ended with agreements not to strike.[2] The Senate Report, *supra*, p. 16 states:

> If unions can break agreements with relative impunity, then such agreements do not tend to stabilize industrial relations. The execution of an agreement

---

1. International Ladies' Garment Workers' Union v. Jay-Ann Co., 228 F. 2d 632 (C.A. 5th Cir.), *semble*; United Steelworkers v. Galland-Henning Mfg. Co., 241 F. 2d 323, 325 (C.A. 7th Cir.); Mercury Oil Refining Co. v. Oil Workers' Union, 187 F. 2d 980, 983 (C.A. 10th Cir.).

2. S. Rep. No. 105, 80th Cong., 1st Sess., pp. 17–18 states:

"Statutory recognition of the collective agreement as a valid, binding, and enforceable contract is a logical and necessary step. It will promote a higher degree of responsibility upon the parties to such agreements, and will thereby promote industrial peace.

"It has been argued that the result of making collective agreements enforceable against unions would be that they would no longer consent to the inclusion of a no-strike clause in a contract.

"The argument is not supported by the record in the few States which have enacted their own laws in an effort to secure some measure of union responsibility for breaches of contract. Four States—Minnesota, Colorado, Wisconsin, and California—have thus far enacted such laws and, so far as can be learned, no-strike clauses have been continued about as before.

"In any event, it is certainly a point to be bargained over and any union with the status of 'representative' under the NLRA which has bargained in good faith with an employer should have no reluctance in including a no-strike clause if it intends to live up to the terms of the contract. The improvement that would result in the stability of industrial relations is, of course, obvious."

does not by itself promote industrial peace. The chief advantage which an employer can reasonably expect from a collective labor agreement is assurance of uninterrupted operation during the term of the agreement. Without some effective method of assuring freedom from economic warfare for the term of the agreement, there is little reason why an employer would desire to sign such a contract.

Consequently, to encourage the making of agreements and to promote industrial peace through faithful performance by the parties, collective agreements affecting interstate commerce should be enforceable in the Federal courts. Our amendment would provide for suits by unions as legal entities and against unions as legal entities in the Federal courts in disputes affecting commerce.

Thus collective bargaining contracts were made "equally binding and enforceable on both parties." *Id.,* p. 15. As stated in the House Report, *supra,* p. 6, the new provision "makes labor organizations equally responsible with employers for contract violations and provides for suit by either against the other in the United States district courts." To repeat, the Senate Report, *supra,* p. 17, summed up the philosophy of § 301 as follows: "Statutory recognition of the collective agreement as a valid, binding, and enforceable contract is a logical and necessary step. It will promote a higher degree of responsibility upon the parties to such agreements, and will thereby promote industrial peace."

Plainly the agreement to arbitrate grievance disputes is the *quid pro quo* for an agreement not to strike. Viewed in this light, the legislation does more than confer jurisdiction in the federal courts over labor organizations. It expresses a federal policy that federal courts should enforce these agreements on behalf of or against labor organizations and that industrial peace can be best obtained only in that way.

To be sure, there is a great medley of ideas reflected in the hearings, reports, and debates on this Act. Yet, to repeat, the entire tenor of the history indicates that the agreement to arbitrate grievance disputes was considered as *quid pro quo* of a no-strike agreement. And when in the House debate narrowed to the question whether § 301 was more than jurisdictional, it became abundantly clear that the purpose of the section was to provide the necessary legal remedies. Section 302 of the House bill, the substantial equivalent of the present § 301, was being described by Mr. Hartley, the sponsor of the bill in the House:

> MR. BARDEN. Mr. Chairman, I take this time for the purpose of asking the Chairman a question, and in asking the question I want it understood that it is intended to make a part of the record that may hereafter be referred to as history of the legislation.

> It is my understanding that section 302, the section dealing with equal responsibility under collective bargaining contracts in strike actions and proceedings in district courts contemplates not only the ordinary lawsuits for damages but also such other remedial proceedings, both legal and equitable, as might be appropriate in the circumstances; in other words, proceedings could, for example, be brought by the employers, the labor organizations, or interested individual employees under the Declaratory Judgments Act in order to secure declarations from the Court of legal rights under the contract.

> MR. HARTLEY. The interpretation the gentleman has just given of that section is absolutely correct. 93 Cong. Rec. 3656–3657.

It seems, therefore, clear to us that Congress adopted a policy which placed sanctions behind agreements to arbitrate grievance disputes,[3] by implication rejecting the common-law rule, discussed in Red Cross Line v. Atlantic Fruit Co., 264 U.S. 109, against enforcement of executory agreements to arbitrate.[4] We would undercut the Act and defeat its policy if we read § 301 narrowly as only conferring jurisdiction over labor organizations.

The question then is, what is the substantive law to be applied in suits under § 301 (a)? We conclude that the substantive law to apply in suits under § 301 (a) is federal law, which the courts must fashion from the policy of our national labor laws. See Mendelsohn, *Enforceability of Arbitration Agreements Under Taft-Hartley Section 301*, 66 YALE L. J. 167. The Labor Management Relations Act expressly furnishes some substantive law. It points out what the parties may or may not do in certain situations. Other problems will lie in the penumbra of express statutory mandates. Some will lack express statutory sanction but will be solved by looking at the policy of the legislation and fashioning a remedy that will effectuate that policy. The range of judicial inventiveness will be determined by the nature of the problem. See Board of Commissioners v. United States, 308 U.S. 343, 351. Federal interpretation of the federal law will govern, not state law. Cf. Jerome

---

3. Assn. of Westinghouse Employees v. Westinghouse Electric Corp., 348 U.S. 437, is quite a different case. There the union sued to recover unpaid wages on behalf of some 4,000 employees. The basic question concerned the standing of the union to sue and recover on those individual employment contracts. The question here concerns the right of the union to enforce the agreement to arbitrate which it has made with the employer.

4. We do not reach the question, which the Court reserved in Red Cross Line v. Atlantic Fruit Co., *supra,* p. 125, whether as a matter of federal law executory agreements to arbitrate are enforceable, absent congressional approval.

v. United States, 318 U.S. 101, 104. But state law, if compatible with the purpose of § 301, may be resorted to in order to find the rule that will best effectuate the federal policy. See Board of Commissioners v. United States, *supra*, at 351–352. Any state law applied, however, will be absorbed as federal law and will not be an independent source of private rights.

It is not uncommon for federal courts to fashion federal law where federal rights are concerned. See Clearfield Trust Co. v. United States, 318 U.S. 363, 366–367; National Metropolitan Bank v. United States, 323 U.S. 454. Congress has indicated by § 301 (a) the purpose to follow that course here. There is no constitutional difficulty. Article III, § 2, extends the judicial power to cases "arising under ... the Laws of the United States." The power of Congress to regulate these labor-management controversies under the Commerce Clause is plain. Houston & Texas R. Co. v. United States, 234 U.S. 342; Labor Board v. Jones & Laughlin Corp., 301 U.S. 1. A case or controversy arising under § 301 (a) is, therefore, one within the purview of judicial power as defined in Article III.

The question remains whether jurisdiction to compel arbitration of grievance disputes is withdrawn by the Norris-LaGuardia Act, 47 Stat. 70, 29 U.S.C. § 101. Section 7 of that Act prescribes stiff procedural requirements for issuing an injunction in a labor dispute. The kinds of acts which had given rise to abuse of the power to enjoin are listed in § 4. The failure to arbitrate was not a part and parcel of the abuses against which the Act was aimed. Section 8 of the Norris-LaGuardia Act does, indeed, indicate a congressional policy toward settlement of labor disputes by arbitration, for it denies injunctive relief to any person who has failed to make "every reasonable effort" to settle the dispute by negotiation, mediation, or "voluntary arbitration." Though a literal reading might bring the dispute within the terms of the Act (see Cox, *Grievance Arbitration in the Federal Court*, 67 Harv. L. Rev. 591, 602–604), we see no justification in policy for restricting § 301 (a) to damage suits, leaving specific performance of a contract to arbitrate grievance disputes to the inapposite[5] procedural requirements of that Act. Moreover, we held in Virginian R. Co. v. System Federation, 300 U.S. 515, and in Graham v. Brotherhood of Firemen, 338 U.S. 232, 237, that the Norris-LaGuardia Act does not deprive federal courts of jurisdiction to compel compliance with the mandates of the Railway Labor Act.

The mandates there involved concerned racial discrimination. Yet those decisions were not based on any peculiarities of the Railway Labor Act. We followed the same course in Syres v. Oil Workers International Union, 350 U.S. 892, which was governed by the National Labor Relations Act. There an injunction was sought against racial discrimination in application of a collective bargaining agreement; and we allowed the injunction to issue. The congressional policy in favor of the enforcement of agreements to arbitrate grievance disputes being clear,[6] there is no reason to submit them to the requirements of § 7 of the Norris-LaGuardia Act.

A question of mootness was raised on oral argument. It appears that since the date of the decision in the Court of Appeals respondent has terminated its operations and has contracted to sell its mill properties. All work in the mill ceased in March, 1957. Some of the grievances, however, ask for back pay for increased workloads; and the collective bargaining agreement provides that "the Board of Arbitration shall have the right to adjust compensation retroactive to the date of the change." Insofar as the grievances sought restoration of workloads and job assignments, the case is, of course, moot. But to the extent that they sought a monetary award, the case is a continuing controversy.

The judgment of the Court of Appeals is reversed and the cause is remanded to that court for proceedings in conformity with this opinion.

Reversed.

The dissent by Justice Frankfurter is a masterly presentation of the arguments against the result and rationale of the majority. It is well worth reading for the light it sheds on the legislative history of § 301, among other things. It is omitted, however, because of its great length and the fact that it is of little value in the development of the doctrines begun with the *Lincoln Mills* case.

In General Electric Co. v. Local 205, United Electrical Workers, 353 U.S. 547, a companion

---

5. See Judge Magruder in Local 205 v. General Electric Co., 233 F. 2d 85, 92.

6. Whether there are situations in which individual employees may bring suit in an appropriate state or federal court to enforce grievance rights under employment contracts where the collective bargaining agreement provides for arbitration of those grievances is a question we do not reach in this case. Cf. Assn. of Westinghouse Employees v. Westinghouse Electric Corp., 348 U.S. 437, 460, 464; Moore v. Illinois Central R. Co., 312 U.S. 630; Slocum v. Delaware, L. & W. R. Co., 339 U.S. 239; Transcontinental Air v. Koppal, 345 U.S. 653.

case, the Court affirmed the court of appeals judgment that an arbitration clause was specifically enforceable. However, that court had based its conclusion upon the United States Arbitration Act. The Court said: "We follow *in part* a different path ... though we reach the same result" (based upon § 301) (emphasis added). And in Goodall-Sanford v. United Textile Workers, 353 U.S. 550, another companion case, the Court declined to follow precedents on the non-appealability of an order directing arbitration decided under the United States Arbitration Act.

B.

The Allocation of Authority Between Court and Arbitrator—The Trilogy

UNITED STEELWORKERS OF AMERICA
v.
AMERICAN MANUFACTURING CO.
363 U.S. 564 (1960)

Opinion of the Court by MR. JUSTICE DOUGLAS, announced by MR JUSTICE BRENNAN.

This suit was brought by petitioner union in the District Court to compel arbitration of a "grievance" that petitioner, acting for one Sparks, a union member, had filed with the respondent, Sparks' employer. The employer defended on the ground (1) that Sparks is estopped from making his claim because he had a few days previously settled a workmen's compensation claim against the company on the basis that he was permanently partially disabled, (2) that Sparks is not physically able to do the work, and (3) that this type of dispute is not arbitrable under the collective bargaining agreement in question.

The agreement provided that during its term there would be "no strike," unless the employer refused to abide by a decision of the arbitrator. The agreement sets out a detailed grievance procedure with a provision for arbitration (regarded as the standard form) of all disputes between the parties "as to the meaning, interpretation and application of the provisions of this agreement."[1]

The agreement reserves to the management power to suspend or discharge any employee "for cause."[2] It also contains a provision that the employer will employ and promote employees on the principle of seniority "where ability and efficiency are equal."[3] Sparks left his work due to an injury and while off work brought an action for compensation benefits. The case was settled, Sparks' physician expressing the opinion that the injury had made him 25 per cent "permanently partially disabled." That was on September 9. Two weeks later the union filed a grievance which charged that Sparks was entitled to return to his job by virtue of the seniority provision of the collective bargaining agreement. Respondent refused to arbitrate and this action was brought. The District Court held that Sparks, having accepted the settlement on the basis of permanent partial disability, was estopped to claim any seniority or employment rights and granted the motion for summary judgment. The Court of Appeals affirmed, 264 F. 2d 624, for different reasons. After reviewing the evidence it held that the grievance is "a frivolous, patently baseless one, not subject to arbitration under the collective bargaining agreement." *Id.,* at 628. The case is here on a writ of certiorari, 361 U.S. 881.

---

1. The relevant arbitration provisions read as follows:

"Any disputes, misunderstandings, differences or grievances arising between the parties as to the meaning, interpretation and application of the provisions of this agreement, which are not adjusted as herein provided, may be submitted to the Board of Arbitration for decision. . . .

"The arbitrator may interpret this agreement and apply it to the particular case under consideration but shall, however, have no authority to add to, subtract from, or modify the terms of the agreement. Disputes relating to discharges or such matters as might involve a loss of pay for employees may carry an award of back pay in whole or in part as may be determined by the Board of Arbitration.

"The decision of the Board of Arbitration shall be final and conclusively binding upon both parties, and the parties agree to observe and abide by same."

---

2. "The Management of the works, the direction of the working force, plant layout and routine of work, including the right to hire, suspend, transfer, discharge or otherwise discipline any employee for cause, such cause being: infraction of company rules, inefficiency, insubordination, contagious disease harmful to others, and any other ground or reason that would tend to reduce or impair the efficiency of plant operation; and to lay off employees because of lack of work, is reserved to the Company, provided it does not conflict with this agreement."

3. This provision provides in relevant part:

"The Company and the Union fully recognize the principle of seniority as a factor in the selection of employees for promotion, transfer, lay-off, re-employment, and filling of vacancies, where ability and efficiency are equal. It is the policy of the Company to promote employees on that basis."

Section 203 (d) of the Labor Management Relations Act, 1947, 61 Stat. 154, 29 U.S.C. § 173 (d), states, "Final adjustment by a method agreed upon by the parties is hereby declared to be the desirable method for settlement of grievance disputes arising over the application or interpretation of an existing collective-bargaining agreement." That policy can be effectuated only if the means chosen by the parties for settlement of their differences under a collective bargaining agreement is given full play.

A state decision that held to the contrary announced a principle that could only have a crippling effect on grievance arbitration. The case was International Assn. of Machinists v. Cutler-Hammer, Inc., 271 App. Div. 917, 67 N.Y.S. 2d 317, aff'd 297 N.Y. 519, 74 N.E. 2d 464. It held that "If the meaning of the provision of the contract sought to be arbitrated is beyond dispute, there cannot be anything to arbitrate and the contract cannot be said to provide for arbitration." 271 App. Div., at 918, 67 N.Y.S. 2d, at 318. The lower courts in the instant case had a like preoccupation with ordinary contract law. The collective agreement requires arbitration of claims that courts might be unwilling to entertain. In the context of the plant or industry the grievance may assume proportions of which judges are ignorant. Yet, the agreement is to submit all grievances to arbitration, not merely those that a court may deem to be meritorious. There is no exception in the "no strike" clause and none therefore should be read into the grievance clause, since one is the *quid pro quo* for the other.[4] The question is not whether in the mind of the court there is equity in the claim. Arbitration is a stabilizing influence only as it serves as a vehicle for handling any and all disputes that arise under the agreement.

The collective agreement calls for the submission of grievances in the categories which it describes, irrespective of whether a court may deem them to be meritorious. In our role of developing a meaningful body of law to govern the interpretation and enforcement of collective bargaining agreements, we think special heed should be given to the context in which collective bargaining agreements are negotiated and the purpose which they are intended to serve. See Lewis v. Benedict Coal Corp., 361 U.S. 459, 468. The function of the court is very limited when the parties have agreed to submit all questions of contract interpretation to the arbitrator. It is confined to ascertaining whether the party

seeking arbitration is making a claim which on its face is governed by the contract. Whether the moving party is right or wrong is a question of contract interpretation for the arbitrator. In these circumstances the moving party should not be deprived of the arbitrator's judgment, when it was his judgment and all that it connotes that was bargained for.

The courts, therefore, have no business weighing the merits of the grievance,[5] considering whether there is equity in a particular claim, or determining whether there is particular language in the written instrument which will support the claim. The agreement is to submit all grievances to arbitration, not merely those which the court will deem meritorious. The processing of even frivolous claims may have therapeutic values of which those who are not a part of the plant environment may be quite unaware.[6]

The union claimed in this case that the company had violated a specific provision of the contract. The company took the position that it had not violated that clause. There was, therefore, a dispute between the parties as to "the meaning, interpretation and application" of the collective bargaining agreement. Arbitration should have been ordered. When the judiciary undertakes to determine the merits of a grievance under the guise of interpreting the grievance procedure of collective bargaining agreements, it usurps a function which under that regime is entrusted to the arbitration tribunal.

Reversed.

MR. JUSTICE FRANFURTER concurs in the result.

MR. JUSTICE WHITTAKER, believing that the District Court lacked jurisdiction to determine

---

4. Cf. Structural Steel & Ornamental Iron Assn. v. Shopmens Local Union, 172 F. Supp. 354, where the employer sued for breach of the "no strike" agreement.

5. See New Bedford Defense Products Division v. Local No. 1113, 258 F. 2d 522, 526 (C.A. 1st Cir.).

6. Cox, *Current Problems in the Law of Grievance Arbitration*, 30 ROCKY MT. L. REV. 247, 261 (1958), writes:

"The typical arbitration clause is written in words which cover, without limitation, all disputes concerning the interpretation or application of a collective bargaining agreement. Its words do not restrict its scope to meritorious disputes or two-sided disputes, still less are they limited to disputes which a judge will consider two-sided. Frivolous cases are often taken, and are expected to be taken, to arbitration. What one man considers frivolous another may find meritorious, and it is common knowledge in industrial relations circles that grievance arbitration often serves as a safety valve for troublesome complaints. Under these circumstances it seems proper to read the typical arbitration clause as a promise to arbitrate every claim, meritorious or frivolous, which the complainant bases upon the contract. The objection that equity will not order a party to do a useless act is outweighed by the cathartic value of arbitrating even a frivolous grievance and by the dangers of excessive judicial intervention."

the merits of the claim which the parties had validly agreed to submit to the exclusive jurisdiction of a Board of Arbitrators (Textile Workers v. Lincoln Mills, 353 U.S. 448), concurs in the result of this opinion.

MR. JUSTICE BLACK took no part in the consideration or decision of this case.

MR. JUSTICE BRENNAN, with whom MR. JUSTICE HARLAN joins, concurring.*

While I join the Court's opinions in Nos. 443, 360 and 538, I add a word in Nos. 443 and 360.

In each of these two cases the issue concerns the enforcement of but one promise—the promise to arbitrate in the context of an agreement dealing with a particular subject matter, the industrial relations between employers and employees. Other promises contained in the collective bargaining agreements are beside the point unless, by the very terms of the arbitration promise, they are made relevant to its interpretation. And I emphasize this, for the arbitration promise is itself a contract. The parties are free to make that promise as broad or as narrow as they wish, for there is no compulsion in law requiring them to include any such promises in their agreement. The meaning of the arbitration promise is not to be found simply by reference to the dictionary definitions of the words the parties use, or by reference to the interpretation of commercial arbitration clauses. Words in a collective bargaining agreement, rightly viewed by the Court to be the charter instrument of a system of industrial self-government, like words in a statute, are to be understood only by reference to the background which gave rise to their inclusion. The Court therefore avoids the prescription of inflexible rules for the enforcement of arbitration promises. Guidance is given by identifying the various considerations which a court should take into account when construing a particular clause—considerations of the milieu in which the clause is negotiated and of the national labor policy. It is particularly underscored that the arbitral process in collective bargaining presupposes that the parties wanted the informed judgment of an arbitrator, precisely for the reason that judges cannot provide it. Therefore, a court asked to enforce a promise to arbitrate should ordinarily refrain from involving itself in the interpretation of the substantive provisions of the contract.

_____

*[This opinion applies also to No. 443, United Steelworkers of America v. Warrior & Gulf Navigation Co., and No. 538, United Steelworkers of America v. Enterprise Wheel & Car Corp.]

To be sure, since arbitration is a creature of contract, a court must always inquire, when a party seeks to invoke its aid to force a reluctant party to the arbitration table, whether the parties have agreed to arbitrate the particular dispute. In this sense, the question of whether a dispute is "arbitrable" is inescapably for the court.

On examining the arbitration clause, the court may conclude that it commits to arbitration any "dispute, difference, disagreement, or controversy of any nature or character." With that finding the court will have exhausted its function, except to order the reluctant party to arbitration. Similarly, although the arbitrator may be empowered only to interpret and apply the contract, the parties may have provided that any dispute as to whether a particular claim is within the arbitration clause is itself for the arbitrator. Again the court, without more, must send any dispute to the arbitrator, for the parties have agreed that the construction of the arbitration promise itself is for the arbitrator, and the reluctant party has breached his promise by refusing to submit the dispute to arbitration.

In *American,* the Court deals with a request to enforce the "standard" form of arbitration clause, one that provides for the arbitration of "[a]ny disputes, misunderstandings, differences or grievances arising between the parties as to the meaning, interpretation and application of this agreement." Since the arbitration clause itself is part of the agreement, it might be argued that a dispute as to the meaning of that clause is for the arbitrator. But the Court rejects this position, saying that the threshold question, the meaning of the arbitration clause itself, is for the judge unless the parties clearly state to the contrary. However, the Court finds that the meaning of that "standard" clause is simply that the parties have agreed to arbitrate any dispute which the moving party asserts to involve construction of the substantive provisions of the contract, because such a dispute necessarily does involve such a construction.

The issue in the *Warrior* case is essentially no different from that in *American,* that is, it is whether the company agreed to arbitrate a particular grievance. In contrast to *American,* however, the arbitration promise here excludes a particular area from arbitration—"matters which are strictly a function of management." Because the arbitration promise is different, the scope of the court's inquiry may be broader. Here, a court may be required to examine the substantive provisions of the contract to ascertain whether the parties have provided that contracting out shall be a "function of management." If a court may delve into the merits to the extent of inquiring whether the parties have expressly agreed whether or not contracting out was a "function of management," why was it error for the lower court here to evaluate the evidence of bargaining history for the same purpose? Neat logical distinctions do not provide the answer. The Court rightly concludes that appropriate regard for the national labor policy and the special factors relevant to the labor arbitral process, admonish that judicial inquiry into the merits of this grievance should be limited to the search for an explicit provision which brings the grievance under the cover of the exclusion clause since "the exclusion clause is vague and arbitration clause quite broad." The hazard of going further into the merits is amply demonstrated by what the courts below did. On the basis of inconclusive evidence, those courts found that *Warrior* was in no way limited by any implied covenants of good faith and fair dealing from contracting out as it pleased—which would necessarily mean that *Warrior* was free completely to destroy the collective bargaining agreement by contracting out all the work.

The very ambiguity of the *Warrior* exclusion clause suggests that the parties were generally more concerned with having an arbitrator render decisions as to the meaning of the contract than they were in restricting the arbitrator's jurisdiction. The case might of course be otherwise were the arbitration clause very narrow, or the exclusion clause quite specific, for the inference might then be permissible that the parties had manifested a greater interest in confining the arbitrator; the presumption of arbitrability would then not have the same force and the Court would be somewhat freer to examine into the merits.

The Court makes reference to an arbitration clause being the *quid pro quo* for a no-strike clause. I do not understand the Court to mean that the application of the principles announced today depends upon the presence of a no-strike clause in the agreement.

MR. JUSTICE FRANKFURTER joins these observations.

In reality, there is no "standard" grievance or arbitration provision. According to the preceding Bureau of Labor Statistics study of contracts covering 1,000 or more employees groups, roughly half the collective agreements studied, covering half the employees in the sample, specified that all disputes were subject to the grievance procedure, while the other half limited grievances to disputes over contract provisions. Not all arbitration provisions are coextensive with grievance procedures; where they differ, the arbitration clause usually is more narrow. Hence, many matters of potential dispute do not come within the ambit of arbitration clauses. The lower courts frequently characterize clauses similar to that in the main case as "the standard arbitration clause."

UNITED STEELWORKERS OF AMERICA v. WARRIOR & GULF NAVIGATION CO.
363 U.S. 574 (1960)

Opinion of the Court by MR. JUSTICE DOUGLAS, announced by MR. JUSTICE BRENNAN.

Respondent transports steel and steel products by barge and maintains a terminal at Chickasaw, Alabama, where it performs maintenance and repair work on its barges. The employees at that terminal constitute a bargaining unit covered by a collective bargaining agreement negotiated by petitioner union. Respondent between 1956 and 1958 laid off some employees, reducing the bargaining unit from 42 to 23 men. This reduction was due in part to respondent contracting maintenance work, previously done by its employees, to other companies. The latter used respondent's supervisors to lay out the work and hired some of the laid-off employees of respondent (at reduced wages). Some were in fact assigned to work on respondent's barges. A number of employees signed a grievance which petitioner presented to respondent, the grievance reading:

> We are hereby protesting the Company's actions, of arbitrarily and unreasonably contracting out work to other concerns, that could and previously has been performed by Company employees.
>
> This practice becomes unreasonable, unjust and discriminatory in lieu [*sic*] of the fact that at present there are a number of employees that have been laid off for about 1 and ½ years or more for allegedly lack of work.
>
> Confronted with these facts we charge that the Company is in violation of the contract by inducing a partial lock-out, of a number of the employees who would otherwise be working were it not for this unfair practice.

The collective agreement had both a "no strike" and a "no lockout" provision. It also had a grievance procedure which provided in relevant part as follows:

> Issues which conflict with any Federal statute in its application as established by Court procedure or matters which are strictly a function of management shall not be subject to arbitration under this section.
>
> Should differences arise between the Company and the Union or its members employed by the Company as to the meaning and application of the

provisions of this Agreement, or should any local trouble of any kind arise, there shall be no suspension of work on account of such differences but an earnest effort shall be made to settle such differences immediately in the following manner:

A. For Maintenance Employees:

First, between the aggrieved employees, and the Foreman involved;

Second, between a member or members of the Grievance Committee designated by the Union, and the Foreman and Master Mechanic.

Fifth, if agreement has not been reached the matter shall be referred to an impartial umpire for decision. The parties shall meet to decide on an umpire acceptable to both. If no agreement on selection of an umpire is reached, the parties shall jointly petition the United States Conciliation Service for suggestion of a list of umpires from which selection will be made. The decision of the umpire shall be final.

Settlement of this grievance was not had and respondent refused arbitration. This suit was then commenced by the union to compel it.

The District Court granted respondent's motion to dismiss the complaint. 168 F. Supp. 702. It held after hearing evidence, much of which went to the merits of the grievance, that the agreement did not "confide in an arbitrator the right to review the defendant's business judgment in contracting out work." *Id.*, at 705. It further held that "the contracting out of repair and maintenance work, as well as construction work, is strictly a function of management not limited in any respect by the labor agreement involved here." *Ibid.* The Court of Appeals affirmed by a divided vote, 269 F. 2d 633, the majority holding that the collective agreement had withdrawn from the grievance procedure "matters which are strictly a function of management" and that contracting out fell in that exception. The case is here on a writ of certiorari. 361 U.S. 912.

We held in Textile Workers v. Lincoln Mills, 353 U.S. 448, that a grievance arbitration provision in a collective agreement could be enforced by reason of § 301 (a) of the Labor Management Relations Act and that the policy to be applied in enforcing this type of arbitration was that reflected in our national labor laws. *Id.*, at 456–457. The present federal policy is to promote industrial stabilization through the collective bargaining agreement.[1] *Id.*, at 453–454.

A major factor in achieving industrial peace is the inclusion of a provision for arbitration of grievances in the collective bargaining agreement.[2]

Thus the run of arbitration cases, illustrated by Wilko v. Swan, 346 U.S. 427, becomes irrelevant to our problem. There the choice is between the adjudication of cases or controversies in courts with established procedures or even special statutory safeguards on the one hand and the settlement of them in the more informal arbitration tribunal on the other. In the commercial case, arbitration is the substitute for litigation. Here arbitration is the substitute for industrial strife. Since arbitration of labor disputes has quite different functions from arbitration under an ordinary commercial agreement, the hostility evinced by courts toward arbitration of commercial agreements has no place here. For arbitration of labor disputes under collective bargaining agreements is part and parcel of the collective bargaining process itself.

The collective bargaining agreement states the rights and duties of the parties. It is more than a contract; it is a generalized code to govern a myriad of cases which the draftsmen cannot wholly anticipate. See Shulman, *Reason, Contract, and Law in Labor Relations*, 68 HARV. L. REV. 999, 1004–1005. The collective agreement covers the whole employment relationship.[3] It calls into being a new common law—the

---

1. In § 8 (d) of the National Labor Relations Act, as amended by the 1947 Act, 29 U.S.C. § 158 (d), Congress indeed provided that where there was a collective agreement for a fixed term the duty to bargain did not require either party "to discuss or agree to any modification of the terms and conditions contained in" the contract. And see Labor Board v. Sands Mfg. Co., 306 U.S. 332.

2. Complete effectuation of the federal policy is achieved when the agreement contains both an arbitration provision for all unresolved grievances and an absolute prohibition of strikes, the arbitration agreement being the "*quid pro quo*" for the agreement not to strike. Textile Workers v. Lincoln Mills, 353 U.S. 448, 455.

3. "Contracts which ban strikes often provide for lifting the ban under certain conditions. Unconditional pledges against strikes are, however, somewhat more frequent than conditional ones. Where conditions are attached to no-strike pledges, one or both of two approaches may be used: certain *subjects* may be exempted from the scope of the pledge, or the pledge may be lifted after certain *procedures* are followed by the union. (Similar qualifications may be made in pledges against lockouts.)

"Most frequent conditions for lifting no-strike pledges are: (1) the occurrence of a deadlock in wage reopening negotiations; and (2) violation of the contract, especially non-compliance with the grievance procedure and failure to abide by an arbitration award.

"No-strike pledges may also be lifted after compliance with specified procedures. Some contracts permit the union to strike after the grievance procedure has been exhausted without a settlement, and where arbitration is not prescribed as the final recourse. Other contracts permit a strike if mediation efforts fail, or after a specified cooling-off period.', COLLECTIVE BARGAINING, NEGOTIATIONS AND CONTRACTS' BUREAU OF NATIONAL AFFAIRS, INC., 77:101.

common law of a particular industry or of a particular plant. As one observer has put it: [4]

> ... [I]t is not unqualifiedly true that a collective-bargaining agreement is simply a document by which the union and employees have imposed upon management limited, express restrictions of its otherwise absolute right to manage the enterprise, so that an employee's claim must fail unless he can point to a specific contract provision upon which the claim is founded. There are too many people, too many problems, too many unforeseeable contingencies to make the words of the contract the exclusive source of rights and duties. One cannot reduce all the rules governing a community like an industrial plant to fifteen or even fifty pages. Within the sphere of collective bargaining, the institutional characteristics and the governmental nature of the collective-bargaining process demand a common law of the shop which implements and furnishes the context of the agreement. We must assume that intelligent negotiators acknowledged so plain a need unless they stated a contrary rule in plain words.

A collective bargaining agreement is an effort to erect a system of industrial self-government. When most parties enter into contractual relationship they do so voluntarily, in the sense that there is no real compulsion to deal with one another, as opposed to dealing with other parties. This is not true of the labor agreement. The choice is generally not between entering or refusing to enter into a relationship, for that in all probability pre-exists the negotiations. Rather it is between having that relationship governed by an agreed-upon rule of law or leaving each and every matter subject to a temporary resolution dependent solely upon the relative strength, at any given moment, of the contending forces. The mature labor agreement may attempt to regulate all aspects of the complicated relationship, from the most crucial to the most minute over an extended period of time. Because of the compulsion to reach agreement and the breadth of the matters covered, as well as the need for a fairly concise and readable instrument, the product of negotiations (the written document) is, in the words of the late Dean Shulman, "a compilation of diverse provisions: some provide objective criteria almost automatically applicable; some provide more or less specific standards which require reason and judgment in their application; and some do little more than leave problems to future consideration with an expression of hope and good faith." Shulman, *supra*, at 1005. Gaps may be left to be filled in by reference to the practices of the particular

industry and of the various shops covered by the agreement. Many of the specific practices which underlie the agreement may be unknown, except in hazy form, even to the negotiators. Courts and arbitration in the context of most commercial contracts are resorted to because there has been a breakdown in the working relationship of the parties; such resort is the unwanted exception. But the grievance machinery under a collective bargaining agreement is at the very heart of the system of industrial self-government. Arbitration is the means of solving the unforeseeable by molding a system of private law for all the problems which may arise and to provide for their solution in a way which will generally accord with the variant needs and desires of the parties. The processing of disputes through the grievance machinery is actually a vehicle by which meaning and content are given to the collective bargaining agreement.

Apart from matters that the parties specifically exclude, all of the questions on which the parties disagree must therefore come within the scope of the grievance and arbitration provisions of the collective agreement. The grievance procedure is, in other words, a part of the continuous collective bargaining process. It, rather than a strike, is the terminal point of a disagreement.

The labor arbitrator performs functions which are not normal to the courts; the considerations which help him fashion judgments may indeed be foreign to the competence of courts.

> A proper conception of the arbitrator's function is basic. He is not a public tribunal imposed upon the parties by superior authority which the parties are obliged to accept. He has no general charter to administer justice for a community which transcends the parties. He is rather part of a system of self-government created by and confined to the parties. Shulman, *supra*, at 1016.

The labor arbitrator's source of law is not confined to the express provisions of the contract, as the industrial common law—the practices of the industry and the shop—is equally a part of the collective bargaining agreement although not expressed in it. The labor arbitrator is usually chosen because of the parties' confidence in his knowledge of the common law of the shop and their trust in his personal judgment to bring to bear considerations which are not expressed in the contract as criteria for judgment. The parties expect that his judgment of a particular grievance will reflect not only what the contract says but, insofar as the collective bargaining agreement permits, such factors as the effect upon productivity of a particular

4. Cox, *Reflections Upon Labor Arbitration*, 72 HARV. L. REV. 1482, 1498 (1959).

result, its consequence to the morale of the shop, his judgment whether tensions will be heightened or diminished. For the parties' objective in using the arbitration process is primarily to further their common goal of uninterrupted production under the agreement, to make the agreement serve their specialized needs. The ablest judge cannot be expected to bring the same experience and competence to bear upon the determination of a grievance, because he cannot be similarly informed.

The Congress, however, has by § 301 of the Labor Management Relations Act, assigned the courts the duty of determining whether the reluctant party has breached his promise to arbitrate. For arbitration is a matter of contract and a party cannot be required to submit to arbitration any dispute which he has not agreed so to submit. Yet, to be consistent with congressional policy in favor of settlement of disputes by the parties through the machinery of arbitration, the judicial inquiry under § 301 must be strictly confined to the question whether the reluctant party did agree to arbitrate the grievance or did agree to give the arbitrator power to make the award he made. An order to arbitrate the particular grievance should not be denied unless it may be said with positive assurance that the arbitration clause is not susceptible of an interpretation that covers the asserted dispute. Doubts should be resolved in favor of coverage.[5]

We do not agree with the lower courts that contracting-out grievances were necessarily excepted from the grievance procedure of this agreement. To be sure, the agreement provides that "matters which are strictly a function of management shall not be subject to arbitration." But it goes on to say that if "differences" arise or if "any local trouble of any kind" arises, the grievance procedure shall be applicable.

Collective bargaining agreements regulate or restrict the exercise of management functions; they do not oust management from the performance of them. Management hires and fires, pays and promotes, supervises and plans. All these are part of its function, and absent a collective bargaining agreement, it may be exercised freely

except as limited by public law and by the willingness of employees to work under the particular, unilaterally imposed conditions. A collective bargaining agreement may treat only with certain specific practices, leaving the rest to management but subject to the possibility of work stoppages. When, however, an absolute no-strike clause is included in the agreement, then in a very real sense everything that management does is subject to the agreement, for either management is prohibited or limited in the action it takes, or if not, it is protected from interference by strikes. This comprehensive reach of the collective bargaining agreement does not mean, however, that the language, "strictly a function of management," has no meaning.

"Strictly a function of management" might be thought to refer to any practice of management in which, under particular circumstances prescribed by the agreement, it is permitted to indulge. But if courts, in order to determine arbitrability, were allowed to determine what is permitted and what is not, the arbitration clause would be swallowed up by the exception. Every grievance in a sense involves a claim that management has violated some provision of the agreement.

Accordingly, "strictly a function of management" must be interpreted as referring only to that over which the contract gives management complete control and unfettered discretion. Respondent claims that the contracting out of work falls within this category. Contracting out work is the basis of many grievances; and that type of claim is grist in the mills of the arbitrators.[6] A specific collective bargaining agreement may exclude contracting out from the grievance procedure. Or a written collateral agreement may make clear that contracting out was not a matter for arbitration. In such a case a grievance based solely on contracting out would not be arbitrable. Here, however, there is no such provision. Nor is there any showing that the parties designed the phrase "strictly a function of management" to encompass any and all forms of contracting out. In the absence of any express provision excluding a particular grievance from arbitration, we think only the most forceful evidence of a purpose to exclude the claim from arbitration

---

5. It is clear that under both the agreement in this case and that involved in American Manufacturing Co., the question of arbitrability is for the courts to decide. Cf. Cox *Reflections Upon Labor Arbitration*, 72 HARV. L. REV. 1482, 1508. Where the assertion by the claimant is that the parties excluded from court determination not merely the decision of the merits of the grievance but also the question of its arbitrability, vesting power to make both decisions in the arbitrator, the claimant must bear the burden of a clear demonstration of that purpose.

6. See Celanese Corp. of America, 33 LAB. ARB. REP. 925, 941 (1959), where the arbiter in a grievance growing out of contracting out work said:

"In my research I have located 64 published decisions which have been concerned with this issue covering a wide range of factual situations but all of them with the common characteristic—*i.e.*, the contracting-out of work involved occurred under an Agreement that contained no provision that specifically mentioned contracting-out of work."

can prevail, particularly where, as here, the exclusion clause is vague and the arbitration clause quite broad. Since any attempt by a court to infer such a purpose necessarily comprehends the merits, the court should view with suspicion an attempt to persuade it to become entangled in the construction of the substantive provisions of a labor agreement, even through the back door of interpreting the arbitration clause, when the alternative is to utilize the services of an arbitrator.

The grievance alleged that the contracting out was a violation of the collective bargaining agreement. There was, therefore, a dispute "as to the meaning and application of the provisions of this Agreement" which the parties had agreed would be determined by arbitration.

The judiciary sits in these cases to bring into operation an arbitral process which substitutes a regime of peaceful settlement for the older regime of industrial conflict. Whether contracting out in the present case violated the agreement is the question. It is a question for the arbiter, not for the courts.

Reversed.

MR. JUSTICE FRANKFURTER concurs in the result.

MR. JUSTICE BLACK took no part in the consideration or decision of this case.

[For opinion of MR. JUSTICE BRENNAN, joined by MR. JUSTICE FRANFURTER and MR. JUSTICE HARLAN, see *ante*.]

MR. JUSTICE WHITTAKER, dissenting.

Until today, I have understood it to be the unquestioned law, as this Court has consistently held, that arbitrators are private judges chosen by the parties to decide particular matters specifically submitted;[1] that the contract under which matters are submitted to arbitrators is at once the source and limit of their authority and power;[2] and that their power to decide issues with finality, thus ousting the normal functions of the courts, must rest upon a clear, definitive agreement of the parties, as such powers can never be implied. United States v. Moorman,

338 U.S. 457, 462;[3] Mercantile Trust Co. v. Hensey, 205 U.S. 298, 309.[4] See also Fernandez & Hnos. v. Rickert Rice Mills, 119 F. 2d 809, 815 (C.A. 1st Cir.);[5] Marchant v. Mead-Morrison Mfg. Co., 252 N.Y. 284, 299, 169 N.E. 386, 391;[6] Continental Milling & Feed Co. v. Doughnut Corp., 186 Md. 669, 676, 48 A. 2d 447, 445;[7] Jacob v. Weisser, 207 Pa. 484, 489, 56 A. 1065, 1067.[8] I believe that the Court today departs from the established principles announced in these decisions.

Here, the employer operates a shop for the normal maintenance of its barges, but it is not equipped to make major repairs, and accordingly the employer has, from the beginning of its operations more than 19 years ago, contracted out its major repair work. During most, if not all, of this time the union has represented

---

1. "Arbitrators are judges chosen by the parties to decide the matters submitted to them." Burchell v. Marsh, 17 How. 344, 349.

2. "The agreement under which [the arbitrators] were selected *was at once the source and limit of their authority*, and the award, to be binding, must, in substance and form, conform to the submission." (Emphasis added.) Continental Ins. Co. v. Garrett, 125 F. 589, 590 (C.A. 6th Cir.)—Opinion by Judge, later Mr. Justice, Lurton.

3. "It is true that *the intention of parties to submit their contractual disputes to final determination outside the courts should be made manifest by plain language.*" (Emphasis added.) United States v. Moorman, 338 U.S. 457, 462.

4. "To make such [an arbitrator's] certificate conclusive *requires plain language in the contract.* It is not to be implied." (Emphasis added.) Mercantile Trust Co. v. Hensey, 205 U.S. 298, 309.

5. "A party is never required to submit to arbitration any question which he has not agreed so to submit, and contracts providing for arbitration *will be carefully construed in order not to force a party to submit to arbitration a question which he did not intend to be submitted.*" (Emphasis added.) Fernandez & Hnos. v. Rickert Rice Mills. 119 F. 2d 809, 815 (C.A. 1st Cir.).

6. In this leading case, Judge, later Mr. Justice, Cardozo said:

"The question is one of intention, to be ascertained by the same tests that are applied to contracts generally.... No one is under a duty to resort to these conventional tribunals, however helpful their processes, *except to the extent that he has signified his willingness.* Our own favor or disfavor of the cause of arbitration is not to count as a factor in the appraisal of the thought of others." (Emphasis added.) Marchant v. Mead-Morrison Mfg. Co., 252 N.Y. 284, 299, 169 N.E. 386, 391.

7. In this case, the Court, after quoting Judge Cardozo's language in *Marchant, supra,* saying that "the question is one of intention," said:

"Sound policy demands that the terms of an arbitration agreement *must not be strained to discover power to pass upon matters in dispute, but the terms must be clear and unmistakable to oust the jurisdiction of the Court, for trial by jury cannot be taken away in any case merely by implication.*" (Emphasis added.) Continental Milling & Feed Co. v. Doughnut Corp., 186 Md. 669, 676, 48 A. 447, 450.

8. "But, under any circumstances, before the decision of an arbitrator can be held final and conclusive, it must appear, as was said in Chandley Bros. v. Cambridge Springs, 200 Pa. 230, 49 Atl. 772, *that power to pass upon the subject-matter, is clearly given to him. 'The terms of the agreement are not to be strained to discover it. They must be clear and unmistakable to oust the jurisdiction of the courts; for trial by jury cannot be taken away by implication merely in any case'.*" (Emphasis added.) Jacob v. Weisser, 207 Pa. 484, 489, 56 A. 1065, 1067.

the employees in that unit. The District Court found that

> [t]hroughout the successive labor agreements between these parties, including the present one, . . . [the union] has unsuccessfully sought to negotiate changes in the labor contracts, and particularly during the negotiation of the present labor agreement, . . . which would have limited the right of the [employer] to continue the practice of contracting out such work. 168 F. Supp. 702, 704–705.

The labor agreement involved here provides for arbitration of disputes respecting the interpretation and application of the agreement and, arguably, also some other things. But the first paragraph of the arbitration section says: "[M]atters which are strictly a function of management shall not be subject to arbitration under this section." Although acquiescing for 19 years in the employer's interpretation that contracting out work was "strictly a function of management," and having repeatedly tried—particularly in the negotiation of the agreement involved here—but unsuccessfully, to induce the employer to agree to a covenant that would prohibit it from contracting out work, the union, after having agreed to and signed the contract involved, presented a "grievance" on the ground that the employer's contracting out work, at a time when some employees in the unit were laid off for lack of work, constituted a partial "lockout" of employees in violation of the antilockout provision of the agreement.

Being unable to persuade the employer to agree to cease contracting out work or to agree to arbitrate the "grievance," the union brought this action in the District Court, under § 301 of the Labor Management Relations Act, 29 U.S.C. § 185, for a decree compelling the employer to submit the "grievance" to arbitration. The District Court, holding that the contracting out of work was, and over a long course of dealings had been interpreted and understood by the parties to be, "strictly a function of management," and was therefore specifically excluded from arbitration by the terms of the contract, denied the relief prayed, 168 F. Supp. 702. The Court of Appeals affirmed, 269 F. 2d 633, and we granted certiorari. 361 U.S. 912.

The Court now reverses the judgment of the Court of Appeals. It holds that the arbitrator's source of law is "not confined to the express provisions of the contract," that arbitration should be ordered "unless it may be said with positive assurance that the arbitration clause is not susceptible of an interpretation that covers the asserted dispute," that "[d]oubts of arbitrability] should be resolved in favor of cover-

age," and that when, as here, "an absolute no-strike clause is included in the agreement, then . . . everything that management does is subject to [arbitration]." I understand the Court thus to hold that the arbitrators are not confined to the express provisions of the contract, that arbitration is to be ordered unless it may be said with positive assurance that arbitration of a particular dispute is excluded by the contract, that doubts of arbitrability are to be resolved in favor of arbitration, and that when, as here, the contract contains a no-strike clause, everything that management does is subject to arbitration.

This is an entirely new and strange doctrine to me. I suggest, with deference, that it departs from both the contract of the parties and the controlling decisions of this Court. I find nothing in the contract that purports to confer upon arbitrators any such general breadth of private judicial power. The Court cites no legislative or judicial authority that creates for or gives to arbitrators such broad general powers. And I respectfully submit that today's decision cannot be squared with the statement of Judge, later Mr. Justice, Cardozo in *Marchant* that "No one is under a duty to resort to these conventional tribunals, however helpful their processes, *except to the extent that he has signified his willingness.* Our own favor or disfavor of the cause of arbitration is not to count as a factor in the appraisal of the thought of others" (emphasis added), 252 N.Y., at 299, 169 N.E., at 391 ; nor with his statement in that case that "[t]he question is one of intention, to be ascertained by the same tests that are applied to contracts generally," *id.* ; nor with this Court's statement in *Moorman,* "that the intention of the parties to submit their contractual disputes to final determination outside the courts *should be made manifest by plain language*" (emphasis added), 338 U.S., at 462 ; nor with this Court's statement in *Hensey* that: "To make such [an arbitrator's] certificate conclusive *requires plain language in the contract. It is not to be implied.*" (Emphasis added.) 205 U.S., at 309. "A party is never required to submit to arbitration any question which he has not agreed so to submit, and *contracts providing for arbitration will be carefully construed in order not to force a party to submit to arbitration a question which he did not intend to be submitted.*" (Emphasis added.) Fernandez & Hnos. v. Rickert Rice Mills, *supra,* 119 F. 2d, at 815 (C.A. 1st Cir.).

With respect, I submit that there is nothing in the contract here to indicate that the employer "signified [its] willingness" (*Marchant, supra,* at 299) to submit to arbitrators whether it must cease contracting out work. Certainly no such intention is "made manifest by plain language" (*Moorman, supra,* at 462), as the law "requires," because such consent "is not to be implied." *Hensey, supra,* at 309.) To the contrary, the parties by their conduct over many years interpreted the contracting out of major repair work to be "strictly a function of management," and if, as the concurring opinion suggests, the words of the contract can "be understood only by reference to the background which gave rise to their inclusion," then the interpretation given by the parties over 19 years to the phrase "matters which are strictly a function of management" should logically have some significance here. By their contract, the parties agreed that "matters which are strictly a function of management shall not be subject to arbitration." The union over the course of many years repeatedly tried to induce the employer to agree to a covenant prohibiting the contracting out of work, but was never successful. The union again made such an effort in negotiating the very contract involved here, and, failing of success, signed the contract, knowing, of course, that it did not contain any such covenant, but that, to the contrary, it contained, just as had the former contracts, a covenant that "matters which are strictly a function of management shall not be subject to arbitration." Does not this show that, instead of signifying a willingness to submit to arbitration the matter of whether the employer might continue to contract out work, the parties fairly agreed to exclude at least that matter from arbitration? Surely it cannot be said that the parties agreed to such a submission by any "plain language." *Moorman, supra,* at 462, and *Hensey, supra,* at 309. Does not then the Court's opinion compel the employer "to submit to arbitration [a] question which [it] has not agreed so to submit"? (*Fernandez & Hnos., supra,* at 815.)

Surely the question whether a particular subject or class of subjects is or is not made arbitrable by a contract is a judicial question, and if, as the concurring opinion suggests, "the court may conclude that [the contract] commits to arbitration any [subject or class of subjects]," it may likewise conclude that the contract does not commit such subject or class of subjects to arbitration, and "[with that finding the court will have exhausted its function" no more nor less by denying arbitration than by ordering it. Here the District Court found, and the Court of Appeals approved its finding, that by the terms of the contract, as interpreted by the parties over 19 years, the contracting out of work was "strictly a function of management" and "not subject to arbitration." That finding, I think,

should be accepted here. Acceptance of it requires affirmance of the judgment.

I agree with the Court that courts have no proper concern with the "merits" of claims which by contract the parties have agreed to submit to the exclusive jurisdiction of arbitrators. But the question is one of jurisdiction. Neither may entrench upon the jurisdiction of the other. The test is: Did the parties in their contract "manifest by plain language" (*Moorman, supra,* at 462) their willingness to submit the issue in controversy to arbitrators? If they did, then the arbitrators have exclusive jurisdiction of it, and the courts, absent fraud or the like, must respect that exclusive jurisdiction and cannot interfere. But if they did not, then the courts must exercise their jurisdiction, when properly invoked, to protect the citizen against the attempted use by arbitrators of pretended powers actually never conferred. That question always is, and from its very nature must be, a judicial one. Such was the question presented to the District Court and the Court of Appeals here. They found the jurisdictional facts, properly applied the settled law to those facts, and correctly decided the case. I would therefore affirm the judgment.

WARRIOR AND GULF NAVIGATION CO.
and
UNITED STEELWORKERS OF AMERICA

Steelworkers Arbitration Bulletin 6549 (1961)
Opinion of the Arbitrator, J. Fred Holly:

COMPANY CONTENTIONS

The Company contends that the subject grievance should be dismissed since it does not present an issue which is arbitable under the Labor Agreement. When the Supreme Court held that the language in the Labor Agreement did not prevent arbitration, it left the basic question of arbitrability for the Arbitrator to decide. The following comment taken from a recent issue of the YALE LAW JOURNAL substantiates this point.[1]

> The *Warrior* test does not require that the Court finally determine arbitrability, but only that the Court satisfy itself that the dispute is not unequivocably barred from arbitration. The Court's attitude suggests that a judicial finding of subject matter arbitrability will not preclude the Arbitrator from reaching an opposite conclusion, because presumably the Arbitrator will not be bound by the same rule of strict construction. Thus, in *Warrior,*

---

1. 70 YALE LAW JOURNAL, March 1961, pp. 614–17.

the dispute went to arbitration because the Court did not regard the employer's interpretation as the only possible reasonable construction of the Collective Bargaining Agreement, but that decision did not foreclose the Arbitrator, construing the Agreement in greater detail, from agreeing with the employer that contracting out was not a proper subject matter for arbitration.

Section 10 of the Labor Agreement provides "Issues ... which are strictly a function of Management shall not be subject to arbitration." In the first Company-Union negotiations (1952) the Union attempted to obtain a restriction limiting the right of the Company to contract out work. The Company strongly opposed this proposal, contending that the practice of contracting out was "strictly a function of Management." In the 1954 negotiations the Union again proposed a limitation on contracting out and the Company took the same position as in 1952. In these negotiations, however, the Company succeeded in inserting the following language in Section 10: "Issues ... which are strictly a function of Management shall not be subject to arbitration." This clause has been retained in all subsequent labor agreements. Thus, the history of negotiations establishes that beginning in 1952 the parties equated contracting out with "strictly a function of Management." Company negotiators and Company minutes of the negotiations verify this as a fact. Moreover, Union negotiators present at the hearing did not take the stand to contradict the Company testimony regarding this fact. In the negotiations of 1956 and 1958 the Union repeated its earlier attempts to limit contracting out, but failed to achieve such limitations. Curiously, at the hearing the Union advanced the argument that its chief negotiator had always taken the position in these negotiations that present Contract language provided an implied limitation on contracting out and that additional language was unnecessary. Despite Company denials of this, the Union negotiators who were present at the hearing did not take the stand.

Also, except in the aforementioned negotiations, there were no discussions between the parties regarding contracting out. Moreover, no grievances were filed on this subject prior to the filing of the instant one on August 22, 1958. Thus, despite repeated instances of contracting out over a period of six years, no formal protest came from the employees or the Union. The only reasonable conclusion from this is that both the employees and their leaders understood that contracting out was not a proper subject for a grievance. Therefore, the express language of the Contract and the bargaining history since the beginning of the collective bargaining relationship clearly shows that a grievance protesting contracting out is not arbitrable.

Finally, the Company argument that the Arbitrator should dismiss this grievance on the basis that it does not present an arbitrable issue is supported by precedent. In support of this point the Company cites portions of three papers presented at the Ninth and Thirteenth Annual Meetings of the National Academy of Arbitrators by Messrs. Jules J. Justin, Mark L. Kahn, and Donald A. Crawford. The first two of these papers emphasize that the Arbitrator should not consider matters that are outside the Contract.

> When Mr. Crawford in his article on "The Arbitration of Disputes over Sub-Contracting" ... states that where the contract is silent as to contracting out there is no question of arbitrability, he is not talking about a contract such as ours; for though there is no specific reference in the Contract to contracting out, there is this express language withdrawing from the grievance-arbitration procedure "matters which are strictly a function of Management," and the genesis of that language is in the negotiations on the precise subject of contracting out.

Also, the Company cites the following arbitration awards in support of its position. *Marion Power Shovel Company* (34 LA 709); *Black-Clawson Company* (34 LA 215); and *Operating Engineers v. Standard Oil Company* (46 LRRM 2997).

UNION CONTENTIONS

The Supreme Court of the United States (363 U.S. 584, 80 S.Ct. 1354) said:

> Accordingly, "strictly a function of Management" must be interpreted as referring only to that over which the Contract gives Management complete control and unfettered discretion. Respondent claims that the contracting out of work falls within this category. Contracting out work is the basis of many grievances; and that type of claim is grist in the mills of the Arbitrators. A specific Collective Bargaining Agreement may exclude contracting out from the grievance procedure. Or a written collateral agreement may make clear that contracting out was not a matter for arbitration. In such a case a grievance based solely on contracting out would not be arbitrable. Here, however, there is no such provision. Nor is there any showing that the parties designed the phrase "strictly a function of Management" to encompass any and all forms of contracting out. In the absence of any express provision excluding a particular grievance from arbitration, we think only the most forceful evidence of a purpose to exclude the claim from arbitration can prevail, particularly where, as here, the exclusion clause is vague and the arbitration clause quite broad.

While this should have disposed of the arbitrability issue, the Company attempted in the hearing to show that "strictly a function of Management" encompassed any and all forms of contracting out. This phrase did not even appear in the 1952 Contract, but the Company testimony purported to show that the two were equated in those negotiations. The same Company witness who so testified also indicated his opinion that such language in the Contract was "completely unnecessary." Company notes on the 1952 negotiations indicate that the top Management representative therein said, "The Company would always consider paying a little more than a job might cost outside, where convenience in having the work performed in its own shops was an element, and the cost was not too far out of line." These notes also indicate that this representative also stated, "Will not contract out work unless strictly a matter of dollars and cents and even then Company will make some allowance for convenience of having work performed at its own Plant." These notes also indicate that Company representatives stressed that contracting out would not be subject to the grievance procedure. The Company witness testified that the Union never agreed to this proposition. No evidence was presented to indicate that when, in 1954, the phrase "strictly a function of Management" found its way into the Contract, that the parties in any way made it encompass contracting out.

In the 1954 negotiations Union representatives stressed that the recognition clause of the Contract prevented the Company from undermining the bargaining unit by contracting out. The Company representative did not deny that this was said. Also, the Company actually considered another grievance concerning contracting out at the very meeting in which it claimed that the instant grievance was not subject to the grievance procedure. Further, rather than acquiescing in the Management practice of contracting out, the Union made this a repeated subject of discussion in every negotiation. This fact is not denied by the Company.

Finally, Arbitrators generally hold that a Union does not waive the right to file a grievance by its failure to file grievances in earlier situations involving identical facts. (See: *Menasco Manufacturing Company*, 32 LA 406; *Bethlehem Steel Company*, 15 LA 688; and *Union Carbide and Carbon Chemicals Corporation*, 16 LA 811.)

DISCUSSION

The Arbitrator holds that the phrase excluding from the grievance procedure those matters that are "strictly a function of Management" does not effectively exclude the subject of contracting out of work. The Company notes covering the 1952 negotiations dispose of this issue. The notes covering the negotiations on September 3, 1952, on page 2 state:

> A brief attempt was made by the Union to discuss where work should be performed but Mr. Guthens (Company Vice President) and Mr. Winschel (Company Counsel) were adamant that such matters were a function of Management.

If the matter had been left here there would be considerable justification for the contentions of the Company, but the matter was not left here. Before adjourning this session the Union indicated that it would carry a report of the day's session to the rank and file and report back on the next day. On September 4, 1952, the Union Committee reported that the rank and file had rejected the Company offer, and the meeting thereupon recessed. Negotiations were resumed on September 5, 1952, with a Federal Mediation and Conciliation Service representative present. The Company notes for that day indicate the following:

> (7) *Union Request: Classification of Company Position on Matter of Contracting Work Out:*
> Company position: The Company has the right and will continue to have the right to run its operations to the best advantage of the owners. Will not contract work out unless strictly a matter of dollars and cents and even then Company will make some allowance for convenience of having work performed at its own Plant.
> The Conciliator asked what would be the procedure if the Union felt that the Company should not contract a certain piece of work.
> Company position: The Company would be perfectly willing to explain its decision to the Grievance Committee. However, any decision in the matter of contracting work out is strictly a function of Management and this Company could not in any way relinquish this function. This position was backed by Mr. Winschell, Attorney, who said that such matters are a function of Management.

Following the negotiation session of September 5, 1952, the Company drew up a memorandum outlining the status of negotiations. The following note appears therein:

> *Contracting Work Out:* The Union request that the Company should not contract out any work that is normally performed by employees was approached from several angles but it was pointed out that this was a Management function and that the Company would always consider paying a little more than a job might cost outside, where convenience in having the work performed in its own

shops was an element, and the cost was not too far out of line. It was further agreed by the Company that they would discuss this informally but that this was a Management function and one which would not be put into the Contract and handled as a grievance.

This explanation seemed to suffice and apparently this request has been satisfied.*

The foregoing statements must be interpreted in the light of concurrent events. The Company made the point that one of the major Union selling points in organizing the employees in 1952 "was that the Union was going to protect the employees from layoff by getting a contract limiting the practice of contracting out." (*Company Brief,* p. 13.) When the Union made such a proposal on September 3, 1952, the Company took an adamant position in opposition as recorded above. Then, the rank and file rejected the Company position on this and other matters. On the following day of negotiations, as recorded above, the Company modified its position on contracting out by stating that such contracting out would not be engaged in "unless strictly a matter of dollars and cents and even then Company will make some allowance for convenience of having work performed at its own Plant." This represents a considerable change from the adamant position of two days earlier, and can be interpreted only to mean that the Company agreed that some limitations existed on contracting out. The later statements of the Company to the effect that, despite this, contracting out is a function of Management, have a hollow sound. Also, note the concluding remarks in the Company notes to the effect that "apparently this request has been satisfied." It is unlikely that it could have been satisfied unless the Union representatives interpreted the Company statement to mean that limitations on contracting out had been recognized. Now, since this analysis leads to the conclusion that the parties jointly recognized a limitation on contracting out in 1952, the Company claim, that when the phrase "strictly a function of Management" was added to the Contract in 1954 barred such matters from the grievance procedure, must be denied. Accordingly, the instant grievance cannot be dismissed on the grounds that it is non-arbitrable. Therefore, the grievance must be considered on its merits.

[* This sentence would seem to belong to the bargaining memorandum, but does not so appear in the Bulletin.]

The Grievance

UNION CONTENTIONS

1. It is well established in arbitration that collective bargaining contracts which are silent on the subject of contracting out limit Management's power to contract out. Therefore, when Management fails to obtain an exclusive right to contract out, it does so with the full knowledge that its powers to contract out are limited. Such knowledge must have been available and known to this Company which is a subsidiary of the United States Steel Corporation. In 1952 the Union proposed a limitation on the right of the Steel Corporation to contract out work. The Wage Stabilization Board recommended that the Union withdraw its proposal, stating: "The proposal is not needed to prevent contracting-out which would have the effect of unreasonably narrowing the bargaining unit; the Board of Arbitration under the United States Steel Contract has ruled that the expired Contract, without the proposed claim, prohibits such contracting-out." (18 LA 120.) This ruling was handed down in March 1952 some six months prior to the 1952 negotiations herein involved.

On this same point the Union relies heavily on the findings of Arbitrator Crawford who made an intensive study of arbitration awards on sub-contracting.[2] The Union emphasizes the following summation made in this study:

> To put it too boldly and too simply, the decision measured against the underlying factual situations seem quite consistent and quite logical. Rightly or wrongly, up to now, the published awards convey that the issue as to contracting out is:
>
> First, is the contracting out apparently based on economies available to the subcontractor of lower wage rates including fringe benefits rather than other economies of operation or special advantage? If so, the contracting out will be found in violation of the limitation implied from the Recognition Clause.
>
> Second, if not, is permanent continuing work being contracted out?
>
> If not, the work may be contracted out.
>
> If so, is the contracting out of the permanent work based on *compelling* logic or economies of operation that justify such action?
>
> The doctrine seems to be that the Company cannot undermine the status of the collective bargaining agent by contracting out work primarily to beat the Union prices, nor can the Company contract out permanent work without compelling reasons other than a seeming desire to reduce the status of the exclusive agent.

2. Donald A. CRAWFORD, *The Arbitration of Disputes over Subcontracting* in Jean T. McKELVEY, editor, CHALLENGES TO ARBITRATION (Washington: Bureau of National Affairs, 1960), pp. 51–72.

Otherwise and generally, therefore, contracting out is a Management decision since the status of the bargaining agent is not involved.

2. The Company has unreasonably narrowed the scope of the bargaining unit and undermined the Union by its contracting out practices. When this case was before the Supreme Court, the Court found: [3]

> Respondent between 1956 and 1958 laid off some employees, reducing the bargaining unit from 42 to 23 men. This reduction was due in part to respondent contracting maintenance work, previously done by its employees, to other companies. The latter used respondent's Supervisors to lay out the work and hired some of the laid-off employees of respondent (at reduced wages).

While this should have settled the matter, the Company now contends that it introduced inaccurate statistics in court because of improper preparation. The figures submitted in court indicated that the dollar volume of work contracted out almost doubled between 1955 and 1958, while the number of employees was reduced by nearly 50 per cent. The figures introduced by the Company at the hearing show a reduction of contracting out between 1955 and 1958. The Arbitrator should reject the Company Exhibit filed in support of this trend (Company Exhibit No. 10).

The Company advances two explanations for the reduction of the maintenance work force. (1) The reduction resulted from the termination of a construction program which was inaugurated in 1947. (2) The Company listed a number of labor saving innovations that enable the Company to further reduce the number of maintenance employees. These arguments will not stand up, however, for the following reasons. In 1947, the Company had one-third less repair work in its yard than in 1958; yet, the number of employees in 1947 was double those of 1958. Also, the termination of the construction program had little to do with the curtailment. Two Company witnesses gave three different years for the termination date and one stated that it made no difference when the construction period ended—"We had lots of work that had fell behind on account of these other boats had been set aside." Also, the Company's list of innovations indicate the elimination of 14.10 men; yet, using the Company's own data there would still be a need for 32.9 maintenance men instead of the 22 actually used in 1958. One can only conclude that the contracting out practices of the Company contributed to a substantial reduction

of the bargaining unit. Company witnesses even verify this fact, and their testimony, along with that of Union witnesses, verify that the purpose was to undermine the Union.

3. Company representatives refused to offer any explanation for contracting out any specific work, but gave many general reasons for such action. Some of these general reasons were good, and some were bad. The Union agrees that the Company can contract out in the following situations:

a. When an emergency occurs.

b. When the work must be done somewhere else to permit a transportation unit to keep its commitments.

c. When the Chickasaw facilities are tied up, for example, when a repair requires dry docking and the one dry dock at Chickasaw is in use.

d. When the equipment and facilities at Chickasaw are not adequate for the task.

e. When Management can get the job done cheaper somewhere else because of savings other than lower wages including fringe benefits.

f. When the work to be performed is true construction work such as building barges.

g. When the type of repair work has never been done at Chickasaw.

h. When a collision with a vessel belonging to another company necessitated the repairs.

i. When the work force is at full strength.

j. When materials are readily available to other firms but not to Warrior and Gulf.

k. When the work has never been necessary before and will probably not be necessary again during the life of the equipment.

The following reasons for contracting out are clearly improper.

a. When the reason is to take advantage of the subcontractors lower wages and fringe benefits.

b. When work is contracted out when doing the work at Chickasaw would make it necessary to call men off layoff.

c. When contracting out is done under the guise of assuring that other firms will perform emergency services for Warrior and Gulf when it is necessary.

4. The evidence shows that the employees laid off in December 1956 and January 1957 would have been called back had the Company not been contracting out work at their expense, and that certain specific jobs performed at other yards after the filing of the grievance should have been performed at the Chickasaw facility.

---

3. Steelworkers v. Warrior and Gulf Navigation Company, 363 U.S. 575 (U.S. Sup. Ct.).

5. The Union proposes the following remedy:

a. Move the layoff dates of all employees laid off in December 1956 and January 1957 up to the date of the trial in court—October 30, 1958. This remedy is designed to protect the seniority rights of those laid-off employees.

b. Pay the number of Mechanics and Helpers laid off in late 1956 and early 1957 who would have been needed if the five inner bottom jobs and four outer bottom jobs complained of had been done on the Company's yard.

c. Pay the appropriate number of Mechanics and Helpers laid off in December 1956 and January 1957 the same as if they had done the work for all jobs (if any) contracted to other firms for any reason not specifically approved in Item 3 (a) through (k) above.

The Union proposes that the Arbitrator order the parties to consult and agree on the employees affected by the second and third proposed remedies. In the event that the parties are unable to agree as proposed, the Union recommends that the items in dispute should be referred back to the Arbitrator, within a reasonable period of time, for final determination.

COMPANY CONTENTIONS

1. If the Arbitrator should find that this grievance is arbitrable, he must, nevertheless, dismiss the grievance because the Contract does not restrict Management's function of contracting out. In the first place, the Contract contains no express prohibition or limitation of contracting out. Secondly, there is no implied restriction or prohibition on contracting out in the Contract. In the early arbitration cases concerning this topic it was held that a Company has the right to subcontract work unless the contract specifically restricts the right. This right has been subjected to scrutiny in later cases, lest it be abused, as where a Company uses it as a pretext "merely (as) an excuse to hurt the Union." Of course, such situations must be proven. The recognition, seniority and other general clauses exist for other purposes and do not give the employees exclusive jurisdiction to all of the work.

2. If any limitation on contracting out can be construed from the Agreement, it is a narrow one limited only to an act of bad faith or to anti-Union motivation and the facts in this case would not support a finding of a violation of such an obligation. The arbitration cases in which an implied limitation on Management's right to contract out has been found are virtually unanimous in requiring a showing of bad faith or anti-Union animus as a basis for such implied limitation. Since contracting out is not a *per se* violation of the Agreement, the burden of showing that the contracting out constitutes a Contract violation falls on the Union and the Union carries the burden of showing that the Company action was in bad faith or was in derogation of the Union.

3. The facts in this case do not bring it within the narrow area in which Arbitrators have found contracting out to be in violation of the labor agreement. In the first place, the layoffs complained of were the natural result of the conclusion of the Company's capital expansion program of 1947–1956. At the conclusion of this program it was necessary to restore the maintenance work force to the normal level. In addition, the operations of the Company have de-emphasized its participation in the collateral maintenance and repair function while concentrating upon its primary function of providing a transportation service. Moreover, the contracting out of work by the Company has not appreciably affected the total number of unionized personnel in this and other bargaining units within the Company. There is an absence of lack of good faith in connection with the Company's actions.

4. The Company is in the transporation business and is not in the ship repair business. A great number of arbitration awards are based on a determination of whether the work contracted out was a portion of the principal business of the Company or whether it was a function apart from the Company's normal business.

5. Past practice plays an important part in the decisions of Arbitrators when they deal with this subject. Here it must be recognized that the Company has always contracted out maintenance and repair work, and did so without the filing of a grievance from 1952 to 1958.

6. The practice of contracting out to independent ship repair yards of the type of work here involved is virtually without exception in the industry. Sound reasons exist for this uniform practice. In order to keep barges in constant operating condition, the barge lines must rely upon those who have ready facilities, ready know-how, and the over-all ability to put the barges and tow-boats back into operation as quickly as possible.

> If carriers like Warrior and Gulf cannot provide all of these (repair) services, they cannot be sure of providing any at any given time to any substantial degree, so they are left with the choice of having a small skeletal maintenance crew for routine repairs, or with doing no maintenance work whatsoever.

7. "It has also been the uniform practice of Warrior and Gulf to contract out work of the

nature involved here except when the existence of a large force for capital improvement permitted some of the work to be done in Warrior and Gulf's yard, and this is the only practical and efficient way for the Company to operate." Unless the Company were to operate a repair yard open to the public, the Company cannot piece out repair work at its terminal without great cost and inconvenience. Such a change would also force the firm to enter a new industry.

8. Finally, in this dispute the Union has failed to specify a Contract violation or to indicate any appropriate relief. The following quotation, taken from pages 39–41 of the *Company Brief*, amplifies this point.

> In the foregoing sections of this brief, the Company has demonstrated the insupportability of any contention that the Company is prohibited from contracting out or in any way limited in this right.
>
> But, the Union argues, the objection is not to contracting out *per se*; the grievance is addressed to arbitrary and discriminatory contracting out, but for which these layoffs would not have occurred. This complaint ignores the industry practice of contracting out *all* such work, the fact that the larger work force was hired for new construction, the fact that the men were laid off as the new construction was completed, and, finally, the fact that there is no proof that in *any* instance of work contracted out one or more important economic reasons such as cost, quick turn-around, absence of facilities or know-how, etc., did not require it. The burden of proving arbitrary action ("bad faith") is upon the Union in view of the Management right or prerogative of contracting out or making any other changes in its business operations even though the working force is adversely affected thereby. Arbitrators have, without exception, expressed their agreement with this requirement.
>
> The starting point of the Union's contentions is its grievance (Joint Exhibit No. 2), in which it makes certain general charges. In other grievances mentioned at the hearing it did what is inevitably done— it pointed to the specific matter for which it sought relief, and it asked for specific relief; in the Willcutt discharge case several years earlier the relief sought was reinstatement; in the grievance (as yet not pressed) which was filed in August 1958, about the same time as this one, relating to work in our yard by a Hamilton Machine Shop employee, the relief asked was two days' pay for one man.
>
> But the grievance here is of a general nature, and it charges no instance of contracting out to be in violation of the Labor Agreement—it does not, therefore, ask for any specific relief, because there is no specific charge or evidence on which specific relief could be granted. Its general charge that an "unreasonable, unjust and discriminatory" *practice* constitutes a Contract violation is novel in the large body of arbitration decisions regarding contracting out. The other cases all refer to specific items of contracting out or a specific *kind* of work contracted out. This general charge, and all of the Union's evidence, show a very revealing purpose: To get an arbitration award requiring the Company to discuss with the Union, before or in grievance proceedings, all jobs contracted or to be contracted out which the Union thinks should be done in our yard. This is precisely the limitation sought by the Union in the negotiation of the 1952, 1954 and 1956 Contracts —according to Messrs. Black and Rodriguez (see Court record, especially); this was the express limitation proposed in writing by the Union in the negotiation of the 1956 Contract under which this grievance was filed. *This is then a belated attempt by the Union to get an Arbitrator to write into the parties' Labor Agreement that which the parties themselves have fought out and left out.* No additional citations of authority are needed to show that the Arbitrator lacks authority to grant such a request.

DISCUSSION

Although there is no specific clause in the Contract dealing with contracting out, it is apparent that implied limitations exist on contracting out. As stated in the above discussion of arbitrability, the 1952 bargaining history "leads to the conclusion that the parties jointly recognize a limitation on contracting out." Also, Company witness and the Company *Brief* indicate several situations wherein contracting out has possible limitations, as follows:

1. Where the contracting out is in bad faith.
2. Where the purpose of contracting out is to subvert the Union.
3. When it is costlier and less convenient to have the work done elsewhere.
4. When the contracting out is less efficient.
5. When Company employees and facilities are presently available to do the work.

In addition, the Union also emphasized a number of situations in which contracting out was clearly improper. Thus, it is concluded that both parties recognize that implied limitations exist on the Company's right to contract out work. As a result, it becomes necessary to examine the practices of the Company in an effort to determine whether the Company has violated the implied limitation on its rights.

[The arbitrator's summary of the parties' contentions and discussion of the evidence on this issue is omitted.]

The Arbitrator holds that while he is not empowered to rule on events subsequent to the grievance, he can use those events for the purpose of casting light on events which transpired prior to and at the time of the grievance. The Union presented two types of work that had been contracted out and subsequent to the grievance. One type involved the turning of barges and the installation of new outer bottoms on those barges. The second type involved the contracting out of the installation of new inner bottoms. The testimony indicates that each of these operations at prior times had been done at the Company's terminal and at times had been contracted out. The Arbitrator holds that the evidence is sufficient to prove that the turning of barges at Chickasaw would be inadvisable. Such barge turning has not been performed by the Company since about 1952 and the present traffic at the terminal would not permit the resumption of such an activity on any sizable scale. Moreover, the dock facilities at the terminal are such that modern barge turning equipment cannot be installed. On the other hand, inner bottoms can be installed at the terminal at any time when there is available dock space and maintenance personnel. Although no specific example was cited regarding such work between 1956 and 1958, the record makes it apparent that such work or work of a similar nature had been contracted out. The Company's explanations of this contracting out were inadequate, however, since specific reasons for such contracting out were not forthcoming, and the general explanations fail to account for all types of subcontracting. In other words, the Company's reasons as advanced are inadequate to explain the volume of subcontracting and the decline of the workforce. Management's claims were vague and general. It is necessary for the Company to come forth with evidence showing that such contracting out was either necessary or permissible. This the Company failed to do while contending that there was no implied limitation on its right to contract out. This situation demands an explanation of the failure of the Company to replace employees in what had been described as a "normal" size workforce and at the same time to increase the dollar volume of work contracted out. In the absence of proof that work was properly contracted out, the Arbitrator can only conclude that at least one type of improper contracting out occurred between the dates of the protested layoffs and the filing of the grievance.

Having reached this conclusion, what relief is available? The Union seeks three types of relief: (1) a restoration of seniority rights for laid-off employees, (2) pay for those laid-off employees who were deprived of the right to do the work contracted out subsequent to the grievance, and (3) pay for those laid-off employees "the same as if they had done the work for all jobs (if any) contracted to other firms for any reason not specifically approved in Section VI" (of the Union *Brief*.) The Arbitrator's jurisdiction does not extend to events subsequent to the filing of the grievance, except as previously noted. Accordingly, he is not empowered to grant relief on subsequent events. Secondly, the Arbitrator does not possess the authority to order the parties to accept his criteria for contracting out and to require them to examine all past instances of contracting out in the light of these standards. To do this, the Arbitrator would be assuming a negotiation function and would be guilty of legislating where the parties have not legislated. On the other hand, there are firm grounds for advancing the seniority of those employees who were laid off in December 1956 and January 1957. Since the conclusion has been reached that some contracting out was improper between December 1956 and the date of the grievance, it naturally follows that some employees were entitled to recall and this would have provided seniority rights for at least two additional years. It is impossible to determine which employees would have been entitled to recall, but it will not damage the parties to have the lay-off dates of these two groups advanced to the date of the grievance.

Finally, the Arbitrator is well aware of the fact that this holding does not settle the problem of contracting out. He is convinced, however, that in view of the nature of the grievance and the evidence he is powerless to do more. Now that the conclusion has been reached that implied limitations exist on the right of the Company to contract out work, the parties can proceed to resolve the problem to their own interests and satisfaction.

UNITED STEELWORKERS OF AMERICA
v.
ENTERPRISE WHEEL & CAR CORP.
363 U.S. 593 (1960)

Opinion of the Court by MR. JUSTICE DOUGLAS, announced by MR. JUSTICE BRENNAN.

Petitioner union and respondent during the period relevant here had a collective bargaining agreement which provided that any differences "as to the meaning and application" of the agreement should be submitted to arbitration and that the arbitrator's decision "shall be final and binding on the parties." Special provisions were included concerning the suspension and discharge of employees. The agreement stated:

> Should it be determined by the Company or by an arbitrator in accordance with the grievance procedure that the employee has been suspended unjustly or discharged in violation of the provisions

of this Agreement, the Company shall reinstate the employee and pay full compensation at the employee's regular rate of pay for the time lost.

The agreement also provided:

> ... It is understood and agreed that neither party will institute *civil suits or legal proceedings* against the other for alleged violation of any of the provisions of this labor contract; instead all disputes will be settled in the manner outlined in this Article III—Adjustment of Grievances.

A group of employees left their jobs in protest against the discharge of one employee. A union official advised them at once to return to work. An official of respondent at their request gave them permission and then rescinded it. The next day they were told they did not have a job any more "until this thing was settled one way or the other."

A grievance was filed; and when respondent finally refused to arbitrate, this suit was brought for specific enforcement of the arbitration provisions of the agreement. The District Court ordered arbitration. The arbitrator found that the discharge of the men was not justified, though their conduct, he said, was improper. In his view the facts warranted at most a suspension of the men for 10 days each. After their discharge and before the arbitration award the collective bargaining agreement had expired. The union, however, continued to represent the workers at the plant. The arbitrator rejected the contention that expiration of the agreement barred reinstatement of the employees. He held that the provision of the agreement above quoted imposed an unconditional obligation on the employer. He awarded reinstatement with back pay, minus pay for a 10-day suspension and such sums as these employees received from other employment.

Respondent refused to comply with the award. Petitioner moved the District Court for enforcement. The District Court directed respondent to comply. 168 F. Supp. 308. The Court of Appeals, while agreeing that the District Court had jurisdiction to enforce an arbitration award under a collective bargaining agreement,[1] held that the failure of the award to specify the amounts to be deducted from the back pay rendered the award unenforceable. That defect, it agreed, could be remedied by requiring the parties to complete the arbitration. It went on to hold, however, that an award for back pay subsequent to the date of termination of the collective bargaining agreement could not be enforced. It also

---

[1]. See Textile Workers v. Cone Mills Corp., 208 F. 2d 920 (C.A. 4th Cir.).

held that the requirement for reinstatement of the discharged employees was likewise unenforceable because the collective bargaining agreement had expired. 269 F. 2d 327. We granted certiorari. 361 U.S. 929.

The refusal of courts to review the merits of an arbitration award is the proper approach to arbitration under collective bargaining agreements. The federal policy of settling labor disputes by arbitration would be undermined if courts had the final say on the merits of the awards. As we stated in United Steelworkers of America v. Warrior & Gulf Navigation Co., *ante,* decided this day, the arbitrators under these collective agreements are indispensable agencies in a continuous collective bargaining process. They sit to settle disputes at the plant level—disputes that require for their solution knowledge of the custom and practices of a particular factory or of a particular industry as reflected in particular agreements.[2]

When an arbitrator is commissioned to interpret and apply the collective bargaining agreement, he is to bring his informed judgment to bear in order to reach a fair solution of a problem. This is especially true when it comes to formulating remedies. There the need is for flexibility in meeting a wide variety of situations. The draftsmen may never have thought of what specific remedy should be awarded to meet a particular contingency. Nevertheless, an arbitrator is confined to interpretation and application of the collective bargaining agreement; he does not sit to dispense his own brand of industrial justice. He may of course look for guidance from many sources, yet his award is legitimate

---

[2]. "Persons unfamiliar with mills and factories—farmers or professors, for example—often remark upon visiting them that they seem like another world. This is particularly true if, as in the steel industry, both tradition and technology have strongly and uniquely molded the ways men think and act when at work. The newly hired employee, the 'green hand,' is gradually initiated into what amounts to a miniature society. There he finds himself in a strange environment that assaults his senses with unusual sounds and smells and often with different 'weather conditions' such as sudden drafts of heat, cold, or humidity. He discovers that the society of which he only gradually becomes a part has of course a formal government of its own—the rules which management and the union have laid down—but that it also differs from or parallels the world outside in social classes, folklore, ritual, and traditions.

"Under the process in the old mills a very real 'miniature society' had grown up, and in important ways the technological revolution described in this case history shattered it. But a new society or work community was born immediately, though for a long time it developed slowly. As the old society was strongly molded by the *discontinuous* process of making pipe, so was the new one molded by the *continuous* process and strongly influenced by the characteristics of new high-speed automatic equipment." Walker, *Life in the Automatic Factory,* 36 Harv. Bus. Rev. 111, 117.

only so long as it draws its essence from the collective bargaining agreement. When the arbitrator's words manifest an infidelity to this obligation, courts have no choice but to refuse enforcement of the award.

The opinion of the arbitrator in this case, as it bears upon the award of back pay beyond the date of the agreement's expiration and reinstatement, is ambiguous. It may be read as based solely upon the arbitrator's view of the requirements of enacted legislation, which would mean that he exceeded the scope of the submission. Or it may be read as embodying a construction of the agreement itself, perhaps with the arbitrator looking to "the law" for help in determining the sense of the agreement. A mere ambiguity in the opinion accompanying an award, which permits the inference that the arbitrator may have exceeded his authority, is not a reason for refusing to enforce the award. Arbitrators have no obligation to the court to give their reasons for an award. To require opinions[3] free of ambiguity may lead arbitrators to play it safe by writing no supporting opinions. This would be undesirable for a well-reasoned opinion tends to engender confidence in the integrity of the process and aids in clarifying the underlying agreement. Moreover, we see no reason to assume that this arbitrator has abused the trust the parties confided in him and has not stayed within the areas marked out for his consideration. It is not apparent that he went beyond the submission. The Court of Appeals' opinion refusing to enforce the reinstatement and partial back pay portions of the award was not based upon any finding that the arbitrator did not premise his award on his construction of the contract. It merely disagreed with the arbitrator's construction of it.

The collective bargaining agreement could have provided that if any of the employees were wrongfully discharged, the remedy would be reinstatement and back pay up to the date they were returned to work. Respondent's major argument seems to be that by applying correct principles of law to the interpretation of the collective bargaining agreement it can be determined that the agreement did not so provide, and that therefore the arbitrator's decision was not based upon the contract. The acceptance of this view would require courts, even under the standard arbitration clause, to review the merits of every construction of the contract. This plenary review by a court of the merits would make meaningless the provisions that the

arbitrator's decision is final, for in reality it would almost never be final. This underlines the fundamental error which we have alluded to in United Steelworkers of America v. American Manufacturing Co., decided this day. As we there emphasized, the question of interpretation of the collective bargaining agreement is a question for the arbitrator. It is the arbitrator's construction which was bargained for; and so far as the arbitrator's decision concerns construction of the contract, the courts have no business overruling him because their interpretation of the contract is different from his.

We agree with the Court of Appeals that the judgment of the District Court should be modified so that the amounts due the employees may be definitely determined by arbitration. In all other respects we think the judgment of the District Court should be affirmed. Accordingly, we reverse the judgment of the Court of Appeals except for that modification, and remand the case to the District Court for proceedings in conformity with this opinion.

It is so ordered.

MR. JUSTICE FRANKFURTER concurs in the result.

MR. JUSTICE BLACK took no part in the consideration or decision of this case.

MR. JUSTICE WHITTAKER (dissenting). Claiming that the employer's discharge on January 18, 1957, of 11 employees violated the provisions of its collective bargaining contract with the employer—covering the period beginning April 5, 1956, and ending April 4, 1957—the union sought and obtained arbitration, under the provisions of the contract, of the issues whether these employees had been discharged in violation of the agreement and, if so, should be ordered reinstated and awarded wages from the time of their wrongful discharge. In August 1957, more than four months after the collective agreement had expired, these issues, by agreement of the parties, were submitted to a single arbitrator, and a hearing was held before him on January 3, 1958. On April 10, 1958, the arbitrator made his award, finding that the 11 employees had been discharged in violation of the agreement and ordering their reinstatement with back pay at their regular rates from a time 10 days after their discharge to the time of reinstatement. Over the employer's objection that the collective agreement and the submission under it did not authorize nor empower the arbitrator to award reinstatement or wages for any period after the date of expiration of the contract (April 4, 1957), the District Court ordered

---

3. See Jalet, *Judicial Review of Arbitration: The Judicial Attitude*, 45 CORNELL L. Q. 519, 522.

enforcement of the award. The Court of Appeals modified the judgment by eliminating the requirement that the employer reinstate the employees and pay them wages for the period *after* expiration of the collective agreement, and affirmed it in all other respects, 269 F. 2d 327, and we granted certiorari, 361 U.S. 929.

That the propriety of the discharges, under the collective agreement, was arbitrable under the provisions of that agreement, even after its expiration, is not in issue. Nor is there any issue here as to the power of the arbitrator to award reinstatement status and back pay to the discharged employees to the date of expiration of the collective agreement. It is conceded, too, that the collective agreement expired by its terms on April 4, 1957, and was never extended or renewed.

The sole question here is whether the arbitrator exceeded the submission and his powers in awarding reinstatement and back pay for any period after expiration of the collective agreements. Like the Court of Appeals, I think he did. I find nothing in the collective agreement that purports to so authorize. Nor does the Court point to anything in the agreement that purports to do so. Indeed, the union does not contend that there is any such covenant in the contract. Doubtless all rights that accrued to the employees under the collective agreement during its term, and that were made arbitrable by its provisions, could be awarded to them by the arbitrator, even though the period of the agreement had ended. But surely no rights *accrued* to the employees under the agreement after it had expired. Save for the provisions of the collective agreement, and in the absence, as here, of any applicable rule of law or contrary covenant between the employer and the employees, the employer had the legal right to discharge the employees at will. The collective agreement, however, protected them against discharge, for specified reasons, during its continuation. But when that agreement expired, it did not continue to afford rights *in futuro* to the employees—as though still effective and governing. After the agreement expired, the employment status of these 11 employees was terminable at the will of the employer, as the Court of Appeals quite properly held, 269 F. 2d, at 331, and see Meadows v. Radio Industries, 222 F. 2d 347, 349 (C.A. 7th Cir.) ; Atchison, T. & S. F. R. Co. v. Andrews, 211 F. 2d 264, 265 (C.A. 10th Cir.) ; Warden v. Hinds, 163 F. 201 (C.A. 4th Cir.), and the announced discharge of these 11 employees then became lawfully effective.

Once the contract expired, no rights continued to accrue under it to the employees. Thereafter

they had no contractual right to demand that the employer continue to employ them, and *a fortiori* the arbitrator did not have power to order the employer to do so ; nor did the arbitrator have power to order the employer to pay wages to them after the date of termination of the contract, which was also the effective date of their discharges.

The judgment of the Court of Appeals, affirming so much of the award as required reinstatement of the 11 employees to employment status and payment of their wages until expiration of the contract, but not thereafter, seems to me to be indubitably correct, and I would affirm it.

ENTERPRISE WHEEL AND CAR CORP. and UNITED STEELWORKERS OF AMERICA

Steelworkers Arbitration Bulletin 4403 (1958)
Opinion of the Arbitrator, Milton H. Schmidt:

THE GRIEVANCE AND ISSUE

This grievance, filed by 11 employees on January 23, 1957, challenges the action of the Company in discharging them on January 18, 1957. It is claimed that the discharge was without good cause and was not procedurally proper in that the grievants were not first suspended as required by Article IV of the Agreement. Reinstatement with retroactive compensation for all lost pay is requested.

Hearing of the grievance was delayed pending determination by the United States District Court for the Southern District of West Virginia of the enforceability of the arbitration provisions of the Agreement, the Company having refused to arbitrate on the claim that the Arbitration Agreement was not enforceable under the West Virginia law. The Court ruled that the arbitration clause was valid and specifically enforceable, relying upon the recent decisions of the United States Supreme Court in Textile Workers of America v. Lincoln Mills of Alabama, 353 U.S. 448 ; General Electric Company v. Local 205, United Electrical, Radio and Machine Workers of America, 353 U.S. 545 ; and Goodall Sanford, Inc. v. United Textile Workers of America, 353 U.S. 350.

The Company asserts that the grievants quit their employment voluntarily by participating in an unlawful and unauthorized strike ; that in any event, even if the termination could be considered a discharge, it was for good cause ; and finally that the grievance is moot since the Agreement between the Company and the Union expired by its terms on April 4, 1957.

FACTS AND DECISION

The parties entered into a Collective Bargaining Agreement on April 5, 1956, to continue until midnight, April 4, 1957. No Agreement has been entered into by the parties since the latter date.

Article III of the Agreement provided for the settlement of disputes by the usual four-step grievance procedure with final arbitration of unresolved grievances.

Article IV, Section 1, provided that no employee would be peremptorily discharged, but that in all cases where Management determined that an employee's conduct justified discharge, he would first be suspended for not more than five days, with a right to a hearing, during the five-day period, on the question of the propriety of the suspension and whether it should be modified or concerted into discharge.

This Section further provides in part:

> Should it be determined by the Company or by an Arbitrator in accordance with the grievance procedure that the employee has been suspended unjustly or discharged in violation of the provisions of this Agreement, the Company shall reinstate the employee and pay full compensation at the employee's regular rate of pay for time lost.

The Company had 53 employees in December, 1956, and 52 employees in January, 1957, within the bargaining unit.

On January 17, 1957, a committee of the Union came to the office of the President and Manager of the Company to protest the action of the Company in discharging an employee, Medley, for alleged repeated absences. This meeting took place about 12:30 p.m., during the lunch hour. The President stated that he would not alter his previous decision concerning Medley, and that, if the Union considered the action improper, a grievance could be filed. There is some evidence that members of the committee rejected this suggestion. It is claimed that some members of the committee stated, in substance, "We have a better way of handling that" (Tr. 37, 75) but this statement is denied by the Union witnesses who were present at the meeting (Tr. 66, 67, 73).

After a few minutes' discussion the men left the office and returned to the Plant. About 1 p.m. the President, Mr. Kraehenbuehl, went into the Plant and the 11 grievants were congregated in the washroom discussing the subject of their prior conference. After answering a telephone call the President returned and told the men either to go back to work or to ring out and go outside and figure it out (Tr. 77). Thereupon, the 11 employees punched out their time cards and walked outside.

The President stated that at that time he had made no decision to terminate the employment of these men (Tr. 44, 45).

Upon leaving the Plant one of the grievants called the Staff Representative and told him about the situation. The Staff Representative advised them to return to the Plant and inform the President that they would file a grievance on the Medley matter and return to work.

Shortly thereafter, that is about 30 to 35 minutes after leaving the Plant, the grievants went back to the President's office, told him that they had conferred by telephone with the Staff Representative and that they had decided to submit the Medley dispute to the grievance procedure.

The President testified:

> They wanted to know whether they could come back to work and I said "No, not with Medley." Medley couldn't come back. They said "How about if we keep Medley out, can the rest of us come back in the morning?" And I said "Yes." And so they left ... (Tr. 45.)

The President then, within five minutes, called the Company attorney to tell him what had happened. The attorney advised him that he was under no obligation to take the men back since they had quit their jobs. The President then went into the Plant and informed the President of the Union that the 11 men who had gone out "would not be permitted to return at the present time." (Tr. 46.)

The Union President, who was laid off at the time of the hearing, did not testify. One of the grievants, Insco, testified that the Union President did not advise the men that the previous understanding that they were to return to work the following day had been cancelled (Tr. 53, 54).

The following morning, January 18, as the men reported to work they found that their time cards had been removed from the rack. The President of the Company who was in the clock house, told them they "didn't have any job there any more until this thing was settled one way or the other." (Tr. 53.) They were ordered off the property.

The grievants then picketed the Plant from January 21 to January 25. The evidence is not clear as to whether they carried picket signs or banners. Other employees respecting the picket line did not report for work during that week (Tr. 41).

The Company introduced evidence that about a month previous to the instance covered by this grievance, there had been a wildcat or unauthorized strike for two days in which most of the grievants and some other employees joined. The men, however, returned to work and no disciplinary action was taken against them.

The men were not expressly told at any time that they were discharged, nor did they receive a preliminary suspension notice.

These facts present the question whether the grievants voluntarily quit their jobs, or, in the alternative, whether their employment was properly terminated for good cause.

The evidence is clear that the men were not discharged when they first left the Plant. They were told by the President either to go back to work or ring out and go outside and discuss their problem. He did not consider or state to the men at that time that if they left the Plant their act of leaving would be construed as quitting their jobs. Upon their return within a half hour, the President admittedly told them they could return to work the following day. No penalty was suggested or inferred. Presumably the matter was settled at this point. The men left the premises with the assurance of the President that their jobs were not in jeopardy.

Under these circumstances I am unable to conclude from the evidence that the men had quit their jobs. Or, if their previous leaving could be construed as an intention to quit, then the Company through the President, had excused this brief walkout by agreeing that they should return to work the following day.

The President, after this agreement, changed his mind upon advice of his counsel, and informed the President of the Union that the men would not be taken back. This second decision was carried out the following day by excluding the men who reported for work from the Plant. I interpret these facts to constitute discharge of the grievants.

The grievants were in error in not immediately filing a grievance in the Medley dispute matter, rather than taking the action they did.

As soon as they checked with the Union Staff Representative they corrected their previous mistake and promptly informed Management that they would process the Medley dispute under grievance procedure. As a compromise and settlement of the problem Management agreed to permit them to continue their jobs and directed them to report for work the next morning.

Under these circumstances, it is my judgment that the penalty of discharge was not justified. In any event, the contractual obligation of the Company to suspend prior to discharge was ignored. The walkout of December 6, 1956, cannot justify the action taken on January 18, since that event was past history and waived by the Company. At least it was not asserted as a justifiable basis or ground for the termination of employment.

The action of the men should not be condoned, despite the first decision of Management to have them return to work without penalty. At most, however, the facts warrant the imposition of a disciplinary penalty of suspension of 10 days for each of the grievants.

I cannot agree with the Company's contention that this grievance is moot since the Agreement terminated on April 4, 1957, and no new Agreement has been entered into. Not only was the Agreement effective during and for several months after the grievance arose, but, even after that, the Union continued as the representative and collective bargaining agent for the grievants and all other employees in the unit. Their status as employees continued, during the subsequent period of negotiations for contract renewal. They were protected by the law from improper discrimination or termination of their employment without good cause. Their grievance presented a continuing controversy as to rights of employment reinstatement and back pay.

Article IV of the Agreement imposes an unconditional obligation on the Company to compensate an employee wrongfully discharged or suspended for time lost.

The decision of the Regional Director of the NLRB refusing to issue a complaint on the charge of the Union that the Company had committed unfair labor practices in violation of Section 8 of the National Labor Relations Act involved different issues than those raised here. This action is therefore no bar to the arbitration of this grievance.

In view of the foregoing, therefore, it is my judgment that the grievants were discharged without good or proper cause; that the discharge be reduced to a suspension for 10 days for each of the grievants; that they be reinstated to their former status of employees; that they be compensated for such time as they would have worked, less the suspension period and less such sums as each may have received from other employment.

AWARD

The grievance is allowed as follows:

1. The discharge of each of the grievants which occurred on January 18, 1957, is set aside and reduced to a disciplinary penalty of 10 days' suspension for each of the grievants. The 10-day period is to be calculated from January 18, 1957.

2. The Company shall reinstate each of the grievants who desire reinstatement to the status

of employees with their classifications and seniority status as of the date of their discharge, January 18, 1957.

3. The Company shall reimburse the grievants for all time actually lost from work which they would otherwise have had from the Company at the regular rate of pay for each grievant, less the 10-day suspension period and less such amounts as each has received for other employment since 10 days after January 18, 1957.

C.

The Issue of Strikes in the Context of Arbitration

LOCAL 174, TEAMSTERS v.
LUCAS FLOUR CO.
369 U.S. 95 (1962)

STEWART, J. The petitioner and the respondent (which we shall call the union and the employer) were parties to a collective bargaining contract within the purview of the National Labor Relations Act. The contract contained the following provisions, among others:

Article II

The Employer reserves the right to discharge any man in his employ if his work is not satisfactory.

Article XIV

Should any difference as to the true interpretation of this agreement arise, same shall be submitted to a Board of Arbitration of two members, one representing the firm, and one representing the Union. If said members cannot agree, a third member, who must be a disinterested party shall be selected, and the decision of the said Board of Arbitration shall be binding. It is further agreed by both parties hereto that during such arbitration, there shall be no suspension of work.

Should any difference arise between the employer and the employee, same shall be submitted to arbitration by both parties. Failing to agree, they shall mutually appoint a third person whose decision shall be final and binding.

In May of 1958 an employee named Welsch was discharged by the employer after he had damaged a new fork-lift truck by running it off a loading platform and onto some railroad tracks. When a business agent of the union protested, he was told by a representative of the employer that Welsch had been discharged because of unsatisfactory work. The union thereupon called a strike to force the employer to rehire Welsch. The strike lasted eight days.[1] After the strike was over, the issue of Welsch's discharge was submitted to arbitration. Some five months later the Board of Arbitration rendered a decision, ruling that Welsch's work had been unsatisfactory, that his unsatisfactory work had been the reason for his discharge, and that he was not entitled to reinstatement as an employee.

In the meantime, the employer had brought this suit against the union in the Superior Court of King County, Washington, asking damages for business losses caused by the strike. After a trial that court entered a judgment in favor of the employer in the amount of $6,501.60.[2] On appeal the judgment was affirmed by Department One of the Supreme Court of Washington. 57 Wash. 2d 95, 356 P. 2d 1.

Whether, as a matter of federal law, the strike which the union called was a violation of the collective bargaining contract is thus the ultimate issue which this case presents. It is argued that there could be no violation in the absence of a no-strike clause in the contract explicitly covering the subject of the dispute over which the strike was called. We disagree.

The collective bargaining contract expressly imposed upon both parties the duty of submitting the dispute in question to final and binding arbitration.[3] In a consistent course of decisions the Courts of Appeals of at least five Federal Circuits have held that a strike to settle a dispute which a collective bargaining agreement provides shall be settled exclusively and finally by compulsory arbitration constitutes a violation of the agreement.[4] The National Labor Relations Board

---

1. The strike was terminated by a temporary injunction issued by the state court.

2. The amount of damage is not in issue here.

3. It appears that this would be true whether the dispute be considered as a "difference as to the true interpretation of this agreement" or as a difference "between the employer and the employee" under Article XIV of the contract. See p. 96, *supra*. The union not only now concedes that the dispute as to Welsch's discharge was subject to final and binding arbitration, but, indeed, after the strike, the dispute was so arbitrated.

4. See Local 25, Teamsters Union v. W. L. Mead, Inc., 230 F. 2d 576, 583–584 (C.A. 1st Cir.); United Construction Workers v. Haislip Baking Co., 223 F. 2d 872, 876–877 (C.A. 4th Cir.); Labor Board v. Dorsey Trailers, Inc., 179 F. 2d 589, 592 (C.A. 5th Cir.); Lewis v. Benedict Coal Corp., 259 F. 2d 346, 351 (C.A. 6th Cir.); Labor Board v. Sunset Minerals, 211 F. 2d 224, 226 (C.A. 9th Cir.).

has reached the same conclusion. W. L. Mead, Inc., 113 **N.L.R.B.** 1040. We approve that doctrine.[5] To hold otherwise would obviously do violence to accepted principles of traditional contract law. Even more in point, a contrary view would be completely at odds with the basic policy of national labor legislation to promote the arbitral process as a substitute for economic warfare. See United Steelworkers v. Warrior & Gulf Nav. Co., 363 U.S. 574.

What has been said is not to suggest that a no-strike agreement is to be implied beyond the area which it has been agreed will be exclusively covered by compulsory terminal arbitration. Nor is it to suggest that there may not arise problems in specific cases as to whether compulsory and binding arbitration has been agreed upon, and, if so, as to what disputes have been made arbitrable.[6] But no such problems are present in this case. The grievance over which the union struck was, as it concedes, one which it had expressly agreed to settle by submission to final and binding arbitration proceedings. The strike which it called was a violation of that contractual obligation.

Affirmed.

BLACK, J. (dissenting). The petitioner local union and the respondent company entered into a written collective bargaining agreement containing an express provision for the arbitration of disputes growing out of differences as to the proper application of the agreement in the following terms:

> Should any difference arise between the employer and the employee, same shall be submitted to arbitration by both parties. Failing to agree, they shall mutually appoint a third person whose decision shall be final and binding.

The Court now finds—out of clear air, so far as I can see—that the union, without saying so in the agreement, not only agreed to arbitrate such differences, but also promised that there would be no strike while arbitration of a dispute was pending under this provision. And on the basis of its "discovery" of this additional

unwritten promise by the union, the Court upholds a judgment awarding the company substantial damages for a strike in breach of contract.

That the Court's decision actually vacates and amends the contract that the parties themselves had made and signed is shown, I think, by the very face of that original contract. The arbitration provision covering disputes growing out of the application of the contract immediately follows another quite different arbitration provision —one covering disputes "as to the true interpretation of this agreement" in the following terms.

> Should any difference as to the true interpretation of this agreement arise, same shall be submitted to a Board of Arbitration of two members, one representing the firm, and one representing the Union. If said members cannot agree, a third member, who must be a disinterested party shall be selected, and the decision of the said Board of Arbitration shall be binding. *It is further agreed by both parties hereto that during such arbitration, there shall be no suspension of work.* (Emphasis supplied.)

In view of the fact that this latter provision contains an explicit promise by the union "that during such arbitration, there shall be no suspension of work," it seems to me plain that the parties to this contract, knowing how to write a provision binding a union not to strike, deliberately included a no-strike clause with regard to disputes over broad questions of contractual interpretation and deliberately excluded such a clause with regard to the essentially factual disputes arising out of the application of the contract in particular instances. And there is not a word anywhere else in this agreement which indicates that this perfectly sensible contractual framework for handling these two different kinds of disputes was not intended to operate in the precise manner dictated by the express language of the two arbitration provisions.

The defense offered for the Court's rewriting of the contract which the parties themselves made is that to allow the parties' own contract to stand "would obviously do violence to accepted principles of traditional contract law" and "be completely at odds with the basic policy of national labor legislation to promote the arbitral process." I had supposed, however—though evidently the Court thinks otherwise—that the job of courts enforcing contracts was to give legal effect to what the contracting parties actually agree to do, not to what courts think they ought to do. In any case, I have been unable to find any accepted principle of contract law— traditional or otherwise—that permits courts to

---

5. Deciding the case as we do upon this explicit ground, we do not adopt the reasoning of the Washington court. Insofar as the language of that court's opinion is susceptible to the construction that a strike during the term of a collective bargaining agreement is *ipso facto* a violation of the agreement, we expressly reject it.

6. With respect to such problems, compare United Mine Workers v. Labor Board, 103 U.S. App. D.C. 207, 257 F. 2d 211, with Lewis v. Benedict Coal Corp., 259 F. 2d 346 (affirmed on this question by an equally divided Court, 361 U.S. 459), for differing interpretations of an identical contract.

change completely the nature of a contract by adding new promises that the parties themselves refused to make in order that the new court-made contract might better fit into whatever social, economic, or legal policies the courts believe to be so important that they should have been taken out of the realm of voluntary contract by the legislative body and furthered by compulsory legislation.

The mere fact that the dispute which brought about this strike was subject to "final and binding" arbitration under this contract certainly does not justify the conclusion that the union relinquished its right to strike in support of its position on that dispute. The issue here involves, not the nature of the arbitration proceeding, but the question of whether the union, by agreeing to arbitrate, has given up all other separate and distinct methods of getting its way. Surely, no one would suggest that a provision for final and binding arbitration would preclude a union from attempting to persuade an employer to forego action the union was against, even where that action was fully within the employer's rights under the contract. The same principle supports the right of the union to strike in such a situation for historically, and as was recognized in both the Wagner and Taft-Hartley Acts, the strike has been the unions' most important weapon of persuasion. To say that the right to strike is inconsistent with the contractual duty to arbitrate sounds like a dull echo of the argument which used to be so popular that the right to strike was inconsistent with the contractual duty to work—an argument which frequently went so far as to say that strikes are inconsistent with both the common law and the Constitution.

The additional burden placed upon the union by the Court's writing into the agreement here a promise not to strike is certainly not a matter of minor interest to this employer or to the union. The history of industrial relations in this country emphasizes the great importance to unions of the right to strike as well as an understandable desire on the part of employers to avoid such work stoppages. Both parties to collective bargaining discussions have much at stake as to whether there will be a no-strike clause in any resulting agreement. It is difficult to believe that the desire of employers to get such a promise and the desire of the union to avoid giving it are matters which are not constantly in the minds of those who negotiate these contracts. In such a setting, to hold—on the basis of no evidence whatever—that a union, without knowing it, impliedly surrendered the right to strike by virtue of "traditional contract law" or anything else is to me just fiction. It took more than 50 years for unions to have written into federal legislation the principle that they have a right to strike. I cannot understand how anyone familiar with that history can allow that legislatively recognized right to be undercut on the basis of the attenuated implications the Court uses here.

I do not mean to suggest that an implied contractual promise cannot sometimes be found where there are facts and circumstances sufficient to warrant the conclusion that such was the intention of the parties. But there is no factual basis for such a conclusion in this case and the Court does not even claim to the contrary. The implication of a no-strike clause which the Court purports to find here—an implication completely at war with the language the parties used in making this contract as well as with the normal understanding of the negotiation process by which such contracts are made—has not been supported by so much as one scrap of evidence in this record. The implication found by the Court thus flows neither from the contract itself nor, so far as this record shows, from the intention of the parties. In my judgment, an "implication" of that nature would better be described as a rigid rule of law that an agreement to arbitrate has precisely the same effect as an agreement not to strike—a rule of law which introduces revolutionary doctrine into the field of collective bargaining.

I agree that the Taft-Hartley Act shows a congressional purpose to treat collective bargaining contracts and agreements for arbitration in them as one important way of insuring stability in industrial production and labor relations. But the fact that we may agree, as I do, that these settlements by arbitration are desirable is no excuse whatever for imposing such "contracts," either to compel arbitration or to forbid striking, upon unwilling parties. That approach is certainly contrary to the industrial and labor philosophy of the Taft-Hartley Act. Whatever else may be said about that Act, it seems plain that it was enacted on the view that the best way to bring about industrial peace was through voluntary, not compelled, labor agreements. Section 301 is torn from its roots when it is held to require the sort of compulsory arbitration imposed by this decision. I would reverse this case and relegate this controversy to the forum in which it belongs—the collective bargaining table.

ATKINSON v. SINCLAIR REFINING CO.
370 U.S. 238, 82 S.Ct. 1318 (1962)

WHITE, J. The respondent company employs at its refinery in East Chicago, Indiana, approximately 1,700 men, for whom the petitioning international union and its local are bargaining agents, and 24 of whom are also petitioners here. In early February 1959, the respondent company docked three of its employees at the East Chicago refinery a total of $2.19. On February 13 and 14, 999 of the 1,700 employees participated in a strike or work stoppage, or so the complaint alleges. On March 12, the company filed this suit for damages and an injunction, naming the international and its local as defendants, together with 24 individual union member-employees.

Count I of the complaint, which was in three counts, stated a cause of action under § 301 of the Taft-Hartley Act (29 U.S.C. § 185) against the international and its local. It alleged an existing collective bargaining agreement between the international and the company containing, among other matters, a promise by the union not to strike over any cause which could be the subject of a grievance under other provisions of the contract. It was alleged that the international and the local caused the strike or work stoppage occurring on February 13 and 14 and that the strike was over the pay claims of three employees in the amount of $2.19, which claims were properly subject to the grievance procedure provided by the contract. The complaint asked for damages in the amount of $12,500 from the international and the local.

Count II of the complaint purported to invoke the diversity jurisdiction of the District Court. It asked judgment in the same amount against 24 individual employees, each of whom was alleged to be a committeeman of the local union and an agent of the international, and responsible for representing the international, the local, and their members. The complaint asserted that on February 13 and 14, the individuals,

> contrary to their duty to plaintiff to abide by said contract, and maliciously confederating and conspiring together to cause the plaintiff expense and damage, and to induce breaches of the said contract, and to interfere with performance thereof by the said labor organizations and the affected employees, and to cause breaches thereof, individually and as officers, committeemen and agents of the said labor organizations, fomented, assisted and participated in a strike or work stoppage.

Count III of the complaint asked for an injunction but that matter need not concern us here since it is disposed of in Sinclair Refining Co. v. Atkinson, decided this day.

The defendants filed a motion to dismiss the complaint on various grounds and a motion to stay the action for the reasons (1) that all of the issues in the suit were referable to arbitration under the collective bargaining contract and (2) that important issues in the suit were also involved in certain grievances filed by employees and said to be in arbitration under the contract. The District Court denied the motion to dismiss Count I, dismissed Count II, and denied the motion to stay (187 F. Supp. 225). The Court of Appeals upheld the refusal to dismiss or stay Count I, but reversed the dismissal of Count II (290 F. 2d 312), and this Court granted certiorari (368 U.S. 937).

I

We have concluded that Count I should not be dismissed or stayed. Count I properly states a cause of action under § 301 and is to be governed by federal law. Local 174 v. Lucas Flour Co., 369 U.S. 95, 102–104 ; Textile Workers Union v. Lincoln Mills, 353 U.S. 448. Under our decisions, whether or not the company was bound to arbitrate, as well as what issues it must arbitrate, is a matter to be determined by the Court on the basis of the contract entered into by the parties.

> The Congress . . . has by § 301 of the Labor Management Relations Act, assigned the courts the duty of determining whether the reluctant party has breached his promise to arbitrate. For arbitration is a matter of contract and a party cannot be required to submit to arbitration any dispute which he has not agreed so to submit.

United Steelworkers v. Warrior & Gulf Nav. Co., 363 U.S. 574, 582. See also United Steelworkers v. American Mfg. Co., 363 U.S. 564, 570–571 (concurring opinion). We think it unquestionably clear that the contract here involved is not susceptible to a construction that the company was bound to arbitrate its claim for damages against the union for breach of the undertaking not to strike.

While it is quite obvious from other provisions of the contract[1] that the parties did not intend

---

1. The no-strike clause (Article III) provides that "[T]here shall be no strikes . . . (1) For any cause which is or may be the subject of a grievance . . . or (2) For any other cause, except upon written notice by Union to Employer. . . ." Article XXVII, covering "general disputes," provides that disputes which are general in character or which affect a large number of employees are to be negotiated between the parties; there is no provision for arbitration. Moreover, the management-prerogative clause (Article XXXI) recognizes that "operation of the Employer's facilities and the direction of the working forces, including the right to hire, suspend or discharge for good and sufficient cause and pursuant to the seniority Article of this agreement, the right to relieve employees from duties because of lack of work, are among the sole prerogatives of the Employer; provided, however, that . . . such suspensions and discharges shall be subject to the grievance and arbitration clause.

to commit all of their possible disputes and the whole scope of their relationship to the grievance and arbitration procedures established in Article XXVI,[2] that article itself is determinative of the issue in this case since it precludes arbitration boards from considering any matters other than employee grievances.[3] After defining a grievance as "any difference regarding wages, hours or working conditions between the parties hereto or between the Employer and an employee covered by this working agreement," Article XXVI provides that the parties desire to settle employee grievances fairly and quickly and that therefore a stated procedure "must be followed." The individual employee is required to present his grievance to his foreman, and if not satisfied there, he may take his grievance to the plant superintendent who is to render a written decision. There is also provision for so-called Workmen's Committees to present grievances to the local management. If the local superintendent's decision is not acceptable, the matter is to be referred for discussion between the President of the International and the Director of Industrial Relations for the company (or their representatives), and for decision by the Director alone. If the Director's decision is disputed, then "upon request of the President or any District Director" of the international, a local arbitration board may be convened and the matter finally decided by this board.

Article XXVI then imposes the critical limitation. It is provided that local arbitration boards "shall consider only individual or local employee or local committee grievances arising under the application of the currently existing agreement." There is not a word in the grievance and arbitration article providing for the submission of grievances by the company. Instead, there is the express, flat limitation that arbitration boards should consider only employee grievances. Furthermore, the article expressly provides that arbitration may be invoked only at the option of the union. At no place in the contract does the union agree to arbitrate at the behest of the company. The company is to take its claims elsewhere, which it has now done.

The union makes a further argument for a stay. Following the strike, and both before and after the company filed its suit, 14 of the 24 individual defendants filed grievances claiming reimbursement for pay withheld by the employer. The union argues that even though the company need not arbitrate its claim for damages, it is bound to arbitrate these grievances; and the arbitrator, in the process of determining the grievants' right to reimbursement, will consider and determine issues which also underlie the company's claim for damages. Therefore, it is said that a stay of the court action is appropriate.

We are not satisfied from the record now before us, however, that any significant issue in the damage suit will be presented to and decided by an arbitrator. The grievances filed simply claimed reimbursement for pay due employees for time spent at regular work or processing grievances. Although the record is a good deal less than clear and although no answer has been filed in this case, it would appear from the affidavits of the parties presented in connection with the motion to stay that the grievants claimed to have been disciplined as a result of the work stoppage and that they were challenging this disciplinary action. The company sharply denies in its brief in this Court that any employee was disciplined. In any event, precisely what discipline was imposed, upon what grounds it is being attacked by the grievants, and the circumstances surrounding the withholding of pay from the employees are unexplained in the record. The union's brief here states that the important issue underlying the arbitration and the suit for damages is whether the grievants instigated or participated in a work stoppage contrary to the collective bargaining contract. This the company denies and it asserts that no issue in the damage suit will be settled by arbitrating the grievances.

The District Court must decide whether the company is entitled to damages from the union for breach of contract. The arbitrator, if arbitration occurs, must award or deny reimbursement in whole or in part to all or some of the 14 employees. His award, standing alone, obviously would determine no issue in the damage suit. If he awarded reimbursement to the employees and if it could be ascertained with

---

2. Article XXVI is set out in full *infra* as an Appendix.

3. We do not need to reach, therefore, the question of whether, under the contract involved here, breaches of the no-strike clause are "grievances," *i.e.*, "difference[s] regarding wages, hours or working conditions," or are "grievances" in the more general sense of the term. See Hoover Express Co. v. Teamsters Local, No. 327, 217 F. 2d 49 (C.A. 6th Cir.). The present decision does not approve or disapprove the doctrine of the Hoover case or the Sixth Circuit cases following it (*e.g.*, Vulcan-Cincinnati, Inc., v. United Steelworkers, 289 F. 2d 103; United Auto Workers v. Benton Harbor Indus., 242 F. 2d 536). See also cases collected in Yale & Towne Mfg. Co. v. Local Lodge No. 1717, 299 F. 2d 882, 883–884 n. 5, 6 (C.A. 3d Cir.). In Drake Bakeries, Inc., v. Local 50, decided this day, the question of arbitrability of a damages claim for breach of a no-strike clause is considered and resolved in favor of arbitration in the presence of an agreement to arbitrate "all complaints, disputes or grievances arising between them [*i.e.*, the parties] involving . . . any act or conduct or relation between the parties."

any assurance[4] that one of his subsidiary findings was that the 14 men had not participated in a forbidden work stoppage—the critical issue according to the union's brief—the company would nevertheless not be foreclosed in court since, even if it were bound by such a subsidiary finding made by the arbitrator, it would be free to prove its case in court through the conduct of other agents of the union. In this state of the record, the union has not made out its case for a stay.[5]

For the foregoing reasons, the lower courts properly denied the union's motion to dismiss Count I or stay it pending arbitration of the employer's damage claim.

II

We turn now to Count II of the complaint, which charged 24 individual officers and agents of the union with breach of the collective bargaining contract and tortious interference with contractual relations. The District Court held that under § 301 union officers or members cannot be held personally liable for union actions, and that therefore "suits of the nature alleged in Count II are no longer cognizable in state or federal courts." The Court of Appeals reversed, however, ruling that "Count II stated a cause of action cognizable in the courts of Indiana and, by diversity, maintainable in the District Court."

We are unable to agree with the Court of Appeals, for we are convinced that Count II is controlled by federal law and that it must be dismissed on the merits for failure to state a claim upon which relief can be granted.

Under § 301 a suit for violation of the collective bargaining contract in either a federal or state court is governed by federal law (Local 174 v. Lucas Flour Co., 369 U.S. 95, 102–104;

Textile Workers Union v. Lincoln Mills, 353 U.S. 448), and Count II on its face charges the individual defendants with a violation of the no-strike clause. After quoting verbatim the no-strike clause, Count II alleges that the 24 individual defendants "contrary to their duty to plaintiff to abide by" the contract fomented and participated in a work stoppage in violation of the no-strike clause. The union itself does not quarrel with the proposition that the relationship of the members of the bargaining unit to the employer is "governed by" the bargaining agreement entered into on their behalf by the union. It is universally accepted that the no-strike clause in a collective agreement at the very least establishes a rule of conduct or condition of employment the violation of which by employees justifies discipline or discharge (Mastro Plastics Cor. v. Labor Board, 350 U.S. 270, 280 & n. 10; Labor Board v. Rockaway News Co., 345 U.S. 71, 80; Labor Board v. Sands Mfg. Co., 306 U.S. 332; Labor Board v. Draper Corp., 145 F. 2d 199 (C.A. 4th Cir.); United Biscuit Co. v. Labor Board, 128 F. 2d 771 (C.A. 7th Cir.); see R. R. Donnelley & Sons Co., 5 LAB. ARB. 16; Ford Motor Co., 1 LAB. ARB. 439). The conduct charged in Count II is therefore within the scope of a "violation" of the collective agreement.

As well as charging a violation of the no-strike clause by the individual defendants, Count II necessarily charges a violation of the clause by the union itself. The work stoppage alleged is the identical work stoppage for which the union is sued under Count I and the same damage is alleged as is alleged in Count I. Count II states that the individual defendants acted "as officers, committeemen and agents of the said labor organizations" in breaching and inducing others to breach the collective bargaining contract. Count I charges the principal, and Count II charges the agents for acting on behalf of the principal. Whatever individual liability Count II alleges for the 24 individual defendants, it necessarily restates the liability of the union which is charged under Count I, since under § 301 (b) the union is liable for the acts of its agents, under familiar principles of the law of agency (see also § 301 (e)). Proof of the allegations of Count II in its present form would inevitably prove a violation of the no-strike clause by the union itself. Count II, like Count I, is thus a suit based on the union's breach of its collective bargaining contract with the employer, and therefore comes within § 301 (a). When a union breach of contract is alleged, that the plaintiff seeks to hold the agents liable in-

---

4. Arbitrators generally have no obligation to give their reasons for an award. United Steelworkers v. Enterprise Corp., 363 U.S. 593, 598; Bernhardt v. Polygraphic Co., 350 U.S. 198, 203. The record of their proceedings is not as complete as it is in a court trial. *Ibid.*

5. The union also argues that the preemptive doctrine of cases such as San Diego Bldg. Trades Council v. Garmon, 359 U.S. 236, is applicable and prevents the courts from asserting jurisdiction. Since this is a § 301 suit, that doctrine is inapplicable. Local 174 v. Lucas Flour Co., 360 U.S. 95, 101.

We put aside, since it is unnecessary to reach them, the questions of whether the employer was excused from arbitrating the damage claim because it was over breach of the no-strike clause (see Drake Bakeries, Inc., v. Local 50, decided this day) and whether the underlying factual or legal determination, made by an arbitrator in the process of awarding or denying reimbursement to 14 employees, would bind either the union or the company in the latter's action for damages against the union in the District Court.

stead of the principal does not bring the action outside the scope of § 301.[6]

Under any theory, therefore, the company's action is governed by the national labor relations law which Congress commanded this Court to fashion under § 301 (a). We hold that this law requires the dismissal of Count II for failure to state a claim for which relief can be granted —whether the contract violation charged is that of the union or that of the union plus the union officers and agents.

When Congress passed § 301, it declared its view that only the union was to be made to respond for union wrongs, and that the union members were not to be subject to levy. Section 301 (b) has three clauses. One makes unions suable in the courts of the United States. Another makes unions bound by the acts of their agents according to conventional principles of agency law (cf. § 301 (e)). At the same time, however, the remaining clause exempts agents and members from personal liability for judgments against the union (apparently even when the union is without assets to pay the judgment). The legislative history of § 301 (b) makes it clear that this third clause was a deeply felt congressional reaction against the *Danbury Hatters* case (Loewe v. Lawlor, 208 U.S. 274 ; Lawlor v. Loewe 235 U.S. 522), and an expression of legislative determination that the aftermath (Loewe v. Savings Bank of Danbury, 236 F. 444 (C.A. 2d Cir.)) of that decision was not to be permitted to recur. In that case, an antitrust treble damage action was brought against a large number of union members, including union officers and agents, to recover from them the employer's losses in a nationwide, union-directed boycott of his hats. The union was not named as a party, nor was judgment entered against it. A large money judgment was entered, instead, against the individual defendants for participating in the plan "emanating from headquarters" (235 U.S., at 534), by knowingly authorizing and delegating authority to the union officers to do the acts involved. In the debates, Senator Ball, one of the Act's sponsors, declared that § 301, "by providing that the union may sue and be sued as a legal entity, for a violation of contract, and that

liability for damages will lie against union assets only, will prevent a repetition of the *Danbury Hatters* case, in which many members lost their homes" (93 Cong. Rec. 5014). See also 93 Cong. Rec. 3839, 6283 ; S. Rep. No. 105, 80th Cong., 1st Sess. 16.

Consequently, in discharging the duty Congress imposed on us to formulate the federal law to govern § 301 (a) suits, we are strongly guided by and do not give a niggardly reading to § 301 (b). "We would undercut the Act and defeat its policy if we read § 301 narrowly" (Lincoln Mills, 353 U.S., at 456). We have already said in another context that § 301 (b) at least evidences "a congressional intention that the union as an entity, like a corporation, should in the absence of agreement be the sole source of recovery for injury inflicted by it" (Lewis v. Benedict Coal Corp., 361 U.S. 459, 470). This policy cannot be evaded or truncated by the simple device of suing union agents or members, whether in contract or tort, or both, in a separate count or in a separate action for damages for violation of a collective bargaining contract for which damages the union itself is liable. The national labor policy requires and we hold that when a union is liable for damages for violation of the no-strike clause, its officers and members are not liable for these damages. Here, Count II, as we have said, necessarily alleges union liability but prays for damages from the union agents. Where the union has inflicted the injury it alone must pay. Count II must be dismissed.[7]

The case is remanded to the District Court for further proceedings not inconsistent with this opinion.

It is so ordered.

MR. JUSTICE FRANKFURTER took no part in the consideration or decision of this case.

Appendix to Opinion of the Court

Article XXVI provides:

GRIEVANCE AND ARBITRATION PROCEDURE

DEFINITION

1. A grievance is defined to be any difference

---

6. Swift & Co. v. United Packinghouse Workers, 177 F. Supp. 511 (D. Colo.). Contra, Square D Co. v. United E., R & M. Wkrs., 123 F. Supp. 776, 779–781 (E.D. Mich.). See also Morgan Drive Away, Inc., v. Teamsters Union, 166 F. Supp. 885 (S.D. Ind.), concluding, as we do, that the complaint should be dismissed because of §§ 301 (b) and 301 (c), but for want of jurisdiction rather than on the merits. Our holding, however, is that the suit is a § 301 suit; whether there is a claim upon which relief can be granted is a separate question. See Bell v. Hood, 327 U.S. 678.

7. In reaching this conclusion, we have not ignored the argument that Count II was drafted in order to anticipate the possible union defense under Count I that the work stoppage was unauthorized by the union, and was a wildcat strike led by the 24 individual defendants acting not in behalf of the union but in their personal and nonunion capacity. The language of Count II contradicts the argument, however, and we therefore do not reach the question of whether the count would state a proper § 301 (a) claim if it charged unauthorized, individual action.

regarding wages, hours or working conditions between the parties hereto or between the Employer and an employee covered by this working agreement which might arise within any plant or within any region of operations.

GRIEVANCE PROCEDURE

It is the sincere desire of both parties that employee grievances be settled as fairly and as quickly as possible. Therefore, when a grievance arises, the following procedure must be followed:

2. For the purpose of adjusting employee grievances and disputes as defined above, it is agreed that any employee, individually or accompanied by his committeeman, if desired shall:

(a) Seek direct adjustment of any grievance or dispute with the foreman under whom he is employed. Such meeting will be without loss of time to the employee and/or his committeeman during regular working hours for time spent in conference with the foreman. The foreman shall reply to said employee within three (3) working days (Saturday, Sunday and Holidays excluded) from the date on which the grievance was first presented to him;

(b) If the question is not then settled, the employee may submit his grievance in writing, on forms supplied by Union, to a committee selected as hereinafter provided for the particular plant or region in which such employee is employed. Such committee shall investigate said complaint and if in its opinion the grievance has merit it shall have the right to meet with the local company superintendent or his representative, who shall receive the committee for this purpose. Written decisions shall be made by the local superintendent or his representative within ten (10) days after meeting with the committee, provided that prior to the time of or at the meeting with the committee such complaint or grievance has been submitted in writing to the local superintendent or his representative.

(c) In exceptional cases, Workmen's Committees shall have the right to institute grievances concerning any alleged violation of this Agreement by filing written complaint with the official locally in charge.

(d) Any grievance filed with or by the local Workmen's Committee can only be withdrawn with the Workmen's Committee's consent.

3. No complaint or grievance shall be considered hereunder unless it is presented to the superintendent or official locally in charge within sixty (60) days from the date on which the complaint or grievance arose, or from the date on which the employee or employees concerned first learned of the cause of complaint.

4. The committee above mentioned shall be selected from among and by employees of the Employer who are members of the Union. No official, foreman, or employee having authority to hire or discharge men shall serve on the committee.

5. In case of discharge or lay-off, employees who may desire to file complaints must present such complaints within one (1) week after the effective date of discharge or lay-off to the committee mentioned in this Article. Before any such employee is to be discharged for cause, other than flagrant violation of rules, or is to be laid off, he shall be given a written notice, dated and signed by his foreman or other respresentative of the Employer, setting forth the reason for such discharge or lay-off. In the event an employee has been discharged for a flagrant violation of a company rule, he shall subsequently, upon request, be given a written notice, dated and signed by his foreman or other representative of the Employer setting forth the reason for such discharge. The Workmen's Committee will be furnished with a copy of the statement furnished to the employee, both where the discharge or lay-off is for cause or for flagrant violation of a Company rule. Any grievance to be filed under this section must be filed within forty (40) days from the effective date of the discharge or lay-off.

6. In the event the decision of the superintendent or his representative shall not be satisfactory to the committee, it is agreed that the President of the Oil, Chemical and Atomic Workers International Union, AFL–CIO, or someone designated by him, shall, not later than forty-five (45) days after such decision, have the right to confer with the Director of Industrial Relations for the Sinclair Companies, or someone designated by him, for the purpose of discussing grievances or disputes and of obtaining decisions thereon. It is agreed that the Director of Industrial Relations for the Sinclair Companies, or someone designated by him, shall render a decision to the President of the Oil, Chemical and Atomic Workers International Union, AFL—CIO, within twenty (20) days after grievances or disputes have been so submitted to him in writing.

7. If such decision is not satisfactory, then, upon request of the President or any District Director of the Oil, Chemical and Atomic Workers International Union, AFL–CIO and within sixty (60) days from the posting date of the final appeal answer, there shall be set up a local Arbitration Board, and such grievances and disputes submitted to it within ten (10) days after formation of such Board. Such local boards may be set up at each refinery to deal with cases arising therefrom; cases arising from Sinclair Oil & Gas Company shall be heard and determined at Tulsa, Oklahoma; Fort Worth, Texas; Midland, Texas; or Casper, Wyoming; cases arising from Sinclair Pipe Line Company shall be heard and determined at the cities previously named or at Kansas City, Missouri; Toledo, Ohio; Houston, Texas; Chicago, Illinois; Philadelphia, Pennsylvania; or Independence, Kansas. These local Arbitration Boards shall consider only individual or local employee or local committee grievances arising under the application of the currently existing agreement, or supplements thereto, and local wage and classification disputes submitted on the initiative of the President or any District Director of the Oil, Chemical and Atomic Workers International Union, AFL-CIO. In this connection, Employer agrees to give consideration to local classification rate inequity complaints existing by reason of a comparison with the average of competitive rates of pay for like jobs

having comparable duties and responsibilities being paid by agreed-upon major competitive companies in the local area. Such requests for adjustments of classification rate inequities, if any, shall be made not more frequently than twice annually, to be effective on February 1st and August 1st. Such requests to be submitted at least thirty (30) days prior to such semi-annual dates.

8. The above mentioned local Arbitration Board shall be composed of one person designated by Employer and one designated by the President or District Director of the Oil, Chemical and Atomic Workers International Union, AFL–CIO. The board shall be requested by both parties to render a decision within seven (7) days from date of submission. Should the two members of the Board selected as above provided, be unable to agree within seven (7) days, or to mutually agree upon an impartial third arbitrator, an impartial third member shall be selected within seven (7) days thereafter by the employer or employee member of the Arbitration Board, or such two parties jointly, requesting the Federal Mediation and Conciliation Service to submit a panel of arbitrators from which the third member of the board will be selected in accordance with the procedure of such Federal Mediation and Conciliation Service.

9. The decision of the Board aforesaid, as pro-, vided in Section 8 hereof, shall be final. However if the rules and conditions existing at the time a given case originated are subsequently changed, it is understood that the arbitration award rendered under former rules and conditions shall not act to prohibit consideration of a complaint originating under the changed rules and conditions.

10. Cases arising from the Gasoline Plants shall be considered as coming within the Producing Division in which they are located.

11. The fee and expense of the impartial arbitrator selected as above provided shall be divided equally between the parties to such arbitration. The Parties agree to attempt to hold the arbitrator's fees to a reasonable basis.

DRAKE BAKERIES, INC. v. LOCAL 50, AMERICAN BAKERY & CONFECTIONERY WORKERS
370 U.S. 254, 82 S.Ct. 1346 (1962)

WHITE, J. The petitioning company brought this action for damages in the District Court under § 301 (a) of the Taft-Hartley Act, alleging that the respondent union had violated the no-strike clause of the collective bargaining contract between the union and the company. The sole question in the case is whether the District Court was correct in holding that the employer's claim was an arbitrable matter under the contract and in ordering a stay of the action pending completion of arbitration. The Court of Appeals for the Second Circuit affirmed the judgment of the District Court by an equally divided vote. This Court granted certiorari (368 U.S. 975), and set the cause of argument immediately following Atkinson v. Sinclair Refining Co., ante, decided this day.

The company's business is baking and selling cakes and other bakery products. On December 16, 1959, the company notified the union and its employees that because Christmas and New Year's would fall on Fridays and because it was desirable to have fresh bakery products to sell on the Mondays following the holidays, employees would not work on the Thursdays before Christmas and New Year's but would work on the Saturdays following those holidays. Meetings between the union and the company on December 18 and December 22 ensued, the company's position being that it was exercising management's prerogative in rescheduling work, the union's that the proposed work schedule violated the collective bargaining contract and that the employees were not obligated to work on December 26 or January 2. A compromise arrangement was worked out for December 26, and 80 out of 190 employees reported on that day, a sufficient number to allow production to proceed. Further conversations on December 28 were not fruitful, however, and on Saturday, January 2, the company was unable to produce its goods because only 26 employees reported for work. The company promptly filed this damage action on January 4, 1960, alleging that the union instigated and encouraged its members to strike or not to report for work on January 2, all in violation of the no-strike clause contained in the collective bargaining contract. No answer has been filed by the union but the union's affidavit in support of the motion for stay stated what its answer would contain and specifically denied that the union had instigated a strike or encouraged its members not to work on January 2.

As was true in Atkinson, supra, the issue of arbitrability is a question for the courts and is to be determined by the contract entered into by the parties. "[A] party cannot be required to submit to arbitration any dispute which he has not agreed so to submit." United Steelworkers v. Warrior & Gulf Nav. Co., 363 U.S. 574, 582. But the contract here is much different from the agreement in Atkinson. Under Article

V[1] of the contract: "The parties agree that they will promptly attempt to adjust all complaints, disputes or grievances arising between them involving questions of interpretation or application of any clause or matter covered by this contract or any act or conduct or relation between the parties hereto, directly or indirectly."

This is broad language, indeed, and the procedure thereafter provided in Article V does not, as it did in *Atkinson,* exclude claims or complaints of the employer. It is provided that in the first instance the union will be represented by a committee and the shop chairman, and the employer by the shop manager. Failing adjustment at this stage, the issue is required to be submitted in writing by "the party claiming to be aggrieved to the other party," whereupon the union and the plant manager are to attempt to reach a satisfactory agreement. If agreement is not reached within seven days from the time the issue is submitted in writing, either party "shall have the right to refer the latter to arbitration."

Article V does not stop with disputes "involving questions of interpretation or application of any clause or matter" covered by the contract. The adjustment and arbitration procedures are to apply to all complaints, all disputes and all grievances involving any act of either party, or any conduct of either party, or any relation between the parties, directly or indirectly. The company asserts that there was a strike by the union in violation of the no-strike clause. It therefore has a "complaint" against the union concerning the "acts" or "conduct" of the union. There is also involved a "dispute" between the union and the company, for the union denies

that there was a strike at all, denies that it precipitated any strike, denies that the employees were obligated under the contract to work on that January 2, and itself claims that the employer breached the contract in scheduling work for the holidays.[2] Article V on its face easily reaches the employer's claim against the union for damages caused by an alleged strike in violation of the contract.

The company earnestly contends that the parties cannot have intended to arbitrate so fundamental a matter as a union strike in breach of contract, and that only an express inclusion of a damage claim by the employer would suffice to require arbitration. But it appears more reasonable to us to expect such a matter, if it is indeed so fundamental and so basic to the company under the contract, to have been excluded from the comprehensive language of Article V if the parties so intended. In Article VII[3] which contains the no-strike provisions, the parties prohibited strikes, insulated the union, its officers and members from damages for strikes which the union did not authorize, and agreed that even in the case of unauthorized strikes, the company would arbitrate disciplinary action taken against the strikers. In the face of the

---

1. "Article V—Grievance Procedure

"(a) The parties agree that they will promptly attempt to adjust all complaints, disputes or grievances arising between them involving questions of interpretation or application of any clause or matter covered by this contract or any act or conduct or relation between the parties hereto, directly or indirectly.

"In the adjustment of such matters the Union shall be represented in the first instance by the duly designated committee and the Shop Chairman and the Employer shall be represented by the Shop Management. It is agreed that in the handling of grievances there shall be no interference with the conduct of the business.

"(b) If the Committee and the Shop Management are unable to effect an adjustment, then the issue involved shall be submitted in writing by the party claiming to be aggrieved to the other party. The matter shall then be taken up for adjustment between the Union and the Plant Manager or other representative designated by management for the purpose. If no mutually satisfactory adjustment is reached by this means, or in any event within seven (7) days after the submission of the issue in writing as provided above, then either party shall have the right to refer the matter to arbitration as herein provided."

2. Immediately before the Christmas weekend in 1959, petitioner and respondent exchanged telegrams, in the course of which exchange respondent charged:

"We have informed you that we did not agree with, or accept your proposal to amend or alter past practice concerning holiday week-ends. Your proposed schedule and your threats of disciplinary penalties violates contract and practice. . . . If you do not retract position we shall demand arbitration."

3. "Article VII—No Strikes

"(a) There shall be no strike, boycott, interruption of work, stoppage, temporary walk-out or lock-out for any reason during the terms of this contract except that if either party shall fail to abide by the decision of the Arbitrator, after receipt of such decision, under Article 6 of this contract, then the other party shall not be bound by this provision.

"(b) The parties agree as part of the consideration of this agreement that neither the International Union, the Local Union, or any of its officers, agents or members, shall be liable for damages for unauthorized stoppage, strikes, intentional slowdowns or suspensions of work if:

"(a) The Union gives written notice to the Company within twenty-four (24) hours of such action, copies of which shall be posted immediately by the Union on the bulletin board that it has not authorized the stoppage, strike, slowdown or suspension of work, and

"(b) if the Union further cooperates with the Company in getting the employees to return and remain at work.

"It is recognized that the Company has the right to take disciplinary action, including discharge, against any employee who engages in any unauthorized strike or work stoppage, subject to the Union's right to submit to arbitration in accordance with the agreement the question of whether or not the employee did engage in any unauthorized strike or work stoppage."

comprehensive language of Article V, it would have been most appropriate at this point for the parties to have excluded from the arbitration procedures the company's claim for strike damages, if they had intended to do so. Instead, the inclusive coverage of Article V was left intact.

Of significance also are certain events which occurred in August 1959. At that time the company took issue with union conduct in connection with overtime work. Labeling this conduct an "overtime strike" and a "breach of contract," the company wrote a letter to the State Mediation Board of New York saying that the contract with the union provided for arbitration of disputes before an arbitrator appointed by the Board and requesting the appointment of an arbitrator to "determine the question of breach of contract and damages suffered by" the company as a result of the strike. An award of damages against the union was requested, as was injunctive relief against a continuance of the overtime strike.[4] It would appear, then, that the company, just four months earlier in 1959, considered that the fundamental matter of a union-led strike was a dispute to be arbitrated under the provisions of the contract.[5]

The company further asserts that even if it agreed in the contract to arbitrate union violations of the no-strike clause, it is excused by the union's breach from pursuing the post-breach remedies called for in the contract. The company does not deny that grievance and arbitration procedures under this contract—as is true generally (United Steelworkers v. Warrior & Gulf Nav. Co., 363 U.S. 574, 584)—contemplate as a matter of course the arbitration of many alleged breaches of contract. Indeed, central to the company's position is its assertion that the union was bound to arbitrate, rather than strike over, its claim that the company breached the contract by scheduling Saturday work. But in its view, the union's violation of the no-strike clause is *sui generis* and so basic to what the employer bargained for in the contract and so inherently and "fundamentally inconsis-

tent with" the grievance and arbitration procedures that the faithful observance of the no-strike clause by the union is a condition precedent to the employer's duty to arbitrate (even though he has promised to do so), or that the union must be deemed to have waived, or to be estopped from asserting, its right to arbitrate.

However, this Court has prescribed no such inflexible rule rigidly linking no-strike and arbitration clauses of every collective bargaining contract in every situation.[6] The company has not attempted, or claimed the right, either to terminate the entire contract or to extinguish permanently its obligations under the arbitration provisions. Instead, it has sued for damages for an alleged strike and, as far as this record reveals, the contract continued in effect, as did the promises of the parties to arbitrate and the promise of the union not to strike. Moreover, in this case, under this contract, by agreeing to arbitrate all claims without excluding the case where the union struck over an arbitrable matter, the parties have negatived any intention to condition the duty to arbitrate upon the absence of strikes. They have thus cut the ground from under the argument that an alleged strike, automatically and regardless of the circumstances, is such a breach or repudiation of the arbitration clause by the union that the company is excused from arbitrating, upon theories of waiver, estoppel, or otherwise.[7] Arbitration provisions, which themselves have not been repudiated, are meant to survive breaches of contract, in many

---

4. Apparently the employer's thought was that the federal law should borrow the New York rule which is that an arbitrator may award relief in the nature of an injunction, enforceable in the courts regardless of the New York statute similar to the Norris–LaGuardia Act. Ruppert v. Egelhofer, 3 N.Y. 2d 576, 148 N.E. 2d 129.

5. The union opposed arbitration of this dispute, claiming that there was no arbitrable controversy as to the claimed existence of an obligation to work overtime. The parties settled the controversy without conclusive determination of the arbitrability dispute.

6. We do not understand the opinions in Textile Workers Union v. Lincoln Mills, 353 U.S. 448, 455, or United Steelworkers v. American Mfg. Co., 363 U.S. 564, 567, to enunciate a flat and general rule that these two clauses are properly to be regarded as exact counterweights in every industrial setting, or to justify either party to the contract in wrenching them from their context in the collective agreement on the ground that they are mutually dependent covenants which are severable from the other promises between the parties.

7. In Local 174 v. Lucas Flour Co., 369 U.S. 95, 105–106, it was held that a clause requiring the parties to submit disputes to final determination by arbitration implied an obligation not to strike over such disputes. Accordingly, the Court upheld an employer's § 301 breach of contract suit against the union for strike damages due to a walkout over an arbitrable dispute. In that case, unlike the present one, the union conceded that there had been a strike over a grievance which the union had agreed to submit to arbitration. The only question in dispute was liability *vel non*. The union did not contend that, and the Court did not consider whether, the employer's damage claim should have been taken to an arbitrator. And, of course, the Court did not consider whether the union's breach of the no-strike clause constituted a repudiation or waiver of arbitration of the damage claim.

contexts, even total breach;[8] and in determining whether one party has so repudiated his promise to arbitrate that the other party is excused the circumstances of the claimed repudiation are critically important.[9] In this case the union denies having repudiated in any respect its promise to arbitrate, denies that there was a strike, denies that the employees were bound to work on January 2 and asserts that it was the company itself which ignored the adjustment and arbitration provisions by scheduling holiday work.

In passing § 301, Congress was interested in the enforcement of collective bargaining contracts since it would "promote a higher degree of responsibility upon the parties to such agreements, and will thereby promote industrial peace" (S. Rep. No. 105, 80th Cong., 1st Sess. 17). It was particularly interested in placing "sanctions behind agreements to arbitrate grievance disputes" (Textile Workers Union v. Lincoln Mills, 353 U.S. 448, 456). The preferred method for settling disputes was declared by Congress to be "[f]inal adjustment by a method agreed upon by the parties" (§ 203 (d) of the Act, 29 U.S.C. § 173 (d)). "That policy can be effectuated only if the means chosen by the parties for settlement of their differences under a collective bargaining agreement is given full play" (United Steelworkers v. American Mfg. Co., 363 U.S. 564, 566). Under our federal labor policy, therefore, we have every reason to preserve the stabilizing influence of the collective bargaining contract in a situation such as this. We could enforce only the no-strike clause by refusing a stay in the suit for damages in the District Court.

We can enforce both the no-strike clause and the agreement to arbitrate by granting a stay until the claim for damages is arbitrated. This we prefer to do.[10]

Petitioner relies upon decisions by various Courts of Appeals denying stays of damage suits for breach of no-strike clauses for want of arbitrability of the dispute.[11] Most of them, however, involved far more narrowly drawn arbitration clauses than that which is involved here.[12] And in at least two Court of Appeals decisions involving clauses of comparable breadth to that of the instant case, violations of no-strike clauses have been held to be arbitrable and suits for damages have been stayed pending arbitration.[13]

This Court held in Mastro Plastics Corp. v. Labor Board, 350 U.S. 270, that the employer did not have the right to replace employees who had struck over employer unfair labor practices, in the face of an absolute no-strike clause. It was said that, despite the broad prohibition of strikes in the contract, the parties could not have intended to waive the employees' right to strike over a flagrant unfair labor practice, absent an express statement in the contract to that effect. The company urges that *Mastro* precludes the result we have reached in this case. *Mastro*, however, involved a flagrant unfair

---

8. See In re Pahlberg Petition, 131 F. 2d 968 (C.A. 2d Cir.); Kulukundis Shipping Co. v. Amtorg Trading Corp., 126 F. 2d 978 (C.A. 2d Cir.); Pennsylvania Greyhound Lines v. Amalgamated Assn., 98 F. Supp. 789 (W.D. Pa.), rev'd on other grounds, 193 F. 2d 327 (C.A. 3d Cir.); Batter Bldg. Mats. Co. v. Kirschner, 142 Conn. 1, 110 A. 2d 464; Heyman v. Darwins, Ltd., [1942] A.C. 356 (H.L.) (disapproving Jureidini v. National Br. & Ir. Ins. Co., [1915] A.C. 499, 505 (H.L.)). See also Shanferoke Coal Corp. v. Westchester Serv. Corp., 70 F. 2d 297, 299 (C.A. 2d Cir.), aff'd, 293 U.S. 449, 453–454.

9. 6 CORBIN, CONTRACTS § 1443 (1961 Supp., n. 34, pp. 192–193) states:

"The effect of a repudiation upon the repudiator's right to arbitration should depend on the character of his so-called 'repudiation' and the reasons given for it. One who flatly repudiates the provision for arbitration itself should have no right to the stay of a court action brought by the other party. But mere nonperformance, even though unjustified, is not *per se* a 'repudiation.' One who asserts in good faith that the facts justify him in refusing performance of other provisions in the contract should not thereby lose his right to arbitration that he would otherwise have had. There is no inconsistency in his demanding arbitration at the same time that he asserts his legal privilege not to proceed with performance."

10. Cf. Boone v. Eyre, 1 Bl. H. 273, 126 Eng. Rep. 160 (K.B. 1777) (L. Mansfield): ". . . [W]here mutual covenants go to the whole of the consideration on both sides, they are mutual conditions, the one precedent to the other. But where they go only to a part, where a breach may be paid for in damages, there the defendant has a remedy on his covenant, and shall not plead it as a condition precedent." See also Dermott v. Jones, 23 How. 220, 231.

11. These cases are collected in the withdrawn decision of the three-judge panel of the Court of Appeals, 287 F. 2d 155, 158 n. 4. See also Vulcan-Cincinnati, Inc., v. United Steelworkers, 289 F. 2d 103 (C.A. 6th Cir.).

12. E.g., United Furniture Workers v. Colonial Hardwood Co., 168 F. 2d 33 (C.A. 4th Cir.), where arbitration was limited to employee grievances over wages, hours, or working conditions, as in Atkinson v. Sinclair Refining Co., *ante*, and United Automobile Workers v. Benton Harbor Indus., 242 F. 2d 536 (C.A. 6th Cir.); Cuneo Press, Inc., v. Kokomo Union, 235 F. 2d 108 (C.A. 7th Cir.), where arbitration was limited to employee grievances. But see United E., R. & M. Wkrs. v. Miller Metal Prods., Inc., 215 F. 2d 221 (C.A. 4th Cir.) ("[a]ll differences, disputes and grievances that may arise between the parties to this contract with respect to the matters covered in this agreement"); Markel Elec. Prod., Inc., v. United E., R. & M. Wkrs., 202 F. 2d 435 (C.A. 2d Cir.) ("differences . . . as to the meaning and application of the provisions of this agreement, or . . . any trouble of any kind . . . in the plant").

13. Signal-Stat Corp. v. Local 475, 235 F. 2d 298 (C.A. 2d Cir.); Yale & Towne Mfg. Co. v. Local 1717, 299 F. 2d 882 (C.A. 3d Cir.). See *id.*, at 883–884 n. 5, collecting authorities from lower courts. Under New York law, broad arbitration clauses permit arbitrators to award damages. See In re Publishers Assn., 8 N.Y. 2d 414, 171 N.E. 2d 323.

labor practice by the company threatening the very existence of the union itself. A strike in violation of contract is not *per se* an unfair labor practice and there is no suggestion in this record that the one-day strike involved here was of that nature. We do not decide in this case that in no circumstances would a strike in violation of the no-strike clause contained in this or other contracts entitle the employer to rescind or abandon the entire contract or to declare its promise to arbitrate forever discharged or to refuse to arbitrate its damage claims against the union. We do decide and hold that Article V of this contract obligates the company to arbitrate its claims for damages from forbidden strikes by the union and that there are no circumstances in this record which justify relieving the company of its duty to arbitrate the consequences of this one-day strike, intertwined as it is with the union's denials that there was any strike or any breach of contract at all.

If the union did strike in violation of the contract, the company is entitled to its damages ; by staying this action, pending arbitration, we have no intention of depriving it of those damages. We simply remit the company to the forum it agreed to use for processing its strike damage claims. That forum, it is true, may be very different from a courtroom,[14] but we are not persuaded that the remedy there will be inadequate. Whether the damages to be awarded by the arbitrator would not normally be expected to serve as an "effective" deterrent to future strikes, which the company urges, is not a question to be answered in the abstract or in general terms. This question, as well as what result will best promote industrial peace, can only be answered in the factual context of particular cases. Here, the union claims it did not call a strike and that the men were not bound to work on January 2, basing its claim upon years of past practice under the contract. The dispute which this record presents appears to us to be one particularly suited for arbitration, if the parties have agreed to arbitrate. We hold that they did so agree and will hold the company to its bargain.

A final matter is the company's suggestion that the union is not entitled to a stay because it has not proceeded with dispatch in seeking arbitration. The District Court held that the union was not in default, and we agree. If the company had a claim for damages, the contract provided for the company's attempting to adjust its claim by consulting with the union. Failing this, either party could take the matter to arbitration. The

company's claim arose out of events which occured on January 2. This case was filed on January 4. This was the first occasion for the union to insist upon its right to arbitrate the employer's claim for damages. This it promptly did by moving for a stay in the District Court.[15] As its conduct shows in a previous situation, the employer was aware of the procedure to be followed.[16] It should have followed it here.

For the foregoing reasons, the judgment affirming the opinion of the District Court was correct, and, on the merits, the panel decision properly withdrawn.

Affirmed.

MR. JUSTICE FRANKFURTER took no part in the consideration or decision of this case.

HARLAN, J. (dissenting). The question presented in this case is whether the parties to this collective bargaining agreement intended that a court, rather than an arbitrator, should decide the employer's claim that the union had violated the no-strike clause of the agreement. Whether a strike in breach of contract has occurred and, if so, what damages have been suffered, are matters with respect to which a court of law can hardly be deemed less competent, as an adjudicator, than an arbitrator. There is no special reason to suppose that the parties preferred to submit this kind of a dispute to an arbitrator whose expertise is more likely to be in the area of employees' grievance claims, as in United Steelworkers v. Warrior & Gulf Navigation Co., 363 U.S. 574, 580–582 ; United Steelworkers v. Enterprise Wheel & Car Corp., 363 U.S. 593, 597–598. The less so, from the standpoint of the employer, when it is recognized that any damages awarded by an arbitrator would not be self-enforcing.

It would require more persuasive evidence than either this collective agreement or record affords to persuade me that it was contemplated that the employer would forego his statutory remedy under § 301 respecting alleged violations of the no-strike clause of the collective agreement. I would reverse the judgment below substantially for the reasons given in the panel opinion of the Court of Appeals, 287 F. 2d 155.

_____

14. Bernhardt v. Polygraphic Co., 350 U.S. 198, 203.

_____

15. Compare Shanferoke Coal Corp. v. Westchester Serv. Corp., 70 F. 2d 297, 299 (C.A. 2d Cir., L. Hand, J.), aff'd, 293 U.S. 449, 453–454, with Lane, Ltd. v. Larus & Bro. Co., 243 F. 2d 364 (C.A. 2d Cir.).

16. See text accompanying notes 4–5, *supra*.

A COMMENT ON EMPLOYER INITIATION OF ARBITRATION

The BLS Arbitration Study reported:

Approximately 90 per cent (1,445) of the 1,609 contracts permitted either party to refer unsettled disputes to arbitration. The remaining 164 contracts provided for initiation of arbitration by the aggrieved party, by the union, or only by mutual consent of the parties (46). The requirement of mutual consent means that one party can block arbitration.

Most of the 1,445 contracts explicitly stated that arbitration could be initiated by either party.

The contracts studied predated *Drake*. Reportedly some companies, notably in the steel industry, sought and procured contract changes precluding employer resort to the grievance arbitration procedure. Some employers clearly prefer to have courts pass upon alleged violations of the no-strike clause in the belief, possibly well-founded, that they will be less tender than arbitrators in making damage awards. Indeed, some arbitrators seem to prefer not to handle such questions. However, before such a choice is made, an employer might well consider whether it prefers the prospect of a large court damage judgment against the possibly speedy injunction by award against continuation of a strike. See Chapter XIV, "The Remedy Power."

LOCAL 721, UNITED PACKINGHOUSE WORKERS v. NEEDHAM PACKING CO. 376 U.S. 247 (1964)

HARLAN, J. This case, which was brought here from the Supreme Court of Iowa, 374 U.S. 826, presents a problem concerning the relationship between an arbitration clause and a no-strike clause in a collective bargaining agreement.

Although this case comes to us on the pleadings and some disputed questions of fact are still to be resolved, we accept as true the following facts for the purposes of our decision. The petitioner, Local Union No. 721, United Packinghouse, Food and Allied Workers, AFL-CIO, and the respondent, Needham Packing Co., had an agreement which included provisions of both kinds, set out hereafter. On May 11, 1961, Needham discharged Anton Stamoulis, an employee represented by the union. In response, on the same day about 190 other employees left work. During the next few days Needham advised the employees to return to work, stating that if they did not their employment would be regarded as terminated and that the discharge of Stamoulis would be treated under the grievance procedures

of the collective agreement. The employees did not return to work.

On July 5, 1961, the union presented to Needham written grievances on behalf of Stamoulis and the other employees, asserting that they had been "improperly discharged" and requesting their reinstatement with full seniority rights and pay for lost time. By letter dated July 11, 1961, Needham refused to process the grievances. The letter stated that the union and its members had by their conduct "repudiated and terminated the labor agreement" with the company. In addition, Needham stated that it would not have further dealings with the union and did not recognize the union as majority representative of Needham employees.

This suit by the union under § 301 (a) of the Labor Management Relations Act, 29 U.S.C. § 185 (a), to compel arbitration of the two grievances followed. Needham alleged as a defense that the union and its members had struck on May 11, 1961, and that this breach of the no-strike clause of the collective bargaining agreement had been and was treated by Needham as having terminated its obligations under the agreement. In addition, Needham filed a counterclaim, alleging that it had been damaged in the amount of $150,000 by the union's breach of the no-strike clause. The union denied such breach. At the close of the pleadings, in accordance with Iowa procedure, Needham moved for a ruling on points of law and a final order denying the union's petition to compel arbitration.[1] Deciding solely on the basis of matters raised in the pleadings as to which there was no dispute, the trial court ruled in Needham's favor and issued an order against the union. The union obtained an appeal. The Supreme Court of Iowa affirmed the holding below that "the Union had waived its right to arbitrate the grievances filed by its walkout." 119 N.W. 2d 141, 143.[2]

---

1. Rule 105 of the Iowa Rules of Civil Procedure provides:

"The court may in its discretion, and must on application of either party, made after issues joined and before trial, separately hear and determine any point of law raised in any pleading which goes to the whole or any material part of the case. It shall enter an appropriate final order before trial of the remaining issues, adjudicating the point so determined, which shall not be questioned on the trial of any part of the case of which it does not dispose. If such ruling does not dispose of the whole case, it shall be deemed interlocutory for purposes of appeal."

2. Although Rule 105 provides that a final order entered under it shall be "deemed interlocutory for purposes of appeal," the order which is entered is a "final order . . . adjudicating the point so determined, which shall not be questioned on the trial of any part of the case of which it does not dispose." See *supra*, note 1. Accordingly, our jurisdiction was properly invoked.

In the present posture of this case, we must answer the question whether acts of the union relieved Needham of its contractual obligation to arbitrate almost entirely on the basis of the agreement itself. We think it plain that, seen from that perspective, the judgment below must be reversed.

The two controlling provisions of the collective bargaining agreement are written in comprehensive terms. The no-strike clause provides:

> It is agreed that during the period of this agreement the employees shall not engage in and the Union shall not call or sanction any slow down, work stoppage or strike. . . .

The grievance provisions include typical procedures for the resolution of a dispute preliminary to arbitration. They then provide:

> In the event a dispute shall arise between the Company and the Union with reference to the proper interpretation or application of the provisions of this contract and such dispute cannot be settled by mutual agreement of the parties, such dispute shall be referred to a board of arbitration upon the request of the Union.

It is evident from the above as well as other provisions of the agreement[3] that the grievance procedures were intended largely, if not wholly, for the benefit of the union.

A state court exercising its concurrent jurisdiction over suits under § 301 (a) applies federal substantive law. Charles Dowd Box Co., Inc., v. Courtney, 368 U.S. 502. The law which controls the disposition of this case is stated in Drake Bakeries, Inc., v. Local 50, American Bakery & Confectionery Workers International, AFL-CIO, 370 U.S. 254. In that case, the employer had filed an action for damages under § 301 (a), alleging that the union had "instigated and encouraged its members to strike or not to report for work," in violation of a no-strike clause. Id., at 256. The collective bargaining agreement contained a broad arbitration clause covering "all complaints, disputes or grievances arising between . . . [the parties] involving questions of interpretation or application of any clause or matter covered by this contract or any act or conduct or relation between the parties hereto, directly or indirectly." Id., at 257.

The employer argued that the promise not to strike was so basic to the collective bargain and breach of the no-strike clause so completely inconsistent with the provision for arbitration that the employer's duty to arbitrate was excused by the union's breach. This argument, which is essentially that of Needham here, was rejected on grounds fully applicable to this case. Although the Court relied in part on the employer's apparent intention not to terminate the contract altogether, more central to its conclusion was the view that there was no "inflexible rule rigidly linking no-strike and arbitration clauses of every collective bargaining contract in every situation." Id., at 261 (Footnote omitted.) We said:

> . . . [U]nder this contract, by agreeing to arbitrate all claims without excluding the case where the union struck over an arbitrable matter, the parties have negatived any intention to condition the duty to arbitrate upon the absence of strikes. They have thus cut the ground from under the argument that an alleged strike, automatically and regardless of the circumstances, is such a breach or repudiation of the arbitration clause by the union that the company is excused from arbitrating, upon theories of waiver, estoppel, or otherwise. Arbitration provisions, which themselves have not been repudiated, are meant to survive breaches of contract, in many contexts, even total breach; and in determining whether one party has so repudiated his promise to arbitrate that the other party is excused the circumstances of the claimed repudiation are critically important. In this case the union denies having repudiated in any respect its promise to arbitrate, denies that there was a strike, denies that the employees were bound to work on January 2 and asserts that it was the company itself which ignored the adjustment and arbitration provisions be scheduling holiday work. Id., at 262–263 (Footnotes omitted.)

Continuance of the duty to arbitrate is, if anything, clearer here than it was in Drake Bakeries, where one of the issues was whether an alleged strike was within the intended scope of the arbitration clause. There is no question in this case that the union's claim of wrongful discharge is one which Needham agreed to arbitrate.[4] Nothing in the agreement indicates an intention to except from Needham's agreement to arbitrate disputes concerning the "interpretation or application" of the agreement any dispute which involves or follows an alleged breach of the no-strike clause. That the no-strike clause does not itself carry such an implication is the holding of Drake Bakeries.

The fact that the collective bargaining agreement does not require Needham to submit its

---

3. For example, the agreement provides that grievances must be presented within 14 days "of the occurrence giving rise to such grievance" or within 14 days "of the time the Union has knowledge, or should have had knowledge of such grievance. . . ."

---

4. In effect, the union's grievance involved the "interpretation or application" of § 8 (a) of the collective bargaining agreement, which provided that Needham could discharge employees "for just cause."

claim to arbitration, as the employer was required to do in *Drake Bakeries*, and indeed appears to confine the grievance procedures to grievances of the union, does not indicate a different result. Needham's claim is the subject of a counterclaim in the Iowa courts; nothing we have said here precludes it from prosecuting that claim and recovering damages.[5] That Needham asserts by way of defense to the union's action to compel arbitration the same alleged breach of the no-strike clause which is the subject of the counter-claim does not convert the union's grievance into Needham's different one.

Nor do we believe that this case can be distinguished from *Drake Bakeries* on the ground that that case involved only a "one-day strike," *id.*, at 265. Whether a fundamental and long-lasting change in the relationship of the parties prior to the demand for arbitration would be a circumstance which, alone or among others, would release an employer from his promise to arbitrate we need not decide, since the undeveloped record before us reveals no such circumstance. Compare *Drake Bakeries, supra*, at 205. The passage of time resulting from Needham's refusal to arbitrate cannot, of course, be a basis for releasing it from its duty to arbitrate.

Needham's allegations by way of defense and counterclaim that the union breached the no-strike clause, supported by such facts as were undisputed on the pleadings, did not release Needham from its duty to arbitrate the union's claim that employees had been wrongfully discharged. On that basis, we reverse and remand to the Iowa Supreme Court for further proceedings.

It is so ordered.

NO-STRIKE, NO-LOCKOUT PROVISIONS*

Restrictions on strikes and lockouts over disputes arising during the term of the agreement were found in 1,537 of the 1,717 contracts analyzed. Slightly less than half (757 of the 1,537) specified an absolute ban. The remainder of the provisions (780) mainly limited the strike ban to disputes subject to grievance and/or arbitration procedures; waived the ban for specific violations of the agreement; or permitted strikes after exhaustion of the grievance procedure. The

5. Here, as in Atkinson v. Sinclair Refining Co., 370 U.S. 238, we find it unnecessary to decide what effect, if any, factual or legal determinations of an arbitrator would have on a related action in the courts. See *id.*, at 245, note 5.

*Excerpted from BLS Arbitration Study.

latter group consisted of agreements with no provision for arbitration, or which provided for arbitration by mutual consent only.

With the exception of the communication industry, strike restrictions were found in the majority of the agreements in each industry, and were slightly more prevalent in manufacturing than in nonmanufacturing. In communications, only 24 of 80 agreements analyzed provided strike restrictions. Although nearly all of the agreements in this industry included grievance and arbitration machinery, only one-fourth of the agreements which provided for such machinery considered all disputes subject to arbitration.

Absolute Strike Ban. All of the 757 contracts with an absolute ban on strikes included grievance procedures, and all but 9 provided for arbitration. Even though 594 of these contracts excluded some issues from arbitration, strikes over the excluded issues also were prohibited by the absolute ban. All disputes were arbitrable under 154 contracts; and only specific issues were excluded from arbitration in 59. Arbitration was limited to disputes involving interpretation, application, or violation of the contract in 529; and further exclusions were listed in 6.

Absolute strike ban provisions were incorporated in contracts negotiated by many unions. The following tabulation lists those unions which have negotiated at least 10 major contracts with an absolute ban, accounting for one-half or more of the major contracts negotiated by each union.

Table X-I

Union	Total agreements examined	Total agreements with absolute strike or lockout ban
Steelworkers	120	98
Machinists	94	47
IBEW	92	56
IUE	47	25
Oil, Chemical	31	20
Textile Workers Union	24	13
Mine Workers (Dist. 50)	20	15
Building Services	19	11
Papermakers	17	15

Reflecting the problem of agreement compliance and enforcement among large numbers of small employers, only 30 per cent of the multi-employer contracts covered in this study stipulated an absolute ban on strikes and lockouts as against 60 per cent of the single-employer agreements.

Limited Strike Ban. All but two of the remaining 780 contracts with strike restrictions limited the prohibition in some manner short of an absolute ban. The two agreements, one multiplant and one multiemployer, gave no details on such restrictions, but referred to strike and lockout provisions to be negotiated at the local level. Of these 780 agreements, 62 failed to provide for arbitration.

The strike ban in 351 agreements applied to disputes subject to grievance and/or arbitration. Only two contracts in this group did not provide for arbitration. In 64, all disputes were subject to arbitration, hence the strike ban in these was equivalent to a no-strike pledge for the term of the agreement. The remaining 285 contracts in this group limited the disputes that were subject to arbitration, thereby presumably limiting the strike prohibition. Although relatively few (44) of these explicitly stated that strikes would be permitted over disputes not subject to grievance and arbitration procedures or disputes subject to arbitration by mutual consent only, the right to strike over excluded disputes was not explicitly withdrawn in the remaining contracts. Explicit permission to strike over excluded issues is contained in the following clauses:

> As to any disputes subject to arbitration, the union agrees that it will not cause nor will its members take part in any strike or work stoppage, and the company agrees that it will not cause any lockout.
>
> As to any dispute not subject to arbitration, no strike, work stoppage, or lockout will be caused or sanctioned until negotiations have continued for at least 5 days at the final step of the bargaining procedure described in article＿. Thereafter any strike which occurs under such circumstances shall not be deemed to be a violation of this agreement, which shall continue to remain in full force notwithstanding such strike.

> There shall be no interruption or impeding of the work, work stoppage, strike, slowdown, or lockout during the term of this agreement except that the union shall have the right to strike only to resolve a grievance concerning a new or changed incentive standard or the day or base rates for a new or changed job classification in the event it strictly complies with the following procedure:
> (a) The grievance shall have been timely filed and processed through the third step of the grievance procedure in article＿.
> (b) Within 30 days from the receipt of the company's answer in the third step (or, in case such answer is not rendered within the time limit, from the date such answer was due), the union shall notify the company in writing that Local＿ and the international union have each authorized (as provided in the union constitution) a strike of all employees in the unit as defined in section ＿hereof concerning such grievance and fixing

a time not earlier than 5 working days or later than 10 working days after the receipt by the company of said notice on which said strike will begin.

The following is a typical clause which appears to open the possibility of a strike over disputes excluded from grievance and/or arbitration procedures. This clause was taken from a contract which extended the grievance procedure to all grievances, but limited arbitration to grievance disputes involving interpretation and application of the contract.

> Should any grievance or misunderstanding arise, an earnest effort shall be made to settle the matter promptly . . .
>
> If no satisfactory settlement is reached within a reasonable time and if the grievance relates to the interpretation or application of the provisions of this agreement, it shall be referred, at the request of either party, to arbitration. . . .
>
> During the life of this master agreement, no strike in connection with disputes arising hereunder shall be caused or sanctioned in any of the plants or other appropriate bargaining units covered by this agreement by the union or by any members thereof, and no lockouts shall be ordered by the company in connection with such dispute.
>
> In the event that the company or the union shall fail or refuse to arbitrate any grievance or dispute which is subject to arbitration by the terms of this agreement, or should refuse to abide by the award of the arbitrators within 3 days after its issuance, the union shall have the unqualified right to strike and the company shall have the unqualified right to lock out the employees in addition to whatever other legal remedies either party may have.

In the event a member of the association refuses to abide by a decision of the impartial chairman, the union shall give the association notice in writing of the refusal of its member to comply. If at the expiration of 48 hours after such notice has been given by the union to the association, the violating member of the association still refuses to comply with the decision of the impartial chairman, the union may at its option consider all its obligations under this contract terminated with respect to the violating member of the association.

In the event a member of the union refuses to abide by a decision of the impartial chairman, the association shall give the union notice in writing of the refusal of its member to comply. If at the expiration of 48 hours after such notice has been given by the association to the union, the violating member of the union still refuses to comply with the decision of the impartial chairman, the employer may at his option discharge such a member of the union from the job.

. . . it is agreed that the union and its members, individually and collectively, will not, during the term of this agreement, tolerate, cause, encourage, support, permit, or participate or take part in any strike, picketing, sitdown, stayin, slowdown, or other curtailment or restriction of production or interference with work in or about the company's premises, but will avail itself exclusively of the procedure herein provided for the settlement of grievances, unless the company refuses to abide by an arbitration award.

More than one specific exemption was cited in many of the contracts, including a number of provisions which waived the strike ban because of grievance and arbitration violations. Most prevalent of the reasons cited for such exemptions were the failure of the employer to fulfill health and welfare plan obligations and to make proper wage or related payments.

Among other exemptions which lifted the strike ban were the following:

Violation of the union security provision
Changes without union approval:
    Addition of new machines
    Establishment of new rates on new work
    Adjustment of job classification
Violation of shop regulations
Unfair labor practices, as determined by outside parties
Employer insistence on workers disregarding picket line
Employment of nonunion contractors (apparel industry)

Waiver clauses were most prevalent in association contracts in industries such as apparel, transportation, retail trade, and construction.

The four remaining provisions did not fall into any of the above categories. Two agreements mentioned earlier—one multiplant and other multi-employer—stated that strike and lockout provisions would be negotiated at local levels. One agreement permitted strike action for any "justifiable" reason ; and the other prohibited strikes during the first year of a 2-year agreement. The latter contract did not provide for arbitration.

No Ban on Strikes. Of the 180 contracts which did not contain any explicit strike restrictions, 161 provided grievance procedures and 143 also included arbitration. Nineteen agreements, all multiemployer, failed to provide for grievance or arbitration procedures.

Since arbitration is a mechanism through which disputes may be settled without strikes, the scope of arbitration in the 143 contracts, as shown in the following tabulation [Table X-2] also may define the area of strike prohibition. Only 25 contracts guaranteed arbitration for any and all disputes.

Table X-2

	Agreements	Workers (in thousands)
Total	180	609.1
With grievance and arbitration provisions	143	510.0
Type of disputes subject to arbitration:		
All disputes	25	81.8
All disputes, with specific exclusions	5	11.2
Interpretation, application and/or violation of agreement	48	131.7
Interpretation, application and/or violation of agreement, with specific exclusions	64	283.8
Not clear	1	1.8
Without arbitration provision	37	99.1
With grievance procedure	18	50.3
Without grievance procedure	19	48.8

NOTE: Because of rounding, sums of individual items may not equal totals.

Table X-3

How Strikes May Occur During the Term of Agreements Without Violating the Agreements (1,717 major agreements)

Strikes banned	Strikes possible
Absolute ban on strikes (757)	
Not all possible disputes subject to grievance and/or arbitration (594)	
No arbitration (9)	
All disputes subject to arbitration (154)	
Limited ban on strikes (780)	
All disputes subject to arbitration (64)	Strikes banned over disputes subject to arbitration but not all possible disputes subject to grievance and/or arbitration (285)
	Arbitration provided but strike ban waived if agreement violated (331)
	Arbitration required mutual consent (35)
	No arbitration (62)
	Other (3)
No ban on strikes (180)	
All disputes subject to arbitration (25)	Arbitration provided but not all possible disputes subject to grievance and/or arbitration (118)
	No arbitration (37)
Total agreements (846)	(871)

STRIKES AND LOCKOUTS DURING THE TERM OF THE AGREEMENT

Despite the widespread prevalence of grievance and arbitration procedures and no strike-lockout pledges, a strike not constituting a violation of the letter of the agreement is possible in about half of all major agreements [Table X-3].

Clauses which permitted termination of the contract in the event of contract violation were incorporated in 101 contracts, covering nearly one million workers. The meaning of contract cancellation clauses is difficult to assess in relation to the previous discussion. Presumably, if a union has grounds to cancel, and does cancel, the contract of an employer member of an association agreement, or even perhaps of the association as a whole, a shutdown is almost certain to follow. This also may be the case when a single-employer contract is canceled by the union. On the other hand, in the event of employer cancellations the results are much less certain.

Violation of the strike or lockout clause was specified in nearly half of the cancellation clauses with some of the concentration in transportation equipment and apparel contracts. A few clauses were found in electrical machinery, rubber, communications, utilities and service industries ; the remaining were scattered through various other industries, mainly manufacturing.

Frequently, the contracts set a time limit after the "illegal" strike or lockout occurred before the contract could be terminated. This was typical in the transportation equipment industry, as illustrated in the following excerpt from the General Motors agreement:

> During the life of this agreement, the corporation will not lock out any employees until all of the bargaining procedure as outlined in this agreement has been exhausted and in no case on which the umpire shall have ruled, and in no other case on which the umpire is not empowered to rule until after negotiations have continued for at least 5 days at the third step of the grievance procedure. In case a lockout shall occur the union has the option of cancelling the agreement at any time between the 10th day after the lockout occurs and the date of its settlement.
>
> ...In case a strike or stoppage of production shall occur, the corporation has the option of cancelling the agreement at any time between the 10th day after the strike occurs and the day of its settlement.

In the apparel industry, cancellation because of violation of the strike or lockout clause generally was limited to failure of the union in its obligation to end any work stoppage, and of

management in its responsibility for ending a lockout. In either case, the existence of a substantial violation was to be determined by the impartial chairman before the contract could be terminated.

A few contracts did not specify a time limit before termination of some or all clauses of the contract.

Over 50 contracts permitted cancellation because of other contract violations. In addition, a few of those which specified strike or lockout violations also permitted cancellation for other contract violations.

Violations frequently cited were the failure to exhaust the grievance and/or arbitration procedure, or to abide by the awards.

Some of the contracts set a time limit for compliance before cancellation could be effected. A few agreements included the option to strike or terminate the contract.

Violation of the health and welfare or pension provisions was cause for termination under several contracts. In most instances, the violation was limited to failure to make proper contributions to the fund.

A few included any violation of the welfare plan as grounds for cancellation.

Other grounds for cancellations included failure to make wage payments ; granting by the union of more favorable terms to other companies ; requiring employees to handle struck work ; and violation of the union security provision, of established working hours, or of work rules.

Most of these agreements specified one or two causes for cancellation. An exception was found in a few electrical contracting association agreements with the International Brotherhood of Electrical Workers. These agreements, in addition to specifying as causes for cancellation default in wage or employee benefit payments, rebating of wages, and subletting of labor services to any workman, included violation of the international union's work rules.

Two other exceptions permitted cancellation for any substantial or for any deliberate violations, after proper investigation. Some agreements, however, excluded work assignments involved in jurisdictional disputes as a cause for cancellation.

The issue of injunctions against strikes in violation of no-strike clauses in agreements containing provisions for arbitration is considered in Chapter XIV, "The Remedy Power."

D.

Contracts Subject to Section 301

LOCALS NOS. 128 and 633, RETAIL CLERKS INT'L ASS'N v. LION DRY GOODS, INC.
369 U.S. 17 (1962)

BRENNAN, J. Section 301 (a) of the Labor Management Relations Act, provides that

> Suits for violation of contracts between an employer and a labor organization representing employees in an industry affecting commerce as defined in this chapter, or between any such labor organizations, may be brought in any district court of the United States having jurisdiction of the parties, without respect to the amount in controversy or without regard to the citizenship of the parties.

The questions presented in this case are: (1) Does the scope of "contracts" within § 301 (a) include the agreement at bar, claimed to be not a "collective bargaining contract" but a "strike settlement agreement"? (2) If otherwise includible, is the "strike settlement agreement" cognizable under § 301 (a), although the petitioners, the labor-organization parties to the agreement, acknowledged that they were not entitled to recognition as exclusive representatives of the employees of the respondents?

The opinions below appear to rest upon alternative holdings, answering in the negative each of these questions. The District Court's conclusion that it lacked jurisdiction over the subject matter, 179 F. Supp. 564, was affirmed in a brief *per curiam* by the Court of Appeals, saying:

> The contract here involved is not a collective bargaining agreement between an employer and a labor organization representing its employees. We think that the trial court was correct in reaching the conclusion that collective bargaining contracts between a union and an employer are the only contracts intended to be actionable in a United States District Court under the provisions of section 301 (a). 286 F. 2d 235.

We granted certiorari because of the importance of the questions to the enforcement of the national labor policy as expressed in § 301 (a). 366 U.S. 917. We hold that the lower courts erred and remand the cause for trial and further proceedings consistent with this opinion.

The petitioners, local unions of the Retail Clerks International Association, brought this action on the sole jurisdictional basis of § 301 (a) and (b), seeking to compel respondents' compliance with two allegedly binding arbitration awards. Respondents are two department stores in Toledo, Ohio, covered by the Labor Management Relations Act. For some years prior to 1957, petitioners had been the collective bargaining representatives of respondents' employees and had been parties to collective bargaining agreements with respondents. In November 1957, negotiations for renewal contracts ended in impasse. A strike ensued against one of the respondents, Lasalle's, and continued until December 24, 1958; the dispute with the other respondent, Lion Dry Goods, continued during the whole of those 13 months although no strike occurred. On December 24, 1958, the parties ended their dispute with the aid of the Toledo Labor-Management-Citizens' Committee (hereinafter, L–M–C), a local mediation and arbitration body.[1] Negotiations by means of L–M–C mediation had produced a "Statement of Understanding"[2] satisfactory to all parties.

---

1. Before 1957, the respondents and two other downtown Toledo department stores, through an organization, Retail Associates, Inc., recognized the petitioners as representatives of their employees and executed collective bargaining agreements with the petitioners on a multi-employer basis. When the 1957 impasse developed, the petitioners struck one of those two other stores and it promptly contracted separately with the petitioners. Respondents and the second of the two other stores petitioned the National Labor Relations Board to conduct an election among the employees of the three stores as a single bargaining unit. The petitioners reacted with a demand that each store negotiate separately. Simultaneously, the petitioners called the strike at respondent Lasalle's. The dispute produced considerable litigation. See Local 128, Retail Clerks v. Leedom, 42 LRR Man. 2031; Retail Associates, Inc., 120 N.L.R.B. 388; Retail Clerks Assn. v. Leedom, 43 LRR Man. 2004, 2029.

A few days before December 24, 1958, the L–M–C proposed a plan for settling the dispute. Discussions ensued between the Committee and the respondents, and between the Committee and the petitioners. At no time were direct negotiations carried on between petitioners and the respondents. Each side made known to the L–M–C the conditions under which it was willing to resolve the dispute and the L–M–C discussed these conditions with the other side. In this manner a basis for settlement was fashioned which was embodied in the Statement referred to in the text.

2. The Lasalle's Statement of Understanding (exhibits omitted) reads as follows:

"1. Employees of Lasalle's, who have been absent due to the strike, will be re-instated without discrimination because of any strike activities and without loss of seniority provided they make application for reinstatement in the form and manner provided for by the employer within fifteen days of receipt of notice from the employer.

The Statement contained such key points of settlement as the unions' acknowledgment that they were not then entitled to recognition as

"2. All such employees who have complied with the provisions of Paragraph 1 above, will be returned to work not later than February 2, 1959, as scheduled by the Company, in their former position classifications if vacant or in positions comparable in duties and earning opportunities.

".... No employee will be discriminated against, by reason of Union activities, membership or non-membership. All employees will continue to have job security and no employee will be discharged except for just cause.

"5. Neither the Company nor the Union will interfere with the employee's right to join or not to join a union, as provided and guaranteed by the Labor-Management-Relations Act. Nothing contained herein is to be construed as giving recognition to the union unless at some future time within the discretion of the union, the union is certified as having been chosen by a majority of employees in a single store unit election conducted by the National Labor Relations Board.

"6. The Union agrees that it will not request bargaining rights unless it proves its right to represent the employees as provided in Paragraph 5 above; nor will the employer recognize any union except upon certification by the N.L.R.B.; nor will the Company file a petition for election unless a claim for representation is made upon the employer. Nothing herein shall preclude an employee representative from entering areas of the store which are open to customers; or from communicating with employees, provided such communication is on the employee's non-working time and in no way interferes with the operating of the business.

"7. Any individual employee who may have a grievance involving an interpretation or application of or arising under the terms of this understanding with the L–M–C, and who has presented such grievance to his supervisor and the Personnel Department without reaching a satisfactory solution, may take his case to the chairman of the L–M–C who in turn shall refer the case to a panel of the L–M–C, whose majority decision and order shall be final and binding. The panel shall render its decision and order within fifteen days after the grievance has been submitted to it. The procedure regulating the hearing of the grievance by the L–M–C panel shall be determined by the panel.

"8. The Union will agree that immediately upon receipt of this statement of understanding by the Toledo Labor-Management-Citizens Committee it will cease all picketing, boycotting or other interference with the business of Lasalle's, or R. H. Macy & Co., Inc. wherever located. The Union, the strikers, and the Company shall withdraw forthwith all petitions, unfair labor practice charges and litigation before the National Labor Relations Board and the Courts and further agree not to institute in the future any litigation involving or arising out of the instant dispute. The Union and the Employer shall execute mutually satisfactory releases, releasing and discharging each other, the International Union, the local unions involved, and representatives of the union in their representative or individual capacity, labor papers, and all other labor organizations or their representatives who acted in concert or cooperation in connection with the dispute, from any and all claims, demands, causes of action, of whatever nature or description arising out of the labor dispute, including but not limited to the strikes, picketing, boycotting, and all other activities which may have taken place up to the present date.

"9. This understanding shall become effective in accordance with the letter of transmittal dated December 24, 1958."

The Lion Store's Statement is identical except for the omission of paragraphs 1, 2 and 3.

exclusive representatives, and would not seek such recognition unless and until certified as so entitled in single store unit elections conducted by the National Labor Relations Board, and Lasalle's agreement to reinstate striking employees without discrimination. Both stores also agreed to continue in effect detailed wage and hour schedules and provisions as to working conditions and other benefits, incorporated as exhibits to the Statement. All terms of employment had been in force prior to December 24, 1958, except an agreement by the stores to provide and pay fully for specified insurance coverage. The stores wrote the L–M–C delivering the Statement, calling it "the basis on which the heretofore existing dispute between [the Locals] and our compan[ies] is to be fully and finally resolved," and specifying that "The conditions to be performed and met by us are, of course, subject to and conditioned upon the receipt by your organization of guarantees from the respective labor organizations to make the principles enumerated [in the Statement] completely effective." A few days later the Locals wrote the L–M–C that "we herewith agree to the conditions and guarantees of the Statement of Understanding." The conditions to be performed by each side were performed and the dispute was terminated. In a few months, however, new grievances arose, including the two that generated this case. *First.* The unions claimed under the Statement the right of access to the employees' cafeteria in order to communicate with employees during their non-working time. The stores claimed that Statement ¶ 6 gave no right of access to the employees' cafeterias, for these are not "areas of the store which are open to customers."[3] *Second.* Two Lasalle's employees, salesladies in the men's furnishings department, had been fully reinstated except that the saleslady formerly assigned to sell men's shirts was assigned to sell men's sweaters, and the other saleslady, who had been selling sweaters, now was assigned to sell shirts. The Locals submitted these matters to the L–M–C under the procedure of Statement ¶ 7; the stores and the Locals participated fully in the ensuing arbitration proceedings; and the award went to the Locals on both grievances. The stores' refusal to accede to those awards prompted this suit.

The District Court viewed as crucial the question whether the Statement given by the stores to the L–M–C and then concurred in by the

3. The parties' trial stipulation says, *inter alia:* "[T]he employee cafeterias in the downtown stores of the defendants ... are located in areas in each of the stores not open to customers; ..."

Locals, constituted "such a contract as is contemplated by Section 301 (a)." 179 F. Supp., at 567. Although the opinion is somewhat ambiguous, we read it as holding that there was a contract between the Locals and the stores but that only certain kinds of contracts are within the purview of § 301 (a) and this was not one of them.[4] We interpret the District Court as holding that to be within § 301 (a), contracts must be "collective bargaining contracts, or agreements arrived at through collective bargaining," *ibid.*; and further, must be with a union that is the recognized majority representative of the employees. The court found that the Statement of Understanding met neither test.[5] The Court of Appeals' brief affirmance, *supra*, fails to make clear whether it agreed with both of those limitations on § 301 (a), or with only one and if so which one.

It is argued that Congress limited § 301 (a) jurisdiction to contracts that are "collective bargaining contracts," meaning, so runs the argument, only agreements concerning wages, hours,

---

4. Apart from the question of its cognizability under § 301 (a), it is clear that the Statement constitutes a contract between the parties. This is so, although they did not negotiate directly but through a mediator, and did not conjoin their signatures on one document. The record makes obvious that neither the parties nor L–M–C contemplated two independent agreements, one by each side with L–M–C only, unenforceable by either side against the other.

The parties stipulated as to the arbitration proceedings that it was "assumed by all parties in attendance to be a meeting of a panel chosen . . . to perform proper functions delegated to such a panel under the provisions of . . . [the] Statements of Understanding. . . ." They further stipulated that "nothing . . . [herein] is to preclude the Court from finding that the settlement of December 24, 1958, was a collective bargaining agreement." In their answer in the District Court, respondents denied "that there is in existence any contract between the plaintiffs, or either of them, and the defendants, or either of them, or that there is in existence any agreement between the parties, collectively or singly, whereby the [L–M–C] is given any right or authority to arbitrate any grievance which the plaintiffs might claim to have." Petitioners claim and the respondents do not deny that at no time prior to their answer had respondents suggested there was no contract: they complied with the conditions for ending the dispute, they continued following the old wage and hour schedules and other provisions, they participated in the arbitration proceedings and they asked the L–M–C to reconsider their awards on the merits.

Respondents' contention throughout, whether because of the stipulation or otherwise, has been not to negate the existence of any contract at all, but rather to deny that there is a contract of the kind contemplated by § 301 (a). The District Court so construed the defense, 179 F. Supp., at 565. The Court of Appeals appears to have agreed; see *supra*. And at no point in their brief in this Court do respondents argue that no contract exists; they agree that the only issue is jurisdictional.

5. The court emphasized that the Statement disclaimed the Locals' right to be recognized as exclusive bargaining agent until so certified by the National Labor Relations Board.

---

and conditions of employment concluded in direct negotiations between employers and unions entitled to recognition as exclusive representatives of employees.

The words of § 301 (a) require no such narrow construction as is suggested; rather, they negate it. *First.* The Section says "contracts" though Congress knew well the phrase "collective bargaining contracts," see, *e.g.*, § 8 (d), § 9 (a), § 201 (c), § 203 (d), § 204 (a) (2), § 211 (a). Had Congress contemplated a restrictive differentiation, we may assume that it would not have eschewed "collective bargaining contracts" unwittingly. Moreover, Congress provided in § 211 (a):

> For the guidance and information of interested representatives of employers, employees, and the general public, the Bureau of Labor Statistics . . . shall maintain a file of copies of all available collective bargaining agreements and other available agreements and actions thereunder settling or adjusting labor disputes.

Whatever the proper construction of that Section, insofar as it reflects upon § 301 (a) at all, it supports the inference that "contracts" does include more than "collective bargaining agreements," at least as respondents would define them. *Second.* If "contracts" means only collective bargaining contracts, the subsequent words "or between any such labor organizations" are superfluous, for if there is a collective bargaining agreement between unions it follows that as to that agreement, one union is the employer and the other represents employees. See Office Employes Union v. Labor Board, 353 U.S. 313. Congress was not indulging in surplusage: A federal forum was provided for actions on other labor contracts besides collective bargaining contracts. See, *e.g.*, United Textile Workers v. Textile Workers Union, 258 F. 2d 743 (no-raiding agreement). But, it is urged, though Congress meant that labor organizations could sue one another in federal courts on other contracts between themselves, suits between employers and unions were still limited to actions on collective bargaining contracts. The provision for suits between labor organizations was inserted in Conference. Differing House and Senate bills were reconciled in Conference. The House bill spoke of suits involving a violation of "an agreement between an employer and a labor organization or other representative of employees." The Senate bill read "contracts concluded as the result of collective bargaining between an employer and a labor organization." It is urged that the Conference compromise upon the word "contracts" reflects a desire to use one word to cover both suits between employers and unions, and suits between unions. But it seems obvious that had Congress intended any limiting differentiation, this would have been accomplished by retaining the Senate bill's phrasing for agreements between employers and unions and then providing specifically for the application of the statute to "contracts between any such labor organizations." *Third.* A 1959 enactment, § 8 (f), explicitly contemplates contracts that would not fit respondents' concept of "collective bargaining agreements." It authorizes contracting with unions that represent persons not yet even hired by the employer. Such a contract might cover only hiring procedures and not wages, hours, and conditions of employment. Nothing supports the improbable congressional intent that the federal courts be closed to such contracts.

We find, then, from a reading of the words of § 301 (a), both in isolation and in connection with the statute as a whole, no basis for denying jurisdiction of the action based upon the alleged violation of the "strike settlement agreement."

Furthermore, the statute's purpose would be defeated by excluding such contracts from "contracts" cognizable under § 301 (a). See Charles Dowd Box Co. v. Courtney, 368 U.S. 502. If this kind of strike settlement were not enforceable under § 301 (a), responsible and stable labor relations would suffer, and the attainment of the labor policy objective of minimizing disruption of interstate commerce would be made more difficult. It is no answer that in a particular case the agreement might be enforceable in state courts: a main goal of § 301 was precisely to end "checkerboard jurisdiction," Seymour v. Schneckloth, 368 U.S. 351, at 358. See Charles Dowd Box Co. v. Courtney, *supra.*

Lastly, legislative history refutes the argument that Congress intended to omit agreements of the kind in suit from "contracts" falling within the purview of § 301 (a).

We need not decide whether or not this strike settlement agreement is a "collective bargaining agreement" to hold, as we do, that it is a "contract" for purposes of § 301 (a). "Contract in labor law is a term the implications of which must be determined from the connection in which it appears." J. I. Case Co. v. Labor Board, 321 U.S. 332, 334. It is enough that this is clearly an agreement between employers and labor organizations significant to the maintenance of labor peace between them. It came into being as a means satisfactory to both sides for terminating a protracted strike and labor dispute. Its terms affect the working conditions of the employees of both respondents. It effected the end of picketing and resort by the labor organizations to other economic weapons, and restored strikers to their jobs. It resolved a controversy arising out of, and importantly and directly affecting, the employment relationship. Plainly it falls within § 301 (a). "[F]ederal courts should enforce these agreements on behalf of or against labor organizations and ... industrial peace can be best obtained only in that way." Textile Workers Union v. Lincoln Mills, 353 U.S. 448, 455.

Only a few words are necessary to dispose of respondents' second contention, that even if this agreement were otherwise within § 301 (a), petitioners' disclaimer of entitlement to recognition as exclusive representatives puts them out of court. This issue does not touch upon whether minority unions may demand that employers enter into particular kinds of contracts or the circumstances under which employers may accord recognition to unions as exclusive bargaining agents. The question is only whether "labor organization representing employees" in § 301 (a) has a meaning different from "labor organization which represents employees" in § 301 (b).* In United States v. Ryan, 350 U.S. 299, we rejected the argument that § 301 (b)* was limited to majority representatives. Neither the words, purpose, nor history of the statute suggests any reason for a different construction of the virtually identical words of subsection (a). Nor can "labor organization representing employees" in § 301 (a) be read as differing from "any such labor organizations" in that subsection's very next phrase, and plainly, in suits between labor organizations, their right to recognition as exclusive representatives *vis-à-vis* employers has no relevance whatever.

"Members only" contracts have long been recognized. See, *e.g.,* Consolidated Edison Co. v. Labor Board, 305 U.S. 197. Had Congress thought that there was any merit in limiting federal jurisdiction to suits on contracts with exclusive bargaining agents, we might have expected Congress explicitly so to provide, for example, by enacting that § 301 (a) should be read with § 9 (a). Compare § 8 (a) (3), § 8 (a) (5), § 8 (b) (3), § 8 (b) (4), § 8 (d). Moreover, § 8 (f), the 1959 amendment considered *supra,* contemplates contracting with unions that would not represent a majority. Lastly, if the federal courts' jurisdiction under § 301 (a) required a preliminary determination of the representative status of the labor organization involved, potential conflict with the National Labor Relations Board would be increased, cf. La Crosse Telephone Corp. v. Wisconsin Employment Relations Board, 336 U.S. 18; Amazon

---

*[The Court must have meant § 302 (b).]

Cotton Mill Co. v. Textile Workers Union, 167 F. 2d 183, and litigation would be much hindered.

We conclude that the petitioners' action for alleged violation of the strike settlement agreement was cognizable by the District Court under § 301 (a). The judgment of the Court of Appeals is reversed and the cause is remanded to the District Court for further proceedings consistent with this opinion.

It is so ordered.

FRANKFURTER, J. (concurring). I wholly agree with the Court in rejecting the restrictive meaning given by the Court of Appeals to "contracts" in § 301 (a) of the Labor Management Relations Act. I have, however, serious doubt whether the "statement of understanding" on the basis of which the strike was settled was in fact a contract, in the sense of a consensual arrangement between the Retail Clerks and Lion Dry Goods, rather than a formulation of the results of the intercession of a public-spirited intermediary on the basis of which each side was prepared to lay down its arms. However, on a matter of construing a particular document, in light of the surrounding circumstances, I do not desire to dissent.

On remand, the Court of Appeals held (2–1) that the strike settlement agreement conferred the right to invoke arbitration upon individual employees with grievances but not upon the union. 341 F. 2d 715, *cert. den.,* 382 U.S. 839 (1965).

The AFL–CIO no-raiding agreement is a contract "between any such labor organizations" within the meaning of Section 301 (a). International Ass'n of Machinists v. International B'hd of Firemen and Oilers, (D.C. N.D. Ga. 1964) 234 F. Supp. 858 (1964). But the courts have been reluctant to treat union constitutions or local charters as contracts of this sort, for the reasons put forward in Note, *Applying the "Contracts Between Labor Organizations" Clause of Taft-Hartley Section 301: A Plea for Restraint,* 69 YALE L. J. 299 (1959).

LOCAL 89, GENERAL DRIVERS v. RISS & CO., INC.
372 U.S. 517 (1963)

PER CURIAM. Petitioners are a union and six of its members employed by the respondent interstate motor freight common carrier. The present action was brought in the United States District Court for the Western District of Kentucky, and jurisdiction was predicated on § 301 of the Labor Management Relations Act, 1947, 29 U.S.C. § 185. In their complaint, petitioners alleged that the respondent had refused to comply with a ruling of the Joint Area Cartage Committee, directing that the individual petitioners be reinstated with full seniority and back pay. The Committee's ruling was asserted to have been handed down in accordance with the grievance procedures established in the collective bargaining agreement between the union and employer. The relief demanded in the complaint included the reinstatement of the individual petitioners, with full back pay and fringe benefits to the time of reinstatement.

Respondent, after filing its answer, moved to dismiss the complaint. The District Court granted the motion on the pleadings as supplemented at pretrial conference by excerpts from the Local Cartage Agreement between the union and the employer. The District Court's ground for dismissing the complaint was want of federal jurisdiction, a result deemed compelled by our decision in Association of Westinghouse Salaried Employees v. Westinghouse Elec. Corp., 348 U.S. 437. The Court of Appeals for the Sixth Circuit affirmed, 298 F. 2d 341, but added two more grounds in support of the order of dismissal: (1) That the determination of the Joint Area Cartage Committee was not an arbitration award and so not enforceable under § 301; (2) That on the merits petitioners were not entitled to the relief ordered by the Joint Area Cartage Committee. We granted certiorari, 371 U.S. 810. We reverse and remand to the District Court for trial.

According to the allegations of the complaint, the six individual petitioners were discharged because they chose to respect and did respect a picket line established by another union at a place of business of respondent. Contending that such discharge violated Article IX of the Local Cartage Agreement, which provides in part that "it shall not be cause for discharge if any employee or employees refuse to go through the picket line of a union," petitioners invoked the grievance machinery set up by the Agreement, and processed their grievances through the provided channels culminating in the Joint Area Cartage Committee's determination. Article VIII, § 1 (e), of the Agreement provides: "It is agreed that all matters pertaining to the interpretation of any provisions of this contract shall be referred, at the request of any party at any time, for final decision to the Joint Area Cartage Committee."

If, as petitioners allege, the award of the Joint Area Cartage Committee is under the collective bargaining agreement final and binding, the District Court has jurisdiction under § 301 to enforce it, notwithstanding our Westinghouse decision. See Textile Workers v. Lincoln Mills, 353 U.S. 448, 456, n. 6; United Steelworkers v. Pullman-Standard Car Mfg. Co., 241 F. 2d 547, 551–552 (C.A. 3d Cir. 1957). Plainly, this allegation cannot be rejected on the basis merely of what the present record shows. It is not enough that the word "arbitration" does not appear in the collective bargaining agreement, for we have held that the policy of the Labor Act "can be effectuated only if the means chosen by the parties for settlement of their differences under a collective bargaining agreement is given full play." United Steelworkers v. American Mfg. Co., 363 U.S. 564, 566; cf. Retail Clerks v. Lion Dry Goods, Inc., 369 U.S. 17. Thus, if the award at bar is the parties' chosen instrument for the definitive settlement of grievances under the Agreement, it is enforceable under § 301. And if the Joint Area Cartage Committee's award is thus enforceable, it is of course not open to the courts to reweigh the merits of the grievance. American Mfg. Co., *supra*, at 567–568.

Of course, if it should be decided after trial that the grievance award involved here is not final and binding under the collective bargaining agreement, no action under § 301 to enforce it will lie. Then, should petitioners seek to pursue the action as a § 301 suit for breach of contract, there may have to be considered questions unresolved by our prior decisions. We need not reach those questions here. But since the courts below placed so much reliance on the *Westinghouse* decision, we deem it appropriate to repeat our conclusion in Smith v. Evening News Assn., 371 U.S. 195, 199, that "subsequent decisions ... have removed the underpinnings of *Westinghouse* and its holding is no longer authoritative as a precedent."

Reversed and remanded.

In Smith v. Union Carbide Corp., (6th Cir. 1965) 350 F. 2d 258, an employee given a "medical termination" applied for pension benefits, apparently claiming eligibility as one totally disabled. The pension plan provided that in the event of a dispute between the company and an employee as to whether he is thus disabled "within the meaning of the Pension Plan" the dispute was to be settled by examination by physicians, the company and the union each selecting one. After their examination, if they disagreed, the doctors were to select a third, who after examining the employee and consulting with the two other doctors, was to "decide the question." The party-selected doctors agreed that the plaintiff was not disabled by organic disease but wanted the issue of disability by virtue of mental illness decided by a specialist. The physician they selected decided that Smith was not permanently disabled, but he did not consult with the other two doctors in reaching this conclusion. The district judge held that the "arbitration" procedure was not followed and proceeded to decide the merits, finding the plaintiff disabled. The court of appeals reversed, holding that the case should have been remanded to the "arbitrators," *i.e.* the doctors.

A union-company employee pension agreement was to expire in late 1962. In April 1961 the company closed its plant. It claimed that the closing terminated its obligation under the agreement; the union contended that the obligations continued until the 1962 termination date and sued for certain payments. While the suit was pending an employee applied for early retirement to the Joint Board established to administer the agreement. A company Board member opposed granting the application on grounds of failure to follow prescribed procedure; the union moved to arbitrate the issue under a pension-agreement provision calling for the vote of an impartial chairman to break union-management deadlocks. The court held that the provision was enforceable under § 301 although the term "arbitration" did not occur in the provision. And, the court went on:

> In the present contract one of the employer's primary obligations was to pay to the trust fund certain sums in conformance with the requirements of Article IV, paragraph one. The point in time at which that obligation terminated is the disputed question which gave rise to this lawsuit. Another obligation imposed by the agreement, binding on both parties, is that of administering the plan, *i.e.*, receiving and approving or rejecting applications for retirement and authorizing the dispersement [*sic*] of funds.
>
> The termination of the aforementioned two

obligations, one unilateral and the other bilateral, need not necessarily occur at the same point in time. It is conceded that certain pension rights survive the agreement. To the Court it appears reasonable to assume that the scheme which the parties have by mutual consent provided for the fulfillment of those rights should also survive.

The conduct of the parties since the closing of the employer's plant confirms this interpretation. The joint board has continued to function. According to plaintiff's brief, thirty-seven applications for benefits have been received by the board and acted upon. Although the foregoing is not verified by affidavit, exhibits attached to plaintiff's request for admission of facts indicate that the board authorized payments to at least eight applicants in 1962, four applicants in 1963, and the same number in 1964. The last authorization was made on October 28, 1964. All of these actions occurred subsequent to the plant closing. And all of them were necessarily undertaken under the authority and pursuant to the applicable provisions of the pension agreement. Thus, the parties themselves have demonstrated by their conduct the existence of a mutual duty to administer the pension agreement at the time the eligibility dispute arose. The final step in that administration is submittal of disputed issues to a neutral chairman.

For the foregoing reasons the union's motion for an order directing the defendant to arbitrate the matter of the eligibility dispute which has arisen since the institution of this lawsuit will be allowed. And because it appears that the arbitrable dispute is not only relevant to this lawsuit but a determination in the company's favor may render this suit without purpose, the union's further motion for a stay will also be granted.

Local 459, United Automobile Workers v. Defiance Industries, Inc., (N.D. Ohio, W.D. 1966) 251 F. Supp. 650.

LOCAL 60, LUGGAGE WORKERS UNION v. MAJOR MOULDERS, INC.
11 A.D. 2d 668, 204 N.Y.S. 2nd 77
(1st Dept. 1960)

Appellant entered into an agreement with the union wherein it was provided that within 30 days from the date thereof, the parties would enter into a "full length collective bargaining agreement with the Union upon the same terms and conditions as provided in the Union's contracts with Employers in the Industry generally, except in the following specific respects." No copy of the so-called general industry contract was annexed. No such later agreement was entered into. Any dispute which might arise under the initial agreement was to be "settled in the same manner as will be provided in the collective bargaining agreement to be entered into as hereinabove stated." In effect, the union was seeking arbitration under a collective agreement that was never consummated. That unexecuted agreement was to contain the provisions for the machinery of arbitration. Without such a binding collective agreement, there was no effective commitment by the parties to arbitrate.

Concur—BREITEL, J. P., RABIN, VALENTE AND BERGAN, JJ.

CHAPTER XI

AFTERMATH OF THE TRILOGY

The three Steelworker cases mark a dividing line almost as important as *Lincoln Mills*. They had a possibly profound effect, if not upon what people were doing in arbitration, then upon what some courts had been doing. The other major cases that followed (set out in the preceding chapter) filled in important details.

Chief among the effects of the Trilogy was an outpouring of criticism of the three opinions. While many critics did not take issue with the results of the decisions, the extravagance of language and the purported breadth of the arbitrator's role they prescribed were sharply questioned. (Citations to this literature emerge in the foot-notes to the cases and in the materials that comprise this chapter.)

As will be seen, the effects have been diverse. Some, such as the amendment of the New York Act, probably were caused by the same forces as those that led to the Trilogy.

Some of what follows deals with problems that go beyond those dealt with in the Trilogy and the other major cases. One set of problems, injunctions against strikes, deriving from the "second trilogy" (*Drake, Atkinson v. Sinclair, Sinclair v. Atkinson*) is dealt with in the subsequent chapter on remedies.

A.

Some Reactions in the States

In 1962 the New York Civil Practice Act was amended by adding § 1448-a:

> In determining any matter arising under this article, the court or judge shall not consider whether the claim with respect to which arbitration is sought is tenable, or otherwise pass upon the merits of the dispute.

The avowed purpose of this amendment, which became the last sentence of CPLR § 7501 by amendment in 1963, was to "overrule" the Cutler-Hammer doctrine. See Report of the Law Revision Commission, Leg. Doc. (1962) No. 65 (F).

The last phrase of the amendment could be read as applying to postaward proceedings. However, the legislative history shows concern only with pre-arbitration proceedings. Different considerations should guide the judicial role in pre- and post-arbitration stages. The policy of the statute argues, at the least, for judicial restraint at the review stage.

MATTER OF EMPIRE STATE MASTER HAIRDRESSERS' ASS'N. (JOURNEYMEN BARBERS) (Kings Cty. 1962) (51 LRRM 2153)

Low, J. Petitioner is an association of beauty shop owners in the Borough of Brooklyn, City of New York. Respondent is a labor union representing employees in the beauty service industry. On May 15, 1955, petitioner and respondent entered into a collective bargaining agreement setting forth wages, hours and other terms and conditions of employment for the employees in the beauty service industry. The agreement runs for a period of five years and is automatically renewable for an additional period of three years.

Article IX of the agreement provides as follows:

> Article IX—Duration of Agreement—This agreement goes into effect immediately and shall remain binding until the 15th day of May, 1963. It is further agreed that either party hereto may give the other party written notice two months prior to the expiration of this agreement of its intention or desire to terminate or to change or alter any of the provisions of this agreement, and the failure of both parties to give such notice shall operate as a renewal of this agreement and all its provisions for a further period of 3 years. Provided, further, that one year after this agreement becomes effective, and annually thereafter, either party hereto shall have the privilege of proposing changes in the provisions of this agreement, by giving 30 days' notice to the other party and changes in the terms of this agreement may thereafter be effected by mutual consent after negotiation. If both parties are unable to agree within two weeks after said notice, either may demand the arbitration of such controversy and the parties hereto agree to submit to such arbitration. In the event that arbitration shall be demanded by either party, the arbitrator shall be appointed by the Board of Mediation of the Department of Labor of the State of New York. The decision of the arbitrator shall be final and binding upon both parties, but any revision under this clause shall not lower the wages or increase the number of hours of labor established herein.

No changes in the agreement were made or proposed by either of the parties until February 7, 1962, when the petitioner-union sent to respondent-association a written proposal, pursuant to the provisions of Article IX of the agreement, seeking a *change* thereof by inserting a provision for contributions to be paid by the employer to the association towards a health and welfare fund for its members. This proposal was at first rejected by the association. Representatives of the union and the association attempted to negotiate the union's proposal, but were unable to come to any agreement. Consequently, the union requested arbitration of the dispute by the New York State Board of Mediation and forwarded a notice therefor to the respondent-association.

Petitioner now moves to stay the arbitration on the ground that the alleged controversy between the parties is not arbitrable within the term of the collective bargaining agreement.

Article IX of the agreement between the parties provides that the agreement may be reopened annually for the proposal of *changes* therein by either party. It also provides that any dispute or controversy arising between them concerning such proposed changes shall be submitted to arbitration on request of either party. Petitioner argues that the union's proposal for health and welfare fund contributions, not being covered by the agreement, constitutes a new provision, outside the letter and spirit of the agreement, and not a *change* contemplated by the terms of the agreement, and consequently is beyond the scope of the arbitration clause thereof.

The 1962 Legislature of the State of New York passed and on April 9, 1962, the Governor signed an amendment to the Civil Practice Act, known as section 1448-a, which reads as follows.

> *Arbitrability not to depend upon merits of claims.* In determining any matter arising under this article, the court or judge shall not consider whether the claim with respect to which arbitration is sought is tenable, or otherwise pass upon the merits of the dispute.

The purpose of this amendment was to abrogate the rule under which the courts were required to examine into the merits of disputes before deciding whether the arbitration should be directed (Matter of Internat. Ass'n of Machinists [Cutler-Hammer, Inc.] 297 N.Y. 519, 20 LRRM 2445). This is no longer the rule in this state.

Under the new provision the function of the court is confined to ascertaining whether a party seeking arbitration has a prima facie claim governed by the contract and is not to consider the merits or the tenability of the claim sought to be arbitrated. The amendment changed the law of this state to conform to that expressed by the United States Supreme Court in United Steel

Workers of America v. Warrior & Gulf Navigation Co. (363 U.S. 574, 46 LRRM 2416).

The court is of the opinion that the express provision for the annual reopening of the collective bargaining agreement for the purpose of effectuating any *changes* therein is sufficiently broad to include the change proposed by the petitioner and that any dispute with respect to such change is arbitrable under the provisions of Article IX of said agreement and vests the arbitrator with power to impose a new agreement on the parties. Welfare and pension contributions and similar fringe benefits are the proper subject of collective bargaining negotiations within the wage provisions of collective bargaining agreements.

Accordingly, the motion to stay the arbitration is denied. Settle order on notice.

MATTER OF FITZGERALD
(GENERAL ELEC. CO.)
23 A.D. 2d 288, 260 N.Y.S. 2d 470 (1965)

McNALLY, J. In this proceeding to compel arbitration in accordance with provision therefor in a collective bargaining agreement, the question presented is whether the grievances involve arbitrable disputes.

The collective bargaining agreement between petitioner and respondent dated October 27, 1960 provides for grievance procedure as to any dispute or grievance, and for arbitration thereof if it remains unsettled and involves "the interpretation or application of a provision of this Agreement," with the provision that if either party advises the American Arbitration Association that the grievance does not raise an arbitrable issue then it shall not have the authority to process the request for arbitration until a court has adjudicated the issue of arbitrability. Pending any grievance or dispute, the union covenants not to cause any strike or related action.

Respondent's janitors, porters and charwomen, within bargaining units of respondent's Baltimore and Fort Edward plants, are represented by petitioner's Locals 120 and 332. On or about January 10, 1961 and March 2, 1961, Local 120 initiated grievances charging respondent with violations of Articles I and XII of the agreement in that it subcontracted the work theretofore performed by members of Local 120. The relevant portion of Article I is respondent's recognition of the petitioner and its certified locals as the exclusive bargaining representatives of its employees within the certified units. The perti-

nent portion of Article XII requires the application of certain factors in respect of layoffs or transfers, the major one being seniority.

The grievance procedures were exhausted. Petitioner requested arbitration on March 8, 1961 as to the grievance initiated in January, 1961, and on March 29, 1961 as to the one initiated in March, 1961. In each case the respondent advised the arbitration forum it was of the opinion the grievance did not raise an arbitrable issue. Petitioner on September 19, 1961 instituted this proceeding to compel arbitration. The order appealed from entered July 2, 1962 dismisses the petition on the ground that the disputes do "not involve interpretation or application of any provision of the collective bargaining agreement." By stipulation of the parties argument of this appeal was deferred pending the application for certiorari before the United States Supreme Court in International Union of Electrical, Radio & Machine Workers, AFL–CIO v. General Electric Co. (*infra*).

The agreement provides its interpretation and application shall be governed by the law of the State of New York. Federal and New York State law are alike in respect of arbitration pursuant to collective bargaining agreements. (Matter of Long Island Lumber Co. v. Martin, 15 N.Y. 2d 380, 259 N.Y.S. 2d 142, 207 N.E. 2d 190 [decided April 15, 1965].)

"It is only where the parties have employed language which clearly rebuts the presumption of arbitrability, *e.g.,* by stating that an issue either as to procedure or as to substance is *not* to be determined by arbitration, that the matter may be determined by the courts. In the absence of such unmistakably clear language, as here, the matter is sent to the arbitrator for his determination on the merits. (See United Steelworkers of America v. Enterprise Wheel & Car Corp., 363 U.S. 593, [80 S.Ct. 1358, 4 L.Ed. 2d 1424] [1960])." (Matter of Long Island Lumber Co. v. Martin, p. 385, 259 N.Y.S. 2d p. 146, 207 N.E. 2d p. 193, *supra*.)

The agreement here provides for arbitration of "any dispute." The reservation of exclusive management authority in the respondent contained in Article XXVII thereof does not serve to exclude from the all-inclusive provision for arbitration the grievances here involved. (United Steelworkers v. Warrior & Gulf Co., 363 U.S. 574, 583, 80 S.Ct. 1347, 4 L.Ed. 2d 1409.) The petitioner's precontract demand for a limitation of the respondent's subcontracting practice is irrelevant. (See dissenting opinion of Whittaker, J., in United Steelworkers v. Warrior & Gulf Co., *supra*, p. 588, 80 S.Ct. 1354.) (International Union of Electrical, Radio & Machine Workers,

AFL–CIO v. General Electric Co., 2 Cir., 332 F. 2d 485, 488–490, cert. denied 379 U.S. 928, 85 S.Ct. 324, 13 L.Ed. 2d 341.)

On this record arbitration may not be denied because the disputes in issue are within the scope of the broad provision for arbitration and no provision of the contract serves to exclude them from arbitration. Moreover, if there were doubt, it would be "resolved in favor of coverage." (United Steelworkers v. Warrior & Gulf Co., *supra*, 363 U.S., p. 583, 80 S.Ct. 1347 ; Matter of Long Island Lumber Co. v. Martin, *supra*.)

The order should be reversed, on the law, with costs and disbursements to petitioner-appellant, and the motion to direct arbitration granted.

All concur except BREITEL, J. P., who dissents in a dissenting opinion.

BREITEL, J. P. (dissenting). I dissent. The majority holding is predicated on the premise that the parties agreed to submit "any dispute" to arbitration. That holding requires arbitration of an issue that the parties never agreed to submit to arbitration. Despite the parties' express stipulation in the arbitration clause in this collective bargaining agreement that a court must first pass on the arbitrability of a dispute, this Court now leaves that very issue of arbitrability to be determined by the arbitrators. The Court does so without so much as examining the scope of the agreement to arbitrate.

The Court concludes, despite earlier references to a limitation, that the agreement provides for arbitration of "any dispute." On the contrary, the agreement, so far as it is here applicable, requires arbitration only of "any grievance . . . which involves . . . the interpretation or application of a provision of this Agreement."[1] Thus

the right to arbitration was not extended broadly to any dispute or controversy that might arise between the parties, nor even to any dispute that might arise in the performance of the contract. It was explicitly limited to issues of construction of the agreement. Presumably all other issues were to be resolved through the normal processes of collective bargaining, or, where legal rights would be involved, through litigation.

The agreement recognizes, moreover, that threshold issues of arbitrability may easily arise under this limited arbitration clause. The clause goes on to provide, therefore, that these threshold issues must first be resolved by the court in favor of arbitration before the arbitrators are vested with jurisdiction to decide the substantive dispute. The agreement accomplishes this by conferring jurisdiction on the arbitrators "only after a final judgment of a Court has determined that the grievance upon which arbitration has been requested raises arbitrable issues and has directed arbitration of such issues."[2]

In view of the limited scope of the arbitration agreement now before the Court, decisions involving broad clauses are not in point. As this Court stated in Matter of Uddo [Taormina], 21 A.D. 2d 402, 405, 250 N.Y.S. 2d 645, 647:

> Confusion may arise from the holdings interpreting broad clauses in agreements which provide as arbitrable any question that may arise under or in connection with the making, meaning or performance of the particular contract.

Patently, Mtr. of Long Island Lumber Co. v. Martin, 15 N.Y. 2d 380, 259 N.Y.S. 2d 142,

---

1. The text of Article XVII, section 1 is:

"1. Any grievance which remains unsettled after having been fully processed pursuant to the provisions of Article XVI, and which involves either,

    (a) the interpretation or application of a provision of this Agreement, or

    (b) a disciplinary penalty (including discharge) imposed on or after the effective date of this Agreement, which is alleged to have been imposed without just cause,

shall be submitted to arbitration upon written request of either the Union or the Company, provided that such request is made within 30 days after the final decision of the Company has been given to the Union pursuant to Article XVI, Section 1(c) (5). The Union may withdraw from arbitration any grievance it submits if within ten days from the date the Company advises the Union in writing that the grievance so submitted does not, in the opinion of the Company, raise an arbitrable issue, the Union notifies the Company in writing that it withdraws the grievance from arbitration. A failure on the part of the Union to withdraw a grievance during said 10 day period shall

preclude withdrawal at a later date and *thereafter all questions concerning arbitrability shall be determined in accordance with the procedures set forth in Section 2(b) of this Article.* For the purpose of proceedings within the scope of (b), above, the standard to be applied by an arbitrator to cases involving disciplinary penalties (including discharge) is that such penalties shall be imposed only for just cause." (Emphasis supplied, and the Article to which the emphasized material refers is set forth in the next footnote following.)

2. Article XVII, Section 2(b), provides:

"It is further expressly understood and agreed that the American Arbitration Association shall have no authority to process a request for arbitration or appoint an arbitrator if either party shall advise the Association that such request arises under Section 1(a) of this Article, but that the grievance desired to be arbitrated does not, in its opinion, raise an arbitrable issue. In such event, the Association shall have authority to process the request for arbitration and appoint an arbitrator in accordance with its rules only after a final judgment of a Court has determined that the grievance upon which arbitration has been requested raises arbitrable issues and has directed arbitration of such issues. The foregoing part of this subsection (b) shall not be applicable if by its terms the request for arbitration requests only relief from a disciplinary penalty or discharge alleged to have been imposed without just cause."

207 N.E. 2d 190, is not in point, as there the agreement requiring arbitration of "all grievances" without limitation was unquestionably broad enough to cover the substantive issue, namely, the applicability of a wage agreement to a particular individual. The arbitration clause covering, as it did, the substantive dispute, the Court held that compliance with procedural prerequisites was to be determined by the arbitrator. The substantive scope of the arbitration clause was simply not an issue.

Thus, Judge Burke wrote in the *Lumber* case that "In the light of these cases, questions of timeliness and compliance with step-by-step grievance procedures, prior to formal and final binding arbitration, are questions of 'procedural arbitrability'. Now it is clear that such questions must be left to the arbitrator" (p. 386, 259 N.Y.S. 2d p. 147, 207 N.E. 2d p. 193). And again: "But, as we have indicated above, the rule which we have recognized and followed leaves *all* procedural questions for the arbitrator to consider along with the substantive issues involved in the arbitration claims" (p. 387, 259 N.Y.S. 2d p. 147, 207 N.E. 2d p. 193). Because the substantive clause in the case was broad and unlimited, none of this reasoning has pertinence for the instant case.

Where there is an arbitration clause as to interpretation, without any express stipulation for judicial finding of arbitrability, and any question of interpretation of the agreement arises, the situation is simpler. Thus, in United Steelworkers v. American Mfg. Co., 363 U.S. 564, 80 S.Ct. 1343, 4 L.Ed. 1403, the court was faced with a collective bargaining agreement, which, not unlike the one at bar, required arbitration of

> [a]ny disputes, misunderstandings, differences or grievances arising between the parties as to the *meaning, interpretation and application* of the provisions of the agreement. (363 U.S. 565, 80 S.Ct. 1345, fn. 1) (Emphasis added).

The substantive issue on which the union sought arbitration was whether an injured employee, who had settled a compensation claim on his attorney's representation that he had a permanent partial disability, was entitled to return to his job (for a statement of facts, see 6 Cir., 264 F. 2d 624). This, of course, raised an arbitrable question of interpretation, as the contract allowed management to discharge an employee "for cause", and required the company to recognize the principle of seniority as a factor in re-employment "where ability and efficiency are equal." The majority opinion recognized the existence of a dispute as to interpretation, and

reversed the judgment below, which dismissed a complaint to compel arbitration, on the ground that even frivolous claims should proceed to arbitration. The Court thus rejected the "Cutler-Hammer" doctrine, which is, of course, no longer the law of New York (CPLR 7501; 8 WEINSTEIN-KORN-MILLER, N.Y. CIV. PRAC. ¶ 7501.20).

Of critical significance to the instant case, however, is the Supreme Court's holding in United Steelworkers v. American Mfg. Co. that the scope—the substantive scope—of the arbitration clause is for the court, not the arbitrator. Thus the Court stated, at 363 U.S. 567–568, 80 S.Ct. 1346:

> The function of the court is very limited when the parties have agreed to submit all questions of contract interpretation to the arbitrator. It is confined to ascertaining whether the party seeking arbitration is making a claim which on its face is governed by the contract.

Thus the court may not look behind the face of the claim and examine the merits of the claim or even decide whether the dispute is different from what the party seeking arbitration says it is. It must take the claim as framed by the party and determine whether that claim raises an issue of interpretation of the contract. This question of groundless but included disputes is a different problem from that of procedural limitations in arbitration, and, of course, it is yet again different from that of limitations in arbitration clauses on the substantive scope.

That the court must itself determine whether the parties have agreed to arbitrate the particular dispute is also the law of this State (Matter of Lipman [Haeuser Shellac Co.], 289 N.Y. 76, 80, 43 N.E. 2d 817, 819, 142 A.L.R. 1088; Mtr. of Rosenbaum [Amer. Sur. Co., N.Y.], 11 N.Y. 2d 310, 314, 229 N.Y.S. 2d 375, 377, 183 N.E. 2d 667, 668; Mtr. of Carey v. Westinghouse Elec., 11 N.Y. 2d 452, 456, 230 N.Y.S. 2d 703, 704, 184 N.E. 2d 298, 299, rev'd on other grds., 375 U.S. 261, 84 S.Ct. 401, 11 L.Ed. 2d 320). It is, consequently, unnecessary to determine whether the express contract provision, present in the instant collective bargaining agreement, that New York law is to govern could override an inconsistent rule adopted by the Supreme Court under Section 301 of the Labor Management Relations Act of 1947, 29 U.S.C. § 185 (see Textile Workers etc. v. Lincoln Mills, 353 U.S. 448, 77 S.Ct. 912, 1 L.Ed. 2d 972).

An examination of the substantive claim as framed by petitioner-union shows that it does not raise an included issue as to interpretation or application of the contract. Both grievances submitted by the union charge that the company assigned or contracted out cleaning work previously done by company employees to an outside firm. One grievance declared this to be a violation of Articles I and XII of the agreement and the other charged a violation of only Article I.

Article I does not have any relationship to this or any other contracting out issue. Article I merely requires the company to recognize the union as the exclusive bargaining agent of employees within certified bargaining units. Moreover the union's petition states that the individuals who were to do the work, as contracted out by the company, were not even within the collective bargaining unit. Thus the real issue, as well as the issue framed by the union, does not involve questions of union recognition requiring an interpretation or application of Article I.

Article XII deals solely with the procedure to be followed and the factors to be considered in determining which employees are to be laid off or transferred "due to lack of work." Seniority is the major factor to be considered. Although a "seniority" issue, or other such issue under Article XII, may well have attended or followed the company's decision to contract out certain work, the grievances and petition are wholly barren of any such allegation, as is the company's answer. In the absence of any such allegation there is not even the pretense of an arbitrable issue.

In briefing this matter on appeal the union has not even attempted to show that the contracting out dispute is "governed by the contract," to use the Supreme Court's test (United Steelworkers v. American Mfg. Co., 363 U.S. 564, 568, 80 S.Ct. 1343, *supra*). It obviously is not. If, nevertheless, ambiguity were to remain, the prior negotiations demonstrate that the contract was not intended to forbid contracting out (*i.e.*, to "govern" contracting out). In these negotiations the union sought, but was unable to obtain a contract provision against contracting out.

The mere reference to Articles I and XII in the demand for arbitration and conclusory allegations that they were violated do not make the issue an arbitrable one of interpretation. It is true that under United Steelworkers v. American Mfg. Co. (*supra*) it is entirely the role of the party seeking arbitration to frame the dispute in any way it pleases. It may frame its demand to exclude part or all of the real dispute, and it may even, under that holding, demand arbitration of a claim that is obviously and totally devoid of merit. The Supreme Court teaches that the processing of even frivolous claims in

arbitration may have "therapeutic values" (United Steelworkers v. American Mfg. Co., 363 U.S. 564, 568, 80 S.Ct. 1343). It is also true that under New York arbitration law the merits of the dispute are for the arbitrators not the court (CPLR 7501, 8 Weinstein-Korn-Miller, N.Y. Civ. Prac. ¶ 7501.20). These rules forbidding the court to examine the merits of the dispute do not even purport to change the well-established rule that the court must, in the first instance, determine whether the claim is one that the parties have agreed to arbitrate.

It follows from what has been said that a party may compel arbitration of any claim (however meritless) under a *broad* agreement to arbitrate, but may not compel arbitration of any claim (however meritorious) under a *limited* arbitration agreement by falsely characterizing that claim in order that it fall within an included category. It is always for the court, in the case of a limited arbitration clause, to reject a specious characterization of the claim actually made, regardless of its merits—indeed, even if of the greatest merit—and to determine whether there was an agreement to arbitrate that claim in its true category. This is particularly so where, as here, the parties have expressly bargained for a judicial examination of the nature of the claim. Any other view would mean that parties are powerless to limit the scope of arbitration, and that just is not so.

The *Bridgeport* case (International Union of Elec., R. & M. Wkrs. v. General Elec. Co., 332 F. 2d 485, cert. den. 379 U.S. 928, 85 S.Ct. 324, 13 L.Ed. 2d 341) decided by a divided court, if in point, is neither controlling nor persuasive. Although the union in this case describes the agreement involved in that case as "virtually" identical with the agreement in this case, the Court in the Bridgeport case never discussed the express provision, if there was one, for judicial advance determination of arbitrability. Such a provision is of vital significance.

There is no doubt that an agreement may contain limitations on the rights of the parties as distinguished from limitations on the right to arbitrate, or perhaps in rare cases even on the right to arbitrate, which are addressed to the arbitrators alone to govern their determinations. Such provisions are distinguishable from those in an agreement which are addressed to limiting the jurisdiction or power of the arbitrators to make determinations and which, therefore, are addressed to the court. This distinction creates the subtlest problems most difficult of resolution where the parties have not expressly related the issue to judicial determination. When the parties have stipulated that the limitation is one for judicial determination, as was done here, both the subtlety and difficulty of resolution disappear. (The distinction is made incisively by Mr. Justice Brennan in his concurring opinion in United Steelworkers v. American Mfg. Co., 363 U.S. 564, 571–572, 80 S.Ct. 1343, *supra*.)

By compelling arbitration of this matter the Court does the cause of labor arbitration, and more important, of labor peace, a disservice. The parties have bargained for a limited arbitration clause and for a court determination of the threshold question of arbitrability. Perhaps one party, or both, would not otherwise have agreed to any arbitration clause at all. If so, the prevailing holding may serve as a warning to the labor-relations bar that the Court will not examine the scope of a limited arbitration clause. The gravity of the problem is undoubtedly greater under industry arrangements where there are permanent arbitrators or impartial chairmen. Unless a party, fearful of unlimited arbitration, can anticipate all disputes that may arise in the future and obtain the other side's agreement to clauses expressly defining and forbidding arbitration of all such possible disputes, it must, and will, decline any arbitration agreement whatsoever. A rule of law throwing such an obstacle in the path of limited agreements to arbitrate does not forward, but actually thwarts, voluntary recourse to the arbitral forum for resolution of labor disputes. Instead of fostering labor peace, which is the expressed ground for the Supreme Court's policy in collective bargaining cases, recently espoused by our Court of Appeals in Mtr. of Long Island Lumber Co. v. Martin, 15 N.Y. 2d 380, 259 N.Y.S. 2d 142, 207 N.E. 2d 190, *supra*, the result would discourage the use of limited arbitration clauses and thus encourage labor strife where the parties are unable to agree on unlimited arbitration.

Accordingly, I dissent and vote to affirm the order of Special Term dismissing the petition to compel arbitration.

POSNER v. GRUNWALD-MARX, INC.
56 Cal. 2d 169, 14 Cal. Rptr. 297, 363 P. 2d 313
(1961)

PETERS, J. Petitioner union brought these proceedings to compel the defendant employer, Grunwald-Marx, Inc., to arbitrate the question of vacation pay for 1957 and holiday pay for May 30, 1957 (Decoration Day), which pay the union contends is owed to its members.

Both the union and the employer rely on a collective bargaining agreement entered into on October 1, 1953, and which, on October 23, 1956, was renewed and extended through September 30, 1959. Among other things, the agreement provided for a one-week vacation in each calendar year, based on hours and days worked during a period computed as ending with the last pay period in June of each year, which vacation was to be taken in the first week of July in the absence of a mutual agreement as to some other period. It also provided that, as a requirement of eligibility for the paid vacation, an employee must have been on the company pay roll nine months prior to the commencement of the vacation period and at the commencement of the vacation period; and that any employee who quit or was discharged for cause prior to the vacation period lost his rights to vacation pay. The agreement provided for May 30 (Decoration Day) as a paid holiday and required for eligibility that an employee must work the last working day before the holiday and the first working day after the holiday. Under the agreement an employee was entitled to holiday pay if he did not work any of these days due to illness or layoff.

On or about May 29, 1957, defendant employer moved its plants from Los Angeles County to Phoenix, Arizona, and "terminated" its employees. The collective bargaining agreement did not expressly provide for the contingency of the plant's removal or the "termination" of the employees.

The arbitration provision of the collective bargaining agreement provided, in part, that:

> A complaint, grievance or dispute arising between the parties relating directly or indirectly to the provision[s] of this agreement whether concerning discharges or any other terms thereof shall in the first instance be taken up for adjustment by a representative of the Union and a representative of the Company. In the event that they are unable to adjust the same then such matters shall be submitted to arbitration.

Upon the refusal of Grunwald-Marx, Inc., to pay vacation pay for 1957, or holiday pay for May 30, 1957, or to arbitrate these matters, the union, pursuant to section 1282 of the Code of Civil Procedure, filed a petition for an order directing arbitration. The petition was then withdrawn because the employer voluntarily agreed to arbitrate, and then again filed when the employer refused to proceed with the arbitration.

The trial court denied the petition and ordered the proceedings dismissed. It concluded that Grunwald-Marx, Inc., was not in default under the arbitration provisions of the collective bargaining agreement because "The wording of the collective bargaining agreement is without ambiguity as to vacation pay and holiday pay."

In thus limiting the arbitration clause of the agreement, the trial court adopted the older of two conflicting rules for the interpretation of such provisions found in collective bargaining agreements. It purported to apply the so-called "Cutler-Hammer" doctrine, which is that:

> While the contract provides for arbitration of disputes as to the "meaning, performance, non-performance or application" of its provisions, the mere assertion by a party of a meaning of a provision which is clearly contrary to the plain meaning of the words cannot make an arbitrable issue. . . . If the meaning of the provision of the contract sought to be arbitrated is beyond dispute, there cannot be anything to arbitrate and the contract cannot be said to provide for arbitration.

(International Assn. of Machinists v. Cutler-Hammer, Inc., 271 App. Div. 917 [67 N.Y.S. 2d 317, 318], affd. 297 N.Y. 519 [74 N.E. 2d 464].) This doctrine has never been affirmed by this court. It has received sharp academic criticism and little "academic" support.

An entirely different rule was adopted by the United States Supreme Court in a series of three significant cases decided last June [citing the Trilogy]. This rule is to the effect that, where the collective bargaining agreement provides for arbitration of all disputes pertaining to the meaning, interpretation and application of the collective bargaining agreement and its provisions, any dispute as to the meaning, interpretation and application of any specific matter covered by the collective bargaining agreement is a matter for arbitration. Doubts as to whether the arbitration clause applies are to be resolved in favor of coverage. The parties have contracted for an arbitrator's decision and not for that of the courts. The high court declared that

> The function of the court is very limited when the parties have agreed to submit all questions of contract interpretation to the arbitrator. It is confined to ascertaining whether the party seeking arbitration is making a claim which on its face is governed by the contract. Whether the moving party is right or wrong is a question of contract interpretation for the arbitrator. In these circumstances the moving party should not be deprived of the arbitrator's judgment, when it was his judgment and all that it connotes that was bargained for.

(United Steelworkers v. American Mfg. Co., *supra*, 363 U.S. 564, 567–568.) The court also carefully pointed out that the parties may exclude a particular grievance from arbitration either in the collective bargaining agreement or in a written collateral agreement. (United Steel-

workers v. Warrior & Gulf Navigation Co., *supra*, 363 U.S. 574, 584–585.)

This federal rule is not binding on this court in the instant case because petitioner failed to allege that the employer was engaged in interstate commerce. Moreover, the trial court found the employer's allegation (in an affirmative defense) that it was engaged in interstate commerce to be false. (See Textile Workers Union v. Lincoln Mills, 353 U.S. 448, 456 [77 S.Ct. 912, 1 L.Ed. 2d 972] ; McCarroll v. Los Angeles County etc. Carpenters, 49 Cal. 2d 45, 59–60 [312 P. 2d 322].) [2a]. But there are strong policy reasons why the federal rule is preferable. Certainly, uniformity is desirable. In view of the complex state of industry in this country, the majority of the major collective bargaining agreements necessarily relate to interstate commerce, and so they, of course, are governed by the federal rules. And, as petitioner union pointed out at oral argument, most large unions utilize a standard contract which they seek to have signed by the various employers whether such employers are engaged in either intrastate or interstate commerce. Certainly it would seem that in reference to the interpretation, scope and application of such contracts, uniformity is to be desired. It must also not be forgotten that "arbitration agreements in labor contracts are primarily designed to prevent strikes and other expressions of unrest by a prompt and equitable settlement of labor disputes, and not merely, as in the case with other arbitration agreements, to avoid the formalities, the delay, the expense, and vexation of ordinary litigation." (31 AM. JUR., Labor, § 114, p. 479.) [2b] Moreover, in favor of the federal rule it should be noted that the "Cutler-Hammer" doctrine is based on a strict and technical application of ordinary contract law, while the rule adopted by the United States Supreme Court properly takes into consideration the peculiar nature of the collective bargaining agreement. In this regard, the Supreme Court, in the *American Manufacturing Company* case noted that "[S]pecial heed should be given to the context in which collective bargaining agreements are negotiated and the purpose which they are intended to serve" and that "The collective agreement requires arbitration of claims that courts might be unwilling to entertain. In the context of the plant or industry the grievance may assume proportions of which judges are ignorant. Yet, the agreement is to submit all grievances to arbitration, not merely those that a court may deem to be meritorious." (363 U.S. at p. 567.)

[The court went on to cite Cox, Chamberlain, Shulman and the Trilogy in favor of the role for arbitration outlined in those cases; it also found in the state arbitration statute evidence that "our state policy favors arbitration provisions in collective bargaining agreements."]

From the above analysis, it can be safely stated that it is a fundamental part of both federal and California public policy to promote industrial stabilization through the medium of collective bargaining agreements. Certainly, it can be said that, in the instant case, both parties intended to secure, if possible, industrial stabilization. To obtain this end the parties expressed their intent to include within the arbitration clauses of the agreement all clauses of the contract, and all disputes arising under the agreement. The action of Grunwald-Marx, Inc., in first proceeding to arbitrate is some evidence in support of the inference that it intended the vacation pay and holiday pay provisions to be arbitrable in the event of removal of its plants and "termination" of its employees. This being so, the federal rule to the effect that in such cases all disputes as to the meaning, interpretation and application of any clause of the collective bargaining agreement, even those that *prima facie* appear to be without merit, are the subject of arbitration, is adopted by this court.

This does not mean that we adopt all of the implications of the federal cases. There is some general language in those three cases that can be interpreted as indicating a complete judicial retreat from the field of arbitration in collective bargaining cases, which could result in the arbitrary remaking of the collective bargaining agreement by an arbitrator contrary to the intentions of the parties. These implications have been criticized.[1] Certainly, such implications would be contrary to the rules already adopted in this state, and we have no intent at the present time of changing these rules.

The proper rule is that the arbitrator of a collective bargaining agreement entered into by a labor union and an employer "serves their pleasure only, to administer the rule of law established by their collective agreement." (Shulman, *"Reason, Contract and Law in Labor Relations," supra,* 68 HARV. L. REV. 999 [1955].) The United States Supreme Court, in fact, in the

Enterprise case, seemed to recognize this principle when it stated that:

> The draftsmen [of the collective bargaining agreement] may never have thought of what specific remedy should be awarded to meet a particular contingency. Nevertheless, an arbitrator is confined to interpretation and application of the collective bargaining agreement; he does not sit to dispense his own brand of industrial justice. He may of course look for guidance from many sources, yet his award is legitimate only so long as it draws its essence from the collective bargaining agreement. When the arbitrator's words manifest an infidelity to this obligation, courts have no choice but to refuse enforcement of the award. (363 U.S. at p. 597.)

Professor Kagel, an authority in the field of arbitration, has pointed out that the collective bargaining agreement

> is a codification of much of the industrial common law, *i.e.*, the practices of the industry or plant. Some Agreements specifically provide whether or not remaining unrecorded practices are to be recognized as additional and a substantive part of the Agreement.
>
> Where the parties have not made such specific provisions then to the extent that the unrecorded industrial common law does not negate or is not inconsistent with the written Agreement it becomes a substantive part of the Agreement for the purpose of interpreting that writing. Thus industrial common law, *i.e.*, practices, are used in the grievance procedure to aid in resolving ambiguities in the written Agreement. But not to add new or contradictory terms to the Agreement.

Thus, the federal rule, at least limited as suggested above, is in conformity with the California cases and results in enforcing the intent of the parties.

But even if we were not to adopt the federal rule, as thus limited, and were to adopt the "Cutler-Hammer" doctrine, nevertheless the dispute here involved would be subject to arbitration. This is so because it would be unreasonable to conclude from the face of the collective bargaining agreement that the controversy between petitioner union and Grunwald-Marx Inc., does not fall within the scope of arbitration agreed upon by both parties. In other words, it cannot be said from a reading of the holiday and vacation provisions that their meaning is so clear that there is nothing to arbitrate. The holiday pay provision requires employment on the last working day before, and the first working day after a holiday; the vacation pay provision requires (1) length of service, (2) employment at a specific date or period and (3) the taking of the vacation at a specific time. It would seem clear that the purpose of these pro-

1. Hays, *The Supreme Court and Labor Law October Term, 1959* (1960), 60 Columb. L. Rev. 901, 919–935; Davey, *The Supreme Court and Arbitration: The Musings of an Arbitrator* (1961), 36 NOTRE DAME LAW. 138; and Note (1961), 46 CORNELL L. Q. 336.

But see *The Supreme Court, 1959 Term* (1960), 74 Harv. L. Rev. 81, 178–181; Comment (1960), 34 So. CAL. L. REV. 63; Note (1960), 59 MICH. L. REV. 454; Note (1960), 49 GEO. L. J. 873; and Note (1960), 36 NOTRE DAME LAW. 63.

visions is to offer a reward of additional wages for constant and continuous service. As Judge Magruder in Goodall-Sanford, Inc. v. United Textile Workers, 233 F. 2d 104, pointed out, there is an "increasingly complex use of compensation in the form of 'fringe benefits,' some types of which inherently are not payable until a time subsequent to the work which earned the benefits." (233 F. 2d at p. 110.)

In a case that applied the "Cutler-Hammer" doctrine (Botany Mills, Inc. v. Textile Workers Union (1958), 50 N.J. Super. 18 [141 A. 2d 107]), the interpretation of a vacation provision in a collective bargaining agreement, similar to the one before us, and its application to "terminated" employees was deemed to be a question for arbitration. In that case the employer contended that complete performance of a condition precedent was necessary before the employees could recover and the union contended that vacation payments as deferred compensation are payable if there is a rendition of substantial services. The court concluded that the dispute arose under the contract and both disputants were advancing positions that were reasonably tenable in the light of the contract language and relevant extrinsic circumstances.

In the instant case, it can also be argued that the vacation provisions do not require complete performance, but that the doctrine of substantial performance is applicable.

Reversed.

B.

Arbitrability Revisited

In United Brick and Clay Workers v. A. P. Green Fire Brick Co. a disagreement arose about the meaning of a contract provision immediately after the execution of the collective agreement by the company. The company informed the union three days after signing it that if the union construed the agreement to provide for overtime for Saturday work even if no hours over forty were worked there had been no meeting of the minds and no contract. The district judge found: "it is clear that the Company never agreed to arbitrate the present dispute" and "looking at the extrinsic evidence ... it is evident that there was no intention to arbitrate the question." 232 F. Supp. 223 (D.C.E.D. Mo. 1964). The court of appeals reversed, noting that the union claimed a violation of a contract provision and that this gave rise to a controversy that "involves the interpretation or application of the provisions of the agreement," thus making an arbitrable issue. (8th Cir. 1965) 343 F. 2d 590.

LOCAL 30, PHILADELPHIA LEATHER WORKERS' UNION v. HYMAN BRODSKY & SON CORP.
243 F. Supp. 728 (E.D. Pa. 1964)

KIRKPATRICK, D. J. This lawsuit was precipitated when the defendant company permanently discontinued all its operations on three days notice, thereby terminating the employment of some 70 employees represented by the plaintiff union. The union then served upon the company a demand for arbitration, based upon its collective bargaining agreement, of a number of issues[1] arising from the company's discontinuance of its operations. Upon the company's refusal to arbitrate, the union filed its complaint in this suit in which it asked certain action from the court in regard to a pension fund and an order requiring the defendant to arbitrate the issues set forth in the demands.[2] These issues have now been boiled down to three, to wit: severance pay, the employer's action in shutting down its plant and its failure to give notice of the shut-down, and the claimed "Pension Plan."

Presently before the court are the defendant's motion to dismiss on the ground that the complaint fails to state a cause of action upon which relief can be granted and the plaintiff's motion for summary judgment, together with a supporting affidavit. The motion to dismiss presents the defendant's contention that none of the issues referred to above are arbitrable and the motion for summary judgment that they all are.

The arbitration clause of the collective bar-

---

1. Set out with greater specificity in a later demand.

2. It is not suggested that the company's going out of business was a step taken in anything but good faith, and it is not charged that it was a maneuver for the purpose of avoiding obligations under the collective bargaining agreement.

gaining agreement, or so much of it as is pertinent, is as follows:

> In the event of . . . a dispute concerning the meaning or application of any provision of this agreement . . . either party may refer the same to a Board of Arbitration . . .

The plaintiff's contention as to the law governing arbitration articles in labor contracts is, in substance, as follows: The courts will compel arbitration under section 301 of *any* dispute where the collective bargaining agreement contains a "No Strike" clause and a broad arbitration clause and which does not by its terms exclude the dispute. This proposition derives from a statement by Mr. Justice Douglas in the opinion of the Supreme Court in United Steelworkers of America v. Warrior and Gulf Navigation Co., 363 U.S. 574, 584, 585.

> In the absence of any express provision excluding a particular grievance from arbitration, we think only the most forceful evidence of a purpose to exclude the claim from arbitration can prevail, particularly where, as here, the exclusion clause is vague and the arbitration clause quite broad.

The agreement in the present case has what may properly be called a "broad" arbitration clause (although that term is not definitive) and it contains no clause excluding from arbitration any of the three issues referred to. The plaintiff contends in effect that under the above principle the question whether any of the points for which arbitration is demanded is arbitrable at all is one of the matters to be determined by the arbitrator. I think that the plaintiff has taken too broad a view of the *Warrior* case, *supra.* The quoted excerpt from the opinion indicates plainly enough that even in the absence of an express exclusion arbitration will be denied provided "the most forceful evidence of a purpose to exclude" is adduced.

The latest pronouncement of the Supreme Court upon the question is to be found in John Wiley & Sons, Inc., v. David Livingston, [49 LC ¶ 18,846] March 30, 1964, in which the Court, quoting from Atkinson v. Sinclair Refining Co., 370 U.S. 238, 241, said

> Under our decisions, whether or not the company was bound to arbitrate, as well as what issues it must arbitrate, is a matter to be determined by the Court on the basis of the contract entered into by the parties.

The arbitration clause in the collective bargaining agreement in the *Wiley* case is even broader than the corresponding clause in the present agreement, covering as it does not only disputes concerning the meaning or application of the provisions of the agreement but "any and all acts or omissions claimed to have been committed by either party during the term of this agreement."

The arbitration clause in the present case is limited to disputes concerning the meaning or application of provisions of the contract and it does not include the matters covered by the contract of the *Wiley* case, nor by the even broader agreement in Drake Bakeries v. Bakery Workers, 370 U.S. 254, 257, which covered "any act or conduct or relation between the parties."

Inasmuch as the duty to arbitrate is contractual and since the contract in this case is to arbitrate matters concerning the meaning and application of the provisions of the collective bargaining agreement, we must look to that agreement to find provisions concerning whose meaning or application the dispute as to the three points mentioned exists.

As to the pension plan dispute, there are provisions in the contract concerning a pension plan. Whether or not the plan ever came into effect or whether or not the union has any claim under it is not a matter for this court. The parties having agreed that both meaning and application of this article shall be submitted to arbitration, it would be improper for me to express my views upon the subject.

As to the company's action in shutting down the plant and its failure to give advance warning of its intention to do so, the plaintiff has not been able to point to any provision in the contract that it seeks to have applied or interpreted, and, from an examination of it, I find no provision that could be applied or interpreted. As a result, I cannot find that the parties have agreed to arbitrate this matter.

As to the claim for severance pay because of the employees' loss of their jobs, the same situation is presented—no provision to be applied or interpreted. I, therefore, cannot order this dispute arbitrated.

Contracts in Force

There have been three collective bargaining agreements. The basic agreement "A" was dated January 1, 1959, and expired by its own terms December 31, 1961. Another agreement "B," also ending December 31, 1961, stating that it supplements and extends the "A" agreement for a two-year term beginning January 1, 1960, was entered into, for what reason is not clear. On October 24, 1961, the union notified the company of its "desire to terminate the present contract" and indicated a desire to negotiate with the company for a new agreement. These negotiations resulted in an undated supplement "C" (apparently entered into after December 31, 1961) which recited that it amended, added to, and extended "the presently-existing contract and the Supplemental Agreement thereto which expired as of December 31, 1961." The defendant argues that since at the time of the execution of supplement "C" both existing agreements had expired, the language quoted referred to nothing and, therefore, only the provisions of supplement "C" are in effect. Supplement "C" did not contain any arbitration clause.

I cannot agree. Not only is it usually the aim of the parties that collective bargaining agreements should be continuous, but these parties have expressly stated that they regarded their agreement as an addition and amendment to their prior agreements. They certainly meant this language to be given effect and I, therefore, conclude that the contract between the parties consists of the basic contract "A," supplement "B," and supplement "C."

Appropriate orders may be submitted.

LOCAL 483 INT'L. BHD. OF BOILERMAKERS

v.

SHELL OIL CO.

(7th Cir. 1966) 369 F. 2d 526

Before Duffy, Knoch and Kiley, Circuit Judges.

Kiley, C. J. The district court dismissed plaintiff-Union's action, under section 301 (a) of the Labor Management Relations Act, 29 U.S.C. § 185 (a), to compel arbitration of a grievance under its bargaining agreement with defendant, the Shell Oil Company. The Union has appealed. We affirm in part and reverse in part.

The grievance arose from Shell's contracting out to Nooter Corporation of St. Louis, Missouri, the five-million-dollar work involved in a "turn-around" renovation and construction project in September and October of 1963 at Shell's Wood River, Illinois, Refinery. The Union claimed that Shell had, in contracting out the work, discriminated against boilermaker members and improperly assigned the work to persons outside the unit. It demanded arbitration of the grievance, the demand was rejected, and this suit followed.

We think the first issue to be decided is, as stated by the Union, whether the question of Shell's right to contract out the work is arbitrable.[1] We hold that the district court correctly decided that the bargaining agreement did not "forbid or limit" Shell's contracting out of the work and consequently there was "no application or interpretation" of the agreement to be arbitrated under Article 18 of the bargaining agreement.[2]

The Union claims that the district court substituted itself for the arbitrator by its application and interpretation of the bargaining agreement with respect to contracting out of the work in excess of its function delineated in United Steelworkers of America v. American Mfg. Co., 363 U.S. 564, 567–569, 80 S.Ct. 1343, 4 L.Ed. 2d 1403 (1960). The claim has no merit.

The district court did not decide the merits of the Union's grievance, but decided that the claimed grievance—plaintiff claimed defendant violated the Preamble, Article 5 (Seniority), Article 8 (Working Hours) and Article 23 (Discrimination)—fell outside any promise of Shell's in the agreement. The question the court decided was not whether there was a violation of a provision, but whether there was a provision in the contract. As the court found, and Shell argues here, Article 18, the arbitration clause before us, is not a broad clause, such as the broad "any disagreement" clause in Local Union No. 702, IBEW v. Central Ill. Pub. Serv. Co., 324 F. 2d 920, 921 (7th Cir. 1963), but is limited to "application or interpretation of this Agreement." Here the Union is making a claim which "on its face" is not governed by the agreement. In United Steelworkers of America v. American Mfg. Co., 363 U.S. at 568, 80 S.Ct. at 1346, the rule stated is that the function of the court is to decide whether the claim is on its face governed by the contract.

The district court found that the bargaining history between Shell and the Union shows that the Union had sought without success to have Shell agree to a provision in the agreement "specifically prohibiting or limiting" Shell's right to contract out work, and that each proposal

---

1. The grievance filed by the Union states: "The Company has taken the maintenance and repair work on the cat cracker, properly belonging to the Boilermakers group, has discriminated against the men in the Boilermakers group in assignment of this work and the Company has further made improper assignment of such work to persons outside the unit."

2. Article 18 of the agreement provides: 1. "In the event complaints or controversies arising out of the application or interpretation of this Agreement remain unsettled after full compliance with the procedure set forth in Article 17 preceding, such may be settled by arbitration as follows: [a representative of the Employer, and one of the Union, select a third person to act as umpire, and his findings are final and binding on the parties.]"

was rejected by Shell and none included in the agreement. This finding has substantial support in the record.

The Union proposed limitations on Shell's freedom to contract out work for the 1958 and 1960 bargaining agreements. It proposed, for the 1962 agreement before us, that "the company will contract out such work only to the extent it cannot be performed by existing Company forces without prolonged over-time and working on existing classifications within the scope of this Agreement...." Shell consistently rejected the proposals and they were omitted from the agreements. The rejection of the 1962 proposal was a ground for the strike which began August 18, 1962, and ended February 3, 1963. Renewed proposals were made August 18, August 29, September 24, November 19, and November 21, 1962. Finally, on November 26, the Union proposed a "package" to settle the strike.

The package contained a proposal that the Union would consider a letter from Shell to the effect that Shell reserved its freedom to contract out maintenance and operational work, but in accordance with past practice would consider available qualified employees. On December 13, 1962, Shell responded with a letter which omitted any reference to past practice, claiming its determination to decide "whether any work will be assigned to employees or contracted," but stating it would give what it considered appropriate consideration to laid off employees with seniority. The letter was re-dated and included in a package proffered by Shell in January, 1963. The Union made no response to the letter. The agreement ending the strike contained no provision respecting Shell's right to contract out work.

Shell's consistent refusal, in three bargaining agreements, to agree to limit its freedom to contract out the work, the settlement of the strike and that issue without acceding to the Union demand, and the Union's tacit acceptance of Shell's position in its December, 1962, letter distinguish contracting out cases in which courts have compelled arbitration. *E.g.,* Procter & Gamble Independent Union of Port Ivory, N.Y. v. Procter & Gamble Mfg. Co., 298 F. 2d 644 (2d Cir. 1962). The evidence before us indicates "beyond peradventure of doubt" that contracting out in itself was not intended to be a subject of grievance. Thus the case comes within the rule stated in the Procter & Gamble case, 298 F. 2d at 646.

And we do not think that the same court's views in International Union of Elec. Radio & Mach. Workers v. General Elec. Co., 332 F. 2d 485, 490 (2d Cir.), cert. denied, 379 U.S. 928,

85 S.Ct. 324, 13 L.Ed. 2d 341 (1964), upon use of bargaining history, militate against our conclusion. The bargaining history here of unsuccessful Union attempts is capped by the Union's tacit acceptance of Shell's letter reserving freedom to contract out work and promising to give "such consideration as in its opinion is appropriate" to employment opportunities to employees with seniority. We think that nothing in the beneficent purpose of the labor-management arbitration process can fairly accommodate the Union's contention and also that there is here the "most forceful evidence of a purpose to exclude" this part of the grievance from arbitration. United Steelworkers of America v. Warrior & Gulf Nav. Co., 363 U.S. 574, 585, 80 S.Ct. 1347, 1354, 4 L.Ed. 2d 1409 (1960).

We think the district court properly relied upon this court's decision in Independent Petroleum Workers of America v. American Oil Co., 324 F. 2d 903 (7th Cir. 1963), aff'd, 379 U.S. 130, 85 S.Ct. 271, 13 L.Ed. 2d 333 (1964), in deciding in favor of Shell. There are some differences, of course, in the facts. But fundamentally the question decided there, and here, is that where arbitration is limited in the bargaining agreement to questions involving the application and interpretation of the agreement, and the agreement does not limit the freedom of the employer to contract out work, a court should not compel arbitration. This court there considered the Supreme Court cases (the "Steelworkers Trilogy") relied upon here and found that those cases did not change the principle "that compulsory arbitration cannot be properly awarded absent a contract between the parties agreeing thereto." 324 F. 2d at 906. The court there considered as having "some significance" the bargaining history between the parties, which showed the Union's lack of success in gaining an agreement prohibiting or limiting the company's right to contract out work, and the silence of the contract on the point. The history before us is stronger for Shell because of the final letter written by Shell. The district court could have found, with support in the evidence, that it was accepted by the Union's failure to reject it orally or in writing. There was testimony that union spokesman Harrelson said of the letter that it "is the best we can get, we'd better take it." Harrelson was not called to rebut this testimony.

The letter bound Shell only to give consideration when contracting out the "turn-around" and construction work to the hiring of plaintiff's boilermaker members with seniority. It renders inapplicable the rule from United Steelworkers of America v. Warrior & Gulf Nav. Co., 363

U.S. 574, 585, 80 S.Ct. 1347, 1354, 4 L.Ed. 2d 1409 (1960), that where there is no clause expressly excluding contracting out, or "most forceful evidence of a purpose to exclude," the arbitrator, and not the court, should interpret the agreement to determine whether the parties intended the claimed grievance to be arbitrable.[3]

We conclude that the district court correctly decided the contracting out issue.

But this conclusion does not remove the question of discrimination under Article 23 of the agreement from the scope of the arbitration provision. Article 23, entitled "Coercion, Intimidation and Discrimination," provides: "There shall be no coercion, intimidation or discrimination practiced by the Employer or Unions against any employee because of membership or non-membership in any Union." The tacit acceptance of the company's final statement upon the contracting out issue does not preclude the Union from asserting a grievance with respect to a claimed violation of Article 23 in the exercise of the "freedom" reserved by the company in its final statement.

This part of the grievance states that the company "has discriminated against the men in the Boiler-Makers group in assignment of this [maintenance and repair] work." The Complaint for Injunction filed by the Union alleged the filing of a grievance alleging, among others, a violation of Article 23 in that the company "has discriminated against the men in the Boilermakers group in assignment of this work," and that the defendant has refused to submit the grievance to arbitration in accordance with the provisions of Article 18. The prayer of the complaint sought submission of the "unresolved grievances to arbitration."

The district court made no finding on or reference to this demand for arbitration on the issue of discrimination in violation of Article 23, at the trial or after alternative motions for new trial or amendment of findings and judgment called the omission to the court's attention.

Since Article 23 is part of the bargaining agreement, and its violation is alleged in the grievance, this is within the scope of Article 18, *i.e.,* arbitration for "controversies arising out of the application or interpretation" of the agreement.

It is not for this court to decide on the facts developed at trial that the Union cannot prevail in arbitration of this part of the grievance. Thus whether the Union claim is a "sham," in fact frivolous or moot, as Shell contends, is for the arbitrator. Neither was the Union required to present proof in the district court to show that its arbitrable grievance had merit. United Steelworkers of America v. American Mfg. Co., 363 U.S. 564, 568, 80 S.Ct. 1343, 4 L.Ed. 2d 1403 (1960). That question also is for the arbitrator. The agreement shows on its face that the claim is covered by the contract and is a matter of "application or interpretation" of the agreement as a matter of law. The court erred in not ruling on this part of the grievance and not ordering that it be submitted to arbitration in accordance with Article 18 of the agreement.[4] The question whether Shell maintained control of the hiring and firing of Nooter's boilermaker-employees is embraced in the discrimination issue.

We hold that the district court erroneously declined to decide the question whether the claimed grievance in Shell's alleged discrimination in contracting out the work is arbitrable under Articles 23 and 18 of the agreement, that as a matter of law that claim is arbitrable, and that dismissal of this part of the Union's complaint was reversible error.

For the reasons given, the judgment of dismissal is affirmed so far as it concerns the issue of Shell's right to contract out work. As to the discrimination issue we reverse and remand for entry of judgment for plaintiff-Union granting the relief as prayed.

KNOCH, C. J. (dissenting). It seems to me inconsistent to sustain the District Court's decision on the issue of arbitration of Shell's right to contract out work and then to destroy the effect of that decision by holding that Shell must nevertheless arbitrate that part of the stated grievance which accuses Shell of discrimination against some employees on account of their union membership by contracting out work to a firm which hires other members of the same union.

I would affirm the decision of the District Court in toto.

In Boeing Co. v. United Autoworkers and UAW Local 1069, (E.D. Pa. 1964) 231 F. Supp.

---

3. See generally Smith & Jones. *The Supreme Court and Labor Dispute Arbitration: The Emerging Federal Law,* 63 MICH. L. REV. 751 (1965).

4. The Union also argues that the district court's finding of fact "9" is clearly erroneous in stating that "the *plaintiff* informed the *defendant* that contracting of maintenance and construction work was not a proper subject for arbitration under Article 18 . . ." (Emphasis added.) The record is devoid of evidence to support that finding, which is contrary to the Union's consistent position. Both parties agree that there was an inadvertent mistake, and that the italicized words should be interchanged, *i.e.,* "the defendant informed the plaintiff . . ."

930, the company sought a declaratory judgment that it was not obligated to arbitrate a dispute over the elimination of company distribution of turkeys to employees at Christmastime. The practice, begun in 1954, was eliminated by the company in 1963. The union, which became the collective-bargaining agent, contended that the practice was a form of remuneration and, although not specified in the collective agreement, had been bargained over and was considered to be part of the agreement. The arbitration provision of the agreement provided for arbitration only of a grievance "involving the interpretation or application of this agreement which has been processed through Step 4 of the grievance procedure" and said that "the jurisdiction of the arbitrator shall be limited to a determination of the facts and the interpretation and application of the specific provisions of this agreement at issue"; the provision contained the conventional language that he cannot add to, subtract from, amend, or modify its provisions. *Held*: No contract provision dealt with Christmas turkeys; because the arbitration provision was limited to "interpretation and application of specific provisions" the dispute was not arbitrable. Also rejected was the union contention that arbitrability was a question for the arbitrator. Summary judgment, on the court's own motion, entered for plaintiff company. Affirmed, *per curiam*, 349 F. 2d 412 (3d Cir. 1965).

COMMUNICATIONS WORKERS v. NEW YORK TELEPHONE CO.
327 F. 2d 94 (2d Cir. 1964)

[The district court had denied the union's motion to compel arbitration.]

Before MEDINA, WATERMAN and MARSHALL, CIRCUIT JUDGES.

WATERMAN, C. J. The dispute sought to be arbitrated involves the proper criteria to be used by defendant company in deciding which employees to promote. It is the union's position that all promotions, whether temporary or permanent, must be based on seniority if all other relevant qualities of employee candidates are substantially equal. The company disagrees, maintaining that the parties' collective bargaining agreement requires that consideration of the seniority of employees is applicable to permanent promotions only, and, though requested by the union to do so, refused to arbitrate the dispute.

Resolution of the differences between petitioner and the company depends upon the proper con-

struction of two sections of the parties' collective bargaining agreement.

The section of the contract which provoked the disagreement over the proper method of handling promotions is Section 9.08 of Article 9, which states:

> 9.08. In selecting employees for promotion to occupational classifications within the bargaining unit, seniority shall govern if other necessary qualifications are substantially equal. In no event shall any grievance or dispute arising out of this Section 9.08 be subject to the arbitration provisions of this Agreement.

The bargaining agreement's basic arbitration provision, which the plaintiff union maintains requires arbitration of the dispute, is Section 12.01 of Article 12. That section provides as follows:

> 12.01. Either the Union or the Company may arbitrate a grievance regarding the true intent and meaning of a provision of this Agreement, or a grievance involving a claim referable to arbitration as provided in Articles 7, 8, 10 and 15, provided in all cases that the grievance has been processed in accordance with the provisions of Article 11 and has not been adjusted, and that written notice of intention to arbitrate is given to the other party within thirty (30) calendar days after the review in Step 4 of Article 11 has been completed. It is understood that the right to require arbitration does not extend to any matters other than those expressly set forth in this Article.

Parties to a labor agreement containing an arbitration clause may, of course, exclude certain types of disputes from arbitration. But an exclusionary clause, to be effective, must be clear and unambiguous.

It is difficult to imagine a clearer or more direct exclusionary clause than the one in Section 9.08 above set forth. It expressly provides that "in no event" shall "*any* grievance or dispute" arising out of the section be subject to the contract's arbitration provisions. (Emphasis supplied.) We believe these words convey a clear and unambiguous directive that no Section 9.08 disputes of any kind are arbitrable.

The union, nevertheless, seeks to saddle the exclusionary clause of Section 9.08 with ambiguity, by arguing that it only definitely forecloses review by an arbitrator of the company's estimate of the comparative abilities of employees eligible for promotion. According to the union, the clause does not clearly prohibit arbitral inquiry into the true meaning of the terms used in the section. Thus, the union's argument amounts to pointing out two types of disputes which might arise under Section 9.08, and then contending that the section's exclusionary clause clearly covers but one of them.

One obvious difficulty with this argument is that Section 9.08 states that arbitration proceedings shall not be invoked with regard to *"any grievance or dispute"* arising under the section. (Emphasis supplied.) But there is another reason, relating to the only way in which the contract's arbitration clause could cover Section 9.08 disputes absent an exclusionary clause, for rejecting the argument. Section 12.01, above quoted, the basic arbitration provision, is so drawn as to compel arbitration in two categories of cases: (1) those involving claims referable to arbitration as provided in Articles 7, 8, 10 and 15 of the contract; and (2) those involving disputes as to the true intent and meaning of any provision in the contract.

For the exclusionary clause of Section 9.08 to have any meaning at all, it must be regarded as referring to that part of Section 12.01 which, except for that clause, would extend to disputes under Section 9.08. Since Section 9.08 is in Article 9 (and not Article 7, 8, 10 or 15), the only way disputes under it could be arbitrable would be through application of Section 12.01's "true intent and meaning" clause. Therefore, the exclusionary clause of Section 9.08, unless we hold it to be devoid of any meaning whatever, must be viewed as referring to and foreclosing disputes as to the meaning of the terms used in that section. And as this is precisely the sort of dispute the union argues is not covered by Section 9.08's exclusionary clause we find no merit in its argument.

We are not unmindful of the "federal policy of promoting industrial peace and stability, especially with reference to arbitration procedures set up in collective bargaining agreements." Livingston v. John Wiley & Sons, Inc., *supra*, 313 F. 2d at 56. The advantages of arbitration are obvious and compelling indeed, and absent a legitimate contractual restriction prohibiting it, the most desirable method of resolving this dispute would no doubt be through its submission to arbitration. But, if the strong presumption in favor of arbitrability established in the *Steelworkers* cases is not to be made irrebuttable, we cannot close our eyes to the plain meaning of the words used in this contract. The union also argues that if the company is not compelled to arbitrate this grievance it will be able to exercise almost unlimited discretion over the operation of matters arising under an entire section of the agreement. This argument does not impress. We cannot bring ourselves to accept this invitation to ignore the plain meaning of the Section 9.08 exclusionary clause, and to find ambiguity where none exists, by indulging ourselves in speculation as to what types of disputes

a union might be likely to require an employer to settle by arbitration. The union concedes it intended to give the company unlimited discretion with respect to certain facets of Section 9.08's operation. If, at the bargaining table, the union's true intent was to reserve a different sort of Section 9.08 question for an arbitrator, it should not have consented to the incorporation into that section of an exclusionary clause so broad and sweeping.

Affirmed.

MEDINA, C. J. (dissenting). I dissent. For centuries philosophers and others have been puzzled and sometimes even amused at the proclivities of lawyers and judges to weave a web of confusion around some perfectly simple proposition, and in the process come out with a result that defies common sense. This case is a perfect illustration.

The collective bargaining agreement contains a clause providing that in selecting employees for "promotion" seniority shall govern; and there is to be no arbitration of grievances or disputes arising out of this particular clause. Along comes the employer who says "promotion" means only "permanent promotion." Had it been to the economic advantage of the employer to do so, I suppose it could have taken the directly contrary position, to the effect that "promotion" means only "temporary promotion."

As the employees have no other way of procuring a decision by a court on the point, the dispute is processed as a grievance and the Union comes into a federal court asking for arbitration.

It is hornbook law that it is the function of the court in these arbitration cases first to construe the meaning of the agreement. All we have to do, and what in my judgment we should do, is to say that, as as we construe the contract, "promotion" means "promotion," and that includes a "temporary promotion" as well as a "permanent promotion." Thus there is nothing to arbitrate and it turns out that the Union was right from the beginning.

DESERT COCA COLA BOTTLING CO. v. LOCAL 14, GENERAL SALES DRIVERS (IBT)
335 F. 2d 198 (9th Cir. 1964)

Before BARNES, CIRCUIT JUDGE, MADDEN, JUDGE OF THE COURT OF CLAIMS, and BROWNING, CIRCUIT JUDGE.

BARNES, C. J.

[Employers moved to compel arbitration of a union claim for overtime payments to driver-salesmen for hours worked in excess of forty hours in a week. The district court denied the motion. The arbitration clause of the collective agreement provided in part:]

> (d) The decision of the arbitrator or a majority of said Board of Arbitration, upon any issue concerning the terms of this Agreement shall be final, binding and conclusive upon all parties concerned.
>
> (e) Pending such decision, there shall be no cessation or stoppage of work because of such controversy, dispute or disagreement.
>
> (f) Any expense jointly incurred, as a result of arbitration, shall be borne one-half by the Employer and one-half by the Union.
>
> It is understood that the above shall not apply in any way concerning wages.

The foregoing would seem, down to the last sentence, to be a conventional, broad and inclusive arbitration provision. Paragraph (d) would quite clearly make the instant dispute arbitrable, unless the last sentence of the entire arbitration provision quoted above is applicable to the current dispute and removes it from the generality of paragraph (d). What we have said indicates our view that that last sentence, "It is understood that the above shall not apply in any way concerning wages," is of crucial importance to the determination of whether the parties had agreed to arbitrate disputes of the type of the current dispute.

Where shall one look for evidence as to whether or not the parties intended to so agree? If the language of the entire arbitration provision, including the last sentence, were perfectly clear and could bear only one meaning, we would look no further, and adopt that plain meaning. But it is a common experience to find that language which, read in isolation, seems to have only one possible meaning was, in its context in a larger writing and in the circumstances in which it was written, intended to mean something quite different.

In the instant case the union points to the last sentence of the arbitration provision and says that it plainly removes from arbitration the dispute as to whether driver-salesmen should receive overtime pay, since the dispute is a dispute "concerning wages."

The employers urge that a court must approach the question which is before us with a strong presumption that when a labor agreement contains an arbitration provision, that provision is intended to have the most inclusive coverage that its language, interpreted in the light of all circumstances relevant to its meaning, will bear.

The district court broadly interpreted the word "wages" as commensurate with "compensation," quoting 92 C.J.S. p. 1035. But the word "wages" can also be given a narrower definition, commensurate only with "wage scale." Although hours, overtime, and vacations all can affect one's income for tax purposes, the word "wages" in the contract might well only have been intended to mean the general wage scale. Here the arbitration clause, paragraph (d), was broad, and the exclusion clause, on its face, uncertain, if not vague. Can we say the issue here presented clearly "concerns wages" any more than the total number of hours to be worked each day or week "concerns wages," and would hence be beyond arbitration?

By the contract, time and a half is payable after eight hours work in one day or after forty hours work in one week. Suppose the employer claimed those hours worked after Sunday midnight should apply on the next week's total hours, rather than those of the preceding week. If the former, the second week might well go into overtime, and the first not. Or the opposite might be true. Or neither week might get into overtime by an allocation of such hours of employment to one week or another. If the employee disputed the week to which such hours could be credited, the resolution of such differences might well result in a different total compensation for the two-week period. To the extent it changes the total compensation, it "concerns" compensation, yet the amount of wages paid per hour—the general wage scale—is not involved.

In other words, can a dispute affect compensation without affecting wages? We think it can fairly and honestly be thought that it can. We cannot hold that the term is "clear and unambiguous," or say "with positive assurance that the arbitration clause is not susceptible of an interpretation that covers the asserted dispute."

MADDEN, J. (dissenting). The court is right, of course, in concluding that it is obliged, under the binding precedents, to lean strongly in the direction of arbitration. But I think the court has leaned farther than the Supreme Court's impulsion *a tergo* requires it to do. I think the union, when it insisted upon the addition to the conventional language of the contract of the sentence: "It is understood that the above shall not apply *in any way* concerning wages," (the italics are mine), meant that, so far as the wages which an employee should draw at the end of the week, such a question should be determined on a strictly legalistic basis, and not in the discretionary or mediatory fashion in which an arbitrator is free to act. The words "in any way" concerning wages ought to be pointed enough to include a dispute as to whether an employee's pay envelope should, or should not, include some dollars for the overtime which he worked. If the question were whether one, under the contract, is entitled to straight time or to time and a half for overtime, that would, the court indicates, be a "wages" question, since it relates to the "general wage scale." The instant question whether he gets nothing, or something, for overtime work seems to me to relate to the wage scale.

The District Court took the view which I take on the arbitrability question. It decided that it had jurisdiction to decide the dispute on the merits of the overtime pay question, and it decided that question. That action, if this court had allowed it to stand, would have wound up a lengthy and costly litigation. I think there should be a considerable tendency, in an appellate court, to lean in the direction of sustaining such a beneficent result, rather than requiring the parties to thresh again the same old straw before another type of moderator.

Strauss v. Silvercup Bakers, Inc., 353 F. 2d 555 (2d Cir. 1965) also involved an employer's motion to compel arbitration denied by the district court. The company planned to switch from a six-day to a five-day-a-week basis for deliveries; the change would have eliminated fifty-five jobs. The union objected, contending that the contract prohibited such a change without its agreement and it would not agree. The arbitration provision applied to "all disputes which may arise between the parties." Article 24 declared the union's and company's recognition of the problems of competition and the possibilities of changes "in delivery, merchandising and compensation methods." As to them, the employer was to meet and negotiate with the union. "In the event the parties are unable to agree, the dispute shall not be subject to ... Arbitration." The company and union differed as to the kind of changes in delivery covered by Article 24, and the court of appeals noted that neither interpretation was "patently impossible or unreasonable"; nor was the exclusionary provision as unambiguously applicable as the clause it found to be so in *New York Telephone.* The opinion (by Judge Moore for a panel in-

cluding Judge Waterman and Friendly) went on:

> But the mere fact that neither of two proffered interpretations of an exclusionary clause, one of which would permit arbitration, the other of which would prevent it, is frivolous or unreasonable on its face, does not mean, as the trial court apparently believed, that the court must order the parties to proceed to arbitration. We believe that the trial court should have accepted proffered proof relevant to the intentions of the parties at the time they drafted their agreement. The duty to arbitrate being contractual in origin, the court must make an effort to construe the extent of that contractual duty, rather than force arbitration even of arbitrability upon parties who did not bind themselves to such a submission. Further inquiry may well enable the trial court to say with "positive assurance" that the exclusionary clause covers this dispute, so that the request for an order compelling arbitration should be denied. On the other hand, further inquiry may also indicate that the trial court cannot positively declare that the parties intended to exclude the dispute from arbitration—in which case, the trial court must issue an order directing the parties to proceed to arbitration.
>
> We are aware of the danger that courts will become "entangled in the construction of the substantive provisions of a labor agreement ... through the back door of interpreting the arbitration clause" (citing *Warrior & Gulf*).
>
> We have accordingly refused to permit inquiries into bargaining history that would draw us into the merits of a labor dispute without shedding much light on the extent of the duty to arbitrate. In Local 12298, Dist. 50, UMW v. Bridgeport Gas Co., 328 F. 2d 381 (2d Cir. 1964), we did not allow an employer resisting arbitration to show that the union had failed in an attempt to cover the subject matter of the dispute in the collective bargaining agreement. But the inquiry here is directly connected with the extent of the duty to arbitrate, and does not touch upon the merits of the dispute. The ultimate issue is whether the court can say with positive assurance that the exclusionary clause applies to the dispute sought to be arbitrated. We reverse and remand for an inquiry into the intention of the parties as to the scope of the exclusionary clause.

Reversed and remanded.

In *Bridgeport Gas* (mentioned in the preceding opinion) the employer had not posted a job vacancy, which the union claimed violated two provisions requiring posting and governing the method of filling such a vacancy. The company claimed the unreviewable right to blank the job when it determined the position surplus to its needs under a management-rights provision giving it exclusive authority "to relieve employees from duty because of lack of work" and "to discharge for proper cause." Judges Smith and Waterman reversed the trial court's summary judgment for the company. Judge Moore dissented, expressing the view that the parties should have been permitted to present testimony on the issue of practice and bargaining history to enable the court to decide as a matter of law whether the subject was one they had agreed to arbitrate.

A collective agreement negotiated after a strike specifically excluded from arbitration all grievances predating the agreement whether or not an employee had been permanently replaced. The grievance at issue here was filed on behalf of thirty-eight former employees whose names had appeared on a pre-agreement company list of those it had replaced permanently; the company allegedly had violated their seniority rights. None had worked since the strike. The district court denied the union's motion to compel arbitration. The union asserted that some company action had occurred since the agreement's execution that affected their status. Evidence that such a claim existed consisted of an IBM print-out of employees for whom the company had checked off union dues.

> Assuming that this piece of evidence was admissible over the objection of the Employer, it does not carry the day for the Union. Since the Union in seeking court enforcement of arbitration had to show that there was a controversy "on the face" of the asserted grievance, it necessarily opened up the evidence as it bore on that restricted, limited phase. While the Court is not permitted to weigh conflicting evidence, it had a right and duty to determine whether there was *any* evidence showing a grievance which the parties had agreed to arbitrate. From that standpoint the evidence was simply uncontradicted. The evidence from the Employer, the Union witnesses, and the stipulations of its own counsel, showed without a doubt that not a single one of these 38 men either had done a single minute's work between July 1 and the date of the grievance, or that they had been called back by the Employer to do so. None had any moral, legal or equitable claim for any compensation whatever.
>
> The exclusionary terms used in the contract were emphatic. Under no circumstances was the status of persons displaced prior to the execution of the contract to be the subject of the grievance machinery and arbitration. This was stated in dual terms. One excluded the question of status as "permanently replaced or not." The second, even more broadly, excluded any grievance "the basis for which occurred prior to the date of the signing of this agreement." While the Union had contrived a beguiling theory to make this appear to be something other than

what it really is, the effect is to allow arbitration of a dispute categorically excluded. Since in point of positive fact none has been an employee subsequent to the signing of the contract, never performed a single day's work or received, or was entitled to receive, a single cent as wages for services performed subsequent to July 1, the only basis for an arbiter's award would be one occurring prior to July 1. The parties by the plainest of language excluded this controversy and all of those growing out of it from the grievance machinery.

The district court's ruling was affirmed. Local 787, Int'l Union of Electrical Workers v. Collins Radio Co., 317 F. 2d 214 (5th Cir. 1963).

Was this grievance patently excluded or was it unmeritorious?

As the court pointed out, there would be considerable doubt that the IBM print-out constituted an admission. Yet, as those familiar with cases of this sort can attest, employees and union officials frequently regard any fragment of action or language inconsistent with the employer's asserted position as if it *were* an admission. The court in discussing the dubious nature of the occurrence as an admission observed that the law of agency would apply. Conceivably an arbitrator could explain the nonprobative character of the occurrence in terms more comprehensible. Obviously the employer (as advised by counsel) did not desire the advantages of such an explanation. Should they be "conferred upon him" nonetheless?

On occasion "discharge for cause" grievances, clearly arbitrable, collide with involuntary retirements under pension plans, which often are expressly made not subject to arbitration. In at least one such case the court ordered arbitration. Local 1011, Int'l B'hd of Electrical Workers v. Bell Telephone of Nevada 254 F. Supp. 462 (Nev. 1966). Company evidence of practice consistent with its interpretation of the retirement provision was held not "the most forceful evidence of a purpose to exclude" the claim from arbitration; the issue was for the arbitrator.

In Socony Vacuum Tanker Men's Association v. Socony Mobil Oil Co., Inc., (2d Cir. 1966) 369 F. 2d 480, the arbitration clause provided that: "The statement of the question to be arbitrated shall be mutually agreed upon." But the parties could not agree. The court of appeals, in affirming the district court order, declared that the provision requires "the parties to make a reasonable effort to agree on the statement of the issue to be submitted. As reasonable efforts were made and were unsuccessful, the court may state the question to be arbitrated." And it did.

What if the party resisting arbitration had been unreasonable? Would that forestall arbitration?

In most cases the grieving party controls formulation of the issue. Here an attempt was made to confine that initiative. As a matter of logic it would seem to give the complained-against party a veto, which this court refused to honor. Is such a provision meaningless and useless? Perhaps it does enable the resisting party to exercise some influence over the grieving party.

Should the court have defined the issue, or is the arbitrator, presumably more competent to decide the issue once formulated, better equipped by background—and by the benefit of a full hearing—to define the issue?

C.

The Award as *Res Judicata:* Effect upon a Related Grievance

TODD SHIPYARDS CORP. v. LOCAL 15, MARINE AND SHIPBUILDING WORKERS (D.N.J. 1965) 242 F. Supp. 606

SHAW, D. J. This is an action by plaintiff as employer against defendant union for declaratory judgment pursuant to 28 U.S.C. § 2201. Defendant, acting as the collective bargaining agent of employees of plaintiff, demanded arbitration of an alleged grievance. Plaintiff contends that the grievance asserted "presents no issue properly arbitrable" because the subject matter thereof had previously been determined by arbitration. Defendant denies that the Court has jurisdiction to determine the issue of arbitrability alleging that the grievance in question is not the same as the one previously presented for arbitration and it seeks by way of counterclaim: (1) an order compelling plaintiff to arbitrate the grievance in question, and (2) to vacate and set aside the prior award in arbitration in so far as it purports to dispose of the grievance now in question.

The matter has been submitted to the Court for disposition upon the pleadings and stipulated facts. The precise question presented is whether a previous arbitration award precludes arbitration of the grievance now asserted. Jurisdiction exists by virtue of Section 301 of the Labor Management Relations Act, 29 U.S.C. § 185.

The pertinent facts may be briefly summarized as follows:

Plaintiff is a New York corporation which operates ship repair yards in Brooklyn, New York and Hoboken, New Jersey. Defendant is a labor organization having its principal office at 1312 Washington Street, Hoboken, New Jersey. It has been the bargaining agent for employees of plaintiff at the Hoboken yard since August 18, 1942, the first collective bargaining agreement having been made between defendant and Todd Hoboken Drydock, Inc., the predecessor corporation of the present plaintiff. The particular collective bargaining agreement, provisions of which are applicable to the pending litigation, was made on July 29, 1960. It was a joint labor agreement with plaintiff to which defendant and an affiliate union, Local 39, were parties. Members of defendant union were employed at the Hoboken yard of plaintiff. Members of the affiliate union, Local 39, were employed at the Brooklyn yard. For purposes of grievance and arbitration procedure, employees of plaintiff in the Hoboken yard are represented by defendant. Employees at the Brooklyn yard are represented by the affiliate union, Local 39.

Robert Bateman, an employee of plaintiff and a member of the defendant union, had been employed for many years by plaintiff at its Hoboken yard and had attained a seniority status as defined by the labor agreement. On April 18, 1961, his employment at the Hoboken yard was terminated by plaintiff on the ground of alleged disability due to loss of hearing.

As a consequence of the termination of the employment of Robert Bateman, defendant submitted a grievance on April 25, 1961. The labor agreement provided for a grievance procedure and for arbitration if the grievance was not satisfactorily adjusted and could not be settled between plaintiff and defendant. It also contained provision barring strikes or lockouts.

The grievance submitted on behalf of Robert Bateman on April 25, 1961 designated as 32–1961 read as follows:

> On Tuesday, April 18, 1961, R. Bateman badge 88006, department 24, night shift, employed since March 1943, was laid off.
>
> The Union demands that R. Bateman be returned to work and be paid for all time lost.

Plaintiff denied the grievance by letter dated May 1, 1961 wherein it stated:

> As we advised the Union representatives verbally on April 18, 1961, Mr. Bateman was being laid-off effective that date because of his physical deficiency in hearing (25 per cent binaural loss of hearing), which makes it unsafe for both himself and his fellow employees to continue working in his occupation in our shipyard.
>
> The action taken was proper in our opinion and the Union's claim is therefore denied.
>
> It will be recalled that it was agreed that Steps II and III of the grievance procedure would be waived and that we would proceed to a prompt arbitration on the matter.

The parties then designated Richard T. Davis, Esq. as sole arbitrator to hear and decide the grievance. He conducted a hearing on June 22, 1961 and made an award in favor of plaintiff on August 11, 1961. He found that plaintiff had a right to rely on the opinion of its physician that "Mr. Bateman's *discharge* was medically indicated." (Emphasis supplied.)

Bateman applied for further employment with plaintiff at its Hoboken yard on August 18, 1961 and his application was denied by plaintiff. The union responded by filing a second grievance designated as 55–1961 which read as follows:

> On August 18, 1961 this man applied to the Todd Shipyards Corporation of Hoboken, N.J., for employment, doing any kind of work which he was capable of performing.
>
> He was flatly refused and was told he could never be employed by the Todd Corporation again.
>
> This is a violation of Article XI, Section 7, of the existing Labor Agreement.
>
> Bateman had previously been terminated by the Company because of a physical impairment resulting from his 18 years of employment at Todd.
>
> He still retains his seniority, plus the physical ability to perform many and various types of jobs in the ship repair yard.
>
> The Union demands that Bateman be assigned employment immediately to work which is "within his capacity to perform." Article XI, Section 7.
>
> The Union also seeks payment to Bateman for all time lost by him, from the date this grievance is presented until he is assigned to work "within his capacity to perform."

Article XI, Section 7 of the labor agreement referred to in the grievance provides:

> Where an employee has been injured while employed on Company work and remains subject to partial disability or limitation, the Company, in so far as its operations permit, will endeavor to transfer such employee to some work which is within his then capacity to perform.

Plaintiff rejected the second grievance and defendant, after processing the same through the grievance procedure, requested arbitration and designated its member to serve on a board of arbitration. Plaintiff also designated its member to serve on the board but without prejudice to any right which it might have to dispute arbitrability. This litigation followed.

Parenthetically, it might be noted that Bateman did work at Todd's Brooklyn yard on October 1, 1961 for 8 hours and he shaped up at this yard on five other occasions during October and November, 1961. Finally he was removed from the payroll there on November 27, 1961 because of his failure to shape up for twelve days as required by the labor agreement. The fact that he did work for plaintiff on October 1, 1961 for 8 hours and shaped up subsequently at the Brooklyn yard is not considered to have any particular significance in connection with the basic issue here, to wit: Whether plaintiff had the right to refuse employment at the Hoboken yard by virtue of the arbitrator's disposition of grievance 32–1961.

Bateman's application for employment at plaintiff's Brooklyn yard was made on September 25, 1961 and he was hired as a machinist rigger without having taken a complete physical examination. His application made no reference to previous employment by plaintiff at its Hoboken yard. Personnel administration at the Brooklyn yard was separate and distinct from that at the Hoboken yard until November 9, 1961, after which the Personnel Director at the Brooklyn division acted as Personnel Director at the Hoboken division. It has been stipulated that it would have been futile for Bateman to shape up for work at the Hoboken yard after the award of the arbitrator in favor of plaintiff. It should also be mentioned that Article IX of the labor agreement relating to transfers is not applicable to Bateman's case. There has been argument with respect to the terms "laid off" and "discharged" as they were used in connection with Bateman's termination as of April 18, 1961 and in the transcript of the proceedings before the arbitrator and reference thereto in his written opinion. Ordinarily the term "laid off" indicates a temporary cessation of employment and the terms "discharged" or "dismissed" indicate a complete and final termination. Plaintiff argues that Bateman's employment was completely and finally terminated on April 18, 1961 and that this termination was upheld by the arbitrator. Defendant contends that Bateman was merely laid off on April 18, 1961 and that, therefore, his rights under the labor agreement to have a further grievance processed continued. Whether the term "laid off" or the term "discharged" was used in describing the action that plaintiff took on April 18, 1961 is not of controlling significance.

Inquiry must be directed to the substance of the action as understood by the parties rather than to the choice of literal terms describing it. Hence, the Court must look to the intent of defendant in framing the issue for arbitration as made known to plaintiff by the language defendant chose to employ. In conjunction with this, the Court must also examine the record of the arbitration proceedings to determine if the evidence adduced by each of the parties reflects common accord and understanding of the particularly defined grievance which the arbitrator deemed in his opinion to be the matter in issue. Disappointment with the result plus afterthought of a more narrow grievance that could have been presented is of no consequence. Defendant, in framing the issue of grievance and at the hearing thereon, could have limited it to the narrow question it now urges if it had desired to do so.

Defendant was aware of the fact that Bateman's employment was terminated because of his impairment of hearing "which makes it unsafe for both himself and his fellow employees to continue working in his occupation in our ship yard." The overall tenor of the evidence adduced at hearing related to a discharge because of the environmental element of noise prevalent in ship yard operations. It was developed at that hearing that Bateman had done practically every type of job in a ship yard so that his occupation was more in the nature of a ship yard worker than that of an employee particularly assigned to one specified class of work. The arbitrator in his opinion refers to the issue developed at hearing as one of whether the company had good and substantial cause to *discharge* Mr. Bateman. He concludes, "The fact that Mr. Bateman's discharge was in accord with Dr. Pflug's opinion was confirmed at the hearing when Dr. Pflug took the stand to give the opinion that Mr. Bateman's discharge was medically indicated." Dr. Pflug was the plaintiff's physician and he fixed a range of up to 18 per cent binaural loss of hearing as non-hazardous. The employment of those having binaural loss of hearing in excess of 18 per cent was not recommended. Bateman's impairment of hearing was in excess of 18 per cent.

Article XI, Section 1[1] of the labor agreement imposes upon plaintiff the obligation to maintain safe and healthful working conditions. Article XI, Section 7 of the agreement provides for transfers of employees suffering from disability only "in so far as ... operations permit." The arbitration clause[2] conferring decisional authority on the arbitrator is broad in scope and it cannot be said here that the result reached constituted an abuse of the discretion entrusted to him by the parties.

As indicated, defendant contends that the instant grievance is a new and different grievance than the one previously submitted to arbitration. This Court cannot agree. The substance of the first grievance involved the right of Bateman to be employed at the Hoboken yard of plaintiff. This encompassed a right to be continued on the payroll regardless of the particular work to which he might be assigned. The arbitrator, construing the application of the pertinent portions of the labor agreement, concluded that plaintiff had a right to terminate Bateman's employment when the action taken was in accordance with the standard of health and safety fixed by plaintiff's physician.

Ordinarily, where there is a broad arbitration clause as here, a grievance which arguably comes within the clause should be submitted to arbitration. United Steelworkers of America v. Warrior & Gulf Navigation Company, 363 U.S. 574, 80 S.Ct. 1347, 4 L.Ed. 2d 1409 (1960). There is no dispute that, absent the first award, arbitration would clearly be required. Instead, the Court is faced with the problem of determining the effect of a previous award on the arbitrability of a subsequent grievance. Counterbalancing the liberal policy favoring arbitration is the policy favoring finality of arbitration awards. The harmony sought by arbitration as a substitute for work stoppage and elimination of industrial strife between labor and management could be jeopardized if repetitive submission to arbitration of the same grievance was permitted. Unless there is finality to an arbitration award as contemplated by the parties, there would be no inducement to accept a provision for arbitration in the labor agreement.

---

1. "The Company will continue to exert every effort to provide and maintain safe and healthy working conditions and the Union will cooperate to that end and will encourage its members to work in a safe manner."

2. Article XXIII, Arbitration: In the event of any dispute or difference of opinion between the parties hereto as to any matter or thing arising out of, or relating to, this Agreement or any provision hereof, or the construction or application hereof, including a grievance of any employee not satisfactorily adjusted according to the procedure prescribed by Article XXII of this Agreement, which cannot be settled between the parties themselves, either party may require the matter in dispute to be submitted to arbitration by three arbitrators to be designated as provided in this Article. . . .

The decision of any two of the three arbitrators thus chosen or appointed, when reduced to writing and signed by them, shall be final, conclusive and binding upon both parties hereto.

It is suggested by defendant that it is not within the jurisdiction of this Court to determine that the previous award in arbitration is *res adjudicata*. Defendant argues that *res adjudicata* is a defense on the merits and one for an arbitrator to determine on hearing of the instant grievance. In conjunction with this, it was also suggested that instead of construing the effect of the arbitration award by Davis, the Court remand to him to "rewrite it within limits to be indicated by the *Court's judgment*." (Emphasis supplied.) Further, it should be noted that defendant seeks to invoke arbitration of its instant grievance by a three-member arbitration board.

The contention that *res adjudicata* is a defense on the merits would be persuasive in a situation where in the application of the doctrine it is necessary to resolve a genuine issue of material fact. Such is not the case here. The opinion of Arbitrator Davis is clear and unambiguous, precisely covering the subject matter of the grievance presented by defendant, *i.e.*, Bateman's discharge from employment with plaintiff at its Hoboken yard. An award of an arbitrator acting within the scope of his authority has the effect of a judgment and is conclusive as to all matters submitted for decision at the instance of the parties. Panza v. Armco Steel Corp., 316 F. 2d 69 (3rd Cir. 1963) ; See 5 AM. JUR. 2d, Arbitration and Award, § 147. Moreover, finality of disposition of a grievance by arbitration is what the parties here contemplated by express provision in the labor agreement.

Summarized, defendant urges on the one hand by way of relief sought that the Court adjudicate its second grievance as arbitrable and disassociate it entirely from its previous grievance. But it recognizes that the decision of the arbitrator disposing of the first grievance might very well be construed as dispositive of the second grievance. Therefore, defendant urges in the alternate that the Court modify the effect of the decision made by the arbitrator or remand to him with direction to rewrite it.

Consonant with the limitation on the power of the Court to interfere with any determination of the arbitrator reasonably reached on the merits of a grievance, remand to the arbitrator is appropriate where there is reasonable ground for disagreement as to what he actually did decide. See International Association of Machinists, etc. v. Crown Cork and Seal Co., 300 F. 2d 127 (3rd Cir. 1962) ; Transport Workers Union of Phila., Local 234 v. Philadelphia Transportation Company, 228 F. Supp. 423 (E.D. Pa. 1964). But the power to remand should not be exercised unless there is patent ambiguity in the decision of the arbitrator or the text of it is not germane to the issue presented as reflected by the record of the proceedings before him. To remand under any other circumstances would be to suggest to the arbitrator that the Court differed in opinion with the result on the merits which had been reached by the arbitrator and would constitute an intrusion upon his exclusive function to pass upon the merits of the grievance.

There is no basis upon which this Court can reasonably conclude that the decision of the arbitrator is ambiguous or that it constitutes a determination which went beyond and covered matter not encompassed within the issue of the particular grievance presented by defendant. Accordingly, the award of the arbitrator as written holding that plaintiff had a right to discharge Bateman will be enforced and the counterclaim of defendant dismissed.

An appropriate order for entry of judgment in favor of plaintiff and against defendant consistent herewith will be presented.

D.

The Issue of Contract Formation

GENESCO v. JOINT COUNCIL, UNITED SHOE WORKERS
341 F. 2d 482 (2d Cir. 1965)

Before FRIENDLY and SMITH, CIRCUIT JUDGES, and BLUMENFELD, DISTRICT JUDGE.

FRIENDLY, C. J. Genesco sought damages for a strike in breach of a no-strike clause in an alleged collective bargaining contract dated as of October 31, 1962. The union moved to dismiss on the ground that by the alleged contract "the parties agreed that any issue or dispute arising out of an alleged breach thereof shall be settled by arbitration" ; the motion stated that "the defendants specifically reserve the right, at a future time and in the appropriate forum to assert the defense that no collective bargaining agreement was in fact entered into by the defendants covering the period in question."

After hearing the motion, the judge entered an order reciting that "the existence of the col-

lective bargaining agreements presents a threshold issue which must be determined before defendant's motion ... can be decided" and directed
a hearing before him "for the sole purpose
of taking testimony with respect to the existence
of collective bargaining agreements" during the
period of the strike. We do not understand why
this was thought necessary. The court's jurisdiction was not in issue ; even if the first cause of
action were viewed alone, and apart from the
allegation of diversity, the claim of a contract
between an employer and a labor organization
gave jurisdiction under § 301 (a) of the Taft-
Hartley Act, although the plaintiff must prove the
existence of a contract to obtain relief. Since
the contract pleaded by the employer had an
arbitration clause, the union was entitled to raise
the question whether an action was not barred
by its very terms, while reserving the right to
deny the existence of the contract if the court
decided adversely, F.R.Civ.P. 8 (e).

What seems to have happened is that the judge,
perhaps recognizing that the existence of an arbitration clause would normally not warrant dismissal as contrasted with a stay, see American
Sugar Ref. Co. v. Anaconda, 138 F. 2d 765, 767
(5 Cir. 1943), aff'd, without discussion of this
point, 322 U.S. 42, 64 S.Ct. 863, 88 L.Ed. 1117
(1944) ; Swartz & Funston, Inc. v. Bricklayers
Union, 319 F. 2d 116 (3 Cir. 1963) ; Gilmour v.
Wood Lathers Union, 223 F. Supp. 236, 244
(N.D. Ill. 1963) ; but see Bonnot v. Congress of
Independent Unions, 331 F. 2d 355, 359 (8 Cir.
1964), treated the case in effect as if he had denied the motion and the union had proffered the
alternative defense that no contract existed,
which it had reserved. We should have difficulty
in approving this course if it had impaired any
substantial rights. Not only is it better to let a
party do its own pleading, but the collapsing
process may have obscured the right to a trial
by jury. Whatever the right to jury trial may be
when the existence of a contract giving rise to
substantive rights is undenied and the dispute,
arising on a request for arbitration or for a
stay, is solely over the existence of an agreement to arbitrate, it can scarcely be doubted that
Genesco was entitled to a jury trial on the existence of the contract on which all of its rights
to damages hung. However, no one made any
objection to the procedure the judge propounded,
and a full evidentiary hearing was had ; indeed,
although Genesco objects in this court to the
procedure that was followed, it still has not
complained of deprivation of jury trial. We therefore treat the case as if the union had denied
the existence of a collective bargaining agree-

ment and, in the absence of a jury demand, the
court had found in its favor.

Genesco was a member of the Shoe Manufacturers Board of Trade of New York, Inc.,
an association of employers, which for many
years had acted for its members in bargaining
with the union through a negotiating committee
on which each member was represented. On
August 29, 1962, the union addressed identical
letters to the members of the Board of Trade,
giving notice of the termination of the current
contract on October 31 and offering to meet the
members at the office of the Board to negotiate
a new one. At the same time it sent a copy of
the notice to Benjamin Seligman, attorney for
the Board of Trade, and recited its understanding that the members "will be represented by
your organization in the coming negotiations for
a collective bargaining contract."

In addition to the issues common to all the
members, Genesco had a particular problem with
the union, namely, whether manufacture of a
shoe called "Act II," by its I. Miller & Sons
Co. division, should continue at its plant on
11th St. in Long Island City or be transferred
to its plant on 23rd St.—an issue which concerned the union because of a radical decrease
of production at the 23rd St. plant where there
were many senior employees. Two union officials testified that after several unsuccessful efforts
to discuss this question with Genesco's local
plant manager, they had met at his suggestion
with Seligman, who assured them that if agreement could be reached on other matters, Genesco would not stand a strike on the place of
manufacture of Act II ; Seligman denied this,
and the judge did not resolve the conflict. Upon
the expiration of the contracts on October 31,
the union struck all members of the Board of
Trade.

A day or so later the union informed Seligman
of a settlement with another group of shoe
manufacturers. On November 5, the Board of
Trade sent the union a telegram saying that
this settlement was acceptable and "we will meet
with you to work out contract language" ; the
union was asked to have the employees back at
work on November 6.

Later on November 5 officers of the union
appeared at Seligman's law office with a number
of unsigned contracts. The form, providing for a
two-year extension of the basic agreement with
various modifications, was entitled "Memorandum of Understanding ... between   on
behalf of its members and Joint Council No.
13, USWA, AFL–CIO," and concluded with a
blank subscribed "Firm" and a line for an officer's signature, and "Joint Council 13, United

Shoe Workers of America, AFL–CIO, By
" Whatever ambiguity may have ex-
isted in the form, the practice was to have contracts executed individually by each member
firm. Seligman read the form and pronounced
it acceptable to the Board of Trade. As the
union officers began to sign the contracts, they
informed him that none would be entered into
with the two I. Miller factories unless the Act II
issue was settled as they desired. Seligman insisted that the union was already committed to
Genesco; at the same time, however, he arranged for a vice-president to come from its
Nashville headquarters for a conference in New
York the following morning. The union officers
left the signed contracts with Seligman. They
testified he promised these would not be presented to Genesco for signature; he denied this.
Although the judge made no specific finding as
to such a promise, we gather from his decision
that he found the union had made quite clear
its unwillingness to contract unless the Act II
question was settled. The conference on November 6 proved fruitless. On that day the employees
of the other Board of Trade members returned
to work, but I. Miller's did not. On November 6
also I. Miller sent a long telegram to the union,
taking the position that a contract had been
made and that the continued strike was in breach
of its no-strike clause. The next day the Board
of Trade despatched a telegram along the same
lines, and Seligman transmitted to the union
the contracts signed by the employers, including
the two with I. Miller. The union promptly returned the latter.

On November 15 Genesco notified the union
that it considered the contracts terminated by
the union's material breach and that it had been
compelled by the union's action to withdraw
from the Board of Trade. Later it filed a charge
with the National Labor Relations Board, whose
Regional Director, on Feb. 28, 1963, issued a
complaint alleging, inter alia, that the union had
refused to sign a collective bargaining contract
with Genesco to which it had agreed and by
this and other acts had violated §§ 8(b) (1) (A),
8(b) (1) (B), and 8(b) (3) of the National Labor
Relations Act. In April, the Regional Director
approved a settlement, consented to by the union
and the employer, wherein the union, disclaim-
ing any admission it had violated the Act, agreed
that it would not refuse to bargain with the
Board of Trade by striking to compel I. Miller
"to modify any collective bargaining agreements, during the effective term thereof, by requiring the transfer" of the place of manufacture of the Act II shoes, that it would not
strike, without compliance with § 8(d) of the

National Labor Relations Act, "to compel I.
Miller to modify any collective bargaining
agreements, during the effective term thereof"
by requiring such transfer, and that it would
not insist on a release from liability as a condition to entering into a collective bargaining
agreement with I. Miller.

If the issue is to be determined by applying
ordinary principles of contract law, we would
conclude that no agreement between the union
and Genesco was reached. Certainly none was
made by the despatch of the Board of Trade's
telegram on November 5, which indicated agreement in principle but proposed a meeting to
work out contract language. See Lees v. Akshun
Mfg. Co., 205 F. 2d 577, 578 (7 Cir. 1953);
Ryan v. Schott, 109 Ohio App. 317, 159 N.E. 2d
907 (1953). A closer question would be whether
contracts were made when Seligman pronounced
the language satisfactory, just before the union
officers reiterated their demand as to Act II,
since the member firms had already approved
the substance and Seligman had authority to
approve the form. Cf. NLRB v. Winchester Elec-
tronics, Inc., 295 F. 2d 288, 290–291 (2 Cir.
1961). That the parties plan later to sign an
agreement does not preclude prior formation of
the contract by signifying assent to an unsigned
paper; the issue is one of intention, Mississippi
& Dominion S.S. Co. v. Swift, 86 Me. 248, 29
A. 1063 (1894); Restatement (Second), Contracts
§ 26 (Tent. Draft No. 1, 1964), 1 CORBIN, CON-
TRACTS § 30 (1963); Llewellyn, On Our Case-Law
of Contract: Offer and Acceptance, I, 48 YALE
L. J. 1, 14 (1938). Considering the importance attached to signed contracts in the field of
collective bargaining, H. J. Heinz Co. v. NLRB,
311 U.S. 514, 523–526, 61 S.Ct. 320, 85 L.Ed.
309 (1941), and § 8(d) of the Act, 29 U.S.C.
§ 158(d), the long-standing practice here of having contracts signed by the individual employers,
the fact that the instant contracts were to be
an extension and modification of contracts so
signed, and the doubtful enforceability of a two-
year oral contract, we think no one really believed that the parties would be bound until the
contracts were fully executed and delivered. This
is so even though the employers asked that the
men return to work before these steps were
completed. Once this is decided, it is clear that
delivery to Seligman of the forms signed by the
union officers on condition that the contracts
with Genesco should not be consummated until
resolution of the Act II issue, did not permit
formation of a contract unless the condition
was met. See Dickey v. Hurd, 33 F. 2d 415,
419 (1 Cir.), cert. denied, 280 U.S. 601, 50 S.Ct.
82, 74 L.Ed. 646 (1929); Detroit Football Co. v.

Robinson, 186 F. Supp. 933 (E.D. La.), aff'd on other grounds, 283 F. 2d 657 (5 Cir. 1960) ; 1 WILLISTON, CONTRACTS § 77 (3d ed. Jaeger 1957) ; 3A CORBIN, CONTRACTS § 629A (1964 Supp.).

Genesco advances the interesting contention that ordinary contract principles are not the proper criterion in the light of Mr. Justice Douglas' statement in Textile Workers' Union v. Lincoln Mills, 353 U.S. 448, 456–457, 77 S.Ct. 912, 918, 1 L.Ed. 2d 972, 980 (1957), "that the substantive law to apply in suits under § 301(a) is federal law, which the courts must fashion from the policy of our national labor laws." It argues that when a union's refusal to sign a contract would constitute an unfair labor practice, compare Chicago Stevedoring Co., 125 N.L.R.B. 61 (1959), modified sub nom. NLRB v. Local 19, Int'l Bhd. of Longshoremen, 7 Cir., 286 F. 2d 661, cert. denied, 368 U.S. 820, 82 S.Ct. 36, 7 L.Ed. 2d 25 (1961), courts should hold that a contract exists, no matter how clearly a party has indicated it does not intend to be bound until a formal contract is signed. A court applying federal labor contract law would thus regard as done what it thinks the Labor Board would think ought to be done or, at least, what it thinks the Labor Board would order to be done. The justification for this, in addition to the authority of the Supreme Court's statement, would lie in reinforcing the principles of bargaining developed by the Board and in avoiding duplicitous judicial and administrative proceedings—the latter of which the aggrieved party could never compel and which might be impossible in some instances due to self-imposed limitations on the Board's jurisdiction, § 14(c) (1).

The argument ought not be rejected merely on a mechanical view that federal power attaches only when a contract has been made, so that the "federal law" doctrine expounded in Lincoln Mills and enforced in Local 174, Teamsters, Chauffeurs, Warehousemen & Helpers of America v. Lucas Flour Co., 369 U.S. 95, 82 S.Ct. 571, 7 L.Ed. 2d 593 (1962), can apply only to interpretation of collective bargaining contracts as contrasted with their formation. Yet the distinction has force as a point of substance, although it has none as one of federal power. Where the parties have reached an agreement embodied in a signed contract, one of the prime aims of national labor policy, it is altogether reasonable that courts or arbitrators should hold them to it even though they may have to pass on the same conduct as the NLRB might have to consider in the trial of an unfair labor practice complaint ; the doctrine of San Diego Building Trades Council v. Garmon, 359 U.S. 236, 79 S.Ct. 773, 3

L.Ed. 2d 775 (1959), has been shunted aside to that extent. See Smith v. Evening News Ass'n, 371 U.S. 195, 196–198, 83 S.Ct. 267, 9 L.Ed. 2d 246 (1962) ; Carey v. General Elec. Co., 315 F. 2d 499, 508–511 (2 Cir. 1963), cert. denied, 377 U.S. 908, 84 S.Ct. 1162, 12 L.Ed. 2d 179 (1964). Utilizing national labor policy as a new source of law to govern the formation of labor contracts raises more serious problems. The Third Circuit, sitting *in banc,* divided evenly on the issue whether national labor policy should be deemed to nullify the doctrine of Pym v. Campbell, El. & Bl., 370, 374, 119 Eng. Rep. 903, 905 (1856), that "evidence to show that there is not an agreement at all is admissible" despite the parol evidence rule. Lewis v. Mears, 297 F. 2d 101 (3 Cir.), cert. denied, 369 U.S. 873, 82 S.Ct. 1142, 8 L.Ed. 2d 276 (1962). See also Chief Judge Sobeloff's dissent in Lewis v. Lowry, 295 F. 2d 197, 201–202 (4 Cir. 1961), cert. denied. 368 U.S. 977, 82 S.Ct. 478, 7 L.Ed. 2d 438 (1962). But an affirmative holding on that issue would have a much readier application, and would entail far less danger of judicial and administrative conflict, than a general principle that a court would consider a contract to have been made whenever it believes that failure to execute the contract is an unfair labor practice. Such a principle would place the courts—state as well as federal—in the center of the very area, the definition of unfair labor practices, which Congress staked out for the Labor Board ; moreover it would mean that the courts would be forced to decree contract formation, and this with retroactive effect, in all such cases, although the Board, with the wide choice of remedies given by § 10(c) of the Act, might think a lesser sanction appropriate. Evidently, as its action in this very matter may bear witness, the Board does not always direct the execution of a contract even when it considers that a party ought to have signed ; the difference between the settlement of the unfair labor practice complaint approved in this case and an order to sign a contract as of November 5, 1962, is crucial to the very controversy at issue.

The problem bears some resemblance to the reception of principles of equity into contract law. The common law courts did not hurry to accept equity principles but allowed some time for the chancellor to work out his doctrines, so that a fair degree of certainty would exist ; and even then they left equitable remedies to the chancery. Similar restraint seems desirable in integrating principles of national labor policy into labor contract law ; courts must be careful not to go further than the agency to which Congress has given prime responsibility. It suffices for decision here that we are by no means certain that the Board would find that the union's refusal to sign the contracts with Genesco was an unfair labor practice, and still less certain that the Board would have directed it to sign them as of November 5, 1962.

The union's refusal to acknowledge itself as bound to an extension agreement with Genesco might be deemed an unfair labor practice on two scores. One would be that the place of manufacture of the Act II shoe was not an issue relating "to wages, hours, and other terms and conditions of employment" within § 8(d), on which alone the union could permissibly bargain to an impasse. Until very recently we should have thought that was rather clearly so. See NLRB v. Rapid Bindery, Inc., 293 F. 2d 170 (2 Cir. 1961) and other cases cited in Mr. Justice Stewart's concurring opinion in Fibreboard Paper Prods. Corp. v. NLRB, 85 S.Ct. 398 n. 7 (1964). But, in Mr. Justice Stewart's phrase, the majority opinion in *Fibreboard,* although not the actual decision, "radiates implications of such disturbing breadth," 85 S.Ct. at 406, that we no longer feel certain about this.

The other point, more strongly pressed by Genesco and apparently the sole subject of the General Counsel's complaint, is that the union could not lawfully withdraw from multi-employer bargaining by a last minute particularized demand on one employer. See Retail Associates, Inc., 120 N.L.R.B. 388 (1958). Compare Kasco Trucking Co., 133 N.L.R.B. 627 (1960). There surely can be no general principle that multi-employer bargaining prevents either side from bargaining about or even from insisting on a solution of a mandatory subject peculiar to a particular plant; we should suppose that any such principle would very likely result in curtailment or abandonment of a practice deemed important to industrial peace. See NLRB v. Truck Drivers Local 449, 353 U.S. 87, 77 S.Ct. 643, 1 L.Ed. 2d 676 (1957). The considerations and authorities pertinent to this issue have just been exceedingly well reviewed by Judge McGowan in Retail Clerks Union No. 1550 v. NLRB, 117 U.S. App. D.C. 336, 330 F. 2d 210, 216, cert. denied, 379 U.S. 828, 85 S.Ct. 59, 13 L.Ed. 2d 39 (1964). Dealing with an employer's insistence on separate treatment of a particular bargainable issue, he said that where the departure from uniformity "is not surreptitious, or accompanied by a refusal to bargain on an individual basis, the Board may well conclude that the accused employer has not failed to meet the standards which Congress has set for him in treating with his employees." Multi-employer bargaining does not altogether preclude demand for specialized treatment of special problems; what is required, if an employer or a union is unwilling to be bound by a general settlement, is that the particularized demand be made early, unequivocally and persistently. See NLRB v. Jeffries Banknote Co., 9 Cir., 281 F. 2d 893 (1960). If the testimony of the union officers here is credited, its conduct met that test; we are by no means certain that if the complaint had gone to hearing, the Board would not have concluded that the union had acted properly and that Genesco had lulled it into a false security that the Act II issue would be settled as it wished. And, both on this point and on the mandatorily bargainable character of the issue, we are even less confident that the Board would have found the union's conduct to be such that it would have directed signature of the contract as of a date preceding the strike, with the possibly serious financial consequences to the union flowing therefrom.

We thus do not find the radiations "from the policy of our national labor laws" giving such clear signals in this case as to justify our holding the union to be bound by a contract which it would not be considered to have made on ordinary principles of contract law.

Affirmed.

Note, *Section 301 (a) and The Federal Common Law of Labor Agreements,* 75 YALE L. J. 877 (1966) concludes that "had *Genesco* been decided by considering the dictates of national labor policy, a different result would have been reached." Judge Friendly's "first mistake," says the Note, was improper deference to the NLRB on the question of whether a contract had been formed. Under the company's proffered theory it would have been necessary to decide whether the union's refusal to conclude a collective agreement with one member of the association constituted a refusal to bargain within Section 8(b) (3) of the National Labor Relations Act. Courts should and do decide such issues despite possible conflict with the Board, the Note observes, citing Sovern, *Section 301 and the Primary Jurisdiction of the NLRB,* 76 HARV. L. REV. 529 (1963) and Carey v. Westinghouse Elec. Corp., 375 U.S. 261 (1964). Judge Friendly's "mistake" led him into the second "error" of using ordinary contract principles rather than national labor policy, including consideration of industry practice. The promotion of collective bargaining, a prime goal of that policy, would militate toward a holding that the contract was formed. That issue could not be fobbed off on an arbitrator, it was argued, because *Wiley* teaches that rarely does an arbitrator have the power to decide his own authority (a subject on which he is not disinterested) ; rather that issue is for the court.

DECIDING THE ISSUE OF CONTRACT FORMATION, EXTENSION, AND ARBITRABILITY—A PROPOSAL

If it is desirable, or unavoidable, for the court to decide the issue of contract formation in a case such as *Genesco* (a similar issue could arise as to whether a collective agreement had or had not been extended past its stated termination date), the next question would seem to be *how* it should discharge that obligation. Although contract making is legal stuff on which courts are expert, it may be argued that they are no more expert on the issue of contract formation than they are in regard to contract interpretation. (The issue, for the moment, is institutional fitness, not whether the parties have confided the question to the arbitrator.) Indeed, the argument might be made with equal force in both labor and nonlabor disputes in recognition of the fact that the methods and mores of contract formation vary widely among different trades and in the many different kinds of labor-management relationships that can be found.

Would the court be well advised to designate the arbitrator chosen by the parties (*i.e.* according to the procedure specified in their contract) to take evidence, sift it, and rule initially on the threshold issue subject to court review?

In addition to making available to the court whatever expertise the arbitrator brings to the task, such a course would also serve another purpose. The merits of the controversy may, and often will, be intertwined with the jurisdictional question. In *Genesco* the two issues were almost co-extensive. Mainly for this reason the Trilogy directs courts to send disputes to the arbitrators in most cases, and *Wiley* commands that issues of procedural arbitrability be decided by arbitrators.

Where such overlap exists, the arbitrator would be empowered to hear the merits in the interests of saving time and preventing duplication, although he might well defer issuing the ruling on them until the court, if a party presented it with a request to review the arbitrator's initial ruling, has disposed of the jurisdictional question so as not to cloud that issue. Alternatively, an arbitrator might finesse the jurisdictional problem if he finds the grievance were not meritorious, thus sparing the parties the effort and cost of pursuing their dispute in court.

Conceivably, a similar device could be used where contract formation is not in dispute but arbitrability of the issue tendered is. Again, the arbitrator could deal with the merits if the overlap of jurisdiction and merits was large enough to recommend that course ; or, he could defer consideration of the merits if that seemed the more economical course. (The latter situation will occur; I have had cases that appeared to me to be in that category where a resolution of the jurisdictional issue before reaching the merits seemed preferable because of the complexity of the fact issues.)

Such a procedure would provide an initial decision by a presumably more competent tribunal, subject to the protections afforded by courts against dragooning a party into arbitration when he has not consented to arbitrate. However, the availability of such a procedure might stimulate resort to the courts. The answer may be that the litigious will litigate and that it is preferable to minimize court involvement in issues to which they bring comparatively little competence and also to make more readily available a procedure whereby reluctant parties may obtain a ruling on their jurisdictional doubts with the least inconvenience.

Note that this procedure does not harmonize with New York practice, under which a party may be precluded from raising the jurisdictional issue if he is served with a notice of intention to arbitrate in the requisite way and does not move to stay arbitration, thereby precipitating the jurisdictional issue *before* the arbitration gets under way. Note also that *Layne-Minnesota* managed in a similar format to defer court resolution of the arbitrability issue until after the arbitration was held.

E.

Post-Award Review

LOCAL 77, AMERICAN FEDERATION OF MUSICIANS, AFL–CIO v. PHILADELPHIA ORCHESTRA ASSOCIATION
252 F. Supp. 787 (E.D. Pa. 1966)

LORD, D. J. Defendant is the Philadelphia Orchestra Association, hereafter called the *Association*. Plaintiff is the union representing the musicians of the Orchestra, hereafter called the *Union*. The Association has planned a concert tour of South and Central America, which hereafter will be called the *Tour*. The scheduled Tour cannot be made unless the orchestra travels by air.

On September 9, 1963, the parties entered into a collective bargaining agreement which is presently in force—hereafter called the *Contract*. This Contract contains in Article 15(B) certain provisions concerning travel requirements for out of town concerts. It has not been contended, however, that such provision or any other part of the Contract specifically mentions air travel as such.

Sometime in the summer of 1965, the Association let it be known that it was scheduling this Tour as part of the regular season encompassed by the Contract, and that the musicians —which is to say the membership of the Union —would be required to travel by aircraft.

The Union objected; there was submission to arbitration by mutual agreement, and the Arbitrator decided in a manner which the Union challenges in the present civil action.

At any rate it is clearly agreed that there is no dispute as to any matters of fact pertinent to resolution of the present litigation. The parties agree that the question should be decided purely as a matter of law.

Comprehensive briefs have been filed by both parties, and counsel have also presented their respective positions with great skill and sincerity on oral argument. Having had the benefit of these briefs and arguments, points and authorities—and having studied the pleadings and accompanying exhibits, the Court is prepared to rule upon the motions.

The complaint of Union does not attack the fact of arbitration or the form of the reference of the question. For that matter, the agreement of both parties to such arbitration is shown by the correspondence submitted with Association's Answer as Exhibits A and B thereto. One of those exhibits is a letter of Union's counsel to the American Arbitration Association dated January 28, 1966. In that letter he first disclaims acquiescence in certain characterizations of the dispute and its background which are contained in the letter (Exhibit A) of Association's counsel to the same arbitration association. But then he goes on to say:

> ...We are in accord that the narrow issue to be determined is *whether under the collective bargaining agreement the musicians may be required to fly.* (Exhibit B; emphasis added).

The essence of the resulting Award of Arbitrator is contained in its first paragraph (Appendix A, *infra*):

> Under the contract, the Association may require members of the Orchestra to travel by airplane on the forthcoming tour of South and Central America, except that individual members who can show a genuine physical or psychological incapacity for flying shall be excused, without pay, from making the tour.

In paragraph 16 of the Complaint, and also in paragraph 13 of the Motion for Preliminary Injunction, Union says:

> Said award and opinion is invalid and should be set aside in that:
> a. The arbitrator exceeded his powers, authority and jurisdiction.
> b. The arbitrator modified and amended the existing provisions of the agreement in contravention of the specific limitation imposed by Paragraph 25 of the agreement.
> c. The arbitrator rendered an award and opinion which on its face is not based on the contract, but is in direct conflict with the contract and is no more than a proposed offer of settlement which had in fact been rejected by Plaintiff as is reflected in the affidavit attached hereto and marked Exhibit "C".
> d. The arbitrator rendered an award and opinion upon subject matter which was not submitted to him.

Jurisdiction is obtained under the Labor Management Relations Act of 1947 as amended, Sec. 301, 29 U.S.C.A. § 185; and also under the Act of July 30, 1947, 61 Stat. 669, 9 U.S.C.A. § 10 relating to arbitration.

Association points out, however, that the

Union's burden in seeking to set aside the award of the Arbitrator is overwhelming. The circumstances of the reference to arbitration have already been mentioned. In the collective bargaining agreement (Sec. 25) there is the Union's own commitment that the decision of the Arbitrator shall be "final and binding upon all parties." Association points to the language of the court in Local 453, I. U. of E. R. & M. Workers, etc. v. Otis Elevator Co., 314 F. 2d 25, 28 (2nd Cir. 1963):

> Having bargained for the decision of the arbitrator . . . the parties are bound by it, even if it be regarded as unwise or wrong on the merits . . .

Union counters by saying that the Arbitrator did not fulfill his obligation; that he abused the power conferred upon him. The text upon which this argument rests is a certain passage from United Steelworkers of America v. Enterprise Wheel and Car Corp., 363 U.S. 593, 80 S.Ct. 1358, 4 L.Ed. 2d 1424 (1960), consisting of the last three sentences of the first full paragraph of the opinion of the Court at page 597, 80 S.Ct. at page 1361:

> . . . Nevertheless, an arbitrator is confined to interpretation and application of the collective bargaining agreement; he does not sit to dispense his own brand of industrial justice. He may of course look for guidance from many sources, yet his award is legitimate only so long as it draws its essence from the collective bargaining agreement. When the arbitrator's words manifest an infidelity to this obligation, courts have no choice but to refuse enforcement of the award.

Appended hereto is the award and the accompanying 12-page opinion of the Arbitrator (Appendices A & B)* It must be understood that by attaching the Arbitrator's writings hereto, this Court is in no sense purporting to pass upon the merits thereof. Courts may not look into the merits of an arbitrable matter. International Tel. & Tel. Corp. v. Local 400, etc., 286 F. 2d 329, 331 (3rd Cir. 1961). More cases are collected in H. K. Porter Co. v. United Saw, File and Steel Prod. Wkrs., 217 F. Supp. 161, at 164 (E.D. Pa. 1963); affirmed in this respect (under same caption) 333 F. 2d. 596, 600 (3rd Cir. 1964).

The opinion last cited is not only a familiar one, but also is peculiarly pertinent to the present problem. Three decisions are involved in that case, with the same parties in each: the Union, being the United Saw, File and Steel Products Workers of America, Federal Labor Union No. 22254, AFL–CIO, and the Employer-company, being the H. K. Porter Company, Diss-

---

[*Omitted]

ton Division. After Porter acquired the Disston plant, it moved it from Philadelphia to Danville, Virginia. Agreement as to severance pay and pension rights of affected employees was held arbitrable in United Saw, File and Steel Products Workers v. H. K. Porter Co., 190 F. Supp. 407 (E.D. Pa. 1960). The arbitrator's award which resulted was challenged as not within the scope of arbitration, but upheld in H. K. Porter Co. v. United Saw, File and Steel Prod. Workers, 217 F. Supp. 161 (E.D. Pa. 1963).

Part I of the Ruling of the Arbitrator concerned employees whose jobs had been terminated by removal of the plant, and who had not attained the age of 65 years, but had rendered the Company more than 25 years of service. The contract simply provided that

> . . . Basic yearly allowance . . . shall be paid a retired employee who has reached the age of 65 with at least 25 years of continuous service with the company. (See 217 F. Supp. at 165).

On appeal from the District Court's affirmance of the Arbitrator's Award, the Court said in H. K. Porter Co. v. United Saw, File and Steel Products Workers, 333 F. 2d 596, 601 (3rd Cir. 1964):

> In the margin is a list of the [20] instances examined by the Arbitrator where the length of service had influenced the Pension Board of Disston to grant pensions to employees notwithstanding the failure of strict compliance with the eligibility clause of sixty-five years of age and twenty-five years of continuous service. Under the circumstances of this case these practices formed a source of guidance to which the Arbitrator was authorized to look, in interpreting the eligibility clause of the agreement. The Arbitrator acted entirely within his competence in granting the pensions based on duration of service. The District Court properly approved these findings and conclusions.

In part II of the Award, the Arbitrator had also made awards to employees who had reached age 65 without 25 years of continuous service (age 65 but less than 25 years of service—as opposed to 25 years of service but age less than 65). No background or precedent of practice for awards of any kind in such case was found, and it was held that to this extent the award had been erroneously affirmed below. That part of the award was a violation of the stricture that "the Arbitrator may not administer his own brand of industrial justice." Porter Co. v. United Saw, File and Steel Products Workers, 333 F. 2d 596, 602 (3rd Cir. 1964).

The factual parallel is quite close. The sale and closing of the Disston plant there was obviously not in contemplation when the saw workers and the former employer reached their bargain. In the same way, the contemplated Tour was not in mind when the Association and the Union revised and renewed their contract in 1963. The instant Contract does not mention air travel nor, for that matter, does it mention intercontinental travel, by ocean or by air.

To turn back now to the Union's position, it will be remembered its argument relies heavily upon a passage of three sentences quoted from the case of United Steelworkers of America v. Enterprise Wheel and Car Corp., 363 U.S. 593, 80 S.Ct. 1358, 4 L.Ed. 2d 1424 (1960) which have already been quoted above. It would be well now to consider the first part of the paragraph in which those admonitions against arbitrator's private industrial justice appeared, i.e.:

> When an arbitrator is commissioned to interpret and apply the collective bargaining agreement, he is to bring his informed judgment to bear in order to reach a fair solution of a problem. This is especially true when it comes to formulating remedies. *There the need is for flexibility in meeting a wide variety of situations.* The draftsmen may never have thought of what specific remedy should be awarded to meet a particular contingency. Nevertheless, an arbitrator is confined [etc., as quoted earlier]. United Steelworkers of America v. Enterprise Wheel and Car Corp., 363 U.S. 593, 597, 80 S.Ct. 1358, 1361 (1960) [emphasis added].

While the cases quoted here, and the authorities collected therein, may not contain all the law and the prophets on this subject, they suffice to show that there is but one inquiry here. It is not whether this Court approves the Arbitrator's award; or whether the award and opinion contain surplusage or on the other hand are too condensed. The question is whether the award is based on the contract. In that light the Award and Opinion, Appendices A & B hereafter, will not be re-examined.

Concentrating upon that precise question, the answer is abundantly clear: the Arbitrator did indeed carry out with fidelity his obligation to interpret and apply the contract. This is apparent as one reviews the opinion, page by page. The first page delineates the problem and its history in the first two paragraphs, and commences discussion of the contract in the third—first stating the position of the Union in that respect. On page 2 the most nearly relevant paragraph of the contract is quoted, and the Union's argument with respect thereto is briefly stated, with the Association's counter argument.

On page 3 the history of air travel with respect to orchestras generally and, since 1955, with respect to this Orchestra in particular, is discussed. The Philadelphia Orchestra has made over thirty trips by air since 1955, and the respective arguments of the Union and the Association as to whether that history establishes an acquiescence by the Union in air travel under the Contract and its predecessors is thoroughly analyzed. Circumstances of the particular trips are detailed, and the Arbitrator finds on page 4 that

> ... Only one trip (to Havana in 1958) found all the members flying without any special agreement having been negotiated.

Down through the center of page 6 of the opinion (Appendix B), the possible significance of bargaining history and negotiation—as argued by both sides—is carefully considered. The Arbitrator concludes that the contract is not so clear and unambiguous, on the subject of air travel, as to support the Union's argument that there is no room for consideration of evidence on the subject. That result is supported by reason and analysis; it is not to be deemed capricious or arbitrary.

On page 7 and 8 the custom and practice regarding air travel is considered against the background of the contract, or so much of it as is pertinent, in the following words (Appendix B, p. 8).

> In my judgment, this history indicates that the parties have recognized and accepted air travel as an acceptable and permissible mode of travel. To that extent I think there *has* been shown a mutual intent and understanding, to the effect that travel by airplane, just as much as travel by railroad, is a proper mode of transportation for out-of-town tours under the contract. It has been accepted, if you will, as meeting the contractual obligation to provide "first class transportation."

Beyond that, the Arbitrator does no more than to decide that

> Under the contract, the Association may require members of the Orchestra to travel by airplane on the forthcoming tour of South and Central America, except

The Union argues that the exception is gratuitous —that there are sick-leave provisions in the contract which make it unnecessary for any Arbitrator to provide the following exclusion, and machinery for its implementation (i.e.):

> except that individual members who can show a genuine physical or psychological incapacity for flying shall be excused, without pay, from making the tour.

I have already determined that the Award is one which draws its essence from the contract with respect to the submitted question: whether under the collective bargaining agreement the musicians may be required to fly.

As to any other aspects of the case: it must be recalled that the matter is one of urgency—it is conceded that the disposition of the Motion for Preliminary Injunction is the essence of this case. That is, tour departure is imminent; there is no time for full scale hearing on the merits of the complaint even were such relief available under the law. Again, prospective application of the Contract is of no concern, since counsel for the Union have stated that the Contract will be renegotiated in September of this year.

For the purposes of a Motion for Preliminary Injunction, accordingly, the requirements of a showing which would justify the extraordinary remedy of injunction must be considered. The Union alleges that there is no adequate remedy at law; and that the Union members are threatened with irreparable harm in that they will be required to sacrifice either jobs, seniority, employment rights or leave the country for six weeks with compulsory air travel.

I hold that there is no equity in the Motion of the Union as to Union's allegation that the award of the Arbitrator went beyond the submission and was not based upon the terms of the contract. I so decide because:

(1) It resolved the exact question which was submitted, and—as heretofore shown—in terms of the Contract and its interpretation; it is therefore not subject to reexamination on the merits.

(2) As to the allegation that its provisions for excusing those incapable of making the Tour go beyond the terms of the submission, I find that objection invalid for the foregoing reasons, and also for want of equity in that should any members of the Union be aggrieved thereby they would, under the very terms of that award, suffer no irreparable injury.

For all the foregoing reasons, the Motion of the plaintiff, Union, to Vacate Award of Arbitrator and for Preliminary Injunction is denied and it is so ordered.

And for the further reasons heretofore shown, the Motion to Dismiss of the defendant, the Association, is granted and the Complaint is dismissed for failure to state a claim upon which relief can be granted, and it is so ordered.

———————

Thus does a court perform the delicate task of inquiring whether the arbitrator exceeded his jurisdiction without inquiring into the merits. *Query*: How unreasonable can the arbitrator's opinion be before a court will decide that the award is insupportable by the collective agreement?

———————

In Hyland v. United Airlines, (N.D. Ill. E.D. 1966) 254 F. Supp. 367, provisions regarding seniority were in conflict. The court said:

> It is, in short, ambiguous; its words standing alone do not justify the arbitrator's result; but similarly they do not support a change in seniority status for plaintiffs. Both results are inconsistent with the words of some portion of the Agreement. An arbitrator is employed to pierce this opaque veil, if he can, and discover what it was the parties intended when they wrote the conflicting words. This is the ordinary process of interpretation, well within the authority of an arbitrator. This is what Dr. Mark L. Kahn did; he did it thoroughly, properly and well and his award is consequently final, binding and immune to attack here.

———————

For an example of the use of *American Manufacturing* and *Warrior & Gulf* in a proceeding to enforce an award, see Local 52, Nat'l B'hd of Packinghouse Wkrs. v. Western Iowa Pork Co., (S.D. Ia. W.D. 1965) 247 F. Supp. 367.

———————

The arbitrator found the grievant guilty of falsifying his work-hour records and properly subject to discipline but held that discharge was an excessive penalty and awarded reinstatement without back pay. The collective agreement provided for "discharge for proper cause" and required a written warning for misconduct but excluded dishonesty and drunkenness from the warning requirement. Among the arbitration provisions was this language:

> the arbitration board shall not substitute its judgment for that of the management and shall only reverse the action or decision of the management if it finds that the Company's complaint against the employee is not supported by the facts, and that the management has acted arbitrarily and in bad faith or in violation of the express terms of this Agreement.

No finding of bad faith or contract violation appeared in the findings or award. The court held that the reinstatement award exceeded the arbitrator's powers and refused to enforce the order of reinstatement. The court also observed:

> Appellant makes a further claim of error on the part of the trial court in receiving, over objection, testimony as to the reason why Owings was discharged. Under the bargaining agreement between the parties, it was necessary to know the reason for the discharge before the court could determine whether the arbitrator exceeded his authority. We find no error.

Local 784, Truck Drivers' Union v. Ulry-Talbert Co., 330 F. 2d 562 (8th Cir. 1964). What issue made the evidence necessary to the court's opinion? Would a remand to the arbitrator for findings have been permissible? Or should the court have decided the issue on the basis of the omission from the brief "findings" of any specific conclusion that the employer was "arbitrary" or otherwise in violation of the agreement? Is it conceivable that the arbitrator thought the employer (or a supervisor) arbitrary and did not want to say so in just so many words in consideration of the fact that both the supervisor and the employee would be working together again?

AMERICAN ARBITRATION ASSOCIATION
VOLUNTARY LABOR ARBITRATION TRIBUNAL

THE TORRINGTON CO. v.
METAL PRODUCTS WORKERS UNION
Local 1645, UAW, AFL–CIO
Award of Arbitrator

The undersigned arbitrator, having been designated in accordance with the Arbitration Agreement entered into by the above-named Parties, and dated January 18, 1964 and having been duly sworn and having duly heard the proofs and allegations of the Parties, awards, as follows:

1. The issue of whether the company is obliged to grant time off with pay to employees who request it to vote on Election Day is arbitrable.

2. The benefit of time off with pay up to a maximum of one hour for the purpose of voting on Election Day had become a firmly established practice at this company which could be changed by the company only by negotiating it with the union.

3. In the 1963–1964 labor negotiations, which culminated in the current labor contract, the parties did *not* reach an agreement to discontinue this practice.

4. The company erred in refusing to grant this benefit to employees on Election Day, November 3, 1964.

5. Employees who took time off to vote on November 3, 1964 shall be paid up to a maximum of one hour and all other employees who worked during the election hours on that Election Day and who were paid this benefit on November 6, 1962 shall be paid for the same amount of time off for Election Day 1964 as they received for Election Day 1962.

DATED: June 25, 1965

THOMAS KENNEDY

Pay for Time Off for Voting

The Issue. At the arbitration hearing which was held at the company's plant in Torrington, Connecticut on May 19, 1965 the parties were unable to agree on a statement of the issue. Therefore the arbitrator accepted as the issue to be decided the grievance filed by the union on December 17, 1964 which is as follows:

> Under established contractual past practice, the company is required to grant time off with pay to employees who request it on Election Day in order that they may cast their votes. This contractual practice was violated when the company informed the union that employees would not be granted time off with pay for the purpose of voting on November 3, 1964 and by supervisors' threats that any employee who left work before the end of his shift on that day for the purpose of voting would be subject to discipline.

Background. On November 1, 1962 the company posted the following bulletin:

> Voting hours at all voting places in Torrington will be from 6 a.m. until 7 p.m.
>
> Registered Torrington voters will be allowed up to one hour off with pay for the purpose of voting. Any such time off must be arranged in advance with the appropriate supervisor so as to keep the disruption of operations to a minimum. The right to vote is every citizens duty as well as his most valuable privilege. Vote for the candidate of your own choice—but vote!

The message in this bulletin was in line with a well-established past practice at this company. For some twenty years or more employees had been given time off with pay on election days, although this benefit was not specifically stated in the labor agreements.

In late 1962 the company decided to change its practice with respect to paying employees for time off to vote. It appears that the company's intention to make this change was stated first in the December issue of the Torrington Company Newsletter. On February 20, 1963 the president of the union wrote to the company asking to be officially informed regarding the company's position on this matter.

On March 8, 1963 the company replied to the union president that it had changed its policy for economic reasons and also because in its opinion conditions had so changed that the time off was no longer necessary to enable employees to vote. The company's letter which dealt also with pay for time lost from work for the purpose of negotiating the collective bargaining agreement ended with the following paragraph.

> Since you doubtlessly feel that the question of continuing or discontinuing both of the above past

practices is subject to negotiations between the company and the union, I suggest that you consider this as an invitation to so bargain. We will be available at any mutually convenient time for the purpose of such good faith bargaining, or if you prefer, the matters in question may await the contract renegotiations which, presumably, will begin on or about July 27, 1963.

On April 9, 1963 the union filed with the NLRB a charge of unfair labor practices against the company. Among the unfair labor practices claimed by the union was that of "making a unilateral change in its established policy of paid time off for voting for bargaining unit employees." In an amended charge filed on April 29, 1963 and in a second amended charge filed on May 22, 1963 the union continued to include the voting-time issue. However, on June 10, 1963 the union filed a third amended charge in which this issue did not appear. On July 29, 1963 the Acting Regional Director of the NLRB dismissed the charge, as amended.

The old contract between the parties was due to expire on September 27, 1963, so in August the parties began to hold meetings to negotiate a new contract. The first meeting was held evidently on August 14. At that time the company informed the union orally that it did not intend to pay for time off for voting in the future. The union did not present its demands at the first meeting. At a later meeting the union did present a list of demands including the following: "Company will allow one hour with pay for Election Day."

By September 26, 1963, the day before the old contract was scheduled to terminate, no agreement had been reached. A number of issues, including time off with pay for voting which the union continued to include in its list of demands, remained in dispute. On that date, September 26, the company presented a written proposal which began as follows:

> The company respectfully proposes that the current collective bargaining agreement and the pension agreement between itself and the union, be extended until September 27, 1966 but with the following amendments.

There followed twenty-two proposed changes in the contract; none of which made any reference to time off with pay for voting. However, the company's proposal was not acceptable to the union and further negotiations failed to produce an agreement prior to the termination date. On September 27, therefore, the union called the employees out on strike.

Negotiations were continued during the strike and on October 25, 1963 the union made a written proposal to the company. The October 25, 1963 union proposal began as follows:

> The union proposes that the collective bargaining agreement and the pension agreement which expired September 27, 1963 be reinstated with the following amendments.

Among the amendments no reference was made to time off with pay in order to vote on Election Day.

The October 25 proposal did not result in an agreement and the strike continued through the November 1963 Election Day. Some bargaining unit employees worked during the strike but they did not receive paid time off to vote on the November, 1963 Election Day.

The strike continued for seventeen weeks until January 18, 1964, at which time the parties reached agreement on the current labor contract which became effective on that date. No language was included in the new contract with respect to time off with pay for voting.

On November 2, 1964 the union issued a flier to its members in which it was stated that "The Torrington Company has again stated that you will *not* be allowed the one hour time off for voting this year." The flier urged the employees to vote. The following day, November 3, 1964, which was Election Day, employees were not given time off with pay to vote.

On December 17, 1964 the union filed the grievance which constitutes the issue in this case. By mutual agreement the grievance was passed directly to the third step of the grievance procedure. However, the parties were unable to reach an agreement on the issue and the union then requested arbitration as provided in Article V of the 1964 labor contract.

Pertinent Contract Clauses. The following clauses in the current labor agreement between the parties, dated January 18, 1964 are applicable to this case:

ARTICLE V, Arbitration

Section 1

If a grievance is not settled after it has been processed through the three (3) steps described in Article IV above, and if it is a grievance with respect to the interpretation or application of any provisions in this contract and is not controlled by Section 1 of Article XIV (Management) it may be submitted to arbitration in the manner herein provided.

Section 3

The arbitrator shall be bound by and must comply with all of the terms of this agreement and he shall have no power to add to, delete from, or modify, in any way, any of the provisions of this agreement. The arbitrator shall not have the authority to determine the right of employees to merit increases. The arbitrator shall have no authority to set or determine wages except as provided by Section 21 of Article VI, Wages.

ARTICLE XIV, Management Rights

Section 1

The management of the company shall have the exclusive rights to determine from time to time the places and products (in Torrington or elsewhere) of manufacture, to sub-contract and to establish the methods and processes of manufacture. The company's right to establish methods and processes of manufacture shall not derogate or diminish any rights of employees otherwise specifically provided by this agreement.

Section 2

The management of the company shall have all other rights of management, including, but not limited to, the direction of the working force, the right to hire, transfer, suspend, promote, retain, discipline or discharge for proper cause, to maintain quality and efficient operations, and to layoff employees because of lack of work or other proper cause: subject only to the specific provisions herein contained dealing with those subject matters.

Discussion

1. *Arbitrability.* At the outset of the hearing the company raised the question of arbitrability. It argued that the grievance is not arbitrable because the payment for time off for voting was never a matter of contract obligation ; the union included this matter in an unfair labor practice charge before the NLRB and later withdrew it ; and the matter was negotiated off the table in the last contract negotiations, the union having included it among its demands and later having withdrawn it.

We do not believe that the inclusion of and later the withdrawal of an item from an unfair labor practice charge removes that item from being an arbitrable issue. In fact some items may be withdrawn from a charge for the very reason that they are arbitrable under a contract. Whether the payment for time off for voting was a matter of contract obligation is not clear on the face of it. The same can be said of the statement that the issue was bargained off the table in the recent negotiations. For these reasons we are of the opinion that the issue is arbitrable. The arbitrator must decide whether the payment for time off for voting was a contract obligation and, if so, whether that obligation was bargained off the table in the negotiations which resulted in the current labor agreement.

2. *The Substantive Issue.* There was no clause which called for the payment of time off for voting in the earlier labor contracts and there

is no such clause in the current contract. However, by 1962 this benefit had become a firmly established practice. It had been available to employees for approximately 20 years. We believe that a *benefit* of this nature, continued as it had been without change over a period of so many years, must be considered to have become an implied part of the contract.

We emphasize that it is a *benefit*. We distinguish between a past practice involving a *benefit* of this type and a past practice involving method of operation or direction of the working force. In a recent award at the Torrington Company we upheld the company's right to unilaterally change a method of operation. The latter we believe is a right which management clearly has under the management clause in this contract in order to promote efficient operation. On the other hand, we do not believe that the management clause gives to the company the right to discontinue unilaterally a *benefit* which has become an implied part of the contract. In brief, we conclude that the company did have an obligation under the contract to continue to pay for time off for voting until such time as it negotiated a change in the matter. The company recognized its responsibility in this respect when, in its letter of March 8, 1963, it proposed to the union that negotiations on the matter be undertaken.

The union's inclusion of this issue in an unfair labor practice charge and its later withdrawal of it from the charge can have little bearing on this arbitration decision. The union's inclusion of the issue in the charge did indicate that it was aware that the company intended to discontinue this benefit. However, its withdrawal of the issue did not indicate that the union had accepted the company's right to discontinue it. Likewise, the union's action did not foreclose its right to bargain about and to arbitrate this issue. The parties both recognized that it was still a bargainable issue when they included it in their original demands in August, 1963.

It was the company which introduced the matter of pay for time off for voting at the first contract negotiations meeting on August 14, 1963. At that time, the company made it clear that it was insisting on a change in this practice. The union then followed by including the continuance of such time off with pay among its demands. These two conflicting demands evidently remained on the table until September 26.

The company's proposal of September 26, however, in our opinion constituted a significant change in the bargaining position of the parties with respect to this issue. That proposal suggested that the old agreement "be extended until September 27, 1966" except for twenty-two amendments. No mention was made of time off with pay for voting among the twenty-two amendments. It may be that the company intended that its earlier oral statement regarding discontinuance of such time off with pay should continue to be considered part of its demands. However, the union had reason to believe that the September 26 proposal meant that the company was dropping its demand for a change in this past practice.

The October 25, 1963 proposal of the union also began with the statement that the "collective bargaining Agreement and the Pension Agreement which expired September 27, 1963 *be reinstated* with the following amendments." There followed then half a dozen or so changes which did not include time off with pay for voting. We believe that the fact that the union did not list this issue among its demands in the October 25 proposal cannot be considered as a withdrawal of the issue by the union and an agreement not to continue this practice. There is no evidence that any union representative ever stated that the union was withdrawing its demand in favor of the company's demand on this issue. In our opinion the company's proposal of September 26 by its failure to mention the company's demand for a change in this practice removed it from the table. Therefore, it was no longer necessary for the union to continue its counterdemand. Thus, by October 25 both parties agreed that the old contract was to be continued except for certain changes among which was *not* a change in the practice of giving time off with pay for voting.

The strike continued following the above proposals and on Election Day in November 1963 the company did not give time off with pay for the purpose of voting to its employees who were still coming to work including some bargaining unit employees. Since no contract was in effect at the time, the company was free to change the employee benefits which had been either stated or implied in the earlier contract. We do not find, however, that the failure to provide the benefit under such conditions affected in any way the bargaining position of the parties. It did not create a precedent under a contract.

We have no evidence that the position of the parties on this issue was changed or that the issue was ever discussed after the exchange of the written proposals of September 26 and October 25. We must conclude, therefore, that the final bargain between the parties did not include an agreement to discontinue the practice of allowing time off with pay for voting—a benefit which had become firmly established by past practice

under the old contract. We find, therefore, that the company was in violation of the contract when it refused to pay this benefit to employees on Election Day 1964.

3. *Remedy.* Prior to the November 1964 Election Day, the employees had been informed that the company would not pay them for time off for voting up to a maximum of one hour, as it had done under prior labor agreements. As a result, most employees did not take the time off, and those who did were not paid for it.

In 1962 and earlier years, when the company did pay this benefit, not all employees asked for and received it. As a result, it is difficult to devise a remedy which will be fair to both parties because we cannot be sure which employees would have claimed and received time off with pay if the company had offered it on Election Day 1964. However, we believe that substantial justice will be achieved if those employees who actually took time off to vote on Election Day 1964 are paid up to the maximum of one hour's pay and if all other employees who received this benefit in 1962 and who were working during the election hours on Election Day 1964 are paid for the same amount of time for 1964 as they were paid in 1962.

THE TORRINGTON CO. v. LOCAL 1645, METAL PRODUCTS WORKERS UNION, UAW, AFL–CIO
362 F. 2d 677 (2d Cir. 1966)

Before Lumbard, Chief Judge, and Kaufman and Feinberg, Circuit Judges.

Lumbard, C. J. This appeal presents the question whether an arbitrator exceeded his authority under the collective bargaining agreement between The Torrington Company (Torrington) and Metal Products Workers Union Local 1645, UAW, AFL–CIO (the Union), in ruling that the agreement contained an implied provision, based upon prior practice between the parties, that Torrington would allow its employees up to one hour off with pay to vote each election day. The District Court for the District of Connecticut held that "the arbitrator exceeded and abused his authority when he attempted to read into the agreement this implied contractual relationship," and it vacated and set aside the arbitrator's award. We affirm.

In its company newsletter of December 1962, Torrington announced that it was discontinuing its twenty-year policy of permitting employees time off with pay to vote on election days.[1] This policy had been unilaterally instituted by the company and was not a part of the then-existing collective bargaining agreement, which contained an extremely narrow arbitration provision. The Union did not attempt to arbitrate this issue. Rather, on April 9, 1963, it filed a many-faceted complaint with the National Labor Relations Board which included a charge that the unilateral change of election day policy constituted an unfair labor practice.

The Union later dropped this charge, and the Board dismissed the entire complaint on July 29, 1963. In August, the parties began negotiations for a new collective bargaining agreement, as the old contract was due to expire September 27, 1963. At the first meeting, Torrington informed the Union that it did not intend to re-establish its paid time off for voting policy. The Union responded by including a contrary provision in its written demands presented at a meeting in August or early September.

At this point, the record is somewhat unclear as to the circumstances surrounding the negotiations. We know that in the written proposals made by Torrington (September 26) and by the Union (October 25), *each* suggested that the old contract be continued with specific amendments, none of which involved the election day policy. We know that a long and costly strike began when the old contract expired on September 27, that some employees worked during the strike, and that those employees were not given paid time off for the November 1963 elections. And it is conceded by all that the current contract, signed on January 18, 1964, contained, like the old, no mention of paid time off for voting.

When the 1964 elections became imminent. Torrington's understanding of its rights under the new contract was revealed by a union flier to the employees dated November 2, 1964. The Union reported that, "The Torrington Company has again stated that you will *not* be allowed the one hour time off for voting this year." This time, however, the Union was armed with a new weapon, for the new contract contained a much less restrictive arbitration clause. Thus, on December 17, 1964, the Union filed the grievance which underlies this case. When no solution was reached by the parties, application was made to the American Arbitration Association for determination under its Voluntary Labor Arbitration Rules, and the arbitrator was selected by

the parties. A hearing was held on May 19, 1965.

In his written decision, the arbitrator first held that the dispute was arbitrable under the new contract's arbitration clause even though the contract contained no express provision for paid time off for voting, a decision which is not challenged. See, *e.g.,* United Steelworkers of America v. Warrior & Gulf Nav. Co., 363 U.S. 574, 80 S.Ct. 1347, 4 L.Ed. 2d 1409 (1960); Procter & Gamble Independent Union of Port Ivory v. Procter & Gamble Mfg. Co., 298 F. 2d 644 (2 Cir. 1962). Compare Metal Prods. Workers Union, etc. v. Torrington Co., 358 F. 2d 103 (2 Cir. 1966). He then ruled that the benefit of paid time off to vote was a firmly established practice at Torrington, that the company therefore had the burden of changing this policy by negotiating with the Union, and that in the negotiations which culminated in the current bargaining agreement the parties did not agree to terminate this practice. Finding further that this employee benefit was not within management's prerogative under the "management functions" clause of the contract,[2] the arbitrator held that employees who took time off to vote on November 3, 1964, or who worked on that day and had received an election benefit in 1962 must be paid a comparable benefit for Election Day 1964.

The company petitioned to vacate the award. Judge Clarie agreed with the arbitrator that the practice at issue had been long established at Torrington prior to 1963. But he also found that, "Throughout the negotiations [of 1963–1964], the plaintiff employer persistently reiterated its position not to grant this benefit [in the new contract]." Commenting that, "Labor contracts generally affirmatively state the terms which the contracting parties agree to; not what practices they agree to discontinue," Judge Clarie held that the arbitrator had gone outside the terms of the contract and thus had exceeded his authority by reading the election day benefit into the new contract after the parties had negotiated the issue but had made no such provision in that contract.

The essence of the Union's argument on appeal is that, in deciding that the arbitrator exceeded his authority in making this award, the District Court exceeded the scope of its authority and improperly examined the merits of the arbi-

---

1. Torrington's brief on appeal explains that this decision was made because "in the light of the extension of voting hours and the substitution of voting machines for paper ballots . . . it was no longer necessary to permit employees time off to vote."

2. Section 1 of Article XIV gives management exclusive right to determine the places and products of manufacture, the methods and processes to be used, and whether work shall be sub-contracted out. Section 2 leaves with the company "all other rights of management." Torrington does not contend that Article XIV is applicable to this dispute.

trator's award. The Union relies on the language in United Steelworkers of America v. Enterprise Wheel & Car Corp., 363 U.S. 593, 596, 80 S.Ct. 1358, 1360, 4 L.Ed. 2d 1424 (1960), the third of the famous *Steelworkers* trilogy in which the Supreme Court outlined the proper role of the judiciary in labor arbitration cases, to the effect that the courts are not "to review the merits of an arbitration award."

I

It is now well settled that a grievance is arbitrable "unless it may be said with positive assurance that the arbitration clause is not susceptible of an interpretation that covers the asserted dispute." United Steelworkers of America v. Warrior & Gulf Nav. Co., 363 U.S. at 582–583, 80 S.Ct. at 1353.[3] A less settled question is the appropriate scope of judicial review of a specific arbitration award. Although the arbitrator's decision on the merits is final as to questions of law and fact, his authority is contractual in nature and is limited to the powers conferred in the collective bargaining agreement. For this reason, a number of courts have interpreted *Enterprise Wheel* as authorizing review of whether an arbitrator's award exceeded the limits of his contractual authority. See H. K. Porter Co. v. United Saw, File & Steel Prods. Workers, 333 F. 2d 596 (3 Cir. 1964); Truck Drivers & Helpers Union Local 784 v. Ulry-Talbert Co., 330 F. 2d 562 (8 Cir. 1964); I. A. M. v. Hayes Corp., 296 F. 2d 238, 242–243 (5 Cir. 1961). The precise question seems not to have arisen in this Circuit, compare Local 453, Intern. Union of Electrical, etc. v. Otis Elevator Co., 314 F. 2d 25 (2 Cir.), cert. denied, 373 U.S. 949, 83 S.Ct. 1680, 10 L.Ed. 2d 705 (1963), where the arbitrator's power to settle the dispute was clear, but we have plainly intimated that the arbitrator's authority to render a given award is subject to meaningful review. See Carey v. General Elec. Co., 315 F. 2d 499, 508 (2 Cir. 1963). We agree

with *Carey* that this is an appropriate question for judicial review.

Torrington contends that the arbitrator exceeded his authority in this case by "adding" the election day bonus to the terms of the January 1964 agreement. However, the arbitrator held that such a provision was implied by the prior practice of the parties. In some cases, it may be appropriate exercise of an arbitrator's authority to resolve ambiguities in the scope of a collective bargaining agreement on the basis of prior practice, since no agreement can reduce all aspects of the labor-management relationship to writing. However, while courts should be wary of rejecting the arbitrator's interpretation of the implications of the parties' prior practice, the mandate that the arbitrator stay within the confines of the collective bargaining agreement, footnote 3 *supra,* requires a reviewing court to pass upon whether the agreement authorizes the arbitrator to expand its express terms on the basis of the parties' prior practice. Therefore, we hold that the question of an arbitrator's authority is subject to judicial review, and that the arbitrator's decision that he has authority should not be accepted where the reviewing court can clearly perceive that he has derived that authority from sources outside the collective bargaining agreement at issue. See Textile Workers Union of America v. American Thread Co., 291 F. 2d 894 (4 Cir. 1961).[4]

II

Unfortunately, as the dissenting opinion illustrates, agreeing upon these general principles does not make this case any easier. Certain it is that Torrington's policy of paid time off to vote was well established by 1962. On this basis, the arbitrator ruled that the policy must continue during the 1964 agreement because Torrington did not negotiate a contrary policy into that

---

3. It has been argued that this standard should be broadened to render not arbitrable any situation where "a frivolous claim [is made] that a grievance is within the scope of the agreement." Freidin, *Discussion of a paper by Sam Kagel,* in ARBITRATION AND PUBLIC POLICY 10, 14 (Proceedings of the Fourteenth Annual Meeting, National Academy of Arbitrators (1961). However, while plausible, such a position was not adopted by the Supreme Court, primarily because there is real advantage in sending even frivolous claims to arbitration. Moreover, as a long-time labor arbitrator and member of this court has said, "No great harm is done by applying a liberal rule as to arbitrability, if the court carefully scrutinizes what the arbitrator later decides." Paul R. Hays, LABOR ARBITRATION, A DISSENTING VIEW 80 (1966).

4. Of course, it can be argued that our decision authorizes an impermissible review of the "merits" in a case where the principal issue was whether the arbitrator should find an implied substantive obligation in the contract, see Meltzer, *The Supreme Court, Arbitrability, and Collective Bargaining,* 28 U. CHI. L. REV. 464, 484–85 (1961), but we think this position is contrary to *Enterprise Wheel.* See note 3 *supra.* The question of the arbitrator's authority is really one of his contractual jurisdiction, and the courts cannot be expected to place their stamp of approval upon his action without making some examination of his jurisdiction to act. As stated above, we think more exhaustive judicial review of this question is appropriate after the award has been made than before the award in a suit to compel arbitration; in this way, the court receives the benefit of the arbitrator's interpretive skills as to the matter of his contractual authority. See Livingston v. John Wiley & Sons, Inc., 313 F. 2d 52, 59 n. 5 (2 Cir. 1963), aff'd, 376 U.S. 543, 84 S.Ct. 909, 11 L.Ed. 2d 898 (1964).

agreement. To bolster his decision, the arbitrator noted that Torrington's written demands of September 26, 1963, constituted the first occasion on which either party did not expressly insist that its election day position be adopted. Therefore, he concluded, it was the company which removed this question "from the table" and the company cannot complain if its policy under the old contract is now continued.

We cannot accept this interpretation of the negotiations. In the first place, as Judge Clarie stated, labor contracts generally state affirmatively what conditions the parties agree to, more specifically, what restraints the parties will place on management's freedom of action. While it may be appropriate to resolve a question never raised during negotiations on the basis of prior practice in the plant or industry, it is quite another thing to assume that the contract confers a specific benefit when that benefit was discussed during negotiations but omitted from the contract.

> [I]n entering into a collective agreement, in the negotiations for which as much care and deliberateness were exercised in respect to the omission as to the inclusion of various restraints and obligations, neither party agreed to submit to an arbitrator the question of whether it should be subjected to the very restraint or obligation which in negotiations the parties, by omitting it from the contract, agreed the contract should *not* subject it to. Freidin, *supra* note 3, at p. 12.

The arbitrator's primary justification for reading the election day benefit into the 1964 agreement was that such a benefit corresponded to the parties' prior practice. But in this the arbitrator completely ignored the fact that the company had revoked that policy almost ten months earlier, by newsletter to the employees in December 1962 and by formal notice to the Union in April 1963. It was within the employer's discretion to make such a change since the narrow arbitration clause in the previous collective bargaining agreement precluded resort to arbitration by the Union.[5] And there was no showing that

Torrington's announcement was merely a statement of bargaining position and was not a seriously intended change in policy.

In light of this uncontroverted fact, and bearing in mind that the arbitrator has no jurisdiction to "add to" the 1964 agreement, we do not think it was proper to place the "burden" of securing an express contract provision in the 1964 contract on the company. At the start of negotiations, Torrington announced its intent to *continue* its previous change of election day policy. This was an express invitation to the Union to bargain with respect to this matter. After the Union failed to press for and receive a change in the 1964 agreement, the company was surely justified in applying in November 1964 a policy it had rightfully established in 1962, and had applied in November 1963 (during the strike).

In our opinion, the Union by pressing this grievance has attempted to have "added" to the 1964 agreement a benefit which it did not think sufficiently vital to insist upon during negotiations for the contract which ended a long and costly strike. We find this sufficiently clear from the facts as found by the arbitrator to agree with the district court that the arbitrator exceeded his authority by ruling that such a benefit was implied in the terms of that agreement. As Judge Brown has written for the Fifth Circuit:

> But if full rein is to be given to this device as a means thought best able to achieve industrial peace, it must be enforced with an even hand. That which the parties have committed to the arbiter is for the arbiter alone, not the Court. Courts must assure that. But it is equally important to assure that neither party—through one guise or another—may obtain the intervention of an arbiter when the contract clearly excludes it from the reach of the grievance machinery. Local Union No. 787, I.U.E. v. Collins Radio Co., 317 F. 2d 214, 220 (1963).

Far from having the disruptive effect upon the finality of labor arbitration which results when courts review the "merits" of a particular remedy devised by an arbitrator, we think that the limited review exercised here will stimulate voluntary resort to labor arbitration and thereby strengthen this important aspect of labor-management relations by guaranteeing to the parties to a collective

---

5. Article V, § 3 of the prior contract provided: "The arbitrator is bound by and must comply with all the terms of this agreement, and he shall not have any power whatsoever to arbitrate away any part of the agreement, nor add to, delete from, or modify, in any way, any of the provisions of this agreement. The Company's decisions will stand and will not be overruled by any arbitrator unless the arbitrator can find that the Company misinterpreted or violated the express terms of the agreement." The Union concedes that the scope of arbitration under this contract was "strictly limited," but it contends that the modification of the above provision in the 1964 agreement, see footnote 2 *supra*, "necessarily impels" the conclusion that the parties intended to confer upon the arbitrator the authority exercised

in this case. It is true that under the 1964 agreement the arbitrator is no longer bound by the Company's decision in all cases where the Company has not "misinterpreted or violated the express terms of the agreement." However, the new agreement retained the prohibition against an arbitrator "adding to" its provisions, and we do not think that the parties intended to confer upon the arbitrator unreviewable power to determine the scope of his authority with respect to a particular grievance.

bargaining agreement that they will find in the arbitrator not a "philosopher king" but one who will resolve their disputes within the framework of the agreement which they negotiated.

The judgment is affirmed.

FEINBERG, C. J. (dissenting): I respectfully dissent.

I start with the proposition, accepted by the majority, that an arbitrator's award may be reviewed by the courts only to see if "it draws its essence from the collective bargaining agreement" and whether "the arbitrator's words manifest an infidelity to this obligation." See United Steelworkers of America v. Enterprise Wheel & Car Corp., 363 U.S. 593, 597, 80 S.Ct. 1358, 1361, 4 L.Ed. 2d 1424 (1960). But this inquiry is a very limited one and, so limited, should lead to reversal of the court below.

The arbitrator in this case concluded that both parties agreed at the bargaining table to continue the prior practice of paid time off for voting. It is clear that the new contract did not by its terms deal with the time off for voting issue. But the arbitrator reasoned that it was the company, not the union, that was trying to change the twenty-year old practice. It was the company that introduced the issue into the bargaining at the first negotiation meeting in August 1963, and insisted on a change in the practice. Thereafter, according to the arbitrator, the company "removed ... [this demand] from the table ... Thus ... both parties agreed that the old contract was to be continued except for certain changes among which was *not* a change in the practice of giving time off with pay for voting."

The arbitrator assumed that a collective bargaining agreement can include terms or conditions not made explicit in the written contract. This proposition is correct. In a prior appeal involving these same parties and this same contract, this court said that the arbitration clause of the agreement could be applicable to a recall grievance if there were "some special agreement making it applicable or ... some custom or common understanding which has that effect." Torrington Co. v. Metal Prods. Workers, 347 F. 2d 93, 95 (2d Cir.), cert. denied, 382 U.S. 940, 86 S.Ct. 394, 15 L.Ed. 2d 351 (1965). This is a clear statement of the view that it is proper to look beyond the terms of a labor contract in interpreting it. In United Steelworkers of America v. Warrior & Gulf Nav. Co., 363 U.S. 574, 580, 80 S.Ct. 1347, 1352, 4 L.Ed. 2d 1409 (1960), the Supreme Court said: "Gaps [in the "written document"] may be left to be filled in by reference to the practices of the particular industry and of the various shops covered by the agree-

ment." Moreover, the difference between the earlier (1961–1963) and the new contract in this case is most significant. The arbitration article in the earlier contract contained the following limitations on the arbitrator's power:

> The Company's decisions will stand and will not be over-ruled by any arbitrator unless the arbitrator can find that the Company misinterpreted or violated the express terms of the agreement.

> No point not covered by this contract shall be subject to arbitration.

After a 16-week strike in which the scope of the arbitration clause was an important issue (which, in itself, is unusual), these limitations on the arbitrator's power were excluded in the new contract. This was a clear recognition by the parties that there can be "implied" as well as "express" terms in the agreement. In this case, the arbitrator held that pay for time off for voting was a benefit which was such "an implied part of the contract." If so, then, of course, the arbitrator did not "add to, delete from, or modify, in any way, any of the provisions of this agreement" in violation of the arbitration clause.

Thus, the arbitrator looked to prior practice, the conduct of the negotiation for the new contract and the agreement reached at the bargaining table to reach his conclusion that paid time off for voting was "an implied part of the contract." From all of this, I conclude that the arbitrator's award "draws its essence from the collective bargaining agreement" and his words do not "manifest an infidelity to this obligation." Once that test is met, the inquiry ends. Whether the arbitrator's conclusion was correct is irrelevant[1] because the parties agreed to abide by it, right or wrong. Nevertheless, the majority has carried the inquiry further and concerned itself with a minute examination of the merits of the award, which we are enjoined not to do. Thus, the majority opinion states that the arbitrator "ignored the fact that the company had revoked [its] ... policy almost ten months earlier." Of course, the arbitrator was aware of the company's actions in December 1962 and April 1963 and referred to them in his opinion. And I would suppose that what significance to attach to these acts—*e.g.*, whether the company could "revoke" its policy unilaterally—and to the bargaining held thereafter is exactly the sort of question the parties left to the arbitrator to decide.

Supreme Court decisions are quite clear that the courts should not leap into the arbitration

---

1. I by no means imply that I think the arbitrator was wrong here on the merits.

process too quickly. I need not repeat here the reasons for this approach; they are set out in detail in the famous trilogy. United Steelworkers of America v. Enterprise Wheel & Car Corp., *supra*; United Steelworkers of America v. Warrior & Gulf Nav. Co., *supra*; United Steelworkers of America v. American Mfg. Co., 363 U.S. 564, 80 S.Ct. 1343, 4 L.Ed. 2d 1403 (1960). It used to be that the attempt to obtain court review of the merits of an arbitration award was made under the guise that the issue was so clear it was not arbitrable. But the trilogy settled that old fight. This case shows the same attempt under the guise that the arbitrator has exceeded his authority, and it should meet with no greater success.

———

In the text to note 5 the court declares that the employer was free to make a unilateral change in a benefit not affirmatively required by the text of the collective agreement because the arbitrator could "overrule" the company only if he found the employer had "misinterpreted or violated the express terms of the agreement." Do you agree? If the arbitration clause contained no such limitation, would the employer be prohibited from making such a change? Does the National Labor Relations Act affect the employer's power? Is it in turn affected by the arbitration clause described?

———

In 1964 the American Bar Association's House of Delegates adopted the following resolution on the recommendation of the Section of Labor Relations Law: *

Resolved, That the American Bar Association recommends to the Congress that Section 301 of the Labor Management Relations Act of 1947 be amended by adding the following subparagraph thereto, to be known as subparagraph (f), in the following language:

(f) Where suit is brought under this section to compel the performance of an agreement to arbitrate contained in a collective bargaining agreement, the court will direct arbitration only if the court is convinced that the dispute sought to be arbitrated is one which the language of the collective bargaining agreement clearly makes arbitrable, and, in any order directing arbitration, will specify the issue or issues which are appropriate for arbitration under the language of the collective bargaining agreement; and, where suit is brought under this

*50 A.B.A.J. 393 (1964).

section to enforce the award of an arbitrator, the court will grant enforcement only if, and to the extent that, the arbitrator has conformed to the jurisdictional area permissible under the controlling collective bargaining agreement.

A Note on Review of the Arbitrator's Award:

Two major problems are involved in deciding whether an arbitrator's award should be reviewed: whether he has decided an issue not governed by the agreement and whether he has made a mistake on the merits. By now it should be clear that the two issues may be interwoven. In *Torrington* the two issues seem to be inseparable.

One procedure to guard against arbitral mistake, suggested earlier (see p. 148), is the tentative award. Its utility is attested to by Sylvester Garrett in his presidential address during the Proceedings of the Seventeenth Annual Meeting of the National Academy of Arbitrators. Edgar Jones also recommends it in *Arbitration and the Dilemma of Possible Error,* 11 LAB. L. J. 1023 (1960).

Some few arbitral arrangements provide for internal appellate review, as do some trade associations. (For a brief description consult Dallas Jones and Russell Smith, *Management and Labor Appraisals and Criticisms of the Arbitration Process: A Report with Comments,* 62 MICH. L. REV. 1116 (1960). Apparently this procedure is little used.)

Torrington probably will embolden some to resort to the courts who otherwise might have been discouraged by the pulsating overtones of *Enterprise* that post-award review is to be minimal; indeed, to some *Enterprise* indicates that no serious court review is to be expected. That interpretation leaves the nagging question as to when the courts are to exercise their power to decide, at the least, whether a dispute is arbitrable. In fact, the courts have performed that task, in *Atkinson,* for example, as well as other cases preceding this note. That opinions on whether they have done the task well may differ is only to be expected. But given the *Warrior & Gulf* tests, my own view is that some courts have intervened too far and too vigorously and beyond their competence.

Some few believe that if court intrusion is to be minimized at the pre-arbitration stage, then the courts must redeem their responsibility to supervise this process at the post-award stage, at least to insure that a party has not been required to arbitrate something he never agreed to arbitrate. Professor Wellington argues for this in his *Judicial Review of the Promise to Arbit-*

rate, 37 N.Y.U.L. REV. 471 (1962), where he suggests:

> serious judicial review of whether the parties agreed to arbitrate the particular dispute in a post-arbitration proceeding. This does not mean, of course, that the court will examine the question *de novo.* It does mean that the arbitrator must be required to write a reasoned and unambiguous opinion. It does mean that the court will review the arbitrator's award to determine whether it is reasonable in light of the language and purpose of the collective bargaining agreement and the common law of the enterprise as revealed in the opinion of the arbitrator.

Of course, the proposal poses some difficulties. In many cases, there is no transcript because the parties did not wish to incur the expense. There are no pleadings to speak of. The record then must often consist of the collective agreement and the arbitrator's opinion. Wellington indicates that it is in the logic of the arbitrator's "reasoned and unambiguous opinion" that a court is to discover whether he has gone beyond his charter.

One need not agree with Mr. Justice Douglas' expressed fear that requiring a persuasive arbitral opinion may frighten arbitrators out of writing any to see some difficulties with the suggestion.

The arbitrator's opinion is written for the parties. Professor Wellington would have them written for the court. One does not have to suspect arbitrators of hypocrisy to observe that the two messages may be dissimilar. Reasoning that may assuage the judicial mind may sound alien and unwelcome to the parties. Whereas some things are better left unsaid if the parties are to live together in harmony, arbitrators may be forced to be more explicit. (We have seen the often baleful effects upon NLRB Trial Examiners' intermediate reports of the need to explain and justify in detail their conclusions.)

Nor is logic the heart of the arbitrators' art. Informed judgment is what the parties want, and although that should be amenable to logical explication, logic often is quite unnecessary for the parties' purposes. And, indeed, the judgment may defy adequate explanation. For example, one arbitrator could say that "In this industry among parties of the sophistication and bargaining history of these parties a custom becomes part of the collective agreement and stays part of it until it is explicitly negotiated out." Coming from an arbitrator of the experience of the arbitrator in *Torrington,* who had decided cases between the same parties, that might strike many as quite enough. Equally, another arbitrator might observe that "Custom is a ticklish thing in this

industry and lasts only until the employer disowns it. That's the way it's done in this business." Logic, reason and lack of ambiguity do not have much to do with it unless the courts are to write a set of rules of contract for collective agreements, which is what the majority in *Torrington* seems to have set about.

Finally, ambiguity is at the heart of some arbitrator's art. As with some musicals of questionable artistic depth, most of the audience leaves happy and humming. Must we insist that at least the losers leave utterly enlightened and chastened? On occasion the arbitrator's job is to let the loser down easily, sometimes implying that he had a much better case than he had. An opinion with such a goal is not easily compatible with one whose spanking logic will show the court that the loser's argument on arbitrability was beneath contempt.

Aside from the American Bar Association Labor Section's 1964 resolution (*supra*), there seems to be little support for rigorous review of awards even on the issue of arbitrability.

Some observers feel that the courts will refuse enforcement to awards infected by egregious error while generally eschewing post-arbitral review.

Dallas Jones and Russell Smith observe (*op. cit.,* at 1121–1122):

> It seems obvious, however, that the commonly accepted values of the arbitration process will apply inversely with the extent of resort to the courts to avoid either the use or the results of the process. This is not to say that the courts should not be available—indeed, under our law they must be—to prevent assumptions of authority by the arbitrator which the parties clearly intended to withhold from him. But we seriously question whether the risk of improvident, unsound, or insupportable decisions, either in issues of arbitral authority or on the merits of the issue of contract interpretation or application—and such risk there undoubtedly is—should be "remedied" through increased availability of resort to the courts, at least as our judicial system is now constructed in relation to such questions.

LOCAL 133, UNITED AUTO WORKERS v. FAFNIR BEARING CO.
151 Conn. 650, 201 A. 2d 656 (1964)

Plaintiff union moved to vacate an award on the grounds that the arbitrator either exceeded his powers or so imperfectly executed them that a final and definite award was not made. Defendant company cross-applied for confirmation or modification or correction and confirmation of the resulting award. The submission posed two questions: (1) "Did the company violate the agreement [by described conduct]?" and "If so, to what remedy are these employees entitled?" The arbitrator's award read: "Grievance No. 62–96 is denied." The trial court admitted the arbitrator's opinion and corrected the award by adding: "The answer to Question No. 1 as submitted is 'No'."

> Under the circumstances, and even without an examination of the arbitrator's memorandum of decision, there can be no doubt as to the meaning of the language of the award that "Grievance No. 62–96 is denied." We conclude that the modification was proper. It was simply the addition of clarifying language to state expressly what was already obvious. The addition was merely technical and formal in nature.
>
> There was no error in the ruling of the court admitting as an exhibit the arbitration decision. It is true that the award rather than the finding and conclusions of fact controls and, ordinarily, the memorandum of an arbitrator is irrelevant. American Brass Co. v. Torrington Brass Workers' Union, 141 Conn. 514, 522, 107 A. 2d 255 (1954); Von Langendorff v. Riordan, 147 Conn. 524, 527, 163 A. 2d 100 (1960). There is no legal doctrine, however, which dictates the exclusion of an arbitrator's opinion or which forbids its examination in the determination whether an award should be corrected under § 52–419 or whether an arbitrator in his award has demonstrated infidelity to his obligation.

AMERICAN BOSCH ARMA CORP. v. LOCAL 794, INT'L UNION OF ELECTRICAL WORKERS
243 F. Supp. 493 (N.D. Miss. E.D. 1965)

[A grievance sought pay for thirteen employees alleged to have been improperly kept from working on specified assembly line work on June 4, 1964. The arbitrator's opinion restated the claim (including the date); his award granted the relief sought for a denial of the work on June 5, 1964. The employer's motion to vacate was denied.]

It is quite true that the formal language of the grievance as filed did not make a specific claim for pay for June 5, 1964, the day for which the arbitrator ordered pay for the complaining workers. But, it has never been required that grievances be submitted in language comparable to that used in formal court proceedings. Even if this were true, the addition of the lawyer's crutch "on or about" would have made this particular grievance not only acceptable lawyer-wise, but also broad enough to cover the specific award of pay for the day next following June 4, 1964.

It has never been the proper function of courts in cases such as this to look over the shoulder of an arbitrator and relitigate in detail all or any of the issues properly submitted to him for his decision under such a contract as the one here. Even the case upon which the plaintiff company places its greatest reliance does not say so. In Kansas City Luggage & Novelty Workers Union, etc. v. Neevel Luggage Manufacturing Company, Inc., 325 F. 2d 992 (8th Cir. 1964), a grievance was submitted for arbitration on the question of whether or not the lay-off of certain employees was improper under the terms of the contract. *No question of pay or back pay was included in this submission.* The arbitrator found that the lay-offs were improper and then entered an award not only ordering the employees reinstated but also ordering certain back pay for the time lost. The company sought a rehearing before the arbitrator, which was refused, and the matter was submitted to the United States District Court for the Western District of Missouri on the petition of the union to enforce the arbitrator's award. The district court refused to enforce the award with respect to back pay, stating that it was not based upon the grievance and granted as to this the employer's motion for summary judgment. The Court of Appeals affirmed the judgment of the district court, saying, *inter alia*:

> [I]t is true, as the trial court said, that the back pay issue was not specifically or necessarily included in the subject matter submitted to arbitration.
>
> It is the law that "arbitration is a matter of contract and a party cannot be required to submit to arbitration any dispute which he has not agreed so to submit."

That court also said:

> In our opinion, this does not mean that every arbitration award may be subjected to an exhaustive postmortem in the hope of salvaging for further controversy some subsidiary question of no controlling practical consequence, it if was not specifically included in the problem as it was submitted to the arbitrator for determination. Whether the post-award back pay question raised by the Company in this case actually merits or requires that that portion of the award be not enforced may be questionable.

In the case here, the basic underlying purpose of the grievance was pay for a time when the workers claimed that work was available and that the company had wrongfully declined to give them employment for eight hours. The very basis of the submission to the arbitrator was to determine what pay, if any, was owed to the complaining employees. He decided that they were due eight hours pay for June 5, 1964, rather than the date mentioned in the protesting part of the grievance of June 4, 1964. Hence, *Kansas City Luggage* has no factual application here.

The union and company agreed to submit to arbitration the question whether the company violated the collective agreement's seniority provisions in recalling employees after a strike. The arbitrator ruled that it had. His opinion noted that the agreement's seniority provisions "extend over several pages ... there are no specific provisions relating to order of recalling employees after strikes." The company resisted enforcement of the award and asked summary judgment on the ground that the arbitrator's award was outside the scope of the issues submitted. The court rejected that contention, observing that the provisions for recall after a "curtailment" might have been the basis for the arbitrator's conclusion and that such an application (or interpretation) of "curtailment" would sustain the award even if the court disagreed with it.

The parties had agreed to work out the amounts of back pay due but had not done so. The union asked the court to make the findings and computations in regard to back pay, but the court ordered the parties to "complete the arbitration," thereby assigning the arbitrator a task beyond that specified in the parties' submission. Great Falls Mill Union v. Anaconda Co., (Mont. 1966) 260 F. Supp. 445. What alternatives were there?

In O'Malley v. Petroleum Maintenance Co., 48 Cal. 2d 107, 308 P. 2d 9 (1957), a lower court had ordered arbitration on the merits of a disputed discharge, after which the parties entered into a submission agreement. That agreement submitted two issues: (1) whether the dispute over the discharge was arbitrable and (2) the merits of that dispute. A majority of the arbitrators held that because of the lower court's order the discharge was arbitrable, although they would not have found it so on the basis of the parties' contract. Motion to confirm award ordering the dischargee's reinstatement granted. The arbitrators did not exceed their powers even if they decided the arbitrability issue erroneously. That issue having been submitted to the arbitrators, the merits of the arbitrator's award is not subject to judicial review. The dissent characterized the arbitrators' action as an imperfect exercise of their power; the arbitrators did not decide the arbitrability issue on its own merits but proceeded on the erroneous belief that the original court order precluded their inquiry into that issue.

F.

The Interrelation of Sections 301 and 303

OLD DUTCH FARMS, INC. v. MILK DRIVERS UNION No. 584
359 F. 2d 598 (2d Cir. 1966)

MOORE, C. J. The appellee, Milk Drivers and Dairy Employees Local Union No. 584 (the union), is the collective bargaining representative for employees working in the New York metropolitan area milk industry. The union and the appellant, Old Dutch Farms, Inc. (the employer), were parties to an industry-wide collective bargaining agreement. In December 1962, a dispute arose between the employer and the union concerning whether the employer, by opening a milk "depot" in Brooklyn for the retail sale of milk and milk products, had violated Section 66A of the collective bargaining agreement. This dispute was submitted to arbitration in the spring of 1963 pursuant to arbitration procedures pro-

vided for in the collective agreement. Subsequently, in May 1963, the union proceeded to induce employees of a neutral employer (a supplier of Old Dutch Farms, Inc.) to engage in work stoppages, and to threaten such employer, in an effort to cause such employer to cease doing business with Old Dutch Farms, Inc. Thereafter, Old Dutch Farms, Inc. filed a petition with the National Labor Relations Board (the NLRB) alleging that the union was engaged in unlawful secondary activity. On October 9, 1963, the NLRB held that the union had violated Section 8 (b) (4) (i) & (ii) (B) of the Labor Management Relations Act (the LMRA), 29 U.S.C.A. § 158(b) (4) (i) & (ii) (B), 146 N.L.R.B. 509 (1964), and its decision was enforced by this court in January 1965. NLRB v. Milk Drivers & Dairy Employees Local Union No. 584, 341 F. 2d 29 (2d Cir. 1965).

In March 1965 the employer commenced the present action in the United States District Court for the Eastern District of New York, pursuant to Section 303[1] to collect damages for business injuries sustained as a result of the union's allegedly unlawful activity. The union made a motion to stay all proceedings in the action pending arbitration of the damage claim on the ground that the disputes came within the purview of the general arbitration clause contained in the collective agreement. The arbitration clause provided that

> any and all disputes and controversies arising under or in connection with the terms and provisions of this agreement, or in connection with or relating to the application or interpretation of any of the terms or provisions hereof, or in respect to anything not herein, expressly provided but germane to the subject matter of this agreement . . . shall be submitted for arbitration to an arbitrator.

The trial court granted the motion finding that the employer's statutory action presented a controversy which was "within the inclusive description of the arbitrable disputes," 243 F. Supp. 246, 247, set forth in the arbitration clause and concluded that "the dispute . . . arises out of the contract relation not only because it centred on the 'depot' clause in the contract, but also because Section 17 contained a no-strike clause which forbade the Union to 'call . . . any sympathetic strike of its members'" 243 F. Supp. 246, 248. We reverse on the ground that the employer is not precluded by the arbitration clause in the parties' collective agreement from asserting in the district court a claim for tort damages based on the alleged unlawful secondary activity of the union and forced to rely upon arbitration for relief.

It is well established that whether an employer is required to arbitrate, as well as what issues he must arbitrate, "is a matter to be determined by the Court on the basis of the contract entered into by the parties." Atkinson v. Sinclair Refining Co., 370 U.S. 238, 241, 82 S. Ct. 1318, 1320, 8 L.Ed. 2d 462 (1962). Moreover, an employer "cannot be required to submit to arbitration any

dispute which he has not agreed so to submit." United Steelworkers of America v. Warrior & Gulf Nav. Co., 363 U.S. 574, 582, 80 S. Ct. 1347, 1353, 4 L. Ed. 2d 1409 (1960); see John Wiley & Sons v. Livingston, 376 U.S. 543, 547, 84 S. Ct. 909, 11 L. Ed. 2d 898 (1964). Thus, the principal issue raised by this appeal is whether the employer's tort damage claim constitutes an arbitrable issue within the meaning of the broad arbitration clause contained in the parties' collective bargaining agreement.[2]

This action arises under Section 303(a) and (b). It is in no way based on an alleged breach of contract and neither invokes nor needs to invoke the contract. The employer asserts that it was "injured in its business or property" and seeks damages solely for the injuries caused by the union's allegedly unlawful activity. Both the union and the district court maintain, however, that the employer's tort damage claim is an arbitrable dispute on the ground that it is connected with and "germane to the subject matter of" the collective agreement. Their theory is that the dispute is intimately related to Section 66A of the collective agreement since the business injury which forms the basis for the employer's Section 303 damage claim was caused by union activity which was originally provoked by an alleged breach of that section. They argue that since the union's secondary activity constituted a response to an alleged breach of contract by the employer, the damage claim is inextricably connected with the interpretation of the contract provision which it allegedly violated. But, this action bears no meaningful connection with the terms, conditions or subject matter of the parties' collective bargaining agreement. The fact that the union activity which forms the basis for this Section 303 damage suit was provoked by an alleged breach of contract by the employer is no reason to conclude that this suit arises under or is connected with the interpretation of the collective agreement within the meaning of the arbitration clause. This is so, not only because this suit rests solely on Section 303 and cannot be considered as a contract claim[3] but, more significantly, because

1. § 303 of the LMRA, 29 U.S.C. § 187 provides:
(a) It shall be unlawful, for the purpose of this section only, in an industry or activity affecting commerce, for any labor organization to engage in any activity or conduct defined as an unfair labor practice in section 8 (b) (4) of the National Labor Relations Act, as amended.
(b) Whoever shall be injured in his business or property by reason of any violation of subsection (a) may sue therefor in any district court of the United States subject to the limitations and provisions of Section 301 hereof without respect to the amount in controversy, or in any other court having jurisdiction of the parties, and shall recover the damages by him sustained and the cost of the suit.

2 It should be noted that the present suit constitutes a special case under § 303 in that there is a contractual relationship between the parties to the suit. § 303 provides an employer with a federal right to sue any union that damages him by engaging in activity proscribed by § 8 (b) (4) irrespective of whether a contractual relationship exists between them.
3. Judge Dooling's partial reliance on the no-strike clause in the parties' collective agreement to support his conclusion that the present action arose under the contract is erroneous. 243 F. Supp. 246, 248 (E.D.N.Y. 1965). This action is not based in any way on an alleged violation of that clause by the union or, for that matter, on any violation of the contract by the union.

whether or not the employer violated Section 66A of the collective agreement has no bearing on the validity of the Section 303 suit and the determination of the issues it presents, *viz.,* whether the union violated Section 8(b) (4) of NLRA and whether and to what extent the employer sustained actual damages as a result of the union activity. Quite apart from the agreement and its arbitration clause, the present action arises under the terms and conditions of specific federal labor statutes, *i.e.,* Section 303 of the LMRA and Section 8(b) (4) of the NLRA and is concerned only with their interpretation and application. Moreover, nothing in the broad arbitration clause involved here commits to arbitration disputes which are unrelated to the interpretation of particular provisions of the collective agreement or to the subject matter of the agreement. It cannot be said that the present dispute is germane, *i.e.,* relevant, see *Webster's New International Dictionary* (2d ed. 1961), to the subject matter of the collective agreement for there is no indication either in the record or in the contract itself that the subject of tort damages suffered by either party to the contract ever was discussed or referred to by the parties when they negotiated their industrial code. Reason dictates that for a dispute to be characterized as germane to the subject matter of the contract it must at the very least raise some issue, the resolution of which requires a reference to, or construction of, some portion of the contract involved. Thus, "whatever other effect the agreement to arbitrate may have had, the agreement did not even suggest that the question of violation (or not) of § 303 was arbitrable." United States Steel Corp. v. Seafarers' International Union, 237 F. Supp. 529, 532 (E.D. Pa. 1965). In *Seafarers' International Union, supra,* the court in like manner dismissed a motion to stay a Section 303 damage claim pending arbitration, although it was admittedly confronted with a narrower arbitration clause than the one involved here. There the union argued that the employer's Section 303 damage claim should be submitted to arbitration on the basis of an arbitration clause which provided that "any alleged violations or disputes arising under this Agreement" shall be submitted to an arbitrator. The court concluded that the Section 303 action was not embraced in the arbitration agreement and, thus, refused to order arbitration pointing out that "parties cannot be compelled to go to arbitration on issues which they have not agreed to submit to arbitration." *Id.* at 532. See Twin

Excavating Co. v. Local Union No. 731, 337 F. 2d 437 (7th Cir. 1964).[4]

There is a strong national labor policy favoring arbitration as a means of resolving disputes between parties to collective bargaining agreements concerning the interpretation or application of those agreements and, as a result, arbitration clauses that relate to such disputes should be liberally construed. *E.g.,* United Steelworkers of America v. Warrior & Gulf Nav. Co., *supra ;* see Smith & Jones, *The Supreme Court and Labor Dispute Arbitration. The Emerging Federal Law,* 63 Mich. L. Rev. 751 (1965); cf. Section 203(d) of the LMRA, 29 U.S.C. § 173(d). Contrary to the union's position, however, such principles do not have any direct bearing on the issue presented here since they were formulated in the context of actions arising under Section 301(a), which authorizes suits for the violation of collective bargaining contracts, 29 U.S.C. § 185(a), and pertain to the desirability of *contract* arbitration as a means for insuring industrial peace. The interpretation and application of the terms of a collective bargaining agreement is a function that traditionally has been considered to be within the peculiar province of labor arbitrators and, therefore, it is reasonable to presume that when parties to a collective agreement insert a broad arbitration clause in it, they intend all disputes which require performance of that function to be determined by an arbitrator, unless they specifically exclude them from arbitration. Such reasoning, however, does not apply with equal force to suits, like the present one, which arise under Section 303 since the issues raised in such a proceeding are the kind which have traditionally been determined by courts and concern matters to which the expertise of labor arbitrators does not necessarily extend.

The resolution of the present controversy requires (1) a determination of whether the union

---

4. In *Twin Excavating Co.,* the Seventh Circuit affirmed the denial of a motion to stay a § 303 suit pending arbitration. The rationale of the court, however, does not clearly emerge from its two-page opinion. On one hand, the court raised serious questions about the validity of the arbitration clause in the collective agreement invoked by the union and, thus, its comments with respect to the arbitrability of § 303 claims can justifiably be treated as dictum. On the other hand, the decision can be construed as saying that the usual arbitration clause contained in collective agreements is not broad enough to encompass an action under § 303, for the court stated the issue before it as whether the LMRA "contemplated an arbitration proceeding as a substitute for a court hearing in a suit for damages under § 303," *id.* at 438, and the arbitration clause before the court provided only that all the conditions and articles of the collective agreement were to be enforced by a committee selected by the parties to the contract.

violated Section 8(b) (4) of the NLRA, and (2) an assessment of the actual business injuries sustained by the employer. Courts hardly can be considered less competent than a labor arbitrator, whose forte is more likely to be in the area of contract disputes and "employee's grievance claims," . . . Drake Bakeries v. Local 50, 370 U.S. 254, 267, 82 S. Ct. 1346, 8 L. Ed. 2d 474 (1962) (Harlan, J., dissenting), to determine whether particular union activities violate a federal labor statute or to assess the extent of an employer's business injuries. See Fleming, *Arbitrators and the Remedy Power*, 48 VA. L. REV. 1199, 1220 (1962). Thus, there is no special reason to presume that the parties to a collective bargaining contract desire to submit to an arbitrator disputes concerned with an employer's statutory right to recover damages caused by specific union unfair labor practices which is entirely separate from any right conferred on him by Section 301, see United Const. Workers, etc. v. Laburnum Const. Corp., 347 U.S. 656, 667, 74 S. Ct. 883, 98, L. Ed. 1025 (1954) ; 2 LEGIS. HISTORY OF THE MANAGEMENT RELATIONS ACT OF 1947, 1371 (1948). "The less so, from the standpoint of the employer, when it is recognized that any damages awarded by an arbitrator would not be self-enforcing." Drake Bakeries v. Local 50, *supra*, 370 U.S. at 268, 82 S. Ct. at 1354 (Harlan, J., dissenting). This leads to the conclusion that absent a clear, explicit statement in the collective bargaining contract directing an arbitrator to hear and determine the validity of tort damage claims by one party against another, it must be assumed that the employer did not intend to forego his rights under Section 303 and that the parties did not intend to withdraw such disputes from judicial scrutiny.

The Supreme Court's decision in Drake Bakeries v. Local 50, 370 U.S. 254, 82 S. Ct. 1346 (1962), holding that a claim for damages based on a breach of a no-strike provision in a collective bargaining agreement under Section 301 should be submitted to arbitration does not suggest a contrary result. Although as a result of that decision the arbitrator may be called on to assess contract damages (assuming he finds that the parties intended to delegate that function to him), the primary question submitted to the arbitrator in *Drake Bakeries* was whether the strike activity on the part of the union violated a no-strike provision in the collective bargaining contract—a question which the Court stated "appears to us to be one particularly suited for arbitration." *Id*. at 266, 82 S. Ct. at 1353. In other words, whether the employer was entitled to contract damages turned on a question of contract interpretation which "was peculiarly within the expertise of an arbitrator." Smith & Jones, *supra*, at 767. By direct contrast, the present suit under Section 303 does not raise any question of contract interpretation which can be characterized as particularly suited for arbitration. Rather, the validity of the employer's claim for tort damages turns solely on issues which are particularly suited for judicial adjudication.

Since nothing in the record or collective agreement involved here provides a basis for finding that the employer and the union agreed to submit the employer's damage claim to an arbitrator, we reverse the decision of the district court.

G.
"Successor" Employers — and "Procedural Arbitrability"

JOHN WILEY & SONS v. LIVINGSTON
The Court. 376 U.S. 543 (1964)

HARLAN, J. This is an action by a union, pursuant to § 301 of the Labor Management Relations Act, 61 Stat. 136, 156, 29 U.S.C. § 185, to compel arbitration under a collective bargaining agreement. The major questions presented are (1) whether a corporate employer must arbitrate with a union under a bargaining agreement between the union and another corporation which has merged with the employer, and, if so, (2) whether the courts or the arbitrator is the appropriate body to decide whether procedural prerequisites which, under the bargaining agreement, condition the duty to arbitrate have been met. Because of the importance of both questions to the realization of national labor policy, we granted certiorari (378 U.S. 908) to review a judgment of the Court of Appeals directing arbitration (313 F. 2d 52), in reversal of the District Court which had refused such relief (203 F. Supp. 171). We affirm the judgment below, but, with respect to the first question above, on grounds which may differ from those of the Court of Appeals, whose answer to that question is unclear.

I.

District 65, Retail, Wholesale and Department Store Union, AFL–CIO, entered into a collective bargaining agreement with Interscience Publishers, Inc., a publishing firm, for a term expiring on January 31, 1962. The agreement did not contain an express provision making it binding on successors of Interscience. On October 2, 1961, Interscience merged with the petitioner, John Wiley & Sons, Inc., another publishing firm, and ceased to do business as a separate entity. There is no suggestion that the merger was not for genuine business reasons.

At the time of the merger Interscience had about 80 employees, of whom 40 were represented by this Union. It had a single plant in New York City, and did an annual business of somewhat over $1,000,000. Wiley was a much larger concern, having separate office and warehouse facilities and about 300 employees, and doing an annual business of more than $9,000,000. None of Wiley's employees was represented by a union.

In discussions before and after the merger, the Union and Interscience (later Wiley) were unable to agree on the effect of the merger on the collective bargaining agreement and on the rights under it of those covered employees hired by Wiley. The Union's position was that despite the merger it continued to represent the covered Interscience employees taken over by Wiley, and that Wiley was obligated to recognize certain rights of such employees which had "vested" under the Interscience bargaining agreement. Such rights, more fully described below, concerned matters typically covered by collective bargaining agreements, such as seniority status, severance pay, etc. The Union contended also that Wiley was required to make certain pension fund payments called for under the Interscience bargaining agreement.

Wiley, though recognizing for purposes of its own pension plan the Interscience service of the former Interscience employees, asserted that the merger terminated the bargaining agreement for all purposes. It refused to recognize the Union as bargaining agent or to accede to the Union's claims on behalf of Interscience employees. All such employees, except a few who ended their Wiley employment with severance pay and for whom no rights are asserted here, continued in Wiley's employ.

No satisfactory solution having been reached, the Union, one week before the expiration date of the Interscience bargaining agreement, commenced this action to compel arbitration.

II.

The threshold question in this controversy is who shall decide whether the arbitration provisions of the collective bargaining agreement survived the Wiley-Interscience merger, so as to be operative against Wiley. Both parties urge that this question is for the courts. Past cases leave no doubt that this is correct.[1] "Under our decisions, whether or not the company was bound to arbitrate, as well as what issues it must arbitrate, is a matter to be determined by the Court on the basis of the contract entered into by the parties." Atkinson v. Sinclair Refining Co., 370 U.S. 238, 241. Accord, e.g., United Steelworkers v. Warrior & Gulf Navigation Co., 363 U.S. 574, 582. The problem in those cases was whether an employer, concededly party to and bound by a contract which contained an arbitration provision, had agreed to arbitrate disputes of a particular kind. Here, the question is whether Wiley, which did not itself sign the collective bargaining agreement on which the Union's claim to arbitration depends, is bound at all by the agreement's arbitration provision. The reason requiring the courts to determine the issue is the same in both situations. The duty to arbitrate being of contractual origin, a compulsory submission to arbitration cannot precede judicial determination that the collective bargaining agreement does in fact create such a duty. Thus, just as an employer has no obligation to arbitrate issues which it has not agreed to arbitrate, so a fortiori, it cannot be compelled to arbitrate if an arbitration clause does not bind it at all.

The unanimity of views about who should

---

1. Wiley argues that the Court of Appeals decided that the effect of the merger on the obligation to arbitrate was a question for the arbitrator. The opinion below is unclear. It first states that "the question of 'substantive arbitrability' is for the court not for the arbitrator to decide." 313 F. 2d, at 55. At another point, it says: "We merely hold that, as we interpret the collective bargaining agreement before us in the light of Supreme Court decisions enunciating the federal policy of promoting industrial peace and stability, especially with reference to arbitration procedures set up in collective bargaining agreements, we cannot say that it was intended that this consolidation should preclude this Union from proceeding to arbitration to determine the effect of the consolidation on the contract and on the rights of the employees arising under the contract." 313 F. 2d, at 56–57. Elsewhere, however, the opinion states: ". . . [W]e think and hold . . . that it is not too much to expect and require that this employer proceed to arbitration with the representatives of the Union to determine whether the obligation to arbitrate regarding the substantive terms of the contract survived the consolidation on October 2, 1961, and, if so, just what employee rights, if any, survived the consolidation." 313 F. 2d, at 57 (footnote omitted). Judge Kaufman, concurring separately, plainly thought that the court had left to the arbitrator the question of whether Wiley was obligated to arbitrate at all. 313 F. 2d, at 65, 66.

decide the question of arbitrability does not, however, presage the parties' accord about what is the correct decision. Wiley, objecting to arbitration, argues that it never was a party to the collective bargaining agreement, and that, in any event, the Union lost its status as representative of the former Interscience employees when they were mingled in a larger Wiley unit of employees. The Union argues that Wiley, as successor to Interscience, is bound by the latter's agreement, at least sufficiently to require it to arbitrate. The Union relies on § 90 of the N.Y. Stock Corporation Law, which provides, among other things, that no "claim or demand for any cause" against a constituent corporation shall be extinguished by a consolidation.[2] Alternatively, the Union argues that, apart from § 90, federal law requires that arbitration go forward, lest the policy favoring arbitration frequently be undermined by changes in corporate organization.

Federal law, fashioned "from the policy of our national labor laws," controls. Textile Workers Union v. Lincoln Mills, 353 U.S. 448, 456. State law may be utilized so far as it is of aid in the development of correct principles or their application in a particular case, id., at 457, but the law which ultimately results is federal. We hold that the disappearance by merger of a corporate employer which has entered into a collective bargaining agreement with a union does not automatically terminate all rights of the employees covered by the agreement, and that, in appropriate circumstances, present here, the successor employer may be required to arbitrate with the union under the agreement.

This Court has in the past recognized the central role of arbitration in effectuating national labor policy. Thus, in *Warrior & Gulf Navigation Co., supra,* at 578, arbit-

ration was described as "the substitute for industrial strife," and as "part and parcel of the collective bargaining process itself." It would derogate from "the federal policy of settling labor disputes by arbitration," United Steelworkers v. Enterprise Wheel & Car Corp., 363 U.S. 593, 596, if a change in the corporate structure or ownership of a business enterprise had the automatic consequence of removing a duty to arbitrate previously established; this is so as much in cases like the present, where contracting employer disappears into another by merger, as in those in which one owner replaces another but the business entity remains the same.

Employees, and the union which represents them, ordinarily do not take part in negotiations leading to a change in corporate ownership. The negotiations will ordinarily not concern the well-being of the employees, whose advantage or disadvantage, potentially great, will inevitably be incidental to the main considerations. The objectives of national labor policy, reflected in established principles of federal law, require that the rightful prerogative of owners independently to rearrange their businesses and even eliminate themselves as employers be balanced by some protection to the employees from a sudden change in the employment relationship. The transition from one corporate organization to another will in most cases be eased and industrial strife avoided if employees' claims continue to be resolved by arbitration rather than by "the relative strength . . . of the contending forces," *Warrior & Gulf, supra,* at 580.

The preference of national labor policy for arbitration as a substitute for tests of strength between contending forces could be overcome only if other considerations compellingly so demanded. We find none. While the principles of law governing ordinary contracts would not bind to a contract an unconsenting successor to a contracting party,[3] a collective bargaining agreement is not an ordinary contract. "[I]t is generalized code to govern a myriad of cases which the draftsmen cannot wholly anticipate . . . . The collective agreement covers the whole employment relationship. It calls into being a new common law—the common law of a particular industry or of a particular plant." *Warrior & Gulf, supra* at 578–579 (footnotes omitted). Central to the peculiar status and function of a collective bargaining agreement is the fact, dictated both by circumstance, see *id.,* at 580, and

---

2. "The rights of creditors of any constituent corporation shall not in any manner be impaired, nor shall any liability or obligation due or to become due, or any claim or demand for any cause existing against any such corporation or against any stockholder thereof be released or impaired by any such consolidation; but such consolidated corporation shall be deemed to have assumed and shall be liable for all liabilities and obligations of each of the corporations consolidated in the same manner as if such consolidated corporation had itself incurred such liabilities or obligations. The stockholders of the respective constituent corporations shall continue subject to all the liabilities, claims and demands existing against them as such, at or before the consolidation; and no action or proceeding then pending before any court or tribunal in which any constituent corporation is a party, or in which any such stockholder is a party, shall abate or be discontinued by reason of such consolidation, but may be prosecuted to final judgment, as though no consolidation had been entered into; or such consolidated corporation may be substituted as a party in place of any constituent corporation, by order of the court in which such action or proceeding may be pending."

3. But cf. the general rule that in the case of a merger the corporation which survives is liable for the debts and contracts of the one which disappears. 15 FLETCHER, PRIVATE CORPORATIONS (1961 rev. ed.), § 7121.

by the requirements of the National Labor Relations Act, that it is not in any real sense the simple product of a consensual relationship. Therefore, although the duty to arbitrate, as we have said, *supra,* pp. 546–547, must be founded on a contract, the impressive policy considerations favoring arbitration are not wholly overborne by the fact that Wiley did not sign the contract being construed.[4] This case cannot readily be assimilated to the category of those in which there is no contract whatever, or none which is reasonably related to the party sought to be obligated. There was a contract, and Interscience, Wiley's predecessor, was party to it. We thus find Wiley's obligation to arbitrate this dispute in the Interscience contract construed in the context of a national labor policy.

We do not hold that in every case in which the ownership or corporate structure of an enterprise is changed the duty to arbitrate survives. As indicated above, there may be cases in which the lack of any substantial continuity of identity in the business enterprise before and after a change would make a duty to arbitrate something imposed from without, not reasonably to be found in the particular bargaining agreement and the acts of the parties involved. So too, we do not rule out the possibility that a union might abandon its right to arbitration by failing to make its claims known. Neither of these situations is before the Court. Although Wiley was substantially larger than Interscience, relevant similarity and continuity of operation across the change in ownership is adequately evidenced by the wholesale transfer of Interscience employees to the Wiley plant, apparently without difficulty. The Union made its position known well before the merger and never departed from it. In addition, we do not suggest any view on the questions surrounding a certified union's claim to continued representative status following a change in ownership. See, *e.g.,* Labor Board v. Aluminum Tubular Corp., 299 F. 2d 595, 598–600 ; Labor Board v. McFarland, 306 F. 2d 219 ; Cruse Motors, Inc., 105 N.L.R.B. 242, 247. This Union does not assert that it has any bargaining rights independent of the Interscience agreement ; it seeks to arbitrate claims based on that ageement, now expired, not to negotiate a new agreement.[5]

---

4. Compare the principle that when a contract is scrutinized for evidence of an intention to arbitrate a particular kind of dispute, *national labor policy* requires, within reason, that "an interpretation that covers the asserted dispute," *Warrior & Gulf, supra,* pp. 582–583, be favored.

5. The fact that the Union does not represent a majority of an appropriate bargaining unit in Wiley does not prevent it from representing those employees who are covered by the agreement which is in dispute and out of which Wiley's duty to arbitrate arises. Retail Clerks Int'l Assn., Local

III.

Beyond denying its obligation to arbitrate at all, Wiley urges that the Union's grievances are not within the scope of the arbitration clause. The issues which the Union sought to arbitrate, as set out in the complaint, are:

(a) Whether the seniority rights built up by the Interscience employees must be accorded to said employees now and after January 30, 1962.

(b) Whether, as part of the wage structure of the employees, the Company is under an obligation to continue to make contributions to District 65 Security Plan and District 65 Security Plan Pension Fund now and after January 30, 1962.

(c) Whether the job security and grievance provisions of the contract between the parties shall continue in full force and effect.

(d) Whether the Company must obligate itself to continue liable now and after January 30, 1962 as to severance pay under the contract.

(e) Whether the Company must obligate itself to continue liable now and after January 30, 1962 for vacation pay under the contract.

Section 16.0 of the collective bargaining agreement provides for arbitration as the final stage of grievance procedures which are stated to be the "sole means of obtaining adjustment" of "any differences, grievance or dispute between the Employer and the Union arising out of or relating to this agreement, or its interpretation or application, or enforcement." There are a number of specific exceptions to the coverage of the grievance procedures, none of which is applicable here.[6] Apart from them, the intended

---

Unions Nos. 128 & 633, v. Lion Dry Goods, Inc., 369 U.S. 17. There is no problem of conflict with another union, cf. L. B. Spear & Co., 106 N.L.R.B. 687, since Wiley had no contract with any union covering the unit of employees which received the former Interscience employees.

Problems might be created by an arbitral award which required Wiley to give special treatment to the former Interscience employees because of rights found to have accrued to them under the Interscience contract. But the mere possibility of such problems cannot cut off the Union's right to press the employees' claims in arbitration. While it would be premature at this stage to speculate on how to avoid such hypothetical problems, we have little doubt that within the flexible procedures of arbitration a solution can be reached which would avoid disturbing labor relations in the Wiley plant.

6. Section 16.5 provides:
"It is agreed that, in addition to other provisions elsewhere contained in this agreement which expressly deny arbitration to specific events, situations or contract provisions, the following matters shall not be subject to the arbitration provisions of this agreement:
"(1) the amendment or modification of the terms and provisions of this agreement;
"(2) salary or minimum wage rates as set forth herein;
"(3) matters not covered by this agreement; and
"(4) any dispute arising out of any question pertaining to the renewal or extension of this agreement."
Other provisions of the agreement "which expressly deny arbitration to specific events" are §§ 4.2, 4.4, 6.4.1, 14.4, 16.9.

wide breadth of the arbitration clause is reflected by § 16.9 of the agreement which provides, with an irrelevant exception:

> [T]he arbitration procedure herein set forth is the sole and exclusive remedy of the parties hereto and the employees covered hereby, for any claimed violations of this contract, and for any and all acts or omissions claimed to have been committed by either party during the term of this agreement, and such arbitration procedure shall be (except to enforce, vacate, or modify awards) in lieu of any and all other remedies, forums at law, in equity or otherwise which will or may be available to either of the parties.

All of the Union's grievances concern conditions of employment typically covered by collective bargaining agreements and submitted to arbitration if other grievance procedures fail. Specific provision for each of them is made in the Interscience agreement.[7] There is thus no question that had a dispute concerning any of these subjects, such as seniority rights or severance pay, arisen between the Union and Interscience prior to the merger, it would have been arbitrable. Wiley argues, however, that the Union's claims are plainly outside the scope of the arbitration clause: first, because the agreement did not embrace post-merger claims, and, second, because the claims relate to a period beyond the limited term of the agreement.

In all probability, the situation created by the merger was one not expressly contemplated by the Union or Interscience when the agreement was made in 1960. Fairly taken, however, the Union's demands collectively raise the question which underlies the whole litigation: What is the effect of the merger on the rights of covered employees? It would be inconsistent with our holding that the obligation to arbitrate survived the merger were we to hold that the fact of the merger, without more, removed claims otherwise plainly arbitrable from the scope of the arbitration clause.

It is true that the Union has framed its issues to claim rights not only "now"—after the merger but during the term of the agreement—but also after the agreement expired by its terms. Claimed rights during the term of the agreement, at least, are unquestionably within the arbitration clause; we do not understand Wiley to urge that the Union's claims to all such rights have become moot by reason of the expiration of the agree-ment.[8] As to claimed rights "after January 30, 1962," it is reasonable to read the claims as based solely on the Union's construction of the Interscience agreement in such a way that, had there been no merger, Interscience would have been required to discharge certain obligations notwithstanding the expiration of the agreement.[9] We see no reason why parties could not if they so chose agree to the accrual of rights during the term of an agreement and their realization after the agreement had expired. Of course, the Union may not use arbitration to acquire new rights against Wiley any more than it could have used arbitration to negotiate a new contract with Interscience, had the existing contract expired and renewal negotiations broken down.

Whether or not the Union's demands have merit will be determined by the arbitrator in light of the fully developed facts. It is sufficient for present purpose that the demands are not so plainly unreasonable that the subject matter of the dispute must be regarded as nonarbitrable because it can be seen in advance that no award to the Union could receive judicial sanction. See *Warrior & Gulf, supra,* at 582–583.

IV.

Wiley's final objection to arbitration raises the question of so-called "procedural arbitrability." The Interscience agreement provides for arbitration as the third stage of the grievance procedure. "Step 1" provides for "a conference between the affected employee, a Union Steward and the Employer, officer or exempt supervisory person in charge of his department." In "Step 2," the grievance is submitted to "a conference between an officer of the Employer, or the Employer's representative designated for that purpose, the Union Shop Committee and/or a representative of the Union." Arbitration is reached under "Step 3" "in the event that the grievance shall not have been resolved or settled in 'Step 2.'"[10] Wiley argues that since Steps 1 and 2 have not been followed, and since the duty to arbitrate arises only in Step 3, it has no

---

7. See Art. VI: Seniority; Art. XV: Welfare Security Benefits; Art. VII: Discharges and Lay-offs; Art. XXIII: Severance Pay; Art. XII: Vacations.

8. Wiley apparently concedes the possibility that a right to severance pay might accrue before the expiration of the contract but be payable "at some future date." Brief. p. 38.

9. Wiley apparently so construes at least part of one of the Union's claims. See note 8, *supra.*

10. All of these provisions are contained in § 16.0 of the Interscience agreement.

duty to arbitrate this dispute.[11] Specifically, Wiley urges that the question whether "procedural" conditions to arbitration have been met must be decided by the court and not the arbitrator.[12]

We think that labor disputes of the kind involved here cannot be broken down so easily into their "substantive" and "procedural" aspects. Questions concerning the procedural prerequisites to arbitration do not arise in a vacuum; they develop in the context of an actual dispute about the rights of the parties to the contract or those covered by it. In this case, for example, the Union argues that Wiley's consistent refusal to recognize the Union's representative status after the merger made it "utterly futile—and a little bit ridiculous to follow the grievance steps as set forth in the contract." Brief, p. 41. In addition, the Union argues that time limitations in the grievance procedure are not controlling because Wiley's violations of the bargaining agreement were "continuing." These arguments in response to Wiley's "procedural" claim are meaningless unless set in the background of the merger and the negotiations surrounding it.

Doubt whether grievance procedures or some part of them apply to a particular dispute, whether such procedures have been followed or excused, or whether the unexcused failure to follow them avoids the duty to arbitrate cannot ordinarily be answered without consideration of the merits of the dispute which is presented for arbitration. In this case, one's view of the Union's responses to Wiley's "procedural" arguments depends to a large extent on how one answers questions bearing on the basic issue, the effect of the merger; e.g., whether or not the merger was a possibility considered by Interscience and the Union during the negotiation of the contract. It would be a curious rule which required that

intertwined issues of "substance" and "procedure" growing out of a single dispute and raising the same questions on the same facts had to be carved up between two different forums, one deciding after the other. Neither logic nor considerations of policy compel such a result.

Once it is determined, as we have, that the parties are obligated to submit the subject matter of a dispute to arbitration, "procedural" questions which grow out of the dispute and bear on its final disposition should be left to the arbitrator. Even under a contrary rule, a court could deny arbitration only if it could confidently be said not only that a claim was strictly "procedural," and therefore within the purview of the court, but also that it should operate to bar arbitration altogether, and not merely limit or qualify an arbitral award. In view of the policies favoring arbitration and the parties' adoption of arbitration as the preferred means of settling disputes, such cases are likely to be rare indeed. In all other cases, those in which arbitration goes forward, the arbitrator would ordinarily remain free to reconsider the ground covered by the court insofar as it bore on the merits of the dispute, using the flexible approaches familiar to arbitration. Reservation of "procedural" issues for the courts would thus not only create the difficult task of separating related issues,. but would also produce frequent duplication of effort.

In addition, the opportunities for deliberate delay and the possibility of well-intentioned but no less serious delay created by separation of the "procedural" and "substantive" elements of a dispute are clear. While the courts have the task of determining "substantive arbitrability," there will be cases in which arbitrability of the subject matter is unquestioned but a dispute arises over the procedures to be followed. In all of such cases, acceptance of Wiley's position would produce the delay attendant upon judicial proceedings preliminary to arbitration. As this case, commenced in January 1962 and not yet committed to arbitration, well illustrates, such delay may entirely eliminate the prospect of a speedy arbitrated settlement of the dispute, to the disadvantage of the parties (who, in addition, will have to bear increased costs) and contrary to the aims of national labor policy.

No justification for such a generally undesirable result is to be found in a presumed intention of the parties. Refusal to order arbitration of subjects which the parties have not agreed to arbitrate does not entail the fractionating of disputes about subjects which the parties do wish to have submitted. Although a party may resist arbitration once a grievance has arisen, as does

---

11. In addition to the failure to follow the procedures of Steps 1 and 2, Wiley objects to the Union's asserted failure to comply with § 16.6, which provides:

Notice of any grievance must be filed with the Employer and with the Union Shop Steward within four (4) weeks after its occurrence or latest existence. The failure by either party to file the grievance within this time limitation shall be construed and be deemed to be an abandonment of the grievance.

12. The Courts of Appeals have disagreed on this issue. The First and Seventh Circuits have held that the courts determine whether procedural conditions to arbitration have been met. Boston Mutual Life Ins. Co. v. Insurance Agents' Int'l Union, 258 F. 2d 516; Brass & Copper Workers Federal Labor Union No. 19322 v. American Brass Co., 272 F. 2d 849. The Third, Fifth, and Sixth Circuits agree with the Second Circuit's decision in this case that the question of "procedural arbitrability" is for the arbitrator. Radio Corporation of America v. Association of Professional Engineering Personnel, 291 F. 2d 105; Deaton Truck Line, Inc., v. Local Union 612, 314 F. 2d 418; Local 748 v. Jefferson City Cabinet Co., 314 F. 2d 192.

Wiley here, we think it best accords with the usual purpose of an arbitration clause and with the policy behind federal labor law to regard procedural disagreements not as separate disputes but as aspects of the dispute which called the grievance procedures into play.

With the reservation indicated at the outset, the judgment of the Court of Appeals is

Affirmed.

MR. JUSTICE GOLDBERG took no part in the consideration or decision of this case.

The collective bargaining agreement provided for arbitration, and the pension agreement provided for an appeals procedure. These agreements expired after fruitless bargaining for new agreements. Thereafter the employer rejected employee claims for severance and vacation benefits under the collective agreements and benefits under the pension agreement. The union sought arbitration. Motion to compel arbitration granted; the rights asserted arose, if at all, under the expired agreements, and such rights are to be determined under the dispute procedures those agreements provide. The court referred to the benefits sought as "vested rights" but also noted that whether the claims were meritorious was for the arbitrator to decide. United Steelworkers of America v. H. K. Porter Co., Inc. (W. D. Pa. 1966) F. Supp. (64 LRRM 2201).

WACKENHUT CORP. v. LOCAL 151 UNITED PLANT GUARD WORKERS
(9th Cir. 1964) 332 F. 2d 954

The company purchased General Plant's business as an operating unit before the expiration date of the seller's collective agreement with the plaintiff union. The business was operated without noticeable change.]

There are statements in the opinion of the Supreme Court in *Wiley* which, considered separately, might appear to indicate that the fact that the change of employers had been accomplished by a merger, rather than by a sale and purchase of assets as in our case, was a controlling factor in reaching the result indicated. Reading the opinion as a whole, however, we are convinced that the Supreme Court did not rest the decision in *Wiley* on that narrow ground, but upon a broader view dictated by the policy of the national labor laws.

What the Supreme Court did in *Wiley* was to balance the rightful prerogative of owners independently to rearrange their businesses and even eliminate themselves as employers against the necessity of affording some protection to the employees covered by a collective bargaining agreement containing an arbitration clause, from a sudden change in the employment relationship. Having in view the objectives of national labor policy reflected in established principles of federal law, the court held the described interest of the employees outweighs that of the employer, and must prevail.

The specific rule which we derive from *Wiley* is that where there is substantial similarity of operation and continuity of identity of the business enterprise before and after a change in ownership, a collective bargaining agreement containing an arbitration provision, entered into by the predecessor employer is binding upon the successor employer.

In *Wiley* as in our case, the successor employer was substantially larger than the predecessor and there, as here, substantially all of the employees of the predecessor were accepted as employees of the successor. It follows that the observation made in *Wiley*, 376 U.S. at page 551, 84 S. Ct. at page 915, that

> relevant similarity and continuity of operation across the change in ownership is adequately evidenced by the wholesale transfer of Interscience employees to the Wiley plant, apparently without difficulty,

is equally applicable here. It follows that under the rule of *Wiley*, Wackenhut is bound by the collective bargaining agreement entered into by General Plant, and is bound thereunder to arbitrate the union grievances as ordered by the district court.

UNITED STEELWORKERS of AMERICA v. RELIANCE UNIVERSAL, INC.
(3d Cir. 1964) 335 F. 2d 891

[The predecessor sold its plant to the defendant under an FTC order to divest itself of the unit and sell it as a going concern. This was done before the expiration date of the plaintiff-union's collective agreement with the seller.]

In one respect the union's case here is stronger than in *Wiley*. There the plant was closed and its productive activity and some of its employees were absorbed in a pre-existing larger plant. Obviously, difficulties might be experienced in adapting plantwide commitments, which were appropriate for the closed plant to the situation of employees transferred to and integrated into the work force in another plant. Here, however, the problem does not exist because the original operation remained intact. However, the two cases are different in another detail which, in the new employer's view, should make the *Wiley* case inapplicable here. *Wiley* was a merger case. In the present case the plant was sold as a going concern. Appellee argues that a merger is a sort of succession in which it is more reasonable to impose a carry over of obligations between labor and management than in the case of an outright sale of a business. However, a contrary view is clearly indicated by the following language of the *Wiley* opinion:

> It would derogate from "[t]he federal policy of settling labor disputes by arbitration," United Steelworkers of America v. Enterprise Wheel & Car Corp., 363 U.S. 593, 596, 80 S.Ct. 1358, 1360, 4 L.Ed. 2d 1424, if a change in the corporate structure or ownership of a business enterprise had the automatic consequence of removing a duty to arbitrate previously established; this is so as much in cases like the present, where the contracting employer disappears into another by merger, as in those in which one owner replaces another but the business entity remains the same. 376 U.S. at 549, 84 S.Ct. at 914.

Moreover, unless the original corporate operator and the corporation into which it merges were already related before the merger, a fact which does not appear in the *Wiley* opinion, the legal and equitable considerations involved in imposing a predecessor's obligations upon an independent successor are no different in a merger case than in a sale of business case. We have no doubt that the result the court reached in the *Wiley* case would have been the same had the transfer there been accomplished by a sale of the business instead of by merger.

One important matter remains. The opposing parties here have argued for and against the proposition that the collective bargaining agreement is unqualifiedly binding upon Reliance, as would have been the case if there had been an assignment or novation substituting Reliance as a party to the instrument. But, in the *Wiley* case, the Supreme Court seems to have been careful to avoid so broad a ruling. It merely reasoned and decided that federal labor law imposed upon a succeeding proprietor a duty to arbitrate those questions which his predecessor was bound to arbitrate under his labor contract. The fact that the plant covered by the labor contract had been closed and its employees mingled with other workers with independent and perhaps different rights at another plant may

well have influenced this careful limitation of the *Wiley* holding.

In any event, we find implicit in the guarded language of the *Wiley* opinion, recognition and concern that new circumstances created by the acquisition of a business by a new owner may make it unreasonable or inequitable to require labor or management to adhere to particular terms of a collective bargaining agreement previously negotiated by a different party in different circumstances. Although the pre-existing labor contract indicates the structure of labor relations and the established practice of the shop at the beginning of the new proprietorship, an arbitrator of a subsequent complaint charging unwarranted departure from that scheme may properly consider any relevant new circumstances arising out of the change of ownership, as well as the provisions of and practices under the old contract, in achieving a just and equitable settlement of the grievance at hand. The requirements of the contract remain basic guides to the law of the shop, but the arbitrator may find that equities inherent in changed circumstances require an award in a particular controversy at variance with some term or terms of that contract. We do not imply that any departure from what was established under the old contract is justified by any special circumstances of this case. We do not know. And, in any event, this is a matter for the arbitrator's determination.

While this is not spelled out in the *Wiley* case, the power heretofore recognized in arbitrators to achieve justice in situations not contemplated by or not adequately covered in an existing collective bargaining agreement leads us to believe that analogous power exists here. Cf. United Steelworkers of America v. Warrior & Gulf Navigation Co., 1960, 363 U.S. 574, 80 S. Ct. 1347, 4 L. Ed. 2d 1409 ; United Steelworkers of America v. Enterprise Wheel & Car Corp., 363 U.S. 593, 80 S. Ct. 1358, 4 L. Ed. 2d 1424. And see Cox, *Reflections on Labor Arbitration,* 1959, 72 HARV. L. REV. 1482.

Our conclusion, therefore, is that the 1962 collective bargaining agreement, as an embodiment of the law of the shop, remained the basic charter of labor relations at the Bridgeville plant after the change of ownership. But, in the arbitration of any grievance asserted thereunder, the arbitrator may properly give weight to any change of circumstances created by the transfer of ownership which may make adherence to any term or terms of that agreement inequitable.

The judgment will be reversed and the cause remanded for further proceedings consistent with this opinion.

McGUIRE v. HUMBLE OIL & REFINING COMPANY
355 F. 2d 352 (2d Cir. 1966)

Before MEDINA, WATERMAN and HAYS, CIRCUIT JUDGES.

MEDINA, C. J. This case involves an appraisal of the extent to which the principles of John Wiley & Sons, Inc. v. Livingston, 1964, 376 U.S. 543, S. Ct. 909, 11 L. Ed. 2d 898 are applicable where, instead of a merger, there has been a purchase of part of the business of another concern, and where there is another union representing the employees of the purchasing corporation. Judge Tenney in the Southern District of New York (247 F. Supp. 113) has held the terms of collective bargaining agreements requiring arbitration of disputes between Local 553 and Weber & Quinn, the seller, binding on Humble Oil & Refining Company, the purchaser. Humble appeals from the judgment requiring it to submit to arbitration. We reverse.

While the contentions of the parties cover a wide range, we think it necessary to discuss only two aspects of the case. First, as this is a purchase of part of a business and not a merger, are the circumstances such as to indicate that

> the lack of any substantial continuity of identity in the business enterprise before and after a [the] change would make a duty to arbitrate something imposed from without, not reasonably to be found in the particular bargaining agreement and the acts of the parties involved?

John Wiley & Sons, Inc. v. Livingston, *supra*, 376 U.S. at p. 551, 84 S. Ct. at p. 915. See also Piano & Musical Instrument Workers Union, v. W. W. Kimball Co., 1964, 379 U.S. 357, 85 S. Ct. 441, 13 L. Ed. 2d 541, reversing Per Curiam 333 F. 2d 761 (7 Cir. 1964).

We agree with the recent holdings by the Third and Ninth Circuits that the mere fact that we are here dealing with a purchase and sale rather than a merger does not of itself make the principles of *Wiley* inapplicable. Wackenhut Corp. v. International Union, United Plant Guard Workers, 1964, 9 Cir., 332 F. 2d 954; United Steelworkers of America v. Reliance Univ., Inc., 3 Cir., 1964, 335 F. 2d 891. Indeed, Mr. Justice Harlan's opinion in *Wiley* states in so many words that the duty to arbitrate cannot be automatically removed by "a change in the corporate structure *or ownership* of a business enterprise" (376 U.S. at p. 549, 84 S. Ct. at p. 914). (Emphasis supplied.) Nor would it seem to be decisive that the transfer was of something less than the business as a whole or of all the assets of the seller. Here, however, the precise terms of the contract

of purchase and sale are not before us. Only 13 of the former employees of Weber & Quinn were integrated into the group of 260 truck drivers and 95 mechanics employed by Humble. There are other factors. For example, Local 553 might have sought protection of the rights of the former Weber & Quinn employees by prosecuting arbitration proceedings against Weber & Quinn which the proofs disclose as still in existence and functioning.

In any event, as we have decided the case on the second point, namely the theory that the presence of another union at Humble, Industrial Employees Association, Inc., and the decision of the National Labor Relations Board, to which reference will be made below, make the enforcement of the arbitration clauses as against Humble unpractical and inequitable, we do not decide whether, if there was no union representing all the employees of Humble, including those previously in the employ of Weber & Quinn, the decision to compel arbitration could be sustained. We think it better to avoid crossing that bridge until it is necessary to do so.

As we find the union features of the case dispositive of the issues, we shall now discuss the facts in some detail.

I.

Prior to the transaction of purchase and sale on August 7, 1964, Weber & Quinn owned and operated a retail coal and fuel oil business at 73 Ninth Street, Brooklyn, N.Y. Burdi Fuel Co., Inc. had a similar business at 242 Central Avenue in Brooklyn. The partnership of Weber & Quinn bought out Burdi and the corporation was dissolved, but Weber & Quinn continued to use the Burdi name. There were in effect four collective bargaining agreements with the union, Coal, Gasoline, Fuel Oil Teamsters, Chauffeurs, Oil Burner Installation, Maintenance, Servicemen and Helpers of New York City and Vicinity, Nassau and Suffolk Counties, New York, N.Y., Local Union 553, affiliated with the International Brotherhood of Teamsters, Chauffeurs, Warehousemen and Helpers of America; *i.e.* one agreement for drivers and one agreement for servicemen with Weber & Quinn and with Burdi. We may disregard the separate agreement with Burdi as the terms of the agreements were identical. The agreement with Weber & Quinn expired on December 15, 1965. It established Local 553 as the exclusive bargaining agent of the employees of Weber & Quinn and contained numerous provisions relative to seniority, the processing of grievances, pension and welfare rights, job security and other matters. Weber &

Quinn, including Burdi, employed 10 drivers and 14 mechanics.

Humble, on the other hand, is a fully integrated oil company. In its New York Area, which includes Westchester, New York City and Long Island, Humble distributes substantial quantities of gasoline, fuel oil and other petroleum products to thousands of gasoline stations, commercial establishments and homes. Deliveries are made from bulk plants where large quantities of gasoline and fuel oil are kept in storage tanks. These distribution activities are carried on principally by motor truck salesmen, truck drivers, mechanics and bulk plant operators. Since 1937 these employees have been represented by the Association above referred to. The collective bargaining agreement between Humble and the Association at the time of the purchase and sale will continue in effect until April 30, 1966. The Association, while not certified, is made the exclusive bargaining agent for all the employees "with respect to rates of pay, wages, hours of work and other conditions of employment," and provision is made for the modification of the agreement prior to its date of expiration, upon 15 days notice by Humble or by the union. This collective bargaining agreement also contains numerous provisions affecting seniority, the processing of grievances and job security. In addition, provision is made for disability protection, retirement annuities and other welfare benefits. As of December 31, 1964 this agreement covered 518 employees. Of these 260 are truck drivers and 95 are mechanics in the New York Area.

The agreement of purchase and sale contained an express disclaimer by Humble of any obligations of Weber & Quinn to its employees, whether arising out of collective bargaining agreements or otherwise; and it contained no promise on the part of Humble to employ the former employees of Weber & Quinn. What Humble bought was "certain assets," including some trucks and equipment, but "principally" the Weber & Quinn fuel oil accounts in Brooklyn. Of the 10 Weber & Quinn drivers, 4 voluntarily entered the employ of Humble. Of the 14 Weber & Quinn mechanics, 9 voluntarily entered the employ of Humble. In his opinion denying the motion of Local 553 for a temporary injunction, Judge Sugarman found: "Certain other Weber-Quinn employees either refused an offer of employment from Humble or failed to pass Humble's regular physical examination and were not hired."

The process of integrating the former Weber & Quinn employees into the Humble organization had been planned in advance and was consummated immediately after the closing. The trucks were removed and repainted, and none of the employees formerly covered by the Local 553 agreements were kept on the premises of Weber & Quinn after August 7, 1964. Interim arrangements were made for receiving orders over the telephone, and receipts for deliveries bearing the names of Weber & Quinn and Burdi were used for a time, solely for certain accounting purposes connected with the terms of the sale.

Local 553 promptly demanded arbitration. As the arbitration clause of the Local 553 agreements provided for arbitration by a designee of the New York State Board of Mediation, the items claimed to be subject of arbitration are set forth in a letter of September 10, 1964 to the Board from counsel for Local 553. The judgment appealed from directs the parties to proceed to arbitration "of the disputes noticed for arbitration before the New York State Board of Mediation on September 10, 1964," and we have set forth in the margin the letter of September 10, 1964, in which 26 items of dispute are enumerated.

Humble's refusal to arbitrate was followed on December 23, 1964 by the commencement of this action to compel Humble to submit to arbitration, pursuant to Section 301 of the Labor-Management Relations Act of 1947, as amended, 29 U.S.C., Section 185. On January 20, 1965 Humble filed with the National Labor Relations Board a petition for clarification "of the appropriate bargaining unit represented by the Association, so as to make clear that such unit includes the former employees of Weber." On July 11, 1965 the Board granted Humble's petition and ruled that the former Weber & Quinn employees being "effectively merged . . . into the New York unit currently represented by Industrial [the Association] . . . cannot now be considered a separate appropriate unit." Humble Oil & Refining Co., 1965, 153 N.L.R.B. No. 111. Although expressly disavowing any view on the question of Humble's contractual obligations to Local 553, the Board held that the Association is now the exclusive bargaining representative of the former Weber & Quinn employees.

II.

It is elementary in these arbitration cases that *in limine* the court shall decide whether there is a duty to arbitrate. That is precisely the question before us. The only differentiating feature is that, instead of interpreting the language used in a particular arbitration clause of a written contract, we are now fashioning a feature of federal labor law in the context of the policy to be deduced from the integration of the various relevant Acts of the Congress and the decisions of the courts in the field of labor law. Just as *Wiley* broke new ground and did so in the light of the existing body of federal law on the subject, so must we now put the strands of this case together and arrive at a reasoned conclusion consistent with the spirit and tenor of the principles already developed. In the light of *Wiley* we do not see how we can arrive at any other conclusion than that to direct arbitration here would disturb the harmony of the existing body of feeral labor law and tend to foster rather than prevent industrial strife and unrest.

It is the failure of the court below to realize that all the facts, including the union features of the case, are to be taken into consideration in deciding the primary and controlling question of whether or not there is an obligation or "agreement" to arbitrate binding on Humble that led to the judgment that we are constrained to reverse.

We begin with footnote 5 at page 551 of 376 U.S., at page 915 of 84 S.Ct., in *Wiley*:

> The fact that the Union does not represent a majority of an appropriate bargaining unit in Wiley does not prevent it from representing those employees who are covered by the agreement which is in dispute and out of which Wiley's duty to arbitrate arises. Retail Clerks Int'l Assn., Local Unions Nos. 128 & 633 v. Lion Dry Goods, Inc., 369 U.S. 17 [82 S.Ct. 541, 7 L.Ed. 2d 503]. There is no problem of conflict with another union, cf. L. B. Spear & Co., 106 N.L.R.B. 687, since Wiley had no contract with any union covering the unit of employees which received the former Interscience employees.

In this case we not only have another union representing the Humble employees; we also have the decision of the Labor Board in the clarification proceeding establishing the fact that the Humble union, the Association, is the exclusive bargaining representative of all the present Humble employees, including those formerly employed by Weber & Quinn. This order of the Labor Board has not been challenged in the courts, and so it has become final and binding on all concerned. Moreover, it would seem not necessary to do more than to mention in passing that the order of the Labor Board in the clarification proceeding was made in the exercise of its primary and exclusive jurisdiction.

The consequences that flow from the Association's exclusive bargaining representation of all the Humble employees are decisive of the case.

A.

If the judgment below should be affirmed and the arbitration proceedings commence, there would be an obvious conflict between the interests of the Humble employees as a whole and the interests of the 13 Humble employees who formerly worked for Weber & Quinn. If it be assumed that in the arbitration proceeding Local 553 would continue to represent the former employees of Weber & Quinn, it is not unlikely that they would press for an award giving these employees preferential treatment in the matter of seniority, job security, working conditions and other benefits that would adversely affect the other Humble employees. The result might well be unrest and dissatisfaction among the vast majority of workers in the plant. Such a burdening of the collective bargaining relationship is clearly to be avoided, as a matter of national labor policy. The combination of the two unions, one representing all the employees and the other representing a minority, is on its face an anomaly. Indeed, a mere glance at the 26 enumerated items of dispute proposed for arbitration will show that perhaps the principal purpose behind this action is to preserve the status of Local 553 as at least in some respects the bargaining representative of the former Weber & Quinn employees.

It is no answer to say, as does Local 553, that the Association's collective bargaining agreement will not expire until April 30, 1966 and that there will be nothing for the Association to bargain about with Humble until that agreement is about to terminate. The bargaining process is a continuing affair. The agreement of the Association itself provides for modification during the term of the agreement on 15 days notice by either side. The processing of grievances is also an integral part of the entire scheme of the collective bargaining. The arbitration of the 26 disputes demanded by Local 553 could be a source of endless exacerbation and conflict for all concerned.

B.

But in view of the decision of the Labor Board in the clarification proceeding, it is not even clear that Local 553 would be entitled to represent the former employees of Weber & Quinn before the arbitrator. Thus an order to Humble to arbitrate might force Humble to commit an unfair labor practice by "bargaining" with a minority union when a majority union is in existence. See Modine Mfg. Co. v. Grand Lodge Int'l Ass'n of Machinists, 6 Cir., 1954, 216 F. 2d 326; American Seating Co., 1953, 106 N.L.R.B. 250; cf. Glendale Mfg. Co. v. Local 520, 4 Cir., 1960, 283 F. 2d 936, cert. denied, 1961, 366 U.S. 950, 81 S.Ct. 1902, 6 L.Ed. 2d 1243; Hughes Tool Co. v. N.L.R.B., 5 Cir., 1945, 147 F. 2d 69; Hotel Corp. of Puerto Rico, Inc., 1963, 144

N.L.R.B. 728. But cf. Douds v. Local 1250, 2 Cir., 1949, 173 F. 2d 764. Compare Black-Clawson Co., etc. v. International Ass'n of Machinists Lodge 355, 2 Cir., 1962, 313 F. 2d 179 ; Plasti-Line, Inc. v. NLRB, 6 Cir., 1960, 278 F. 2d 482.

Arbitration of grievances is clearly a part of the collective bargaining process as defined in Section 8(d) of the National Labor Relations Act:

> [T]o bargain collectively is the performance of the mutual obligation of the employer and the representative of the employees to meet at reasonable times and confer in good faith with respect to . . . the negotiation of an agreement, *or any question arising thereunder.* 29 U.S.C., Section 158(d) (emphasis added).

Indeed, in the course of its discussion of the favored place arbitration occupies in our national labor policy, the Supreme Court has recognized that "arbitration of labor disputes under collective bargaining agreements in part and parcel of the collective bargaining process itself."

A duty of the employer under the Act is to bargain with the collective bargaining representative of a majority of the employees in the unit. 29 U.S.C., Section 158(a) (5). Such representative, moreover, has the right to be bargained with exclusively ; the duty to bargain with the employees' agent under Section 8(a) (5) imposes "the negative duty to treat with no other." N.L.R.B. v. Jones & Laughlin Steel Corp., 1937, 301 U.S. 1, 44, 57 S.Ct. 615, 628, 81 L.Ed. 893 ; 29 U.S.C., Section 159(a) ; see Modine Mfg. Co. v. Grand Lodge Int'l Ass'n of Machinists, *supra,* 216 F. 2d 326 ; cf. American Seating Co., *supra,* 106 N.L.R.B. 250 ; Admin. Ruling of N.L.R.B. General Counsel, Case No. F–1132. 1959, 44 L.L.R.M. 1338. And this duty to bargain applies whether the collective-bargaining representative is certified or not. See 29 U.S.C. Sections 158(a) (5), 159(a) ; Irving Air Chute Co. v. N.L.R.B., 2 Cir., 1965, 350 F. 2d 176.

Conclusion

Thus we conclude that, because of the union features of this case, there is no implied or constructive duty or agreement on the part of Humble to arbitrate with Local 553 any of the 26 items in controversy. The complaint is dismissed.

We express no opinion relative to the rights of Local 553 against Weber & Quinn.

Reversed.

———————————

Local 553 sought arbitration of alleged viola-

tions of the agreement in regard to its status as exclusive representative ; provisions governing wages, overtime, Sunday and holiday pay ; the purchaser's failure to pay insurance and welfare benefits ; and its failure to make specified fringe benefit payments to specified funds. Many of these items are like those in *Wiley.*

What "result" (in first paragraph under A) does Judge Medina believe "might well be unrest and dissatisfaction among the vast majority of workers in the plant"? Is it Local 553's "pressing" for preferential treatment, or does he foresee that the arbitrator will grant it? ; the latter seems to be just the kind of question left to the arbitrator in *Wiley.* Does it seem preferable to have an "inexpert" court (albeit in this instance a panel including the quite expert Judge Hays) decide that nothing survives from the former contract simply because another union represents the unit into which the former company's employees have been merged? Or might a more discriminating resolution be left to an arbitrator? For example, one of Local 553's claims was over the company's refusal to grant vacations under Local 553's agreement. Many arbitrators and courts look upon that particular benefit as "earned" during the pre-vacation work period. Is it essential to wash out such a claim in its entirety in order to protect the integrity of the majority representative in the new unit? Is it sufficient that such a claim (for the money equivalent of ungranted vacations) could be pressed against Weber and Quinn? What if Weber and Quinn had been a corporation that no longer was functioning?

What if a claim arose under the former representative's and company's pension plan continued for just the former company's employees? That does happen, often to the benefit of the successor company. *E.g.,* Gorr v. Consolidated Food Corp., 253 Minn. 375, 91 N.W. 2d 772 (1958). For just such an effect, in the absence of unions, see BERNSTEIN, THE FUTURE OF PRIVATE PENSIONS, Ch. V. especially pp. 115–116 (1964).

Acquisitions and mergers are a common feature of current industrial relations. Might it not be argued that expert arbitrators can make an especially useful contribution if their decisions accommodate the many different interests of the several parties? One possible difficulty is that the arbitral machinery may have a bias against nonparties to the original agreement. (In this case, for example, certain alleged violations would have been referrable to the Fuel Industry Union and Management Committee). Could a court deal with that specific difficulty by naming a substitute arbitrator?

———————————

During the term of a collective bargaining agreement the sole owner sold the business to a corporation in which he held a controlling interest. The corporation discharged four employees, who thereupon grieved. The matter went to arbitration, over the protests of the old and new employer, and the arbitrator ordered reinstatement and back pay against both employers. The Court of Appeals held that the Appellate Division improperly vacated the award and the judgment enforcing it. Under *Wiley* the successor was bound by its predecessor's agreement. Nor was back pay beyond the stated termination of the agreement improper because under the broad "all dispute" arbitration provision the arbitrator could decide whether the agreement in fact had terminated. Burt Bldg. Materials Corp. v. Local 1205, Teamsters Union, 18 N.Y. 2d 556, 223 N.E. 2d 884 (1966).

Discussions of some of the issues presented by these cases and other related ones (such as the impact of *Wiley* upon NLRB successorship-bargaining doctrine) can be found in Platt, *The NLRB and the Arbitrator in Sale and Merger Situations* in CHRISTENSEN (ed.), PROCEEDINGS OF N.Y.U. 19th ANNUAL CONFERENCE ON LABOR 375 (1967) ; and Note, *The Contractual Obligations of a Successor Employer under the Collective Bargaining Agreement of a Predecessor*, 113 U. PA. L. REV. 914 (1965).

In Glendale Mfg. Co. v. Local 520, Int'l Ladies Garment Workers, 283 F. 2d 936 (4th Cir. 1960), the collective agreement entered into on October 15, 1955 for a term of almost three years contained a clause permitting wage reopening annually if the Consumer Price Index fluctuated 5 per cent. After reopening and failure to agree upon an increase, the disagreement was to be treated as a dispute and processed through the contract's dispute-adjustment machinery. After the CPI rose 7.31 per cent, the union sought reopening on April 29, 1958. The company contended that reopening was possible only on contract anniversary dates, but the union claimed that its demand was timely. The union took the dispute to arbitration. The arbitrator refused to set a wage ; he held that the reopening claim was timely and must be negotiated to a disagreement before the contract empowered him to set new wage rates. The decision was issued on September 24, 1958 ; the contract expired six days later. On October 1, 1958, the union lost an NLRB representation election, and the Board decertified the union. The court of appeals rejected the employer contention that the issue involved in the award was moot. But it also declined to enforce the award as issued because that would require the employer to negotiate with the union, which no longer represented a majority of the employees and whose loss of majority status was not caused by employer unfair labor practices. It said:

> Under the circumstances, it seems appropriate to refer the entire matter back to the arbitrator who may reframe the award in the light of subsequent developments. Unless the substantive right of negotiation has been foreclosed by other events, he may order the employer to negotiate the wage question with the employees directly or with any properly constituted committee or representative of the employees. The specific procedures to implement his award should be developed by the parties in interest or prescribed by the arbitrator after inquiry. Those remedial procedures which, in the light of current conditions, are most practical and most likely to facilitate a resolution of the question may thus be employed.

Despite the broad language employed [in *Wiley*], it is not clear that the Court will give the arbitrator full discretion to determine whether to dismiss a grievance because of some alleged purely procedural defect in the presentation or processing of the complaint [grievance]. The doubt arises from the excerpt [reproduced immediately following] and from the fact that the Union's failure to follow strictly the procedural requirements of the agreement may have been caused by the uncertainty which existed with respect to survival of the agreement. Possibly a different conclusion as to the role of the courts would be reached where, for example, the arbitration clause states explicitly that an arbitrator has no jurisdiction over a grievance which has not been processed in the manner provided by the contract, especially if there is no question as to the applicability of the agreement.

Russell Smith and Dallas Jones, *The Supreme Court and Labor Dispute Arbitration: The Emerging Federal Law,* 63 MICH. L. REV. 751 (1965). The passage in *Wiley* referred to read:

> Once it is determined, as we have, that the parties are obligated to submit the subject matter of a dispute to arbitration, "procedural" questions which grow out of the dispute and bear its final disposition should be left to the arbitrator. *Even under a contrary rule, a court could deny arbitration only if it could confidently be said not only that a claim was strictly "procedural," and therefore within the purview of the court, but also that it should operate to bar arbitration altogether*, and not merely limit or qualify an arbitral award.

The buyer claimed numerous defects in a ship within six months of its delivery in 1959 by the builder. Many of the complaints were settled between the parties. As to others that remained, buyer demanded arbitration in 1962. Builder asserted the defenses of laches and waiver. The district court ordered arbitration, impliedly holding that the issue of waiver of the right to arbitrate was a question for the arbitrator. In affirming, the court of appeals cited *Wiley* and several other labor cases in which procedural questions were referred by the courts to the arbitrators. World Brilliance Corp. v. Bethlehem Steel Co., (2d Cir. 1965) 342 F. 2d 362, 365.

In Matter of Straight Line Foundry and Machine Corp. (Wojcik) 25 M. 2d 1039, 204 N.Y.S. 2d 29, aff'd mem. 10 AD 816, 200 N.Y.S. 2d 398, aff'd mem. 9NY 2d 867, 216 NYS 2d 690 (1961), it was undisputed that a written grievance was not filed within forty-eight hours of discharge. The union claimed that there were oral protests and discussion and that it followed the same procedure that was customary under that contract for fourteen years. Held: Question of "waiver" by employer of filing of written grievance was for the arbitrator.

MATTER of WILAKA CONSTRUCTION CO. (NEW YORK CITY HOUSING AUTHORITY) 17 N.Y. 2d 195, 216 N.E. 2d 696 (1966)

KEATING, J. By permission of this court, the New York City Housing Authority appeals from an order of the Appellate Division, First Department, unanimously affirming, without opinion, an order of the Supreme Court, New York County (LYMAN, J.), which, on motion of the respondent, Wilaka Construction Co., directed the parties to arbitrate a dispute for extra compensation arising out of a construction contract between them.

The contract contains certain conditions precedent to invoking arbitration, and it is the alleged failure of Wilaka to abide by them which gives rise to the present controversy.

On this appeal, both parties agree that Special Term erred in holding that the fulfillment of conditions precedent to arbitration is a question for the arbitrator. That question is for the court. (Matter of Exercycle Corp. [Maratta], 9 N.Y. 2d 329, 214 N.Y.S. 2d 353, 174 N.E. 2d 463; Matter of Rosenbaum [American Sur. Co.], 11 N.Y. 2d 310, 229 N.Y.S. 2d 375, 183 N.E. 2d

667; Matter of Lipman [Haeuser Shellac Co.], 289 N.Y. 76, 43 N.E. 2d 817, 142 A.L.R. 1088; Matter of Board of Educ. [Heckler Elec. Co.], 7 N.Y. 2d 476, 199 N.Y.S. 2d 649, 166 N.E. 2d 666.)

The facts are undisputed, and the primary questions of law presented are whether the contractor, Wilaka, failed to comply with time requirements of the contract for invoking arbitration of a claim and, if it did, whether the claim may nonetheless be arbitrated because the Housing Authority waived compliance.

Before turning to the facts, we briefly outline the pertinent provisions of the contract.

Wilaka undertook to serve as general contractor for the construction of a housing project known as West Brighton Houses.

Article 15 of the contract deals with disputes. Section a makes time of the essence, and it accordingly provides, in substance, that all work directed by the Authority shall be performed by Wilaka without delay "reserving to the parties the right to have determined by the method in this Contract provided all questions relating to compensation, damages, or other payments of money."

Subdivision (1) of section b deals with "*Disputes as to Money Payment or for Damages ...Conditions Precedent to Recovery.*" If the contractor claims that any direction involves "Extra Work entailing extra cost," he must, within five days after receipt of such instructions and before executing the work,

> file with the Authority written notice of his intention to make a claim for extra compensation.

> The filing by the Contractor of a notice of claim ... within the time limited herein, shall be a condition precedent to the settlement of any claim or to the right of appeal to arbitration as hereinafter provided.

Subdivision (2) of section b gives the Authority power to determine whether work required is extra work or whether the contractor is entitled to compensation for damages and such determination shall be final, subject to the provisions of the paragraphs entitled "Appeal from Decision" and "Arbitration." Until a determination is made following a claim by the contractor "as above provided" for extra work, the contractor shall not proceed with the work.

Section c is entitled "*Appeal from Decision.*" It provides that the decision of the Authority "made upon the notice of claim" "shall be conclusive and binding upon the Contractor unless within ten (10) days from the service upon the Contractor of written notification of such decision, the Contractor files with the Authority

...a notice of intention to arbitrate." The failure of the Authority to make a decision within 30 days shall be deemed a denial of the claim, and the contractor has 10 days thereafter to demand arbitration.

> In default of such notice of intention to arbitrate within the time limited herein, the Contractor shall be deemed to have ratified such decision and to have waived any and all rights and remedies which he might otherwise have had, and the service of such notice of intention to arbitrate within the time limited, shall be a condition precedent to the right to appeal to arbitration.

Section d deals with the arbitration procedure itself but, for our purposes, it need not be considered.

We turn now to the facts.

The contract was made on September 29, 1960, and, among other things, it required Wilaka to construct the framework "true and plumb" within certain tolerances. Wilaka engaged Lafayette Ironworks, Inc., to perform this work.

On May 16, 1961 the Authority informed Wilaka that columns in certain buildings were out of plumb. It asked what corrective measurements would be taken and stated, "Any remedial work which may be necessary is to be done by you without added cost to the Authority."

Wilaka answered on July 6, 1961 that it was enclosing a technical report from a consulting firm employed by Lafayette along with three letters from Lafayette all dated June 8, 1961. The letter from Wilaka to the Authority asks the Authority to consider the technical report and the letters, and to inform Wilaka so that it may proceed with corrective measures. The letters from Lafayette to Wilaka and the technical report make it clear that Lafayette attributed the problem to faulty construction plans.

The Authority wrote back on July 14, 1961, acknowledging receipt of Wilaka's letter and the technical report, but indicating that Wilaka had forgotten to enclose the letters from Lafayette to Wilaka. "In any event," wrote the Authority, "it should be emphasized that no contractual relationship exists between [Lafayette] and the Authority." "We wish to remind you, in this connection, that any corrective work that is need...must be done at your cost and expense," notwithstanding the technical report which attributed fault to the Authority's plans.

The extra expenses allegedly incurred by Layfayette form the basis of Wilaka's claim here.

Wilaka responded on July 24, 1961 and requested a meeting "for the purpose of resolving, if possible, the question of responsibility for the existing condition and a determination as to the nature and extent of the corrective work required."

The Authority answered on August 8, 1961. They acknowledged the conflict on the question of responsibility, reiterated their position that corrective work must be done at "your [Wilaka's] cost and expense", refused to consider the claim by Lafayette "with whom we have no contractual relationship", and stated, "Such claims, if made, should be made by you in writing in accordance with the provisions of the contract."

Ten days later on August 18, 1961, Wilaka again wrote to the Authority. To avoid further misunderstanding, Wilaka made it clear that, in forwarding the technical report and letters from Lafayette, it was acting on behalf of itself as well as Lafayette, and it would "in due course, submit [a] claim for all of the increased costs incurred", but in the meantime "to resolve the existing impasse, we are prepared to proceed with the suggested remedial measures". Such work, however would be done "without prejudice and subject to later determination as to responsibility for the increased costs".

The final letter of significance here was sent by the Authority to Wilaka, dated August 22, 1961. The crucial portions state:

"We have received your letter of August 18, 1961...

"We note your statement...that you will submit your claim of increased costs incurred by your structural steel contractor [and that] you were acting on behalf of your subcontractor as well as yourselves.

"We herewith direct you to proceed in accordance with your proposed corrective measures...

> In accordance with our interpretation of the Contract you are responsible for all increased costs due to lack of plumbness... *However, we will give your claim consideration in accordance with the terms of the Contract, when received.* (Emphasis added.)

The letters which follow deal primarily with the technical aspects of the corrective work.

The steel work was completed by the end of January, 1962. The buildings were completed and occupied between August and December, 1962. Layfayette submitted its claim to Wilaka the following month (January 22, 1963). Wilaka forwarded the claim to the Authority on February 5, 1963. The Authority rejected the claim on March 15, 1963; and Wilaka, seven days later, on March 22, 1963, gave the Authority formal written notice of intention to arbitrate the dispute in accordance with section 15 (article) of the contract. This letter went unanswered, as did subsequent letters of June 7, 1963 and July 18, 1963, requesting the Authority to comply with the arbitration provisions. On August 5, 1963 Wilaka commenced this proceeding to compel arbitration.

The claim is for $291,786.04 for the extra work performed by Lafayette, and $37,500 representing a claim by Wilaka for additional compensation.

Upon these facts, the question of law is on what date did petitioner first claim that a direction from the Authority involved "Extra Work entailing extra cost." Subdivision (1) of section b dealing with disputes allows but five days thereafter in which to serve notice of intentions to make a claim for extra compensation.

Ordinarily, the question of whether the contractor has complied with the condition precedent to arbitration, namely, the filing requirement imposed upon it by the agreement, is for Special Term. Here, however, there is no need to remit to that court since examination of the documents establishes, as a matter of law, that the condition precedent was satisfied.

The Authority's letter of May 16, 1961 created neither a dispute nor an extra claim. Indeed Wilaka had no first-hand information on the alleged matter, and first had to contact its subcontractor, Lafayette.

Wilaka's answer of July 6, 1961 merely supplied the requested information and asked for further instructions. The tenor of the letter itself refutes any indication of a dispute. To the extent that Lafayette's letters, included thereafter, suggested a claim, the Authority was already, in fact, being given notice of possible claim.

The Authority's letter of July 14, 1961 reiterated the need for corrective work at Wilaka's expense, and Wilaka 10 days later, requested a meeting to resolve the question of responsibility and determine the extent of extra work required.

When this meeting was refused by the Authority's letter of August 8, Wilaka wrote to the Authority on August 18, made it clear beyond question that they intended "to make a claim for extra compensation" and would proceed with the work, without prejudice, *as soon as the Authority approved the remedies suggested by the subcontractor.*

The only conclusion possible, therefore, is that Wilaka's letter of August 18 was a timely assertion of its intention to make a claim for extra compensation. All of the letters which preceded it failed, in one way or another to satisfy the circumstances under which Wilaka was required to file—and not until this date was there a *dispute* in which Wilaka *knew* that there would be an extra work claim. In fact, it could be argued that

the five-day period did not start to run until the Authority's letter followed on August 22, 1961, since only that letter constitutes a *direction* to do work and gives the necessary approval of the proposed corrective measures to be taken.

After giving notice of intention to make a claim, Wilaka was required by the contract to give further notice of intention to arbitrate if the claim was rejected by the Authority within a specified period. Those provisions, however, were clearly waived by the Authority in its letter of August 22, 1961 when it stated "However, we will give your claim consideration in accordance with the terms of the Contract, when received." Read in the context of the letters preceding and following it, both parties intended that the work be proceeded with and that the Authority would consider the claim "when received." The phrase, "in accordance with the Contract," does not bar a waiver. In context, it relates to the merits only.

The Authority's rejection of the claim, dated March 15, 1963, followed by Wilaka's notice of intention to arbitrate, dated March 22, complied, as indicated above, with the time provisions of the agreement and, therefore, this court is warranted in concluding that Wilaka is entitled to have the claim heard on its merits at arbitration.

The Authority raises two other objections to arbitration.

It claims first that the dispute sought to be arbitrated does not come within the class of those things which it agreed to arbitrate. The argument is based on the assertion that, while Wilaka alleges a claim for *extra* work, it is really seeking to recover for *corrective* work. The answer to this depends on whether fault is ultimately placed with the Authority for faulty plans or with Layfayette for faulty work, and that issue is for the arbitrators, not for the courts. Moreover, the arbitration provision, authorizing as it does submission of "all questions relating to compensation, damages, or other payments of money" is quite broad.

The Authority also contends that the alleged disagreement is not bona fide within the meaning of the *Cutler-Hammer* doctrine (Matter of International Assn. of Machinists etc., [Cutler-Hammer, Inc.], 271 App. Div. 917, 67 N.Y.S. 2d 317, affd. 297 N.Y. 519, 74 N.E. 2d 464) and that it is, therefore, not an arbitrable dispute.

Without passing on this assertion of non bona fide, it is sufficient to point out that the so-called *Cutler-Hammer* doctrine has been overruled by CPLR 7501 (formerly Civil Practice Act, § 1448–a). Under this provision, the court may not consider "whether the claim with respect to which arbitration is sought is tenable, or otherwise pass upon the merits of the dispute."

The contention that CPLR 7501 does not apply to the arbitration agreements entered into before its effective date seems equally lacking in merit. This statutory section affords no new rights—it merely affects the jurisdiction of the court to consider a particular question and it speaks in the mandatory present tense, without any indication that it is not to be applied by arbitration agreements entered into before its effective date. (See Matter of Berkovitz v. Arbib & Houlberg, 230 N.Y. 261, 130 N.E. 288 [1921].)

DESMOND, C. J., and FULD, VAN VOORHIS, BURKE, SCILEPPI and BERGAN, JJ. concur.

Order affirmed.

The collective agreement required grievances to be filed "no later than three (3) days following the occurrence or knowledge of the dispute." It also required the grievance to be signed by the employee and a union committeeman. The grievance was filed within the stipulated time but without the grievant-dischargee's signature. After the three day period his signature was added. The arbitrator denied the grievance on the ground that it was untimely filed. Wolf Range Corp. v. Stove, Furnace and Appliance Workers, 64–2 ARB. para. 8552 (1964).

H. K. PORTER & CO. and INT'L BHD of ELECTRICAL WORKERS, LOCAL 1073, 47 Lab. Arb. 408, 412–413 (1966)

In 1963 the company transferred work from a company subsidiary to the plant covered by Local 1073's collective agreement and hired new employees to do the work. Local 1073's collective agreement provided that "The service of any employee who fails to make application for membership in the Union immediately after thirty days after employment shall be automatically terminated." When new employees did not apply after their first thirty days on the job, the union made inquiry and was told that more employees were to be hired and that after the new unit was all set up, the entire crew, except for one supervisor, would apply. The agreement in force in 1963 came to an end, and after a strike a new agreement was executed; it contained the membership requirement quoted above. Before the strike the company stated its readiness to

agree to union membership for the new employees if the union would assure continuity of their work in a strike. The union declined to make an arrangement for the group apart from a new contract for all the people it represented. The company argued that the new agreement, effective in May 1965, did not cover the group. When the new employees refused to apply for membership, the union grieved. The company declined to treat the grievance as a proper one; after unsuccessful attempts to secure company consideration at several levels, the matter was quiescent for four months. Then the instant grievance was filed. The company claimed that the former grievance had not been appealed to higher levels and thus was "settled" under a provision of the agreement dealing with unsettled, unappealed grievances.

The arbitrator said:

> This grievance must clearly be sustained unless, as the Company argues, decision on the merits is barred by procedural considerations. It is true that Paragraph 59 provides definite time limitations, all of which appear to be customary and well within the range one ordinarily finds in a labor agreement. Obviously such limitations are desirable to avoid proliferation and repetition of grievances. Under this contract a grievance must be submitted within seven working days "of the date the grievance occurred." It seems proper to deem this grievance background as occurring each and every day non-union employees worked in the Data Processing Department after the agreement to such work had been withdrawn—that is to say, after early 1965. It could be argued with a semblance of truth that the Union slept on its rights for some months after the strike and the signing of the new contract, but Paragraph 4 is substantive and clear and requires union membership by these employees. The parties knew this when they signed the contract and they *also* knew that the company had attempted to gain, and failed to obtain, some consideration in the form of strike protection—a *quid pro quo* that Paragraph 4 rendered unnecessary. It follows that each passing day when non-union employees worked furnished renewed subject matter for a grievance. Thus, the December 3, 1965, grievance was timely.

One would be hard put to generalize from this discussion when a contract violation is a continuing one so as to escape the ban of the agreement's statute of limitations. Compare Bryan Mfg. Co. v. NLRB, 362 U.S. 411 (1960). Regarding the limitation as waived by the company's assurances might have avoided the problem of characterization. This experienced arbitrator obviously felt that the merits should be reached, although he recognized the utility of the time limitation.

His conclusion makes labor relations sense even if the rationale on procedural grounds may be logically unsatisfying.

Despite the considerable published criticism of the Trilogy and the many private exchanges among labor specialists that Mr. Justice Douglas really did not know what he was talking about in the more extravagant passages of the Trilogy opinions, no observable revulsion with labor arbitration has taken place. On the contrary, its use continues apparently unabated. The now generally common use of arbitration and grow-ing experience with it, however, have tended to focus more attention upon details of organization and procedure that some find unsatisfactory. The evaluations and palliatives vary according to situations and taste. For an informed report on the standing of arbitration among experienced practitioners and their views of shortcomings and possible cures, consult Dallas Jones and Russell Smith, *Management and Labor Appraisals and Criticism of the Arbitration Process: A Report with Comments,* 62 MICH. L. REV. 1116 (1964).

A valuable review of post-Trilogy developments will be found in RUSSELL SMITH and DALLAS JONES, *The Impact of the Emerging Federal Law of Grievance Arbitration on Judges, Arbitrators and Parties,* 52 VA. L. REV. 831 (1966).

CHAPTER XII

ARBITRATION AND THE NLRB

A.

NLRB Policies and Practice

NATIONAL LABOR RELATIONS BOARD v. WALT DISNEY PRODUCTIONS
146 F. 2d 44 (9th Cir. 1945)

Because respondent's collective bargaining agreement with Union contains a grievance and arbitration procedure for the settlement of disputes, respondent contends that the unfair labor practice alleged, namely the discharge of Babbitt for his union activities, could not affect interstate commerce and therefore that the Board had no jurisdiction over the proceeding. According to respondent's theory the collective bargaining agreement provides a peaceable means of settling labor disputes; the tranquil disposition of such disputes negatives the possibility of burdening or obstructing interstate commerce; therefore there exists no unfair labor practice over which the Board has jurisdiction under the Act. The Board found the contention without merit.

The basic purpose of the Act is to free interstate commerce of obstructions resulting from industrial unrest by protecting the rights of self-organization and collective bargaining, 29

U.S.C.A. § 151; National Labor Relations Board v. Fansteel Metallurgical Corp., 1939, 306 U.S. 240, 247, 59 S. Ct. 490, 83 L. Ed. 627, 123 A.L.R. 599. By 29 U.S.C.A. § 160(a) the Act authorizes the Board "to prevent any person from engaging in any unfair labor practice (listed in section 158) affecting commerce." Within its grant of power the Board acts in the public interest to enforce a public right. Amalgamated Utility Workers v. Consolidated Edison Co., 1940, 309 U.S. 261, 60 S. Ct. 561, 84 L. Ed. 738; National Licorice Co. v. National Labor Relations Board, 1940, 309 U.S. 350, 366, 60 S. Ct. 569, 84 L. Ed. 799.

Without restriction the Board may exercise jurisdiction over any situation involving an unfair labor practice affecting commerce under the terms of § 160(a). Whether or not a collective bargaining agreement has been reached as between an employer and the representative of a group of employees is immaterial, for collective bargaining agreements do not necessarily accomplish peace; they are not a guaranty that no further unfair labor practices will occur or that such practices will not burden commerce. In point of possibility it may be said that arbitration decisions themselves may burden commerce. The instant case is proof enough that even the establishment of a grievance and arbitration procedure in a collective bargaining agreement may not eradicate serious disputes in an organization engaged in interstate commerce.

The Act itself contemplates a continuing jurisdiction by the Board over employer-employee relationships, for § 160 (a) includes a provision that the Board's power over unfair labor practices "shall be exclusive, and shall not be affected by any other means of adjustment or prevention that has been or may be established by agreement, code, law, or otherwise." Clearly, agreements between private parties cannot restrict the jurisdiction of the Board. National Labor Relations Board v. Newark Morning Ledger Co., 3 Cir., 1941, 120 F. 2d 262, 267–268, 137 A.L.R. 849; National Labor Relations Board v. Prettyman, 6 Cir., 1941, 117 F. 2d 786, 792; National Labor Relations Board v. General Motors Corp., 7 Cir., 1940, 116 F. 2d 306, 312. Therefore, we believe the Board may exercise jurisdiction in any case of an unfair labor practice when in its discretion its inteference is necessary to protect the public rights defined in the Act. The Board, then, had discretionary power to exercise its jurisdiction in the instant case.

Respondent argues that it is the policy of the National War Labor Board (NWLB) in the case of a discriminatory discharge dispute between employer and employees to require a resort to any such grievance and arbitration procedure as may have been established in a collective bargaining agreement and that the National Labor Relations Board (NLRB) should follow the same policy in the instant case since, according to respondent, the two boards have concurrent jurisdiction over disputes involving discriminatory discharges. Assuming that the policy of the NWLB is as defined by respondent, we think the NLRB is under no compulsion to conform to that policy. We mention again that the NLRB acts in the public interest to free interstate commerce from the burdens of specified unfair labor practices, including discriminatory discharges, and is given exclusive jurisdiction over such practices by 29 U.S.C.A. § 160(a) despite the existence of any other means devised for the settling of labor disputes. Consistently, the War Labor Disputes Act expressly directs that the NWLB decisions shall conform to the provisions of the National Labor Relations Act, 50 U.S.C.A. Appendix § 1507(a) (2) ; and Executive Order 9017, dated January 12, 1942, 50 U.S.C.A. Appendix, following § 1507, creating the NWLB prescribes in paragraph 7 that "Nothing herein shall be construed as superseding or in conflict with the provisions of . . . the National Labor Relations Act." The result is inevitable that the NLRB may exercise its jurisdiction over the discriminatory discharge dispute herein in issue and is in no way governed by the NWLB policy favoring arbitration.

Our opinion in Consolidated Aircraft Corp. v. National Labor Relations Board, 1944, 141 F. 2d 785, 787, does not support respondent's position. Therein, the court merely pointed out that the employer acted in good faith in asserting its view as to the wage rate controlling the Sunday morning work of its third shift and concluded that the employer had not interfered with, restrained, or coerced its employees' rights of collective bargaining guaranteed in 29 U.S.C.A. § 157. No inference can be drawn from such a conclusion that where an unfair labor practice within the terms of the National Labor Relations Act exists, the grievance and arbitration procedures established in a prevailing collective bargaining agreement must be exhausted before the NLRB will accept jurisdiction over the matter.

SPIELBERG MANUFACTURING COMPANY AND HAROLD GRUENBERG
112 N.L.R.B. 1080 (1955)

As part of the settlement of a strike of the Respondent's employees called by Luggage and Leather Workers Local 160, herein called the Union, the Respondent and the Union agreed to arbitrate the question of whether the four strikers, whom the Respondent did not wish to reinstate because of conduct they assertedly engaged in on the picket line, should be reinstated.

Thereafter, the union membership ratified the contract negotiated by the Union and the Respondent, which provided, *inter alia*, that the arbitration would be held. An agreement executed by the Respondent and the Union simultaneously with the collective-bargaining contract described the method of choosing a three-man arbitration panel and provided that the parties would be bound by the decision of the panel majority.

Shortly thereafter, as described in the Intermediate Report, the arbitration proceeding was held. The Respondent submitted evidence. Three of the four strikers appeared personally and testified. All four were represented by an attorney who filed a brief in their behalf. In these circumstances, it is clear that the four individuals concerned, as well as the Union, actively participated and acquiesced in the arbitration proceeding.

The arbitration award, by a majority of the panel, with the union member dissenting, held that the Respondent was not obligated to reinstate these four employees. Thereafter, they filed a charge, and the complaint upon which this proceeding is based issued. In finding that the Respondent's refusal to reinstate these four strikers violated the Act, the Trial Examiner rejected the defense based on the arbitration award, on the ground that the Board is not bound by such an award.

We agree with the Trial Examiner that the Board is not bound, as a matter of law, by an arbitration award. As the court said in the *Disney* case:

> Clearly, agreements between private parties cannot restrict the jurisdiction of the Board. We believe the Board may exercise jurisdiction in any case of an unfair labor practice when in its discretion its interference is necessary to protect the public rights defined in the Act.

The Board has exercised its discretion in the past to remedy an unfair labor practice even though the parties had used arbitration to dispose of an issue. In so doing, in the *Monsanto* case,[1] the Board said:

> There can be no justification for deeming ourselves bound, as a policy matter, by an arbitration award which is at odds with the statute. We shall therefore disregard the award in this case.

And in the *Wertheimer* case,[2] the Board pointed out that where the arbitration had been carried out over the opposition of the individual involved the circumstances were not such as to warrant the Board, in the exercise of its discretion, to decline to assert its jurisdiction.

In the instant case factors which impelled the Board to exercise its jurisdiction in *Monsanto* and *Wertheimer* are not present. Thus, the arbitration award is not, as it was *Monsanto,* at odds with the statute. This does not mean that the Board would necessarily decide the issue of the alleged strike misconduct as the arbitration panel did. We do not pass upon that issue. And unlike *Wertheimer,* all parties had acquiesced in the arbitration proceeding. In summary, the proceedings appear to have been fair and regular, all parties had agreed to be bound, and the decision of the arbitration panel is not clearly repugnant to the purposes and policies of the Act. In these circumstances we believe that the desirable objective of encouraging the voluntary settlement of labor disputes will best be served by our recogni-

tion of the arbitrators' award. Accordingly, we find that the Respondent did not violate the Act when, in accordance with the award, it refused to reinstate the four strikers.[3] We shall therefore dismiss the complaint in its entirety.

[The Board dismissed the complaint.]

[From the Trial Examiner's Intermediate Report]:

The Arbitration Proceedings

Kavner* and Packman† agreed upon Felix Kraft as the third member of the board of arbitration. In brief, Kraft, a public accountant, testified that he had known Packman for some 20 years, that they had represented mutual clients, not including the Company, and that he had no prior experience in matters of this kind. In agreeing to act as arbitrator Kraft said he understood from Packman that the proceedings "wouldn't last long" and he "got the impression that it would be more or less of a formality."

On October 5, the board met in Packman's office with Burzinsky, Dalton, Hocher, Attorney Harold Gruenberg, Deans, Baris, and the Spielbergs present. Henthorne was informed of the meeting but was sick and unable to attend. The evidence pertaining to the events at this meeting is to the effect, as stated by Baris, that at the outset Gruenberg, who acted as counsel for the Union, questioned Kraft's qualifications to act as arbitrator and announced he would not be bound by any decision of the board. Baris and Packman then showed him the memorandum agreement of September 22, and Gruenberg, after conferring with Deans, agreed to proceed with the matter. The meeting lasted about 2 hours during which Saul Spielberg read a statement giving his position and the 3 discriminatees were asked some questions by counsel.

As appears above, a majority of the board, Kraft and Packman, entered a written decision which merely states that the Company was justified in refusing to reinstate the four individuals. Kavner said he disagreed with the majority.

The discriminatees were notified of the decision and thereafter, about October 26, met with Gruenberg, Kavner, Deans, and Gibbons, at the latter's office. Dalton asked why they were not being reinstated and Gibbons told her, "Well, in a case like this some people have to sacrifice their job to get a union contract in, that is what

1. Monsanto Chemical Company, 97 N.L.R.B. 157, enfd. 205 F. 2d 763 (C.A. 8).

2. Wertheimer Stores Corp., 107 N.L.R.B. 1434.

3. As noted above, we do not, by this decision, express any opinion as to the legality of the picket-line conduct.

*A union official.

†The company attorney.

happened here." Gibbons concluded by saying the only thing that could be done would be to find new jobs for them. Burzinsky, Hocher, and Henthorne corroborated Dalton's testimony concerning her conversation with Gibbons.

Deans said Gibbons told them it was regrettable but "they ought to look on the fact their jobs were now lost as a sacrifice for the overall good of the rest of the workers."

At this hearing the International Union took the position that although they disagreed with the decision they would honor their agreement with the Company and abide by its terms.

HONOLULU STAR-BULLETIN, LTD.
123 N.L.R.B. 395 (1959)

We agree, for the reasons set forth in the Intermediate Report, that Anthony Van Kralingen, Jr., was discharged because of his distribution of his November 12 campaign release and because of the ideas expressed therein, rather than for his alleged violation of office rule 15. We also agree that in disseminating his ideas by means of his distribution of his letters in connection with his campaign for union office, Van Kralingen was engaged in protected concerted activities within the Union. Although, as the Respondent and the Union contended, some of the policies advocated by Van Kralingen were in conflict with the provisions of the National Labor Relations Act, his efforts were directly solely to expressing his views to his fellow employees within the scope of his campaign. He made no demand upon management, and his activities did not place Respondent in any danger of yielding to an unlawful demand.

Like the Trial Examiner, we reject the contention that the arbitration award upholding Van Kralingen's discharge is binding upon the Board. As set forth by the Trial Examiner, the Board has paramount jurisdiction to prevent unfair labor practices which is not affected by the existence of any other means of adjustment or prevention. However, the Board may, in its discretion, refrain from concerning itself with certain controversies between management and labor. Where it can do so without abandoning its duties to protect rights which the statute guarantees to employers, bargaining representatives, individual employees, or the public, the Board, as a matter of policy, favors the adoption of arbitration awards. But, the Board refuses to honor an arbitration award which is at odds with or repugnant to the Act. Such a situation exists where, as here, the Board is not satisfied

as to the fairness and regularity of the arbitration proceeding,* and the decision is clearly repugnant to the purposes and policies of the Act.

HERSHEY CHOCOLATE CORPORATION
129 N.L.R.B. 1052 (1960)

Like the Trial Examiner, we find that the arbitration award of July 18, 1959, is no defense to the unfair labor practices committed by Respondents. Counsel for the 20 employees, whose cases Respondent Union brought before the arbitrator, and whose interests were adverse to the Union, specifically advised the arbitrator of their intention to seek other legal recourse should the arbitrator's decision be unfavorable. The employees named in the August 5, 1959, letter did not have their cases arbitrated at all, as the Union did not seek their discharge until after the arbitrator's award. It is thus sufficiently evidenced, in our opinion, that none of the employees involved herein agreed to be bound by the arbitration proceeding. In any case, we fully agree with the Trial Examiner's reasoning and conclusion that the arbitrator's award was contrary to law. It is quite apparent, as the Board has held, that under a "maintenance of membership" clause, members of one union may not lawfully be required to maintain membership in another union. In the prior representation case, the Board by its schism determination specifically found the seperate identity of the two locals, and the present record in fact supports that conclusion. Accordingly, we find that the arbitrator's decision, that members of Local 464, B.C.W. (Bakery and Confectionary Workers International Union of America, Independent) were required to maintain membership in Local 464, A.B.C. (American Bakery and Confectionary Workers International Union, AFL–CIO), was repugnant to the provisions of the Act.

DENVER-CHICAGO TRUCKING
COMPANY, INC.
132 N.L.R.B. 1416 (1961)

The Trial Examiner found the Respondent discharged Emmet Kirk and David Timmerman in violation of Section 8 (a) (3) and (1) of the Act.

---

*The dischargee's counsel was not permitted to enter the room at the arbitration proceeding, let alone to participate. He also attempted to record the proceedings but was not permitted to do so. Incomplete "minutes" were taken by the secretary of a member of the panel.

We disagree. At the time these drivers were discharged Local Union No. 710, International Brotherhood of Teamsters, represented Respondent's employees under a collective-bargaining contract running from February 1, 1958, to January 31, 1961. Kirk was shop steward for Local 710 and Timmerman was a driver for Respondent and a member of 710. The testimony relating to the cause for discharge is sharply disputed by the parties and the issue of credibility was resolved by the Trial Examiner in favor of the dischargees. However, we do not consider it necessary to reach that issue.

The aforementioned collective-bargaining contract contained, in articles VII and VIII, lengthy grievance provisions which need not be set forth in full. That part of article VII, which is pertinent herein, reads:

Section 1. The operators and the Union in each of the following states shall together create a permanent Joint State Committee for such state: [the States are then named, Illinois being among them]. The joint State Committee shall consist of an equal number appointed by Employers and Unions but no less than three from each group. Each member may appoint an alternate in his place. The Joint State Committee shall at its first meeting formulate rules of procedure to govern the conduct of its proceedings. Each Joint State Committee shall have jurisdiction over disputes and grievances involving Local Unions or complaints by Local Unions located in its state.

* * * * *

Section 4. It shall be the function of the various committees above-referred-to to settle disputes *which cannot be settled* between the Employers and the Local Unions in accordance with the procedure established in Section 1 of Article VIII. [Emphasis supplied.]

That part of article VIII, which is pertinent herein, reads:

Section 1. The Employer and the Union agree that there shall be no strike, lockout, tie-up, or legal proceedings without first using all possible means of a settlement, as provided for in this Agreement, of any controversy which might arise. Disputes shall first be taken up between Employer and the Local Union involved.

Failing adjustment by these parties, the following procedure shall then apply:

(a) Where a Joint State Committee, by a majority vote, settles a dispute, no appeal may be taken to the Joint Area Committee. *Such a decision shall be final and binding on both parties.* [Emphasis supplied.]

Kirk and Timmerman were both discharged from Respondent's employ as a result of telephone calls made by them from Angola, Indiana, on May 23, 1959. Kirk was there because his truck had broken down and he was waiting relief

and Timmerman was en route to Buffalo on a "single" run. They met at the Round-Up Cafe. According to Timmerman, he had stopped at his home in Gary after leaving Chicago and found his wife unconscious on the floor. He telephoned his dispatcher asking to be relieved of his run, a request which was refused. After calling a doctor and neighbor he continued until he met Kirk at Angola. Kirk telephoned Operations Manager Nolte at Chicago and, according to Kirk, explained Timmerman's situation to Nolte and suggested sending relief for Timmerman. Nolte's version is that Kirk called and protested letting Timmerman make the single run to Buffalo and, as shop steward, refused to let Timmerman proceed. Nolte then discharged Kirk under article III of the contract and, when Timmerman refused to continue, told him he had quit. Article III of the contract provides, in part, as follows:

Job stewards and alternates have no authority to take strike action or any other action interrupting the Employer's business in violation of this agreement, except as authorized by official action of the Union. The Employer recognizes this limitation upon the authority of job stewards and their alternates. The Employer, in so recognizing such limitation, shall have the authority to render proper discipline, including discharge without recourse, to such job steward or his alternate, if he be an employee, in the event the job steward or his alternate has taken unauthorized strike action, slow down or work stoppage in violation of this agreement.

Following their discharges the Union took their grievance to the Joint State Committee, which heard the cases at a hearing on June 30 to July 1, 1959. The cases were presented by Mike Healy, the Union's business representative, who customarily presented Local 710 cases. Subsequently, the Joint State Board issued decisions in some 30 grievances heard on those days. In Case No. 23—G its decision read as follows:

The company is upheld in its discharge of Emmet Kirk for violation of Article III in that he took action beyond the authority and duties permitted in such Article which action resulted in a work stoppage and interruption of the company's business and operation.

In case No. 23—H its decision read:

The company is upheld in its termination of D. Timmerman for willful and deliberate refusal to carry out a normal work assignment to the point of rejecting his employment with the company.

Thus, we are confronted squarely with the question whether the Board will honor the findings of the Joint Committee in accordance with the principles of the *Spielberg* case. It is clear, however, that the Board's jurisdiction over unfair labor practices is exclusive under the Act and that the Board is not, therefore, bound by an arbitration decision or by grievance procedures established by a collective-bargaining contract between the parties. In the *Spielberg* case the issue of the reinstatement of four strikers was submitted to arbitration by agreement between the Union and Respondent. A hearing was thereafter held at which three of the strikers appeared and testified and were represented by an attorney who submitted a brief on their behalf. The Board held that it was clear that the strikers, as well as the Union, actively participated and acquiesced in the arbitration. Distinguishing the facts in *Spielberg* from those in *Monsanto Chemical Company,* 97 NLRB 517, in which the decision of the arbitrators was contrary to the statute, and from those in *Wertheimer Stores Corp.,* 107 NLRB 1434, where the arbitration proceedings were carried out over the opposition of the individual involved, the Board concluded in *Spielberg*:

> In summary, the proceedings appear to have been fair and regular, all parties had agreed to be bound, and the decision of the arbitration panel is not clearly repugnant to the purposes and policies of the Act. In these circumstances we believe the desirable objective of encouraging the voluntary settlement of labor disputes will best be served by our recognition of the arbitrator's award.

The question presented here is whether the proceedings before the Joint Committee meets the *Spielberg* standards of fairness and regularity. We note that both Kirk and Timmerman testified, at the Board hearing, that they had not been given a fair hearing before the Joint Committee. Kirk testified that he had not been given an opportunity to state his case in full but had been interrupted while the Joint Committee interrogated one of his witnesses. He also testified that the Joint Committee gave him and his witness a "tongue lashing." (No reason nor explanation was given for this by Kirk.) He also stated that he tried to present a doctor's certificate certifying Timmerman's wife was sick on the date Timmerman was fired but that the Joint Committee refused to accept it on the ground they accepted the fact that his wife was sick. Kirk was asked to leave the room while his case was being decided and recalled when the Joint Committee announced its decisions in all the Denver-Chicago cases. When his decision was announced, Kirk inquired as to the reasons and

was told, "That's none of your business," after which he was led from the room.[1]

Timmerman's testimony was that he attended the hearing and that Union Representative Healy and Kirk were present, that he was asked no questions and made no request to speak, and that he made no protest during the hearing. After the hearing he asked if "we were supposed to speak up" but it is not clear to whom he addressed this remark except that it was not addressed to either Healy or any member of the Joint Committee. Healy, who presented the cases for Kirk and Timmerman, was not called by the General Counsel as a witness. The General Counsel admitted Healy was available.

The Respondent called Barney Cushman, president of Cushman Motors Company, to testify to the procedure of hearings before the Joint Committee. Cushman, who had been a member of the Joint Committee for 18 years, described the Joint Committee's procedure as follows:

> We first listened to the driver's story, as presented by him or his business agent, or both, hear all of the evidence. The driver is then requested by any member of the committee—he is then questioned by any member of the committee on the evidence as presented and then the employer presents his side in exactly the same manner. When the employer gets through with the presentation, every member of the committee is afforded an opportunity to question him on any subject during the testimony as presented. When the testimony is all in, all the principals are requested to leave the room, and the committee goes into executive session.
>
> At that time we go over all of the evidence as presented by both sides, and it takes a majority to get a decision, a majority of 4 votes out of 6.

Cushman testified that he had no recollection as to whether he sat on the panel which decided the Kirk and Timmerman cases which is not strange in view of the fact that the grievance hearings took place more than 9 months prior to his testifying in the present Board hearing and the Kirk and Timmerman cases were only 2 of some 30 heard at the June meeting of the Joint Committee. (The Joint Committee met once a month.) In fact, the Trial Examiner discounted

---

1. Kirk testified that he had appeared at a Joint Committee hearing as a grievant following discharge by the Respondent only a few months before the instant hearing. At that time he stated he listened to the Company's witnesses, told his own story, was told to leave the room while the Joint Committee deliberated, was called back when the decision was announced, and was awarded reinstatement and backpay. He directed no complaint to the fairness of this hearing before the same Joint Committee. Kirk also testified that during the period he was union steward he had occasion to file grievances before the Joint Committee and that he had been upheld in 98 per cent of the cases.

the grievance procedure on the ground that 30 cases had been heard in 2 days whereas the Board hearing in the instant case took 5 days.[2] Since the two other criteria of *Spielberg* were clearly met, *i.e.*, the parties had participated and agreed to be bound (no claim of reservation was made by either Kirk or Timmerman) and the decision of the panel was not repugnant to the statute, we are confined to passing on the sufficiency of the hearing. In so doing we note that the grievance procedure had been followed by the parties for 18 years and that it presumably satisfied both the employers and the unions as serving its purpose. We also note that no claim was made by either Kirk or Timmerman that the hearings in their cases differed procedurally from established practice nor was any claim of collusion asserted. Under these circumstances, failure to adopt the decision of the Joint Committee would imply an obligation to fix standards of formality in procedure on the part of grievance and arbitration panels which must be met before their awards could receive endorsement. We consider it enough under *Spielberg* if the procedures adopted meet normal standards as to sufficiency, fairness, and regularity. As to these, each case must rest on its own bottoms. Where, as here, the parties have found that the machinery which they have created for the amicable resolution of their disputes has adequately served its purpose, we shall accept such a resolution absent evidence of irregularity, collusion, or inadequate provisions for the taking of testimony.[3]

GATEWAY TRANSPORTATION CO.
137 N.L.R.B. 1763 (1962)

The Trial Examiner concluded that it would not accord with Board policy to give effect to the arbitration award, upholding Willey's discharge. We agree with that conclusion but for different reasons.

---

2. The Board hearing, however, embraced many issues besides that of the discharge of Kirk and Timmerman and included an exhaustive history of the relations between Respondent and Kirk as shop steward during the 9 months he held that position.

3. We do not agree with the Trial Examiner that it is essential that a public member sit on grievance panels and we note that in the instant case the General Counsel stipulated that there was balanced representation on the Joint Committee which heard the Kirk and Timmerman cases. See also Max B. Oscherwitz, *et al.*, doing business as J. Oscherwitz and Sons, 130 N.L.R.B. 1078 (Member Kimball dissenting); International Association of Machinists, AFL–CIO, *et al.* (The New Britain Machine Company), 116 N.L.R.B. 645; Consolidated Aircraft Corporation, 47 N.L.R.B. 694, enfd. as mod. 141 F. 2d 785 (C.A. 9).

As found by the Trial Examiner, on September 24 Willey received his discharge notice; on September 26 he received a telegram advising that on September 28 the arbitration board established by the contract would hold a hearing on his "discharge appeal"; and on September 28 such a hearing was held, despite Willey's protest that he had not had sufficient time to prepare for it. The record further established that the "discharge appeal" was filed by the Union, as the contract apparently required, and not by Willey; the attorney who represented the Union at the arbitration hearing declined to present Willey's case because "Mr. Willey has never come up to the Local Union to object to his discharge"; and that Willey's expressed reason for protesting the hearing was his desire for time in which to call certain drivers as witnesses in support of his position.

In the *Spielberg* case, the Board stated in substance that it would give effect to arbitration awards if certain conditions were satisfied; one of these conditions is that the proceedings be fair and regular. As explicated in the *Denver-Chicago* case, "the procedures adopted [must] meet normal standards as to sufficiency, fairness and regularity and there must not be "evidence of irregularity, collusion or inadequate provisions for the taking of testimony." In this case, as set forth above, Willey was forced to a hearing, with no more than 48 hours' notice, on the basis of an appeal which he did not initiate; union counsel, although present at the hearing, declined to represent him; and his request for a continuance, in order that he might prepare his case and call necessary witnesses, was rejected. Such a procedure, in our opinion, does not satisfy the required standards of fairness and regularity, and it is for that reason that we agree that no effect should be given to the arbitration award involved herein. Accordingly, we deem it unnecessary to consider whether this award should be rejected for the reasons which have impelled the Trial Examiner to reject it.

INTERNATIONAL HARVESTER CO.
138 N.L.R.B. 923 (1962)

Thee Trial Examiner found, in substance, that the Respondent Local Union 98 and its agent, Barnard, violated Section 8(b) (2) and (1) (A) of the Act by pursuing a grievance to arbitration to compel the Respondent Company to fulfill its contractual obligation to discharge employee Ramsey for failing to pay his union membership dues during the term of a valid union-security agreement, and by insisting that the Company put into effect a rendered arbitration award which subsequently resulted in Ramsey's layoff in an economic reduction in force. The Trial Examiner further found that the Respondent Company violated Section 8(a) (3) and (1) of the Act by reducing Ramsey's seniority in compliance with the arbitration award and thereafter laying him off. Without passing upon the merits of the alleged unfair labor practices, we find that the Trial Examiner erred in not honoring the arbitration award and dismissing the complaint herein.

The facts pertinent to our determination may be summarized as follows: The Respondents were parties to a collective-bargaining agreement which was executed in 1955 for a term expiring on August 1, 1958. This agreement contained a valid union-security provision requiring employees, as a condition of employment, to join the Union and maintain membership for the duration of the contract to the extent of paying an initiation fee and regular periodic dues. In addition, the agreement provided for a voluntary dues checkoff. In compliance with the terms of this agreement, Ramsey reluctantly joined the Union and authorized the Company in writing to deduct his periodic dues from his wages. Regular deductions were made through April 1958 and forwarded to the Union. Thereafter the Company discontinued this practice on the basis of a letter it had received from Ramsey which it interpreted as a request to cancel his checkoff authorization. The Company gave prompt notice to both Ramsey and the Union of the action thus taken. Ramsey did not disapprove the cancellation.

Although fully apprised that dues were no longer being deducted, Ramsey made no effort to meet his dues obligation. Thereupon the Union sought to collect the accrued dues from the Company under the checkoff authorization but met with no success. As a result, the Union on July 1 certified to the Company that Ramsey was more than 60 days in arrears and requested that "appropriate action be taken against this employee." Under the contract, Ramsey was thereby allowed 10 more working days to comply with the union-shop requirements of the contract. When Ramsey failed to rectify his default, the Union, on July 21, filed a grievance with the Company, complaining that the Company had violated its contract obligation in not discharging Ramsey. On August 6, following the expiration of the contract, the Company informed the Union that it rejected its grievance because a State court order—of dubious validity[1] —prohibited it from enforcing the union-security provisions of the contract. The Company also directed the Union's attention to the fact that upon the expiration of the contract these provisions became inoperative by reason of Indiana's right-to-work law. The Union thereupon promptly took its grievance to arbitration as provided in the contract.

In May 1960, following several fruitless attempts to settle the Union's grievance, the matter was heard by David L. Cole, the permanent arbitrator appointed under the contract. On August 12, the arbitrator issued his decision sustaining the Union's grievance that the Company had failed to perform its contractual obligation to discharge Ramsey during the contract term for nonpayment of union dues. However, because Indiana's right-to-work law barred union-shop agreements at the plant in question after the contract's expiration on August 1, 1958, the arbitrator, with the Union's consent, treated Ramsey as having been reemployed as of that date with his seniority unbroken for all purposes except job tenure. Thereafter, the Company notified Ramsey it was reducing his seniority in compliance with the award. As a consequence of this reduction in seniority, Ramsey was laid off when the Company curtailed operations.

As indicated above, the Trial Examiner found the Respondents guilty of unfair labor practices essentially because the Union pursued its contractual remedy to arbitration and the Company complied with the award rendered by the arbitrator. Unlike the Trial Examiner, we find that it will effectuate the purposes and policies of the Act to honor this award.

---

1. As discussed in the Intermediate Report, this referred to a declaratory judgment rendered on February 4, 1957, in a suit instituted against the Company and a sister local of Respondent Local 98 by employees of another plant which was covered by the same contract as the one here involved (Snavely v. International Harvester Company). The court there simply decreed that the union-security provisions were null and void and unenforceable under Indiana's Anti-Injunction Act of 1933. However, on June 20, 1957, in another action involving General Motors Corporation and the Respondent International, the Appellate Court of Indiana found contrary to the lower court in the Snavely case and held that the 1933 Anti-Injunction Act did not invalidate the union shop (Smith v. General Motors Corporation, 143 N.E. 2d 441). In addition, that court ruled that the Indiana right-to-work law, which was passed in 1957, was not retroactive to invalidate contracts in existence at the time of its passage, as was the contract involved in the present case. The Snavely decision was appealed, but the appeal was dismissed in 1959 on the ground of mootness because the contract had expired in the meantime. In this connection, it appears that a declaratory judgment under Indiana law is not self-executing but requires the institution of another action to enforce rights decreed thereunder (Brindley v. Meara, 198 N.E. 310).

There is no question that the Board is not precluded from adjudicating unfair labor practice changes even though they might have been the subject of an arbitration proceeding and award. Section 10(a) of the Act[2] expressly makes this plain, and the courts have uniformly so held.[3] However, it is equally well established that the Board has considerable discretion to respect an arbitration award and decline to exercise its authority over alleged unfair labor practices if to do so will serve the fundamental aims of the Act.

The Act, as has repeatedly been stated, is primarily designed to promote industrial peace and stability by encouraging the practice and procedure of collective bargaining. Experience has demonstrated that collective-bargaining agreements that provide for final and binding arbitration of grievance and disputes arising thereunder, "as a substitute for industrial strife," contribute significantly to the attainment of this statutory objective. Approval of the arbitral technique, which has become an effective and expeditious means of resolving labor disputes, finds expression in Section 203(d) of the Labor Management Relations Act, 1947. That provision declares: "Final adjustment by a method agreed upon by the parties is hereby declared to be the desirable method for settlement of grievance disputes arising over the application or interpretation of an existing collective bargaining agreement." The Board has often looked to this declaration as a guideline in administering its Act.

Recognizing arbitration as an instrument of national labor policy for composing contractual differences, which it found imbedded in the quoted statutory provision and other Federal legislation and sources, the Supreme Court of the United States has given this policy meaningful substance. In the landmark decision in *Lincoln Mills* and related cases, it held that in suits under Section 301 of the Act, courts were empowered to compel parties to observe their arbitral commitments and the mere expiration of the contract did not relieve the parties of their obligation to arbitrate grievances arising during the contract term. So important a role did the Court regard arbitration as playing in the national labor scheme as "a stabilizing influence" the Court in later cases cautioned the lower courts in Section 301 suits to refrain from passing on the merits of the grievances under the guise of determining the question of arbitrability, but to construe contractual arbitration provisions expansively if "congressional policy in favor of settlement of disputes by the parties through the machinery of arbitration" is to be realized.

If complete effectuation of the Federal policy is to be achieved, we firmly believe that the Board, which is entrusted with the administration of one of the many facets of national labor policy, should give hospitable acceptance to the arbitral process as "part and parcel of the collective bargaining process itself," and voluntarily withhold its undoubted authority to adjudicate alleged unfair labor practice charges involving the same subject matter, unless it clearly appears that the arbitration proceedings were tainted by fraud, collusion, unfairness, or serious procedural irregularities or that the award was clearly repugnant to the purposes and policies of the Act. As the Court has reminded the Board in another context but in language equally applicable to the situation here presented:[4]

> ... that the Board has not been commissioned to effectuate the policies of the Labor Relations Act so single-mindedly that it may wholly ignore other and equally important Congressional objectives. Frequently the entire scope of Congressional purpose calls for careful accommodation of one statutory scheme to another, and it is not too much to demand of an administrative body that it undertake this accommodation without excessive emphasis upon its immediate task.

Consistent with this reminder, and aware of the underlying objectives of the Act, the Board in the appropriate case has not permitted parties to bypass their specially devised grievance-arbitration machinery for resolving their disputes and where an arbitration award had already been rendered has held them to it.

From what has been said previously, it is quite clear that, in pursuing its grievance to arbitration, the Union in the present case was simply exercising a contractual right to have that tribunal vindicate its claim that the Company breached its obligation by refusing to enforce their concededly valid union-shop agreement to

---

2. Section 10 (a) provides that the Board's power to prevent unfair labor practices affecting commerce "shall not be affected by any other means of adjustment or prevention that has been, or may be established by agreement, law or otherwise...."

3. N.L.R.B. v. Walt Disney Productions, 146 F. 2d 44, 48 (C.A. 9), cert. denied 324 U.S. 877; NLRB v. Hershey Chocolate Corporation, *et al.*, 297 F. 2d 286, 293–294 (C.A. 3). However, in the *Hershey* case, the court added that it had "serious doubts whether the Board in this instance wisely rejected the arbitration decision.... It seems to us that such course would have resulted in the effectuation of the final adjustment policy declared desirable by Section 203 (d) of the Labor-Management Relations Act, 1947..."

4. Southern Steamship Company v. NLRB, 316 U.S. 31, 47.

discharge Ramsey for failing to pay his regular membership dues. The Company did not challenge the Union's right to resort to arbitration and properly so, for this was the very procedure which the parties had agreed in their contract was "adequate to provide a fair and final determination of all grievances arising under the terms of this Contract," and which justified the Union's no-strike commitment.[5] Furthermore, it is apparent that the parties' submission of their controversy was not only required by their agreement, but also, under established law, was mandatory and survived the contract term.

The record is clear that the issue of the Company's contractual obligation to comply with the Union's demand for Ramsey's discharge was fully and fairly litigated before an impartial arbitrator. In a well-reasoned and informed decision, the arbitrator sustained the Union's grievance. There is certainly not the slightest suggestion—nor is such a contention even urged —of fraud, collusion, or other irregularity on the part of any party to "railroad" Ramsey out of his job. Admittedly, Ramsey was in default in his dues payments which, under the contract at least, made him vulnerable to discharge. Although Ramsey was not given notice of the arbitration hearing, his interests were vigorously defended there by the Company, which had at all times supported Ramsey's position that he was not legally required to maintain his union membership and stubbornly resisted the Union's efforts to secure his removal from his job. For these reasons, we find no serious procedural infirmities in the arbitration proceedings which warrant disregarding the arbitrator's award.[6] After all is said and done, "procedural regularity [is] not ... an end in itself, but [is] ... a means of defending substantive interests."

Nor do we find, as the Trial Examiner did, that the resolution of the legal issue before him

5. Article X, section 2. In Textile Workers Union of America, AFL–CIO v. Lincoln Mills of Alabama, 352 U.S. 448, 455, the Court observed: "Plainly the agreement to arbitrate grievance disputes is the *quid pro quo* for an agreement not to strike."

6. The present case is plainly distinguished from Gateway Transportation Co., 137 N.L.R.B. 1763, where the Board refused to give effect to an arbitration award because the arbitration proceeding did not measure up to the standards of fairness. There, unlike here, the employee contested the employer's right to discharge him and, although neither the union nor anyone else sponsored his cause, he was denied the opportunity to do so himself. In the present case, on the other hand, the Company was aligned in interest with Ramsey and both before and at the arbitration proceeding strenuously resisted the Union's asserted right to demand Ramsey's discharge. Indeed, the arbitration proceeding was initiated by the Union because the Company refused to heed its demand.

was at variance with settled law and therefore clearly repugnant to the purposes of the Act. In the light of recent Board decisions and the rapidly developing body of Federal labor law reflected in the *Lincoln Mills* line of cases, the decisions relied upon by the Trial Examiner to support his finding are not conclusive. For example, they do not answer basic questions respecting the Union's contractual right to pursue arbitration to enforce its demand, first made *during the contract term*, for the discharge of Ramsey for failing to make dues payments as required by a concededly valid union-security agreement. However, we need not decide these questions in determining to accept the arbitrator's award since it plainly appears to us that the award is not palpably wrong. To require more of the Board would mean substituting the Board's judgment for that of the arbitrator, thereby defeating the purposes of the Act and the common goal of national labor policy of encouraging the final adjustment of disputes, "as part and parcel of the collective bargaining process."

In sum, while an arbitrator's award concededly cannot oust the Board of its jurisdiction to adjudicate unfair labor practice charges, we conclude that, under the facts and circumstances herein, it will effectuate the policies of the Act to respect the award and dismiss the complaint in its entirety.

[The board dismissed the complaint.]

MEMBER RODGERS (dissenting): I disagree with my colleagues' decision to dismiss this complaint, and I would find, as did the Trial Examiner, that the Respondent Union unlawfully caused the Respondent to discriminate against employee Ramsey.

The facts are not in dispute. Employee Ramsey became delinquent in his dues payable to the Union under a union-security clause in its contract with the Company, and the Union, pursuant to that contract, filed a grievance seeking Ramsey's discharge. On August 1, 1958, and before anything else occurred, *the contract expired*. Although the contract was no longer in effect and Indiana's right-to-work law made it unlawful for the Company and Union to enter into any new union-security agreement, the Union continued to press for Ramsey's discharge. At one point, the Union rejected an offer which would have given it all back dues owed by Ramsey, adamantly insisting that Ramsey be discharged. The matter was ultimately considered by the permanent arbitrator appointed under the contract. The arbitrator sustained the Union's position that the Company should have discharged Ramsey. Because of Indiana's right-to-work law, the arbitrator ruled that Ramsey "be regarded as having been reemployed on August 1, 1958." The effect of this award was to deprive Ramsey of 15 or 16 years' seniority, and within a few days after the Company notified Ramsey it was complying with that award, Ramsey was caught in a layoff because of reduced seniority brought about by this award.

In reversing the Trial Examiner and dismissing the complaint, the majority rely on the fact that we have here an arbitrator's award, and that it was pursuant to this award that Ramsey lost his seniority rights and perforce his job. It must be noted that the majority does not say that Ramsey suffered no unlawful discrimination. They do not say that in pressing for this arbitrator's award the Union was acting within the law. They do not say that the award itself was one consonant with rights secured to employees under the National Labor Relations Act. The majority has avoided these basic issues and has chosen to "honor" the award solely because that "award is not palpably wrong." I disagree.

Under established Board precedent, a union cannot lawfully demand an employee's discharge for nonpayment of union dues absent *the existence* of a valid union-security agreement. Material here, of course, is the word "existence." The Board has consistently held that a union can justify such a demand for a discharge only by showing that a permissible union-security agreement was in effect *at the moment* the attempted or actual discharge action is taken, and the fact that the employee may have failed to satisfy dues obligations accrued under a *prior* union-security agreement does not make the discharge demand lawful. The facts recited above show that after the contract expired the Union continued to press for, and ultimately succeeded in obtaining, Ramsey's "discharge." Since no union-security agreement existed during this period, the Union had no lawful basis for pressing for Ramsey's discharge, and, it follows, the arbitrator's award upholding the Union's position conflicted with Ramsey's rights guaranteed under the Act. The award being so clearly at odds with the statute is not one which I think the Board should honor.

For the foregoing reasons, I would sustain the Trial Examiner and find the violations alleged.

MEMBER FANNING (dissenting): I would affirm the Trial Examiner for the reasons set forth in his Intermediate Report.

LUMMUS COMPANY
142 N.L.R.B. 517 (1963)

The agreement contains a provision which provides that when an applicant or a registrant believes that he has not received fair treatment at the hiring hall, he may file a written appeal to a joint hiring committee that is composed of equal members of Employer and Union representatives. The appellant appears before the committee which then decides his appeal. In the event of a deadlock, the appellant may take his appeal to an impartial umpire whose decisions are final. Respondents contend that the Board should not have entertained this case in the first instance because the Kivlins did not use the appeal procedure. Unlike our dissenting colleague, Member Brown, we find this contention to be without merit. The evidence, in our opinion, refutes the assumption that the Kivlins had actual "knowledge" of the appeal procedure.* While the Kivlins were long-standing union members, it seems quite clear from the record in this case that they did not know what course to pursue after being denied an opportunity to register at Local 80's hiring hall. They were, rather, denied the benefit of Gibson's attempted explanation through the threats of Local 80's steward. In these circumstances, we cannot agree with our dissenting colleague that the "record does not disclose any justification for the failure to invoke the available contractual grievance machinery."

Moreover, Members Rodgers and Leedom find Respondents' contention to be without merit for an additional reason. It is true that the Board has exercised its discretion in the past in recognizing an arbitration award which appears to have been conducted pursuant to fair and regular proceedings with all parties agreeing to be bound and the decision is not clearly repugnant to the purposes and policies of the Act. *Spielberg Manufacturing Company,* 112 N.L.R.B. 1080, 1082. However, we are not faced with such a situation here. There has been no request for arbitration by the aggrieved parties. We are dealing only with primary jurisdiction and the interposition of the agreement in itself cannot oust the Board from its primary jurisdiction over unfair labor practices. In effect, the Respondents here would seek to have the aggrieved parties submit, exclusive of all other procedures, to the jurisdiction of a private tribunal composed, at least in part, of the perpetrators of the unfair labor practices involved herein. In situations like that presented in the instant case, the common interest

*They were members of a sister local.

of the employer and the union representatives could be expected to militate against the likelihood of a deadlock and thus preclude access to an impartial tribunal. Under such circumstances, we do not feel that the Kivlins should be penalised for failing to employ such a remedy.

ROADWAY EXPRESS, INC.
145 N.L.R.B. 513 (1963)

In resting our decision on the merits of the fully litigated 8 (a) (3) issue rather than the Joint Area Committee's judgment as to whether Burns, contrary to company rules and specific instructions, was away from his equipment during its repair, we are not departing from the principles set forth in *Spielberg Manufacturing Company*, nor from our decision in *Denver-Chicago Trucking Company, Inc.*

In *Denver-Chicago*, we considered an award rendered by a bipartite committee, and ruled that the absence of an impartial public member on the arbitration panel did not necessarily invalidate such an award under the *Spielberg* standards of fairness and regularity. However, the record in the case did not suggest a division-in-interest between the entire committee and the aggrieved employees.

In the ordinary arbitration proceeding the parties, being unable to adjust a dispute under grievance procedures, submit it to an impartial third party for decision under the terms of their contract. In such circumstances, the interests of the parties are in conflict and we have given binding effect to the arbitrator's determination. Where contract grievance procedures simply provide for the submission of a dispute to a bipartite committee, composed of representatives of the contracting parties, the absence of a public, or impartial, member will not necessarily foreclose the exercise of our discretion to give binding effect to decisions of the committee, for each representative is customarily prepared to argue for or against the merits of the employee's grievance. However, where in addition to the absence of an impartial or public member it appears from the evidence that all members of the bipartite panel may be arrayed in common interest against the individual grievant, strong doubt exists as to whether the procedures comport with the standards of impartiality that we expect to find in arbitration. In the instant case, Burns' vigorous opposition to the Teamsters Union, underscored by his formation and becoming first president of the Rebel Teamsters Union for the purpose of providing employees in the truck-

ing industry an alternative to his own Local 710 and its sister locals affiliated with the International Brotherhood of Teamsters, together with his repeated and widely publicized attacks upon the trucking industry in general, strongly support the conclusion that the arbitration tribunal was constituted with members whose common interests were adverse to the grievant, Burns. For such reasons, we do not in the present circumstances rest our decision upon the award of the Joint Area Committee, but adopt, instead, the Trial Examiner's finding on the merits that the Respondent did not violate Section 8(a) (3) and (1) of the Act in discharging Burns.

[The Board dismissed the complaint.]

MEMBER FANNING (concurring). I concur in my colleagues' adoption of the Trial Examiner's independent findings on the merits that Burns was discharged for cause rather than for engaging in antiunion activity, and that the Respondent did not violate Section 8(a) (3) of the Act by separating him from its employ. In view of these factual findings as to the reason for Burns' discharge, I see no need to consider whether the arbitration award of the Joint Area Committee satisfied the standards of acceptability set forth in the *Spielberg* decision. Hence, I do not subscribe to my colleagues' observations as to that award, or to their generalizations concerning the composition of arbitral boards or the manner in which they should function.

To be sure, the binding effect of an arbitration award should always depend upon a close examination of the circumstances under which it was rendered whenever rights under the Act may be at stake. *Spielberg* has long embodied that caution.

RALEY'S SUPERMARKETS
143 N.L.R.B. 256 (1963)

Upon a petition duly filed under Section 9(c) of the National Labor Relations Act, a hearing was held before M. C. Dempster, hearing officer. The hearing officer's rulings made at the hearing are free from prejudicial error and are hereby affirmed.

Upon the entire record in this case, the Board finds:

1. The Employer is engaged in commerce within the meaning of the Act.
2. The labor organization [*sic*] involved claim to represent certain employees of the Employer.
3. No question affecting commerce exists con-

cerning the representation of employees of the Employer within the meaning of Section 9(c) (1) and Section 2 (6) and (7) of the Act for the following reasons:

The Petitioner seeks a unit of 14 janitors and 3 bottle sorters employed at the Employer's 12 retail food stores located in the Sacramento, California, metropolitan area. The janitors mop and sweep the floors, clean the glass doors, and carry refuse to a disposal point outside the stores. They work an 8-hour day but begin about 3 hours before the clerks do. The bottle sorters sort empty bottles in sheds outside the stores. Other employees of the Employer have been represented by the Intervenor for more than 20 years on a multiemployer basis with retail store employees of a number of other employers in the area. With respect to these employees, bargaining is conducted through the Sacramento Valley Employers' Council, herein called the Council, and the Council and the Intervenor are currently parties to a collective-bargaining agreement, effective from May 1, 1961, to April 30, 1964. As described more fully below, the contract unit consists of all nonsupervisory employees of the Employer, excluding meat department employees.

In July 1962, shortly after the Employer decided to hire janitors and bottle sorters on a full-time basis, the Petitioner and the Employer entered into a contract covering the Employer's janitors. At about the same time, the Intervenor requested that the Employer include janitors and bottle sorters under their current multiemployer contract. The Employer refused, advising the Intervenor of its contract with the Petitioner. On September 6, 1962, the Intervenor filed unfair labor practice charges against the Employer alleging that the Employer had unlawfully dominated and assisted the Petitioner. After an investigation revealing that the Petitioner did not represent a majority of the Employer's janitors, a settlement agreement was approved by the Regional Director of the Twentieth Region on October 2, 1962, which nullified the contract between the Petitioner and the Employer covering the janitors. The Employer also agreed not to recognize the Petitioner as representative of the janitors, absent Board certification. In October 1962, the Intervenor, pursuant to the arbitration clause of the contract between the Council and the Intervenor, obtained an order from a State court requiring the Employer to arbitrate the question whether janitors and bottle sorters were covered by that contract. The instant petition was filed on December 4, 1962. On January 15, 1963, an award was handed down by an arbitrator, holding that employees of the Employer performing janitorial services and bottle sorting were covered by the contract between the Employer and the Intervenor.

The Intervenor contends that its contract with the Employer covers the employees sought herein, and that since the instant petition is not timely filed with respect to such a contract, the petition should be dismissed. In this connection, the Intervenor would have the Board give effect to the above-described arbitration award in which the arbitrator found that the multiemployer contract covers the employees involved herein. The Petitioner, relying particularly on the fact that janitors and bottle sorters are not mentioned in the contract, contends that the contract does not cover the employees sought in the petition. The Employer takes no position. For the reasons hereinafter set forth, we find merit in the Intervenor's contention that the Board should honor the arbitration award and conclude that the contract covers the Employer's janitors and bottle sorters, that the petition is not timely filed with respect to the contract, and that the petition should be dismissed.

In the recently decided *International Harvester Company* case, a majority of the Board indicated that it would give "hospitable acceptance to the arbitral process" in order "to promote industrial peace and stability by encouraging the practice and procedure of collective bargaining." Relying on various statutory provisions, particularly Section 203(d) of the Labor Management Relations Act, 1947, and on decisions of the United States Supreme Court which recognize arbitration as "an instrument of national labor policy for composing contractual differences," the Board concluded that it would withhold its undoubted authority to adjudicate unfair labor practice charges and give effect to arbitration awards involving the same subject matter "unless it clearly appears that the arbitration proceedings were tainted by fraud, collusion, or serious procedural irregularities or that the award was clearly repugnant to the purposes and policies of the Act." While it is true that *International Harvester,* as well as other cases in which the Board honored arbitration awards, involved unfair labor practice proceedings, we believe that the same considerations which moved the Board to honor arbitration awards in unfair labor practice cases are equally persuasive to a similar acceptance of the arbitral process in a representation proceeding such as the instant one. Thus, where, as here, a question of contract interpretation is in issue, and the parties thereto have set up in their agreement arbitration machinery for the settlement of disputes arising under the contract, and an award has already been rendered which meets Board requirements applicable to arbitration awards, we think that it would further the underlying objectives of the Act to promote industrial peace and stability to give effect thereto. It is true, of course, that under Section 9 of the Act the Board is empowered to decide questions concerning representation. However, this authority to decide questions concerning representation does not preclude the Board in a proper case from considering an arbitration award in determining whether such a question exists.

We are satisfied that the award upon which the Intervenor relies meets the above-mentioned requirements applicable to arbitration awards for the following reasons: The arbitration proceeding was conducted pursuant to a provision in the agreement between the Intervenor and the Employer. The parties to the arbitration proceeding were the Employer and the Intervenor. The issue presented to the arbitrator was whether employees of the Employer performing janitorial services and bottle sorting were covered by the agreement. The Intervenor took the position that this contract covered janitors and bottle sorters. The Employer vigorously contended that the contract did not cover these employees. In his award of January 15, 1963, the arbitrator held that employees of the Employer performing janitorial services and bottle sorting were covered by the contract.

The arbitrator decided essentially the same issue as to the scope of the contract that confronts the Board in the instant representation case. We perceive nothing in the arbitrator's decision, relating to the contract coverage of janitors and bottle sorters, that is repugnant to the purposes and policies of the Act. Indeed, in circumstances substantially identical with those in the instant case, the Board has held that the employees involved were an accretion to the contract unit and were therefore covered by the contract. In addition, the arbitration proceeding was fair and regular and free from any procedural infirmity which might render the award unacceptable.[1]

---

1. While the Petitioner was not a party to the arbitration, as already indicated, its position was vigorously defended by the Employer, which at all times maintained, in agreement with the Petitioner, that the contract did not cover the employees sought herein. See *International Harvester, supra.*

Although Member Fanning dissented in *International Harvester* because of his agreement with the Trial Examiner, who had relied, *inter alia*, on the absence of the alleged discriminatee from the arbitration proceedings even though his position had been vigorously espoused by the company, he is of the view that the circumstances of this case are so different from *International Harvester* that the absence of the Petitioner from the arbitration proceedings here does not bar its acceptance by the Board.

In view of the foregoing, we find it will effectuate the policies and purposes of the Act to honor the arbitration award. We, accordingly, find that the contract between the Employer and the Intervenor covers the employees sought herein, and that, since the petition is untimely with respect to such contract, the contract is a bar to the petition.

[The Board dismissed the petition.]

MEMBERS RODGERS and BROWN took no part in the consideration of the above Decision and Order.

CLOVERLEAF DIV. OF ADAMS DAIRY CO., 147 N.L.R.B. 1410 (1964)

The Trial Examiner found that although Respondent might have violated Section 8(a) (5) by changing the working conditions of some of its drivers without notifying or consulting with the Union in advance, the complaint should be dismissed because the Union had not resorted to the arbitration provisions of the existing contract. We do not agree.

The contract subject to its arbitration procedures only such disputes as concern "the interpretation or application of the terms of this Agreement." But in the instant case, the precise union claim, which is the subject of the complaint before us, does not relate to the meaning of any established term or condition of the contract, or to any asserted misapplication thereof by Respondent. It is directed instead at Respondent's denial to it of a statutory right guaranteed by Section 8(d) of the Act, namely, the right to be notified and consulted in advance, and to be given an opportunity to bargain, about substantial changes in the working conditions of unit employees in respects *not covered by the contract.* As the particular dispute between the Union and Respondent now before us thus involves basically a disagreement over statutory rather than contractual obligations, the disposition of the controversy is quite clearly within the competency of the Board, and not of an arbitrator who would be without authority to grant the Union the particular redress it seeks and for which we provide below in our remedial order. (*The Timken Roller Bearing Co.*)

We are not unmindful of the fact that the resolution of the unfair labor practice issue in this case has required our consideration, as a subsidiary issue, of Respondent's claim that it was impliedly authorized under the contract to take unilateral action on the matters complained of—a claim we have rejected as without merit. We may assume that this claim gave rise to a difference over the meaning of contractual provisions that might have been submitted for consideration under the contract's arbitration procedures. Nevertheless, we do not consider that reason enough for us to refuse either to entertain the instant unfair labor practice proceeding, or to provide the necessary redress for the violation found. It is quite clear that the Board is not precluded from resolving an unfair labor practice issue, which may call for appropriate relief under the Act, simply because as an incident to such violation it may be necessary to construe the scope of a contract which an arbitrator is also empowered to construe. Section 10(a) of the Act expressly provides with respect to the Board's power to prevent unfair labor practices that "[t]his power shall not be affected by any other means of adjustment or prevention that has been or may be established by agreement, law, or otherwise."

Nor in our view is the situation presented by this case such as to move us in the exercise of our discretion to withhold our own remedial processes in deference to the arbitration processes the parties have agreed upon for the settlement of contract disputes. None of the considerations that have impelled us to do so in other cases is present here. In the instant case, it does not appear that there is already in existence an arbitration award passing on matters that bear on the ultimate issue we must decide, and to which we are asked to give weight or effect. Indeed, it affirmatively appears that neither party has even so much as sought to invoke arbitration. Nor is this a case involving an alleged unfair labor practice, the existence of which turns primarily on an interpretation of specific contractual provisions, unquestionably encompassed by the contract's arbitration provisions, and coming to us in a context that makes it reasonably probable that arbitration settlement of the contract dispute would also put at rest the unfair labor practice controversy in a manner sufficient to effectuate the policies of the Act.

B.

The Problem of Primary Jurisdiction—The Board's and the Arbitrator's

SMITH v. EVENING NEWS ASSOCIATION
371 U.S. 195 (1962)

WHITE, J. Petitioner is a building maintenance employee of respondent Evening News Association, a newspaper publisher engaged in interstate commerce, and is a member of the Newspaper Guild of Detroit, a labor organization having a collective bargaining contract with respondent. Petitioner, individually and as assignee of 49 other similar employees who were also Guild members, sued respondent for breach of contract in the Circuit Court of Wayne County, Michigan.[1] The complaint stated that in December 1955 and January 1956 other employees of respondent, belonging to another union, were on strike and respondent did not permit petitioner and his assignors to report to their regular shifts, although they were ready, able and available for work. During the same period, however, employees of the editorial, advertising and business departments, not covered by collective bargaining agreements, were permitted to report for work and were paid full wages even though there was no work available. Respondent's refusal to pay full wages to petitioner and his assignors while paying the non-union employees, the complaint asserted, violated a clause in the contract providing that "there shall be no discrimination against any employee because of his membership or activity in the Guild."

The trial court sustained respondent's motion to dismiss for want of jurisdiction on the ground that the allegations, if true, would make out an unfair labor practice under the National Labor Relations Act and hence the subject matter was within the exclusive jurisdiction of the National Labor Relations Board. The Michigan Supreme Court affirmed, 362 Mich. 350, 106 N.W. 2d 785, relying upon San Diego Trades Council v. Garmon, 359 U.S. 236, and like pre-emption cases. Certiorari was granted, 369 U.S. 827, after the decisions of this Court in Local 174, Teamsters v. Lucas Flour Co., 69 U.S. 95, and Dowd Box Co. v. Courtney, 368 U.S. 502.

Lucas Flour and *Dowd Box*, as well as the later Atkinson v. Sinclair Refining Co., 370 U.S. 238, were suits upon collective bargaining con-

---

1. There was no grievance arbitration procedure in this contract which had to be exhausted before recourse could be had to the courts. Compare Atkinson v. Sinclair Refining Co., 370 U.S. 238; Drake Bakeries Inc. v. Local 50, American Bakery Workers, 370 U.S. 254.

tracts brought or held to arise under § 301 of the Labor Management Relations Act and in these cases the jurisdiction of the courts was sustained although it was seriously urged that the conduct involved was arguably protected or prohibited by the National Labor Relations Act and therefore within the exclusive jurisdiction of the National Labor Relations Board. In *Lucas Flour* as well as in *Atkinson* the Court expressly refused to apply the pre-emption doctrine of the *Garmon* case; and we likewise reject that doctrine here where the alleged conduct of the employer, not only arguably, but concededly, is an unfair labor practice within the jurisdiction of the National Labor Relations Board. The authority of the Board to deal with an unfair labor practice which also violates a collective bargaining contract is not displaced by § 301, but it is not exclusive and does not destroy the jurisdiction of the courts in suits under § 301. If, as respondent strongly urges, there are situations in which serious problems will arise from both the courts and the Board having jurisdiction over acts which amount to an unfair labor practice, we shall face those cases when they arise. This is not one of them, in our view, and the National Labor Relations Board is in accord.

We are left with respondent's claim that the predicate for escaping the *Garmon* rule is not present here because this action by an employee to collect wages in the form of damages is not among those "suits for violation of contracts between an employer and a labor organization," as provided in § 301. There is support for respondent's position in decisions of the Courts of Appeals, and in Association of Westinghouse Salaried Employees v. Westinghouse Corp., 348 U.S. 437, a majority of the Court in three separate opinions concluded that § 301 did not give the federal courts jurisdiction over a suit brought by a union to enforce employee rights which were variously characterized as "peculiar in the individual benefit which is their subject matter," "uniquely personal" and arising "from separate hiring contracts between the employer and each employee." Id., at 460, 461, 464.

However, subsequent decisions here have removed the underpinnings of *Westinghouse* and its holding is no longer authoritative as a precedent. Three of the Justices in that case were driven to their conclusion because in their view § 301 was procedural only, not substantive, and therefore grave constitutional questions would be raised if § 301 was held to extend to the controversy there involved. However, the same three Justices observed that if, contrary to their belief, "Congress has itself defined the law or authorized the federal courts to fashion the judicial

rules governing this question, it would be self-defeating to limit the scope of the power of the federal courts to less than is necessary to accomplish this congressional aim." *Id.,* at 442, Textile Workers v. Lincoln Mills, 353 U.S. 448, of course, has long since settled that § 301 has substantive content and that Congress has directed the courts to formulate and apply federal law to suits for violation of collective bargaining contracts. There is no constitutional difficulty and § 301 is not to be given a narrow reading. *Id.,* at 456, 457. Section 301 has been applied to suits to compel arbitration of such individual grievances as rates of pay, hours of work and wrongful discharge, Textile Workers v. Lincoln Mills, *supra*; General Electric Co. v. Local 205, UEW, 353 U.S. 547; to obtain specific enforcement of an arbitrator's award ordering reinstatement and back pay to individual employees, United Steelworkers v. Enterprise Wheel & Car Corp., 363 U.S. 593; to recover wage increases in a contest over the validity of the collective bargaining contract, Dowd Box Co. v. Courtney, *supra*; and to suits against individual union members for violation of a no-strike clause contained in a collective bargaining agreement. Atkinson v. Sinclair Refining Co., *supra*.

The concept that all suits vindicate individual employee rights arising from a collective bargaining contract should be excluded from the coverage of § 301 has thus not survived. The rights of individual employees concerning rates of pay and conditions of employment are a major focus of the negotiation and administration of collective bargaining contracts. Individual claims lie at the heart of the grievance and arbitration machinery, are to a large degree inevitably intertwined with union interests and many times precipitate grave questions concerning the interpretation and enforceability of the collective bargaining contract on which they are based. To exclude these claims from the ambit of § 301 would stultify the congressional policy of having the administration of collective bargaining contracts accomplished under a uniform body of federal substantive law. This we are unwilling to do.

The same considerations foreclose respondent's reading of § 301 to exclude all suits brought by employees instead of unions. The word "between," it suggests, refers to "suits," not "contracts," and therefore only suits between unions and employers are within the purview of § 301. According to this view, suits by employees for breach of a collective bargaining contract would not arise under § 301 and would be governed by state law, if not pre-empted by *Garmon*, as this one would be, whereas a suit by a union for the same breach of the same contract would be a § 301 suit ruled by federal law. Neither the language and structure of § 301 nor its legislative history requires or persuasively supports this restrictive interpretation, which would frustrate rather than serve the congressional policy expressed in that section. "The possibility that individual contract terms might have different meanings under state and federal law would inevitably exert a disruptive influence upon both the negotiation and administration of collective agreements." Local 174, Teamsters v. Lucas Flour Co., *supra,* at 103.

We conclude that petitioner's action arises under § 301 and is not pre-empted under the *Garmon* rule.[2] The judgment of the Supreme Court of Michigan is reversed and the cause remanded for further proceedings not inconsistent with this opinion.

Reversed and remanded.

BLACK, J. (dissenting). I would affirm the Michigan Supreme Court's holding that Michigan courts are without jurisdiction to entertain suits by employees against their employers for damages measured by "back pay" based on discrimination, which discrimination § 8(a) of the National Labor Relations Act makes an unfair labor practice and which § 10(b) and (c) subject to the jurisdiction of the Labor Board with power after hearings to award "back pay." It is true that there have been expressions in recent cases which indicate that a suit for the violation of a collective bargaining contract may be brought in a state or federal court even though the conduct objected to was also arguably an unfair labor practice within the Labor Board's jurisdiction. It seems clear to me that these expressions of opinion were not necessary to the decisions in those cases[3] and that neither these prior decisions nor § 301 of the Labor

Management Relations Act requires us to hold that either employers or unions can be made to defend themselves against governmental regulation and sanctions of the same type for the same conduct by both courts and the Labor Board. Such duplication of governmental supervision over industrial relationships is bound to create the same undesirable confusion, conflicts, and burdensome proceedings of the National Labor Relations Act was designed to prevent, as we have interpreted that Act in prior cases like San Diego Building Trades Council v. Garmon, 359 U.S. 236 (1959).

One example is enough to show how Congress' policy of confining controversies over unfair labor practices to the Labor Board might well be frustrated by permitting unfair labor practice claimants to choose whether they will seek relief in the courts or before the Board. Section 10(b) of the Act provides that "no complaint shall issue based upon any unfair labor practice occurring more than six months prior to the filing of the charge with the Board." In contrast, the statute of limitations in Michigan governing breach of contract suits like this is six years. The Court's holding thus opens up a way to defeat the congressional plan, adopted over vigorous minority objection, to expedite industrial peace by requiring that both the complaining party and the Board act promptly in the initiation of unfair labor practice proceedings. Instead, by permitting suits like this one to be filed, it is now not only possible but highly probable that unfair labor practice disputes will hang on like festering sores that grow worse and worse with the years. Of course this Court could later, by another major statutory surgical operation, apply the six-months Labor Board statute of limitations to actions for breach of collective bargaining contracts under § 301. But if such drastic changes are to be wrought in the Act that Congress passed, it seems important to me that this Court should wait for Congress to perform that operation.

There is another reason why I cannot agree with the Court's disposition of this case. In the last note on the last page of its opinion, the Court says:

> The only part of the collective bargaining contract set out in this record is the no-discrimination clause. Respondent does not argue here and we need not consider the question of federal law of whether petitioner, under this contract, has standing to sue for breach of the no-discrimination clause nor do we deal with the standing of other employees to sue upon other clauses in other contracts.

---

2. The only part of the collective bargaining contract set out in this record is the no-discrimination clause. Respondent does not argue here and we need not consider the question of federal law of whether petitioner, under this contract, has standing to sue for breach of the no-discrimination clause nor do we deal with the standing of other employees to sue upon other clauses in other contracts.

3. Atkinson v. Sinclair Rfg. Co., involved a strike by union members over pay claims, in violation of an agreement to arbitrate grievances. Local 174, Teamsters Union v. Lucas Flour Co., concerned a strike by the union over the discharge of an employee, in violation of an agreement to arbitrate such disputes. Dowd Box Co. v. Courtney, was an action by union officers against a company for failure to put into effect pay increases and vacation benefits provided in a collective bargaining agreement. In my view, none of the activities in any of these cases were even arguably unfair labor practices subject to the Labor Board's jurisdiction, and the Court did not suggest that they were.

Unless my reading of this note is wrong, the Court purports to reserve the question of whether an employee who has suffered the kind of damages here alleged arising from breach of a collective bargaining agreement can file a lawsuit for himself under § 301. Earlier in its opinion the Court decides that a claim for individual wages or back pay is within the subject-matter jurisdiction of courts under § 301, that is, that such a claim is of the type that the courts are empowered to determine. The Court then rejects respondent's argument that an individual employee can never under any circumstances bring a § 301 suit. But it seems to me that the Court studiously refrains from saying when, for what kinds of breach, or under what circumstances an individual employee can bring a § 301 action and when he must step aside for the union to prosecute his claim. Nor does the Court decide whether the suit brought in this case is one of the types an individual can bring. This puzzles me. This Court usually refrains from deciding important questions of federal law such as are involved in this case without first satisfying itself that the party raising those questions is entitled (has standing) to prosecute the case. It seems to me to be at least a slight deviation from the Court's normal practice to determine the law that would be applicable in a particular lawsuit while leaving open the question of whether such a law-suit has even been brought in the particular case the court is deciding. This Court has not heretofore thought itself authorized to render advisory opinions. Moreover, I am wholly unable to agree that the right of these individuals to bring this lawsuit under § 301 was not argued here.

Finally, since the Court is deciding that this type of action can be brought to vindicate workers' rights, I think it should also decide clearly and unequivocally whether an employee injured by the discrimination of either his employer or his union can file and prosecute his own lawsuit in his own way. I cannot believe that Congress intended by the National Labor Relations Act either as originally passed or as amended by § 301 to take away rights to sue individuals have freely exercised in this country at least since the concept of due process of law became recognized as a guiding principle in our jurisprudence. And surely the Labor Act was not intended to relegate workers with lawsuits to the status of wards either of companies or of unions.

NLRB v. C & C PLYWOOD CORP.
385 U.S. 421 (1967)

STEWART, J. The respondent employer was brought before the National Labor Relations Board to answer a complaint that its inauguration of a premium pay plan during the term of a collective agreement, without prior consultation with the union representing its employees, violated the duties imposed by §§ 8(a) (5) and (1) of the National Labor Relations Act. The Board issued a cease-and-desist order, rejecting the claim that the respondent's action was authorized by the collective agreement. The Court of Appeals for the Ninth Circuit refused, however, to enforce the Board's order. It reasoned that a provision in the agreement between the union and the employer, which "arguably" allowed the employer to institute the premium pay plan, divested the Board of jurisdiction to entertain the union's unfair labor practice charge. 351 F. 2d 224. We granted certiorari to consider a substantial question of federal labor law. 384 U.S. 903.

In August 1962, the Plywood, Lumber, and Saw Mill Workers Local No. 2405 was certified as the bargaining representative of the respondent's production and maintenance employees. The agreement which resulted from collective bargaining contained the following provision:

Article XVII

WAGES

A. A classified wage scale has been agreed upon by the Employer and Union, and has been signed by the parties and thereby made a part of the written agreement. The Employer reserves the right to pay a premium rate over and above the contractual classified wage rate to reward any particular employee for some special fitness, skill, aptitude or the like. The payment of such a premium rate shall not be considered a permanent increase in the rate of that position and may, at the sole option of the Employer, be reduced to the contractual rate.

The agreement also stipulated that wages should be "closed" during the period it was effective[1] and that neither party should be obligated to bargain collectively with respect to any matter not specifically referred to in the contract. Grievance machinery was established, but no ultimate arbitration of grievances or other disputes was provided.

---

1. Article XVII: "B. It is mutually agreed that the attached classified wage scale shall be effective upon the signing of this Working Agreement with wages closed for the term of that agreement...."

Less than three weeks after this agreement was signed, the respondent posted a notice that all members of the "glue spreader" crews would be paid $2.50 per hour if their crews met specified biweekly (and later weekly) production standards, although under the "classified wage scale" referred to in the above quoted Art. XVII of the agreement, the members of these crews were to be paid hourly wages ranging from $2.15 to $2.29, depending upon their function within the crew. When the union learned of this premium pay plan through one of its members, it immediately asked for a conference with the respondent. During the meetings between the parties which followed this request, the employer indicated a willingness to discuss the terms of the plan, but refused to rescind it pending those discussions.

It was this refusal which prompted the union to charge the respondent with an unfair labor practice in violation of §§ 8 (a) (5) and (1). The trial examiner found that the respondent had instituted the premium-pay program in good-faith reliance upon the right reserved to it in the collective agreement. He, therefore, dismissed the complaint. The Board reversed. Giving consideration to the history of negotiations between the parties, as well as the express provisions of the collective agreement, the Board ruled the union had not ceded power to the employer unilaterally to change the wage system as it had. For while the agreement specified different hourly pay for different numbers of the glue spreader crews and allowed for merit increases for "particular employee[s]," the employer had placed all the members of these crews on the same wage scale and had made it a function of the production output of the crew as a whole.

In refusing to enforce the Board's order, the Court of Appeals did not decide that the premium-pay provision of the labor agreement had been misinterpreted by the Board. Instead, it held the Board did not have jurisdiction to find the respondent had violated § 8(a) of the Labor Act, because the "existence . . . of an unfair labor practice [did] not turn entirely upon the provisions of the Act, but arguably upon a good-faith dispute as to the correct meaning of the provisions of the collective bargaining agreement." 351 F. 2d, at 228.

The respondent does not question the proposition that an employer may not unilaterally institute merit increases during the term of a collective agreement unless some provision of the contract authorizes him to do so. See NLRB v. J. H. Allison & Co., 165 F. 2d 766 (C. A. 6th Cir.),

cert. denied, 335 U.S. 814. Cf. Beacon Piece Dyeing Co., 121 N.L.R.B. 953 (1958). The argument is, rather, that since the contract contained a provision which *might* have allowed the respondent to institute the wage plan in question, the Board was powerless to determine whether the provision *did* authorize the respondent's action, because the question was one for a state or federal court under § 301 of the Act.

In evaluating this contention, it is important first to point out that the collective bargaining agreement contained no arbitration clause. The contract did provide grievance procedures, but the end result of those procedures, if differences between the parties remained unresolved, was economic warfare, not "the therapy of arbitration." Carey v. Westinghouse Corp., 375 U.S. 261, 272. Thus, the Board's action in this case was in no way inconsistent with its previous recognition of arbitration as "an instrument of national labor policy for composing contractual differences." International Harvester Co., 138 N.L.R.B. 923, 926 (1962), aff'd sub nom., Ramsey v. NLRB, 327 F. 2d 784 (C. A. 7th Cir.), cert. denied, 377 U.S. 1003.

The respondent's argument rests primarily upon the legislative history of the 1947 amendments to the National Labor Relations Act. It is said that the rejection by Congress of a bill which would have given the Board unfair labor practice jurisdiction over all breaches of collective bargaining agreements shows that the Board is without power to decide any case involving the interpretation of a labor contract. We do not draw that inference from this legislative history.

When Congress determined that the Board should not have general jurisdiction over all alleged violations of collective bargaining agreements and that such matters should be placed within the jurisdiction of the courts, it was acting upon a principle which this Court had already recognized:

> The Railway Labor Act, like the National Labor Relations Act, does not undertake governmental regulation of wages, hours, or working conditions. Instead it seeks to provide a means by which agreement may be reached with respect to them.

Terminal Railroad Assn. v. Brotherhood of Railroad Trainmen, 318 U.S. 1, 6. To have conferred upon the National Labor Relations Board generalized power to determine the rights of parties under all collective agreements would have been a step toward governmental regulation of the terms of those agreements. We view

Congress' decision not to give the Board that broad power as a refusal to take this step.[2]

But in this case the Board has not construed a labor agreement to determine the extent of the contractual rights which were given the union by the employer [sic]. It has not imposed its own view of what the terms and conditions of the labor agreement should be. It has done no more than merely enforce a statutory right which Congress considered necessary to allow labor and management to get on with the process of reaching fair terms and conditions of employment— "to provide a means by which agreement may be reached." The Board's interpretation went only so far as was necessary to determine that the union did not agree to give up these statutory safeguards. Thus, the Board, in necessarily construing a labor agreement to decide this unfair labor practice case, has not exceeded the jurisdiction laid out for it by Congress.

This conclusion is reenforced by previous judicial recognition that a contractual defense does not divest the Labor Board of jurisdiction. For example, in Mastro Plastics Corp. v. NLRB, 350 U.S. 270, the legality of an employer's refusal to reinstate strikers was based upon the Board's construction of a "no strike" clause in the labor agreement, which the employer contended allowed him to refuse to take back workers who had walked out in protest over his unfair labor practice. The strikers applied to the Board for reinstatement and back pay. In giving the requested relief, the Board was forced to construe the scope of the "no strike" clause. This Court, in affirming, stressed that the whole case turned "upon the proper interpretation of the particular contract." 350 U.S., at 279. Thus, Mastro Plastics stands squarely against the respondent's theory as to the Board's lack of power in the present case.

If the Board in a case like this had no jurisdiction to consider a collective agreement prior to an authoritative construction by the courts, labor organizations would face inordinate delays in obtaining vindication of their statutory rights. Where, as here, the parties have not provided for arbitration, the union would have to institute a court action to determine the applicability of the premium pay provision of the collective bar-

gaining agreement.[3] If it succeeded in court, the union would then have to go back to the Labor Board to begin an unfair labor practice proceeding. It is not unlikely that this would add years to the already lengthy period required to gain relief from the Board. Congress cannot have intended to place such obstacles in the way of the Board's effective enforcement of statutory duties. For in the labor field, as in few others, time is crucially important in obtaining relief. Amalgamated Clothing Workers v. Richman Bros. Co., 348 U.S. 511, 526 (dissenting opinion).

The legislative history of the Labor Act, the precedent interpreting it, and the interest of its efficient administration thus all lead to the conclusion that the Board had jurisdiction to deal with the unfair labor practice charge in this case. We hold that the Court of Appeals was in error in deciding to the contrary.

The remaining question, not reached by the Court of Appeals, is whether the Board was wrong in concluding that the contested provision in the collective agreement gave the respondent no unilateral right to institute its premium pay plan. In reaching this conclusion, the Board relied upon its experience with labor relations and the Act's clear emphasis upon the protection of free collective bargaining. We cannot disapprove of the Board's approach. For the law of labor agreements cannot be based upon abstract definitions unrelated to the context in which the parties bargained and the basic regulatory scheme underlying that context. See Cox, *The Legal Nature of Collective Bargaining Agreements,* 57 MICH. L. REV. 1 (1958). Nor

---

2. Congress was also concerned with the possibility of conflicting decisions that would result from placing all questions of contract interpretation before both the Board and the courts. See 93 Cong. Rec. 4153, 2 LEGIS. HISTORY OF LMRA 1043 (remarks of Senator Murray); 93 CONG. REC. 6600, 2 LEGIS. HISTORY OF LMRA 1539. But such a possibility does not arise in a case like the present one, since courts have no jurisdiction to enforce the union's statutory rights under §§ 8 (a) (5) and (1).

3. The precise nature of the union's case in court is not readily apparent. If damages for breach of contract were sought, the union would have difficulty in establishing the amount of injury caused by respondent's action. For the real injury in this case is to the union's status as bargaining representative, and it would be difficult to translate such damage into dollars and cents. If an injunction were sought to vindicate the union's contractual rights, the problem of the applicability of the Norris-LaGuardia Act would have to be faced. A federal injunction issuing from a court with § 301 jurisdiction might be barred by § 7 of that Act. See International Union of Electrical Workers v. General Electric Co., 341 F. 2d 571 (C.A. 2d Cir.); Local No. 861 v. Stone & Webster Corp., 163 F. Supp. 894 (D.C.W.D.La.). Cf. Sinclair Refining Co. v. Atkinson, 370 U.S. 195; Publishers' Assn. v. New York Mailers' Union, 317 F. 2d 624 (C.A. 2d Cir.), cert. granted, 375 U.S. 901, judgment vacated in part for dismissal as moot, 376 U.S. 775. Whether a state injunction might be similarly barred in suits governed by federal labor law, Teamsters Local v. Lucas Flour Co., 369 U.S. 95, is an open question. See Charles Dowd Box Co. v. Courtney, 368 U.S. 502, 514, n. 8. Thus, it may be that the only remedy in court which would be available to the union would be a suit for a declaratory judgment, assuming such a suit in these circumstances would be maintainable under state or federal law.

can we say that the Board was wrong in holding that the union had not foregone its statutory right to bargain about the pay plan inaugurated by the respondent. For the disputed contract provision referred to increases for "particular employee[s]," not group of workers. And there was nothing in it to suggest that the carefully worked out wage differentials for various members of the glue spreader crew could be invalidated by the respondent's decision to pay all members of the crew the same wage.

The judgment is accordingly reversed and the case is remanded to the Court of Appeals with directions to enforce the Board's order.

Reversed and remanded.

NLRB v. ACME INDUSTRIAL CO.
385 U.S. 432 (1967)

STEWART, J. In NLRB v. C. & C Plywood, decided today, we dealt with one aspect of an employer's duty to bargain during the term of a collective bargaining agreement. In this case we deal with another—involving the obligation to furnish information that allows a union to decide whether to process a grievance.

In April 1963, at the conclusion of a strike, the respondent entered into a collective bargaining agreement with the union which was the certified representative of its employees. The agreement contained two sections relevant to this case. Article 1, § 3, provided, "It is the Company's general policy not to subcontract work which is normally performed by employees in the bargaining unit where this will cause the layoff of employees or prevent the recall of employees who would normally perform this work." In Art. VI, § 10, the respondent agreed that

> [i]n the event the equipment of the plant . . . is hereafter moved to another location of the Company, employees working in the plant . . . who are subject to reduction in classification or layoff as a result thereof may transfer to the new location with full rights and seniority, unless there is then in existence at the new location a collective bargaining agreement covering . . . employees at such location.

A grievance procedure culminating in compulsory and binding arbitration was also incorporated into the collective agreement.

The present controversy began in January 1964, when the union discovered that certain machinery was being removed from the respondent's plant. When asked by union representatives about this movement, the respondent's foremen replied that there had been no violation of the collective agreement and that the company, therefore, was not obliged to answer any questions regarding the machinery. After the rebuff, the union filed 11 grievances charging the respondent with violations of the above quoted clauses of the collective agreement. The president of the union then wrote a letter to the respondent, requesting "the following information at the earliest possible date:

> 1. The approximate dates when each piece of equipment was moved out of the plant.
> 2. The place to which each piece of equipment was moved and whether such place is a facility which is operated or controlled by the Company.
> 3. The number of machines or equipment that was moved out of the plant.
> 4. What was the reason or purpose of moving the equipment out of the plant.
> 5. Is this equipment used for production elsewhere."

The company replied by letter that it had no duty to furnish this information since no layoffs or reductions in job classification had occurred within five days (the time limitation set by the contract for filing grievances) prior to the union's formal request for information.

This refusal prompted the union to file unfair labor practice charges with the Board. A complaint was issued, and the Board, overruling its trial examiner, held the respondent had violated § 8(a) (5) of the Act by refusing to bargain in good faith. Accordingly, it issued a cease-and-desist order. The Board found that the information requested was "necessary in order to enable the Union to evaluate intelligently the grievances filed" and pointed out that the agreement contained no "clause by which the Union waives its statutory right to such information."

The Court of Appeals for the Seventh Circuit refused to enforce the Board's order. 351 F. 2d 258. It did not question the relevance of the information nor the finding that the union had not expressly waived its right to the information. The court ruled, however, that the existence of a provision for binding arbitration of differences concerning the meaning and application of the agreement foreclosed the Board from exercising its statutory power. The court cited United Steelworkers v. Warrior & Gulf Navig. Co., 363 U.S. 574, and United Steelworkers v. American Mfg. Co., 363 U.S. 564, as articulating a national labor policy favoring arbitration and requiring the Board's deference to an arbitrator when construction and application of a labor agreement are in issue. We granted certiorari to consider the substantial question of federal labor law thus presented. 383 U.S. 905.

There can be no question of the general obligation of an employer to provide information that is needed by the bargaining representative for the proper performance of its duties. NLRB v. Truitt Mfg. Co., 351 U.S. 149. Similarly, the duty to bargain unquestionably extends beyond the period of contract negotiations and applies to labor-management relations during the term of an agreement. NLRB v. C & C Plywood Co.; NLRB v. F. W. Woolworth Co., 352 U.S. 938. The only real issue in this case, therefore, is whether the Board must await an arbitrator's determination of the relevancy of the requested information before it can enforce the union's statutory rights under § 8(a) (5).

The two cases upon which the court below relied, and the third of the *Steelworkers* trilogy, United Steelworkers v. Enterprise Wheel & Car Corp., 363 U.S. 593, do not throw much light on the problem. For those cases dealt with the relationship of courts to arbitrators when an arbitration award is under review or when the employer's agreement to arbitrate is in question. The weighing of the arbitrator's greater institutional competency, which was so vital to those decisions, must be evaluated in that context. 363 U.S., at 567, 581–582, 596–597. The relationship of the Board to the arbitration process is of a quite different order. See Carey v. Westinghouse, 375 U.S. 261, 269–272. Moreover, in assessing the Board's power to deal with unfair labor practices, provisions of the Labor Act which do not apply to the power of the courts under § 301, must be considered. Section 8(a) (5) proscribes failures to bargain collectively in only the most general terms, but §8(d) amplifies it by defining "to bargain collectively" as including "the mutual obligation of the employer and the representative of the employees to meet at reasonable times and confer in good faith with respect to . . . . any question arising [under an agreement]."[1] And § 10(a)[2] provides: "The Board is empowered . . . to prevent any person from engaging in any unfair labor practice. . . . This power shall not be affected by any other means of adjustment or prevention that has been or may be established by agreement, law or otherwise." Thus, to view the *Steelworkers* decisions as automatically requiring the Board in this case to defer to the primary determination of an

arbitrator[3] is to overlook important distinctions between those cases and this one.

But even if the policy of the *Steelworkers Cases* were thought to apply with the same vigor to the Board as to the courts, that policy would not require the Board to abstain here. For when it ordered the employer to furnish the requested information to the union, the Board was not making a binding construction of the labor contract. It was only acting upon the probability that the desired information was relevant, and that it would be of use to the union in carrying out its statutory duties and responsibilities. This discovery-type standard decided nothing about the merits of the union's contractual claims.[4] When the respondent furnishes the requested information, it may appear that no subcontracting or work transfer has occurred, and, accordingly, that the grievances filed are without merit. On the other hand, even if it appears that such activities have taken place, an arbitrator might uphold the respondent's contention that no breach of the agreement occurred because no employees were laid off or reduced in grade within five days prior to the filing of any grievance. Such conclusions would clearly not be precluded by the Board's threshold determination concerning the potential relevance of the requested information. Thus, the assertion of jurisdiction by the Board in this case in no way threatens the power which the parties have given the arbitrator to make binding interpretations of the labor agreement.

Far from intruding upon the preserve of the arbitrator, the Board's action was in aid of the arbitral process. Arbitration can function properly only if the grievance procedures leading to it can sift out unmeritorious claims. For if all claims originally initiated as grievances had to be processed through to arbitration, the system would be woefully overburdened. Yet, that is precisely what the respondent's restrictive view would require. It would force the union to take a grievance all the way through to arbitration without providing the opportunity to evaluate the

---

1. Cf. United Steelworkers v. Warrior & Gulf Co., 363 U.S. 574, 581: "The grievance procedure is, in other words, a part of the continuous collective bargaining process."

2. 29 U.S.C. § 160 (a) (1964 ed.).

---

3. See Sinclair Refining Co. v. NLRB, 306 F. 2d 569, 570 (C.A. 5th Cir.).

4. Cf. 4 MOORE, FEDERAL PRACTICE, ¶ 26.16[1], 1175–1176 (2d ed.): "[I]t must be borne in mind that the standard for determining relevancy at a discovery examination is not as well defined as at the trial. . . . Since the matters in dispute between the parties are not as well determined at discovery examinations as at the trial, courts of necessity must follow a more liberal standard as to relevancy."

Id., at 1181: "Examination as to relevant matters should be allowed whether or not the theory of the complaint is sound or the facts, if proved, would support the relief sought."

merits of the claim.[5] The expense of arbitration might be placed upon the union only for it to learn that the machines had been relegated to the junk heap. Nothing in federal labor law requires such a result.

---

5. See Fafnir Bearing Co. v. NLRB, 362 F. 2d 716: 721: "By preventing the Union from conducting these studies [for an intelligent appraisal of its right to grieve], the Company was, in essence, requiring it to play a game of blind man's buff."

We hold that the Board's order in this case was consistent both with the express terms of the Labor Act and with the national labor policy favoring arbitration which our decisions have discerned as underlying that law. Accordingly, we reverse the judgment and remand the case to the Court of Appeals with directions to enforce the Board's order.

Reversed and remanded.

C.

Arbitral Agreements Purporting to Exclude NLRB Jurisdiction

LODGE Nos. 743 and 1746, INT'L ASS'N OF MACHINISTS v. UNITED AIRCRAFT CORP.
337 F. 2d 5 (2d Cir. 1964)

WATERMAN, C. J. Appellees (hereinafter the Union) brought suit in the United States District Court for the District of Connecticut under § 301(a) of the Labor Management Relations Act, 29 U.S.C. § 185(a), alleging that appellants (hereinafter the Company) had violated a strike settlement agreement dated August 11, 1960. The Company counterclaimed, also under § 301(a), alleging a violation by the Union of a subsequent arbitration submission agreement dated August 24, 1960, and requesting declaratory relief, injunctive decrees, and damages. The Union, joined by the National Labor Relations Board as an intervenor, moved to dismiss the counterclaim on several grounds, including failure to state a claim upon which relief could be given, and on August 1, 1963 the motion was granted. The opinion below is reported at 220 F. Supp. 19. The Company appeals to this court under 28 U.S.C. § 1292(a) (1), which, insofar as it is relevant, authorizes appeals from interlocutory orders denying injunctive relief.[1]

The claims and counterclaims in this suit arose out of a strike called by the Union at four Company plants in June, 1960. The strike ended in failure two months later with the conclusion of a settlement agreement which provided, in part, for the recall to work of the strikers according to a complex formula. The Company, however, refused to apply the agreement to fifty employees whom it accused of misconduct during the strike. The Union, in response, contended that

---

1. This appeal therefore concerns only the denial of injunctive relief, and not the dismissal of the Company's request for a declaratory judgment and damages.

these employees had not engaged in conduct which merited them less favorable treatment than the other strikers received. Unable to reach an understanding, the parties executed an arbitration submission agreement which provided in part:

> To resolve this issue ... finally and completely, and without recourse whatsoever to any appeal or review under any State or federal laws by the Unions, or by the Company, or by any individual employee whose name is listed on Exhibit C attached hereto, the Unions (acting for and on behalf of themselves and in their capacity as representatives of the said individual employees so listed) and the Company agree as follows:
> 1. The Honorable Raymond E Baldwin, Chief Justice of the Supreme Court of Errors for the State of Connecticut, may appoint, and is hereby requested to appoint, a panel of three retired judges of the said Court (including a fourth judge to act as an alternate in this matter) to sit as an impartial board of arbitration to hear and decide finally and completely the aforesaid issue concerning the reinstatement rights of each of the striking employees whose names are listed on Exhibit C.
>
> 4. The panel shall have no jurisdiction or authority to award back pay to any employee involved in this matter, or to assess against any of the parties any monetary award or penalty, but shall have full, complete and final jurisdiction and authority to determine and decide whether any individual whose name is listed on Exhibit C attached hereto should, under all of the circumstances, be accorded all, or any part, or none of the rights and privileges accorded other striking employees under the strike settlement agreements.

By the time of the arbitration hearing fourteen names had been dropped from the list, and during the hearing the Union withdrew its claims in behalf of six others. As for the remaining thirty employees, the arbitrators found them guilty of strike misconduct and deprived them of some or all their rights under the strike settlement agreement.

Undaunted, beginning in December 1960, the Union filed unfair labor practice charges with the National Labor Relations Board under § 8(a) (3) and § 8(a) (1) of the National Labor Relations Act, 29 U.S.C. §§ 158(a) (3), 158(a) (1), alleging that the Company was discriminating against approximately 3,500 employees, including the thirty-six whose names remained on the list at the start of the arbitration hearing, by denying them reinstatement rights because of their participation in the strike. In February, 1963, the General Counsel of the Board issued a complaint based on the Union's charges, and in May, 1963, a hearing began before a trial examiner.

Meanwhile, the Union had also brought suit under § 301(a) in December, 1961, claiming a violation by the Company of the strike settlement agreement. In response, the Company, in May, 1963, filed the counterclaim at issue in this appeal, alleging that the Union had violated the arbitration submission agreement by charging the Company with an unfair labor practice as to the thirty-six employees. The Company relied on the provision of the arbitration agreement · which sanctioned a final determination of the rights of the thirty-six employees, "without recourse whatsoever to any appeal or review under any State or federal laws." As injunctive relief, the Company requested a decree requiring the Union to withdraw its unfair labor practice charges regarding the thirty-six employees, and another decree forbidding the Union from attacking the arbitration award in any other way.

In dismissing the counterclaim for failure to state a claim upon which relief could be granted, the court below held:

> Insofar as the arbitration agreement of August 24, 1960, attempted to preclude by contract the Union or its members from filing unfair labor practice charges against the company with the National Labor Relations Board, it is contrary to Federal law and is unenforceable. 220 F. Supp. 19, 23.[2]

At the outset we are faced with a question concerning interpretation of the arbitration agreement. The Union argues that it was not the intent of the parties to bar the filing of unfair labor practice charges before the Board, or at least the filing of charges such as are involved in this case. Alternatively, even if the provision of the agreement can be construed as a waiver of the right to file unfair labor practice charges, the Union contends it was not sufficiently clear and unmistakable to be given legal effect. These arguments, however, raise in part questions of

fact as to the circumstances of the agreement that cannot be dealt with on a motion to dismiss.[3] For the purposes of this appeal we must accept the allegation of the Company that the arbitration agreement effectively barred the filing of unfair labor practice charges in connection with the refusal of the Company to grant the thirty-six employees full reinstatement rights.

Turning now to the nub of the case, we must decide whether § 301(a) authorized the lower court to grant enforcement of the arbitration agreement as interpreted above. In performing this task, the Supreme Court has instructed us to consult "the policy of our national labor laws," including "express statutory mandates." Textile Workers Union v. Lincoln Mills. We conclude that the policy and the express mandates of the National Labor Relations Act are opposed to the enforcement of that part of the arbitration agreement which bars the Union from maintaining unfair labor practice charges before the Board.

The standard rule in cases such as this, enunciated in numerous decisions of the Supreme Court, this court, and the courts of other circuits, is that the right to resort to the Board for relief against unfair labor practices cannot be foreclosed by private contract. For example, see J. I. Case Co. v. N.L.R.B., 321 U.S. 332, 336–339, 64 S. Ct. 576, 88 L. Ed. 762 (1944); National Licorice Co. v. N.L.R.B., 309 U.S. 350, 359–361, 60 S. Ct. 569, 84 L. Ed. 799 (1940); N.L.R.B. v. Radio Officers' Union, 196 F. 2d 960, 965 (2 Cir. 1952), aff'd 347 U.S. 17, 74 S. Ct. 323, 98 L. Ed. 455 (1954); **NLRB v E. A. Laboratories, Inc.**, 188 F. 2d 885, 887 (2 Cir. 1951), cert. denied, 342 U.S. 871, 72 S. Ct. 110, 96 L. Ed. 655 (1951); International Union of Elec. Workers v. NLRB 328 F. 2d 723, 727 (3 Cir. 1964); NLRB v. Threads, Inc., 308 F. 2d 1, 8 (4 Cir. 1962). Nor is an arbitration award of any greater effect in this respect. **NLRB v. Bell Aircraft Corp.**, 206 F. 2d 235, 237 (2 Cir. 1953); **NLRB v. Hershey Chocolate Corp.**, 297 F. 2d 286, 293 (3 Cir. 1961); **NLRB v. International Union, UAW**, 194 F. 2d 698, 702 (7 Cir. 1952).

These decisions are based on the express language of § 10(a), of the National Labor Relations Act, 29 USC § 160(a), which provides in part:

> The Board is empowered . . . to prevent any person from engaging in any unfair labor practice . . . affecting commerce. This power shall not be affected by any other means of adjustment or prevention that has been or may be established by agreement, law, or otherwise: . . .

---

2. The lower court's decision thus related only to inhibitions on the filing and pursuit of unfair labor practice charges, and not to other kinds of legal recourse by the Union.

3. According to the record on appeal, there was no trial of the Company's counterclaim, but only oral argument and the filing of briefs.

This express statutory mandate, in turn, reflects the theory enunciated by the Supreme Court in National Licorice Co. v. NLRB: "The Board asserts a public right vested in it as a public body, charged in the public interest with the duty of preventing unfair labor practices." 309 U.S. at 364, 60 S. Ct. at 577. This public interest in preventing unfair labor practices cannot be entirely foreclosed by a purely private arrangement, no matter how attractive the arrangement may appear to be to the individual participants. Moreover, as the court below pointed out, "The Board was designed to prevent any unfair economic pressure or expedient arrangements condoning unfair labor practices." 220 F. Supp. at 24. The aim of the act to give special protection to the economically vulnerable would be defeated if contracts entered into because of that very vulnerability were enough to preclude enforcement of the act.

The Company acknowledges that such has been the law, but it contends that recent judicial trends require reconsideration of these propositions. First, it points to a number of cases which apparently hold that rights under the National Labor Relations Act can be waived by private contract. One line of these cases cited by the Company endorses the waiver by unions through collective bargaining agreements of their right to obtain information for use in collective bargaining under § 8(a) (5), 29 U.S.C. § 158(a) (5); N.L.R.B. v. Perkins Machine Co., 326 F. 2d 488 (1 Cir. 1964); Timken Roller Bearing Co. v. N.L.R.B., 325 F. 2d 746, 751 (6 Cir. 1963), cert. denied 376 U.S. 971, 84 S.Ct. 1135, 12 L.Ed 2d 85 (1964). There are cases in this court to the same effect. N.L.R.B. v. New Britain Machine Co., 210 F. 2d 61 (2 Cir. 1954); N.L.R.B. v. Otis Elevator Co., 208 F. 2d 176, 179 (2 Cir. 1953).

Another line of cases sanctions the waiver by unions through no-raiding agreements with other unions of their right under § 9(c) of the Act, 29 U.S.C. § 159(c), to petition the Board for certification as a collective bargaining agent: United Textile Workers v. Textile Workers Union, 258 F. 2d 743 (7 Cir. 1958); Local 2608, Lumber & Sawmill Workers v. Millmen's Local 1495, 169 F. Supp. 765 (N.D. Cal. 1958); contra, International Union of Doll & Toy Workers v. Metal Polishers, etc. Union, 180 F. Supp. 280 (S.D. Cal. 1960). Still another case cited by the Company is Retail Clerks Int'l Ass'n v. Lion Dry Goods, Inc., 369 U.S. 17, 82, S.Ct. 541, 7 L. Ed. 2d 503 (1962), in which the Supreme Court held that a strike settlement agreement, which among other things obligated the parties to withdraw all unfair labor practice charges before the Board and to refrain from filing any new ones on account of the strike, was cognizable under § 301(a).

Taking these instances of waiver in reverse order, we agree with the Union and the NLRB that the Lion Dry Goods decision was concerned only with the general question of whether a strike settlement agreement, including one executed by a union not entitled to be an exclusive bargaining agent, was a "contract" enforceable under § 301(a), 369 U.S. at 18, 82 S. Ct. 541. It did not pass on the enforceability of specific provisions of the agreement. Likewise, the citation in the Lion Dry Goods decision to United Textile Workers v. Textile Workers Union, supra, alleged by the Company to constitute an endorsement of the full holding in that case, merely signified approval of the proposition that § 301(a) provides a federal forum "for actions on other labor contracts besides collective bargaining contracts." 369 U.S. at 26, 82 S. Ct. at 547.

As for the United Textile Workers decision itself, it too seems to have focused almost exclusively on the general question of whether contracts between unions which are not collective bargaining agreements are "contracts" enforceable under § 301(a). 258 F. 2d at 748–749. It did not squarely face the problem of possible conflict with the policies of the National Labor Relations Act. When in a later case this problem was forcefully presented to the same Court of Appeals, it intimated that it might not apply the rule laid down in the United Textile Workers decision in every suit under § 301(a) requesting enforcement of a no-raiding agreement. N.L.R.B. v. Weyerhaeuser Co., 276 F. 2d 865, 875–876 (7 Cir. 1960), cert. denied, 364 U.S. 879, 81 S. Ct. 168, 5 L. Ed. 2d 102 (1960).

Even more important for our purposes, the United Textile Workers decision concerned restraints on representation proceedings rather than on unfair labor practice cases. Whereas the latter, as shown above, enjoy express statutory protection from infringement by private agreements, the former do not. Thus, that decision is clearly distinguishable.

Similarly, the cases cited above that deal with the waiver by unions of their right to obtain information for use in collective bargaining are not controlling. It is noteworthy that none of these cases found such a waiver.[4] Thus their acknowledgment of the validity of this kind of waiver is not entirely conclusive. Nor has the

---

4. The Company also cites Sinclair Refining Co. v. N.L.R.B., 306 F. 2d 569 (5 Cir. 1962). The case is not in point. It concerned a dispute over the relevance of the information sought by the Union, and not a waiver of the Union's right to admittedly relevant information.

Board, to our knowledge, taken the position that such a waiver is inherently invalid, as it does in the present case with respect to a waiver of the right to change an employer with anti-union discrimination. The Board's attitude on this point has presumably influenced the decisions to some extent.

Apart from the weakness of the authorities, there is reason to distinguish these two types of waivers. The obligation of an employer to disclose certain information to his employees' representative is only an extrapolation from the generalized prohibition contained in § 8(a) (5) against refusal "to bargain collectively." By contrast, the right of employees to be free from anti-union discrimination by their employer is expressly proclaimed in § 8(a) (3). Having the explicit sanction of Congress behind it, the latter may well be entitled to greater respect than the former when a court is called upon to invalidate a private agreement in the name of so vague a legal principle as "the public interest."

Second, the Company relies on a spate of recent Supreme Court decisions exalting the role of private agreements and private machinery in procuring industrial peace. One line of such cases ordains an extreme laissez-faire policy on the part of the courts in reviewing arbitration awards, lest they discourage resort to private methods of settling labor disputes. The most famous of these are the so-called *Steelworkers* Trilogy. The mood of these decisions was reaffirmed again by the Supreme Court in its most recent term. John Wiley & Sons, Inc. v. Livingston, 376 U.S. 543, 84 S. Ct. 909, 11 L. Ed. 2d 898 (1964).

The other line of cases cited by the Company holds that enforcement of private agreements under § 301(a) is not barred simply because the suit is also within the jurisdiction of the Board. Local 174, Teamsters, etc. Union v. Lucas Flour Co., 369 U.S. 95, 101 n. 9, 82 S. Ct. 571, 7 L. Ed. 2d 593 (1962); Smith v. Evening News Ass'n, 371 U.S. 195, 197–198, 83 S. Ct. 267, 9 L. Ed. 2d 246 (1962); Humphrey v. Moore, 375 U.S. 335, 84 S. Ct. 363, 11 L. Ed. 2d 370 (1964) Carey v. Westinghouse Elec. Corp., 375 U.S. 261, 84 S. Ct. 401, 11 L. Ed. 2d 320 (1964).

These very cases, however, also explicitly affirm that the jurisdiction of the Board is not ousted because the suit arises under § 301(a). As the Union and the Board point out, the fact that Board jurisdiction is non-exclusive does not mean that it has been altogether preempted by private contract enforcement. As for the cases which, in general, warn courts to abstain from meddling with arbitration awards, they are inapplicable to the Board which, unlike the courts, is charged with vindicating a body of public rights set forth in the National Labor Relations Act. It is concern for these rights which precludes enforcement here of the arbitration agreement between the Union and the Company.

The final contention of the Company is that a waiver of the right to file unfair labor practice charges, contained in an arbitration agreement, should at least be enforced in those cases in which it is the declared policy of the Board to defer to prior arbitration awards. According to a recent restatement of this policy, the Board will so defer "unless it clearly appears that the arbitration proceedings were tainted by fraud, collusion, unfairness, or serious procedural irregularities or that the award was clearly repugnant to the purposes and policies of the Act." International Harvester Co., 138 N.L.R.B. 923, 927 (1962), aff'd sub nom. Ramsey v. N.L.R.B., 327 F. 2d 784 (7 Cir. 1964). The Company claims that the General Counsel of the Board has not proved, nor has he even alleged, that there was any such flaw in the award of the arbitrators in this case.

The most obvious answer to this objection is that the policy described above was adopted by the Board in the exercise of its own discretion to dispose of cases already before it. The courts ought not to transmute this Board policy into a rule of law and thereby prevent unfair labor practice charges from ever reaching the Board. However, the Company's contention does point up one fact relevant to the present proceedings before the Board. In the ordinary case, as the Supreme Court has noted approvingly, "the weight of the arbitration award is likely to be considerable, if the Board is later required to rule on phases of the same dispute." Carey v. Westinghouse Elec. Corp., 375 U.S. 261, 271, 84 S. Ct. 401, 409 (1964). The arbitration award in this case, having been rendered by three former Chief Justices of the Supreme Court of Errors of the State of Connecticut, carries unusual weight. Presumably the Board will take this fact into consideration, if it has not already done so, in deciding whether to apply its policy of self-restraint.

The order of the lower court dismissing the Company's counterclaim for injunctive relief, insofar as such relief would bar the Union from maintaining unfair labor practice charges before the Board is affirmed.

HAYS, C. J. (concurring). Rather than suggesting that the arbitration award carries "unusual" weight, I would remind the Board that we expect it to discharge its public duty under the statute without regard to the award.

I concur in the result.

———————

Donald Rothschild, *Arbitration and the National*

Labor Relations Board: An Examination of Preferences and Prejudices and their Relevance, 28 OHIO ST. L. J. 195 (1967). The author interviewed arbitrators, union and management lawyers, and NLRB officials. He explores the relevance of the views they expressed to the assignment of various roles to the courts, the Board and arbitrators.

D.

Arbitration of Jurisdictional Disputes

THE BASIC PROBLEM*

MERTON BERNSTEIN

A jurisdictional dispute concerns, at the minimum, three parties—two unions and the employer. It is rare for the same arbitral arrangements to govern the contract relations of an employer and unions with possibility competing claims; only the Construction Joint Board provides such an arrangement and its coverage falls far short of the universal. In "industries" with umpires with power over many employers and many unions, such disputes probably are rare. Hence the basic difficulty is how to achieve a resolution of such a three-cornered dispute speedily, expertly and fairly. Arbitration seems a logical candidate for the task. When it works well it is speedy, the arbitrator is expert, and both the arbitrator and the procedure have fairness as a principal goal. But most arrangements for arbitration contemplate only two parties— the employer and one contracting union. Arbitral provisions differ; most importantly perhaps, so do arbitrators.

There is little or no problem if all the parties can agree upon an arbitration of the jurisdictional dispute in which all participate. Often, however, one or another will have reasons not to do so. For example, the union whose members have been assigned the disputed work has no grievance. Frequently it will stand pat. The employer often will have the same position visa-vis that organization, which I shall call "the other union." When the union whose member does not have the work grieves, the dilemma then becomes whether to proceed with a two party (bilateral) arbitration between the claiming union, or to leave the resolution to inter-union arbitral machinery where it exists, or to manip-

ulate the arbitral machinery so as to induce or require "the other union" to get into the arbitral fray, or to declare arbitration inadequate to the task and resort to other more certain means of resolution, to wit a § 10(k) proceeding before the NLRB.

Some special arrangements exist which offer alternatives to an employer–one union bilateral arbitration proceeding.

The Joint Board for the Settlement of Jurisdictional Disputes operates within the construction industry. However, not all contractors have agreed to be bound by its determinations and some unions have been less than obedient to its decisions. In the past the Joint Board has deemed itself lacking in enforcement power and the parties, apparently, have not sought court enforcement. Whether the Board as reconstituted in the spring of 1965 will overcome these limitations remains to be seen. The Joint Board *is* expeditious, rendering decisions sometimes within as little as 24 hours. It is expert, which is not to say that it may not make mistakes.

The AFL–CIO Internal Disputes Agreement, embedded in the body of the merged federation's constitution, is an outgrowth of the "no raiding" pact which was so central a condition of the merger itself. It is not notably speedy; its emphasis has been upon protecting existing bargaining relationships, but it has dealt—decisively —with disputes over the allocation of new work. The employer is not a party and so his interests are not a central concern. However, he may achieve a final and binding decision by agreeing to abide by the outcome; this may be insufficient to his needs and sometimes will be less desirable than either an employer-one union procedure or a 10(k) proceeding.

The NLRB's superiority is found in the compulsory nature of its authority in this area—it can proceed with all parties participating. However, its processes are often slow. Its 10(k) procedures are available only if § 8(b) (4) (D) has

———

*Excerpted from Bernstein, *Arbitration of Jurisdictional Disputes*, REFERENCE MANUAL, 1965 MIDWEST LABOR CONFERENCE 6.01. Reprinted with permission.

been violated, *i.e.,* the claiming union has struck to obtain assignments for its members as against another union's members or it has engaged in threats, restraint or coercion to that end. Moreover, from the claiming union's point of view, the 10(k) proceeding is undesirable, or decidedly less desirable than having its own bilateral arbitration, because the Board decisions heavily favor the employer's assignment.

CAREY v. WESTINGHOUSE ELEC. CORP.
375 U.S. 261 (1964)

DOUGLAS, J. The petitioner union (IUE) and respondent employer (Westinghouse) entered into a collective bargaining agreement covering workers at several plants including one where the present dispute occurred. The agreement states that Westinghouse recognizes IUE and its locals as exclusive bargaining representatives for each of those units for which IUE or its locals have been certified by the National Labor Relations Board as the exclusive bargaining representative ; and the agreement lists among those units for which IUE has been certified a unit of "all production and maintenance employees" at the plant where the controversy arose, "but excluding all salaried technical . . . employees." The agreement also contains a grievance procedure for the use of arbitration in case of unresolved disputes, including those involving the "interpretation, application or claimed violation" of the agreement.

IUE filed a grievance asserting that certain employees in the engineering laboratory at the plant in question, represented by another union, Federation, which had been certified as the exclusive bargaining representative for a unit of "all salaried, technical" employees, excluding "all production and maintenance" employees, were performing production and maintenance work. Westinghouse refused to arbitrate on the ground that the controversy presented a representation matter for the National Labor Relations Board. IUE petitioned the Supreme Court of New York for an order compelling arbitration. That court refused. The Appellate Division affirmed, one judge dissenting, 15 App. Div. 2d 7, 221 N.Y.S. 2d 303. The Court of Appeals affirmed, one judge dissenting, holding that the matter was within the exclusive jurisdiction of the Board since it involved a definition of bargaining units. 11 N.Y. 2d 452, 230 N.Y.S. 2d 703. The case is here on certiorari. 372 U.S. 957.

We have here a so-called "jurisdictional" dispute involving two unions and the employer. But the term "jurisdictional" is not a word of a single meaning. In the setting of the present case this "jurisdictional" dispute could be one of two different, though related, species: either—(1) a controversy as to whether certain work should be performed by workers in one bargaining unit or those in another ; or (2) a controversy as to which union should represent the employees doing particular work. If this controversy is considered to be the former, the National Labor Relations Act (61 Stat. 136, 73 Stat. 519, 29 U.S.C. § 151 *et seq.*) does not purport to cover all phases and stages of it. While § 8(b) (4) (D) makes it an unfair labor practice for a union to strike to get an employer to assign work to a particular group of employees rather than to another,[1] the Act does not deal with the controversy anterior to a strike nor provide any machinery for resolving such a dispute absent a strike. The Act and its remedies for "jurisdictional" controversies of that nature come into play only by a strike or a threat of a strike. Such conduct gives the Board authority under § 10(k) to resolve the dispute.[2]

Are we to assume that the regulatory scheme contains a hiatus, allowing no recourse to arbitration over work assignments between two unions but forcing the controversy into the strike stage before a remedy before the Board is available?

---

1. § 8 (b) (4) (D):

"It shall be an unfair labor practice for a labor organization or its agents—

"(4) (i) to engage in, or to induce or encourage any individual employed by any person engaged in commerce or in an industry affecting commerce to engage in, a strike or a refusal in the course of his employment to use, manufacture, process, transport, or otherwise handle or work on any goods, articles, materials, or commodities or to perform any services; or (ii) to threaten, coerce, or restrain any person engaged in commerce or in an industry affecting commerce, where in either case an object thereof is—

"(D) forcing or requiring any employer to assign particular work to employees in a particular labor organization or in a particular trade, craft, or class rather than to employees in another labor organization or in another trade, craft, or class, unless such employer is failing to conform to an order or certification of the Board determining the bargaining representative for employees performing such work." 29 U.S.C. (Supp. IV) § 158 (b) (4) (D).

2. Section 10 (k) provides:

"Whenever it is charged that any person has engaged in an unfair labor practice within the meaning of paragraph (4) (D) of section 8 (b), the Board is empowered and directed to hear and determine the dispute out of which such unfair labor practice shall have arisen, unless, within ten days after notice that such charge has been filed, the parties to such dispute submit to the Board satisfactory evidence that they have adjusted, or agreed upon methods for the voluntary adjustment of, the dispute. Upon compliance by the parties to the dispute with the decision of the Board or upon such voluntary adjustment of the dispute, such charge shall be dismissed." 29 U.S.C. § 160 (k).

The Board, as admonished by § 10 (k),[3] has often given effect to private agreements to settle disputes of this character; and that is in accord with the purpose as stated even by the minority spokesman in Congress—"that full opportunity is given the parties to reach a voluntary accommodation without governmental intervention if they so desire." 93 Cong. Rec. 4035 ; 2 Leg. Hist. L.M.R.A. (1947) 1046. And see Labor Board v. Radio Engineers, 364 U.S. 573, 577.

As Judge Fuld, dissenting below, said: "The underlying objective of the national labor laws is to promote collective bargaining agreements and to help give substance to such agreements through the arbitration process." 11 N.Y. 2d 452, 458, 230 N.Y.S. 2d 703, 706.

Grievance arbitration is one method of settling disputes over work assignments ; and it is commonly used, we are told. To be sure, only one of the two unions involved in the controversy has moved the state courts to compel arbitration. So unless the other union intervenes, an adjudication of the arbiter might not put an end to the dispute. Yet the arbitration may as a practical matter end the controversy or put into movement forces that will resolve it. The case in its present posture is analogous to Whitehouse v. Illinois Central R. Co., 349 U.S. 366, where a railroad and two unions were disputing a jurisdictional matter, when the National Railroad Adjustment Board served notice on the railroad and one union of its assumption of jurisdiction. The railroad, not being able to have notice served on the other union, sued in the courts for relief. We adopted a hands-off policy, saying, "Railroad's resort to the courts has preceded any award, and one may be rendered which could occasion no possible injury to it." Id., at 373.

Since § 10(k) not only tolerates but actively encourages voluntary settlements of work assignment controversies between unions, we conclude that grievance procedures pursued to arbitration further the policies of the Act.

What we have said so far treats the case as if the grievance involves only a work assignment dispute. If however, the controversy be a representational one, involving the duty of an employer to bargain collectively with the representative of the employees as provided in §8(a) (5), further considerations are necessary.

If this is truly a representation case, either IUE or Westinghouse can move to have the certificate

clarified. But the existence of a remedy before the Board for an unfair labor practice does not bar individual employees from seeking damages for breach of a collective bargaining agreement in a state court, as we held in Smith v. Evening News Assn., 371 U.S. 195. We think the same policy considerations are applicable here ; and that a suit either in the federal courts, as provided by § 301(a) of the Labor Management Relations Act of 1947 (61 Stat. 156, 29 U.S.C. § 185(a); Textile Workers v. Lincoln Mills, 353 U.S. 448), or before such state tribunals as are authorized to act (Charles Dowd Box Co. v. Courtney, 368 U.S. 502; Teamsters Local v. Lucas Flour Co., 369 U.S. 95) is proper, even though an alternative remedy before the Board is available, which, if invoked by the employer, will protect him.

The policy considerations behind Smith v. Evening News Assn., supra, are highlighted here by reason of the blurred line that often exists between work assignment disputes and controversies over which of two or more unions is the appropriate bargaining unit. It may be claimed that A and B, to whom work is assigned as "technical" employees, are in fact "production and maintenance" employees ; and if that charge is made and sustained the Board, under the decisions already noted, clarifies the certificate. But IUE may claim that when the work was assigned to A and B, the collective agreement was violated because "production and maintenance" employees, not "technical" employees, were entitled to it. As noted, the Board clarifies certificates where a certified union seeks to represent additional employees ; but it will not entertain a motion to clarify a certificate where the union merely seeks additional work for employees already within its unit.

As the Board's decisions indicate, disputes are often difficult to classify. In the present case the Solicitor General, who appears amicus, believes the controversy is essentially a representational one. So does Westinghouse. IUE on the other hand claims it is a work assignment dispute. Even if it is in form a representation problem, in substance it may involve problems of seniority when layoffs occur (see Sovern, Section 301 and the Primary Jurisdiction of the NLRB, 76 Harv. L. Rev. 529, 574–575 (1963)) or other aspects of work assignment disputes. If that is true, there is work for the arbiter whatever the Board may decide.

If by the time the dispute reaches the Board, arbitration has already taken place, the Board shows deference to the arbitral award, provided

3. Section 10 (k), supra, note 2, provides that the Board shall determine the dispute, "... unless ... the parties to such dispute submit to the Board satisfactory evidence that they have adjusted, or agreed upon methods for the voluntary adjustment of, the dispute."

the procedure was a fair one and the results were not repugnant to the Act.

> There is no question that the Board is not precluded from adjudicating unfair labor practice charges even though they might have been the subject of an arbitration proceeding and award. Section 10 (a) of the Act expressly makes this plain, and the courts have uniformly so held. However, it is equally well established that the Board has considerable discretion to respect an arbitration award and decline to exercise its authority over alleged unfair labor practices if to do so will serve the fundamental aims of the Act.
>
> The Act, as has repeatedly been stated, is primarily designed to promote industrial peace and stability by encouraging the practice and procedure of collective bargaining. Experience has demonstrated that collective-bargaining agreements that provide for final and binding arbitration of grievance and disputes arising thereunder, "as a substitute for industrial strife," contribute significantly to the attainment of this statutory objective. International Harvester Co., 138 N.L.R.B. 923, 925–926.

Thus the weight of the arbitration award is likely to be considerable, if the Board is later required to rule on phases of the same dispute. The Board's action and the awards of arbiters are at times closely brigaded. Thus where grievance proceedings are pending before an arbiter, the Board defers decisions on the eligibility of discharged employees to vote in a representation case, until the awards are made. See Pacific Tile & Porcelain Co., 137 N.L.R.B. 1358, 1365–1367, overruling Dura Steel Products Co., 111 N.L.R.B. 590. See 137 N.L.R.B., p. 1365, n. 11.

Should the Board disagree with the arbiter, by ruling, for example, that the employees involved in the controversy are members of one bargaining unit or another, the Board's ruling would, of course, take precedence; and if the employer's action had been in accord with that ruling, it would not be liable for damages under § 301. But that is not peculiar to the present type of controversy. Arbitral awards construing a seniority provision (Carey v. General Electric Co., 315 F. 2d 499, 509–510), or awards concerning unfair labor practices, may later end up in conflict with Board rulings. See International Association of Machinists, 116, N.L.R.B. 645; Monsanto Chemical Co., 97 N.L.R.B. 517. Yet, as we held in Smith v. Evening News Assn., *supra,* the possibility of conflict is no barrier to resort to a tribunal other than the Board.

However the dispute be considered—whether one involving work assignment or one concerning representation—we see no barrier to use of the arbitration procedure. If it is a work assignment dispute, arbitration conveniently fills a gap and avoids the necessity of a strike to bring the matter to the Board. If it is a representation matter, resort to arbitration may have a pervasive, curative effect even though one union is not a party.

By allowing the dispute to go to arbitration its fragmentation is avoided to a substantial extent; and those conciliatory measures which Congress deemed vital to "industrial peace" (Textile Workers v. Lincoln Mills, *supra,* at 455) and which may be dispositive of the entire dispute, are encouraged. The superior authority of the Board may be invoked at any time. Meanwhile the therapy of arbitration is brought to bear in a complicated and troubled area.

Reversed.

HARLAN, J. (concurring). I join the Court's opinion with a brief comment. As is recognized by all, neither position in this case is without its difficulties. Lacking a clear-cut command in the statute itself, the choice in substance lies between a course which would altogether preclude any attempt at resolving disputes of this kind by arbitration, and one which at worst will expose those concerned to the hazard of duplicative proceedings. The undesirable consequences of the first alternative are inevitable, those of the second conjectural. As between the two, I think the Court at this early stage of experience in this area rightly chooses the latter.

BLACK, J., joined by CLARK, J. (dissenting). The International Union of Electrical Workers (IUE), of which petitioner is president, and another union, the Federation, each have collective bargaining contracts with and are certified bargaining agents for employees of the respondent, Westinghouse Electric Corporation. IUE's contract covers "all production and maintenance" employees, but not "salaried technical" employees. Federation's contract covers "all salaried, technical" employees but not "production and maintenance" employees. IUE demanded that Westinghouse stop permitting a number of Federation employees to do certain work, claiming that what they were doing was "production and maintenance" work and that therefore IUE's members, not Federation's, were entitled to these jobs. Westinghouse refused to make the change, whereupon IUE, instead of filing an appropriate proceeding to have the dispute decided by the National Labor Relations Board (as I understand the Court to hold that it could have done), called on Westinghouse to arbitrate the dispute with IUE. This demand rested on a provision of the IUE-Westinghouse contract agreeing to arbitration of grievances growing out of the "interpretation, application or claimed violation" of the contract. Westinghouse resisted arbitration, contending that the dispute ought to be resolved by the National Labor Relations Board, and the Court of Appeals of New York, agreeing with Westinghouse, refused to compel Westinghouse to arbitrate.[1]

I agree with the New York court and would affirm its judgment. Stripped of obscurantist arguments, this controversy is a plain, garden-variety jurisdictional dispute between two unions. The Court today holds, however, that the National Labor Relations Act not only permits but compels Westinghouse to arbitrate the dispute with only one of the two warring unions. Such an arbitration could not, of course, bring about the "final and binding arbitration of grievance[s] and disputes" that the Court says contributes to the congressional objectives in passing the Labor Act. Unless all the salutary safeguards of due process of law are to be dissipated and obliterated to further the cause of arbitration, the rights of employees belonging to the Federation should not, for "policy considerations," be sacrificed by an arbitration award in proceedings between IUE and Westinghouse alone. Although I do not find the Court's opinion so clear on the point as I would like, I infer that it is not holding that this misnamed "award" would be completely final and binding on the Federation and its members. What the Court does plainly hold, however— that "the weight of the arbitration award is likely to be considerable, if the Board is later required to rule on phases of the same dispute"—seems only a trifle less offensive to established due process concepts. And this means, I suppose, that this same award, *ex parte* as to Federation, must be given the same or greater weight in any judicial review of the Board's final order involving the same "phases of the same dispute."

Moreover, the Court holds that suits for damages can be filed against the employer in state courts or federal courts under § 301 of the Taft-Hartley Act,, 29 U.S.C. § 185, for the "unfair labor practice" of failing to bargain with the right union when two unions are engaged in a jurisdictional dispute. The employer, caught in that jurisdictional dispute, is ordinarily in a helpless position. He is trapped in a cross-fire between two unions. All he can do is guess as to which union's members he will be required by an arbitrator, the Labor Board, or a court to assign to the disputed jobs. If he happens to guess wrong, he is liable to be mulcted in damages. I assume it would be equally difficult for him to prophesy what award an arbitrator, the Labor Board, or a judge will make as to guess

how big a verdict a court or a jury would give against him. It must be remembered that the employer cannot make a choice which will be binding on either an arbitrator, the Board, or a court. The Court's holding, thus subjecting an employer to damages when he has done nothing wrong, seems to me contrary to the National Labor Relations Act as well as to the basic principles of common everyday justice.

The result of all this is that the National Labor Relations Board, the agency created by Congress finally to settle labor disputes in the interest of industrial peace is to be supplanted in part by so-called arbitration which in its very nature cannot achieve a final adjustment of those disputes. One of the main evils it had been hoped the Labor Act would abate was jurisdictional disputes between unions over which union members would do certain work.[2] The Board can make final settlements of such disputes. Arbitration between some but not all the parties cannot. I fear that the Court's recently announced leanings to treat arbitration as an almost sure and certain solvent of all labor troubles has been carried so far in this case as unnecessarily to bring about great confusion and to delay final and binding settlements of jurisdictional disputes by the Labor Board, the agency which I think Congress intended to do that very job.

I would affirm.

The NLRB declined to clarify the complaining union's certification when requested to do so by the company *after* the Supreme Court decision but delayed decision pending the outcome of the arbitration. This may have been because of the Court's enforcement of the obligation to arbitrate. Compare *Standard Register Co.,* 146 N.L.R.B. 1043 (1964).

In the *Westinghouse* arbitration the company sought to have the arbitrator force the joinder of the absent union, which had disclaimed an interest in intervening. The arbitrator declined to do so.

After the award the company and the second union renewed efforts before the Board. The NLRB held, as had the arbitrator, that the controversy was not a jurisdictional dispute but concerned representation. It observed that the second union was not a party to the arbitration and had not participated in it. The record, and hence the arbitrators' decision, the Board said, was deficient

---

1. 11 N.Y. 2d 452, 184 N.E. 2d 298, 230 N.Y.S. 2d 703

2. See Labor Board v. Radio & Television Broadcast Engineers Union, 364 U.S. 573; cf. Order of Railway Conductors v. Pitney, 326 U.S. 561, 567.

on some pertinent aspects of the controversy, such as the bargaining history of the absent union's unit. "... while we give some consideration to the award, we do not think it would effectuate the statutory policy to defer to it entirely." The Board's unit decision in favor of the second union was inconsistent with the arbitrator's award.

Professor Edgar Jones has proposed that an arbitrator confronted by a claim of contract violation by one union because of the award of work to employees in another union's unit should seek the views of the absent union and, indeed, should attempt to achieve a "trilateral" arbitration by directing the grieving union to attempt to "interplead" the other union. Its refusal to do so would result in the arbitrator's declaration that the grieving union's claim is not arbitrable. For presentation of his views, see Jones, *Autobiography of a Decision: The Function of Innovation in Labor Arbitration and the National Steel Orders of Joinder and Interpleader,* 10 U.C.L.A. L. REV. 987 (1963). For a criticism of his proposals, see Bernstein, *Nudging and Shoving All Parties to a Jurisdictional Dispute into Arbitration: The Dubious Procedure of National Steel,* 78 HARV. L. REV. 784 (1965). Professor Jones replied in, *On Nudging and Shoving the National Steel Arbitration into a Dubious Procedure,* 79 HARV. L. REV. 327 (1965). The final (?) round in the controversy came in Bernstein and Jones (severally) in, *Jurisdictional Dispute Arbitration: The Jostling Professors,* 14 U.C.L.A. L. REV. 347 (1966). For another view, and a comprehensive pre-Carey analysis of the problems of this Chapter, consult Sovern, *Section 301 and the Primary Jurisdiction of the NLRB,* 76 HARV. L. REV. 529 (1963).

In *E. R. Wagner Co.,* 43 LAB. ARB. 210 (1964), Arbitrator Robben Fleming declined to follow the Jones plan; he indicated his willingness to hear the case as a bilateral dispute but directed the union and company, which already had invited the absent union to participate without success, to invite it once more. Possibly going beyond that, the Wisconsin Employment Relations Board directed the parties to invite the absent union; the report does not indicate how agreeable they were to the procedure. Bakery and Confectionery Workers (William M. Heineman Bakeries, Inc., 60 LRRM 1164 (1965).

An employer awarded work to one union, and then another union prevailed in a bilateral arbitration proceeding. The General Counsel of the NLRB declined to issue a refusal-to-bargain complaint against the employer. Neither obeying the arbitrator's award nor failing to give notice to the first union of the arbitration proceeding in which the employer defended its original assignment constituted a refusal to bargain. 61 LRR 250 (1966).

In Local 17, New Orleans Typographical Union v. NLRB, (5th Cir. 1966) 368 F. 2d 755, the court was called upon to enforce an NLRB order awarding jurisdiction of the disputed work to one union and an arbitrator's award (enforced by the district court before the NLRB's decision issued) directing the employer to have the work performed by the members of another union (ITU). The court held the NLRB order to warrant enforcement although questionable in some respects; the court noted that the Board had not confined itself to contract considerations, and properly so. Finding the judgment enforcing the award incompatible with the NLRB decision, it reversed the district court and refused enforcement of the arbitrator's award.

If, as is possible, the contract of the party losing in an NLRB proceeding was breached in the opinion of an arbitrator, why should not that party (and the employees it represented) receive compensatory damages? A problem of procedure arises when the award has been issued before the NLRB's dispute determination. In a proceeding to enforce the award, the court could remand to the arbitrator to set the damage figure.

In Transportation-Communications Employees v. Union Pacific R.R. Co., 385 U.S. 157 (1966), a case arising under the Railway Labor Act, the Court held that the National Railroad Adjustment Board, a statutory body before whom contract violation disputes between unions and carriers must be brought (but see Walker v. Southern Ry. Co., *infra*), could not decide one union's claim to work in the absence of the other union. In an earlier case the Court had held that the absent other union was entitled to notice. But the Railway Labor Executives Association agreed that the absent union should stay out and press its claim in a separate proceeding. Under the Court's new ruling both unions must participate.

Cases of that sort hereafter will go to the NRAB, composed of an equal number of union and carrier members. The cases go to a neutral for decision only if the partisan members deadlock. What if a union representative on the Board votes with all the carrier representatives to award the work to his union?

Some commentators believe that this decision casts doubt upon the continued vitality of *Carey*. It may. Or it may be distinguishable on the ground that the Adjustment Board's role is more like that of the NLRB in deciding a 10(k) dispute than like an arbitrator selected by some of the parties.

For a comprehensive and thoughtful discussion of problems considered in this chapter and recent trends consult, Comment, *The NLRB and Deference to Arbitration,* 77 YALE L. J. 1191 (1968).

For a discussion of some related problems, see SHAPIRO, *Some Thoughts on Intervention Before Courts, Agencies and Arbitrators,* 81 HARV. L. REV. 721 (1968).

CHAPTER XIII

INDIVIDUAL RIGHTS IN THE GRIEVANCE ARBITRATION PROCEDURE

A.

Individual Rights, "Fair Representation," and the Bargaining Representative's Authority to Settle Grievances

UNION NEWS CO. v. HILDRETH
295 F. 2d 658 (6th Cir. 1961)

O'SULLIVAN, C.J. This is an appeal by defendant-appellant, Union News Company, from a judgment for $5,000.00 entered upon a jury verdict in favor of plaintiff-appellee, Gladys Hildreth. Her complaint charged that she had been discharged from defendant's employ without just cause, in breach of a collective bargaining agreement between defendant and the Hotel and Restaurant Employees and Bartenders International Union, AFL, Detroit Local Joint Executive Board, hereinafter referred to as the Union. Damages awarded included wages lost by plaintiff between her discharge and the time of trial and damages she claims she will suffer through loss of seniority as defendant's employee.

Defendant operated a soda fountain and lunch counter at the Michigan Central Railroad terminal at Detroit. Plaintiff was one of a crew of eleven or twelve persons employed at said counter. She had been employed at the Detroit terminal for about ten years, and was a member of the Union. During the period of plaintiff's employment, the Union was the designated exclusive bargaining representative of defendant's employees. The current agreement between the Union and defendant, dated October 15, 1957, was to run for one year with the usual provisions for automatic yearly renewals unless terminated by either party.

Material and relevant to the issues on this appeal are the following paragraphs of the Collective Bargaining Agreement:

14. No regular employee covered by this Agreement shall be discharged except for just cause. In the event of a claim by the Union that an employee has been discharged without just cause, such claim must be filed with the manager of the unit within five (5) days and disposed of by him within five (5) days thereafter. If the matter cannot be satisfactorily

adjusted between the Union and the employer's manager, the same shall be promptly referred to the employer's home office at 131 Varick Street, New York City.

15. Any and all questions and discussions which at any time may arise affecting the employees of the employer shall be taken up with the manager of the unit involved at such time and place as will be mutually agreed upon between the Union and the manager.

17. During the term of this agreement, any question arising hereunder which cannot be directly and satisfactorily adjusted between the Union and the employer shall be referred to a Committee which shall consist of one member representing the Union, one representing the employer, and a third member to be mutually agreed upon by the employer and the Union, and the decision of any two (2) members of such Committee shall be final and binding upon the parties hereto.

On March 14, 1958, plaintiff was laid off by defendant. Her layoff matured into a discharge as discussed hereinafter. For a period of nine to twelve months prior to plaintiff's discharge, the manager of defendant's enterprise was concerned about its cost experience at the counter where plaintiff worked. There was evidence that in the type of business there being carried on, efficient and honest work by counter employees should result in food costs being something less than 40 per cent of the amount of gross sales ; that a percentage of 35 per cent to 37 per cent in that regard is considered good ; and that where the cost of merchandise reaches a figure above 40 per cent of the amount of gross sales, it is indicative of a "poor operation" resulting from mishandling of merchandise and money by employees. Such mishandling could include dishonesty. From January, 1957, through February, 1958, this percentage was running rather uniformly above the 40 per cent figure and was the cause of continuing discussions between defendant's manager and the Union. Defendant was unable to ascertain which of, and how many of, its counter employees were guilty of the misconduct causing its bad experience. Its manager suggested to the Union that the only solution was the replacement of all, or some of, the crew. The Union refused at first, suggesting less drastic measures such as talking to the girls and telling defendant's manager to "do the best you can and we will look into it further." Conditions did not improve, and in early 1958 defendant's manager opened its books to the business agents of the Union who made their own examination and analysis of defendant's continuing problem. In February, 1958, the food cost percentage was the highest, but one, of any of the preceding twelve months. Union representatives made their own analysis of the records of defendant and concluded that some action had to be taken to remedy the situation. Defendant's manager suggested that the entire crew on the soda and lunch counter be replaced. The Union representative felt that such action was too drastic and between the Union agent and defendant's manager, it was agreed that five of the counter employees be given a three day layoff and be replaced by new employees. There was then to be a trial period of ten days to two weeks to see whether such change of crew would bring about an improvement. It was agreed that if improvement came it would demonstrate that the laid off employees were, at least partially, the cause of the trouble. In such case, the laid off employees would not be rehired. It was further agreed that if conditions did not improve following the layoff, such experience would exculpate the laid off employees of fault and they would be rehired and paid the wages lost during the period of the lay-off. The laid off employees were replaced by other members of the Union. Following the replacement of the five employees, one of whom was the plaintiff, defendant's operation did improve and for the month of March the percentage of food costs to sales dropped from 43.46 per cent for February to 39.90 per cent for March and to 35.90 per cent for April. This percentage remained below 40 per cent for the entire balance of 1958, except for the month of August. In the week following the layoff, the cash receipts of the counter in question were $250.00 more than the final week with the old crew. After about ten days of the new operation, the Union agreed with defendant that it had proved its point and the replacement of the five employees became permanent. On the trial, plaintiff, to some extent, challenged the validity of the conclusions of the Union and defendant as to the significance of the food cost figures. However, there was no evidence of bad faith in the reliance of the Union and defendant upon such analysis.

After learning that she had been replaced, plaintiff took the matter up with her Union. On March 24th, a meeting was had at which the Union and defendant's representatives were present, as well as plaintiff and the other replaced employees. At this meeting, defendant's representative told plaintiff that she was laid off under Code No. 12, which meant "change of crew without prejudice." Such a termination of employment, the company representative said, would not disqualify plaintiff for unemployment compensation. When first laid off, she was told that it was for the good of the Union News Company, with mention being made of the bad condition at the fountain. She was told that the matter had already been cleared with the Union. Except for this meeting of March 24, plaintiff made no further contact with defendant until her attorney wrote a letter to it some months later. Plaintiff continued for a time to press for action by her Union. She was told that the Union was convinced that her discharge was for just cause. With the other discharged girls, she met with Union officers at the various levels of authority, and with the Union's grievance committee. This committee referred the matter to the Executive Board of the Union, and final consideration of it was had at a meeting of the Executive Board in June following the discharge. Plaintiff was present at this meeting. No action was taken by the Board and no grievance was ever presented by the Union on Plaintiff's behalf.

Between May 6, 1958, and November 14, 1958, there was an exchange of correspondence between plaintiff's attorney, the Union News Company, and the latter's counsel. Plaintiff's attorney, on May 6, 1958, and on behalf of plaintiff and the other discharged employees, demanded that the Union News Company "meet with us for the purpose of continuing the processing of the grievance in accordance with their rights under the law." This letter was unanswered and on May 31 the attorney advised the Union News that unless it set a time for a meeting, "with the above named persons and the writer, to process their grievances arising out of their wrongful discharge by you, legal action will be instituted to enforce their rights." This letter advised that a copy of it was being sent to the Union "in accordance with the provisions of Sec. 9 of the Taft-Hartley Act, to enable them to be present, but they will not participate in said grievance processing." In October, defendant's counsel advised that it was willing to proceed with grievance and arbitration proceedings as provided for in the bargaining agreement. Plaintiff's counsel however, advised that, "It is the intention of the grievants to process their own grievances, as provided by the Taft-Hartley Act (29 U.S.C.A. § 159) assisted by myself." Nothing further was done in this regard.

On July 11, 1958, the complaint in this case was filed. Its prayer for relief asked:

A. That defendant may be ordered to meet with plaintiff for the purpose of processing her grievance out of her wrongful discharge, as provided by 29 U.S.C.A. Sec. 159.

B. That defendant, Union News Company, may be ordered to pay to plaintiff Thirty Thousand Dollars, plus the loss of her wages to the date of trial, as compensation for the damages suffered by her.

It concluded with a prayer for general relief. The remedy sought under above paragraph A was not pursued in the trial court and is not involved here.

Plaintiff's complaint averred, inter alia, that the Union Local 705 was her "statutory collective bargaining representative and agent"; that her cause of action was bottomed upon the Union's contract with defendant; that she was discharged on March 14, 1958, "without just cause in violation of the terms and conditions of said contract of employment"; that "plaintiff has made numerous and several attempts to invoke the remedies provided by the grievance procedure, including arbitration, but defendant Union News Company has wholly refused, failed and neglected to discuss said grievance with plaintiff's collective bargaining representative or to permit plaintiff to present her grievance to it as provided by 29 U.S.C.A. § 159, commonly known as the Taft-Hartley Act."

The defendant's answer, with amendment thereto, denied that plaintiff was discharged without cause; denied that it refused to discuss plaintiff's grievance or to permit her to present her grievance; and affirmatively averred that plaintiff was guilty of carelessness "amounting to dishonesty or malfeasance in the handling of funds and merchandise of the defendant, which resulted in financial loss to defendant" and that the discharge of plaintiff "was agreed and consented to by . . . Local 705."

A first trial of the cause resulted in a verdict and judgment of no cause of action. A new trial was ordered which ended in the judgment for plaintiff before us on this appeal.

Upon trial, plaintiff testified that after her discharge on March 14, 1958, she sought other employment but that she was "obviously pregnant at the time." Her only child was born on October 22, 1958, plaintiff then being 39 years old. She stated that she had planned to work until about September 1, 1958, and that she had expected to be off work for about six and one-half months, including time before and after her confinement; that had she retained her job with defendant, she would have had an aunt look after her child while she worked. Plaintiff testified to no efforts to seek work after the birth of her child. Objection was sustained to defendant's effort to show that at the time of, and following, plaintiff's discharge, there was constant demand for the services of counter girls and waitresses in Detroit, and that the Union was regularly filling requests for such employment, but that plaintiff, although requested so to do, failed to go to the Union office for placement in another job. Defendant made such an offer of proof, supported by evidence upon a segregated record, after plaintiff's objection was sustained because defendant had not pleaded as an affirmative defense plaintiff's failure to mitigate her damages. The trial court denied defendant's motion (made following the sustaining of the foregoing objection) to amend its answer to include such an affirmative defense.

Before discussion of the legal questions involved, we should add that there was no proof directly connecting plaintiff individually, with dishonesty, wrong-doing, or malfeasance. We further, preliminarily, observe that in our opinion there was no evidence from which a jury could find that in agreeing to lay off and then discharge plaintiff and her co-workers in an effort to solve defendant's problems, there was any fraud, bad faith or collusion on the part of, or between, the Union's and defendant's agents. We do not think that the inability of defendant to place individual responsibility for its difficulties on plaintiff impairs the validity of our conclusion in this regard, nor prevents the discharge of plaintiff and her fellow workers being "for just cause." An employer should not be fore-closed from applying a remedy to stop a continuing loss merely because it cannot identify and isolate the particular source, or sources, of such loss. We state also that what was done by the Union and defendant after plaintiff's discharge could not, in our opinion, be relied upon as evidence of fraud, bad faith or collusion in the prior mutual agreement to terminate plaintiff's employment.

Defendant's motion for a directed verdict at the close of plaintiff's evidence, renewed after proofs were closed, was denied. This ruling, with others, makes up the questions involved on this appeal. Because we are of the opinion that defendant was entitled to a directed verdict of no cause of action, we do not reach other errors charged as ground for reversal.

It is our conclusion that, considering the statutory authority of the Union as the bargaining agent, the language of the collective bargaining agreement, and the undisputed facts as to the good faith bargaining between the Union and the defendant, it was within the authority of the Union as bargaining agent to agree with defendant that there was just cause for plaintiff's discharge. Her discharge following, and pursuant to, such agreement was not a breach of contract by defendant.

Plaintiff is a resident of Michigan and was there employed by defendant. The collective bargaining contract was made in Michigan and the events here involved occurred there. Under like circumstances, we have held that "the law of Michigan is important, if not, indeed controlling." Elder v. New York Central Railroad Co., 6 Cir., 1945, 152 F. 2d 361, 365. Under the law of Michigan, in accord with the weight of authority, an employer has the right to discharge an employee at will, unless such right is restricted or qualified by contract or statute. Lynas v. Maxwell Farms, 279 Mich. 684, 273 N.W. 315 ; Cortez v. Ford Motor Company, 349 Mich. 108, 84 N.W. 2d 523 ; United States Steel Corporation v. Nichols, 6 Circ., 1956, 229 F. 2d 396, 399, 55 A.L.R. 2d 980, certiorari denied 351 U.S. 950, 76 S.Ct. 846, 100 L.Ed. 1474 ; N.L.R.B. v. Standard Coil Products Co., 1 Cir., 1955, 224 F. 2d 465, 470 ; 35 AM. JUR. "Master and Servant" § 34, p. 469. Plaintiff's right of action, if any, must arise from the terms of the contract between the Union and the employer. Not only the sentence of that contract which provides against discharge without cause, but all other relevant provisions of the contract and existing law, must be respected in determining whether, in this case, plaintiff has established a cause of action for breach of such contract. Mastro Plastics Corp. v. N.L.R.B., 350 U.S. 270, 279, 76 S. Ct. 349, 100 L. Ed. 309, 318. Michigan, again in accord with general law, holds that seniority rights, which for this purpose we equate with protection against discharge without cause, do not arise as an incident to employment, but exist only by virtue of contract. Hartley v. Brotherhood, 283 Mich. 201, 206, 277 N.W. 885; Ryan v. New York Central Railroad Co., 267 Mich. 202, 208, 255 N.W. 365; Cortez v. Ford Motor Co., 349 Mich. 108, 112, 84 N.W. 2d 523; Elder v. New York Central, 6 Cir., 1945, 152 F. 2d 361, 365. Whatever protection against discharge inured to plaintiff was the consequence of the *collective* action of plaintiff's Union. The Union, chosen as the statutory bargaining agent of plaintiff and defendant's other employees, is declared by statute to "be the exclusive representative(s) of all of the employees (in such unit) for the purposes of collective bargaining in respect to rates of pay, wages, hours of employment, or other conditions of employment." (Title 29 U.S.C.A. § 159[a]).

The question, then, for decision here is whether such statutory power, in combination with the terms of the bargaining contract, authorized the Union and defendant to mutually conclude, as a part of the bargaining process, that the circumstances shown by the evidence provided just cause for the layoff and discharge of plaintiff and other of defendant's employees. We conclude that it did. Unless such bilateral decisions, made in good faith, and after unhurried consideration between a Union and an employer, be sustained in court, the bargaining process is a mirage, without the efficacy contemplated by the philosophy of the law which makes its use compulsory.

Neither the right of a Union to bargain for its members nor the correlative duty of an employer to recognize and bargain with such agent ends upon the signing of a contract. "For the collective bargaining power is not exhausted by being once exercised." Elgin, Joliet and Eastern Railway Co. v. Burley, 325 U.S. 711, 739, 65 S. Ct. 1282, 1297, 89 L. Ed. 1886, 1903. In this cited case, the majority of the Supreme Court held that a bargaining agent could not, through retroactive compromise, settle or wipe out a vested and already existing grievance or cause of action of an employee. Mr. Justice Rutledge was careful, however, to distinguish between the right of a Union to agree to prospective action and its power to dispose retroactively of existing grievances. "For it is precisely the difference between making settlements effective only for the future and making them effective retroactively to conclude rights claimed as having already accrued which marks the . . . boundary between collective bargaining and the settlement of grievances." The collective bargaining authority is likewise not limited to the negotiations which periodically precede the making of new or successive contracts. The employer is required to deal with the bargaining agent in between times concerning working conditions and the carrying out of existing contracts. In National Labor Relations Board v. J. H. Allison & Co., 6 Cir., 1948, 165 F. 2d 766, 3 A.L.R. 2d 990, we held that an employer's duty to consult with the bargaining agent continued between contract negotiations. We there quoted from Order of Railroad Telegraphers v. Railway Express Agency, Inc., 321 U.S. 342, 346, 347, 64 S. Ct. 582, 585, 88 L. Ed. 788, 791, where Justice Jackson said, "Hence effective collective bargaining has been generally conceded to include the right of the representatives of the unit *to be consulted and to bargain* about the exceptional as well as the routine rates, rules, and working conditions." In Steele v. Louisville & N.R.R. Co., 323 U.S. 192, 202, 65 S. Ct. 226, 232, 89 L. Ed. 173, 183, dealing with the powers of one of the railroad brotherhoods under the Railway Labor Act, the Supreme Court said, "Congress has seen fit to clothe the bargaining representative with powers comparable to those possessed by a legislative body both to create and restrict the rights of those whom it represents."

The National Labor Relations Board emphasizes the continuing duty of the employer to bargain concerning the administration of a contract, "It is now well settled that the statutory duty to bargain collectively does not close with the execution of the collective agreement. The employer is under the further duty to negotiate with the accredited bargaining agency concerning the modification, *interpretation and administration* of the *existing* agreement." Carroll's Transfer Co., 56 N.L.R.B. 935, 937. "[T]he execution of a collective contract does not end the process of collective bargaining . . . the *interpretation* and *administration* of a contract already made and the settlement of disputes arising under any such contract are properly regarded as within the sphere of collective bargaining." Consolidated Aircraft Corp., 47 N.L.R.B. 694, 706. Professor Archibald Cox in his learned and comprehensive treatise *Rights Under a Labor Agreement* (69 HARV. L. REV. 601, 622) says, "It is also settled law that the Union's right to bargain and the employer's correlative duties are not limited to the negotiation of an agreement. Both the N.L.R.B. and the courts have consistently held that to refuse to discuss grievances and questions of contractual interpretation violates Section 8(a) (5)."

The *interpretation* of a contract by the parties thereto is not done as a matter of academic interest or in a vacuum. Interpretation is employed where there are facts to which such an interpretation is to be applied. Here the contract forbade discharge except for just cause. A condition arose which called for an interpretation of such clause. The employer disclosed to the Union the facts which the company felt would constitute just cause for the discharge of some of its employees. After an investigation and appraisal of such facts, the bargaining agent agreed that such facts constituted just cause. For our conclusion we do not rely upon the fact that, after plaintiff's discharge, the Union failed to present or process a grievance on her behalf, nor upon the then expressed opinion of its representatives that her discharge was for just cause. We are aware of the authorities which have held that the collective bargaining agent's authority does not extend to a retroactive determination that a discharge was for just cause or to the waiver or settlement of an existing grievance. Elgin, Joliet & Eastern Railway Co. v. Burley, 325 U.S. 711, 761, 65 S. Ct. 1282, 89 L. Ed. 1886; Woodward Iron Company v. Ware et al., 5 Cir., 1958, 261 F. 2d 138, 139; In re Norwalk Tire and Rubber Co., D.C., 100 F. Supp. 706; and cases gathered in note in 18 A.L.R. 2d 352. Neither do we rely upon authorities which have held that under such a contract as the one here involved only the Union can process a grievance and if a Union refuses or neglects to do so, an aggrieved employee is without remedy against his employer.

We turn, then to the specific terms of the contract in this case to see whether what was done here was within the power of the contracting parties. The first sentence of paragraph 14 contains the prohibition against discharge "except for just cause." The next sentence of the paragraph provides that "[i]n the event of a claim *by the Union* that an employee has been discharged without just cause" certain procedures are to follow. Nothing is said about a claim by the *employee* to the same effect. Paragraph 15 provides that "any and all questions and discussions which at any time may arise *effecting the employees* of the employer *shall* be taken up with the manager of the unit involved at such time and place as will be mutually agreed upon between *the Union* and the manager." The discussion between the representatives of the Union and defendant concerning the prospective layoff and discharge of some of defendant's employees was a matter "affecting the employees' and obeyed the command of such paragraph.

Paragraph 17 provides that "[d]uring the term of this agreement *any question* arising hereunder which cannot be directly and satisfactorily adjusted between *the Union and the employer* shall be referred to a committee." Such committee is given authority to make a binding determination. It should be noted that the responsibility of implementing the contract's terms is, in each case, placed with the Union. Procedure to call into question a discharge is provided only in the event "of a claim *by the Union* that an employee has been discharged without just cause." We are impressed that a fair reading of these provisions discloses the contract's intent that the parties thereto had authority to do what was done here. The employer, is keeping with its duty to bargain on all matters, presented its problems to the Union. It did not act hastily or unilaterally. The Union, on behalf of its members, refused initially to permit the discharge of defendant's employees. It urged further and less drastic methods. Discussion of defendant's problems continued for many months with submission by defendant to the Union of data which defendant asserted demonstrated that some discharges had to be made. The Union made its own study of this material and concluded that action had to be taken. It refused, however, to allow the defendant to discharge all of the employees in the unit and suggested a layoff of half of them with their ultimate discharge if their replacement with new employees proved the company's point. The defendant acquiesced in the Union's suggestion and the layoffs and discharges were carried out in strict compliance with the programme agreed upon. We consider that the Union was acting in the *collective* interest of those who by law and contract the Union was charged with protecting.

We think the case of Cortez v. Ford Motor Co., 349 Mich. 108, 84 N.W. 2d 523, while not providing an exact analogy for our decision, is supportive of our conclusion. There a group of female employees sought damages for claimed illegal and discriminatory layoffs. The propriety of the layoffs was the subject of extensive negotiation between the company and the Union. Such negotiations, ended in an accord between them that the layoffs were proper although to some extent a departure from the strict seniority provisions of a collective bargaining agreement. It is apparent that the Union and management agreed in advance as to the matter of layoffs, but the Union did present grievances on plaintiffs' behalf to the employer's foreman for disposition. It did not press such grievances further. In affirming a dismissal of the plaintiff's declaration on motion, Mr. Justice Edwards said,

> Our Court has repeatedly held that proper exercise of such discretion over grievances and *interpretation of contract terms* in the interest of all its members is vested in authorized representatives of the Union, subject to challenge after exhaustion of the grievance procedure only on grounds of bad faith, arbitrary action or fraud. 349 Mich. 108, at page 121, 84 N.W. 2d 523, at page 529.

Justice Edwards quoted from Ford Motor Co. v. Huffman, 345 U.S. 330, 337, 73 S. Ct. 681, 686, 97 L. Ed. 1048, where the Supreme Court made reference to the quality and extent of the collective bargaining agent's authority as follows:

> Any authority to negotiate derives its principal strength from a delegation to the negotiators of a discretion to make such concessions and accept such advantages as, in the light of all relevant considerations, they believe will best serve the interests of the parties represented.

In Hartley v. Brotherhood of Railway & Steamship Clerks, etc., 283 Mich. 201, 206, 277 N.W. 885, 887, a female employee was laid off by her railroad employer contrary to her acquired seniority. This was as a consequence of an agreement between the railroad and the Brotherhood (bargaining agent for the railroad employees) whereby married women were to be relieved from the service irrespective of seniority. The Supreme Court of Michigan held that it was within the power of the Brotherhood to modify the existing agreement, saying:

> This agreement was executed for the benefit of all the members of the Brotherhood, and not for the individual benefit of plaintiff. When, by reason of changed economic circumstances, it became apparent that the earlier agreement should be modified in the general interest of all members of the Brotherhood it was within the power of the latter to do so, notwithstanding the result thereof to plaintiff. The Brotherhood had the power by agreement with the Railway to create the seniority rights of plaintiff, and it likewise to the same method had the power to modify or destroy these rights in the interest of all the members.

We approved the holding of that case and the quoted language in Elder v. New York Central Railroad Co., 6 Cir., 1945, 152 F. 2d 361, 365.

The fact that in the case at bar the agreement by the Union to permit defendant to discharge plaintiff and others was not reduced to a written agreement or memorandum does not detract from its legality.

Professor Cox reviews what has been decided by the courts to date on this subject (69 HARV. L. REV. 601) and what that distinguished scholar considers desirable in labor contracts and in courts' construction of rights growing out of them. He says:

> All this suggests that the bargaining rights of the majority representatives are as broad *in the administration of a collective agreement as in its negotiation.* (p. 622.)
>
> In my judgment the interests of the individual will be better protected on the whole by first according legal recognition to the group interest in contract administration and then strengthening the representative's awareness of its moral and legal obligations to represent all employees fairly than by excluding the union in favor of an individual cause of action. Consequently, I would lean toward finding such an intention in an ambiguous agreement. (p. 657.)

We find no precise precedent for our decision, but believe it comports with legal principle and is consonant with the beneficial objectives of collective bargaining, now so important a tool in the continuing efforts to strengthen the position of the individual through collective action. Unless those upon whom is placed the responsibility for protecting collective interests are given the authority needed to discharge such responsibility, the entire process is of doubtful worth. Under the philosophy of collective responsibility an employer who bargains in good faith should be entitled to rely upon the promises and agreements of the Union representatives with whom he must deal under the compulsion of law and

contract. The collective bargaining process should be carried on between parties who can mutually respect and rely upon the authority of each other.

No motion for judgment notwithstanding the verdict was made by the defendant-appellant and this court is, therefore, limited upon reversal to granting of a new trial. Cone v. West Virginian Pulp & Paper Co., 330 U.S. 212, 67 S. Ct. 752, 91 L. Ed. 849. The judgment of the district court is reversed and a new trial ordered.

What are the collective interests at stake in this case? Was the result necessary to their vindication?

STEELE v. LOUISVILLE & NASHVILLE R.R. CO.
323 U.S. 192 (1944)

STONE, CH. J. The question is whether the Railway Labor Act, 48 Stat. 1185, 45 U.S.C. §§ 151 *et seq.*, imposes on a labor organization, acting by authority of the statute as the exclusive bargaining representative of a craft or class of railway employees, the duty to represent all the employees in the craft without discrimination because of their race, and, if so, whether the courts have jurisdiction to protect the minority of the craft or class from the violation of such obligation.

The issue is raised by demurrer to the substituted amended bill of complaint filed by petitioner, a locomotive fireman, in a suit brought in the Alabama Circuit Court against his employer, the Louisville & Nashville Railroad Company, the Brotherhood of Locomotive Firemen and Enginemen, an unincorporated labor organization, and certain individuals representing the Brotherhood. The Circuit Court sustained the demurrer, and the Supreme Court of Alabama affirmed. 245 Ala. 113, 16 So. 2d 416. We granted certiorari, 322 U.S. 722, the question presented being one of importance in the administration of the Railway Labor Act.

The allegations of the bill of complaint, so far as now material, are as follows: Petitioner, a Negro, is a locomotive fireman in the employ of respondent Railroad, suing on his own behalf and that of his fellow employees who, like petitioner, are Negro firemen employed by the Railroad. Respondent Brotherhood, a labor organization, is, as provided under § 2, Fourth of the Railway Labor Act, the exclusive bargaining representative of the craft of firemen employed by the Railroad and is recognized as such by it and the members of the craft. The majority of the firemen employed by the Railroad are white and are members of the Brotherhood, but a substantial minority are Negroes who, by the constitution and ritual of the Brotherhood, are excluded from its membership. As the membership of the Brotherhood constitutes a majority of all firemen employed on respondent Railroad, and as under § 2, Fourth the members because they are the majority have the right to choose and have chosen the Brotherhood to represent the craft, petitioner and other Negro firemen on the road have been required to accept the Brotherhood as their representative for the purposes of the Act.

On March 28, 1940, the Brotherhood, purporting to act as representative of the entire craft of firemen, without informing the Negro firemen or giving them opportunity to be heard, served a notice on respondent Railroad and on twenty other railroads operating principally in the southeastern part of the United States. The notice announced the Brotherhood's desire to amend the existing collective bargaining agreement in such manner as ultimately to exclude all Negro firemen from the service. By established practice on the several railroads so notified only white firemen can be promoted to serve as engineers, and the notice proposed that only "promotable," *i.e.* white, men should be employed as firemen or assigned to new runs or jobs or permanent vacancies in established runs on jobs.

On February 18, 1941, the railroads and the Brotherhood, as representative of the craft, entered into a new agreement which provided that not more than 50 per cent of the firemen in each class of service in each seniority district of a carrier should be Negroes; that until such percentage should be reached all new runs and all vacancies should be filled by white men; and that the agreement did not sanction the employment of Negroes in any seniority district in which they were not working. The agreement reserved the right of the Brotherhood to negotiate for further restrictions on the employment of Negro firemen on the individual railroads. On May 12, 1941, the Brotherhood entered into a supplemental agreement with respondent Railroad further controlling the seniority rights of Negro firemen and restricting their employment. The Negro firemen were not given notice or opportunity to be heard with respect to either of these agreements, which were put into effect before their existence was disclosed to the Negro firemen.

Until April 8, 1941, petitioner was in a "pass-enger pool," to which one white and five Negro firemen were assigned. These jobs were highly desirable in point of wages, hours and other considerations. Petitioner had performed and was performing his work satisfactorily. Following a reduction in the mileage covered by the pool, all jobs in the pool were, about April 1, 1941, declared vacant. The Brotherhood and the Railroad, acting under the agreement, disqualified all the Negro firemen and replaced them with four white men, members of the Brotherhood, all junior in seniority to petitioner and no more competent or worthy. As a consequence petitioner was deprived of employment for sixteen days and then was assigned to more arduous, longer, and less remunerative work in local freight service. In conformity to the agreement, he was later replaced by a Brotherhood member junior to him, and assigned work on a switch engine, which was still harder and less remunerative, until January 3, 1942. On that date, after the bill of complaint in the present suit had been filed, he was reassigned to passenger service.

Protests and appeals of petitioner and his fellow Negro firemen, addressed to the Railroad and Brotherhood, in an effort to secure relief and redress, have been ignored. Respondents have expressed their intention to enforce the agreement of February 18, 1941 and its subsequent modifications. The Brotherhood has acted and asserts the right to act as exclusive bargaining representative of the firemen's craft. It is alleged that in that capacity it is under an obligation and duty imposed by the Act to represent the Negro firemen impartially and in good faith; but instead, in its notice to and contracts with the railroads, it has been hostile and disloyal to the Negro firemen, has deliberately discriminated against them, and has sought to deprive them of their seniority rights and to drive them out of employment in their craft, all in order to create a monopoly of employment for Brotherhood members.

The bill of complaint asks for discovery of the manner in which the agreements have been applied and in other respects; for an injunction against enforcement of the agreement made between the Railroad and the Brotherhood; for an injunction against the Brotherhood and its agents from purporting to act as representative of petitioner and others similarly situated under the Railway Labor Act, so long as the discrimination continues, and so long as it refuses to give them notice and hearing with respect to proposals affecting their interests; for a declaratory judgment as to their rights; and for an award of damages against the Brotherhood for its wrongful conduct.

The Supreme Court of Alabama took jurisdiction of the cause but held on the merits that petitioner's complaint stated no cause of action. It pointed out that the Act places a mandatory duty on the Railroad to treat with the Brotherhood as the exclusive representative of the employees in a craft, imposes heavy criminal penalties for willful failure to comply with its command, and provides that the majority of any craft shall have the right to determine who shall be the representative of the class for collective bargaining with the employer, see Virginian R. Co. v. System Federation, 300 U.S. 515, 545. It thought that the Brotherhood was empowered by the statute to enter into the agreement of February 18, 1941, and that by virtue of the statute the Brotherhood has power by agreement with the Railroad both to create the seniority rights of petitioner and his fellow Negro employees and to destroy them. It construed the statute, not as creating the relationship of principal and agent between the members of the craft and the Brotherhood, but as conferring on the Brotherhood plenary authority to treat with the Railroad and enter into contracts fixing rates of pay and working conditions for the craft as a whole without any legal obligation or duty to protect the rights of minorities from discrimination or unfair treatment, however gross. Consequently it held that neither the Brotherhood nor the Railroad violated any rights of petitioner or his fellow Negro employees by negotiating the contracts discriminating against them.

If, as the state court has held, the Act confers this power on the bargaining representative of a craft or class of employees without any commensurate statutory duty toward its members, constitutional questions arise. For the representative is clothed with power not unlike that of a legislature which is subject to constitutional limitations on its power to deny, restrict, destroy or discriminate against the rights of those for whom it legislates and which is also under an affirmative constitutional duty equally to protect those rights. If the Railway Labor Act purports to impose on petitioner and the other Negro members of the craft the legal duty to comply with the terms of a contract whereby the representative has discriminatorily restricted their employment for the benefit and advantage of the Brotherhood's own members, we must decide the constitutional questions which petitioner raises in his pleading.

But we think that Congress, in enacting the Railway Labor Act and authorizing a labor union, chosen by a majority of a craft, to represent the craft, did not intend to confer plenary power upon the union to sacrifice, for the bene-

fit of its members, rights of the minority of the craft, without imposing on it any duty to protect the minority. Since petitioner and the other Negro members of the craft are not members of the Brotherhood or eligible for membership, the authority to act for them is derived not from their action or consent but wholly from the command of the Act. Section 2, Fourth provides:

> Employees shall have the right to organize and bargain collectively through representatives of their own choosing. The majority of any craft or class of employees shall have the right to determine who shall be the representative of the craft or class for the purposes of this Act.

Under §§ 2, Sixth and Seventh, when the representative bargains for a change of working conditions, the latter section specifies that they are the working conditions of employees "as a class." Section 1. Sixth of the Act defines "representative" as meaning "Any person or . . . labor union . . . designated either by a carrier or group of carriers or by its or their employees, to act for it or them." The use of the word "representative," as thus defined and in all the contexts in which it is found, plainly implies that the representative is to act on behalf of all the employees which, by virtue of the statute, it undertakes to represent.

By the terms of the Act, § 2. Fourth, the employees are permitted to act "through" their representative, and it represents them "for the purposes of" the Act. Sections 2, Third, Fourth, Ninth. The purposes of the Act declared by § 2 are the avoidance of "any interruption to commerce or to the operation of any carrier engaged therein," and this aim is sought to be achieved by encouraging "the prompt and orderly settlement of all disputes concerning rates of pay, rules, or working conditions." Compare Texas & New Orleans R. Co. v. Brotherhood of Clerks, 281 U.S. 548, 569. These purposes would hardly be attained if a substantial minority of the craft were denied the right to have their interests considered at the conference table and if the final result of the bargaining process were to be the sacrifice of the interests of the minority by the action of a representative chosen by the majority. The only recourse of the minority would be to strike, with the attendant interruption of commerce, which the Act seeks to avoid.

Section 2, Second, requiring carriers to bargain with the representative so chosen, operates to exclude any other from representing a craft. Virginian R. Co. v. System Federation, *supra,* 545. The minority members of a craft are thus deprived by the statute of the right, which they would otherwise possess, to choose a representative of their own, and its members cannot bargain individually on behalf of themselves as to matters which are properly the subject of collective bargaining. Order of Railroad Telegraphers v. Railway Express Agency, 321 U.S. 342, and see under the like provisions of the National Labor Relations Act J. I. Case Co. v. Labor Board, 321 U.S. 332, and Medo Photo Supply Corp. v. Labor Board, 321 U.S. 678.

The labor organization chosen to be the representative of the craft or class of employees is thus chosen to represent all of its members, regardless of their union affiliations or want of them. As we have pointed out with respect to the like provision of the National Labor Relations Act in J. I. Case Co. v. Labor Board, *supra,* 338:

> The very purpose of providing by statute for the collective agreement is to supersede the terms of separate agreements of employees with terms which reflect the strength and bargaining power and serve the welfare of the group. Its benefits and advantages are open to every employee of the represented unit.

The purpose of providing for a representative is to secure those benefits for those who are represented and not to deprive them or any of them of the benefits of collective bargaining for the advantage of the representative or those members of the craft who selected it.

As the National Mediation Board said in In The Matter of Representation of Employees of the St. Paul Union Depot Company, Case No. R635:

> Once a craft or class has designated its representative, such representative is responsible under the law to act for all employees within the craft or class, those who are not members of the represented organization, as well as those who are members.

Unless the labor union representing a craft owes some duty to represent non-union members of the craft, at least to the extent of not discriminating against them as such in the contracts which it makes as their representative, the minority would be left with no means of protecting their interests or, indeed, their right to earn a livelihood by pursuing the occupation in which they are employed. While the majority of the craft chooses the bargaining representative, when chosen it represents, as the Act by its terms makes plain, the craft or class, and not the majority. The fair interpretation of the statutory language is that the organization chosen to represent a craft is to represent all its members, the majority as well as the minority, and it is to act for and not against those whom it represents.[1] It is a principle of general application that the exercise of a granted power to act in behalf of others involves the assumption toward them of a duty to exercise the power in their interest and behalf, and that such a grant of power will not be deemed to dispense with all duty toward those for whom it is exercised unless so expressed.

We think that the Railway Labor Act imposes upon the statutory representative of a craft at least as exacting a duty to protect equally the interests of the members of the craft as the Constitution imposes upon a legislature to give equal protection to the interests of those for whom it legislates. Congress has seen fit to clothe the bargaining representative with powers comparable to those possessed by a legislative body both to create and restrict the rights of those whom it represents, cf. J. I. Case Co. v. Labor Board, *supra,* 335, but it has also imposed on the representative a corresponding duty. We hold that the language of the Act to which we have referred, read in the light of the purposes of the Act, expresses the aim of Congress to impose on the bargaining representative of a craft or class of employees the duty to exercise fairly the power conferred upon it in behalf of all those for whom it acts, without hostile discrimination against them.

This does not mean that the statutory representative of a craft is barred from making contracts which may have unfavorable effects on some of the members of the craft represented. Variations in the terms of the contract based on differences relevant to the authorized purposes of the contract in conditions to which they are to be applied, such as differences in seniority, the type of work performed, the competence and skill with which it is performed, are within the scope of the bargaining representation of a craft, all of whose members are not identical in their interest or merit. Cf. Carmichael v. Southern Coal Co., 301 U.S. 495, 509–510, 512 and cases cited; Washington v. Superior Court, 289 U.S. 361, 366; Metropolitan Casualty Co. v. Brownell, 294 U.S. 580, 583. Without attempting to mark the allowable limits of differences in the terms of contracts based on differences of conditions to which they apply, it

---

1. Compare the House Committee Report on the N.L.R.A. (H. Rep. No. 1147, 74th Cong., 1st Sess., pp. 20–22) indicating that although the principle of majority rule "written into the statute books by Congress in the Railway Labor Act of 1934" was to be applicable to the bargaining unit under the N.L.R.A., the employer was required to give "equally advantageous terms to non-members of the labor organization negotiating the agreement." See also the Senate Committee Report on the N.L.R.A. to the same effect. S. Rep. No. 573, 74th Cong., 1st Sess., p. 13.

is enough for present purposes to say that the statutory power to represent a craft and to make contracts as to wages, hours and working conditions does not include the authority to make among members of the craft discriminations not based on such relevant differences. Here the discriminations based on race alone are obviously irrelevant and invidious. Congress plainly did not undertake to authorize the bargaining representative to make such discriminations. Cf. Yick Wo. v. Hopkins, 118 U.S. 356; Yu Cong Eng v. Trinidad, 271 U.S. 500; Missouri ex rel. Gaines v. Canada, 305 U.S. 337; Hill v. Texas, 316 U.S. 400.

The representative which thus discriminates may be enjoined from so doing, and its members may be enjoined from taking the benefit of such discriminatory action. No more is the Railroad bound by or entitled to take the benefit of a contract which the bargaining representative is prohibited by the statute from making. In both cases the right asserted, which is derived from the duty imposed by the statute on the bargaining representative, is a federal right implied from the statute and the policy which it has adopted. It is the federal statute which condemns as unlawful the Brotherhood's conduct. "The extent and nature of the legal consequences of this condemnation, though left by the statute to judicial determination, are nevertheless to be derived from it and the federal policy which it has adopted." Deitrick v. Greaney, 309 U.S. 190, 200–201; Board of County Commissioners v. United States, 308 U.S. 343; Sola Electric Co. v. Jefferson Co., 317 U.S. 173, 176–7; cf. Clearfield Trust Co. v. United States, 318 U.S. 363.

So long as a labor union assumes to act as the statutory representative of a craft, it cannot rightly refuse to perform the duty, which is inseparable from the power of representation conferred upon it, to represent the entire membership of the craft. While the statute does not deny to such a bargaining labor organization the right to determine eligibility to its membership, it does require the union, in collective bargaining and in making contracts with the carrier, to represent non-union or minority union members of the craft without hostile discrimination, fairly, impartially, and in good faith. Wherever necessary to that end, the union is required to consider requests of non-union members of the craft and expressions of their views with respect to collective bargaining with the employer and to give to them notice of and opportunity for hearing upon its proposed action.

Nor are there differences as to the interpretation of the contract which by the Act are committed to the jurisdiction of the Railroad Adjustment Board.

Section 3, First (i), which provides for reference to the Adjustment Board of "disputes between an employee or group of employees and a carrier or carriers growing out of grievances or out of the interpretation or application of agreements," makes no reference to disputes between employees and their representative. Even though the dispute between the railroad and the petitioner were to be heard by the Adjustment Board, the Board could not give the entire relief here sought. The Adjustment Board has consistently declined in more than 400 cases to entertain grievance complaints by individual members of a craft represented by a labor organization. "The only way that an individual may prevail is by taking his case to the union and causing the union to carry it through to the Board." Administrative Procedure in Government Agencies, S. Doc. No. 10, 77th Cong., 1st Sess., Pt. 4, p. 7. Whether or not judicial power might be exerted to require the Adjustment Board to consider individual grievances, as to which we express no opinion, we cannot say that there is an administrative remedy available to petitioner or that resort to such proceedings in order to secure a possible administrative remedy, which is withheld or denied, is prerequisite to relief in equity. Further, since § 3, First (c) permits the national labor organizations chosen by the majority of the crafts to "prescribe the rules under which the labor members of the Adjustment Board shall be selected" and to "select such members and designate the division on which each member shall serve," the Negro firemen would be required to appear before a group which is in large part chosen by the respondents against whom their real complaint is made. In addition § 3, Second provides that a carrier and a class or craft of employees, "all acting through their representatives, selected in accordance with the provisions of this Act," may agree to the establishment of a regional board of adjustment for the purpose of adjusting disputes of the type which may be brought before the Adjustment Board. In this way the carrier and the representative against whom the Negro firemen have complained have power to supersede entirely the Adjustment Board's procedure and to create a tribunal of their own selection to interpret and apply the agreements now complained of to which they are the only parties. We cannot say that a hearing, if available, before either of these tribunals would constitute an adequate administrative remedy. Cf. Tumey v. Ohio, 273 U.S. 510. There is no administrative means by which the Negro firemen can secure separate representation for the purposes of collective bargaining. For the Mediation Board "has definitely ruled that a craft or class of employees may not be divided into two or more on the basis of race or color for the purpose of choosing representatives."

In the absence of any available administrative remedy, the right here asserted, to a remedy for breach of the statutory duty of the bargaining representative to represent and act for the members of a craft, is of judicial cognizance. That right would be sacrificed or obliterated if it were without the remedy which courts can give for breach of such a duty or obligation and which it is their duty to give in cases in which they have jurisdiction. Switchmen's Union v. National Mediation Board, *supra,* 300 ; Stark v. Wickard, 321 U.S. 288, 306–7. Here, unlike General Committee v. M.-K.-T. R. Co., *supra,* and General Committee v. Southern Pacific Co., *supra,* there can be no doubt of the justiciability of these claims. As we noted in General Committee v. M.-K.-T. R. Co., *supra,* 331, the statutory provisions which are in issue are stated in the form of commands. For the present command there is no mode of enforcement other than resort to the courts, whose jurisdiction and duty to afford a remedy for a breach of statutory duty are left unaffected. The right is analogous to the statutory right of employees to require the employer to bargain with the statutory representative of a craft, a right which this Court has enforced and protected by its injunction in Texas & New Orleans R. Co. v. Brotherhood of Clerks, *supra,* 556–557, 560, and in Virginian R. Co. v. System Federation, *supra,* 548, and like it is one for which there is no available administrative remedy.

We conclude that the duty which the statute imposes on a union representative of a craft to represent the interests of all its members stands on no different footing and that the statute contemplates resort to the usual judicial remedies of injunction and award of damages when appropriate for breach of that duty.

The judgment is accordingly reversed and remanded for further proceedings not inconsistent with this opinion.

Reversed.

[Mr. Justice Murphy concurred; he declared that the constitutional issue should have been decided and that he believed the Brotherhood's discriminations to offend the Fifth Amendment.]

In a case decided the same day, the court held that the same rationale applied where the person discriminated against was a member of the defendant union ; in addition, the court held that the right to "fair representation" was a federal right implied in the Railway Labor Act and conferred federal-question jurisdiction upon the federal district courts. Tunstall v. Bhd of Locomotive Firemen & Enginemen, 323 U.S. 210 (1944).

Several cases involving racial discrimination in railroad employment have applied the *Steele* doctrine. For the most part, the successful assertion of a breach of the statutory representative's duty of fair representation has been limited to cases of racial discrimination. A few cases affirmatively extend the doctrine to nonracial discrimination. The doctrine has been involved in many nonracial cases and discussed by courts as applicable to nonracial aspects of employment under the National Labor Relations Act. These cases will be considered hereafter.

ELGIN, JOLIET & EASTERN RY. CO. v. BURLEY
325 U.S. 711 (1945)

RUTLEDGE, J. This cause, arising upon an amended complaint, brings for decision novel and important questions concerning the authority of a collective bargaining representative, affecting the operation of the Railway Labor Act of 1934. 48 Stat. 1185, 45 U.S.C. § 151 ff. The ultimate issues are whether such an agent has authority, by virtue of the Act or otherwise, either to compromise and settle accrued monetary claims of ten employees or to submit them for determination by the National Railroad Adjustment Board to the exclusion of their right, after the settlement and after the Board's adverse decision, to assert them in a suit brought for that purpose. The claims are for "penalty damages" for alleged violation of the starting time provisions of a collective agreement, varying from $3,500 to $14,000, and in the aggregate amounting to $65,274.00.[1]

The District Court rendered summary judgment for the carrier, holding that the Board's award was a final adjudication of the claims, within the union's power to seek and the Board's to make, precluding judicial review. The Court

---

1. The record sets forth no provision for penalty damages. But the complaint alleges that under the terms of the agreement each of the plaintiffs is entitled to "pay for an additional day, at time and one-half, at the regular daily rate" for each day he was required to work contrary to the agreement's terms.

of Appeals reversed the judgment, 140 F. 2d 488, holding that the record presented a question of fact whether the union had been authorized by respondents "to negotiate, compromise and settle" the claims. We granted certiorari, 323 U.S. 690, in order to resolve the important questions affecting application and operation of the Act.

A statement of the more important facts will put the issues in sharper perspective. The controversy relates to operations in petitioner's so-called "Whiting Yard." Prior to July 24, 1934, respondents, or some of them, were employed by the Standard Oil Company to do private intra-plant switching in its Whiting, Indiana, plant. On that date this work was taken over by petitioner. Until then Standard Oil's switching crews began work each day at hours fixed in advance by the management, which varied as plant operations required.

Prior to 1934 petitioner's crews at all yards in Indiana and Illinois began work daily in accordance with starting time provisions contained in Article 6 of a collective agreement made in 1927 between petitioner and the Brotherhood of Railroad Trainmen, governing rules, working conditions and rates of pay of yardmen.

Upon transfer of the Whiting yard switching to petitioner, respondents therefore employed by Standard Oil became employees of petitioner and members of the Brotherhood. On July 24, 1934, company officials conferred with representatives of the engineers, the firemen and the yardmen concerning terms of employment. The Brotherhood acted for the yardmen. Apparently agreement was reached on all matters except starting time but, as to that, versions of what transpired differ.

Whichever version is true, a long controversy resulted. The carrier continued to follow the former practice, although departures from the schedule were reduced, as it claims, in conformity with the oral undertaking to observe it as far as possible. The work went on without interruption. But numerous complaints on account of departures were made through local officers of the Brotherhood. Time slips were filed by the employees. Frequent negotiations took place. None however resulted in a settlement prior to October 31, 1938.

In this state of affairs, respondents authorized the Brotherhood to file complaint with the National Railroad Adjustment Board for violation of Article 6. This was done on November 23, 1936. The "statement of claim" was signed and filed by Williams, chairman of the general grievance committee. It asserted that the carrier, having "placed the employees under the agreement of the yardmen," had "failed to put into effect the starting time provisions" of Article 6, and denied that violation was justified either because the carrier had agreed with the Engineers to follow the formerly prevailing practice or by the carrier's claim that the work could be done in no other way. The submission was intended to secure compliance. There was no prayer for money damages. Petitioner maintained that Article 6 was not applicable.

The Board, following its customary procedure, docketed the claim as No. 3537, notified the carrier and the union that the case, with many others docketed at the same time, was "assumed to be complete," and forwarded to each copies of the other's submissions. The record does not disclose what followed until nearly two years later.

On October 31, 1938, Williams and Johnson, secretary of the Brotherhood, two of the grievance committee's three members, accepted an offer made by petitioner's president, Rogers, to settle the claim. The settlement took the form of a proposal, made in a letter by Rogers to Williams, to settle some 61 different claims, including "Labor Board Docket No. 3537—Starting time of switch engines in Whiting S. O. Yard." Williams and Johnson endorsed acceptance for the Brotherhood and the yardmen on the letter. Because of its importance, pertinent portions are set forth in the margin.[2] On the day

2. The letter was addressed to Williams, as general chairman of the Brotherhood, and dated October 28, 1938. It stated:

"Since my letter of August 18th in which I tentatively proposed settlement of certain matters of grievance we have had further correspondence and conferences which have modified our decision in some cases. Therefore, in order that the whole matter be placed in concrete form I am outlining below our proposals to settle all of the cases except as otherwise specified.

"Case No. 5—Labor Board Docket #3537—Starting time of switch engines in Whiting S.O. Yard.

"Settled by agreement that *the starting times for a ninety day trial period* commencing November 15th, 1938, *shall be the times provided for in Article 6 of the Yardmen's* Agreement *instead of the starting times heretofore agreed upon and now being followed.* If at the end of the ninety day trial period the Railway Company or its employees claim that the starting times as fixed in Article 6 do not result in efficient and economical operation and in satisfaction to our employees and to the industry served, then representatives of the Railway Company and representatives of the Yardmen, and representatives of the Engineers and representatives of the Fireman *will sit down and work out a schedule of starting time best suited for meeting the special requirements of the industry.*

"We have by this letter given you a complete résumé of all of the claims which have not heretofore been disposed of, filed by you on behalf of the employees whom you represent and have proposed in this letter a very liberal disposition of all the cases involved. The settlements proposed are predicated on *a complete settlement and withdrawal of all cases now pending* either before the board, *or under discussion with this office except Case No. 4, which it is*

the settlement was concluded Rogers and Williams advised the Board of it by letter and jointly requested that the case be withdrawn from the docket, which accordingly was done.

Notwithstanding the settlement, a further dispute arose. In March, 1939, the Brotherhood, through Williams, requested the carrier to furnish a complete list of crews in the Whiting yard started at times other than those fixed by Article 6 from August 27, 1934, to November 15, 1938, when the settlement became effective. The company declined to furnish the list, stating it was at a loss to understand the reason for the request in view of the settlement.

The upshot of the dispute was the filing of another claim with the Board, Docket No. 7324, on May 18, 1939, by Williams, acting for the Brotherhood. This submission was

> for one day's pay at time and one-half for each foreman and each helper for each day they were required to work in yard service in the Whiting (Standard Oil Company) Yard, in violation of the fixed starting time provided for in Article No. 6 of the Yardmen's Agreement ... effective January 1, 1927, and applicable to Whiting (Standard Oil Company) Yardmen, July 27, 1934, from dates of August 27, 1934, until November 14, 1938, inclusive.

The submission not only maintained the applicability of Article 6 and accrual of the individual claims asserted. It also maintained that the settlement of October 31, 1938, was effective only to fix the starting time for the future and had no effect to waive or determine individual claims for penalty damages accrued prior to the settlement.

The carrier's submission reiterated its position in Case No. 3537. It also relied upon the settlement as precluding later assertion of any claim, individual or collective, based upon occurrences prior to the date of the settlement.

The matter went to decision by the Board. Under the procedure prescribed in case of deadlock, cf. § 3 First (1), a referee was called in. The award was made by the First Division on September 6, 1940. It sustained the Board's jurisdiction, found that "the parties to said dispute

---

understood will be left to a decision by the National Railroad Adjustment Board, *and it is further understood that in the event these settlements are accepted that the claims listed in this letter cover all claims of a similar nature, and that no other claims covering the same or like situations will be presented when such claims arise from causes occurring prior to the date of this settlement.* [Emphasis added.]

"Yours truly,
"S. M. Rogers, *President.*
"Accepted for the Yardmen: Oct. 31, 1938.
"C. H. Williams, General Chairman, B. of R.T.
"S. F. Johnson, Secretary, B. of R.T."

were given due notice of hearing thereon," and held that "the evidence shows that the parties to the agreement disposed of the claim here made by the letter of carrier dated October 28, 1938, accepted by employees October 31, 1938." Accordingly the claim was "denied per findings."

Thereafter, on November 19, 1940, the present suit was instituted. As has been noted, the case comes here after a summary judgment rendered on the carrier's motion, supported by the affidavit of its vice president. This in effect set up the compromise agreement and the award in Case No. 7324 as bases for the judgment sought.

The range and precise nature of the issues may be summarized best perhaps as they were shaped upon respondents' opposition to the carrier's motion. They denied that either Williams or the union had authority to release their individual claims or to submit them for decision by the Board. They relied upon provisions of the Brotherhood's constitution and rules, of which the carrier was alleged to have knowledge, as forbidding union officials to release individual claims or to submit them to the Board "without specific authority so to do granted by the individual members themselves"; and denied that such authority in either respect had been given.

The issues are not merely, as the Court of Appeals assumed, whether the Brotherhood had authority to compromise and settle the claims by agreement with the carrier and whether on the record this presents a question of fact. For petitioner insists, and the District Court held, that the award of the Board was validly made, and is final, precluding judicial review. We do not reach the questions of finality, which turn upon construction of the statutory provisions and their constitutional validity as construed. Those questions should not be determined unless the award was validly made, which presents, in our opinion, the crucial question. Respondents attack the validity and legal effectiveness of the award in three ways. Two strike at its validity on narrow grounds. Respondents say the Brotherhood had no power to submit the dispute for decision by the Board without authority given by each of them individually and that no such authority was given. They also maintain that they were entitled to have notice individually of the proceedings before the Board and none was given.

I

The difference between disputes over grievances and disputes concerning the making of collective agreements is traditional in railway labor affairs. It has assumed large importance in the

Railway Labor Act of 1934, substantively and procedurally. It divides the jurisdiction and functions of the Adjustment Board from those of the Mediation Board, giving them their distinct characters. It also affects the parts to be played by the collective agent and the represented employees, first in negotiations for settlement in conference and later in the quite different procedures which the Act creates for disposing of the two types of dispute. Cf. §§ 3, 4.

The statute first marks the distinction in § 2, which states as among the Act's five general purposes

> (4) to provide for the prompt and orderly settlement of all disputes concerning rates of pay, rules, or working conditions; (5) to provide for the prompt and orderly settlement of all disputes growing out of grievances or out of the interpretation or application of agreements covering rates of pay, rules, or working conditions.

The two sorts of dispute are sharply distinguished, though there are points of common treatment. Nevertheless, it is clear from the Act itself, from the history of railway labor disputes and from the legislative history of the various statutes which have dealt with them, that Congress has drawn major lines of difference between the two classes of controversy.

The first relates to disputes over the formation of collective agreements or efforts to secure them. They arise where there is no such agreement or where it is sought to change the terms of one, and therefore the issue is not whether an existing agreement controls the controversy. They look to the acquisition of rights for the future, not to assertion of rights claimed to have vested in the past.

The second class, however, contemplates the existence of a collective agreement already concluded or, at any rate, a situation in which no effort is made to bring about a formal change in terms or to create a new one. The dispute relates either to the meaning or proper application of a particular provision with reference to a specific situation or to an omitted case. In the latter event the claim is founded upon some incident of the employment relation, or asserted one, independent of those covered by the collective agreement, *e.g.*, claims on account of personal injuries. In either case the claim is to rights accrued, not merely to have new ones created for the future.

In general the difference is between what are regarded traditionally as the major and the minor disputes of the railway labor world. The former present the large issues about which strikes ordinarily arise with the consequent interruptions of traffic the Act sought to avoid. Because they more often involve those consequences and because they seek to create rather than to enforce contractual rights, they have been left for settlement entirely to the processes of noncompulsory adjustment.

The so-called minor disputes, on the other hand, involving grievances, affect the smaller differences which inevitably appear in the carrying out of major agreements and policies or arise incidentally in the course of an employment. They represent specific maladjustments of a detailed or individual quality. They seldom produce strikes, though in exaggerated instances they may do so. Because of their comparatively minor character and the general improbability of their causing interruption of peaceful relations and of traffic, the 1934 Act sets them apart from the major disputes and provides for very different treatment.

Broadly, the statute as amended marks out two distinct routes for settlement of the two classes of dispute, respectively, each consisting of three stages. The Act treats the two types of dispute alike in requiring negotiation as the first step toward settlement and therefore in contemplating voluntary action for both at this stage, in the sense that agreement is sought and cannot be compelled. To induce agreement, however, the duty to negotiate is imposed for both grievances and major disputes.

Beyond the initial stages of negotiation and conference, however, the procedures diverge. "Major disputes" go first to mediation under the auspices of the National Mediation Board; if that fails, then to acceptance or rejection of arbitration, cf. § 7; Trainmen v. Toledo, P. & W. R. Co., 321 U.S. 50; and finally to possible presidential intervention to secure adjustment. § 10. For their settlement the statutory scheme retains throughout the traditional voluntary processes of negotiation, mediation, voluntary arbitration, and conciliation. Every facility for bringing about agreement is provided and pressures for mobilizing public opinion are applied. The parties are required to submit to the successive procedures designed to induce agreement. § 5 First (b). But compulsions go only to insure that those procedures are exhausted before resort can be had to self-help. No authority is empowered to decide the dispute and no such power is intended, unless the parties themselves agree to arbitration.

The course prescribed for the settlement of grievances is very different beyond the initial stage. Thereafter the Act does not leave the parties wholly free, at their own will, to agree or not to agree. On the contrary, one of the main purposes of the 1934 amendments was to provide a more effective process of settlement.

The procedure adopted is not one of mediation and conciliation only, like that provided for major disputes under the auspices of the Mediation Board. Another tribunal of very different character is established with "jurisdiction" to determine grievances and make awards concerning them. Each party to the dispute may submit it for decision, whether or not the other is willing, provided he has himself discharged the initial duty of negotiation. § 3 First (i). Rights of notice, hearing, and participation or representation are given. § 3 First (j). In some instances judicial review and enforcement of awards are expressly provided or are contemplated. § 3 First (p) ; cf. § 3 First (m). When this is not done, the Act purports to make the Board's decisions "final and binding." § 3 First (m).

II

The collective agent's power to act in the various stages of the statutory procedures is part of those procedures and necessarily is related to them in function, scope and purpose.

The statute itself vests exclusive authority to negotiate and to conclude agreements concerning major disputes in the duly selected collective agent. Cf. *Virginian R. Co. v. System Federation, supra.* Since the entire statutory procedure for settling major disputes is aimed only at securing agreement and not decision, unless the parties agree to arbitration, this exclusive authority includes representation of the employees not only in the stage of conference, but also in the later ones of mediation, arbitration and conciliation.

Whether or not the agent's exclusive power extends also to the settlement of grievances, in conference or in proceedings before the Board, presents more difficult questions. The statute does not expressly so declare. Nor does it explicitly exclude these functions. The questions therefore are to be determined by implication from the pertinent provisions. These are the ones relating to rights of participation in negotiations for settlement and in proceedings before the Board. They are in part identical with the provisions relating to major disputes, but not entirely so ; and the differences are highly material.

The questions of power to bargain concerning grievances, that is, to conclude agreements for their settlement, and to represent aggrieved employees in proceedings before the Board are not identical. But they obviously are closely related in the statutory scheme and in fact. If the collective agent has exclusive power to settle grievances by agreement, a strong infer-

ence, though not necessarily conclusive, would follow for its exclusive power to represent the aggrieved employee before the Board. The converse also would be true. According it will be convenient to consider the two questions together.

The primary provisions affecting the duty to treat are found in § 2 First and Second, imposing the duty generally as to all disputes, both major and minor, and §§ 2 Sixth and 3 First (i), together with the proviso to § 2 Fourth, which apply specially to grievances. These sections in material part are set forth in the margin,[3] except the proviso which is as follows:

> Provided, That nothing in this Act shall be construed to prohibit a carrier from permitting *an employee, individually,* or local representatives of employees *from conferring* with management during working hours *without loss of time,* or to prohibit a carrier from furnishing free transportation to its employees while engaged in the business of a labor organization. [Emphasis added.]

Relating to participation in the Board's proceedings, in addition to the concluding sentence

---

3. By § 2 First, "*It shall be the duty of all* carriers, their officers, agents, and *employees* to exert every reasonable effort to make and maintain agreements concerning rates of pay, rules, and working conditions, and *to settle all disputes,* whether arising out of *the application* of such agreements or otherwise, in order to avoid any interruption to commerce . . ." By § 2 Second, "*All* disputes between a carrier or carriers and its or their employees *shall be considered, and, if possible, decided,* with all expedition, in conference *between representatives designated and authorized* so to confer, respectively, by the carrier or carriers and *by the employees thereof interested in the dispute.*" [Emphasis added.] These are the basic sections creating the duty, applicable to all disputes, major or minor, and to carriers and employees alike.

Section 2 Sixth applies specially to grievances, as does § 3 First (i). The former provides: "In case of a dispute between a carrier or carriers and its or their employees, *arising out of grievances or out of the interpretation or application of agreements* concerning rates of pay, rules, or working conditions, *it shall be the duty of the designated representative* or representatives of such carrier or carriers and *of such employees,* within ten days after the receipt of notice of a desire on the part of either party *to confer* in respect to such dispute, to specify a time and place . . ." Section 3 First (i) is as follows: "The disputes between *an employee* or group of employees and a carrier or carriers growing out of grievances or out of the interpretation or application of agreements concerning rates of pay, rules, or working conditions, including cases pending and unadjusted on the date of approval of this Act, *shall be handled in the usual manner up to and including* the chief operating officer of the carrier designated to handle such disputes; but, *failing to reach an adjustment in this manner, the disputes may be referred by petition of the parties or by either party to the appropriate division of the Adjustment Board* with a full statement of the facts and all supporting data bearing upon the disputes." [Emphasis added.]

of § 3 First (i), see note 26, in § 3 First (j), as follows.

> Parties may be heard either *in person*, by counsel, or by other representatives, as they may respectively elect, and the several divisions of the Adjustment Board shall give due notice of all hearings *to the employee* or employees and the carrier or carriers involved in any dispute submitted to them. [Emphasis added.]

Petitioner urges that, notwithstanding the proviso and § 3 First (j), the effect of the provisions taken as a whole is to make the collective agent the employees' exclusive representative for the settlement of *all* disputes, both major and minor, and of the latter "whether arising out of the application of such [collective] agreements or otherwise." The argument rests primarily upon §§ 2 First, Second, Third, Fourth, Sixth, and 3 First (i). It emphasizes the carrier's duty to treat with the collective representative, as reinforced by §§ 2 Eighth and Tenth.

Petitioner does not squarely deny that the aggrieved employee may confer with the carrier's local officials either personally or through *local* union representatives in accordance with the proviso to § 2 Fourth. But this right, if it exists, is regarded apparently as at most one to be heard, since in petitioner's view the power to make settlement by agreement is vested exclusively in the collective agent. Cf. §§ 2 Sixth and 3 First (i).

The collective agent, as the carrier conceives the statute, is the "representative[s], designated and authorized to confer" within the meaning of § 2 Second, without distinction between major and minor disputes. It is likewise the "representative, for the purposes of this Act," again without distinction between the two types of dispute, in the selection of which by "the respective parties" § 2 Third forbids the other to interfere. It is also "the designated representative" of the employees with whom, by § 2 Sixth, the carrier is required to treat concerning grievances in conference, a provision considered to carry over into § 3 First (i). The latter requires that disputes over grievances "shall be handled in the usual manner up to and including the chief operating officer of the carrier designated to handle such disputes."

In accordance with this view "either party," within the further provision of § 3 First (i) authorizing reference of the dispute to the Adjustment Board "by petition of the parties or by either party," refers to the carrier or the collective agent, not to the aggrieved employee acting otherwise than by the collective agent. Hence, "parties" as used in § 3 First (j) is given similar meaning. Consequently the collective agent also has exclusive power to submit the dispute to the Board and to represent aggrieved employees before it.

Petitioner's view has been adopted, apparently, in the general practice, if not the formally declared policy of the Adjustment Board. And this, it seems, has been due to the position taken consistently by the employees' representatives on the Board, over the opposition of carrier representatives. The unions, apparently, like petitioner in this case, interpret the Act as not contemplating two distinct systems for the settlement of disputes, one wholly collective for major disputes, the other wholly individual for minor ones. In this view the collective agent becomes a party to the collective agreement by making it, and its interest as representative of the collective interest does not cease when that function ends. It remains a party to the agreement, as such representative, after it is made; and consequently, in that capacity and for the protection of the collective interest, is concerned with the manner in which the agreement may be interpreted and applied.

Accordingly, petitioner urges that the statute, both by its terms and by its purpose, confers upon the collective agent the same exclusive power to deal with grievances, whether by negotiation and contract, or by presentation to the Board when agreement fails, as is given with respect to major disputes. And the aggrieved employee's rights of individual action are limited to rights of hearing before the union and possibly also by the carrier.

We think that such a view of the statute's effects, in so far as it would deprive the aggrieved employee of effective voice in any settlement and of individual hearing before the Board, would be contrary to the clear import of its provisions and to its policy.

It would be difficult to believe that Congress intended, by the 1934 amendments, to submerge wholly the individual and minority interests, with all power to act concerning them, in the collective interest and agency, not only in forming the contracts which govern their employment relation,[4] but also in giving effect to them and to all other incidents of that relation. Acceptance of such a view would require the clearest expression of purpose. For this would mean that Congress had nullified all preexisting rights of workers to act in relation to their employment, including perhaps even the fundamental right to consult with one's employer, except as the collective agent might permit. Apart from questions

---

4. Cf. Steele v. Louisville & N. R. Co., 323 U.S. 192; Tunstall v. Brotherhood of Locomotive Firemen, 323 U.S. 210; Wallace Corp. v. Labor Board, 323 U.S. 248.

of validity, the conclusion that Congress intended such consequences could be accepted only if it were clear that no other construction would achieve the statutory aims.[5]

The Act's provisions do not require such a construction. On the contrary they appear expressly to preclude it. The proviso to § 2 Fourth in terms reserves the right of "an employee *individually*" to confer with management; and § 3 First (j) not only requires the Board to give "due notice of all hearings *to the employee* ... involved in any dispute *submitted*" but provides for "parties" to be heard "either *in person,* by counsel, or by other representatives, as they may respectively elect."

These provisions would be inapposite if the collective agent, normally a labor union and an unincorporated association, exclusively were contemplated. Such organizations do not and cannot appear and be heard "in person." Nor would the provision for notice "to *the employee* ... involved in any dispute" be either appropriate or necessary. If only the collective representative were given rights of submission, notice, appearance and representation, language more aptly designed so to limit those rights was readily available and was essential for the purpose.

This conclusion accords fully with the terms of the proviso to § 2 Fourth. It appears to be intended as a qualification, in respect to loss of time and free transportation, of the section's preceding prohibitions against the carrier's giving financial and other aid to labor organizations and to employees in an effort to influence their union affiliations.[6] However, the language clearly contemplates also that the individual employee's right to confer with the management about his own grievance is preserved. There is some indication in the legislative history to this effect. The

right is so fundamental that we do not believe the purpose was to destroy it. Cf. 40 Op. Atty. Gen., No. 59, pp. 5, 6 (Dec. 29, 1942); Hughes Tool Co. v. Labor Board, 147 F. 2d 69.

Rights of conference are not identical with rights of settlement. But the purpose of conference and the duty to treat is to bring about agreement. The right and the obligation to share in the negotiations are relevant to their aim. Conceivably the statute might confer the right to participate in the negotiations, that is, to be heard before any agreement is concluded, either upon the collective agent or upon the aggrieved employee or employees, at the same time conferring upon the other the final voice in determining the terms of the settlement. This is, in effect, the position taken by each of the parties in this case. But they differ concerning where the final say has been vested. Petitioner maintains it has been given to the union. Respondents say it has been left with them.

In the view we take the Act guarantees to the aggrieved employee more than merely the right to be heard by the union and the carrier. We cannot say that the terms of the proviso to § 2 Fourth and of § 3 First (j) are so limited. Moreover, § 3 First (p) expressly states that the statutory suit to enforce an award in favor of an aggrieved employee may be brought by "the petitioner," presumably the collective agent or by the employee. All of these provisions contemplate effective participation in the statutory procedures by the aggrieved employee.

His rights, to share in the negotiations, to be heard before the Board, to have notice, and to bring the enforcement suit, would become rights more of shadow than of substance if the union, by coming to agreement with the carrier, could foreclose his claim altogether at the threshold of the statutory procedure. This would be true in any case where the employee's ideas of appropriate settlement might differ from the union's But the drastic effects in curtailment of his pre-existing rights to act in such matters for his own protection would be most obvious in two types of cases: one, where the grievance arises from incidents of the employment not covered by a collective agreement, in which presumably the collective interest would be affected only remotely, if at all; the other, where the interest of an employee not a member of the union and the collective interest, or that of the union itself, are opposed or hostile. That the statute does not purport to discriminate between these and other cases furnishes strong support for believing its

---

5. In this connection it is important to recall that the Act does not contemplate the existence of closed shops, to the extent at any rate that the carrier is forbidden to make such agreements. Cf. § 2 Fourth; 78 Cong. Rec. 12,402; 40 Op. Atty. Gen., No. 59 (Dec. 29, 1942). Accordingly the interests of unorganized workers and members of minority unions are concerned in the solution. These are not always adverse to the interests of the majority or of the designated union. But they may be so or even hostile. Cf. the authorities cited in note 30*. To regard the statute as so completely depriving persons thus situated of voice in affairs affecting their very means of livelihood would raise very serious questions.
[*Note 4 in this edited version.]

6. This undoubtedly was the primary object. The language in the concluding clause, "while engaged in the business of a labor organization," applies literally only to employees travelling upon union business, and has no apparent application to the preceding provision relating to the individual employee's right to confer with management.

purpose was not to vest final and exclusive power of settlement in the collective agent.[7]

We need not determine in this case whether Congress intended to leave the settlement of grievances altogether to the individual workers, excluding the collective agent entirely except as they may specifically authorize it to act for them, or intended it also to have voice in the settlement as representative of the collective interest. Cf. Matter of Hughes Tool Co., 56 N.L.R.B. 981, modified and enforced, Hughes Tool Co. v. Labor Board, *supra*. The statute does not expressly exclude grievances from the collective agent's duty to treat or power to submit to the Board. Both collective and individual interests may be concerned in the settlement where, as in this case, the dispute concerns all members alike, and settlement hangs exclusively upon a single common issue or cause of dispute arising from the terms of a collective agreement.[8] Those interests combine in almost infinite variety of relative importance in relation to particular grievances, from situations in which the two are hostile or in which they bear little or no relation of substance to each other and opposed to others in which they are identified.

Congress made no effort to deal specifically with these variations. But whether or not the collective agent has rights, independently of the aggrieved employee's authorization, to act as representative of the collective interest and for its protection in any settlement, whether by agreement or in proceedings before the Board, an award cannot be effective as against the aggrieved employee unless he is represented individually in the proceedings in accordance with the rights of notice and appearance or representation given to him by § 3 First (j). Those rights are separate and distinct from any the collective agent may have to represent the collective interest. For an award to affect the employee's rights, therefore, more must be shown than that the collective agent appeared and purported to act for him. It must appear that in some legally sufficient way he authorized it to act in his behalf.[9]

Petitioner's contrary view, as has been indicated, regards the settlement of grievances as part of the collective bargaining power, indistinguishable from the making of collective agreements. The assumption ignores the major difference which the Act has drawn between those functions, both in defining them and in the modes provided for settlement.

To settle for the future alone, without reference to or effect upon the past, is in fact to bargain collectively, that is, to make a collective agreement. That authority is conferred independently of the power to deal with grievances, as part of the power to contract "concerning rates of pay, rules, or working conditions." It includes the power to make a new agreement settling for the future a dispute concerning the coverage or meaning of a preexisting collective agreement. For the collective bargaining power is not exhausted by being once exercised; it covers changing the terms of an existing agreement as well as making one in the first place.

But it does not cover changing them with retroactive effects upon accrued rights or claims. For it is precisely the difference between making settlements effective only for the future and making them effective retroactively to conclude rights claimed as having already accrued which marks the statutory boundary between collective bargaining and the settlement of grievances. The latter by explicit definition includes the "interpretation or application" of existing agreements. To regard this as part of the collective bargaining power identifies it with making new agreements having only prospective operation; and

---

7. It is to be doubted that Congress by the generally inclusive language used concerning grievances intended, for instance, to give the collective agent exclusive power to settle a grievance arising independently of the collective agreement, affecting only nonunion men to whose claim the union and the majority were hostile.

8. But whether or not the carrier's violation affects all the members of the group immediately and alike, so as to create a present basis for claims by each, the violation, though resulting from misinterpretation, would constitute a present threat to the similar rights of all covered by the contract. Cf. Hughes Tool Co. v. Labor Board, *supra*, 72, 74; 40 Op. Atty. Gen., No. 59, pp. 4, 5 (Dec. 29, 1942).

To leave settlements in such cases ultimate' to the several choices of the members, each according his own desire without regard to the effect upon the collective interest, would mean that each affected worker would have the right to choose his own terms and to determine the meaning and effect of the collective agreement for himself. Necessarily, the carrier would be free to join with him in doing so and thus to bargain with each employee for whatever terms its economic power, pitted against his own, might induce him to accept. The result necessarily would be to make the agreement effective, not to all alike, but according to whatever varied interpretations individual workers, from equally varied motivations, might be willing to accept. To give the collective agent power to make the agreement, but exclude it from any voice whatever in its interpretation would go far towards destroying its uniform application.

9. Authority might be conferred in whatever ways would be sufficient according to generally accepted or "common law" rules for the creation of an agency, as conceivably by specific authorization given orally or in writing to settle each grievance, by general authority given to settle such grievances as might arise, or by assenting to such authority by becoming a member of a union and thereby accepting a provision in its constitution or rules authorizing it to make such settlements.

by so doing obliterates the statute's basic distinction between those functions.[10]

The Brotherhood had power, therefore, as collective agent to make an agreement with the carrier, effective for the future only, to settle the question of starting time, and that power was derived from the Act itself. In dealing within its scope, the carrier was not required to look further than the Act's provisions to ascertain the union's authority. But it does not follow, as petitioner assumes, that it had the same right to deal with the union concerning the past. That aspect of the dispute was not part of the collective agent's exclusive statutory authority.

If to exclude it severs what otherwise might be considered organic, the severance clearly is one which Congress could make and is one we think it has made, by its definition of grievances and by the provisions for individual participation in their settlement. If, moreover, as petitioner urges, this may make the settlement less convenient than if power to deal with grievances were vested exclusively in the collective agent, that consequence may be admitted. But it cannot outweigh the considerations of equal or greater force which we think Congress has taken into account in preserving the individual workman's right to have a voice amounting to more than mere protest in the settlement of claims arising out of his employment.

From the fact that the Brotherhood occupied the position of collective bargaining agent and as such had power to deal for the future, therefore, petitioner was not entitled to make any assumption concerning its authority to settle the claims accrued for the past or to represent the claimants exclusively in proceedings before the Board. Accordingly for the union to act in their

---

10. The distinction holds true although "interpretation or application" may look to the future as well as the past, as it often does. It goes to the source of the right asserted, whether in an antecedent agreement or only to one presently sought. The difference is important for other issues as well as those presently involved, *e.g.*, application of statutes of limitations.

The distinction is not to be ignored or wiped out merely because a particular dispute or agreement may look both to the past and to the future. The special procedure for settling grievances was created because it was intended they should be disposed of differently from disputes over "rates of pay, rules, or working conditions," which were committed exclusively to the collective agent's authority. One important difference preserved the aggrieved employee's rights to participate in all stages of the settlement. Congress therefore, when it preserved those rights, contemplated something more than collective representation and action to make the settlement effective for the past. It follows that the individual employee's rights cannot be nullified merely by agreement between the carrier and the union. They are statutory rights, which he may exercise independently or authorize the union to exercise in his behalf.

behalf with conclusive effect, authorization by them over and above any authority given by the statute was essential.

III

Petitioner urges that, apart from the statute, the facts of record show as a matter of law that respondents authorized the Brotherhood to settle claims, to submit them to the Board, and to represent them in its proceedings. Respondents deny that authority in any of these respects was given, either by individual authorization or by virtue of the Brotherhood's constitution and rules; and they insist that the record presents these questions as issues of fact.

It is apparent that the parties are at odds upon the inferences to be drawn from the facts and their legal effects rather than upon the facts themselves. Respondents deny, and petitioner apparently does not claim, that they at any time individually and specifically authorized the Brotherhood or its officials to compromise their claims for money due or to act for them exclusively in Board proceedings concerning those claims. If there is an issue in this respect it is obviously one of fact concerning which evidence and findings would be required.

The real issues, as we view the record, come down to whether respondents assented, in legal effect, to the final settlement of their claims by the union or to exclusive representation by it in any of the following ways: (1) by making complaints through local union officials; (2) by authorizing the Brotherhood to submit the complaint in Docket No. 3537; (3) by virtue of the Brotherhood's regulations; (4) by virtue of the collective agreement.

The collective agreement could not be effective to deprive the employees of their individual rights. Otherwise those rights would be brought within the collective bargaining power by a mere exercise of that power, contrary to the purport and effect of the Act as excepting them from its scope and reserving them to the individuals aggrieved. In view of that reservation the Act clearly does not contemplate that the rights saved may be nullified merely by agreement between the carrier and the union.

Nor can we say as a matter of law that the mere making of complaints through local Brotherhood officials amounted to final authorization to the union to settle the claims or represent the employees before the Board. Neither the statute nor the union's regulations purported to give these effects to that conduct. The time slips apparently were filed by the employees themselves. The record shows only the general fact that complaints concerning departures were made through local officials. More than this would be required to disclose unequivocal intention to surrender the individual's right to participate in the settlement and to give the union final voice in making it together with exclusive power to represent him before the Board. The making of complaints in this manner was only preliminary to negotiation and equivocal at the most.

Nor can we say, in the present state of the record, that the union's regulations unequivocally authorized the general grievance committee or its chairman either to settle the claims or to act as exclusive representative before the Board.

Because both factual and legal inferences would be involved in determining the effects of the regulations to bring about a surrender of the individual rights to take part in the settlement and in the Board's proceedings, those effects cannot be determined as a matter of law in the first instance here.

Since upon the total situation we cannot say as a matter of law that respondents had authorized the Brotherhood to act for them in Docket No. 7324, whether in submitting the cause or in representing them before the Board; since it is conceded also that they were not given notice of the proceedings otherwise than as the union had knowledge of them; and since further they have denied that they had knowledge of the proceedings and of the award until after it was entered, the question whether the award was effective in any manner to affect their rights must be determined in the further proceedings which are required. The crucial issue in this respect, of course, will be initially whether respondents had authorized the Brotherhood in any legally sufficient manner to represent them, individually, in the Board's proceedings in Docket No. 7324.

Until that question is determined, it is not necessary for us to pass upon the important issue concerning the finality and conclusive effect of the award, or to determine the validity and legal effect of the compromise agreement. We accordingly express no opinion concerning those issues.

The judgment is affirmed. The cause is remanded for further proceedings in conformity with this opinion.

FRANKFURTER, J., (dissenting). But respondents claim that irrespective of the authority of the Brotherhood officials to handle claims for the enforcement of the agreed starting time, Williams did not have authority to present to the Adjustment Board the claim for damages due to respondents for petitioner's alleged past violation of the starting-time agreement. They insist that there is no relation between a claim for money resulting from the violation of a collective agreement and a claim for the enforcement of a collective agreement. But surely this is to sever that which is organic. It wholly disregards the nature of such a collective agreement, its implications and its ramifications. In passing on the claim for money damages arising out of the yard agreement, any tribunal would have to examine, interpret and apply the collective agreement precisely as it would if the issue were the duty to observe the agreement in the future. An award based on the application of the collective agreement would, quite apart from technical questions of *res judicata,* affect future claims governed by the same collective agreement whatever the particular forms in which the claims may be cast. To find here merely an isolated, narrow question of law as to past liability is to disregard the ties which bind the money controversy to its railroad environment. Such a view is blind to the fact that "all members of the class or craft to which an aggrieved employee belongs have a real and legitimate interest in the dispute. Each of them, at some later time, may be involved in a similar dispute." 40 Ops. Atty. Gen., No. 59 (Dec. 29, 1942) pp. 4–5. Indeed, such a view leaves out of consideration not only the significant bearing of the construction of the same collective agreement on parts of the carrier's lines not immediately before the Court. It overlooks the relation of a provision in a collective agreement with one railroad to comparable provisions of collective agreements with other roads.

[On rehearing at the next term, 327 U.S. 661 (1946), the court "adhered" to its earlier decision and devoted an additional opinion to the question of employee authorization to the collective bargaining representative to settle his claim or represent him before the adjustment Board.]

For whether the collective agent has authority is a question which may arise in many types of situations involving the grievances either of members of the union or of nonmembers, or both, and necessarily therefore no all-inclusive rule can be formulated for all such situations. But neither does this mean that an equally all-exclusive rule must be followed, namely, that authority can be given or shown only in some particular way.

The question whether the collective agent has authority, in the two pertinent respects, does not turn on technical agency rules such as apply in the simple, individualistic situation where P deals with T through A about the sale of Blackacre. We are dealing here with problems in a specialized field, with a long background of custom and practice in the railroad world. And the fact that § 3 First (i) provides that disputes between carriers and their employees arising out of grievances or out of the interpretation or application of agreements concerning rates of pay, rules or working conditions "shall be handled in the usual manner" up to and including the chief operating officer of the carrier, indicates that custom and usage may be as adequate a basis of authority as a more formal authorization for the union, which receives a grievance from an employee for handling, to represent him in settling it or in proceedings before the Board for its determination.[1]

Moreover, when an award of the Adjustment Board involving an employee's individual grievance is challenged in the courts, one who would upset it carries the burden of showing that it was wrong. Its action in adjusting an individual employee's grievance at the instance of the collective bargaining agent is entitled to presumptive weight. For, in the first place, there can be no presumption either that the union submitting the dispute would undertake to usurp the aggrieved employee's right to participate in the proceedings by other representation of his own choice, or that the Board knowingly would act in disregard or violation of that right. Its duty, and the union's, are to the contrary under the Act.

Furthermore, the Board is acquainted with established procedures, customs and usages in the railway labor world. It is the specialized agency selected to adjust these controversies. Its expertise is adapted not only to interpreting a collective bargaining agreement, but also to ascertaining the scope of the collective agent's authority beyond what the Act itself confers, in view of the extent to which this also may be affected by custom and usage.

We also pointed out that the Act imposes correlative affirmative duties upon the carrier, the collective agent and the aggrieved employee to make every reasonable effort to settle the dispute. It would be entirely inconsistent for the

Act to require the carrier and the union to negotiate concerning the settlement of the grievance and, while withholding power from them to make that settlement effective finally as against the employee, to relieve him altogether of obligation in the matter. Not only is he required to take affirmative steps. His failure to do so may result in loss of his rights.

It is not likely that workingmen having grievances will be ignorant in many cases either of negotiations conducted between the collective agent and the carrier for their settlement or of the fact that the dispute has been submitted by one or the other to the Adjustment Board for determination. Those negotiations, as the Act requires, are conducted on the property. § 2 Sixth. Ordinarily submissions are not, and the statute contemplates that they shall not be, made to the Board until after all reasonable efforts to reach an agreement have been exhausted in good faith.

In view of these facts there cannot be many instances in which an aggrieved employee will not have knowledge or notice that negotiations affecting his claim are being conducted or, if they fail, the proceedings are pending before the Board to dispose of it. Although under our ruling his rights to have voice in the settlement are preserved, whether by conferring with the carrier and, having seasonably done so, refusing to be bound by a settlement reached over his protest, or by having representation before the Board according to his own choice, we did not rule, and there is no basis for assuming we did, that an employee can stand by with knowledge or notice of what is going on with reference to his claim, either between the carrier and the union on the property, or before the Board on their submission, allow matters to be thrashed out to a conclusion by one method or the other, and then come in for the first time to assert his individual rights. No such ruling was necessary for their preservation and none was intended.

FRANKFURTER, J., (dissenting). The Court now announces that it "adheres" to its decision. But as we read the Court's interpretation of its original opinion, it "adheres" to it by extracting from it almost all of its vitality. We say "almost" because the one thing that remains is the conclusion that the determination by the Adjustment Board that the recognized union represented its members is allowed to be reopened not before the Board but anew in the courts, State or federal, in an independent suit by a member of the union against the carrier. To be sure, the prospects for redetermination are largely illusory because the Court now erects a series of hurdles which will

---

1. Furthermore, so far as union members are concerned, and they are the only persons involved as respondents in this cause, it is altogether possible for the union to secure authority in these respects within well established rules relating to unincorporated organizations and their relations with their members, by appropriate provisions in their by-laws, constitution or other governing regulations, as well as by usage or custom. There was nothing to the contrary in our former opinion. We only ruled that on the showing made in this respect, which included controverted issues concerning the meaning and applicability of the union's regulations, and the effects of customs and usage, we could not say as a matter of law that the disputed authority had been given.

be, and we assume were intended to be, almost impossible for an employee to clear. But since litigation is authorized and hope springs eternal in a litigant's breast, the far-reaching mischief of unsettling non-litigious modes of adjustment under the machinery of the Railway Labor Act largely remains. When peaceful settlements between carriers and the Brotherhoods are subject to such hazards, the carrier can hardly be expected to negotiate with a union whose authority is subject to constant challenge.

———

Interestingly, the Solicitor General, the Railway Labor Executives Association (composed of the standard railroad labor organizations), and the C.I.O. presented amicus briefs criticizing the original opinion as disruptive of normal grievance settlement procedures. Excerpts appear in the Frankfurter dissent.

After the second opinion, in response to footnote 1 (2 in the original), unions amended constitutions or by-laws declaring, in essence, that membership constituted authorization of the union to represent the member in grievance matters and to settle claims. At the time of the opinion and these amendments neither the closed nor the union shop was permitted on the railroads. But in 1951 the Railway Labor Act was amended to permit carrier-union agreements requiring union membership, after sixty days of employment or the agreement was made, in essentially the same terms as the union shop proviso to Section 8(a) (3) of the National Labor Relations Act. In effect both require no more than payment of initiation fees and dues. They *seem* to require membership, and in most cases employees under such agreements do join a union whose agreement contains such a requirement for continued employment. Membership under such an arrangement probably cannot perform the authorizing function that pre-amendment membership combined with constitution and by-law provisions did.

A NOTE ON GRIEVANCE SETTLING PRACTICE

As indicated in *Elgin v. Burley,* unions and management often attempt to settle a number of accumulated grievance cases by compromising and trading off claims. Such sessions often are known by such names as "bargain day" or "wholesale day." The settlements often are agreed to be without precedent value. Obviously such arrangements serve the institutional interests of union and may help remove irritations between employees and supervision. Wholesale settlement sometimes occurs as part of the process of negotiating a new agreement. Some employees get more than they are entitled to, some get about their due (and sooner than if the whole grievance-arbitration procedure were exhausted), and some get less than full enforcement of the agreements would avail them. In *Elgin v. Burley* the "settlement" seems to have been fairly advantageous to the grieving employees. They sought application of the agreement to their starting time (they did not initially seek money), and they obtained, through the union's "settlement," a trial for ninety days of the starting time they wanted plus an undertaking to negotiate further on the subject. Could it not be argued that the settlement was essentially a bargaining arrangement looking to the future in return for which the union gave up the claim to have the agreement starting time govern? Would it be appropriate to allow *one* of the ten claimants to block a settlement that thus governs future working conditions and pay rates of the group? Assuming that the claim was only colorable but not assuredly correct, the elimination of a point of contention and embarking upon an agreed course to achieve arrangements mutually satisfactory to employer and employees would seem not only desirable but what collective bargaining is supposed to achieve when it is working well.

———

B.

Section 9(a) of the National Labor Relations Act and the "Nature" of the Collective Agreement

The Possible Pertinence of Elgin v. Burley to Employee Grievance-Arbitration Rights under the NLRA

The Rutledge opinion leans heavily upon the language of the Railway Labor Act and especially the statutory provisions concerning the National Railroad Adjustment Board. However, several factors give *Elgin* relevance to employee rights under the National Labor Relations Act and Section 301. The Wagner Act (the original National Labor Relations Act which, as amended, became Title I of the Labor-Management Relations Act of 1947) drew heavily upon the Railway Labor Act. So, for example, the proviso to Section 2 Fourth of the latter (referred to in *Elgin*) is echoed in the proviso to Section 8 (2) of the Wagner Act which remains in the present Section 8(a) (2). The concept that the union chosen by a majority of the employees is the *exclusive* bargaining representative of the group, including those who voted against it, derives from the Railway Labor Act. This common element made the applicability of *Steele* to non-railroad union-member relationships an easy one. But, of course, there are innumerable differences not only in statutory language but in the organization of unions, the extent of bargaining, the methods of processing grievances, the statutory Adjustment Board procedure, and others. Nonetheless, it can be argued that the basic dichotomy of bargaining and agreement administration are essentially the same and that institutional and individual interests are much the same in both settings. And, perhaps most importantly, some legislative history of the 1947 amendments to Section 9 of the National Labor Relations Act indicates a congressional intent to import *Elgin*. The following shows the changes made by the 1947 amendment of the Wagner Act (unchanged language in roman, additions in italics):

> Sec. 9. (a) Representatives designated or selected for the purposes of collective bargaining by the majority of the employees in a unit appropriate for such purposes, shall be the exclusive representatives of all the employees in such unit for the purposes of collective bargaining in respect to rates of pay, wages, hours of employment, or other conditions of employment: *Provided*, That any individual employee or a group of employees shall have the right at any time to present grievances to their employer [.] *and to have such grievances adjusted, without the intervention of the bargaining representative, as long as the adjustment is not inconsistent with the terms of a collective-bargaining contract or agreement then in effect: Provided further, That the bargaining representative has been given opportunity to be present at such adjustment.*

The amendment to the first proviso was added by the House Committee and remained unchanged in the bill passed by the House. The second proviso originated in the Senate Committee, the Senate passed bill contained it, and it was adopted in conference.

EMPLOYEE PARTICIPATION IN THE GRIEVANCE ASPECT OF COLLECTIVE BARGAINING*

BERNARD DUNAU

The further proviso, [to section 9(a)] which explicitly affords the representative an opportunity to be present at the grievance adjustment, was added in evident response to the severe criticism levelled at the revision by the NLRB in a statement filed by Chairman Herzog with the Senate Labor Committee. The NLRB feared that the revision would result in "serious impingement on the authority of the exclusive representative to act for the whole unit" in that it would encourage "individual bargaining" and provide a ready device for "playing off individual employees against the group"; it further argued that "there is no provision for determining whether the individual bargain . . . [on a grievance] violates the collective agreement, nor does the bill say who shall make that determination"; and finally, that it would "destroy the rule of the *Hughes Tool* case." Unimpressed with the statement, except insofar as it may have induced the further proviso, the proponents of the amendment were convinced of the need to reinvigorate the independent right of employees to redress

---

*From 50 COLUM. L. REV. 731, 744–49 (1950). Reprinted with permission.

their grievances. The "present bill," stated the House Report, "permits the employees and their employer to *settle* the grievances," "the revised language," stated the Senate Report, "would make it clear that the employee's right to present grievances exists *independently* of the rights of the bargaining representative"; and the Senate Minority Report, otherwise strident in its criticism, stated that the revision "spelled out desirable grievance procedures."

The most instructive comment occurred in an interchange on the floor of the House during the only time that the measure was actively debated in either forum. In a broadside attack echoing the NLRB's criticism, Representative Lanham charged that the revision negated the "principle of collective bargaining and majority rule"; that it granted "individual employees the right to present and settle grievances which relate to wages, hours, and conditions of employment without permitting the representative . . . to participate in the conference and join in any adjustment"; that it would "create rivalry, dissension, suspicion, and friction among employees," "permit employers to play off one group of employees against another," "confuse the employees," and "be disastrous." In reply, in a statement fully endorsed by Representative Hartley, the leading House proponent of the amendments, Representative Owens disclaimed the meaning imputed to the revision and stated it was designed in adherence to the principle expressed in *Elgin*.

With the return to *Elgin* via congressional reassertion under the NLRA of the employee's independent standing to adjust grievances, the full circle is completed. But the problem of accommodating the individual and collective interest recurs, for restoration of the employees' autonomous status was accompanied by acknowledgment of the representative's parallel concern in grievance disposition. Any settlement of a grievance founded upon a collective agreement must be consistent with its terms, and beyond that, whatever the nature of the grievance, the representative must be given an opportunity to be present at its adjustment. The statement of the limitations is easier than its translation into reality. The process of adjusting grievances without the intervention of the representative, but in its presence, so long as the adjustment is consistent with agreement, is hardly self-evident in its operability. Resort to the legislative history to ascertain the interrelation of the parts, an elusive quest at best, gives no help, for apart from confirming the dominant purpose of the provision to be the reestablishment of the employees' status, it does not advance the task of implementation beyond what the words in themselves, unaided by the

gloss, suggest. Those words, however, when related to their purpose and to the milieu in which they are expected to operate, yield a workable result.

The first task is to elucidate the line drawn between the intervention and the presence of the representative. Preclusion of intervention was designed to undo the *Hughes Tool* rule by restoring the power of decision in grievance disposition to the employee and divesting the representative of it. Without the intervention of the representative means, therefore, vesting the employee with the final say in the settlement of a grievance. The extent of the representative's remaining participation in grievance adjustment, insofar as it rests only on the right to be present, depends on the role alloted it by that qualification.

Verbally to be present is consistent either with the right to be heard or the right to observe. If it means only to observe, it casts the representative in the role of a passive auditor empowered perhaps to grunt its displeasure without articulating it. The picture of a gagged representative is too ludicrous to accept. It is hardly commensurate with the dignity of its position and with its legitimate concern in the administrative aspect of the employment relationship. It partakes of the same incongruity as the rejected suggestion under the pre-amendment NLRA that the right of employees to present grievances meant no more than to draw attention to their existence, and it undercuts the premise of the *Elgin* case which assumed that the representative had at least "the right to participate in the negotiations, that is, to be heard before any agreement is concluded." The opportunity afforded the representative to be present appears therefore to contemplate the right to be heard.

This conclusion is fortified by Section 8(d) of the amended NLRA which defines the duty to bargain collectively as "the performance of the mutual obligation of the employer and the representative" to "confer in good faith" with respect, among other things, to "any question arising" under an agreement. *Non constat* the wish of the employee, both the employer and the representative can at the very least require each other to confer about a grievance founded upon an agreement, for any such grievance raises a "question arising thereunder." Upon this analysis, the difference between the representative's intervention and presence is the distinction between the power to decide and the right to be heard.

The representative's right to be heard extends to every grievance whatever its nature, but where the grievance is founded upon the claimed denial of a job right granted by collective agreement, the representative possesses more than the mere opportunity to confer. It is excluded from intervention only "as long as the adjustment is not inconsistent with the terms of a collective-bargaining contract or agreement then in effect." This qualification recognizes a right of intervention in the representative if the adjustment deviates from the terms of the agreement. Literally speaking, the condition precedent to intervention is a determination of inconsistency. Realistically speaking, the establishment of this precondition by a feasible method is an impossibility. There is no magic caliper which measures agreement observance, and however seemingly consonant with the agreement the adjustment may appear to be either to the employer, the employee, or the representative, the other may in all sincerity raise an issue of conformity. To be given effect, therefore, the right of intervention must depend on no more than the representative's own determination that a question of deviation exists.

The necessity for this conclusion is apparent from a consideration of the reason for and the scope of intervention. On its face the right of intervention is bottomed on the need to maintain the integrity and uniformity of the agreement, for the protection of which the representative's participation in conference without more is insufficient. To be meaningful, intervention must enlarge on the already existing right to be heard, but to prevent displacement of the employee's power of decision, it must encompass less than exclusive authority to settle the grievance on the employee's behalf. The middle ground is to grant the representative and the employee an equal voice in determining the question of conformity. On this basis, although the right to intervene adheres as soon as the issue of conformity is raised, disposition of a grievance, insofar as the requirement of conformity with the terms of agreement is concerned, requires the tripartite agreement of the employer, the employee, and the representative.

The legitimacy of requiring tripartite concurrence on the issue of conformity is emphasized by the nature of a grievance founded upon an agreement. The aspect of the grievance which gives the employee his independent standing to redress it is the accrued character of the claim, and to that end he is entitled to press his understanding of the agreement in support of his matured interest. But, on the other hand, the employee has no standing to participate in thrashing out the interpretation of an existing employment standard to the extent that it purports to settle the future scope of a disputed existing right. Insofar as it operates prospectively, the interpretation of a standard, no less than its form-

ulation, is within the exclusive province of the representative, for the interpretative process is a policy-making function which calls for the imaginative and informed choice of available alternatives in construing an agreement. Whether the result is termed an interpretation or a change of the agreement, its essence is to imbue it with a new meaning to which the employees are bound in the future.

But this is the nub of the difficulty, for as Mr. Justice Frankfurter observed in dissent in *Elgin:* "In passing on the claim" as to

> past liability, ... any tribunal would have to examine, interpret and apply the collective agreement precisely as it would if the issue were the duty to observe the agreement in the future. An award based on the application of the collective agreement, would ... affect future claims governed by the same collective agreement whatever the particular forms in which the claims may be cast.

Thus, the employee in redressing his past claim influences the future construction of the agreement. His standing, however, cannot be divested by showing that " 'interpretation or application' may look to the future as well as the past," because his status rests on "*the source of the right asserted,* whether in an antecedent agreement or only to one presently sought." The only way to cut the Gordian knot is to require tripartite agreement on the question of consistency, and thereby prevent dilution of the agreement through disparate interpretation and preserve the representative's exclusive status from diminution.

The requirement of tripartite agreement brings into sharp relief the question of breaking an impasse over the disposition of a grievance when the disputants fail to reach accord through negotiation. If the grievance does not have its foundation in a collective agreement, a deadlock can arise between only the employer and the employee, because the representative's participation is limited to a right to be heard without a share in decision. But, if the grievance is founded on a collective agreement, a deadlock may involve all three on the question of consistency with the agreement, although it can involve only the employer and the employee on any other question, such as the existence of a fact pertinent to the dispute, or the willingness to compromise a money claim. In the absence of a grievance procedure ending in final and binding arbitration, the three alternatives available to break the deadlock are (1) to submit to the employer's last offer, (2) to resort to self-help to induce the employer to yield his position, or (3) to litigate the issue in court. None are desirable methods of grievance adjustment.

The salutary answer to the question of deadlock lies in the negotiation by the representative and the employer of a grievance procedure ending in final and binding arbitration before an impartial arbiter through which all can process a grievance to a definitive conclusion. The value of the method is enhanced because it fits into the customary industrial practice of negotiating the procedural mode of grievance disposition as an integral adjunct to the substantive rights which the agreement creates.

If an individual's contract claim cannot be settled without his "consent" (within the meaning of *Elgin v. Burley*), may it be litigated in arbitration only upon notice and opportunity to participate in the hearing? Or does the doctrine of fair representation afford sufficient protection to the individual so that other accommodations in arbitration practice need not be made?

Does the procedure of the National Labor Relations Board provide a parallel? The General Counsel (a public official) has unreviewable discretionary power to issue a complaint on a charge or to refrain from doing so. He has unreviewable power to settle the charges (but a settlement is not *res judicata* as to an alleged breach of contract based on the same facts). If a complaint is issued, the charging party is given notice and may intervene and participate as a party, but the General Counsel has control of the plaintiff's case. The intervenor-charging party may appeal from the Trial Examiner's decision and recommended order and the Board's decision and order.

BLACK CLAWSON CO., INC. v. INTERNATIONAL ASSOCIATION OF MACHINISTS
313 F. 2d 179 (2d Cir. 1962)

KAUFMAN, C. J. The plaintiff, Black-Clawson Company, Inc., (hereafter referred to as Black-Clawson or the employer) is engaged in the manufacture of machinery for the paper-making industry in various states. In July 1959, Black-Clawson entered into a collective bargaining agreement with the International Association of Machinists, Lodge 355, District 137 (hereafter referred to as the Union), which served as the exclusive bargaining representative for certain production and maintenance employees in the plaintiff's Watertown, New York plant. One member of the unit represented by the Union was Theodore A. Best who, along with the Union, was joined as a defendant in the court below in a suit for a declaratory judgment brought by Black-Clawson. Best was an employee of the company from June 4, 1951 until May 8, 1961, when his employment was terminated by a written notice informing him that the cause for discharge was his failure to return to work at the end of a protracted period of sick leave. The collective bargaining agreement between Black-Clawson and the Union established a four-step grievance procedure, terminating in arbitration, for resolution of employee grievances. Best, purporting to have complied with the preliminary steps of the grievance procedure, demanded that the employer go to arbitration in order to remedy what Best contended was a wrongful discharge in violation of the collective agreement. [The employer brought action for a declaratory judgment that the dispute was not arbitrable. The portion of the opinion holding that a declaratory judgment action may be brought under § 301 is omitted.]

The heart of the controversy presented on appeal is the interpretation of those sections of the collective bargaining agreement between Black-Clawson and the Union which deal with the resolution of grievances. Article XX, entitled "Grievance Procedures," defines a grievance as "any dispute between the Company and the Union, or between the Company and any employee," and goes on to establish a four-step procedure for the solution of such disputes. Step one provides that the "grievance shall be taken up orally by the aggrieved employee and a member of the Union Committee if he so desires with the Department Foreman within three (3) days after the grievance becomes known by the aggrieved employee or by the Shop Committee." Within two working days, the foreman must give his answer to the grievance, and if no settlement is reached, the grievance is to be reduced to written form, upon which the foreman will record his answer. Step two is in the hands of the Shop Committee which, within two days, may present the written grievance to the Plant Superintendent, who must meet with the Committee and give his written answer within four working days. If no settlement of the grievance is achieved at this stage, mounting to step three is again in the hands of the Shop Committee, which may, within four days, request a meeting with the Director of Personnel, whose answer must be forthcoming before ten days pass. Step four of the grievance procedure is described as follows:

> In the event the grievance or dispute is not settled in a manner satisfactory to the grieving party then the grieving party may submit such grievance or dispute to arbitration. Whomever requests arbitration shall serve notice to the other party and submit letter of notification of intent to arbitrate to the Federal Mediation and Conciliation Service within fifteen (15) days after receiving the written answer from the Director of Personnel or his designee.

After Best's employment was terminated on May 8, 1961, both he and the Union purported to comply with the first three steps of the grievance procedure. Judge Brennan, in the court below, held that they had in fact failed to comply with the letter of the collective bargaining agreement. In any event, on July 5, 1961, Best mailed a letter to Black-Clawson's Director of Personnel, invoking step four of the grievance procedure and requesting arbitration. The employer indicated on several occasions that it did not consider the matter to be arbitrable.

Best contends that not only is the issue arbitrable but the terms of the contract are such as to permit him personally to request arbitration and to compel it by an action in a court of law. We disagree, and hold that the terms of Article XX of the collective bargaining agreement give no standing to Best, as an individual employee, to compel arbitration.

It matters not that "grievance" is defined in one sense as a "dispute . . . between the Company and any employee"; that is merely a definition in the contract and does not in any way govern the proper procedure for settling the grievance. It is clear that the rights of the individual employee with regard to the grievance procedure are limited to step one, confrontation with the Department Foreman. From that point on, the right to progress from one step to the next is vested in the Union and ultimately in the employer as well. Best contends that step four permits the "grieving party" to invoke arbitration, and that this clearly refers to the individual employee. But by doing no more than placing this phrase in its context, we are drawn ineluctably to the conclusion that "party" in step four means what it means throughout the entire collective bargaining agreement—either Black-Clawson or the Union. Step four itself requires that notice of intention to submit to arbitration be given "to the other party." "Each party" must bear its respective expenses during arbitration. Article XX also provides that "either party to this agreement shall be permitted to call employee witnesses" in administering the grievance procedure. The words "either party" recur too frequently in

Article XX to permit of any construction other than that we here adopt. Our conclusion is reinforced by the fact that the drafters of the collective bargaining agreement were apparently well aware of the difference between a "grieving party" and an "aggrieved employee," for the latter phrase was used unequivocally when assigning rights during the course of the grievance procedure to individual employees.[1]

The collective agreement we have before us is typical in language and structure of many such agreements in the field of labor-management relations. Similar language in an agreement almost identical in form to the one before us caused this Court to conclude only recently:

> The right to arbitrate under a collective agreement is not ordinarily a right incident to the employer-employee relationship, but one which is incident to the relationship between employer and union. Under the collective agreement between the parties, it was the union which had the right to take grievances to arbitration, not the individual employees. See Black-Clawson Co. v. International Ass'n of Machinists, 212 F. Supp. 818 (N.D.N.Y. 1962) . . . The wording of the grievance clause as a whole clearly indicates that only the union or the employer can demand arbitration. Procter and Gamble Independent Union v. Procter & Gamble Mfg. Co., 312 F. 2d 181 (2d Cir., 1962).

The Supreme Court's recent holding in Smith v. Evening News Ass'n, 371 U.S. 195, 83 S.Ct. 267, 9 L.Ed. 2d 246 (1962) convinces us that henceforth, actions between employees and employers brought under section 301(a) will be governed by "federal law, which the courts must fashion from the policy of our national labor laws," Textile Workers of America v. Lincoln Mills of Ala., 353 U.S. at 456, 77 S.Ct. at 917. Lincoln Mills further held that "state law, if compatible with the purpose of §301, may be resorted to in order to find the rule that will best effectuate the federal policy." 353 U.S. at 457, 77 S.Ct. at 918. We conclude that the terms of the grievance procedure in the collective bargaining agreement before us give the employee Best no right to compel Black-Clawson to submit to arbitration, and that this conclusion must be reached by applying federal law and by resorting to reasoned state precedent for guidance. See Ostrofsky v. United Steelworkers, etc., 171 F. Supp. 782 (D. Md. 1959), aff'd, 273 F. 2d 614 (4th Cir.), cert. denied, 363 U.S. 849, 80 S.Ct. 1628, 4 L.Ed.

---

1. "Step 1. The dispute or grievance shall be taken up orally by the aggrieved employee and a member of the Union Committee if he so desires."
   "Section 3. The Company will pay the members of the Shop Committee and aggrieved employees at their regular hourly rate, for time spent in processing grievances."

2d 1732 (1960); United States v. Voges, 124 F. Supp. 543 (E.D.N.Y. 1954); Parker v. Borock, 5 N.Y. 2d 156, 162, 182 N.Y.S. 2d 577, 581, 156 N.E. 2d 297, 300 (1959) (concurring opinion of Fuld, J.); Bianculli v. Brooklyn Union Gas Co., 14 Misc. 2d 297, 115 N.Y.S. 2d 715 (Sup. Ct. 1952); Falsetti v. Local Union No. 2026, United Mine Workers of America, 400 Pa. 145, 161 A. 2d 882 (1960).

Appellant Best also contends that his right to compel arbitration is guaranteed by section 9(a) of the Labor Management Relations Act, 29 U.S.C. § 159(a)—which authorizes the presentation and adjustment of grievances by the individual employee independently of the bargaining representative—and by the terms of the grievance procedure of the collective bargaining agreement —which adopt section 9(a) of the act and provide that any such individual adjustment be processed in accordance with the terms of the contract. We disagree and hold that section 9(a) does not confer upon an individual grievant the power, enforceable in a court of law, to compel the employer to arbitrate his grievance.

That section reads as follows:

Representatives designated or selected for the purposes of collective bargaining by the majority of the employees in a unit appropriate for such purposes, shall be the exclusive representatives of all the employees in such unit for the purposes of collective bargaining in respect to rates of pay, wages, hours of employment, or other conditions of employment: *Provided*, That any individual employee or a group of employees shall have the right at any time to present grievances to their employer and to have such grievances adjusted, without the intervention of the bargaining representative, as long as the adjustment is not inconsistent with the terms of a collective-bargaining contract or agreement then in effect: *Provided further*, That the bargaining representative has been given opportunity to be present at such adjustment.

Best seizes upon the first proviso to the section, which affords to the employee "the right at any time to present grievances" to the employer and to have them adjusted. Despite Congress' use of the word "right", which seems to import an indefeasible right mirrored in a duty on the part of the employer, we are convinced that the proviso was designed merely to confer upon the employee the privilege to approach his employer on personal grievances when his union reacts with hostility or apathy. Prior to the adoption of this proviso in section 9(a), the employer had cause to fear that his processing of an individual's grievance without consulting the bargaining rep-

resentative would be an unfair labor practice; section 9(a) made the union the exclusive representative of the employees in the bargaining unit, and section 8(a) (5) made a refusal to bargain with the exclusive representative an unfair labor practice. The proviso was apparently designed to safeguard from charges of violation of the act the employer who voluntarily processed employee grievances at the behest of the individual employee, and to reduce what many had deemed the unlimited power of the union to control the processing of grievances.

The few elucidating passages in the legislative history of section 9(a) give support to the construction here adopted. Thus, the Report of the House Committee on Education and Labor sets out the function of the section:

The bill further adds to the freedom of workers by *permitting* them not only to present grievances to their employers, as the old Board heretofore has permitted them to do, but also to settle the grievances when doing so does not violate the terms of a collective-bargaining agreement, which the Board has not allowed. H. Rep. No. 245, 80th Cong., 1st Sess. 7 (1947). [Emphasis added.]

When the bill emanated from the Conference Committee, that Committee reported that

Both the House bill and the Senate amendment amended section 9 (a) of the existing law to specifically *authorize* employers to settle grievances presented by individual employees or groups of employees, so long as the settlement is not inconsistent with any collective bargaining contract in effect. H. Rep. No. 510, 80th Cong., 1st Sess. 46 (1947), U.S. Code Congressional Service 1947, p. 1152. [Emphasis added.]

It seems clear, therefore, that rather than conferring an indefeasible right upon the individual employee to compel compliance with the grievance procedure up to and including any arbitration provision, section 9(a) merely set up a buffer between the employee and his union, "permitting" the employee to take his grievances to the employer, and "authorizing" the employer to hear and adjust them without running afoul of the "exclusive bargaining representative" language of the operative portion of section 9(a).[2] This construction also best comports with the structure of the section. "The office of a proviso is seldom to create substantive rights and obliga-

---

2. See also 93 Cong. Rec. 4904 (1947): "In further protection of the rights of employees and to insulate employers from possible charges of unfair bargaining practices, we have . . . clarified the right of individuals or groups to settle and adjust grievances under section 9 (a) of the act whenever the bargaining agent, although given the opportunity to participate, nonetheless does not indicate a desire to take part in the adjustment."

tions; it carves exceptions out of what goes before." Cox, *Rights Under a Labor Agreement*, 69 HARV. L. REV. 601, (1956).

As applied to the case before us, section 9(a) of the Labor Management Relations Act, and its adoption by Black-Clawson and the Union in their collective bargaining agreement, assured Best the privilege of presenting his grievance to the employer even without the cooperation of the Union, and with the consent of Black-Clawson to have those grievances adjusted, so long as the adjustment was not inconsistent with the terms of the collective agreement. See Ostrofsky v. United Steelworkers, etc., 171 F. Supp. 782, 791 (D. Md. 1959), aff'd, 273 F. 2d 614 (4th Cir.), cert. denied, 363 U.S. 849, 80 S.Ct. 1628, 4 L.Ed. 2d 1732 (1960); Arsenault v. General Elec. Co., 147 Conn. 130, 157 A. 2d 918 (1960). See also General Cable Corp., 20 Lab. Arb. 443 (Hays, 1953).[3] Best is therefore without power to compel Black-Clawson to arbitrate the grievance stemming from his accusation of wrongful discharge. The Union is the sole agency empowered to do so by the statute and by the terms of the contract before us.

Our conclusion is dictated not merely by the terms of the collective bargaining agreement and by the language, structure, and history of section 9(a), but also by what we consider to be a sound view of labor-management relations. The union represents the employees for the purposes of negotiating and enforcing the terms of the collective bargaining agreement. This is the modern means of bringing about industrial peace and channeling the resolution of intra-plant disputes. Chaos would result if every disenchanted employee, every disturbed employee, and every employee who harbored a dislike for his employer, could harass both the union and the employer by processing grievances through the various steps of the grievance procedure and ultimately by bringing an action to compel arbi-

tration in the face of clear contractual provisions intended to channel the enforcement remedy through the union. See Stewart v. Day & Zimmermann, Inc., 294 F. 2d 7, 11 n. 6 (5th Cir. 1961); Ostrofsky v. United Steelworkers, *supra*; United States v. Voges, *supra*; Bianculli v. Brooklyn Union Gas Co., *supra*. "A union's right to screen grievances and to press only those it concludes should be pressed is a valuable right. Ostrofsky v. United Steelworkers, 171 F. Supp. at 790, and inures to the benefit of all the employees.

Our conclusion is in complete accord with the latest utterances of this Court:

> [T]he right to arbitrate is in no sense an incident or a "condition" of the employer-employee relationship as such, but depends, in exactly the same degree as does the union's right to arbitrate, on the existence of an agreement to arbitrate. In the absence of such an agreement no employee has the right to compel his employer to arbitrate any matter whatsoever. Procter & Gamble Independent Union v. Procter and Gamble Mfg. Co., 312 F. 2d 181 (2d Cir., Dec. 10, 1962).

If employer and union deem it consonant with the efficient handling of labor disputes to repose power in the individual employee to compel the employer to arbitrate grievances, then they may do so, by incorporating such a provision in clear language in the collective bargaining agreement. They have not done so here.

For these reasons, we affirm the judgment of the District Court.

PROCTER & GAMBLE INDEPENDENT UNION v. PROCTER & GAMBLE MFG. CO.
312 F. 2d 181 (2d Cir. 1962)

[The union sought to compel arbitration of grievances that arose after the collective agreement expired by its terms and before a new agreement was achieved.]

The district court held that in spite of the expiration of the old agreement, "the relationship of employer-employee continued," and that one of the "conditions" of the continuing relationship was the right to arbitrate grievances.

The right to arbitrate under a collective agreement is not ordinarily a right incident to the employer-employee relationship, but one which is incident to the relationship between employer and union. Under the collective agreement between the parties, it was the union which had the right to take grievances to arbitration, not the individual employees.

The agreement provides that "in the event that

---

3. "Although the situation with respect to presentation of grievances by employees is referred to in Section 9 (a) as a 'right,' the Act itself nowhere provides protection for this right. The language appears to be used in such a way as to create an exception to the employer's duty to bargain exclusively with the majority representatives. The act does not make it an unfair labor practice for the employer to refuse to entertain grievances from individual employees (Adm. Ruling, Gen. Counsel, Case No. 317 (1952), 30 L.R.R.M. 1103; Case No. 418 (1952), 31 L.R.R.M. 1039), and there seems to be no other method of enforcement available either in the Act or otherwise." 20 Lab. Arb. at 445.

See Gen. Counsel's Adm. Dec. No. 317, 30 L.R.R.M. 1103 (1952): "An individual employee is merely granted 'permission' to present a grievance. An employer is not 'required' to meet with a minority group of employees to adjust or discuss a grievance."

the arbitration is called for by either party hereto, the Employer and the Union, shall appoint an arbitrator." The wording of the grievance clause as a whole clearly indicates that only the union or the employer can demand arbitration.

Moreover the right to arbitrate is in no sense an incident or a "condition" of the employer-employee relationship as such, but depends, in exactly the same degree as does the union's right to arbitrate, on the existence of an agreement to arbitrate. In the absence of such an agreement no employee has the right to compel his employer to arbitrate any matter whatsoever. Thus even if it could be argued that employees had any right to compel arbitration under the collective agreement, which expired on April 30 or May 14, there would be no more reason to hold that that right survived the expiration of the agreement to arbitrate than there would be to hold that the union's right so survived. The attempt to argue for a transfer of the right to arbitrate from union to employees upon the expiration of the collective agreement finds no support whatever in authority or logic.

The language of the court is perhaps especially influential because it was written by Circuit Judge Paul R. Hays, an authority on labor law and arbitration and, indeed, a sharp critic of labor arbitration.

The BLS Arbitration Study reports:

Approximately 90 per cent (1,445) of the 1,609 contracts permitted either party to refer unsettled disputes to arbitration. The remaining 164 contracts provided for initiation of arbitration by the aggrieved party, by the union, or only by mutual consent of the parties (46). The requirement of mutual consent means that one party can block arbitration.

Most of the 1,445 contracts explicitly stated that arbitration could be initiated by either party, as in the following: "If the [grievance] procedure has failed to settle a grievance, ... it shall, if requested by either party, be submitted to arbitration."

Most of the 46 clauses which limited the right of invoking arbitration to the aggrieved party were similar to the following: "the issue may be submitted in writing for final determination to arbitration by the party aggrieved, within 30 calendar days, to a board of arbitration."

A few of the 46 specified the employee involved or the aggrieved employee, rather than the union.

Occasionally, the employee was given the choice of initiating arbitration on his own or through his union.

In the event the grievance is not settled in step 3, then within, but not later than, 10 calendar days after the company shall have rendered its decision the grievance may be submitted by the employee or employees involved for arbitration.

Any employee who is not satisfied with the decision on his grievance or complaint at step 5 of the grievance procedure may, individually or through his union grievance representative, file with the impartial arbitrator at any time within 15 days after said decision has been made at step 5, a demand that the impartial arbitrator give his opinion and make his determination with respect to the said grievance or complaint.

The 72 agreements which specified only the union as the referral agent presumably barred management from taking this step, should such an occasion ever arise, but also may be interpreted as barring the aggrieved employee from taking this action on his own.

If the grievance is not settled satisfactorily in accordance with the foregoing procedure, and involves a question of interpretation or application of the terms of this agreement, the union may refer the matter to arbitration by written notice to the company not later than 10 days after decision in stage 3.

If the grievance or dispute is not settled as a result of the foregoing, then the union shall have the right to request arbitration thereof.

In the event the grievance shall not have been settled satisfactorily, the matter may be referred to arbitration for final and binding determination, provided referral of the grievance to arbitration shall have been reviewed by the district director of the international union under whose jurisdiction the plant involved is located. If the union decides to arbitrate it will make its appeal in writing as promptly as possible, but in no case more than 30 days after the receipt of the company's 4th step answer.

BELK v. ALLIED AVIATION SERVICE CO.
315 F. 2d 513 (2d Cir.), [cert. denied, 375 U.S. 847 (1963)]

Before Clark, Moore, and Kaufman, Circuit Judges.

Moore, C. J. Plaintiff James Belk, a resident of New York, was employed by Allied Aviation Service Company of New Jersey, Inc. (Allied) as a Sky Cap Porter at the Municipal Airport, Newark, New Jersey. He is a member of Local

297 of the United Transport Service Employees (the Union), the recognized bargaining agent for plaintiff, and is subject to a collective bargaining contract between Allied and the Union. While working on September 29, 1961, Belk received a letter terminating his services without giving him notice of a hearing as required in such cases under the terms of the contract.

Without any effort to obtain redress for his discharge through his Union, Belk brought suit directly against Allied in the Southern District of New York for damages as a result of the alleged breach. Jurisdiction was founded on diversity of citizenship. The Court below granted defendant's motion to dismiss and Belk appeals.

The contractual provisions for the settlement of disputes are contained in Article 20 of the collective agreement. In summary that article provides that no employee who has been in service for ninety days will be dismissed without a fair and impartial hearing before the employer. The initial stages of this grievance procedure are prosecuted by the employee himself, although he is entitled to the presence of his Union representative if he so desires. The contract further states that if the Union feels that the Company's ultimate determination is unfair, the Company and Union shall endeavor to settle the issue, and failing this either may demand arbitration.

Appellant argues that the failure of the Company to offer him a hearing was a breach of the agreement entitling him to damages in a suit on the contract. He further contends that since the Union does not enter the procedure until the Company has made a determination of his status after a hearing and, since the Union can request arbitration only if it feels that the decision is unfair, recourse to arbitration through the Union before suit is not only unnecessary but is foreclosed under the contract since no such determination after a hearing has been made.

The broad coverage and intent of the contract to seek "amicable adjustment" instead of court litigation is apparent from the opening clause of the Article 21: "No Strike—No Lockout", reading:

"As this agreement provides for the amicable adjustment of any and all disputes and grievances, ..." Assuming that failure to give notice made the specific provisions of Article 20 (d) unavailable, Article 20 (e) provides that:

> When a dispute or claim involving the application, construction, interpretation or performance of the rules of this agreement occurs, the parties agree that they shall endeavour in good faith, first to adjust and settle such disputes between themselves after a fair hearing. Failing such adjustment or settlement between themselves, either party may demand arbitration by an arbitrator designated by the Federal Mediation and Conciliation Service; the other party must agree thereto, and the decision and award of said arbitrator shall be final and binding upon the parties. The cost of any arbitration, if any, shall be borne equally by the parties hereto.

Although the preliminary procedures prescribed in this contract for the prosecution of cases of wrongful discharge may be somewhat unusual, a dispute over the Company's breach of the notice and hearing provisions constitutes a dispute involving "performance of the rules of this agreement." Any collective agreement is intended to secure rights for individual employees; notice and a hearing after discharge are merely examples of such rights. They are no different from provisions with respect to seniority, vacations or overtime pay. Under the broad arbitration clause set out above, controversies concerning these matters were clearly intended to be submitted to arbitration as agreed upon in the contract. So too the breach of contract alleged in this case.

That a matter of procedure rather than one of substance is involved is of no significance. In fact, we recently held that the question of compliance with the procedural prerequisites to arbitration set forth in the collective agreement is to be decided by the arbitrator and not the court. Livingston v. John Wiley & Sons, Inc., 313 F. 2d 52 (Jan. 11, 1963). What effect is to be given this breach by the employer, whether the arbitrator would require that the employer give Belk a hearing or whether he would find jurisdiction to deal with this discharge on the merits are all questions that the contract contemplates will be submitted to the arbitrator.

This being the case, the remaining question is the effect of the arbitration clause on the individual's right to sue for breach of contract. Since this is a diversity case, there is no question of this court's jurisdiction to entertain this action. Even were this not so, the Supreme Court in Smith v. Evening News Association, 371 U.S. 195, 83 S.Ct. 267, 9 L.Ed. 2d 246 (1962), held that suits by individuals are cognizable in the federal courts under Section 301. In addition, that Court held that all such suits are to be governed by federal law. However, the opinion in that case indicates in no uncertain terms that the Court was not striking down arbitration in favor of suits by individual employees in the courts because the Court specifically said, "There was no grievance arbitration procedure in this contract which had to be exhausted before recourse could be had to the courts." 371 U.S. 196, n. 1 83 S.Ct. 271, and invited comparison with its recent decisions in Atkinson v. Sinclair Refining Co., 370 U.S. 238, 82 S.Ct. 1318, 8 L.Ed. 2d 462, and Drake Bakeries, Inc. v. Local 50, American Bakery Workers, 370 U.S. 254, 82 S.Ct. 1346, 8 L.Ed. 2d 474, Conversely, if, as here, there is grievance arbitration procedure provided for, there should be recourse to it before the individual employee is permitted to bring a court action.

The Supreme Court by virtue of *Evening News* has now committed the federal courts to fashioning a body of law encompassing the rights of all parties concerned in the bargaining process. State courts, the lower federal courts at least in diversity cases, and numerous commentators have heretofore struggled to construct an adequate legal theory to deal with the relationship between employee, union, employer and the collective bargaining contract. See Cox, *The Legal Nature of Collective Bargaining Agreements*. 57 Mich. L. Rev. 1 (1958). They have flirted with the theory of a third party beneficiary contract, with a finding of an agency relationship between union and employee, and with application of the principles of the law of trusts. See discussion of these theories in Association of Westinghouse Salaried Employees v. Westinghouse Electric Corp., 210 F. 2d 623, 625–627 (3d Cir., 1954), aff'd 348 U.S. 437, 75 S.Ct. 489, 99 L.Ed. 510 (1955). Strict use of any one of these analogies leads to insurmountable difficulties, arising primarily from the fact that collective bargaining agreements are to a large degree *sui generis*. That is not to say that resort to established principles of law in these areas cannot at times be useful, but only that these agreements do not fit snugly into any one category. For example, a collective agreement is made for the benefit of the employees (at least in part), but a third party beneficiary is not bound by the contract under usual third party beneficiary rules. Certainly such a rule in the labor field might well lead to chaos and would be totally inconsistent with the purpose of such agreements.

We need not at this juncture try to resolve all these problems even assuming (which we do not) that such a herculean effort were possible because the case before us does not require it. We decide only that where the collective agreement provides for arbitration by the Union of the subject matter of the employee's suit, the employee must look to his union initially for the vindication of his rights. If every employee is to be free to institute suits directly against his employer for every incident which he claims to be a violation of some right under the collective bargaining agreement, little benefit is to be gained by any of the parties either from union representation

or arbitration clauses. Where his remedy lies when his union refuses to prosecute his claim we leave to future cases as they arise. [The court then noted the duty of fair representation and also cited cases denying and allowing suit by individual employees.]

This result is in complete harmony with Drake Bakeries, Inc. v. Local 50, American Bakery & Confectionery Workers, *supra*. There the Company action for breach of a no-strike provision was dismissed, the Court holding that arbitration of this alleged breach was a prerequisite to suit. The Court rejected the argument that breach of a no-strike clause, often viewed as the *quid pro quo* for the arbitration provision (see Textile Workers Union v. Lincoln Mills, 353 U.S. 448, 455, 77 S. Ct. 912, 1 L. Ed. 2d 972 (1957)), was a sufficient ground for avoiding the Company's duty to arbitrate. Atkinson v. Sinclair Refining Co., *supra, does not apply here*. The Supreme Court there merely held that since the arbitration clause in question only allowed the Union and not the employer to request arbitration, the Company had on [*sic*] duty to resort to arbitration before bringing suit for breach.

The entire import of the Supreme Court cases beginning with *Lincoln Mills,* through the trilogy of the *Steelworker* cases to *Drake* at their last term is that arbitration, when agreed upon by the parties, is the best method for reconciliation of disputes arising out of collective agreements. Where an arbitration clause admits of a construction including the dispute in question within its ambit, recourse to the courts before any effort is made to process the dispute through arbitration is to be looked upon with disfavor. As we said recently:

> The union represents the employees for the purposes of negotiating and enforcing the terms of the collective bargaining agreement. This is the modern means of bringing about industrial peace and channeling the resolution of intra-plant disputes. Chaos would result if every disenchanted employee, every disturbed employee, and every employee who harbored a dislike for his employer, could harass both the union and the employer by processing grievances through the various steps of the grievance procedure and ultimately by bringing an action to compel arbitration in the face of clear contractual provisions intended to channel the enforcement remedy through the union. Black-Clawson Co. v. International Association of Machinists, 313 F. 2d 179 (2d Cir., Dec. 22, 1962).

Affirmed.

CLARK, C. J. (concurring). Of course noncompliances with procedural provisions of the arbitration clauses in collective bargaining agreements should be subjects of arbitration. See Livingston

v. John Wiley & Sons, 2 Cir., 313 F. 2d 52; Carey v. General Electric Co., 2 Cir., 315 F. 2d 499; Note, *Procedural Requirements of a Grievance Arbitration Clause: Another Question of Arbitrability*, 70 YALE L. J. 611 (1961). The problem for me is that Black-Clawson Co. v. International Asso. of Machinists Lodge 355, Dist. 137, 2 Cir., 313 F. 2d 179, closed to individual employees the sort of provision (see Article 20.e of the collective bargaining agreement, quoted in note 1 of the majority opinion) which my brothers now hold up to this employee as their reason for refusing to entertain his case. I would have preferred that the individual employee should not be left solely to the mercies of his employer and his union. See Summers, *Individual Rights in Collective Agreements and Arbitration*, 37 N.Y.U.L. REV. 362 (1962). For we have seen in recent years that, in some cases, a sweet harmony develops between the two that proves a bitter lockout of the solitary employee who finds his contractual rights going unprotected. Here Belk was dismissed in flagrant violation of Article 20 of the collective bargaining agreement, and it remains doubtful to say the least whether he will ever have redress of this wrong in the event of his eventual reinstatement or even more if he is not reinstated.

But the law of the circuit has apparently been determined to the contrary, and so I shall join in my brothers' disposition of this case, adding only the hope that Belk's union may yet act to rectify his wrong.

Two aspects of the case warrant comment. The grievance procedure contains elements of railroad and industrial grievance dispute procedure. The employer may have been influenced by the procedures followed by air carriers subject to the Railway Labor Act. It is quite common for railroad employee discharge cases to be handled initially by a hearing on charges before some employer official. It also is common to have only the procedure subject to review by the Adjustment Board. However, airline practice frequently differs, especially in the use of arbitrators chosen by the parties or by some neutral agency, often the National Mediation Board.

Note also that arbitration does not follow demand as a matter of right. "Either party may demand" it, and "the other party must agree thereto." The apparent misreading of the contract provision by the court does not invalidate the "exhaustion" approach implicit in the result. The court's apparent unawareness of the probable derivation of the grievance procedure pattern and the misreading of the arbitration provision, however, demonstrate how innocent and mistaken courts can be in this area. Often plaintiff's counsel in this kind of case are not specialists in labor matters, and leave undeveloped potential case and policy arguments. Courts can not be expected to decide cases differently depending upon the apparent experience of counsel. But they might proceed with somewhat greater caution where inexperience of counsel may result in less than a full development of the issues.

C.

The Different Interests Under a Collective Agreement

PARKER v. BOROCK
5 N.Y. 2d 156, 156 N.E. 2d 297 (1959)

Plaintiff's action is for damages for wrongful discharge. For aught that appears, plaintiff's contract of employment was not a hiring for a specific term. Hence, standing alone, it was terminable at will, and would not give rise to a cause of action. (Watson v. Gugino, 204 N.Y. 535.) But here there is an additional factor—the collective agreement. There has been a growing recognition by the courts that the collective agreement can modify the terms of the contract of hiring. (See WILLISTON, CONTRACTS, §39A [3d ed.], and §379A [Rev. ed.]: TELLER, LABOR DISPUTES

AND COLLECTIVE BARGAINING, §§ 166–169 and supplements thereto.)

In this jurisdiction, it is clear that wage provisions in the collective bargaining agreement inure to the direct benefit of employees and may be the subject of a cause of action (Barth v. Addie Co., 271 N.Y. 31; Gulla v. Barton, 164 App. Div. 293; cf. Canton v. Palms, Inc., 152 Misc. 347; Morrison v. Gentler, 152 Misc. 710; Mesloh v. Schulte, 151 Misc. 750).

More recently, the courts of this State have been concerned with the effect of provisions in the collective bargaining which prohibit the discharge of an employee, except for cause, on his contract of employment. There are two basic problems presented in these cases: (1) were the "no discharge without cause" provisions intended to benefit directly the employee? (2) assuming an affirmative answer to the first question, what effect does the language used have on the employee's contract of hiring?

We conclude that the employee is the direct beneficiary of such provisions (see Gulla v. Barton, *supra*). Unlike Rotnofsky v. Capitol Distrs. Corp. (262 App. Div. 521), these clauses were not inserted to insure the retention of union men by the company. In the present agreement, there are other specific provisions for a union shop and for releasing of employees who do not join the union.

Our main task then is to ascertain the effect to be ascribed to these provisions.

In Barth v. Addie Co. (271 N.Y. 31, *supra*) the plaintiff, discharged without cause, sought to recover wages from the date of his discharge to the date of the expiration of the collective contract. The agreement provided that the employer would not discharge any member of the union whose salary was payable weekly, unless the employer gave two weeks' notice in writing of such an intention to the union, except that an employee may be discharged on payment of two weeks' salary. It was held that plaintiff's recovery was limited to two weeks' salary. Implicit in this ruling is the finding that the contract of employment can be modified by a collective agreement limiting the right to discharge an employee. (See also, Rolandez v. Star Liq. Dealers, 257 App. Div. 97; cf. Hudak v. Hornell Ind., 304 N.Y. 207; Marranzano v. Riggs Nat. Bank, 184 F. 2d 349.)

Certainly, then, if such clauses in the present agreement are to have meaning, we must arrive at a similar conclusion.

However, a fundamental proposition in construing instruments is the entire writing must be considered. All the provisions of the agreement are to be given effect. Thus, while we have arrived at a different conclusion than the Appellate Division as to the significance of the "no discharge without cause" provisions, we are of the opinion, nevertheless, that the granting of defendant's motion for summary judgment must be sustained.

The collective agreement concludes: "This Agreement shall be binding on the employer, its successors and assigns, and upon the Union and its officers, representatives and members." Plaintiff is a member of the union and, therefore, is bound by the agreement. By its terms, the collective bargain "inured" to the members of the union. (Ott v. Metropolitan Jockey Club, 282 App. Div. 946, affd. 307 N.Y. 696.) In the *Ott*

case, as here, the employee could not avail himself of the arbitration procedure since that right was granted only to the union and the employer by the terms of the collective agreement. Hence, plaintiff here is bound by and limited to the provisions of the agreement. (See also, Triboro Coach Corp. v. State Labor Relations Bd., 286 N.Y. 314; Barth v. Addie Co., *supra*; Rolandez v. Star Liq. Dealers, *supra*.)

Incidentally the agreement in Hudak v. Hornell Ind. (*supra*) did not contain this limiting provision.

A reading of the existing agreement indicates that plaintiff has entrusted his rights to his union representative. It may be that the union failed to preserve them. As was said in Donato v. American Locomotive Co. (283 App. Div. 410, 417, affd. 306 N.Y. 966):

> the only conclusion which logically follows is that the employee is without any remedy, except as against his own union, if he claims that the union mishandled the arbitration proceeding or improperly failed to move to vacate the award. If this conclusion is reached upon the premise here set forth, this is not an exaltation of procedure over substance; it rests rather upon a proposition of substantive law limiting the right of the individual employee under a collective bargaining agreement.

The judgment of the Appellate Division granting defendant's motion for summary judgment should be affirmed, with costs.

FULD, J. (concurring). I agree with the conclusion reached by the court and, in the main, with Judge Burke's opinion. However, because I believe that the result is dictated as much by policy considerations as by the language of the collective bargaining agreement, I would add these few words.

Discharge cases arises in the course of the administration of a collective bargaining agreement. They may raise countless questions, such as interpretation of the agreement, reasonableness of plant rules and regulations and conformity with past practices. The exclusive representative is in the best position, after investigating the truth and merits of the employee's complaint and after weighing the many factors involved, to determine whether uniformity in the administration of the agreement and protection of the group interests of the majority of employees require it to press or abandon the case. Accordingly, absent specific language giving the employee the right to act on his own behalf, it is my conclusion that, under a collective bargaining agreement such as the one before us—which contains provision for the submission of unsettled disputes to arbitration—the union alone has a right to control the prosecution of discharge cases. (See Cox, *Rights Under a Labor Agreement,* 69 HARV. L. REV. 601.)

To the contention that this may subject the individual employee to capricious or discriminatory action by the union, it is sufficient to observe, as Judge Burke has intimated, that the employee has a remedy against the union for breach of fiduciary duty if it unfairly discriminated against him. (See, *e.g.,* Donato v. American Locomotive Co., 306 N.Y. 966, affg. 283 App. Div. 410, 417; Conley v. Gibson, 355 U.S. 41, 45 *et seq.*)

VAN VOORHIS, J. (concurring). The clause in this labor contract that no regular employee shall be discharged or disciplined without good and sufficient cause, is not equivalent to providing term employment for each employee until the expiration date of the collective bargaining agreement.

The union may not have a beneficial interest in the job tenure of employees. Such a holding would enable a labor union in its discretion to prevent any of its members from receiving the benefit of union wage scales or other individual property rights secured to the employees by collective bargaining agreements. Where such an agreement enures to the direct benefit of employees (Barth v. Addie Co., 271 N.Y. 31; Gulla v. Barton, 164 App. Div. 293), a union cannot exert power over its members by attempting to provide in the contract that what the union obtains for them the union can also take away. In the pending action, however, as the Appellate Division has held, this labor contract provides for no term of employment enforcible by anyone, and the clause in question is solely for the benefit of the union in order to prevent attacks upon it by discrimination in the discharge of union members. For this reason I vote to affirm the order of the Appellate Division.

CHIEF JUDGE CONWAY and JUDGES DESMOND, DYE and FROESSEL concur with JUDGE BURKE; JUDGES FULD and VAN VOORHIS concur in separate opinions.

Judgment affirmed.

Prior to the enactment of Section 301 some courts found it difficult to regard collective bargaining agreements as enforceable, especially in suits brought by individual employees. They stumbled on the conceptual difficulty that because employees were not bound by such agreements to work for the employer, such agreements arguably lacked mutuality. However, many courts overcame this difficulty. The question for them remained whether individual employees could sue under the bargaining agreement. Many held that they could provided that the provision invoked was for their benefit rather than the union's. Cases are collected in 18 A.L.R. 2d 348 (1951). Of course, other considerations enter into the problem of employee rights *vis-a-vis* the grievance-arbitration provisions of an agreement. Even here, some substantive collective agreement provisions solely or primarily involve the union's institutional interest. Indeed, in the Cox article, excerpted hereafter, most grievances are argued to involve important union interests.

FALSETTI v. LOCAL 2026, UNITED MINE WORKERS OF AMERICA 400 Pa. 145, 161 A. 2d 882 (1960)

[Plaintiff, an employee allegedly discharged in violation of his seniority rights under the collective agreement, sought reinstatement with damages for loss of wages.]

By his claim against appellee Company and the individual appellees[*] for an allegedly wrongful discharge in violation of his seniority rights, appellant seeks enforcement of third-party rights under the collective bargaining agreement (Agreement) between the International Union and the Company. Although generally a third party beneficiary may enforce rights flowing to him from a contract,[1] whether he may so enforce a collective bargaining agreement raises serious problems not heretofore faced by our Court. The issue involved is of great importance to labor, to management and to the countless number of employees governed by seniority provisions in collective bargaining agreements.

A collective bargaining agreement, it is impor-

---

[*] Local union officials.

1. The law of Pennsylvania in regard to the rights of a third-party beneficiary to a contract was clearly set forth in Williams v. Paxson Coal Co., 346 Pa. 468, 471, 31 A. 2d 69 (1943), wherein we stated: "The foundation of any right the third party may have, whether he is a donee beneficiary or a creditor of the promisee, is the promisor's contract. Unless there is a valid contract, no right can arise in favor of anyone. Moreover, the rights of the third person, like the rights of the promisee, must be limited by the terms of the promise. . . . Broadly speaking, not only must any formal requirements be complied with, but the beneficiary also takes subject to the due performance of all express and implied conditions affecting the promise in which he is interested: 2 WILLISTON ON CONTRACTS (Revised Ed.), § 364 (a)." See also Rose v. Rose, 385 Pa. 427, 123 A. 2d 693 (1956); CORBIN ON CONTRACTS, §§ 817–819, 821–823; Restatement, Contracts, § 140; 8 P.L.E., Contracts § 164, p. 213.

tant to note, is simply a contract, and any rights and remedies the appellant possesses must be derived solely from the Agreement itself. The complaint indicates that the Agreement between the International and the signatory coal companies was first entered into on June 19, 1941. This Agreement was executed by the International on behalf of the various local unions and the individual members thereof, including the appellant. Seniority rights were expressly recognized therein. Said Agreement was amended several times in subsequent years, significantly so in regard to seniority rights on September 29, 1952. It is the seniority rights acquired under this Agreement that appellant now seeks to enforce.

We have carefully read the entire Agreement and can find *no* provision which authorizes appellant to enforce it. Although the seniority provisions relied upon inure directly for the benefit of the appellant-employee and do not exist simply to protect the interests of the Union, appellant's cause of action is precluded by a contractual grievance and arbitration procedure which, by its very terms, limits access thereto to the Union. The parties in drafting this Agreement provided for a simple, expeditious and inexpensive grievance procedure to be administered by persons intimately familiar therewith. The procedure outlined was designed not only to promote settlement, but also to foster more harmonious employer-employee and employer-union relations. The parties expressly sought to avoid litigation, recognizing that the courts are particularly ill-equipped to assume the role of umpire in industrial disputes. Cf. Slocum v. Delaware, Lackawanna & Western R. Co., 339 U.S. 239, 70 S.Ct. 577, 94 L.Ed. 795 (1950). It should be noted that after the first step in the five outlined in the grievance procedure, the complaint is to be processed by representatives of the Union. The ultimate responsibility in discharge cases is thereby left not to individual members, but rather to their trustee in these matters. The result we reach thus flows as a matter of course from the face of the Agreement. In effect, the appellant is a beneficiary of the appellee Company's promises as to seniority rights, but the Company has limited those promises by refusing to entertain claims based on such rights (beyond the initial complaint stage) unless brought by the other party to the Agreement, the trustee Union. The limited character of the Company's promises serves to defeat any attempt to get redress individually.

To view this type of agreement otherwise would lead to chaos and a breakdown in the entire scheme of collective bargaining for which the parties have provided and contracted. Instead of being able to rely on the disposition of employee grievances through the established machinery, the Company would face the constant threat of attempted individual enforcement through litigation. Union responsibility would be diminished and all parties would suffer. For these reasons, most, if not all, Union-management agreements of any magnitude in force throughout the Commonwealth are similarly drafted, with an eye toward reposing enforcement responsibility in the labor organization concerned.

The aggrieved member-employee, limited to seeking relief against the Union, is not without effective remedy. In entering into this Agreement, the Union has assumed the role of trustee for the rights of its members and other employees in the bargaining unit. The employees, on the other hand, have become beneficiaries of fiduciary obligations owed by the Union. As a result, the Union bears a heavy duty of fair representation to all those within the shelter of its protection. See Syres v. Oil Workers Union, 350 U.S. 892, 76 S.Ct. 152, 100 L.Ed. 785 (1955), reversing per curiam 223 F. 2d 739 (5th Cir. 1955); Ford Motor Co. v. Huffman, *supra* at 337-339; Cox, *supra* at 632-638. If the Union, in processing an employee's grievance, does not act in good faith, in a reasonable manner and without fraud, it becomes liable in damages for breach of duty. In this way, the employee is recompensed for the harm he had suffered, and yet the process of collective bargaining in the industry is meaningfully preserved.

MATTER OF SOTO (GOLDMAN)
7 N.Y. 2d 397, 165 N.E. 2d 855 (1960)

DYE, J. In this proceeding commenced by an order to show cause, the respondent-appellant union appeals by permission from an order vacating an award of the New York State Board of Mediation, rendered in an arbitration between the respondent Lenscraft Optical Corp. (Rayex), as employer, and appellant union, as collective bargaining agent, under an agreement then in full force and effect, the validity of which had previously been upheld (cf. Rayex Corp. v. Sanchez, 6 A.D. 2d 902, motion for reargument denied 6 A.D. 2d 1044, motion for leave to appeal to the Court of Appeals dismissed 5 N.Y. 2d 915). The award permitted the employer to discharge the petitioners-respondents for conduct violative of the contract conditions, a deliberate slowdown.

The basic issue is whether the petitioners-respondents have status, within the meaning of subdivision 3 of section 1462 of the Civil Practice Act, to initiate the proceeding.

The court below accepted the petitioners' contention that they had been prejudiced by the mediator's refusal to allow them to be independently represented at the arbitration by counsel of their own choosing. In so deciding, the Appellate Division deemed the petitioners had status as parties since—because their jobs were at stake—they were either third-party beneficiaries of the collective contract or in the position of beneficiaries of a trust. This was a wrong approach. The award, having been rendered in a controversy between the parties to a valid collective agreement, could be vacated only at the initiation of a party to the arbitration in the manner and for the reasons provided by section 1462 of the Civil Practice Act. The misconduct of an arbitrator, contemplated by the statute, and warranting the setting aside of an award, is that "by which the rights of any *party* have been prejudiced" (§ 1462, subd. 3; emphasis supplied). The petitioners, not being parties to the agreement, may not avail themselves of rights which under the Civil Practice Act are limited to parties; an exception to such limitation may not be created by judicial application of equitable principles, nor may a basis for vacatur be supplied by implication. Such a result can be accomplished only by appropriate legislative action. Furthermore, the ruling complained of was well within the reach and scope of our recent decision in Parker v. Borock (5 N.Y. 2d 156). There we made it clear that an employee could not avail himself of the arbitration procedure provided in the collective bargaining agreement since there, as here, the contract granted such right only to the union and to the employer (cf. Hudak v. Hornell Ind., 304 N.Y. 207). This was in the interest of maintaining orderly procedure under accepted principles of substantive law. At the same time, an employee is not foreclosed, in an appropriate case, from pursuing any remedy at law that might be available for breach of fiduciary duty owing by the union.

The order of the Appellate Division should be reversed and the arbitrator's award reinstated.

FROESSEL, J. (dissenting). Seven employees (herein called petitioners), each earning about $42 per week, were threatened with discharge by their employer, Lenscraft Optical Corporation, for having allegedly caused slowdown activities at the latter's plant. At the instance of appellant, petitioners' union Local No. 122, which had a collective bargaining agreement with the employer, the provisions of which are not before us, arbitration was had with the employer and the matter was submitted to the New York State Board of Mediation.

About two hours before the arbitration hearing was scheduled, the employer delivered letters to petitioners informing them that the hearing was to be held at 2.00 P.M. on that day, March 8, 1957, and that the letters were "being handed" to them so that they "may appear before the Board *and be heard* at the hearing" [emphasis supplied]. The union also asked them to be present.

At 2.00 P.M. petitioners attended the hearing with an attorney, Henry Brickman. The latter on behalf of his clients applied for an adjournment because of the short two hours' notice, and pointed out that the union lawyer then present was the same attorney who appeared as of counsel to the attorneys for the employer in an injunction proceeding seeking to enjoin *these very petitioners* and others from picketing in December, 1956; that this same attorney appeared again as of counsel to the employer in an employer's application to punish officials of another union for contempt. He further stated to the arbitrator that, absent proper representation by an attorney of their own selection, petitioners would be in effect defendants in a kangaroo court. His application was resisted by the same union attorney.

The arbitrator granted a short four-day adjournment (from Friday to Tuesday, March 12th), and reserved decision as to Brickman's right to represent petitioners, who were the specific individuals involved in the dispute before the arbitrator. On Monday the arbitrator telephoned Brickman that petitioners could not be represented by independent counsel, whereupon Brickman advised him that "that would be the same as not having any lawyer". On the following Thursday the arbitrator informed Brickman that the employer had put in its case, that the union interposed no defense, and that on the record he was impelled to award the employer the right to discharge the seven petitioners. Whether or not petitioners deserved to be discharged is of course not before us.

Thereafter, petitioners succeeded in having the award vacated at Special Term in the present proceedings, and the Appellate Division has unanimously affirmed. Upon the record, we agree with the courts below. The Appellate Division has collated the cases in this and the lower courts in this somewhat unsettled area of the law. Ordinarily, it may be said that a union, as the employees' bargaining agent, may control the presentation and prosecution of grievances under a standard collective bargaining agreement. Respondents recognize this rule which is based on sound policy. But the rule is not inflexible. Where, for example, employees, as to specific rights, are in effect the designated third-party beneficiaries under such an agreement, they may sue the employer directly (Hudak v. Hornell Ind., 304 N.Y. 207). And where as here the rights of specific employees are directly involved, and a determination in an arbitration proceeding voluntarily initiated by the employer and the union will in effect be binding upon the employees, it would be contrary to every principle of justice and fair dealing to have them or their union represented by counsel who has in related matters also acted as counsel for the employer. Implicit in the general rule above stated is the requirement that such representation must be free from fraud, collusion, double-dealing or like conduct; otherwise a workman would be wholly at the mercy of a conspiracy against him between his union and his employer. How, indeed, could one reasonably require these petitioners, who were invited to come to the hearing and be heard, to submit to representation by union counsel who represented the employer in litigation affecting these same petitioners? Upon the plainest principles of elementary justice, the policy of the courts in formulating the general rule cannot be deemed to embrace such a situation (see Matter of Iroquois Beverage Corp. [International Union], 14 Misc 2d 290; Manson, *Labor Relations Law*, 32 N.Y.U.L. Rev. 1374; *Rights of Individual Workers in Union-Management Arbitration Proceedings*, 66 Yale L. J. 946; Pattenge v. Wagner Iron Works, 275 Wis. 495).

This is not a case where the union by inaction declines to demand arbitration as in Parker v. Borock (5 N.Y. 2d 156). Nor is it a situation where the employee sought to vacate an award by a plenary action in equity, as in Donato v. American Locomotive Co. (283 App. Div. 410, 417, affd. 306 N.Y. 966). In that case it was strongly intimated that the employee might intervene in the arbitration proceeding and move to vacate the award (p. 416) under the provisions of sections 1459 and 191–193-b of the Civil Practice Act.

If a union under a collective bargaining agreement assumes to represent its members, it must do so fairly and in good faith. When it supplies counsel who has also acted for the employer in labor matters and who merely goes through the form of an arbitration proceeding affecting substantial rights of specific individuals, of all of which the arbitrator had notice, the award may properly be vacated. Petitioners had no time to seek leave from the Supreme Court to intervene, for they had but two hours' notice of the hearing and but 24 hours' notice that they could not be represented by independent counsel. They properly sought redress under section 1462 of the Civil Practice Act.

As the Appellate Division stated below:

> Enough was shown to negative the possibility of fair representation of the interests of petitioners by Local 122. The denial of the right to independent representation, under the special circumstances of this case, vitiated the award rendered in the absence of the petitioners at the hearings, particularly since the evidence which they were seeking to adduce on the question of collusion went directly to the issues to be decided by the arbitrator. There was no invalid exercise of power and no abuse of discretion in vacating the award.

The order of the Appellate Division should be affirmed with costs.

Chief Judge Desmond and Judges Fuld, Burke and Foster concur with Judge Dye; Judge Froessel dissents in an opinion in which Judge Van Voorhis concurs.

Order reversed, without costs, and matter remitted to Special Term for further proceedings in accordance with the opinion herein.

Note that the union, which supposedly provided the attorney to appear on behalf of the discharged employees, appealed from the lower court decisions vacating the award upholding the discharges.

CLARK v. HEIN-WERNER CORP.
8 Wis. 2d 264, 99 N.W. 2d 132 (1959)
[*cert. denied*,
362 U.S. 962 (1960)]

Action by 17 employees of the Hein-Werner Corporation to have a labor arbitration award declared null and void and to enjoin the employer corporation and International Association of Machinists, Local 1377, A.F.L.–C.I.O., from applying such award to the accumulated seniority of the plaintiffs.

The facts were stipulated by counsel for the plaintiffs, the employer, and the union. The employer is a Wisconsin corporation operating a factory in the city of Waukesha and is engaged in interstate commerce. On October 22, 1956, it entered into a collective-bargaining contract with the union effective from September 18, 1956, to September 18, 1959. There was included in such contract a provision for handling grievances and for final disposition of these grievances by arbitration between the employer and the union.

In September, 1957, a grievance arose concerning the seniority of four employees who had been laid off when certain supervisory employees were demoted from their supervisory positions and transferred back into the bargaining unit. Such supervisory employees had originally held nonsupervisory positions in the bargaining unit before they had been promoted to their supervisory positions. The clause in the contract covering seniority read as follows: "Seniority is an employee's length of service with the company in years, months, and days."

The question raised by the grievance was whether such former supervisory employees had continuous seniority measured from the date they had entered the service of the company, or whether there should be excluded from such period of continuous service the time they had spent in their supervisory positions. The company had interpreted and applied the seniority clause in accordance with the first of such two stated alternatives, while the union contended that the latter was the correct interpretation.

The grievance was processed in accordance with the grievance procedure stated in the contract and it ended in arbitration before a single arbitrator. Such arbitrator conducted a hearing in the city of Waukesha in which both the union and the employer were represented by counsel. The arbitrator received evidence, and heard witnesses. Counsel presented oral argument and briefs were filed. However, none of the demoted supervisory employees were notified of the time and place of such hearing and none were present or participated in the arbitration proceedings.

On March 10, 1958, the arbitrator made his award in writing. Such award upheld the union's position and, among other things, provided that employees while employed in job classifications outside of the bargaining unit could not accumulate seniority for such period. The award also ordered that the four employees laid off be made whole for any wage loss sustained by reason of the employer's giving seniority credit to supervisory employees for time worked outside of the bargaining unit.

Subsequent to the award a meeting of the employees in the bargaining unit was held at which time the award was read and explained. In the words of the stipulation, "A determination at this meeting was had that no change would be made in seniority as set forth in the arbitrator's award." All of the plaintiff's participated in this meeting. The employer proceeded to change the seniority list in accordance with the

award, and paid some of the affected employees' back pay in accordance therewith.

There were 29 demoted supervisory employees adversely affected by the award but only 17 instituted the instant circuit court action. Because the relief sought was equitable in nature, the action was tried to the court without a jury. Judgment in favor of the plaintiffs was rendered.

The plaintiff employees were not parties to the collective-bargaining contract and under the grievance procedure set forth therein were given no right to initiate arbitration or to participate in the arbitration once it was set in motion. The instant appeal presents the problem of when, if ever, can judicial protection of the rights of individual employees through the arbitral process be invoked. This is a problem which has greatly troubled the courts and legal writers.

So long as the union is fighting the battle of the employees through the arbitration proceeding the employees' interests are being represented and there is no need for courts to provide protection to the employees. Sound public policy dictates that a court should not interfere with or disturb the orderly working of the arbitration process unless a compelling reason for invoking the court's equitable powers is presented. One of the principal purposes of arbitration is to reach a speedy final result and to avoid protracted litigation.

However, as pointed out in a comment in 6 U.C.L.A. Law Review (1959), 603, 628,

> Often the substantial interests of the individual employee and the union diverge. At this point it is difficult for the union to adequately represent the individual's interest. This may occur when he is a non-union member of the collective-bargaining unit, or he belongs to a minority faction of the union, or he is the "square peg in the round hole" type, or merely because the union officials do not believe in his claim.

It is in such a situation that some courts have extended judicial protection to the employees whose interests are actually not being represented by the union in the arbitral process.

The test of fair representation employed by the court in the *Soto Case* is the one advocated by Prof. Cox in his article, *Rights Under a Labor Agreement* in 69 Harvard Law Review (1956), 601, 638:

> The relationship between law and industrial relations will be improved, and collective bargaining will work better, in my opinion, without any sacrifice of the interests of individual employees, if contracts which contemplate active administration through a grievance and arbitration procedure controlled by the union are held to vest the power to settle grievances

in the collective-bargaining representative, *subject to its fiduciary duty of fair representation.* [Emphasis supplied.]

We deem such test of fair representation, in determining when to grant court protection to the rights of an individual employee under the collective-bargaining contract, to be sound in principle and we adopt the same. In most situations whether the union is performing its fiduciary duty of fair representation in an arbitration proceeding presents a question of fact. However, where the interests of two groups of employees are diametrically opposed to each other and the union espouses the cause of one in the arbitration, it follows as a matter of law that there has been no fair representation of the other group. This is true even though, in choosing the cause of which group to espouse, the union acts completely objectively and with the best of motives. The old adage, that one cannot serve two masters, is particularly applicable to such a situation.

This court applied the test of fair representation in giving judicial relief to individual employees in Pattenge v. Wagner Iron Works (1957) 275 Wis. 495, 82 N.W. (2d) 172. There the court entertained a suit by the employees to recover vacation pay due under a collective-bargaining contract without the union's having invoked the grievance procedure, the end step of which was arbitration. The rationale of such holding is stated in the opinion as follows (p. 500):

> We do not construe the contract or the law as requiring an individual employee to invoke this grievance procedure to assert an accrued pecuniary claim in circumstances where it is reasonably apparent that the union is hostile to him and will not give him adequate representation. To do so would place the employee's accrued rights against his employer more or less at the mercy of an unfriendly union. Both congress and the Wisconsin legislature have shown solicitude to protect employees from such consequences, by the provisions of the 1947 Federal Labor Management Act, 61 U.S. Stats. at L., p. 143, sec. (9) (a), and the Wisconsin Employment Peace Act, sec. 111.05 (1), that any individual employee shall have the right at any time to present grievances to the employer. See discussion and authorities cited in Lenhoff. *The Effect of Arbitration Clauses upon the Individual,* 9 ARBITRATION JOURNAL, 3, and Elgin J. & E. R. Co. v. Burley, 325 U.S. 711, 733, 736, 65 Sup. Ct. 1282, 89 L.Ed. 1886.

Under the holding in Soto v. Lenscraft Optical Corp., *supra,** if the plaintiff employees in the instant case had applied to the arbitrator to inter-

vene in the arbitration proceeding, it would have been his duty to have granted it. Such right of intervention would be valueless, however, if the plaintiffs were not given adequate notice of the arbitration hearing. In view of our holding that there was no fair representation of the plaintiffs by the union at such hearing, to hold that they would be bound by the arbitrator's adverse award contravenes our concept of due process.

While the plaintiff employees had no seniority rights at common law, and such rights were created solely by reason of the labor contract negotiated in their behalf by the union, nevertheless they constitute a valuable property right and cannot be divested without due process of law. Estes v. Union Terminal Co. (5th Cir. 1937), 89 Fed. (2d) 768, and Primakow v. Railway Express Agency (D. C. Wis. 1943), 56 Fed. Supp. 413.[1] It is the contention of the union that no due-process problem is present, in holding the award binding upon the plaintiffs' seniority rights, because the plaintiffs were represented by the union in the arbitration proceedings. The leading case on due process as applied to class representation is Hansberry v. Lee (1940), 311 U.S. 32, 61 Sup. Ct. 115, 85 L.Ed. 22, 132 A.L.R. 741, in which the opinion was written by Mr. Justice (later Chief Justice) Stone. The opinion expressed the conclusion that, where the substantial interests of the representative are not necessarily or even probably the same as those he purports to represent, due process militates vigorously against giving the decision effect upon them. Here the interests of the union espoused in the arbitration were in direct opposition to those of the plaintiffs.

The union advances the further argument that plaintiffs' rights were adequately represented before the arbitrator because the employer's position in the arbitration proceedings was identical to that of the plaintiffs. While such contention might be material on the issue of due process, we deem it to be beside the point on the issue of whether the plaintiffs were entitled to notice of the hearing, and an opportunity to intervene, as a matter of sound labor policy.

---

* [At the Appellate Division level.]

1. The brief *amicus curiae* contends that there is no issue of due process under the Fourteenth amendment present because of the absence of any state action, citing Ross v. Ebert (1957), 275 Wis. 523, 82 N.W. (2d) 315. However, the case of Dunphy Boat Corp. v. Wisconsin E. R. Board (1954), 267 Wis. 316, 64 N.W. (2d) 866, clearly demonstrates that state action is present. This is because, as pointed out therein, the Employment Peace Act (secs. 111.01 to 111.19, Stats.) makes it an unfair labor practice not to carry out the arbitration clause of a collective-bargaining contract. At common law in Wisconsin such an arbitration clause was unenforceable. Local 1111 v. Allen-Bradley Co. (1951), 259 Wis 609, 49 N.W. (2d) 720.

Employees not fairly represented by the union should never be put in the position of having to solely depend upon the employer's championing their rights under the collective-bargaining contract.

We find it unnecessary to ground our holding, that the award should be held not binding upon the plaintiffs because of lack of notice to them of the arbitration hearing, upon lack of due process. Courts of equity traditionally have the power to grant relief in situations which offend the court's sense of justice and fair play. We are herein confronted with a new situation in which it is incumbent upon us to adopt such rule of law as we deem to be in the best interests of sound public policy. We do not believe that the requiring of the giving of notice, and an opportunity to intervene, to those employees not being fairly represented in the arbitration by the union, as a condition to the award being binding on such employees, will prove disruptive of the arbitration process. We are inclined to believe that in the vast majority of labor arbitrations no question of fair representation will ever arise.

We have intentionally avoided discussion of whether the employees' right to fair representation is derived from a theory of agency, third-party beneficiary doctrines, or a trustee and cestui relationship. As well stated in 66 YALE LAW JOURNAL (1957), at page 951,

> labor-management relations pose special problems that should be resolved with a view to the needs of contemporary labor policy. In short whether employees are entitled to protection in union management arbitrations, and whether participation, a stay or an attack upon the award is the proper remedy should be viewed as questions of labor policy.

PER CURIAM (on motion for rehearing). The brief of the appellant union, in support of its motion for rehearing, contends that federal labor law controls the instant case and not state law, because of the fact that the employer is substantially engaged in interstate commerce. We find it unnecessary to pass on this contention because several of the authorities relied upon in our opinion are federal cases. The United States supreme court has not yet spoken on the principal point decided. When it does, we can perceive of no reason why the same policy considerations which are discussed in our original opinion and which caused us to reach the result we did, should not carry equal weight with that court.

The second point advanced by the union in support of its motion for rehearing is that our original decision interferes with the union's rights derived from the Labor Management Relations Act of 1947, as amended, to be the exclusive collective-bargaining agent for the plaintiff employees in matters affecting their seniority rights. In support of such contention Ford Motor Co. v. Huffman (1953), 345 U.S. 330, 73 Sup. Ct. 681, 97 L.Ed. 1048, is cited. That case dealt with preferential seniority rights of employees, who had been in military service, arising under a collective-bargaining contract negotiated by the union as the collective-bargaining agent. The argument now advanced seems to be this: Because the union in the first instance could have negotiated a contract with the employer giving the plaintiff employees unfavorable seniority rights, the union can accomplish the same result in the arbitration proceeding.

We deem the foregoing to be a fallacious argument. Once the rights of employees have become fixed in the collective-bargaining contract, the union does not possess the right to barter them away before an arbitrator. The cases of Estes v. Union Terminal Co. (5th Cir. 1937), 89 Fed. (2d) 768, and Primakow v. Railway Express Agency (D. C. Wis. 1943), 56 Fed. Supp. 413, deal with rights arising under the National Railway Labor Act. Those cases hold that employees have vested seniority rights under their collective-bargaining contract, which entitle them to notice of, and the right to participate in, an arbitration proceeding instituted to pass on such rights. We do not deem that seniority rights negotiated under the Labor Management Relations Act, and embodied in a collective-bargaining contract, should be accorded any lesser protection.

The motion for rehearing is denied without costs.

The union sought arbitration of its demand to discharge five employees pursuant to a union shop agreement. The five had worked on behalf of a rival union ; they sought a stay of arbitration. The court held that they lacked standing because they were not "parties" to the agreement. The court relied upon *In re Soto,* among other cases. In Re McKevitt (Arrow Co.) (S.Ct. Westchester Cty.) 57 LRRM 2282 (1964). While *Soto* does not squarely say so, the potential dischargees apparently had no right to intervene under New York Law.

JENKINS v.
WM. SCHULDERBERG-T. J. KURDLE CO.
217 Md. 556, 144 A. 2d 88 (1958)

[The union was not a party to this suit.]

Section 1(B) of the agreement provides that "No employee shall be unjustly discharged or laid off." The appellant claims that she was unjustly discharged and that the employer has committed a breach of the agreement.

There no longer seems to be any doubt that in certain situations an individual employee may sue his employer for the breach of a collective bargaining agreement. Several theories have been advanced to explain this result. One view is that although the agreement gives no rights to individual workers, whenever a man goes to work, his individual contract incorporates the union agreement as a local custom or usage so that every breach of the collective agreement is also a breach of the individual contract of employment. A second theory holds that a collective bargaining agreement is a contract with the employer as promisor, the union as promisee, and the employees as third party beneficiaries. A third view is that the collective bargaining agreement is like a trust, with the union holding the employer's promises in trust for the benefit of the individuals. Under any of these theories, the individual may sue the employer for infringement of his individual rights.

The general rule is that before an individual employee can maintain a suit, he must show that he has exhausted his contractual remedies.

We think that under the provisions of the agreement now before us the Employer is generally entitled to immunity from suits by individual employees, that the Union is to consider carefully and fairly the alleged grievances of its members, that it is likewise to exercise its judgment and discretion fairly on behalf of its individual members in determining upon what terms it believes any grievances of theirs should be adjusted and whether such grievances should be carried to arbitration, if negotiations for settlement or adjustment fail. It is conceded in the present case that, but for the prohibition against unjust discharge contained in the collective bargaining agreement, the plaintiff would have no claim at all against the Employer. We think that she must take the bitter with the sweet and cannot select and rely upon one provision of the agreement which is to her advantage and at the same time reject or ignore another which limits or is a condition to the exercise of the provision which she invokes.

But, accepting that premise, the question is whether or not she is barred from redress through litigation for allegedly wrongful discharge by the Union's refusal to carry her claim to arbitration, notwithstanding that the Union's refusal is due to conduct which, on the pleadings before us, must be taken as wilful, arbitrary and discriminatory.

A number of these cases deal with failure of the employee to exhaust contractual procedure.

In Pattenge v. Wagner Iron Works, 275 Wis. 495, 82 N.W. 2d 172 (1957), discharged employees brought an action against the employer for vacation pay allegedly due under the collective bargaining agreement. The contract even provided that the grievance procedure "shall be the sole means of disposing of grievances." However, it was held that these employees, who had been discharged for supporting a rival union, were not required to use the grievance procedure before bringing suit against the employer since it was "reasonably apparent that the [incumbent] union is hostile to him and will not give him adequate representation." The court felt that to require exhaustion of the contractual remedy "would place the employee's accrued rights against his employer more or less at the mercy of an unfriendly union." The court also emphasized the fact that the individual could not demand arbitration as a matter of right.

In United Protective Workers v. Ford Motor Co., 223 F. 2d 49 (7th Cir. 1955), a suit for reinstatement and back pay by an employee against his employer was upheld despite the employee's failure first to follow the grievance procedure of the collective bargaining agreement. This did not bar his recovery in court, "because the Company's attitude . . . made it obvious that pursuit of the grievance procedure would have availed [him] nothing." On a previous appeal, United Protective Workers v. Ford Motor Co., 194 F. 2d 997 (7th Cir. 1952), the court had similarly found that although the collective bargaining agreement established a grievance procedure, if the employer refused to participate in this procedure in a wrongful discharge case, the employee need not exhaust the contractual remedies.

In Nichols v. National Tube Co., 122 F. Supp. 726 (N.D. Ohio 1954), an individual employee recovered damages for a discharge resulting from his employer's violating the collective agreement by compelling him to retire, even though the union had waived all claims for past violations in negotiating a retirement policy. The court said:

> [I]t would seem . . . completely futile to have instituted grievance proceedings in such circumstances. The retired employee had not the slightest

change of remedial consideration; there was no basis for relief. According to the defendant, the policy of retirement was inflexible and no one in the Company had the right to make exceptions; it was not an arbitral grievance; consequently, it would not be expected that the plaintiff should be required to do a vain thing as a prerequisite to a suit. (p. 729).

In Youmans v. Charleston & W.C. Ry., 175 S.C. 99, 178 S.E. 671 (1935), where the employer refused to grant a hearing and made it impossible for the employee to pursue the course prescribed under the collective agreement, the employee's failure to exhaust his contractual remedy was no defense to his suit.

In many cases where it has been held that an employer can not be sued until the contractual remedies have been exhausted, the facts show that the employee had initiated the grievance procedure but the union rejected the claim *on its merits* as unworthy, and these cases are the converse of the exception suggested by Professor Cox, which we have quoted.

Thus, in DiSanti v. United Glass and Ceramic Workers, 33 CCH Lab. Cas. 94, 785 (Pa. C.P. 1957), the plaintiff claimed seniority over another worker who was taken off the job. The other worker initiated a grievance claim under the contract machinery and eventually the plaintiff was removed from his job. Plaintiff then sued the employer for wrongful removal. The union and the other worker were joined as parties defendant. Against plaintiff's contention that it would have been futile to exhaust his remedy under the contract because of the prior adjudication, the court held that plaintiff was bound by the union's actions in settling the dispute when the other worker had brought his grievance. The Court distinguished the situation there found to exist from such a situation as is alleged in the present case and said (p 94, 789):

> In stating that plaintiff is bound by decisions arrived at according to the provisions of the contract, the Court does not mean to imply that a member of a collective bargaining agency can never seek the protection of the courts for wrongs done him. Certainly where it is made clear that the decision was *arbitrary* or *capricious* or where fraud is sufficiently set forth, the courts are open to redress such wrong. However, such is not the case here. [Emphasis added.]

Chacko v. Pittsburgh Steel Co., 32 CCH Lab. Cas. 94, 452, 105 Pitt. L.J. 429 (Pa. C.P. 1957) was a suit to enjoin an employer from depriving the plaintiff of proper seniority rights. The grievance machinery was similar to the procedure in the agreement in the present case. The court there found that the union refused to process either grievance any further because it felt that they had no merit, and went on to say:

> Under the collective bargaining agreement, the Union alone has authority to demand arbitration and is entitled to exercise its honest discretion in deciding whether or not an employee has a grievance which justifies appeal to arbitration . . . At best, plaintiff's own case indicates that his Union used sound judgment in refusing to take his grievance to arbitration. (p. 94, 455).

In Garner v. KMTR Radio Corp., 146 Cal. App. 2d 441, 303 P. 2d 825 (1956), a local union of electrical workers was the exclusive bargaining agent of radio technicians employed by the defendant. The plaintiff, a technician, was discharged by the defendant because he failed to report for duty, whereupon the union, which alone had authority to demand arbitration on the plaintiff's behalf, ascertained through investigation that the plaintiff was then in jail and would be there for some time, and determined that the discharge was justified and not wrongful. It was held that plaintiff could not thereafter sue the defendant-employer. Plaintiff did not deny that the grievance procedure was exclusive, and he did not suggest "that the union did not make a complete and fair investigation or that its decision was unjust in any respect."

In Terrell v. Local Lodge 758, 141 Cal. App. 2d 17, 296 P. 2d 100 (1956), a suit against an employer for wrongful discharge where plaintiff initiated the grievance procedure but the union decided not to go to arbitration, the court said:

> The union . . . as the representative of appellant, exercised its discretion in this case and elected not to proceed to arbitration under the step four procedure. It therefore failed to exhaust the grievance procedure which is, by the contract, the exclusive method for adjusting claims or disputes of an employee against the company. (p. 103).

See also Terrell v. Local Lodge 758, 150 Cal. App. 2d 24, 309 P. 2d 130 (1957), where the employee's action against the union for failure to appeal the plaintiff's grievance to arbitration was dismissed.

A case often cited is Cone v. Union Oil Co., *supra,* 129 Cal. App. 2d 558, 277 P. 2d 464 (1954). There an employee sued his employer for loss of wages and seniority rights. The plaintiff's bill did not allege that she ever made any demand on the union to pursue her grievance under the collective agreement. The employer-defendant filed a motion for summary judgment with accompanying affidavits setting up the existence of the grievance procedure and the plaintiff's failure to ask the union to press her grievance. The motion for summary judgment was granted.

Cortez v. Ford Motor Co., 349 Mich. 108, 84 N.W. 2d 523 (1957) involved a dispute in which 108 women claimed that they were laid off from work in violation of their seniority rights. The employees filed grievances with the union. The claims of the employees were rejected, and they sued the employer and the union. Although the plaintiffs claimed that the union "refused" to file and process their grievance, their pleadings and exhibits clearly showed that the union and its representatives received and considered plaintiffs' grievance at great length and that the general problem with which the grievance was concerned was the subject of extensive negotiation between the union and the company. The court said:

> The essence of plaintiffs' complaint is really that the union failed to accept plaintiffs' position upon this grievance . . . [T]he contract makes amply clear that union representatives have discretion to receive, pass upon and withdraw grievances presented by individual employees.
>
> Our Court has repeatedly held that proper exercise of such discretion over grievances and interpretation of contract terms in the interest of all its members is vested in authorized representatives of the union, subject to challenge after exhaustion of the grievance procedure only on grounds of bad faith, arbitrary action or fraud. (p. 529).

See also Zdero v. Briggs Mfg. Co., 388 Mich. 549, 61 N.W. 2d 615 (1953) where a suit for reinstatement was denied. There was no "failure on the part of the respective local unions to do all in their power to aid and assist Zdero in securing reinstatement. There is a complete absence of any testimony indicating that the defendants, Local Unions Nos. 212 and 272, acted in bad faith or in an arbitrary or negligent manner."

A case most heavily relied upon by appellee is Taschenberger v. Celanese Corp., 26 CCH Lab. Cas. 86, 944 (1954), decided by the Circuit Court for Allegany County, Maryland. There, the discharged plaintiff presented his grievance to the union. A hearing was held, after which the employer filed with the employer notice of its intention to arbitrate plaintiff's case. Subsequent investigation by the union, however, disclosed that there was not sufficient evidence to warrant arbitration. Plaintiff decided not to appeal this refusal to arbitrate to the executive board of the union, but instead sued the employer. His declaration did not, so far as appears from the report of the case, allege that the union had acted arbitrarily with respect to his grievance. The employer's motion for summary judgment which showed the facts above was granted.

A slim minority of cases grants the employee relief even though the union has rejected his grievance on the merits.

Alabama Power Co. v. Haygood, 266 Ala. 194, 95 So. 2d 98 (1957) was an action by an employee against the employer and the union for a declaratory judgment of his rights under the collective agreement which he claimed were violated by his wrongful discharge. In his amended bill, plaintiff alleged that he followed the first step in the grievance machinery, but that the Union "failed or refused" to carry his grievance to the second step. A demurrer to the bill was overruled. The Court held that

> when the Union failed or refused to act, in effect it cut off the appellee's [plaintiff's] right to settle the grievance under step two and exhausted the administrative remedies thereunder for the appellee. Since we reach the conclusion that the appellee has in effect complied with the administrative remedies in the contract, he is entitled to have his bill for a declaratory judgment submitted to the courts. (p. 101).

This case definitely represents the minority view since there was no allegation of arbitrary or fraudulent conduct by the union. The opinion did not cite any authorities from other jurisdictions.

In Moore v. Illinois Central R. R., 180 Miss. 276, 176 So. 593 (1937), a suit by employee against his employer for wrongful discharge, the contract provided for the presentation of grievances to the superintendent and then to the officers of the employer. Plaintiff abandoned this grievance machinery in mid-stream. It was held that he could bring his action in the courts. There was no allegation of arbitrary action here. Mississippi has followed this case and today holds that the court remedy is concurrent with the contractual remedy. See Dufour v. Continental Southern Lines, 219 Miss. 296, 68 So. 2d 489 (1953).

One other case supporting the minority position is In re Norwalk Tire & Rubber Co., 100 F. Supp. 706 (D. Conn. 1951). This was a suit by two employees for wrongful discharge against the trustee in reorganization proceedings of the employer. After the discharges, the plaintiffs requested an investigation through the grievance machinery of the collective bargaining agreement. After these meetings, the union committee settled the grievance in favor of the employer and refused to take the case to arbitration. The plaintiffs thereupon sued the employer. The defendant claimed that the settlement under the grievance procedure was a bar to this suit. It was held that since the collective agreement did not expressly make the union's position binding upon the employee, the employee could reject this position and bring suit against the employer. The bargaining agreement provided that the results of arbitration should be binding on all parties but it did not make this provision with regard to the results of mere negotiation. Against the argument that it would have been academic to provide for a negotiation procedure in the handling of grievances if the results of the negotiation were not to be binding, the court felt that even if the negotiations broke down, they still had the salutary effect of preventing strikes. Finally, the court referred to the danger that an individual's rights could be traded off by a union in its handling of grievances and took the view that they therefore could be adequately protected only by the courts. We are of the opinion that the rule suggested by Professor Cox, referred to above, is sound. This is that as a general rule grievance procedures provided by a collective bargaining agreement should be a bar to suits by individuals against the Employer based upon alleged violation of the agreement, but that such suits are not barred if the Union acted unfairly towards the employee in refusing to press the employee's claim through to, and including, arbitration under the collective bargaining agreement. We accordingly hold that under the agreement here involved, the plaintiff is not barred from bringing this suit against her employer for allegedly wrongful discharge, where, on the facts alleged (and admitted by the demurrer) the Union acted arbitrarily and in a discriminatory manner in refusing to press the plaintiff's grievance to arbitration under the agreement. The order and judgment appealed from will therefore be reversed and the case remanded.

RIGHTS UNDER A LABOR AGREEMENT*

ARCHIBALD COX

While the interests affected and their relative importance vary so sharply from case to case as to make generalization hazardous, it seems fair to say that the interests potentially affected by a grievance fall into five categories:

(1) the interests of the union as an organization in recognition, the union shop, the checkoff, consultation concerning changes in working conditions, and any form of discrimination against union stewards or members;

(2) the unassorted interests of employees as a group, such as are involved in preserving the

*Excerpted from 69 HARV. L. REV. 601 (1956). Copyright 1956 by the Harvard Law Review Association and reprinted with the permission of the Association and the author.

work "belonging to" the bargaining unit or some segment thereof;

(3) the future interests affected by the law-making aspects of grievance adjustment;

(4) the present interests of employees who may be in competition with the immediate grievant or who, through the force of comparison, may gain or lose from the adjustment of the grievance;

(5) the interests of the individual who claims that he has not been paid correctly or that he has been damaged by the employer's failure to perform his contract obligations. Manifestly each worker has a strong and intensely personal interest in his compensation. He did the work. The money will be his, if recovered. His right is vested in the sense that the events giving rise to the employer's obligations are past and the claim is accrued. The law's traditional concern for such rights is testimony to the importance which society accords them.

In the final analysis the respective rights of the individual and union under a collective bargaining agreement turn upon a judgment as to the best way to secure a just measure for each class of interests outlined above.

The legal rights of the individual employees and bargaining representative in the enforcement of a labor agreement turn upon three questions, of which the first is most important.

First. Who may make a binding settlement of a claim that the contract has been violated? May it be done by the union alone, the individual alone, or only by both together?

Second. Who may maintain an action to enforce the promise, either by way of specific performance or declaratory judgment, or through an action for damages? Are the union and employee both necessary parties, or may one sue without the other?

Third. If the collective agreement establishes a grievance procedure ending in final and binding arbitration, may an individual sue to recover damages for a violation without first resorting to the contract procedure? If he does pursue the administrative machinery, may he challenge an adverse award?

The answers are plain enough with respect to claims of contract violation relating to the status of the union. Promises relating to such things as recognition, union security, the deduction of dues, the use of bulletin boards, and access to the plant all run to the union. Performance directly benefits the union as an organization. The employees are incidental beneficiaries who may gain from the strength of their representative but whose personal interests are not immediately affected. Wherever labor agreements are treated as binding contracts, the union is the proper party to enforce these obligations and an individual does not have standing to sue. Despite the lack of precedent, it seems safe also to conclude that the union alone has power to compromise or release claims for past violations.[1]

Laying aside this small and relatively simple class of promises, the range of possible claims under a collective agreement forms a continuum in which the interests of the union, of general groups of employees, and of identifiable individuals may be arrayed into infinite combinations and permutations of relative importance, conflict, and coincidence. At one extreme is the simple claim to wages which turns on a question of fact. At the other end are such contract rights as an employer's promises not to engage in subcontracting or to cooperate in making an elaborate job evaluation realigning the internal wage structure prospectively and retroactively.

Conceivably the law might approach these questions by giving fixed answers applicable to all employment under collective bargaining agreements. The difficulty is that no single rule seems to fit all cases—certainly not so clearly as to say that labor and management must conform to it regardless of their own appraisal. The procedure best suited to a simple dispute over whether a man worked eight or nine hours may be an individual suit, but the same procedure is ill-adapted to the administration of job evaluation plans and entirely unworkable in the case of obligations which cannot be shown to affect an identifiable person. Similarly, while claims at one end of the range might be left to the individual to prosecute or settle without much risk of injury to others, only the group representative is in a position to enforce those at the other.

Another conceivable solution is for the law to appraise *ad hoc* the several practical interests affected by a claim and then decide eclectically whether to allow the union or the individual to control its prosecution. The fatal weakness in so particularistic an approach is that it produces uncertainty in a field in which it is highly important to know the ground rules in advance. Is there to be one set of rules applicable to discharges and another to promises intended to preserve the pool of work available? Would the rule applicable to a promise not to engage in subcontracting depend upon whether the breach caused layoffs resulting in damage to identifiable individuals? Perhaps some promises relating to compensation for work would be enforceable by the union and some by the individual, for the balance of interests, as we have seen, differs according to the circumstances and the precise point at issue. Since no two cases would be quite alike, no one could say for certain whether the union or the individual had the right to handle the prosecution or adjustment of a particular claim of contract violation. Yet unless the parties are simply to disregard the law, the courts must formulate an approach which makes it possible to know *in the plant* whether the individual or the union controls the grievance. Thus, while differences would be tolerable from company to company and even from plant to plant, there is great need for uniformity of procedure in handling claims within a single establishment.

In my opinion the needs of the industrial community would be served best by leaving management and union free to determine by the terms of their collective bargaining agreement what shall be the respective rights of the union and the individual in its administration. The law could fill any gap resulting from the parties' failure to manifest a reasonably clear intention by formulating presumptions based upon considerations of fairness and convenience mixed with an informed hunch as to the "intent" of the transaction. If this approach is sound, it should embrace three propositions.

(1) The employer and bargaining representative are free to determine by contract in the collective agreement who shall have the right to enforce and settle claims arising out of the employer's failure to observe the agreed conditions of employment. In other words, the power to compromise claims, the right to sue for breach of contract, and the necessity of exhausting a grievance procedure shall be determined by asking what character of rights the parties intended to create when they negotiated the agreement.

(2) Unless a contrary intention is manifest, the employer's obligations under a collective bargaining agreement which contains a grievance procedure controlled by the union shall be deemed to run solely to the union as the bargaining representative, to be administered by the union in accordance with its fiduciary duties to employees in the bargaining unit. The representative can enforce the claim. It can make reasonable, binding compromises. It is liable for

---

1. The text oversimplifies several problems. An employer's promise not to discriminate against employees because of union activities belongs in the category of obligations benefiting the union as an organization, but the individual would seem to have the same kind of interest which he has in the ordinary obligation not to discharge without just cause. Provisions giving top seniority to union officials probably have this double aspect.

breaches of trust in a suit by the employee beneficiaries.

(3) Unless a contrary intention is manifest, a collective agreement which contains no grievance procedure shall be deemed a bilateral contract between the employer and union which contemplates the execution of further bilateral contracts of employment between the employer and individual workers incorporating the wage scale and other conditions of employment set forth in the collective agreement. The union may sue on the collective agreement to enforce the closed shop, check-off, and similar provisions inuring to its benefit as an organization, but only individuals may prosecute or settle claims based upon failure to observe the stipulated conditions of employment.

There is no lack of legal concepts suitable to describe these arrangements and their consequences. One is essentially the analysis pursued by Mr. Justice Reed and the majority of the court of appeals in the *Westinghouse* litigation. The other parallels the traditional trust, a legal technique frequently invoked when the obligee must play a continuing part in the administration of a contract intended for the benefit of a large and ever-changing group of beneficiaries who may have divergent interests. Massachusetts business trusts and mortgage indentures covering public bond issues furnish convenient illustrations. Under such an arrangement the trustee is normally the only proper party to bring an action on the contract and the judgment binds the beneficiaries. The trustee can enter into binding settlements with the obligor, and the beneficiary's remedy is to show a breach of fiduciary obligations. There would be room for another direct bilateral contract between the employer and an individual employee with respect to matters outside the scope of the collective agreement, as in the case of employment for a term or on supplemental conditions not covered by the master contract, but the usual hiring at will would simply designate the employee as a beneficiary under the agreement between the employer and the bargaining representative.[2]

Prior to the Wagner Act employers had no legal obligation to receive grievances from individuals. Generally speaking, that act was not intended to enlarge the rights of individuals, and the failure to provide any remedy for a refusal to receive their complaints suggests that no enforceable right was intended. The sponsors of the Taft-Hartley amendments were more concerned with protecting individual employees against the union, but nothing was done to change section 9(a) in any respect relevant to the immediate issue. The omission is entirely consistent with the general Taft-Hartley policy of enlarging the employer's rights and privileges with respect to the union in order to make him the protector of the individual employee. The office of a proviso is seldom to create substantive rights and obligations ; it carves exceptions out of what goes before. In my opinion, therefore, section 9(a) is entirely consistent with the view that an employer may lawfully promise the union not to process individual grievances and may also give the union the only legal right to compromise or enforce substantive obligations.

Many grievances result from failure to foresee a problem at the time of contract negotiations. When the contingency arises and conflicting views are asserted, the issue is nominally framed by the past but the truly important question may be, "What rule shall hereafter govern our conduct in these circumstances?" The group may be affected by the future implications of the ruling to an extent that far outweighs the individual claims to damages.

The union is the natural spokesman for future implications. Nor can adjudication of past rights be separated from rule making for the future. Both pertain to the interstices of the contract. The parties—and when they fail, an arbitrator—can successfully project general standards upon specific occasions because they are required to make their determinations within a given framework. The process works precisely because the same decision must be both an adjudication of the past and a rule for the future. To separate the two would either take the rule-making function out of the framework of the contract or else produce the unacceptable incongruity of two interpretations upon the same set of facts.

Many claims of contract violation affect employees other than those who were directly damaged by nonperformance.

Vesting the union with control of all grievances increases the likelihood of uniformity and therefore reduces "a potential source of competitions and discriminations that could be destructive of the entire structure of labor relations in the plant."[3] To deny the majority representative

---

2. No doubt it is wise to channelize all individual grievances into the established procedure if the individual has an Hohfeldian right to present them, but I find it difficult to read into the statute a command that the employer and union must permit the right to be exercised through any machinery they establish to handle union grievances even though both are unwilling. Most decisions hold that the individual cannot invoke contract machinery which is created to resolve disputes between the company and the union.

3. Douglas Aircraft Co., 25 War Lab. Rep. 57, 64–65 (1945).

power to control the presentation of grievances offers dissident groups, who may belong to rival unions, the opportunity "to press aggressively all manner of grievances, regardless of their merit, in an effort to squeeze the last drop of competitive advantage out of each grievance and to use the settlement even of the most trivial grievances as a vehicle to build up their own prestige. Imaginary grievances could be conjured up and others which, under ordinary circumstances, would be dropped at the first step could be magnified out of all proportion to their importance. The settlement of grievances could become the source of friction and competition and a means for creating and perpetuating employee dissatisfaction instead of a method of eliminating it."[4]

Competition between rival groups of employees can be troublesome to an employer not only because of the resulting unrest in the plant but also because it deters the bargaining representative from taking what the employer may consider a "responsible position." Public officials and arbitrators no less than employers constantly remind union officials that they have a duty to discountenance disruptive and frivolous claims.

When the interests of several groups conflict, or future needs run contrary to present desires, or when the individual's claim endangers group interests, the union's function is to resolve the competition by reaching an accommodation or striking a balance. The process is political. It involves a melange of power, numerical strength, mutual aid, reason, prejudice and emotion. Limits must be placed on the authority of the group, but within the zone of fairness and rationality this method of self-government probably works better than the edicts of any outside arbiter. A large part of the daily grist of union business is resolving differences among employees poorly camouflaged as disputes with the employer.

A study of broad industrial agreements reveals that these practical considerations have usually persuaded employers and bargaining representatives to give the union complete control over the prosecution of grievances.

The utility of these standard forms of grievance procedure largely depends upon the effectiveness of adjustments agreed upon between company and union representatives at the lower levels. Today their practical effectiveness is considerable because doubt concerning the governing legal principle, expense, inertia, and fear of reprisals discourage individual employees from seeking to upset the negotiated adjustments. To hold the adjustments legally ineffective would widen the gulf between industrial practice and the law. It would also increasingly undermine the practical effectiveness of settlements in the very situations in which there is the greatest danger to labor-management relations, for rival unions engaged in raiding and dissident internal factions are the most likely source of the energy, material resources, and legal talent necessary to upset an adjustment satisfactory to the company and to the established bargaining representative. Once it was clear that such challenges could succeed, their number would increase and the number of compromise settlements would diminish.

Applying the duty of fair representation to the settlement of grievances involves a further, more difficult inquiry. Where the sum is plainly due, the collective bargaining representative should have no power to waive or compromise the claim of one group of employees in return for a concession supposed to benefit a larger number. Such dickering in vested rights is simply taking money from one group to give to another. Even a legislature has no power thus to redistribute the wealth. In constitutional law, however, the rule is not absolute. The courts sustained the provisions of the Portal-to-Portal Act which wiped out vested employee claims for past wages potentially totaling many million dollars.

Part of the justification for the qualification is the fallacy in our conventional assumption that a legal claim is either valid or invalid once the events have passed because existing law covers every point and every instrument has a fixed meaning. In truth, the adjudication of disputable claims may involve a large measure of law making, and the interpretation of contracts often requires supplying a "fictitious" intent in order to provide a rule for a situation the parties did not anticipate. The repercussions of the new law may reach beyond the immediate parties to the surrounding community, where the impact may be more important than the private quarrel. In the Portal-to-Portal Act cases, moreover, the employees' claims were an unexpected windfall. No one could be supposed to have worked in reliance upon a right to pay for travel time not established by contract or usage or to have altered his position when the claim was called to his attention.

Might not similar criteria be applied to the compromise of grievances by a bargaining representative? Where the intent of the collective agreement is to give only rights which can be enforced and compromised by the union, the adjustment should be binding unless the compromise arbitrarily gives away the "property" (*i.e.,*

---

4. *Id.* at 61–62.

the claim to compensation or damages) of the individual worker. In judging whether the compromise is arbitrary one should take into account the fact that negotiation of the collective contract was the result of a group endeavor, and also such other circumstances as the merits of the claim, the effect upon other employees, the future implications of the settlement, and any evidence of discrimination or arbitrary "horse trading."

In practice, the value of the theoretical right to fair representation must be heavily discounted because only small sums are likely to be involved, because this branch of labor law is full of uncertainties, and because individual workers often have difficulty in obtaining skilled and imaginative legal services. Without meaning to minimize these very serious difficulties, however, I doubt whether the obstacles are any greater than those which confront the individual employees when they are legally free to prosecute suits directly against the employer. And there is some reason to suppose that unions would be more sensitive to the interests of individuals under a principle that gave them power to make settlements which were binding if fair than under a rule that although the union might bind itself not to prosecute a grievance, the settlement would not affect the legal rights of individuals. Under the latter rule union officials may shrug off responsibility by pointing to the employee's right to sue despite the settlement.

As can be seen, the Cox article has had a powerful influence upon the courts. Perhaps its rationale was shaped by the *Westinghouse* decision, whose many opinions badly needed rationalization. The article attempts to work out a system as to when unions can enforce an agreement and when contract rights are "uniquely personal." Perhaps its classification scheme loses much of its validity by the later court declarations that *Westinghouse* is a dead letter. However, this would not be the first doctrine that outlived its cause.

INDIVIDUAL RIGHTS IN COLLECTIVE AGREEMENTS AND ARBITRATION*

CLYDE W. SUMMERS

[Referring to Section 9 (a) of the National Labor Relations Act]:

The bare words of the statute make plain four elementary propositions concerning the status of

*Excerpted from 37 N.Y.U.L. Rev. 362 (1962). Reprinted with permission.

the union in enforcing the collective agreement: (1) The statutory right of the union to represent the employees in negotiating an agreement is different from its statutory right in settling grievances arising under the agreement. (2) The statute does not give the union the right of exclusive representation in settling grievances, for the proviso expressly permits grievances to be presented by individual employees and to be adjusted without intervention of the union. (3) The union has a valid interest in all grievances and cannot, against its will, be excluded from the adjustment. (4) The union can insist that all grievance settlements be consistent with the terms of the collective agreement.

These four propositions do not meet squarely the crucial question whether the union and the employer can, by agreement, vest in the union greater control over settling individual grievances than that granted by the statute. However, the words of the proviso to section 9(a), if given their natural meaning, would seem to speak to this question. The proviso declares that the individual "shall have the right at any time to present grievances to their employer and to have such grievances adjusted." These words, on their face, declare that an individual has a statutory right to process his grievance to final adjustment. "Without intervention of the bargaining representative" would seem to make it clear that the union may not bar the individual's asserting a claim or block his obtaining an adjustment.

It has been strongly argued, however, that in spite of its words, the proviso does not create any rights in the individual employee, but only makes plain that the employer's duty to bargain with the majority union is not violated if he chooses to hear and adjust grievances with individuals. The proviso is not placed in the statute in the section stating affirmative rights, but is placed in section 9(a) as a qualification of the majority union's right to represent. Section 8(a)(5) defines the employer's duty to bargain as "subject to the provisions of section 9(a)." Therefore, it is argued, the proviso merely states an exception to the employer's duty to bargain with the majority union as exclusive representative. Furthermore, the employer has no legal obligation to hear the grievances of his employees when there is no statutory bargaining agent. He should therefore be free to agree with the union not to process individual grievances. Finally, it is said, no sanction is provided for this claimed right, so it would be a right without a remedy, a legal contradiction which confirms that the word "right" was used loosely and not in a Hohfeldian sense.

These arguments which limit the effect of the

proviso to granting the employer freedom to hear individual grievances lack persuasiveness for the following reasons:

First, the argument views the role of section 9(a) in the statutory scheme too narrowly, for it treats the section as relevant only to the union's rights against the employer. The function of section 9(a) is much more wide ranging and profound—it establishes the majority union as statutory bargaining agent. That status relates not only to the employer but to other unions and to the employees. Thus, it affects the rights of other unions to picket or to bargain[1] for their members. Without that status the union violates the individual's statutory right if it pretends to bargain for him without his consent; with that status the union can make an agreement which truncates his right to refrain from union activity. And the status may simultaneously affect different parties in different ways. Thus, if an individual employee and his employee and his employer make an employment contract which conflicts with the collective agreement, the employee would merely be barred from enforcing the contract but the employer would be guilty of an unfair labor practice.

The broad function of section 9(a) is to establish the status of the majority union, and the purpose of the *proviso* is to define that status, not only with reference to the employer but also with reference to the employees. The proviso ought not to be viewed merely as a misplaced part of section 8(a) (5), nor should its words granting rights to individuals be construed solely to confer a privilege upon employers. It speaks directly to the relative rights of the union and the individual in the enforcement of the collective agreement.

Second, the argument that because the employer can refuse to hear individual grievances when there is no majority union, he can agree with the union not to hear such grievances, does not meet the critical issue.[2] Although the em-

ployer may refuse to listen, he cannot by turning a deaf ear bar the individual from legally enforcing his employment contract. Whether the employer can agree with the union to listen only through the established grievance procedure is a subsidiary problem with which we are not here principally concerned. The critical issue is whether the employer by such an agreement can use the union's silence to bar the individual from legally enforcing his claim. If the employer could so agree, then the individual would have fewer legal rights than before. The end result would be that although the collective agreement prescribed the terms of the individual employment contract, the employee would have no enforceable rights under his employment contract. In practice, if not in theory, the rights would belong solely to the union.

Third, the absence of sanctions to enforce the "right" stated in the proviso does not prevent that proviso from being given effect when an individual brings suit under section 301 to enforce his rights under the collective agreement. The individual seeks to use the proviso only to nullify a term of the collective agreement, which he claims the union as bargaining agent had no authority to make. In outlining the sources of substantive law to be applied, Mr. Justice Douglas explained, "Other problems will lie in the penumbra of express statutory mandates. Some will lack express statutory sanction but will be solved by looking at the policy of the legislation and fashioning a remedy that will effectuate that policy."

Fourth, there may in fact be sanctions to enforce this right. If the function of the proviso is, as has been suggested above, to strike a balance between the power of the union and the rights of the individual, and to mark the limits of the union's authority, then various sanctions are available to keep the union within those limits. Where the union negotiates an agreement which oversteps its statutory authority to the injury of individual rights, the courts can use their broad equitable power to enjoin application of the offensive provisions, or the NLRB can use the administrative remedy of removing certification. In addition, violation of the right granted by the proviso may be an unfair labor practice. Section 7 guarantees employees not only the right to bargain collectively and engage in other concerted activities, but also "the right to refrain from any or all such activities." These rights are obviously qualified by section 9(a) to the extent that the statutory status of the majority union circumscribes the individual's right to refrain from bargaining collectively. If the proviso is read as limiting the union's authority

---

1. In the absence of a majority union, a minority union can bargain for its own members. Consolidated Edison Co. v. NLRB, 305 U.S. 197 (1938). When a majority union is present, a minority union cannot represent its members, even in processing grievances. Hughes Tool Co. v. NLRB, 147 F. 2d 69 (5th Cir. 1945).

2. The General Counsel of the NLRB has ruled that § 9 (a) does not require an employer to deal with a minority group of employees who request a wage increase, Admin. Ruling of the NLRB Gen. Counsel, Case No. 317, 30 L.R.R.M. 1103 (June 2, 1952), or meet with a discharged employee and his lawyer to discuss the discharge, Admin. Ruling of the NLRB Gen. Counsel, Case No. 418, 31 L.R.R.M. 1039 (Nov. 3, 1952). Neither of these reaches the question of the validity or legal effect of contractual provisions purporting to give the union exclusive control over grievances.

over the individual, any agreement between the union and the employer which gives the union greater control over disposition of grievances invades the individual's right to refrain from bargaining collectively as guaranteed by section 7, and may therefore be a violation of sections 8(a) (1) and 8(b) (1).[3] The plain words of the proviso creating an affirmative right can not be brushed aside as lacking enforcing sanctions.

The words of the proviso in section 9(a), when viewed in the context of the total statutory structure, point strongly in the direction of giving the individual a right to enforce substantive provisions in a collective agreement without being subject to the union's veto.

Two cases are important not as authoritative statements of federal labor policy or irreversible precedents, but as integral parts of the legislative history of section 9(a) in its present form. They help frame the purposes of the Taft-Hartley amendment and thereby illuminate the congressional policy to be effectuated in suits under section 301.

The purposes of adding [the proviso] are clouded by the customary imprecision of committee reports and legislative debates, but through the clouds three guideposts emerge quite clearly. First, the discussion was almost entirely in terms of the individual's rights, and the proviso was viewed through the eyes of the individual employee. Concern focused not on the duty of the employer to bargain, but on the relative rights of the individual and the union. Second, the words added to the proviso were framed with explicit reference to the prior decisions. The *Hughes Tool* case was in the forefront of congressional debates; and the effect of the proviso was measured against the Supreme Court's decision in Elgin, Joliet & Eastern R.R. v. Burley. Third, at a very minimum Congress intended to secure by statute the individual rights recognized by the Board in *Hughes Tool*, and to adopt the principle of *Elgin, Joliet.*

One of the dominant themes in the enactment of Taft-Hartley was to protect the individual employee from being wholly submerged by the collective bargaining structures. The proviso of section 9(a) was listed by Representative Hartley as a part of a "bill of rights" for individual workers, along with the right to choose the majority representative, the right not to be discharged when expelled from the union, and the right to vote on union security contracts. These were not shadow rights protected only when championed by the employer; they were rights protected against both union and employer and not destructible by their collective agreement.

Both the external evidence of legislative history and the internal evidence of the words of section 9(a), read in the context of the statutory structure, point in the same general direction. From the words and legislative history emerge guidelines for fashioning the federal substantive law under section 301:

(1) The individual employee has rights under the collective agreement, the enforcement of which are not subject to the union's exclusive control.

(2) The union and the employer cannot block the enforcement of these rights by agreeing between themselves that those rights can be compromised or ignored without the individual employee's consent or authorization.

(3) The individual rights are limited by the substantive terms of the collective agreement.

(4) The union has an interest in all terms of the collective agreement and a right to insist on the enforcement of the agreement.

Additional guidance in delineating the rights of individual employees under the collective agreement can be drawn from the Railway Labor Act. This act, which was the precursor of the Wagner Act, established as national labor policy the primary principle that the majority union should be the exclusive representative for purposes of collective bargaining. The federal courts, in applying the statute, have been confronted with problems comparable to those which will arise under section 301, and have sought to develop working rules which will balance the needs and interests of the union and the individual.

The most relevant difference between the two statutes is that the Railway Labor Act requires that grievances which the parties are unable to adjust by the usual process of negotiation be submitted to the National Railroad Adjustment Board for determination. Those determinations are enforceable in the federal courts. But even this difference can be overstated, for the function of the statutorily created Adjustment Board is generally comparable to that of contractually

---

3. See Sherman, *The Individual and His Grievance— Whose Grievance Is It?*, 11 U. PITT. L. REV. 35, 53–54 (1949); *ABA Report on Individual Grievances* 33, 62–63, 50 Nw. U.L. REV. at 178–79 (1955). Giving the union such control to enforce or waive the provisions of the collective agreement which benefit the individual and govern his terms and conditions of employment might also be a violation of §§ 8 (a) (3) and 8 (b) (2). This would be equivalent to giving the union unilateral control over seniority, which has been held to be unlawful. NLRB v. Dallas Gen. Drivers, 228 F. 2d 702 (5th Cir. 1956); NLRB v. International Bhd. of Teamsters, 225 F. 2d 343 (8th Cir. 1955).

created grievance arbitration enforced under section 301.

Prior to 1945, the unions insisted that the individual employee had no right to process his grievance and carry it to the Adjustment Board. They insisted that they were the exclusive representatives not only for negotiating agreements but also for settling grievances arising under such agreements. In Elgin, Joliet & Eastern R.R. v. Burley, the Supreme Court, relying on statutory language far less explicit than the proviso to section 9(a), squarely rejected this view. So far as grievances were concerned, the individual had rights "to share in the negotiations, to be heard before the Board, to have notice, and to bring the enforcement suit." These rights could not be foreclosed by the union's settling his claim without his consent. Nor could an award of the Board be effective as against him unless he had authorized the union to present his case or had been given notice and opportunity to be heard.

The holding in Elgin, Joliet that the union does not have exclusive power to settle or appeal an employee's grievance has required the federal courts to develop rules governing the individual's processing and enforcing his own claim. It now seems generally accepted, both by the parties and the courts, that the individual can file his grievance without going through the union. However, he must process it "in the usual manner," which means that he must follow the contractual grievance procedure. Thus, in the lower steps he may not be entitled to be represented by counsel or by a minority union unless the contract so permits, and the bargaining representative is entitled to receive notice and to participate in accordance with the contract. Moreover, the individual may not settle the grievance without the union's consent, for as the Court recognized in Elgin, Joliet, both collective and individual interests are involved when the dispute arises from the terms of a collective agreement. The process thus required is remarkably similar to that described by the NLRB in Hughes Tool.

When the individual has exhausted the grievance procedure in seeking to enforce his claim, his resort is not to the courts but to the Adjustment Board, for it has exclusive primary jurisdiction over individual claims as well as claims of unions and employers. As the Supreme Court pointed out in Pennsylvania R.R. v. Day, the "need for experience and expert knowledge" and the "need for uniformity of interpretation and orderly adjustment of differences" is the same regardless of who is the claimant. In the proceedings before the Adjustment Board, the union is an interested party representing the collective interests of other employees in the interpretation of the contract. The individual is entitled at this stage to be represented by any person or union of his choice.

The individual employee may not only carry his own case to the Adjustment Board, but he is also entitled to notice and the opportunity to be heard in proceedings which effectively adjudicate his rights under the collective agreement. In Estes v. Union Terminal Co., the union filed a grievance claiming that one employee, Lane, had improperly been given seniority over certain other employees. It carried the case to the Board and won, but the company refused to comply with the award on the grounds that Lane had been given no notice. To the argument that Lane was not entitled to notice, the court replied:

> [E]very person who may be adversely affected by an order entered by the Board should be given reasonable notice of the hearing...No man should be deprived of his means of livelihood without a fair opportunity to defend himself. Plainly, that is the intent of the law. The case at bar illustrates how a single employee may be caught between the upper and nether millstones in a controversy to which only a labor organization and a carrier are parties before the Board.

This right to notice and hearing was solidified by Elgin, Joliet, and has been applied in subsequent cases involving competing claims of groups of employees.

The unifying purpose of these decisions under the Railway Labor Act is to provide the individual employee procedural due process in having his substantive rights under the collective agreement determined. The very essence of procedural due process is to have those rights determined by an impartial tribunal. In Edwards v. Capital Airlines, the union protested that two pilots had been given seniority status greater than to which they were entitled, and carried the dispute to a system board of adjustment. The two pilots appeared with lawyers who argued in their behalf, but the system board, made up only of representatives of the union and the carrier, ruled against them. In a suit to enjoin enforcement of the award, the court held that the collective contract provision making the board's award final and binding could not foreclose the rights of a minority group when the union representing the interests of the many was actively an adversary party. "Persons in their situation must have available to them, at some point, an impartial look at a decision, thus made, denying their claims to substantial rights. This is the time-honored function of an equity court." Recognizing that the award was "presumptively valid," the court nonetheless declared the seniority provisions to be clear, interpreted them, and modified the decision of the system board. Even a decision of the Adjustment Board itself can be reviewed on the grounds that members of the Board, as officers of the union, had adverse interests such as to justify an inference of bias.

Both the National Labor Relations Act and the Railway Labor Act express the basic national policy of reliance on collective bargaining as a system of industrial government. Section 301 is but a segment of the statutory framework supporting and shaping that system, and the courts in constructing rules to govern the rights of individual employees should seek to further, not frustrate, the purposes of collective bargaining. But the purposes to be furthered are not simply those of the collective entities—union and management. The controlling purposes are those of the statute, for collective bargaining, a private institution, is charged with a public function.[4]

Collective bargaining as conceived by the statute vests in the union collective power to enable it to bargain effectively with the employer, but the purpose of giving the union that power is to benefit the employees. The function of the collective agreement is not only to stabilize the relationship of the collective parties, but also to establish terms and conditions of employment for the employees. Nor are the interests of the employees conceived in narrow economic terms, for one of the dominant purposes of collective bargaining is to protect employees from arbitrary or unequal treatment—to bring a sense of justice to the workplace. The role of the collective agreement is to substitute general rules for unchanneled discretion; wages are not based on whimsy but on established rates, layoffs are not governed by favoritism but by seniority provisions, discharges are not based upon vindictive bias but upon just cause found after objective inquiry. As the Labor Study Group of the Committee for Economic Development has so well stated:

> A major achievement of collective bargaining, perhaps its most important contribution to the American workplace, is the creation of a system of industrial jurisprudence, a system under which employer and employee rights are set forth in

contractual form and disputes over the meaning of the contract are settled through a rational grievance process usually ending, in the case of unresolved disputes, with arbitration. The gains from this system are especially noteworthy because of their effect on the recognition and dignity of the individual worker.

The needs of collective bargaining, thus conceived, inevitably look two ways—toward the interests of the collective parties and their relationship, and toward the interests of the employees and their individual rights. The need for an effective union to obtain benefits and establish rules carries with it a need for individuals to receive those benefits according to the rules. The need for the collective parties to resolve disputes and meet changed conditions during the contract has a concurrent need for the individual to be fairly treated according to general rules. In framing the legal rules, the multiple needs of collective bargaining cannot be fully served by looking only to the collective relationship; for one of the major functions of collective bargaining may be frustrated if the employees' interest in fair and equal treatment under established rules is not given significant weight.

If the law looks only to the needs and desires of union and management, it may give little protection to the individual. Both of the collective parties are primarily concerned with managing their relationship, and that is simplified by giving the union exclusive control over the prosecution of grievances. Three uses of the grievance procedure in managing the collective relationship are particularly relevant in defining individual rights. First, the grievance procedure is used to complete the collective agreement. Contract provisions may be intentionally silent or vague, or they may unwittingly leave gaps, include inconsistent terms, or fail to foresee future problems. Whatever its source, ambiguity reveals that the agreement is incomplete and requires continued bargaining. The forum for bargaining is the grievance procedure, and the unsettled rule is illustrated by a particular grievance. The process of completion is akin to the original negotiation of the agreement, and the collective parties have primary interests in evolving the general rule to fill out the agreement. But this bargaining process is more confined than the original negotiation, for the parties normally expect that the grievance will be settled within the range of reasonable interpretations which can be drawn from guides in the agreement, and if they are unable to settle the dispute, it will be resolved by arbitration.

Second, the grievance procedure may be used to change the collective agreement and serve

---

4. Congress, in amending § 9 (a), made clear that it did not believe that exclusive control by the union over grievances was essential for collective bargaining to fulfill the statutory purpose. At the very least, § 9 (a) upholds contracts which deny unions such exclusive control. Indeed, the legislative history makes it unmistakably clear that Congress considered such contracts preferable.

the needs of flexibility.[5] During cut-backs in employment the employer may lay off all women employees and retain men with lesser seniority or impose layoffs instead of spreading the work as required by the seniority clause. The union, by refusing to appeal the grievances, accepts an informal modification of the agreement. The purposes of both collective parties are served by the freedom to improvise exceptions to the general rules of the agreement. Of course, the line between changing the contract and completing the contract is indistinct, but the line is crossed when the settlement is beyond the range of reasonable interpretation of the agreement or contravenes a previously established rule. The indistinctness of the dividing line does not obliterate the essential difference in the two uses of the grievance procedure.

Third, the grievance procedure may be used as a clearing house for balancing off unrelated claims. Grievances may be bargained against each other, the employer granting one in return for the union's surrendering another. This may serve a useful and legitimate function, but also can raise serious problems. In Guzzo v. United Steelworkers, the union called a strike during the contract term. The employer sued the union for damages and singled out one employee for discharge. The union protested the discharge as discriminatory and processed the employee's grievance up to arbitration, but at that point the union agreed to withdraw the grievance in return for the employer's dropping his suit against the union. When the grievance procedure becomes clogged, large numbers of grievances may be settled in a wholesale exchange. Thus in *Elgin, Joliet*, the union's surrender of back pay claims was part of a package settlement of sixty-one different grievances.

From the union's institutional viewpoint, exclusive control over grievances enhances the union's prestige and authority. Through the prosecution of grievances it can daily demonstrate its effectiveness as guardian of the employee's interests ; successful settlement builds bonds of

loyalty from those benefited ; and refusal to process underscores the union's authority. Conversely, grievances settled with individuals or other unions makes the majority union appear unnecessary, if not ineffective, and creates conflicting loyalties. More importantly, the union as representative of all of the employees has a collective interest in the individual's claim. If the claim is granted, it may be at the expense of other employees—seniority, promotion, and job assignment cases are only the most obvious examples. If the claim is denied, it may provide a precedent which casts a cloud over other employees' rights. The union has not only an interest but a responsibility to protect the other employees' rights. In addition, it has a separable institutional interest that the bargain it has made not be remade or frittered away by individual action.

From management's viewpoint, vesting exclusive control over grievances in the union simplifies contract administration. Friction and distrust on the part of the union are reduced, and all grievances are funneled through a single established procedure which orders appeals up the chain of management control. Most important, it simplifies management's obtaining definite answers to questions arising under the collective agreement. Grievances settled with the union cannot return to haunt management in the form of individual claims ; dispensations granted by union officers cannot be challenged by individual employees. The employer can proceed with full security, for the union's control over the grievance procedure shields him from possible liability to his employees.

These needs and desires of the collective parties, and their use of the grievance procedure to manage their collective relationship are all served by giving the union exclusive control over the grievance procedure. Obviously, not all of these needs are equally compelling nor the desires worthy of fulfillment in the same measure. More important, however, many of these needs do not require such totality of union control, or may be adequately met through other methods. The purpose here is only to identify the principal collective needs, not to prescribe the measure or method of meeting them. That must be done through specifying the design of the substantive law.

The needs of collective bargaining look also to the interests of the employees and their individual rights. In simple economic terms, the individual's interest is often of first magnitude, for more than three-fourths of the cases coming to the courts involve seniority rights or disciplinary discharges. The individual's very liveli-

---

5. One of the arguments most commonly used against recognition of individual rights under the collective agreement is that "a prime function of the grievance procedure is to secure uniformity in interpreting the agreement and building up a 'law of the plant' with respect to matters not spelled out in the agreement." Ostrofsky v. United Steelworkers, 171 F. Supp. 782, 790 (D. Md. 1959). See discussion in Cox, *Individual Enforcement of Collective Bargaining Agreements*, 8 LAB. L. J. 850, 855 (1957). This argument puts the shoe on the wrong foot, for it is the individual who insists on uniformity—that he be treated according to the "law of the plant" which governs all others under the agreement. It is the collective parties who insist on exceptions, variations and departure from uniformity.

hood is at stake. In personal terms, loss of seniority undermines his sense of security, and discharge darkens his good name. Making the union the exclusive representative for processing grievances subordinates those interests of individual employees and endangers interests which collective bargaining purposes to protect.

The grievance procedure is particularly susceptible to abuse, for through it individuals or groups may be singled out for arbitrary treatment. In DiSanti v. United Glass Workers,[6] a former union officer bid for and was given a promotion. The grievance committee, dominated by his political rival, insisted that he be removed from the job and management complied. And in Woodward Iron Co. v. Ware,[7] two employees who had been discharged sought to persuade the union to process their grievances but their request was summarily rejected by hostile members. Seniority grievances are especially vulnerable to discrimination. In Edward v. Capital Airlines,[8] two pilots who had been reinstated found themselves pitted against all those lower on the seniority list; the union officers cast aside the contract and embraced the majority. And in Cortez v. Ford Motor Co.,[9] women who were systematically laid off in violation of the seniority provision found that the local union president had informally arranged with the employer that regardless of the contract, men should have preference. The danger of unfairness is magnified and its presence obscured when the grievance depends on a disputed issue of fact. Thus, in *Cortez,* the union thinly veiled its discrimination by claiming that the jobs were too heavy for women; and in *Matter of Soto* the union conceded that unwanted employees had engaged in a slowdown. Most grievances involve some factual issue, and the union, by rejecting the employees' version, can act "responsible" and wear the face of fairness.

The individual's interest may more often be vitiated without vindictiveness or deliberate discrimination. In complete investigation of the facts, reliance on untested evidence, or colored evaluation of witnesses may lead the union to reject grievances which more objective inquiry would prove meritorious. Union officials burdened with institutional concerns may be willing to barter unrelated grievances or accept wholesale settlements if the total package is advantageous, even though some good grievances are lost. Concern for collective interests and the

6. 40 L.R.R.M. 2548 (Pa. Ct. C.P. 1957).

7. 261 F. 2d 138 (5th Cir. 1958).

8. 176 F. 2d 755 (D.C. Cir. 1949).

9. 349 Mich. 108, 84 N.W. 2d 523 (1957).

needs of the enterprise may dull the sense of personal injustice. [Omitted is a summary of Union News Co. v. Hildreth.]

Although the frequence of unfairness in grievance handling is impossible to measure, there is no doubt that the danger to the individual can be substantial. Within union groups cliques are not uncommon, political rivalries are often sharp and factional fights are bitter. Refusal to process grievances or "botching" them is a subtle but effective weapon. Seniority grievances are vulnerable to group pressures, and "horse-trading" of grievances can become commonplace. That these are real dangers is evidenced by the few studies made and confirmed by leading commentators.

Beyond these dangers of malice, majority intolerance, or official insensitivity, there are less tangible, but more pervasive values. One of the functions of collective bargaining is to replace vagrant discretion with governing rules. The individual, by his ability to insist that those general rules be observed, gains an assurance of fair and equal treatment and a sense of dignity and individual worth. If the union, by *ad hoc* settlement, can set aside the rule and bar the aggrieved individual from access to any neutral tribunal, these values are denied. What is involved, and what collective bargaining seeks to bring to industrial life, are elemental notions of due process—the right of a person to be governed by the law of the land and the right to be heard in his own cause.

[As to how individual interests should be protected, Professor Summers observed]:

First, the individual employee is bound by the substantive terms of the collective agreement. He cannot bargain individually to vary the contract or set it aside; he can only demand compliance with its terms. He cannot deny the union's power to make a binding agreement; he can only insist that when the agreement is made, he shall not be denied its benefits. The very essence of the individual's claim is that the terms and conditions of his employment are governed by the collective agreement and that neither he, nor the union, nor the employer can refuse to live by it.

The collective agreement by which the individual and the collective parties are governed is not limited to the four corners of the written instrument. It is the whole agreement, including industrial customs, established practices, understandings and precedents which infuse the contractual words with life and meaning. The collective agreement inevitably includes incomplete terms and unresolved ambiguities; and the individual's rights, like those of the collective parties, are subject to these gaps and uncertainties. The individual whose claim is disputed cannot insist on his interpretation; he can only insist on access to an appropriate procedure through which that dispute can be resolved. In this sense, the individual's right under a collective agreement is essentially procedural—the right of access to a tribunal, court or arbitrator, to have his substantive claims determined and enforced.

Second, the union has a substantial interest in the settlement of all individual claims arising under the collective agreement. The employee and the employer cannot make a binding settlement without the consent of the union, nor can they submit their dispute to a tribunal without making the union a party. The union has a right to be heard on behalf of other employees and its institutional interests.

But this right of the union has more than procedural significance, particularly when the individual's claim arises out of a gap or ambiguity in the collective agreement. If the union supports management's interpretation, this will be highly persuasive to the court or arbitrator so long as the interpretation is within the range of reasonableness as determined by the words, practices and precedents of the parties. Thus the collective parties will retain a dominant voice in completing the terms of the agreement, thereby satisfying in substantial measure this need of collective bargaining.

Third, the collective parties can change the general rules governing the terms and conditions of employment, either by negotiating a new agreement or by formally amending the old. The individual has no right to have the contract remain unchanged; his right is only to have it followed until it is changed by proper procedures. Although contract making (or amending) and contract administration are not neatly severable, they are procedurally distinct processes. Most union constitutions prescribe the method of contract ratification, and it is distinct from grievance settlement; the power to make and amend contracts is not placed in the same hands as the power to adjust grievances. Indeed, many union constitutions expressly bar any officer from ratifying any action which constitutes a breach of any contract. Through the ability to change the agreement, the collective parties retain a measure of flexibility. They are not free, however, to set aside general rules for particular cases, nor are they free by informal processes to replace one general rule with a contrary one.

These three basic guides go far toward defining in broad terms the relative status of the individual and the union, fulfilling the essential purposes of the federal statutes and accommodating some of the most pressing needs of the collective parties in managing their collective relationship. Within this framework it is necessary to sketch some of the details of the design of the federal substantive law, for it is in those details that the national labor policy is expressed and the multiple needs of collective bargaining finally accommodated. In marking out the rights of the individual, it is helpful to examine separately his rights: (1) when the union supports his claim; (2) when the union refuses to support or actively opposes his claim; and (3) when the union carries a case to arbitration that directly affects his interests. All have common considerations, but each raises distinctive problems.

1. *The Rights of the Individual When the Union Supports His Claim.* An employee may seek to present and process his own grievance even though the union is ready and willing to press it on his behalf. He may distrust the union and fear that it will make but a half-hearted presentation; he may actively dislike unions and wish to avoid involvement or obligation; or he may favor a rival union and prefer that it shall obtain the credit. The evidence available indicates that the third reason is the main motivation in the great majority of cases in which an individual seeks to by-pass a ready and willing majority union. The proviso of section 9(a) clearly precludes an individual from processing his grievance through a minority union, but he can have a "more experienced friend" speak for him, and this is often an officer or attorney for the rival union.

Such grievances inevitably undermine the prestige of the statutory representative and can sow seeds of disruptive tension. Moreover, a poor presentation and unfavorable settlement may create a damaging precedent. The union must then bear the burden of appealing and is saddled with the handicaps of overcoming an adverse decision. Such grievances also present problems for management, for dealing with an individual invites distrust by the union, and settlement may ultimately require consultation with the union.

The intersecting needs and desires of the parties would seem to be best accommodated by requiring the employee to file his grievance through the statutory representative and have it processed through the regular channels. By giving the individual a right to be present and an opportunity to add what he believed necessary, he would be assured that his claim had been forcefully argued. Whether the proviso in section 9(a) requires that the individual be given greater rights is unclear, for neither the words nor the legislative history distinguish sharply between the proviso's two functions—limiting the employer's duty to bargain, and limiting the union's control over the individual employee. The legislative history makes it reasonably clear that an employer can legally bargain for the freedom to deal with individuals on grievances and restrict the union's role to protesting the adjustment. However, there is no compelling evidence that the right of the individual as against the collective parties was intended to be more than the right to participate and the right not to be bound by the settlement without consent. The pattern under the Railway Labor Act has been that the individual may be limited to these rights at the lower steps of the grievance procedure, but before the National Railroad Adjustment Board, he has free choice of representatives.

2. *The Rights of the Individual When the Union Refuses to Press or Actively Opposes His Claim.* The union may refuse to process an employee's grievance because it disbelieves his version of the facts, disagrees with his interpretation of the agreement, believes the grievance is too trivial, or because of personal hostility or political pressures. In cases such as those involving seniority, the union may actively oppose the individual's claim or even press a grievance on behalf of competing claims. All of the cases, however, have the common element that the union accepts a result which the individual believes violates his rights under the collective agreement and he seeks to enforce those rights himself. The effort to enforce presents a cluster of subordinate problems which must be resolved in the light of the statutory policies and the needs of collective bargaining.

(a) What procedures must the individual follow in enforcing his claim? The successive steps of the grievance procedure provide an established and orderly process for consideration and review of disputes arising under the collective agreement. It is designed to aid in resolving those disputes, and ends with appeal to the highest level of authority. All grievances, regardless of who is the grievant, should be channeled through this process, for it simplifies the administrative work of management; provides the maximum opportunity for settlement; and helps insure that the substantive terms of the settlements will be uniform. If the union processes the grievance through some of the steps and then withdraws, the individual should be required to appeal through the succeeding steps. If the collective

parties bar his grievance, then further appeals should be excused, for an individual's rights cannot be conditioned on his exhaustion of non-existent remedies.

The grievance procedure in such a case may become three-cornered in nature, for the union continues to be a party. In some cases, such as discipline, the union may be neutral, torn between hoping for the individual's hopeless cause and fearing the embarrassment of his possible victory. In others, such as seniority, the union may be more opposed to the individual's claim than the management. No binding settlement is possible without the agreement of all three parties.

Conceivably there may be more than two competing claims—three or more employees may seek the same promotion, or three groups of employees may each claim top seniority. Such cases are in fact less common than often imagined; only one reported case appears to have involved such a dispute. When such a case does arise, it would seem that all claims should be represented in the grievance procedure, whether by the union, management or other spokesmen, so that any settlement would be final and binding on all.

(b) What tribunal should determine the individual's unsettled grievance? The union and the employer are entitled to have a uniform body of rules govern their relationship, and the very core of the individual's claim is his right to equal treatment. But such uniformity and equality cannot be achieved if individual grievances are adjudicated by courts and union grievances are decided by arbitrators. As the Supreme Court has said:

> The labor arbitrator performs functions which are not normal to the courts; the considerations which help him fashion judgments may indeed be foreign to the competence of courts.
>
> . . . .
>
> The ablest judge cannot be expected to bring the same experience and competence to bear upon the determination of a grievance, because he cannot be similarly informed.

This mirrors the view of the parties that the deciding of disputes by an arbitrator is a part of the very substance of the agreement. More than that, it expresses the larger federal policy, as enunciated by the Supreme Court, that disputes under collective agreements should be resolved through arbitration and that courts ought not substitute their judgment for that of arbitrators. All of these considerations point unmistakably to arbitration as the proper forum for individual grievances.

These considerations have been largely ignored by the courts in applying state law. Arbitration rests solely on contract, they reason, and the arbitration clause is worded as giving only the union and the employer the right to demand arbitration. The individual employee, therefore, has no right to arbitration. Often, as in Parker v. Borock, this logic is but a prelude to denying him any rights under the collective agreement—essentially what the collective parties intended when they denied him access to arbitration. Whether they intended that if he had rights under the collective agreement his claims should be adjudicated by a court rather than an arbitrator seems much more doubtful. The more serious weakness in the logic, however, is that it severs labor arbitration from its special context and cramps it into common contract molds. If the collective parties cannot by agreement prevent an individual employee from acquiring substantive rights under collective agreement, they ought not be able to bar him from the procedure which they have chosen to help give the agreement life and meaning, nor should he be free to choose another forum. This again is the pattern of the Railway Labor Act—the Adjustment Board has primary and exclusive jurisdiction over disputes arising under the collective agreement, whether brought by unions or individuals.

(c) How shall the arbitrator for individual claims be chosen? If arbitration is the proper forum, it might be argued that individual claims should come before the same arbitrator as union grievances. But this would mean that the individual would face an arbitrator named by his opponents. The more appropriate solution is an arbitrator acceptable to all three parties. If the collective agreement contemplates *ad hoc* arbitration, such tri-partite selection of the arbitrator would not affect the substance of the agreement. If the collective agreement contemplates a permanent umpire, his personal experience, attitudes and judgment may be more of the substance of the bargain. However, the individual employee, aware that the arbitrator's tenure depends on the collective parties, may have less than full confidence in his fairness, even though he may in fact be more independent than an *ad hoc* arbitrator. The umpire himself may find his judgment disturbed by doubts as to his own objectivity. A substitute for the particular case may, therefore, be necessary, and though the specially selected arbitrator is not the same person, he will bring to the case much the same attitudes, considerations and competence.[10]

Experience under the union shop amendment to the Railway Labor Act is instructive. Shortly after the passage of the amendment, a presidential emergency board recognized that appeal to the Adjustment Board was not adequate protection to an employee discharged under a union shop clause. It recommended that the individual should have the right to request arbitration and should have an equal right with the union and carrier in selecting the arbitrator. A number of unions and carriers have included provisions for such arbitration in their union shop agreements, several arbitrations have been held under these provisions, some resulting in reinstatement of improperly discharged employees.

3. *The Right of the Individual to Intervene in Arbitration.* The practical objections commonly raised to allowing an individual to demand arbitration of his grievance have little or no application when the individual seeks to intervene in arbitration initiated by the union or the employer. The collective parties' freedom to agree is not circumscribed, for the arbitration manifests their ability to agree. They are not drawn unwillingly into the procedure nor saddled with a wholly uninvited burden. At most, the costs may be increased a fraction by the addition of an intervenor. Selection of the arbitrator poses little problem, for the intervening individual will normally be bound by the collective parties' choice. Even if the policy considerations favored allowing the union to settle the employee's grievances against his will, it does not follow that the individual should be excluded from the arbitration of his unsettled grievance. He has important interests at stake—whether or not they are denominated rights—and a substantial claim to being heard.

Court decisions denying the right of the individual to intervene have most often used the sterile and unresponsive contract analysis that the arbitration clause did not make the individual a party to the arbitration, drawing no distinction between the right to compel and the right to intervene. In Bailer v. Local 470, Teamsters,[11] the court also saw practical difficulties in intervention. In September, 1957, Bailer seconded a motion that the local oppose the election of

10. The special arbitrator would normally follow relevant precedents of the umpire. However, the umpire would not feel equally bound to follow the special arbitrator's decision. The use of outside arbitrators for special cases in an umpire system is no novel device. See, *e.g.*, Ostrofsky v. United Steelworkers, 171 F. Supp. 782 (D. Md. 1959).

11. 400 Pa. 188, 161 A. 2d 343 (1960).

Hoffa as president of the international. The local president refused to put the motion to a vote and declared that the local's vote would be for Hoffa. Bailer and others then circulated a petition to the joint council asking it to order the local president to conduct the union's affairs in a democratic manner. The day that Hoffa was elected, Bailer was discharged on the grounds that he had been circulating the petition during working hours. The local submitted the case to arbitration, but denied Bailer's request to have his own counsel represent him at the arbitration. When the arbitrator upheld the discharge, Bailer claimed that the adverse decision was the result of the union's failure to represent him in good faith before the arbitrator. Said the court:

> Were each aggrieved employee permitted to be represented at an arbitration by private counsel who has the right to question witnesses and otherwise participate fully in the proceedings, the Local, as a trustee representative, would be effectively unable to perform its duty. Union officials and private counsel might well be at complete loggerheads over what witnesses to present, in what order to present them, the efficacy of cross-examination of a particular witness, or over any one of the myriad decisions that enter into the conduct of a trial proceeding.

Such reasons lose persuasiveness when confronted with the realities of modern procedural rules allowing liberal intervention and joinder of parties. In unfair labor practice proceedings before the National Labor Relations Board, employers or unions who file charges are allowed to participate fully along with the Board's counsel in prosecuting the complaint. It is a strange lack of confidence in the adaptability of informal arbitration procedure to argue that it cannot cope with such problems when the way has been shown by the courts and administrative agencies.

Intervention may be sought in three types of cases. *Bailer v. Local 470* represents the first type of case. The individual may fear that the union in presenting his claim will not make out the best possible case—either out of incompetence, indifference or malice.

Clark v. Hein-Werner Corp. represents the second type of case—the individual (or group) interest is actively opposed by the union and supported by the employer. Grievances rooted in seniority rights are commonly of this character. When the issue is the right of supervisors to seniority upon return to the production unit, management has strong interests and may be a vigorous spokesman; but when the issue is simply the order of layoff, transfers, or even promotion, management's interest may reach little beyond saving face and back pay. Employees in an organized plant ought not to be compelled to look to the employer as their defender, and they might understandably have less than full confidence in the employer as counsel. Again, practical problems of proof and the burden of a second proceeding weigh against inquiring into the question whether the employer will adequately represent the employee's interest. Much simpler and much more productive of fairness and the sense of fairness is to allow the individual or group to intervene and be heard on their own behalf.

Iroquois Beverage[12] represents the third type of case. The employer gave work to group A, the union insisted it should go to group B, and at arbitration group C sought to intervene, claiming it had seniority over both other groups. Obviously, without intervention the interests of this group will not be represented, and the arbitrator may not be fully informed of the ramifications of his decision. Theoretically, the arbitration could become multi-sided and the proceedings cumbersome, but this will in fact rarely occur, for the dispute will almost always narrow down to the two or three most plausible interpretations. The arbitration will probably never become as complicated as proceedings which courts commonly confront in litigation arising out of decedents' estates, trusts, partnerships or corporate ownership.

The right to intervene need be extended only to those directly affected by the outcome of the case.

DONNELLY v. UNITED FRUIT CO., 40 N.J. 61, 190 A.2d 825 (1963)

[A unanimous court embraced the Dunau and Summers analysis of Section 9(a), reading it into Section 301. Plaintiff Donnelly was discharged by the defendant company. The union, after inquiry, declined to invoke the formal grievance procedure and proceed to arbitration because it was persuaded that Donnelly was discharged for cause.]

He [the employee] may intervene in arbitration proceedings and obtain independent representation, if the union is acting adversely to his interests as they appear in, or derive from, the collective bargaining contract.

On the other hand, if a union at the request

---

12. Matter of Arbitration between Iroquois Beverage Corp. and International Brewery Workers, 14 Misc. 2d 290, 159 N.Y.S. 2d 256 (Sup. Ct. 1955).

of an employee prosecutes his claim of improper discharge fairly and impartially through the various steps of the grievance machinery set forth in the collective bargaining agreement, the result is binding on all parties concerned.

But what are the rights of the employee under the contract when the union declines to process the discharged employee's grievance? His livelihood, his economic life, are at stake. The function of a bargaining agreement is not only to stabilize union-management relations ; it also adjusts substantial job interests of the employees. If the protection of those employees' interests is left wholly to the unlimited discretion of the union, then in a particular situation an important part of the security the employee hoped to gain by union membership, and which on the face of the bargaining contract he appeared to have gained, might be lost without a fair opportunity to defend himself or to realize upon the benefits granted to him by the contract. And such loss would occur even though the union acted in good faith in declining to use the grievance procedure to contest the validity of his discharge from employment. Summers, *Individual Rights in Collective Agreements and Arbitration,* 37 N.Y.U.L. REV. 362, 391–95 (1962).

It is true the employee is not a nominal or formal party to a collective agreement. But the rights, duties and benefits of his employment are so created and controlled by the agreement made in his behalf by his statutory representative, the union, that for some purposes, at least, he ought to be regarded as a third-party beneficiary in substance as well as in spirit, or as possessing independent rights under section 9(a) of the Labor Management Relations Act, *supra,* which ought to be considered as part of every such contract by operation of law. In this connection, for conceptual purposes it is not amiss to revert to the common law notion of the amorphous character of an unincorporated association, such as a labor union. So considered, it lacks jural personality ; it does not exist apart from its members. A contract in its assumed business name is the agreement of all of its members. That concept of an association and its contracts has some relevance as perspective in evaluating the nature of the labor-management contract and the enforceable personal benefits which flow therefrom to the individual employee.

On the other hand, there is much persuasive force to the suggestion that unions should be left to manage their own households exclusively, so long as in acting as bargaining agent, they proceed fairly and in good faith in asserting the interests of the employees.

As has been noted above, section 9(a), in be-

stowing on the employee the right to present his grievance personally and to have it adjusted, forbids an adjustment inconsistent with the collective bargaining agreement. Although the Congressional requirement for consistency was probably concerned primarily with substance rather than procedure, nevertheless it is entirely reasonable to conclude from the legislation that the demanded consistency also contemplated vindication of the employee's substantive right though use of the grievance procedure set forth in the agreement, unless unfeasible. Sound development of the law in this area calls for adherence to the contractual mode of processing grievances by the individual employee, as well as by the union. In our judgment such a Congressional intention floods the four corners of the statute.

Moreover, requiring individual grievances to be handled through to arbitration in accordance with the agreed code of the plant not only will effectuate the Congressional purpose shown in section 9(a), but at the same time will harmonize it with the pattern of procedure commonly followed in labor-management relations. And if, perchance, in a particular case, the necessary impartiality cannot be achieved for the individual employee under the collective agreement, because of the nature or control of one or more of the steps outlined in the grievance mechanism, and the parties cannot agree upon a substitute measure, judicial inventiveness can be counted on to fill the breach. "The range of judicial inventiveness will be determined by the nature of the problem." Textile Workers Union v. Lincoln Mills, *supra,* 353 U.S., at p. 457, 77 S.Ct., at p. 918, 1 L.Ed. 2d 972. In such situation a proper court "can exercise its vast equitable powers and grant the relief which the circumstances dictate." (Cf. Cooper v. Nutley Sun Printing Co., Inc., 36 N.J. 189, 198 (1961) ; and see, Textile Workers Union v. American Thread Co., 113 F. Supp. 137, 141–142 (D.C. Mass. 1953) ; *i.e.,* such substitutionary *cy-pres* measures as will preserve, as nearly as possible, the procedure established by the collective agreement.

It seems unlikely that the position outlined herein for the protection and prosecution of individual grievances will interfere unduly with normal management-union administration of the collective employee interests. There are few businesses so entirely local that their operations do not affect interstate commerce within the contemplation of section 10 of the Labor Management Relations Act, 29 U.S.C.A. § 160 ; National Labor Relations Board v. Fainblatt, 306 U.S. 601, 59 S.Ct. 668, 83 L.Ed. 1014 (1939) ; National Labor Relations Board v. Denver Bldg. & Constr. T. Council, 341 U.S. 675, 684, 685, 71 S.Ct. 943,

949, 950, 95 L.Ed. 1284, 1293 (1951). Thus, our rule accommodates itself with what we discern to be the controlling legislative purpose *i.e.,* establishment of a uniform body of federal law in this expanding field. It leaves undisturbed the doctrine of immunity of the union from damage suits by employee members for failure or refusal to process grievances, where the failure or refusal is grounded in good faith and fair treatment toward the individual employee. At the same time, it gives necessary recognition to the federal right granted to the employee by section 9(a), but does so within the collective agreement pattern established by management and union.

In administration, the right of the individual to process his grievance must be subject to the principle espoused by this court in Jorgensen v. Pennsylvania R. R. Co., *supra.* That is, initially, for purposes of obtaining reinstatement and back pay or simply back or lost pay where reinstatement is not asked, the individual must pursue or attempt in good faith to pursue the grievance procedure set forth in the collective bargaining contract before seeking a court remedy. Belk v. Allied Aviation Service Co. of New Jersey, *supra.* If the union refuses to handle the matter for him or if it has a conflicting interest, the employee should request the employer to take up the grievance with him according to the contractually-prescribed mode, but with the employee in control of the procedural steps wherever necessary to achieve a just determination. On refusal, recourse may be had to the courts for specific performance of the agreement to process the dispute through to arbitration or, at the option of the employee, for damages suffered by him because of the employer's conduct (for example, discharge without cause) which gave rise to the grievance.

During the argument before us, questions were raised as to where the burden of costs would rest when, in order to obtain relief, an employee finds it necessary to "present" his grievance personally. If the matter is pressed to the final stage of arbitration, decision as to expenses may be left to the arbitrator. Obviously, the union should not be saddled with costs of arbitrating worthless or petty claims of disputatious employees. On the other hand, if the employee is successful and the grievance is one which in the judgment of the arbitrator should have been handled by the union, presumably, costs would follow the course fixed in the collective agreement or usually followed by custom or practice. Further, even if the employee is unsuccessful after arbitration, if his cause is colorable and presented in good faith, and in the judgment of the arbitrator refusal of the union to press it was unfair and arbitrary, he should be relieved of costs. But if he fails and has no colorable claim of a substantial nature, he must shoulder the costs. Such treatment of expenses would be consistent with the existing union-management code of the plant and would serve to integrate further the section 9(a) right of the employee with that code.

[The court held that the company did not refuse access to the grievance procedure, that the plaintiff never sought to pursue his contract remedies on his own rather than through the union, that the "union's conclusion was an independent one and there is no proof that it was induced by improper influence of the employer or by a wrongful conspiracy of union and employer" and so summary judgment for the defendants was proper.]

In Scaglione v. Yale Express System, Inc., 50 CCH Lab. Cas. ¶ 51, 133 (N.J. Sup. Ct. Ch. 1964), the union initiated arbitration on behalf of the plaintiffs who had been discharged. The plaintiffs attempted to participate in the hearings through their own attorney; the employer insisted that they had no right to do so and that only the union had access to the arbitration procedure. The court interpreted *Donnelly* as limiting the right of employees to representation in "grievance proceedings" to situations in which "there appears a conflict of interest between the employee and his union." The employers, who were willing to arbitrate as long as the union represented the plaintiffs, were upheld in their objection to arbitrating directly with the discharged employees.

D.

The Supreme Court Speaks

HUMPHREY v. MOORE
375 U.S. 335 (1964)

WHITE, J. The issue here is whether the Kentucky Court of Appeals properly enjoined implementation of the decision of a joint-employer-employee committee purporting to settle certain grievances in accordance with the terms of a collective bargaining contract. The decision of the committee determined the relative seniority rights of the employees of two companies, Dealers Transport Company of Memphis, Tennessee, and E & L Transport Company of Detroit, Michigan. We are of the opinion that the Kentucky court erred and we reverse its judgment.

Part of the business of each of these companies was the transportation of new automobiles from the assembly plant of the Ford Motor Company in Louisville, Kentucky. In the face of declining business resulting from several factors, the two companies were informed by Ford that there was room for only one of them in the Louisville operation. After considering the matter for some time, the two companies made these arrangements: E & L would sell to Dealers its "secondary" authority out of Louisville, the purchase price to be a nominal sum roughly equal to the cost of effecting the transfer of authority; E & L would also sell to Dealers its authority to serve certain points in Mississippi and Louisiana; and Dealers would sell to E & L its initial authority out of Lorain, Ohio, along with certain equipment and terminal facilities. The purpose of these arrangements was to concentrate the transportation activities of E & L in the more northerly area and those of Dealers in the southern zone. The transfers were subject to the approval of regulatory agencies.

The employees of both Dealers and E & L were represented by the same union, General Drivers, Warehousemen and Helpers, Local Union No. 89. Its president, Paul Priddy, as the result of inquiry from E & L by his assistant, understood that the transaction between the companies involved no trades, sales, or exchanges of properties but only a withdrawal by E & L at the direction of the Ford Motor Company. He consequently advised the E & L employees that their situation was precarious. When layoffs at E & L began three E & L employees filed grievances claiming that the seniority lists of

Dealers and E & L should be "sandwiched" and the E & L employees be taken on at Dealers with the seniority they had enjoyed at E & L. The grievances were placed before the local joint committee, Priddy or his assistant meanwhile advising Dealers employees that they had "nothing to worry about" since E & L employees had no contract right to transfer under these circumstances.

The collective bargaining contract involved covered a multi-employer, multi-local union unit negotiated on behalf of the employers by Automobile Transporters Labor Division and on behalf of the unions by National Truckaway and Driveaway Conference. Almost identical contracts were executed by each company in the unit and by the appropriate local union. According to Art. 4, § 1 of the contract "seniority rights for employees shall prevail" and "any controversy over the employees' standing on such lists shall be submitted to the joint grievance procedure...." Section 5 of the same article, of central significance here, was as follows:

> In the event that the Employer absorbs the business of another private, contract or common carrier, or is a party to a merger of lines, the seniority of the employees absorbed or affected thereby shall be determined by mutual agreement between the Employer and the Unions involved. Any controversy with respect to such matter shall be submitted to the joint grievance procedure.

Article 7 called for grievances to be first taken up between the employer and the local union and, if not settled, to be submitted to the local joint committee where the union and the employer were to have equal votes. Failing settlement by majority vote of the members of the local committee, the matter could be taken to the Automobile Transporters Joint Conference Committee upon which the employers and the unions in the overall bargaining unit had an equal number of representatives. Decisions of the Joint Conference Committee were to be "final and conclusive and binding upon the employer and the union, and the employees involved." However, if the Joint Conference Committee was unable to reach a decision the matter was to be submitted to arbitration as provided in the contract.

Article 7 also provided that:

> (d) It is agreed that all matters pertaining to the interpretation of any provision of this Agreement, whether requested by the Employer or the Union, must be submitted to the full Committee of the Automobile Transporters Joint Conference Committee, which Committee, after listening to testimony on both sides, shall make a decision.

Other provisions of the contract stated that it was "the intention of the parties to resolve all questions of interpretation by mutual agreement" and that the employer agreed "to be bound by all of the terms and provisions of this Agreement, and also agrees to be bound by the interpretations and enforcement of the Agreement."

The grievances of the E & L employees were submitted directly to the local joint committee and endorsed "Deadlocked to Detroit for interpretation" over the signatures of the local union president and the Dealers representative on the committee. Later, however, the local union, having been more fully advised as to the nature of the transaction between the two companies, decided to recommend to the Joint Conference Committee that the seniority lists of the two companies be dovetailed and the E & L employees be employed at Dealers with seniority rights based upon those which they had enjoyed at E & L. The three shop stewards who represented the Dealers employees before the Joint Conference Committee meeting in Detroit were so advised by the union immediately prior to the opening of the hearing. After hearing from the company, the union and the stewards representing Dealers employees, the Joint Conference Committee thereupon determined that "in accordance with Article 4 and particularly sub-sections 4 and 5" of the agreement the employees of E & L and of Dealers should "be sandwiched in on master seniority boards using the presently constituted seniority lists and the dates contained therein."

Since E & L was an older company and most of its employees had more seniority than the Dealers employees, the decision entailed the layoff of a large number of Dealers employees to provide openings for the E & L drivers.

Respondent Moore, on behalf of himself and other Dealers employees, then brought this class action in a Kentucky state court praying for an injunction against the union and the company to prevent the decision of the Joint Conference Committee from being carried out. Damages were asked in an alternative count and certain E & L employees were added as defendants by amendment to the complaint. The complaint alleged that Dealers employees had relied upon the union to represent them, that the president of Local 89, Paul Priddy, assured Dealers employees that they had nothing to worry about and that precedent in the industry provided that when a new business is taken over, its employees do not displace the original employees of the acquiring company; it further alleged that Priddy had deliberately "deadlocked" the local joint committee and that the Dealers employees learned for the first time before the Joint Conference Committee in Detroit, that Priddy favored dovetailing the seniority lists. Priddy's actions, the complaint went on, "in deceiving these plaintiffs as to his position left them without representation before the Joint Conference Committee." The decision, according to the complaint, was "contrived, planned and brought about by Paul Priddy" who "has deceived and failed completely to represent said employees" and whose "false and deceitful action" and "connivance ... with the employees of E & L" threatened the jobs of Dealers employees. The International union is said to have "conspired with and assisted the defendant, Local No. 89, and its president, Paul Priddy, in bringing about this result." The decision of the Joint Conference Committee was charged to be arbitrary and capricious, contrary to the existing practice in the industry and violative of the collective bargaining contract.

After hearing, the trial court denied a temporary and permanent injunction.[1] The Court of Appeals of the Commonwealth of Kentucky reversed and granted a permanent injunction, two judges dissenting. 356 S.W. 2d 241. In the view of that court, Art. 4, § 5 could have no application to the circumstances of this case since it came into play only if the absorbing company agreed to hire the employees of the absorbed company. The clause was said to deal with seniority, not with initial employment. Therefore, it was said, the decision of the Joint Conference Committee was not binding because the question of employing E & L drivers was not "arbitrable" at all under this section. The Court of Appeals, however, went on to hold that even if it were otherwise, the decision could not stand since the situation involved antagonistic interests of two sets of employees represented by the same union advocate. The result was inadequate representation of the Dealers employees in a context where Dealers itself was essentially neutral. Against such a backdrop, the erroneous decision of the board became "arbitrary and violative of natural justice." Kentucky cases

---

1. The denial of a temporary injunction by the trial court was set aside and temporary injunction ordered by the Court of Appeals. Thereafter the trial court dismissed the complaint, but the Court of Appeals reversed and made the temporary injunction permanent.

were cited and relied upon. We granted both the petition filed by the E & L employees in No. 17 and the petition in No. 18, filed by the local union. 371 U.S. 966, 967.

I.

Since issues concerning the jurisdiction of the courts and the governing law are involved, it is well at the outset to elaborate upon the statement of the Kentucky court that this is an action to enforce a collective bargaining contract, an accurate observation as far as we are concerned.

First, Moore challenges the power of the parties and of the Joint Conference Committee to dovetail seniority lists of the two companies because there was no absorption here within the meaning of § 5 of Art. 4 and because, as the court below held, that section granted no authority to deal with jobs as well as seniority. His position is that neither the parties nor the committee has any power beyond that delegated to them by the precise terms of § 5. Since in his view the Joint Committee exceeded its power in making the decision it did, the settlement is said to be a nullity and his impending discharge a breach of contract.

Second, Moore claims the decision of the Committee was obtained by dishonest union conduct in breach of its duty of fair representation and that a decision so obtained cannot be relied upon as a valid excuse for his discharge under the contract. The undoubted broad authority of the union as exclusive bargaining agent in the negotiation and administration of a collective bargaining contract is accompanied by a responsibility of equal scope, the responsibility and duty of fair representation. Syres v. Oil Workers Union, 350 U.S. 892, reversing 223 F. 2d 739; Brotherhood of Railroad Trainmen v. Howard, 343 U.S. 768; Tunstall v. Brotherhood of Locomotive Firemen & Enginemen, 323 U.S. 210; Steele v. Louisville & N. R. Co., 323 U.S. 192. "By its selection as bargaining representative, it has become the agent of all the employees, charged with the responsibility of representing their interests fairly and impartially." Wallace Corp. v. Labor Board, 323 U.S. 248, 255. The exclusive agent's obligation "to represent all members of an appropriate unit requires [it] to make an honest effort to serve the interests of all of those members, without hostility to any" and its powers are "subject always to complete good faith and honesty of purpose in the exercise of its discretion." Ford Motor Co. v. Huffman, 345 U.S. 330, 337–338.

In the complaint which Moore filed here, the union is said to have deceived the Dealers employees concerning their job and seniority rights, deceitfully connived with the E & L drivers and with the International union to deprive Moore and others of their employment rights and prevented the latter from having a fair hearing before the Joint Committee by espousing the cause of the rival group of drivers after having indicated that the interests of the men at Dealers would be protected by the union. These allegations are sufficient to charge a breach of duty by the union in the process of settling the grievances at issue under the collective bargaining agreement.

Both the local and international unions are charged with dishonesty, and one-half of the votes on the Joint Committee were cast by representatives of unions affiliated with the international. No fraud is charged against the employer; but except for the improper action of the union, which is said to have dominated and brought about the decision, it is alleged that Dealers would have agreed to retain its own employees. The fair inference from the complaint is that the employer considered the dispute a matter for the union to decide. Moreover, the award had not been implemented at the time of the filing of the complaint, which put Dealers on notice that the union was charged with dishonesty and a breach of duty in procuring the decision of the Joint Committee. In these circumstances, the allegations of the complaint, if proved, would effectively undermine the decision of the Joint Committee as a valid basis for Moore's discharge.[2]

For these reasons this action is one arising under § 301 of the Labor Management Relations Act and is a case controlled by federal law, Textile Workers Union v. Lincoln Mills, 353 U.S. 448, even though brought in the state court. Local 174, Teamsters v. Lucas Flour Co., 369 U.S. 95; Smith v. Evening News Assn., 371 U.S. 195. Although there are differing views on whether a violation of the duty of fair representation is an unfair labor practice under the Labor Management Relations Act, it is not necessary for us to resolve that difference here. Even if it is, or arguably may be, an unfair labor practice, the complaint here alleged that Moore's discharge would violate the contract and was therefore within the cognizance of federal and state courts, Smith v. Evening News Assn., *supra*, subject, of course, to the applicable federal law.

We now come to the merits of this case.

---

2. In its brief filed here Dealers does not support the decision of the Joint Committee. It suggests, rather, that the matter be finally settled by arbitration under the terms of the contract.

If we assume with Moore and the courts below that the Joint Conference Committee's power was circumscribed by § 5 and that its interpretation of the section is open to court review, Moore's cause is not measurably advanced. For in our opinion the section reasonably meant what the Joint Committee said or assumed it meant. There was an absorption here within the meaning of the section and that section did deal with jobs as well as with seniority.[3]

Prior to this transaction both E & L and Dealers were transporting new cars out of Louisville for the Ford Motor Company. Afterwards, only one company enjoyed this business, and clearly this was no unilateral withdrawal by E & L. There was an agreement between the companies, preceded by long negotiation. E & L's authority to engage in the transportation of new cars out of Louisville was sold to Dealers. The business which E & L had done in that city was henceforth to be done by Dealers. While there was no sale of tangible assets at that location, the Joint Conference Committee reasonably concluded that there was an absorption by Dealers of the E & L business within the meaning of § 5 of the contract.

It was also permissible to conclude that § 5 dealt with employment as well as seniority. Mergers, sales of assets and absorptions are commonplace events. It is not unusual for collective bargaining agreements to deal with them, especially in the transportation industry where the same unions may represent the employees of both parties to the transaction. Following any of such events, the business of the one company will probably include the former business of the other; and the recurring question is whether it is the employees of the absorbed company or those of the acquiring company who are to have first call upon the available work at the latter concern. Jobs, as well as seniority, are at stake; and it was to solve just such problems that § 5 was designed. Its interpretation should be commensurate with its purposes.

---

3. We also put aside the union's contention that Art. 7, § (d)—providing that all matters of interpretation of the agreement be submitted to the Joint Conference Committee —makes it inescapably clear that the committee had the power to decide that the transfer of operating authority was an absorption within the scope of § 5. But it is by no means clear that this provision in Art. 7 was intended to apply to interpretations of § 5, for the latter section by its own terms appears to limit the authority of the committee to disputes over seniority in the event of an absorption. Reconciliation of these two provisions, going to the power of the committee under the contract, itself presented an issue ultimately for the court, not the committee, to decide. Our view of the scope and applicability of § 5, *infra*, renders an accommodation of these two sections unnecessary.

Seniority has become of overriding importance, and one of its major functions is to determine who gets or who keeps an available job. Here § 5 provided for resolving the seniority of not only those employees who are "absorbed," but all who were "affected" by the absorption. Certainly the transaction "affected" the E & L employees; and the seniority of these drivers, which the parties or the Joint Conference Committee could determine, was clearly seniority at Dealers, the company which had absorbed the E & L business. The parties very probably, therefore, intended the seniority granted an E & L employee at Dealers to carry the job with it, just as seniority usually would. If it did not and if Dealers unilaterally could determine whether to hire any E & L employee, it might decide to hire none, excluding E & L employees from any of the work which they had formerly done. Or if it did hire E & L employees to fill any additional jobs resulting from the absorption of the E & L business, it might select E & L employees for jobs without regard to length of service at E & L or it might insist on an agreement from the union to grant only such seniority as might suit the company. Section 5 would be effectively emasculated.

The power of the Joint Conference Committee over seniority gave it power over jobs. It was entitled under § 5 to integrate the seniority lists upon some rational basis, and its decision to integrate lists upon the basis of length of service at either company was neither unique nor arbitrary. On the contrary, it is a familiar and frequently equitable solution to the inevitably conflicting interests which arise in the wake of a merger or an absorption such as occurred here. The Joint Conference Committee's decision to dovetail seniority lists was a decision which § 5 empowered the committee to make.

Neither do we find adequate support in this record for the complaint's attack upon the integrity of the union and of the procedures which led to the decision. Although the union at first advised the Dealers drivers that they had nothing to worry about but later supported the E & L employees before the Joint Conference Committee, there is no substantial evidence of fraud, deceitful action or dishonest conduct. Priddy's early assurances to Dealers employees were not well founded, it is true; but Priddy was acting upon information then available to him, information received from the company which led him to think there was no trade or exchange involved, no "absorption" which might bring § 5 into play. Other sections of the contract, he thought, would protect the jobs of Moore and his fellow drivers. Consistent with this view, he also advised E & L employees that the situation appeared unfavorable for them. However, when he learned of the pending acquisition by Dealers of E & L operating authority in Louisville and of the involvement of other locations in the transaction, he considered the matter to be one for the Joint Committee. Ultimately he took the view that an absorption was involved, that § 5 did apply and that dovetailing seniority lists was the most equitable solution for all concerned. We find in this evidence insufficient proof of dishonesty or intentional misleading on the part of the union. And we do not understand the court below to have found otherwise.

The Kentucky court, however, made much of the antagonistic interests of the E & L and Dealers drivers, both groups being represented by the same union, whose president supported one group and opposed the other at the hearing before the Joint Conference Committee. But we are not ready to find a breach of the collective bargaining agent's duty of fair representation in taking a good faith position contrary to that of some individuals whom it represents nor in supporting the position of one group of employees against that of another. In Ford Motor Co. v. Huffman, 345 U.S. 330, the Court found no breach of duty by the union in agreeing to an amendment of an existing collective bargaining contract, granting enhanced seniority to a particular group of employees and resulting in layoffs which otherwise would not have occurred.

> Inevitably differences arise in the manner and degree to which the terms of any negotiated agreement affect individual employees and classes of employees. The mere existence of such differences does not make them invalid. The complete satisfaction of all who are represented is hardly to be expected. A wide range of reasonableness must be allowed a statutory bargaining representative in serving the unit it represents, subject always to complete good faith and honesty of purpose in the exercise of its discretion.

Id., at 338. Just as a union must be free to sift out wholly frivolous grievances which would only clog the grievance process, so it must be free to take a position on the not so frivolous disputes. Nor should it be neutralized when the issue is chiefly between two sets of employees. Conflict between employees represented by the same union is a recurring fact. To remove or gag the union in these cases would surely weaken the collective bargaining and grievance processes.

As far as this record shows, the union took its position honestly, in good faith and without hostility or arbitrary discrimination. After Dealers absorbed the Louisville business of E & L, there were fewer jobs at Dealers than there were Dealers and E & L drivers. One group or the other was going to suffer. If any E & L drivers were to be hired at Dealers either they or the Dealers drivers would not have the seniority which they had previously enjoyed. Inevitably the absorption would hurt someone. By choosing to integrate seniority lists based upon length of service at either company, the union acted upon wholly relevant considerations, not upon capricious or arbitrary factors. The evidence shows no breach by the union of its duty of fair representation.

There is a remaining contention. Even though the union acted in good faith and was entitled to take the position it did, were the Dealers employees, if the union was going to oppose them, deprived of a fair hearing by having inadequate representation at the hearing? Dealers employees had notice of the hearing; they were obviously aware that they were locked in a struggle for jobs and seniority with the E & L drivers, and three stewards representing them went to the hearing at union expense and were given every opportunity to state their position. Thus the issue is in reality a narrow one. There was no substantial dispute about the facts concerning the nature of the transaction between the two companies. It was for the Joint Conference Committee initially to decide whether there was an "absorption" within the meaning of § 5 and, if so, whether seniority lists were to be integrated and the older employees of E & L given jobs at Dealers. The Dealers employees made no request to continue the hearing until they could secure further representation and have not yet suggested what they could have added to the hearing by way of facts or theory if they had been differently represented. The trial court found it "idle speculation to assume that the result would have been different had the matter been differently presented." We agree.

Moore has not, therefore, proved his case. Neither the parties nor the Joint Committee exceeded their power under the contract and there was no fraud or breach of duty by the exclusive bargaining agent. The decision of the committee, reached after proceedings adequate under the agreement, is final and binding upon the parties, just as the contract says it is. Drivers Union v. Riss & Co., 372 U.S. 517.

The decision below is reversed and the cases are remanded for further proceedings not inconsistent with this opinion.

It is so ordered.

DOUGLAS, J. (concurring). I agree for the reasons stated by my Brother GOLDBERG that this litigation was properly brought in the state court but on the merits I believe that no cause of action has been made out for the reasons stated by the Court.

GOLDBERG, J., joined by BRENNAN, J. (concurring). I concur in the judgment and in the holding of the Court that since "Moore has not ... proved his case," the decision below must be reversed. *Supra.* I do not, however, agree that Moore stated a cause of action arising under § 301 (a) of the Labor Management Relations Act, 61 Stat. 156, 29 U.S.C. § 185 (a). It is my view rather that Moore's claim must be treated as an individual employee's action for a union's breach of its duty of fair representation—a duty derived not from the collective bargaining contract but from the National Labor Relations Act, as amended, 61 Stat. 136, 29 U.S.C. § 141 *et seq.* See Syres v. Oil Workers Int'l Union, 350 U.S. 892, reversing 223 F. 2d 739 ; Brotherhood of Railroad Trainmen v. Howard, 343 U.S. 768 ; Tunstall v. Brotherhood of Locomotive Firemen & Enginemen, 323 U.S. 210 ; Steele v. Louisville & N. R. Co., 323 U.S. 192. Cf. International Association of Machinists v. Central Airlines, Inc., 372 U.S. 682.

The complaint does not expressly refer either to § 301 (a) of the Labor Management Relations Act or to the National Labor Relations Act as the source of the action. Since substance and not form must govern, however, we look to the allegations of the complaint and to the federal labor statutes to determine the nature of the claim.

The opinion of the Court correctly describes Moore's complaint as alleging that the decision of the Joint Conference Committee dovetailing the seniority lists of the two companies violated Moore's rights because: (1) the Joint Committee exceeded its powers under the existing collective bargaining contract in making its decision dovetailing seniority lists, and (2) the decision of the Committee was brought about by dishonest union conduct in breach of its duty of fair representation.

Neither ground, it seems to me, sustains an action under § 301(a) of the L.M.R.A. A mutually acceptable grievance settlement between an employer and a union, which is what the decision of the Joint Committee was, cannot be challenged by an individual dissenting employee under § 301 (a) on the ground that the parties exceeded their contractual powers in making the settlement. It is true that this Court, in a series of decisions dealing with labor arbitrations, has recognized that the powers of an arbitrator arise from and are defined by the collective bargaining agreement. "For arbitra-

tion," as the Court said in United Steelworkers of America v. Warrior & Gulf Navigation Co., 363 U.S. 574, 582, "is a matter of contract and a party cannot be required to submit to arbitration any dispute which he has not agreed so to submit." Thus the existing labor contract is the touchstone of an arbitrator's powers. But the power of the union and the employer jointly to settle a grievance dispute is not so limited. The parties are free by joint action to modify, amend, and supplement their original collective bargaining agreement. They are equally free, since "[t]he grievance procedure is ... a part of the continuous collective bargaining process," to settle grievances not falling within the scope of the contract. *Id.,* at 581. In this case, for example, had the dispute gone to arbitration, the arbitrator would have been bound to apply the existing agreement and to determine whether the merger-absorption clause applied. However, even in the absence of such a clause, the contracting parties—the multiemployer unit and the union—were free to resolve the dispute by amending the contract to dovetail seniority lists or to achieve the same result by entering into a grievance settlement. The presence of the merger-absorption clause did not restrict the right of the parties to resolve their dispute by joint agreement applying, interpreting, or amending the contract. There are too many unforeseeable contingencies in a collective bargaining relationship to justify making the words of the contract the exclusive source of rights and duties.

These principles were applied in Ford Motor Co. v. Huffman, 345 U.S. 330. There the union and the employer during a collective bargaining agreement entered into a "supplementary agreement" providing seniority credit for the preemployment military service of veterans, a type of seniority credit not granted in the original agreement. *Id.,* at 334, n. 6. Huffman, on behalf of himself and other union members whose seniority was adversely affected, brought suit to have the supplementary provisions declared invalid and to obtain appropriate injunctive relief against the employer and the union. There was no doubt that Huffman and members of his class were injured as a result of the "supplementary agreement" ; they were subjected to layoffs that would not have affected them if the seniority rankings had not been altered. Despite the change in rights under the prior agreement, this Court held that the existing labor agreement did not limit the power of the parties jointly, in the process of bargaining collectively, to make new and different contractual arrangements affecting seniority rights.

It necessarily follows from *Huffman* that a

settlement of a seniority dispute, deemed by the parties to be an interpretation of their agreement, not requiring an amendment, is plainly within their joint authority. Just as under the *Huffman* decision an amendment is not to be tested by whether it is within the existing contract, so a grievance settlement should not be tested by whether a court could agree with the parties' interpretation. If collective bargaining is to remain a flexible process, the power to amend by agreement and the power to interpret by agreement must be coequal.

It is wholly inconsistent with this Court's recognition that "[t]he grievance procedure is . . . a part of the continuous collective bargaining process," United Steelworkers of America v. Warrior & Gulf Navigation Co., 363 U.S., at 581, to limit the parties' power to settle grievances to the confines of the existing labor agreement, or to assert, as the Court now does, that an individual employee can claim that the collective bargaining contract is violated because the parties have made a grievance settlement going beyond the strict terms of the existing contract.

I turn now to the second basis of the complaint, *viz.,* that the decision of the Joint Conference Committee was brought about by dishonest union conduct in breach of its duty of fair representation. In my view, such a claim of breach of the union's duty of fair representation cannot properly be treated as a claim of breach of the collective bargaining contract supporting an action under § 301 (a). This is particularly apparent where, as here, "[n]o fraud is charged against the employer." *Ante,* at 343.

This does not mean that an individual employee is without a remedy for a union's breach of its duty of fair representation. I read the decisions of this Court to hold that an individual employee has a right to a remedy against a union breaching its duty of fair representation —a duty derived not from the collective bargaining contract but implied from the union's rights and responsibilities conferred by federal labor statutes. See Syres v. Oil Workers Int'l Union, *supra* (National Labor Relations Act); Brotherhood of Railroad Trainmen v. Howard, *supra* (Railway Labor Act); Tunstall v. Brotherhood of Locomotive Firemen & Enginemen, *supra* (Railway Labor Act); Steele v. Louisville & N. R. Co., *supra* (Railway Labor Act). Cf. International Association of Machinists v. Central Airlines, Inc., *supra* (Railway Labor Act). There is nothing to the contrary in Smith v. Evening News Assn., 371 U.S. 195. In that case the gravamen of the individual employee's § 301 (a) action was the employer's discharge of employees in violation of the express terms of the collective bargaining agreement. No breach of the union's duty of fair representation was charged. To the contrary, the union supported the employee's suit which was brought as an individual suit out of obeisance to what the union deemed to be the requirements of Association of Westinghouse Salaried Employees v. Westinghouse Electric Corp., 348 U.S. 437.

The remedy in a suit based upon a breach of the union's duty of fair representation may be extended to the employer under appropriate circumstances. This was recognized in Steele v. Louisville & N. R. Co., *supra,* where the Court extended the remedy against the union to include injunctive relief against a contract between the employer and the union. There the employer willfully participated in the union's breach of its duty of fair representation and that breach arose from discrimination based on race, a classification that was held "irrelevant" to a union's statutory bargaining powers. The Court observed:

> [I]t is enough for present purposes to say that the statutory power to represent a craft and to make contracts as to wages, hours and working conditions does not include the authority to make among members of the craft discriminations not based on . . . relevant differences. *Id.,* at 203.

The Court distinguished classifications and differences which are "relevant to the authorized purposes of the contract . . . such as differences in seniority, the type of work performed, [and] the competence and skill with which it is performed," *Ibid.* Where the alleged breach of a union's duty involves a differentiation based on a relevant classification—in this case seniority rankings following an amalgamation of employer units—and where the employer has not willfully participated in the alleged breach of the union's duty, the collective bargaining agreement should not be open to the collateral attack of an individual employee merely because the union alone has failed in its duty of fair representation. We should not and, indeed, we need not strain, therefore, as the Court does, to convert a breach of the union's duty to individual employees into a breach of the collective bargaining agreement between the employer and the union.

I do not agree with the Court that employer willfulness was claimed in this case by "[t]he fair inference from the complaint" that Dealers "considered the dispute a matter for the union to decide." *Ante,* at 343. Nor can I agree that willfulness could be predicated on the rationale that since "the award had not been implemented at the time of the filing of the complaint,"

Dealers was "put...on notice that the union was charged with dishonesty and a breach of duty in procuring the decision of the Joint Committee." *Ibid*. Dealers may indeed have been neutral when the case was presented to the Joint Conference Committee but the Court overlooks that the employer-party to the collective bargaining contract was the multiemployer unit whose representatives—acting on behalf of both Dealers and E & L—fully participated in the Joint Committee's decision resolving the dispute. Furthermore, an employer not willfully participating in union misconduct should not be restrained from putting a grievance settlement into effect merely by being "put ... on notice" that an individual employee has charged the union with disonesty. Such a rule would penalize the honest employer and encourage groundless charges frustrating joint grievance settlements. Finally, it is difficult to conceive how mere notice to an employer of union dishonesty can transform the union's breach of its duty of fair representation into a contractual violation by the employer.

In summary, then, for the reasons stated, I would treat Moore's claim as a *Syres-Steele* type cause of action rather than as a § 301 (a) contract action. So considering it, I nevertheless conclude, as the Court does, that since "there was no fraud or breach of duty by the exclusive bargaining agent," *ante*, at 351, Moore is not entitled to the relief sought.

I have written at some length on what may seem a narrow point. I have done so because of my conviction that in this Court's fashioning of a federal law of collective bargaining, it is of the utmost importance that the law reflect the realities of industrial life and the nature of the collective bargaining process. We should not assume that doctrines evolved in other contexts will be equally well adapted to the collective bargaining process. Of course, we must protect the rights of the individual. It must not be forgotten, however, that many individual rights, such as the seniority rights involved in this case, in fact arise from the concerted exercise of the right to bargain collectively. Consequently, the understandable desire to protect the individual should not emasculate the right to bargain by placing undue restraints upon the contracting parties. Similarly, in safeguarding the individual against the misconduct of the bargaining agent, we must recognize that the employer's interests are inevitably involved whenever the labor contract is set aside in order to vindicate the individual's right against the union. The employer's interest should not be lightly denied where there are other remedies available to insure that a union will respect the rights of its constitutents. Nor should trial-type hearing standards or conceptions of vested contractual rights be applied so as to hinder the employer and the union in their joint endeavor to adapt the collective bargaining relationship to the exigencies of economic life. I have deemed it necessary to state my views separately because I believe that the Court's analysis in part runs contrary to these principles.

HARLAN, J., (concurring in part and dissenting in part). I agree with the Court's opinion and judgment insofar as it relates to the claim that the Joint Conference Committee exceeded its authority under the collective bargaining agreement. Although it is undoubtedly true as a general proposition that bargaining representatives have power to alter the terms of a contract with an employer, the challenge here is not to a purported exercise of such power but to the validity of a grievance settlement reached under proceedings allegedly not authorized by the terms of the collective agreement. Moreover, a committee with authority to settle grievances whose composition is different from that in the multiunion-multiemployer bargaining unit cannot be deemed to possess power to effect changes in the bargaining agreement. When it is alleged that the union itself has engaged or acquiesced in such a departure from the collective bargaining agreement, I can see no reason why an individually affected employee may not step into the shoes of the union and maintain a § 301 suit himself.

But insofar as petitioners' claim rests upon alleged unfair union representation in the grievance proceeding, I agree with the views expressed in the concurring opinion of my Brother GOLDBERG (*ante,* 355–358) (except that I would expressly reserve the question of whether a suit of this nature would be maintainable under § 301 where it is alleged or proved that the employer was a party to the asserted unfair union representation). However, the conclusion that unilateral unfair union representation gives rise only to a cause of action for violation of a duty implicit in the National Labor Relations Act brings one face-to-face with a further question: Does such a federal cause of action come within the play of the preemption doctrine, San Diego Trades Council v. Garmon, 359 U.S. 236, contrary to what would be the case were such a suit to lie under § 301, Smith v. Evening News Assn., 371 U.S. 195? Short of deciding that question, I do not think it would be appropriate to dispose of this case simply by saying that no unfair union representation was shown in this instance. For if there be preemption in this situation, *Garmon* would not only preclude state court jurisdiction but would also require this Court initially to defer to the primary jurisdiction of the Labor Board.

The preemption issue is a difficult and important one, carrying ramifications extending far beyond this particular case. It should not be decided without our having the benefit of the views of those charged with the administration of the labor laws. To that end I would reverse the judgment of the state court to the extent that it rests upon a holding that the Joint Conference Committee acted beyond the scope of its authority, set the case for reargument on the unfair representation issue, and invite the National Labor Relations Board to present its views by brief and oral argument on the preemption question. Cf. Retail Clerks International Assn. v. Schermerhorn, 373 U.S. 746, 757; 375 U.S. 96.

The third circuit court of appeals agreed with a district court that an individual has standing to bring suit for breach of the duty of fair representation (for failure to prosecute plaintiff's grievance against the company's alleged breach of the seniority provisions of the collective agreement) and a § 301 count alleging that the company and union conspired to discharge him in violation of the agreement. The court did no more than cite Smith v. Evening News and Humphrey v. Moore. Falsetti v. Local 2026, United Mine Workers, 355 F. 2d 658 (3rd Cir. 1966).

In Simmons v. Union News Co., 341 F. 2d 531 (6th Cir.) cert. denied, 382 U.S. 884 (1965), the court of appeals reaffirmed the views it held in *Hildreth*; citing *Humphrey v. Moore,* the court said that applying federal law made no difference. Mr. Justice Black, in a dissent joined by Chief Justice Warren, expressed the fear that the denial of certiorari in this case and *Hildreth* would be taken to mean that the court approved "forfeiture of contractual claims of individual employees" by union-management agreement. He declared that he could not construe the National Labor Relations Act as giving a union and an employer "any such power over members." He expressed the belief that

Maddox preserved the right of an employee to sue

> if his union refused to press his grievance . . . If the construction of the labor law given by the courts below is to stand, it should be clearly and unequivocally announced by this court so that Congress can, if it sees fit, consider this question and protect the just claims of employees from the joint power of employers and unions.

REPUBLIC STEEL CORP v. MADDOX
379 U.S. 650 (1965)

HARLAN, J. Respondent Maddox brought suit in an Alabama state court against his employer, the Republic Steel Corporation, for severance pay amounting to $694.08, allegedly owed him under the terms of the collective bargaining agreement existing between Republic and Maddox's union. Maddox had been laid off in December 1953. The collective bargaining agreement called for severance pay if the layoff was the result of a decision to close the mine, at which Maddox worked, "permanently."[1] The agreement also contained a three-step grievance procedure to be followed by binding arbitration, but Maddox made no effort to utilize this mode of redress. Instead, in August 1956, he sued for breach of the contract. At all times material to his claim. Republic was engaged in interstate commerce within the meaning of the Labor Management Relations Act, and Republic's industrial relations with Maddox and his union were subject to the provisions of that Act.

The case was tried on stipulated facts without a jury. Judgment was awarded in favor of Maddox, and the appellate courts of Alabama affirmed on the theory that state law applies to suits for severance pay since, with the employment relationship necessarily ended, no further danger of industrial strife exists warranting the application of federal labor law. Moore v. Illinois Central R. Co., 312 U.S. 630 (1941), and Transcontinental & Western Air, Inc. v. Koppal,

---

1. The section of the contract dealing with severance allowance provided in relevant part:

"When, in the sole judgment of the Company, it decides to close permanently a plant or discontinue permanently a department of a mine or plant, or substantial portion thereof and terminate the employment of individuals, an Employee whose employment is terminated either directly as a result thereof because he was not entitled to other employment with the Company under the provisions of Section 9 of this Agreement—Seniority and Subsection C of this Section 14, shall be entitled to a severance allowance in accordance with and subject to the provisions hereinafter set forth in this Section 14."

345 U.S. 653 (1953), cases decided under the Railway Labor Act, were cited to support the proposition. Furthermore, it was held that under Alabama law Maddox was not required to exhaust the contract grievance procedures. We granted Republic's petition for certiorari, 377 U.S. 904, to determine whether the rationale of Moore v. Illinois Central R. Co. carries over to a suit for severance pay on a contract subject to § 301 (a) of the Labor Management Relations Act. We conclude that the state judgment must be reversed.

I.

As a general rule in cases to which federal law applies, federal labor policy requires that individual employees wishing to assert contract grievances must *attempt* use of the contract grievance procedure agreed upon by employer and union as the mode of redress.[2] If the union refuses to press or only perfunctorily presses the individual's claim, differences may arise as to the forms of redress then available. See Humphrey v. Moore, 375 U.S. 335; Labor Board v. Miranda Fuel Co., 326 F. 2d 172. But unless the contract provides otherwise, there can be no doubt that the employee must afford the union the opportunity to act on his behalf. Congress has expressly approved contract grievance procedures as a preferred method for settling disputes and stabilizing the "common law" of the plant. LMRA § 203 (d), 9 U.S.C. § 173 (d); § 201 (c), 29 U.S.C. § 171 (c) (1958 ed.) Union interest in prosecuting employee grievances is clear. Such activity complements the union's status as exclusive bargaining representative by permitting it to participate actively in the continuing administration of the contract. In addition, conscientious handling of grievance claims will enhance the union's prestige with employees. Employer interests, for their part, are served by limiting the choice of remedies available to aggrieved employees. And it cannot be said, in the normal situation, that contract grievance procedures are inadequate to protect the interests of an aggrieved employee until the employee has attempted to implement the procedures and found them so.

A contrary rule which would permit an individual employee to completely sidestep available grievance procedures in favor of a lawsuit has little to commend it. In addition to cutting across the interests already mentioned, it would deprive employer and union of the ability to establish a uniform and exclusive method for orderly settlement of employee grievances. If a grievance procedure cannot be made exclusive, it loses much of its desirability as a method of settlement. A rule creating such a situation "would inevitably exert a disruptive influence upon both the negotiation and administration of collective agreements." Teamsters Local v. Lucas Flour Co., 369 U.S. 95, 103.

II.

Once it is established that the federal rule discussed above applies to grievances in general, it should next be inquired whether the specific type of grievance here in question—one relating to severance pay—is so different in kind as to justify an exception. Moore v. Illinois Central R. Co., and Transcontinental & Western Air, Inc. v. Koppal, *supra*, are put forward for the proposition that it is.

In *Moore,* the Court ruled that a trainman was not required by the Railway Labor Act to exhaust the administrative remedies granted him by the Act before bringing suit for wrongful discharge. Mr. Justice Black, for the Court, based the decision on the use of permissive language in the Act—disputes "may be referred ... to the ... Adjustment Board." Mr. Justice Black wrote again in Slocum v. Delaware, L. & W. R. Co. 339 U.S. 239 (1950), a declaratory judgment suit brought in a state court by a railroad company against two unions to resolve a representation dispute. The Court held that jurisdiction of the Adjustment Board to resolve such disputes was exclusive. *Moore* was distinguished thus:

> Moore was discharged by the railroad. He could have challenged the validity of his discharge before the Board, seeking reinstatement and back pay. Instead he chose to accept the railroad's action in discharging him as final, thereby ceasing to be an employee, and brought suit claiming damages for breach of contract. As we there held, the Railway Labor Act does not bar courts from adjudicating such cases. A common-law or statutory action for wrongful discharge differs from any remedy which the Board has power to provide, and does not involve questions of future relations between the railroad and its other employees. 339 U.S. 239, at 244.

---

2. Smith v. Evening News Assn., 371 U.S. 195, 196, n. 1 (by implication); Belk v. Allied Aviation Service Co., 315 F. 2d 513, cert. denied, 375 U.S. 847; see Cox, *Rights Under a Labor Agreement*, 69 HARV. L. REV. 601, 647–648 (1956). The proviso of § 9 (a) of the National Labor Relations Act, as amended, 29 U.S.C. § 159 (a) (1958 ed.), is not *contra;* Black-Clawson Co. v. Machinists, 313 F. 2d 179.

This distinction was confirmed in Transcontinental & Western Air, Inc. v. Koppal, *supra*:

> Such [a wrongfully discharged] employee may proceed either in accordance with the administrative procedures prescribed in his employment contract or he may resort to his action at law for alleged unlawful discharge if the state courts recognize such a claim. Where the applicable law permits his recovery of damages without showing his prior exhaustion of his administrative remedies, he may so recover, as he did in the *Moore* litigation, *supra*, under Mississippi law. 345 U.S. 653, at 661.

Federal jurisdiction in both *Moore* and *Koppal* was based on diversity; federal law was not thought to apply merely by reason of the fact that the collective bargaining agreements were subject to the Railway Labor Act. Since that time the Court has made it clear that substantive federal law applies to suits on collective bargaining agreements covered by § 204 of the Railway Labor Act, International Assn. of Machinists v. Central Airlines, Inc., 372 U.S. 682, and by § 301 (a) of the LMRA, Textile Workers v. Lincoln Mills, 353 U.S. 448. Thus a major underpinning for the continued validity of the *Moore* case in the field of the Railway Labor Act, and more importantly in the present context, for the extension of its rationale to suits under § 301 (a) of the LMRA, has been removed.

We hold that any such extension is incompatible with the precepts of *Lincoln Mills* and cannot be accepted. Grievances depending on severance claims are not critically unlike other types of grievances. Although it is true that the employee asserting the claim will necessarily have accepted his discharge as final, it does not follow that the resolution of his claim can have no effect on future relations between the employer and other employees. Severance pay and other contract terms governing discharge are of obvious concern to all employees, and a potential cause of dispute so long as any employee maintains a continuing employment relationship. Only in the situation in which no employees represented by the union remain employed, as would be the case with a final and permanent plant shutdown, is there no possibility of a work stoppage resulting from a severance-pay claim. But even in that narrow situation, if applicable law did not require resort to contract procedures, the inability of the union and employer at the contract negotiation stage to agree upon arbitration as the exclusive method of handling permanent shutdown severance claims in all situations could have an inhibiting effect on reaching an agreement. If applicable law permitted a court suit for severance pay in any circumstances without prior recourse to available contract remedies, an employer seeking to limit the modes of redress that could be used against him could do so only by eliminating contract grievance procedures for severance-pay claims. The union would hardly favor the elimination, for it is in the union's interest to afford comprehensive protection to those it represents, to participate in interpretations of the contract, and to have an arbitrator rather than a court decide such questions as whether the company has determined to "close permanently."

There are, then, positive reasons why the general federal rule should govern grievances based on severance claims as it does others. Furthermore, no positive reasons appear why the general federal rule should not apply. "Comprehensiveness is inherent in the process by which the law is to be formulated under the mandate of *Lincoln Mills*," and "the subject matter of § 301 (a) 'is peculiarly one that calls for uniform law.'" Teamsters Local v. Lucas Flour Co., 369 U.S., at 103. Maddox' suit in the present case is simply on the contract, and the remedy sought, award of $694.08, did not differ from any that the grievance procedure had power to provide. Federal law governs "Suits for violation of contracts between an employer and a labor organization representing employees in an industry affecting commerce as defined in this chapter." Section 301 (a) of the LMRA, 29 U.S.C. § 185 (a) (1958 ed.), Textile Workers v. Lincoln Mills, *supra*. The suit by Maddox clearly falls within the terms of the statute and within the principles of *Lincoln Mills*, and because we see no reason for creating an exception, we conclude that the general federal rule applies.[3]

III.

The federal rule would not of course preclude Maddox' court suit if the parties to the collective bargaining agreement expressly agreed that arbitration was not the exclusive remedy. The section of this contract governing grievances provides, *inter alia*:

> It is the purpose of this Section to provide procedure for prompt, equitable adjustment of claimed grievances. It is understood and agreed that unless

---

3. By refusing to extend Moore v. Illinois Central R. Co. to § 301 suits, we do not mean to overrule it within the field of the Railway Labor Act. Consideration of such action should properly await a case presented under the Railway Labor Act in which the various distinctive features of the administrative remedies provided by that Act can be appraised in context, *e.g.*, the make-up of the Adjustment Board, the scope of review from monetary awards, and the ability of the Board to give the same remedies as could be obtained by court suit.

otherwise specifically specified elsewhere in this Agreement grievances to be considered hereunder must be filed within thirty days after the date on which the fact or events upon which such alleged grievance is based shall have existed or occurred.

Any Employee who has a complaint may discuss the alleged complaint with his Foreman in an attempt to settle it. Any complaint not so settled shall constitute a grievance within the meaning of this Section. "Adjustment of Grievances."
 Grievances shall be handled in the following manner:
 STEP 1. Between the aggrieved Employee, his Grievance Committeeman or Assistant Grievance Committeeman and the Foreman.

The procedure calls for two more grievance-committee steps capped with binding arbitration of matters not satisfactorily settled by the initial steps.

The language stating that an employee "may discuss" a complaint with his foreman is susceptible to various interpretations; the most likely is that an employee may, if he chooses, speak to his foreman himself without bringing in his grievance committeeman and formally embarking on Step 1. Use of the permissive "may" does not of itself reveal a clear understanding between the contracting parties that individual employees, unlike either the union or the employer, are free to avoid the contract procedure and its time limitations in favor of a judicial suit. Any doubts must be resolved against such an interpretation. See United Steelworkers v. Warrior & Gulf Navigation Co., 363 U.S. 574; Belk v. Allied Aviation Service Co., 315 F. 2d 513, cert. denied, 375 U.S. 847.

Finally, Maddox suggests that it was not possible for him to make use of the grievance procedure, the first step of which called for a discussion within 30 days of his discharge with his foreman, because a mine that has permanently closed has no foreman—indeed, no employees of any kind. This casuistic reading of the contract cannot be accepted. The foreman did not vanish; and it is unlikely that the union grievance procedure broke down within 30 days of Maddox' discharge. In any event, the case is before us on stipulated facts; in neither the facts nor the pleadings is there any suggestion that Maddox could not have availed himself of the grievance procedure instead of waiting nearly three years and bringing a court suit.

Reversed.

BLACK, J. (dissenting). This is an ordinary, common, run-of-the-mill lawsuit for breach of contract brought by respondent Charlie Maddox an iron miner employed by petitioner Republic Steel, to recover $694.08 of wages which he said the company owed him. This amount he said was due by the terms of a contract made between the company and the union representing workers at the mine at which Maddox worked, a contract which provided that if any employee should be discharged because the company "permanently" closed the mine, he should continue to be paid the amount of his regular wages for a number of weeks after the discharge. The mine closed down, Maddox lost his job, but the company nevertheless refused to continue to pay him the wages he said it had obligated itself to pay under the contract. To collect the money he hired a lawyer and went to court. The trial court in Alabama awarded him the $694.08 (the stipulated amount due, if any) and the Supreme Court of the State affirmed. This Court now reverses. It holds that because the contract, agreed to by the union, provided for binding arbitration of all "grievances," federal law has deprived Maddox of his right to hire his own lawyer and to sue in a court of law for the balance of wages due, and has instead left him with only the remedies set out in the contract: a long, involved grievance procedure, controlled by the company and the union, followed by compulsory arbitration, with his claim put in the hands of union officials and union lawyers whether he wants them to handle it or not.

In thus deciding on its own, or deciding that Congress somehow has decided, to expand apparently without limit the kinds of claims subject to compulsory arbitration, to include even wage claims, and in thus depriving individual laborers of the right to handle their wage claims for themselves, today's decision of the Court interprets federal law in a way that is revolutionary. Yet the Court disposes of this case as easily as it would reach the conclusion that 2 plus 2 equal 4. First the Court says that the contract between the union and the company provides that a laborer who wants to assert a "contract grievance" is bound to attempt to use the contract grievance procedure, which requires several stages of company-union meetings, negotiations, etc., to be followed by submitting the dispute for final decision to an arbitrator "appointed by mutual agreement" of the union and the company. Next the Court labels Maddox' claim for wages due him a "grievance" —and, indeed, no one would deny that Maddox was unhappy about the company's failure to pay him what it had promised. Finally the Court, citing as its authority § 301 (a) of the Labor Management Relations Act, lays down for this and future cases the flat rule that no matter what his contractual claim—or "grievance," as the Court prefers to call it—an individual laborer, even though no longer an employee, has no choice but to follow the long, time-consuming, discouraging road to arbitration set out in the union-company contract, including having the union represent him whether he wants it to or not and whether or not he is still in its good graces. And of course the Court's logic leads irresistibly to the conclusion (although it has not yet had occasion to say so) that if instead of seeking wages due on discharge an employee wants to sue his employer for unpaid wages while he is still working, he cannot do that either, but must instead wait until the union processes his claim through the interminable stages of "grievance procedure" and then turns him over to the arbitrator, whom he does not want. Employees are thus denied a judicial hearing and state courts have their ancient power to try simple breach-of-contract cases taken away from them—taken away, not by Congress, I think, but by this Court. Today's holding is in my judgment completely unprecedented, and is the brainchild of this Court's recent consistently expressed preference for arbitration over litigation in all types of cases, and for accommodating the wishes of employers and unions in all things over the desires of individual workers. Since I do not believe that Congress has passed any law which justifies any inference at all that workers are barred from bringing and courts from deciding cases like this one, and since I am not sure that it constitutionally could, it is impossible for me to concur in this decision.

I think one crucial flaw in the Court's logical presentation is that it treats things as the same which are in fact different. "Grievance" is a word of many meanings in many contexts, and yet the Court uses it without any discrimination among them. As used in the industrial field "grievance" generally signifies something that has happened that is unsatisfactory to employers or employees in connection with their work. Failure to settle serious and widespread grievances has sometimes brought about industrial tensions, strikes and violence, often disrupting the peace and doing irreparable harm to the economy of the Nation. In order to try to prevent such widespread disastrous results to the public, arbitration has come to be accepted as a good way to settle such semi-public controversies, which are more in the nature of power struggles between giants than ordinary justiciable controversies involving individual laborers. When a contract provided for arbitration to settle disputes which affected many workers and

which could lead to strikes, this Court approved it and held that since both sides—company and union—had agreed to this method of peaceful settlement, federal law would honor and enforce it. Textile Workers Union v. Lincoln Mills, 353 U.S. 448. But to hold that the union and company can bind themselves to arbitrate a dispute of general importance affecting all or many of the union's members and vitally threatening the public welfare is a far cry from saying, as the Court does today, that an ordinary laborer whose employer discharges him and then fails to pay his past-due wages or wage substitutes must, if the union's contract with the employer provides for arbitration of grievances, have the doors of the courts of his country shut in his face to prevent his suing the employer to get his own wages for breach of contract. *Lincoln Mills* was a case involving a real and active collective bargaining dispute between union and employer over general working conditions; but the present case is a controversy not about general working conditions but about whether the company will pay one individual his wages.

For the individual, whether his case is settled by a professional arbitrator or tried by a jury can make a crucial difference. Arbitration differs from judicial proceedings in many ways: arbitration carries no right to a jury trial as guaranteed by the Seventh Amendment; arbitrators need not be instructed in the law; they are not bound by rules of evidence; they need not give reasons for their awards; witnesses need not be sworn; the record of proceedings need not be complete; and judicial review, it has been held, is extremely limited. To say that because the union chose a contract providing for grievance arbitration an individual employee freely and willingly chose this method of settling any contractual claims of his own which might later arise is surely a transparent and cruel fiction. And even if the employee could with any truth be regarded as having himself agreed to such a thing, until recently this Court refused to recognize and enforce contracts under which individuals were to be denied access to courts and instead left to the comparatively standardless process of arbitration. An insurance company cannot enforce a contract made with its insured to arbitrate all disputes which might arise in the future, this Court said, since such an agreement would be "an attempt to oust the courts of jurisdiction by excluding the assured from all resort to them for his remedy." Riddlesbarger v. Hartford Ins. Co., 7 Wall. 386, 391. Cf. Insurance Co. v. Morse, 20 Wall. 445. The Court holds today, however, that a union representing a worker in a mine or factory can by the union's contract take away from that worker his right to sue, which he would not be able to contract away himself unless the *Riddlesbarger* case is to be overruled. Compare Moseley v. Electronic & Missile Facilities, Inc., 374 U.S. 167, 172–173 (concurring opinion). And there is nothing in the legislative history of § 301 which indicates any congressional purpose to overrule or avoid the *Riddlesbarger* rule. Moreover, there is not one word in § 301 about agreements to arbitrate. It is true that this Court said in *Lincoln Mills*, "Plainly the agreement to arbitrate grievance disputes is the *quid pro quo* for an agreement not to strike," and "the entire tenor of the history indicates that the agreement to arbitrate grievance disputes was considered as *quid pro quo* of a no-strike agreement." In that case, however, the Court expressly recognized that its decision and reasoning did "not reach" the right of individual employees to bring suit in court on their individual claims. Forcing Charlie Maddox who is out of a job, to submit his claim to arbitration is not going to promote industrial peace. Charlie Maddox is not threatening to go out in the street by himself and stage a strike against the Republic Steel Corporation to get his unpaid wages. Merely because this Court in *Lincoln Mills* has expressed its preference for arbitration when used to avoid industrial warfare by heading off violent clashes between powerful employers and powerful unions, it does not follow that § 301 should be expanded to require a worker to arbitrate his wage claim or to surrender his right to bring his own suit to enforce that claim in court. Such an expansion would run counter to this Court's long-established policy of preserving the ancient, treasured right to judicial trials in independent courts according to due process of law.

The past decisions of this Court which are closest to the case before us are not *Lincoln Mills* and cases like it, which involved broad conflicts between unions and employers with reference to contractual terms vital to settlement of genuine employer-union disputes. The cases really in point are those which involved agreements governed by the Railway Labor Act and which expressly refused to hold that a discharged worker must pursue collective bargaining grievance procedures before suing in a court for wrongful discharge. Transcontinental & Western Air, Inc. v. Koppal, 345 U.S. 653 ; Moore v. Illinois Central R. Co., 312 U.S. 630. While those were wrongful-discharge cases and the suit here is for wages due on a contract after discharge, the principle of those cases is precisely applicable here, since as was pointed out in Slocum v. Delaware, L. & W. R. Co.,

339 U.S. 239, 244, the claim of a person no longer employed will almost never involve questions substantially affecting future relations between an employer and the remaining employees. The Court recognizes the relevance of *Moore* and *Koppal* and, while declining expressly to overrule them in this case, has raised the overruling axe so high that its falling is just about as certain as the changing of the seasons. Yet although members of Congress and alert counsel for the national unions and employers are bound to have been familiar with *Moore* at the time the comprehensive labor statute of which § 301 is a part was enacted, Congress did not see fit to disown the *Moore* rule and did not express a preference for a different policy with reference to individual suits on collective bargaining agreements covered by the LMRA.

The Court's opinion manifests great concern for the interests of employers and unions, but not, I fear, enough understanding and appreciation for an individual worker caught in the plight Maddox is in. The Court refers with seeming approval to the " 'common law' of the plant," and directs attention to the clear interest that the union has in handling employees' grievances in order to "enhance the union's prestige with employees." It also refers to the great interest that an employer has (and I agree) in having a complicated procedural system which dissatisfied employees are here compelled to follow, which ends up in binding arbitration and which relieves the employer of a lawsuit. The Court then expresses its view that allowing this former employee to sue without going through the grievance procedure and arbitration, as he would be permitted to do in this case by the law of his State, has "little to commend it" and "would deprive *employer* and *union* of the ability to establish a uniform and exclusive method for orderly settlement of employee grievances." I emphasize the words "employer" and "union" to point out that here, as elsewhere in the opinion, theirs seem to be the chief interests on which the Court's attention is focused. The procedure *they* (employer and union) want must be "made exclusive," or else *they* might not like it.[1] Individual workers are to take some comfort, I suppose, in the Court's statement that "it cannot be said, in the normal situation, that contract grievance procedures are inadequate to protect the interests of an aggrieved employee until the employee has attempted to implement the procedures and found them so." I think it can be said, however, and I say it. I

---

1. The AFL–CIO has filed an *amicus* brief supporting the employer in this case.

think an employee is just as capable of trying to enforce payment of his wages or wage substitutes under a collective bargaining agreement as his union, and he certainly is more interested in this effort than any union would likely be. This is particularly true where the employee has lost his job and is most likely outside the union door looking in instead of on hand to push for his claim. Examples certainly have not been wanting from which the Court might learn that often employees for one reason or another have felt themselves compelled to sue the union as a prerequisite to obtaining any help from the union at all. See, *e.g.*, Humphrey v. Moore, 375 U.S. 335; Syres v. Oil Workers Int'l Union, 350 U.S. 892; Brotherhood of R. Trainmen v. Howard, 343 U.S. 768; Tunstall v. Brotherhood of Locomotive Firemen & Enginemen, 323 U.S. 210; Steele v. Louisville & N. R. Co., 323 U.S. 192. But, says the Court, the employee attempting to recover wages owed him must, unless the collective bargaining contract of the company and the union provides otherwise, "afford the union the opportunity to act on his behalf." The Court then implies that if the union "refuses to press or only perfunctorily presses the individual's claim," there may be some form of redress available to the worker, but we are left in the dark as to what form that redress might take. It may be that the worker would be allowed to sue after he had presented his claim to the union and after he had suffered the inevitable discouragement and delay which necessarily accompanies the union's refusal to press his claim. But I cannot agree that this is the sort of remedy a worker should have to invoke to bring a simple lawsuit.

I am wholly unable to read § 301 as laying any such restrictive burdens on an employee. And I think the difference between my Brethren and me in this case is not simply one concerning this Court's function in interpreting or formulating laws. There is also apparently a vast difference between their philosophy and mine concerning litigation and the role of courts in our country. At least since Magna Carta people have desired to have a system of courts with set rules of procedure of their own and with certain institutional assurances of fair and unbiased resolution of controversies. It was in Magna Carta, the English Bill of Rights, and other such charters of liberty, that there originally was expressed in the English-speaking world a deep desire of people to be able to settle differences according to standard, well-known procedures in courts presided over by independent judges with jurors taken from the public. Because of these deep-seated desires, the right to sue and be sued in courts according to the "law of the land," known later as "due process of law," became recognized. That right was written into the Bill of Rights of our Constitution and in the constitutions of the States. See Chambers v. Florida, 309 U.S. 227, 235–238. Even if it be true, which I do not concede, that Congress could force a man in this country to have his ordinary lawsuit adjudicated not under due process of law, *i.e.*, without the constitutional safeguards of a court trial, I do not think that this Court should ever feel free to infer or imply that Congress has taken such a step until the words of the statute are written so clearly that no one who reads them can doubt. Cf. United States ex rel. Toth v. Quarles, 350 U.S. 11; United States v. Lovett, 328 U.S. 303; Duncan v. Kahanamoku, 327 U.S. 304; Reid v. Covert, 354 U.S. 1, 5–10 (opinion announcing judgment); Barsky v. Board of Regents, 347 U.S. 442, 456 (dissenting opinion); Stein v. New York, 346 U.S. 156, 197 (dissenting opinion); Shaughnessy v. United States ex rel. Mezei, 345 U.S. 206, 216 (dissenting opinion); Galloway v. United States, 319 U.S. 372, 396 (dissenting opinion). Maddox has a justiciable controversy. He has not agreed since the controversy arose, or even for that matter before it arose, to arbitrate it, and so he should not have the doors of the courts shut in his face. Nor do I believe that he or any other member of the union should be treated as an incompetent unable to pursue his own simple breach-of-contract losses. I cannot and do not believe any law Congress has passed provides that when a man becomes a member of a labor union in this country he thereby has somehow surrendered his own freedom and liberty to conduct his own lawsuit for wages. Of course this is not the worst kind of servitude to which a man could be subjected, but it is certainly contrary to the spirit of freedom in this country to infer from the blue that workers lose their rights to appeal to the courts for redress when they believe they are mistreated. Compare Smith v. Evening News Assn., 371 U.S. 195, 204–205 (dissenting opinion).

I would affirm.

In Walker v. Southern Ry. Co., 385 U.S. 196, (1966), an individual employee sued the carrier for unlawful discharge. The district court decided that it had jurisdiction based upon *Moore* and succeeding cases. The court of appeals reversed, holding that *Maddox* required the employee to exhaust his administrative remedies before the National Railroad Adjustment Board, a statutory body established by the Railway Labor Act for deciding railroad disputes as to the meaning and application of "rules" (i.e., collective bargaining) agreements between railroad labor unions and carriers. The Supreme Court held that as of the time Walker was discharged and sued, the Adjustment Board procedures entailed such delay that the discharged employee was excused from following the *Maddox* exhaustion doctrine. However, it intimated that the 1966 legislation to improve Adjustment Board procedures made *Maddox* applicable to railroad contract-interpretation disputes after the June 20, 1966, effective date of the new law. The court observed as to *Maddox*:

> We held that contract grievance procedures voluntarily incorporated by the parties in collective bargaining agreements subject to the LMRA, unless specified by the parties to be nonexclusive, must be exhausted before direct legal redress may be sought by the employee.
>
> Provision for arbitration of a discharge grievance, a minor dispute, is not a matter of voluntary agreement under the Railway Labor Act; the Act compels the parties to arbitrate minor disputes before the National Railroad Adjustment Board established under the Act.

The significance of this comparison was not explicated by the Court. The potentialities of this differentiation remain to be seen. The Court did not say that seldom do the parties select the neutral referee who in fact decides the disputes; rather he is appointed by the National Mediation Board. It is believed, however, that either a union or carrier can blackball a referee for future service. Whatever effect that practice might have upon awards, it is not the equivalent of voluntary choice of an arbitrator or the voluntary selection of the system. It is at least open to discussion whether the rationale of the Trilogy should be applied to a compulsory system even though the Adjustment Board referees are, by and large, quite expert in railroad labor practice. (Observe, however, that in the Transportation-Communications Employees v. Union Pacific, 385 U.S. 157 (1966), the Court indicated that its view of railroad rules agreement derived from *Wiley* and *Warrior and Gulf*.) Mr. Justice Fortas, in dissent, reminded the Court that railroad labor-management relations have been considered quite different from those in other industries.

The 1966 amendment to the Railway Labor Act provides a procedure for setting up auxiliary "special adjustment boards." It also eliminates the provision for judicial review of only a money award at the instance of a carrier and makes all Adjustment Board awards open to limited judicial review "for failure ... to comply with the requirements of this Act, for failure of the order to conform, or confine itself, to matters within the scope of the division's jurisdiction, or for fraud or corruption by a member of the division making the award." P. L. 89-456 (1966). The Senate Report noted that the Committee considered and rejected a proposal to provide for setting aside an award because of "arbitrariness or capriciousness" so as to avoid judicial interference on the merits. "This was done on the assumption that a Federal Court would have the power to decline to enforce an award which was actually and indisputably (sic) without foundation in reason or fact, and the committee intends that, under this bill, the courts will have that power." S. Rept. No. 1201, 89th Cong. 2d Sess. (1966). Also see H. Rept. No. 1114, 89th Cong., 1st Sess. (1965) for a description of the Adjustment Board composition and procedures and the Committee discussion of its processes as "arbitration."

In Broniman v. Great Atlantic and Pacific Tea Co., 353 F. 2d 559 (6th Cir. 1965), cert. denied, 384 U.S. 907 (1966), an employee on layoff filed a grievance on May 11, 1961, alleging violation of his seniority rights on the ground that other less senior employees remained at work. On the following August 7 he was informed that he had been discharged on May 22. (A discharge for cause required two written warnings, which had not been given.) He alleged that the union steward, who was to handle grievances at the first step, had failed to take action on his layoff grievance. The agreement provided that if the steward is unable to settle the grievance, it "shall be submitted" to the business agent. The court affirmed the district court grant of summary judgment for the employer. Section 9(a) does not entitle an employee to an affirmative order directing the employer to process his grievance, citing *Black-Clawson*. And, under *Maddox* the plaintiff, seeking damages for contract violation, had not exhausted his remedies because he should have submitted the grievance to the business agent, treating the steward's inaction as a failure to achieve a settlement.

Serra v. Pepsi-Cola General Bottlers, Inc., 248 F. Supp. 684 (N.D. Ill. E.D. 1965), reviewing the major federal cases, concluded that after an employee attempts to invoke the grievance procedure and is rebuffed by the union and the employer, he has standing to bring suit under § 301. The court also noted that suit against the union for unfair representation is inadequate where the employee seeks reinstatement. It was held further that the union is not an indispensable party in the suit against the employer.

In Allied Oil Workers Union v. Ethyl Corp., 341 F. 2d 47 (5th Cir. 1965), the union sought a declaratory judgment that the employer breached an agreement by insisting that employees work overtime. The collective agreement contained a grievance procedure; it provided for arbitration only if union and company "mutually agree ... Neither the company nor the union shall be compelled to arbitrate any difference." The company argued that the clause relegated the union to self-help (strike) and that the court was not open to it under § 301. The court rejected that view, holding it inimical to the declaration that § 301 confers substantive rights to judicial enforcement of the collective agreement. And, it added, the provision serves its essential purpose, the avoidance of industrial conflict, in just such a situation.

In Int'l B'ld of Telephone Workers v. New England Tel. & Tel. Co., 240 F. Supp 426 (D. Mass. 1965), the court expressed its agreement with the Fifth Circuit in the preceding case and entertained a breach of contract suit by both the union and discharged employee. It adopted the Summers' view of the individual's right to enforce the collective agreement; perhaps it cast some slight doubt on the breadth of its adoption by stating "where the union and the discharged employee have pursued the bargained-for grievance procedure and are both claiming that the contract was breached by the employer, both are proper plaintiffs." Without defining the difference from his normal role, the judge "assumed the arbitrator's responsibility" as suggested by Cox. He did a good job, too.

HAYNES v. U.S. PIPE & FOUNDRY CO.,
__F. 2d.__ (5th Cir. 1966) (62 LRRM 2389)

The absence of an arbitration clause from the grievance procedure did not permit the grieving employee on whose behalf the union had exhausted the prescribed procedure to resort to court suit under § 301. The unusual method provided by the collective agreement was a multi-stage union-management conference culminating with an international vice president and plant manager. If the latter denied the grievance, the union could give notice of intent to strike over the grievance. After processing this dispute to that level (with no hint of anything but good faith) the union did not give strike notice. The court reasoned that national labor policy gives preference to dispute-settlement methods of the parties' own choice. The union representative can by agreement prescribe the method of dispute settlement to the exclusion of resort to the courts.

> As previously noted, the Supreme Court has said that the policy of § 203 (d) "can be effectuated only if the means chosen by the parties for settlement of their differences under a collective bargaining agreement is given full play." United Steelworkers v. American Mfg. Co. The policy contemplates whatever means the union and the employer may have chosen to settle grievances. See Drivers Union v. Riss & Co., 1963, 372 U.S. 517, 9 L. Ed. 2d 918, 83 S.Ct. 789, where the method of settling grievances fell short of an arbitration clause. There the court said that where the agreement provides that the decision made is final and binding, the District Court has jurisdiction under § 301 to enforce the award. See also Humphrey v. Moore, 1964, 375 U.S. 335, 84 S.Ct. 363, 11 L.Ed. 2d 370. Moreover, the national labor policy inherent in the *Lincoln Mills-Maddox* line of cases is that an employee is bound by such grievance remedies as his union may negotiate. The means chosen here did not include arbitration but it is binding on the employee. It was his remedy and the next question presented is whether the doors of the court opened to him when he exhausted that remedy.

The court rejected the implication of *Maddox* that once the contract method is exhausted the employee can resort to court. Citing *Hildreth* and *Simmons,* the court reasoned that here the union's decision not to strike amounted to a final disposition of the grievance, which, like a settlement, bars suit by the individual employee.

Allied Oil Workers v. Ethyl Corp. was not mentioned.

In 1958 this court decided Woodward Iron Co. v. Ware, 261 F. 2d 138, in which the union refused to carry grievances to arbitration. The court took the view that the common-law right of an employee to sue for breach of contract was not extinguished. The court seems in *Haynes* to be on a different tack. How much difference does it make that the union in *Woodward* was arrayed against the employee-grievant and apparently on his side, but with limits, in *Haynes*?

In Miranda Fuel Co., 140 N.L.R.B. 181 (1962), the N.L.R.B. found that Section 8(b)(1)(A) of the National Labor Relations Act was violated by the union's successful demand upon the employer to reduce the employee's seniority for no apparently valid reason. The court of appeals refused enforcement. 326 F. 2d 172 (2d Cir. 1963). However, the Board apparently intends to adhere to its *Miranda* view, applying it to a refusal to process the grievance of a Negro employee by a segregated white local in Independent Metal Workers Union, No. 11 Hugh Tool Co. 147 N.L.R.B. 1573 (1964). (The split within the Board over nice questions of the applicability of various sections of its statute is beyond our purview here.)

Also see: Local 1376, International Longshoremens Union, 148 N.L.R.B. 897 (1964); Automobile Workers Union, 149 N.L.R.B. 482 (1964).

Prior to 1962 several Negro employees had been laid off while less-senior white employees were retained in employment and hired because separate white and Negro seniority rosters were maintained and white employees had precedence over more-senior Negroes as a matter of "custom." The local union refused to process grievances based upon these and other racially discriminatory practices. In 1962, under governmental pressure, the union and company agreed to abandon these "customs." Thereafter, the union again refused to present the Negroes' grievance for back pay for pre-March 1962 discriminations. The court upheld the National Labor Relations Board's conclusion that the union thereby violated its duty of fair representation and thus restrained and coerced employees in the rights guaranteed them by the National Labor Relations Act. The court also declared that where, as here, the employee does not claim that the union breached the collective agreement but failed in its representative duty, the NLRB's primary jurisdiction attaches to the exclusion of the courts. It enforced the Board's order directing the union to process the grievances to arbitration. Local 12, United Rubber Workers v. NLRB (5th Cir. 1966) 368 F. 2d 12. (opinion by Thornberry, C. J.).

One commentator suggests that union refusal to process grievances should be decided by the National Labor Relations Board. Yablonski, *Refusal to Process a Grievance, The NLRB and*

The Duty of Fair Representation, 26 U. Pitt. L. Rev. 593, 615 (1965):

> The problem today is not one of standards, but one of implementation, for the standards, as they have been applied by the courts, have been ineffective. This ineffectiveness of application has led to the creation of many available forums where a disgruntled grievant can seek redress. In *Miranda*, the Board applied virtually the same standards as were announced in *Steele* and found a breach of the "duty." Even the *Miranda* standard—action based upon considerations which are "irrelevant, invidious, or unfair"—sounds like *Steele's* pronouncement that "discriminations based on race are obviously irrelevant and invidious." Although the courts have failed to propose tests under the *Steele* rationale in other than racial cases, and to properly apply them, the Board in *Miranda* has indicated that it can apply the standards and that it is willing to do so. In lieu of applying *Steele* in non-racial cases the Court has resorted to the expansion of the number of available forums, all of which eventually must turn to *Steele* for guidance. This is the heart of the problem. There are too many forums available, few of which can properly dispense the requested remedy. The Board, having shown that it is equal to the task, should be vested with the power to resolve this type of dispute.
>
> Even if the Court should choose to accept the *Miranda* rationale and grant NLRB jurisdiction, it will not be enough. In order properly to resolve the problem, the Court must make Board jurisdiction exclusive, thereby eliminating the diverse, ineffective and inefficient operation of the courts which not only have failed to properly administer the principles of fair representation but have interfered with the collective bargaining process. The application of the pre-emption doctrine will place the sole responsibility of ensuring fair representation upon the Board.

The subject of union refusal to process a member's grievance as a possible violation of the Labor-Management Reporting and Disclosure Act (Landrum-Griffin) is not considered here. For a case raising the issue, see Scovile v. Watson, 338 F. 2d 678 (7th Cir. 1944) cert. denied, 380 U.S. 963 (1964).

VACA v. SIPES
386 U.S. 171 (1967)

White, J. On February 13, 1962, Benjamin Owens filed this class action against petitioners, as officers and representatives of the National Brotherhood of Packinghouse Workers and of its Kansas City Local No. 12 (the Union), in the Circuit Court of Jackson County, Missouri. Owens, a Union member, alleged that he had been discharged from his employment at Swift & Company's (Swift) Kansas City Meat Packing Plant in violation of the collective bargaining agreement then in force between Swift and the Union, and that the Union had "arbitrarily, capriciously and without just or reasonable reason or cause" refused to take his grievance with Swift to arbitration under the fifth step of the bargaining agreement's grievance procedures.

Petitioners' answer included the defense that the Missouri courts lacked jurisdiction because the gravamen of Owens' suit was "arguably and basically" an unfair labor practice under § 8(b) of the National Labor Relations Act, as amended 29 U.S.C. § 158(b), within the exclusive jurisdiction of the National Labor Relations Board (NLRB). After a jury trial, a verdict was returned awarding Owens $7,000 compensatory and $3,300 punitive damages. The trial judge set aside the verdict and entered judgment for petitioners on the ground that the NLRB had exclusive jurisdiction over this controversy, and the Kansas City Court of Appeals affirmed. The Supreme Court of Missouri reversed and directed reinstatement of the jury's verdict,[1] relying on this Court's decisions in International Assn. of Machinists v. Gonzales, 356 U.S. 617, and in Automobile Workers v. Russell, 356 U.S. 634, 397 S.W. 2d 658. During the appeal, Owens died and respondent, the administrator of Owens' estate, was substituted. We granted certiorari to consider whether exclusive jurisdiction lies with the NLRB and, if not, whether the finding of Union liability and the relief afforded Owens are consistent with governing principles of federal labor law, 384 U.S. 969. The American Federation of Labor and Congress of Industrial Organizations (AFL–CIO), Swift, and the United States have filed *amicus* briefs supporting petitioners. Although we conclude that state courts have jurisdiction in this type of case, we hold that federal law governs, that the governing federal standards were not applied here, and that the judgment of the Supreme Court of Missouri must accordingly be reversed.

I.

In mid-1959, Owens, a long-time high blood pressure patient, became sick and entered a hospital on sick leave from his employment with Swift. After a long rest during which his weight and blood pressure were reduced, Owens was certified by his family physician as fit to resume his heavy work in the packing plant. However, Swift's company doctor examined Owens upon his return and concluded that his blood pressure was too high to permit reinstatement. After securing a second authorization from another outside doctor, Owens returned to the plant, and a nurse permitted him to resume work on January 6, 1960. However, on January 8, when the doctor discovered Owens' return, he was permanently discharged on the ground of poor health.

Armed with his medical evidence of fitness, Owens then sought the Union's help in securing reinstatement, and a grievance was filed with Swift on his behalf. By mid-November 1960, the grievance had been processed through the third and into the fourth step of the grievance procedure established by the collective bargaining agreement.[2] Swift adhered to its position that Owens' poor health justified his discharge, rejecting numerous medical reports of reduced blood pressure proffered by Owens and by the Union. Swift claimed that these reports were not based upon sufficiently thorough medical tests.

On February 6, 1961, the Union sent Owens to a new doctor at Union expense "to see if we could get some better medical evidence so that we could go to arbitration with his case." R., at 182. This examination did not support Owens' position. When the Union received the report, its executive board voted not to take the Owens grievance to arbitration because of insufficient medical evidence. Union officers suggested to Owens that he accept Swift's offer of referral to a rehabilitation center, and the grievance was suspended for that purpose. Owens rejected this alternative and demanded that the Union take his grievance to arbitration, but the Union refused. With his contractual remedies thus stalled at the fourth step, Owens brought this suit. The grievance was finally dismissed by the Union and Swift shortly before trial began in June 1964.[3]

2. The agreement created a five-step procedure for the handling of grievances. In steps one and two, either the aggrieved employee or the Union's representative presents the grievance first to Swift's department foreman, and then in writing to the division superintendent. In step three, grievance committees of the Union and management meet, and the company must state its position in writing to the Union. Step four is a meeting between Swift's general superintendent and representatives of the National Union. If the grievance is not settled in the fourth step, the National Union is given power to refer the grievance to a specified arbitrator.

3. No notice of the dismissal was given to Owens, who by that time had filed a second suit against Swift for breach of contract. The suit against Swift is still pending in a pretrial stage.

1. Punitive damages were reduced to $3,000, the amount claimed by Owens in his complaint.

In his charge to the jury, the trial judge instructed that petitioners would be liable if Swift had wrongfully discharged Owens and if the Union had "arbitrarily ... and without just cause or excuse ... refused" to press Owens' grievance to arbitration. Punitive damages could also be awarded, the trial judge charged, if the Union's conduct was "willful, wanton and malicious." However, the jury must return a verdict for the defendants, the judge instructed, "if you find and believe from the evidence that the union and its representatives acted reasonably and in good faith in the handling and processing of the grievance of the plaintiff." R., at 259–261. The jury then returned the general verdict for Owens which eventually was reinstated by the Missouri Supreme Court.

II.

Petitioners challenge the jurisdiction of the Missouri courts on the ground that the alleged conduct of the Union was arguably an unfair labor practice and within the exclusive jurisdiction of the NLRB. Petitioners rely on Miranda Fuel Co., 140 N.L.R.B. 181 (1962), enforcement denied, 326 F. 2d 172 (C. A. 2d Cir. 1963), where a sharply divided Board held for the first time that a union's breach of its statutory duty of fair representation violates N.L.R.A. § 8(b), as amended. With the NLRB's adoption of Miranda Fuel, petitioners argue, the broad pre-emption doctrine defined in San Diego Building Trades Council v. Garmon, 359 U.S. 236, becomes applicable. For the reasons which follow, we reject this argument.

It is now well established that, as the exclusive bargaining representative of the employees in Owens' bargaining unit, the Union had a statutory duty fairly to represent all of those employees, both in its collective bargaining with Swift, see Ford Motor Co. v. Huffman, 345 U.S. 330 ; Syres v. Oil Workers International Union, 350 U.S. 892, and in its enforcement of the resulting collective bargaining agreement, see Humphrey v. Moore, 375 U.S. 335. The statutory duty of fair representation was developed over 20 years ago in a series of cases involving alleged racial discrimination by unions certified as exclusive bargaining representatives under the Railway Labor Act, see Steele v. Louisville & N. R. R. 323 U.S. 192 ; Tunstall v. Brotherhood of Locomotive Firemen, 323 U.S. 210, and was soon extended to unions certified under the N.L.R.A., see Ford Motor Co. v. Huffman, supra. Under this doctrine, the exclusive agent's statutory authority to represent all members of a designated unit includes a statutory obligation

to serve the interests of all members without hostility or discrimination toward any, to exercise its discretion with complete good faith and honesty, and to avoid arbitrary conduct. Humphrey v. Moore, 375 U.S., at 342. It is obvious that Owens' complaint alleged a breach by the Union of a duty grounded in federal statutes, and that federal law therefore governs his cause of action. E.g., Ford Motor Co. v. Huffman, supra.

Although N.L.R.A. § 8 (b) was enacted in 1947, the NLRB did not until Miranda Fuel interpret a breach of a union's duty of fair representation as an unfair labor practice. In Miranda Fuel, the Board's majority held that N.L.R.A. § 7 gives employees "the right to be free from unfair or irrelevant or invidious treatment by their exclusive bargaining agent in matters affecting their employment," and "that Section 8 (b) (1) (A) of the Act accordingly prohibits labor organizations, when acting in a statutory representative capacity, from taking action against any employee upon considerations or classifications which are irrelevant, invidious, or unfair." 140 N.L.R.B., at 185. The Board also held that an employer who "participates" in such arbitrary union conduct violates § 8 (a) (1), and that the employer and the union may violate §§ 8 (a) (3) and 8 (b) (2), respectively, "when, for arbitrary or irrelevant reasons or upon the basis of an unfair classification, the union attempts to cause or does cause an employer to derogate the employment status of an employee."[4] Id. at 186.

The Board's Miranda Fuel decision was denied enforcement by a divided Second Circuit, 326 F. 2d 172 (1963). However, in Local 12, United Rubber Workers v. NLRB, 368 F. 2d 12 (Nov. 9, 1966), the Fifth Circuit upheld the Board's Miranda Fuel doctrine in an opinion suggesting that the Board's approach will pre-empt judicial cognizance of some fair representation duty suits. In light of these developments, petitioners argue that Owens' state court action was based upon Union conduct that is arguably proscribed by N.L.R.A. § 8 (b), was potentially enforceable by the NLRB, and was therefore pre-empted under the Garmon line of decisions.

A. In Garmon, this Court recognized that the broad powers conferred by Congress upon the National Labor Relations Board to interpret and to enforce the complex Labor Management Relations Act necessarily imply that potentially

---

4. See also Cargo Handlers, Inc., 159 N.L.R.B. No. 17; Local 12, United Rubber Workers, 150 N.L.R.B. 312, enforced, No. 22239 (C.A. 5th Cir. Nov. 9, 1966); Maremont Corp., 149 N.L.R.B. 482; Galveston Maritime Assn., Inc., 148 N.L.R.B. 897; Hughes Tool Co., 147 N.L.R.B. 1573.

conflicting "rules of law, of remedy, and of administration" cannot be permitted to operate. 359 U.S., at 242. In enacting the National Labor Relations Act and later the Labor Management Relations Act,

> Congress did not merely lay down a substantive rule of law to be enforced by any tribunal competent to apply law generally to the parties. It went on to confide primary interpretation and application of its rules to a specific and specially constituted tribunal. . . . Congress evidently considered that centralized administration of specially designed procedures was necessary to obtain uniform application of its substantive rules and to avoid these diversities and conflicts likely to result from a variety of local procedures and attitudes towards labor controversies. . . . A multiplicity of tribunals and a diversity of procedures are quite as apt to produce incompatible or conflicting adjudications as are different rules of substantive law. Garner v. Teamsters Union, 346 U.S. 485, 490–491.

Consequently, as a general rule, neither state nor federal courts have jurisdiction over suits directly involving "activity [which] is arguably subject to § 7 or § 8 of the Act." San Diego Building Trades Council v. Garmon, 359 U.S., at 245.

This pre-emption doctrine, however, has never been rigidly applied to cases where it could not fairly be inferred that Congress intended exclusive jurisdiction to lie with the NLRB. Congress itself has carved out exceptions to the Board's exclusive jurisdiction: Section 303 of the Labor Management Relations Act, 29 U.S.C. § 187, expressly permits anyone injured by a violation of N.L.R.A. § 8 (b) (4) to recover damages in a federal court even though such unfair labor practices are also remediable by the Board; § 301 of that Act, 29 U.S.C. § 185, permits suits for breach of a collective bargaining agreement regardless of whether the particular breach is also an unfair labor practice within the jurisdiction of the Board, see Smith v. Evening News Assn., 371 U.S. 195; and N.L.R.A. § 14, as amended by Title VII, § 701 (a) of the Labor-Management Reporting and Disclosure Act of 1959, 73 Stat. 541, 29 U.S.C. § 164 (c), permits state agencies and courts to assume jurisdiction "over labor disputes over which the Board declines, pursuant to paragraph (1) of this subsection, to assert jurisdiction." Compare Guss v. Utah Labor Relations Board, 353 U.S. 1.

In addition to these congressional exceptions, this Court has refused to hold state remedies pre-empted

> where the activity regulated was a merely peripheral concern of the Labor Management Relations Act . . . [or] touched interests so deeply rooted in local feeling and responsibility that, in the absence of

compelling congressional direction, we could not infer that Congress has deprived the States of the power to act.

San Diego Building Trades Council v. Garmon, 359 U.S., at 243–244. See, *e.g.,* Linn v. United Plant Guard Workers, 383 U.S. 53 (libel); United Automobile Workers v. Russell, 356 U.S. 634 (violence); International Assn. of Machinists v. Gonzales, 356 U.S. 617 (wrongful expulsion from union membership); Electrical Workers v. Wisconsin Employment Relations Board, 315 U.S. 740 (mass picketing). See also Hanna Mining Co. v. Marine Engineers Beneficial Assn., 382 U.S. 181. While these exceptions in no way undermine the vitality of the pre-emption rule where applicable, they demonstrate that the decision to pre-empt federal and state court jurisdiction over a given class of cases must depend upon the nature of the particular interests being asserted and the effect upon the administration of national labor policies of concurrent judicial and administrative remedies.

A primary justification for the pre-emption doctrine—the need to avoid conflicting rules of substantive law in the labor relations area and the desirability of leaving the development of such rules to the administrative agency created by Congress for that purpose—is not applicable to cases involving alleged breaches of the union duty of fair representation. The doctrine was judicially developed in *Steele* and its progeny, and suits alleging breach of the duty remained judicially cognizable long after the NLRB was given unfair labor practice jurisdiction over union activities by the L.M.R.A.[5] Moreover, when the Board declared in *Miranda Fuel* that a union's breach of its duty of fair representation would henceforth be treated as an unfair labor practice, the Board adopted and applied the doctrine as it had been developed by the federal courts. See 140 N.L.R.B., at 184–186. Finally, as the dissenting Board members in *Miranda Fuel* have pointed out, fair representation duty suits often require review of the substantive positions taken and policies pursued by a union in its negotiation of a collective bargaining agreement and in its handling of the grievance machinery; as these matters are not normally within the Board's unfair labor prac-

---

5. See Ford Motor Co. v. Huffman, 345 U.S. 330, 332, n. 4. In Huffman, the NLRB submitted an *amicus* brief stating that it had not assumed pre-emptive jurisdiction over fair representation duty issues. Mem. for the NLRB, Nos. 193 and 194, Oct. Term, 1952. In Syres v. Oil Workers International Union, 350 U.S. 892, the Court reversed the dismissal of a suit which claimed breach of the duty of fair representation despite express reliance by one respondent on exclusive NLRB jurisdiction. Brief for Resp. Gulf Oil Corp., No. 390, Oct. Term, 1955.

tice jurisdiction, it can be doubted whether the Board brings substantially greater expertise to bear on these problems than do the courts, which have been engaged in this type of review since the *Steele* decision.[6]

In addition to the above considerations, the unique interests served by the duty of fair representation doctrine have a profound effect, in our opinion, on the applicability of the pre-emption rule to this class of cases. The federal labor laws seek to promote industrial peace and the improvement of wages and working conditions by fostering a system of employee organization and collective bargaining. See N.L.R.A. § 1, as amended, 29 U.S.C. § 151. The collective bargaining system as encouraged by Congress and administered by the NLRB of necessity subordinates the interests of an individual employee to the collective interests of all employees in a bargaining unit. See, *e.g.,* J. I. Case Co. v. N.L.R.B., 321 U.S. 332. This Court recognized in *Steele* that the congressional grant of power to a union to act as exclusive collective bargaining representative, with its corresponding reduction in the individual rights of the employees so represented, would raise grave constitutional problems if unions were free to exercise this power to further racial discrimination. 323 U.S., at 198–199. Since that landmark decision, the duty of fair representation has stood as a bulwark to prevent arbitrary union conduct against individuals stripped of traditional forms of redress by the provisions of federal labor law. Were we to hold, as petitioners and the government urge, that the courts are pre-empted by the NLRB's *Miranda Fuel* decision of this traditional supervisory jurisdiction, the individual employee injured by arbitrary or discriminatory union conduct could no longer be assured of impartial review of his complaint, since the Board's General Counsel has unreviewable discretion to refuse to institute an unfair labor practice complaint. See United Electrical Contractors Assn. v. Ordman, No. 29879, C. A. 2d Cir., Sept. 23, 1966, cert. denied, 35 U.S.L. Week 3243 (Jan. 17, 1967).[7] The exist-

ence of even a small group of cases in which the Board would be unwilling or unable to remedy a union's breach of duty would frustrate the basic purposes underlying the duty of fair representation doctrine. For these reasons, we cannot assume from the NLRB's tardy assumption of jurisdiction in these cases that Congress, when it enacted N.L.R.A. § 8 (b) in 1947, intended to oust the courts of their traditional jurisdiction to curb arbitrary conduct by the individual employee's statutory representative.

B. There are also some intensely practical considerations which foreclose pre-emption of judicial cognizance of fair representation duty suits, considerations which emerge from the intricate relationship between the duty of fair representation and the enforcement of collective bargaining contracts. For the fact is that the question of whether a union has breached its duty of fair representation will in many cases be a critical issue in a suit under L.M.R.A. § 301 charging an employer with a breach of contract. To illustrate, let us assume a collective bargaining agreement that limits discharges to those for good cause and that contains no grievance, arbitration or other provisions purporting to restrict access to the courts. If an employee is discharged without cause, either the union or the employee may sue the employer under L.M.R.A. § 301. Under this section, courts have jurisdiction over suits to enforce collective bargaining agreements even though the conduct of the employer which is challenged as a breach of contract is also arguably an unfair labor practice within the jurisdiction of the NLRB. *Garmon* and like cases have no application to § 301 suits. Smith v. Evening News Assn., 371 U.S. 195.

The rule is the same with regard to pre-emption where the bargaining agreement contains grievance and arbitration provisions which are intended to provide the exclusive remedy for breach of contract claims.[8] If an employee is discharged without cause in violation of such an agreement, that the employer's conduct may be an unfair labor practice does not preclude a suit by the union[9] against the employer to compel arbitration of the employee's grievance;

---

6. See Hughes Tool Co., 147 N.L.R.B. 1573, 1589–1590 (Chairman McCulloch and Member Fanning, dissenting in part).

7. The public interest in effectuating the policies of the federal labor laws, not the wrong done the individual employee, is always the Board's principal concern in fashioning unfair labor practice remedies. See N.L.R.A. § 10 (c), as amended, 29 U.S.C. § 160 (c); Phelps Dodge Corp. v. N.L.R.B., 313 U.S. 177. Thus, the General Counsel will refuse to bring complaints on behalf of injured employees where the injury complained of is "insubstantial." See Administrative Decision of the General Counsel, Case No. K–610, Aug. 13, 1956, in CCH N.L.R.B. Decisions, 1956–1957, at ¶ 54,059.

8. If a grievance and arbitration procedure is included in the contract, but the parties do not intend it to be an exclusive remedy, then a suit for breach of contract will normally be heard even though such procedures have not been exhausted. See Republic Steel Corp. v. Maddox, 379 U.S. 650, 657–658; 6A CORBIN, CONTRACTS § 1436 (1962).

9. Occasionally, the bargaining agreement will give the aggrieved employee, rather than his union, the right to invoke arbitration. See Retail Clerks v. Lion Dry Goods, Inc., 341 F. 2d 715, cert. denied, 382 U.S. 839.

the adjudication of the claim by the arbitrator ; or a suit to enforce the resulting arbitration award. See, *e.g.,* Steelworkers v. American Mfg. Co., 363 U.S. 564.

However, if the wrongfully discharged employee himself resorts to the courts before the grievance procedures have been fully exhausted, the employer may well defend on the ground that the exclusive remedies provided by such a contract have not been exhausted. Since the employee's claim is based upon breach of the collective bargaining agreement, he is bound by terms of that agreement which govern the manner in which contractual rights may be enforced. For this reason, it is settled that the employee must at least attempt to exhaust exclusive grievance and arbitration procedures established by the bargaining agreement. Republic Steel Corp. v. Maddox, 379 U.S. 650. However, because these contractual remedies have been devised and are often controlled by the union and the employer, they may well prove unsatisfactory or unworkable for the individual grievant. The problem then is to determine under what circumstances the individual employee may obtain judicial review of his breach-of-contract claim despite his failure to secure relief through the contractual remedial procedures.

An obvious situation in which the employee should not be limited to the exclusive remedial procedures established by the contract occurs when the conduct of the employer amounts to a repudiation of those contractual procedures. Cf. Drake Bakeries Inc. v. Bakery Workers, 370 U.S. 254, 260–263. See generally 6A CORBIN, CONTRACTS § 1443 (1962). In such a situation (and there may of course be others), the employer is estopped by his own conduct to rely on the unexhausted grievance and arbitration procedures as a defense to the employee's cause of action.

We think that another situation when the employee may seek judicial enforcement of his contractual rights arises if, as is true here, the union has sole power under the contract to invoke the higher stages of the grievance procedure, *and* if, as is alleged here, the employee-plaintiff has been prevented from exhausting his contractual remedies by the union's *wrongful* refusal to process the grievance. It is true that the employer in such a situation may have done nothing to prevent exhaustion of the exclusive contractual remedies to which he agreed in the collective bargaining agreement. But the employer has committed a wrongful discharge in breach of that agreement, a breach which could be remedied through the grievance process to

the employee-plaintiff's benefit were it not for the union's breach of its statutory duty of fair representation to the employee. To leave the employee remediless in such circumstances would, in our opinion, be a great injustice. We cannot believe that Congress, in conferring upon employers and unions the power to establish exclusive grievance procedures, intended to confer upon unions such unlimited discretion to deprive injured employees of all remedies for breach of contract. Nor do we think that Congress intended to shield employers from the natural consequences of their breaches of bargaining agreements by wrongful union conduct in the enforcement of such agreements. Cf. Richardson v. Texas & N.O.R.R., 242 F. 2d 230, 235–236 (C. A. 5th Cir.).

For these reasons, we think the wrongfully discharged employee may bring an action against his employer in the face of a defense based upon the failure to exhaust contractual remedies, provided the employee can prove that the union as bargaining agent breached its duty of fair representation in its handling of the employee's grievance.[10] We may assume for present purposes that such a breach of duty by the union is an unfair labor practice, as the NLRB and the Fifth Circuit have held. The employee's suit against the employer, however, remains a § 301 suit, and the jurisdiction of the courts is no more destroyed by the fact that the employee, as part and parcel of his § 301 action, finds it necessary to prove an unfair labor practice by the union, than it is by the fact that the suit may involve an unfair labor practice by the employer himself. The court is free to determine whether the employee is barred by the actions of his union representative, and, if not, to proceed with the case. And if, to facilitate his case, the employee joins the union as a defendant, the situation is not substantially changed. The action is still a § 301 suit, and the jurisdiction of the courts is not pre-empted under the *Garmon* principle. This, at the very least, is the holding of Humphrey v. Moore with respect to pre-emption, as petitioners recognize in their brief. And, insofar as adjudication of the union's breach of duty is concerned, the result should be no different if the employee, as Owens did

---

10. Accord, Hiller v. Liquor Salesmen's Union, 338 F. 2d 778 (C.A. 2d Cir.); Hardcastle v. Western Greyhound Lines, 303 F. 2d 182 (C.A. 9th Cir.), cert. denied, 341 U.S. 920; Fiore v. Associated Transport, Inc., 255 F. Supp. 596; Bieski v. Eastern Automobile Forwarding Co., 231 F. Supp. 710, aff'd, 354 F. 2d 414 (C.A. 3d Cir.); Ostrofsky v. United Steelworkers, 171 F. Supp. 782, aff'd per curiam, 273 F. 2d 614 (C.A. 4th Cir.), cert. denied, 363 U.S. 849; Jenkins v. Wm. Schluderberg-T. J. Kurdle Co., 217 Md. 556, 144 A. 2d 88.

here, sues the employer and the union in separate actions. There would be very little to commend a rule which would permit the Missouri courts to adjudicate the Union's conduct in an action against Swift but not in an action against the Union itself.

For the above reasons, it is obvious that the courts will be compelled to pass upon whether there has been a breach of the duty of fair representation in the context of many § 301 breach-of-contract actions. If a breach of duty by the union and a breach of contract by the employer are proven, the court must fashion an appropriate remedy. Presumably, in at least some cases, the union's breach of duty will have enhanced or contributed to the employee's injury. What possible sense could there be in a rule which would permit a court that has litigated the fault of employer and union to fashion a remedy only with respect to the employer? Under such a rule, either the employer would be compelled by the court to pay for the union's wrong—slight deterrence, indeed, to future union misconduct—or the injured employee would be forced to go to two tribunals to repair a single injury. Moreover, the Board would be compelled in many cases either to remedy injuries arising out of a breach of contract, a task which Congress has not assigned to it, or to leave the individual employee without remedy for the union's wrong.[11] Given the strong reasons for not pre-empting duty of fair representation suits in general, and the fact that the courts in many § 301 suits must adjudicate whether the union has breached its duty, we conclude that the courts may also fashion remedies for such a breach of duty.

It follows from the above that the Missouri courts had jurisdiction in this case. Of course, it is quite another problem to determine what remedies may be recovered from the Union if a breach of duty is proven. See Part IV, *infra.* But

----

11. Assuming for the moment that Swift breached the collective bargaining agreement in discharging Owens and that the Union breached its duty in handling Owens' grievance, this case illustrates the difficulties that would result from a rule pre-empting the courts from remedying the Union's breach of duty. If Swift did not "participate" in the Union's unfair labor practice, the Board would have no jurisdiction to remedy Swift's breach of contract. Yet a court might be equally unable to give Owens full relief in a § 301 suit against Swift. Should the court award damages against Swift for Owens' full loss, even if it concludes that part of that loss was caused by the Union's breach of duty? Or should it award Owens only partial recovery hoping that the Board will make him whole? These remedy problems are difficult enough when one tribunal has all parties before it; they are impossible if two independent tribunals, with different procedures, time limitations, and remedial powers must participate.

the unique role played by the duty of fair representation doctrine in the scheme of federal labor laws, and its important relationship to the judicial enforcement of collective bargaining agreements in the context presented here, render the *Garmon* pre-emption doctrine inapplicable.

III.

Petitioners contend, as they did in their motion for judgment notwithstanding the jury's verdict, that Owens failed to prove that the Union breached its duty of fair representation in its handling of Owens' grievance. Petitioners also argue that the Supreme Court of Missouri, in rejecting this contention, applied a standard that is inconsistent with governing principles of federal law with respect to the Union's duty to an individual employee in its processing of grievances under the collective bargaining agreement with Swift. We agree with both contentions.

A

In holding that the evidence at trial supported the jury's verdict in favor of Owens, the Missouri Supreme Court stated:

> The essential issue submitted to the jury was whether the union . . . arbitrarily . . . refused to carry said grievance . . . through the fifth step.

> We have concluded that there was sufficient substantial evidence from which the jury reasonably could have found the foregoing issue in favor of plaintiff. It is notable that no physician actually testified in the case. Both sides were content to rely upon written statements. Three physicians certified that plaintiff was able to perform his regular work. Three other physicians certified that they had taken plaintiff's blood pressure and that the readings were approximately 160 over 100. It may be inferred that such a reading does not indicate that his blood pressure was dangerously high. Moreover, plaintiff's evidence showed that he had actually done hard physical labor periodically during the four years following his discharge. We accordingly rule this point adversely to defendants. 397 S.W. 2d, at 665.

Quite obviously, the question which the Missouri Supreme Court thought dispositive of the issue of liability was whether the evidence supported Owens' assertion that he had been wrongfully discharged by Swift, regardless of the Union's good faith in reaching a contrary conclusion. This was also the major concern of the plaintiff at trial: the bulk of Owens' evidence was directed at whether he was medically fit at the time of discharge and whether he had performed heavy work after that discharge.

A breach of the statutory duty of fair representation occurs only when a union's conduct toward a member of the collective bargaining unit is arbitrary, discriminatory, or in bad faith. See Humphrey v. Moore, *supra*; Ford Motor Co. v. Huffman, *supra*. There has been considerable debate over the extent of this duty in the context of a union's enforcement of the grievance and arbitration procedures in a collective bargaining agreement. See generally Blumrosen, *The Worker and Three Phases of Unionism: Administrative and Judicial Control of the Worker-Union Relationship* 61 MICH. L. REV. 1435 (1963); Comment, *Federal Protection of Individual Rights under Labor Contracts* 73 YALE L. J. 1215 (1964). Some have suggested that every individual employee should have the right to have his grievance taken to arbitration.[12] Others have urged that the Union be given substantial discretion (if the collective bargaining agreement so provides to decide whether a grievance should be taken to arbitration, subject only to the duty to refrain from patently wrongful conduct such as racial discrimination or personal hostility.[13]

Though we accept the proposition that a union may not arbitrarily ignore a meritorious grievance or process it in perfunctory fashion, we do not agree that the individual employee has an absolute right to have his grievance taken to arbitration regardless of the provisions of the applicable collective bargaining agreement. In L.M.R.A. § 203 (d), U.S.C. § 173 (d), Congress declared that "Final adjustment by a method agreed upon by the parties themselves is ... the desirable method for settlement of grievance disputes arising over the application or interpretation of an existing collective bargaining agreement." In providing for a grievance and arbitration procedure which gives the union discretion to supervise the grievance machinery and to invoke arbitration, the employer and the union contemplate that each will endeavor in good faith to settle grievances short of arbitration. Through this settlement process, frivolous grievances are ended prior to the most costly and time-consuming step in the grievance

procedures. Moreover, both sides are assured that similar complaints will be treated consistently, and major problem areas in the interpretation of the collective bargaining contract can be isolated and perhaps resolved. And finally, the settlement process furthers the interest of the union as statutory agent and as coauthor of the bargaining agreement in representing the employees in the enforcement of that agreement. See Cox, *Rights Under a Labor Agreement,* 69 HARV. L. REV. 601 (1956).

If the individual employee could compel arbitration of his grievance regardless of its merit, the settlement machinery provided by the contract would be substantially undermined, thus destroying the employer's confidence in the union's authority and returning the individual grievant to the vagaries of independent and unsystematic negotiation. Moreover, under such a rule, a significantly greater number of grievances would proceed to arbitration.[14] This would greatly increase the cost of the grievance machinery and could so overburden the arbitration process as to prevent it from functioning successfully. See NLRB v. Acme Ind. Co., 385 U.S. 432 (1967); Ross, *Distressed Grievance Procedures and Their Rehabilitation,* in LABOR ARBITRATION AND INDUSTRIAL CHANGE, Proceedings of the 16th Annual Meeting, National Academy of Arbitrators 104 (1963). It can well be doubted whether the parties to collective bargaining agreements would long continue to provide for detailed grievance and arbitration procedures of the kind encouraged by L.M.R.A. § 203 (d), *supra,* if their power to settle the majority of grievances short of the costlier and more time-consuming steps was limited by a rule permitting the grievant unilaterally to invoke arbitration. Nor do we see substantial danger to the interests of the individual employee if his statutory agent is given the contractual power honestly and in good faith to settle grievances short of arbitration. For these reasons, we conclude that a union does not breach its duty of fair representation, and thereby open up a suit by the employee for breach of contract, merely

---

12. See Donnelly v. United Fruit Co., 40 N.J. 61, 190 A. 2d 825; 1954 REPORT OF COMMITTEE ON IMPROVEMENT OF ADMINISTRATION OF UNION-MANAGEMENT AGREEMENTS, INDIVIDUAL GRIEVANCES, 50 Nw. U. L. REV. 143 (1955); Murphy, *The Duty of Fair Representation under Taft-Hartley,* 30 Mo. L. REV. 373, 389 (1965); Summers, *Individual Rights in Collective Agreements and Arbitration,* 37 N. Y. U. L. REV. 362 (1962).

13. See Sheremet v. Chrysler Corp., 372 Mich. 626, 127 N.W. 2d 313; Wyle, *Labor Arbitration and the Concept of Exclusive Representation,* 7 B. C. IND. & COM. L. REV. 783 (1966).

14. Under current grievance practices, an attempt is usually made to keep the number of arbitrated grievances to a minimum. An officer of the National Union testified in this case that only one of 967 grievances filed at all of Swift's plants between September 1961 and October 1963 was taken to arbitration. And the AFL–CIO's *amicus* brief reveals similar performances at General Motors Company and United States Steel Corporation, two of the Nation's largest unionized employers: less than .05 per cent of all written grievances filed during a recent period at General Motors required arbitration, while only 5.6 per cent of the grievances processed beyond the first step at United States Steel were decided by an arbitrator.

because it settled the grievance short of arbitration.

For these same reasons, the standard applied here by the Missouri Supreme Court cannot be sustained. For if a union's decision that a particular grievance lacks sufficient merit to justify arbitration would constitute a breach of the duty of fair representation because a judge or jury later found the grievance meritorious, the union's incentive to settle such grievances short of arbitration would be seriously reduced. The dampening effect on the entire grievance procedure of this reduction of the union's freedom to settle claims in good faith would surely be substantial. Since the union's statutory duty of fair representation protects the individual employee from arbitrary abuses of the settlement device by providing him with recourse against both employer (in a § 301 suit) and union, this severe limitation on the power to settle grievances is neither necessary nor desirable. Therefore, we conclude that the Supreme Court of Missouri erred in upholding the verdict in this case solely on the ground that the evidence supported Owens' claim that he had been wrongfully discharged.

B.

Applying the proper standard of union liability to the facts of this case, we cannot uphold the jury's award, for we conclude that as a matter of federal law the evidence does not support a verdict that the Union breached its duty of fair representation. As we have stated, Owens could not have established a breach of that duty merely by convincing the jury that he was in fact fit for work in 1960; he must also have proved arbitrary or bad-faith conduct on the part of the Union in processing his grievance. The evidence revealed that the Union diligently supervised the grievance into the fourth step of the bargaining agreement's procedure, with the Union's business representative serving as Owens' advocate throughout these steps. When Swift refused to reinstate Owens on the basis of his medical reports indicating reduced blood pressure, the Union sent him to another doctor of his own choice, at Union expense, in an attempt to amass persuasive medical evidence of Owens' fitness for work. When this examination proved unfavorable, the Union concluded that it could not establish a wrongful discharge. It then encouraged Swift to find light work for Owens at the plant. When this effort failed, the Union determined that arbitration would be fruitless and suggested to Owens that he accept Swift's offer to send him to a heart association for rehabilitation. At this point, Owens' grievance

was suspended in the fourth step in the hope that he might be rehabilitated.

In administering the grievance and arbitration machinery as statutory agent of the employees, a union must, in good faith and in a non-arbitrary manner, make decisions as to the merit of particular grievances. See Humphrey v. Moore, 375 U.S. 335, 349–350; Ford Motor Co. v. Huffman, 345 U.S. 330, 337–339. In a case such as this, when Owens supplied the Union with medical evidence supporting his position, the Union might well have breached its duty had it ignored Owens' complaint or had it processed the grievance in a perfunctory manner. See Cox, *Rights under Labor Agreement,* 69 HARV. L. REV., at 632–634. But here the Union processed the grievance into the fourth step, attempted to gather sufficient evidence to prove Owens' case, attempted to secure for Owens less vigorous work at the plant, and joined in the employer's efforts to have Owens rehabilitated. Only when these efforts all proved unsuccessful did the Union conclude both that arbitration would be fruitless and that the grievance should be dismissed. There was no evidence that any Union officer was personally hostile to Owens or that the Union acted at any time other than in good faith.[15] Having concluded that the individual employee has no absolute right to have his grievance arbitrated under the collective bargaining agreement at issue, and that a breach of the duty of fair representation is not established merely by proof that the underlying grievance was meritorious, we must conclude that that duty was not breached here.

IV.

In our opinion, there is another important reason why the judgment of the Missouri Supreme Court cannot stand. Owens' suit against the Union was grounded on his claim that Swift had discharged him in violation of the applicable collective bargaining agreement. In his complaint, Owens alleged "that, as a direct result of said wrongful breach of said contract, by em-

---

15. Owens did allege and testify that petitioner Vaca, President of the Kansas City local, demanded $300 in expenses before the Union would take the grievance to arbitration, a charge which all the petitioners vigorously denied at trial. Under the collective bargaining agreement, the local union had no power to invoke arbitration. See Note 2 *supra.* Moreover, the Union's decision to send Owens to another doctor at Union expense occurred after Vaca's alleged demand, and the ultimate decision not to invoke arbitration came later still. Thus, even if the jury believed Owens' controverted testimony, we do not think that this incident would establish a breach of duty by the Union.

ployer ... Plaintiff was damaged in the sum of Six Thousand, Five Hundred ($6,500.00) Dollars per year, continuing until the date of trial." For the Union's role in "preventing Plaintiff from completely exhausting administrative remedies," Owens requested, and the jury awarded, compensatory damages for the above-described breach of contract plus punitive damages of $3,000. R., at 6. We hold that such damages are not recoverable from the Union in the circumstances of this case.

The appropriate remedy for a breach of a union's duty of fair representation must vary with the circumstances of the particular breach. In this case, the employee's complaint was that the Union wrongfully failed to afford him the arbitration remedy against his employer established by the collective bargaining agreement. But the damages sought by Owens were primarily those suffered because of the employer's alleged breach of contract. Assuming for the moment that Owens had been wrongfully discharged, Swift's only defense to a direct action for breach of contract would have been the Union's failure to resort to arbitration, compare Republic Steel Corp. v. Maddox, 379 U.S. 650, with Smith v. Evening News Assn., 371 U.S. 195, and if that failure was itself a violation of the Union's statutory duty to the employee, there is no reason to exempt the employer from contractual damages which he would otherwise have had to pay. The difficulty lies in fashioning an appropriate scheme of remedies.

Petitioners urge that an employee be restricted in such circumstances to a decree compelling the employer and the union to arbitrate the underlying grievance.[16] It is true that the employee's action is based on the employer's alleged breach of contract plus the union's alleged wrongful failure to afford him his contractual remedy of arbitration. For this reason, an order compelling arbitration should be viewed as one of the available remedies when a breach of the union's duty is proved. But we see no reason inflexibly to require arbitration in all cases. In some cases, for example, at least part of the employee's damages may be attributable to the union's breach of duty, and an arbitrator may have no power under the bargaining agreement to award such damages against the union. In other cases, the arbitrable issues may be substantially resolved in the course of trying the fair representation controversy. In such situations, the court should be free to decide the contractual claim and to award the employee appropriate damages or equitable relief.

A more difficult question is, what portion of the employee's damages may be charged to the union: in particular, may an award against a union include, as it did here, damages attributable solely to the employer's breach of contract? We think not. Though the union has violated a statutory duty in failing to press the grievance, it is the employer's unrelated breach of contract which triggered the controversy and which caused this portion of the employee's damages. The employee should have no difficulty recovering these damages from the employer, who cannot, as we have explained, hide behind the union's wrongful failure to act; in fact, the employer may be (and probably should be) joined as a defendant in the fair representation suit, as in Humphrey v. Moore, *supra*. It could be a real hardship on the union to pay these damages, even if the union were given a right of indemnification against the employer. With the employee assured of direct recovery from the employer, we see no merit in requiring the union to pay the employer's share of the damages.[17]

The governing principle, then, is to apportion liability between the employer and the union according to the damage caused by the fault of each. Thus, damages attributable solely to the employer's breach of contract should not be charged to the union, but increases if any in those damages caused by the union's refusal to process the grievance should not be charged to the employer. In this case, even if the Union had breached its duty, all or almost all of Owens' damages would still be attributable to his allegedly wrongful discharge by Swift. For these reasons, even if the Union here had properly been found liable for a breach of duty, it is clear that the damage award was improper.

Reversed.

---

16. Obviously, arbitration is an appropriate remedy only when the parties have created such a procedure in the collective bargaining agreement.

17. We are not dealing here with situations where a union has affirmatively caused the employer to commit the alleged breach of contract. In cases of that sort where the union's conduct is found to be an unfair labor practice, the NLRB has found an unfair labor practice by the employer, too, and has held the union and the employer jointly and severally liable for any back pay found owing to the particular employee who was the subject of their joint discrimination. *E.g.*, Imparato Stevedoring Corp., 113 N.L.R.B. 883 (1955); Squirt Distrib. Co., 92 N.L.R.B. 1667 (1951); H. M. Newman, 85 N.L.R.B. 725 (1949). Even if this approach would be appropriate for analogous § 301 and breach-of-duty suits, it is not applicable here. Since the Union played no part in Swift's alleged breach of contract and since Swift took no part in the Union's alleged breach of duty, joint liability for either wrong would be unwarranted.

FORTAS, J., with whom THE CHIEF JUSTICE and HARLAN J., join (concurring). 1. In my view, a complaint by an employee that the union has breached its duty of fair representation is subject to the exclusive jurisdiction of the NLRB. It is a charge of unfair labor practice. See Miranda Fuel Co., 140 N.L.R.B. 181 (1962);[1] Local 12, United Rubber Workers, 150 N.L.R.B. 312, enforced, No. 22239 (C. A. 5th Cir., Nov. 9, 1966).[2] As is the case with most other unfair labor practices, the Board's jurisdiction is pre-emptive. Garner v. Teamsters Union, 346 U.S. 485 (1953); Guss v. Utah Labor Board, 353 U.S. 1 (1957); San Diego Building Trades Council v. Garmon, 359 U.S. 236 (1959); Local 438, Constr. Laborers v. Curry, 371 U.S. 542 (1963); Plumbers' Union v. Borden, 373 U.S. 690 (1963); Iron Workers v. Perko, 373 U.S. 701 (1963); Liner v. Jafco, Inc., 375 U.S. 301 (1964). Cf. Woody v. Sterling Alum. Prods. Inc., No. 18,083 (C. A. 8th Cir., Sept. 2, 1966, petition for certiorari pending, No. 946, O. T. 1966). There is no basis for failure to apply the pre-emption principles in the present case, and, as I shall discuss, strong reason for its application. The relationship between the union and the individual employee with respect to the processing of claims to employment rights under the collective bargaining agreement is fundamental to the design and operation of federal labor law. It is not "merely peripheral," as the Court's opinion states. It "presents difficult problems of definition of status, problems which we have held are precisely 'of a kind most wisely entrusted initially to the agency charged with the day-to-day administration of the Act as a whole.'" Iron Workers v. Perko, *supra,* 373 U.S. at 706. Accordingly, the judgment of the Supreme Court of Missouri should be reversed and the

complaint dismissed for this reason and on this basis. I agree, however, that if it were assumed that jurisdiction of the subject matter exists, the judgment would still have to be reversed because of the use by the Missouri court of an improper standard for measuring the union's duty, and the absence of evidence to establish that the union refused further to process Owens' grievance because of bad faith or arbitrarily.

2. I regret the elaborate discussion in the Court's opinion of problems which are irrelevant. This is not an action by the employee against the employer, and the discussion of the requisites of such an action is, in my judgment, unnecessary. The Court argues that the employee could sue the employer under NLRB § 301; and that to maintain such an action the employee would have to show that he has exhausted his remedies under the collective bargaining agreement, or alternatively that he was prevented from doing so because the union breached its duty to him by failure completely to process his claim. That may be; or maybe all he would have to show to maintain an action against the employer for wrongful discharge is that he demanded that the union process his claim to exhaustion of available remedies, and that it refused to do so.[3] I see no need for the Court to pass upon that question, which is not presented here, and which, with all respect, lends no support to the Court's argument. The Court seems to use its dicussion of the employee-employer litigation as somehow analogous to or supportive of its conclusion that the employee may maintain a court action against the union. But I do not believe that this follows. I agree that the NLRB's unfair labor practice jurisdiction does not preclude an action under § 301 against the employer for wrongful discharge from employment. Smith v. Evening News Assn., 371 U.S. 195 (1962). Therefore, Owens might maintain an action against his employer in the present case. This would be an action to enforce the collective bargaining agreement, and Congress has authorized the courts to entertain

---

1. This decision of the NLRB was denied enforcement by the Court of Appeals for the Second Circuit but on a basis which did not decide the point relevant here. NLRB v. Miranda Fuel Co., 326 F. 2d 172 (C.A. 2d Cir. 1963). Only one judge, Judge Medina, took the position that the NLRB had incorrectly held violation of the duty of fair representation to be an unfair labor practice. As an alternative ground for decision, he held that the NLRB had not had sufficient evidence to support its finding of breach of the duty. Judge Lumbard agreed with this latter holding, and explicitly did not reach the question whether breach of the duty is an unfair labor practice. Judge Friendly dissented. He would have affirmed the NLRB both on the sufficiency of the evidence and on the holding that breach of the duty of fair representation is an unfair labor practice as to which the NLRB can give relief.

2. The opinion by Judge Thornberry for the Fifth Circuit supports the views expressed herein. See also Cox, *The Duty of Fair Representation*, 2 VILLANOVA L. REV. 151, 172–173 (1957): Wellington, *Union Democracy and Fair Representation: Federal Responsibility in a Federal System*, 67 YALE L. J. 1327 (1958).

3. Cf. my Brother Black's dissenting opinion in this case. Cf. also Brown v. Sterling Alum. Prods. Inc., 365 F. 2d 651, 656–657 (C. A. 8th Cir. 1966, petition for certiorari pending, No. 946, O.T. 1966). Republic Steel Corp. v. Maddox, 379 U.S. 650 (1965), does not pass upon the issue. The Court states that "To leave the employee remedyless" when the union wrongfully refuses to process his grievance, "would . . . be a great injustice," I do not believe the Court relieves this injustice to any great extent by requiring the employee to prove an unfair labor practice as a prerequisite to judicial relief for the employer's breach of contract. Nor do I understand how giving the employee a cause of action against the *union* is an appropriate way to remedy the injustice which would exist if the union were allowed to foreclose relief against the *employer*.

actions of this type. But his claim against the union is quite different in character, as the Court itself recognizes. The Court holds—and I think correctly if the issue is to be reached—that the union could not be required to pay damages measured by the breach of the employment contract, because it was not the union but the employer that breached the contract. I agree ; but I suggest that this reveals the point for which I contend: that the employee's claim against the union is not a claim under the collective bargaining agreement, but a claim that the union has breached its statutory duty of fair representation. This claim, I submit, is a claim of unfair labor practice and it is within the exclusive jurisdiction of the NLRB. The Court agrees that "one of the available remedies [obtainable, the Court says, by court action] when a breach of the Union's duty is proved" is "an order compelling arbitration." This is precisely and uniquely the kind of order which is within the province of the Board. Beyond this, the Court is exceedingly vague as to remedy: "appropriate damages or other equitable relief" are suggested as possible remedies, apparently when arbitration is not available. Damages against the union, the Court admonishes, should be gauged "according to the damage caused by its fault"—*i.e.,* the failure to exhaust remedies for the grievance. The Court's difficulty, it seems to me, reflects the basic awkwardness of its position: It is attempting to force into the posture of a contract violation an alleged default of the union which is not a violation of the collective bargaining agreement but a breach of its separate and basic duty fairly to represent all employees in the unit. This is an unfair labor practice, and should be treated as such.[4]

3. If we look beyond logic and precedent to the policy of the labor relations design which Congress has provided, court jurisdiction of this type of action seems anomalous and ill-advised. We are not dealing here with the interpretation of a contract or with an alleged breach of an employment agreement. As the Court in effect acknowledges, we are concerned with the subtleties of a union's statutory duty faithfully to represent employees in the unit, including those who may not be members of the union. The Court—regrettably, in my opinion—ventures to state judgments as to the metes and bounds of the reciprocal duties involved in the relationship between the union and the employee. In my opinion, this is precisely and especially the kind of judgment that Congress intended to entrust to the Board and which is well within the preemption doctrine that this Court has prudently stated.[5] See cases cited, *supra,* especially the *Perko* and *Borden* cases, the facts of which strongly parallel the situation in this case. See also Linn v. Plant Guard Workers, 383 U.S. 53, 72 (1966) (dissenting opinion). The nuances of union-employee and union-employer relationship are infinite and consequential, particularly when the issue is as amorphous as whether the union acted "in bad faith or arbitrarily" which the Court states as the standard applicable here. In all reason and in all good judgment, this jurisdiction should be left with the Board and not be placed in the courts, especially with the complex and necessarily confusing guidebook that the Court now publishes.

Accordingly, I join the judgment of reversal, but on the basis stated.

BLACK, J. (dissenting). The Court today opens slightly the courthouse door to an employee's incidental claim against his union for breach of its duty of fair representation, only to shut it in his face when he seeks direct judicial relief for his underlying and more valuable breach-of-contract claim against his employer. This result follows from the Court's announcement in this case, involving an employee's suit against his union, of a new rule to govern an employee's suit against his employer. The rule is that before an employee can sue his employer under § 301 of the L.M.R.A. for a simple breach of his employment contract, the employee must prove not only that he attempted to exhaust his contractual remedies, but that his attempt to exhaust them was frustrated by "arbitrary, discriminatory or ... bad faith" conduct on the part of

---

4. The Court argues that since the employee suing the employer for breach of the employment contract would have to show exhaustion of remedies under the contract, and since he would for this purpose have to show his demand on the union and, according to the Court, its wrongful failure to prosecute his grievance, the union could be joined as a party defendant; and since the union could be joined in such a suit, it may be sued independently of the employer. But this is a *non sequitur*. As the Court itself insists, the suit against the union is not for breach of the employment contract, but for violation of the duty fairly to represent the employee. This is an entirely different matter. It is a breach of statutory duty—an unfair labor practice—and not a breach of the employment contract.

5. In a variety of contexts the NLRB concerns itself with the substantive bargaining behavior of the parties. For example: (a) the duty to bargain in good faith, see, *e.g.,* Fibreboard Corp. v. Labor Board, 379 U.S. 203 (1964): (b) jurisdictional disputes, see, *e.g.,* Labor Board v. Radio Engineers, 364 U.S. 573 (1961); (c) secondary boycotts and hot cargo clauses, see, *e.g.,* Orange Belt District Council of Painters No. 48 v. NLRB, 328 F. 2d 534 (C.A.D.C. Cir. 1964).

his union. With this new rule and its result, I cannot agree.

The Court recognizes, as it must, that the jury in this case found at least that Benjamin Owens was fit for work, that his grievance against Swift was meritorious, and that Swift breached the collective bargaining agreement when it wrongfully discharged him. The Court also notes in passing that Owens has a separate action for breach of contract pending against Swift in the state courts. And in Part IV of its opinion, the Court vigorously insists that "there is no reason to exempt the employer from contractual damages which he would otherwise have had to pay," that the "employee should have no difficulty recovering these damages from the employer" for his "unrelated breach of contract," and "the employee [is] assured of direct recovery from the employer." But this reassurance in Part IV gives no comfort to Owens, for Part IV is based on the assumption that the union breached its duty to Owens, an assumption which, in Part III of its opinion, the Court finds unsupported by the facts of this case. What this all means, though the Court does not expressly say it, is that Owens will be no more successful in his pending breach-of-contract action against Swift than he is here in his suit against the union. For the Court makes it clear "that the question of whether a union has breached its duty of fair representation will ... be a critical issue in a suit under L.M.R.A. § 301," that "the wrongfully discharged employee may bring an action against his employer" only if he "can prove that the union ... breached its duty of fair representation in its handling of the employee's grievance," and "that the employee, as part and parcel of his § 301 action, finds it necessary to prove an unfair labor practice by the union." Thus, when Owens attempts to proceed with his pending breach-of-contract action against Swift, Swift will undoubtedly secure its prompt dismissal by pointing to the Court's conclusion here that the union has not breached its duty of fair representation. Thus, Owens, who now has obtained a judicial determination that he was wrongfully discharged, is left remediless, and Swift, having breached its contract, is allowed to hide behind, and is shielded by, the union's conduct. I simply fail to see how it should make one iota of difference, as far as the "unrelated breach-of-contract" by Swift is concerned, whether the union's conduct is wrongful or rightful. Neither precedent nor logic support the Court's new announcement that it does.

Certainly, nothing in Republic Steel Corp v. Maddox, 379 U.S. 650, supports this new rule.

That was a case where the aggrieved employee attempted to "completely sidestep available grievance procedures in favor of a lawsuit." *Id.*, at 653. Noting that "it cannot be said ... that contract grievance procedures are inadequate to protect the interests of an aggrieved employee until the employee has attempted to implement the procedures and found them so," *ibid.*, the Court there held that the employee "must *attempt* use of the contract grievance procedure," *id.*, at 652, and "must afford the union the opportunity to act on his behalf," *id.*, at 653. I dissented on the firm belief that an employee should be free to litigate his own lawsuit with his own lawyer in a court before a jury, rather than being forced to entrust his claim to a union which, even if it did agree to press it, would be required to submit it to arbitration. And even if, as the Court implied, "the worker would be allowed to sue after he had presented his claim to the union and after he had suffered the inevitable discouragement and delay which necessarily accompanies the union's refusal to press his claim," *id.*, at 669. I could find no threat to peaceful labor relations or to the union's prestige in allowing an employee to bypass completely contractual remedies in favor of a traditional breach-of-contract lawsuit for backpay or wage substitutes. Here, of course, Benjamin Owens did not "completely sidestep available grievance procedures in favor of a lawsuit." With complete respect for the union's authority and deference to the contract grievance procedures, he not only gave the union a chance to act on his behalf, but in every way possible tried to convince it that his claim was meritorious and should be carried through the fifth step to arbitration. In short, he did everything the Court's opinion in *Maddox* said he should do, and yet now the Court says so much is not enough.

In *Maddox,* I noted that the "cases really in point are those which involved agreements governed by the Railway Labor Act and which expressly refused to hold that a discharged worker must pursue collective bargaining grievance procedures before suing in a court for wrongful discharge. Transcontinental & Western Air, Inc. v. Koppal, 345 U.S. 653 ; Moore v. Illinois Central R. Co., 312 U.S. 630." 379 U.S., at 666. I also observed that the Court's decision in *Maddox* "raised the overruling axe so high [over those cases] that its falling is just about as certain as the changing of the seasons." *Id.,* at 667. In the latter observation I was mistaken. The Court has this Term, in Walker v. Southern R. Co., 385 U.S. 196, refused to overrule in light of *Maddox* such cases as *Moore* and *Koppal.*

Noting the long delays attendant upon exhausting administrative remedies under the Railway Labor Act, the Court based this refusal on "the contrast between the administrative remedy" available to Maddox and that available to Walker. If, as the Court suggested, the availability of an administrative remedy determines whether an employee can sue without first exhausting it, can there be any doubt that Owens who had no administrative remedy should be as free to sue as Walker who had a slow one? Unlike Maddox, Owens attempted to implement the contract grievance procedures and found them inadequate. Today's decision, following in the wake of Walker v. Southern R. Co., merely perpetuates an unfortunate anomaly created by *Maddox* in the law of labor relations.

The rule announced in *Maddox*, I thought, was a "brainchild" of the Court's recent preference for arbitration. But I am unable to subscribe any such genesis to today's rule, for arbitration is precisely what Owens sought and preferred. Today the Court holds that an employee with a meritorious claim has no absolute right to have it either litigated or arbitrated. Fearing that arbitrators would be overworked, the Court allows unions unilaterally to determine not to take a grievance to arbitration—the first step in the contract grievance procedure at which the claim would be presented to an impartial third party—as long as the union decisions are neither "arbitrary" nor "in bad faith." The Court derives this standard of conduct from a long line of cases holding that "a breach of the statutory duty of fair representation occurs only when a union's conduct toward a member of the collective bargaining unit is arbitrary, discriminatory, or in bad faith." What the Court overlooks is that those cases laid down this standard in the context of situations where the employee's sole or fundamental complaint was against the union. There was not the slightest hint in those cases that the same standard would apply where the employee's primary complaint was against his employer for breach of contract and where he only incidentally contended that the union's conduct prevented the adjudication, by either court or arbitrator, of the underlying grievance. If the Court here were satisfied with merely holding that in this situation the employee cannot recover damages from the union unless the union breached its duty of fair representation, then it would be one thing to say that the union did not do so in making a good-faith decision not to take the employee's grievance to arbitration. But if, as the Court goes on to hold, the employee cannot sue his employer for breach of contract unless his failure to exhaust contractual remedies is due to the union's breach of its duty of fair representation, then I am quite unwilling to say that the union's refusal to exhaust such remedies—however nonarbitrary—does not amount to a breach of its duty. Either the employee should be able to sue his employer for breach of contract after having attempted to exhaust his contractual remedies, or the union should have an absolute duty to exhaust contractual remedies on his behalf. The merits of an employee's grievance would thus be determined by either a jury or an arbitrator. Under today's decision it will never be determined by either.

And it should be clear that the Court's opinion goes much further than simply holding that an employee has no absolute right to have the union take his grievance to arbitration. Here, of course, the union supervised the grievance through the fourth step of the contract machinery and dropped it just prior to arbitration on its belief that the outcome of arbitration would be unfavorable. But limited only by the standard of arbitrariness, there was clearly no need for the union to go that far. Suppose, for instance, the union had a rule that it would not prosecute a grievance even to the first step unless the grievance were filed by the employee within 24 hours after it arose. Pursuant to this rule, the union might completely refuse to prosecute a grievance filed several days late. Thus, the employee, no matter how meritorious his grievance, would get absolutely nowhere. And unless he could prove that the union's rule was arbitrary (a standard which no one can define), the employee would get absolutely no consideration of the merits of his grievance—not by a jury, nor by an arbitrator, nor by the employer, nor by the union. The Court suggests three reasons for giving the union this almost unlimited discretion to deprive injured employees of all remedies for breach of contract. The first is that "frivolous grievances" will be ended prior to time-consuming and costly arbitration. But here no one, not even the union, suggests that Benjamin Owens' grievance was frivolous. The union decided not to take it to arbitration simply because the union doubted the chance of success. Even if this was a good-faith doubt, I think the union had the duty to present this contested, but serious claim to the arbitrator whose very function is to decide such claims on the basis of what he believes to be right. Second, the Court says that allowing the union to settle grievances prior to arbitration will assure consistent treatment of "major problem areas in interpretation of collective bargaining contract." But can it be argued that whether Owens was "fit to work" presents a major problem in the interpretation of the collective bargaining agreement? The problem here was one of interpreting medical reports, not a collective bargaining agreement, and of evaluating other evidence of Owens' physical condition. I doubt whether consistency is either possible or desirable in determining whether a particular employee is able to perform a particular job. Finally, the Court suggests that its decision "furthers the interests of the union as statutory agent." I think this is the real reason for today's decision which entirely overlooks the interests of the injured employee, the only one who has anything to lose. Of course, anything which gives the union life and death power over those whom it is supposed to represent furthers its "interests." I simply fail to see how the union's legitimate role as statutory agent is undermined by requiring it to prosecute all serious grievances to a conclusion or by allowing the injured employee to sue his employer after he has given the union a chance to act on his behalf.

Henceforth, in almost every § 301 breach-of-contract suit by an employee against an employer, the employee will have the additional burden of proving that the union acted "arbitrarily or in bad faith." The Court never explains what is meant by this vague phrase or how trial judges are intelligently to translate it to a jury. Must the employee prove that the union in fact acted arbitrarily, or will it be sufficient to show that the employee's grievance was so meritorious that a reasonable union would not have refused to carry it to arbitration? Must the employee join the union in his § 301 suit against the employer, or must he join the employer in his unfair representation suit against the union? However these questions are answered, today's decision, requiring the individual employee to take on both the employer and the union in every suit against the employer and to prove not only that the employer breached its contract, but that the union acted arbitrarily, converts what would otherwise be a simple breach-of-contract action into a three-ring donnybrook. It puts an intolerable burden on employees with meritorious grievances and means they will frequently be left with no remedy. Today's decision, while giving the worker an ephemeral right to sue his union for breach of its duty of fair representation, creates insurmountable obstacles to block his far more valuable right to sue his employer for breach of the collective bargaining agreement.

HILLER v. LIQUID SALESMEN'S UNION LOCAL NO. 2
338 F. 2d 778 (2d Cir. 1964)

HAYS, C. J. Plaintiffs are the administrators of the estate of Louis L. Hiller. The complaint in the action alleges, in effect, that Hiller was unlawfully discharged in 1959 from his employment with The American Distilling Company, Inc. and in 1960 from his employment with Popper-Morson Corporation, and that these discharges were with the knowledge, consent and connivance of the Liquor Salesmen's Union, Local No. 2, of which Hiller was a member in good standing, that Hiller was unlawfully deprived of certain disability insurance and other benefits, that during his employment by Popper-Morson, Hiller was paid less than the salary provided for in the collective bargaining agreement between Popper-Morson and the Union, that this was with the Union's knowledge, consent and connivance, that The American Distilling Company, Inc. coerced Hiller into accepting a compromise of certain rights to commissions and seniority rights, and into signing a letter of resignation, all in violation of the collective bargaining agreement and all with the knowledge, consent and connivance of the Union. The plaintiffs demand damages totalling $48,690.

In the district court, the defendants moved for a stay pending arbitration and their motion was granted. 226 F.Supp. 161 (1964). This was error.

However inartistically stated, the amended complaint seeks to set forth a claim based upon denial by the Union of the right of fair representation. See Syres v. Oil Workers Int'l Union, 350 U.S. 892, 76 S.Ct. 152, 100 L.Ed. 785, reversing per curiam 223 F. 2d 739 (5th Cir. 1955); Brotherhood of Railroad Trainmen v. Howard, 343 U.S. 768, 72 S.Ct. 1022, 96 L.Ed. 1283 (1952); Tunstall v. Brotherhood of Locomotive Firemen, 323 U.S. 210, 65 S.Ct. 235, 89 L.Ed. 187 (1944); Steele v. Louisville & N. R.R., 323 U.S. 192, 65 S.Ct. 226, 89 L.Ed. 173 (1944); cf. Ford Motor Co. v. Huffman, 345 U.S. 330, 337, 73 S.Ct. 681, 97 L.Ed. 1048 (1953). When as is alleged here an employer joins with the union to defraud the employee of his rights, both union and employer are liable. See Ford Motor Co. v. Huffman, *supra*; Steele v. Louisville & N. R.R., *supra*; Richardson v. Texas & N. O. R.R., 242 F. 2d 230 (5th Cir. 1957); Central of Georgia Ry. v .Jones, 229 F. 2d 648 (5th Cir.), cert. denied, 352 U.S. 848, 77 S.Ct. 32, 1 L.Ed. 2d 59 (1956).

It is true that the collective bargaining agreements contain arbitration clauses and that if this were simply a suit for wrongful discharge, the arbitration clauses would be available to the employers as a defense. Larsen v. American Airlines, Inc., 313 F. 2d 599 (2d Cir. 1963); Henderson v. Eastern Gas and Fuel Co., 290 F. 2d 677 (4th Cir. 1961). But where the employee's case is based upon a conspiracy between his union and his employer to deprive him of his rights he cannot be forced to submit that issue to an arbitration between the employer and the union. Such a procedure would fail completely to settle the issues between the union member and his union. It would entrust representation of the employee to the very union which he claims refused him fair representation, and it would present as adversaries in the arbitration procedure the two parties who, the employee claims, are joined in a conspiracy to defraud him.

PART III

EMERGING PROBLEMS AND POTENTIALITIES

CHAPTER XIV

REMEDY POWER

An arbitration proceeding culminates in an award. In many cases the claimant does not prevail, and the award is one dismissing or denying the claim or grievance. Often a claim is found meritorious in whole or in part. The question then becomes whether the arbitrator has power to provide for a remedy and, if so, what kind.

Some submissions and arbitration agreements make it reasonably clear that the arbitrator's task ends with the determination of who is "right." Some agreements indicate nothing one way or the other. Some are very explicit. Unfortunately, we lack data on what patterns are. The Bureau of Labor Statistics 1966 study does not deal with the subject, and no modern study of commercial contract remedy provisions has been unearthed. Information should be gathered and published.

The American Arbitration Association rules for both commercial and labor cases are both comprehensive and explicit. (See appendices).

A.

The Arbitrator's Power to Shape Remedies

REFINERY EMPLOYEES UNION OF LAKE CHARLES v. CONTINENTAL OIL CO.
(5th Cir.) 268 F. 2d 447
[cert. denied, 361 U.S. 896 (1959)]

Before HUTCHESON, CHIEF JUDGE, and BROWN and WISDOM, CIRCUIT JUDGES.

[The union complained that a foreman made an erroneous overtime assignment and it claimed pay equal to the overtime earned for the employee who should have been awarded the work. At first the company admitted an error and offered to assign the employee to "make-work" overtime, thereby maintaining the company policy of "no work—no pay", giving the grieved employee his pay, and not reducing the overtime that would be worked by others. The union insisted that the grievant was entitled to the pay he would have earned if the proper assignment had been made. The company there-

569

after denied the contract breach. The court held that the assignment dispute was arbitrable.]

The difficult question in this case is whether the district court correctly limited the arbitrable issue in holding that the parties to the collective bargaining contract did not intend to submit to arbitration the remedy for misassignment of overtime work, including authority to award wages for work not performed.

This Court is committed to the policy that "private arbitration in the labor-management field is to be afforded broad liberalities." Lodge No. 12, Dist. No. 37, International Association of Machinists v. Cameron Iron Works, 5 Cir., 1958, 257 F. 2d 467, 474, certiorari denied 358 U.S. 880, 79 S.Ct. 120, 3 L.Ed. 2d 110. But this policy does not permit the Court to find agreement where there is no agreement.

The arbitration clause in the case at bar[1] is not a broad grant of authority to the arbitrators,[2] a *quid pro* for giving up the right to strike. The Union expressly reserved the right to strike during the term of the agreement. The arbitration clause in question is a limited clause that does not purport to cover "any or all" disputes. It covers: "*Only* differences relating to the interpretation or performance of this agreement." The contract is silent as to the remedy, if any, for misassigned overtime. The arbitration clause is silent as to the power of arbitrators to provide a remedy or to impose a penalty.

The underlying problem as to whether the overtime work was assigned to an employee in the proper classification is plainly a difference expressly covered by the arbitration clause. The real dispute as to whether the Company should pay for time not worked, as a penalty imposed on the Company to discourage future violations, is plainly not covered in the contract—unless, giving a broad interpretation to the arbitration clause, the Court should hold that the authority of an arbitrator to make awards and fix damages is implied in the arbitration of every grievance.

There is a difference between arbitration of a commercial dispute and arbitration of a labor dispute. That difference is not so great when there is a limited arbitration clause, as in this case. In Marchant v. Mead-Morrison the court found that the parties did not intend to arbitrate "every difference having its genesis in the contract", but only differences as to the "construction" and "performance" of the contract.[3] Such a submission withholds from the arbitrators authority to give consequential damages. Citing this case as authority, several courts have held squarely that "unless the arbitrator is [expressly] given the power to award damages . . . an award attempting to do this is void as beyond the power of the Board [of arbitrators]." Lone Star Cotton Mills v. Thomas, Tex. Civ. App., 1959, 227 S.W. 2d 300, 307. Guidry v. Gulf Oil Corporation, Tex. Civ. App., 1959, 320 S.W. 2d 691, is to the same effect. "It is not lawful for arbitrators to fix damages arising out of the matters submitted to them unless the issue of such damages is also specifically submitted." Publishers' Association of New York City v. New York Typographical Union No. 6, 1938, 168 Misc. 267, 5 N.Y.S. 2d 847, 853.

The precise question at issue, however, has

---

1. Section 21, entitled "Arbitration," provides: "21–1 Only differences relating to the interpretation or performance of this agreement which cannot be adjusted by mutual agreement, after processing through the grievance procedure may upon written notice by one party to the other, not later than sixty (60) days after the date of the decision of the regional manager of manufacturing be submitted to arbitration."

2. Compare the arbitration clause recommended by the American Arbitration Association: "The American Arbitration Association recommends the following general arbitration clause in labor agreement; 'Any dispute, claim or grievance arising out of or relating to this agreement shall be submitted to arbitration under the Voluntary Labor Arbitration Rules, then obtaining, of the American Arbitration Association. The parties agree to abide by the award, subject to such regulations as any Federal agency having jurisdiction may impose. The parties further agree that there shall be no suspension of work when such dispute arises and while it is in process of adjustment or arbitration'." DEPT. OF LABOR BULL., 908–16, at p. 858.

"Even though an arbitration clause covering only 'disputes concerning the interpretation and application' of the collective agreement cannot mean barely the translation of words, it must impose some limit. The phrasing of the arbitration clause is often an important issue in collective bargaining. Experienced negotiators are thoroughly aware of their ability to choose between the comparatively narrow clause noted above and a wide-open undertaking to arbitrate 'any dispute, difference, disagreement or controversy of any nature or character' which may arise during the term of the agreement. When the former clause is selected, the company believes that a limit has been imposed upon the power of the arbitrator. . . . The contrast between the wide-open clause and the conventional phraseology is too plain to put down to inadvertence. The apparent purpose is to confine the power of the arbitrator. Apparently the parties choose it because one party, usually the employer, distrusts arbitration at least to the point of insisting upon the inclusion of some safeguard against the arbitrator's imposition of significant obligations not contemplated by the agreement and quite beyond its scope. The clause does not tell what the arbitrator should not do. It tells what he cannot do." Cox, *Reflections Upon Labor Arbitration*, 72 HARV. L. REV. 1483, 1500, 1509 (1959).

3. In Marchant v. Mead-Morrison the court found a limited submission. In later cases, New York courts have held that when an arbitrator is given power to decide a controversy in its entirety, "any and all controversies," the arbitrator has an implied power to award damages. Utility Laundry Service v. Sklar, 1949, 300 N.Y. 255, 90 N.E. 2d 178, 180.

not been decided in any reported decision, as far as our research goes.[4] In United Electrical Radio & Machine Workers of America v. Miller Metal Products, 4 Cir., 1954, 215 F. 2d 221 and in International Union United Furniture Workers of America v. Colonial Hardwood Flooring Co., 4 Cir., 1948, 168 F. 2d 33, 35, the court held that claims for damages for breach of a no-strike clause are not arbitrable, since the arbitration clause contemplates matters subject to the grievance procedure and not such controversies as strikes and secondary boycotts which are entirely foreign to the grievance procedure. "It would have been possible," Judge Parker held in *Colonial Hardwood,*

> for the parties to provide for the arbitration of any dispute which might arise between them; but they did not do this, and the rule *noscitur a sociis* applies to the arbitration clause in the grievance procedure to limit its application to controversies to which the grievance procedure was intended to apply.

A similar result was reached with reference to a claim for consequential damages in a contract clause referring to a dispute over hiring and transferring employees. Council of Western Electric Technical Employees National v. Western Electric Co., 2 Cir., 1956, 238 F. 2d 892. In these and other cases that might be cited, the federal courts have been fully aware of the force of the considerations supporting a broad commitment of labor disputes to arbitration, but have adhered firmly to the principle that remedies (damages) are not arbitrable unless there is clear contractual authority for their arbitrability. See especially Local No. 149 of American Federation of Technical Engineers (A.F.L.) v. General Electric Company, 1 Cir., 1957, 250 F. 2d 922, 926, 930.

The contract in the instant case covers forty-two pages, detailing wages and hours of work, overtime, premium time, shifts and shifts differentials, job classification, seniority, craft senior-

---

4. Few arbitrators, however, have had any doubts as to the extent of their jurisdiction in awarding damages for breach of contract. International Harvester Company, 1947, 9 L.A. 894; Standard Lime and Cement Company, 1956, 26 L.A. 468; Bridgeport Grass Company, 1952, 19 L.A. 690; International Harvester Company, 1950, 14 L.A. 430; Ingersoll-Rand Company, 1947, 7 L.A. 564; Bethlehem Steel Company, 1947, 7 L.A. 493; United States Rubber Company, 1949, 13 L.A. 840; Phillips Chemical Company, 1951, 17 L.A. 721; Mississippi Aluminium Corporation, 1956, 27 L.A. 625; Vanette Hosiery Mills, 1951, 17 L.A. 349; American Machine and Foundry Company, 1950, 15 L.A. 822. Various reasons are given: (1) the company must be given a penalty, to discourage future contract violations; (2) the job classification and work assignment provisions are valueless, unless an award (damages) is given for their breach; (3) like any other contract violation or tort, damages are inseparably connected with the claim; (4) the aggrieved employee, in an overtime case, is entitled to work the overtime hours when they are available, not at some later time. Some arbitrators have held, however, that equivalent work at the same pay is the proper means of disposing of the dispute since it "satisfies the dominant intention of the parties" and enables the error to be "equitably rectified." Celanese Corporation of America, 1954, 24 L.A. 168; Goodyear Atomic Corporation, 1956, 27 L.A. 634.

The International Harvester Company decision is considered the leading case on the authority of arbitrators to make money awards. In this case employees were given new piece-work assignments but were not informed of the piece-work price until after they had worked on them some time. The contract required that employees be notified of the rate in advance. The arbitrator held that the employees were entitled to be paid at average earnings rather than at the price on the jobs involved. The case has a special bearing here because the decision was based in part on the company's practice (policy) in the past of making adjustments on the basis of average earnings. The case did not involve payment for work not performed. The language of the arbitrator has been quoted in a number of cases and legal articles: "The conclusion that no money arbitration award is proper regarding contract provisions which do not specifically provide for it would have two effects. The first would be

the substitution of some other method of settlement in the place of arbitration. The second would be cluttering up of the contract with a lot of 'liquidated damage' provisions which would invite more trouble than they could ever be expected to prevent. It will be unfortunate if collective bargaining agreements develop along the lines of the revenue laws, with provision necessarily being made for every little hair-line question which may arise between adverse parties pressing conflicting interests. They will lose their effectiveness when they become so involved that laymen cannot follow or understand them. It would contribute dangerously to that tendency if it were required that every contract clause had to contain a damages provision. This is the kind of thing which it must be assumed the parties intended would be handled in the light of the applicability of a particular clause to the particular problems that might arise under it."

Phillips Chemical Company, 1951, 17 L.A. 721 was an arbitration of a claim for overtime. "The purpose of arbitration is to settle disputes justly and fully, as a substitute for strikes and lock-outs. If a grievance has no merit, relief is denied; but if it has merit adequate relief should be granted. That is what the parties contemplate. Anything less than that would not effect justice and would not satisfy the complaining party. Therefore, it is implied in the arbitration section that the arbitration board has power to grant adequate relief. The power merely to decide that the agreement has been violated, without power to redress the injury, would be futility in the extreme. Furthermore, Article 14 provides 'The arbitration board should have jurisdiction over all the disputes arising under the terms of this agreement;' and jurisdiction means power to grant relief. ¶ "Hence, it is implied that where breach of the agreement has caused a money loss, the board has power to award the proper amount as compensatory damages. A specific clause to that effect would of course make that power clearer, but a clause is not essential. Therefore, making such an award is not adding a term to the agreement; it is merely carrying out the clearly implied purpose of arbitration, viz., to grant proper relief for meritorious grievances. In the courts, the customary relief is money damages; it is not surprising that frequently in arbitration cases the same relief is required."

ity preference lists, military leave, holidays, vacations, jury duty, severance notice and pay, annuities and benefits, funeral leave, grievance procedure, arbitration, strikes and lock-outs, working conditions, and other matters. With all of that, there is no list of job classifications and rate ranges and, as in Local No. 149 of American Federation of Technical Engineers (A.F.L.) v. General Electric Company, "no language by way of job descriptions which could be interpreted or applied for the purpose of determining whether the duties performed by a particular employee fall within any particular grade." It is unlikely that the omission was accidental. It seems to us that such a contract, involving a large, complicated, modern refinery, contemplates play in the joints—a number of instances when there will be disagreement between company and union as to job classification. The refinery cannot cease operating while the parties decide what employee should do a particular job. Instead, the company representative assigns the work according to his best judgment and if the assignment is incorrect, as the Union might see it, the question may be settled by the grievance procedure and arbitration. The settlement of a job classification is sufficient justification in itself for resort to arbitration. There is no reason to assume that the parties must have intended a penalty to be implied in order to make the contract operative. And there is no basis for asserting that without damages the union has a right but not a remedy: the remedy is settlement of the classification or proper assignment. The union is not in the position of an ordinary private litigant asserting a claim for breach of contract. Here, for example, as we read the correspondence between the Union and the Company, whatever interest the particular aggrieved employee may have had in receiving equivalent work at the same pay, instead of damages, was lost in the shuffle, overridden by the company-union struggle over the principle of paying for work not performed.

Section 8-1 provides that "work peculiar to a classification shall be performed by employees assigned to that classification". Nowhere in Section 8 is there any provision for a penalty or for damages for a misassignment. But a remedy is expressly provided or probably implied in other sections of the contract, such as those dealing with vacations, jury duty, severance pay, annuities, and funeral leaves. Section 5-7, dealing with overtime, states: "It is the intent of the Company to equalize overtime among employees of the same job classification insofar as it may be practical." This provision declares that the Company intends to equalize "overtime" (work),

but it imposes no absolute obligation, refers to no remedy, and contains no inference that damages will be awarded in case of misassignment. (In making this statement, and in the opinion generally, this Court is not passing on any remedy the aggrieved employee or the Union may have for misassigned overtime work. That issue is not before us. We are simply pointing out that the contract contains no express or implied provision covering a money award for misassignment of overtime, from which might be drawn the inference that the remedy was a matter of "interpretation" or "performance" of the contract and therefore an arbitrable issue.)

We return to our starting point. The Company did not agree to submit all differences to arbitration but "only differences relating to the interpretation or performance" of the agreement. The Company policy is against paying two employees for overtime worked by one. Granted broad approval of arbitration, this Court must consider whether the parties intended a third person to alter basic Company policy through the medium of an arbitration procedure. The correctness of the work assignment is a matter of concern to the individual aggrieved employee. It is also a matter of concern to a union interested in strict observance of craft lines and generally equal distribution of overtime benefits. But subjecting the Company to punitive damages in order to discourage future misassignments and overturning the Company's policy of paying only for work performed goes beyond rectifying individual grievances and beyond the ordinary arbitrative process. There is not much of a contract between the parties and there is not much stability of the company-union relationship, if an important term may be added to a contract and a fundamental change made in the operation of a plant because a dispute is traceable to its genesis in an individual grievance.

The real difference between the parties is over the company policy: no work—no pay. The bone of contention between the Company and the Union is whether a mistake in work assignment should be rectified by damages to the aggrieved employee or by equivalent pay for work performed. This is an over-all labor-management issue that involves, on the one hand, efficient plant management and the economics of production, and, on the other hand, protection of an individual worker through union organization. The proper forum for settlement of the dispute is the bargaining table. The proper persons to make the settlement are the representatives of the Union and the Company, not some third arbitrator.[5] So, at least, was the intention of the parties as we read the contract we are required to interpret. In reaching this conclusion we have sought to escape the binds of a narrow, stultifying construction of a legal document. We have sought to construe the contract as a collective bargaining agreement to be read in the context of (1) the collective bargaining process, (2) the background of the particular dispute, (3) the nature of labor arbitration, and (4) the mandate of the Supreme Court in *Lincoln Mills*.

Judgment is affirmed.

[In concurring Chief Judge Hutcheson agreed with the court and read his dissenting colleague a stern and sharp lecture on the perils of being "pioneer, teacher and guide in the role of judicial activist."]

BROWN, C. J. (dissenting). Running through the Court's opinion is the idea that a supposed policy of "no work—no pay" is evidence of an intent not to allow a third party to award damages. Of course, the fact of this case, as the Court acknowledges, is that a worker had a right to a specific task; the company wrongfully deprived him of it; what he seeks is what he would have earned at it. A court of law would award him no less and would pay scant heed to the suggestion that this was paying for work not done. Everyone who risks a claim of breach of con-

tract understands that if a court rejects his denial of breach, he may end up paying twice. He will find no judicial succor on the plea that this is punitive.

The idea of a person deciding a controversy so that his decision may then become the subject of a new and further one—*i.e.,* controversy in bargaining—is repugnant to the scheme of an orderly disposition of disputes before they ripen into the seeds of industrial conflict.

LODGE 12, INTERNATIONAL ASSOCIATION OF MACHINIST v. CAMERON IRON WORKS, INC.
(5th Cir.) 292 F. 2d 112
[*cert. denied,* 368 U.S. 926 (1961)]

Before TUTTLE, CH. J. and HUTCHESON and BROWN, C. J.

BROWN, C. J. We deal here with the question of whether arbitration of a labor dispute pursuant to a collective bargaining agreement may comprehend an award of a money sum equivalent to back pay for time lost due to an unauthorized discharge. The District Court answered it in the negative. We disagree and reverse:

The case is here for the second time. On its former appearance, in there reversing the District Court, we held that a grievance within the terms of the arbitration clause was presented concerning the discharge of 15 employees for misconduct during the preceding strike. Lodge No. 12, etc. v. Cameron Iron Works, Inc., 5 Cir., 1958, 257 F. 2d 467, certiorari denied, 358 U.S. 880, 79 S.Ct. 120, 3 L.Ed. 2d 110. On remand the Court, without a jury, heard the case. The Employer's effort to establish that in the settlement of the strike the parties had expressly agreed not to arbitrate this controversy having failed, there was nothing left for the Court to do save order arbitration. This it did. But in so doing, the Court expressly directed that the "scope of arbitration, however, may extend only to the issue of reinstatement of the employees and may not include the award of back pay for time lost." [183 F. Supp. 148.] The Court presumably had two things in mind. First, since the "grievance sought to be arbitrated is the reinstatement of the employees," such controversy "may be settled by the board upon terms and conditions not necessarily involving the award of back pay." Second, and more important, it held that there "is no clear authority in the contract for the award of back pay as a remedy in arbitration,"

---

5. In Douds v. Local 1250, Retail Wholesale Department Store Union, 2 Cir., 1949, 173 F. 2d 764, 768, 7 A.L.R. 2d 685, Judge Hand referred to a Fifth Circuit holding that grievances "must be understood to be limited to questions of minor importance." Hughes Tool Co. v. National Labor Relations Board, 5 Cir., 1945, 147 F. 2d 69, 158 A.L.R. 1165. On rehearing he felt that Elgin, Joliet & Eastern Ry. Co. v. Burley, 1945, 325 U.S. 711, 65 S.Ct. 1282, 1290, 89 L.Ed. 1886, confirmed this view on the principal matter, and, in this case, Mr. Justice Rutledge distinguished between disputes concerning the making of collective agreements and those over grievances or interpretations. "The first relates to disputes over the formation of collective agreements or efforts to secure them," continued Justice Rutledge. "They arise where there is no such agreement or where it is sought to change the terms of one, and therefore the issue is not whether an existing agreement controls the controversy. They look to the acquisition of rights for the future, not to assertion of rights claimed to have vested in the past. The second class, however, contemplates the existence of a collective agreement already concluded or, at any rate, a situation in which no effort is made to bring about a formal change in terms or to create a new one. The dispute relates either to the meaning or proper application of a particular provision with reference to a specific situation or to an omitted case. In the latter event the claim is founded upon some incident of the employment relation, or asserted one, independent of those covered by the collective agreement, *e.g.*, claims on account of personal injuries. In either case the claim is to rights accrued, not merely to have new ones created for the future."

and "such a remedy cannot be implied from a grant of authority to arbitrate" any difference as prescribed in the collective bargaining agreement. The Judge cited and without a doubt relied heavily on our recent decision in Refinery Employees Union v. Continental Oil Co., 5 Cir., 1959, 268 F. 2d 447, certiorari denied, Nov. 16, 1959, 361 U.S. 896, 80 S.Ct. 199, 4 L.Ed. 2d 152.

The collective bargaining agreement reflected the mutual purpose of settling "problems or grievances." In contract terms which have been characterized as the standard clause, United Steel Workers v. American Manufacturing Co., 1960, 363 U.S. 564, at page 565, 80 S.Ct. 1343, 4 L.Ed. 2d 1403, the parties bound themselves to arbitrate "any difference ... between the Company and any employee as to the meaning, application or interpretation of the provisions of" the agreement. Arbitration machinery comprehended the selection of arbitrators and their function, the selection of the disinterested member, and the powers of the Board of Arbitration so constituted.[1]

After the District Court announced its decision, the Supreme Court handed down the three Steel Workers opinions on June 20, 1960. The Union by timely motion for revision of findings, F.R. Civ. P. 59(e), 28 U.S.C.A., brought these to the attention of the Trial Court. Presumably the Court considered them of no substantial significance. We think their importance has been too much minimized and without attempting to cast it in terms of the impact of these cases upon our *Continental Oil* case, 268 F. 2d 447, we think these intervening decisions point in a compelling way to a reversal.

The Employer insists in its brief that the 63 printed page contract with its minute details of rates of pay, hours of work, and conditions of employment is a "mundane and specific contract that seeks to spell out the details of the agreement." Consequently, it urges it "is no broad and 'generalized code of industrial self-government'" nor an "ambiguous and amorphous charter to bring into being an undefined 'common law of the shop.'" But this is really no answer.

[The court then reviewed some highlights of the Trilogy.]

At the outset is the nature of the grievance,

---

1. Article V then continues: "Section 2. The Board of Arbitration shall render a decision within fifteen (15) days from the date the hearing is completed. The terms and conditions of settlement shall be within the sole discretion of the Board and the decision of a majority of the Board shall be final and binding on the parties; provided, however, the Board shall have no authority to violate, contravene, disregard or supplement the terms of this agreement."

that is the controversy over which there was a dispute. It covered two things. The first was the claim that each of the 15 men was wrongfully denied reinstatement and hence wrongfully discharged. The second aspect was the demand that each be reinstated "with all rights unimpaired and with pay for all time lost." This latter facet was an integral part of the controversy over the substantive rights accorded by the collective bargaining agreement. It was not a mere dispute over the nature or operation of the arbitration machinery or the power of the arbitrator. It was, therefore, a "difference ... as to the meaning, application or interpretation of the provisions" of the contract.

The Arbitration Board in reaching what is called a "settlement" rather than, say, an adjudication, is not to act as a mediator in working out a new agreement on something not previously covered at all. That is what would result if a "settlement" were forced on the parties which would, as the clause states, "violate" or "contravene" the agreement. So far as the term "supplement" is concerned it can not be read literally to rule out the right of arbitrators—just as would a court—to find substantive rights, obligations and duties which are implied though not expressed. The alternative to this would make the agreement to arbitrate superfluous for the sole inquiry would then be: is it expressed in the contract? If not, then to read it into the contract is to "supplement" it, and this is forbidden.

Once this interpretation of the exclusionary clause is made by the Court, what substantive matter is thereafter considered to be within or without the express or implied terms of the agreement is a decision for the arbitrators. For this would present a "difference ... as to the meaning, application or interpretation of the provisions" of the agreement.

Likewise, whether it is thought to be a part of the substantive right or more a part of the grievance procedure, in the absence of clearly restrictive language, great latitude must be allowed in fashioning the appropriate remedy constituting the arbitrator's "decision."

> When an arbitrator is commissioned to interpret and apply the collective bargaining agreement, he is to bring his informed judgment to bear in order to reach a fair solution of a problem. This is especially true when it comes to formulating remedies. There the need is for flexibility in meeting a wide variety of situations.

363 U.S. 593, at page 597, 80 S.Ct. 1358, at page 1361. And particularly should latitude in fashioning the remedy be allowed when the grievance itself comprehends demands both for reinstatement and back pay so that on its face

the controversy is a "difference ... as to the meaning, application or interpretation" of the agreement.

Applying these principles to this contract which in a sweeping grant of authority specifies that the "terms and conditions of settlement shall be within the sole discretion of the Board," we find no such positive declaration as would exclude from the arbitrators the power to determine whether the award of back pay is or is not within the terms of the agreement, and if so, whether it is or is not an appropriate remedy.[2]

The whole grievance complaining of wrongful refusal to reinstate and to reimburse the dischargees for back pay is for the Board of Arbitration. The Trial Court's order compelling arbitration should be without the restrictions imposed. In order that arbitration of this 1957 controversy may now go forward, the order is modified by deleting the restriction and as modified, affirmed. 28 U.S.C.A. § 2106.

Modified and as modified affirmed.

HUTCHESON, C. J., concurs in the result.

———————

In Selb Mfg. Co. v. District 9, International Association of Machinists (8th Cir. 1962) 305 F. 2d 177, the union had grieved over the company's removal of equipment from its St. Louis plant, claiming that this violated a contract limitation upon subcontracting. The arbitrator ordered the equipment returned from Arkansas and Colorado and the reinstatement of employees without loss of seniority or pay. On the basis of the *Trilogy* the court affirmed the lower court order enforcing the award despite the "debatable" "validity and coverage" of the subcontracting clause. Subsequently the case was settled for a cash payment to the union, which divided the sum among the employees affected.

———————

As noted in *Continental Oil*, arbitrators generally do not doubt their power to grant back pay and other monetary claims as part of their

———————

2. It is fundamentally erroneous to approach this as merely a grievance over reinstatement. The controversy involves both reinstatement and back pay under the contract. Each is a substantive matter under the contract. It is not merely a question of what remedy, as such, is permitted for a single substantive claim. "The function of the court is very limited when the parties have agreed to submit all questions of contract interpretation to the arbitrator. It is confined to ascertaining whether the party seeking arbitration is making a claim which on its face is governed by the contract." 363 U.S. 564, at pages 567–568, 80 S.Ct. 1343, at page 1346.

awards. On some occasions, dispute submissions explicitly limit the issue before the arbitrator to the correctness of a company or union position, but that would seem to be the exceptional case.

Monetary awards frequently are quite general in terms, do not specify exact amounts (which seldom are a matter of contest), and often do not specify what account should be taken of earnings during the period of wrongful discharge or layoff or unemployment compensation.

For an example of how complex the other earnings issue can be see, In re U.S. Steel Corp. and United Steelworkers, 40 LAB. ARB. 1036 (1963), in which earnings were held not to be deductible under the language of the agreement and the compensation patterns involved. Experienced arbitrator Sidney Wolff in *The Power of the Arbitrator to Make Monetary Awards* (in KAHN (ed.)), LABOR ARBITRATION—PERSPECTIVES AND PROBLEMS 176 (1964), denounced nondeductibility as inappropriate in the arbitral assessment of damages. But a discussant of the Wolff paper, David Feller (then counsel to the Steelworkers and now professor of law) suggested that Arbitrator Wolff posed the wrong question. Feller contended that the question is not how damages should be computed but how a given contract should be interpreted. *Id.* at 193–201. The court in United Furniture Workers v. Virco Mfg. Co., (E.D. Ark. W.D. 1962) 257 F. Supp. 138, 144, indicated that a difference over deduction would call for resubmission to the arbitrator to take "into consideration the extent, if any, to which the award ... should be reduced on account of sums earned."

In labor arbitration monetary awards generally do not include interest from the time the payment became due. For a critical commentary see, Youngdahl, *Awarding Interest in Labor Arbitration Cases,* 54 KY. L. J. 717 (1966). However, this area may be in the process of change. We lack survey data.

MATTER OF PUBLISHERS' ASSOCIATION OF NEW YORK CITY (NEW YORK STEREOTYPERS' UNION No. 1) 8 N.Y. 2d 414, 171 N.E. 2d 323 (1960)

DESMOND, CH. J. These are two separate arbitrations under two successive collective bargaining agreements between these parties. The first proceeding arose under the agreement which covered the period from December, 1956 to December, 1958. We agree with the Appellate Division that sections 57 and 62 of that contract were properly applied to the situation presented and that it was correct to order the union to participate in the selection of a fifth member of the Joint Conference Committee.

The second above-entitled appeal brings up the interpretation of the 1958–1960 contract between these parties and calls for more extended discussion.

The arbitration provision in the second contract says that there shall be a Joint Conference Committee of four members, two selected by each party, and "To this Committee shall be referred for settlement any matter arising from the application of this agreement if such matter cannot be settled by conciliation between the Union and the Publisher involved." In the early morning hours of February 18, 1959 (or so it is claimed by the association), about 60 stereotypers employed at the *New York Times* engaged in a work stoppage at the direction, it is said, of the "Chapel Chairman" who is a sort of a shop steward of the stereotypers. The Publishers' Association later sent a telegram to the President of the Stereotypers' Union announcing that the association was filing a grievance because of this work stoppage, the telegram asserting that the stoppage was a violation of certain provisions of the contract and giving notice that at the hearing of the grievance before the Joint Conference Committee the association would demand damages. The union by answering letter wrote that it would participate in the selection of a fifth or independent arbitrator and would arbitrate the question of whether this work stoppage was a violation. It insisted, however, that there was no basis for arbitration "as to the matter contained in the balance of the telegram." In other words, the union said that it was not required to and would not arbitrate the question of damages. The association then brought this proceeding for an order to direct the union to proceed to an arbitration of the whole matter.

At Special Term the motion was granted by an order which stated: "The arbitration clause in the current agreement of the parties is sufficiently broad to include therein as an arbitrable issue the matter of damages arising from the alleged breach of the agreement." The Appellate Division, First Department, unanimously affirmed without opinion and we granted leave to appeal.

The arbitration clause of this collective bargaining contract does not include the word "damages" but it is a broad covenant providing that there shall be referred to the Joint Conference Committee "any matter arising from the application of this agreement." We know that innumerable arbitrations of damage questions are held pursuant to arbitration agreements which do not directly mention "damages." No

reason appears for a different result here. Our own records show that under a similar agreement between these same two parties the question of damages was arbitrated and litigated although, because of insufficient proof (but not because of contract limitations), no damages were in fact awarded by the arbitrators in that instance (Matter of Publishers' Assn. of New York City [New York Stereotypers' Union], 1 A.D. 2d 941, motion for stay denied 1 N.Y. 2d 860).

The landmark arbitration case of Matter of Marchant v. Mead-Morrison Mfg. Co. (252 N.Y. 284, 298–299) says that an agreement in a contract that all controversies growing out of it should be arbitrated—or any equivalent agreement—authorizes the arbitrators to assess damages. The *Marchant* case held, as did other cases (Matter of Utility Laundry Serv. [Sklar], 300 N.Y. 255; De Lillo Constr. Co. v. Lizza & Sons, 7 N.Y. 2d 102), that a general arbitration clause regardless of precise language ordinarily authorizes arbitration of damages. Of course, we are not discussing consequential damages since no such question is before us. Appellant cites Matter of New York Mirror (Potoker) (5 A.D. 2d 423 ; see, also, Matter of Potoker [Brooklyn Eagle], 2 N.Y. 2d 553) but the *Potoker* decisions have no particular bearing on our problem. The union is really arguing here that, while the arbitrators can decide whether or not there is a violation and a breach, any claim for damages as a result of a violation or a breach so found would have to be the subject of a separate suit at law. There is no reason to think that the parties contemplated successive litigations arising out of one violation.

The other argument made by appellant union bases itself on section 876-a of the Civil Practice Act and Martin v. Curran (303 N.Y. 276). That is, the union points out that under section 876-a and other New York statutes an unincorporated association cannot be held liable except on proof which would make all the members liable individually. The union says that, with this statutory immunity in existence, the intent of this agreement could not have been to authorize an award of damages for violation which actually involved only about 60 of the union's 1,100 members. There are at least two answers to this. First, Matter of Ruppert (Egelhofer) (3 N.Y. 2d 576) held that arbitrators under appropriate language in an agreement could order an injunction even though section 876-a would prevent a court from issuing an injunction on the same facts. The second and more general answer is that the question of arbitration clause coverage is one of intent, damages are a most common feature of arbitration awards and nothing before us suggests that these parties intended their arbitrations to result in futile declarations only. If the parties intended to prohibit the arbitrators from exercising the customary function of fixing damages, they probably would have said so, especially since, under an earlier but apparently identical form of arbitration agreement between these same parties, the association had sought damages and the question of damages had been tried out before arbitrators with no complaint from the union (see Matter of Publishers' Assn. of New York City [New York Stereotypers' Union], motion for stay denied 1 N.Y. 2d 860 [1956], *supra*).

Both orders appealed from should be affirmed, with costs.

JUDGES DYE, FULD, FROESSEL, VAN VOORHIS, BURKE and FOSTER concur.

Orders affirmed.

B.

Reinstatement in Discharge Cases

THE ARBITRATION OF DISCHARGE CASES: WHAT HAPPENS AFTER REINSTATEMENT*

ARTHUR M. ROSS†

I. Introduction

Law and statistics are notoriously uncongenial. While the original "Brandeis brief" was filed almost fifty years ago, and while some courts are increasingly willing to take notice of economic and sociological data (particularly the Supreme Court in constitutional cases), concepts and principles remain the staple item of diet. So it is in arbitration. Since arbitration is a private system of contract enforcement, and is manned to a growing extent by attorneys, it is not surprising that rules, maxims and precedents are so prominent.

Doubtless this state of affairs will continue in large measure. But logic and legitimacy are not the only tests of a doctrine. The question of how it actually works out is also of interest.

In labor arbitration there is much to be gained from studies of experience after the award. For example, we are frequently called upon to decide whether particular employees are qualified for particular jobs on which seniority rights are being asserted. We have developed various tests of capability; we consider certain types of evidence as relevant. We decide that some of the employees are qualified, and order that they be assigned, promoted or recalled to the jobs in question. Are they *really* qualified? It would be instructive, and not very difficult, to learn how many of them actually "make out" on the jobs.

I am reporting today on a study of experience under arbitration awards in which discharged employees have been reinstated. For arbitrators there ought to be an unusual degree of interest in how these reinstatements have worked out. The principal reason is that arbitrators themselves have created the standards of decision for this type of case. This has been a matter of necessity rather than preference; we are a timid lot for the most part. We have had to invent standards because none have been furnished. In no field of arbitration can less guidance be had from general legal doctrines or from the language of contracts and submission agreements than in the field of industrial discipline.

To be sure, an arbitrator is applying the terms of a collective bargaining agreement when he decides a discharge case. Typically the agreement recites that the employer will not discharge without proper cause, and the arbitrator makes a judgment as to whether there *was* proper cause. Technically this is contractual interpretation. But it is contractual interpretation in the same sense as it was statutory interpretation when the O.P.A. decided that $1.00 was a "fair and equitable" ceiling price for a peck of winter potatoes.

It is true that some collective agreements afford more guidance than the familiar rubrics of "just cause," "proper cause," or just plain "cause." The contract may incorporate a list of disciplinary offenses with the corresponding penalties. It may specify that certain derelictions, such as persistent absenteeism or falsification of production records, will be grounds for discharge. The submission agreement may limit the arbitrator to finding whether the grievant was guilty of the offense for which he was terminated. The contract or submission agreement may instruct the arbitrator as to whether he is authorized to mitigate the penalty, as an alternative to up-

*Abridged from MCKELVEY, ed., CRITICAL ISSUES IN LABOR ARBITRATION (1957). Reprinted with the permission of the Bureau of National Affairs, Inc.

†Director, Institute of Industrial Relations, University of California, Berkeley.

holding it or rescinding it altogether. In these and other ways the parties may "structure" the situation, as the sociologists would say. Ordinarily they do not.

Certainly the antecedent Law of Contracts offers little help. At common law the employer generally had an unrestricted right to discharge, just as the employee had an unlimited right to quit his job.

Perhaps the developing standards of "just cause" for discharge under a collective bargaining contract could be translated into more traditional categories such as failure of consideration; but it is not clear that such a translation would accomplish much and, in any case, it has never been attempted.

There were additional reasons for studying the aftermath of the reinstatement award. Although the discharge case is probably not the most important type of grievance brought to arbitration, from some standpoints it is almost certainly the most numerous type. During a recent year, for example, about 25 per cent of all arbitration appointments made by the Federal Mediation and Conciliation Service were in discharge matters.

Many discharge cases are charged with emotion and generate strong feelings among the parties. In fact, the parties may have stronger feelings about the discharge or reinstatement of a single employee than about a wage case involving large numbers of employees and great sums of money.

Some widely divergent theories about the subsequent career of the reinstated employee are current. One theory runs something as follows: He is a marked man, or he never would have been discharged in the first place. His number was up. Management will nail him again soon, and make it stick. Reinstating him merely throws him back into an impossible situation. His best bet will be to pick up his retroactive pay and find himself another job. At the other extreme, it is said that he was probably discharged by an impetuous supervisor in a fit of anger. Everyone is relieved when the arbitrator slaps him on the wrist and puts him back to work. Having been discharged once, he will now get religion and keep his nose clean. In fact he will become a model employee. Neither of these popular theories, nor any of the intermediate positions, has ever been tested statistically.

2. The Arbitrators' Approach to Industrial Discipline

In their search for principles of industrial discipline, the arbitrators have turned not to the Law of Contracts but to modern concepts of enlightened personnel administration, sprinkled with elements of procedural due process in criminal cases. This is not the place to present a full-blown theory of industrial discipline. For the present purpose it will suffice to list a few of the major tenets which are stressed in the literature of personnel administration and in the thinking of arbitrators concerning disciplinary grievances.

1. The employer is entitled to prescribe reasonable rules of conduct. What rules are necessary will vary from one establishment to another, and the employer enjoys considerable discretion in making this determination.

2. The employee has a right to know what is expected of him. Therefore the employer has an obligation to give adequate notice of the rules, unless they are so self-evident as not to require notice. This requirement gives rise to a number of chronic issues, such as (a) whether a particular rule has been promulgated with sufficient notoriety, and (b) whether violations have been condoned to such an extent as to make the rule invalid.

3. The employer has no jurisdiction over the employee's private life, and no right to impose discipline for behavior off company time and property—this being a task for the civil authorities. The exception occurs when the employee's actions away from the job have the effect of damaging or seriously jeopardizing the employer's legitimate interests. The problem in cases of this type is to decide whether the employer's interests were sufficiently involved as to justify his intervention.

4. The employee must conform with valid rules in good faith and with serious purpose. He must comport himself as a disciplined individual; otherwise goods or services cannot be produced with any degree of efficiency.

5. The employer must avoid arbitrary, hasty or capricious action when confronted with unsatisfactory conduct. The tendency for supervisors to "over-react" against what they regard as a challenge to their authority is one of the persistent problems of industrial discipline. To guard against this tendency, collective agreements frequently provide that an employee will not be discharged until after a preliminary suspension, or until after consultation with the union.

6. Disciplinary policies should be applied consistently and even-handedly. This standard is clear enough in disparaging capricious decisions and discriminatory purposes. It does not mean, however, that a mechanical uniformity of treatment must be achieved, regardless of differences

in the background or circumstances of particular cases. What is important, as Benjamin Aaron has stressed, is consistent purposes rather than uniform penalties.

7. The punishment should fit the crime. There is a controversy among arbitrators as to whether they have authority to mitigate penalties where the employee is guilty of the offense charged but the penalty is regarded as excessive. In 70 per cent of the reinstatement cases covered by the present survey, workers were reinstated with partial back pay or no back pay.

8. Proper industrial discipline is corrective rather than punitive. The purpose is to instill self-discipline in the working force. Both employer and employee lose when the employee is terminated. The employer must recruit and train a replacement, and must often reckon with ill will on the part of the discharged employee's fellow workers; while the employee loses his seniority and all the valuable rights associated with it. Therefore discharge should normally be invoked only as a last resort, after it has become clear that corrective measures will not succeed.

9. It follows that the evaluation of a given penalty will depend not only on the immediate offense but also on the employee's previous disciplinary record. It also follows that, in the normal case, a series of disciplinary measures—including interviews, formal reprimands, and disciplinary layoffs—should be applied with gradually increasing severity before discharge is considered. "Capital punishment" should not be levied until it has been established that the employee will not respond to lesser penalties. Doubtless many cases of mitigated penalties represent the arbitrator's attempt to apply this principle to a firm which does not make a practice of assigning disciplinary layoffs. Whether the arbitrator should, in effect, impose such a practice on a firm which has never used it is subject to much controversy.

3. Summary of Findings

It was said of the late Dr. Kinsey that no one could study a matter so long and so intensively without developing a certain amount of enthusiasm for his subject. Nevertheless, it is not my purpose to endorse—or disparage, for that matter—the prevalent practices in disciplinary cases. My objective is limited to reporting what they are.

The reinstatement cases analyzed here were found in the printed volumes of LABOR ARBITRATION REPORTS covering the years 1950–1955. Exactly 207 [reinstated] individual grievants in 145 establishments were found.

SENIORITY STATUS AT THE TIME OF DISCHARGE

The discharge problem seems to be concentrated among relatively junior employees. To the extent that seniority information is available, 28 per cent of the reinstated workers had two years or less seniority on the date of discharge. Another 23 per cent had from three to five years. Thus, more than half can be classified as junior, if five years or less will serve as a definition of junior status. Only 18 per cent had eleven years or more of seniority at the time of discharge.

While official probationary periods in industry usually run from thirty days to six months, it is well known that a considerably longer period elapses before an employee becomes permanent in the full sense of the word. The first few years of employment are a period of trial and error. Many studies have shown that a large proportion of workers who quit their jobs have low seniority. Layoffs for lack of work are normally concentrated among workers with relatively recent hiring dates. It now appears that the majority of discharged employees are also fairly new. By the time that employees have accumulated substantial seniority, they have likewise accumulated important rights which they are careful to protect. They have become valued members of the work force, and will not be discharged hastily. They have adjusted to their supervisors; the supervisors have adjusted to them. They have arrived, and are likely to remain.

GROUNDS FOR DISCHARGE

A majority of the employees were discharged for overt and dramatic types of misbehavior. Twenty-seven per cent were discharged for illegal strikes, strike violence, or deliberately restricting production.

Another twenty-two per cent were accused of refusing to perform job assignments, refusing to work overtime, and similar forms of insubordination. Nine per cent were teminated on the scores of fighting, assaults, horse-play and trouble-making. Thus, almost 60 per cent of the cases involved these three types of offenses. All of them represent an open challenge to the authority of management, as viewed by management, or a breach of peace inside the plant.

The quieter, less conspicuous and more gradual forms of dereliction did not account for such a large proportion of all the terminations. Eleven per cent were discharged for absenteeism, tardiness or leaving early; 8 per cent for incompetence, negligence, poor workmanship or violation of safety rules; and 5 per cent for dishonesty, theft or falsification of records. The remaining eighteen per cent were scattered among numerous categories, including intoxication, disloyalty, gambling, loafing and miscellaneous rule violations.

If a similar distribution of all discharged employees were made, including those *not* reinstated, the proportions would be somewhat different. Nevertheless, it seems evident that the drastic and shocking episode, such as a fight, an illegal strike or an act of defiance, puts the greatest strain on the employment relationship. Quieter problem like absenteeism and poor workmanship do not produce a crisis in the shop, do not mobilize emotions, and are more likely to be resolved without resort to the sanction of discharge. It may be that the modern theory of corrective discipline, which emphasizes patient educational effort with the delinquent employee, is widely accepted in industry insofar as the less dramatic offenses are concerned ; and that fighting, illegal strikes, etc., are regarded by employers as "capital crimes," justifying immediate discharge notwithstanding the employee's previous record. The proper application of corrective discipline to these kinds of offenses has never been fully explored or explained.

PRINCIPAL REASONS FOR REINSTATEMENT

In each of the 207 cases, the arbitration opinion has been analyzed to determine the arbitrator's principal ground for reinstating the grievant. It is instructive that the question of literal guilt or innocence has not been decisive in the majority of the cases. The reason most frequently invoked has been the existence of mitigating circumstances. For example, the grievant did assault a fellow worker, but had been sorely provoked. Or the grievant did refuse an overtime assignment, but had worked a great deal of overtime in recent months. Or the grievant's long service and previously unblemished disciplinary record should have been given more weight. In 50 cases, or 24 per cent of the total, discharged employees were reinstated because of mitigating circumstances.

A closely related ground for reinstatement was that discharge was an excessive penalty for the offense. This ground was assigned in 39 cases, or 19 per cent of the total. Here again, the grievants were not held innocent of blame. Rather the arbitrators found they had been dealt with too harshly: that the punishment did not fit the crime.

In 20 cases (10 per cent), arbitrators held that the employer had failed to meet his own obligations.

In nineteen cases (9 per cent), employees were reinstated on the ground of unequal treatment.

They were singled out for discharge although other employees, guilty of identical or similar conduct, were not terminated. The employer's actions were held to be capricious or discriminatory.

Among the remaining seventy-nine cases, forty-three grievants were reinstated on the ground of insufficient evidence to support the charge against them. Sixteen were reinstated because their actions were found partly or wholly justified. Twenty were reinstated for miscellaneous reasons.

Thus, in over 60 per cent of the cases, the crucial issue was not whether the grievant had misbehaved. The issue was whether discharge was a fair and reasonable penalty in view of the nature of the misbehavior, the surrounding circumstances, the employee's previous record and the employer's policy in handling similar cases. Some arbitrators, it is true, accord the employer more leeway than others. Some will uphold a penalty if it is within an area of reasonable discretion. Others will uphold it only if they are personally convinced that it was fair. In either case, apparently the typical discharge hearing is not so much a trial of guilt or innocence as a review of the reasonableness of managerial action.

TERMS OF REINSTATEMENT

In view of what has been shown, it is not surprising that only a minority of the grievants were reinstated with complete retroactivity. (In practically every case, of course, the unions asked that they be made whole.) Sixty-three, or 30 per cent, were reinstated with full back pay ; 60, or 29 per cent, with partial back pay ; and 84, or 41 per cent, with no back pay at all.

The extent of back pay varied with the original charge. Most of the grievants who had been accused of insubordination were reinstated without back pay. The same was true in cases of fighting, assaults, etc. On the other hand, the larger group of those charged with strike leadership or violence or deliberately restricting production were reinstated with full back pay.

As one would expect, the extent of back pay also varied with the arbitrators' reasons for reinstatement. Where mitigating circumstances were found, the largest group was restored without retroactivity, the second-largest with partial back pay, and only a few were made whole. The same is true of cases in which discharge was deemed an excessive penalty. Where the employer had failed to present sufficient evidence to sustain the charge, the majority of grievants were restored with full back pay.[1]

People will have different opinions concerning the frequency of no-back-pay or partial-back-pay decisions. Some will accuse the arbitrator of compromising instead of facing the issue. Some will say that he strained the facts to get the grievant back on the payroll by hook or by crook. In defense, it will be argued that in these cases there was just cause for some punishment, but not for the ultimate sanction of discharge; that the arbitrator should not be required to select between two equally unfair results; and that he should not be stigmatized as a "compromiser" when he finds a reasonable solution. In any event, it is clear that the majority of arbitrators believe they have authority to mitigate penalties when not prevented by the contract, the submission agreement, or perhaps the previous practice of the parties.

HOW LONG DID THEY STAY?

We come now to the after-history of the reinstatement decision. First, do the reinstated actually return; and if so, how long do they stay? We have this information for 123 employees covered by the employer questionnaires.

Twelve employees never returned to work. Six of these had less than two years of seniority. Seniority information concerning the remaining six is lacking, but presumably most of them were short-service men. The probable inference is that the employees who failed to take advantage of reinstatement were too new to have established roots in the plant. Incidentally, eleven of the twelve were ordered reinstated without retroactivity [back pay].

Of those who returned, thirteen were terminated, for one reason or another, within six months; twenty-two within a year; and thirty-two within two years. Among the entire group of 123, sixty-three are still employed in the same establishment and sixty are no longer there. Thirty-five have quit since the date of reinstatement, including the twelve who never returned. Seventeen have been discharged a second time, including nine within the first year. Eight are dead, have retired, or were laid off in the permanent closing of a plant.

Among those reinstated in 1950, the majority are no longer in the establishment. Of those reinstated from 1951 to 1954, about half have left and half have remained. Most of the workers reinstated in 1955 are still employed in the same establishment. Naturally, the more time passes, the more likely it is that a given employee will resign, retire, die or be discharged.

Most of the employees who have been terminated since the date of reinstatement were short-service men (to the extent that we have information concerning seniority status). Conversely, a majority of the short-service men have been terminated. Most of the long-service men (six years or more of seniority) are still employed. *Only one of these has been discharged a second time since being reinstated. Only three have quit.*

The implications are obvious. The reinstated long-service employee will probably last. The reinstated short-service employee is not so likely to remain.

With respect to the short-service employees, however, the statistics must be interpreted with great caution. My own view is that the reinstated short-service employee is not more likely to quit than others with similar seniority. He is more likely to be discharged, however.

THE REINSTATED EMPLOYEE AS SEEN BY HIS EMPLOYER

Employers were requested to state whether the grievant has been a satisfactory worker since reinstatement; whether he has made normal occupational progress in terms of promotions, merit increases, etc.; whether there has been a recurrence of disciplinary problems; whether further disciplinary action has been necessary; how his supervisors have felt towards him; and what has been the grievant's attitude.

Has the grievant been a satisfactory employee since reinstatement? "Yes": 65 per cent. "No": 35 per cent. Of those employees deemed satisfactory, two-thirds are still employed. Of those regarded as unsatisfactory, about sixty per cent have left—primarily by the discharge route. Practically all the "unsatisfactory" employees had less than five years' seniority at the time of the original discharge. A majority had less than two years. Only three with six years or more where classified "unsatisfactory."

Has the grievant made normal occupational progress? "Yes": 64 per cent. "No": 35 per cent. Of those still employed, however, more than 70 per cent have made normal progress,

---

1. At first blush, it seems difficult to understand why some of the arbitrators denied back pay after finding insufficient evidence to support the charge. Analysis of such decisions indicates that in the majority of cases, the grievant was accused of several delinquencies. The principal accusation was not supported, but some of the minor charges were admitted or established. Regrettably, however, there were a few cases in which the arbitrators apparently concluded that (a) the grievants were guilty, but (b) the employers had not proved it. This curious concept of "proof," as being something different from persuasion, is widely held by lay juries but has not been characteristic of persons in a judicial role. In one or two cases it is possible that the arbitrators resolved their genuine doubts by splitting the award, an expedient requiring no comment.

according to the employer. Of course there is more room for advancement in some plants than in others. Some of the grievants are in the same jobs which they held at the time of discharge, but are still described as having made "normal progress." But many workers who have never been discharged are assigned to the same jobs for long periods of time. For those employees who failed to make normal progress, another question is whether they failed because of personal deficiencies or because they were working under a cloud. Analysis of the questionnaires does not furnish any clear answer. It is likely, however, that the reinstated employee has a somewhat diminished chance of being promoted.

Has there been a recurrence of disciplinary problems? Have any disciplinary penalties been imposed since reinstatement? The answers to these questions deserve careful scrutiny. As noted above, it is sometimes said that the reinstated employee will be particularly careful to keep out of trouble thereafter; others feel that the difficulty will probably recur, and that supervisors will endeavor to "nail" him a second time.

A total of 123 reinstated employees are covered by the employer questionnaires. No information on subsequent disciplinary history is reported for twenty-seven. With respect to the remaining ninety-six, employers state that sixty-seven, or seventy per cent have presented no subsequent disciplinary problems. Eight have repeated the same offense for which they were originally terminated; four of these have been discharged again. Twenty-one, the employers state, have been guilty of some different offense, and eleven of these have been discharged.

Once more the influence of seniority is striking. Practically all of the "repeaters" were short-service men with five years or less of seniorty at the time of their original discharge. So far as we have information, only three employees with six years or more have experienced further difficulties, and none with eleven years or more. Apparently the employee with considerable seniority is almost certain to stay out of trouble after being reinstated.

How have the supervisors felt toward the reinstated employee? In 71 per cent of the cases, the responses can be classified as favorable or neutral. In the remaining 29 per cent, supervisors were reported as holding an unfavorable or resentful attitude.

Needless to say, a supervisor will not be overjoyed when a discharged employee is reinstated in his work group. The employee stands as a symbol of two unpleasant facts: that the supervisor's authority is limited, and that the arbi-

trators disagreed with his judgment. Many employers emphasize, however, that the supervisors have attempted to let bygones be bygones and deal with the grievant as with any other employee. Some employers report that the supervisors have been unhappy over the need to reinstate employees whom they consider unacceptable.

What has been the grievant's attitude since reinstatement? The responses can be classified as follows:

"Attitude good": 54 per cent—mostly still employed. In twenty-eight cases, employers state definitely that the disciplinary crisis had a favorable effect on the grievants' behaviour.

"Attitude unchanged": 14 per cent—mostly still employed. The significance of this response is not too clear. Presumably what is meant is that the attitude continued unsatisfactory, or else that the original problem was not one of attitude.

"Attitude poor": 30 per cent, about half of whom are still employed. Some employers state that the reinstated employees now consider themselves above the law.

It would be only human if the employers were somewhat more charitable in describing the attitudes of the supervisors than in characterizing those of the reinstated employees. Nevertheless, it is significant that about three-quarters of the supervisors are reported and a strong majority of the grievants are reported as having satisfactory attitudes. These reports indicate a generally sound adjustment to the difficult human problems attending reinstatement after discharge.

THE ARBITRATION AWARD AS VIEWED BY THE EMPLOYER

The final question addressed to the employers reads as follows: "Looking back on the incident, do you believe the arbitrator made the right decision in reinstating this employee? Please give reasons."

Of the 110 [responses] employers believe the decision was correct in forty-three cases (39 per cent), and wrong in sixty-seven cases (61 per cent).

Many of the affirmative responses are explained by the favorable effects of the award. A number of practical benefits were noted. Several employers noted that the grievant became a satisfactory employee after reinstatement. Other employers believe the decision supported or clarified the company's disciplinary policy.

Still others agreed with the decision because they considered it correct on the merits, although some felt the outcome would have been different if the evidence had been fully or properly presented.

As noted above, employers still disagree with the awards in sixty-seven cases. The reasons assigned mostly relate to the merits of the decisions, as seen by the employers, rather than the practical outcome.

In a minority of cases the employer criticizes the decision on the ground of its bad effects. In seven cases, the weakening of supervisory authority is stressed.

And in seven other cases, the objection is that the grievant's poor attitude was only reinforced by his being reinstated.

On the other hand, several employers who disagree with the decision frankly concede that the employee has turned out well.

As a point of purely scientific interest, it might be noted that the employer's reaction to the decision is not greatly affected by the conditions of reinstatement. Employers believe the decision was correct in 35 per cent of the cases providing full back pay, 47 per cent providing partial back pay, and 37 per cent providing no back pay.

The employers' reasons for approving or disapproving the decisions have been summarized above. There is considerable correlation, however, between these evaluations, on the one hand, and the practical outcome after reinstatement, on the other.

Favorable experience after reinstatement does not guarantee that the employer will approve the decision, however. In numerous cases the employee has been satisfactory, has made normal progress, has kept out of further trouble, etc.; but the employer continues to disagree with the decision on its merits or because of its supposed long-run effects. About all that can be said is that the employer is more likely to approve a reinstatement that works out well, and is almost certain to disapprove of one that works out poorly.

OUTCOME OF REINSTATEMENT AS SEEN BY UNIONS

Only thirty-eight union questionnaires had been returned at the time it became necessary to tabulate the results. Because of this rather small response (18 per cent, as compared with 60 per cent of the employer questionnaires), it was not practical to make such an elaborate analysis of the material. However, it has proved helpful for certain purposes.

The first question which arises is whether the union questionnaires are comparable with the larger group of employer questionnaires, or with all the cases originally selected for the survey. In some respects these 38 cases are quite representative.

The major difference is that most of these thirty-eight cases are ones which turned out well after reinstatement, in view of the employers as well as the unions. That is, in the vast majority of these particular cases, employers reported that the grievants proved satisfactory after reinstatement, made normal occupational progress, encountered no further disciplinary trouble, etc.

The union's view of the outcome of these cases is even rosier. In some instances the unions were not able to reply to all questions, because of lack of detailed familiarity with conditions in the shop. But to the extent that replies were forthcoming, they were almost uniformly favorable.

The unions were asked to explain their opinions as to whether it was worthwhile to arbitrate these cases. The largest number replied that the grievant had been unjustly accused, so that it was the union's duty as bargaining representative to oppose his discharge; that the grievant was justified in what he did; and that the grievant was worthy, as confirmed by his conduct after reinstatement. Another sizable group explained that the decision enhanced the union's position and vindicated the principle of unionism. One respondent stated that the grievance lacked merit, and one said that the decision had a bad effect on union-management relations.

Needless to say, the soundness of a decision cannot be tested primarily by whether the litigants are happy. If they wish to be assured of a happy solution, they are free to negotiate one themselves and stay out of arbitration. Nevertheless, the prevalent theory of corrective discipline does involve a judgment as to whether the grievant is potentially a useful and acceptable employee. When a reinstatement is based on the theory of corrective discipline, presumably the arbitrator has made an affirmative judgment of this type; or at least, he believes the negative has not been sufficiently established. Therefore it should be of interest to know whether his conclusion is borne out.

The most significant variable revealed in the questionnaires is seniority status. A majority of the grievants had five years or less seniority at the time of discharge. A majority of the short-service men did not take advantage of reinstatement, or were terminated after reinstatement. Those reinstated employees deemed unsatisfactory were practically all relatively junior, and a majority had less than two years at the time of discharge. Almost all the employees who encountered disciplinary troubles after reinstatement were in the junior group.

About 60 per cent of the grievants were discharged over dramatic and conspicuous episodes such as illegal strikes, assaults and acts of insubordination. The theory of corrective discipline has never been satisfactorily expounded in relation to this kind of offense, although it is clear enough with respect to continuing problems of a gradual character.

The decision to reinstate was not typically based on a finding of innocence, or a refusal to find guilt. The most common grounds for reinstatement were that mitigating circumstances should be recognized, that discharge was an excessive penalty, and that the employer had failed to pursue a consistent disciplinary policy. Moreover, about 70 per cent of the grievants were reinstated with no back pay or only partial retroactivity. Thus it is apparent that the discharge case most frequently becomes a review of the reasonableness of management's action rather than a trial of guilt or innocence.

Ten per cent of the employees did not return. Another 20 per cent lasted less than a year. Fifty per cent are no longer employed. But the normal rate of labor turnover in industry must be taken into account. Probably the reinstated employee is not more likely than other employees to resign* but is more likely to be discharged again.

From an operational standpoint, about two-thirds of the cases have worked out well. Employers say that two-thirds of the reinstated employees have proved satisfactory. About 60 per cent have reportedly made normal occupational progress, although there is reason to believe that the reinstated employee is less likely to be promoted. Seventy per cent have presented no further disciplinary problems. The attitude of supervisors has been favorable or neutral in about 70 per cent of the cases. The reinstated employee's attitude is described as good in about 60 per cent of the cases. Since reinstatement creates a delicate human situation in the shop at best, these responses indicate a generally mature and far-sighted adjustment to the difficulties.

A rather small proportion of the union questionnaires was returned.

Nonetheless, it is surely of some significance that the unions did not complain of unfair treatment in a single case. In virtually every case the union reported that supervisors as well as grievants have displayed sound and favorable attitudes.

Employers now believe that the decision to reinstate was correct in 39 per cent of the cases. By way of explanation, they stress principally the favorable outcome of the reinstatements. Employers disagree with 61 per cent of the decisions, chiefly on the merits as they stood at the time of discharge. Thus the employer is more likely to approve of a reinstatement that works out well, and almost certain to disapprove of one that works out poorly.

The unions agreed with the decision, and considered it worthwhile to have arbitrated the grievance, in almost every case. Unions believe they have a primary duty to support a discharged employee unless the merits of the discharge are clear.

Perhaps the foregoing report has somewhat illuminated the processes of discharge and reinstatement under collective bargaining agreements. To avoid a distorted impression, please bear in mind that not every discharged employee is reinstated.

C.

Penalties

IN THE MATTER OF EAST INDIA TRADING CO. (HALARI)
280 App. Div. 420, 117 N.Y.S. 2nd 93
(First Dept. 1952)

PECK, P. J. The questions presented on this appeal are whether the successful party in an arbitration proceeding is entitled to interest on the award for the period from the date thereof to the entry of judgment and (2) whether a provision in the arbitration rules of a trade association, under which the arbitration is held, providing that whenever it shall be decided that a party has failed to fulfill the terms of a contract and is in default, the defaulting party shall pay a "penalty," as determined by the arbitrators, of not less than 2 per cent and not more than 10 per cent of the market value established as of the date of the default, is enforcible. In this case a 2 per cent "penalty" of $436.80 was included in the arbitrators' award.

The learned court at Special Term disallowed both the item of interest and the penalty.

We are unanimous in holding that the item of interest should have been allowed (Civ. Prac. Act, §§ 1464, 480). The majority of the court

---

*But short-term employees do have a greater propensity to leave jobs and are more vulnerable to layoff than their seniors.

thinks that the "penalty" should also have been allowed.

The decision of the "penalty" issue should not be made on the basis of nomenclature. The true nature and justification of the "penalty" assessment, rather than the verbal characterization of it, should be regarded. If there is any rational and proper basis for the provision it should be recognized, for so long as public policy is not offended the contract of the parties and the award of the arbitrators are entitled to respect. We think that the "penalty" provision is justified and inoffensive.

Judicial notice can be taken of the expense of litigation and the inadequacy of ordinary costs. While we have not adopted a policy of awarding compensatory costs in our court system, there is no reason why in the private forums of trade arbitration a reasonable system of compensatory costs or something of that nature should not be established and recognized. Furthermore, the difference between the contract price and market price may not reflect the full measure of damage and giving the arbitrators some latitude to add to that amount is fair. The limited additional authority and discretion given to the arbitrators, which presumably will be exercised conformally to the merits of a case, does not appear to have any improper purpose and at least is defensible. We think that it was within the province of the trade association to incorporate this provision in its arbitration system and that it was within the province of the parties voluntarily to adopt it.

The order appealed from should be modified to allow the item in question and, as so modified, affirmed, with $20 costs and disbursements to appellant.

COHN, J. (dissenting in part). The law is settled that stipulated damages or penalties which are disproportionate to the loss sustained or greater than the damages which may be estimated with reasonable certainty are regarded as illegal and unenforcible (1 SEDGWICK ON DAMAGES [9th ed.], §407; Seidlitz v. Auerbach, 230 N.Y. 167).

The written contract between the parties specifically provided that all questions and controversies and all claims arising under the contract shall be submitted to and settled by arbitration under the rules of the American Spice Trade Association, which rules were printed on the reverse side of the written contract. Rule 12 of these rules contains the arbitration provision involved in this appeal. So far as pertinent it reads:

> 12. Default:—Whenever it shall be admitted by the Buyer or the Seller, or decided by arbitration that either party has failed to fulfill the terms of the contract, and is therefore in default, the contract shall be settled as follows: Arbitrators shall determine the difference between the contract price and the market value on the day of default, such difference to be payable to the Seller or to the Buyer, as the case may be, within 10 days from the date of the Arbitration Award. The defaulting party *shall pay a penalty*, as determined by arbitration, *of not less than 2 per cent and not more than 10 per cent of the market value* established as of the date of the default. [Emphasis supplied.]

The contract was for the sale of pepper. A default occurred during a rising market when the goods were available. The measure of damages in such a situation in a court of law is the difference between the contract price and the market price on the date of default. (Personal Property Law, § 148.)

Under rule 12 embodied in the contract it is provided that in addition to damages awarded on the basis of the actual loss sustained as represented by the difference between the contract price and the market value on the day of default, "The defaulting party *shall pay* a penalty, as determined by arbitration, of not less than 2 per cent and not more than 10 per cent of the market value established as of the date of the default." In compliance with this command, which directed the fixation of a penalty within the limits stated, the arbitrators selected 2 per cent of the market value, which amounted to $436.80 and added this sum to the amount arrived at by ascertaining the difference between the contract price of the pepper and the market value on the day of default.

The penalty provision in the rules as enforced by the arbitrators in this case was clearly illegal. While the use of the term "penalty" is not conclusive as to its character, the payment required by the rules was in excess of actual damage, and without reasonable relation to any possible damage which might follow a breach; the intention of the parties was to impose a forfeit or monetary punishment upon the violator in addition to the actual damages and is therefore a penalty, in fact as well as in name. Provisions for a penalty are invalid in any contract. (3 WILLISTON ON CONTRACTS [Rev. ed.], §§ 776, 777.) Even though they be denominated as liquidated damages, penalties may not be enforced. (Kothe v. R. C. Taylor Trust, 280 U.S. 224, 226; Wirth & Hamid Fair Booking v. Wirth, 265 N.Y. 214, 223; Weinstein & Sons v. City of New York, 264 App. Div. 398 [1st Dept.], affd. 289 N.Y. 741.)

A payment pursuant to an *in terrorem* term of a contract can have no more legal effect in arbitration proceedings than it would have in a court of law. Extrajudicial tribunals, such as boards of arbitration, have no power to disregard the settled public policy of our State. Boards of arbitration may not give legal effect to void or illegal obligations. (Matter of Western Union Tel. Co. [Amer Communications Assn.], 299 N.Y. 177, 185 ; 6 C.J.S., Arbitration and Award, § 12 ; STURGES ON COMMERCIAL ARBITRATIONS AND AWARDS § 61 ; Matter of Gale [Hilts], 176 Misc. 277, revd. on other grounds 262 App. Div. 834 ; Matter of Metro Plan [Miscione], 257 App. Div. 652.) The effect here is to nullify the arrangement for the penalty payment specified without affecting the validity of the contract as a whole. The Special Term was right in striking down this penalty provision as illegal and in modifying the award to that extent. I am in accord, however, with the view of the majority that the Special Term should have awarded interest from the date of the award to the date of the entry of judgment.

The order should, accordingly, be modified by the inclusion of interest from the date of the award to the date of the entry of judgment, and otherwise affirmed.

DORE and CALLAHAN, JJ., concur with PECK, P. J. ; COHN, J. dissents in part in opinion.

Order modified so as to allow the items in question and, as so modified, affirmed, with $20 costs and disbursements to the appellant. Settle order on notice.

Penalty versus liquidated damages: When the provision is one that will be enforced by the court, the amount specified therein is called liquidated damages. In cases where enforcement is denied, it is said that the parties have provided for a penalty or a forfeiture. 5 CORBIN, CONTRACTS § 1058, at 283 (1951).

Note that United States Court of Appeals, 2d Cir., Rule 26(b), 28 U.S.C.A. provides that where appeal delays a final result and the appeal "shall appear to have been sued out merely for delay" damages up to 10 per cent, in addition to interest, may be added to the judgment.

In South East Atlantic Shipping, Ltd. v. Garnac Grain Co., 365 F. 2d 189 (2d Cir. 1966) the court observed:

Finally, although the panel majority's opinion indicates that they were morally outraged by Garnac's conduct in repudiating the contract and then in attempting to hedge its position by the counter-proposal of January 4, we agree with Judge Palmieri that the award was not punitive. Moreover, we think it within the arbitrators' power to consider such questions of business morality in determining whether to award Atlantic the full extent of its loss regardless of whether some of that loss, in retrospect, might have been avoided. Such an award, however liberal, does not amount to an "unlawful" assessment of punitive damages.

PRIVATE LAWMAKING BY TRADE ASSOCIATIONS*

In working out standard sales forms, trade associations have developed remedies especially adapted to business needs. Among these is "cover," which allows the buyer to purchase substitute goods at the seller's expense if there is a default in delivery. This remedy has proved so useful that it has been incorporated into the Commercial Code. Another type of standard clause allows the seller to replace nonconforming goods, and thus relieves him of costly damage claims for breach of warranty without depriving the buyer of adequate remedy.

In providing remedies for breach of contract, the law recognizes only an interest in compensation and forbids punitive damages. However, breaches of contract may not only damage the other party, but also involve an injury to the industry as a whole. Thus, refusal of buyers to fulfill their obligations on a falling market may accelerate the deflationary spiral. Recognition of the tort element in breach of a business contract is evidenced by the penalty clauses in some standard forms. Penalty clauses may be used as a lever to dislodge certain practices regarded by the trade association as undesirable. For example, in the cotton industry an especially severe penalty is provided if the seller's default consists in the delivery of reginned or reprocessed cotton as raw cotton.

MATTER OF PUBLISHERS' ASS'N OF NEW YORK CITY (NEWSPAPER & MAIL DELIVERERS' UNION)
280 App. Div. 500, 114 N.Y.S. 2d 401 (First Dept. 1952)

BERGAN, J. The question presented by this appeal is the enforcement by the judicial power

*Excerpted from 62 HARV. L. REV. 1346, 1358, 1942. Reprinted with permission. Copyright © 1942 Harvard Law Review Association.

of the State of a penalty imposed by arbitrators as punishment for a breach of contract. The arbitrators fixed the actual damage arising from the breach and assessed an additional amount which they denominated "punitive damages or money penalty."

The contract pursuant to which the arbitration was had gave express authority to the arbitrators "to impose damages, money or other penalties upon any party hereto found guilty of a violation" of the agreement. The court at Special Term has entered an order and judgment in conformity with the award.

The contract is a collective bargaining agreement between the Publishers' Association of New York and the Newspaper and Mail Deliverers' Union of New York and Vicinity, effective November 1, 1950. One of the provisions of the contract is that there shall be "No strikes, lockouts or other cessation of work" during its term. On February 14, 1951, there was a strike at the plant of the News Syndicate Co., Inc., publisher of the New York Daily News. This publisher was one of the group for whose benefit the publishers' association had made the collective bargaining agreement with the union.

This arbitration proceeding was thereupon instituted by the association for the benefit of the News, and the arbitrators, constituted in the agreement as the "Board of Adjustment," found that the union had violated the no-strike provision of the contract "by authorizing and sanctioning" the strike of February 14, 1951, and had further violated the provisions of the contract by authorizing and sanctioning "interference with work" in the News plant between February 14th and April 12th of that year.

"Actual damages" found to have arisen from these violations were fixed and awarded in the sum of $2,000. "Punitive damages" were fixed and awarded additionally in the sum of $5,000. The "punitive damages," however, were not to be payable by the union "unless and until" the adjustment board "finds or awards" that the union has "again" violated the contract, upon which finding the $5,000 shall "instantly" become payable.

The "instantly" payable obligation of the award, in turn, is to be operative only at the "option" of the News. In commenting in his opinion on this phase of the decision, the impartial chairman observed that "This suspension of the collectibility of the punitive damages" should "serve both as a warning and an inducement" to the union to conform to the contract.

In its historic conception and early formulation, the action at common law on contract not under seal had a somewhat penal cast. Assumpsit, which took form about 1500, treated the breach of the condition of a contract in the sense of a wrong, and, indeed, was itself an action in tort.

Assumpsit has been described as "an action in tort which by a stroke of genius ... became the remedy for all contracts, whether written or verbal, other than those made under seal." (Levy-Ullmann, The English Legal Tradition, p. 71, citing Jenks, Digest of English Civil Law [1st ed.], Book V, 1910, preface, p. xv). The theory of this and some similar civil actions, remarked Lévy-Ullmann, was "quasi-criminal." (P. 329.)

There are, or at any rate until very recently there were, vestiges of the idea of redress for wrong implicit in many pleadings on the contract, as the survival of the word "breach" itself suggests; but no modern judge would regard damage as a punishment for breach, or as an object lesson to encourage future due performance, as an admissible basis of a judgment for nonperformance of a contract, or as constituting a statement of a good cause of action in contract.

From the very earliest stages of the action at law on contract, there has been maintained a very close correlation between the damage allowed and the actual loss to the complaining party; and the ascertainment of the loss was kept as close as it was found to be feasible to the actualities of the case.

There is more involved here than whether parties can agree between themselves on a scale of punishments to be mutually operative if they fail to carry out their contractual undertakings. There is involved also the question whether the court must impose automatically the penalties privately agreed upon; or whether in a controversy in which it would not itself grant any such relief under any circumstances, the court might reserve the right not to feel required to do so in obedience to a private contractual arrangement.

The trouble with an arbitration admitting a power to grant unlimited damages by way of punishment is that if the court treated such an award in the way arbitration awards are usually treated, and followed the award to the letter, it would amount to an unlimited draft upon judicial power. In the usual case, the court stops only to inquire if the award is authorized by the contract; is complete and final on its face; and if the proceeding was fairly conducted.

Actual damage is measurable against some objective standard—the number of pounds, or days, or gallons or yards; but punitive damages take their shape from the subjective criteria involved in attitudes toward correction and reform, and courts do not accept readily the delegation of that kind of power. Where punitive damages have been allowed for those torts which are still regarded somewhat as public penal wrongs as well as actionable private wrongs, they have had rather close judicial supervision. If the usual rules were followed there would be no effective judicial supervision over punitive wards in arbitration.

Under the terms of the contract before us, and as both parties construe it, there could be returned against either party an award for punitive damages in any amount—that could be stated in millions as well as thousands of dollars—and if the petitioner-respondent is right about the legal argument it pursues, the court would be required unquestioningly to direct entry of its judgment for whatever amount the award states on its face. Delegation in this scope should be approached with some reservation.

In the case before us the words defining the scope of the powers of the arbitrators not only made it quite explicit that it was the intention of the contracting parties to give them the right to impose punitive damages for a breach of terms of the written agreement; but in actual operation and in the terms and effect of the award, the arbitrators allowed punitive damages, not in form merely, but actually.

As the New York contract cases are examined, it becomes apparent at once that the problem was nearly always whether the words which said "liquidated damages" or their equivalents actually meant punitive damages. There is no hesitancy observable in a very long period of consistent judicial policy in New York not to enforce that part of a contract which departed from the reasonably responsive and appropriate in damage for its breach and fixed damages by way of penalty, punishment or example. The judges took it quite for granted that if this kind of a condition became manifest and clear they would not allow damage of that kind.

The theory behind the judicial policy, so often merely implicit in judicial opinions, was expressed with a sharp clarity by Judge Gray in Ward v. Hudson Riv. Bldg. Co. (125 N.Y. 230–235). The purpose of the court to relieve parties of stipulated penalties was that if they were disproportionate to readily ascertainable loss, the court would regard the sum stated in the contract, "not of the essence of the agreement" but "in the nature of a security for performance."

The penalty was therefore regarded as severable and not treated as damages, but as a matter collateral to the contract. This separation became the basis of the policy, upon a long line of cases cited, beginning with the judgment by Lord Mansfield in Lowe v. Peers (4 Burr. 2225, 2228,

2229). Judge Cowen, expressing quite a different basis of objection to exemplary damages, in Hoag v. McGinnis (22 Wend. 163) felt that the "use of penalties" as damages in the unlimited discretion of the parties would be "oppressive" (p. 166).

In many of the cases on this subject it was found by the court that the fixed damages stated to be "liquidated damages" were in fact quite appropriate to the loss from the breach. In Curtis v. Van Bergh (161 N.Y. 47) Judge Vann carefully restated the rule; but the very essence of his treatment of the subject is that unless the damages could be found thus to be appropriate and in true proportion they would not be allowed (p. 51).

The decision at General Term in Laurea v. Bernauer (33 Hun 307) is an example of a case where the penal nature of the damage was found from the language of the agreement itself and recovery was confined to the damages actually sustained. Judge Dykman was of opinion that language of an agreement actually using the term "penalty" was commonly regarded by the court as conclusive in respect of its meaning (p. 309). Another example is Caesar v. Rubinson (174 N.Y. 492) which treats a deposit on rent in the nature of a penalty, waived on re-entry by the landlord. The subject is well discussed, consistently with the current of authority, in Richards v. Edick (17 Barb. 260).

The court has always regarded itself competent to inquire whether the result that arbitrators have worked out has been consistent with the public and legal policy of the community. A few examples will point the direction. An award which would sanction, under the interpretation of it given by the arbitrators, a refusal to deliver messages which would violate the Penal Law was vacated in Matter of Western Union Tel. Co. (ACA) (299 N.Y. 177).

Arbitration was stayed in Matter of Levinsohn Corp. (Cloak, etc. Union) (273 App. Div. 469) where the court was of opinion that the purpose of the contract was to break other contracts, i.e., a "purpose" to "bring about the violation of existing contractual relationships" (p. 474). Here, surely, was the imposition of judicial policy against the effectiveness of an arbitration agreement. Reversal and remission of the decision (299 N.Y. 454) turned upon a different view taken by the Court of Appeals of the merits of the question of the legality of the acts involved and not upon the power of the court to vacate an award under circumstances where the invalidity of the acts were not in doubt.

A parallel case is Matter of Hill (Hill) (199 Misc. 1035) where the Special Term felt that arbitration provisions of a separation agreement were not binding on the court in relation to the custody of children. In Matter of Metro Plan, Inc. v. Miscione (257 App. Div. 652) this court held that if a chattel mortgage was found to be usurious, the arbitration provisions of the contract fall. In labor arbitration agreements, it has likewise been the common practice of the court to inquire whether the damage has been liquidated and reasonably appropriate to the loss (Matter of Mencher [Geller & Sons], 276 App. Div. 556 ; Maisel v. Sigman, 123 Misc. 714, 731).

In Matter of Kingswood Management Corp. (Salzman), decided in this court in 1947 (272 App. Div. 328), an interesting light is thrown on the question of judicial policy affecting the right to arbitration. There, a cause of action for treble damages and for attorneys' fees for violation of a price control act created by statute, to be prosecuted in any court of competent jurisdiction, was held not the proper subject for determination by arbitration because where a remedy is given by statute for violation of a right created by the same statute, the remedy given was regarded as exclusive. The intervention of a strong public policy may sometimes put an end entirely to the arbitrable nature of the dispute so that it is no longer deemed a "controversy" arising out of contract, as in the case of the insinuation of the price administrator's order into the price arrangements of the parties. (Matter of Kramer & Uchitelle, Inc., 288 N.Y. 467).

In reading Matter of Marchant v. Mead-Morrison Mfg. Co. (252 N.Y. 284) where the arbitrators, having powers to deal with the construction, the terms and the performance of a contract, were excluded from allowing consequential damages which otherwise might seem proper enough, a compelling inference must be drawn that on the question of the scope of their powers in respect of the measure of damage, arbitrators are held closely, not only to the language of the contract under which they function, but to a consistency with general legal rules in respect of damage.

The classic statement of Judge Cardozo in Loucks v. Standard Oil Co. (224 N.Y. 99, 112) that "We have no public policy that prohibits exemplary damages or civil penalties" is pressed upon us. It would require violent separation, text from context, to bring about an apposite employment of those words to this case. The court was there dealing with a cause of action in tort which arose in Massachusetts and was considering the effect of the application of exemplary damages allowable under Massachusetts law in an action prosecuted in New York.

New York, has, of course, allowed punitive damages for a few willful or wanton torts. But neither the Legislature nor the judges have ever given any legal sanction to the enforcement according to the tenor of its terms of any contractual undertaking calling for damages for actual loss due to a breach, and beyond that an entirely separate, additional and unlimited measure of damage directed solely toward punishment for the same breach.

It has been seen that in an action at law the court would not send any such agreed measure of damage to a jury. The court would rule that in such a case it would allow the actual, but not the punitive, measure ; and the test for statutory arbitration is a controversy which "may be the subject of an action." (Civ. Prac. Act, § 1448). This definition sweeps in "a written labor contract" which is "likewise" valid and enforcible.

We are of opinion that the penalty provision of the contract is unenforcible under any admissible theory under our law even though a separable finding of actual damage for breach could be made. The general rule that arbitrators are not bound by technical rules of law, and under a broad enough submission may interpret law as well as fact, is no adequate answer to this kind of legal infirmity which attaches itself to the nature of the submission itself. The court will not lend its power to the enforcement of the kind of a decision in arbitration which would neither allow nor enforce as the subject of an action maintained before it directly. We do not read the words "must grant" in section 1461 of the Civil Practice Act as requiring the court to confirm in its entirety the award before us when article 84 of the statute is read in full context.

The form of this award in respect of its punitive damages also is such that it is not final and definite within subdivision 4 of section 1462 of the Civil Practice Act and this would require in any event that the award be vacated. To make operative the $5,000 punitive part of the award, three additional events, each uncertain and unpredictable, must conjoin at some indefinite future time ; (a) there must be a new violation of the contract by the Union ; (b) there must be a finding of a new violation by the Adjustment Board ; and (c) the News must exercise an "option" to make the punitive damages effective. This is neither final nor definite.

In vacating part of the award, however, our decision is based on the broader ground that the allowance of punitive damages is not enforcible with the aid of the judicial power, rather than on the absence of finality under the form of the award.

Nothing in this opinion is inconsistent with the holding by the court in Matter of East India Trading Co. (Halari) (280 App. Div. 420) where, upon the facts, the court found that no penalty as such was imposed.

The order entered February 19, 1952, and the order and judgment entered March 12, 1952, should be modified by reversing so much thereof as confirms the award for $5,000 punitive damages and by vacating such part of the award, and, as so modified the order and the order and judgment so appealed from should be affirmed, with costs to the appellant.

CALLAHAN and HEFFERNAN, JJ. (dissenting). We are in accord with the views expressed by the Special Term as to the enforcibility of the provisions of the collective bargaining agreement permitting the Adjustment Board presided over by an Impartial Chairman as arbitrators to impose "damages, money or other penalties" for breaches of said agreement. We construe such provision to be no broader than one permitting the assessment of punitive damages. Neither such a contractual provision nor the awarded penalty of $5,000 imposed tentatively as a deterrent against future violations of the collective bargaining agreement would seem to conflict with the public policy of the State (Loucks v. Standard Oil Co., 224 N.Y. 99 ; Matter of Mencher [Geller & Sons] 276 App. Div. 556; Matter of East India Trading Co. [Halari], 280 App. Div. 420; Civ. Prac. Act, §§ 1448, 1462). We see no adequate reason why this court should decline to affirm such award.

Special Term confirmed the award both as to the compensatory and punitive damages. The sole question presented on this appeal is the enforcibility by the court of that part of the award providing for the $5,000 penalty or punitive damages. It seems to us that only two points require consideration: (1) as to whether the contract provisions for and the award of a penalty or punitive damages should be refused enforcement by the courts as against public policy, and (2) whether the award is sufficiently mutual, final and definite to justify enforcement by judgment.

The majority view appears to be that the courts will decline to enforce the penalty provision, because it would not allow or enforce such provision in an action at law for breach of the contract maintained before the court directly.

It seems to us that this adopts too narrow a view of the court's duty in this matter.

We are dealing with an award in arbitration as to which the legal rules of damage have no application. Arbitrators are not bound to recognize the distinction made by the courts as to the damages properly awarded in actions in contract as distinguished from those in tort.

It would serve little purpose to discuss at length the historical background of the rules applied by the courts as to the proper measure of damages in actions at law for breach of contract. We agree that in actions at law the penalty imposed by the arbitrators here would not be assessed. But the rules limiting damages in civil actions grow out of judicial interpretation. Arbitrators have no rule of *stare decisis*. One of these judicial rules affecting damages is that punitive damage is not to be allowed for breach of contract. Even this rule has had an exception in actions for breach of contract to marry. It does not follow that such a rule of law as to plenary actions establishes a rule of public policy limiting the power of an arbitrator. It is just as much the public policy of this State that arbitration awards within the limit of the submission are not to be impeached for misconception of the law (Matter of Marchant v. Mead-Morris Mfg. Co., 252 N.Y. 284, 302). Historically, the amount or nature of the damage to be awarded even in cases of breach of contract was first considered to be solely the affair of the jury, and the courts were reluctant to interfere with the punishment imposed (1 SEDGWICK ON DAMAGES, [9th ed.], §§ 347–352, 370). The courts from time to time and step by step narrowed this rule, including a restriction against punitive damages for a breach of contract. But, as we have noted, in arbitration the interpretation of the law as well as the facts is for the arbitrators, and they are limited solely by the extent of their jurisdiction under the submission and against an award that would offend the public policy of the State. An award that might contravene the penal laws of the State is an example of one that might offend our public policy (Matter of Western Union Tel. Co. [ACA], 299 N.Y. 177).

There would appear to be no such offense where arbitrators within the power expressly conferred by the parties impose a contingent penalty of $5,000 to deter unwarranted industrial warfare in the future. In fact, it would seem to us that the public policy is as much, if not more, concerned with the maintenance of industrial peace as it is with the inflexibility of any judge-made rule of damages in contract actions brought in the courts. The collective bargaining agreement here concerns complex relations of employer and employee, and not a casual conflict between buyer and seller over how much one should pay to the other for violating a contract of sale. The parties by their voluntary agreement charged the arbitrators with the duty of maintaining the integrity of their contract and peace in the industry, and gave them the broadest power of action in accomplishing this end, including the right to impose penalties. The tentative penalty or fine of $5,000 in the event of recurrence of an improper act might well be found by those charged with such duty as the one sure way of maintaining observance of the collective bargaining agreement. It seems to us that the courts should not decline to enforce such a penalty on any theory or ground that it calls upon the judicial branch of the Government or approval of an act offending its sense of propriety.

The Legislature of the State has determined the validity of a contract to arbitrate, except as to certain instances not relevant here (Civ. Prac. Act, § 1448). It has directed that the courts must confirm and enforce an award, unless it is vacated upon certain grounds of illegality specifically enumerated in the statute (Civ. Prac. Act, § 1462). No ground of excessive or improper damage is specified as a basis for vacating an award.

We consider it our duty to follow the legislative directive and confirm the award so long as the arbitrators kept within the limit of their conferred powers, even though a court might not award damages in the same amount or of the same nature in an action at law. We are not faced with any situation where there has been the imposition of confiscatory or oppressive damages by way of unwarranted penalties fixed in the millions instead of the thousands. Thus, we find that there has not been imposed any unlimited draft upon the judicial power. When an occasion arises that the penalty is so oppressive as to offend our sense of public justice to enforce it, then it will be time enough to consider the question of the extent of our right to refuse to do so.

The duty of the court in respect to confirming and enforcing arbitrators' awards is prescribed by statute, and we may not lightly disregard the statutory mandates upon any theory of separation of powers. At least, we may not do so in this particular case where its confirmation of the award would so little offend any exercise of the judicial power.

As to the second question concerning the finality, definiteness and mutuality of the award, we are of the opinion that it is enforcible. This award specifically states the conditions under which the $5,000 becomes payable. There is nothing more for the arbitrators to do except to say that there has been a recurrence of a strike in violation of section 16P. Thus the strike that already occurred defines the event, the recurrence of which makes the penalty payable. In any event, it would seem to us that the union is not aggrieved if payment of a sum is postponed, when it might have been presently required.

Accordingly, we dissent and vote to affirm the order and judgment confirming the award.

COHN, J. P., and VAN VOORHIS, J., concur with BERGAN, J.; CALLAHAN and HEFFERNAN, JJ., dissent and vote to affirm, in opinion.

Thereafter the Publishers Association members adopted a policy that a grievance stoppage against one member in violation of their agreement could, upon consultation, lead to suspension of operations by the other members until the original stoppage terminated. The publishers invoked this arrangement several times. See New York Mailers Union v. National Labor Relations Board (2d Cir. 1964) 327 F. 2d 292, holding that the NLRB justifiably dismissed the complaint alleging that the employer's activities constituted unfair labor practices (discrimination and restraint). The court agreed with the Board characterization that the publishers' conduct was justifiable defensive activity.

Is such an arrangement preferable to the conditional "punitive damages" disallowed by the Appellate Division? It should be noted that although the publishers ordered half a dozen shut downs none required sending employees from work or in loss of pay; at worst, editions were delayed for short periods.

Punitive damages for violation of no-strike Clause held permissible under § 301. Sidney Wanzer & Sons v. Milk Drivers' Union, 249 F. Supp. 664 (N.D. Ill. 1966). But cf., Local 127, United Shoe Workers v. Brooks Shoe Mfg. Co. 298 F. 2d 277 (3rd Cir. 1962). In a critical Note, 52 VA. L. REV. 1377 (1966) the court's lack of understanding of the "peculiar nature of labor disputes" was said to be one of the reasons for disapproving the ruling. Does an arbitrator's freedom from such a reproach argue for arbitral power to impose punitive damages?

D.

Non-Monetary Remedies

IN THE MATTER OF
POCKETBOOK UNION (CENTRA CORP.)
14 Misc. 2d 268, 149 N.Y.S. 2nd 56
(N.Y. Cty. 1956)

STEUER, J. The motion and cross motion, the former to confirm and the latter to vacate the award of an arbitrator, reveal some trivial and certain very important questions. It would be simple to dispose of the former variety first. Objection is made to the award in that the complete machinery of adjustment was not exhausted prior to demanding arbitration. The occasion of the dispute was whether respondent was in fact removing its plant from New York City to Oklahoma. The omission complained of was that this question was not first taken up, on the shop steward level. Obviously this objection lacks substance. Upon the question here involved discussion on the level suggested would be less than a formality. The contract must be read with that in mind and the obvious construction is that it does not require what would be useless.

The second objection is not significant legally, though its social implications are ever looming larger. It concerns the impartiality of the arbitrator. As in many industries, the arbitrator is a permanent official called the "impartial chairman." The title, of course, represents a sincere hope and doubtless it is realized as closely as is humanly possible where the tenure in office depends on continuing to be generally acceptable to the stronger party. Respondent claims that the chairman's partiality was demonstrated throughout the proceedings, particularly with regard to a press release almost simultaneous with the decision. The instances demonstrate nothing and the arbitrator's manners are as unsusceptible of review as are his findings.

Coming now to the important questions, the arbitrator disposed of the matter by enjoining the respondent from moving outside the city, directing that it procure the return of machinery already shipped out and making provisions for the wages of those people who are losing work due to the absence of this machinery. Admittedly this is an award of equitable relief in a primary degree and not as an incident to other relief. The question is whether such relief can be had in arbitration, a question which also concerned the

arbitrator as he discusses it in his opinion. He takes the position that the contract so provides and the provision has the sanction of judicial decision.

The pertinent clauses of the contract are:

> 27d. The impartial chairman is hereby given the powers of determining all complaints or controversies arising out of the terms of this agreement, and of determining the damages that the employer may be obliged to pay to the union, or to the workers, for the violation of any clause under this agreement.
>
> g. It is the sense of this agreement that the machinery of adjustment provided for in this agreement is the exclusive means of adjusting all complaints, disputes and grievances between the employer, the workers and the union.
>
> 30b. The union shall be entitled, as a matter of right, to equity relief enjoining and restraining the employer from breaching or threatening to breach the provisions of this agreement during the term provided for in this agreement.

Of the above, the first two paragraphs are a portion of section 27, entitled "Machinery of Adjustment" and the last is from section 30, entitled "Strikes and Lockouts."

The purposes of the last provision must be that in the event the union wishes to apply to a court for injunctive relief it will not be faced with the argument that the expression "all controversies" in the earlier clause makes arbitration the sole forum and deprives the court of jurisdiction and, further, it is an expression of the intent of the parties that specific performance of the contract may be enforced. But the jurisdiction of the arbitrator is neither increased nor limited by this provision and the arbitrator's conclusion that it is, is erroneous. What is meant is that whatever is arbitrable according to law should be so heard. The contract being of no peculiar aid in this respect, inspection of the law is called for.

The fact that an arbitration contemplates or involves equitable relief does not in and of itself make it nugatory. (Matter of Freydberg Bros. v. Corey, 177 Misc. 560, affd. 263 App. Div. 805.) But in such cases it is the court that fashions the decree based on the determination of the arbitrator. (Matter of Albert, 160 Misc. 237.) And equity will not "render a decree which shocks good conscience or is otherwise offensive to equity.' (Matter of Young [Deschler], 202 Misc. 811, 813.) Here certain difficulties, practical and logical, are encountered. Arbitrators make no findings and are not required to have minutes made of their proceedings. In ignorance of the testimony and without a guide as to how any particular issue was resolved by the forum, how is it to be determined whether the result is or is not shocking to the conscience? And as the arbitrator is not bound by rules of law he may order a decree where equity would refuse relief. Is this offensive to equity? While in this instance there are minutes and the arbitrator's opinion is a possible substitute for findings, the second horn of the dilemma above set out is presented. The respondent did not participate in the arbitration. There was ample proof as to the contentions and declarations of its officers. As to that branch of the relief which enjoins their removal from the city there is nothing either in the state of the proof or in the relief afforded which would give pause to the conscience of the chancellor. But it is not the same with that part of the award which consists of a mandatory injunction directing respondent to move back to New York all machinery heretofore removed in violation of the contract. The contract does not prohibit the removal of machinery except as this may be an incident of changing the locality of the shop. On this application respondent has by affidavit stated the removal was of machinery used in the manufacture of plastic bags, an operation which was so unprofitable that respondent desired to discontinue it. Respondent was in debt for an advance and the lender agreed to take this machinery in part payment of the loan. The circumstances are not without question and the arbitrator's prior experience with this respondent might well induce in him the belief that its contentions were not entitled to credence but, aside from that mistrust of their actions and elements of possible suspicion of the *bona fides* of the alleged transaction, there is nothing in the record which contradicts the respondent's version. Doubtless an arbitrator in rendering a money judgment could do so on a record in this condition, whereas a court could not. Here a court is requested to enter a judgment requiring a person to do something on pain of incarceration, as to which there is no proof satisfactory to the court that it is in the person's power to comply. Few instances will be so clear that what is "offensive to equity" will ever be more than a subjective concept, but to this court the situation presented is in excess of what the proven facts would warrant and an injunction to the extent indicated would be denied.

Motion granted, cross motion denied, settle judgment as indicated.

IN THE MATTER OF RUPPERT (EGELHOFER)
3 N.Y. 2d 576 148 N.E. 2d 129 (1958)

DESMOND, J. Appellants, Brewery Workers Local Unions of the International Brotherhood of Teamsters, appeal here as of right from a unanimous modification by the Appellate Division, Firt Department, of a Special Term order. The Special Term order had granted the motion of petitioners-respondents (five separate brewing corporations) to confirm an award made by an arbitrator and had denied, also, the cross motion of the unions to vacate the arbitration award. The Appellate Division's modifications was merely as to the title of the proceeding and the designations of defendants but this modification authorizes an appeal to this court as of right (Civ. Prac. Act, § 588, subd. 1, par. [b], cl. [ii]).

The principal law points argued by appellants dispute the authority of the arbitrator to order an injunction against appellants.

Arbitration and adjustment procedures are prescribed by Part V and Part VI of the general collective bargaining agreement between the breweries and the unions and the collective bargaining agreement, among other things, forbids any "slowdown" (or any lockout or strike). On March 1, 1956 the brewery companies, alleging that the unions and the workers were engaging in a slowdown, demanded of the American Arbitration Association that the association proceed immediately with the appointment of an arbitrator and with the scheduling of a hearing to be held within 24 hours. This was a resort to the so-called "speedy arbitration" procedure which is described in the collective bargaining agreement in section 1(b) of Part VI. Earlier parts of this agreement, being Part V and section 1 of Part VI, describe possible proceedings before an adjustment committee and before a board of arbitration. However, Part VI, in sections 1(b) and 2, makes it clear that whenever a violation of the prohibition against strikes, slow-downs, etc., is alleged, either party may waive the adjustment and arbitration provisions referred to in earlier parts of the agreement and thereupon the dispute shall be submitted to arbitration within 24 hours after receipt of notice by the American Arbitration Association, and the award in such cases shall be issued not later than 48 hours after the conclusion of the hearing. Those speedy procedures were carried out in this instance with the result that on March 2, 1956, the next day after the companies invoked the speedy procedure, hearings were held before the arbitrator. On March 4, 1956 the arbitrator handed up his opinion and award in which he found that there were slowdowns at the breweries in violation of the agreement. He therefore enjoined the local unions from continuing the slowdowns and directed the local unions to take necessary steps to stop the slowdowns.

Besides questioning the power of the arbitrator to issue an injunction, the unions, appellants, make other points: first, that there was failure to comply with a condition precedent to arbitration; and, second, that there was no sufficient proof before the arbitrator that the unions had ordered and conducted a slowdown.

The first and most important question is as to whether the arbitrator exceeded his powers in including an injunction in his award. The collective bargaining agreement does not directly affirm or deny such a power but in general terms authorizes arbitration and says that the arbitrators' decision "shall be final and binding upon all parties to the given dispute". However, it is apparent that nothing short of an injunction would have accomplished the evident intent of these parties that there be speedy and immediately effective relief against strikes, lockouts and slowdowns. True, we find no decision in this court confirming an arbitration award containing an injunction but we have upheld awards which commanded employers to rehire or retain employees—that is, mandatory injunctions (Matter of Devery [Daniels & Kennedy, Inc.], 292 N.Y. 596; Matter of United Culinary Bar & Grill Employees [Schiffman], 299 N.Y. 577). The whole question is as to the intent of the parties (see Dodds v. Hakes, 114 N.Y. 260). Traditionally, arbitrators have been licensed to direct such conduct of the parties as is necessary to the settlement of the matters in dispute (see 6 WILLISTON ON CONTRACTS [rev. ed.], p. 5392 et seq.; see authorities cited in 5 C. J., Arbitration and Award, p. 131, n. 34, and in 6 C. J. S., Arbitration and Award, p. 225).

On this injunction question, appellants say further that, even if injunctions are not necessarily and always unlawful in arbitration awards, this particular injunction was forbidden by section 876-a of the Civil Practice Act. That well-known statute forbids the issuance of an injunction by a court or judge in a labor dispute except after the making of findings not made here. This award was confirmed by Special Term (and affirmed by the Appellate Division) and so in the broadest sense, although not in the sense of the statute, the courts have ordered this particular injunction. But, once we have held that this particular employer-union agreement not only did not forbid but contemplated the inclusion of an injunction in such an award, no ground remains for invalidating this injunction. Section 876-a, like its prototype the Federal Norris-La Guardia Act, was the result of union resentment against the issuance of injunctions in labor strifes. But arbitration is voluntary and there is no reason why unions and employers should deny such powers to the special tribunals they themselves create. Section 876-a and article 84 (Arbitration) are both in our Civil Practice Act. Each represents a separate public policy and by affirming here we harmonize those two policies.

We are cited to certain Federal court cases (Bull S. S. Co. v. Seafarers' Int. Union, 250 F. 2d 326; Bull S. S. Co. v. National Mar. Engineers' Beneficial Assn., 250 F. 2d 332; Trainmen v. Chicago R. & I. R. R. Co., 353 U.S. 30) but all those decisions construe particular language in particular Federal statutes. None of them control our decision or suggest an answer to our problem.

We next take up the assertion of appellants that this whole arbitration was invalid since, according to them, there was lack of jurisdictional prerequisite in that there was no compliance with section 1 of Part V, which states in its second paragraph that all disputes shall be settled if possible by agreement and that if not so settled shall be submitted to the adjustment committee. Section 2 of Part V sets up the adjustment committee. Part VI then provides for formal arbitration. Appellants concede that when the "speedy" method of section 1(b) of Part VI is invoked, the adjustment committee may be by-passed. They insist, however, that a serious effort by the parties to settle disputes by agreement is a necessary preliminary to any arbitration, even of the "speedy" sort. We do not think that the language of section 1 of Part V admits of this meaning and we are sure that if it did it would produce an impossible result. The obvious purpose of this "speedy" method of Part VI is to have an immediate arbitration with an immediate decision, a result that was accomplished in this case. To say that the vague general language of paragraph 2 of section 1 of Part V requires that for some indeterminate period there be some unspecified amount of parleying before the "speedy" procedures may be utilized would be a contradiction in terms.

The last position taken by appellants is that there was no proof of a slowdown and no proof that if there were a slowdown it was caused by the unions. However, the transcript in this record of the proceedings before this arbitrator, while containing no common-law proof that there had been a slowdown, does show what amounts to testimony by representatives of all the brewing companies that there had been a slowdown with no denial by the unions. A reading of the transcript shows that this fact was not really in dispute at all and the present contention of appellants that there was no sufficient proof of a slowdown seems to be an afterthought.

The judgment appealed from should be affirmed, with costs.

CHIEF JUDGE CONWAY and JUDGES DYE, FULD, FROESSEL, VAN VOORHIS and BURKE concur.

Judgment affirmed.

IN THE MATTER OF
STAKLINSKI (PYRAMID ELEC. CO.)
6 N.Y. 2d 159, 188 N.Y.S. 2d 541 (1959)

DESMOND, J. We see nothing illegal about this arbitration award and no reason for vacating it. Petitioner was for years appellant's president and in charge of its production and engineering and one of its directors and largest stockholders. In 1954 appellant entered into an 11-year contract employing petitioner as manager in charge of production and engineering at a large salary plus a percentage of net profits. Included was a covenant that, if petitioner should be declared permanently disabled, he would receive reduced compensation for the next three years and then the contract would end. The contract provided that any controversy arising out of it should be settled by arbitration in accordance with American Arbitration Association rules and the rules of that Association in so many words authorized an arbitrator to grant equitable relief including "specific performance of a contract."

In June, 1956 the corporation's directors made a determination that appellant was permanently disabled and that his services should be terminated. Petitioner disputed the finding of permanent disability. The resulting difference of opinion was just such a controversy as the parties had agreed to submit to arbitration and to arbitration it went. The arbitrators held in favor of petitioner on the issue and ordered petitioner's reinstatement. That, of course, put beyond reach of the courts the question thus conclusively determined by arbitration as to whether petitioner was in fact permanently disabled. It is now asserted, however, that it is against public policy to compel a corporation to continue the services of an officer whose services are unsatisfactory to the directors. But we must remember that this corporation made a valid long-term employment contract with this man and agreed that any disputes would go to arbitrators who would be empowered to order specific performance. Since the contract was indisputably valid, so is the arbitration award. The power of an arbitrator to order specific performance in an appropriate case has been recognized from early times (see Justice Story in McNeil v. Magee, Fed. Cas. No. 8915 [1829]).

In Matter of Ruppert (Egelhofer) (3 N.Y. 2d 576) we upheld the grant by arbitrators of an injunction against a strike in a labor dispute, and we cited a number of precedents therefor. A supposed "public policy" against such an injunction was urged on us in *Ruppert* since there we had a specific statute (Civ. Prac. Act, § 876-a) which would have made it impossible for a court to grant that same injunction. However, we held in *Ruppert* that the parties had agreed not only to submit their controversies to arbitration but had validly authorized the arbitrators to issue an injunction. The same is true here. Whether a court of equity could issue a specific performance decree in a case like this (see Matter of Buffalo & Erie Ry. Co., 250 N.Y. 275, 280–281) is beside the point. There is no controlling public policy which voids an arbitration agreement like this one and the courts are not licensed to announce a new public policy to fit the supposed necessities of the case (see Matter of Rhinelander, 290 N.Y. 31, 36).

The judgment should be affirmed, with costs.

FROESSEL, J. (concurring). I concur for affirmance. I do not, however, read the arbitrator's award or the judgment entered thereon as directing "specific performance" of a personal service contract.

The only dispute submitted to arbitration was whether petitioner was "permanently disabled", so as to entitle the corporation to terminate its liability to him after making specified payments for three years from the date of disability. All the arbitrators decided was that petitioner was not "permanently disabled", and hence was improperly discharged under the "permanent disability" clause of the contract. In directing the corporation to reinstate him in his position, the arbitrators awarded the natural and logical relief called for by the nature of the dispute submitted to them.

Future performance will depend upon future events which cannot now be foreseen. The board of directors of the corporation may discharge petitioner for good cause, and any discharge without good cause will be at the peril of damages.

BURKE, J. (dissenting). An arbitrators' award of specific performance of a contract for personal services directing the issuance of a mandatory injunction against a foreign employer in behalf of a nonresident employee who has been wrongfully discharged is without precedent and violates settled principles of equity. In such a situation, the courts of this State are not bound to uphold an arbitration award that offends established principles of law and public policy.

While a public corporation may be liable in damages for a breach of a long-term contract of employment (Douglass v. Merchants' Ins. Co., 118 N.Y. 484 ; Cuppy v. Stollwerck Bros., 216 N.Y. 591 ; 2 FLETCHER'S CYCLOPEDIA CORPORATIONS [Perm. ed.], § 353, p. 151 ; § 363, p. 177), we have found no case wherein a court has decreed specific performance of these contracts. The reason is that equity has traditionally declined to afford such relief (Cuppy v. Ward, 227 N.Y. 603 ; 81 C.J.S., Specific Performance, § 82).

While no statute expressly defines the arbitrators' powers to grant relief, the provisions of section 1448 of the Civil Practice Act, making valid and enforcible arbitration submissions and contracts, suggests the adoption of the common-law concept of remedies. This follows from the fact that an arbitration submission and agreements to arbitrate must be capable of being the subject of an action (Civ. Prac. Act, § 1448; Matter of Burkin [Katz], 1 N.Y. 2d 570).

Where equitable relief has been granted in an arbitration proceeding, it is the *court* that fashions the decree based on the determination of the arbitrator (Matter of Ruppert [Egelhofer], 3 N.Y. 2d 576 ; Matter of Albert, 160 Misc. 237) Heretofore, we have refused to confirm arbitrators' awards where such were illegal or violative of some well-defined public policy. (See *e.g.*, Matter of Western Union Tel. Co. [American Communications Assn.], 299 N.Y. 177; Matter of Publishers' Assn. [Newspaper Union], 280 App. Div. 500.)

In this case the mandatory injunction exceeded the powers of the arbitrator and the decree enforcing it violates both the statutory policy confiding to directors the management of public corporations and the principles of equity barring injunctive relief of this nature. We do not believe that, under a general grant of equitable powers, arbitrators may disregard equitable principles and issue an award not possible either at law or equity. As Judge Pound said, dissenting in Matter

of Buffalo & Erie Ry. Co. (250 N.Y. 275, 280–281)

> It by no means follows that the findings of the arbitrators may be enforced by the court by the remedy of specific performance. *No man may be compelled to work for another or to continue another in his employment.* I hold merely that industrial disputes as to future wages may be submitted to arbitration where the parties so agree. [Emphasis added.]

Cases involving collective bargaining agreements are inapposite here. The reason for this conclusion was stated by the United States Supreme Court in Case Co. v. Labor Bd., (321 U.S. 332, 334–335) wherein the court stated that:

> Collective bargaining between employer and representatives of a unit, usually a union, results in an accord as to terms which will govern hiring and work and pay in that unit. The result is not, however, a contract of employment except in rare cases; no one has a job by reason of it and no obligation to any individual ordinarily comes into existence from it alone. The negotiations between union and management result in what often has been called a trade agreement, rather than a contract of employment.

Further, it has become clear both under the State and National Labor Relations Acts, as well as in arbitration, that specific performance is frequently essential to maintain and further the collective relationships involved. (See Goldman v. Cohen, 222 App. Div. 631.)

However, the reasons compelling the courts and arbitrators to grant both specific performance and injunctive relief in collective bargaining agreements do not apply to contracts such as the one in question. A decree for the reinstatement of a nonresident manager in a public corporation is subject to all the obstacles and objections equity has always recognized, and is not justified by the special considerations that make this type of relief desirable in the collective bargaining area.

Matter of Ruppert (Egelhofer) (*supra*), involving a collective bargaining agreement, is cited as upholding an arbitrators' award of equitable relief (injunction) where a court, under the same circumstances, would be powerless to act. However, as we view *Ruppert,* it is neither determinative nor controlling of the issues here.

Implicit in the *Ruppert* decision was a finding (p. 581) that not only had the parties authorized the imposition of equitable relief but that "nothing short of an injunction would have accomplished the evident intent of these parties that there be a speedy and immediately effective relief against strikes, lockouts and slowdowns."

Even if the agreement here authorizes specific performance of this contract, we are still of the opinion that the injunctive relief should not have been granted by the arbitrators. (Matter of Publishers' Assn. [Newspaper Union], *supra*.) To hold otherwise is to state in effect that under this agreement the corporation itself could seek specific performance of a recalcitrant employee and that arbitrators could award specific performance compelling the employee to work for the corporation. Such a result would be clearly undesirable.

On a motion to confirm an award, the court does not sit as an administrative rubber stamp over an arbitrator's determination, but rather as a court of equity applying equitable principles and enjoys a certain latitude of discretion. (Cf. Matter of Lipschutz [Gutwirth], 304 N.Y. 58, 63; Matter of Feuer Transp. [Local No. 445], 295 N.Y. 87; Western Union Tel. Co. v. Selly, 295 N.Y. 395.) In Matter of Finsilver, Still & Moss v. Goldberg, Maas & Co. (253 N.Y. 382, 392), this court wrote (per Cardozo, Ch. J.): "The motion to confirm is equivalent to a suit in equity to carry into effect the terms of the agreement and the arbitration had thereunder." Proceedings involving arbitration have always been considered as equitable in nature "and the practice of equity as to relief should be followed." (Matter of Feuer Transp. [Local No. 445], *supra*, p. 92.)

We conclude that the confirmation of an award compelling reinstatement of a nonresident official in a foreign corporation in the form of specific performance of a contract for personal services should not be made by this court even though the parties may have provided for it.

Accordingly, the judgment of the Appellate Division and that of Special Term should be reversed and the motion to vacate the award should be granted.

JUDGES DYE and FULD concur with JUDGE DESMOND; JUDGE FROESSEL concurs in a separate memorandum; JUDGE BURKE dissents in an opinion in which JUDGE VAN VOORHIS concurs; CHIEF JUDGE CONWAY taking no part.

Judgment affirmed.

Matter of Exercycle (Maratta). See Chapter VI, C.

IN THE MATTER OF GRAYSON-ROBINSON STORES (IRIS CONST. CO)
8 N.Y. 2d 133, 168 N.E. 2d 377 (1960)

DESMOND, CH. J. Again, as in Matter of Staklinski (Pyramid Elec. Co.) 6 N.Y. 2d 159), the courts are called upon to confirm an arbitration award which, conformably to the express powers given by the parties to the arbitrators, directed specific performance of a contract. Appellant, defaulting in performance and losing its case before the arbitrators, now argues to the courts, as did the losing party in Staklinski and in Matter of Ruppert (Egelhofer) (3 N.Y. 2d 576), that enforcement of this award would be contrary to public policy. Specific performance of a contract to construct a building, argues appellant, is never ordered by courts of equity because of the necessity of continuous judicial supervision and control of performance. Therefore, so the argument runs, the same courts will not confirm and enforce an arbitration award which decrees specific performance of the same kind of agreement. We disagree. There is no hard and fast rule against applying the remedy of specific performance to such contracts, especially when the parties have by agreement provided for just that remedy.

In 1955 appellant Iris, owner of vacant land in Levittown, Nassau County, entered into a written agreement with respondent Grayson (later assigned by Grayson to its subsidiary respondent Klein) whereby Iris undertook to erect on the Iris tract a building (part of a "shopping center") to be rented by Iris to Grayson for use as a retail department store for a term of 25 years after completion with certain optional provisions for renewals of the term. Possession was to be turned over to Grayson "on or before September 1, 1957, time being of the essence." The agreement called for arbitration of all disputes and incorporated the rules of the American Arbitration Association which in terms empower the arbitrator in his award to grant any just or equitable remedy or relief "including ... specific performance."

There were several amendments and extensions of the original contract, but none of these are relevant to our discussion. The plans and specifications for the building were completed or practically completed, a public ground-breaking ceremony was held and excavation commenced, then Iris notified Grayson-Klein that, because of difficulties in getting mortgage money, Iris could not go further unless Grayson-Klein agreed to increase the agreed rent. The tenant declined to pay more. The building has never been completed.

It was, apparently, always the intention of Iris to obtain by mortgage loan the money it needed for construction but there is nothing in the agreement relieving Iris of its obligation, in the event it should find such borrowing to be difficult or impossible. At the arbitration and in the courts Iris has argued "impossibility" but the arbitrators disposed of that issue by ordering Iris to "proceed forthwith with the improvements of the leased premises in accordance with the terms of the said lease, as amended." There was no proof before the arbitrators of any physical or actual impossibility as distinguished from difficulty of financing or additional expense of construction.

It would be quite remarkable if, after these parties had agreed that arbitrators might award specific performance and after the arbitrators had so ordered, the courts would, contrary to the command of article 84 of the Civil Practice Act, frustrate the whole arbitration process by refusing to confirm the award. The only ground suggested for such a refusal is that confirmation would involve the court in supervision of a complex and extended construction contract. We hold that this apprehension or speculation is no deterrent to confirmation by the courts.

There is, of course, an old tradition or approach according to which courts have been reluctant to enforce "Contracts which require the performance of varied and continuous acts, or the exercise of special skill, taste and judgment" because "the execution of the decree would require such constant superintendence as to make judicial control a matter of extreme difficulty" (Standard Fashion Co. v. Siegel-Cooper Co., 157 N.Y. 60, 66). In some instances courts of equity in other States have for some such reasons refused to order specific performance of building contracts (McCormick v. Proprietors of Cemetery of Mt. Auburn, 285 Mass. 548 ; see discussion in McDonough v. Southern Oregon Min. Co., 177 Ore. 136, 150). Other courts of equity have gone the other way (see Jones v. Parker, 163 Mass. 564, which also was a contract to build for a lessee). "There is no universal rule that courts of equity never will enforce a contract which requires some building to be done. They have enforced such contracts from the earliest days to the present time" (Jones v. Parker, *supra,* p. 567). On varying facts our New York decisions take one or the other position (Strauss v. Estates of Long Beach, 187 App. Div. 876 ; Post v. West Shore R. R. Co., 123 N.Y. 580, 591 ; Jones v. Seligman, 81 N.Y. 190 ; Beck v. Allison, 56 N.Y. 366 ; Conger v. West Shore R. R. Co., 120 N.Y. 29, 32). Modern writers think that the "difficulty

of enforcement" idea is exaggerated and that the trend is toward specific performance (5 CORBIN, CONTRACTS [1951 ed.], § 1172; 5 WILLISTON, CONTRACTS [rev. ed.], p. 3977 ; RESTATEMENT, CONTRACTS, § 371, comment *a*). Clearly there is no binding rule that deprives equity of jurisdiction to order specific performance of a building contract. At most there is discretion in the court to refuse such a decree. And here we do not even have an equity suit but a motion made as of right to confirm a completely valid arbitration award conforming in all respects to the express conferral of authority on the arbitrators and meeting all statutory requirements for confirmation (see Civ. Prac. Act, §§ 1461, 1462, 1462-a).

Assuming that the equity court in an original suit would have discretion to refuse specific performance, and even making the very large assumption that the court would have similar discretionary power to refuse to confirm this award, it remains that such discretion, if any, was exercised the other way in this case, and unanimously affirmed by the Appellate Division. That exercise of discretion was justified on the facts. There is nothing extraordinary about this ordinary building contract. Appellant is simply being required to fulfill its promise. If it fails or refuses to obey the judgment, the remedy is in section 773 of the Judiciary Law.

Arbitration is by consent and those who agree to arbitrate should be made to keep their solemn, written promises. Such is New York State's public policy, plainly written in article 84 of the Civil Practice Act. The courts should follow a "liberal policy of promoting arbitration both to accord with the original intention of the parties and to ease the current congestion of court calendars" (Lawrence Co. v. Devonshire Fabrics, 271 F. 2d 402, 410).

The judgment should be affirmed, with costs.

VAN VOORHIS, J. (dissenting). If "Arbitration is not merely a step in judicial enforcement of a claim nor auxiliary to a main proceeding, but the full relief sought" (Goodall-Sanford v. Textile Workers, 353 U.S. 550, 551), it would relieve the courts if the arbitrators enforced their own awards in specific performance instead of delegating that essential function to the courts after they have been discharged from further duty. Only recently was it settled that an arbitration award will be enforced by the courts which grants, under an appropriate arbitration clause, equitable relief by injunction (Matter of Ruppert [Egelhofer], 3 N.Y. 2d 576). More recently it was held that our courts would enforce specific performance of an employment contract on an arbitration award (Matter of Staklinski [Pyramid Elec. Co.], 6 N.Y. 2d 159) even though a court of equity would not compel a man to work for another or to continue another in his employment (see dissenting opinion by Judge Burke] in Matter of Staklinski [Pyramid Elec. Co.], *supra*, p. 165). The decision in the present case lends the enforcement machinery of the courts, to implement specific performance directed by arbitration that extends beyond any equitable relief which the courts have heretofore granted either on arbitrations or after trial.

The mechanism for enforcement of this award of specific performance of a complicated construction contract for the erection of a building estimated to cost $5,000,000, is a judgment to be entered following confirmation of the award under section 1466 of the Civil Practice Act which provides that "The judgment so entered has the same force and effect, in all respects as, and is subject to all the provisions of law relating to, a judgment in an action; and it may be enforced as if it had been rendered in an action in the court in which it is entered." This signifies not that the arbitrators but that the court is the agency which will be called upon to supervise the construction of this elaborate and expensive building, and which will be required to do so by the very inappropriate remedy of punishment as for contempt of court. The plans and specifications, whether they have been finally approved by the parties or not, are not before the court and have been materially changed since the contract was made. They have been the subject of long and acrimonious disputes between the parties which are not likely to end with the entry of a judgment on this award for specific performance.

Respondents' brief admits that the enforcement of this building contract will be the responsibility of the court and not that of the arbitrators (pp. 17–18). In a case of this kind, that circumstance closes the gap between what courts and boards of arbitration can do in specific performance where the objection to that form of court relief is impossibility of adequate enforcement. That is the basis on which courts have traditionally declined to grant specific performance of elaborate and time-consuming building construction contracts (Beck v. Allison, 56 N.Y. 366, 370; Standard Fashion Co. v. Siegel-Cooper Co., 157 N.Y. 60; McCormick v. Proprietors of Cemetery of Mt. Auburn, 285 Mass. 548; Jones v. Parker, 163 Mass. 564; RESTATEMENT, CONTRACTS, § 371). This section of the RESTATEMENT says:

> Specific enforcement will not be decreed if the performance is of such a character as to make effective enforcement unreasonably difficult or to require such long-continued supervision by the court as is disproportionate to the advantages to be gained from such a decree and to the harm to be suffered in case it is denied.

Where difficulty of enforcement is the reason for nonintervention by courts of equity, it is equally a reason on account of which restraint should be exercised in confirming and entering judgment upon arbitration awards where the difficulty of enforcement is precisely the same whether the judgment has been entered on the decision of a court or on an award in arbitration. This objection to the confirmation of this award is not based upon any threatened usurpation by the court of the jurisdiction of the arbitrators. This objection does not arise out of anything which the arbitrators did or omitted in the performance of their functions, but springs from difficulty in enforcement problems which devolve upon the court under the arbitration article of the Civil Practice Act which is invoked by respondents in moving to confirm the award. It was well said by Frank E. Johnson, J., in Queens Plaza Amusements v. Queens Bridge Realty Corp. (22 Misc 2d 315, revd. on other grounds 265 App. Div. 1057).

> It is a fundamental limitation upon the jurisdiction of any equity court that it will not entertain demands that are inherently unenforcible by it. A decree *in personam* is enforced by contempt and whether or not there had been default would involve the trial of a question of fact as to plans, specifications, construction details, etc.; the enormous detail indicated by this contract would put the court in a position of a building superintendent and an architect, passing upon an incredible number of problems arising on a building construction large enough to warrant the mortgage of $140,000. This is so plainly outside of the power and function of a Justice of this court that supervision of the performance of such agreements cannot be entertained; they are outside of the practicable limits of equity jurisdiction.

These problems are neither solved nor diminished by the circumstance that this responsibility of supervision of the construction of this building has to be undertaken by the court as the result of an arbitration. If the arbitrators were to remain upon the scene and supervise and enforce the building operations which courts are not created to handle, the result might be different. Once the award has been confirmed and judgment of specific performance entered, the arbitrators depart and the court has to enforce the building contract by contempt proceedings against the appellant and the persons of its officers and agents. The court cannot look to the arbitrators to resolve disputes arising in the erection of this building, either of interpretation of the building contract, plans or specifications, or concerning performance. The theory on which judgment will be entered is that the award is final and definite so that the acts to be performed can be clearly ascertained and the court determine whether or not the performance rendered is in accord with the contractual duty assumed (Civ. Prac. Act, §§ 1461–1462; 5 CORBIN, CONTRACTS, pp. 756–760). In order to punish deviation from the specific performance directed, or to decide whether or in what respects there has been performance, substantial performance or nonperformance, the court will be unable to call in the arbitrators to interpret its decree or subrogate them to vindicate its dignity if its decree is violated.

The court cannot appoint a receiver as an arm of the court to take possession of the property and cause the work to be done as was pointed out in Beck v. Allison (supra). The unsatisfactoriness of contempt of court as the means of enforcement of transactions of this kind is augmented by the inability of the court to punish defaults that are not willful or deliberate (Staples v. Staples, 206 App. Div. 196; see opinion by McGivern, J., in Matter of Chassman [Probyn], 1 Misc 2d 766).

While "There is no universal rule that courts of equity never will enforce a contract which requires some building to be done", in the words of Justice Holmes in Jones v. Parker (supra), the "question is practical rather than a matter of precedent" and specific performance of construction projects can be decreed, said Justice Holmes, where the possible differences between the parties over the performance of the undertaking are such as lie "within a narrow compass and which can be adjusted by the court." All that was involved there was the installation of heating and lighting apparatus for the benefit of a lessee. Jones v. Parker is "A decision which has often been cited far more than it held" (164 A. L. R. 802, 822). A similar holding was made in Strauss v. Estates of Long Beach (187 App. Div. 876) in directing the specific performance of a covenant to construct a sewer in a street in a subdivision in which the plaintiff had already purchased a lot from the defendant. A highway crossing was required to be constructed across a railroad in Post v. West Shore R. R. Co. (123 N.Y. 580). Professor Corbin enumerates in section 1172 of his work on Contracts situations where a court "has ordered performance of building repairs and other construction work," relating to such relatively simple matters as the enforcement of contractual obligations for the construction of highway bridges, digging wells, repairing houses, laying sidewalks in subdivisions or refilling excavations after mining or gravel pit operations have been completed. But because this can be done in some instances does not mean that it can be done in all, nor does equitable jurisdiction in arbitrators signify that the courts will enforce anything that arbitrators may do—especially if it is of a nature that has been held to be unenforcible by judicial decree. None of the projects just enumerated approximate the complexity and magnitude of the building operation involved here.

The board of arbitration, without doubt, would have had jurisdiction to award damages to petitioners for any breach of this construction contract which has occurred but they were not asked to award damages. Petitioners told the arbitrators that they did not want damages but specific performance, which it is evident that the arbitrators granted pro forma because the contract said that a building was to be erected, and without considering whether the construction of this building by appellant had become impossible. They appear not to have understood that specific performance is not granted mechanically, that equity does not enforce idle ceremonies, that before making an award of this kind they had to rule upon whether performance had become impossible (Saperstein v. Mechanics & Farmers Sav. Bank, 228 N.Y. 257) and that if it was impossible petitioners would be relegated to damages. The record before us indicates that appellant applied unsuccessfully to 27 different leading institutions in order to obtain the necessary mortgage money with which to erect this building. Petitioners appear to recognize that for this reason the building may not be constructed by appellant even after the entry of a specific performance decree. They profess an intention of suing for damages by the recovery of a fine to be imposed on appellant under section 773 of the Judiciary Law in case appellant is adjudged in contempt (petitioners-respondents' brief, pp. 17–18). This contention presents a double anomaly in that (1) if it is impossible for appellant to construct the building, its failure to do so would not be willful and, therefore, would not subject it to punishment for contempt, and (2) the board of arbitration is deprived of its function to assess damages which should have been claimed and awarded in the first instance in case they found specific performance by appellant to be impossible.

Therefore, even if confirmation were not denied to the specific performance award on account of difficulty in enforcement, the award should be vacated and the matter remitted to the arbitrators to rule upon whether specific performance by appellant is possible and, if they find it is not, to decide upon the question of damages.

JUDGES DYE, FULD and FROESSEL concur with CHIEF JUDGE DESMOND; JUDGE VAN VOORHIS dissents in an opinion in which JUDGES BURKE and FOSTER concur.

Judgment affirmed.

Presumably an arbitrator can give a "declaratory judgment" contract interpretation wherever a court could. Where justiciability is not required, may an arbitrator pass on an issue where a court could not (*e.g.,* because the differences between the parties have not ripened into a "controversy")?

E.

The Issue of Strikes—II: Enjoining a Strike Allegedly in Breach of a No-Strike Clause

McCARROLL v. LOS ANGELES COUNTY DIST. COUN. OF CARPENTERS
49 Cal. 2d 45, 315 P. 2d 322 (1957)

TRAYNOR, J. Plaintiffs are engaged in the contracting business in the Los Angeles area. They brought the present action against defendant labor unions and their officers for damages and injunctive relief against strikes allegedly called by defendants.

In their second amended complaint plaintiffs allege that plaintiffs and defendants are parties to a collective bargaining agreement known as the BCA-AF of L Master Labor Agreement. This agreement provides that a contractor shall have complete freedom in hiring workmen, except that he must first call on the local union having jurisdiction over the area in which the contracting work is to be done to satisfy his need for labor. The local union must immediately furnish the required number of competent and skilled workmen, and if after forty-eight hours notice it has failed to do so, the contractor is free to obtain workmen from any available source. Furthermore, the contractor is permitted to transfer workmen up to 10 per cent of his current requirements in any craft from the jurisdiction of one local union to the jurisdiction of another local union. He may transfer more than 10 per cent if permitted by the constitution and by-laws of the craft at the time the collective bargaining agreement was entered into. The by-laws of the Los Angeles County District Council of Carpenters permit such a transfer up to 50 per cent of a contractor's requirements, and also require a local union to honor a contractor's request for specific workmen. The agreement also provides that the unions will not call a strike

against a contractor during the life of the agreement, but that all grievances or disputes over the interpretation or application of the terms of the agreement will be settled by a specified grievance procedure and by arbitration.

The complaint further alleges that plaintiffs entered into contracts to do the carpentry work on various construction projects in the Los Angeles area. Pursuant to the collective bargaining agreement, plaintiffs called on defendant local unions to supply them with workmen. The workmen sent to plaintiffs were, however, unskilled and incompetent, and furthermore defendants informed plaintiffs that they would not be permitted to transfer workmen from the jurisdiction of one local union to the jurisdiction of another local union in excess of 10 per cent of their current requirements. Defendants also refused to honor plaintiffs' requests for named workmen or to permit plaintiffs to transfer their regular workmen from different parts of Los Angeles County to specific construction projects. Defendants ordered strikes of plaintiffs' employees on specific construction projects, and finally brought about a strike of all plaintiffs' employees.

The complaint alleges that the only reasons defendants gave for their conduct were that plaintiffs are labor contractors and are violating state safety regulations; that in fact plaintiffs are not labor contractors since they undertake to do complete carpentry jobs and not merely to furnish workmen, and that in any event labor contracting is prohibited neither by law nor by the collective bargaining agreement; that a state safety inspector found that plaintiffs were not violating any state safety regulations; and that defendants' purpose in calling strikes was to harass plaintiffs and totally destroy their business.

Plaintiffs seek to state three causes of action: breach of the collective bargaining agreement through a violation of the no-strike clause, a tortious attempt to destroy plaintiffs' business without any legitimate labor objective, and a violation of the Cartwright Act (Bus. & Prof. Code, §§ 16700–16758) by restraining trade without any legitimate labor objective. On the basis of the complaint, testimony, and numerous affidavits, the trial court issued a preliminary injunction against defendants' calling or continuing a strike against plaintiffs, and it is from this order that defendants appeal. In view of our conclusion that the issuance of the injunction was justified by the breach of the collective bargaining agreement, we do not find it necessary to consider the second and third causes of action stated in the complaint.

Defendants first contend that the trial court was without jurisdiction to issue its injunction because the National Labor Relations Board has exclusive jurisdiction over the conduct alleged in the complaint. It is now well established that if conduct may be reasonably deemed to fall within the provisions of the Labor Management Relations Act defining unfair labor practices (29 U.S.C.A. § 158(a)—(b)), a state court has no jurisdiction to grant injunctive relief under either state or federal law, even if the National Labor Relations Board has declined to exercise jurisdiction over the controversy. Weber v. Anheuser-Busch, Inc., 348 U.S. 468, 481, 75 S.Ct. 480, 99 L.Ed. 546 ; Guss v. Utah Labor Relations Bd., 351 U.S. 1, 77 S.Ct. 598, 1 L.Ed. 2d 601 ; Charles H. Benton, Inc., v. Painters Union, 45 Cal. 2d 677, 681, 291 P. 2d 13. The conduct alleged in the present case, however, cannot reasonably be deemed to fall within any of the provisions of section 8(b) of the federal act defining unfair labor practices by unions. 29 U.S.C.A. § 158(b).

If the allegations in the complaint are true, the reason for the strike in the present case was either defendants' contention that plaintiffs are labor contractors and are violating state safety regulations, or the personal hostility of some of the individual defendants toward plaintiffs. At no time did defendants express dissatisfaction with the terms of the contract between the parties or inform plaintiffs of a desire to modify it in any regard. The object of the strike appears to have concerned a subject wholly ungoverned by the contract and outside the usual sphere of collective bargaining. Since it was not a strike to terminate or modify the contract it did not constitute the unfair labor practice of refusing to bargain.

Since defendants' conduct as alleged cannot reasonably be deemed an unfair labor practice under any of the provisions of section 8(b), it is unnecessary for us to decide whether a court has jurisdiction to enjoin conduct that is in breach of a collective bargaining agreeement and at the same time may be reasonably deemed an unfair labor practice. See Independent Petroleum Workers v. Esso Standard Oil Co., 3 Cir., 235 F. 2d 401; Textile Workers, etc., v. Arista Mills Co., 4 Cir., 193 F. 2d 529 ; Dunau, *Contractual Prohibition of Unfair Labor Practices: Jurisdictional Problems,* 57 COLUM. L. REV. 52 ; but see N.L.R.B. v. Wagner Iron Works and Bridge Workers, 7 Cir., 220 F. 2d 126, 137, certiorari denied, 350 U.S. 981, 76 S.Ct. 466, 100 L.Ed. 850.

Defendants contend that even if this is not a case over which the National Labor Relations Board has exclusive jurisdiction, since it is an action for breach of a collective bargaining agreement it is within the exclusive jurisdiction of the federal courts under section 301(a) of the Labor Management Relations Act. 29 U.S.C.A. § 185(a). Section 301(a) provides that:

> Suits for violations of contracts between an employer and a labor organization representing employees in an industry affecting commerce . . . may be brought in any district court of the United States having jurisdiction of the parties, without respect to the amount in controversy or without regard to the citizenship of the parties.

From the time of its enactment the federal courts were in continual disagreement as to whether section 301 required the creation of a characteristically federal decisional law to govern collective bargaining agreements affecting interstate commerce, or merely provided a federal forum for the enforcement of substantive rights grounded in the law of the states. The majority of the lower federal courts held that section 301 created substantive rights based on federal law, and did not merely confer jurisdiction. Some were persuaded to this view by the fear that if section 301 were construed merely to extend the jurisdiction of the federal courts, it would confer upon them jurisdiction over cases not arising under the laws of the United States, and thus exceed the scope of the judicial power of the United States as defined in article III of the Federal Constitution. See Signal-Stat. Corp. v. Local 475, United Elecc. Workers, 2 Cir., 235 F. 2d 298, 300, certiorari denied, 77 S.Ct. 1293 ; Shirley-Herman Co. v. International Hod Carriers, 2 Cir., 182 F. 2d 806, 808–809; International Union of Operating Engineers v. Dahlem Const. Co., 6 Cir., 193 F. 2d 470, 475 ; United Elec. Workers v. Oliver Corp., 8 Cir., 205 F. 2d 376, 384–385.

Recently the Court of Appeals for the First Circuit took the position that the supposed constitutional difficulty did not exist, since even if an action under 301 is based on state law, the case arises under the laws of the United States for the purposes of article III. Federal court jurisdiction is necessary to implement a congressional policy governing collective bargaining agreements affecting interstate commerce. International Brotherhood of Teamsters v. W. L. Mead, Inc., 1 Cir., 230 F. 2d 576, 580–582, certiorari dismissed, 352 U.S. 802, 77 S.Ct. 21, 1 L.Ed. 2d 37. This view could have prepared the way for an interpretation of 301 that preserved the application of state law but provided a federal forum for suits against unions that because of procedural obstacles could not be sued as entities in the courts of many states. The extremely fragmentary legislative history and almost total absence of any direction in the statute as to the content of a federal substantive law gave considerable support to such an interpretation. Textile Workers Union, etc., v. American Thread Co., D.C. Mass., 113 F. Supp. 137, 139–141; see Association of Westinghouse Salaried Employees v. Westinghouse Elec. Corp., 348 U.S. 437, 441–459, 75 S.Ct. 488, 99 L.Ed. 510 (Mr. Justice Frankfurter concurring and dissenting) ; Wollett and Wellington, *Federalism and Breach of the Labor Agreement,* 7 STAN. L. REV. 455 ; Cox, *Some Aspects of the Labor Management Relations Act,* 1947, 61 HARV. L. REV. 274, 303–305.

The United States Supreme Court, however, has now authoritatively declared that section 301 creates a federal substantive law governing collective bargaining agreements affecting interstate commerce. Textile Workers v. Lincoln Mills of Alabama, 77 S.Ct. 912. Although the case before the Court concerned only the power of a federal court to give a remedy not available under state law—specific enforcement of an agreement to arbitrate—the majority opinion broadly states that "the substantive law to apply in suits under § 301(a) is federal law which the courts must fashion from the policy of our national labor laws."

Federal interpretation of the federal law will govern, not state law. [Citation.] But state law, if compatible with the purpose of § 301, may be resorted to in order to find the rule that will best effectuate the federal policy. [Citation.] Any state law applied, however, will be absorbed as federal law and will not be an independent source of private rights. 77 S.Ct. 918.

It does not necessarily follow from a decision that federal law governs the rights of the parties that state courts are ousted of jurisdiction to enforce those rights. As Mr. Justice Bradley stated in Claflin v. Houseman, 93 U.S. 130, 136, 23 L.Ed. 833,

[I]f exclusive jurisdiction [in the federal courts] be neither express nor implied, the State courts have concurrent jurisdiction [to enforce federal rights] whenever, by their own constitution, they are competent to take it." Concurrent jurisdiction exists "where it is not excluded by express provision, or by incompatability in its exercise arising from the nature of the particular case."

See Gerry of California v. Superior Court, 32 Cal. 2d 119, 122–123, 194 P. 2d 689.

Section 301 does not expressly exclude state courts. On the contrary, it merely declares that an action for breach of a collective bargaining agreement may be brought in a federal court. Surely if Congress had intended to exclude state courts it would have used more forthright language. Nor does enforcement of collective bargaining agreements in state courts conflict with any federal policy embodied in section 301 or any other part of the federal statute. Defendants contend that the rationale of Garner v. Teamsters Union, 346 U.S. 485, 74 S.Ct. 161, 98 L.Ed. 228, and Weber v. Anheuser-Busch, Inc., 348 U.S. 468, 75 S.Ct. 480, 99 L.Ed. 546, which excludes state court jurisdiction over unfair labor practices in order that the National Labor Relations Board may be free to develop a consistent federal policy, applies equally to exclude state court jurisdiction over actions that could be brought under section 301. Section 301, however, does not confine jurisdiction to one expert tribunal for the development of federal policy, but on the contrary gives jurisdiction to all the federal district courts. The possibility of conflict between state and federal courts is no greater than the possibility of conflict among the federal courts themselves, with uniformity ultimately dependent in either case on review by the United States Supreme Court. Moreover, federal courts are no more expert than state courts in the interpretation of contracts. See Philadelphia Marine Trade Ass'n v. International Longshoremen's Ass'n, 382 Pa. 326, 115 A. 2d 733, 736–737, certiorari denied, 350 U.S. 843, 76 S.Ct. 84, 100 L.Ed. 751 ; General Elec. Co. v. International Union United Automobile Workers, 93 Ohio App. 139, 108 N.E. 2d 211, 219–222, appeal dismissed, 158 Ohio St. 555, 110 N.E. 2d 424 ; Wollett and Wellington. *Federalism and Breach of the Labor Agreement,* 7 STAN. L. REV. 445, 452–455 ; but cf. International Plainfield Motor Co. v. Local 343, International Union United Automobile Workers, D.C.N.J., 123 F. Supp. 683, 692 ; Note, 57 YALE L. J. 630, 637 n. 24.

State courts therefore have concurrent jurisdiction with federal courts over actions that can be brought in the federal courts under section 301. It is obvious that in exercising this jurisdiction state courts are no longer free to apply state law, but must apply the federal law of collective bargaining agreements, otherwise the scope of the litigants' rights will depend on the accident of the forum in which the action is brought. What the substantive federal law of collective bargaining agreements is we cannot now know. Until it is elaborated by the federal courts we assume it does not differ significantly from our own law.

If in the present case it is not necessary to determine wherein the substantive federal law differs from the law we have until now applied, another problem does press for resolution: what remedies are available in a state court vindicating rights created by section 301? It can be argued that since federal courts in actions brought under 301 cannot enjoin strikes in breach of a collective bargaining agreement because of the prohibitions of the Norris-LaGuardia Act (29 U.S.C.A. §§ 101, 104), state courts enforcing rights created by 301 likewise cannot issue an injunction and give a remedy not available in the federal courts.

Some courts have broadly suggested that section 301 authorizes even federal courts to use injunctive process for the "full enforcement of the substantive rights created by section 301(a), apparently notwithstanding the restrictions of the Norris-LaGuardia Act. Milk and Ice Cream Drivers Union v. Gillespie Milk Products Corp., 6th Cir., 203 F. 2d 650, 651. Although we do not pause to decide this question, the better view would seem to be that the inclusion of specific instances in the Labor Management Relations Act in which injunctive relief is expressly authorized negatives any general repeal of the Norris-LaGuardia Act in respect to the enforcement of collective bargaining agreements. See W. L. Mead, Inc., v. International Brotherhood of Teamsters, 1 Cir., 217 F. 2d 6, 8–10, certiorari dismissed, 352 U.S. 802, 77 S.Ct. 21, 1 L.Ed. 2d 37 ; Associated Tel. Co. v. Communication Workers, D.C.S.D. Cal., 114 F. Supp. 334, 340–341 ; United Packinghouse Workers v. Wilson & Co., D.C.N.D. Ill., 80 F. Supp. 563 ; 567–568. By its holding in Textile Workers v. Lincoln Mills of Alabama, 77 S.Ct. 912, that the Norris-LaGuardia Act was never intended to prohibit specific enforcement of agreements to arbitrate, the Supreme Court has not suggested otherwise ; strike injunctions clearly were intended to fall under the ban of the act.

If it is assumed that federal courts cannot enjoin strikes in actions under section 301 save in compliance with the strict requirements of the Norris-LaGuardia Act, state courts enforcing federal rights are not necessarily subject to the same restraint. In the first place it is not entirely clear that Congress can compel a state court to withhold a remedy that would be available if the action arose under the contract law of the state. Congress can compel a state court to enforce a federal right and give a prescribed remedy when it is essential to the full realization of the right, and the state court would be competent under its own law to give a remedy of like character for a right based on state law. Testa v. Katt, 330 U.S. 368, 67 S.Ct. 810, 91 L.Ed. 967 ; Miller v. Municipal Court, 22 Cal. 2d 818, 836–851, 142 P. 2d 297. Moreover, in cases brought in state courts under the Federal Employers' Liability Act (45 U.S.C.A. § 51 et seq.), an area in which the most vexing problems of state enforcement of federal rights have arisen, it has been held that state procedure must give way if it impedes the uniform application of the federal statute essential to effectuate its purpose, even though the procedure would apply to similar actions arising under state law. E.g. Dice v. Akron, Canton & Youngstown R. R., 342 U.S. 359, 362–364, 72 S.Ct. 312, 96 L.Ed. 398.

It would be a step beyond these decisions, however, to hold that a state enforcing a federal right can be compelled to withhold a remedy usually available in its courts, although it might be said that since Congress can completely exclude state jurisdiction it can dictate that certain remedies be withheld if necessary to implement federal policy. Some light is thrown on this question by Brown v. Gerdes, 321 U.S. 178, 64, S.Ct. 487, 88 L.Ed. 659. In that case the court held that the Federal Bankruptcy Act deprived a state court of power to fix or grant fees to counsel for trustees, even though they had performed services in actions before the court and under state law were entitled to a lien on their client's cause of action. See also Hines v. Lowrey, 305 U.S. 85, 59 S.Ct. 31, 83 L.Ed. 56. This decision, however, does not settle the precise issue before us, and a strong argument can be made that Congress must take the state courts as it finds them in regard to the availability of equitable remedies, and can require only that they not discriminate against litigants enforcing federal rights.

In the converse situation, when a federal court enforced a state-created right and jurisdiction was based on diversity of citizenship, it was established that the court could give an equitable remedy not available under state law, Guffey v.

Smith, 237 U.S. 101, 35 S.Ct. 526, 59 L.Ed. 856; see Guaranty Trust Co. v. York, 326 U.S. 99, 105–106, 65 S.Ct. 1464, 89 L.Ed. 2079, or withhold a remedy that was available under state law. Pusey & Jones Co. v. Hanssen, 261 U.S. 491, 494–499, 43 S.Ct. 454, 67 L.Ed. 763. Considerable doubt has been cast on the vitality of this doctrine by decisions stressing more and more that the goal of diversity jurisdiction is substantial similarity of outcome whether an action is brought in a state or federal court, and that remedies often go to the substance of the right. *E.g.* Bernhardt v. Polygraphic Co., 350 U.S. 198, 202–204, 76 S.Ct. 273, 100 L.Ed. 199; cf. Angel v. Bullington, 330 U.S. 183, 191–192, 67 S.Ct. 657, 91 L.Ed. 832. Whatever the implications of diversity jurisdiction, however, they do not necessarily determine whether a state court, under the compulsion of the supremacy clause, must withhold a specific remedy. A state court enforcing a federal right is not simply another federal court. Minneapolis & St. Louis R. R. Co. v. Bombolis, 241 U.S. 211, 222, 36 S.Ct. 595, 60 L.Ed. 961.

The difficulties that inhere in the question of congressional power to control equitable remedies available in state courts strengthen our conviction that, whether or not Congress could deprive state courts of the power to give such remedies when enforcing collective bargaining agreements, it has not attempted to do so either in the Norris-LaGuardia Act or section 301.

The Norris-LaGuardia Act is in terms drawn as a limitation on the courts of the United States. "No court of the United States," declares section 1, "shall have jurisdiction to issue any . . . injunction in a case involving or growing out of a labor dispute," and a court of the United States is defined in section 13(d) as "any court of the United States whose jurisdiction has been or may be conferred or defined or limited by Act of Congress, including the courts of the District of Columbia." 29 U.S.C.A. §§ 101, 113(d). The statute aimed to restrict the federal equity power, and was justified constitutionally on the basis of Congress' power to regulate the jurisdiction of the federal courts. Brotherhood of R. R. Trainmen v. Toledo, Peoria & Western R. R., 321 U.S. 50, 58, 63, 64 S.Ct. 413, 88 L.Ed. 534; Lauf v. E. G. Shinner & Co., 303 U.S. 323, 330, 58 S.Ct. 578, 82 L.Ed. 872. It did not limit the remedial power of the state courts (see United Elec., Radio & Mach. Workers v. Westinghouse Elec. Corp. D.C. E.D. Pa., 65 F. Supp. 420, 422; General Bldg. Contractors' Ass'n v. Local Unions, 370 Pa. 73, 87 A. 2d 250, 254, 32 A.L.R. 2d 822; Markham & Callow, Inc., v. International Woodworkers, 170 Or. 517, 135 P. 2d 727, 746, citing FRANKFURTER and GREENE, THE LABOR INJUNC-

TION at 220; 39 Ops. U.S. Atty. Gen. 242, 246), and could not constitutionally have done so since its prohibition was not restricted to injunctions in labor disputes affecting interstate commerce or any other subject over which Congress has paramount power.

Section 301 of the Labor Management Relations Act does not embody any policy that requires a state court enforcing rights created by that section to withhold injunction relief. The principal purpose of section 301 was to facilitate the enforcement of collective bargaining agreements by making unions suable as entities in the federal courts, and thereby to remedy the one-sided character of existing labor legislations. See United Packinghouse Workers v. Wilson & Co., D.C.N.D. Ill., 80 F. Supp. 563, 568. We would give altogether too ironic a twist to this purpose if we held that the actual effect of the legislation was to abolish in state courts equitable remedies that had been available, and leave an employer in a worse position in respect to the effective enforcement of his contract than he was before the enactment of section 301.

Nothing in the nature of the rights created by section 301 requires that injunctive relief be denied in their enforcement. Such relief would of course not impair any federal contract right, nor would it expand it in conflict with any policy that we have been able to discern in the statute. To the contrary, the principal purpose of the statute is to encourage the formation and effective enforcement of collective bargaining agreements. See Textile Workers v. Lincoln Mills of Alabama, 77 S.Ct. 912. The restriction on the remedies available in the federal courts arises not from any policy in the Labor Management Relations Act itself but from the Norris-LaGuardia Act, and the policy of that statute as we have seen is confined to the federal courts. See Associated Tel. Co. v. Communication Workers, D.C., S.D. Cal., 114 F. Supp. 334, 341; Philadelphia Marine Trade Ass'n v. International Longshoremen's Ass'n, 382 Pa. 326, 115 A. 2d 733, 735, certiorari denied, 350 U.S. 843, 76 S.Ct. 84, 100 L.Ed. 751; Wollett and Wellington, *Federalism and Breach of the Labor Agreement*, 7 STAN. L. REV. 445.

Finally, there is no invariable requirement, implicit in the federal system, that a state court enforcing a federal right must not go beyond the remedies available in a federal court. Uniformity in the determination of the substantive federal right itself is no doubt a necessity, but such uniformity is not threatened because a state court can give a more complete and effective remedy. Several federal courts, proceeding on the hypothesis that substantive rights in actions under section 301 arise out of state law, have concluded that the federal court is not confined to the remedies available in the state courts. Local 205, United Elec. Workers v. General Elec. Co., 233 F. 2d 85, 94–95, affirmed on other grounds, 77 S.Ct. 921, Textile Workers Union, etc. v. American Thread Co., D.C. Mass., 113 F. Supp. 137, 141 ; see Cox, *Grievance Arbitration in the Federal Courts,* 67 HARV. L. REV. 591. We cannot see why, under the opposite hypothesis, it is not equally true that a state court is not confined to remedies available in a federal court when the restriction on the federal court does not flow from the statute creating the federal right.

As a final attack on the jurisdiction of the trial court, defendants contend that plaintiffs are precluded from maintaining the present action because the issue involved is referable to arbitration under the collective bargaining agreement. The issue defendants contend must be arbitrated is whether the strike was in breach of the contract.

Article III(A) of the contract provides that:

> it is the purpose and intent of the parties hereto that all grievances or disputes arising between them over the interpretation or application of the terms of this Agreement shall be settled by the procedure set forth in Article V hereof, and that during the term of this Agreement the Unions . . . shall not . . . call or engage in, sanction, or assist in a strike against . . . the Contractors.

Article V is entitled, "Procedure For Settlement of Grievances and Disputes." In paragraph A it provides that employees are to present grievances and disputes to their craft steward, who will report them to a special representative. The special representative will then attempt to adjust the dispute with the contractor. Paragraphs C and D provide that if this method of settlement fails, the dispute or grievance may be referred to a Joint Conference Board and from there to a Joint Arbitration Committee. If a majority vote of the Joint Arbitration Committee cannot be obtained, the grievance or dispute is to be submitted to an arbiter whose award is final and binding. Paragraph E repeats the provision of article III that all disputes or grievances arising out of the interpretation or application of any of the terms or conditions of the contract shall be determined by the procedure set forth in article V.

The arbitrability of a dispute may itself be subject to arbitration if the parties have so provided in their contract. In this situation the court should stay proceedings pending the arbiter's determination of his own jurisdiction unless it is clear that the claim of arbitrability is wholly groundless. See International Union, United Automobile Workers v. Benton Harbor Malleable Industries, 6 Cir., 242 F. 2d 536, 539, petition for certiorari filed, 25 U.S.L. Week 3361 (U.S. May 24, 1957), Local 205, United Elec. Workers v. General Elec. Co., 1 Cir., 233 F. 2d 85, 101 affirmed, 77 S.Ct. 921 ; Scoles, *Review of Labor Arbitration Award on Jurisdictional Grounds,* 17 U. CHI. L. REV. 616, 621. Of course, even when the parties have conferred upon the arbiter the unusual power of determining his own jurisdiction, the court cannot avoid the necessity of making a certain threshhold determination of arbitrability, namely, whether the parties have in fact conferred this power on the arbiter. There is no indication in the present contract that the parties intended any such result. It may be that leaving to an arbiter the question of arbitrability is a desirable procedure from the point of view of harmonious labor relations (see Arbitrability, 1951 Report of the Committee on Improvement of Administration of Union-Employer Contracts, Section of Labor Relations Law, American Bar Ass'n, in READINGS ON LABOR LAW 172, 192–194 (REYNARD ed. 1955)), although some have expressed fear that the procedure may be used to bring about unbargained for changes in the relations of the parties. (See minority report in *id.* at 201.) Whatever the merits of the procedure, we think it sufficiently outside the usual understanding of the relations of court and arbiter and their respective functions to assume that the parties expected a court determination of arbitrability unless they have clearly stated otherwise. See Philadelphia Marine Trade Ass'n v. International Longshoremen's Ass'n, 382 Pa. 326, 115 A. 2d 733, 738, certiorari denied, 350 U.S. 843, 76 S.Ct. 84, 100 L.Ed. 751. 751.

Plaintiffs take the position that defendants' breach of contract is not an issue referable to arbitration because by striking in violation of the no-strike clause defendants have themselves repudiated the arbitration procedure. The argument misconceives the question since it assumes that defendants have in fact breached the no-strike provision, the very issue that defendants dispute and say must go to arbitration. All strikes during the life of a contract are not necessarily violations of a no-strike clause, even though on its face the prohibition appears to be absolute. (See The No-Strike Clause, 1952 Report of the Committee on Improvement of Administration of Union-Employer Contracts, Section of Labor Relations Law, American Bar Ass'n, in READINGS ON LABOR LAW 255, 275–277 (REYNARD ed. 1955).) The question is whether the collective bargaining agreement requires arbitration to determine if defendants' conduct violates the no-strike clause, or whether the court itself may make this determination. As with all problems of contract interpretation, the answer must reflect the intention of the parties.

This same question has been before the lower federal courts on numerous occasions. Many of the decisions, although helpful, are not determinative of the problem before us because they turn on the language of a particular collective bargaining agreement. Some of the decisions are in irreconcilable conflict.

We think the trial court was right in concluding that the parties to the contract in the present case did not contemplate arbitration of a breach of the no-strike clause. It is true that the language of the arbitration provision is broad, stating that "all grievances or disputes arising between . . . [the parties] over the interpretation or application of the terms of this Agreement shall be settled by the procedure set forth in Article V." If this were the only provision to be considered, it might reasonably be argued that the question of whether a strike is in breach of contract is arbitrable since it involves interpretation of a term of the contract. The contract, however, must be read as a whole and the grievance and arbitration procedure viewed in the light of its purpose.

The grievance procedure set forth in article V is designed primarily to cope with the usual employee complaints concerning working conditions, wrongful discharge, and the like. The first steps in the procedure require a grievance to be submitted to a craft steward and then reported to a special representative for adjustment. It is inconceivable that the parties thought an employer would be required to follow these steps in prosecuting his objection to a strike. It is possible that they expected employer complaints to be presented directly to the Joint Conference Board or the Joint Arbitration Committee. The later steps in the grievance procedure, however, and arbitration itself, appear to be integrated parts of a single scheme for the settlement of disputes. They are to be resorted to when the earlier steps in the procedure have failed to yield a settlement, and purport to dispose of the same disputes and grievances that are the subject of the earlier steps.

A more persuasive consideration, however, is the relation between the grievance and arbitration procedure and no-strike guarantee. The grievance and arbitration procedure is an alternative to the strike as a means of settling disputes, and it is clear that the parties bound themselves to resort to this procedure for the very purpose of avoiding the possibility of a strike. The parties' intention is shown by the fact that defendants' promise in article III not to resort to a strike follows immediately after their promise to use the grievance procedure. Moreover, the preamble to the contract states that

> it is the desire of the parties hereto to provide, establish and put into practice effective methods for the settlement of misunderstandings, disputes or grievances between the parties hereto to the end that the Contractors are assured continuity of operation and the members of the Unions are assured continuity of employment, and industrial peace is maintained.

The grievance and arbitration procedure assumes that work goes on. Resort to the procedure is designed to avoid the necessity of a strike, not to adjudicate a strike once it has occurred, and the purpose of the procedure limits its applicability. See International Union United Automobile Workers v. Benton Harbor Malleable Industries, 6 Cir., 242 F. 2d 536, 540–541, petition for certiorari filed, 25 U.S.L.WEEK 3361 (U.S. May 24, 1957).

It is urged that arbitration provisions in collective bargaining agreements should when possible be construed broadly to cover all disputes between the parties to the end that the contract will provide a complete system of government for the parties, a system far more satisfactory than any the courts can provide and, because established by the parties themselves, more likely to lead to industrial peace. We do not dispute the attractiveness of the ideal, but it does not justify overriding the parties' intentions and forcing on them a method of decision wholly unexpected in its application. As Mr. Justice Cardozo pointed out in Marchant v. Mead-Morrison Mfg. Co., 252 N.Y. 284, 169 N.E. 386, 391, 393,

> Courts are not at liberty to shirk the process of construction under the empire of a belief that arbitration is beneficent, any more than they may shirk it if their belief happens to be the contrary. No one is under a duty to resort to these conventional tribunals, however helpful their processes, except to the extent that he has signified his willingness. . . . [The contracting parties] . . . are not to be trapped by a strained and unnatural construction of words of doubtful import into an abandonment of legal remedies, unwilled and unforeseen.

Finally, there was sufficient evidence to justify the issuance of the preliminary injunction. Defendants do not deny the strike, nor on this appeal do they contend, as they did in the trial court, that the contract was not in force at the time of the strike or that plaintiffs were not parties to it. The reasons for the strike are obscure. There is some indication that defendants objected to plaintiffs on the grounds that they were labor contractors and violating state safety regulations. Defendants failed, however, to explain precisely what labor contracting is, to show that plaintiffs were engaged in it, or even if they were, that defendants were justified in striking rather than resorting to the grievance procedure. The evidence tended to show that plaintiffs had not violated any state safety regulation. There was substantial evidence to support plaintiffs' claim that the strike was in breach of contract and that they would be irreparably injured if it continued.

The order is affirmed.

GIBSON, C.J., and SPENCE and McCOMB, JJ., concur.

SHENK and SCHAUER, JJ., concur in the judgment.

CARTER, J. I dissent.

In this case the majority holds that where there is a collective bargaining agreement between a union and employer, with a no-strike provision, which has been violated by the union, but there has been no unfair labor practice under the Labor Management Relations Act (29 U.S.C.A. § 151 et seq.) a state court has jurisdiction to give preventive relief against such violation; but, however, the federal substantive law (29 U.S.C.A. § 185) is exclusively controlling in rights and duties under such collective bargaining agreements where interstate commerce is affected (Textile Workers Union of America v. Lincoln Mills of Alabama, 353 U.S. 448, 77 S.Ct. 912, 1 L.Ed. 2d 972); that state courts have jurisdiction generally of proceedings under section 301 of the Labor Management Relations Act although they must apply the federal substantive law; *that in applying such law they* (state courts) *may give whatever form of relief they deem proper, for example, injunctive relief enjoining the violation of a no-strike provision of the bargaining agreement as in the case at bar.* I cannot agree with this latter holding. On the contrary, it is my view that a state court may not give any more stringent or different relief than could be given by a federal court.

The rights under the bargaining agreement being controlled by federal law, that law must also measure the remedies available for otherwise the federal law is not being applied. Turning to the federal law, it is conceded by the majority that federal courts could not give injunctive relief under section 301 of the Labor Management Relations Act. The Norris-LaGuardia Act (29 U.S.C.A. § 101 et seq.) to which reference is made prohibits injunctive relief generally or demands

compliance with certain requirements before it may be granted. If it is applicable it is conceded that an injunction would not be available in this case if the action were in the federal court. The majority reasons, however, that the Norris-LaGuardia Act relates only to the jurisdiction of federal courts, but there is nothing in section 301 of the Labor Management Relations Act which forbids an injunction and the purpose of uniformity in the disposal of labor relations matters affecting interstate commerce is not involved. There are several reasons why those arguments are not persuasive.

In Textile Workers Union of America v. Lincoln Mills of Alabama, *supra,* 77 S.Ct. 912, 916, the United States Supreme Court held that substantive federal law must apply to an action under section 301 to specifically enforce an arbitration provision in a bargaining agreement (the action was in a federal district court) and the Norris-LaGuardia Act was not a bar because the failure to arbitrate was not one of the abuses the Norris Act was aimed at and the policy in favor of enforcing such agreements expressed in the Labor Management Relations Act was clear, but in the course of its opinion there is a clear indication that in declaring the federal substantive law applicable it was also including so-called procedural matters of importance such as injunctive relief.

For illustration, the court said:

> Both the Senate and the House took pains to provide for "the usual processes of the law" by provisions which were the substantial equivalent of § 301 (a) in its present form. Both the Senate Report and the House Report indicate a primary concern that unions as well as employees should be bound to collective bargaining contracts. But there was also a broader concern—*a concern with a procedure* for making such agreements enforceable in the courts by either party....
>
> Plainly the agreement to arbitrate grievance disputes is the *quid pro quo* for an agreement not to strike. Viewed in this light, the legislation does more than confer jurisdiction in the federal courts over labor organizations. It expresses a federal policy that *federal courts should enforce* these agreements on behalf of or against labor organizations and that industrial peace can be best obtained only in that way.... And when in the House the debate narrowed to the question whether § 301 was more than jurisdictional, it became abundantly clear that the purpose of the section was to provide the necessary *legal remedies....*
>
> It seems, therefore, clear to us that Congress adopted a policy which placed *sanctions* behind agreements to arbitrate grievance disputes ... Other problems will lie in the penumbra of express statutory mandates. Some will lack express statutory sanction but will be solved *by looking at the policy*

of the legislation and *fashioning a remedy* that will effectuate that policy. The range of judicial inventiveness will be determined by the nature of the problem. . . . Any state law applied, however, will be absorbed as federal law and will not be an independent source of private rights. [Emphasis added.]

Indeed, the issue involved in the *Textile* case was whether section 301 authorized a particular *remedy,* specific enforcement, in case of breach of a bargaining agreement. I deduce from this that the federal law including the remedies available or not available is to be applied when the action is in the state court under section 301.

Moreover, there is additional reason why the remedy, such as injunction, should not be given by the state court if it may not be given by a federal court. Such a remedy is more than mere procedure. It goes to the very essence of the right itself. In many instances it would make the difference of whether or not the right could be truly realized. This is especially true in injunctions in labor disputes, such as an injunction against a strike. The case is usually won or lost at the preliminary injunction stage, even before the hearing on the application for a permanent injunction—the final judgment. If a preliminary injunction is obtained, economic circumstances may break the strike and render impotent the efforts of the union to secure the goals sought by it. If it is not secured, management and labor continue their bargaining in the manner contemplated by the law. The purpose of the Norris-LaGuardia Act is to prevent injunctive restraints in such disputes with the thought that management and labor may have a free hand to iron out their problems.

A state court, in enforcing rights measured by federal law (rights here under collective bargaining agreement) cannot obstruct or give greater or lesser relief than would be available in a federal court. It is said in Brown v. Western R. of Alabama, 338 U.S. 294, 296, 70 S.Ct. 105, 106, 94 L.Ed. 100, where the question was whether the pleading was sufficient in an action in a Georgia court under the Federal Employer's Liability Act:

> The argument is that while state courts are without power to detract from "substantive rights" granted by Congress in FELA cases, they are free to follow their own rules of "practice" and "procedure." To what extent rules of practice and procedure may themselves dig into "substantive rights" is a troublesome question at best as is shown in the very case on which respondent relies. Central Vermont R. Co. v. White, 238 U.S. 507, 35 S.Ct. 865, 59 L.Ed. 1433. Other cases in this Court point up the impossibility of laying down a precise

rule to distinguish "substance" from "procedure." Fortunately, we need not attempt to do so. A long series of cases previously decided, from which we see no reason to depart, makes it our duty to construe the allegations of this complaint ourselves in order to determine whether petitioner has been denied a right of trial granted him by Congress. *This federal right cannot be defeated by the forms of local practice.* [Emphasis added.]

And it is said:

> It follows also from the rule as to supremacy of the United States within its proper sphere that the individual states may not in any way impair, qualify, or disturb the enjoyment of federal constitutional or statutory rights. Accordingly, a state may not impose any condition requiring relinquishment of a right guaranteed by the federal Constitution; nor may it impose such conditions as it sees fit with respect to rights created and causes of action conferred by an act of congress, or defeat a federal right by forms of local practice.

81 C.J.S. States § 7. It is said in United Mine Workers etc. v. Arkansas Flooring Co., 351 U.S. 62, 75, 76 S.Ct. 559, 567, 100 L.Ed. 941,

> Such being the case, the state court is governed by the federal law which has been applied to industrial relations, like these, affecting interstate commerce and the state court erred in enjoining the peaceful picketing here practiced. *A "State may not prohibit the exercise of rights which the federal Acts protect."* [Emphasis added.]

In the case at bar the right to be not enjoined under the Norris-LaGuardia Act (see, also, 29 U.S.C.A. § 163) is a part of the federal right—a part and parcel of the rights which may be exercised with reference to bargaining agreements. Certainly a state court cannot give more relief (in fact, relief which will be the end of the case) than a federal court when administering federal law. If it may, the requirement that the federal law be applied may well dwindle to nothing and there will be no uniformity as is sought by the federal act in labor relations affecting interstate commerce. The right will be no greater than the remedy afforded for its protection which may vary from state to state. If as in Brown v. Western R. of Alabama, *supra,* 338 U.S. 294, 70 S.Ct. 105, the mere matter of state rules of pleading may not control in the enforcement of a federal law by a state court, then certainly the important and fundamental matter of allowing an injunction under state law cannot stand if the federal law forbids it. In short the federal law is exclusive in the field of bargaining agreements affecting commerce. When a state entertains jurisdiction and applies that law it should be bound by all the important restrictions including those embraced in the

Norris-LaGuardia Act. It would not be doubted that if section 301 which gives federal courts jurisdiction over actions involving collective bargaining agreements where interstate commerce is affected, but also provided that no injunctive relief was available then no such relief would be proper if the action is in a state rather than federal court. The fact that the Norris-LaGuardia Act is in a separate statute should not alter the result.

I would therefore reverse the order granting a preliminary injunction.

Rehearing denied; CARTER, J., dissenting.

"Whether a state injunction may be ... barred [by the Norris-LaGuardia Act] in suits governed by federal labor law ... is an open question" (citing *Dowd Box*) NLRB v. C & C Plywood Corp., U.S. 385 U.S. 421 (1967) note 15.

SINCLAIR REFINING CO. v. ATKINSON
370 U.S. 195 (1962)

BLACK, J. delivered the opinion of the Court.

The question this case presents is whether § 301 of the Taft-Hartley Act, in giving federal courts jurisdiction of suits between employers and unions for breach of collective bargaining agreements, impliedly repealed § 4 of the pre-existing Norris-LaGuardia Act, which, with certain exceptions not here material, barred federal courts from issuing injunctions "in any case involving or growing out of any labor dispute."[1]

The complaint here was filed by the petitioner Sinclair Refining Company against the Oil, Chemical and Atomic Workers International Union—

and Local 7–210 of that union and alleged: that the International Union, acting by and with the authority of the Local Union and its members, signed a written collective bargaining contract with Sinclair which provided for compulsory, final and binding arbitration of "any difference regarding wages, hours or working conditions between the parties hereto or between the Employer and an employee covered by this working agreement which might arise within any plant or within any region of operations"; that this contract also included express provisions by which the unions agreed that "there shall be no slowdowns for any reason whatsoever" and "no strikes or work stoppages ... [f]or any cause which is or may be the subject of a grievance"; and that notwithstanding these promises in the collective bargaining contract the members of Local 7–210 had, over a period of some 19 months, engaged in work stoppages and strikes on nine separate occasions, each of which, the complaint charged, grew out of a grievance which could have been submitted to arbitration under the contract and therefore fell squarely within the unions' promises not to strike. This pattern of repeated, deliberate violations of the contract, Sinclair alleged, indicated a complete disregard on the part of the unions for their obligations under the contract and a probability that they would continue to "subvert the provisions of the contract" forbidding strikes over grievances in the future unless they were enjoined from doing so. In this situation, Sinclair claimed, there was no adequate remedy at law which would protect its contractual rights and the court should therefore enter orders enjoining the unions and their agents

> preliminarily at first, and thereafter permanently, from aiding, abetting, fomenting, advising, participating in, ratifying, or condoning any strike, stoppage of work, slowdown or any other disruption of, or interference with normal employment or normal operation or production by any employee within the bargaining unit at plaintiff's East Chicago, Indiana refinery covered by the contract between the parties dated August 8, 1957, in support of, or because of, any matter or thing which is, or could be, the subject of a grievance under the grievance procedure of the said contract, or any extension thereof, or any other contract between the parties which shall contain like or similar provisions.[2]

The unions moved to dismiss this complaint on the ground that it sought injunctive relief

---

1. "No court of the United States shall have jurisdiction to issue any restraining order or temporary or permanent injunction in any case involving or growing out of any labor dispute to prohibit any person or persons participating or interested in such dispute (as these terms are herein defined) from doing, whether singly or in concert, any of the following acts:

"(a) Ceasing or refusing to perform any work or to remain in any relation of employment;

.   .   .   .   .   .

"(e) Giving publicity to the existence of, or the facts involved in, any labor dispute, whether by advertising, speaking, patrolling, or by any other method not involving fraud or violence;

.   .   .   .   .   .

"(i) Advising, urging, or otherwise causing or inducing without fraud or violence the acts heretofore specified...." 47 Stat. 70, 29 U.S.C. § 104.

2. The suit filed by Sinclair was in three counts, only one of which, Count 3, is involved in this case. Counts 1 and 2, upon which Sinclair prevailed below, are also before the Court in No. 430. See Atkinson v. Sinclair Refining Co., decided today.

which United States courts, by virtue of the Norris-LaGuardia Act, have no jurisdiction to give. The District Court first denied the motion, but subsequently, upon reconsideration after full oral argument, vacated its original order and granted the unions' motion to dismiss. In reaching this conclusion, the District Court reasoned that the controversy between Sinclair and the unions was unquestionably a "labor dispute" within the meaning of the Norris-LaGuardia Act and that the complaint therefore came within the proscription of § 4 of that Act which "withdraws jurisdiction from the federal courts to issue injunctions to prohibit the refusal 'to perform work or remain in any relation of employment' in cases involving *any* labor dispute." The Court of Appeals for the Seventh Circuit affirmed the order of dismissal for the same reasons. Because this decision presented a conflict with the decision on this same important question by the Court of Appeals for the Tenth Circuit,[3] we granted certiorari.

We agree with the courts below that this case does involve a "labor dispute" within the meaning of the Norris-LaGuardia Act. Section 13 of that Act expressly defines a labor dispute as including

> any controversy concerning terms or conditions of employment, or concerning the association or representation of persons in negotiating, fixing, maintaining, changing, or seeking to arrange terms or conditions of employment, regardless of whether or not the disputants stand in the proximate relation of employer and employee.

Sinclair's own complaint shows quite plainly that each of the alleged nine work stoppages and strikes arose out of a controversy which was unquestionably well within this definition.

Nor does the circumstance that the alleged work stoppages and strikes may have constituted a breach of a collective bargaining agreement alter the plain fact that a "labor dispute" within the meaning of the Norris-LaGuardia Act is involved. Arguments to the contrary proceed from the premise that § 2 of that Act, which expresses the public policy upon which the specific anti-injunction provisions of the Act were based, contains language indicating that one primary concern of Congress was to insure workers the

right "to exercise actual liberty of contract" and to protect "concerted activities for the purpose of collective bargaining."[4] From that premise, Sinclair argues that an interpretation of the term "labor dispute" so as to include a dispute arising out of a union's refusal to abide by the terms of a collective agreement to which it freely acceded is to apply the Norris-LaGuardia Act in a way that defeats one of the purposes for which it was enacted. But this argument, though forcefully urged both here and in much current commentary on this question,[5] rests more upon considerations of what many commentators think would be the more desirable industrial and labor policy in view of their understanding as to the prevailing circumstances of contemporary labor-management relations than upon what is a correct judicial interpretation of the language of the Act as it was written by Congress.

---

3. Chauffeurs, Teamsters & Helpers Local No. 795 v. Yellow Transit Freight Lines, 282 F. 2d 345. Both the First and the Second Circuits have also considered this question and both have taken the same position as that taken below. See W. L. Mead, Inc., v. Teamsters Local No. 25, 217 F. 2d 6; Alcoa S.S. Co. v. McMahon, 173 F. 2d 567; *In re Third Ave. Transit Corp.*, 192 F. 2d 971; A. H. Bull Steamship Co. v. Seafarers' International Union, 250 F. 2d 326.

4. "In the interpretation of this Act and in determining the jurisdiction and authority of the courts of the United States, as such jurisdiction and authority are herein defined and limited, the public policy of the United States is hereby declared as follows:

"Whereas under prevailing economic conditions, developed with the aid of governmental authority for owners of property to organize in the corporate and other forms of ownership association, the individual unorganized worker is commonly helpless to exercise actual liberty of contract and to protect his freedom of labor, and thereby to obtain acceptable terms and conditions of employment, wherefore, though he should be free to decline to associate with his fellows, it is necessary that he have full freedom of association, self-organization, and designation of representatives of his own choosing, to negotiate the terms and conditions of his employment, and that he shall be free from the interference, restraint, or coercion of employers of labor, or their agents, in the designation of such representatives or in self-organization or in other concerted activities for the purpose of collective bargaining or other mutual aid or protection; therefore, the following definitions of, and limitations upon, the jurisdiction and authority of the courts of the United States are enacted." 47 Stat. 70, 29 U.S.C. § 102.

5. One of the most forthright arguments for judicial re-evaluation of the wisdom of the anti-injunction provisions of the Norris-LaGuardia Act and judicial rather than congressional revision of the meaning and scope of these provisions as applied to conduct in breach of a collective bargaining agreement is presented in Gregory, *The Law of the Collective Agreement*, 57 MICH. L. REV. 635. That author, in urging that a strike in breach of a collective agreement should not now be held to involve or grow out of a "labor dispute" within the meaning of the Norris-LaGuardia Act, states: "After all, 1932 was a long time ago and conditions have changed drastically. Judges who still confuse violations of collective agreements with § 13 labor disputes and § 4 conduct have, in my opinion, lost contact with reality. The passage of time has operated as a function of many other types of judicial output at the highest level. I do not see why it should not do so in this instance, as well." *Id.*, at 645–646, n. 39. See also Stewart, *No-Strike Clauses in the Federal Courts*, 59 MICH. L. REV. 673, especially at 683; Rice, *A Paradox of our National Labor Law*, 34 MARQ. L. REV. 233.

In the first place, even the general policy declarations of § 2 of the Norris-LaGuardia Act, which are the foundation of this whole argument, do not support the conclusion urged. That section does not purport to limit the Act to the protection of collective bargaining but, instead, expressly recognizes the need of the anti-injunction provisions to insure the right of workers to engage in "concerted activities for the purpose of collective bargaining *or other mutual aid or protection.*" Moreover, the language of the specific provisions of the Act is so broad and inclusive that it leaves not the slightest opening for reading in any exceptions beyond those clearly written into it by Congress itself.[6]

We cannot ignore the plain import of a congressional enactment, particularly one which, as we have repeatedly said, was deliberately drafted in the broadest of terms in order to avoid the danger that it would be narrowed by judicial construction.[7]

Since we hold that the present case does grow out of a "labor dispute," the injunction sought here runs squarely counter to the proscription of injunctions against strikes contained in § 4(a) of the Norris-LaGuardia Act, to the proscription of injunctions against peaceful picketing contained in § 4(e) and to the proscription of injunctions prohibiting the advising of such activities contained in § 4(i). For these reasons, the Norris-LaGuardia Act deprives the courts of the United States of jurisdiction to enter that injunction unless, as is contended here, the scope of that Act has been so narrowed by the subsequent enactment of § 301 of the Taft-Hartley Act that it no longer prohibits even the injunctions specifically described in § 4 where such injunctions are sought as a remedy for breach of a collective bargaining agreement. Upon consideration, we cannot agree with that view and agree instead with the view expressed by the courts below and supported by the Courts of Appeals for the First and Second Circuits that § 301 was not intended to have any such partially repealing effect upon such a long-standing, carefully thought out and highly significant part of this country's labor legislation as the Norris-LaGuardia Act.[8]

The language of § 301 itself seems to us almost if not entirely conclusive of this question. It is especially significant that the section contains no language that could by any stretch of the imagination be interpreted to constitute an explicit repeal of the anti-injunction provisions of the Norris-LaGuardia Act in view of the fact that the section does expressly repeal another provision of the Norris-LaGuardia Act dealing with union responsibility for the acts of agents.[9] If Congress had intended that § 301 suits should also not be subject to the anti-injunction provisions of the Norris-LaGuardia Act, it certainly seems likely that it would have made its intent known in this same express manner. That is indeed precisely what Congress did do in § 101, amending § 10(h) of the National Labor Relations Act, and § 208(b) of the Taft-Hartley Act, by permitting injunctions to be obtained, not by private litigants, but only at the instance of the National Labor Relations Board and the Attorney General, and in § 302(e), by permitting private litigants to obtain injunctions in order to protect the integrity of employees' collective bargaining representatives in carrying out their responsibilities.[10] Thus the failure of Congress to include a provision in § 301 expressly repealing the anti-injunction provisions of the Norris-LaGuardia Act must be evaluated in the context of a statu-

---

6. Thus we conclude here precisely as we did in Lauf v. E. G. Shinner & Co., 303 U.S. 323, 330: "We find nothing in the declarations of policy which narrows the definition of a labor dispute as found in the statutes. The rights of the parties and the jurisdiction of the federal courts are to be determined according to the express provisions applicable to labor disputes as so defined."

7. United States v. Hutcheson, 312 U.S. 219, 234, and cases cited therein.

8. We need not here again go into the history of the Norris-LaGuardia Act nor the abuses which brought it into being for that has been amply discussed on several occasions. See Frankfurter and Greene, The Labor Injunction. And see *e.g.*, United States v. Hutcheson, 312 U.S. 219, 235–236; Milk Wagon Drivers' Union v. Lake Valley Farm Products, Inc., 311 U.S. 91, 102–103. It is sufficient here to note that the reasons which led to the passage of the Act were substantial and that the Act has been an important part of the pattern of legislation under which unions have functioned for nearly 30 years.

9. Section 301 (e) of the Act, 61 Stat. 156, 29 U.S.C. § 185 (e), provides: "For the purposes of this section, in determining whether any person is acting as an 'agent' of another person so as to make such other person responsible for his acts, the question of whether the specific acts performed were actually authorized or subsequently ratified shall not be controlling." This, of course, was designed to and did repeal for purposes of suits under § 301 the previously controlling provisions of § 6 of the Norris-LaGuardia Act, 47 Stat. 71, 29 U.S.C. § 106: "No officer or member of any association or organization, and no association or organization participating or interested in a labor dispute, shall be held responsible or liable in any court of the United States for the unlawful acts of individual officers, members, or agents, except upon clear proof of actual participation in, or actual authorization of, such acts, or of ratification of such acts after actual knowledge thereof."

10. 61 Stat. 157, 29 U.S.C. § 186 (e). That this section, which stands alone in expressly permitting suits for injunctions previously proscribed by the Norris-LaGuardia Act to be brought in the federal courts by private litigants under the Taft-Hartley Act, deals with an unusually sensitive and important problem is shown by the fact that § 186 makes the conduct so enjoinable a crime punishable by both fine and imprisonment.

tory pattern that indicates not only that Congress was completely familiar with those provisions but also that it regarded an express declaration of inapplicability as the normal and proper manner of repealing them in situations where such repeal seemed desirable.

When the inquiry is carried beyond the language of § 301 into its legislative history, whatever small doubts as to the contressional purpose could have survived consideration of the bare language of the section should be wholly dissipated. For the legislative history of §301 shows that Congress actually considered the advisability of repealing the Norris-LaGuardia Act insofar as suits based upon breach of collective bargaining agreements are concerned and deliberately chose not to do so.[11] The section as eventually enacted was the product of a conference between Committees of the House and Senate, selected to resolve the differences between conflicting provisions of the respective bills each had passed. Prior to this conference, the House bill had provided for federal jurisdiction of suits for breach of collective bargaining contracts and had expressly declared that the Norris-LaGuardia Act's anti-injunction provisions would not apply to such suits. The bill passed by the Senate, like the House bill, granted federal courts jurisdiction over suits for breach of such agreements but it did not, like the House bill, make the Norris-LaGuardia Act's prohibition against injunctions inapplicable to such suits. Instead it made breach of a collective agreement an unfair labor practice. Under the Senate version, therefore, a breach of a collective bargaining agreement, like any unfair labor practice, could have been enjoined by a suit brought by the National Labor Relations Board, but no provision of the Senate version would have permitted the issuance of an injunction in a labor dispute at the suit of a private party. At the conference the provision of the House bill expressly repealing the anti-injunction provisions of the Norris-LaGuardia Act, as well as the provision of the bill passed by the Senate declaring the breach of a collective

agreement to be an unfair labor practice, was dropped and never became law. Instead, the conferees, as indicated by the provision which came out of the conference and eventually became § 301, agreed that suits for breach of such agreements should remain wholly private and "be left to the usual processes of the law" and that, in view of the fact that these suits would be at the instance of private parties rather than at the instance of the Labor Board, no change in the existing anti-injunction provisions of the Norris-LaGuardia Act should be made. The House Conference Report expressly recognized that the House provision for repeal in contract actions of the anti-injunction prohibitions of the Norris-LaGuardia Act had been eliminated in Conference:

> Section 302 (e) of the House bill made the Norris-LaGuardia Act inapplicable in actions and proceedings involving violations of agreements between an employer and a labor organization. Only part of this provision is included in the conference agreement. Section 6 of the Norris-LaGuardia Act provides that no employer or labor organization participating or interested in a labor dispute shall be held responsible for the unlawful acts of their agents except upon clear proof of actual authorization of such acts, or ratification of such acts after actual knowledge thereof. This provision in the Norris-LaGuardia Act was made inapplicable under the House bill. Section 301 (e) of the conference agreement provides that for the purposes of section 301 in determining whether any person is acting as an agent of another so as to make such other person responsible for his actions, the question of whether the specific acts performed were actually authorized or subsequently ratified shall not be controlling.

And Senator Taft, Chairman of the Conference Committee and one of the authors of this legislation that bore his name, was no less explicit in explaining the results of the Conference to the Senate: "The conferees ... rejected the repeal of the Norris-LaGuardia Act."[12]

---

11. This fact was expressly recognized by the Court of Appeals for the Second Circuit in A. H. Bull Steamship Co. v. Seafarers' International Union, 250 F. 2d 326, 331–332. See also W. L. Mead, Inc., v. Teamsters Local No. 25, 217 F. 2d 6, 9–10; Comment, *Labor Injunctions and Judge-Made Labor Law: The Contemporary Role of Norris-LaGuardia*, 70 YALE L.J. 70, 97–99. Another commentator, though urging his own belief that a strike in breach of a collective agreement is not a "labor dispute" within the Norris-LaGuardia Act, nevertheless admits that Congress thought it was and deliberately decided to leave the anti-injunction provisions of that Act applicable to § 301 suits. See Rice, *A Paradox of our National Labor Law* 34 MARQ. L. REV. 233, 235.

12. 93 CONG. REC. 6445–6446, II LEG. HIST. 1544. Immediately prior to this remark, Senator Taft had inserted into the Record a written summary of his understanding as to the effect of the conference upon the bill passed by the Senate: "When the bill passed the Senate it also contained a sixth paragraph in this subsection [8 (a)] which made it an unfair labor practice for an employer to violate the terms of a collective-bargaining agreement or the terms of an agreement to submit a labor dispute to arbitration. The House conferees objected to this provision on the ground that it would have the effect of making the terms of every collective agreement subject to interpretation and determination by the Board, rather than by the courts. The Senate conferees ultimately agreed to its elimination as well as the deletion of a similar provision contained in subsection 8 (b) (5) of the Senate amendment which made it an unfair labor practice for a labor organization to

We cannot accept the startling argument made here that even though Congress did not itself want to repeal the Norris-LaGuardia Act, it was willing to confer a power upon the courts to "accommodate" that Act out of existence whenever they might find it expedient to do so in furtherance of some policy they had fashioned under § 301. The unequivocal statements in the House Conference Report and by Senator Taft on the floor of the Senate could only have been accepted by the Congressmen and Senators who read or heard them as assurances that they could vote in favor of § 301 without altering, reducing or impairing in any manner the anti-injunction provisions of the Norris-LaGuardia Act. This is particularly true of the statement of Senator Taft, a man generally regarded in the Senate as a very able lawyer and one upon whom the Senate could rely for accurate, forthright explanations of legislation with which he was connected. Senator Taft was of course entirely familiar with the prohibitions of the Norris-LaGuardia Act and the impact those prohibitions would have upon the enforcement under § 301 of all related contractual provisions, including contractual provisions dealing with arbitration. If, as this argument suggests, the intention of Congress in enacting § 301 was to clear the way for judicial obliteration of that Act under the soft euphemism of "accommodation," Senator Taft's flat statement that the Conference had rejected the repeal of the Norris-LaGuardia Act could only be regarded as disingenuous. We cannot impute any such intention to him.

Moreover, we think that the idea that § 301 sanctions piecemeal judicial repeal of the Norris-LaGuardia Act requires acceptance of a wholly unrealistic view of the manner in which Congress handles its business. The question of whether existing statutes should be continued in force or repealed is, under our system of government, one which is wholly within the domain of Congress. When the repeal of a highly significant law is urged upon that body and the repeal is rejected after careful consideration and discussion, the normal expectation is that courts will be faithful to their trust and abide by that decision. This is especially so where the fact of the controversy over repeal and the resolution of that controversy in Congress plainly appears in the formal legisla-

tive history of its proceedings.[13] Indeed, not a single instance has been called to our attention in which a carefully considered and rejected proposal for repeal has been revived and adopted by this Court under the guise of "accommodation" or any other pseudonym.

Nor have we found anything else in the previous decisions of this Court that would indicate that we should disregard all this overwhelming evidence of a congressional intent to retain completely intact the anti-injunction prohibitions of the Norris-LaGuardia Act in suits brought under § 301. Brotherhood of Railroad Trainmen v. Chicago River & Indiana R. Co.,[14] upon which Sinclair places its primary reliance, is distinguishable on several grounds. There we were dealing with a strike called by the union in defiance of an affirmative duty, imposed upon the union by the Railway Labor Act itself, compelling unions to settle disputes as to the interpretation of an existing collective bargaining agreement, not by collective union pressures on the railroad but by submitting them to the Railroad Adjustment Board as the exclusive means of final determination of such "minor" disputes.[15] Here, on the other hand, we are dealing with a suit under a quite different law which does not itself compel a particular, exclusive method for settling disputes nor impose any requirement, either upon unions or employers or upon the courts, that is in any way inconsistent with a continuation of the Norris-LaGuardia Act's proscription of federal labor injunctions against strikes and peaceful picketing. In addition, in *Chicago River* we were dealing with a statute that had a far different legislative history than the one now before us. Thus there was no indication in the

---

13. The legislative history of the Taft-Hartley Act shows that Congress actually considered and relied upon this normal functioning of the judicial power as insuring that no unintended repeal of the anti-injunction provisions of the Norris-LaGuardia Act would be declared. Thus Senator Taft, when pressed by Senator Morse with regard to the possibility that a provision inserted in § 303 (a) declaring secondary boycotts unlawful might be held to justify an injunction previously forbidden by the Norris-LaGuardia Act, stated: "Let me say in reply to the Senator or anyone else who makes the same argument, that that is not the intention of the author of the amendment. It is not his belief as to the effect of it. It is not the advice of counsel to the committee. Under those circumstances, I do not believe that any court would construe the amendment along the lines suggested by the Senator from Oregon." 93 Cong. Rec. 4872, II Leg. Hist. 1396.

14. 353 U.S. 30.

15. The Court in *Chicago River* expressly recognized and rested its decision upon the differences between provisions for the settlement of disputes under the Railway Labor Act and the Taft-Hartley Act. *Id.*, at 31–32, n. 2. See also Order of Railroad Telegraphers v. Chicago & North Western R. Co., 362 U.S. 330, 338–340.

---

violate the terms of collective-bargaining agreements. The provisions of the Senate amendment *which conferred a right of action for damages* upon a party aggrieved by breach of a collective-bargaining contract, however, were retained in the conference agreement (section 301)." 93 Cong. Rec. 6443, II Leg. Hist. 1539. (Emphasis supplied.)

legislative history of the Railway Labor Act, as there is in the history of § 301, that Congress had, after full debate and careful consideration by both Houses and in Joint Conference, specifically rejected proposals to make the prohibitions of the Norris-LaGuardia Act inapplicable. Indeed, the Court was able to conclude in *Chicago River* "that there was general understanding between both the supporters and the opponents of the 1934 amendment that the provisions dealing with the Adjustment Board were to be considered as compulsory arbitration in this limited field." And certainly no one could contend that § 301 was intended to set up any such system of "compulsory arbitration" as the exclusive method for settling grievances under the Taft-Hartley Act.

Textile Workers Union v. Lincoln Mills,[16] upon which some lesser reliance is placed, is equally distinguishable. There the Court held merely that it did not violate the anti-injunction provisions of the Norris-LaGuardia Act to compel the parties to a collective bargaining agreement to submit a dispute which had arisen under that agreement to arbitration where the agreement itself required arbitration of the dispute. In upholding the jurisdiction of the federal courts to issue such an order against a challenge based upon the Norris-LaGuardia Act, the Court pointed out that the equitable relief granted in that case—a mandatory injunction to carry out an agreement to arbitrate—did not enjoin any one of the kinds of conduct which the specific prohibitions of the Norris-LaGuardia Act withdrew from the injunctive powers of United States courts.[17] An injunction against work stoppages, peaceful picketing or the nonfraudulent encouraging of those activities would, however, prohibit the precise kinds of conduct which subsections (a), (e) and (i) of § 4 of the Norris-LaGuardia Act unequivocally say cannot be prohibited.[18]

Nor can we agree with the argument made in this Court that the decision in *Lincoln Mills*,

---

16. 353 U.S. 448.

17. *Id.*, at 458. See also Order of Railroad Telegraphers v. Chicago & North Western R. Co., 362 U.S. 330, 338–339, where *Lincoln Mills* and other cases not involving an injunction against activity protected by § 4 of the Norris-LaGuardia Act were distinguished on this ground.

18. An injunction against a strike or peaceful picketing in breach of a collective agreement "would require strong judicial creativity in the face of the plain meaning of Section 4," Cox, *Current Problems in the Law of Grievance Arbitration*, 30 ROCKY MT. L. REV. 247, 256, for, indeed, such an injunction "would fly in the face of the plain words of Section 4 of the Norris-LaGuardia Act, the historical purpose of which was to make peaceful concerted activities unenjoinable without regard to the nature of the labor dispute." *Id.*, at 253.

as implemented by the subsequent decisions in United Steelworkers v. American Manufacturing Co., United Steelworkers v. Warrior & Gulf Navigation Co., and United Steelworkers v. Enterprise Wheel & Car Corp., requires us to reconsider and overrule the action of Congress in refusing to repeal or modify the controlling commands of the Norris-LaGuardia Act. To the extent that those cases relied upon the proposition that the arbitration process is "a kingpin of federal labor policy," we think that proposition was founded not upon the policy predilections of this Court but upon what Congress said and did when it enacted § 301. Certainly we cannot accept any suggestion which would undermine those cases by implying that the Court went beyond its proper power and itself "forged . . . a kingpin of federal labor policy" inconsistent with that section and its purpose. Consequently, we do not see how cases implementing the purpose of § 301 can be said to have freed this Court from its duty to give effect to the plainly expressed congressional purpose with regard to the continued application of the anti-injunction provisions of the Norris-LaGuardia Act. The argument to the contrary seems to rest upon the notion that injunctions against peaceful strikes are necessary to make the arbitration process effective. But whatever might be said about the merits of this argument, Congress has itself rejected it. In doing so, it set the limit to which it was willing to go in permitting courts to effectuate the congressional policy favoring arbitration and it is not this Court's business to review the wisdom of that decision.

The plain fact is that § 301, as passed by Congress, presents no conflict at all with the anti-injunction provisions of the Norris-LaGuardia Act. Obedience to the congressional commands of the Norris-LaGuardia Act does not directly affect the "congressional policy in favor of the enforcement of agreements to arbitrate grievance disputes" at all for it does not impair the right of an employer to obtain an order compelling arbitration of any dispute that may have been made arbitrable by the provisions of an effective collective bargaining agreement. At the most, what is involved is the question of whether the employer is to be allowed to enjoy the benefits of an injunction along with the right which Congress gave him in § 301 to sue for breach of a collective agreement. And as we have already pointed out, Congress was not willing to insure that enjoyment to an employer at the cost of putting the federal courts back into the business of enjoining strikes and other related peaceful union activities.

It is doubtless true, as argued, that the right to

sue which §301 gives employers would be worth more to them if they could also get a federal court injunction to bar a breach of their collective bargaining agreements. Strong arguments are made to us that it is highly desirable that the Norris-LaGuardia Act be changed in the public interest. If that is so, Congress itself might see fit to change that law and repeal the anti-injunction provisions of the Act insofar as suits for violation of collective agreements are concerned, as the House bill under consideration originally provided. It might, on the other hand, decide that if injunctions are necessary, the whole idea of enforcement of these agreements by private suits should be discarded in favor of enforcement through the administrative machinery of the Labor Board, as Senator Taft provided in his Senate bill. Or it might decide that neither of these methods is entirely satisfactory and turn instead to a completely new approach. The question of what change, if any, should be made in the existing law is one of legislative policy properly within the exclusive domain of Congress— it is a question for lawmakers, not law interpreters. Our task is the more limited one of interpreting the law as it now stands. In dealing with problems of interpretation and application of federal statutes, we have no power to change deliberate choices of legislative policy that Congress has made within its constitutional powers. Where congressional intent is discernible —and here it seems crystal clear—we must give effect to that intent.[19]

The District Court was correct in dismissing Count 3 of petitioner's complaint for lack of jurisdiction under the Norris-LaGuardia Act. The judgment of the Court of Appeals affirming that order is therefore

Affirmed.

MR. JUSTICE FRANKFURTER took no part in the consideration or decision of this case.

BRENNAN, J., joined by DOUGLAS, J. and HARLAN, J., (dissenting). I believe that the Court has reached the wrong result because it has answered only the first of the questions which must be answered to decide this case. Of course § 301 of the Taft-Hartley Act did not, for purposes of actions brought under it, "repeal" § 4 of the Norris-LaGuardia Act. But the two provisions do coexist, and it is clear beyond dispute that they apply to the case before us in apparently conflicting senses. Our duty, therefore, is to seek out that accommodation of the two which will give the fullest possible effect to the central purposes of both. Since such accommodation is possible, the Court's failure to follow that path leads it to a result—not justified by either the language or history of §301—which is wholly at odds with our earlier handling of directly analogous situations and which cannot be woven intelligibly into the broader fabric of related decisions.

I.

Section 301 of the Taft-Hartley Act, enacted in 1947, authorizes Federal District Courts to entertain "[s]uits for violation of contracts between an employer and a labor organization. . . . ." It does not in terms address itself to the question of remedies. As we have construed § 301, it casts upon the District Courts a special responsibility to carry out contractual schemes for arbitration, by holding parties to that favored process for settlement when it has been contracted for, and by then regarding its result as conclusive. At the same time, § 4 of the Norris-LaGuardia Act, enacted in 1932, proscribes the issuance by federal courts of injunctions against various concerted activities "in any case involving or growing out of any labor dispute." But the enjoining of a strike over an arbitrable grievance may be indispensable to the effective enforcement of an arbitration scheme in a collective agreement; thus the power to grant that injunctive remedy may be essential to the uncrippled performance of the Court's function under § 301.[1] Therefore, to hold that § 301 did not repeal § 4 is only a beginning. Having so held, the Court should—but does not—go on to consider how it is to deal with the surface conflict between the two statutory commands.

---

19. We have not ignored Sinclair's argument that to apply the Norris-LaGuardia Act here would deprive it of its constitutional right to equal protection of the law, both because of an allegedly unlawful discrimination between Taft-Hartley Act employers and Railway Labor Act employers by virtue of the decision in *Chicago River*, and because of an allegedly unlawful discrimination between Taft-Hartley Act employers and unions by virtue of the decision in *Lincoln Mills*. We deem it sufficient to say that we do not find either of these arguments compelling.

1. In Teamsters Local v. Lucas Flour Co., 369 U.S. 95, we held that a strike over a dispute which a contract provides shall be settled exclusively by binding arbitration is a breach of contract despite the absence of a no-strike clause, saying, at p. 105: "To hold otherwise would obviously do violence to accepted principles of traditional contract law. Even more in point, a contrary view would be completely at odds with the basic policy of national labor legislation to promote the arbitral process as a substitute for economic warfare." And in Brotherhood of Railroad Trainmen v. Chicago River R. Co., 353 U.S. 30, 39, we recognized that allowing a strike over an arbitrable dispute would effectively "defeat the jurisdiction" of the arbitrator.

The Court has long acted upon the premise that the Norris-LaGuardia Act does not stand in isolation. It is one of several statutes which, taken together, shape the national labor policy. Accordingly, the Court has recognized that Norris-LaGuardia does not invariably bar injunctive relief when necessary to achieve an important objective of some other statute in the pattern of labor laws. See Brotherhood of Railroad Trainmen v. Chicago River R. Co., 353 U.S. 30; Graham v. Brotherhood of Locomotive Firemen, 338 U.S. 232; Virginian R. Co. v. System Federation, 300 U.S. 515, 562–563. In *Chicago River* we insisted that there "must be an accommodation of [the Norris-LaGuardia Act] and the Railway Labor Act so that the obvious purpose in the enactment of each is preserved."

These decisions refusing inflexible application of Norris-LaGuardia point to the necessity of a careful inquiry whether the surface conflict between § 301 and § 4 is irreconcilable in the setting before us: a strike over a grievance which both parties have agreed to settle by binding arbitration. I think that there is nothing in either the language of § 301 or its history to prevent § 4's here being accommodated with it, just as § 4 was accommodated with the Railway Labor Act.

II.

It cannot be denied that the availability of the injunctive remedy in this setting is far more necessary to the accomplishment of the purposes of § 301 than it would be detrimental to those of Norris-LaGuardia. *Chicago River* makes this plain. We there held that the federal courts, notwithstanding Norris-LaGuardia, may enjoin strikes over disputes as to the interpretation of an existing collective agreement, since such strikes flout the duty imposed on the union by the Railway Labor Act to settle such "minor disputes" by submission to the National Railroad Adjustment Board rather than by concerted economic pressures. We so held, even though the Railway Labor Act contains no express prohibition of strikes over "minor disputes," because we found it essential to the meaningful enforcement of that Act—and because the existence of mandatory arbitration eliminated one of the problems to which Norris-LaGuardia was chiefly addressed, namely, that "the injunction strips labor of its primary weapon without substituting any reasonable alternative."

That reasoning is applicable with equal force to an injunction under § 301 to enforce a union's contractual duty, also binding on the employer, to submit certain disputes to terminal arbitration and to refrain from striking over them. The federal law embodied in § 301 stresses the effective enforcement of such arbitration agreements. When one of them is about to be sabotaged by a strike, § 301 has as strong a claim upon an accommodating interpretation of § 4 as does the compulsory arbitration law of the Railway Labor Act. It is equally true in both cases that "[an injunction] alone can effectively guard the plaintiff's right," Machinists v. Street, 367 U.S. 740, 773. It is equally true in both cases that the employer's specifically enforceable obligation to arbitrate provides a "reasonable alternative" to the strike weapon. It is equally true in both cases that a major contributing cause for the enactment of Norris-LaGuardia—the at-largeness of federal judges in enjoining activities thought to seek "unlawful ends" or to constitute "unlawful means"—is not involved. Indeed, there is in this case a factor weighing in favor of the issuance of an injunction which was not present in *Chicago River*[2]: the express contractual commitment of the union to refrain from striking, viewed in light of the overriding purpose of § 301 to assist the enforcement of collective agreements.

In any event, I should have thought that the question was settled by Textile Workers v. Lincoln Mills, 353 U.S. 448. In that case, the Court held that the procedural requirements of Norris-LaGuardia's § 7, although in terms fully applicable, would not apply so as to frustrate a federal court's effective enforcement under § 301 of an employer's obligation to arbitrate. It is strange, I think, that § 7 of the Norris-LaGuardia Act need not be read, in the face of § 301, to impose inapt procedural restrictions upon the specific enforcement of an employer's contractual duty to arbitrate; but that § 4 must be read, despite § 301, to preclude absolutely the issuance of an injunction against a strike which ignores a union's identical duty.

III.

The legislative history of § 301 affords the Court no refuge from the compelling effect of our prior decisions. That history shows that Congress considered and rejected "the advisability of repealing the Norris-LaGuardia Act insofar as suits based upon breach of collective bargaining agreements are concerned." But congressional rejection of outright repeal certainly does not imply hostility to an attempt by the courts to accommodate all statutes pertinent to the

---

2. It is worth repeating that the Railway Labor Act incorporates no express prohibition of strikes over "minor disputes."

decision of cases before them. Again, the Court's conclusion stems from putting the wrong question. When it is appreciated that there is no question here of "repeal," but rather one of how the Court is to apply the whole statutory complex to the case before it, it becomes clear that the legislative history does not support the Court's conclusion. First, however, it seems appropriate to discuss, as the Court has done, the language of § 301 considered in light of other provisions of the statute.

There is nothing in the words of § 301 which so much as intimates any limitation to damage remedies when the asserted breach of contract consists of concerted activity. The section simply authorizes the District Courts to entertain and decide suits for violation of collective contracts. Taking the language alone, the irresistible implication would be that the District Courts were to employ their regular arsenal of remedies appropriately to the situation. That would mean, of course, that injunctive relief could be afforded when damages would not be an adequate remedy. This much, surely, is settled by *Lincoln Mills*. But the Court reasons that the failure of § 301 explicitly to repeal § 4 of Norris-LaGuardia completely negates the availability of injunctive relief in any case where that provision—in the absence of § 301—would apply. That reasoning stems from attaching undue significance to the fact that express repeal of Norris-LaGuardia provisions may be found in certain other sections of the Taft-Hartley Act—from which the Court concludes "not only that Congress was completely familiar with those provisions but also that it regarded an express declaration of inapplicability as the normal and proper manner of repealing them *in situations where such repeal seemed desirable*." Even on this analysis the most that can be deduced from such a comparative reading is that while repeal of Norris-LaGuardia seemed desirable to Congress in certain other contexts, repeal did not seem desirable in connection with § 301.

Sound reasons explain why repeal of Norris-LaGuardia provisions, acceptable in other settings, might have been found ill-suited for the purpose of § 301. And those reasons fall far short of a design to preclude absolutely the issuance under § 301 of any injunction against an activity included in § 4 of Norris-LaGuardia. Section 10(h) of the Act simply lifts the § 4 barrier in connection with proceedings brought by the National Labor Relations Board—in the Courts of Appeals for enforcement of Board cease-and-desist orders against unfair labor practices, and in the District Courts for interlocutory relief against activities being prosecuted before the

Board as unfair labor practices. This repeal in aid of government litigation to enforce carefully drafted prohibitions already in the Act as unfair labor practices was, obviously, entirely appropriate, definitely limited in scope, predictable in effect, and devoid of any risk of abuse or misunderstanding. Much the same is true of § 208(b) of Taft-Hartley, which simply repeals Norris-LaGuardia in a case where the Attorney General seeks an injunction at the direction of the President, who must be of the opinion—after having been advised by a board of inquiry—that continuation of the strike in question would imperil the national health and safety.

Only in § 302(e) of Taft-Hartley is there found a repeal of Norris-LaGuardia's anti-injunction provisions in favor of a suit by private litigant.[3] The District Courts are there authorized to restrain the payment by employers and the acceptance by employee representatives of unauthorized payments in the nature of bribes. Not only is the problem thus dealt with "unusually sensitive and important," as the Court notes, but the repeal of Norris-LaGuardia is clearly, predictably, and narrowly confined to one kind of suit over one kind of injury; and obviously it presents no possible threat to the important purposes of that Act.

How different was the problem posed by § 301, which broadly authorized District Courts to decide suits for breach of contract. The Congress understandably may not have felt able to predict what provisions would crop up in collective bargaining agreements, to foresee the settings in which these would become subjects of litigation, or to forecast the rules of law which the courts would apply. The consequences of repealing the anti-injunction provisions in this context would have been completely unknowable, and outright repeal, therefore, might well have seemed unthinkable. Congress, clearly, had no intention of abandoning wholesale the Norris-LaGuardia policies in contract suits; but it does not follow that § 301 is not the equal of § 4 in cases which implicate both provisions.

Indeed, it might with as much force be said that Congress knew well how to limit remedies against employee activities to damages when that was what is intended, as the Congress knew how to repeal Norris-LaGuardia when *that* was what it intended. Section 303 of Taft-Hartley author-

---

3. Section 301 (e), 61 Stat. 157, 29 U.S.C. § 185 (e), also mentioned by the Court, has no bearing on injunction problems. It repeals, for its purposes, § 6 of the Norris-LaGuardia Act, which deals with agency responsibility for concerted activities. Its only relevance here is in showing what is clear anyway: That § 301 effected no repeal of the anti-injunction provisions of Norris-LaGuardia.

izes private actions *for damages* resulting from certain concerted employee activities. When that section was introduced on the Senate floor, it provided for injunctive relief as well. Extended debate revealed strong sentiment against the injunction feature which incorporated a repeal of Norris-LaGuardia. The section's supporters, therefore, proposed a different version which provided for damages only. In this form, the section was adopted by the Senate—and later by the Conference and the House. Certainly, after this experience Congress would have used language confining § 301 to damage remedies when it was invoked against concerted activity, if such had been the intention.

The statutory language thus fails to support the Court's position. The inference is at least as strong that Congress was content to rely upon the courts to resolve any seeming conflicts between § 301 and § 4 as they arose in the relatively manageable setting of particular cases, as that Congress intended to limit to damages the remedies court could afford against concerted activities under § 301. The Court then should so exercise its judgment as best to effect the most important purposes of each statute. It should not be bound by inscrutable congressional silence to a wooden preference for one statute over the other.

Nor does the legislative history of § 301 suggest any different conclusion. As the Court notes, the House version would have repealed Norris-LaGuardia in suits brought under the new section. The Senate version of § 301, like the section as enacted, did not deal with Norris-LaGuardia, but neither did it limit the remedies available against concerted activity. Thus any attempt to ascertain the Senate's intention would face the same choices as those I have suggested in dealing with the language of § 301 as finally enacted. It follows that to construe the Conference Committee's elimination of the House repeal as leaving open the possibility of judicial accommodation is at least as reasonable as to conclude that Congress, by its silence, was directing the courts to disregard § 301 whenever opposition from § 4 was encountered.[4]

I emphasize that the question in this case is not whether the basic policy embodied in Norris-

LaGuardia against the injunction of activities of labor unions has been abandoned in actions under § 301; the question is simply whether injunctions are barred against strikes over grievances which have been routed to arbitration by a contract specifically enforceable against both the union and the employer. Enforced adherence to such arbitration commitments has emerged as a dominant motif in the developing federal law of collective bargaining agreements. But there is no general federal anti-strike policy; and although a suit may be brought under § 301 against strikes which, while they are breaches of private contracts, do not threaten any additional public policy, in such cases the anti-injunction policy of Norris-LaGuardia should prevail. Insistence upon strict application of Norris-LaGuardia to a strike over a dispute which both parties are bound by contract to arbitrate threatens a leading policy of our labor relations law. But there may be no such threat if the union has made no binding agreement to arbitrate; and if the employer cannot be compelled to arbitrate, restraining the strike would cut deep into the core of Norris-LaGuardia. Therefore, unless both parties are so bound, limiting an employer's remedy to damages might well be appropriate. The susceptibility of particular concrete situations to this sort of analysis shows that rejection of an outright repeal of § 4 was wholly consistent with acceptance of a technique of accommodation which would lead, in some cases, to the granting of injunctions against concerted activity. Accommodation requires only that the anti-injunction policy of Norris-LaGuardia did not intrude into areas, not vital to its ends, where injunctive relief is vital to a purpose of § 301; it does not require unconditional surrender.

IV.

Today's decision cannot be fitted harmoniously into the pattern of prior decisions on analogous and related matters. Considered in their light, the decision leads inescapably to results consistent neither with any imaginable legislative purpose nor with sound judicial administration.

We have held that uniform doctrines of federal labor law are to be fashioned judicially in suits brought under § 301, Textile Workers v. Lincoln Mills, 353 U.S. 448; that actions based on collective agreements remain cognizable in state as well as federal courts, Dowd Box Co. v. Courtney, 368 U.S. 502; and that state courts must apply federal law in such actions, Teamsters Local v. Lucas Flour Co., 369 U.S. 95.

The question arises whether today's prohibition of injunctive relief is to be carried over

---

4. There is nothing in any Committee Report, or in any floor debate, which even intimates a confinement of § 301 remedies to damages in cases involving concerted activities. The only bit of legislative history which could is the statement of Senator Taft, quoted by the Court at note [12] of its opinion, which he inserted into the Congressional Record. What little significance that isolated insertion might have had has, of course, been laid to rest by *Lincoln Mills*.

to state courts as a part of the federal law governing collective agreements. If so, § 301, a provision plainly designed to *enhance* the responsibility of unions to their contracts, will have had the opposite effect of depriving employers of a state remedy they enjoyed prior to its enactment.

On the other hand if, as today's literal reading suggests[5] and as a leading state decision holds,[6] States remain free to apply their injunctive remedies against concerted activities in breach of contract, the development of a uniform body of federal contract law is in for hard times. So long as state courts remain free to grant the injunctions unavailable in federal courts, suits seeking relief against concerted activities in breach of contract will be channeled to the States whenever possible. Ironically, state rather than federal courts will be the preferred instruments to protect the integrity of the arbitration process, which *Lincoln Mills* and the *Steelworkers* decisions forged into a kingpin of federal labor policy. Enunciation of uniform doctrines applicable in such cases will be severely impeded. Moreover, the type of relief available in a particular instance will turn on fortuities of locale and susceptibility to process—depending upon which States have anti-injunction statutes and how they construe them.

I have not overlooked the possibility that removal of the state suit to the federal court might provide the answer to these difficulties. But if § 4 is to be read literally, removal will not be allowed.[7] And if it is allowed, the result once again is that § 301 will have had the strange consequence of taking away a contract remedy available before its enactment.

V.

The decision deals a crippling blow to the cause of grievance arbitration itself. Arbitration is so highly regarded as a proved technique for industrial peace that even the Norris-LaGuardia Act fosters its use. But since unions cannot be enjoined by a federal court from striking in open defiance of their undertakings to arbitrate, employers will pause long before committing themselves to obligations enforceable against them but not against their unions. The Court

does not deny the desirability, indeed, necessity, for injunctive relief against a strike over an arbitrable grievance.[8] The Court says only that federal courts may not grant such relief, that Congress must amend § 4 if those courts are to give substance to the congressional plan of encouraging peaceable settlements of grievances through arbitration.

IV.

A District Court entertaining an action under § 301 may not grant injunctive relief against concerted activity unless and until it decides that the case is one in which an injunction would be appropriate despite the Norris-LaGuardia Act. When a strike is sought to be enjoined because it is over a grievance which both parties are contractually bound to arbitrate, the District Court may issue no injunctive order until it first holds that the contract *does* have that effect; and the employer should be ordered to arbitrate, as a condition of his obtaining an injunction against the strike. Beyond this, the District Court must, of course, consider whether issuance of an injunction would be warranted under ordinary principles of equity—whether breaches are occurring and will continue, or have been threatened and will be committed; whether they have caused or will cause irreparable injury to the employer; and whether the employer will suffer more from the denial of an injunction than will the union from its issuance.

In the case before us, the union enjoys the contractual right to make the employer submit to final and binding arbitration of any employee grievance. At the same time, the union agrees that "[T]here shall be no strikes...for any cause which is or may be the subject of a grievance."[9] The complaint alleged that the union had, over the past several months, repeatedly engaged in "quickie" strikes over arbitrable grievances. Under the contract and the complaint, then, the District Court might conclude that there have occurred and will continue to occur breaches of contract of a type to which the principle of accommodation applies. It follows that rather than dismissing the complaint's request for an injunction, the Court should remand the case to the District Court with directions to consider whether to grant the relief sought—an injunction against future repetitions. This would

---

5. Section 4 commences: "No court of the United States shall have jurisdiction to issue any restraining order...."

6. McCarroll v. Los Angeles County District Council, 49 Cal. 2d 45, 315 P. 2d 322.

7. Compare note [5], *supra*, with the language of the removal statute, 28 U.S.C. § 1441, allowing removal in cases "of which the district courts of the United States have original jurisdiction."

---

8. The Court acknowledges, of course, that an employer may obtain an order directing a union to comply with its contract to arbitrate. Consistently with what we said in *Lucas, supra,* note [1], a strike in the face of such an order would risk a charge of contempt.

9. See Atkinson v. Sinclair Rfg. Co., decided this day.

entail a weighing of the employer's need for such an injunction against the harm that might be inflicted upon legitimate employee activity. It would call into question the feasibility of setting up *in futuro* contempt sanctions against the union (for striking) and against the employer (for refusing to arbitrate) in regard to prospective disputes which might fall more or less clearly into the adjudicated category of arbitrable grievances. In short, the District Court will have to consider with great care whether it is possible to draft a decree which would deal equitably with all the interests at stake.

I would reverse the Court of Appeals and remand to the District Court for further proceedings consistent with this dissenting opinion.

Shaw Electric Co. v. Int'l Bhd. Electrical Workers, 418 Pa. 1, 208 A. 2d 769 (1965), held that nothing in *Sinclair v. Atkinson* prevents state courts from exercising their traditional jurisdiction, including the power to enjoin strikes, in breach of collective agreement cases. *Accord*: Dugdale Const. Co. v. Operative Plasterers, 257 Ia. 997 (1965), 135 N.W. 2d 656 (1965) (dictum).

Armco Steel Corp. v. Perkins, — Ky. — , (1967) (64 LRRM 2439). State court has power to enjoin rump employee group seeking to process grievances outside collective-agreement grievance procedure. Brief discussion of applicability of Norris-LaGuardia Act but no mention of *Sinclair v. Atkinson*.

PUBLISHERS' ASS'N OF NEW YORK v. NEW YORK MAILERS' UNION NUMBER SIX
317 F. 2d 624 (2d Cir. 1963)

[Under the collective agreement foremen were required to be union members. Another section specified that "the Union shall not discipline the Foreman for carrying out the instructions of the Publisher."

The union, after a membership vote, appointed a committee to investigate charges that a foreman had disciplined a fellow union member. The Publishers' Association moved to compel arbitration of this alleged breach of the agreement and also sought a stay of the union's proceedings against the foreman.]

HAYS, C. J. It is true that in the *Sinclair* case the Court was dealing with alleged contract violations which involved activities removed from federal jurisdiction by § 4 of the Norris-LaGuardia Act, while in the present case the Union must be held to have failed to establish that the activities which have been enjoined are included in any of the categories of § 4. However, § 7 of the Act covers activities which are not covered by § 4. Section 4 withdraws power to issue an injunction against certain activities. Section 7 applies to injunctions in *any* cases involving or growing out of a labor dispute and prohibits the issuance of injunctions in all such cases, without regard to the nature of the activities against which the injunction is sought, unless certain procedural requirements are met and unless the court issuing the injunction makes certain findings. Not only have these requirements not been met in the present case but it would clearly be impossible for the court to make the required findings.

In the *Sinclair* case, the Supreme Court examined the legislative history of § 301 and found there extensive evidence to support the view that Congress in adopting § 301 did not intend to repeal the Norris-LaGuardia Act. While, as we have indicated, *Sinclair* involved activities which fell within Section 4 of the Norris-LaGuardia Act, it would be very difficult indeed to make out from the legislative history, as it is set forth in *Sinclair,* a congressional intent to repeal § 7 of the Act and to leave § 4 intact. There is nothing whatever in that history on which to base any supposition that Congress intended to treat any part of the Norris-LaGuardia Act differently from any other part. Indeed the subtlety of a partial repeal would be even more difficult to derive from the legislative history than would total repeal, the possibility of which the Court rejected.

Moreover there is no ground in reason or policy for assuming that Congress intended to repeal § 7 but not § 4. If we were to assume the contrary we would reach the anomalous result that, while an employer could not enjoin a strike or other § 4 activity in violation of a collective agreement pending arbitration of the violation, he could enjoin any other type of violation. Ordinarily a strike would be far more disruptive of the contract relationship, and far more inimical to the statutory ideal of peaceful solution through the arbitration process than would the type of violation with which we are dealing in the present case. If Congress by adopting § 301 had made any exception to the Norris-LaGuardia Act it would surely have permitted the use of the injunctive remedy against strikes in violation of collective agreements rather than against violations of a much less serious character.

REPORT OF SPECIAL ATKINSON-SINCLAIR COMMITTEE* [sic]

Report of Management Members

On August 7, 1962, the following Resolution was introduced at the annual meeting of the Section of Labor Relations Law:

> RESOLVED that in view of the recent decision of the United States Supreme Court in Sinclair Refining Company v. Atkinson the section on labor relations Law of the American Bar Association urgently recommends that Congress enact a modification to § 4 of the Norris-LaGuardia Act to permit the issuance of a restraining order, temporary or permanent injunction by a Court of the United States in any action brought therein pursuant to § 301 of the Labor Management Relations Act of 1947, as amended, for the purpose of filling the inequitable gap which exists in the law relating to the mutual enforcement of collective bargaining agreements as provided by the Congress under § 301 of the Labor Management Relations Act of 1947, as amended.

The purpose of the Resolution is to permit the granting of injunction relief by Federal Courts to halt the violation by a labor union of its contractual pledge not to strike during the life of a collective bargaining agreement.

We unanimously support the proposed Resolution and urge its adoption by the Council and the Section for the reasons outlined below.

I. A MAJORITY OF THE SUPREME COURT OF THE UNITED STATES SUPPORTS THE PRINCIPLE BEHIND THE RESOLUTION

Rarely in the recent labor law history of the nation's highest tribunal has the Court been more reluctantly dragged to the altar of decision than in Sinclair v. Atkinson Refining Co. Painstakingly, and with a hint of some reservations, a majority of the Court concluded that they were powerless to prevent the arbitrary and unilateral disregard for a contractual obligation freely entered into by one of the parties to a collective bargaining agreement. As their opinion commented:

> The argument . . . seems to rest upon the notion that injunctions against peaceful strikes are necessary

---

*A.B.A., PROCEEDINGS OF THE SECTION OF LABOR RELATIONS LAW, Pt. 2, 226 (1963). Copyright © 1964 American Bar Association. Reprinted by permission of the section and the American Bar Association.

to make the arbitration process effective. But whatever might be said about the merits of this argument, Congress has itself rejected it. In doing so, it set the limit which it was willing to go in permitting courts to effectuate the Congressional policy favoring arbitration and it is not this Court's business to review the wisdom of that decision.

The substance of the majority holding was that Congress had not seen fit to expressly provide for the "accommodation" of the principles behind both the Norris-LaGuardia Act, and § 301 of the Taft-Hartley Act.

In a vigorous and well reasoned dissent for the minority, Justice Brennan (the only member of the Court with actual labor law experience in private practice prior to the recent appointment of Justice Goldberg) argued that the majority mistakenly applied the "accommodation" test and arrived at a result that not only made a mockery of the collective bargaining agreement, but created a chaotic climate for industrial relations.

The Management members of this committee, reassured by what appears to be sentiment from both the majority and minority members of the Court for its position, now seeks to have Congress re-examine its present policies and take the affirmative action proposed in the Resolution.

II. THE TABOO OF THE "LABOR INJUNCTION" IS OBSOLETE IN THE CURRENT ARENA OF LABOR RELATIONS

One of the arguments immediately raised against the Resolution is that it seeks to put an age-old "union busting" weapon back into the hands of Management. Perhaps at one time in this country's history this fear was not without foundation. But its perpetuation in the modern day sophisticated climate of labor relations is unrealistic. It makes as much sense to talk of the "hated injunction" as it does of "conspiracies of employees."

Congress, in enacting the Norris-LaGuardia Act in 1932, was primarily concerned about the indiscriminate use of the labor injunction by conservative-minded federal judges, who, without legislative guidelines, were frustrating the organization efforts of unions by injecting their own economic and political philosophies into labor disputes. To the end of eliminating such interposition, the Norris-LaGuardia Act rejected the injunction as a weapon in labor disputes, declared that the federal courts were not the proper agency of government to formulate a national labor policy and, in effect, repudiated the federal common law of labor relations and established a policy of court neutrality in labor disputes as a means of aiding the development of unions.

However, under appropriate circumstances,

parties have been granted such relief. Thus, Congress has retreated from its original position under Norris-LaGuardia by permitting injunctions to be issued in jurisdictional or work assignment disputes, secondary boycotts, and national emergency strikes. The proposed Resolution would merely extend such relief to those situations in which mutuality of obligation and the integrity of the collective bargaining process require that the pledge to refrain from taking certain action, voluntarily offered by one party to another, not be rendered illusory. Despite the vigorous arguments of the Labor members of the committee, to the contrary, no wholesale attempt is being made to have organized labor bear the injunctive cross at all times and under all circumstances.

III. THE NATURE OF THE COLLECTIVE BARGAINING RELATIONSHIP DEMANDS MUTUALITY OF OBLIGATION THROUGH COURT ENFORCEMENT OF LABOR CONTRACTS

It is axiomatic that both parties to a labor contract should be bound by their commitments and any court decisions which permit either party to void its solemn obligations should be swiftly corrected by Legislative amendments to the laws which permit such interpretation.

Over 90 per cent of the collective bargaining agreements in the United States provide today for the settlement of disputes by arbitration.[1] The employer's promise to arbitrate is fully enforceable in the Federal courts, and the State courts.

Justice Douglas, speaking for the majority in *Lincoln Mills* discussed the Court's concept of the relationship between this promise and the Union's no-strike commitment generally found in collective bargaining agreements:

> Plainly the agreement to arbitrate grievance disputes is the *quid pro quo* for an agreement not to strike. Viewed in this light the legislation does more than confer jurisdiction in the federal courts over labor organizations. It expresses a federal policy that federal courts should enforce these agreements on behalf of *or against* labor organizations and that industrial peace can best be obtained only in that way. [Emphasis supplied.]

The undersigned feel however that *Lincoln Mills* does not fully grasp the nature of *quid pro quo* in the labor agreement. All of the provisions of the contract, save one, are promises by the employer. The *sole* commitment which the Union makes is that it will not strike. This, we submit, is the correct balance. In our view, *all* of the employer's promises, and not just the promise to arbitrate grievances, constitutes the *true quid pro quo* for the union's no-strike pledge. It appears that the courts are by indirection approaching this same conclusion. Thus in the light of the much discussed arbitration trilogy and the Supreme Court's decision in *Drake Bakeries,* management is now required to submit to the grievance procedure and arbitration virtually all disputes under the contract excepting only those matters which are explicitly excluded therefrom. All doubts are decided in favor of arbitrability. Even the question of whether or not an employer can sue for damages for violation of the no-strike clause appears to subject to arbitration[2] which further confuses the issue.

The result of all this is that we now have the rather anomalous situation where under *Lincoln Mills* labor unions can obtain a Federal or State Court order compelling an employer to comply with his contractual commitments on wages, working conditions and other related terms of employment, but under *Sinclair* the employer cannot get a similar order to compel the union to abide by its commitment, the no-strike pledge, under the *same* agreement. The employer is told to bring a suit for damages against the union, a remedy clearly impractical and inadequate to any seasoned observer of the labor-management scene.

IV. AN ACTION FOR DAMAGES IS NOT AN ADEQUATE REMEDY FOR PREVENTING VIOLATIONS OF NO-STRIKE AGREEMENTS

Congress, in passing § 301, had recognized that management's right to discharge employees engaged in unprotected activities, such as strikes in violation of a no-strike clause, was an insufficient deterrent to such activities. As interpreted by the Supreme Court in *Sinclair,* Congress determined that unions would be deterred from strike activity in violation of contract by the threat of an action brought by management for damages resulting from the strike. The intention of Congress to require compliance with collective bargaining agreements voluntarily entered into is clear.

But does an action for damages actually accomplish the purpose sought by Congress? The authorities are almost unanimous in pointing out that damages are, in fact, an insufficient deterrent and unions, in many cases, are willing to risk a

1. *Arbitration Provisions in Collective Bargaining Agreement*, MONTHLY LABOR REVIEW, March 1953, Vol. 76, No. 3, p. 261.

2. Jefferson City Cabinet Co. v. Electrical Workers IUE, Local 748 (CA.6) 313 F. 2d 231, 52 LRRM 2508 cert. den.—U.S.—,53 LRMM 2312 (1963).

difficult-to-calculate damage action tried years later to the vagaries of a jury for the immediate gains which might be secured by strike action, even though in violation of contract.[3]

These same authorities point out that a remedy restricted to damages is inappropriate since the lost orders, customers and goodwill which result from such work interruptions constitute an irreparable injury to the employer which cannot be adequately compensated for in monetary damages. Further, as Archibald Cox observed,[4] an employer can rarely afford to undermine labor-management relations by suing a union made up of his employees after the end of the strike.

In view of these factors, it would appear that an injunction is not only the appropriate remedy, but also the only one which would have any practical significance in securing for management the rights gained through voluntary collective bargaining and deterring unions from striking in violation of contract.

V. THE ACTION PROPOSED BY THE RESOLUTION IS NECESSARY TO PRESERVE THE INTEGRITY OF THE COLLECTIVE BARGAINING PROCESS

The charge has been raised by some of the Labor members of this committee that the Resolution urges "political action" and should not be considered by the Section. Such criticism entirely misses the fundamental problem created by *Sinclair*. Why should management be asked to enter into contracts that are unenforceable *en toto* by both parties, against both parties and with respect to all its provisions? Of what value is such a contract? In this light the no-strike clause is binding only to the extent that the union signatory desires it to be. Once a union voluntarily gives a no-strike pledge, it would appear that elemental fairness requires that some authoritative body, namely the Courts, have the power to immediately halt strike action in violation of the contract.

The very foundation of the collective bargaining process will be slowly undermined by the situation before us. The final step in that process envisions the embodiment of the terms agreed upon in a written contract binding upon both parties during its life.

The Federal Labor Law as set forth in the original Wagner Act states: "It is hereby declared to be the policy of the United States . . .

(to encourage) the practice and procedure of collective bargaining . . ."

The action proposed by this Resolution is not only in the interest of the groups directly affected, labor and management, but also the public which stands to suffer if the collective bargaining process fails as a means of achieving industrial peace.

What is basically involved is the integrity of collective bargaining. It ill behooves the representatives of labor to now charge that action designed to foster the very principles regarding the sanctity of the labor contract which they urged upon the Supreme Court in *Lincoln Mills* are now suspect.

VI. CONCLUSION AND RECOMMENDATION

Remedial legislation of the nature indicated by the Resolution is in the interest of both employers and unions. As the law now stands management has little confidence that entering into a collective bargaining contract and making the necessary concession in order to reach a contract will produce the only benefit the management can obtain from such an instrument, labor stability and peace. We, therefore, urge that the Resolution be adopted.

Report of Members Representing Labor Unions

We are opposed to the adoption of the Resolution as drafted, as well as to the principle it represents.

I.

The Resolution requests the Labor Law Section of the American Bar Association, and subsequently, of course, of the American Bar Association, to take an affirmative position with respect to the jurisdiction of the federal district courts to restrain strikes alleged to be in violation of collective bargaining agreements.[1]

II.

Another pertinent consideration is whether the subject matter of the Resolution deals with a matter of substantial import or weight in the total picture of labor-management relations. Unfortunately, the statistics which are published by the Bureau of Labor Statistics of the United

---

3. See, *e.g.*, Rice, *A Paradox of our National Labor Law*, 34 MARQ. L. R. 233 (1951); Stewart, *No-Strike Clauses in the Federal Courts*, 59 MICH. L. R. 673 (1961).

4. *Current Problems in the Law of Labor Arbitration*, 30 ROCKY MOUNTAIN L. R. 247 (1958).

---

1. We note at the outset that the Resolution is not confined to the *Sinclair* facts, but is couched in the broadest of language avoiding all reference to strikes, breach of contract and arbitration clauses. In accordance with the action of the Council at the Midwinter meeting, this report will be directed to the problem of enjoining strikes during the contract term.

States Department of Labor do not indicate the precise incidence of man-days lost in strikes in violation of contract. Drawing from our own general experience, however, it would be fair to say that either in terms of man-days lost, numbers of employees involved, or duration, we are talking about a very minor irritation in the labor management relationship. This minor irritation is today met by state court injunctive procedures,[2] damage suits,[3] disciplinary suspension or discharge, and, in some instances, by unfair labor practice proceedings premised on violation of Section 8(d) of the National Labor Relations Act.[4]

To say, as the Report of the Management lawyers does, that "The very foundations of the collective bargaining process will be slowly undermined by the situation before us" is to ignore the tremendous vitality of the collective bargaining process during the 30 years since passage of the Norris-LaGuardia Act, and to confuse the issue with "calamity howling" not justified by the facts.

Accordingly, while the issue may be dramatic and academically interesting, there seems to be little reason that the Labor Law Section should become involved in partisan controversy because of it.

III.

Few of the strikes which are alleged to be in violation of contract are actually authorized strikes. They more commonly fall within the classification of "wild-cat strikes." Since wild-cat strikes are neither sanctioned nor supported by the bargaining representative, it is difficult to see just how the right to injunctive relief in the federal courts, running against the individuals involved, can be of any material assistance in settling the dispute. The court cannot require the original "wild-catters" to return to work individually. To command the Union to call off the strike or to urge the strikers to return to work is a mere surplusage, since, by definition, a wild-cat strike is unauthorized to begin with, and the Union has attempted to meet its contractual obligations.

---

2. McCarroll v. Carpenters, 315 P. 2d 322 (Calif. 1957), cert. denied, 355 U.S. 932 (1958). The members of this committee subscribing to this report do not necessarily accept this theory as prevailing or desirable law.

3. Teamsters Unions Local 25 v. Mead, Inc., 320 F. 2d 576 (1st Cir., 1956), cert. denied, 352 U.S. 802 (1956).

4. McCleod v. Sewer Construction Workers, 292 F. 2d 358 (CA2, 1961).

IV.

The question posed in Sinclair Refining Company v. Atkinson, 370 U.S. 195 (1962), was whether Section 301 of the Taft-Hartley Act "in giving federal courts jurisdiction of suits between employers and unions for breach of collective bargaining agreements, impliedly repealed § 4 of the pre-existing Norris-LaGuardia Act, which, . . . barred federal courts from issuing injunctions" in cases involving or growing out of labor disputes. The court found no merit to the argument that the union's refusal to abide by the terms of a collective bargaining agreement did not create a "labor dispute" under the Act, and found, as indeed the legislative history required it to find, that there was no repeal by implication of the Norris-LaGuardia Act in the enactment of § 301 of the Taft-Hartley Act.

During the course of the prevailing opinion Justice Black referred to the Norris-LaGuardia Act as a "long standing, carefully thought out and highly significant part of this country's labor legislation" and apparently found no reason to "go into the history of the Norris-LaGuardia Act nor the abuses which brought it into being for that has been amply discussed on several occasions," other than to note "that the reasons which led to the passage of the Act were substantial and that the Act has been an important part of the pattern of legislation under which Unions have functioned for nearly 30 years." (Footnote 16)

Admittedly, the bare fact that the law has been in existence for thirty years is no justification for opposing, at this time, any revision of its restraints upon the jurisdiction of the federal courts to issue injunctions in cases growing out of labor disputes. But if the substantial reasons for its passage are still extant, then, surely, there should be no tampering with this basic legislation. This of necessity leads to brief reference to the reasons for the passage of the Act.

In THE LABOR INJUNCTION, (FRANKFURTER and GREENE) it is pointed out that:

> The restraining order and preliminary injunction involved in labor disputes reveal the most crucial points of legal maladjustment. Temporary injunctive relief without notice, or, if upon notice relying upon dubious affidavits, serves the important function of staying defendant's conduct *regardless of the ultimate justification of such restraint* . . . The suspension of activities affects only the strikers; the employer resumes his effort to defeat the strike, and resumes them free from the interdicted interferences. Moreover, the suspension of strike activities, even temporarily, may defeat the strike for practical purposes and foredoom its resumption, even if the injunction is later lifted. (Pages 200–201) [emphasis added].

The point is also made that:

> The eagerness of employers to seek injunctions in the federal courts and the diverse channels through which the federal courts enter these controversies, have given the federal labor injunction its political significance. Anything which may seriously impair the prestige of federal courts touches more than the effective administration of law.

And in the *Milk Wagon Drivers'* case, 311 U.S. 91 at 102, the Court emphasized:

> The Norris-LaGuardia Act, passed in 1932, is the culmination of a bitter political, social and economic controversy extending over half a century. Hostility to "government by injunction" had become the rallying slogan of many and varied groups. . . . Thus, the Senate Judiciary Committee, reporting the Norris-LaGuardia Act, said: "That there have been abuses of judicial power in granting injunctions in labor disputes is hardly open to discussion. The use of the injunction in such disputes has been growing by leaps and bounds. . . . For example, approximately 300 were issued in connection with the railway shopmen's strike in 1922."

We see no reason to believe that vesting the federal courts today with jurisdiction to restrain strikes which are allegedly in violation of contract will not give rise to the same abuses.

Nor do we find any substance in the position of the management lawyers that fear of use of the "age-old 'union busting' weapon" is unrealistic "in the modern day sophisticated climate of labor relations." It is precisely this "sophisticated" climate, which underlies our apprehension concerning revival of the labor injunction in federal courts. The apparently equitable appeal to the Chancellor that an injunction against a strike which violates a contractual commitment is a "just" injunction will open the door to the "unjust" injunction as well.

Of course, there may sometimes be "just" grounds for injunction in certain areas, and no doubt there may have been when Norris-LaGuardia was enacted. The Act represented not a criticism of the "just" injunction, but a recognition that too often "unjust" injunctions were issued in the name of justice.

Even today, the judges in our federal district courts have not had not wide exposure to labor cases, and cannot be expected to appreciate the full sweep of our federal labor policy which has developed with such delicate balance over several decades. This difficulty is compounded by the fact that the suit for injunction inevitably requires a quick decision, thus denying the judge the time which would be necessary to research, reflect and acquire that understanding.

The same problems attendant upon the issuance of a preliminary, temporary or permanent injunction in a strike in which no contract is involved are pretty much the same where contracts are involved. Instead of determining whether there is a breach of public statutes such as the Sherman Act, the Clayton Act, the Interstate Commerce Act, or state statutes in diversity cases, the court must make a preliminary determination as to whether there was a breach of a "private statute," that is, the collective bargaining agreement between the parties. These determinations very frequently involve fine questions of contract interpretation which will vary in complexity from one case to the next.

For example, at the threshold there would be involved the question of whether the contract *in haec verba* does contain a "no strike" clause and, if not, whether a pledge not to strike should be "implied," surely an awesome power to be confided to the federal district courts. The "no strike" clause may be a very limited one, and may not apply to all grievances. Not all disputes may be covered by the grievance procedure. There may have been a substantial breach by the employer leading to the right of rescission by the Union or the release of the union from the no-strike clause. The employer may have rescinded, thereby releasing the union. There may have been the commission of a substantial unfair labor practice by the employer. The strike may be protected by § 502 of the Taft-Hartley Act. Indeed, the question may arise as to whether the action itself is in fact or law a strike. The employer may have condoned the strike. The contract containing the no-strike clause may be illegal because made by illegally supported and dominated unions.

Finally, in many instances, an application for an injunction against a strike alleged to be in violation of a contract, and on a matter alleged to be arbitrable under the terms of the contract, requires the Court to determine in the first instance whether there is a breach of contract and whether the dispute is arbitrable, although the parties have confided the right to make determinations to the arbitrator.

Thus, it is begging the question to argue, as some neutral members do, that all that is involved is submission of arbitrable grievances to arbitration. Generally, the problem is whether the issue *is* arbitrable.

A predetermination of any of the above issues by the federal court prior to arbitration, based upon affidavits or abbreviated preliminary hearings, will result in precisely that which the Norris-LaGuardia Act sought to prevent, that is, the curbing of the effective right to strike by temporary suspension pending a final adjudication by either the arbitrators or the courts.

V.

These complex questions, and numerous others which unquestionably will arise in litigation under § 301, strongly suggest that employers be left to their wholly adequate damage remedy, where a wrong decision to issue an equitable remedy will not unsurp the union's basic economic right to strike.

Indeed, measured even by the standards governing injunctions generally, it is doubtful that a case can be made for them under § 301. For the damage suit provides a wholly adequate remedy to the employer who suffers a strike in breach of contract. Damages can impair vitally the financial condition of a union. An injunction cannot compel workers to work. But the danger to the union is manifest, for an injunction improperly issued in the innumerable knotty situations likely to arise will cause irreparable damage, and there is no way to recompense for a strike wrongly interrupted.

Nor is there substance to the oft-repeated charge, reiterated in the Resolution, that application of Norris-LaGuardia provides an "inequitable gap" in the enforcement of § 301. This somewhat elliptical statement may be intended to incorporate the simplistic proposition that if Norris-LaGuardia permits an injunctive order at a union's behest in order to compel arbitration, it should in all equity, permit a corresponding order to be issued, at an employer's request, to enjoin a strike which is in violation of an agreement to use arbitration instead of the strike as a dispute-settling method. Both orders, in this view, are in aid of the arbitration process.

The difficulty with this argument is that it equates the wrong things. The order to arbitrate is an order directed toward an adjudication *after the event*—not an order restraining the employer from acting in violation of the agreement. Under almost all collective agreements the employer is free to act in the first instance—to administer the agreement in accordance with his views as to its meaning. The order to arbitrate does not enjoin him from so doing. It only requires that he submit to an agreed-upon form of adjudication, after the fact, as to whether his actions violated the agreement. The comparable order against a union, alleged to have violated the agreement by striking, only be an order directing it to arbitrate, not an injunctive order preventing it from taking the action which is alleged to be in violation of the agreement. And the Court said in *Sinclair,* 370 U.S. at 214, that such

an order to arbitrate is not barred by Norris-LaGuardia.

There is nothing, therefore, "inequitable" about the present situation. Norris-LaGuardia prevents *either* party from obtaining an order requiring the *other* to conduct itself in accordance with the substantive provisions of the agreement; it permits either party to obtain against the other an order requiring the use of the agreed-upon method of adjudicating whether actions taken are in violation of the agreement.

We doubt that our brethren on the management side would respond favorably to the suggestion by some neutral members that by such amendment to the Norris-LaGuardia the federal district courts will also be open to the unions for temporary injunctive relief to forestall certain management decisions pending resolution of their contractual validity by the arbitrator.

Permitting the court to determine if there is a no-strike clause, if the grievance was arbitrable, and if the action taken is a strike, is permitting the court to *administer* the contract in exactly the same way it would be *administering* the contract if the union could obtain from the court a prior restraint on the employer's promoting, demoting, discharging, making seniority adjustments, assigning overtime, subcontracting, retiming jobs, making work assignments, etc.

VI.

What we have said here is not intended to suggest that we are unsympathetic to the position of the employer whose employees strike in violation of a clear contractual commitment not to do so. We just don't believe that the problem should be subject to the type of treatment suggested by the Resolution. There may be alternatives other than those already available to the employer. For example, in the State of New York it is possible for the employer to obtain an arbitration award directing the immediate termination of a strike in violation of contract and, thereafter, with relative dispatch, have such award enforced by appropriate court order despite New York's little Norris-LaGuardia Act.[5]

While all members signing this report do not necessarily subscribe to this method of handling the problem, all recognize that this approach would permit the arbitrator to fulfill his assigned function, and make the initial, basic determination, as the parties have agreed and intended that he do, and would require the union thereafter to discharge its own obligation under the con-

---

5. In the Matter of Ruppert, 3 N.Y. 2d 576, 148 N.E. 2d 129 (1958).

tract. That is what it agreed to do—to comply with the adjudication of the arbitrator as to the meaning and scope of the contract.

VII.

We take the liberty of suggesting that strikes and stoppages during the term of a collective agreement can be avoided if the parties thereto will include therein the following provisions which constitute a modern, sensible and realistic approach to the resolution of all labor management problems which may arise under the agreement during its terms:

(1) The broadest kind of arbitration provision. This would not only include arbitration of any complaint or grievance relating to the acts or conduct of the employer, his employees or the union, but also any question which may arise regarding the interpretation or application of any of the provisions of the collective agreement.

(2) An additional provision which would state in substance that, in amplification of any and all rights which the arbitrator may have, he may, as part of his decision, issue any and all mandatory directions, prohibitions or orders directed to or against any party breaching the collective agreement or any part thereof.

(3) An expeditious method for the functioning of the grievance machinery and for the effectuation of the award rendered by the arbitrator or arbitrators.

VIII.

We close by reminding the Section of that which they already know, and to which the courts and sophisticated commentators have adverted many times. Analogies between commercial contracts and collective bargaining agreements in the process of application and interpretation cannot and should not easily be drawn. The developing law of collective bargaining agreements is in many aspects unique unto itself and is not always based upon traditional concepts of contract. Accordingly, we cannot agree that in an area as sensitive and as basic as the right to strike, such fundamental labor legislation as the Norris-LaGuardia Act, designed as it was to protect such right from the individual notions and predilections of the federal judiciary, should be amended so as to permit the interpretation, application and enforcement of labor agreements by those unfamiliar with the common law of industrial relations.

Report of the Neutral Members

On August 7, 1962, the following Resolution was introduced at the annual meeting of the Section of the Labor Relations Law:
[Omitted]
Thereafter, a special committee consisting of five neutral members and five representatives from management and labor, respectively, was appointed to consider the Resolution. Upon careful consideration, the neutral members would offer the following comments.

I.

According to the Preliminary Report from the management members, the principal purpose of the Resolution "is to permit the granting of injunction relief by Federal courts to halt the violation by a labor union of its contractual pledge not to strike during the life of a collective bargaining agreement *over issues or disputes which it has agreed will be decided by arbitration.*" [Italics supplied.] The Resolution itself, however, could be interpreted to go further and permit injunctive relief against strikes in breach of contract even where the underlying dispute is not subject to arbitration. The neutral members recommended that the Resolution be amended to reflect more clearly the limited intention of its proponents.

II.

All of the neutral members are agreed that injunctive relief should be available to the employer in cases involving strikes in breach of contract where the underlying dispute is arbitrable. The Supreme Court has declared that § 301 of the Labor Management Relations Act embodies "the basic policy of national labor-legislation to promote the arbitral process as a substitute for economic warfare."[1] The Court has also ruled that a strike over an arbitrable grievance undermines the effectiveness of the arbitral process.[2] Hence, a union which violates its no-strike pledge over a matter that is subject to arbitration not only violates the collective bargaining agreement but directly contravenes the basic policy underlying § 301.

Under existing laws, employers may maintain an action for damages resulting from a strike in breach of contract and may discipline the

---

1. Drake Bakeries, Inc. v. Local 50, American Bakery and Confectionery Workers, 370 U.S. 254, 261 (1962).
2. *Ibid.*

employees involved.[3] In many cases, however, neither of these alternatives will be feasible.[4] Discharge of the strikers is often inexpedient because of a lack of qualified replacements or because of the adverse effect on relationships within the plant. The damage remedy may also be unsatisfactory because the employer's losses are often hard to calculate and because the employer may hesitate to exacerbate relations with the union by bringing a damage action. Hence, injunctive relief will often be the only effective means by which to remedy the breach of the no-strike pledge and thus effectuate federal labor policy.

Any proposal which would subject unions to injunctive relief must take account of the Norris-LaGuardia Act and the opposition expressed in that Act to the issuing of injunctions in labor disputes. Nevertheless, the reasons behind the Norris-LaGuardia Act seem scarcely applicable to the situation under discussion here. The Act was passed primarily because of widespread dissatisfaction with the tendency of judges to enjoin concerted activities in accordance with "doctrines of tort law which made the lawfulness of a strike depend upon judicial views of social and economic policy."[5] Where an injunction is used against a strike in breach of contract, the union is not subjected in this fashion to judicially created limitations on its freedom of action but is simply compelled to comply with limitations to which it has previously agreed. Moreover, where the underlying dispute is arbitrable, the union is not deprived of any practicable means of pressing its claim but is only required to submit the dispute to the impartial tribunal that it has agreed to establish for this purpose. For these reasons, it seems appropriate for Congress to make the Norris-LaGuardia Act inapplicable to cases involving strikes over arbitrable grievances in the same way as it has limited the Act in various other situations where the policies underlying the Act no longer apply. (See *e.g.*, Section 10(h) of the National Labor Relations Act, as amended.)

In opposing the Resolution, the union members have stressed the danger that courts may make erroneous rulings on issues of fact or law and thus may unfairly limit the right to strike. It is doubtless true that no-strike clauses sometimes give rise to difficult issues concerning the scope of the clause, the responsibility of the union for the walkout, etc. Nevertheless, the mere possibility of an erroneous ruling hardly justifies withholding what may often be the only practicable remedy to effectuate an important federal policy. Moreover, the risk of error may be reduced, or at least made more tolerable, by the fact that the no-strike clause will often be interpreted and applied by an arbitrator of the parties' choice rather than a court. The Supreme Court has recently ruled that courts should forbear from passing upon alleged violations of the no-strike clause where the union has asked that the case be submitted to arbitration and where claims involving the no-strike clause are arbitrable under the contract.[6] It is true that this decision is inapplicable where the contract does not provide for arbitration of alleged violations of the no-strike clause. Even in these cases, however, union officials have an opportunity to counteract the danger of erroneous court rulings by seeking to amend the arbitration clause.

If the Resolution is enacted into law, it seems clear that federal courts will specifically enforce an arbitrator's decision holding a strike in breach of contract. It must also be anticipated, however, that courts will grant a temporary injunction in appropriate cases to restrain the strike pending a ruling by the arbitrator.[7] In cases where the alleged breach of the no-strike pledge must be resolved by arbitration, several days or weeks may elapse before an arbitrator is selected and an award handed down. In certain situations, an employer might be forced to resolve the underlying grievance on the union's terms if the strike were allowed to continue pending a determination by the arbitrator. Hence, the granting of equitable relief prior to the arbitrator's decision seems necessary in order to carry out the purposes of the Resolution. It might be pointed out in passing that equitable relief of this kind may work to the benefit of the union as well as the employer, for a temporary injunction could presumably be granted in appropriate cases in order to forestall certain management decisions pend-

3. Under the law in New York, an employer may specifically enforce an arbitrator's order to terminate a strike in breach of contract. Ruppert v. Egelhofer, 3 N.Y. 2d 576, 148 N.E. 2d 129 (1958). In a few jurisdictions, the employer may sue in a state court to enjoin a strike in violation of the contract. See McCarroll v. Los Angeles County District Council, 49 Cal. 2d 45, 315 P. 2d 322 (1957).

4. See Cox, *Current Problems in the Law of Labor Arbitration*, 30 ROCKY MT. L. REV. 247, 255 (1958).

5. Cox, *op. cit.* at p. 256.

6. Drake Bakeries, Inc. v. Local 50, American Bakery and Confectionery Workers, 370 U.S. 245 (1962).

7. Cf. Johnson & Johnson v. Textile Workers, 184 F. Supp. 359 (D.N.J. 1960). (Strike restrained by way of ancillary relief to an order compelling union to comply with arbitration proceedings.) See also American Smelting and Refining Co. v. Tacoma Smeltermen's Union, 175 F. Supp. 750 (W. D. Wash. 1959).

ing resolution of their contract validity by the arbitrator.[8]

To sum up the foregoing discussion, strikes that violate the contract and are precipitated by arbitrable grievances are especially repugnant to the federal policy reflected in § 301. Injunctions against such strikes would plainly not offend the policies underlying the Norris-LaGuardia Act and would provide what may often be the only effective remedy against the union's action. For these reasons, almost all of the impartial authorities who have commented on the question have concluded that the Norris-LaGuardia Act should be amended to permit equitable relief in these circumstances.[9] The neutral members are in accord with this conclusion.

III.

While agreeing that injunctive relief should be available under the circumstances described above, a majority of the neutral members would express reservations concerning the wisdom of taking up in this fashion only one of the many related problems which might be considered in need of legislative reform. Knowledgeable commentators have already pointed out that the matter raised by this Resolution is but one of many similar problems having to do with the current status of the Norris-LaGuardia Act.[10] Moreover, it is difficult to resolve a single problem, such as the strike over arbitrable grievances, without also considering such closely connected questions as whether injunctive relief should be available where the underlying dispute is not arbitrable, whether a strike protesting an arbitrator's award should be enjoinable by a court, whether Congress should amend § 301 simply to repeal § 4 of the Norris-LaGuardia Act or whether §§ 7 and 8 should also be repealed, etc. In the view of a majority of the neutral members, such questions will have to be answered before the problem raised by the Resolution can be finally resolved in a satisfactory manner.

---

8. See Brotherhood of Locomotive Engineers v. Missouri-Kansas-Texas Railroad Co., 363 U.S. 528 (1960).

9. See *e.g.*, Cox, *op. cit. supra* note 3: Summers, *Role of Supreme Court in Labor Relations*, 50 L.R.R.M. 94, 100–102 (1962); Mendelsohn, *Enforceability of Arbitration Agreements under the Taft-Hartley Section 301*, 66 YALE L. J. 167, 179–183 (1956); Note, 76 HARV. L. REV. 205 (1962); 111 U. PA. L. REV. 247 (1962).

10. See AARON, *The Labor Injunction Reappraised*, 10 U.C.L.A. REV. 292 (1963).

INTERNATIONAL LONGSHOREMEN'S ASSOCIATION, LOCAL 1291 v. PHILADELPHIA MARINE TRADE ASSOCIATION
389 U.S. 64 (1967)

MR. JUSTICE STEWART delivered the opinion of the Court.

These cases arise from a series of strikes along the Philadelphia waterfront. The petitioner union, representing the longshoremen involved in those strikes, had entered into a collective bargaining agreement in 1959 with the respondent, an association of employers in the Port of Philadelphia. The agreement included provisions for compensating longshoremen who are told after they report for duty that they will not be needed until the afternoon.[1] The union construed those "set-back" provisions to mean that, at least in some situations, longshoremen whose employment was postponed because of unfavorable weather conditions were entitled to four hours' pay; the association interpreted the provisions to guarantee no more than one hour's pay under such circumstances.

In April, 1965, when this disagreement first became apparent, the parties followed the grievance procedure established by their collective bargaining contract and submitted the matter to an arbitrator for binding settlement.[2] On June 11 the arbitrator ruled that the association's reading

---

1. The 1959 agreement provided in Article 9 (a) that "Men employed from Monday to Sunday, inclusive, shall be guaranteed four (4) hours' pay for the period between 8:00 A.M. and 12:00 Noon, regardless of any condition." Article 9 (h) provided that "If a ship is knocked off on account of inclement weather by the Ship's Master or his authorized representative, the men will be paid the applicable guarantee, but in the event the men knock off themselves, they will be paid only for the time worked, regardless of guarantee provided for in this Agreement."

A Memorandum of Settlement, effective October 1, 1964, provided in Article 10 (5) that "[f]or work commencing at 8 A.M. on Monday or at 8 A.M. on the day following a holiday," employers would "have the right because of non-arrival of a vessel in port to cancel the gangs by 7:30 A.M." Article 10 (6) then stated: "Gangs ordered for an 8 A.M. start Monday through Friday can be set back at 7:30 A.M. on the day of work to commence at 1 P.M. at which time a four hour guarantee shall apply. A one hour guarantee shall apply for the morning period unless employed during the morning period."

Article 16 of the Memorandum of Settlement adopted the provisions of the 1959 agreement by reference, with the proviso that, in cases of conflict, "the provisions of [the Memorandum] shall prevail."

2. Article 28 of the 1959 agreement, unchanged by the Memorandum of Settlement, provided:

"All disputes and grievances of any kind or nature whatsoever arising under the terms and conditions of this agreement, and all questions involving the interpretation of this agreement other than any disputes or grievances arising under the terms and conditions of paragraph 13 (d)

of the set-back provisions was correct.[3] In July, however, a group of union members refused to unload a ship unless their employer would promise four hours' pay for having set back their starting time from 8 a.m. to 1 p.m. The union sought to arbitrate the matter, but the association viewed the original arbitrator's decision as controlling and instituted proceedings in the District Court to enforce it. The complaint alleged that the union had refused "to abide by the terms of the Arbitrator's Award ... resulting in serious loss and damage to [the] Employer ... and to

---

hereof, shall be referred to a Grievance Committee, which shall consist of two members selected by the Employers and two members selected by the Union.... Should the Grievance Committee be unable to resolve the issue submitted and should neither party request an immediate decision from the Arbitrator, then the grievance or dispute shall be submitted to a Joint Grievance Panel consisting of three representatives of the Association and three representatives of the Union. To the end that there shall be no work interruptions and to the end that there shall be limited necessity for arbitration, the Panel shall make every effort to resolve all grievances or disputes which could not be resolved by the Grievance Committee.... Should the Panel be unable to resolve a grievance or dispute which arose in the previous two weeks, or be unable to resolve a grievance or dispute anticipated in the ensuing two weeks, the dispute or grievance, including matters of Interpretation of the contract, shall be referred to an impartial Arbitrator who shall be selected to serve for a period of one year from a panel of five arbitrators to be submitted by the American Arbitration Association.... The Arbitrator thus selected shall conduct his hearings and procedures in accordance with the Rules of the American Arbitration Association, except that he shall be obliged to render his decision within forty-eight hours of the conclusion of his hearings or procedures.... Should the terms and conditions of this agreement fail to specifically provide for an issue in dispute, or should a provision of this agreement be the subject of disputed interpretation, the Arbitrator shall consider port practice in resolving the issue before him. If the Arbitrator determines that there is no port practice to assist him in determining an issue not specifically provided for in the collective bargaining agreement, or no port practice to assist him in resolving an interpretation of the agreement, the issue shall become the subject of negotiation between the parties. There shall be no strike and no lock-out during the pendency of any dispute or issue while before the Grievance Committee, the Joint Panel, or the Arbitrator."

3. The text of the arbitrator's award was this:
"The contention of the Employer, the Philadelphia Marine Trade Association, is hereby sustained and it is the Arbitrator's determination that Section 10 (6) of the Memorandum of Settlement dated February 11, 1965, providing gangs 'ordered for an 8 A.M. start Monday through Friday can be set back at 7:30 A.M. on the day of work to commence at 1 P.M. at which time a 4 hour guarantee shall apply. A 1 hour guarantee shall apply for the morning period unless employed during the morning period,' may be invoked by the Employer without qualification.

"The contention of the Union, the International Longshoremen's Association, Local No. 1291, that Section 10 (6) of the Memorandum of Settlement dated February 11, 1965, referred to above, can only be invoked by the Employer because of non-arrival of a vessel in port, is denied."

the Port of Philadelphia." This refusal, the complaint charged, constituted "a breach of the applicable provisions of the current Collective Bargaining Agreement between the P.M.T.A. and the Union." The complaint concluded with a prayer "that the Court set an immediate hearing and enter an order enforcing the Arbitrator's Award, and that plaintiff may have such other and further relief as may be justified."

Before the court could take any action, the employer had met the union's demands and the men had returned to work. The District Court heard evidence in order to "put the facts on record" but concluded that the case was "moot at the moment" and decided simply to "keep the matter in hand as a judge [and] take jurisdiction ... [i]f anything arises." A similar situation did in fact arise—this time in September. Again, before the District Court could act, the work stoppage ended. The association nonetheless requested

> an order ... to make it perfectly clear to the [union] that it is required to comply with the Arbitrator's award because we cannot operate in this port if we are going to be continually harassed by the Union in taking the position that they are not going to abide by an Arbitrator's award ...

Counsel for the union rejected that characterization of its position. He submitted that the set-back disputes of July and September were distinguishable from the one which occurred in April, and that the arbitrator's decision of June 11, 1965, resolving the April controversy, was not controlling.[4] The District Court expressed no

---

4. The union's position in this regard was twofold. It maintained, first, that even if the July and September disputes had been factually identical to that of April, it was "quite clear ... from past practice and from the agreement itself that ... the award as to [any given] dispute relates only to that dispute and is not controlling so far as any future dispute is concerned." The union contended, second, that the disputes were factually different in at least one crucial respect: In the later disputes, the longshoremen were not notified of the set-back by 7:30 A.M., as required by Article 10 of the Memorandum of Settlement. The arbitrator's award, by its own terms, dealt only with situations in which longshoremen were "set back at 7:30 A.M." Counsel for the association seemingly agreed that the question of notice thus presented an independently arbitrable issue. He said: "[T]he factual issues as far as whether or not there was notice ... should be brought up under the grievance procedure which is in the contract." "The question of notification," he agreed, "was not a matter in the arbitrator's award." He stated that the time and method of notification had not changed from April to September but he conceded that the problem "was never brought to [the arbitrator's] attention by the parties." On this basis, counsel for the union said that his adversary had "admitted on the stand that this situation goes beyond the arbitrator's award." The District Judge thought otherwise: "You have added words to his mouth, my dear boy, and that you can't do."

opinion on any of these contentions but simply entered a decree, dated September 15, 1965, requiring that the arbitrator's award "issued on June 11, 1965, be specifically enforced." The decree ordered the union "to comply with and abide by the said Award." It contained no other command.[5]

When the District Court first indicated that it would issue such a decree, counsel for the union asked the court for clarification:

> "Mr. Freedman: Well, what does it mean, Your Honor?
>
> "The Court: That you will have to determine, what it means.
>
> "Mr. Freedman: Well, I am asking. I have to give my client advice and I don't know what it means. I am asking Your Honor to tell me what it means. It doesn't—
>
> "The Court: You handled the case. You know about it....
>
> "Mr. Freedman: I am telling you very frankly now I don't know what this order means, this proposed order. It says, 'Enforcement of the award.' Now, just what does it mean?... The arbitration... involved an interpretation of the contract under a specific set of facts... Now, how do you enforce it? That case is over and done with. These are new cases. Your Honor is changing the contract of the parties when you foreclose them from going to arbitration on this point again."
>
> "The Court: The Court has acted. This is the order.
>
> "Mr. Freedman: Well, won't Your Honor tell me what it means?
>
> "The Court: You read the English language and I do."

Although the association had expressly told the District Court that it was "not seeking to enjoin work stoppages," counsel for the union asked whether the decree might nonetheless have that effect:

> "Mr. Freedman:... Does this mean that the union cannot engage in a strike or refuse to work or picket?
>
> "The Court: You know what the arbitration was about. You know the result of the arbitration.
>
> .   .   .   .   .
>
> "I have signed the order. Anything else to come before us?

5. The full text of the decree was this:
"ORDER—September 15, 1965
"And Now to Wit, This 15th day of September, 1965, after hearing, it is hereby ordered, adjudged and decreed that the Arbitrator's Award in the matter of arbitration between the Philadelphia Marine Trade Association and International Longshoremen's Association Local 1291, issued on June 11, 1965, be specifically enforced by defendant, International Longshoremen's Association Local 1291, and the said defendant is hereby ordered to comply with and to abide by the said Award.
"By the Court.
"Ralph C. Body, J."

> "Mr. Freedman: I know, but Your Honor is leaving me in the sky. I don't know what to say to my client.
>
> "Mr. Scanlan: No, I have nothing further, Your Honor.
>
> "The Court: The hearing is closed."

Thus, despite counsel's repeated requests, the District Judge steadfastly refused to explain the meaning of the order.

When further set-back disputes disrupted work throughout the Port of Philadelphia in late February 1966, the District Court issued a rule to show cause why the union and its officers should not be held in contempt for violating the order of September 15. Throughout the contempt hearing held on March 1, 1966, counsel for the union sought without success to determine precisely what acts by the union, its officers, or its members were alleged to have violated the court's order. "We have a right to know," he said, "what it is that we are being accused of...." The District Judge refused to comment.[6]

At some points in the proceedings, it appeared that the alleged violation consisted of the work stoppage during the last few days of February; but at other times the inquiry focused upon the union's request for a grievance meeting on February 28 to discuss the latest set-back problem. "Why," counsel for the association asked, did the union seek "to rearbitrate the award...?" As the contempt hearing drew to a close, counsel for the association suggested yet another possibility—that union officials violated the District Court's decree when they "castigated" the arbitrator's award and failed to "tell [the men] that their work stoppage was unauthorized" under the award entered some eight months earlier. "[I]n failing to do that," counsel said, "they have shown that they do not intend to abide by the arbitrator's award which was the essence of the order which Your Honor issued...."

Invited to make a closing argument, counsel for the union said:

> I really don't know what to address myself to because I don't know what it is we are being charged with. Are we being charged because we want to arbitrate or because we asked to invoke the provisions or are we being charged for something else?...

6. At the hearing following the July work stoppage the District Judge had agreed that, as to factual situations going "beyond the arbitrator's award, the union is not bound." The union thus attempted to prove at the contempt hearing on March 1 that the February disputes, like those of the previous July and September, went beyond the arbitrator's award in that they raised a separate question of notice. Cf. n. 4, supra. The District Judge did not comment upon this aspect of the case in holding the union guilty of contempt.

I may say to Your Honor that we have been shooting in the dark here now, trying to guess at what may be an issue ...

But the District Judge evidently felt no need for explanation. After a short recess, the court announced that the dock strike was "illegal ... under the circumstances," and that the union had "violated the order of this Court and therefore shall be adjudged in civil contempt." After extending the contempt holding to "the officers and the men who participated," the court fined the union $100,000 per day, retroactive to 2 p.m., March 1, 1966, when the contempt hearing began, and every day thereafter "as long as the order of this Court is violated." The Court of Appeals affirmed both the original decree of the District Court and its subsequent contempt order, and we granted certiorari to consider the questions presented by these two judgments.

Much of the argument in the Court of Appeals and in this Court has centered upon the District Court's power to issue the order of September 15, 1965.[7] The union maintains that the order was an injunction against work stoppages and points out that in Sinclair Refining Co. v. Atkinson, 370 U.S. 195, we held that, because of the Norris-LaGuardia Act, a federal court cannot enjoin a work stoppage even when the applicable collective bargaining agreement contains a no-strike clause. The association, on the other hand, argues that the order no more than enforced an arbitrator's award, and points out that in Textile Workers Union v. Lincoln Mills, 353 U.S. 448, we held that, under § 301 of the Labor Management Relations Act, a federal court may grant equitable relief to enforce an agreement to arbitrate. The parties have strenuously argued the applicability of Sinclair and Lincoln Mills to the facts before us. We do not, however, reach the underlying questions of federal labor law these arguments present. For whatever power the District Court might have possessed under the circumstances disclosed by this record, the conclusion is inescapable that the decree which the court in fact entered was too vague to be sustained as a valid exercise of federal judicial authority.

On its face, the decree appears merely to enforce an arbitrator's award. But that award contains only an abstract conclusion of law, not an operative command capable of "enforcement." When counsel for the union noted this difficulty and sought to ascertain the District Court's meaning, he received no response. Even at the contempt hearing on March 1, the union

was not told how it had failed to "comply with and ... abide by the [Arbitrator's] Award," in accordance with the District Court's original order.

That court did express the view on March 1 that the February walkouts had been "illegal ... under the circumstances." But such strikes would have been "illegal"—in the sense that they would have been violative of the collective bargaining agreement—even if the District Court had entered no order at all, Teamsters Local v. Lucas Flour Co., 69 U.S. 95, and the record does not reveal what further "circumstances" the court deemed relevant to the conclusion that the union had violated its decree. Thus the September 15 decree, even when illuminated by subsequent events, left entirely unclear what it demanded.

Rule 65 (d) of the Federal Rules of Civil Procedure was designed to prevent precisely the sort of confusion with which the District Court clouded its command. That rule provides:

> Every order granting an injunction and every restraining order shall set forth the reasons for its issuance; shall be specific in terms; shall describe in reasonable detail, and not by reference to the complaint or other document, the act or acts sought to be restrained; and is binding only upon the parties to the action, their officers, agents, servants, employees, and attorneys, and upon those persons in active concert or participation with them who receive actual notice of the order by personal service or otherwise.

Whether or not the District Court's order was an "injunction" within the meaning of the Norris-LaGuardia Act, it was an equitable decree compelling obedience under the threat of contempt and was therefore an "order granting an injunction" within the meaning of Rule 65(d). Viewing the decree as "specifically enforcing" the arbitrator's award would not alter this conclusion. We have previously employed the term "mandatory injunction" to describe an order compelling parties to abide by an agreement to arbitrate,[8] and there is no reason to suppose that Rule 65(d) employed the injunction concept more narrowly. That rule is the successor of § 19 of the Clayton Act. Section 19 was intended to be "of general application," to the end that "[d]efendants ... never be left to guess at what they are forbidden to do...."[9] Consistent with the spirit and purpose

---

7. Other issues have been argued as well. In light of our disposition of these cases, we do not reach them.

8. Textile Workers Union v. Lincoln Mills, 353 U.S. 448, upheld federal judicial power to issue such an enforcement order. In Sinclair Refining Co. v. Atkinson, 370 U.S. 195, we described "the equitable relief granted in" Lincoln Mills as "a mandatory injunction to carry out an agreement to arbitrate." Id., at 212.

9. H.R. Rep. No. 627, 63d Cong., 2d Sess., 26 (1914); S. Rep. No. 698, 63d Cong., 2d Sess., 21 (1914).

of its statutory predecessor, we have applied Rule 65(d) in reviewing a judgment enforcing an order of the National Labor Relations Board, and the courts of appeals have applied the rule not only to prohibitory injunctions but to enforcement orders and affirmative decrees as well. We have no doubt, therefore, that the District Court's decree, however it might be characterized for other purposes, was an "order granting an injunction" for purposes of Rule 65(d).

The order in this case clearly failed to comply with that rule, for it did not state in "specific . . . terms" the acts that it required or prohibited. The Court of Appeals viewed this error as "minor and in no way decisional."[10] We consider it both serious and decisive.

The judicial contempt power is a potent weapon. When it is founded upon a decree too vague to be understood, it can be a deadly one. Congress responded to that danger by requiring that a federal court frame its orders so that those who must obey them will know what the court intends to require and what it means to forbid. Because the decree of this District Court was not so framed, it cannot stand. And with it must fall the District Court's decision holding the union in contempt. We do not deal here with a violation of a court order by one who fully understands its meaning but chooses to ignore its mandate. We deal instead with acts alleged to violate a decree that can only be described as unintelligible. The most fundamental postulates of our legal order forbid the imposition of a penalty for disobeying a command that defies comprehension.

Reversed.

MR. JUSTICE BRENNAN, concurring in result.

I concur in the result. But like my Brother DOUGLAS, I emphasize that today's disposition in no way implies that Sinclair Refining Co. v. Atkinson, 370 U.S. 195, determines the applicability of the Norris-LaGuardia Act to an equitable decree carefully fashioned to enforce the award of an arbitrator authorized by the parties to make final and binding interpretations of the collective bargaining agreement.

MR. JUSTICE DOUGLAS, concurring in part and dissenting in part.

I would reverse in No. 78 and in No. 34 remand the case to the District Court for further proceedings.

If the order of the District Court is an "injunction" within the meaning of Rule 65(d), then I fail to see why it is not an "injunction" within

---

10. 365 F. 2d 295, 301.

the meaning of the Norris-LaGuardia Act. Legal minds possess an inventive genius as great as that of those who work in the physical sciences. Perhaps a form of words could be worked out which would employ the science of semantics to distinguish the Norris-LaGuardia Act problem from the present one. I for one see no distinction ; and since I feel strongly that Sinclair Refining Co. v. Atkinson, 370 U.S. 195, caused a severe dislocation in the federal scheme of arbitration of labor disputes, I think we should not set our feet on a path that may well lead to the eventual reaffirmation of the principles of that case. My Brother STEWART expressly reserves the question whether the present order is an injunction prohibited by the Norris-LaGuardia Act. Despite this qualification, once we have held that the order constitutes an "injunction," the District Court on remand would likely consider Sinclair, which is not overruled, controlling and apply it to preclude the issuance of another order.

We held in Textile Workers Union v. Lincoln Mills 353 U.S. 448, that a failure to arbitrate was not part and parcel of the abuses against which the Norris-LaGuardia Act was aimed. We noted that Congress, in fashioning § 301 of the Labor Management Relations Act, was seeking to encourage collective bargaining agreements in which the parties agree to refrain from unilateral disruptive action, such as a strike, with respect to disputes arbitrable by the agreement. Hence, if unions could break such agreements with impunity, the congressional purpose might well be frustrated. Although § 301 does not in terms address itself to the question of remedies, it commands the District Court to hold the parties to their contractual scheme for arbitration—the "favored process for settlement," as my Brother BRENNAN said in dissent in Sinclair, 370 U.S., at 216. I agree with his opinion that there must be an accommodation between the Norris-LaGuardia Act and all other legislation on the books dealing with labor relations. We have had such an accommodation in the case of railroad disputes. See Brotherhood of Railroad Trainmen v. Chicago R. & I. R. Co., 353 U.S. 30. With respect to § 301, "Accommodation requires only that the anti-injunction policy of Norris-LaGuardia not intrude into areas, not vital to its ends, where injunctive relief is vital to a purpose of § 301; it does not require unconditional surrender." 370 U.S., at 225.

It would be possible, of course, to distinguish Sinclair from the instant case. In this case, the relief sought was a mandate against repetition of strikes over causes covered by the arbitrator's award. The complaint below alleged that the union's "refusal" to comply with the terms of the

Arbitrator's Award constitutes a breach of the applicable provisions of the current Collective Bargaining Agreement. . . ." Respondent asked that the court "enter an order enforcing the Arbitrator's Award, and that plaintiff may have such other and further relief as may be justified." We do not review here, as in *Sinclair,* a refusal to enter an order prohibiting unilateral disruptive action on the part of a union before that union has submitted its grievances to the arbitration procedure provided by the collective bargaining agreement. Rather, the union in fact submitted to the arbitration procedure established by the collective bargaining agreement but, if the allegations are believed, totally frustrated the process by refusing to abide by the arbitrator's decision. Such a "heads I win, tails you lose," attitude plays fast and loose with the desire of Congress to encourage the peaceful and orderly settlement of labor disputes.

The union, of course, may have acted in good faith, for the new dispute may have been factually different from the one which precipitated the award. Whether or not it was, we do not know. To make the accommodation which the *Textile Workers* case visualizes as necessary between the policy of encouraging arbitration on the one hand and the Norris-LaGuardia restrictions on the other, the basic case must go back for further and more precise findings and the contempt case must obviously be reversed. See *Sinclair,* 370 U.S., at 228–229 (dissenting opinion).

NEW ORLEANS STEAMSHIP ASSOCIATION v. GENERAL LONGSHORE WORKERS (5th Cir. 1968) 389 F. 2d 369

GRIFFIN B. BELL, C. J. Appellant New Orleans Steamship Association appeals from an order dismissing its complaint which in substance amounted to a request for a mandatory injunction to enforce an arbitration award. The award directed two local unions, the appellees, and their members to cease and desist work stoppages in violation of a collective bargaining agreement. The District Court was of the view that enforcement of such an order by a federal court was barred by the Norris-LaGuardia Act, 29 U.S.C.A. § 104. We reverse.

Appellant is an association representing various employers who employ longshoremen for the loading and unloading of cargo in the port of New Orleans. These longshoremen are members of and are represented by appellee unions. Appellant and the unions are signatories to a collective bargaining agreement. The parts of the agreement which are involved in this dispute are a no strike clause, an arbitration clause, and a clause em-

powering the arbitrator to issue a desist order. They provide in pertinent part:

"(a) *No Strikes—No Lockouts*

"There shall be no strikes, work stoppages, nor shall there be any lockouts.

"(b) *Disputes Procedure and Arbitration*

"The parties accept the principle that any dispute involving the interpretation or application of the terms of this agreement shall be resolved in an orderly and expeditious manner. They commit themselves to the procedure outlined below. Failure by either party to staff and maintain the permanent disputes committee provided for herein and failure to deal with disputes under the disputes procedure shall constitute a violation of this agreement.

"(c) These steps shall be followed to insure prompt resolution of disputes:

"Step 1. When a problem arises it shall be discussed immediately between the appropriate representatives of the employer and local union involved; if they are unable to reach a satisfactory settlement, either side may request immediate referral of the matter to Step 2. As soon as such request is made known each party shall notify its representatives on the permanent disputes committee.

"Step 2. There shall be established a permanent disputes committee consisting of two representatives of the Association and the presidents of Locals 1418 and 1419. Each member shall have a designated alternate who shall serve in the event a member is unavailable. If the matter is not disposed of in this Step 2 within forty-eight (48) hours of the origin of the dispute, or within such additional time mutually agreed upon, either party may take the dispute to final and binding arbitration."

. . . . .

"(d) Either party to a dispute may by-pass the procedure leading up to arbitration and obtain arbitration forthwith whenever a violation of sections (a) and/or (b) of this Article shall be alleged. In this event, a notice of such allegation shall be made by telegram to the other party and to the arbitrator. The arbitrator shall hold a prompt hearing within seventy-two (72) hours after receipt of the notice and shall render an award within twelve (12) hours after the hearing. In such case, the arbitrator shall make findings of fact concerning the alleged violation and shall prescribe appropriate relief, including an order to desist therefrom."

The arbitrator in this matter served by virtue of his inclusion on a panel of six permanent arbitrators selected by the parties to serve for the duration of the agreement. On October 5, 1965 appellant notified the arbitrator that appellees had engaged in work stoppages and requested a hearing within 72 hours as provided in the agreement, Article XVIII, § (d), *supra.* A four day hearing was held commencing on October 8, 1965. The award was entered on December 13, 1965. The arbitrator found that stoppages had occurred in violation of the contract and sustained appellant's grievance. He directed appellees, their officers, agents, representatives and members to "... cease and desist from work stoppages in violation of their contract...."

Alleging that work stoppages had occurred subsequent to this award, appellant sought relief in the District Court in March 1966 in the form of an order enforcing the award of the arbitrator. The District Court dismissed the complaint, relying on the Norris-LaGuardia Act, *supra,* and the cases of Sinclair Refining Co. v. Atkinson, 1962, 370 U.S. 195, 82 S.Ct. 1328, 8 L.Ed. 2d 440 ; and Gulf & South American Steamship Co. Inc. v. National Maritime Union of America, AFL–CIO, 5 Cir., 1966, 360 F.2d 63.

The court erred in its interpretation of our *Gulf & South American Steamship* case. Our holding there was that the arbitrator exceeded his jurisdiction in making the award and thus there could be no judicial enforcement of the award. We did not reach the question presented here. We held, as had the District Court that Sinclair Refining Company v. Atkinson, *supra,* was direct authority on the question and controlling. Absent jurisdiction in the arbitrator, the case was nothing more than an effort to obtain a federal injunction to enjoin a work stoppage arising out of a labor dispute.

Our decision here turns on a construction of the *Sinclair* holding. That case did not involve an arbitration award. It involved an effort to obtain an injunction to enforce a no strike clause where strikes were ensuing but where there had been no arbitration. The Supreme Court has not considered the precise question with which we are now concerned. Nevertheless, the sweep of *Sinclair* is broad ; the Norris-LaGuardia Act is treated as all encompassing despite § 301 of the Labor-Management Relations Act, 29 U.S.C.A. § 185, and the congressional and national policy enunciated in Textile Workers Union of America v. Lincoln Mills, 1957, 353 U.S. 448, 77 S.Ct. 912, 1 L.Ed. 2d 972, and the *Steelworkers* Trilogy, fostering the arbitration process.

The court stated in Textile Workers Union of America v. Lincoln Mills, *supra,* that the agreement of the employer to arbitrate disputes is the *quid pro quo* for the agreement not to strike. These cases and their progeny now make it settled law that federal courts can compel parties to collective bargaining agreements to carry out their agreements to arbitrate. The court alluded to this in *Sinclair* but stated that such injunctive orders do not conflict with the matters (strikes, work stoppages, and picketing) over which federal courts were deprived of jurisdiction by the Norris-LaGuardia Act.

Meanwhile it has become commonplace for federal courts to enforce arbitration awards by mandatory injunction where matters other than strikes, work stoppages or picketing are involved. See *e.g.,* Minute Maid Co. v. Citrus, Cannery, Food Processing and Allied Workers, Drivers, Warehousemen and Helpers, Local Union # 444, 5 Cir., 1964, 331 F.2d 280, 281 ; Fontainebleau Hotel Corp. v. Hotel Employees' Union Local 255, 5 Cir., 1964, 328 F.2d 310.

In sum the situation to date is that arbitration is encouraged ; it may be compelled where the parties have contractually adopted such a procedure. And the award may be judicially enforced up to the point of those matters proscribed by Norris-LaGuardia.

The question presented now is the power of the District Court to enforce the award of an arbitrator in a setting where the arbitrator, in the exercise of undisputed contractual jurisdiction, has ordered an end to work stoppages. The union has refused to abide by his order and asserts that the court is without jurisdiction to remedy the breach. Practically, this is the ultimate or last step in the arbitration process. The agreement between the parties is valid and the authority of the arbitrator over the subject matter and to enter a desist order is not disputed. We can assume, *arguendo,* that the employer agreed to arbitrate grievances in return for the no work stoppage clause. Does *Sinclair* foreclose relief to the employer? We hold that it does not.

The question was before the court in International Longshoremen's Assn. v. Philadelphia Marine Trade Association, 1967, 389 U.S. 64, 83, S.Ct. 201, 19 L.Ed. 2d 236, but was not reached due to the impreciseness of the injunctive order involved. Justice Douglas, concurring in part and dissenting in part in that case, forecast the problem which the *Sinclair* holding poses in the situation here present where we must accommodate, if possible, two national policies: The proscription of Norris-LaGuardia in labor disputes and the use of arbitration to avoid labor disputes. He considered *Sinclair,* where there had been no arbitration, distinguishable from a case where the arbitration award, as here, is frustrated through a refusal to abide by the decision of the arbitrator.[1] Our approach is to distinguish *Sinclair* on this same basis and on the more than semantical ground that there is a real difference between an ordinary injunction and an order enforcing the award of an arbitrator although the end result is the same.

In this case the parties agreed to the remedy

---

1. At least one state court has considered the same issue. [citing *Ruppert.*]

of a desist order by the arbitrator. Such an order was entered and breached. The court in enforcing such order or award, although injunctive in nature, would be doing no more than enforcing the agreement of the parties. This not unusual action on the part of a court will lie unless the court has been deprived of jurisdiction by the Norris-LaGuardia Act.

Norris-LaGuardia is limited to labor disputes and we consider the instant controversy to be outside the scope of a labor dispute as such. We have before us a contract wherein the parties have ceded their remedy of self-help in a labor dispute to arbitration even to the point of permitting the arbitrator to grant a desist order. Once the arbitration was completed, the matter became ripe for specific performance and fell outside the scope of Norris-LaGuardia.

We think the logic of the arbitration policy compels this result; otherwise one of the parties to a collective bargaining agreement containing arbitration and no strike or work stoppage clauses has a hollow right indeed. He is told: Our national policy is to encourage arbitration; you may contract to arbitrate and obtain a no strike clause as the *quid pro quo* for your agreement to arbitrate; a recalcitrant party will be compelled to arbitrate any dispute arising therefrom; and the arbitrator may be empowered contractually to issue a desist order. We do not believe in light of the body of law which has grown from § 301 that the law will now say to this party that, having done these things, there is no remedy in the event the opposite party decides to ignore the award of the arbitrator to desist the stoppage. No such result should be imputed to Congress: the Supreme Court did not go so far in *Sinclair*.

Our judgment is that the Norris-LaGuardia Act and arbitration under the auspices of § 301 of the Labor-Management Relations Act, construed *in pari materia*, can be meaningfully accommodated. They relate to the same subject matter—labor relations—and they should be construed together. Cf. United States v. Stewart, 1940, 311 U.S. 60, 61 S.Ct. 102, 85 L.Ed. 40. Each has its place in the labor relations arena; the vitality of Norris-LaGuardia is in no wise diminished by the judicial enforcement of the award of an arbitrator made pursuant to a contract.

The District Court had jurisdiction under these circumstances to enforce the award of the arbitrator and erred in dismissing the complaint.

Reversed and remanded for further proceedings not inconsistent herewith.

In Marine Transit Lines v. Curran (S.D.N.Y., 1967) 65 LRRM 2095, the arbitrator issued an award directing the union

> to cease and desist from refusing to allow unlicensed members of the crew to sail the ship forthwith, to provide crewmen who are prepared to sail the ship and to take whatever steps are necessary to bring the strike or work stoppages to a prompt conclusion.

The district court held that Section 4 of the Norris-La Guardia Act, as interpreted in *Sinclair v. Atkinson*, prohibited enforcement of the award. He noted:

> This is a labor dispute. Petitioner does not claim otherwise. The court is being asked to enjoin a work stoppage. This is the reality of the situation whatever may be the form of the proceeding.

AVCO CORP v. AERO LODGE 735, INTERNATIONAL ASSOCIATION OF MACHINISTS
___U.S.___ (1968)

DOUGLAS, J. Petitioner filed a suit in a state court in Tennessee to enjoin respondent and their members and associates from striking at petitioner's plant. The heart of the complaint was a "no-strike" clause in the collective bargaining agreement by which "grievances" were to be settled amicably or by binding arbitration. The eligibility of employees for promotion engendered disputes —allegedly subject to the grievance procedure— which so far as appears involved no violence or trespass but which resulted in work stoppages and a walkout by employees. The state court issued an *ex parte* injunction.

Respondent then moved in the Federal District Court for removal of the case.[1] A motion to remand to the state court was made and denied, the District Court ruling that the action was within its original jurisdiction. The District Court granted respondent's motion to dissolve the injunction issued by the Tennessee court. The Court of Appeals affirmed. 376 F. 2d 337. We granted the

---

1. 28 U.S.C. § 1441, provides in relevant part:

"Actions removable generally

"(a) Except as otherwise expressly provided by Act of Congress, any civil action brought in a State Court of which the district courts of the United States have original jurisdiction, may be removed by the defendant or the defendants, to the district court of the United States for the district and division embracing the place where such action is pending.

"(b) Any civil action of which the district courts have original jurisdiction founded on a claim or right arising under the Constitution, treaties or laws of the United States shall be removable without regard to the citizenship or residence of the parties . . . . "

petition for certiorari (389 U.S. 819) because of an apparent conflict between the decision below and American Dredging Co. v. Local 25, 338 F. 2d 837, from the Third Circuit Court of Appeals.

The starting point is § 301 of the Labor Management Relations Act of 1947, 61 Stat. 156, 29 U.S.C. § 185, which, we held in Textile Workers v. Lincoln Mills, 353 U.S. 448, was fashioned by Congress to place sanctions behind agreements to arbitrate grievance disputes.

An action arising under § 301 is controlled by federal substantive law even though it is brought in a state court.[2] Humphrey v. Moore, 375 U.S. 335 ; Local 174 v. Lucas Flour Co., 369 U.S. 95 ; Charles Dowd Box Co. v. Courtney, 368 U.S. 502. Removal is but one aspect[3] of "the primacy of the federal judiciary in deciding questions of federal law." See England v. Medical Examiners, 375 U.S. 411, 415–416.

It is thus clear that the claim under this collective agreement is one arising under the "laws of the United States" within the meaning of the removal statute. 28 U.S.C. § 1441(b). It likewise seems clear that this suit is within the "original jurisdiction" of the District Court within the meaning of 28 U.S.C. § 1441 (a) and (b). It is true that the Court by a 5-to-3 decision in Sinclair Refining Co. v. Atkinson, 370 U.S. 195, held that although a case was properly in the federal district court by reason of § 301, the Norris-LaGuardia Act bars that court from issuing an injunction in the labor dispute. The nature of the relief available after jurisdiction attaches is, of course, different from the question whether there is jurisdiction to adjudicate the controversy. The relief in § 301 cases varies—from specific performance of the promise to arbitrate (Textile Workers Union v. Lincoln Mills, *supra*), to enforcement or annulment of an arbitration award (United Steel Workers v. Enterprise Wheel & Car Corp., 363 U.S. 593), to an award of compensatory damages (Atkinson v. Sinclair Refining Co., 370 U.S. 238), and the like. See Smith v. Evening

News Assn., 371 U.S. 195, 199–200. But the breadth or narrowness of the relief which may be granted under federal law in § 301 cases is a distinct question from whether the court has jurisdiction over the parties and the subject matter. Any error in granting or designing relief "does not go to the jurisdiction of the court." Swift & Co. v. United States, 276 U.S. 311 331. Cf. Zwickler v. Koota, 389 U.S. 241, 254–255. When the Court in Sinclair Refining Co. v. Atkinson, *supra,* at 215, said that dismissal of a count in the complaint asking for an injunction was correct "for lack of jurisdiction under the Norris-LaGuardia Act," it meant only that the Federal District Court lacked the general equity power to grant the particular relief.[4]

Title 28 U.S.C. § 1337 says that "The district courts shall have original jurisdiction of any civil action or proceeding under any Act of Congress regulating commerce. . . ." It is that original jurisdiction that a § 301 action invokes. Textile Workers v. Lincoln Mills, *supra,* at 457.

Affirmed.

STEWART, J. (with whom MR. JUSTICE HARLAN and MR. JUSTICE BRENNAN join), concurring. I agree that the case before us was removable to the Federal District Court under 28 U.S.C. § 1441.

The District Judge not only denied a motion to remand the case to the state court but also dissolved the state court injunction, and it is only by virtue of the latter order that an appeal was possible at this stage of the litigation. American Dredging Co. v. Local 25, 338 F. 2d 837, 838, n. 2.

As the Court says, it is not clear whether or not the District Judge dissolved the injunction "because it felt that action was required by Sinclair Refining Co. v. Atkinson, 370 U.S. 195," *ante,* at ——, n. 4. Accordingly, the Court expressly reserves decision on the effect of *Sinclair* in the circumstances presented by this case. The Court will, no doubt, have an opportunity to reconsider the scope and continuing validity of *Sinclair* upon an appropriate future occasion.

---

2. We find it unnecessary to rule on the holding of the Court of Appeals below that "the remedies available in State Courts are limited to the remedies available under Federal law." 376 F. 2d, at 343. That conclusion would suggest that state courts are precluded by § 4 of the Norris-LaGuardia Act from issuing injunctions in labor disputes, even though the defendant does not exercise his right—which we confirm today—to remove the case to the District Court under 28 U.S.C. § 1441 (b), and the state court therefore retains jurisdiction over the action. We have no occasion to resolve that matter here, since respondent did elect to have the case removed.

3. See DOBIE, FEDERAL PROCEDURE, 346 (1928); HART & WECHSLER, THE FEDERAL COURTS AND THE FEDERAL SYSTEM, 727-733, 1019-1020 (1953).

---

4. Another question raised here is whether the District Court, to which the action had been removed, should have dissolved the injunction issued by the Tennessee state court. There is, of course, no question of the power of the District Court to dissolve the injunction. See 28 U.S.C. § 1450. Whether it did so because it felt that action was required by Sinclair Refining Co. v. Atkinson, 370 U.S. 195, or because of its equity powers or both is not clear. But the Court of Appeals went much further and said in a dictum that "the remedies available in State Courts are limited to the remedies available under Federal Law." 376 F. 2d, at 343. We reserve decision on those questions.

STATE COURT INJUNCTIONS AND THE FEDERAL COMMON LAW OF LABOR CONTRACTS: BEYOND NORRIS-LaGUARDIA*

HOWARD LESNICK

Had Congress never enacted the 1932 statute, we would long since have seen the development of a corpus of federal rulings dealing with injunctions in labor disputes. Some would have been the product of judicial decisions, others embodied in the Federal Rules, other enacted by the legislature. These principles would govern federal court actions, and the Supreme Court would have authority to decide whether effectuation of the purposes of the extensive federal regulatory scheme in the labor-management field called for similar restrictions on state power to enforce no-strike clauses.

An affirmative answer would often be called for. The federal law whose application *Lincoln Mills* prescribes is one "which the courts must fashion from the policy of our national labor laws." One can, I believe, sum up the themes of federal concern with reasonable accuracy in a few words, although documentation would require a sensitive recollection of two generations of history. The core of the danger is improvident inhibition of protected strikes—in practice not often undone by subsequent lifting of the restraint—through fallible factfinding or overbroad decrees.[1] The development of the preemption doctrine has made clear the central concern, in the Court's perception of national labor policy, that protected concerted activities have "breathing space to survive."[2] There is a strong federal interest in assuring that the remedial scheme by which contract rights are vindicated does not encroach unduly on protected activ-

ities.[3] Breach-of-contract suits are of course not removed from judicial cognizance, whether state or federal, but a state may now vindicate state-created rights only to the extent that they conform to the evolving federal law of labor contracts. Indeed, description of the contract rights in question as "state-created," while doubtless an accurate reflection of the traditions that move a state court to grant or deny a right of action, can probably claim no better legal credentials than those accorded harmless error. Federal law should set the outer limits of the availability of injunctive relief in actions governed by § 301.

The question therefore remains: What is the content of the relevant federal law? Some immediately visible problem areas can be readily perceived. The greater difficulty is to strike a proper balance between the demands of federal labor policy and of state procedural autonomy. The case that seems to me easiest to resolve in favor of federal restraint is the use of ex parte restraining orders. Here lies the greatest danger to federally protected rights.[4] At the same time, the interference with state procedure is relatively slight. I would argue that the spirit of Rule 65(b)[5] and NLRA section 10(l) must be observed, and that restraining orders should not be issuable without notice except on a recitation of immediate need and (more important) should be limited to a short time certain, not renewable ex parte.

More difficulty surrounds the procedure governing preliminary injunctions. One can readily state the requisites of full protection: an opportunity for an evidentiary hearing on demand; appellate or similar review within the state system; capacity of respondents under the restraint of a preliminary injunction to bring the proceedings promptly on for final hearing if desired. Here, however, countervailing consider-

---

*Excerpted from 79 HARV. L. REV. 757 (1966). Copyright © by the Harvard Law Review Association, 1966. Reprinted with permission.

1. To elaborate this problem here would by now be superfluous. See, *e.g.*, Aaron, *Labor Injunctions in the State Courts—Part II: A Critique*, 50 VA. L. REV. 1147, 1156–58 (1964).

2. The phrase is Mr. Justice Brennan's, referring to first amendment rights, in NAACP v. Button, 371 U.S. 415, 433 (1963). In the labor context, see Liner v. Jafco, Inc., 375 U.S. 301, 306–08 (1964) (danger that state law of mootness would hinder NLRB determination of legal status of picketing); Local 438, Construction Union v. Curry, 371 U.S. 542, 550 (1963) (danger that temporary injunction, if not appealable to Supreme Court, would "effectively dispose" of union's right to picket); Garner v. Teamsters Union, 346 U.S. 485, 499 (1953) (danger that state would enjoin picketing that NLRB would permit).

3. Even when state substantive law is permitted to operate, as in the case of "right to work" laws, the Court has proscribed equitable relief against strikes or picketing that is aimed at obtaining a union-security agreement violative of state law, Local 438, Construction Union v. Curry, 371 U.S. 542 (1963), while permitting the state to invalidate or hold actionable a union-security arrangement obtained through collective bargaining. Retail Clerks Int'l Ass'n v. Schermerhorn, 375 U.S. 96 (1963). A substantial reason for holding that state power "begins only with actual negotiation and execution" of the agreement, see *id.* at 105, is the danger of permitting state court litigation about the object of concerted activities to constrain protected conduct "erroneously" found to have a forbidden object. See Garner v. Teamsters Union, 346 U.S. 485, 499 (1953).

4. For the still-classic statement of the problem of "temporary" equitable relief, see FRANKFURTER & GREENE, THE LABOR INJUNCTION 200–02 (1930); on ex parte applications, see *id.* at 223.

5. FED. R. CIV. P. 65 (b).

ations seem stronger. Is it appropriate for federal common law to prescribe a particular allocation of judicial responsibilities within the state system? Assuming the availability of Supreme Court review of injunctions issued by lower state courts and not appealable under state law, does the relative inadequacy of the certiorari mechanism and its procedures for determining the question of a stay pending review warrant federal insistence on a state's creation or expansion of intramural avenues of redress?

The question of the availability of injunction bonds presents, in my view, a relatively weaker federal need. The aim of bond requirements is twofold: to discourage improper resort to equity through a financial deterrent, and to provide some recompense for respondents wrongly denied self-help at the time they chose to resort to it. When the procedures by which a state litigates equity suits are otherwise adequate to safeguard federally protected rights, I would not think that this requirement is so central to the protection of such rights that a state must provide it.

The thesis of this Comment is the presence of "federal law" apart from the Norris-LaGuardia Act. That law asks whether a particular aspect of a state's equity jurisprudence unduly threatens the policy against erosion of federally protected concerted activities. Illustrations are needed to give flesh to the underlying question, and to suggest the process of forming an answer, but it would be premature for me to press the analysis further here.[6] The concept of federal law applicable only in state courts seems a strange one. But the Norris-LaGuardia Act is an uncommon piece of legislation: Its applicability to federal court actions prevented the development of more particularized restrictions on state equity jurisdiction, but its inapplicability to state court actions does not render inapplicable all federal concern. Once the demands of the federal common law are perceived, and the governing considerations expressed, the resolution of specific problems

remains the task of that fallible, indispensable servant, "litigating elucidation."

COMMENT ON ENFORCEMENT OF ARBITRAL "INJUNCTIONS"

If arbitration is to play an effective part in giving employers the benefit of a no-strike clause, some means must be found to afford relief that will encourage its observance and to do so swiftly enough to give substance to the clause in operation.

Where a permanent arbitrator is not available, considerable time (in terms of a strike emergency) can be consumed in the selection of an arbitrator. Special contractual provisions could be written for this exigency empowering a neutral agency to appoint and to empower an arbitrator so appointed to set the time and place of the hearing on extremely short notice. The arbitrator could be empowered to rule without preparing an opinion in advance, although that removes the protection afforded by the necessity of stating cogent reasons for the conclusion reached. Courts could accord such awards presumptive validity sufficient to enforce them by temporary restraining order until any challenge to the award could be heard. Such a procedure removes the tendency of the union to delay the proceeding; indeed, all the pressures are the other way.

A final order of enforcement would be issued only after there had been full opportunity to present objections to the enforcement of the award. Presumably the appropriate grounds for contesting would not include the merits of the arbitrator's determination. Challenges to arbitral procedure and jurisdiction might be entertained by the courts. Perhaps the scope of the order, *e.g.,* enjoining members in the *New Orleans* case, would pose an issue for the court to pass upon. In line with federal labor policy, which still includes the Norris-LaGuardia Act, the courts might well decide that their supervisory role in such cases should be more exacting than where the arbitral machinery proceeds more deliberately.

For a somewhat similar analysis by a management attorney, see Herb Matthews, *Employer Initiated Grievance in the Collective Bargaining Contract: A Friendly View,* 7 SANTA CLARA LAWYER 26 (1966); and also see Merton Bernstein, *Jurisdictional Dispute Arbitration,* 14 U.C.L.A. L. REV. 347, 349–350 (1966).

---

6. Putting aside any supposed "incorporation" of Norris-LaGuardia, it seems clear that a court fashioning federal common law should not adopt a rule absolutely prohibiting specific relief against a strike in breach of contract. See *e.g.*, the discussion in WELLINGTON & ALBERT, Statutory Interpretation and the Political Process, 72 YALE L. J. 1547 (1963).

If state courts are to be permitted the exercise of equity jurisdiction denied to federal judges by the Norris-LaGuardia Act, the removal jurisdiction should not be read to permit an end-run around such jurisdiction. See the discussion in Comment, 113 U. PA. L. REV. 1096, 1097–98 (1965).

CHAPTER XV

CHOOSING APPLICABLE LAW

A large proportion of commercial transactions involves business entities and individuals of different states and, indeed, nations. Arbitration clauses are especially common in agreements involving foreign nationals, *e.g.,* charterparties and import-export trade contracts.

As a result, conflict-of-law problems lurk in many arbitration arrangements, particularly because of the variety of statutory provisions and doctrines regarding arbitration among the states and among nations. Arbitral arrangements have special problems of their own that arise from their peculiarities as a system of private dispute settlement that is sometimes dependent upon the aid of the legal machinery of government to be fully effective.

Often the parties are in different jurisdictions, the transaction touches different jurisdictions, and

the place of arbitration may be in a jurisdiction other than the residence of one or more of the parties. As a result, suits inconsistent with the undertaking to arbitrate may arise ouside the jurisdiction where arbitration should be conducted or arbitration is to take place in a jurisdiction where the respondent cannot be served. And the award may be issued in one jurisdiction (where personal jurisdiction of the respondent is not to be had), but its enforcement may be necessary in another without the possibility of reducing it to judgment in the place of issuance.

Then, too, there is the problem, not unique to arbitration but perhaps more common in commercial arbitration because of its frequently international character, of the extent to which the parties may choose the applicable law.

A.

Enforcing the Agreement to Arbitrate and Enforcing Awards in Multi-State Situations

Estate Property Corp. v. Hudson Coal Co. 132 Misc. 590, 230 N.Y. Supp. 372 (N.Y. Cty. 1928). The complaint alleged failure to maintain fixtures and equipment in proper working order and damage to leased coal mining property

located in Pennsylvania. Although not noting the place of making of the contract, the court held that the motion to stay pending arbitration was governed by Pennsylvania law, found the Pennsylvania Arbitration Act applicable, and said it would "most likely" stay the action if the defendant moved "with reasonable dispatch" to enforce the agreement to arbitrate.

MILLER v. AMERICAN INSURANCE CO.
(D.C. W.D. Ark. 1964)
124 F. Supp. 160

LEMLEY, C. J.

This cause comes on to be heard upon the defendant's plea, set out in the third paragraph of its answer, to the effect that the action has been prematurely brought and should be dismissed for that reason, and has been submitted upon written briefs. The facts necessary for decision are not in dispute and are substantially as follows:

On or about October 4, 1952, Curtis C. Miller, the plaintiff, a citizen of Texas, obtained from the defendant a policy of insurance covering a certain 1952 Model GMC truck owned by him; under the terms of this policy, which policy was written and delivered in Texas, the defendant agreed, among other things, to pay to the plaintiff the actual cash value of any loss of or damage to the truck and its equipment caused by fire. At the time the policy was issued, plaintiff's ownership of the truck was subject to a lien in favor of Yellow Manufacturing Acceptance Corporation, intervenor herein, and said policy contained a loss payable clause in favor of said corporation. On January 19, 1953, while plaintiff was driving the truck along U.S. Highway No. 71 near Mena, Arkansas, the vehicle took fire and was materially damaged. The defendant concedes that at the time of the fire the plaintiff's policy was in full force and effect. The policy contained a provision to the effect that should a loss occur and a disagreement arise as to the amount of such loss, the dispute should be submitted to arbitration. After the fire a dispute did arise between the plaintiff and the defendant as to the amount of loss, and the latter demanded arbitration in accordance with the terms of the policy. The plaintiff, however, refused to submit to such arbitration and commenced this action, after the defendant had refused to pay the amount which he demanded.

It is the contention of the defendant that since the policy in suit was a Texas policy, the validity and effect of the arbitration provision are governed by the law of that state; that under Texas law said provision is reasonable and valid, and that compliance with its terms is a condition precedent to suit. Hence, defendant argues, the plaintiff was required to submit to arbitration,

and since he refused to do so, his action is premature.

The plaintiff does not deny that the policy provision in question was valid under Texas law, nor does he deny that as a general rule the validity of contractual provisions, including provisions contained in an insurance policy, is to be determined by the law of the place where the contract is made. He contends, however, that by virtue of Act 111 of the Acts of the General Assembly of the State of Arkansas for the year 1903, Ark. Stats. 1947, § 66–509, said provision is void in Arkansas[1] that the Arkansas statute manifests a settled public policy of the State hostile to such provisions, and that the arbitration clause here involved is not enforceable in Arkansas, notwithstanding its validity in Texas.[2]

From these contentions of the parties it is clear that the problem here is purely one of conflict of laws; and in solving this problem we are required to ascertain and apply the Arkansas law of conflict of laws. Klaxon Co. v. Stentor Electric Manufacturing Co., Inc., 313 U.S. 487, 61 S.Ct. 1020, 85 L.Ed. 1477. While the Supreme Court of Arkansas has apparently not had occasion to determine whether or not Act 111 of 1903 is applicable to an insurance policy executed in another state in favor of a citizen of such state, we are satisfied from our consideration of the matter that if and when such question is presented to the Court, it will hold that said statute does not apply to an out-

---

1. The language of the statute is as follows: "No policy of insurance shall contain any condition, provision or agreement which shall directly or indirectly deprive the insured or beneficiary of the right to trial by jury on any question of fact arising under such policy, and all such provisions, conditions or agreements shall be void." There is no question that under the terms of this statute an arbitration or appraisal provision in an insurance policy written in Arkansas is void and will not be enforced by the courts of that State. Firemen's Insurance Co. v. Davis, 130 Ark. 576, 198 S.W. 127, Insurance Company of North America. v. Kempner, 132 Ark. 215, 200 S.W. 986, and Papan v. Resolute Insurance Co., 219 Ark. 907, 911, 245 S.W. 2d 565.

2. In 15 C.J.S., Conflict of Laws, § 4, p. 853, it is said: "It is thoroughly established as a broad general rule that foreign law or rights based thereon will not be given effect or enforced if opposed to the settled public policy of the forum." A number of cases, both state and federal, are cited in support of that statement, and counsel for the plaintiff have cited us to certain similar cases, none of which, however, is squarely in point. Prior to the enactment of Act 350 of 1951 the Courts of Arkansas, in the application of this principle, refused to enforce provisions in promissory notes for the payment of attorneys' fees, notwithstanding the validity of such provisions under the laws of the states where the notes were executed or were payable. Arden Lumber Co. v. Henderson Iron Works & Supply Co., 83 Ark. 240, 103 S.W. 185; White-Wilson-Drew Co. v. Egelhoff, 96 Ark. 105, 131 S.W. 208.

of-state policy, and will uphold an arbitration provision in such a policy if valid under the law of the state where the policy was executed; and we so hold in the instant case.

The general rule that a contractual provision which offends the settled public policy of the forum will not be enforced notwithstanding its validity under the *lex loci contracti* is not one of universal application. Such is applicable only in cases where the public policy which is offended is a *strong* public policy of the forum; to hold otherwise would leave practically nothing of the rule that the validity of a contract is governed by the law of the place where the contract is made and would do violence to the doctrine of comity upon which so much of the law of conflict of laws is built.

The mere fact that a contractual provision, valid under the *lex loci contracti,* is violative of a statute of the forum does not necessarily mean, as the plaintiff appears to contend, that said provision will not be enforced at the forum. This is illustrated by the decisions in Dodd v. Axle-Nut Sign Co., 126 Ark. 14, 189 S.W. 663, Smith v. Brokaw, 174 Ark. 609, 297 S.W. 1031, and Swann v. Swann, C.C. Ark., 21 F. 299. In Dodd v. Axle-Nut Sign Co. the defendant executed in Missouri a note evidencing the unpaid purchase price for certain rights in a patented article, which note was secured by a mortgage on Arkansas land; said note was valid under the laws of Missouri but was invalid under the Arkansas law because it did not comply with the provisions of Act 162 of 1891, Ark. Stats. 1947, § 68–901, which required such notes to be executed on a printed form and to show on their face for what they were given. Suit on the note and mortgage was brought in Arkansas, and in allowing recovery the Court applied the law of Missouri notwithstanding the provisions of the Arkansas statute. In the *Brokaw* case a note and a mortgage covering Arkansas land were executed in Oklahoma; the note was valid under Oklahoma law but was absolutely void for usury under the provisions of Article 19, Section 13 of the Arkansas Constitution of 1874, as implemented by Act 56 of 1875, Ark. Stats. 1947, §§ 68–602, 68–603 and 68–608; the Court in allowing recovery applied Oklahoma law. And in *Swann v. Swann* suit was brought in a federal court in Arkansas upon a note executed in Tennessee on a Sunday; the note was valid under Tennessee law but was invalid in Arkansas by virtue of an Arkansas statute, Rev. Stat. Ch. 44, div. 7, art. 2, sec. 1; Ark. Stats. 1947, § 41–3801; the Court allowed recovery by applying the *lex loci contracti.* It will be seen from these decisions that Arkansas has a public policy against Sunday

contracts and a public policy against notes given to evidence the purchase price of patented articles unless such notes are in a certain form, both of which policies are expressed in statutes, and that Arkansas likewise has a public policy against usury, expressed both in her Constitution and in her statutes; none of such policies, however, has been considered sufficiently strong to prompt the Arkansas courts to apply the *lex fori* rather than the *lex loci.*

In 15 C.J.S., Conflict of Laws, § 4 at page 855, it is said that:

> It is usually held that to justify a court in refusing to give effect to or enforce foreign law or rights because it would be against public policy, it must appear that it would be against good morals or natural justice, or for some other reason would be prejudicial to the state or its citizens, the mere fact that the law of two states or nations differs not necessarily implying that the law of one violates the public policy of the other.

There is certainly nothing inherently wrong, immortal or against natural justice in arbitation agreements; on the contrary, the modern tendency of the courts is to look with favor upon such agreements, at least to some extent. See in this connection our opinion in W. R. Grimshaw Co. v. Nazareth Literary & Benevolent Institution, D.C. Ark., 113 F. Supp. 564. Nor do we think that to uphold the arbitration provision included in the policy in suit would in any manner prejudice the State of Arkansas or any of her citizens. Granting that Arkansas has the right to protect her own citizens from policy provisions of this kind, and that she has made void by statute such provisions in insurance policies written in this State, it does not follow that she has any legitimate interest in regulating the dealings between insurance companies and citizens of other states expressed in insurance policies written and delivered elsewhere. On the contrary, it seems to us that to so hold would be to give an unreasonable out-of-state scope to a statute, which we think was designed for the protection of Arkansas people. In this connection we feel that the language of the Court in Dodd v. Axle-Nut Sign Co., *supra,* is applicable here; it was there said:

> This statute was intended for the protection of the citizens of the state, and makes void all notes given for patent rights or territory which are executed in this state and do not comply with the statute.... We do not think, however, the section has any application to the facts of the instant case. The original contract was executed at St. Louis, in the state of Missouri. It was a Missouri contract. No attempt is made to show that the original note and contract was not valid under the laws of the state of Missouri. Consequently the contract was

valid under the laws of that state, and it will be enforced and adjudicated in the courts of this state precisely as it would be adjudicated in the courts of the state of Missouri. 126 Ark. at page 18, 189 S.W. at page 664.

Moreover, there was far more reason in both the *Axle-Nut* case and the *Brokaw* case to apply the rule upon which the plaintiff here relies than there is in the instant case, since the notes sued on in both of those cases were secured by mortgages on Arkansas land, whereas here the only connection between Arkansas and this policy and the truck covered thereby, other than the fact that the suit, a transitory action, has been filed here, arises out of the circumstance that the truck caught fire near Mena. We might point out that if the plaintiff is correct in his argument, the same result would be reached regardless of whether the truck burned in Arkansas, or Texas, or elsewhere ; thus, regardless of where a policy of insurance might be written, or where the insured might live, or where the loss might occur, the insured could nullify the arbitration clause in his policy by the simple device of suing in Arkansas, provided that he could get service. We do not ascribe to the Arkansas Legislature an intent to give to its enactment such a sweeping, and, to our mind, unreasonable extra-territorial effect.

Our decision that the suit has been prematurely brought renders it unnecessary to state or to discuss other issues presented by the pleadings. Let an order be entered dismissing the case, without prejudice to future action after an appraisal has been had.

NIPPON-KI-ITO KAISHA, LTD v. EWING-THOMAS CORPORATION
313 PA. 442, 170 A. 286 (1934)

SIMPSON, J. Plaintiff, a Japanese corporation having an office in the City of New York, by three several written contracts, agreed to sell to defendant, a corporation of this Commonwealth with its principal office in our City of Chester, and the latter agreed to buy one hundred bales of raw silk, of the character and at the prices specified therein. Each of the contracts provided that "All of the terms and provisions of the raw silk rules of the Silk Association of America, Inc., approved and adopted by its board of managers, December 10, 1924, and all subsequent amendments thereto, not inconsistent herewith, are incorporated as a part of this contract"; and each agreement further specified that "Every dispute, of whatever character, arising out of this con-

tract, must be settled by arbitration in New York, to be conducted in the manner provided by the by-laws, rules and regulations of the Silk Association of America, Inc., governing arbitrations."

Plaintiff delivered all the silk provided for in said contracts, but defendant paid less than one-half the contract price, alleging, as its reason for refusing to pay the balance, that the silk was of a quality inferior to that contracted for. Plaintiff denied this, and proposed to defendant that the dispute between them should be "settled by arbitration in New York, to be conducted in the manner provided in the by-laws, rules and regulations of the Silk Association of America, Inc., governing arbitrators," as the several contracts between the parties stipulated "must" be the course pursued under such circumstances. To this defendant refused to agree, whereupon plaintiff filed a petition, as provided by § 3 of our Arbitration Act of April 25, 1927, P. L. 381, setting forth the facts and praying an order on defendant to show cause why this dispute "should not be submitted to arbitration in the manner provided for in said contracts." This section of the statute provides:

> The party aggrieved by the alleged failure, neglect or refusal of another to perform under a written agreement for arbitration, may petition the court of common pleas of the county having jurisdiction for an order to show cause why such arbitration should not proceed in the manner provided for in such agreement.

Defendant, instead of making answer to this petition, filed a counter petition asking the court to "preliminarily determine certain questions of jurisdiction in this case, in accordance with the provisions of the Act of Assembly of March 5, 1925, P. L. 23." Seven such questions were stated therein but they raise only a single point, viz.: "Whether our [Arbitration] Act of April 25, 1927, P. L. 381, is applicable to a proceeding to compel the parties to arbitrate their disputes in a foreign jurisdiction," here in New York. Upon this petition, also, a rule to show cause was granted, and after argument, the court below filed an opinion and made the following order: "And now, to wit, June 1, 1933, it is ordered and decreed that the petition of the defendant raising questions of jurisdiction be and the same is hereby sustained, and it is further ordered and decreed that the plaintiff's petition be and the same is hereby refused." From this order plaintiff appealed. It must be reversed.

Although the same reasons are given by the court below for both parts of its order, a distinct and separate reason exists for reversing the first part, viz., the Act of 1925 does not apply to the existing situation. We have several times said, and the statute clearly shows, that it applies only in cases where the court below has no jurisdiction over the parties or over the subject-matter of the particular litigation: Skelton v. Lower Merion Twp., 298 Pa. 471 ; Gray v. Camac, 304 Pa. 74. Here, both plaintiff and defendant appeared generally before the court, and hence it had jurisdiction over them. It also had jurisdiction to decide whether or not defendant can be required to proceed to arbitration in New York, for § 3 of the Arbitration Act expressly gives it such jurisdiction. That it may ultimately decide it has no power to so require, does not deprive it of jurisdiction to decide the question ; rather it affirms the jurisdiction.

Apparently this matter was not brought to the attention of the court below, possibly because all the points raised by defendant's counter petition were applicable to the questions raised by plaintiff's petition requiring defendant to show cause why it should not submit the dispute to arbitration. This being so, we will treat the facts averred in defendant's petition as an answer to that of plaintiff, and determine the appeal accordingly.

One of the points strenuously argued by defendant, though not referred to in the opinion of the court below, is that even if we should hold the language of our statute was broad enough to compel defendant to go to New York to arbitrate the disputes which had arisen, we should not so construe it, because, under like circumstances, the courts of that state would not compel her citizens to come into Pennsylvania to arbitrate their disputes. It is difficult to see upon what principle we could so decide, even if the courts of New York had so held, since it is our duty to determine all legal questions raised in accordance with the law as we understand it, no matter what the courts of other states may do, unless, indeed, the question raised is as to what is the law of such other state.

The law of New York is not correctly stated by defendant, however. At one time, prior to the passage of their Arbitration Act (which is in all substantial respects and much of it in the same language as ours), it was there held as defendant contends, but the reverse is true since the passage of that statute. The Court of Appeals, in Gilbert v. Burnstine, 255 N.Y. 348,—the latest case on the subject,—by an unanimous vote so decided. [A summary of that case and quotations from the opinion of the Court of Appeals are omitted.]

With this statement of the law we are in entire accord, though we are not required to go so far in the present case. That decision is based upon the doctrine of inviolability of contracts which has been a cardinal principle in the constitutional law of both the nation and the state ever since they have existed as such. As the years go by, and we are brought face to face with many ingenious attempts to evade or qualify it, we are increasingly convinced of the necessity for holding fast to this ancient landmark of our constitutional existence. This is a complete answer to every argument now made to sustain the order of the court below. It might be well, however, to refer, as briefly as we may, to some of those arguments, lest it be thought we have not given due consideration to them.

The principal contention made in the opinion of the Court below, is that our Arbitration Act relates only to arbitrations to be held in Pennsylvania. The statute does not say so, and the argument brought forward to show that under §§ 6, 10 and 11 that conclusion must be implied, is not only both labored and inconclusive, but also wholly overlooks other sections of the act. Moreover it ignores the legal principle that it is our duty to sustain the act, if this can reasonably be done, and not to destroy it either in whole or in part.

The court below calls attention to the fact that § 6 says that if witnesses summoned by the arbitrators "refuse . . . to obey said summons, upon petition, the court of common pleas of the county in which such arbitrators are sitting" may compel them to appear and testify. It does so say, but therefrom there is no justification for the conclusion of the court below "that this clearly indicates that the legislature intended that the act should only apply to situations where the arbitrators were sitting in Pennsylvania." If the arbitrators were sitting in New York and the witnesses were in Pennsylvania, that provision could be applied, but it could not be applied to cases where the witnesses were not in Pennsylvania, no matter where the arbitrators were sitting. Consequently, it might more accurately be inferred "that this [section of the statute] clearly indicates that the legislature intended that the act should only apply to situations where "all the important witnesses in the cause are to be found in Pennsylvania." No one suggests this, however. What the provision under consideration does mean is, that in the case of recalcitrant witnesses, the court of common pleas of the county where the arbitrators are sitting cannot escape acting because the suit is pending in some other county. By this section of the act the former court is given additional jurisdiction under the circumstances stated.

As to §§ 10 and 11 the court below says:

> Furthermore, §§ 10 and 11 indicate that the court should have jurisdiction over the arbitrators themselves [as indeed it does in the many instances provided for in the act]. Section 10 provides that "where an award is vacated . . . the court may, in its discretion, direct a rehearing by the arbitrators." Should this situation later arise, and we should direct a rehearing, we would have no means of enforcing such an order. The legislature certainly never intended that the court should issue a useless order, and it further indicates that the act refers only to cases where the arbitration is proceeding within the State of Pennsylvania. The same reasoning applies to § 11 which provides that "the court may modify and correct the award or resubmit the matter to the arbitrators."

If we assume that all these difficulties are possibilities, defendant is not helped. It was bound to know the law, and yet, notwithstanding that, agreed, for a valuable consideration, to the arbitration out of which these difficulties are conjured. Suppose, as here, the jurisdictional county was Delaware, and the arbitrators chose to sit in Erie, nearly all of the difficulties suggested would exist, exactly as if they were sitting in New York, and in many respects the annoyances would be greater. It has not infrequently occurred, under ealier statutes, that arbitrators have refused to sit, or have disappeared before their first report was completed, or could not be found when the court vacated that report, yet, so far as we are aware, no one ever suggested that those acts were unenforceable. Indeed, all such objections, properly appraised, relate to the entire system of arbitration, which by § 1 of our Arbitration Act is approved as part of the public policy of this Commonwealth. If the statute does not cover every possible situation which may arise,—and this is the basis of these objections,—doubtless the court below and the counsel in the case, especially under the authority contained in other sections of the act, will readily find a way to surmount such difficulties. The proceeding in the court below is, in effect, a bill for specific performance of the arbitration provisions of the contracts (Red Cross Line v. Atlantic Fruit Co., 264 U.S. 109, 124), and the scope of the chancellor's power in that character of case is probably broad enough to overcome all such difficulties.

Section 5 of the act provides that "The respective courts of common pleas shall have the power to make and adopt rules concerning procedure and practice under this act, as shall seem to them proper, except that no rule shall make any provision contrary to the *express* provisions of this act." Section 7 says: "Upon petition, approved by the arbitrators, the court may direct the taking of depositions on behalf of any party, to be used in evidence before the arbitrators, in accordance with existing law with respect to depositions." And § 9 and the later sections appear to cover every point which may arise after the filing of the arbitral award, and give to the court complete control thereover. Without much difficulty these several sections of the statute could probably be utilized to overcome every fearsome doubt, now seemingly harassing appellee and the court below, but if not the remedy is for the legislature and not for the courts.

When, then, plaintiff showed to the court below that the contracts in suit contained a valid provision for arbitration, as binding as any other provision in the contract, and defendant did not allege anything which denied its free execution of the contract, and pointed to no taint in it, but simply denied the right of the court below to enforce it, although defendant had received and was retaining the consideration given for it, the court below should have said to defendant that the constitutional public policy of the nation and the state alike require us to enforce such contracts, and not to aid in defeating them either in whole or in part, especially where, as here, the only antagonistic reasons given are based solely on imaginary fears and not upon facts. Defendant was not compelled to enter into a contract with that provision in it, but, having done so and having received the benefit thereby arising, must stand to that which it voluntarily agreed to do. To hold otherwise would be against the principles of elementary justice, and so the court below should have decided in this case. As it did not do so, we will.

The order of the court below is reversed, defendant's petition is dismissed, and the record is remitted that an order may be forthwith entered in accordance with the prayer of plaintiff's petition, the litigation, thereafter to proceed to final judgment and recovery thereon sec. leg.

MARCHANT v. MEAD-MORRISON MFG. CO.
258 N.Y. 284, 169 N.E. 386 (1929)

CARDOZO, CH. J. By contract dated May 25, 1922, Mead-Morrison Manufacturing Company, a Maine corporation, agreed to sell to Bear Tractors, Inc., a New York corporation, 500 tractors to be manufactured according to specifications and to the delivered in installments. There was an arbitration clause in the following form:

> If for any reason any controversy or difference of opinion shall arise as to the construction of the terms and conditions of this contract, or as to its performance, it is mutually agreed that the matter in dispute shall be settled by arbitration, each party to select an arbitrator, and the two so selected to select a third, and the decision of the majority of such arbitrators given after a full hearing and consideration of the matter in controversy shall be final and binding upon the parties, and a condition precedent to any suit upon or by reason of any such controversy or difference. The cost of such arbitration shall be paid by the party against whom the majority of such arbitrators render such decision.

The contract was closed in East Boston, Mass., and there the tractors were to be manufactured and delivery was to be made.

Bear Tractors, Inc., the buyer, became bankrupt in May, 1924. Two years had then passed since the making of the contract, but of the 500 tractors only part had been received, and these after they were due according to the schedule for deliveries. Seller and buyer each laid the blame upon the other. A controversy having thus arisen as to the performance of the contract, the trustee in bankruptcy made demand that it be settled by arbitration. Each of the parties nominated an arbitrator. The two so selected were unable to agree upon a third. The deadlock, if not broken, would have made the settlement abortive. In this impasse, the trustee moved the court that it designate a third arbitrator in accordance with the statute (Arbitration Law, § 4; Consol. Laws, ch. 72). The seller appeared generally, and opposed the granting of the petition. The chief ground of its resistance was that the arbitration clause should be interpreted as providing for an arbitration in Massachusetts, and nowhere else. The objection was overruled, and the prayer of the petition granted. A third arbitrator was designated by the court to act with the same force and effect as if named in the contract, and the parties were directed to proceed to arbitration before the tribunal thus established. Upon appeal to the Appellate Division, the order was affirmed without opinion (215 App. Div. 759). A motion for leave to appeal to this court was made and denied.

There followed a long contest with twenty-seven hearings, thousands of pages of testimony, and hundreds of exhibits. At its close a majority of the arbitrators filed a report to the effect that the seller had made default in the performance of the contract, and that its default had brought about the bankruptcy of the buyer with a loss of all the capital invested in the enterprise. The capital thus lost, excluding moneys not invested in reliance on the contract, was fixed in the report at $849,006.76. The award was for the amount with the costs of the proceeding.

From the judgment entered on the award there was an appeal to the Appellate Division by the seller, the defendant in the arbitration. The Appellate Division held by a divided court that in respect of a separable provision the award was in excess of the powers of the arbitrators. Buyer and seller, plaintiff and defendant, had been directed to proceed to arbitration in accordance with the contract. The powers of the arbitrators were thus measured by the contract, and did not extend to controversies beyond the terms of the submission. There was power to determine the fact of performance or nonperformance by one party or the other. There was no power to assess the damages resulting to the buyer's business by reason of the breach. The judgment was, therefore, modified by striking out the award of damages, and as modified affirmed.

Cross-appeals are now before us. The seller, the defendant in the arbitration, is dissatisfied because the award has been allowed to stand as an adjudication of its fault. The buyer, the plaintiff in the arbitration, is dissatisfied because the damages, if there have been any, must be assessed and recovered through proceedings in the courts.

The appeal by the defendant is a challenge to the order directing arbitration. The challenge must be heeded even now if the order is merely void, an assumption of unlicensed power. The award can be no stronger than the prop on which it rests. The challenge comes too late, however, if power being present, there has been merely error in the use of it (Fauntleroy v. Lum, 210 U.S. 230, 235; Marin v. Augedahl, 247 U.S. 142, 149; Wagner Co v. Lyndon, 262 U.S. 226, 231) An order for the specific performance of an agreement to arbitrate a controversy is one that finally determines a special proceeding (Hosiery Manufacturers Corp v. Goldston, 238 N.Y. 22, 25, 26). The proceeding thus ended is not a part of the arbitration that is thereby set in motion. It is subject to direct review as a separate controversy. Like any other final order, the mandate, unless void, is not assailable collaterally.

Two reasons are advanced by counsel for the seller why the order has collapsed for defect of jurisdiction.

The order, it is said, is void, because the parties to the contract in agreeing to arbitrate their differences had in view an arbitration in Massachusetts, and not performance somewhere else. Whether this was their meaning was, however, a question of construction, to be determined like any other question of construction by the judge receiving the petition. Jurisdiction was not dependent upon his determining it correctly. We must distinguish between the place of performance in respect of manufacture and delivery and the place of performance for the settlement of differences. The contract was to be performed in Massachusetts to the extent that the things to be sold were to be there manufactured and delivered. The conclusion does not follow of necessity that the remedy prescribed for the settlement of differences was to be sought in the same forum. At common law, general contracts of arbitration, though not specifically enforceable, were not held to be illegal. This is seen from the fact that in case they were broken there might be a recovery of damages (Matter of Berkovitz v. Arbib & Houlberg, Inc., 230 N.Y. 261, 271 ; Red Cross Line v. Atlantic Fruit Co., 264 U.S. 109, 121). The statute of New York does not bring the contract into being, but adds a new implement, the remedy of specific performance, for its more effectual enforcement. This remedy may lawfully be extended to contracts of manufacture made in Massachusetts and there to be performed, unless it is one of the terms of the arbitration clause, implied if not express, that the arbitration shall proceed in a particular locality. Express restriction there is none in the contract now before us. Whether one is to be implied is a question of intention to be determined in the light of context and occasion. That is what was done. The court in the discharge of its judicial function was called upon to declare the implications of the promise. We do not say at this time that the determination was free from error. Enough for present purposes that it is not to be ignored as void.

A second objection, more perplexing, is urged now for the first time. The order, it is said, is void, in so far as it appoints a third arbitrator, not nominated by the other two, but designated by the court. The effect of such an order, we are told, is not merely to give specific performance in New York of a contract to arbitrate made in Massachusetts: the effect is to nullify the contract by exacting a form of arbitration inconsistent with the promise. The parties promised to submit to the decision of two men chosen by themselves and of a third to be chosen by the two. They said nothing in the contract as to the choice of a third if the two could not agree. The statute of New York to the effect that in the event of a lapse for this or other cause a third arbitrator or an umpire may be designated by the court is binding in respect of contracts made in our State or in contemplation of our laws. It is then read into the contract as an implied

term of the engagement. To read it into contracts made in other States and without reference to our laws, is something very different. The law of the forum tells us whether the remedy for the breach of an agreement shall be specific performance or damages. The law of the place of contract defines the content of the agreement upon which the remedy shall operate. A State is without power to modify by its statutes the terms, express or implied, of contracts made in other States in contemplation of their laws. The case may be supposed of an agreement made in Boston that a controversy shall be arbitrated by the Chamber of Commerce of that city, with the express provision that in no event shall there be arbitration by any one else. If the law of Massachusetts refuses to permit the appointment of a substitute, the law of New York may not modify by statute the content of the promise, and designate a substitute in the teeth of the agreement. The defendant would have us hold that this is what was done.

We think the argument is fallacious in assuming as a premise that there has been nullification of a contract under the compulsion of a statute rather than enforcement of the contract by discarding the subordinate and preserving the essential.

A helpful analogy may be found in contracts for the sale of land or for the renewal of leases at a price or a rental to be fixed by appraisers appointed by the parties. The method of selection may fail, and yet the court may give effect to the dominant intention through the agency of appraisers chosen by itself and subject to its scrutiny (Mutual Life Ins. Co. v. Stephens, 214 N.Y. 488, 495). Nice distinctions must then be drawn between a method of selection that is an auxiliary incident and one so wrought into the substance, so much a part of an organic whole, as to be accounted of the essence (Castle Creek Water Co. v. City of Aspen, 146 Fed. Rep. 8, 12 ; Kaufman v. Liggett, 209 Penn. St. 87 ; Grosvenor v. Flint, 20 R. I. 21 ; Kelso v. Kelly, 1 Daly, 419 ; Weir v. Barker, 104 App. Div. 112 ; State Reserve Bank v. Swift & Co., 32 Fed. Rep. [2d] 590 ; Dinham v. Bradford, L. R. [5 Ch. App.] 518 ; FRY ON SPECIFIC PERF. [6th ed.] §§ 355 to 364). The line of division is often shadowy and doubtful.

Contracts to submit to arbitration must answer to like tests, elusive though they be. There may be a dominant intention to arbitrate at all events, the machinery of selection being merely modal and subordinate. If so, the failure of the means will not involve as a consequence the frustration of the end. Equity will give specific performance of the principal engagement with variations of method appropriate to the facts. "It is the privilege of a Court in such circumstances and it is its duty to come to the assistance of parties by the removal of the impasse and the extrication of their rights" (Cameron v. Cuddy, L. R. [1914] App. Cas. 651, 656). On the other hand, the promise to arbitrate may be so wedded to the means that the failure of the one will be the destruction of the other.

We are not required to determine whether there was error in the ruling that the means were in this instance subordinate and incidental rather than indispensable and primary. We are to determine merely this, whether there was a question of intention exacting for its answer the application of the judicial mind, the comparison and appraisal of analogies and precedents. If so, the determination, however erroneous, is proof against attack, unless challenged by direct review (Schuylkill Fuel Corp. v. Nieberg Realty Corp. 250 N.Y. 304, 306). The separating line between nullity and error is not an easy one to draw. If a court were to order arbitration under the mere impulse of a desire to settle a controversy expeditiously and cheaply, reciting, however, in the order that no contract to arbitrate had been made by the contending parties, its determination would be void, for power in such circumstances would be lacking altogether (Vallely v. Northern Fire Ins. Co., 254 U.S. 348, 353 ; Yamashita v. Hinkle, 260 U.S. 199 ; United States v. Walker, 109 U.S. 258, 266). On the other hand, if a court were to find the existence of such a promise upon insufficient evidence, or were to enlarge through misconstruction the scope of a submission, an award dependent upon such an order could not be treated as a nullity (Fauntleroy v. Lum, *supra*). The question like so many others is one of proportion and degree.

With this line of approach, the pathway becomes visible. We assume in favor of the defendant that it is possible to phrase an arbitration clause with a method of selection so transparently essential as to leave no room whatever for the process of construction. This might be so, for illustration, if there were a promise to arbitrate through a named person, and no one else (cf. Matter of Inter-Ocean Food Products, Inc., 206 App. Div. 426). Here, on the contrary, promise and intention are not so free from uncertainty that construction is impossible. In the forefront of the clause is the statement of the dominant purpose that controversies of a given order shall be settled by arbitration. What follows may be figured, at least with a show of reason, as incidental and subsidiary. The error, if it be assumed, is not so utterly indefensible, so free from the possibility of genuine contest

and debate, as to be equivalent to defect of power. If contracts to arbitrate had been subject to specific performance at common law, no one would be likely to urge that under a contract such as this a decree subordinating a method of choice to a supposed dominant intention could be disregarded as a nullity. The result is no different now that specific performance has its basis in the statute. There is significance in the form of order that was upheld by this court in Matter of Berkovitz v. Arbib & Houlberg, Inc. (*supra*), and by the Supreme Court of the United States in Red Cross Line v. Atlantic Fruit Co. (*supra*). Provision was made in each case for the appointment of an umpire to be designated by the court, though the contracts of arbitration made before the adoption of the statute called for an appointment upon the nomination of the arbitrators. True, the point was not urged in those cases any more than it was in this that as to contracts antedating the statue the choice must adhere to the form exacted by the parties. Even so, the orders as entered are pregnant with the assumption that the means might be varied in adaptation to the end. If there was error in the assumption, we think it was not so gross in either case that the decree became a nullity.

IN THE MATTER OF GANTT
(HURTADO & CIA)
297 N.Y. 433, 79 N.E. 2d 815 (1948)

DESMOND, J. Petitioner Gantt is a North Carolina lumber dealer, using the business name of Southland Supply Company. Respondent Hurtado & Cia., Ltda., is a Nicaraguan partnership (or corporation) doing business in that Republic. In July, 1946, at High Point, North Carolina, an authorized representative of Hurtado made two written agreements with "Southland Supply Company," the signatures of the latter being by W. O. Carter, who, in one of those agreements, styled himself "Manager" but whose authority to contract for petitioner Gantt is now disputed by the latter. Each of these July, 1946 writings called for the sale and delivery by Hurtado to "Southland Supply Company," of large quantities of various kinds of tropical woods to be shipped from Nicaraguan ports, at prices f.o.b. those ports, to High Point. Each of those agreements called for the opening by the buyer, for the seller, of an irrevocable letter of credit, the place where such letter of credit was to be obtained not being stated. Both those July, 1946, agreements were modified in various respects by a third document, signed at High Point in September of that year by a representative of Hurtado and by "Southland Supply Company, W. O. Carter." The September pact contained the first mention of arbitration, the language being:

> Any controversy or claims arising out of or relating to this contract or the breach thereof shall be settled by arbitration in accordance with the rules of the Inter-American Commercial Arbitration Commission. This agreement shall be enforceable and judgment upon any award rendered by the arbitrators or a majority of them may be entered in any Court having jurisdiction. The arbitration shall be held in New York, N.Y.

Later in September, 1946, respondent Hurtado, asserting that there had been a violation of contract by Southland Supply Company (or Gantt), in the latter's alleged failure to set up the promised letter of credit, served on Southland a demand for arbitration before the Inter-American Commercial Arbitration Commission. Gantt did not reply to that demand, but commenced in Supreme Court, New York County, the present proceeding to restrain the proposed arbitration, alleging in his petition that Carter had signed the September, 1946, agreement without authority from him (Gantt). Petitioner first applied for a temporary order to restrain the arbitration pending a jury trial, which petitioner requested, of the preliminary question as to Carter's authority (see Civ. Prac. Act, § 1458). That motion was granted at Special Term but immediately afterwards, and before the jury trial could be held (it has not yet been held, we are informed) petitioner Gantt made a further motion, this time for a permanent stay of arbitration, on the ground that the arbitration clause was wholly void by the laws of North Carolina, where the paper in which it appears was signed, and that therefore, according to petitioner, he could not be compelled to enter into any arbitration, anywhere. Special Term denied that second motion, holding that the arbitration clause, in its specific declaration that any arbitration was to "be held in New York, N.Y." amounted to an unconditional consent by the parties to submit their contests to arbitration in New York State under New York arbitration procedures, and that, whether or not such an arbitration covenant could be enforced in North Carolina, it was enforceable under the law of the forum, i.e., New York. The Appellate Division, First Department, unanimously affirmed without opinion but granted petitioner Gantt leave to appeal to this court, certifying to us a question as to whether the order denying petitioner a permanent stay, was properly made.

We deal first with the question of the legality of the arbitration clause, since if it be entirely void, as petitioner argues, the case ends there. North Carolina has an arbitration statute (General Statutes of North Carolina, 1943, div. II, ch. 1, art. 45), but unlike our New York article 84 of the Civil Practice Act, the North Carolina enactment covers and enforces only agreements to submit *existing* controversies to arbitration. It does not mention at all the kind of arbitration covenant we have before us—a covenant to arbitrate controversies thereafter arising—and so we turn (see Tarpley v. Arnold, 226 N.C. 679, 680) to the North Carolina case law to see whether the clause here under scrutiny is good, or bad, in North Carolina. Petitioner says it is totally void for all purposes, under North Carolina law, but his reliance at this point seems to be entirely on the use of the word "void" in Williams v. Branning Mfg. Co. (154 N.C. 205). An examination of that decision, and a number of others in North Carolina's highest court, convinces us that North Carolina's common law does not declare such covenants to be nullities without any legal existence or effect, but merely refuses to compel parties to arbitrate thereunder (see Williams v. Branning Mfg. Co., earlier appeal, 153 N.C. 7, 10; Nelson v. Atlantic Coast Line R. R. Co., 157 N.C. 194, 202, and particularly Tarpley v. Arnold, *supra*, 226 N.C. at p. 680). The second *Williams* case (*supra*), itself, as well as Tarpley v. Arnold (*supra*), and others of the above-cited North Carolina cases, plainly shows that such agreements are given some effect by the North Carolina courts, since awards based thereon may be the subject of suits and defenses. In other words, North Carolina's common law as to arbitration is substantially the same as was the common law in New York before our Legislature dealt with the whole matter of arbitration, and as it was, and is, in other States.

Having thus found that the arbitration treaty we are passing on was not void but unenforceable only, at the place where made, we turn to the question of whether it may be compulsorily enforced by the courts of New York. The place of performance of the arbitration section, though not of the other parts of the September agreement, was to be New York. The New York statute (Civ. Prac. Act, art. 84) provides complete compulsion and full enforcement, as to such promises to arbitrate future-arising disputes. It is the law of the forum which, traditionally, controls as to remedies (M'Elmoyle v. Cohen, 13 Pet. [U.S.] 312; Franklin Sugar Refining Co. v. Lipowicz, 247 N.Y. 465, 469; Mertz v. Mertz, 271 N.Y. 466, 473; RESTATEMENT, CONFLICT OF LAWS § 585). An agreement that all differences arising under a contract shall be submitted to arbitration relates to the law of remedies, and the law that governs remedies is the law of the forum" wrote Judge Cardozo in his concurring opinion in Meacham v. Jamestown, F. & C. R. R. Co. (211 N.Y. 346, 352.) The rule thus expressed is well settled by other decisions (Red Cross Line v. Atlantic Fruit Co., 264 U.S. 109, 124, *supra*; 230 N.Y. at p. 270; Gilbert v. Burnstine, 255 N.Y. 348, 354) and text writers (2 BEALE ON CONFLICT OF LAWS [1935] p. 1158). It may be that, in other States in which there might be future litigation over any award here made, the law in this respect is different. But these parties solemnly promised to arbitrate their controversies in New York, and by case and statue the law of New York then was, and now is, that such an agreement is "a consent of the parties thereto to the jurisdiction of the supreme court of this state to enforce such contract or submission" (Civ. Prac. Act, § 1450—see Matter of Zimmerman v. Cohen, 236 N.Y. 15; Gilbert v. Burnstine, *supra*, 255 N.Y. at p. 354).

Petitioner insists that all this has been changed by Order of Travelers v. Wolfe (331 U.S. 586). We, however, do not think that decision wipes out the old rule that remedies, including arbitration, are regulated by the law of the forum. The *Wolfe* decision (*supra*), as the Supreme Court opinions show, deals with a special situation. The majority opinion itself (at p. 607) says that the court was dealing with a "comparatively narrow issue" and states a distinction between the cause under review and M'Elmoyle v. Cohen (*supra*). Order of Travelers v. Wolfe (*supra*) was an action brought by an Ontario citizen in a South Dakota court for insurance benefits due because of the death of a South Dakota citizen whose life had been insured by the defendant order, an Ohio fraternal society of which the deceased had been a member. A statute of Ohio specifically authorized such a fraternal order to limit the time within which suits could be brought on its certificates. The defendant association had limited the time to six months after acrual, but a South Dakota statute allowed such suits to be brought within six years. The Supreme Court held, as we read the majority opinion, not that the law of the forum (South Dakota) would not, ordinarily, be applicable as to remedies, but only that, under the peculiar set-up of a mutual benefit society, an agreement by its members, expressed in a by-law provisions limiting the time for instituting actions, was so much a part of the members' mutual engagements with one another, that such a by-law would prevail over a statute, otherwise applicable, of the State wherein the suit was brought.

What we have said herein will, we think, serve as an answer to petitioner's contention that the refusal of the permanent stay of this arbitration deprives him of the privileges and immunities he is entitled to under section 2 of article IV of the United States Constitution and his further contention that to allow the arbitration to proceed in New York will be to refuse full faith and credit to the laws of North Carolina. The pertinent North Carolina law, as we have seen, goes only so far as to deny enforceability in its courts to such an arbitration clause, while these parties covenanted that they would, in case of dispute, go into New York State and there submit to an arbitration under the New York statutes; the New York statutes fully enforce such agreements and provide court machinery for compelling the parties to go through with their own arrangements for the settlement of their differences in a private tribunal of their own selection, rather than in a court of law.

The other objection in point of law (briefly referred to at the beginning of this opinion) which petitioner enters against the maintenance of this arbitration, is based on the fact that the agreements were, at least in form, not signed by petitioner but by W. O. Carter, styling himself the "Manager" of "Southland Supply Company." The dispute of fact as to whether Carter was authorized so to contract, was, as we have said, set down, on petitioner's application, for a jury trial. But petitioner goes further and says that a New York statute (Civ. Prac. Act, § 1449) makes entirely illegal in New York an arbitration agreement not signed by the parties themselves. Section 1449 says, in part: "A contract to arbitrate a controversy thereafter arising between the parties must be in writing." Obviously, this contract was in writing. There is no statutory prohibition, in our statute, of signature by an agent, nor any command that, if an agent sign, his authority must be shown in the agreement. We think petitioner's rights are fully protected by the Special Term order sending to a jury trial the question of whether or not Carter was in fact authorized to commit petitioner to the arbitration of such differences as might arise. Much is said in the briefs concerning the second sentence, not applicable here, of section 1449, which second sentence reads: "Every submission to arbitrate an existing controversy is void, unless it or some note or memorandum thereof be in writing, and subscribed by the party to be charged therewith, or by his lawful agent." The case here under review does not justify us in construing that second sentence of section 1449, or analyzing the differences in language as between the first and second sentences. We see no reason for thinking that the requirement in the first sentence of "writing" means anything more than the similar requirement in the Federal Arbitration Act (U.S. Code, tit. 9 § 2) of "a written provision ... to settle by arbitration a controversy thereafter arising."

The order should be affirmed, with costs and the certified question answered in the affirmative.

GILBERT v. BURNSTINE
255 N.Y. 348, 174 N.E. 706 (1931)

O'BRIEN, J. The complaint was dismissed on the merits and the judgment has been affirmed.

The following facts are alleged in the complaint and admitted in the reply: In the year 1925, at New York, defendants, who are citizens and residents of this State, contracted in writing for the sale and delivery to plaintiff within the United States of a quantity of zinc concentrates. By a clause in the contract the parties agreed that all differences arising thereunder should be "arbitrated at London pursuant to the Arbitration Law of Great Britain." Differences arose concerning an alleged failure to deliver in accordance with the terms of the contract and plaintiff served notice upon defendants at New York requesting them to concur in the nomination of a certain named individual or of some other resident of London as sole arbitrator. The notice also stated that in the event of defendants' failure to concur in the nomination of an arbitrator, plaintiff would apply to the High Court of Justice of England for such an appointment pursuant to the provisions of the Arbitration Act of 1889 (52 and 53 Vict., ch. 49). On defendants' failure to comply with this notice, plaintiff obtained from the King's Bench Division an order permitting him to issue a form of process which is described in the complaint as an originating summons. This process was served upon defendants at New York and it directed them to appear at a certain time and place in London before a master chambers so that an arbitrator might be appointed. Defendants again failed to comply and thereupon the master appointed an arbitrator. He issued a notice which was served upon defendants at New York requiring them to furnish him at a specified time and place in London with all documents relevant to the matters in dispute. This notice, like the others, was ignored by defendants. The arbitrator, after causing a peremptory notice to be served upon them, also at New York, proceeded with the arbitration at London and made an award for £46,000

against them. The complaint alleges that all these proceedings were duly had in accordance with the English Arbitration Act of 1889 and demands judgment for the amount of the award. Defendants admit their execution of the arbitration clause in the contract but deny that they ever made submission to arbitration and deny also that the proceedings were had in accordance with the English law. They defend this action on the ground that their agreement is contrary to public policy, that the service of the notices and the originating summons is void, that no court of England ever acquired jurisdiction of their persons or property, that the award was obtained without due process of law and that its enforcement would deprive them of property without due process of law. They argue that the sole question in the case is whether the British court acquired personal jurisdiction in the absence of personal service upon them within British territory.

Settlements of disputes by arbitration are no longer deemed contrary to our public policy. Indeed, our statute encourages them. Contracts directed to that end are now declared valid, enforceable and irrevocable save upon such grounds as exist at law or in equity for the revocation of any contract. (Arbitration Law; Cons. Laws, ch. 72, § 2; Matter of Berkovitz v. Arbib & Houlberg, 230 N.Y. 261; Matter of Zimmerman v. Cohen, 236 N.Y. 15.) Defendants' agreement without reservation to arbitration in London according to the English statute necessarily implied a submission to the procedure whereby that law is there enforced. Otherwise the inference must be drawn that they never intended to abide by their pledge. They contracted that the machinery by which their arbitration might proceed would be foreign machinery operating from the foreign court. No other fair conclusion can be drawn from their language. Their contract constitutes something more than a simple executory one subject to breach. Not only under the foreign statute but also under our own arbitration law, it has become irrevocable in the sense that one of the parties without the consent of the other cannot deprive it of its enforceability. (Matter of Zimmerman v. Cohen, *supra*.) In order, therefore, to determine the issue asserted by defendants that jurisdiction never was acquired, the question must be decided whether their agreement to submit to that jurisdiction is contrary to our public policy.

Generally, extraterritorial jurisdiction of alien tribunals, however vigorously asserted, is denied by us. Of its own force, process issued from the court of a foreign state against our citizen and served upon him here is void. Without his consent he cannot be made subject to it, but whenever he agrees to be bound by its service, his conduct presents a problem. Contracts made by mature men who are not wards of the court should, in the absence of potent objection, be enforced. Pretexts to evade them should not be sought. Few arguments can exist based on reason or justice or common morality which can be invoked for the interference with the compulsory performance of agreements which have been freely made. Courts should endeavor to keep the law at a grade at least as high as the standards of ordinary ethics. Unless individuals run foul of constitutions, statutes, decisions or the rules of public morality, why should they not be allowed to contract as they please? Our government is not so paternalistic as to prevent them. Unless their stipulations have a tendency to entangle national or state affairs, their contracts in advance to submit to the process of foreign tribunals partake of their strictly private business. Our courts are not interested except to the extent of preserving the right to prevent repudiation. In many instances problems not dissimilar from the one presented by this case have been solved. Vigor has been infused into process otherwise impotent. Consent is the factor which imparts power. Text writers have discussed the subject and have concluded from the authorities that non-resident parties may in advance agree to submit to foreign jurisdiction.

Public policy, therefore, would not forbid defendants to appoint an agent to accept service or to confess judgment in their behalf, nor does it after service forbid them in person to acknowledge receipt of it. If the fact be clear that in advance of any form of litigation or arbitration they actually intended to contract that in the event of such a proceeding they would render themselves subject to foreign process, the same policy ought to prevail. That such was their clear intent has been assumed at Special Term and the Appellate Division and the same conclusion now reached by us is plainly supported by the language of the agreement. We will not entertain the theory that, when they agreed to arbitrate at London according to the English Arbitration Act, they contracted with a reservation to refuse to place themselves on English soil and to resist the English law outside that territory. The complaint, after alleging the essential facts, further avers that all proceedings were duly had in accordance with the Arbitration Act of 1889. Merely as a pleading, it states a good cause of action and at this stage it should not be dismissed. Whether its allegations can be sustained must be determined on the trial of the action. The serious problem is whether the proceedings were in fact conducted according to the English statute as interpreted by the English courts. As so interpreted, was the extraterritorial service regularly effected? What is the practice in the English courts? What construction has been put upon the various rules of procedure? These questions raised by the answer must be decided to some extent as issues of fact, for in the ascertainment of foreign law such issues are involved. (Croker v. Croker, 252 N.Y. 24.) After evidence of the facts has been produced then it will be timely for the court to determine (Fitzpatrick v. International Ry. Co., 252 N.Y. 127, 138) whether the English Arbitration Act, taken in connection with the foreign rules of procedure, conforms or conflicts with our public policy.

We do not say that the defendants in subjecting themselves to arbitration in accordance with the British Arbitration Act became bound to submit, not only to the requirements of that act, but of the entire *corpus juris* as developed by the British courts. We do say that there was an implied submission to the terms of the act itself, and to any rules or procedural machinery adopted by competent authority in aid of its provisions. If the arbitration contract had provided that an arbitrator might be named by the London Chamber of Commerce upon notice to the parties, there would be little doubt that notice would be adequate though the defendants were not in Great Britain at the time of its transmission. We cannot say upon this record that any different conclusion ought to follow from notice and nomination at the instance of a judge. The case does not involve the question whether the defendants, staying out of the arbitration, may still challenge in this State the existence of a contract to arbitrate, or the breach of such a contract, unaffected by any adjudication pronounced by the British courts. The case involves no more than this, whether staying out of the arbitration, they are bound by an award, made after due compliance with the requirements of the procedural machinery established by the British statute, unless they are able to show that no contract has been made or broken.

The judgment of the Appellate Division and that of the Special Term should be reversed and defendant's motion for judgment on the pleadings denied, with costs in all courts.

CARDOZO, Ch. J., POUND, CRANE, LEHMAN, KELLOGG and HUBBS, JJ., concur.

Judgments reversed, etc.

IN THE MATTER OF AMTORG TRADING CORP. (CAMDEN FIBRE)
277 App. Div. 531 (First Department, 1950)

PER CURIAM. Petitioner Amtorg Trading Corporation appeals from an order determining that the U.S.S.R. Chamber of Commerce Foreign Trade Arbitration Commission, in Moscow, is disqualified to act as an arbitration board in the determination of a commercial controversy arising under a contract made in 1947, in which it was designated by the parties to act in that capacity. The arbitration proceeding has been directed to proceed before another arbitrator appointed by the court. The other contracting party, a Pennsylvania corporation, now asserts that when it signed this agreement designating the arbitration board, it was ignorant of the fact that the U.S.S.R. Chamber of Commerce Foreign Trade Arbitration Commission had been established by a decree of the Soviet Government, and was composed of persons designated by the Presidium of the All-Union Chamber of Commerce, which in turn is controlled by a governing body largely made up of representatives of various Soviet Government organs. Inasmuch as petitioner is beneficially owned by the Soviet Government, it is contended that an impartial arbitration cannot be had before such a body.

The difficulty with this contention is that unlike judges under § 14 of the Judiciary Law, arbitrators are not disqualified on account of being interested in the result, if that circumstance has been disclosed to the adversary. Although "the courts closely scrutinize the action of an arbitrator whose relation to one of the parties was such as to naturally influence the judgment even of an honest man," such relationship does not necessarily preclude the arbitrator from acting (Sweet v. Morrison, 116 N.Y. 19, 27). In this instance, although respondent may not have known in detail how the U.S.S.R. Chamber of Commerce Foreign Trade Arbitration Commission was constituted, it is chargeable with notice as recently as 1947 that such an organization could not function in the U.S.S.R. unless it were subject to over-all control by the Soviet Government. Having entered into such an arbitration agreement, it does not lie in respondent's mouth at this point to declare that it was ignorant of this matter of common knowledge. No fraud or deception has been shown on the part of Amtorg inducing respondent to agree to the designation of this board of arbitration. The inter-relation between organizations in Russia and the Soviet State is so open and notorious that no business-

man dealing with Amtorg in 1947 could have been unaware of it.

The order appealed from should be modified so as to substitute the arbitration body specifically agreed upon by the parties in their contract, viz., the U.S.S.R. Chamber of Commerce Foreign Trade Arbitration Commission, in place of the arbitrator named in the order, and, as so modified, the order appealed from should be affirmed, with $20 costs and printing disbursements, without prejudice to a renewal of the application in event that visas are not obtainable or if for other reasons it becomes impossible or impracticable to conduct this arbitration in Moscow, U.S.S.R.

CALLAHAN, J. (dissenting). I dissent. I think we would be justified in holding in the present case that there was absolute disqualification of the arbitrator as a matter of law, and of public policy, because of its relationship to one of the parties, and that, therefore, the appointment was void.

But in any event, it seems to me improper to hold upon the present record that the officers of the Camden Fibre Mills, who are merchants, are to be charged with knowledge (the existence of which it denies) that the U.S.S.R. Chamber of Commerce Foreign Trade Arbitration Commission as well as Amtorg Trading Corporation were both instrumentalities of the Russian Government. The use of the words "Chamber of Commerce" as part of the arbitrator's title might well lead an American merchant to believe that such a body would be wholly disassociated from the government. At least, there should be a trial of the existence of such knowledge on the part of Camden before we compel arbitration by one whose relation to one of the parties prevents any hope of an impartial hearing.

Sweet v. Morrison (116 N.Y. 19) is distinguishable. There the person selected by the parties was in the employ of neither party, although he sustained certain relations with both parties which made them stand upon an equal footing before him.

I vote to affirm the order appealed from or to modify the said order by directing a trial of the issue of Camden's knowledge of the relationship of the arbitrator to Amtorg.

PECK, P. J., GLENNON, VAN VOORHIS and SHIENTAG, JJ., concur in PER CURIAM opinion; CALLAHAN, J., dissents in opinion.

[In affirming, the Court of Appeals observed 304 N.Y. 519, 109 N.E. 2d 602 (1952)]

It may be noted that the order of the Appellate Division does not preclude Camden from taking appropriate action should the arbitration in fact deprive it of its fundamental right to a fair and impartial determination. If, as conceded by Amtorg, the arbitration is to be conducted pursuant to the provisions of article 84 of the Civil Practice Act and enforced thereunder, Camden may move to vacate an award in favor of Amtorg for evident partiality of the arbitrators (Civ. Prac. Act, § 1462) or may object to confirmation of such award on that ground (Civ. Prac. Act, §§ 1458, 1461). If such award were to be enforced by action, it would be a valid defense that the proceedings were not conducted in such manner as to result in a fair and impartial determination (Gilbert v. Burnstine, 255 N.Y. 348, 357–358).

In Fox v. The Guiseppe (E.D.N.Y. 1953) 110 F. Supp. 212, a suit in admiralty begun in the Eastern District of New York, the court granted motion to stay the suit pending arbitration. A provision of the agreement provided "Arbitration to be settled in London." The court observed that "It is settled that ... Section 3 [of the U.S.A.A.] applies not only to arbitration in this country, but may also apply to those to be held in a foreign country."

Section 3, once the requisite findings are made, does not seem to grant the court any discretion; the stay seems mandatory. Does the "may" in the preceding quotation imply any element of discretion. Nothing in the statute seems to warrant it.

MATTER OF WOLFF (TULKOFF)
9 N.Y. 2d 356, 174 N.E. 2d 478 (1961)

FULD, J. The novel question presented by this appeal is whether § 1451 of the Civil Practice Act authorizes a stay of proceedings brought in violation of an arbitration contract, where such proceedings are pending, outside of New York State, before an administrative agency of the Federal Government.

The petitioner, Wolff Company, Inc. (a corporation), just as its predecessor, Wolff Company (a partnership), is a broker or agent dealing in perishable agricultural commodities, while the respondent, Tulkoff's Horse Radish Products Co., is a dealer in perishable agricultural commodities. The petitioners, corporation and partnership, doing business in New York, and the respondent, a partnership doing business in Maryland, are licensed pursuant to the provisions of the Perishable Agricultural Commodities Act (U.S. Code, tit. 7, §§ 499a–499s).

In late January, 1959 and early February, 1959, Wolff Company, the partnership, and Tulkoff's engaged in negotiations by telephone concerning the purchase of Japanese horseradish roots. According to an affidavit submitted on behalf of the petitioners, these telephone conversations "were finalized, subject to written confirmation" on or about February 5, 1959 and, shortly thereafter, a letter was sent in which Wolff Company advised Tulkoff's that it would "mail .... as soon as possible copies of Contracts as well as facsimile Credit Letter." On February 6, Wolff Company sent the respondents two "Bought Notes," covering the purchase in question, which contained broad arbitration provisions.

The respondents' version of the sale agrees in all particulars with that of the petitioners except that they insist that the sale was verbal, without any discussion concerning arbitration of future controversies, and they point to the letter of February 5, as well as the "Bought Notes," as confirmation of an already consummated sale. It is on this basis that Tulkoff's urges that no agreement or consent to arbitrate any dispute was ever made.

In March of 1959, the horseradish roots arrived from Japan and were accepted and paid for by Tulkoff's. Thereafter, on May 29, Tulkoff's lodged a preliminary complaint with the United States Department of Agriculture claiming that all shipments failed "to grade according to contract" and that the merchandise was unfit for resale purposes. This preliminary complaint, filed pursuant to subdivision (a) of § 6 of the Perishable Agricultural Commodities Act (U.S. Code, tit. 7, § 499f), was followed in August by a "hearing" before the Agricultural Marketing Service, the purpose of which was to "achieve a settlement between the parties." No settlement was reached, however, and Tulkoff's lodged a formal complaint with the Department of Agriculture in October, 1959.

This complaint, requiring an answer within 20 days, was served on the petitioners in late December, but they requested and received permission to put off their time to answer. However, instead of interposing an answer in the proceeding in the Department of Agriculture, the petitioners, relying on the arbitration provision in the "Bought Notes" which they had sent to the respondents, filed the petition now before us for a stay of the proceedings before the Agriculture Department.

In opposition to the petition for a stay, Tulkoff's alleged (1) that its rights under the Perishable Agricultural Commodities Act may not be vitiated by an arbitration agreement, (2) that the court has no jurisdiction to stay a proceeding pending before a Federal administrative agency; (3) that no agreement or contract exists between the parties requiring arbitration; and (4) that the petitioners have waived any purported right to compel arbitration.

In denying the motion for a stay, the court at Special Term placed its decision upon the ground that it was "without power to stay the Federal proceeding." The Appellate Division affirmed, and the appeal is before us by our permission.

The grant of rights under the Perishable Agricultural Commodities Act was not designed to preclude resort to other statutory or common-law remedies. The statute unequivocally declares that liability under the act "may be enforced either (1) by complaint to the Secretary as hereinafter provided, or (2) by suit in any court of competent jurisdiction," and it goes on to provide that "this section shall not in any way abridge or alter the remedies now existing at common law or by statute, and the provisions of this chapter are in addition to such remedies" (U.S. Code, tit. 7, § 499e; also, § 490o; see Le Roy Dyal Co. v. Allen, 161 F. 2d 152, 157; Krueger v. Acme Fruit Co., 75 F. 2d 67). The question then arises whether the remedy sought by the petitioners, a stay, is available. The respondents claim that it is not, contending that § 1451 of the Civil Practice Act empowers the New York courts to stay only actions or proceedings pending in New York tribunals and that, accordingly, in this case the court had no jurisdiction to stay the administrative proceeding before the United States Department of Agriculture.

The argument lacks merit; the courts of this State possess the power to stay proceedings wherever they may be pending. Had it been the design of our Legislature to limit the stay, as urged by the respondents, words were at hand to reflect that design. The Federal arbitration statute, for instance, sanctions a stay *only* of an action or proceeding "brought in any of the courts of the United States" (U.S. Code, tit. 9, § 3). The broad, unqualified language of the New York statute, in sharp contrast with this, simply recites that "If any action or proceeding be brought upon any issue otherwise referrable to arbitration ... the supreme court ... shall stay all proceedings in the action or proceeding" (Civ. Prac. Act, § 1451). The absence of limiting words is, as suggested, significant, bespeaking as it does an intention that the Supreme Court is empowered to stay actions or proceedings irrespective of where they may have been instituted.

The purpose of a stay is to enforce a contractual obligation to arbitrate by preventing other actions or proceedings inconsistent with that obligation. If our courts may only prevent inconsistent actions or proceedings in the courts or administrative agencies of this State, they will only be providing partial enforcement of the promise to arbitrate; if the court's power to stay were thus limited, the obligation of the contract could easily be frustrated by the prosecution of actions or proceedings in another jurisdiction.

At common law, "Arbitration agreements ... meant very little" because they were not subject to specific enforcement. (See Matter of Feuer Transp. [Local No. 445], 295 N.Y. 87, 91.) It was dissatisfaction with this situation that led to the enactment of our Arbitration Law. And, as this court observed in the *Feuer Transportation* case (295 N.Y., at p. 91), "Under the new statute arbitration became both orderly and enforcible and was made subject in effect to a decree for specific performance." To deny to our courts the power to grant specific performance of an arbitration clause by enjoining the prosecution of foreign proceedings would be a step backward. It would partially reestablish the long-abandoned doctrine that an agreement to arbitrate is revocable. We may not and should not take such a step unless expressly directed to do so by the Legislature.

In short, the petitioners seek an order forbidding the respondents from pursuing their remedy before the Department of Agriculture. If the respondents did agree to arbitrate all differences arising from the sale of Japanese horseradish, and if there has been no waiver of that contractual obligation, neither the New York Arbitration Law nor the Federal Perishable Agricultural Commodities Act stands in the way of specifically enforcing the agreement to arbitrate. (Cf. Watkins v. Hudson Coal Co., 151 F. 2d 311, 320, cert. denied 327 U.S. 777; Donahue v. Susquehanna Collieries Co., 138 F. 2d 3, 6–7.) Having personal jurisdiction over the respondents by reason of the fact, if it is one, that they agreed that "Any controversy or claim ... shall be settled by arbitration in New York, N.Y.," a decree may be entered enjoining the respondents from continued prosecution of their claim before the Department of Agriculture. (Cf. Arpels v. Arpels, 8 N.Y. 2d 339, 341; Garvin v. Garvin, 302 N.Y. 96.)

Since Special Term denied the petitioners' motion on the ground that it was "without power to stay the Federal proceeding," there must be a reversal—unless it is established that the parties either had not entered into a contract to arbitrate or, having done so, the petitioners had waived their right to arbitration. We turn, therefore, to a consideration of these questions.

The factual dispute concerning the making of a

contract to arbitrate, outlined above, consists essentially of a disagreement over whether the parties' initial telephone conversations "closed the deal" or whether they were preliminary, or subject, to the subsequent "Bought Notes" containing the arbitration clause. Whether these facts fall within our holding in Matter of Albrecht Chem. Co. (Anderson Trading Corp.) (298 N.Y. 437) or our holding in Matter of Helen Whiting, Inc. (Trojan Textile Corp.) (307 N.Y. 360) depends on whose version of the sale is accepted. This must be resolved at a hearing to be held at Special Term.

The respondents' further claim, also disputed by the petitioners, that there was a waiver of any rights to arbitration by reasons of laches on the part of the petitioners and their participation in a hearing before the Department of Agriculture likewise involves a determination of fact calling for a hearing and decision by the court at Special Term. (See Matter of Zimmerman v. Cohen, 236 N.Y. 15, 19; cf. Matter of Terminal Auxiliar Maritima, S. A. [Winkler Credit Corp.], 6 N.Y. 2d 294, 299–300; Matter of Haupt v. Rose, 265 N.Y. 108, 110; Nagy v. Arcas Brass & Iron Co., 242 N.Y. 97, 98–99.)

The order of the Appellate Division should be reversed, with costs in this court and in the Appellate Division, and the matter remanded to Special Term for further proceedings in accordance with this opinion.

CHIEF JUDGE DESMOND and JUDGES DYE, FROESSEL, VAN VOORHIS, BURKE and FOSTER concur.

Order reversed, etc.

In H. M. Hamilton and Co. v. American Home Assurance Co., (First Dept. 1964) 21 A.D. 2d 500, 251 N.Y.S. 2d 215 (1964), (aff'd, 15 N.Y. 2d 595, 255 N.Y.S. 2d 262 (mem), the Appellate Division held that Matter of Wolff applied to enjoining the prosecution of a suit in the courts of another state; the decision was reached under CPLR § 7503. The petitioner, a Georgia corporation, was a party to several contracts of reinsurance with several insurance companies, New York corporations; the agreements called for performance in many states. The New York reinsurers demanded inspection of petitioner's book, as they had a right to do under the agreements. When petitioner refused, they instituted suit in Georgia. Petitioner gave notice of intention to arbitrate and shortly thereafter moved to compel arbitration in New York City as the agreements provided and to stay the Georgia

suit. The court made no specific mention of why it was applying New York law, despite a vigorous dissent by Judge Steuer in which, among other things, he said that the agreement to arbitrate in New York did not indicate an intent by the parties to make New York law govern. "The mere fact that in the absence of agreement as to any other site arbitration would be conducted in New York City is neither an agreement to have the contract interpreted by New York law nor any indication of intent to make such an agreement." Impliedly, the majority rejected this view.

I. SAMSON ET AL. v. MICHAEL A. BERGIN
138 Conn. 306, 84 A. 2d 273 (1951)

O'SULLIVAN, J. The plaintiffs brought this action to recover on a judgment in the amount of $1373.50 entered in their favor against the defendant on February 8, 1949, in the Supreme Court of the state of New York. The Court of Common Pleas, to which the present action was returned, rendered judgment for the plaintiffs, and the defendant appealed.

The following facts, found by the court, are undisputed: The plaintiffs live in New York City, where they manufacture clothing. The defendant resides in Wilsonville, Connecticut, and is there engaged in the business of selling woolen goods. During December 1947, he entered into a written contract with the plaintiffs at Wilsonville for the sale of certain fabrics. The contract contained the following provision:

> Any complaint, controversy or question which may arise with respect to this contract that cannot be settled by the parties thereto shall be referred to arbitration. If the controversy concerns the condition or quality of merchandise it shall be referred to the Mutual Adjustment Bureau of the cloth and garment trades pursuant to the rules and regulations thereof. All other controversies shall be submitted to The American Arbitration Association.

When the defendant failed to make the agreed deliveries, the plaintiffs claimed that they had thereby suffered damages and made written demand upon the defendant to arbitrate the matter. The plaintiffs sent a copy of the demand to the American Arbitration Association with a request that it proceed to arbitrate the dispute. Pursuant to its rules, the association sent a list of persons to the parties to obtain an expression of their preference in the selection of the board of arbitrators. After it became apparent that the defendant proposed to take no action to indicate his choice, the association appointed three arbitrators and notified the defendant by registered mail of the date set for a hearing in New York City. The hearing was had at the place and time scheduled, but the defendant failed to appear or take any part therein. On November 30, 1948, the board made its award in favor of the plaintiffs in the amount of $1348.50 and notice thereof was sent by mail to the defendant. An application to confirm the award, subsequently addressed by the plaintiffs to the Supreme Court of the state of New York, was granted, and judgment was entered in their favor. The defendant was not served with process in New York. His knowledge of the step being taken by the plaintiffs came from the receipt of a letter enclosing a copy of the application to confirm. He did not enter his appearance in the Supreme Court and completely ignored the proceeding. The decisive question on this appeal is whether the Court of Common Pleas was correct in holding that the New York court had jurisdiction to render judgment *in personam* against the defendant.

As applied to a court, the word "jurisdiction" means the power to hear and determine a cause.

The question before us does not involve a consideration of jurisdiction of the subject matter since the New York court possessed legislative authority to enter judgment upon the wards of arbitrators. N.Y. Civ. Prac. Act § 1461 et seq. The defendant's grievance lies in his claim that the Supreme Court of New York had not acquired jurisdiction of his person.

Ordinarily, a court obtains jurisdiction of the person of a non-resident by service made upon him in the state of the forum. This may be given in various ways. 44 HARV. L. REV. 1276 n.2. the most usual example is when the defendant voluntarily enters a general appearance. 1 Beale, CONFLICT OF LAWS, § 82.1 ; see G. M. Williams Co. v. Mairs, 72 Conn. 430, 434, 44 A. 729. He may likewise agree, even before litigation arises, to submit to the jurisdiction of a foreign court. 1 Beale, op. cit., § 81.1. It was on this theory that the trial court acted. It concluded that, in entering into the written contract with the plaintiffs, the defendant consented to be bound by the rules of the American Arbitration Association ; that, as these rules permit the association to determine the locality for the arbitration hearing, should the parties be unable to fix it themselves, the defendant agreed to participate in the hearing which eventually was held in New York City ; that, pursuant to § 39 of the rules, the defendant is deemed to have given his consent "to the jurisdiction of the supreme court of [that] state to

enforce such contract or submission." N.Y. Civ. Prac. Act.§ 1450.[1]

The fallacy of this conclusion is that the defendant did not agree to be bound by the rules of the association or to arbitrate in New York. The contract is silent on the situs of arbitration and did not incorporate the rules by reference. To be sure, controversies involving the quality of the merchandise were to be submitted "to the Mutual Adjustment Bureau of the cloth and garment trades pursuant to the rules and regulations thereof." All other controversies were to be submitted to the American Arbitration Association. No mention was made of its rules. The court, however, found that the defendant had "constructive knowledge" of them, and on the basis of this finding it concluded that he had submitted to be bound thereby. We take it that the expression "constructive knowledge" was intended to mean implied knowledge, that is, the knowledge which the court felt that it might reasonably and logically attribute to the defendant from other proven facts. It is the absence of essential facts, however, which shows the lack of sufficient support for this inference. Further, the court did find that the defendant had had no previous experience with the association and knew nothing about its rules. It also found that, when the contract was executed, neither party referred to them in any manner. Indeed, there is nothing in the finding to indicate that the defendant was aware of the existence of any rules at all or of the locality where the association operated. The finding must be corrected by striking out the fact that the defendant had constructive knowledge of the rules of the association. General Petroleum Products, Inc. v. Merchants Trust Co., 115 Conn. 50, 58, 160 A. 296.

Obviously, there was no express consent given by the defendant to arbitrate in New York and thus to subject himself to the courts of that state. Nor, as pointed out above, were any facts found to justify the inference of implied consent or to indicate conduct on his part which would effect the same result. RESTATEMENT, JUDGMENTS § 18, comment g. The cases cited by the plaintiffs are not in point. In most of them, express consent to arbitrate at a specified place was given. Mulcahy v. Whitehill, 48 F. Supp. 917 ; Sturges & Burn Mfg. Co. v. Unit Construction Co., 207 Ill. App. 74 ; Gilbert v. Burnstine, 255 N.Y. 348, 174 N.E. 706 ; Matter of Heyman, Inc. v. Cole Co., 242 App. Div. 362, 275 N.Y.S. 23. In another cited case, the rules of the American Arbitration

---

1. In 1951, the New York legislature added after the word "submission" the following: "and to enter judgment on an award thereon." N.Y. Laws 1951, c. 260.

Association were by reference made a part of the contract. Matter of Bradford Woolen Corporation v. Freedman, 189 Misc. 242, 71 N.Y.S. 2d 257. An interesting article upon the subject under discussion appears in 48 Columbia Law Review 366.

No principle is more universal than that the judgment of a court without jurisdiction is a nullity. The Trial court was in error in failing to hold the New York judgment void for lack of jurisdiction of the defendant.

There is error, the judgment is set aside and the case is remanded with direction to render judgment for the defendant.

BATTLE v. GENERAL CELLULOSE CO.
23 N.J. 538, 129 A. 2d 865 (1957)

Weintraub, J. Plaintiff obtained an arbitration award against defendant in New York City and a judgment thereon in the Supreme Court of New York. He then sued here upon the New York judgment and prevailed on a motion for summary judgment. Defendant appealed to the Appellate Division and we certified on our own motion.

The controversy arose out of an agreement of employment. Plaintiff commenced work on November 2, 1952, as defendant's vice-president and general manager. The terms of employment had not yet been fixed and discussions continued for some period. On January 8, 1953 defendant sent to plaintiff its letter of that date outlining the terms of employment for a year beginning November 1, 1952.

Defendant discharged plaintiff on July 10, 1953. Plaintiff instituted the arbitration proceedings under the following provision of the letter of January 8, 1953: "Any controversy or claim arising out of or relating to this agreement or breach thereof, shall be settled by arbitration according to the rules of the American Arbitration Association."

The employment was contracted in New Jersey and was to be performed here. Plaintiff lived in this State when he was employed and continued to live here until after his discharge when he moved to Indiana, and was a resident of that State when he instituted the arbitration proceedings. Defendant is a corporation of the State of New Jersey and was not subject to service of process within the State of New York.

Defendant declined to participate in the arbitration proceedings or to respond to notice by mail of the application to enter judgment upon the award. In fact, defendant denied the existence

of the contract and advised the American Arbitration Association at once that it disputed its authority to proceed with arbitration until the existence of the alleged contract was first determined in judicial proceedings in New Jersey. Neither party sought to litigate that question before arbitration. Plaintiff acted on his thesis that he was entitled to proceed under the rules of the Association, while defendant rested on its conviction that the award and judgment would be nullities.

Assuming the award was binding, defendant says that nonetheless the judgment of the New York court is not enforceable here because service of the notice was made by mail addressed to defendant in New Jersey. We need not consider whether under the New York statute or under controlling principles of constitutional law New York could thus obtain jurisdiction *in personam* on the basis of an agreement to arbitrate in New York, without more. See Weiss, *Arbitration Award and the Non-Resident: Nuance in New York.* 48 Col. L. Rev. 366 (1948). The *in personam* jurisdiction of the New York court may here be rested on the voluntary agreement of defendant. Matter of Liberty Country Wear, Inc., 197 Misc. 581, 96 N.Y.S. 2d 134 (Sup. Ct. 1950); Merger Fabrics, Inc., v. Coill-Shuman Co., 74 N.Y.S. 2d 76 (Sup. Ct. 1947).

Rule 30 of the Association by which the parties contracted to be bound provides:

> Serving of Notices—Each party to a Submission or other agreement which provides for arbitration under these Rules shall be deemed to have consented and shall consent that any papers, notices or process necessary or proper for the initiation or continuation of an arbitration under these rules and for any court action in connection therewith or for the entry of judgment on any award made thereunder may be served upon such party (a) by mail addressed to such party or his attorneys at his last known address or (b) by personal service, within or without the state wherein the arbitration is to be held (whether such party be within or without the United States of America); provided that reasonable opportunity to be heard with regard thereto has been granted such party.

The intendment of this rule is that an action on the award may be brought in the state wherein the arbitration was held and that process may be served either by mail or personally outside that state. The State of New York having been fixed as the place for arbitration in accordance with another rule by which defendant bound itself, defendant must be held to have agreed that an action on the award may be brought in New York and service of process made in accordance with Rule 30. Bradford Woolen Corporation v.

Freedman, 189 Misc. 242, 71 N.Y.S. 2d 257 (Sup. Ct. 1947). There is no basis for disputing that the notice given pursuant to the rule in fact afforded "reasonable opportunity to be heard." See Republique Francaise v. Cellosilk Manufacturing Co., 309 N.Y. 269, 128 N.E. 2d 750 (Ct. App. 1955).

It is well settled that a personal judgment may be rendered against one who is neither served with process in the state nor domiciled in or a citizen of the state if he consents to jurisdiction over him. Consent may be given in advance of the controversy, and if the terms of the consent are met, the judgment is binding and entitled to full faith and credit.

Defendant stresses the hardship which might conceivably have ensued had the place of arbitration been fixed at a more distant point. But the answer is that defendant need not have contracted to arbitrate at all, or could have specified in the agreement that New Jersey be the situs of the arbitration or the suit on the award or both. Instead, defendant agreed to arbitrate outside this state by its unqualified acceptance of the rules of the Association. Defendant was free so to agree. No public policy of this State or of New York was thereby offended. California Lima Bean Growers Association v. Mankowitz, *supra* (9 N.J. Misc. 362, 154 A. 532), Gilbert v. Burnstine, *supra* (255 N.Y. 348, 174 N.E. 706, 73 A. L. R. 1453) ; cf. Creter v. Davies, 30 N.J. Super. 60 (Ch. Div. 1954), affirmed 31 N.J. Super. 402 (App. Div. 1954). The question whether a controversy between non-residents should be entertained by New York concerns only that state and it is willing, as here, to implement the agreement. Gantt v. Felipe Y. Carlos Hurtado & Cia., *supra* (297 N.Y. 433, 79 N.E. 2d 815) ; Republique Francaise v. Cellosilk Manufacturing Co., *supra* (309 N.Y. 269, 128 N.E. 2d 750).

It accordingly has been held elsewhere that a judgment entered in New York upon an award in circumstances essentially indistinguishable from those of the present case is entitled to full faith and credit, and we agree.

Arnold Bernstein Shipping Co. v. Tidewater Commercial Co. (D.C. Md. 1949) 84 F. Supp. 948. Libelant, a New York corporation, filed libel in Maryland federal district court against respondent, a Maryland corporation. The court held that as the charterparty involved was executed in New York, the issue of the validity of the reassignment of the charterparty was governed by New York law ; it also opined that the legal effect of the arbitration agreement was governed by New York law.

Why the Federal Arbitration Act was not invoked is not at all clear.

CONTINENTAL GRAIN CO. v. DANT & RUSSELL, INC.
118 F. 2d. 967 (9th Cir. 1941)

Proceeding in admiralty by the Continental Grain Company against Dant & Russell, Incorporated, for an order compelling arbitration of certain obligations growing out of a charter party entered into between the parties. From an order directing arbitration within the district where the petition was filed, petitioner appeals.

Before WILBUR, GARRECHT, and STEPHENS, Circuit Judges.

WILBUR, C. J. The appellant invoked the admiralty jurisdiction of the United States District Court for the District of Oregon by applying to that court for an order compelling arbitration of certain obligations growing out of a charterparty entered into between appellant and appellee. The agreement for arbitration is contained in the charterparty and provides that should any dispute arise between the owners and the insurers the matter in dispute shall be referred to three persons in New York, one to be appointed by each of the parties, and the third by the two so chosen. It was provided that "their decision or that of any two of them, shall be final, and for the purpose of enforcing any award, this agreement may be made a rule of the court. The arbitrators shall be commercial men."

The petition showed the nature of the claim made by it upon the appellee for $1,949.04 growing out of the charterparty, that the appellee had refused to pay the sum alleged to be due and that the appellant had demanded arbitration pursuant to the charterparty and had named its arbitrator Geo. M. Bress, 80 Broad Street, New York ; that the appellee had refused to arbitrate or to name an arbitrator. Appellant prayed that the arbitration proceed in accordance with §§ 4 and 5 of the United States Arbitration Act, 9 U.S.C.A. § 4 and 5, for costs and for further relief.

The appellee, after denial of its motion to dismiss the petition, admitted the execution of the charterparty, admitted the existence of a dispute arising therefrom, denied liability, alleged that it refused to arbitrate the matters involved, and that it was unwilling to do so at New York because its place of business was Portland,

Oregon, and that it believed it had a good and meritorious defense to the petitioner's claim; alleged that the witnesses needed to substantiate its claims resided in Portland, and that the appellant had an office and place of business in Portland; alleged it was willing to arbitrate the matter at Portland, Oregon, or within the District of Oregon, but that it would be unfair and unjust to require respondent to be dragged across the country to arbitrate in New York. The court ordered arbitration

in the manner provided for in the agreement, provided the hearing and proceedings under such agreement shall be within the district in which the petition for the order directing such arbitration is filed and provided that petitioner Continental Grain Company fully cooperate therein and proceed with said arbitration.

Appellant gave notice of appeal.

The appellee, without moving to dismiss the appeal for lack of jurisdiction, has suggested that in view of the decision of this court and the Supreme Court in Schoenamsgruber v. Hamburg American Line, 294 U.S. 454, 55 S.Ct. 475, 79 L.Ed. 989; Id., 9 Cir., 70 F. 2d 234, it doubts whether or not the order appealed from is a final order of the court and appealable as such.

It is true, as held in the above case, that where an action has been brought upon an obligation and the defendant, as a defense, invokes an agreement to arbitrate the dispute in order to procure a stay of the trial of the action until the arbitration has been completed, the order for the stay is not a final order because further proceedings are contemplated after the arbitration is completed. 9 U.S.C.A. §§ 3, 5. The appellant is proceeding in conformity with § 4 of the Arbitration Act and the final and only order requested of the court is the order provided for in that section directing "the parties to proceed to arbitration in accordance with the terms of the agreement."

The arbitration agreement herein does not provide for the entry of the award as a judgment of the court as it might have done if the agreement had so provided. 9 U.S.C.A. § 9. In the absence of such an agreement the award cannot be summarily entered as a judgment of the court. Lehigh Structural Steel Co. v. Rust Engineering Co., 61 App. D.C. 224, 59 F. 2d 1038; 9 U.S.C.A. § 9. It follows that the order appealed from is a final order of the court and that this court has jurisdiction of the appeal. The only point raised by the appellant is that the order of arbitration which is requested should have provided for a hearing in New York. This point is not well taken.

The statute expressly provides that the hearing and proceeding shall be within the district in which the petition for the order directing the arbitration is filed. In the statute (Act of Feb. 12, 1925, ch. 213, § 4, 43 Stat. L. pp. 883, 884, 9 U.S.C.A. § 4) the clause under consideration with reference to the place of the arbitration is in the form of a proviso reading as follows:

the court shall make an order directing the parties to proceed to arbitration in accordance with the terms of the agreement: Provided, That the hearing and proceedings under such agreement shall be within the district in which the petition for an order directing such arbitration is filed.

The appellant challenges the right of the court to order the arbitration within the district of Oregon because such an order does not conform to the agreement of the parties for an arbitration in New York. Prior to the enactment of the United States arbitration act (1925) such agreements could not be enforced in the courts of the United States. If there could be any doubt of the power of the legislature to limit the right of arbitration to one conducted within the jurisdiction of the district court ordering the arbitration, it must be dispelled by the consideration that Congress could attach any limitation it desired to the right to enforce arbitration in the federal courts, that it has made a condition that the arbitration be held in the district where the court sits, that the contract in question was executed with a knowledge that Congress had so provided, and that the appellant had invoked the jurisdiction of a court other than that having jurisdiction in New York to enforce the agreement. The appellant, having invoked the jurisdiction of the United States District Court for Oregon is hardly in a position to complain that it has exercised that jurisdiction in accordance with the statute giving it jurisdiction.

The appellee, in aid of the interpretation of the statute as applied by the district court, has called attention to the discussion with reference to that matter on the floor of the United States Senate wherein the proviso above mentioned was added by way of amendment. The reference is to the statement of Senator Sterling, in charge of the bill before the Senate. The appellant contends that the court cannot consider this discussion unless the terms of the act are so ambiguous as to require recourse to such discussion.

It is sufficient for the purposes of this decision to say that the statements invoked merely confirm the clear and obvious meaning of the statute and are not relied upon to change the clearly expressed intent of Congress.

Order affirmed.

AMERICAN LAW INSTITUTE, RESTATEMENT OF THE LAW, SECOND, CONFLICT OF LAWS
Council Draft No. 22 (1968)

§ 186. *Applicable Law.*

In contract actions, the rights and duties of the parties are determined by the law of the state chosen by the parties in accordance with the rule of § 187 and otherwise by the law selected in accordance with the rule of § 188.

§ 187. *Law of the State Chosen by the Parties.*

(1) The law of the state chosen by the parties to govern their contractual rights and duties will be applied if the particular issue is one which the parties could have resolved by an explicit provision in their agreement directed to that issue.

(2) The law of the state chosen by the parties to govern their contractual rights and duties will be applied, even if the particular issue is one which the parties could not have resolved by an explicit provision in their agreement directed to that issue, unless either

(a) the chosen state has no substantial relationship to the parties or the transaction and there is no other reasonable basis for the parties' choice, or

(b) application of the law of the chosen state would be contrary to a fundamental policy of a state which has a materially greater interest than the chosen state in the determination of the particular issue and which, under the rule of § 188, would be the state of the applicable law in the absence of an effective choice of law by the parties.

(3) In the absence of a contrary indication of intention, the reference is to the local law of the state of the chosen law.

Comment:

a. Scope of section. The rule of this Section is applicable only in situations where it is established to the satisfaction of the forum that the parties have chosen the state of the applicable law. When the parties have made such a choice, they will usually refer expressly to the state of the chosen law in their contract, and this is the best way of insuring that their desires will be given effect. But even when the contract does not refer to any state, the forum may nevertheless be able to conclude from its provisions that the parties did wish to have the law of a particular state applied. So the fact that the contract contains legal expressions, or makes reference to legal doctrines, that are peculiar to the local law of a particular state may provide persuasive evidence that the parties wished to have this law applied.

f. Requirement of reasonable basis for parties' choice. The forum will not apply the chosen law to determine issues the parties could not have determined by explicit agreement directed to the particular issue if the parties had no reasonable basis for choosing this law. The forum will not, for example, apply a foreign law which has been chosen by the parties in the spirit of adventure or to provide mental exercise for the judge. Situations of this sort do not arise in practice. Contracts are entered into for serious purposes, and rarely, if ever, will the parties choose a law without good reason for doing so.

When the state of the chosen law has some substantial relationship to the parties or the contract, the parties will be held to have had a reasonable basis for their choice. This will be the case, for example, when this state is that where performance by one of the parties is to take place or where one of the parties is domiciled or has his principal place of business. The same will be the case when this state is the place of contracting except, perhaps, in the unusual situation where this place is wholly fortuitous and bears no real relation either to the contract or to the parties. These situations are mentioned only for purposes of example. There are undoubtedly still other situations where the state of the chosen law will have a sufficiently close relationship to the parties and the contract to make the parties' choice reasonable.

The parties to a multistate contract may have a reasonable basis for choosing a state with which the contract has no substantial relationship. For example, when contracting in countries whose legal systems are strange to them as well as relatively immature, the parties should be able to choose a law on the ground that they know it well and that it is sufficiently developed. For only in this way can they be sure of knowing accurately the extent of their rights and duties under the contract. So parties to a contract for the transportation of goods by sea between two countries with relatively undeveloped legal systems should be permitted to submit their contract to some well-known and highly elaborated commercial law.

§ 188. *Law Governing in Absence of Effective Parties' Choice.*

(1) In contract actions, the rights and duties of the parties with respect to the particular issue are determined by the local law of the state which, as to that issue, has the most significant relationship to the transaction and the parties under the principles stated in § 6.

(2) In the absence of an effective choice of law by the parties (see § 187), the contracts to be taken into account in applying the principles of § 6 to determine the law applicable to an issue include:

(a) the place of contracting,

(b) the place of negotiation of the contract,

(c) the place of performance,

(d) the location of the subject matter of the contract, and

(e) the domicil, residence, nationality, place of incorporation and place of business of the parties.

These contracts are to be evaluated according to their relative importance with respect to the particular issue.

(3) If the place of negotiating the contract and the place of performance are in the same state, the local law of this state will usually be applied, except as otherwise provided in §§ 189–197 and 203.

§ 218. *Validity and Effect of Arbitration Agreement.*

The validity of an arbitration agreement, and the rights created thereby, are determined by the law selected by application of the rules of §§ 187–188. This law determines whether a judicial action brought in violation of the provisions of an arbitration agreement can be maintained.

§ 219. *Method of Enforcement of Arbitration Agreement.*

The method of enforcing an arbitration agreement is determined by the local law of the forum.

§ 220. *Enforcement of Foreign Arbitration Award.*

A foreign arbitration award will be enforced in other states provided:

(1) the award is enforceable in the state of rendition and was rendered by an arbitration tribunal which had personal jurisdiction over the defendant and afforded him reasonable notice of the proceeding and a reasonable opportunity to be heard, and

(2) the forum has judicial jurisdiction over either the defendant or his property and the cause of action on which the award was based is not contrary to the strong public policy of the forum.

B.

The Interaction of Federal Arbitration Law and State Law

1. CASES ARISING UNDER SECTION 301 LMRA

a. The Role of State "Procedure"

COMMENT, "THE APPLICABILITY OF STATE ARBITRATION STATUTES TO PROCEEDINGS SUBJECT TO LMRA SECTION 301"*

Since arbitration procedure varies among the states, a problem will arise. For example, assume an arbitration provision (within a section 301 collective bargaining contract) which fails to specify the manner of appointing the arbitrator should a grievance arise. In Ohio, the state statute provides for court appointment of an arbitrator where no such procedure has been set out in the agreement. In Alabama, the statute provides that the arbitrator is to be chosen by the parties, while in Indiana the statute is silent on the appointment of an arbitrator. If the parties are relying upon section 301 (which the Supreme Court has interpreted as requiring that a federal rule is to be formulated), should different results be permitted? Of what influence is local law in this situation and in other situations where state law is not uniform? Is a "*per se* application," a "*prima facie* application," or a "nonapplication" of state arbitration statues proper? These classifications of the possible methods of applications of state statutes in a section 301 proceeding will subsequently be defined and analyzed.

"*Per se* application" means that the statute is applied without a consideration of any federal labor policy and all the provisions are necessarily applied to the arbitration proceedings. A *per se* application denotes a conclusion that the federal labor policy is not pertinent to the application of the state arbitration procedure statutes, and the statutes are to be applied according to their own legislative intent.

In a "*prima facie* application" the statutes are to be applied unless there is a conflict with the federal labor policy. This policy must necessarily be determined by the court in each situation on

*Excerpted from 21 OHIO ST. L. J. 692 (1966). Reprinted with permission.

a case by case method. If the application of the particular state arbitration provision in question would be at odds with federal labor policy, the provision would not be applied. If there is no clash, the provision would be applied.[1]

Since section 301 does not expressly require any particular arbitration procedure, "non-application" of the state statute would result if it was concluded that, because of the federal policy of favoring arbitration, the state arbitration statutes should only be used by the court as a guideline as to what a general federal "statute" should be. Rather than applying the statute of the particular state, the court would determine from all the statutes what the uniform provisions *should* be.

Thus, it must first be determined how the state arbitration statutes are to be applied. If it is found that the statutes should not be applied *per se,* then it would be necessary for the courts to look at the particular provisions within the statutes.

A. *Per se Application.* The Supreme Court has not yet faced the question of how the national labor policy affects the application of state arbitration statutes in proceedings under section 301. One must look at the legislative history behind section 301, the Supreme Court's interpretation of that legislative history, and court determinations of what the national labor arbitration policies are.

Since federal law is to be applied to cases within section 301, and since arbitration provisions within the collective bargaining agreements are part of the design to promote the achievement of industrial peace, a desire that there be a distinct federal arbitration procedure could be inferred from the *Dowd* case.

Under many arbitration statutes, the arbitrator is given subpoena power. To illustrate the effect of the state statutes assume an arbitration clause in a collective bargaining agreement governed by section 301. A grievance arises, and it has reached the final stage in the grievance procedure—arbitration. During the arbitration proceeding it is learned that the key witness for one of the parties involved in the dispute will not appear voluntarily. If an arguably applicable state arbitration statute contains a subpoena provision, can the arbitrator issue a subpoena to a reluctant witness and have it judicially enforced by relying on section 301? Would it make a difference if the dispute arose in a

second state which does not have such a provision in its arbitration statute? Such questions suggest an interrelationship between state arbitration statutes and the labor arbitration process.

Since the powers of the arbitrators are such a vital part of this favored arbitration system, and since without such powers the effectiveness of the arbitration proceedings would be seriously impaired, why should the arbitration procedures not be governed by federal labor policy? The intent of section 301, to create industrial peace and stability, has fostered a federal labor policy that favors the use of arbitration. Utilization of a state arbitration procedure statute without reference to this federal labor policy would strike at the heart of the stabilization of labor-management relations and thus defeat the thrust of section 301. First, however, there must be a determination of whether the arbitration statute favorably or adversely affects the arbitration proceeding with reference to that federal labor policy.

[The Comment gives no example of a state statute with a provision adverse to federal labor policy other than one lacking a provision conferring subpoena power upon the arbitrator.

An important procedure under New York CPLR may be viewed, however, as irreconcilable with federal policy. Section 7503(c) provides for a "notice of intention to arbitrate." If that section's procedure is not followed, a party "shall thereafter be precluded from objecting that a valid agreement was not made or has not been complied with."

As to the asserted nonexistence of a valid agreement, the federal law might make it a question for the arbitrator in the first instance, subject to later court review. (But *cf.* the *Genesco* case, in Chapter XI, and accompanying text.) However, in a New York case the union contested hiring practices under a strike settlement agreement and took the dispute to arbitration. The company (a large national concern whose activities "affect" interstate commerce) contended before the arbitrators that the strike settlement document contained no arbitration clause, but it participated in the proceeding on the merits. The New York Court of Appeals held that the dispute was covered by the arbitration section of a collective bargaining agreement between the parties that also covered "supplements." It also held that by participating in the arbitration proceeding the Company waived its right to contest arbitrability. Matter of National Cash Register (Wilson) 8 N.Y. 2d 377, 171 N.E. 2d 302 (1960).

And the New York act seems to require court decision before an arbitral hearing if a party

---

1. This type of application must include a *de minimis* proviso or else it would be unmanageable. When the provision only has a minimum adverse effect on the federal policy the provision should still be applied.

raises the issue that procedural prerequisites to arbitration have not been observed, a procedure clearly at odds with the *Wiley* decision.]

B. *Prima Facie Application or Non-application.* The non-application of state statutes would create a steady growth of uniform national arbitration law. Once this national arbitration law has been developed, unions and employers could be assured that arbitration clauses in their national agreements would receive uniform treatment throughout the country. Although this advantage of uniformity will accrue to the negotiators of other labor arbitration agreements as well, it is of particular importance to the national agreements.

The basic question, however, is whether to interpret the Supreme Court's mandate to use state arbitration law as a guideline in a strict or in a liberal sense. Strict interpretation would mean that the statutes must be used only as a guide to a general overview of what is contained in all arbitration statutes and looked at in the light of section 301. This would evolve a form of national labor arbitration law. Non-application, however, in helping fashion a federal policy is not a practical solution. To so apply the state arbitration statutes would possibly result in a conglomeration of various court interpretations as to what should or should not be part of the federal policy. The mandate by the Supreme Court was vague, but that is no reason why the national labor policy fashioned as a result of that mandate must also be vague.

The state courts, as the federal courts, have not faced the problem of the applicability of their arbitration statutes to proceedings subject to section 301 to any great extent.

In *McCarroll*, the court interpreted section 301 to "facilitate the enforcement of collective bargaining agreements by making unions suable as entities in the federal courts, and thereby to remedy the one-sided character of existing labor legislation." The court had misinterpreted the legislative intent of section 301. Making the unions suable was only the *means* to industrial peace and stability, not an end in itself. The court did, however, look first to federal labor policy before determining whether the state court had the right to issue an injunction, realizing that federal law was controlling.

The dissent in *McCarroll* by Justice Carter points out very adequately that in *Lincoln Mills* a remedy was involved—that of specific performance. Justice Carter said that "such remedy [injunctive relief] is more than mere procedure. It goes to the very essence of the right itself. In many instances, it would make the difference

of whether or not the right could be truly realized." He felt that federal law should apply. The provisions of the various state arbitration statutes likewise go to the very essence of this right. The subpoena power of the arbitrator, the power of the court to modify, and other provisions, all affect the outcome of the right asserted under section 301.

A California district court of appeals, in Laufman v. Hall-Mack Co., faced the question of the appealability of an order compelling arbitration. Neither party questioned that the case came within section 301. The problem arose because the order was not appealable under section 1294 of the California Code of Civil Procedure but would be appealable in a federal court.* The court held that because state procedure applied, the order was not appealable. However, the court based its holding upon its finding that federal law encourages arbitration and the California policy behind their state procedure "is even more encouraging of the use of arbitration than is the federal procedure." The court also went on to explain that "if appellant loses in arbitration it then has a statutory right of appeal under section 1294 of the Code of Civil Procedure." Thus, after looking at the federal labor policy and its purpose and concluding that the state procedure was consistent with this federal labor policy, the court applied the state arbitration procedure. The court avoided a direct clash between federal policy and state procedure by finding both were, in reality, supplemental. Such an application by other state courts of their arbitration statutes would require those courts to do as California did; look to the state arbitration statute, determine if the provision in question conformed with the federal labor policy, and if so, apply the statute.

The rationale of the court in *Laufman* is consistent with the Supreme Court's suggestion that "state law, if compatible with the purpose of section 301, may be resorted to in order to find the rule that will best effectuate the federal policy." But the Supreme Court has warned that, any state law applied, "will be absorbed as federal law and will not be an independent source of private rights." To comply properly with the Supreme Court's mandate to apply federal law in section 301 cases and the mandate to adhere to the federal policy of favoring the arbitration process when it is a section 301 col-

---

*[Based upon the Court's holding in Goodall-Sanford v. United Textile Workers, 353 U.S. 550 (1957), a companion case to *Lincoln Mills*, that an order directing arbitration is appealable. Is this 1957 holding under § 301 compatible with the *Trilogy*?]

lective bargaining agreement, the state courts should not indiscriminately apply state arbitration statutes. Those statutes can affect the substance of the controversy and are not *mere* "procedures."

These cases have shown the flexibility and practicality of a *prima facie* application of state arbitration statutes. The *prima facie* application used by the courts, in McCarroll v. Los Angeles County Dist. of Car. (sic) and Laufmann v. Hall-Mack Co., is a more practical approach to the overall problem of application than a *per se* or non-application. It will result in a more uniform handling of labor arbitration in section 301 contracts. The parties need to have some definite rules set down in order to be able to formulate effectively an abitration provision within their collective bargaining contract that best suits their interests. Without the state statutes to look to, the parties would be forced to wait for a case-by-case creation of an arbitration procedure by the courts. A *prima facie* application of the arbitration statutes would give this needed definiteness and would at the same time comply more closely to the Supreme Court's mandate than the other two methods of application.

There will, naturally, be *de minimis* clashes in some situations, but the courts, for the sake of convenience and practicality, should not concern itself with such minimal clashes. For example, time requirements for filing an application to vacate an award might vary from state to state. The advantage of having such statutes of limitation would override any disadvantages arising from the non-uniformity of such statutes between the states.

The practicality of the *prima facie* application of state arbitration statutes is considerable although, naturally, it alone is not determinative of whether such a rule of application can be followed. The attorneys, arbitrators, and parties, as well as the courts involved in the arbitration, need guidelines which can well be supplied by the state statutes. Attorneys, arbitrators, parties, and courts are usually quite familiar with their own individual state statutes and can thus work more effectively under them than they could under a new and foreign set of requirements or under no specific set at all in order to achieve the goal of federal labor policy that encourages arbitration in labor disputes.

A SURVEY OF STATE ARBITRATION PROCEDURE
STATUTES

A. *Statutes That Exclude Labor Arbitration Agreements from Coverage.* [The Comment briefly reviews such statutes and concludes that they must give way before the dominant federal law. Not considered is whether the *"prima facie"* approach, *i.e.,* the use of the state statute's procedure until it collides with federal policy, should be employed when the state statute does not apply to labor arbitration. That would be a bit like using a tail when there is no dog. It is at least arguable that had the state legislature included labor-dispute arbitration it might have provided some procedures differing from those applicable to nonlabor cases. Some few states do make some differentiations. On the other hand, so few states do so and the generality of arbitration provisions are so very similar among statutes of the same generation that it may be regarded as simply looking for trouble for a state to abjure, or federal law to compel, nonuse of the usual state procedures.]

B. *The Subpoena Power of the Arbitrator.* [Assuming that subpoena power in the arbitrator is an important adjunct of effective arbitration and its absence a serious impediment, the Comment in this section concludes that: "the subpoena power should be granted to the arbitrator when the proceedings are subject to section 301, even in states not specifically granting subpoena power in their statutes."

However, the Comment does not discuss whether such a power can be conferred in the absence of a specific statute. Possibly the power exists only when a statute affirmatively confers it. There are obvious problems in looking to Section 7 of the United States Arbitration Act as the source for litigation in state courts. Hence, state statutes may be the only available source. If so, the power would not be present in all states.

Perhaps this problem can be avoided by the bold assertion that Congress meant to confer subpoena power upon section 301 arbitrators, a conclusion derived from the view that subpoena power is an indispensable characteristic of a modern arbitration system.]

C. *Order to Compel or Stay Arbitration ; Stay of Action.* Many state arbitration statutes provide for the application by parties allegedly aggrieved for an order to compel or stay the arbitration or for an order to stay a court action pending the outcome of an arbitrable issue.

The Supreme Court's holding in *Lincoln Mills* removed any doubt about whether courts may order arbitration in controversies covered by arbitration agreements. Whether or not the state arbitration statute provides for such an order by the court, the court should be able to specifically enforce such an agreement. Without the ability to enforce, the court would be deprived of its most effective means of encouraging the arbitration of labor disputes.

Arbitration statutes often contain a provision to stay a pending action if there is an arbitrable issue involved. The courts in the four states studied in detail did not question their right, in the labor arbitration area, to grant a stay of an action pending arbitration. Arguments against judicial grants of stays where the arbitration is subject to section 301 point out that there has been no specific grant of such power to the courts. Traditionally, the courts have only been known to possess the authority to specifically enforce arbitration agreements contained within collective bargaining contracts. Thus, goes the argument, parties have only the section 301 right to enforcement of their contract. But to accept this position is to construe too strictly the substantive rights granted by section 301, a fact evidenced by the Court's liberal approach in *Lincoln Mills.*

The application for a stay of action is treated as an extension of the request for specific performance of an arbitration provision in the *Lincoln Mills* case. There is no doubt that this authority of the court to grant a stay of action comes within section 301 ; any refusal or avoidance of an arbitrable issue being submitted to an arbitration proceeding is a violation of the collective bargaining agreement. The question of whether the court's authority to issue the stay is derived from the state statute or from the federal policy supporting section 301 is more academic than practical. The result in either case is the same. To be consistent with the federal policy, the answer would have to be that the stay power of the state court comes from section 301 itself and the state statute was utilized through a *prima facie* application of that statute.

If there is no stay provision within the statute or there is no arbitration statute at all, the state court should still have the authority to grant a stay in the appropriate cases. The remedy of specific enforcement being available, assuming no waiver of the arbitration provisions by the moving party, there is no logical reason why a stay cannot be granted. Not to grant the stay would be in effect to deny specific performance. Thus the moving party would be deprived of his federal right because of lack of a statutory provision or a state statute. There is no great difficulty in making the jump from allowing the issuance of a stay of a court action, when a statute so permits, to allowing the stay when the statute is silent or absent. Not to allow the jump would conflict with the federal policy.

Some arbitration statutes provide for a stay of arbitration only under certain circumstances. If the purpose of allowing such a stay is only to enforce compliance with a valid agreement against a recalcitrant, it is no more than contract law. Or, if the local statute provides that "the court may stay an arbitration proceeding commenced or threatened on a showing that there is no agreement to arbitrate," the court is merely determining the existence of a valid arbitration contract. Courts would seem to have such authority even in the absence of a statute since the collective bargaining contract contains the arbitration provision which will be stayed. It has been held that no contracting party can be compelled to submit to arbitration any matter which he has not agreed to arbitrate. But since the parties generally have contracted to so arbitrate, the federal policy desires to give effect to such agreements whenever possible and thus a stay of arbitration cannot generally be granted, unless it is upon the basis of general contract law that no agreement exists. To maintain consistency in the arbitration procedures, the test for stay of arbitration should necessarily be the same as that for an action to compel arbitration.

[Section 1218.4 of the California Code has two peculiarities. It seems to require a court order compeling arbitration as a condition to a stay of proceedings in its courts. Although Section 7503 of New York's CPLR also seems to limit stay of proceedings to situations in which the court has "jurisdiction to hear a motion to compel arbitration," the New York courts have not interpreted it so narrowly.) Many of the modern acts, such as the U.S.A.A., require for a stay only that "the issue involved in such suit or proceeding is referable to arbitration under such an agreement."

Should a California court in a section 301 situation decline to stay a case in its courts where it cannot compel arbitration—perhaps because the arbitration is to take place outside California, (which may not be an insuperable obstacle)— and no other court has issued such an order?

The California Code also provides in § 1281.4: "If the issue which is the controversy subject to arbitration is severable, the stay may be with respect to that issue only." Under most modern acts, including the U.S.A.A., severing the issues is not contemplated. Such a provision seems reasonable. Assessing the interrelationship of issues may involve considerable labor-management expertise ; it could be argued that such a determination trenches upon the arbitrator's function. Compare the Supreme Court's view of the interrelationship of court and arbitral proceedings involving alleged violation of no-strike clauses in Atkinson v. Sinclair.]

D. *Vacation or Modification of the Award.* The vast majority of state arbitration statutes contain a provision permitting a court to declare an award void under certain conditions. The existence of this power is generally consistent with section 301. The ability of the court to vacate an award is generally limited to certain specified grounds. Although both parties submit to arbitration as required by an arbitration agreement, the defect might well come when the arbitrator issues the award. The award of the arbitrator is normally final and conclusive, and courts will not review the merits of the dispute. Thus, it is apparent that state legislatures have great faith in the arbitration process. The collective bargaining agreement contemplates an unprejudiced, unbiased award, and it follows that if an award is not made impartially or without bias the agreement has not been fulfilled. Without a procedure for vacation or modification the courts would be at a loss as to correcting the prejudice suffered by either party.

In Keller v. Local 249, Int'l Bhd of Teamsters, 423 Pa. 353, 223 A.2 724 (1966), a party sought vacation of an award in a dispute between the Western Pennsylvania Motor Carriers Association and Local 249. The court held that the common law rules of limited review would be followed rather than the broader review provisions of the 1927 Pennsylvania statute because there was no evidence that the parties intended the 1927 act to apply. No mention was made of section 301, although it seems probable that the Association's activities would be subject to the LMRA.

b. Application of State Statute of Limitations to a Section 301 Suit

AUTOWORKERS v. HOOSIER CARDINAL CORP.
383 U.S. 696 (1966)

Stewart, J. Section 301 of the Labor Management Relations Act, 1947, confers jurisdiction upon the federal district courts over suits upon collective bargaining contracts. Nowhere in the Act, however, is there a provision for any time limitation upon the bringing of an action under § 301. The questions presented by this case arise because of the absence of such a provision.

The petitioner union and the respondent company were parties to a collective bargaining contract within the purview of § 301. The contract contained a section governing vacations. One clause in this section dealt with payment of accumulated vacation pay, by providing: "Employees who qualified for a vacation in the previous year and whose employment is terminated for any reason before the vacation is taken will be paid that vacation at time of termination." On June 1, 1957, prior to the expiration of the contract, the company terminated the employment of employees covered by the agreement, but it did not pay them any accumulated vacation pay. Since that date, two lawsuits have been brought to recover amounts allegedly due. The first was a class action in early 1958, brought against the company in an Indiana court, but the court ruled that such an action was impermissible under Indiana law. In an attempt to remedy this pleading defect, the former employees assigned their vacation pay claims to a union representative who then filed an amended complaint, but this form of action, too, was held improper under Indiana law. Thereafter, by further amended complaints, the employees sought to reform and reinstitute the class action, but once again the trial court held the complaint insufficient as a matter of state law. The court dismissed the suit in June 1960, and the judgment of dismissal was affirmed on appeal. Johnson v. Hoosier Cardinal Corp., 134 Ind. 477, 189 N.E. 2d 592.

Almost four years after the dismissal of that lawsuit by the Indiana trial court, and almost seven years after the employees had left the company, the union filed the present action in the United States District Court for the Southern District of Indiana. On the company's motion, the trial court dismissed the complaint, concluding that the suit was barred by a six-year Indiana statute of limitations. The court regarded this action as based partly upon the written collective bargaining agreement and partly upon the oral employment contract each employee had made, and it held that Indiana would apply to such a hybrid action its six-year statute governing contracts not in writing. Ind. Stat. Ann. § 2–601 (1965 Supp.). 235 F. Supp. 183. The Court of Appeals for the Seventh Circuit affirmed, 346 F. 2d 242, and we granted certiorari, 382 U.S. 808.

We note at the outset that this action was properly brought by the union under § 301. There is no merit to the contention that a union may not sue to recover wages or vacation pay claimed by its members pursuant to the terms of a collective bargaining contract.

Since this suit was properly brought under § 301, the question of its timeliness is squarely presented. It is clearly a federal question, for in § 301 suits the applicable law is "federal law, which the courts must fashion from the policy of our national labor laws." Textile Workers v. Lincoln Mills, 353 U.S. 448, 456. Relying upon that statement and upon the co-ordinate principle that "incompatible doctrines of local law must give way to principles of federal labor law," Teamsters Local v. Lucas Flour Co., 369 U.S. 95, 102, the union contends that this suit cannot be barred by a statute of limitations enacted by a State. We are urged instead to devise a uniform time limitation to close the statutory gap left by Congress. But the teaching of our cases does not require so bald a form of judicial innovation. *Lincoln Mills* instructs that, in fashioning federal law, the "range of judicial inventiveness will be determined by the nature of the problem." 353 U.S., at 457. We do not question that there are problems so vital to the implementation of federal labor policy that they will command a high degree of inventiveness from the courts. The problem presented here, however, is not of that nature.

It is true that if state limitations provisions govern § 301 suits, these suits will lack a uniform standard of timeliness. It is also true that the subject matter of § 301 is "peculiarly one that calls for uniform law." Teamsters Local v. Lucas Flour Co., *supra*. Our cases have defined the need for uniformity, however, in terms that are largely inapplicable here:

> The possibility that individual contract terms might have different meanings under [two systems of law] would inevitably exert a disruptive influence upon both the negotiation and administration of collective agreements. Because neither party could be certain of the rights which it had obtained or conceded, the process of negotiating an agreement would be made immeasurably more difficult by the necessity of trying to formulate contract provisions in such a way as to contain the same meaning under two or more systems of law which might someday be invoked in enforcing the contract. Teamsters Local v. Lucas Flour Co., 369 U.S. 95, 103–104.

The need for uniformity, then, is greatest where its absence would threaten the smooth functioning of those consensual processes that federal labor law is chiefly designed to promote —the formation of the collective agreement and the private settlement of disputes under it. For the most part, statutes of limitations come into play only when these processes have already broken down. Lack of uniformity in this area is therefore unlikely to frustrate in any important way the achievement of any significant goal of labor policy. Thus, although a uniform limitations provision for § 301 suits might well constitute a desirable statutory addition, there is no justification for the drastic sort of judicial

legislation that is urged upon us.[1] See Smith v. Evening News Assn., *supra*, at 203 (Black, J., dissenting).

That Congress did not provide a uniform limitations provision for § 301 suits is not an argument for judicially creating one, unless we ignore the context of this legislative omission. It is clear that Congress gave attention to limitations problems in the Labor Management Relations Act, 1947; it enacted a six months' provision to govern unfair labor practice proceedings, 61 Stat. 146, 29 U.S.C. § 160 (b) (1964 ed.), and it did so only after appreciable controversy. In this context, and against the background of the relationship between Congress and the courts on the question of limitations provisions, it cannot be fairly inferred that when Congress left § 301 without a uniform time limitation, it did so in the expectation that the courts would invent one. As early as 1830, this Court held that state statutes of limitations govern the timeliness of federal causes of action unless Congress has specifically provided otherwise. McCluny v. Silliman, 3 Pet. 270, 277. In 1895, the question was re-examined in another context, but the conclusion remained firm. Campbell v. Haverhill, 155 U.S. 610. Since that time, state statutes have repeatedly supplied the periods of limitations for federal causes of action when federal legislation has been silent on the question. Yet when Congress has disagreed with such an interpretation of its silence, it has spoken to overturn it by enacting a uniform period of limitations. *E.g.,* 69 Stat. 283, 15 U.S.C. 15b (1964 ed.) (Clayton Act); 35 U.S.C. § 286 (Patent Act). See also Herget v. Central Bank Co., 324 U.S. 4. Against this background, we cannot take the omission in the present statute as a license to judicially devise a uniform time limitation for § 301 suits.

Accordingly, since no federal provision governs, we hold that the timeliness of a § 301 suit, such as the present one, is to be determined, as a matter of federal law, by reference

---

1. Our cases have spoken of the federal law applicable to § 301 suits as "substantive," see, *e.g.,* Textile Workers v. Lincoln Mills, 353 U.S., at 456, and the need for uniformity in the "substantive principles" that govern these suits. See Teamsters Local v. Lucas Flour Co., 369 U.S., at 103. In the view we take of the problem presented here, we need not decide whether statutes of limitations are "substantive" or "procedural." See Guaranty Trust Co. v. York, 326 U.S. 99; Burnett v. New York Central R. Co., 380 U.S. 424, 427, note 2. Nor need we rigidly classify them as "primary" or "remedial." To the extent that these terms are useful, we need only notice that lack of uniformity in limitations provisions is unlikely to have substantial effect upon the private definition or effectuation of "substantive" or "primary" rights in the collective bargaining process. See Wellington, *Labor and the Federal System,* 26 U. CHI. L. REV. 542, 556–559.

to the appropriate state statute of limitations.[2] This leaves two subsidiary questions to be decided. Which of Indiana's limitations provisions governs?[3] Does any tolling principle preserve the timeliness of this action?

The union argues that if the timeliness of this action is to be determined by reference to Indiana statutes, federal law precludes reference to the Indiana six-year provision governing contracts not in writing. Reference must be made instead, it is urged, to the Indiana 20-year provision governing written contracts. Ind. Stat. Ann. § 2–602 (1965 Supp.). This contention rests on the view that under federal law this § 301 suit must be regarded as exclusively bottomed upon the written collective bargaining agreement. We agree that the characterization of this action for the purpose of selecting the appropriate state limitations provision is ultimately a question of federal law. Textile Workers v. Lincoln Mills, *supra*; McClane v. Rankin, *supra*. But there is no reason to reject the characterization that state law would impose unless that characterization is unreasonable or otherwise inconsistent with national labor policy. Cf. Reconstruction Finance Corp. v. Beaver County, 328 U.S. 204, 210; De Sylva v. Ballentine, 351 U.S. 570, 580–582.

Applying this principle, we cannot agree that federal law requires that this action be regarded as exclusively based upon a written contract. For purposes of § 301 jurisdiction, we have rejected the view that a suit such as this is based solely upon the separate hiring contracts, frequently oral, between the employer and each

employee. Smith v. Evening News Assn., *supra*. It does not follow, however, that the separate contracts of employment may not be taken into account in characterizing the nature of a specific § 301 suit for the purpose of selecting the appropriate state limitations provision. Indeed, as the present case indicates, consideration of the separate contracts for that purpose is entirely acceptable. The petitioner seeks damages based upon an alleged breach of the vacation pay clause in a written collective bargaining agreement. Proof of the breach and of the measure of damages, however, both depend upon proof of the existence and duration of separate employment contracts between the employer and each of the aggrieved employees. Hence, this § 301 suit may fairly be characterized as one not exclusively based upon a written contract.

Moreover, the characterization that Indiana law imposes upon this action does not lead to any conflict with federal labor policy. Indeed, to the extent that a policy is manifest in the Labor Management Relations Act, it supports acceptance of the characterization adopted here. The six months' provision governing unfair labor practice proceedings, 61 Stat. 146, 29 U.S.C. § 160 (b), suggests that relatively rapid disposition of labor disputes is a goal of federal labor law. Since state statutes of limitations governing contracts not exclusively in writing are generally shorter than those applicable to wholly written agreements, their applicability to § 301 actions comports with that goal. There may, of course, be § 301 actions that can only be characterized fairly as based exclusively upon a written agreement. But since many § 301 actions for wages or other individual benefits will concern employment contracts of the sort involved here, there is no reason to inhibit the achievement of an identifiable goal of labor policy by precluding application of the generally shorter limitations provisions.[4]

Accordingly, we accept the District Court's application of the six-year Indiana statute of limitations to this action. Cf. Bernhardt v. Polygraphic Co., 350 U.S. 198, 204–205; Steele v. General Mills, 329 U.S. 433, 438. Thus, since

---

2. The present suit is essentially an action for damages caused by an alleged breach of an employer's obligation embodied in a collective bargaining agreement. Such an action closely resembles an action for breach of contract cognizable at common law. Whether other § 301 suits different from the present one might call for the application of other rules on timeliness, we are not required to decide, and we indicate no view whatsoever on that question. See, *e.g.*, Holmberg v. Armbrecht, 327 U.S. 392; Moviecolor Limited v. Eastman Kodak Co., 288 F. 2d 80 (C.A. 2d Cir.); 2 MOORE, FEDERAL PRACTICE ¶ 3.07[1]–[3], at 740–764 (2d ed. 1965); Hill, *State Procedural Law in Federal Nondiversity Litigation*, 69 HARV. L. REV. 66, 111–114.

3. The record indicates that Indiana is both the forum State and the State in which all operative events occurred. Neither party has suggested that the limitations provision of another State is relevant. There is therefore no occasion to consider whether such a choice of law should be made in accord with the principle of Klaxon Co. v. Stentor Mfg. Co., 313 U.S. 487, or by operation of a different federal conflict of laws rule. See Richards v. United States, 369 U.S. 1; De Sylva v. Ballentine, 351 U.S. 570; Vanston Bondholders Protective Committee v. Green, 329 U.S. 156; McKenzie v. Irving Trust Co., 323 U.S. 365; D'Oench, Duhme & Co. v. Federal Deposit Ins. Corp., 315 U.S. 447. See also discussion in HART & WECHSLER, THE FEDERAL COURTS AND THE FEDERAL SYSTEM 696 *et seq.*

4. Other questions would be raised if this case presented a state law characterization of a § 301 suit that reasonably described the nature of the cause of action, but required application of an unusually short or long limitations period. See, *e.g.*, N.M. Stat. § 59–3–4 (1953) (an action for wages "must be commenced within sixty [60] days from the date of discharge. . . ."). See Campbell v. Haverhill, 155 U.S. 610, 615; Caldwell v. Alabama Dry Dock & Shipbuilding Co., 161 F. 2d 83 (C.A. 5th Cir.); Mishkin, "The Variousness of 'Federal Law': Competence and Discretion in the Choice of National and State Rules for Decision," 105 U. PA. L. REV. 797, 805–806.

this federal lawsuit was not filed until almost seven years after the cause of action accrued, the cause is barred by the six-year statute unless that statute was somehow tolled by reason of the particularized circumstances of this case.

The contention that some tolling principle saves the life of this action was raised for the first time in this Court. In any event, we find the contention without merit. In Burnett v. New York Central R. Co., 380 U.S. 424, we held that the bringing of a timely action under the Federal Employers' Liability Act in a state court, even though venue was improper, served to toll the statute of limitations contained in that Act. The primary underpinning of *Burnett*, however, is wholly lacking here. As the Court noted in that case, a tolling principle was necessary to implement the national policy of a uniform time bar clearly expressed by Congress when it enacted the FELA limitations provision. 380 U.S., at 434. Section 301 of the Labor Management Relations Act establishes no such policy of uniformity expressed in a national limitations provision. Moreover, unlike the plaintiff in *Burnett* who could no longer bring a timely federal action after the state court dismissed his complaint, the union here had a full three years to bring this lawsuit in federal court after the dismissal of the state court action. Under these circumstances, we have no difficulty in concluding that this cause of action expired in June 1963, six years after it arose.

Affirmed.

c. The Use of the U.S.A.A. in a Section 301 Suit

Innumerable federal cases arising under § 301 apply the procedural prescriptions of the U.S.A.A. apparently without controversy on the point. Yet the Supreme Court, in companion cases to *Lincoln Mills,* made it very clear that § 301 governed such questions as appealability of orders directing arbitration and explicitly rejected the U.S.A.A. as pertinent.

The U.S.A.A. may provide some guidance to the courts on procedural questions however, and its use may be a matter of convenience. As with possibly useful state acts in state courts, however, the proper test would seem to be whether the U.S.A.A. promotes the policies of § 301. Where its provisions may come into conflict, as, for example, the limitations made clear in *Dant & Russell,* above, it should not be controling.

2. COMMERCIAL ARBITRATION

The Supreme Court's decision in *Prima Paint* (set out in Chapter III, Part G) apparently leaves open the question whether the United States Arbitration Act is one of the "laws of the United States" binding upon the states under the Supremacy Clause. The majority opinion speaks repeatedly of the act in relation only to "the federal courts" ["the question is whether Congress may prescribe how federal courts are to conduct themselves with respect to subject matter over which Congress plainly has power to legislate"]. Nor did the majority rise to the bait in the dissent that the Court's opinion left "up in the air" the applicability of the act as federal substantive law "required to be applied by state courts." Only the concurring Justice Harlan explicitly based affirmance upon *Lawrence v. Devonshire.*

Yet it would be rather remarkable to limit the applicability of the United States Arbitration Act, now held to be substantive law for constitutional purposes of federal court jurisdiction, to the federal courts when the act does not itself confer federal court jurisdiction. The statute is unusual, to say the least, in that another independent ground of jurisdiction must be present—"save for such agreement"—in order for the federal courts to take hold in Section 4. And a stay under Section 3 is needed only if a federal court has jurisdiction of the case on some basis other than the act; otherwise dismissal would suffice.

One would suppose that, like Section 301 of the Labor-Management Relations Act (which remarkably enough has *not* been adverted to by the courts in the *Lawrence-Prima* set of cases), Section 2 of the U.S.A.A., declaring agreements to arbitrate in contracts involving interstate commerce and maritime transactions valid, enforceable, and irrevocable, *is* federal substantive law for Supremacy Clause purposes. Although Sections 3 and 4 may be limited to Section 2 agreements, as in *Bernhardt,*[1] it has yet to be decided that if Section 2 is binding upon state courts, the enforcement machinery of Sections 3 (stay of suit), 4 (specific enforcement), 5 (court appointment of arbitrators where parties' method fails), 7 (enforcement of arbitrator's subpoenas), 9, 10, and 11 (confirmation, vacation and modification of awards) accompany it into state courts.

No evidence has come to hand that other non-labor agreements to arbitrate which involve

1. At least one federal court has held a Section 3 stay available in vindication of an arbitration clause valid under New York law. The court conceivably might have reached the same result by using the analogous stay provision of the New York CPLR. (2d Cir. 1966) 364 F. 2d 705. *Capolino Sons Inc. v. Electronic & Missile Facilities, Inc.* (alternate ground).

interstate transactions but do not satisfy federal court jurisdictional criteria are being frustrated. If such a class exists or *Prima* encourages parties to write such agreements which may require enforcement in states hewing to common law arbitration, attempts to invoke section 2 of the U.S.A.A. as substantive law may occur in those states. Insurance companies may decide to seek the shelter of the U.S.A.A. for the arbitration provisions of their uninsured-motorist coverage in states like Arkansas, Oklahoma, and Vermont. Whether individual accident policies "involve" interstate commerce remains to be seen. Judging from the Court's slighting reference in note 9 (note 4 as edited here) to "Contracts ... in which one of the parties characteristically has little bargaining power," the argument that the uninsured-motorist coverage comes under the U.S.A.A. may receive a frosty welcome. On the bargaining power point, see former Justice Goldberg's *A Supreme Court Justice Looks at Arbitration*, 20 ARB. J. (n.s.) 13, 16 (1965). Perhaps a livelier question will be whether federal or state arbitration law will apply in the states with arbitration acts where commercial arbitration is most widely used.

As the dissent points out, if different decisions may result depending upon which court is open to parties in dispute over a contract with a clause that qualifies under section 2, forum shopping of the kind *Bernhardt* and *Erie* were designed to preclude will be encouraged. Surely this is an argument for having the federal statute apply in full in state courts.

But statutory language presents some difficulties to such a course. Section 3, for example, comes into play "If any suit or proceeding be brought in any of the courts of the United States." Even if one were willing to say such courts include state courts, what does one do with section 4, which makes a decree of specific enforcement available from "any United States district court"? Section 5 refers only to "the court," which is to appoint arbitrators when the parties' method miscarries. But power to enforce subpoenas is confided in section 7 "to the United States district court," and so on.

Courts that have learned that what appear to be state procedural rules are to be observed by the federal district courts in diversity cases could also decide that the state courts could adapt what appear to be federal procedural directions in their proceedings.

Or the accommodation could be made on the basis suggested in the *Comment* in the preceding section, *i.e.*, apply the underlying substantive rule of enforcement of agreements to arbitrate and employ the usual state procedures until they interfere with the achievement of federal policy. In the labor sector, the problem has yet to arise, although the potentiality for conflict is there. In the commercial realm, the potentiality for conflict may well be less because arbitration has yet to achieve so favored a position in the Supreme Court's view as that enjoyed by labor arbitration. (Yet commercial arbitration may be operating more successfully, judging from the fact that it generates so little litigation in comparison with section 301.)

A third alternative is to limit the U.S.A.A. to the federal courts and await a demand for legislation to extend its reach to the state courts. Such an extension would not accord with what seems to me to be the predisposition of Congress and would take considerable interest group pressure, which seems to be lacking.[2]

For an early decision dealing with some aspects of this problem, consult California Prune & Apricot Growers' Assn. v. Catz American Co. 60 F. 2d 788 (9th Cir. 1932)

For a pre-*Bernhardt* discussion of this case and associated problems, consult Wesley Sturges and Irving Murphy, *Some Confusing Matters Relating to Arbitration Under the United States Arbitration Act,* 17 LAW AND CONTEMP. PROB. 580, 619–629 (1952).

---

2. When the appropriate committees of the American Bar Association confronted the problems of enforcing the United Nations Convention on the Recognition and Enforcement of Foreign Arbitral Awards, it shrank from suggesting that United States adherence, which it advocated, extend to making arbitration awards and agreement in international transactions enforceable in state courts. A.B.A. Section of International and Comparative Law, REPORT OF THE COMMITTEE ON INTERNATIONAL UNIFICATION OF PRIVATE LAW (1960).

C.

International Arbitration

UNITED NATIONS CONVENTION ON THE RECOGNITION AND ENFORCEMENT OF FOREIGN ARBITRAL AWARDS

Article I

1. This Convention shall apply to the recognition and enforcement of arbitral awards made in the territory of a State other than the State where the recognition and enforcement of such awards are sought, and arising out of differences between persons, whether physical or legal. It shall also apply to arbitral awards not considered as domestic awards in the State where their recognition and enforcement are sought.

2. The term "arbitral awards" shall include not only awards made by arbitrators appointed for each case but also those made by permanent arbitral bodies to which the parties have submitted.

3. When signing, ratifying or acceding to this Convention, or notifying extension under article X hereof, any State may on the basis of reciprocity declare that it will apply the Convention to the recognition and enforcement of awards made only in the territory of another Contracting State. It may also declare that it will apply the Convention only to differences arising out of legal relationships, whether contractual or not, which are considered as commercial under the national law of the State making such declaration.

Article II

1. Each Contracting State shall recognize an agreement in writing under which the parties undertake to submit to arbitration all or any differences which have arisen or which may arise between them in respect of a defined legal relationship, whether contractual or not, concerning a subject matter capable of settlement by arbitration.

2. The term "agreement in writing" shall include an arbitral clause in a contract or an arbitration agreement, signed by the parties or contained in an exchange of letters or telegrams.

3. The court of a Contracting State, when seized of an action in a matter in respect of which the parties have made an agreement within the meaning of this article, shall, at the request of one of the parties, refer the parties to arbitration, unless it finds that the said agreement is null and void, inoperative or incapable of being performed.

Article III

Each Contracting State shall recognize arbitral awards as binding and enforce them in accordance with the rules of procedure of the territory where the award is relied upon, under the conditions laid down in the following articles. There shall not be imposed substantially more onerous conditions or higher fees or charges on the recognition or enforcement of domestic arbitral awards.

Article IV

1. To obtain the recognition and enforcement mentioned in the preceding article, the party applying for recognition and enforcement shall, at the time of the application, supply:

(a) The duly authenticated original award or a duly certified copy thereof;

(b) The original agreement referred to in article II or a duly certified copy thereof.

Article V

1. Recognition and enforcement of the award may be refused, at the request of the party against whom it is invoked, only if that party furnishes to the competent authority where the recognition and enforcement is sought, proof that:

(a) The parties to the agreement referred to in article II were under the law applicable to them, under some incapacity, or the said agreement is not valid under the law to which the parties have subjected it or, failing any indication thereon, under the law of the country where the award was made; or

(b) The party against whom the award is invoked was not given proper notice of the appointment of the arbitrator or of the arbitration proceedings or was otherwise unable to present his case; or

(c) The award deals with a difference not contemplated by or not falling within the terms of the submission to arbitration, or it contains decisions on matters beyond the scope of the submission to arbitration, provided that, if the decisions on matters submitted to arbitration can be separated from those not so submitted, that part of the award which contains decisions on matters submitted to arbitration may be recognized and enforced; or

(d) The composition of the arbitral authority or the arbitral procedure was not in accordance with the agreement of the parties, or, failing such agreement, was not in accordance with the law of the country where the arbitration took place; or

(e) The award has not yet become binding on the parties, or has been set aside or suspended by a competent authority of the country in which, or under the law of which, that award was made.

2. Recognition and enforcement of an arbitral award may also be refused if the competent authority in the country where recognition and enforcement is sought finds that:

(a) The subject matter of the difference is not capable of settlement by arbitration under the law of that country; or

(b) The recognition or enforcement of the award would be contrary to the public policy of that country.

Article VI

If an application for the setting aside or suspension of the award has been made to a competent authority referred to in article V (1) (e), the authority before which the award is sought to be relied upon may, if it considers it proper, adjourn the decision on the enforcement of the award and may also, on the application of the party claiming enforcement of the award, order the other party to give suitable security.

Article VII

[Validity of other multilateral and bilateral agreements not affected; apparently intends them to apply if more favorable to enforcement.] [Also, Geneva Protocol and Convention to be superseded as between States acceding to Convention to the extent that they do so.]

Article VIII

[Ratification]

Article IX

[Accession]

Article X

[Applicability to territories for which State acts internationally—may apply by declaration of State]

Article XI

In the case of a federal or non-unitary State, the following provisions shall apply:

(a) With respect to those articles of this Convention that come within the legislative jurisdiction of the federal authority, the obligations of the federal Government shall to this extent be the same as those of Contracting States which are not federal States;

(b) With respect to those articles of this Convention that come within the legislative jurisdiction of constituent states or provinces which are not, under the constitutional system of the federation, bound to take legislative action, the federal Government shall bring such articles with a favorable recommendation to the notice of the appropriate authorities of constituent states or provinces at the earliest possible moment;

(c) A federal State Party to this Convention shall, at the request of any other Contracting State transmitted through the Secretary-General of the United Nations, supply a statement of the law and practice of the federation and its constituent units in regard to any particular provision of this Convention, showing the extent to which effect has been given to that provision by legislative or other action.

Article XII

[Effective dates]

Article XIII

[Denunciation]

Article XIV

A Contracting State shall not be entitled to avail itself of the present Convention against other Contracting States except to the extent that it is itself bound to apply the Convention.

Articles XV and XVI

[Formal matters re notifications and transla-
tions]

———————

For an excellent discussion of some major
problems of applying the U.N. Convention in
the United States, see Quigley, *Accession to the
United Nations Convention on the Recognition
and Enforcement of Foreign Arbitral Awards*,
70 YALE L. J. 1049 (1961).

On international arbitration problems generally
see MARTIN DOMKE (ed.), INTERNATIONAL TRADE
ARBITRATION (1958). Included are articles on
United States bilateral treaties.

CHAPTER XVI

COMPULSORY, INTEREST, AND ADVISORY ARBITRATION

As with arbitration generally, the subspecies "compulsory arbitration" occurs in different settings and concerns many different problems. It always involves state compulsion to settle disputes. But it need not mean decision by neutrals, although that is the usual connotation of arbitration procedure. The Railway Labor Act of 1934, for example, requires that disputes over contract interpretation and application (the so-called "minor disputes" of the kind involved in the *Elgin* case in Chapter XIII) be submitted to the National Railroad Adjustment Board, which is composed of equal numbers of union and management representatives. Only in case of deadlock are cases referred to neutral referees. In practice, however, the partisan members almost always deadlock, and the cases are in effect decided by nonpermanent *ad hoc* referees (for some reason railroad people do not care for the terms arbitrator or arbitration). The neutrals can be picked by the party representatives and sometimes are; most referees are appointed by the National Mediation Board, a federal agency. In order to expedite these cases, either party can demand a local tripartite board; with the railroader's penchant for giving names that do not quite describe their object, these are called

"Public Law Boards." In 1966 Congress provided for limited review of Adjustment Board and Public Law Board awards. (See references in and accompanying Transportation Communication Employees Union v. Union Pacific R.R. Co., above.)

The Interstate Commerce Commission incorporates arbitration provisions for disputes over the application of employee "protective provisions" included in its orders granting permission for carriers to merge or abandon facilities. Originally such provisions could be short-circuited by the refusal of a union or carrier party to agree upon an arbitrator. The Commission more recently has included deadlock-breaking provisions.

Usually compulsory arbitration refers to an obligatory procedure for setting new contract terms when a union and company (or groups of them) cannot achieve agreement through collective bargaining. Unions and management generally find such procedures unwelcome, although some public utility company officials have endorsed state legislation of this type (see below), and railroad management seems to favor such a mechanism. So far, Congress has enacted such legislation for only two particular disputes and then with great reluctance. In the second case the unions resisted the arbitration but welcomed the outcome while the carriers positions were precisely opposite.

Oddly enough, compulsory arbitration has come into greatest use as a substitute for tort litigation under New York's MVAIC legislation (in which the arbitration clause is mandatory) and similar uninsured-motorist statutes in which the coverage is supposed to be elective (it requires affirmative rejection by an insured taking accident insurance). These cases now make up the largest group of those decided under the auspices of the American Arbitration Association.

And there is the semi-compulsory arbitration of small claims in Pennsylvania under which a court trial *de novo* is available.

Certain aspects of these varying kinds of compulsory arbitration have been considered in earlier portions of the volume. This chapter deals with some of the others.

For description of the National Railroad Adjustment Board and some of the problems encountered in its procedure see Lloyd Garrison, *The National Railroad Adjustment Board: A Unique Administrative Agency,* 46 YALE L. J. 567 (1937); JACOB KAUFMANN, COLLECTIVE BARGAINING IN THE RAILROAD INDUSTRY (1952); Jack Kroner, *Minor Disputes Under the Railway Labor Act: A Critical Appraisal,* 37 N.Y. U. L. REV. 41 (1962).

A.

State Compulsory Arbitration Laws in the Public Utility Field

In the early 1920's a few midwestern states became interested in "Industrial Courts," and Kansas and Nebraska enacted legislation establishing them. The experiment was cut off by the Supreme Court's declaration of unconstitutionality of the Kansas act as applied in Wolff Packing Co. v. Industrial Court, 262 U.S. 522 (1923). A detailed study of its origins and operations can be found in DOMENICO GAGLIARDO, THE KANSAS INDUSTRIAL COURT (1941).

REPORT TO
GOVERNOR ROBERT B. MEYNER

THE GOVERNOR'S COMMITTEE ON LEGISLATION RELATING TO PUBLIC UTILITY LABOR DISPUTES*

(1954)

1. History of the Statute

As originally enacted in 1946 (P.L. 1946, ch. 38), our statute declared that heat, light, power, sanitation, transportation, communication and water are essential for the life of the people and that the possibility of labor strife in such enterprises leading to or threatening interruption of these vital services was a threat to the public health and welfare. Accordingly, the Governor was authorized to take possession of any public utility plant for use and operation by the State

if, in his opinion, this was necessary to insure continuous service.

In its original form, the statute provided for the appointment of members of a panel by the parties or the State Board of Mediation which was to conduct public hearings and report to the Governor its findings of facts and recommendations. There were no sanctions against strikes or lockouts before or during the period of seizure.

In April, 1947, the Act was amended for the purpose of discouraging a strike called by the Traffic-Telephone Workers Federation of New Jersey against the New Jersey Bell Telephone Company. The amendment (P.L. 1947, Ch. 47) forbade strikes or lockouts after seizure and provided for the appointment, within ten days after seizure of a board of arbitration by the Governor which shall hear the dispute, make written findings of fact and promulgate a decision, subject to review by the Appellate Division of the Superior Court. Violations were to be punished by fine or imprisonment, or both, and a civil penalty of $10,000 for each day of violation, recoverable by the State.

The amendment failed to prevent the outbreak of a telephone strike, which started on April 7, 1947. The offices of the Company were picketed and only emergency telephone calls were accepted. The Governor promptly seized the Company, and three telephone operators who had participated in the strike were arrested. The Union obtained a temporary restraining order in the United States District Court in Newark enjoining the State to hold in *status*

---

*Excerpts from pp. 22–28, 41–42. The nine member Committee consisted of three representatives from labor, management and the "public." The partisan members were drawn from the unions and companies in the public utility sector covered by the New Jersey act.

quo all further actions until the constitutionality of the statute could be determined (Traffic Telephone Workers Federation of N. J. v. Driscoll, 71 F. Supp. 681). Because of strong public protest, the legislature soon reconsidered its drastic action; in a second amendment (P.L. 1947, Ch. 75) the provisions for imprisonment were eliminated and the fines were substantially reduced.

The State then commenced a proceeding in the State courts (see Traffic Telephone Workers v. Driscoll, 72 F. Supp. 499) praying for a determination of constitutionality. The strike was settled long before the Supreme Court rendered its final decision holding the provisions for compulsory arbitration unconstitutional "because they delegate legislative power to an administrative agency, without setting up adequate standards to guide the administrative agency in the exercise of the powers delegated to it" (Van Riper v. Traffic Telephone Workers Federation, 2 N.J. 335, 352 (1949)).

The defect found by the Court was immediately corrected by a special session of the Legislature which added a new section providing that, in the case of a dispute concerning the negotiation of a new contract, the board of arbitration shall be required to make its determination on the basis of certain specifically enumerated factors (P.L. 1949, Ch. 308; N.J.S.A. 34:13B-27).

The last amendment of the statute was enacted in 1950; it repealed the provisions for fact-finding panels (P.L. 1950, Ch. 14) on the ground that the Public hearings before these panels had become unnecessary "dress rehearsals for the arbitration proceedings." (N.J. State Board of Mediation, SIXTH ANNUAL REPORT, 1948, p. 20).

2. Judicial Review of Decisions by Arbitration Boards

On two occasions, companies which felt aggrieved by decisions of a statutory arbitration board appealed to the courts. In one case the appeal had been filed after the Supreme Court had held the statute invalid for lack of standards guiding the arbitrators, but before the amendment curing this defect had been enacted. The appeal was, therefore, dismissed on the ground that there was no legal basis to entertain the appeal and the curative amendment had no retroactive effect (Public Service Electric & Gas Company v. Camden Coke and Gas Workers Independent Federation, 5 N.J. Super. 123 (App. Div. 1949)).

In the other case, the Supreme Court set aside and remanded to the arbitration board an award rendered by said board in a statutory proceeding following seizure of the New Jersey Bell Telephone Company (N.J. Bell Telephone Co. v. Communications Workers of America, 5 N.J. 354 (1950)). The decision was based on criticism of the procedure adopted by the arbitrators: The Court held that the arbitrators had disregarded the statutory standards in their determination of wages by referring to "wage trends" (See Matter of New Jersey Bell Telephone Co., 14. L.A. 574, 581); this was, according to the Court, an "illusory" factor which could not properly be considered. Indeed, the Court held that "the Board has not made adequate basic or essential findings to support its conclusions" (5. N.J. 354, at 378) in spite of the fact that the Board's opinion contained repeated references to and comments on the evidence presented to it (14 L.A. 574–593). In addition, the Court pointed out that the Board had filed its "Findings of Fact and Decision" five weeks after it had entered its Order; this "contravenes the orderly process contemplated by the statute to insure substantial justice." The Court also found it objectionable that the three public members of the Board had arrived at their decision in the absence of the labor and industry members (5 N.J. 354, at 380; 14 L.A. 574, at 600). It is thus apparent that the Court insisted on Judicial control over procedure before the Board which goes far beyond the narrow scope of judicial review of arbitration awards rendered pursuant to voluntary arbitration agreements (N.J.S.A. 2A:24–6, 7 and 8).

Procedural questions were, however, not the sole issues determined by the Court in this second Bell Telephone Case. The Court was also asked to determine the constitutionality of the amended statute. Although this part of the Court's opinion would seem to have been superseded by the more recent decision of the U.S. Supreme Court in the *Wisconsin* case, discussed in Part IV of this report, it is, nevertheless necessary to call attention to the Court's holding that the arbitrators had no authority to award a union shop because the New Jersey statute "does not contemplate compulsory arbitration of the unon security questions." (5 N.J. 354, at 368). In the meantime, this requirement of a special election to authorize union shop agreements was replaced by Public Law No. 189, 82nd Cong., 1st Sess. (1951); hence, the Court could probably no longer adhere to this particular ruling if that issue were to come again before it.

3. Administration of the New Jersey Statute; Comments by Representatives of Labor and Industry

The judicial decisions discussed above reflect, of course, only a fragment of the administration of the New Jersey law, since most of the awards rendered by statutory arbitration boards were not challenged in the courts. Therefore, in order to appraise the effect of the statute realistically, it became necessary to ascertain the views of persons with practical experience in the operation of the statute. This task was greatly facilitated by the fact that the members of this Committee had all had such experience. In addition, the Committee asked for and received comments from several prominent representatives of labor and industry throughout New Jersey.

The opinions of responsible spokesmen for industry and labor, which emerged from these consultations, show substantial unanimity of opposition to the statute on the ground that it weakens the vitality of the collective bargaining process by making agreements between labor and management more difficult to reach. (The two published studies of the statute resulted in similar conclusions. FRANCE AND LESTER: COMPULSORY ARBITRATION OF UTILITY DISPUTES IN NEW JERSEY AND PENNSYLVANIA, Princeton, 1951, p. 40 ; MacDonald: *Compulsory Arbitration in New Jersey,* SECOND ANNUAL NEW YORK UNIVERSITY CONFERENCE ON LABOR 625, at 684 (1949). There was also unanimity with respect to the conclusions that the statute was unnecessary because in all the disputes in which it was invoked, agreement would have been reached if the Governor had not intervened, and because no real emergency situation actually threatening the "health and welfare of the people" had ever occurred in New Jersey.

It is appropriate to set forth in more detail the specific information which served as a basis for these general observations. For instance, the Amalgamated Association of Street, Electric Railway and Motor Coach Employees of America was not involved in any strike in New Jersey from 1923 until the advent of the anti-strike law, although the industry was completely organized since 1918. In 1947, for the first time, the Union sensed some reluctance to bargain on the part of Public Service Transportation Company ; nevertheless the Company agreed to voluntary arbitration, waiving its rights under the statute. The Union acknowledged that this created serious difficulties for the Company before the Board of Public Utility Commissioners ; that board would not approve fare increases when the Company voluntarily accepted wage increases. There-

fore, in 1948 and subsequent years, the Company insisted on statutory proceedings, but it accepted a number of statutory awards without judicial review.

In this connection, it was pointed out that strikes are commonly considered unpopular and undesirable in public utilities. In 1946, when the New Jersey law was first enacted, there had accumulated during the stabilization period of the war years strong demands for higher wages. Hence, due to the pressure of temporary postwar conditions, strikes might have been inevitable under any circumstances. The law did not help, because it created a substitute for agreement by collective bargaining. Moreover, according to the Union, the Board of Public Utility Commissioners showed more willingness to grant fare increases to reflect added labor costs when wage increases were ordered by another government agency. When there was no prospect of State intervention, as during the 1954 negotiations, agreement was reached without a strike. The gas strike of January, 1954, ended after five weeks of strike without the law being invoked and significantly, with no serious impairment of service.

According to the Amalgamated, the law has a discriminating effect because it has been invoked mainly in disputes affecting large companies. There have been several strikes against small bus companies who had sought State help ; the Governor's refusal to intervene in such cases was based on his finding that there was no emergency. In fact, the representative of independent bus operators urged us to recommend exemption of bus companies from the law. They contend that bus transportation is now a convenience, and not a necessity, because "the automobile is furnishing stiff competition and riding is declining."

The representative of the electrical workers expressed substantially the same arguments. He said that a one day strike at Public Service Electric and Gas Company in 1945 had caused the demand for this legislation. From 1947 to 1949, agreements were concluded each year, but in 1950 the Company refused the Union's offer of voluntary arbitration of the Union's wage demands. Instead, the Company insisted on its statutory rights, including judicial review of any statutory award. A short strike ensued, and after six days the parties submitted to compulsory arbitration. The Governor then seized the plant because of low fuel supply in generators. In 1952, an agreement was reached voluntarily. In 1954, the parties voluntarily agreed to submit their contract differences to a fact-finding board. The representative of the telephone workers

Table XVI-I—Attitudes and Opinions on Strike-Control Experience

State	Incidents of Strikes Reduced		Effect on Collective Bargaining			Law Approved by						Administration Satisfactory		
						ORGANIZED LABOR		INDUSTRY		PUBLIC				
	Yes	No	LITTLE, IF ANY	ENHANCES	INHIBITS	Yes	No	Yes	No	Yes	No	TO ALL	TO ALL EXCEPT LABOR	TO NONE
Florida														
Labor (1)		1			1		1	1	1	1	1		1	
Utility Management (1)	1			1			1	1	1	1	1		1	
Indiana														
Labor (1)		1	1		1		1			1	1			
Utility Management (2)	2	1	1	1	1		1	1		2		1		
Public (1)			1		1		1		1					
Massachusetts														
Labor (3)		3			3		3	3		2				3
Public (1)			1		1		1	1		1				
Michigan														
Utility Management (2)	2			1	1		2	2		2		2		
Public (2)	1		1		2		1			1		1		
Minnesota														
Labor (1)		1		1	1		1	2		2		1		
Utility Management (2)		1	1	1	1	1	1	2		2		2		
Public (2)	1		1	1	1	2		2		2		2		
Missouri														
Labor (2)	2				2		2	1		1		1	1	
Utility Management (2)	1		1		1		2	2	1	2		1	1	
Public (2)			1				2	2		2		2		
Pennsylvania														
Labor (2)	1				1		2	1	1			2		
Utility Management (1)	1			1			1	1		1		1		
Public (1)		1			1		1	1		1				
Virginia														
Labor (2)		1			2		1	1	1	1				
Management (1)														
Wisconsin														
Labor (1)		1			1		1	1	1	1			1	
Utility Management (1)					1		1	1	1	1			1	
Public (1)			1			1	1	1		1			1	
TOTAL														
Labor	1	11		1	12		12	6	4	6		4	6	
Utility Management	8	1	2	6	4	2	8	11	1	11		7	3	
Public	3	1	3	6	5	2	7	8	2	8		5	1	

NOTE: Totals will not add because of the failure of some respondents to answer all of the questions. Questionnaires returned by officers of two major international unions could not be included in the breakdown because of the general character of the replies.

681

agreed with all of these statements. With respect to the particular conditions of the telephone system, she pointed out that seventy per cent of New Jersey's telephones are now dial operated so that a strike would not now be as serious to the public as in former years. In non-dial areas, the Company used management employees for emergency service and, in addition, the Union has always offered to make emergency crews available.

It thus appears that the representatives of labor believe that the New Jersey statute is unnecessary and should be repealed. Most of them feel that any kind of legislation vesting the Governor with statutory powers would merely "pass the buck" to the Governor, "through the abdication by the parties to him of the duties of settling the dispute." Moreover, they stress the absence of strikes in the utility field before the statute, and the frequency of strikes thereafter. They suggest that "the most practical and efficient treatment of public utility disputes can be realized through a policy of voluntary mediation ..." which "will impose a sense of direct responsibility upon the disputing parties."

The views of leaders of management are, as noted above, practically identical with the views of the Union representatives. Significantly, company representatives shared the view that the mere existence of the law causes the parties to come to the bargaining table with a chip on their shoulders and to "play coy with each other". This attitude "destroys" collective bargaining. Moreover, "so long as supervisors are willing to work (barring sabotage or extreme weather conditions), such disputes need not result in immediate jeopardy to public health and safety." If a real threat to public health and safety should ever occur, the general police power of the State can cope with it. Thus, employers also favor repeal, with the suggestion of strengthening mediation services and, possibly, enactment of a state labor relations act.

The opposition of employers seems to be particularly emphatic with respect to compulsory arbitration. The representative of the New Jersey Bell Telephone Company pointed out that New York, which has no similar statute, has had had no telephone strike, and that New Jersey and Indiana (which has a similar law) suffered much more disruption of telephone service since 1947 than did other states with no such legislation. He was critical of the results of the arbitrations to which his Company had been required to submit. He gave examples to prove that statutory arbitration boards "do much worse than the parties" in arriving at sound wage determinations. There had been no telephone strike

prior to the enactment of this statute since the early nineteen twenties, when tie-ups occured in New England; similarly, the last strike of Public Service Electric and Gas Company employees in New Jersey occurred in 1923. All management representatives agreed that there were no strike-happy unions in this field, and that employees generally have a high sense of public responsibility; that they are anxious not to incur public disfavor. There was also agreement that labor-management relations are better in those states which have no enacted public utility anti-strike laws. One management representative expressed the opinion that enactment of these laws was due to legislative hysteria before the consequences of the strike had even been assessed.

A moderately comprehensive bibliography is to be found in U.S. Department of Labor, COMPULSORY ARBITRATION, Selected References, 1951-1966 (Processed 1966).

OTHER ESSENTIAL SERVICES

New York's Labor Relation Act, § 701(11), was amended to bring nonprofit hospitals and residential care centers within its scope in 1963. In 1965 coverage was extended to include not only employees within New York City, as the 1963 amendment provided, but also those throughout the state. Employees of nonprofit hospitals, through § 713, are prohibited from engaging in any strike, work stoppage, slowdown, or withholding of goods or services. Since they cannot strike, because of § 713's prohibition, § 716 provides compulsory arbitration provisions that are to be read into every collective-bargaining contract, including those that do not contain provisions for such binding determination of grievances, and § 716(3) provides that any such arbitration is to be conducted according to such rules as may be established by the New York State Board of Mediation. The legislation contains no provisions establishing standards to guide arbitrators.

Park Avenue Clinical Hospital v. Jay Kramer, 266 N.Y.S. 2d 1147, 48 Misc. 2d 826 (1966), held that the provision providing for arbitration was not unconstitutional on the ground that it was an unlawful delegation of authority without sufficient standards for the arbitrator's guidance;

but on appeal, 26 A.D. 2d 613, 271 N.Y.S. 2d 747 (1966), the Appellate Division held that although sections banning strikes and lockouts are constitutional, the attack upon the section relating to procedures for resolving grievances was premature because the union had merely petitioned to be certified as the bargaining representative for certain employees. Thus, whether the lack of legislative standards will cause the legislation to be held unconstitutional is still up in the air.

Minnesota's compulsory arbitration act, M.S.A. tit. 13A, §§ 178.35-39 (1966), provides in §179.38 that in the event of the existence of labor disputes that cannot be settled by negotiation between charitable-hospital employers and their employees, issues of maximum hours of work and minimum hourly wage rates shall be submitted to a board of arbitrators, whose determination shall be final and binding. Fairview Hosp. Ass'n v. Public Bldg. Serv. Employees Union, Local 113, 241 Minn. 523, 64 N.W. 2d 16 (1954) held that the provision was constitutional and not an improper delegation of legislative power, although no explicitly stated standards were given. This proposition was affirmed in State v. Johnson, Minn. 134, 139–40, 96 N.W. 2d 9, 13 (1959), which cited *Fairview* with approval for the proposition that where the legislature has defined the general policy of the act and left the adaptation of the policy to administrative bodies, the tendency is to not hold the act in violation of the constitution. A commentator feels that the New York Court of Appeals would not find such a statute constitutional because of the lack of adequate standards for compulsory arbitration and cites the New Jersey experience, stating:

> The New Jersey compulsory arbitration statute in the field of public utilities was originally enacted without standards to guide the arbitrators, and was declared unconstitutional on the ground that it was a delegation of legislative authority without adequate standards. Subsequently, it was amended to include such standards, and as amended, was upheld.

Kevin Reilly, *New York Nonprofit Hospitals and the Labor Relations Act: The Pitfalls of Emergency Legislation,* 17 SYRACUSE L. REV. 482 (1966).

Interestingly enough, as of mid-1966, when *Park Avenue Hospital* was decided, the compulsory arbitration provisions of the New York Act had not been invoked.

B.

Compulsory Arbitration of Small Claims

TRIAL BY LAWYER: COMPULSORY ARBITRATION OF SMALL CLAIMS IN PENNSYLVANIA*

MAURICE ROSENBERG AND MYRA SCHUBIN

I. The Pennsylvania Plan and Its Mechanics

The prototype of the current Pennsylvania procedure was introduced in 1952, when the state legislature enacted a statute permitting the court of common pleas in each county to provide by rule of court for compulsory arbitration in cases involving no more than $1,000 in claimed damages ; actions involving title to real estate were not included. In 1957 the statute was amended to include claims up to $2,000 and to apply to the Municipal Court of Philadelphia as well as the

*Excerpted from 74 HARV. L. REV. 448 (1961). Copyright © 1961 by the Harvard Law Review Association, reprinted with permission of the Association and the authors. The study was made under the auspices of the Columbia University Project for Effective Justice.

common pleas courts. A recent amendment makes the procedure applicable to the County Court of Allegheny County (Pittsburgh).

Under the provisions of the statute, each claim is heard by a panel of three arbitrators who are members of the bar in the judicial district. They are appointed by a court clerk, the prothonotary, from a list of consenting attorneys, within ten days after the case is at issue. Fees ranging from ten to fifty dollars per case for each arbitrator have been set by the courts and are paid by the county. Hearings generally take place within a few weeks of appointment and awards are to be filed within twenty days of hearing. The day, hour, and place of meeting of the arbitrators are fixed by agreement of the parties or, on their failure to agree, by the prothonotary. Commonly, hearings are held in the offices of the chairman of the arbitration board, but the practice seems to vary from county to county. In certain counties local rules of court direct that arbitrators follow the "established" rules of evidence, in others, that they give them liberal construction; the rules of still other counties are silent on the subject. The arbitration award, arrived at by majority vote, has the effect of a final judgment.[1] No record need be kept of the proceedings. Either party has a right of "appeal" as a matter of course—meaning that the appellant may receive a trial *de novo* in court—upon his repayment to the county of the cost of the arbitration proceedings, not to exceed 50 per cent of the amount in controversy. This payment is not a recoverable item of costs even if the appealing party prevails.

In 1955 the constitutionality of the act was unsuccessfully challenged on the grounds that it was a deprivation of property without due process and violated the state's guarantee of trial by jury. The Supreme Court of Pennsylvania upheld the statute; the United States Supreme Court dismissed the appeal.[2] In another action a lower Pennsylvania court rejected the additional claim that the statute violated the state constitutional requirement that all judges be elected.

By June 1956, forty-three of the sixty-seven courts of common pleas had adopted the arbitration rule. In the next two years, the Municipal Court of Philadelphia County and five courts of common pleas accepted it, while five rejected it. Since then, three additional common pleas courts and the County Court of Allegheny County (Pittsburgh) have adopted the system.

II. Objectives of the Pennsylvania Plan

It may be helpful to the consideration by other states of adoption of the Pennsylvania plan, as well as to a general appraisal, to inquire into the precise goals of the plan in its home state and the extent to which they have been achieved. Although the Pennsylvania legislature did not spell out its purposes in enacting the 1952 statute, they have since then been authoritatively set forth. According to the then Chief Justice of the Pennsylvania Supreme Court, speaking in dictum in an opinion upholding the constitutionality of the statute, the purposes were dual: to expedite the processing of smaller claims and to relieve the courts of small cases so that they could concentrate on reducing delay in disposing of the larger ones.

Whatever the effect of the introduction of the arbitration plan may be in retrospect seem to have been, it is plain that not all of the adopting counties could have been intent on using it to reduce trial delay, for in 18 of them jury cases were reported in prearbitration days to be reaching trial within fifteen weeks after commencement of suit. It would seem to follow that these counties were actuated by the other desire, namely, to ease the lot of claimants in small cases. But the postarbitration figures cast doubt on even this explanation, for they show that relatively few small cases were referred to arbitration when the opportunity came.[3] The evidence forces us to conclude that many of the adopting counties were not clear in their own minds why they needed or wanted the arbitration system. In

---

1. Pa. Stat. tit. 5, §§ 51, 54 (1936). *But see* McClure v. Boyle, 141 N.E. 2d 229 (Trumbull County, Ohio C.P. 1957), in which an Ohio court refused to give full faith and credit to a Pennsylvania compulsory-arbitration award. The court there held that the award was not a "judgment" rendered or approved of by a court and was therefore not entitled to protection under the full faith and credit clause.

2. Smith Case, 381 Pa. 223, 112 A. 2d 625, *appeal dismissed sub nom.* Smith v. Wissler, 350 U.S. 858 (1955). In other states, the arbitration plan would likewise have to surmount constitutional objections. In New York, for example, it is not altogether clear that such a plan would be upheld, despite the fact that the state's constitutional guarantee of trial by jury, N.Y. Const. art. 1, § 5, is similar to Pa. Const. art. 1, § 6. The New York appellate courts have, in the past, scrupulously protected the province of the jury. See Grace v. City of New York, 4 App. Div. 2d 1022, 168 N.Y.S. 2d 847 (1st Dep't 1957) (even when the sole witness' testimony on liability is self-contradictory, a question of fact is presented for the jury). See also Measeck v. Noble, 9 App. Div. 2d 19, 189 N.Y.S. 2d 748 (3rd Dep't 1959) (new trial required after juror took ill during deliberations although attorney did not object to unanimous verdict of the remaining jurors and statute permitted verdict by 5/6 of the jurors in civil cases). Nevertheless, the New York Court of Appeals has permitted such jury-limiting devices as additur and remittitur, even when practiced by appellate courts. O'Connor v. Papertsian, 309 N.Y. 465, 131 N.E. 2d 883 (1956). A statute compelling arbitration without appeal of right to a tribunal with a jury would quite clearly be unconstitutional under the New York State Constitution as to issues triable at common law. People *ex rel.* Eckerson v. Trustees, 151 N.Y. 75, 84–85, 45 N.E. 384, 387 (1896); People *ex rel.* Baldwin & Jaycox v. Haws, 37 Barb. 440, 456–57 (N.Y. Sup. Ct. 1862) (alternative holding) (special legislative act compelling the City of New York to submit to arbitration of a claim against it for breach of contract deprives the city of its state constitutional right to a trial "according to the course of the common law"). Whether the Pennsylvania procedure would run afoul of the guarantee would depend on whether the court viewed charging the appellant with the cost of arbitrators' fees as unduly "burdensome." City of Rochester v. Holden, 224 N.Y. 386, 121 N.E. 102 (1918). The guarantee of jury trial contained in the federal constitution has no direct application to trials in the state courts. Wagner Elec. Mfg. Co. v. Lyndon, 262 U.S. 226, 232 (1923) (alternative holding); Olesen v. Trust Co., 245 F. 2d 522 (7th Cir.), cert. denied, 355 U.S. 896 (1957). However, the reasoning in federal cases, *e.g.*, Capital Traction Co. v. Hof, 174 U.S. 1, 43–46 (1899), may be persuasive in analogous state cases.

3. As of March 1, 1956, only 5 out of 40 counties had referred as many as 200 cases to arbitration since their adoption of the rule; one of these courts had been using arbitration for over 5 years, another for $3\frac{1}{2}$ years and two for at least $2\frac{1}{2}$ years.

the others, relief of court delay may have been uppermost in the purposes of some, while speedy and easy disposition of small cases appealed most strongly to the remainder.

III. How the Arbitrated Cases Fare

Two concerted efforts have been made heretofore to analyze the impact of the arbitration system on the cases that have gone through its procedures. One, reported in a Comment in the *Villanova Law Review* in 1957, examines findings compiled in a ten-county survey conducted by Judge William F. Dannehower of the Court of Common Pleas of Montgomery County and the replies from 130 questionnaires recording the observations and opinions of members of the bar of Montgomery and Delaware Counties. The second analysis is a two-part monograph prepared by the Institute of Judicial Administration in July 1956 and supplemented in August 1959. It presents and analyzes answers to questionnaires sent to the courts of common pleas of the sixty-seven Pennsylvania counties, and sets out reports issued by four of the counties in 1955. Not all the items in the questionnaires invited precise answers, but the responses seem to have come from knowledgeable persons and reliable records.

Reports by these and other observers run heavily to the view, with only sporadic dissents, that the arbitrated cases are disposed of more quickly and more easily than in prearbitration days. The evidence of increased speed is impressive. Twenty-one counties now send their cases to arbitration within thirty days of filing. In Philadelphia, cases that formerly had to wait twenty-four to thirty months for trial in the municipal court now wait only five months or less for a hearing before the arbitrators. There have been reports that trial time has been shortened because of the informality of the proceedings and the absence of a jury, and the imminence of trial is said also to expedite settlements. Even in Montgomery County, which has apparently backslid since 1956, the waiting period is substantially less than in prearbitration days. On the negative side, there are reports that arbitration has increased the tendency of attorneys to postpone their smaller cases and that the difficulty of getting five lawyers together at one time has caused numerous continuances. If so, these defects do not seem to have perceptibly slowed the disposition of the majority of small cases. Of course, in the comparatively few cases that are appealed after an arbitration award final disposition must await the conclusion of both proceedings.

To support the claim of greater ease to litigants these points are marshalled: each arbitration hearing is scheduled for a convenient time and place; lawyers, parties, and witnesses do not sit idle waiting for their cases to be called; and witnesses are more at ease than at formal courtroom trials. So far as we know, no one has contradicted these claims of enhanced convenience under the arbitration procedure.

Controversy has flared chiefly over the fairness of the new procedure. Some maintain that arbitration avoids prejudiced juries and sympathy verdicts, but such remarks may merely reflect their utterers' antijury bias. On the other side, doubts arise, even among those who are not opposed in principle to the arbitration system, from the informality of the procedure and the lack of traditional courtroom safeguards. Critics have also expressed fear that attorney-arbitrators tend to become overly involved in the cases before them, are ill-equipped to handle cases out of their fields, are fearful of retribution when roles are reversed, tend to give compromise awards, and generally lack either the sense of public interest or the judicial training needed to reach proper determinations. While some believe these defects will be cured over time, others warn that the low fees paid to arbitrators will intensify the problem by repelling skilled and experienced attorneys once the bar's enthusiasm has worn off.

From the foregoing reports and opinions it seems fair to conclude that on balance the arbitration system permits small cases to be disposed of more quickly and more conveniently than was true under normal court proceedings. But there is no clear agreement that the new system provides a fair means of processing the small cases.

IV. How the Court Fares Under the Arbitration System

Viewed a priori the compulsory-arbitration procedure appears to have high potential as a remedy for delay in the courts. By hypothesis it shunts large numbers of suits from the trial lists and thereby frees judge time to try the remaining cases. As a consequence, trial delay should lessen.

Experience in the Municipal Court of Philadelphia since 1958 provides the most dramatic example of the hypothetical made actual. In one sweep the major part of the court's civil jurisdiction was diverted to arbitration panels; in less than two years delay fell sharply from between twenty-four and thirty months to between three and five months. Outside Philadelphia, where referrals to arbitrators drained off smaller fractions of the business of the courts of common pleas, the expected shrinkage in delay did not, however, always materialize.

The experience of the Philadelphia court is the more striking because there was not merely a siphoning off of the bulk of its case load without substitution of other business, in which event some reduction in delay would have been nearly inevitable. Rather, contemporaneous with adoption of the arbitration procedure, the municipal court's jurisdictional ceiling was increased to $5,000—double the previous limit—and the road was open for larger cases to replace the diverted smaller actions on the court's docket. Nevertheless, as of July 1, 1959, the court could announce that a case would be listed for trial within three months after filing of an order for trial.

We estimate that in its first twenty-two months the new procedure spared the court not only some 1,996 full trials, but an additional 1,000 or so partial trials. Of course, to reflect the net saving, the latter figure would have to be reduced by the number of appealed cases that in fact involved a partial trial—about sixty-seven cases. In passing it may be noted that maintenance by the courts of reliable statistics on such vital subjects as the number of cases reaching trial would obviate the need for guesswork and uncertainty in many of the calculations just made. Even without them, we can say with considerable confidence that the arbitration procedure during its first 22 months spared the municipal court between 2,500 and 4,000 trials, a huge saving of judicial energies.

The saving was not, of course, without certain costs and disadvantages. For many litigants, witnesses, and lawyers, there was the double inconvenience of a trial in the courtroom after a trial before the arbitrators. For the thousands of members of the bar who volunteered their services as arbitrators there was an immense total outlay of time and energy, probably at below normal compensation. In point of sheer volume, by the end of 1959 the Philadelphia program had required some 25,242 "participations" by attorney-arbitrators. This works out to about eight participations by individual lawyers for each full or partial trial that the municipal court was spared. In other words, nearly three arbitration hearings, each presided over by a panel of three lawyers, were needed to avoid one courtroom trial presided over by a judge and also requiring in the majority of cases the services of a twelve-man jury.

One further point must be noted before we leave the subject of whether the arbitration system has basically curtailed the work load (and hence delay) in the Pennsylvania courts. Theoretically, it is conceivable that the introduction of the arbitration system might encourage the bringing of small claims that would otherwise have been abandoned; and that enough of these might return to the courts after arbitration to offset any hypothetical saving. On this entire question, the evidence is equivocal. In Philadelphia there apparently was no increase in small-case litigation after February 1958. During the first and second years of arbitration, an almost identical number of cases reached the trial list, suggesting that the advent of arbitration produced no upward trend in small-case filings. Outside of Philadelphia, 10 of 34 courts reported to the Institute of Judicial Administration that arbitration had noticeably increased the number of smaller actions filed. Considering that all ten counties so reporting had adopted arbitration several years earlier, we infer that the introduction of the plan may have a delayed but discernible tendency to encourage the filing of small claims.

V. Arbitrators v. Juries in Appealed Cases

A matter of obvious importance in assessing the desirability of the arbitration system is whether arbitrators and juries tend to reach different conclusions on the issues they adjudicate. They conceivably might disagree in a given case on the liability issue or the damage issue. Analysis of the appealed cases in Philadelphia sheds some light on the first matter. In appealed trespass cases it appears that the arbitrators were distinctly more favorable to plaintiffs on the liability question than were juries in the same cases. The pattern is much weaker in assumpsit (contract) cases. The following is a summary of the relevant findings on the liability question.

1. As to the frequency with which the arbitrators deviate from the juries' verdicts on appeal, it turned out that, over all, juries reversed arbitrator's findings on liability in 32 per cent of the cases that reached verdict. The largest incidence of "reversals" appeared in the trespass group, where juries disagreed with the arbitrators in 38 per cent of the cases as compared to 25 per cent in the assumpsit group.

2. As to which party benefits from the arbitrators' deviations, it turned out that of the seventy-seven cases in which there was both an arbitration report and a jury verdict, plaintiffs had won sixty arbitration awards but emerged with only forty-seven jury verdicts. Conversely, defendants had won only seventeen awards but ultimately had thirty verdicts. A trend is clearly evident in the trespass cases: defendants went into court with eleven awards and emerged with twenty-two verdicts. In the assumpsit appeals the

juries gave eight of thirty-two decisions to the defendant compared to the arbitrators' 6; but even so plaintiffs took 75 per cent of these verdicts against only 51 per cent of the trespass verdicts.

It appears from the foregoing (assuming that the sample was representative) that arbitrators are markedly more prone to find for plaintiffs in trespass actions than are juries. There is no way of determining which of them is "right." The figures raise the distinct possibility that, for better or worse, almost one-third of the litigants may come out differently before arbitrators than they would have before a jury.[4]

VI. Lessons of and Comments Upon Pennsylvania's Experience

For other jurisdictions plagued with clogged civil dockets there are important lessons in Pennsylvania's experience. Manifestly the more similar the conditions in the adopting jurisdiction, the more cogently the lessons apply. In a state which suffers from the atypical problem of trial delay in a court of *limited* jurisdiction, the Philadelphia case is squarely in point and shows that compulsory arbitration of small claims is a helpful expedient: once the minor cases are deflected from the lesser court's trial lists, they seldom reappear on them.

But suppose that State X has a typical form of the delay affliction, meaning that it suffers from serious backlogs in its courts of *general* jurisdiction. Suppose further that X approves of the Pennsylvania plan in principle and is willing to compel litigants to detour great numbers of cases from court channels to arbitration, subject to a privilege of return by appeal upon paying the arbitration costs. Unless X held the bizarre view that all civil cases should be arbitrated, it would face the need to decide which categories of cases should be sent out to arbitrators. It might choose the small ones, as Pennsylvania did, on the correct assumption that as a matter

of simple economics they would be less prone than larger ones to return to the courts on appeal.[5] Capitalizing on that tendency might seem a logical choice, but on closer examination the benefit proves illusory. The first reason why this is so is that the exiled small cases would probably come from the dockets of lesser courts, so that unless there were quite extraordinary powers in X to transfer judges or cases from court to court the larger courts would not benefit even indirectly. In the second place, even if low-value cases were present in sizable volume on the larger courts' trial lists and all were siphoned off to arbitrators, the benefit to the larger courts would be relatively slight. The explanation for this seeming anomaly is that it is not the removal of mere quantities of cases, but only of "durable" or trial-bound cases that is the key to unburdening the courts; small cases are much less likely to reach trial than large ones.

All this logically suggests that State X should devise an arbitration plan for high-value cases, thereby striking at the core of its delay problem. However, there are stumbling blocks. The basic economic factors that prompt large cases to go to trial with disproportionate frequency would doubtless compel appeals of arbitrators' awards with similar frequency. Accompanying this tendency is a prevailing attitude that, whatever its procedural advantages, arbitration is not an acceptable substitute for the court process where large sums of money are at stake. This attitude is discernible in the fact that Pennsylvania itself has not seen fit to extend the procedure to large cases and is further evidenced by the results of a 1956 opinion poll of Pennsylvania lawyers. If lawyers are convinced that large cases deserve courtroom trials they can be counted on to appeal arbitrators' awards in such cases. The consequence would be an undiminished rate of courtroom trials, a low saving in court energies, and ultimate frustration of the whole purpose of

---

4. This rests on the assumption that the nonappealed cases would have resulted in the same rate of "reversals" as the appealed. We cannot substantiate this belief with any direct evidence. We do know that the appealed cases differ from the nonappealed in regard to the average amount awarded—the former being larger, see note 5, *infra*, but this difference should not produce a different reversal rate.

Despite this evidence that the arbitrators are more favorable to plaintiffs the questionnaire survey by Levin and Woolley indicates that arbitrators apply the contributory-negligence role somewhat more rigorously to defeat plaintiffs than do juries, especially in "clear" cases. LEVIN & WOOLLEY, DISPATCH AND DELAY, A FIELD STUDY OF JUDICIAL ADMINISTRATION IN PENNSYLVANIA 55–56 (1961).

5. The Philadelphia survey provides ample proof that large cases are more likely to be appealed than small. Whereas the average award in the appeals group was $727, for the average arbitrated case it was only $348. Arbitration Commission, *supra* note 64. Table I *infra* shows that under-$1,000 recoveries made up 94 per cent of the awards rendered but only 79 per cent of the appeals. On the assumption that the appeals sample is representative, the difference between the two percentages is persuasive evidence that small awards are not appealed as often as large. Another bit of evidence is of questionable effect: although 11 of the 32 counties that raised the arbitration limit from $1,000 to $2,000 in 1957 reported an increase in appeals attributable to the change, no over-all increase in the ratio of appeals to total number of arbitrations was noted during 1956–1958.

the arbitration program. Only by pegging the cost of appeal at a prohibitively high figure could this result be averted. But then it would become apparent to all that the appeal fee was actually a device to prevent resort to the courts and the whole scheme might capsize as a violation of the state's constitutional guaranty of the right to trial by jury. By contrast, in the small cases the appeal cost can be keyed plausibly to the fees paid the arbitrators and still perform its function of discouraging appeals.

Short of heroic measures to discourage appeals in high-value cases, compulsory arbitration of such cases would not substantially relieve State X's courts of their trial load, and the cases themselves would encounter compounded delay, to say nothing of double trials. Thus, as we evaluate its potential, the arbitration plan has built-in weaknesses as a method of reducing the trial load in major courts. State X would be well advised to look to other means to solve its delay problem in these courts.

Essential to the success of the compulsory-arbitration procedure is the cooperation of the bar in supplying high-quality, part-time adjudicators at low cost. While the desirability of instituting a system involving a large subsidy by lawyers is a policy consideration outside the scope of this article, it is relevant to ask whether the Pennsylvania system, requiring the efforts of eight attorneys for each small-claim trial that the Municipal Court of Philadelphia is spared, is an efficient utilization of the bar's subsidy. Would it be preferable to permit attorneys to serve one at a time as arbitrators, trial referees, or trial masters? In the $100-limit Small Claims Part of the Municipal Court of New York City volunteer attorneys serve as "referees" with apparently satisfactory results.[6] Whether a similar procedure for the higher-value cases arbitrated in Philadelphia would achieve comparable savings without as high a cost in lawyer time as the arbitration system is a question that cannot be answered from the available data.

---

6. This is done by written stipulation and consent of both parties in the night court of the small claims part. N.Y.C. MUNIC. CT. CODE §§ 6 (6), 8 (3); N.Y.C. MUNIC. CT. R. xx-20. These hearings are not considered judicial proceedings but arbitrations. Trager v. Abalene Blouse & Sportswear Corp., 1 Misc. 2d 952, 148 N.Y.S. 2d 682 (Sup. Ct. 1956). In 1958, 374 referees sat in night court in Manhattan and Brooklyn. During this period they heard 5,722 cases. 1958 N.Y.C. MUNIC. CT. ANN. REP. 17–20.

SMITH CASE
381 Pa. 225, 112 A. 2d 625
[appeal dismissed, 350 U.S. 858 (1965)]

The Act of 1952, greatly enlarging, as it does, the scope of the Act of 1836, is of extreme importance in that it effects a decided innovation in procedure for the adjudication of the class of minor claims to which it relates. It has many obvious advantages. It is clearly designed to meet the situation which prevails in some communities of jury lists being clogged to a point where trials can be had only after long periods of delay,— a condition resulting largely from the modern influx of negligence cases arising from automobile accidents in a great number of which no serious personal injuries are involved. Removing the smaller claims from the lists not only paves the way for the speedier trial of actions involving larger amounts, but, what is of equal or perhaps even greater importance, makes it possible for the immediate disposition of the smaller claims themselves, thus satisfying the need for prompt relief in such cases. By the same token, and working to the same end, the use of the Act will free courts for the speedier performance of other judicial functions. Moreover, there will be a saving to claimants of both time and expense by reason of greater flexibility in fixing the exact day and hour for hearings before the arbitrators as compared with the more cumbersome and less adaptable arrangements of court calendars. The operation of the Act has proved eminently successful in all respects, it appearing from statistics gathered in nineteen of the thirty-one counties or more which have thus far put the statute into effect that there were 585 cases tried by arbitrators under its provisons in the period from July 1 to December 28, 1954, in only thirty or 5 per cent of which appeals were taken to the courts of common pleas. It would seem clear, therefore, that the system of arbitration set up by this statute offers encouraging prospects for the speedier administration of justice in the Commonwealth.

What, then, are the objections voiced against it on the alleged ground of unconstitutionality? The main charge is that the Act violates Article I, section 6, of the Constitution that "Trial by jury shall be as heretofore, and the right thereof remain inviolate." It is true, of course, that this provision of the Constitution would be violated by a statute the effect of which was to compel parties to submit to arbitration against their will or without their assent: Cutler & Hinds v. Richley, 151 Pa. 195, 25 A. 96. Indeed compulsory arbitration conflicts also with the 14th

Amendment of the Federal Constitution in that it works a deprivation of property and liberty of contract without due process of law: Chas. Wolff Packing Co. v. Court of Industrial Relations of the State of Kansas, 262 U.S. 522; Dorchy v. State of Kansas, 264 U.S. 286. But this is so only where the statute closes the courts to litigants and makes the decision of the arbitrators the final determination of the rights of the parties; therefore there is no denial of the right of trial by jury if the statute preserves that right to each of the parties by the allowance of an appeal from the decision of the arbitrators or other tribunal: Emerick v. Harris, 1 Binney 416; Capital Traction Co. v. Hof, 174 U.S. 1; 50 C.J.S. 832, 833, § 118. In the *Capital Traction Co.* case it was said (p. 23): "It [the Constitution] does not prescribe at what stage of an action a trial by jury must, if demanded, be had; or what conditions may be imposed upon the demand of such a trial, consistently with preserving the right to it." The only purpose of the constitutional provision is to secure the right of trial by jury before the rights of person or property are *finally* determined. All that is required is that the right of appeal for the purpose of presenting the issue to a jury must not be burdened by the imposition of onerous conditions, restrictions or regulations which would make the right practically unavailable. As to what amounts to such a forbidden restriction it has been held that the constitutional provision is not violated by a requirement of the payment of costs before the entry of an appeal in order to obtain a jury trial: McDonald v. Schell, 6 S. & R. 239; nor by a requirement of giving bail for the payment of cost accrued and to accrue or for the performance of some other duty: Haines v. Levin, 51 Pa. 412; Commonwealth, for use, v. McCann & Co., 174 Pa. 19, 34 A. 299; nor by a requirement of furnishing security for the prosecution of the appeal and satisfaction of the final judgment: Capital Traction Co. v. Hof, 174 U.S. 1, 23, 43-45; nor by a requirement of the payment of a jury fee in advance of trial: Gottschall v. Campbell, 234 Pa. 347, 361, 83 A. 286, 291. There can be no valid objection, therefore, to the provisions of the Act of 1836, unchanged by the Act of 1952, regarding the payment of the accrued costs and the giving of a recognizance for the payment of the costs to accrue in the appellate proceedings as the condition for the allowance of an appeal from the award of the arbitrators.

What the petitioner specifically complains of is the provision of the 1952 Act that the fees of the arbitrators, initially paid by the county, must be repaid to it by the party appealing and shall not be taxed as costs or be recoverable from the adverse party whether or not the appellant be ultimately successful in his appeal. As far as the prohibition of recovery of the fees from the adverse party is concerned, this involves no constitutional violation since the right to recover costs in litigation is purely statutory; it exists only to the extent authorized by legislative enactment (Morganroth's Election Contest Case, 346 Pa. 327, 328, 329, 29 A. 2d 502, 503; Schultz v. Mountain Telephone Company, 364 Pa. 266, 270, 72 A. 2d 287, 289), and if, therefore, the right to recover costs may be withheld by the legislature without infringing on the Constitution, it would seem that the right to recover the compensation paid the arbitrators, which is an administative expense, may similarly be withheld. But the real question is whether the required payment of such fees by the appellant amounts to such a substantial restriction upon the right to present his case to a jury as to constitute a violation of that constitutional right. As already pointed out, no such violation is involved in a requirement of the payment of a jury fee as a condition precedent to the right of such a trial. The problem, however, is one of degree rather than of kind. The rule adopted in Lancaster County which is here under consideration provides for compensation to the arbitrators in the sum of $25, each, or a total of $75, and the necessity of paying that amount as a condition for the right to appeal would seemingly operate as a strong deterrent, amounting practically to a denial of that right, if the case should involve only, as in the present instance, as little as $250. Therefore this rule, as well as the rules adopted or to be adopted by the courts of common pleas of other counties, should take cognizance of this fact and should provide for a lower rate of compensation where only a comparatively small claim is involved. True, this might require an occasional sacrifice on the part of the members of the bar acting as arbitrators in such cases, but it is undoubtedly one that lawyers will cheerfully make in pursuance of those professional ideals which not infrequently lead them, under special circumstances and the observance of long established traditions, to render service to a client without any compensation at all. The requirement that the appellant repay to the county the fees of the arbitrators is obviously designed to serve as a brake or deterrent on the taking of frivolous and wholly unjustified appeals; if there were not such a provision the defeated party would be likely to appeal in nearly all instances and the arbitration proceedings would tend to become a mere nullity and waste of time.

Objection is made by the petitioner to the

limitation of the provisions of the Act to cases where the amount in controversy is $1,000 or less; it is claimed that this amounts to an improper classification in violation of Article III, section 7, of the Constitution forbiding the passage of special laws. It is, however, too well established to require extended discussion or citation of authorities that all that the Constitution demands is that the basis for classification be reasonable and founded upon a genuine and not merely artificial distinction, the test being, not wisdom, but good faith in the classification. Statutory distinctions based on the amount involved in the litigation have been regularly upheld. In Mason-Heflin Coal Co. v. Currie, 270 Pa. 221, 113 A. 202, the Sales Act of May 19, 1915, P.L. 543, was held constitutional in its provision that sale contracts involving a sum of not more than $500 need not be in writing whereas contracts involving a larger amount were enforceable only if evidenced by a memorandum in writing. The court there stated (pp. 225, 226, A. p. 204) that, once it be admitted that there was a valid reason for fixing a dividing line, the exact point at which it should be drawn was for the legislature and not for the courts. The Fiduciaries Act of 1949, P.L. 513, Section 202, the Incompetents' Estates Act of 1951, P.L. 612, Section 201, and the Uniform Commercial Code of 1953, P.L. 3, Section 2–201, all provide for differences in procedure based upon the amounts involved in the proceedings. It is of interest in this connection to note that the Federal Constitution itself provides, in the 7th Amendment, for the preservation of the right of trial by jury only in suits where the value in controversy shall exceed $20. However, it must be pointed out that, since the Act of 1952 authorizes the courts to provide for compulsory arbitration in all cases where the amount in controversy shall be $1000 or less,— that is to say, *all* cases involving less than $1000 —a court may not (as in the case of the Lancaster County rule) limit the submission to arbitra-

tion of cases involving less than $500; the system must either be adopted as an entirety and as prescribed by the Act or not at all. There can be no variances between the counties in that respect.

The fact that the counties may, in pursuance of the authority given by the Act, establish different rates of compensation to the arbitrators is clearly not, as claimed by petitioner, a violation of Article V, section 26, of the Constitution providing for the uniform operation of laws relating to courts; there have never been, and need not be, uniform rates of compensation paid in the various courts to masters, referees, and other members of the bar rendering judicial or quasi-judicial service. And the further objection that the permission given to the courts to establish boards of arbitration represents an unconstitutional delegation of legislative power is obviously untenable, for it is the statute itself which provides for such boards, leaving to the courts only the right to make administrative regulations; all the powers to be exercised by the arbitrators are also granted to them, not by the courts, but by the statute, which powers, incidentally, do not differ from those commonly vested in many of the administrative bodies which are now such important tribunals in the administration of justice.

Our conclusion is that the Act of January 14, 1952, P.L. 2087, is constitutional and in all respects valid, but that Rule 43 of the Court of Common Pleas of Lancaster County should be amended in the two respects herein indicated. Petitioner, however, is not presently affected by either of such directed amendments. His claim is subject to the arbitration provisions of the Act, and accordingly the rule to show cause why a writ of mandamus should not issue directing the court to place the case on the list for trial before a jury, is discharged. Costs to be paid by petitioner.

C.

Voluntary Interest Arbitration

ARBITRATION OF NEW CONTRACT WAGE DISPUTES: SOME RECENT TRENDS*

RICHARD U. MILLER

Analysis of the seventy [voluntary] wage arbitration cases reported above revealed that (1)

*Excerpted from 20 IND. AND LAB. REL. REV. 250 (1967). Reprinted with permission.

little use is made of arbitration in the resolution of wage disputes; (2) those collective bargaining situations in which wage arbitration is resorted to are characterized in the main by small firms, low profit margins, and severe competition; and (3) that awards have become considerably more conservative since the period (1945–1950) studied by [Irving] Bernstein. These three findings, when taken together, seem to indicate that as far as the parties are concerned, the arbitration of wages, unlike the arbitration of grievances, can contribute to collective bargaining only under crisis conditions. Resort is made to a third party only when neither the union nor the company can accept the outcome of either a negotiated settlement or test of endurance.

Also implied in the three findings is that familiarity with the process of wage arbitration will not lead to more widespread usage. Apparently, many of those who experimented with it immediately after World War II abandoned wage arbitration, even while grievance arbitration experienced a surge in popularity. Thus, the prospects for the widespread adoption of third-party resolution of wage disputes in the future would appear very dim, perhaps occurring only under conditions of the greatest economic or governmental pressure.

WINSTON-SALEM PRINTING PRESSMEN v. PIEDMONT PUBLISHING CO.
263 F. Supp. 952 (M.D. No. Car. 1967)

GORDON, D. J. The plaintiff instituted this action on September 27, 1966, to recover damages and to compel the defendant to arbitrate the disputed terms of a new collective bargaining agreement.

On October 18, 1966, defendant filed a motion to dismiss and a motion for summary judgment based on the following contentions:

1. The Court has no jurisdiction to compel arbitration under an agreement which terminates prior to compliance with the contract terms requiring arbitration.

2. The Court has no jurisdiction to compel prospective or quasi-legislative, as distinguished from quasi-judicial, arbitration.

There being no salient facts in dispute, the plaintiff on November 22, 1966, also moved for summary judgment.

Oral argument on both parties' motions for summary judgment was heard December 29, 1966. Having now carefully considered all of counsels' comments, arguments, and contentions, and the reasonable inferences to be drawn therefrom, the Court allows the plaintiff's motion for summary judgment and denies the defendant's motion for summary judgment, and makes Findings of Fact and Conclusions of Law as follows:

Findings of Fact

1. On April 13, 1964, plaintiff Union and defendant Company entered into a collective bargaining agreement, § 15 of which provides:

> This agreement shall continue to and including the 31st day of October, 1965, except that either party on thirty days' notice prior to November 1, 1964, may reopen the agreement for the consideration of wage adjustment only.
>
> Should either party desire to negotiate for changes in any or all of the provisions of this contract as of November 1, 1965, written notice to that effect must be given to the other party on or before September 1, 1965, together with written statement in detail of the changes desired. Otherwise, this agreement shall continue from November 1 through October 31 from year to year and can be changed only by mutual consent or through negotiations started by written notice of one of the parties to the other, on or before September 1st of any succeeding year. Should either party propose such amendments or a new contract, and an agreement proves impossible, the difference or differences shall be arbitrated as herein provided.

Section 1 of the agreement provides a detailed scheme for the arbitration of the differences arising between the parties.

2. By a letter dated August 30, 1965, the plaintiff notified the defendant of its desire to make certain changes and to add new provisions to the agreement. Collective bargaining negotiations were held by the parties on September 29, December 2 and December 3, 1965. A collective bargaining impasse was reached on the latter date and arbitration was mentioned for the first time.

3. On December 7, 1965, plaintiff formally notified the defendant of its desire to submit to arbitration the various provisions of the new collective bargaining agreement then in controversy.

4. Through a letter dated December 13, 1965, from the President of the defendant Company to the representative of the plaintiff Union, the defendant advised the plaintiff that it would not proceed to arbitration on the ground that the collective bargaining agreement had expired on October 31, 1965, and no obligation to arbitrate remained.

Discussion

The first contention of the defendant, that the duty to arbitrate did not exist after the collective bargaining agreement expired on October 31, 1965, is based on the decision in Austin Mailers Union No. 136 v. Newspapers, Inc., 226 F. Supp. 600 (W.D. Tex. 1963), aff'd 329 F. 2d 312 (5 Cir. 1964), cert. den. 377 U.S. 985, 84 S.Ct. 1894, 12 L.Ed. 2d 753 (1964). There the Mailers Union and the Newspaper entered into a collective bargaining agreement effective July 18, 1960, which contained the following provision with regard to the duration of the agreement:

> This contract and scale of wages shall, unless changed by mutual agreement, be in effect from July 15, 1960, for a term of two (2) years, ending July 15, 1962, with the exception of opening for wages after one year from the effective date, and shall continue thereafter within the limitations herein set forth. *Either party hereto desiring to propose a new contract to become effective on or after the expiration date of this agreement*, shall notify the other party in writing of its wishes sixty (60) days prior to the expiration date of this agreement, and accompany such notice with written statement in detail of the changes desired. . . . If notice is not given as above provided, this contract shall run from year to year until terminated or opened for negotiations by the procedure hereinbefore described sixty (60) days before any succeeding anniversary date of expiration. (226 F. Supp. at 601–602.) [Emphasis added.]

The collective bargaining agreement also contained a provision which provided for arbitration of disputes involving the agreement and "any and all disputes arising during the negotiations of any subsequent agreement." (266 F. Supp. at 602)

The Union made a written demand for arbitration on August 14, 1962, and the court held that the right to compel arbitration depends upon a valid and existing collective bargaining contract providing for arbitration and upon compliance with the contractual specifications relative thereto.

The court held that the contract had expired by its own terms on July 15, 1962; therefore, there was no valid and existing contract between the parties when the Union demanded arbitration.

The court concluded by saying:

> This court has no jurisdiction to enforce arbitration under an agreement which terminated prior to compliance with the contract terms requiring arbitration. (226 F. Supp. at 603.)

The defendant urges that the similarity of the facts with the instant case must lead to the same conclusion of law. This Court does not agree.

Even though the terms of the collective bargaining agreement in question and the collective bargaining agreement in the *Austin Mailers* case seem similar at first blush, distinctions exist which dictate a different result. In *Austin Mailers*, the duration provision of the contract explicitly stated that the contract would be in effect for two years, from July 15, 1960, to July 15, 1962. This latter date is specifically referred to as the expiration date of the agreement where it provided that notification had to be given by "[e]ither party hereto desiring to propose a *new*

contract to become effective on or after the *expiration date* of this agreement." (226 F. Supp. at 601). (Emphasis added).

The agreement in question did not spell out a specific period of years that it would exist. The agreement was to continue to and include the 31st day of October, 1965, however this latter date was never referred to as the expiration date. The express language of the contract, wherein it stated, "Should either party desire to negotiate for changes in any or all of the provisions of *this contract* as of November 1, 1965, written notice to that effect must be given," (emphasis supplied) seems to indicate that the contractual relationship between the parties is intended to be a permanent one with a provision for periodic changes in the contract. The *Austin Mailers* case talked of a new contract proposal while this contract talks of changes in the original contract to be effective on the day after, what the defendant contends is, the expiration date. If October 31, 1965, were the expiration date, this provision should talk of a new contract on November 1, 1965, not changes in the existing contract.

The agreement does not state that it will run until October 31, 1965, at which time it will automatically expire nor does it state that either party may give notice of termination of the contract as of that date. The October 31, 1965, date does no more than fix the duration of the specific terms and conditions of the agreement, after which changes may be made through negotiation and that failing, through arbitration.

The parties evidently envisaged a continuing contractual relationship with periodic negotiations to make desired changes in the basic contract. If negotiations were not fruitful, then arbitration was agreed upon to insure a continuity in the relationship. Arbitration was established as the terminal step in implementing such changes after negotiated agreement had proven impossible. Consequently, a bargaining impasse was made the condition precedent to the invocation of the arbitral process. This arbitration provision had been included in agreements between the parties for more than thirty years; therefore, it can be reasonably assumed that the parties could foresee that the bargaining impasse might occur at any time during negotiations, even after the date set in the contract after which changes could be made. The contract did not state that notice to arbitrate must be given before that certain date. The contract simply stated that should agreement prove impossible then the differences shall be arbitrated.

Here notice to make certain changes was given prior to the required date (September 1, 1965) and bargaining sessions were conducted. The impasse which was a prerequisite to arbitration did not occur until December 3, 1965. Notice to arbitrate given prior to October 31, 1965, as the defendant would require, would be premature and on anticipatory action not required of the plaintiff.

From the history of the previous relationship of the parties and the provisions of the agreement before the Court, the parties intended that arbitration would replace a clash of power if agreement through negotiations failed. The voluntary determination to arbitrate was made at the cost of independent action, but it in turn insured the desired stability in the contractual relationship. When changes in the basic contract were requested and negotiations begun, the contract, by its own terms, remained in existence until all differences were settled and this settlement included arbitration, if necessary. The resort to arbitration would have been premature until all other avenues to agreement had been exhausted. However, when that prerequisite had been met, arbitration was properly requested by the plaintiff, and the duty of the defendant to arbitrate exists under the collective bargaining agreement made on April 14, 1964.

The defendant strongly urges that even if the collective bargaining agreement had not expired, this Court lacks jurisdiction of the case and should grant summary judgment to the defendant because § 301 of the Labor Management Relations Act, 1947, does not confer upon the federal courts jurisdiction to compel prospective or quasi-legislative, as distinguished from quasi-judicial, arbitration. This Court agrees that the arbitration requested, that is the terms of a renewal contract, is properly labeled quasi-legislative or prospective arbitration to use these convenient terms. The defendant relies heavily on Boston Printing Pressmen's Union v. Potter Press, 141 F. Supp. 553 (D.C. Mass. 1956), aff'd 241 F. 2d 787 (1 Cir. 1957), cert. den. 355 U.S. 817, 78 S.Ct. 21, 2 L.Ed. 2d 34 (1957). There the District Court found that, although Congress had the constitutional power to authorize the federal courts to enforce such quasi-legislative arbitration provisions, there remained the question of whether the Congress had done so. The court then looked to the United States Arbitration Act as the basis for determining if Congress had intended for such quasi-legislative arbitration to be enforced, and said:

> Hence assuming the constitutionality of a statute which would authorize Federal Courts to enforce legislative awards of arbitrators, I nonetheless conclude that the present United States arbitration statute does not seek to reach that constitutional limit, but is concerned only with the enforcement

of quasi-judicial awards directed at the ascertainment of facts in a past controversy and at the prescription of recoverable damages or other suitable awards for that which has been broken not for that which is to be built. (141 F. Supp. at 557.)

In *Potter Press,* being a case of first impression, the court moved warily and followed the narrow view that if Congress had not included this type of arbitration in the legislation already existing to enforce arbitration, *i.e.,* United States Arbitration Act, then § 301 of the Labor Management Relations Act conferred on the federal courts no jurisdiction to grant a remedy in this unexplored area.

On appeal the First Circuit affirmed, 241 F. 2d 787 (1 Cir. 1957), and stated, as determined by their opinion in Local 205, United Electrical, Radio and Machine Workers of America v. General Electric Company, 233 F. 2d 85 (1 Cir. 1956), that the federal district court was empowered by the co-joint authority of § 301 of the Labor Management Relations Act and of the United States Arbitration Act to decree specific performance in a matter involving grievance arbitration.

Both decisions taken as a whole indicated that § 301 cannot stand alone to confer jurisdiction and provide a proper remedy in this type case; therefore, the United States Arbitration Act must be looked to as the basis for such a remedy, and since it does not envisage such quasi-legislative arbitration the court has no jurisdiction.

Defendant cites other decisions which approved the holding in *Potter Press.* The proper weight to be given these decisions on the point in question must be dictated by the present applicability of the rationale in *Potter Press.*

Plaintiff counters that in the *Potter Press* decision, the court looked for a statutory predicate upon which to base enforcement of the arbitration covenant, and in finding that the United States Arbitration Act did not contemplate this character of dispute, the court determined that it was without authority to enforce the arbitration provision. The plaintiff contends that in doing so, the court proceeded upon the erroneous conception that in enforcing an arbitration covenant, the court had statutory power only, thereby rejecting the proposition that once a court acquires jurisdiction of an action by reason of § 301, the traditional equitable powers of a United States Court are available to enforce contract rights asserted thereunder.

To undermine this restrictive line of reasoning in *Potter Press* and to show it as a misconception, plaintiff points to Textile Workers v. Lincoln Mills, 353 U.S. 448, 77 S.Ct. 912, 1

L.Ed. 2d 972 (1957). This decision specifically held that the authority of the federal courts to enforce arbitration agreements is not derived from any state or federal law (to include the U.S. Arbitration Act), but that such authority can be determined by reference to § 301 itself and the National Labor policy expressed therein, together with the traditional equitable powers of the federal district courts. Even though only grievance arbitration was directly in question, the court concluded that the power to grant a remedy under § 301 was found in § 301 alone; consequently, the courts must fashion a body of federal substantive law without reference to other statutory authority.

The rationale of *Potter Press* is further diminished when the decision in the companion case of *Lincoln Mills* is considered. In General Electric Company v. Local 205, U.E., 353 U.S. 547, 77 S.Ct. 921, 1 L.Ed. 2d 1028 (1957), the court affirmed the First Circuit but distinguished their reasoning, Justice Douglas stating:

> It (the Circuit Court) then held that while § 301 (a) of the Labor Management Relations Act of 1947 gave the District Court Jurisdiction of the cause, it supplied no body of substantive law to enforce an arbitration agreement governing grievances. But it found such a basis in the United States Arbitration Act, which it held applicable to these collective bargaining agreements. It accordingly reversed the District Court judgment and remanded the cause to that court for further proceedings.
> We affirm that judgment and remand the cause to the District Court. We follow in part a different path than the Court of Appeals, though we reach the same result as indicated in our opinion in No. 211, Textile Workers Union of America v. Lincoln Mills of Alabama...We think that § 301 (a) furnishes a body of federal substantive law for the enforcement of collective bargaining agreements. (353 U.S. at 548, 77 S.Ct. at 922, 1 L.Ed. 2d at 1029.)

Thereby the Supreme Court specifically stated that the U.S. Arbitration Act should not provide the basis for a decision involving arbitration, but that such was furnished by § 301 standing alone.

Even though these Supreme Court rulings dealt with grievance arbitration and not arbitration of the terms of future contracts, the rationale in one would of necessity color the other. If § 301 can independently provide jurisdiction and a remedy for grievance (quasi-judicial) arbitration, then reasonably it could provide the needed authority and remedy for the arbitration of renewal contract terms (quasi-legislative arbitration).

Recent decisions cited by the plaintiff have questioned the rationale of *Potter Press* and have found it inapplicable. Division No. 892, etc. v.

M. K. & O. Transit Lines, 210 F. Supp. 351 (N.D. Okla. 1962), rev.´on other grds. 319 F. 2d 488 (10 Cir. 1963), cert. den., 375 U.S. 994, 84 S.Ct. 350, 11 L.Ed. 2d 274 (1963) ; Builders Association v. Kansas City Laborers, etc., 326 F. 2d 867 (8 Cir. 1964), cert. denied, 377 U.S. 917, 84 S.Ct. 1182, 1 2 L.Ed. 2d 186 (1964) ; A. Seltzer & Co. v. Livingston, 253 F. Supp. 509 (S.D. N.Y. 1966) aff'd 361 F. 2d 218 (2 Cir. 1966).

In *M. K. & O. Transit Lines*, the defendant employer contented that it was not required to negotiate a new contract and that such could not be arbitrated regardless of the provisions of a previous agreement. The defendant relied principally on *Potter Press* and to this the Court stated:

> This case (Potter Press) is not in point and is at odds with the rulings of the Supreme Court... This Court has the power to enforce the arbitration provisions of the contract in question even though such enforcement establishes future labor conditions. (210 F. Supp. at 356.)

The Circuit Court found it unnecessary to rule on the applicability of *Potter Press*, because, in reversing the District Court decision, it determined that the union had terminated the contract requiring the employer to arbitrate. Nonetheless, the court noted in passing:

> Even though we believe that the parties contemplated that there might be arbitration of the conditions of a new contract, we do not reach the question of the court's authority or jurisdiction to require such arbitration. It may well be on the latter question that the rationale of the decision in the *Potter Press* case should be reappraised in the light of subsequent decisions of the Supreme Court. Our resolution of this important problem, however, should await a case in which it is squarely presented. (319 F. 2d at 490.)

In *Builders Association,* the defendant contended that the dispute in question (terms of a new trust agreement) was not arbitrable because it concerned the creation of a new agreement, relying upon the decision in *Potter Press*. After discussing the case the court answered:

> It was held (in *Potter Press*) that the federal court was without authority to compel arbitration of the dispute. In the light of what we conceive to be the teachings of the Supreme Court and the cases to which we have referred, we are convinced that the decision in Boston Printing Pressmen's Union v. Potter Press is far too weak a peg upon which to hang a reversal of the judgment in the instant case. (326 F. 2d at 870.)

The most recent case discussing the doctrine of *Potter Press* is *Seltzer & Co.* There the dispute concerned an agreement to enter into a labor contract on the same terms contained in the majority of the union's contracts with other employers and to arbitrate any dispute concerning these terms. The court ultimately decided that the case probably did not involve arbitration of future terms, but not until after it disposed of the plaintiff employers' contention that the *Potter Press* decision relieved it of any duty to arbitrate. The court in discussing this contention noted that the *Potter Press* doctrine had been criticized by text writers, and also pointed out that subsequent to *Potter Press* the Supreme Court had decided the *Steelworkers* cases which emphasized the importance of arbitration as the most appropriate method of resolving employees' grievances. After acknowledging that the recent Supreme Court decisions did not directly touch upon the point decided in *Potter Press* and after citing and discussing the *Builders Association* and the *M. K. & O. Transit* cases, the court reached the conclusion that *Potter Press* is no longer controlling.

The *Seltzer* case was affirmed by the Second Circuit in a per curiam opinion. Consequently aligning the Second Circuit with the Eighth Circuit in questioning the present applicability of the *Potter Press* decision.

Even viewing the defendant's reliance on the rationale of the decision in *Potter Press* from the most favorable aspect, its persuasive force has certainly been diminished by the foregoing decisions. In rulings subsequent to *Potter Press*, the Supreme Court has broadened the scope of § 301 and has encouraged arbitration as a desirable alternative to industrial strife. The parties by the terms of their agreement had freely determined to substitute arbitration for economic warfare in settling labor disputes and had explicitly agreed to arbitrate any differences concerning future contract terms.

This Court therefore rejects the rationale of the *Potter Press* decision and determines that § 301 of the Labor Management Relations Act confers on the Court jurisdiction to compel quasi-legislative as well as quasi-judicial arbitration where such has been voluntarily agreed upon by the parties.

Conclusions Of Law

1. The Court has jurisdiction over the parties and the subject matter of this action.
2. The contract provision requiring arbitration remains valid and requires the defendant to arbitrate with the plaintiff existing unresolved differences regarding the contract.

For further discussion, see Dallas Young, *Arbitration of Terms for New Labor Contracts,* 17 W. RES. L. REV. 1302 (1966) and Note, *Quasi-Legislative Arbitration of Agreements,* 64 COLUM. L. REV. 109 (1964).

For brief surveys of foreign experience and bibliographies, see HERBERT NORTHRUP, COMPULSORY ARBITRATION AND GOVERNMENT INTERVENTION IN LABOR DISPUTES (1966) and National Association of Manufacturers, A STUDY OF COMPULSORY ARBITRATION IN SIX FOREIGN COUNTRIES (processed, 1960).

For a splendid account of the history and results of the first instance of nationally legislated compulsory arbitration of contract terms see David Levinson, *The Locomotive Firemen's Dispute,* 11 LAB. L. J. 671 (1966).

For spirited advocacy of compulsory arbitration of new contract disputes, see Orme Phelps, *Compulsory Arbitration: Some Perspectives,* 18 IND. AND LAB. REL. REV. (1964) in a symposium on "The Strike, the Non-Strike and Compulsory Arbitration." The first article discusses the declining utility of strikes. Professor Phelps argues that compulsory arbitration shares elements in common with court adjudication, NLRB unfair labor practice decisions, and grievance arbitration.

Wage issues predominate among disputes that lead to the impasses that verge on emergencies. There has been considerable wartime experience in the arbitration of such disputes. Probably most commentators would agree that the criteria for decisions are inexact and often slippery. Under the impact of an emergency and the necessity for continued operations both the inexactitude and the involuntary nature of the compulsory resolution may be tolerable. But in the present climate of opinion in the labor-management community, outside the railroad and maritime industries, both seem intolerable in situations that do less than imperil the national economy.

That view, however, fostered in the philosophy of voluntarism that pervaded the group of specialists who achieved their labor-management expertise in World War II's War Labor Board, may give way as the members of that corps are joined and then give way to others who did not share that experience. As the impact of work stoppages becomes more far reaching and economic interrelationships of trades and industries become more complex, the acceptability of strikes may decline and willingness to entertain presently objectionable substitutes may increase.

While experience with voluntary "interest" arbitration is sparse, it may be worth study as the issue of compulsory arbitration revives, as it un-doubtedly will. It is not the only alternative to strikes.

With the rapid spread of collective bargaining and strikes in public employment, interest in compulsory arbitration of new contract terms undoubtedly will grow.

D.

Advisory Arbitration

Finality and enforceability have become the hallmarks of arbitration, so that a dispute-settle-ment procedure lacking these qualities often is regarded as falling outside the category of arbi-tration. In effect, Dean Shulman advocated an advisory procedure as the most desirable kind of arbitration. Few share that view. Yet such a pro-cedure may have its uses.

The decision of an impartial person or panel issued after the presentation of evidence and argument by the interested parties may stimulate a solution of a dispute. Resistance to such an opinion puts a burden upon the recalcitrant party to justify his refusal. Where the pressure for the action that gave rise to the dispute comes from only a segment of an organization, the arbi-trator's opinion may enable other officials or interest groups to overcome the minority with a minimum of bad feeling.

In government, advisory arbitration has been adopted for two basic reasons. One is the legal objection that giving an arbitrator final authority to decide issues involving a public agency is an improper delegation of authority. This view prob-ably is on the wane. The second is the very practical difficulty of meshing an arbitrator's disposition of a dispute with otherwise govern-ing law. For example, some problems have arisen with arbitrators' opinions in federal employee cases because the arbitrators were not sufficiently expert in the arcane subtleties of civil service law and regulations, or at least so some administra-tors have claimed. It is conceivable that as union organization grows in government employment, collective bargaining will actually displace civil service law and regulations.

Experience under the grievance-advisory arbi-tration procedures adopted a few years ago for the Civil Service has been slight. A brief biblio-graphy follows:

Belenker, *Binding Arbitration for Government Employees*, 16 LAB. L. J. 234 (1965).
Blaine, Hagburg, and Zeller, *The Grievance Procedure and its Application in the United States Post Office*, 15 LAB. L. J. 725 (1964).
Harper, *Labor Relations in the Postal Service*, 17 IND. & LAB. REL. REV. 443 (1964).
Hart, *Government Labor's New Frontiers through Presidential Directive*, 48 VA. L. REV. 898 (1962).
———, *The Impasse in Labor Relations in the Federal Civil Service*, 19 IND. & LAB. REL. REV. 175 (1966).
———, *The United States Civil Service Learns to Live with Executive Order 10988: An Interim Appraisal*, 17 IND. & LAB. REL. REV. 205 (1964).
Krislov, *Prospects for the Use of Advisory Grievance Arbitration in Federal Service*, 18 IND. & LAB. REL. REV. 420 (1965).
Schneider, *Collective Bargaining and the Federal Civil Service*, IND. REL., May, 1964, at 97.

APPENDIX A

UNITED STATES ARBITRATION ACT
TITLE 9.—ARBITRATION

This title was enacted by act July 30, 1947, ch. 392, §1, 61 Stat. 669

§ 1. "Maritime transactions" and "commerce" defined; exceptions to operations of title.

"Maritime transactions", as herein defined, means charter parties, bills of lading of water carriers, agreements relating to wharfage, supplies furnished vessels or repairs to vessels, collisions, or any other matters in foreign commerce which, if the subject of controversy, would be embraced within admiralty jurisdiction; "commerce", as herein defined, means commerce among the several States or with foreign nations, or in any Territory of the United States or in the District of Columbia, or between any such Territory and another, or between any such Territory and any State or foreign nation, or between the District of Columbia and any State or Territory or foreign nation, but nothing herein contained shall apply to contracts of employment of seamen, railroad employees, or any other class of workers engaged in foreign or interstate commerce. (July 30, 1947, ch. 392, 61 Stat. 670.)

§ 2. Validity, irrevocability, and enforcement of agreements to arbitrate.

A written provision in any maritime transaction or a contract evidencing a transaction involving commerce to settle by arbitration a controversy thereafter arising out of such contract or transaction, or the refusal to perform the whole or any part thereof, or an agreement in writing to submit to arbitration an existing controversy arising out of such a contract, transaction, or refusal, shall be valid, irrevocable, and enforceable, save upon such grounds as exist at law or in equity for the revocation of any contract. (July 30, 1947, ch. 392, 61 Stat. 670.)

§ 3. Stay of proceedings where issue therein referable to arbitration.

If any suit or proceeding be brought in any of the courts of the United States upon any issue referable to arbitration under an agreement in writing for such arbitration, the court in which such suit is pending, upon being satisfied that the issue involved in such suit or proceeding is referable to arbitration under such an agreement, shall on application of one of the parties stay the trial of the action until such arbitration has been had in accordance with the terms of the agreement, providing the applicant for the stay is not in default in proceeding with such arbitration. (July 30, 1947, ch. 392, 61 Stat. 670.)

§ 4. Failure to arbitrate under agreement; petition to United States court having jurisdiction for order to compel arbitration; notice and service thereof; hearing and determination.

A party aggrieved by the alleged failure, neglect, or refusal of another to arbitrate under a written agreement for arbitration may petition any United States district court which, save for such agreement, would have jurisdiction under Title 28, in a civil action or in admiralty of the subject matter of a suit arising out of the controversy between the parties, for an order directing that such arbitration proceed in the manner provided for in such agreement. Five days' notice in writing of such application shall be served upon the party in default. Service thereof shall be made in the manner provided by the Federal Rules of Civil Procedure. The court shall hear the parties, and upon being satisfied that the making of the agreement for arbitration or the failure to comply therewith is not in issue, the court shall make an order directing the parties to proceed in arbitration in accordance with the terms of the agreement. The hearing and proceedings, under such agreement, shall be within the district in which the petition for an order directing such arbitration is filed. If the making of the arbitration agreement or the failure, neglect, or refusal to perform the same be in issue, the court shall proceed summarily to the trial thereof. If no jury trial be demanded by the party alleged to be in default, or if the matter in dispute is within admiralty jurisdiction, the court shall hear and determine such issue. Where such an issue is raised, the party alleged to be in default may, except in cases of admiralty, on or before the return day of the notice of application, demand a jury trial of such issue, and upon such demand the court shall make an order referring the issue or issues to a jury in the manner provided by the Federal Rules of Civil Procedure, or may specially call a jury for that purpose. If the jury find that no agreement in writing for arbitration was made or that there is no default in proceeding thereunder, the proceeding shall be dismissed. If the jury find that an agreement for arbitration was made in writing and there is a default in proceeding thereunder, the court shall make an order summarily directing the parties to proceed with the arbitration in accordance with the terms thereof. (July 30, 1947, ch. 392, 61 Stat. 671; Sept. 3, 1954, ch. 1263, § 19, 68 Stat. 1233.)

§ 5. Appointment of arbitrators or umpire.

If in the agreement provision be made for a method of naming or appointing an arbitrator or arbitrators or an umpire, such method shall be followed; but if no method be provided therein, or if a method be provided and any party thereto shall fail to avail himself of such method, or if for any other reason there shall be a lapse in the naming of an arbitrator or arbitrators or umpire, or in filling a vacancy, then upon the application of either party to the controversy the court shall designate and appoint an arbitrator or arbitrators or umpire, as the case may require, who shall act under the said agreement with the same force and effect as if he or they had been specifically named therein; and unless otherwise provided in the agreement the arbitration shall be by a single arbitrator. (July 30, 1947, ch. 392, 61 Stat. 671.)

§ 6. Application heard as motion.

Any application to the court hereunder shall be made and heard in the manner provided by law for the making and hearing of motions, except as otherwise herein expressly provided. (July 30, 1947, ch. 392, 61 Stat. 671.)

§ 7. Witnesses before arbitrators; fees; compelling attendance..

The arbitrators selected either as prescribed in this title or otherwise, or a majority of them, may summon in writing any person to attend before them or any of them as a witness and in a proper case to bring with him or them any book, record, document, or paper which may be deemed material as evidence in the case. The fees for such attendance shall be the same as the fees of witnesses before masters of the United States courts. Said summons shall issue in the name of the arbitrator or arbitrators, or a majority of them, and shall be signed by the arbitrators, or a majority of them, and shall be directed to the said person and shall be served in the same manner as subpoenas to appear and testify before the court; if any person or persons so summoned to testify shall refuse or neglect to obey said summons, upon petition the United States district court for the district in which such arbitrators, or a majority of them, are sitting may compel the attendance of such person or persons before said arbitrator or arbitrators, or punish said person or persons for contempt in the same manner provided by law for securing the attendance of witnesses or their punishment for neglect or refusal to attend in the courts of the United States. (July 30, 1947, ch. 392, 61 Stat. 672; Oct. 31, 1951, ch. 655, § 14, 65 Stat. 715.)

§ 8. Proceedings begun by libel in admiralty and seizure of vessel or property.

If the basis of jurisdiction be a cause of action otherwise justiciable in admiralty, then, notwithstanding anything herein to the contrary, the party claiming to be aggrieved may begin his proceeding hereunder by libel and seizure of the vessel or other property of the other party according to the usual course of admiralty proceedings, and the court shall then have jurisdiction to direct the parties to proceed with the arbitration and shall retain jurisdiction to enter its decree upon the award. (July 30, 1947, ch. 392, 61 Stat. 872.)

§ 9. Award of arbitrators; confirmation; jurisdiction: procedure.

If the parties in this agreement have agreed that a judgment of the court shall be entered upon the award made pursuant to the arbitration, and shall specify the court, then at any time within one year after the award is made any party to the arbitration may apply to the court so specified for an order confirming the award, and thereupon the court must grant such an order unless the award is vacated, modified, or corrected as prescribed in sections 10 and 11 of this title. If no court is specified in the agreement of the parties, then such application may be made to the United States court in and for the district

within which such award was made. Notice of the application shall be served upon the adverse party, and thereupon the court shall have jurisdiction of such party as though he had appeared generally in the proceeding. If the adverse party is a resident of the district within which the award was made, such service shall be made upon the adverse party or his attorney as prescribed by law for service of notice of motion in an action in the same court. If the adverse party shall be a nonresident, then the notice of the application shall be served by the marshal of any district within which the adverse party may be found in like manner as other process of the court. (July 30, 1947, ch. 392, 61 Stat. 672.)

§ 10. Same; vacation; grounds; rehearing.

In either of the following cases the United States court in and for the district wherein the award was made may make an order vacating the award upon the application of any part to the arbitration—

(a) Where the award was procured by corruption, fraud, or undue means.

(b) Where there was evident partiality or corruption in the arbitrators, or either of them.

(c) Where the arbitrators were guilty of misconduct in refusing to postpone the hearing, upon sufficient cause shown, or in refusing to hear evidence pertinent and material to the controversy; or of any other misbehavior by which the rights of any party have been prejudiced.

(d) Where the arbitrators exceeded their powers, or so imperfectly executed them that a mutual, final, and definite award upon the subject matter submitted was not made.

(e) Where an award is vacated and the time within which the agreement required the award to be made has not expired the court may, in its discretion, direct a rehearing by the arbitrators. (July 30, 1947, ch. 392, 61 Stat. 672.)

§ 11. Same; modification or correction; grounds; order.

In either of the following cases the United States court in and for the district wherein the award was made may make an order modifying or correcting the award upon the application of any party to the arbitration—

(a) Where there was an evident material miscalculation of figures or an evident material mistake in the description of any person, thing, or property referred to in the award.

(b) Where the arbitrators have awarded upon a matter not submitted to them, unless it is a matter not affecting the merits of the decision upon the matter submitted.

(c) Where the award is imperfect in matter

of form not affecting the merits of the controversy.

The order may modify and correct the award, so as to effect the intent thereof and promote justice between the parties. (July 30, 1947, ch. 392, 61 Stat. 673.)

§ 12. Notice of motions to vacate or modify; service; stay of proceedings.

Notice of a motion to vacate, modify, or correct an award must be served upon the adverse party or his attorney within three months after the award is filed or delivered. If the adverse party is a resident of the district within which the award was made, such service shall be made upon the adverse party or his attorney as prescribed by law for service of notice of motion in an action in the same court. If the adverse party shall be a nonresident then the notice of the application shall be served by the marshal of any district within which the adverse party may be found in like manner as other process of the court. For the purposes of the motion any judge who might make an order to stay the proceedings in an action brought in the same court may make an order, to be served with the notice of motion, staying the proceedings of the adverse party to enforce the award. (July 30, 1947, ch. 392, 61 Stat. 673.)

§ 13. Papers filed with order on motions; judgment; docketing; force and effect; enforcement.

The party moving for an order confirming, modifying, or correcting an award shall, at the time such order is filed with the clerk for the entry of judgment thereon, also file the following papers with the clerk:

(a) The agreement; the selection or appointment, if any, of an additional arbitrator or umpire; and each written extension of the time, if any, within which to make the award.

(b) The award.

(c) Each notice, affidavit, or other paper used upon an application to confirm, modify, or correct the award, and a copy of each order of the court upon such an application.

The judgment shall be docketed as if it was rendered in an action.

The judgment so entered shall have the same force and effect, in all respects, as, and be subject to all the provisions of law relating to, a judgment in an action; and it may be enforced as if it had been rendered in an action in the court in which it is entered, (July 30, 1947, ch. 392 61 Dist. 673.)

§ 14. Contracts not affected.

This title shall not apply to contracts made prior to January 1, 1926. (July 30, 1947, ch. 392, 61 Stat. 673.)

APPENDIX B

NEW YORK CIVIL PRACTICE LAW AND RULES: ARTICLES 75 AND 76

(Effective September 1, 1963)

Article 75: Arbitration

§ 7501. *Effect of arbitration agreement.* A written agreement to submit any controversy thereafter arising or any existing controversy to arbitration is enforceable without regard to the justiciable character of the controversy and confers jurisdiction on the courts of the state to enforce it and to enter judgment on an award. In determining any matter arising under this article, the court shall not consider whether the claim with respect to which arbitration is sought is tenable, or otherwise pass upon the merits of the dispute.

§ 7502. *Applications to the court; venue; statutes of limitation.* (a) Applications to the court, venue. A special proceeding shall be used to bring before a court the first application arising out of an arbitrable controversy which is not made by motion in a pending action. The proceeding shall be brought in the court and county specified in the agreement; or, if none be specified, in a court in the county in which one of the parties resides or is doing business, or, if there is no such county, in a court in any county; or in a court in the county in which the arbitration was held. All subsequent applications shall be made by motion in the pending action or the special proceeding.

(b) *Limitation of time.* If, at the time that a demand for arbitration was made or a notice of intention to arbitrate was served, the claim sought to be arbitrated would have been barred by limitation of time had it been asserted in a court of the state, a party may assert the limitation as a bar to the arbitration on an application to the court as provided in section 7503 or subdivision (b) of section 7511. The failure to assert such bar by such application shall not preclude its assertion before the arbitrators, who may, in their sole discretion, apply or not apply the bar. Except as provided in subdivision (b) of section 7511, such exercise of discretion by the arbitrators shall not be subject to review by a court on an application to confirm, vacate or modify the award.

§ 7503. *Application to compel or stay arbitration; stay of action; notice of intention to arbitrate.* (a) Application to compel arbitration; stay of action. A party aggrieved by the failure of another to arbitrate may apply for an order compelling arbitration. Where there is no substantial question whether a valid agreement was made or complied with, and the claim sought to be arbitrated is not barred by limitation under subdivision (b) of section 7502, the court shall direct the parties to arbitrate. Where any such question is raised, it shall be tried forthwith in said court. If an issue claimed to be arbitrable is involved in an action pending in a court having jurisdiction to hear a motion to compel arbitration, the application shall be made by motion in the action. If the application is granted, the order shall operate to stay a pending or subsequent action, or so much of it as is referable to arbitration.

(b) *Application to stay arbitration.* Subject to the provisions of subdivision (c), a party who has not participated in the arbitration and who has not made or been served with an application to compel arbitration, may apply to stay arbitration on the ground that a valid agreement was not made or has not been complied with or that the claim sought to be arbitrated is barred by limitation under subdivision (b) of section 7502.

(c) *Notice of intention to arbitrate.* A party may serve upon another party a notice of intention to arbitrate, specifying the agreement pursuant to which arbitration is sought and the name and address of the party serving the notice, or of an officer or agent thereof if such party is an association or corporation, and stating that unless the party served applies to stay the arbitration within ten days after such service he shall thereafter be precluded from objecting that a valid agreement was not made or has not been complied with and from asserting in court the bar of a limitation of time. Such notice shall be served in the same manner as a summons or by registered or certified mail, return receipt requested. An application to stay arbitration must be made by the party served within ten days after service upon him of the notice or he shall be so precluded. Notice of such application shall be served in the same manner as a summons or by registered or certified mail, return receipt requested.

§ 7504. *Court appointment of arbitrator.* If the arbitration agreement does not provide for a method of appointment of an arbitrator, or if the agreed method fails or for any reason is not followed, or if an arbitrator fails to act and his successor has not been appointed, the court, on application of a party, shall appoint an arbitrator.

§ 7505. *Powers of arbitrator.* An arbitrator and any attorney of record in the arbitration proceeding has the power to issue subpoenas. An arbitrator has the power to administer oaths.

§ 7506. *Hearing.* (a) *Oath of arbitrator.* Before hearing any testimony, an arbitrator shall be sworn to hear and decide the controversy faithfully and fairly by an officer authorized to administer an oath.

(b) *Time and place.* The arbitrator shall appoint a time and place for the hearing and notify the parties in writing personally or by registered or certified mail not less than eight days before the hearing. The arbitrator may adjourn or postpone the hearing. The court, upon application of any party, may direct the arbitrator to proceed promptly with the hearing and determination of the controversy.

(c) *Evidence.* The parties are entitled to be heard, to present evidence and to cross-examine witnesses. Notwithstanding the failure of a party duly notified to appear, the arbitrator may hear and determine the controversy upon the evidence produced.

(d) *Representation by attorney.* A party has the right to be represented by an attorney and may claim such right at any time as to any part of the arbitration or hearings which have not taken place. This right may not be waived. If a party is represented by an attorney, papers to be served on the party shall be served upon his attorney.

(e) *Determination by majority.* The hearing shall be conducted by all the arbitrators, but a majority may determine may question and render an award.

(f) *Waiver.* Except as provided in subdivision (d), a requirement of this section may be waived by written consent of the parties and it is waived if the parties continue with the arbitration without objection.

§ 7507. *Award; form; time; delivery.* Except as provided in section 7508, the award shall be in writing, signed and acknowledged by the arbitrator making it within the time fixed by the agreement, or, if the time is not fixed, within such time as the court orders. The parties may in writing extend the time either before or after its expiration. A party waives the objection that an award was not made within the time required unless he notifies the arbitrator in writing of his objection prior to the delivery of the award to him. The arbitrator shall deliver a copy of the award to each party in the manner provided in the agreement, or, if no provision is so made, personally or by registered or certified mail, return receipt requested.

§ 7508. *Award by confession.* (a) *When available.* An award by confession may be made for money due or to become due at any time before an award is otherwise made. The award shall be based upon a statement, verified by each party, containing an authorization to make the award, the sum of the award or the method of ascertaining it, and the facts constituting the liability.

(b) *Time of award.* The award may be made at any time within three months after the statement is verified.

(c) *Person or agency making award.* The award may be made by an arbitrator or by the agency or person named by the parties to designate the arbitrator.

§ 7509. *Modification of award by arbitrator.*

On written application of a party to the arbitrators within twenty days after delivery of the award to the applicant, the arbitrators may modify the award upon the grounds stated in subdivision (c) of section 7511. Written notice of the application shall be given to other parties to the arbitration. Written objection to modification must be served on the arbitrators and other parties to the arbitration within ten days of receipt of the notice. The arbitrators shall dispose of any application made under this section in writing, signed and acknowledged by them, within thirty days after either written objection to modification has been served on them or the time for serving said objection has expired, whichever is earlier. The parties may in writing extend the time for such disposition either before or after its expiration.

§ 7510. *Confirmation of award.* The court shall confirm an award upon application of a party made within one year after its delivery to him, unless the award is vacated or modified upon a ground specified in section 7511.

§ 7511. *Vacating or modifying award.* (a) *When application made.* An application to vacate or modify an award may be made by a party within ninety days after its delivery to him.

(b) *Grounds for vacating.*

1. The award shall be vacated on the application of a party who either participated in the arbitration or was served with a notice of intention to arbitrate if the court finds that the rights of that party were prejudiced by:

(i) corruption, fraud or misconduct in procuring the award; or

(ii) partiality of an arbitrator appointed as neutral, except where the award was by confession; or

(iii) an arbitrator, or agency or person making the award exceeded his power or so imperfectly executed it that a final and definite award upon the subject matter submitted was not made; or

(iv) failure to follow the procedure of this article, unless the party applying to vacate the award continued with the arbitration with notice of the defect and without objection.

2. The award shall be vacated on the application of a party who neither participated in the arbitration nor was served with a notice of intention to arbitrate if the court finds that:

(i) the rights of that party were prejudiced by one of the grounds specified in paragraph one; or

(ii) a valid agreement to arbitrate was not made; or

(iii) the agreement to arbitrate had not been complied with; or

(iv) the arbitrated claim was barred by limitation under subdivision (b) of section 7502.

(c) *Grounds for modifying.* The court shall modify the award if:

1. There was a miscalculation of figures or a mistake in the description of any person, thing or property referred to the award; or

2. The arbitrators have awarded upon a matter not submitted to them and the award may be corrected without affecting the merits of the decision upon the issues submitted; or

3. The award is imperfect in a matter of form, not affecting the merits of the controversy.

(d) *Rehearing.* Upon vacating an award, the court may order a rehearing and determination of all or any of the issues either before the same arbitrator or before a new arbitrator appointed in accordance with this article. Time in any provision limiting the time for a hearing shall be measured from the date of such order or rehearing, whichever is appropriate, or a time may be specified by the court.

(e) *Confirmation.* Upon the granting of a motion to modify, the court shall confirm the award as modified; upon the denial of a motion to vacate or modify, it shall confirm the award.

§ 7512. *Death or incompetency of a party.* Where a party dies after making a written agreement to submit a controversy to arbitration, the proceedings may be begun or continued upon the application of, or upon notice to, his executor or administrator or, where it relates to real property, his distributee or devisee who has succeeded to his interest in the real property. Where a committee of the property or of the person of a party to such an agreement is appointed, the proceedings may be continued upon the application of, or notice to, the committee. Upon the death or incompetency of a party, the court may extend the time within which an application to confirm, vacate or modify the award or to stay arbitration must be made. Where a party has died since an award was delivered, the proceedings thereupon are the same as where a party dies after a verdict.

§ 7513. *Fees and expenses.* Unless otherwise provided in the agreement to arbitrate, the arbitrators' expenses and fees, together with other expenses, not including attorney's fees, incurred in the conduct of the arbitration, shall be paid as provided in the award. The court, on application may reduce or disallow any fee or expense it finds excessive or allocate it as justice requires.

§ 7514. *Judgment on an award.* (a) *Entry.* A judgment shall be entered upon the confirmation of an award.

(b) Judgment-roll. The judgment-roll consists of the original or a copy of the agreement and each written extension of time within which to make an award; the statement required by section seventy-five hundred eight where the award was by confession; the award; each paper submitted to the court and each order of the court upon an application under sections 7510 and 7511; and a copy of the judgment.

Article 76: Proceeding to Enforce Agreement for Determination of Issue

§ 7601. *Special proceeding to enforce agreement that issue or controversy be determined by a person named or to be selected.* A special proceeding may be commenced to specifically enforce an agreement, other than one contained in the standard fire insurance policy of the state, that a question of valuation, appraisal or other issue or controversy be determined by a person named or to be selected. The court may enforce such an agreement as if it were an arbitration agreement, in which case the proceeding shall be conducted as if brought under article seventy-five. Where there is a defense which would require dismissal of an action for breach of the agreement, the proceeding shall be dismissed.

APPENDIX C

THE NEW YORK ARBITRATION LAW: ARTICLE 84 OF THE NEW YORK CIVIL PRACTICE ACT

(As in force September 1, 1952)

Section 1448.

Validity of arbitration contracts or submissions. Except as otherwise prescribed in this section, two or more persons may submit to the arbitration of one or more arbitrators any controversy existing between them at the time of the submission, which may be the subject of an action, or they may contract to settle by arbitration a controversy thereafter arising between them and such submission or contract shall be valid, enforceable and irrevocable, save upon such grounds as exist at law or in equity for the revocation of any contract. A provision in a written contract between a labor organization, as defined in subdivision five of section seven hundred one of the labor law, and employer or employers or association or group of employers to settle by arbitration a controversy or controversies thereafter arising between the parties to the contract including but not restricted to controversies dealing with rates of pay, wages, hours of employment or other terms and conditions of employment of any employee or employees of such employer or employers shall likewise be valid, enforceable and irrevocable, save upon such grounds as exist at law or in equity for the revocation of any contract, without regard to the justiciable character of such controversy or controversies.

Such submission or contract may include questions arising out of valuations, appraisals or other controversies which may be collateral, incidental, precedent or subsequent to or independent of any issue between the parties.

A controversy cannot be arbitrated, either as prescribed in this article or otherwise, in either of the following cases:

1. Where one of the parties to the controversy is an infant or a person incompetent to manage his affairs by reason of lunacy, idiocy or habitual drunkenness unless the appropriate court having jurisdiction approve a petition for permission to submit such controversy to arbitration made by the general guardian or guardian ad litem of the infant or by the committee of the incompetent.

2. Where the controversy arises respecting a claim to an estate in real property, in fee or for life.

But where a person capable of entering into a submission or contract has knowingly entered into the same with a person incapable of so doing, as prescribed in subdivision first of this section, the objection on the ground of incapacity can be taken only in behalf of the person so incapacitated.

The second subdivision of this section does not prevent the arbitration of a claim to an estate for years, or other interest for a term of years, or for one year or less, in real property ; or of a controversy respecting the partition of real property between joint tenants or tenants in common ; or of a controversy respecting the boundaries of lands or the admeasurement of dower.

Section 1449.

Form of contract or submission. A contract to arbitrate a controversy thereafter arising between the parties must be in writing. Every submission to arbitrate an existing controversy is void, unless it or some note or memorandum thereof be in writing, and subscribed by the party to be charged therewith, or by his lawful agent.

Section 1450.

Remedy in case of default. The making of a contract or submission for arbitration described in section fourteen hundred forty-eight hereof, providing for arbitrations in this state, shall be deemed a consent of the parties thereto to the jurisdiction of the supreme court of this state to enforce such contract or submission and to enter judgment on an award thereon. A party aggrieved by the failure, neglect or refusal of another to perform under a contract or submission providing for arbitration, described in such section, may petition the supreme court, or a judge thereof, for an order directing that such arbitration proceed in the manner provided for in such contract or submission. Eight days' notice in writing of such application shall be served upon the party in default. Service thereof shall be made in the manner specified in the contract or submission, and if no manner be specified therein, then in the manner provided by law for personal service of a summons, within or without the state, or substituted service of a summons, or upon satisfactory proof that the party aggrieved has been or will be unable with due diligence to make service in any of the foregoing manners, then such notice shall be served in such manner

as the court or judge may direct. The court, or a judge thereof, shall hear the parties and upon being satisfied that there is no substantial issue as to the making of the contract or submission or the failure to comply therewith, the court, or the judge thereof, hearing such application, shall make an order directing the parties to proceed to arbitration in accordance with the terms of the contract or submission.

If evidentiary facts be set forth raising a substantial issue as to the making of the contract or submission or the failure to comply therewith, the court, or the judge thereof, shall proceed immediately to the trial thereof. If no jury trial be demanded by either party, the court, or the judge thereof, shall hear and determine such issue. Where such an issue is raised, any party may, not later than five days after the service of the order directing a trial of such issue, demand a jury trial of such issue, and if such demand be made, the court, or the judge thereof, shall make an order referring the issue or issues to a jury in the manner provided by law for referring to a jury issues in an equity action. Whenever an immediate trial is ordered the order therefor shall provide that if the court, or where a jury has been demanded, the jury, find that a written contract providing for arbitration was made or a submission was entered into, as the case may be, and that there was a failure to comply therewith, the parties shall proceed with the arbitration in accordance with the terms of the contract or submission, and said order shall provide that if the court or jury, as the case may be, find that there was no such contract or submission or failure to comply therewith then the proceeding shall be dismissed.

The procedure herein provided shall be applicable to any motion made under this article in which an issue is raised as to the making of the contract or submission or the failure to comply therewith.

Section 1451.

Stay of proceedings brought in violation of an arbitration contract or submission. If any action or proceeding be brought upon any issue otherwise referable to arbitration under a contract or submission described in section fourteen hundred forty-eight, the supreme court, or a judge thereof, upon being satisfied that the issue involved in such action, or proceeding is referable to arbitration under a contract or submission described in section fourteen hundred forty-eight, shall stay all proceedings in the action or proceeding until such arbitration has been had in accordance with the terms of the contract or submission.

Section 1452.

Provision in case of failure to name arbitrator or umpire. If, in the contract for arbitration or in the submission, described in section fourteen hundred forty-eight, provision be made for a method of naming or appointing an arbitrator or arbitrators or an umpire, such method shall be followed ; but if no method be provided therein, or if a method be provided and any party thereto shall fail to avail himself of such method, or for any reason there shall be a lapse in the naming of an arbitrator or arbitrators or umpire, or in filling a vacancy, then, upon application by either party to the controversy, the supreme court, or a judge thereof, shall designate and appoint an arbitrator or arbitrators or umpire, as the case may require, who shall act under the said contract or submission with the same force and effect as if he or they had been specifically named therein ; and unless otherwise provided, the arbitration shall be by a single arbitrator.

Section 1453.

Appointment of additional arbitrator or umpire. Where a submission or contract is made as prescribed in this article, an additional arbitrator or an umpire cannot be selected or appointed unless the submission or contract expressly so provides. Where a submission or contract made either as prescribed in this article or otherwise, provides that two or more arbitrators therein designated may select or appoint a person as an additional arbitrator, or as an umpire, the selection or appointment must be in writing. An additional arbitrator or umpire must sit with the original arbitrators upon the hearing. If testimony has been taken before his selection, or appointment, the matter must be reheard, unless a hearing is waived in the submission or contract or by the subsequent written consent of the parties or their attorneys.

Section 1454.

Representation by an attorney ; hearings by arbitrators. 1. No waiver of the right to be represented by an attorney in any proceeding or at any hearing before an arbitrator shall be effective unless evidenced by a writing expressly so providing signed by the party requesting such representation, or unless the party fails to assert such right at the beginning of the hearing.

2. Subject to the terms of the submission or contract, if any are specified therein, the arbitrators selected as prescribed in this article must appoint a time and place for the hearing of the matters submitted to them, and must cause notice thereof to be given to each of the parties. They, or a majority of them, may adjourn the hearing from time to time upon the application of either party for good cause shown or upon their own motion, but not beyond the day fixed in the submission or contract for rendering their award, unless the time so fixed is extended by the written consent of the parties to the submission or contract or their attorneys, or the parties have continued with the arbitration without objection to such adjournment.

3. The court shall have power to direct the arbitrators to proceed promptly with the hearing and determination of the controversy.

Section 1455.

Oath of arbitrators. Before hearing any testimony, arbitrators selected either as prescribed in this article or otherwise must be sworn, by an officer authorized by law to administer an oath, faithfully and fairly to hear and examine the matters in controversy and to make a just award according to the best of their understanding, unless the oath is waived by the written consent of the parties to the submission or contract or their attorneys or the parties have continued with the arbitration without objection to the failure of the arbitrators to take the oath.

Section 1456.

Power of arbitrators. The arbitrators selected either as prescribed in this article or otherwise, or a majority of them, may require any person to attend before them as a witness ; and they have, and each of them has, the same powers with respect to all the proceedings before them which are conferred upon a board or a member of a board authorized by law to hear testimony. All the arbitrators selected as prescribed in this article must meet together and hear all the allegations and proofs of the parties ; but an award by a majority of them is valid unless the concurrence of all is expressly required in the submission or contract.

Section 1457.

Fees and expenses of arbitrators. Unless it is otherwise expressly provided in the submission or contract, the award may require the payment, by either party, of the arbitrators' fees, not exceeding the fees allowed to a like number of referees in the supreme court ; and also their expenses.

Section 1458.

Enforceability of award in certain cases. An award shall be valid and enforceable according to its terms and under the provisions of this article, without previous adjudication of the existence of a submission or contract to arbitration, subject, nevertheless, to the provisions of this section ;

1. A party who has participated in the selection of the arbitrators or in any of the proceedings had before them may object to the confirmation of the award only on one or more of the grounds specified in subdivisions one, two, three and four of section fourteen hundred sixty-two and in section fourteen hundred sixty-two-a or (provided that he did not continue with the arbitration with notice of the facts or defects upon which his objection is based) because of a failure to comply with subdivision one of section fourteen hundred fifty-four or with section fourteen hundred fifty-five or because of the improper manner of the selection of the arbitrators.

2. A party who has not participated in the selection of the arbitrators or in any of the proceedings had before them and who has not made or been served with an application to compel arbitration under section fourteen hundred fifty may also put in issue the making of the contract or submission or the failure to comply therewith, either by a motion for a stay of the arbitration or in opposition to the confirmation of the award. If a notice shall have been personally served upon such party of an intention to conduct the arbitration pursuant to the provisions of a contract or submission specified in such notice, then the issues specified in this subdivision may be raised only by a motion for a stay of the arbitration, notice of which motion must be served within ten days after the service of the notice of intention to arbitrate. Such notice must state in substance that unless within ten days after its service, the party served therewith shall serve a notice of motion to stay the arbitration, he shall thereafter be barred from putting in issue the making of the contract or submission or the failure to comply therewith. The arbitration hearing shall be adjourned upon service of such notice pending the determination of the motion. Where such opposing party, either on a motion for a stay or in opposition to the confirmation of an award, sets forth evidentiary facts raising a substantial issue as to the making of the contract or submission or the failure to comply therewith, an immediate trial of the same shall be had, and such party shall have the right to demand a jury trial provided such demand is served with his affidavits. In the event that such party is unsuccessful, he may, nevertheless, participate in the arbitration if the same is still being carried on. Any party may, on or before the return date of the notice of application, demand a jury trial of such issue.

Section 1459.

Arbitration a special proceeding. Arbitration of a controversy under a contract or submission described in section fourteen hundred forty-eight shall be deemed a special proceeding, of which the court specified in the contract or submission, or if none be specified, the supreme court for the county in which one of the parties resides or is doing business, or in which the arbitration was held, shall have jurisdiction.

Any application to the court, or a judge thereof, hereunder shall be made and heard in the manner provided by law for the making and hearing of motions, except as otherwise herein expressly provided.

Section 1460.

Requirements as to award. To entitle the award to be enforced, as prescribed in this article, it must be in writing ; and, within the time limited in the submission or contract, if any, subscribed by the arbitrators making it ; acknowledged or proved, and certified, in like manner as a deed to be recorded, and either filed in the office of the clerk of the court having jurisdiction as provided in section fourteen hundred fifty-nine or delivered to one of the parties or his attorney.

Section 1461.

Motion to confirm award. At any time within one year after the award is made, as prescribed in the last section, any party to the controversy which was arbitrated may apply to the court having jurisdiction as provided in section fourteen hundred fifty-nine for an order confirming the award ; and thereupon the court must grant such an order unless the award is vacated, modified or corrected, as prescribed in the next two sections or unless the award is unenforceable under the provisions of section fourteen hundred fifty-eight. Notice of the motion must be served upon the adverse party or his attorney, as prescribed by law for service of notice of a motion upon an attorney in an action in the same court. In the supreme court, the motion must be made within the judicial district embracing the county where the judgment is to be entered.

Section 1462.

Motion to vacate award. In either of the following cases, the court must make an order vacating the award, upon the application of any party to the controversy which was arbitrated:

1. Where the award was procured by corruption, fraud or other undue means.

2. Where there was evident partiality or corruption in the arbitrators or either of them.

3. Where the arbitrators were guilty of misconduct in refusing to postpone the hearing upon sufficient cause shown, or in refusing to hear evidence pertinent and material to the controversy; or of any other misbehaviour by which the rights of any party have been prejudiced.

4. Where the arbitrators exceeded their powers, or so imperfectly executed them, that a mutual, final and definite award upon the subject-matter submitted was not made.

5. If there was no valid submission or contract, and the objection has been raised under the conditions set forth in section fourteen hundred fifty-eight.

Where an award is vacated, the court, in its discretion, may direct a rehearing before the same arbitrators or before new arbitrators to be chosen in the manner provided in the submission or contract for the selection of the original arbitrators and any provisions limiting the time in which the arbitrators may make a decision shall be deemed applicable to the new arbitration and to commence from the date of the court's order.

Where the court vacates an award, costs, not exceeding twenty-five dollars and disbursements may be awarded to the prevailing party; and the payment thereof may be enforced in like manner as the payment of costs upon a motion in an action.

Section 1462-a.

Motion to modify or correct award. In either of the following cases, the court must make an order modifying or correcting the award, upon the application of any party to the controversy which was arbitrated:

1. Where there was an evident miscalculation of figures, or an evident mistake in the description of any person, thing or property referred to in the award.

2. Where the arbitrators have awarded upon a matter not submitted to them, not affecting the merits of the decision upon the matters submitted.

3. Where the award is imperfect in a matter of form not affecting the merits of the con-

troversy, and, if it had been a referee's report, the defect could have been amended or disregarded by the court.

The order may modify and correct the award so as to effect the intent thereof and promote justice between the parties.

Section 1463.

Notice of motion and stay. Notice of a motion to vacate, modify or correct an award must be served upon the adverse party, or his attorney, within three months after the award is filed or delivered, as prescribed by law for service of notice of a motion upon an attorney in an action; except that in opposition to a motion to confirm an award, any of the grounds specified in section fourteen hundred sixty-two may be set up. For the purpose of the motion, any judge who might make an order to stay the proceedings in an action brought in the same court may make an order, to be served with the notice of motion, staying the proceedings of the adverse party to enforce the award.

Section 1464.

Entry of judgment on award and costs. Upon the granting of an order confirming, modifying or correcting an award, judgment may be entered in conformity therewith, as upon a referee's report in an action, except as is otherwise prescribed in this article. Costs of the application and of the proceedings subsequent thereto, not exceeding twenty-five dollars and disbursements, may be awarded by the court in its discretion. If awarded, the amount thereof must be included in the judgment.

Section 1465.

Judgment roll. Immediately after entering judgment, the clerk must attach together and file the following papers, which constitute the judgment-roll:

1. The submission or contract; the selection or appointment, if any, of an additional arbitrator, or umpire; and each written extension of the time, if any, within which to make the award.

2. The award.

3. Each notice, affidavit or other paper used upon an application to confirm, modify or correct the award, and a copy of each order of the court upon such an application.

4. A copy of the judgment.

The judgment may be docketed as if it was rendered in an action.

Section 1466.

Effect of judgment and enforcement. The judgment so entered has the same force and effect, in all respects as, and is subject to all the provisions of law relating to, a judgment in an action ; and it may be enforced as if it had been rendered in an action in the court in which it is entered.

Section 1467.

Appeals. An appeal may be taken from an order made in a proceeding under this article, or from a judgment entered upon an award. The proceedings upon such an appeal, including the judgment thereupon and the enforcement of the judgment, are governed by the provisions of statute and rule regulating appeals in action as far as they are applicable.

Section 1468.

Death or incompetency of party. Where a party dies after making a submission or contract as prescribed in this article or otherwise, the proceedings may be begun or continued upon the application of, or upon notice to, his executor or administrator, or a temporary administrator of his estate ; or, where it relates to real property, his distributee or devisee who has succeeded to his interest in the real property. Where a committee of the property or of the person of a party to a submission or contract is appointed, the proceedings may be continued upon the application of, or notice to, a committee of the property, but not otherwise. In a case specified in this section, a judge of the court may make an order extending the time within which notice of a motion to confirm, vacate, modify or correct the award must be served. Upon confirming an award, where a party has died since it was filed or delivered, the court must enter judgment in the name of the original party ; and the proceedings thereupon are the same as where a party dies after a verdict.

Section 1469.

Application of this article. This article does not affect any right of action in affirmance, disaffirmance, or for the modification of a submission or contract, made either as prescribed in this article or otherwise, or upon an instrument collateral thereto, or upon an award made or purporting to be made in pursuance thereof. And, except as otherwise expressly prescribed therein, this article does not affect a submission or contract, made otherwise than as prescribed therein, or any proceedings taken pursuant to such a submission or contract, or any instrument collateral thereto.

APPENDIX D

SECTION 301—LABOR-MANAGEMENT RELATIONS ACT, 1947

Suits by and Against Labor Organizations

Sec. 301. (a) Suits for violation of contracts between an employer and a labor organization representing employees in an industry affecting commerce as defined in this Act, or between any such labor organizations, may be brought in any district court of the United States having jurisdiction of the parties, without respect to the amount in controversy or without regard to the citizenship of the parties.

(b) Any labor organization which represents employees in an industry affecting commerce as defined in this Act and any employer whose activities affect commerce as defined in this Act shall be bound by the acts of its agents. Any such labor organization may sue or be sued as an entity and in behalf of the employees whom it represents in the courts of the United States. Any money judgment against a labor organization in a district court of the United States shall be enforceable only against the organization as an entity and against its assets, and shall not be enforceable against any individual member or his assets.

(c) For the purposes of actions and proceedings by or against labor organizations in the district courts of the United States, district courts shall be deemed to have jurisdiction of a labor organization (1) in the district in which such organization maintains its principal office, or (2) in any district in which its duly authorized officers or agents are engaged in representing or acting for employee members.

(d) The service of summons, subpoena, or other legal process of any court of the United States upon an officer or agent of a labor organization, in his capacity as such, shall constitute service upon the labor organization.

(e) For the purposes of this section, in determining whether any person is acting as an "agent" of another person so as to make such other person responsible for his acts, the question of whether the specific acts performed were actually authorized or subsequently ratified shall not be controlling.

APPENDIX E

AMERICAN ARBITRATION ASSOCIATION COMMERCIAL ARBITRATION RULES

CONTENTS

Section 1. Agreement of Parties

The parties shall be deemed to have made these Rules as part of their arbitration agreement whenever they have provided for arbitration by the American Arbitration Association or under its Rules. These Rules and any amendment thereof shall apply in the form obtaining at the time the arbitration is initiated.

Section 2. Name of Tribunal

Any Tribunal constituted by the parties for the settlement of their dispute under these Rules shall be called the Commercial Arbitration Tribunal.

Section 3. Administrator

When parties agree to arbitrate under these Rules, or when they provide for arbitration by the American Arbitration Association and an arbitration is initiated thereunder, they thereby constitute AAA the administrator of the arbitration. The authority and obligations of the administrator are prescribed in the agreement of the parties and in these Rules.

Section 4. Delegation of Duties

The duties of the AAA under these Rules may be carried out through Tribunal Clerks, or such other officers or committees as the AAA may direct.

Section 5. National Panel of Arbitrators

The AAA shall establish and maintain a National Panel of Arbitrators and shall appoint Arbitrators therefrom as hereinafter provided.

Section 6. Office of Tribunal

The general office of a Tribunal is the headquarters of the AAA, which may, however, assign the administration of an arbitration to any of its Regional Offices.

Section 7. Initiation under an Arbitration Provision in a Contract

Arbitration under an arbitration provision in a contract may be initiated in the following manner:

(a) The initiating party may give notice to the other party of his intention to arbitrate (Demand). which notice shall contain a statement setting forth the nature of the dispute, the amount involved, if any, the remedy sought, and

(b) By filing at any Regional office of the AAA two (2) copies of said notice, together with two (2) copies of the arbitration provisions of the contract, together with the appropriate administrative fee as provided in the Administrative Fee Schedule.

The AAA shall give notice of such filing to the other party. If he so desires, the party upon whom the demand for arbitration is made may file an answering statement in duplicate with the AAA within seven days after notice from the AAA, in which event he shall simultaneously send a copy of his answer to the other party. If a monetary claim is made in the answer the appropriate fee provided in the Fee Schedule shall be forwarded to the AAA with the answer. If no answer is filed within the stated time, it will be assumed that the claim is denied. Failure to file an answer shall not operate to delay the arbitration.

Section 8. Change of Claim

After filing of the claim, if either party desires to make any new or different claim, such claim shall be made in writing and filed with the AAA, and a copy thereof shall be mailed to the other party who shall have a period of seven days from the date of such mailing within which to file an answer with the AAA. However, after the Arbitrator is appointed no new or different claim may be submitted to him except with his consent.

Section 9. Initiation under a Submission

Parties to any existing dispute may commence an arbitration under these Rules by filing at any Regional Office two (2) copies of a written agreement to arbitrate under these Rules (Submission), signed by the parties. It shall contain a statement of the matter in dispute, the amount of money involved, if any, and the remedy sought, together with the appropriate administrative fee as provided in the Fee Schedule.

Section 10. Fixing of Locale

The parties may mutually agree on the locale where the arbitration is to be held. If the locale is not designated within seven days from the date of filing the Demand or Submission the AAA shall have power to determine the locale.

Its decision shall be final and binding. If any party requests that the hearing be held in a specfic locale and the other party files no objection thereto within seven days after notice of the request, the locale shall be the one requested.

Section 11. Qualifications of Arbitrator

No person shall serve as an Arbitrator in any arbitration if he has any financial or personal interest in the result of the arbitration, unless the parties, in writing, waive such disqualification.

Section 12. Appointment From Panel

If the parties have not appointed an Arbitrator and have not provided any other method of appointment, the Arbitrator shall be appointed in the following manner: Immediately after the filing of the Demand or Submission, the AAA shall submit simultaneously to each party to the dispute an identical list of names of persons chosen from the Panel. Each party to the dispute shall have seven days from the mailing date in which to cross off any names to which he objects, number the remaining names indicating the order of his preference, and return the list to the AAA. If a party does not return the list within the time specified, all persons named therein shall be deemed acceptable. From among the persons who have been approved on both lists, and in accordance with the designated order of mutual preference, the AAA shall invite the acceptance of an Arbitrator to serve. If the parties fail to agree upon any of the persons named, or if acceptable Arbitrators are unable to act, or if for any other reason the appointment cannot be made from the submitted lists, the AAA shall have the power to make the appointment from other members of the Panel without the submission of any additional lists.

Section 13. Direct Appointment by Parties

If the agreement of the parties names an Arbitrator or specifies a method of appointing an Arbitrator, that designation or method shall be followed. The notice of appointment, with name and address of such Arbitrator, shall be filed with the AAA by the appointing party. Upon the request of any such appointing party, the AAA shall submit a list of members from the Panel from which the party may, if he so desires, make the appointment.

If the agreement specifies a period of time within which an Arbitrator shall be appointed, and any party fails to make such appointment within that period, the AAA shall make the appointment.

If no period of time is specified in the agreement, the AAA shall notify the parties to make the appointment and if within seven days thereafter such Arbitrator has not been so appointed, the AAA shall make the appointment.

Section 14. Appointment of Neutral Arbitrator by Party-Appointed Arbitrators

If the parties have appointed their Arbitrators or if either or both of them have been appointed as provided in Section 13, and have authorized such Arbitrators to appoint a neutral Arbitrator within a specified time and no appointment is made within such time or any agreed extension thereof, the AAA shall appoint a neutral Arbitrator who shall act as Chairman.

If no period of time is specified for appointment of the neutral Arbitrator and the parties do not make the appointment within seven days from the date of the appointment of the last party-appointed Arbitrator, the AAA shall appoint such neutral Arbitrator, who shall act as Chairman.

If the parties have agreed that their Arbitrators shall appoint the neutral Arbitrator from the Panel, the AAA shall furnish to the party-appointed Arbitrators, in the manner prescribed in Section 12, a list selected from the Panel, and the appointment of the neutral Arbitrator shall be made as prescribed in such Section.

Section 15. Nationality of Arbitrator in International Arbitration

If one of the parties is a national or resident of a country other than the United States, the sole Arbitrator or the neutral Arbitrator shall, upon the request of either party, be appointed from among the nationals of a country other than that of any of the parties.

Section 16. Number of Arbitrators

If the arbitration agreement does not specify the number of Arbitrators, the dispute shall be heard and determined by one Arbitrator, unless the AAA, in its discretion, directs that a greater number of Arbitrators be appointed.

Section 17. Notice to Arbitrator of His Appointment

Notice of the appointment of the neutral Arbitrator, whether appointed by the parties or by the AAA, shall be mailed to the Arbitrator by the AAA, together with a copy of these Rules, and the signed acceptance of the Arbitrator shall be filed prior to the opening of the first hearing.

Section 18. Disclosure by Arbitrator of Disqualification

Prior to accepting his appointment, the prospective neutral Arbitrator shall disclose any circumstances likely to create a presumption of bias of which he believes might disqualify him as an impartial Arbitrator. Upon receipt of such information, the AAA shall immediately disclose it to the parties who, if willing to proceed under the circumstances disclosed, shall so advise the AAA in writing. If either party declines to waive the presumptive disqualification, the vacancy thus created shall be filled in accordance with the applicable provisions of these Rules.

Section 19. Vacancies

If any Arbitrator should resign, die, withdraw, refuse, be disqualified or be unable to perform the duties of his office, the AAA shall, on proof satisfactory to it, declare the office vacant. Vacancies shall be filled in accordance with the applicable provisions of these Rules and the matter shall be reheard unless the parties shall agree otherwise.

Section 20. Time and Place

The Arbitrator shall fix the time and place for each hearing. The AAA shall mail to each party notice thereof at least five days in advance, unless the parties by mutual agreement waive such notice or modify the terms thereof.

Section 21. Representation by Counsel

Any party may be represented by counsel. A party intending to be so represented shall notify the other party and the AAA of the name and address of counsel at least three days prior to the date set for the hearing at which counsel is first to appear. When an arbitration is initiated by counsel, or where an attorney replies for the other party, such notice is deemed to have been given.

Section 22. Stenographic Record

The AAA shall make the necessary arrangements for the taking of a stenographic record whenever such record is requested by a party. The requesting party or parties shall pay the cost of such record as provided in Section 49.

Section 23. Interpreter

The AAA shall make the necessary arrangements for the services of an interpreter upon the request of one or more of the parties, who shall assume the cost of such service.

Section 24. Attendance at Hearings

Persons having a direct interest in the arbitration are entitled to attend hearings. The Arbitrator shall otherwise have the power to require the retirement of any witness or witnesses during the testimony of other witnesses. It shall be discretionary with the Arbitrator to determine the propriety of the attendance of any other persons.

Section 25. Adjournments

The Arbitrator may take adjournments upon the request of a party or upon his own initiative and shall take such adjournment when all of the parties agree thereto.

Section 26. Oaths

Before proceeding with the first hearing or with the examination of the file, each Arbitrator may take an oath of office, and if required by law, shall do so. The Arbitrator may, in his discretion, require witnesses to testify under oath administered by any duly qualified person or, if required by law or demanded by either party, shall do so.

Section 27. Majority Decision

Whenever there is more than one Arbitrator, all decisions of the Arbitrators must be at least a majority. The award must also be made by at least a majority unless the concurrence of all is expressly required by the arbitration agreement or by law.

Section 28. Order of Proceedings

A hearing shall be opened by the filing of the oath of the Arbitrator, where required, and by the recording of the place, time and date of the hearing, the presence of the Arbitrator and parties, and counsel, if any, and by the receipt by the Arbitrator of the statement of the claim and answer, if any.

The Arbitrator may, at the beginning of the hearing, ask for statements clarifying the issues involved.

The complaining party shall then present his claim and proofs and his witnesses who shall submit to questions or other examination. The defending party shall then present his defense and proofs and his witnesses, who shall submit to questions or other examination. The Arbitrator may in his discretion vary this procedure but he shall afford full and equal opportunity to all parties for the presentation of any material or relevant proofs.

Exhibits, when offered by either party, may be received in evidence by the Arbitrator.

The names and addresses of all witnesses and exhibits in order received shall be made a part of the record.

Section 29. Arbitration in the Absence of a Party

Unless the law provides to the contrary, the arbitration may proceed in the absence of any party, who, after due notice, fails to be present or fails to obtain an adjournment. An award shall not be made solely on the default of a party. The Arbitrator shall require the party who is present to submit such evidence as he may require for the making of an award.

Section 30. Evidence

The parties may offer such evidence as they desire and shall produce such additional evidence as the Arbitrator may deem necessary to an understanding and determination of the dispute. When the Arbitrator is authorized by law to subpoena witnesses or documents, he may do so upon his own initiative or upon the request of any party. The Arbitrator shall be the judge of the relevancy and materiality of the evidence offered and conformity to legal rules of evidence shall not be necessary. All evidence shall be taken in the presence of all of the Arbitrators and of all the parties, except where any of the parties is absent in default or has waived his right to be present.

Section 31. Evidence by Affidavit and Filing of Documents

The Arbitrator shall receive and consider the evidence of witnesses by affidavit, but shall give it only such weight as he deems it entitled to after consideration of any objections made to its admission.

All documents not filed with the Arbitrator at the hearing, but arranged for at the hearing or subsequently by agreement of the parties, shall be filed with the AAA for transmission to the Arbitrator. All parties shall be afforded opportunity to examine such documents.

Section 32. Inspection or Investigation

Whenever the Arbitrator deems it necessary to make an inspection or investigation in connection with the arbitration, he shall direct the AAA to advise the parties of his intention. The Arbitrator shall set the time and the AAA shall notify the parties thereof. Any party who so desires may be present at such inspection or investigation. In the event that one or both parties are not present at the inspection or investigation, the Arbitrator shall make a verbal or written report to the parties and afford them an opportunity to comment.

Section 33. Conservation of Property

The Arbitrator may issue such orders as may be deemed necessary to safeguard the property which is the subject matter of the arbitration without prejudice to the rights of the parties or to the final determination of the dispute.

Section 34. Closing of Hearings

The Arbitrator shall specifically inquire of all parties whether they have any further proofs to offer or witnesses to be heard. Upon receiving negative replies, the Arbitrator shall declare the hearings closed and a minute thereof shall be recorded. If briefs are to be filed, the hearings shall be declared closed as of the final date set by the Arbitrator for the receipt of briefs. If documents are to be filed as provided for in Section 31 and the date set for their receipt is later than that set for the receipt of briefs, the later date shall be the date of closing the hearing. The time limit within which the Arbitrator is required to make his award shall commence to run, in the absence of other agreements by the parties, upon the closing of the hearings.

Section 35. Reopening of Hearings

The hearings may be reopened by the Arbitrator on his own motion, or upon application of a party at any time before the award is made. If the reopening of the hearing would prevent the making of the award within the specific time agreed upon by the parties in the contract out of which the controversy has arisen, the matter may not be reopened, unless the parties agree upon the extension of such time limit. When no specific date is fixed in the contract, the Arbitrator may reopen the hearings, and the Arbitrator shall have thirty days from the closing of the reopened hearings within which to make an award.

Section 36. Waiver of Oral Hearing

The parties may provide, by written agreement, for the waiver of oral hearings. If the parties are unable to agree as to the procedure, the AAA shall specify a fair and equitable procedure.

Section 37. Waiver of Rules

Any party who proceeds with the arbitration after knowledge that any provision or requirement of these Rules has not been complied with and who fails to state his objection thereto in writing, shall be deemed to have waived his right to object.

Section 38. Extensions of Time

The parties may modify any period of time by mutual agreement. The AAA for good cause may extend any period of time established by these Rules, except the time for making the award. The AAA shall notify the parties of any such extension of time and its reason therefor.

Section 39. Communication with Arbitrator and Serving of Notices

(a) There shall be no communication between the parties and a neutral Arbitrator other than at oral hearings. Any other oral or written communications from the parties to the Arbitrator shall be directed to the AAA for transmittal to the Arbitrator.

(b) Each party to an agreement which provides for arbitration under these Rules shall be deemed to have consented that any papers, notices or process necessary or proper for the initiation or continuation of an arbitration under these Rules and for any court action in connection therewith or for the entry of judgment on any award made thereunder may be served upon such party by mail addressed to such party or his attorney at his last known address or by personal service, within or without the state wherein the arbitration is to be held (whether such party be within or without the United States of America), provided that reasonable opportunity to be heard with regard thereto has been granted such party.

Section 40. Time of Award

The award shall be made promptly by the Arbitrator and, unless otherwise agreed by the parties, or specified by law, not later than thirty days from the date of closing the hearings, or if oral hearings have been waived, from the date of transmitting the final statements and proofs to the Arbitrator.

Section 41. Form of Award

The award shall be in writing and shall be signed either by the sole Arbitrator or by at least a majority if there be more than one. It shall be executed in the manner required by law.

Section 42. Scope of Award

The Arbitrator may grant any remedy or relief which he deems just and equitable and within the scope of the agreement of the parties, including, but not limited to, specific performance of a contract. The Arbitrator, in his award, shall assess arbitration fees and expenses in favor of any party and, in the event any administrative fees or expenses are due to the AAA, in favor of the AAA.

Section 43. Award upon Settlement

If the parties settle their dispute during the course of the arbitration, the Arbitrator, upon their request, may set forth the terms of the agreed settlement in an award.

Section 44. Delivery of Award to Parties

Parties shall accept as legal delivery of the award the placing of the award or a true copy thereof in the mail by the AAA, addressed to such party at his last known address or to his attorney, or personal service of the award, or the filing of the award in any manner which may be prescribed by law.

Section 45. Release of Documents for Judicial Proceedings

The AAA shall, upon the written request of a party, furnish to such party, at his expense, certified facsimiles of any papers in the AAA's possession that may be required in judicial proceedings relating to the arbitration.

Section 46. Applications to Court

(a) No judicial proceedings by a party relating to the subject matter of the arbitration shall be deemed a waiver of the party's right to arbitrate.

(b) The AAA is not a necessary party in judicial proceedings relating to the arbitration.

Section 47. Administrative Fees

As a nonprofit organization, the AAA shall prescribe an administrative fee schedule and a refund schedule to compensate it for the cost of providing administrative services. The schedule in effect at the time of filing or the time of refund shall be applicable.

The administrative fees shall be advanced by the initiating party or parties, subject to final apportionment by the Arbitrator in his award.

When a matter is withdrawn or settled, the refund shall be made in accordance with the refund schedule.

The AAA, in the event of extreme hardship on the part of any party, may defer or reduce the administrative fee.

Section 48. Fee When Oral Hearings are Waived

Where all Oral Hearings are waived under Section 36 the Administrative Fee Schedule shall apply.

Section 49. Expenses

The expenses of witnesses for either side shall be paid by the party producing such witnesses.

The cost of the stenographic record, if any is made, and all transcripts thereof, shall be pro-rated equally among all parties ordering copies unless they shall otherwise agree and shall be paid for by the responsible parties directly to the reporting agency.

All other expenses of the arbitration, including required travelling and other expenses of the Arbitrator and of AAA representatives, and the expenses of any witness or the cost of any proofs produced at the direct request of the Arbitrator, shall be borne equally by the parties, unless they agree otherwise, or unless the Arbitrator in his Award assesses such expenses or any part thereof against any specified party or parties.

Section 50. Arbitrator's Fee

Members of the National Panel of Arbitrators serve without fee in commercial arbitrations. In prolonged or in special cases the parties may agree to the payment of a fee.

Any arrangements for the compensation of a neutral Arbitrator shall be made through the AAA and not directly by him with the parties.

Section 51. Deposits

The AAA may require the parties to deposit in advance such sums of money as it deems necessary to defray the expense of the arbitration, including the Arbitrator's fee if any, and shall render an accounting to the parties and return any unexpected balance.

Section 52. Interpretation and Application of Rules

The Arbitrator shall interpret and apply these Rules insofar as they relate to his powers and duties. When there is more than one Arbitrator and a difference arises among them concerning the meaning or application of any such Rules, it shall be decided by a majority vote. If that is unobtainable, either an Arbitrator or a party may refer the question to AAA for final decision. All other Rules shall be interpreted and applied by the AAA.

Administrative Fee Schedule

The administrative fee of the AAA is based upon the amount of each claim as disclosed when the claim is filed, and is due and payable at the time of filing.

Amount of Claim	Fee
Up to $10,000	3% (minimum $50)
$10,000 to $25,000	$300, plus 2% of excess over $10,000
$25,000 to $100,000	$600, plus 1% of excess over $25,000
$100,000 to $200,000	$1,350, plus $\frac{1}{2}$% of excess over $100,000

The fee for claims in excess of $200,000 should be discussed with the AAA in advance of filing.

When no amount can be stated at the time of filing, the administrative fee is $200, subject to adjustment in accordance with the above schedule if an amount is subsequently disclosed.

If there are more than two parties represented in the arbitration, an additional 10 per cent of the initiating fee will be due for each additional represented party.

Other Service Charges

$30.00 payable by a party causing an adjournment of any scheduled hearing;

$25.00 payable by each party for each hearing after the first hearing;

$5.00 per hour payable by each party for hearings on Saturdays, legal holidays, and after 6:00 P.M. weekdays.

Refund Schedule

If the AAA is notified that a case has been settled or withdrawn before a list of arbitrators had been sent out, all the fee in excess of $50.00 will be refunded.

If the AAA is notified that a case has been settled or withdrawn thereafter but before the due date for the return of the first list, two-thirds of the fee in excess of $50.00 will be refunded.

If the AAA is notified that a case is settled or withdrawn thereafter but at least 48 hours before the date and time set for the first hearing, one-half of the fee in excess of $50.00 will be refunded.

APPENDIX F

FEDERAL MEDIATION AND CONCILIATION SERVICE ARBITRATION POLICIES, FUNCTIONS AND PROCEDURES—Part 1404—Arbitration

Text of Regulations Part 1404, dealing with arbitration policies, functions, and procedures, as last revised by the Director of the Federal Mediation and Conciliation Service, effective January 8, 1957.

Sec.

Authority: Secs. 1404.1 to 1404.13 issued under Sec. 202, 61 Stat. 153, as amended; 29 U.S.C. 172. Interpret or apply Sec. 3, 60 Stat. 238, Sec. 203, 61 Stat. 153; 5 U.S.C. 1002, 29 U.S.C. 173.

Sec. 1404.1—Arbitration

The labor policy of the United States Government is designed to foster and promote free collective bargaining. Voluntary arbitration and factfinding are tools, in appropriate cases, of free collective bargaining and may be desirable alternatives to economic strife. The parties assume broad responsibilities for the success of the private juridical system they have chosen. The Service will assist the parties in their selection of arbitrators.

Sec. 1404.2—Composition of roster maintained by the service

It is the policy of the Service to maintain on

its roster only those arbitrators who are experienced, qualified, and acceptable, and who adhere to ethical standards.

Applicants for inclusion on its roster must not only be well-grounded in the field of labor-management relations, but, also, possess experience in the labor arbitration field or its equivalent. (Arbitrators employed full time as representatives of management or labor are not included on the Service's roster.) After a careful screening and evaluation of the applicant's experience, the Service contracts representatives of both labor and management, as qualified arbitrators must be acceptable to those who utilize its arbitration facilities. The responses to such inquiries are carefully weighed before an otherwise qualified arbitrator is included on the Service's roster.

Sec. 1404.3—Security status

The arbitrators on the Service roster are not employees of the Federal Government, and, because of this status, the Service does not investigate their security status. Moreover, when an arbitrator is selected by the parties, he is retained by them and, accordingly, they must assume complete responsibility for the arbitrator's security status.

Sec. 1404.4—Procedures; how to request arbitration services

The Service prefers to act upon a joint request which should be addressed to the Director of the Federal Mediation and Conciliation Service, Washington 25, D.C. In the event that the request is made by only one party, the Service may act if the parties have agreed that either of them may seek a panel of arbitrators. A brief statement of the nature of the issues in dispute should accompany the request, to enable the Service to submit the names of arbitrators of specialized competence. The request should also include a copy of the collective bargaining agreement or stipulation. In the event that the entire agreement is not available, a verbatim copy of the provisions relating to arbitration should accompany the request.

Sec. 1404.5—Arbitrability

Where either party claims that a dispute is not subject to arbitration, the Service will not decide the merits of such claim. The submission of a panel should not be construed as anything more than compliance with a request.

Sec. 1404.6—Nominations of arbitrators

When the parties have been unable to agree

on an arbitrator, the Service will submit to the parties the names of three, five, seven or more arbitrators, as requested, or will make a direct appointment upon being duly advised that a panel is not desired. Together with the submission of a panel of suggested arbitrators, the Service furnishes a short statement of the background, qualifications, and experience of each of the nominees.

In selecting names for inclusion on a panel, the Service considers many factors, but the desires of the parties are, of course, the foremost consideration. If at any time a company or a union, or both, suggests that a name or names be omitted from a panel, such name or names will generally be omitted. The Service will not, however, place names on a panel at the request of one party unless the other party has knowledge of such request and has no objection thereto, or unless both parties join in such request. If the issue described in the request appears to require special technical experience or qualifications, arbitrators who possess such qualifications will, where possible, be included in the list submitted to the parties. Where the parties expressly request that the list be composed entirely of technicians, or that it be all-local or non-local, such request will be honored, if qualified arbitrators are available.

Two of the methods of selection from a panel are—(1) at a joint meeting, alternately striking names from the submitted panel until one remains, and (2) each party separately advising the Service of its order of preference by numbering each name on the panel. In almost all cases, an arbitrator is chosen from one panel of names. However, if a request for another panel is made, the Service will comply with the request, providing that additional panels are permissible under the terms of the agreement or the parties so stipulate. Subsequent adjustment of disputes is not precluded by the submission of a panel or an appointment. A substantial number of issues are being settled by the parties themselves after the initial request for a panel and after selection of the arbitrator. Notice of such settlement should be sent promptly to the arbitrator and to the Service.

The arbitrator should be compensated whenever he receives insufficient notice of settlement to enable him to rearrange his schedule of arbitration hearings or working hours.

Sec. 1404.7—Appointment of arbitrators

After the parties notify the Service of their selection, the arbitrator is appointed by the director. If any party fails to notify the Service within 15 days after the date of mailing the panel, all persons named therein shall be deemed acceptable to such party. The arbitrator, upon appointment notification, is requested to communicate with the parties immediately to arrange for preliminary matters such as date and place of hearing. There is an advantage to the parties of advising the Service of the arbitrator selected, as the standards and procedure established by the Service, including those governing the range of fees, apply to the appointed arbitrator. Also, the names of arbitrators who have not completed a pending arbitration are not ordinarily included on panels requested by the same parties.

Sec. 1404.8—Status of arbitrators after appointment

After appointment, the legal relationship of arbitrators is with the parties rather than the Service, though the Service does have a continuing interest in the proceedings. Industrial peace and good labor relations are enhanced by arbitrators who function justly, expeditiously and impartially so as to obtain and retain the respect, esteem and confidence of all participants in the arbitration proceedings. The conduct of the arbitration proceeding is under the arbitrator's jurisdiction and control, subject to such rules of procedure as the parties may jointly prescribe. He is to make his own decisions and write his own opinions based on the record in the proceedings. He may not delegate this duty and responsibility to others in whole or in part without the knowledge and prior consent of both parties. The powers of the arbitrators may be exercised by a majority unless otherwise provided by agreement or by law, and, unless prohibited by law, they may proceed in the absence of any party who, after due notice, fails to be present or to obtain a postponement. The award, however, must be supported by evidence as an award cannot be based solely upon the default of a party.

Sec. 1404.9—Prompt decision

Early hearing and decision of industrial disputes is desirable in the interest of good labor relations. The parties should inform the Service whenever a decision is unduly delayed. The Service expects to be notified if and when (1) an arbitrator cannot schedule, hear and determine issues promptly, and (2) he is advised that a dispute has been settled by the parties prior to arbitration. The arbitrator is also expected to keep the Service informed of changes in address, occupation or availability, and of any business connections with or of concern to labor or management.

The award shall be made not later than 30 days from the date of the closing of the hearing, or the receipt of a transcript and any post-hearing briefs, or if oral hearings have been waived, then from the date of receipt of the final statements and proof by the arbitrator, unless otherwise agreed upon by the parties or specified by law. However, a failure to make such an award within 30 days shall not invalidate an award. The Service, however, when nominating arbitrators, takes notice of any arbitrator's failure to comply with its policies and procedures.

The parties can expedite awards. They may advise the Service and the arbitrator if an early decision is desired. If such notice is given, the Service will so advise the arbitrator at the time of his appointment. The parties can also request that an opinion follow the award, or that an opinion be omitted in appropriate cases. The parties may also provide in their agreement or in their arbitration stipulation or request that an award must be rendered within a fixed time after the close of the hearing in order to be valid, unless the time is enlarged by agreement of the parties. Such a provision, however, would operate to nullify an award made after such period of time and should therefore be carefully drafted so as not to cause hasty and ill-considered decisions.

Sec. 1404.10—Importance of impartiality

Interviews with or communications by the arbitrator to and from one party without the knowledge and consent of the other party, are easily misunderstood and should be avoided since they can result in a loss of confidence in the integrity, fairness and judgment of the arbitrator. Likewise, the arbitrator should refrain from giving unsolicited advice in his opinion, or award or other document for the same reason. Arbitrators are called upon to decide issues which the parties have been unable to resolve and, consequently, difficult decisions are inevitable. Their acceptability can be advanced not alone by the soundness of the decisions, but also by the orderly and impartial manner in which the entire arbitration proceeding is conducted.

Sec. 1404.11—Arbitrator's award report

At the conclusion of the hearing and after the award has been submitted to the parties, each arbitrator is required to file a copy with the Service. The Service then evaluates awards with a view to determining whether they meet the accepted professional standards as to form, clarity and logic. The arbitrator is further required to submit a report showing a breakdown of his fees and expense charges so that the Service may be in a position to check conformance with its fee policies. Cooperation in filing both award and report within 15 days after handing down the award is expected of all arbitrators.

It is the policy of the Service not to release arbitration decisions for publication without the consent of both parties. Furthermore, the Service expects the arbitrators it has nominated or appointed not to give publicity to awards they may issue, except in a manner agreeable to both parties.

Sec. 1404.12—Fees of arbitrators

No administrative or filing fee is charged since the Service is required by law to provide such facilities. The current policy of the Service permits its nominees or appointees to charge a fee for their services not exceeding $150 per day. The Service expects its arbitrators in fixing the fee for a case to give due consideration to the financial condition of each party, the accepted standards for the area in which the dispute arises, the complexity of the issues involved and the length of time consumed preliminary to and in the course of the hearing; in the study of the evidence and preparation of the award.

In those rare instances where arbitrators fix wages or other terms of a new contract, the responsibilities involved are so grave that the arbitrators are not subject to the above fee restriction. The parties may prefer to agree with the arbitrator upon a fixed fee in advance of the arbitration. This, however, could result in unnecessarily prolonging an arbitration hearing.

The parties can reduce the cost of arbitration by the careful preparation of exhibits and evidence and by the stipulation of undisputed facts. The parties may also stipulate that the arbitrator devote not more than a specified number of days to the study and preparation of the opinion and award. There is, however, some risk in so doing since the award and opinion may not be satisfactory or sufficiently clear if such restriction is made in other than simple, routine cases.

The Service is not concerned with whether the fees and expenses of the arbitrator are paid by only one of the parties or are divided between them. Nevertheless, unless the parties agree otherwise, (1) the fee and expenses of the arbitrator shall be paid equally by the parties, (2) the expenses of witnesses for either side shall be paid by the parties producing such witnesses, (3) the total cost of the stenographic record, if any is made, and all transcripts thereof, shall be prorated equally by all parties ordering copies, and (4) the expenses of any witnesses or the cost of any briefs produced at the direct request of the arbitrator, shall be borne equally by the parties unless the arbitrator in his award assesses such expenses or any part thereof against any specified party or parties.

Sec. 1404.13—Conduct of hearings

The service does not prescribe detailed or specific rules of procedure for the conduct of an arbitration proceeding because it favors flexibility in labor relations. It believes that the parties and experienced arbitrators know best how arbitration proceedings should be conducted if wise decisions and industrial peace are to be achieved. Questions such as hearing rooms, submission of pre-hearing or post-hearing briefs, and recording of testimony, are left to the discretion of the individual arbitrator and the parties. The Service does, however, expect its arbitrators and the parties to conform to applicable laws, and to be guided by ethical and procedural standards as codified by appropriate professional organizations and generally accepted by the industrial community and experienced arbitrators.

In cities where the Service maintains offices, the parties are welcome upon request to the Service to use its conference rooms when they are available.

APPENDIX G

AMERICAN ARBITRATION ASSOCIATION VOLUNTARY LABOR ARBITRATION RULES[1]

1. Agreement of Parties

The parties shall be deemed to have made these rules a part of their arbitration agreement whenever, in a collective bargaining agreement or submission, they have provided for arbitration by the American Arbitration Association (hereinafter AAA) or under its rules. These rules shall apply in the form obtaining at the time the arbitration is initiated.

2. Name of Tribunal

Any tribunal constituted by the parties under these rules shall be called the Voluntary Labor Arbitration Tribunal.

3. Administrator

When parties agree to arbitrate under these rules and an arbitration is instituted thereunder, they thereby authorize the AAA to administer the arbitration. The authority and obligations of the administrator are as provided in the agreement of the parties and in these rules.

4. Delegation of Duties

The duties of the AAA may be carried out through such representatives or committees as the AAA may direct.

5. National Panel of Labor Arbitrators

The AAA shall establish and maintain a National Panel of Labor Arbitrators and shall appoint arbitrators therefrom, as hereinafter provided.

6. Office of Tribunal

The general office of the Labor Arbitration Tribunal is the headquarters of the AAA, which may, however, assign the administration of an arbitration to any of its regional offices.

7. Initiation Under an Arbitration Clause in a Collective Bargaining Agreement

Arbitration under an arbitration clause in a collective bargaining agreement under these rules

---

1. As amended and in effect Feb. 1, 1965.

may be initiated by either party in the following manner:

(a) By giving written notice to the other party of intention to arbitrate (demand), which notice shall contain a statement setting forth the nature of the dispute and the remedy sought, and

(b) By filing at any regional office of the AAA two copies of said notice, together with a copy of the collective bargaining agreement, or such parts thereof as relate to the dispute, including the arbitration provisions. After the arbitrator is appointed, no new or different claim may be submitted to him except with the consent of the arbitrator and all other parties.

8. Answer

The party upon whom the demand for arbitration is made may file an answering statement with the AAA within 7 days after notice from the AAA, in which event he shall simultaneously send a copy of his answer to the other party. If no answer is filed within the stated time, it will be assumed that the claim is denied. Failure to file an answer shall not operate to delay the arbitration.

9. Initiation under a Submission

Parties to any collective bargaining agreement may initiate an arbitration under these rules by filing at any regional office of the AAA two copies of a written agreement to arbitrate under these rules (submission), signed by the parties and setting forth the nature of the dispute and the remedy sought.

10. Fixing of Locale

The parties may mutually agree upon the locale where the arbitration is to be held. If the locale is not designated in the collective bargaining agreement or submission, and if there is a dispute as to the appropriate locale, the AAA shall have the power to determine the locale and its decision shall be binding.

11. Qualifications of Arbitrator

No person shall serve as a neutral arbitrator in any arbitration in which he has any financial or personal interest in the result of the arbitration, unless the parties, in writing, waive such disqualification.

12. Appointment from Panel

If the parties have not appointed an arbitrator and have not provided any other method of appointment, the arbitrator shall be appointed in the following manner: Immediately after the filing of the demand or submission, the AAA shall submit simultaneously to each party an identical list of names of persons chosen from the labor panel. Each party shall have 7 days from the mailing date in which to cross off any names to which he objects, number the remaining names indicating in order of his preference, and return the list to the AAA. If a party does not return the list within the time specified, all persons named therein shall be deemed acceptable. From among the persons who have been approved on both lists, and in accordance with the designated order of mutual preference, the AAA shall invite the acceptance of an arbitrator to serve. If the parties fail to agree upon any of the persons named or if those named decline or are unable to act, or if for any other reason the appointment cannot be made from the submitted lists, the administrator shall have power to make the appointment from other members of the panel without the submission of any additional lists.

13. Direct Appointment by Parties

If the agreement of the parties names an arbitrator or specifies a method of appointing an arbitrator, that designation or method shall be followed. The notice of appointment with the name and address of such arbitrator, shall be filed with the AAA by the appointing party.

If the agreement specifies a period of time within which an arbitrator shall be appointed, and any party fails to make such appointment within that period, the AAA may make the appointment.

If no period of time is specified in the agreement, the AAA shall notify the parties to make the appointment and if within 7 days thereafter such arbitrator has not been so appointed, the AAA shall make the appointment.

14. Appointment of Neutral Arbitrator by Party-Appointed Arbitrators

If the parties have appointed their arbitrators, or if either or both of them have been appointed as provided in section 13, and have authorized such arbitrators to appoint a neutral arbitrator within a specified time and no appointment is made within such time or any agreed extension thereof, the AAA may appoint a neutral arbitrator, who shall act as chairman.

If no period of time is specified for appointment of the neutral arbitrator and the parties do not make the appointment within 7 days from the date of the appointment of the last party-appointed arbitrator, the AAA shall appoint such neutral arbitrator, who shall act as chairman.

If the parties have agreed that the arbitrators shall appoint the neutral arbitrator from the panel, the AAA shall furnish to the party-appointed arbitrators, in the manner prescribed in section 12, a list selected from the panel, and the appointment of the neutral arbitrator shall be made as prescribed in such action.

15. Number of Arbitrators

If the arbitration agreement does not specify the number of arbitrators, the dispute shall be heard and determined by one arbitrator, unless the parties otherwise agree.

16. Notice to Arbitrator of His Appointment

Notice of the appointment of the neutral arbitrator shall be mailed to the arbitrator by the AAA and the signed acceptance of the arbitrator shall be filed with the AAA prior to the opening of the first hearing.

17. Disclosure by Arbitrator of Disqualification

Prior to accepting his appointment, the prospective neutral arbitrator shall disclose any circumstances likely to create a presumption of bias or which he believes might disqualify him as an impartial arbitrator. Upon receipt of such information, the AAA shall immediately disclose it to the parties. If either party declines to waive the presumptive disqualification, the vacancy thus created shall be filled in accordance with the applicable provisions of these rules.

18. Vacancies

If any arbitrator should resign, die, withdraw, refuse or be unable or disqualified to perform the duties of his office, the AAA shall, on proof satisfactory to it, declare the office vacant. Vacancies shall be filled in the same manner as that governing the making of the original appointment, and the matter shall be reheard by the new arbitrator.

19. Time and Place of Hearing

The arbitrator shall fix the time and place for each hearing. At least 5 days prior thereto the AAA shall mail notice of the time and place of hearing to each party, unless the parties otherwise agree.

20. Representation by Counsel

Any party may be represented at the hearing by counsel or by other authorized representative.

21. Stenographic Record

The AAA will make the necessary arrangements for the taking of an official stenographic record of the testimony whenever such record is requested by one or more parties. The requesting party or parties shall pay the cost of such record directly to the reporting agency in accordance with their agreement.

22. Attendance at Hearings

Persons having a direct interest in the arbitration are entitled to attend hearings. The arbitrator shall have the power to require the retirement of any witness or witnesses during the testimony of other witnesses. It shall be discretionary with the arbitrator to determine the propriety of the attendance of any other persons.

23. Adjournments

The arbitrator for good cause shown may adjourn the hearing upon the request of a party or upon his own initiative, and shall adjourn when all the parties agree thereto.

24. Oaths

Before proceeding with the first hearing, each arbitrator may take an oath of office, and if required by law, shall do so. The arbitrator may, in his discretion, require witnesses to testify under oath administered by any duly qualified person, and if required by law or requested by either party, shall do so.

25. Majority Decision

Whenever there is more than one arbitrator, all decisions of the arbitrators shall be by majority vote. The award shall also be made by majority vote unless the concurrence of all is expressly required.

26. Order of Proceedings

A hearing shall be opened by the filing of the oath of the arbitrator, where required, and by the recording of the place, time and date of hearing, the presence of the arbitrator and parties, and counsel if any, and the receipt by the arbitrator of the demand and answer, if any, or the submission.

Exhibits, when offered by either party, may be received in evidence by the arbitrator. The names and addresses of all witnesses and exhibits in order received shall be made a part of the record.

The arbitrator may, in his discretion, vary the normal procedure under which the initiating party first presents his claim, but in any case shall afford full and equal opportunity to all parties for presentation of relevant proofs.

27. Arbitration in the Absence of a Party

Unless the law provides to the contrary, the arbitration may proceed in the absence of any party, who, after due notice, fails to be present or fails to maintain an adjournment. An award shall not be made solely on the default of a party. The arbitrator shall require the other party to submit such evidence as he may require for the making of an award.

28. Evidence

The parties may offer such evidence as they desire and shall produce such additional evidence as the arbitrator may deem necessary to an understanding and determination of the dispute. When the arbitrator is authorized by law to subpoena witnesses and documents, he may do so upon his own initiative or upon the request of any party. The arbitrator shall be the judge of the relevancy and materiality of the evidence offered and conformity to legal rules of evidence shall not be necessary. All evidence shall be taken in the presence of all of the arbitrators and all of the parties except where any of the parties is absent in default or has waived his right to be present.

29. Evidence by Affidavit and Filing of Documents

The arbitrator may receive and consider the evidence of witnesses by affidavit, but shall give it only such weight as he deems proper after consideration of any objections made to its admission.

All documents not filed with the arbitrator at the hearing but which are arranged at the hearing or subsequently by agreement of the parties to be submitted, shall be filed with the AAA for transmission to the arbitrator. All parties shall be afforded opportunity to examine such documents.

30. Inspection

Whenever the arbitrator deems it necessary, he may make an inspection in connection with the subject matter of the dispute after written notice to the parties who may, if they so desire, be present at such inspection.

31. Closing of Hearings

The arbitrator shall inquire of all parties whether they have any further proofs to offer or witnesses to be heard. Upon receiving negative replies, the arbitrators shall declare the hearings closed and a minute thereof shall be recorded. If briefs or other documents are to be filed, the hearings shall be declared closed as of the final date set by the arbitrator for filing with the AAA. The time limit within which the arbitrator is required to make his award shall commence to run, in the absence of other agreement by the parties, upon the closing of the hearings.

32. Reopening of Hearings

The hearings may be reopened by the arbitrator on his own motion, or on the motion of either party, for good cause shown, at any time before the award is made, but if the reopening of the hearing would prevent the making of the award within the specific time agreed upon by the parties in the contract out of which the controversy has arisen, the matter may not be reopened, unless both parties agree upon the extension of such time limit. When no specific date is fixed in the contract, the arbitrator may reopen the hearings, and the arbitrator shall have 30 days from the closing of the reopened hearings within which to make an award.

33. Waiver of Rules

Any party who proceeds with the arbitration after knowledge that any provision or requirement of these rules has not been compiled with and who fails to state his objection thereto in writing, shall be deemed to have waived his right to object.

34. Waiver of Oral Hearing

The parties may provide, by written agreement, for the waiver of oral hearings. If the parties are unable to agree as to the procedure, the AAA shall specify a fair and equitable procedure.

35. Extensions of Time

The parties may modify any period of time by mutual agreement. The AAA for good cause may extend any period of time established by these rules, except the time for making the award. The AAA shall notify the parties of any such extension of time and its reason therefor.

36. Serving of Notices

Each party to a submission or other agreement which provides for arbitration under these rules shall be deemed to have consented and shall consent that any papers, notices or process necessary or proper for the initiation or continuation of an arbitration under these rules and for any court action in connection therewith or the entry of judgment on an award made thereunder, may be served upon such party (a) by mail addressed to such party or his attorney at his last known address, or (b) by personal service, within or without the state wherein the arbitration is to be held.

37. Time of Award

The award shall be rendered promptly by the arbitrator and, unless otherwise agreed by the parties, or specified by the law, not later than 30 days from the date of closing the hearings, or if oral hearings have been waived, then from the date of transmitting the final statements and proofs to the arbitrator.

38. Form of Award

The award shall be in writing and shall be signed either by the neutral arbitrator or by a concurring majority if there be more than one arbitrator. The parties shall advise the AAA whenever they do not require the arbitrator to accompany the award with an opinion.

39. Award Upon Settlement

If the parties settle their dispute during the course of the arbitration, the arbitrator, upon their request, may set forth the terms of the agreed settlement in an award.

40. Delivery of Award to Parties

Parties shall accept as legal delivery of the award the placing of the award or a true copy thereof in the mail by the AAA, addressed to such party at his last known address or to his attorney, or personal service of the award, or the filing of the award in any manner which may be prescribed by law.

41. Release of Documents for Judicial Proceedings

The AAA shall, upon the written request of a party, furnish to such party at his expense certified facsimiles of any papers in the AAA's possession that may be required in Judicial proceedings relating to the arbitration.

42. Judicial Proceedings

The AAA is not a necessary party in judicial proceedings relating to the arbitration.

43. Administrative Fee

As a nonprofit organization, the AAA shall prescribe an administrative fee schedule to compensate it for the cost of providing administrative services. The schedule in effect at the time of filing shall be applicable.

44. Expenses

The expenses of witnesses for either side shall be paid by the party producing such witnesses.

Expenses of the arbitration, other than the cost of the stenographic record, including required traveling and other expenses of the arbitrator and of AAA representatives, and the expenses of any witnesses or the cost of any proofs produced at the direct request of the arbitrator, shall be borne equally by the parties unless they agree otherwise, or unless the arbitrator in his award assesses such expenses or any party thereof against any specified party or parties.

45. Communication with Arbitrator

There shall be no communication between the parties and a neutral arbitrator other than at oral hearings. Any other oral or written communications from the parties to the arbitrator shall be directed to the AAA for transmittal to the arbitrator.

46. Interpretation and Application of Rules

The arbitrator shall interpret and apply these rules insofar as they relate to his power and duties. When there is more than one arbitrator and a difference arises among them concerning the meaning or application of any such rules, it shall be decided by majority vote. If that is unobtainable, either arbitrator or party may refer the question to the AAA for final decision. All other rules shall be interpreted and applied by the AAA.

Administrative Fee Schedule

INITIAL ADMINISTRATIVE FEE

The initial administrative fee is $30 for each party, due and payable at the time of filing.

EXPENSE ADJUSTMENT

And additional fee of $3 is also payable by each party. This expense adjustment is to reimburse the AAA for postage and telephone expenses.

ADDITIONAL HEARINGS

A fee of $30 is payable by each party for each second and subsequent hearing which is either clerked by the AAA or held in a hearing room provided by the AAA.

POSTPONEMENT FEES

A fee of $5 is payable by a party causing a postponement of any scheduled hearing.

OVERTIME

A fee of $3 per hour is payable by each party for hearings held on Saturdays, legal holidays, or after 6 p.m. on weekdays; provided these hearings are either clerked by the AAA or held in a hearing room provided by the AAA.

TABLE OF CASES

*Cases that are summarized or discussed in text by the author are indicated by asterisks; all not so accompanied are presented in their own text, usually edited. Case names appear in both plaintiff-defendant (petitioner-respondent) and defendant-plaintiff (respondent-petitioner) order. Introductory terms such as "In re" and "In the Matter of" are omitted except in a few special situations, and then the case is alphabetized by the party's name. Respondent names are indicated by parentheses. Union names in this table are listed under the key word indicating craft or industry such as "Autoworkers" or "Teamsters" followed in a few cases by other distinguishing terms (other than Local numbers) in parentheses, e.g., "Drivers (General Sales)." Decisions of the National Labor Relations Board are listed upon the respondent's name, followed by: [NLRB].

SUBJECT INDEX